ID0372408

Russian
Compact Dictionary

Russian – English
English – Russian

Berlitz Publishing
New York · Munich · Singapore

Original edition edited by the Langenscheidt editorial staff

Compiled with contributions by Irina A. Walshe

Inset cover photo: © Punchstock/MedioImages

Neither the presence nor the absence of a designation
indicating that any entered word constitutes a trademark
should be regarded as affecting the legal status thereof.

© 2007 Berlitz Publishing/APA Publications GmbH & Co. Verlag KG
Singapore Branch, Singapore

Trademark Reg. U.S. Patent Office and other countries.
Marca Registrada.
Used under license from Berlitz Investment Corporation.

Berlitz Publishing
193 Morris Avenue
Springfield, NJ 07081
USA

Printed in Germany
ISBN-13: 978-981-246-950-2
ISBN-10: 981-246-950-8

11 10 09 08 07

1. 2. 3. 4. 5.

Preface

This Russian/English Dictionary with its 45,000 references is an ideal tool for all those who work with the Russian and English languages at beginners or intermediate level. The dictionary offers coverage of everyday language and also details the latest developments in Russian and English. Hundreds of up-to-date Russian and English words have been incorporated into the present edition of this dictionary, making it ideal for everyday use in the modern world – in all walks of life and also at school. The dictionary contains the most important terminology from such specialist areas as trade and commerce, technology, and medicine.

Isolated words are often only clearly understood in context. So a large number of multi-word lexical units, loose combinations such as collocations as well as set phrases such as idiomatic expressions, are given to show the full spectrum of a word's meaning and to illustrate how the two languages Russian and English correspond in context.

Translations referring to different word classes of the same headword are indicated by arabic numbers. Synonymous translation variants are seperated by commas, and semantically distinct alternatives by semicolons.

In addition to the main vocabulary, this dictionary contains special quick-reference sections for geographical names and current abbreviations in both Russian and English.

Words need grammar to back them up. This dictionary gives detailed information on the conjugation and declension of Russian verbs, nouns and adjectives. Each Russian verb, noun or adjective in the dictionary includes a reference to a corresponding standard verb, noun or adjective in the grammar appendix, which is then fully conjugated or inflected.

English pronunciation in this dictionary follows the principles laid down by Jones / Gimson and is based on the alphabet of the *International Phonetic Association* IPA.

Russian words can be pronounced properly if the stress is known. Therefore every Russian word has an appropriate stress mark. Shift of stress, as far as it takes place within the inflection, is also indicated. A detailed account of Russian pronunciation with the help of the Symbols of the IPAs phonetic transcription can be found on pages 11–17.

It is hoped that this dictionary will be a rich source of information for you as well as an indispensable part of the materials you use to learn Russian or English.

Contents

How to Use the Dictionary

1. **Arrangement.** Strict alphabetical order has been maintained throughout the dictionary.

   A number of prefixed words, especially verbs, are not explicitly listed because of the limited size of the dictionary, and in such cases it may prove useful to drop the prefix and look up the primary form, e. g.:

   поблагодари́ть → благодари́ть

   Compounds not found at their alphabetical place should be reduced to their second component in order to find out their main meaning, e. g.:

   термоя́дерный → я́дерный = nuclear

   The tilde (~) serves as a mark of repetition. The tilde in bold type replaces either the headword or the part of the headword preceding the vertical bar; e. g.:

   иди́л|л|ия ...; **~и́ческий** = идилли́ческий

   In the English-Russian part the tilde in multi-word lexical units is used to replace the whole headword, e.g.:

   mobil|e ...; *~ phone* = *mobile phone*

   In the Russian-English part the tilde in idioms is used to relace the part preceding the vertical bar, e. g.:

   коль|цево́й ...; *~цо́* ...; *обруча́льное ~цо́* = *обруча́льное кольцо́*

   The tilde with a circle (⁀): when the first letter changes from a capital to a small letter or vice-versa, the usual tilde is replaced by the tilde with a circle.

   In brackets a hyphen (-) has been used instead of the tilde, e. g.:

   брать [беру́, -рёшь; брал, -á ...] = [беру́, берёшь; брал, брала́ ...]

   Of the two main aspects of a Russian verb the imperfective form appears first, in boldface type, followed, in acute-angled brackets < >, by its perfective counterpart.

2. **Pronunciation.** As a rule the pronunciation of individual Russian headwords has been given only in cases and places that differ from the standard pronunciation of Russian vowel and consonant letters, e. g.:

   лёгкий (-xk-) - «гк» is pronounced «хк».

3. **Stress.** The accent mark (´) when is placed above the stressed vowel of a Russian entry (or any other) word with more than one syllable and printed in full, as well as of run-on words, provided their accentuated vowel is not covered by the tilde or hyphen (= marks of repetition), e. g.:

   дока́з|ывать ..., <~а́ть> = <доказа́ть>

   Since ё is always stressed the two dots over it represent implicitly the accent mark.

   Wherever the accent mark precedes the tilde (~) the second-last syllable of the part for which the tilde stands is stressed, e. g.:

   уведом|ля́ть ..., <~и́ть> = <уве́домить>

An accent mark over the tilde (∻) implies that the last (or sole) syllable of the part replaced by the tilde is to be stressed.

Example:

наход|и́ть ...; **∻ка** = **нахо́дка**
прода|ва́ть ..., **<∻ть>** = **<прода́ть>**

In special cases of phonetic transcription, however, the accent mark precedes the stressed syllable, cf. **анте́нна** (-'tɛn-). This usage is in accordance with IPA rules.

Two accents in a word denote two equally possible modes of stressing it, thus:

и́на́че = **ина́че** *or* **и́наче**

Quite a number of predicative (or short) adjectives show a shift, or shifts, of stress as compared with their attributive forms. Such divergences are recorded as follows:

хоро́ший [17; хоро́ш, -а́] = [17; хоро́ш, хороша́, хорошо́ (*pl.* хоро́ши)]

The same system of stress designation applies, to accent shifts in the preterite forms of a number of verbs, e. g.:

да|ва́ть ..., **<∻ть>** [... дал, -а́, -о; ... (дан, -а́)] = [... дал, дала́, да́ло (*pl.* да́ли); ... (дан, дана́, дано́, даны́)]

Insertion of the "epenthetic" o, e, between the two last stem consonants in masculine short forms has been noted in all adjectives where this applies, e. g.:

лёгкий ... [16; лёгок, легка́; *a.* лёгки] = [16; лёгок, легка́, легко́ (*pl.* легки́ *or* лёгки)]

If the stress in all short forms conforms to that of the attributive adjective the latter is merely provided with the abbreviation *sh.* (for *short form*) which indicates at the same time the possibility of forming such predicative forms, e. g.:

бога́тый [14 *sh.*] = [14; бога́т, бога́та, бога́то, бога́ты]

4. **Inflected forms.** All Russian inflected parts of speech appearing in the dictionary are listed in their appropriate basic forms, i. e. nominative singular (nouns, adjectives, numerals, certain pronouns) or infinitive (verbs). The gender of Russian nouns is indicated by means of one of three abbreviations in italics (*m, f, n*) after the headword.* Each inflected entry is followed, in square brackets [ ], by a figure which serves as reference to a definite paradigm within the system of conjugation and declension listed at the end of this book. Any variants of these paradigms are stated after the reference figure of each headword in question.

---

* For users of part II: Any Russian noun ending in a consonant *or* -й is of masculine gender;
those ending in -а *or* -я are of feminine gender;
those ending in -о *or* -е are of neuter gender.
In cases where this rule does not apply, as well as in nouns ending in -ь, the gender is indicated.

Example:

ло́жка *f* [5; *g/pl*.: -жек], like ло́жа *f* [5], is declined according to paradigm 5, except that in the genitive plural the former example inserts the "epenthetic" e between the two last stem consonants: ло́жек; cf. **ло́дка** *f* [5; *g/pl*.: -док] = [*g/pl*.: ло́док].

кусо́к *m* [1; -ска́] = the "epenthetic" o is omitted in the oblique cases of the singular and in all cases of the plural; cf. **коне́ц** *m* [1; -нца́] = [конца́, концу́, etc.].

As the prefixed forms of a verb follow the same inflection model and (with the exception of perfective aspects having the stressed prefix вы-) mode of accentuation as the corresponding unprefixed verb, differences in stress, etc. have in cases of such aspect pairs been marked but once, viz. with the imperfective form.

5. **Government.** Case government, except for the accusative, is indicated with the help of Latin and Russian abbreviations. Emphasis has been laid on differences between the two languages, including the use of prepositions. Whenever a special case of government applies only to one of several meanings of a word, this has been duly recorded in connection with the meaning concerned. To ensure a clear differentiation of person and thing in government, the English and Russian notes to that effect show the necessary correspondence in sequence.

6. **Semantic distinction.** If a word has different meanings and, at the same time, different forms of inflection or aspect, this has been indicated by numbers (e. g. бить, коса́, коси́ть); otherwise a semicolon separates different meanings, a comma mere synonyms. Sense indicators in italics serve to specify individual shades of meanings, e. g. **поднима́ть** ... *трево́гу, пла́ту* raise; *ору́жие* take up; *флаг* hoist; *я́корь* weigh; *паруса́* set; *шум* make; **приёмный** ... *часы́* office; *экза́мен* entrance; *оте́ц, сын* foster.

In a number of Russian verbs the perfective aspect indicated (particularly with the prefixes <за-> and <по->) has, strictly speaking, the connotations "to begin to do s. th." (the former) and "to do s. th. for a (little) while" (the latter); but since these forms are very often rendered in English by means of the equivalent verb without any such additions they have occasionally been given as simple aspect counterparts without explicit indication as to their aforesaid connotations.

7. **Orthography.** In both the Russian and English parts newest spelling standards have been applied, and in the latter differences between American and British usage noted wherever possible and feasible.

Words at the end of a line which are always hyphenated are indicated by repetition of the hyphen (at the end of the first line and the beginning of the next line).

In parts of words or additions given in brackets a hyphen is placed within the bracket.

Abbreviations Used in the Dictionary
English Abbreviations

a.	*also* та́кже	*eccl.*	*ecclesiastical term* церко́вное выраже́ние
abbr.	*abbreviation* сокраще́ние		
ac.	*accusative (case)* вини́тельный паде́ж	*econ.*	*economy* эконо́мика
		educ.	*education* шко́ла, шко́льное де́ло, педаго́гика
adj.	*adjective* и́мя прилага́тельное	*e.g.*	*for example* наприме́р
adv.	*adverb* наре́чие	*el.*	*electrical engineering* электроте́хника
ae.	*aeronautics* авиа́ция		
agric.	*agriculture* се́льское хозя́йство	*esp.*	*especially* осо́бенно
		etc.	*et cetera (and so on)* и т. д. (и так да́лее)
Am.	*Americanism* американи́зм		
anat.	*anatomy* анато́мия	*euph.*	*euphemism* эвфеми́зм
arch.	*architecture* архитекту́ра	*f*	*feminine (gender)* же́нский род
astr.	*astronomy* астроно́мия		
attr.	*attributive usage* атрибути́вное употребле́ние (т. е. в ка́честве определе́ния)	*fig.*	*figurative usage* в перено́сном значе́нии
		fin.	*financial term* фина́нсы, ба́нковое де́ло
Bibl.	*Biblical* библе́йский		
biol.	*biology* биоло́гия	*f/pl.*	*feminine plural* мно́жественное число́ же́нского ро́да
Brt.	*British (English) usage* брита́нское (англи́йское) словоупотребле́ние		
		ft.	*future (tense)* бу́дущее вре́мя
bot.	*botany* бота́ника	*gen.*	*genitive (case)* роди́тельный паде́ж
b.s.	*bad sense* в дурно́м смы́сле		
chem.	*chemistry* хи́мия	*geogr.*	*geography* геогра́фия
cine.	*cinema* кинематогра́фия	*geol.*	*geology* геоло́гия
cj.	*conjunction* сою́з	*ger.*	*gerund* геру́ндий (дееприча́стие)
coll.	*colloquial usage* разгово́рный язы́к		
		g/pl.	*genitive plural* роди́тельный паде́ж мно́жественного числа́
collect.	*collective (noun)* собира́тельное и́мя (существи́тельное)		
		g. pr. (pt.)	*present (past) gerund* дееприча́стие настоя́щего (проше́дшего) вре́мени
com.	*commonly* обыкнове́нно		
comm.	*commercial term* торго́вля	*gr.*	*grammar* грамма́тика
comp.	*comparative (form)* сравни́тельная сте́пень	*hist.*	*history* исто́рия
		hort.	*horticulture* садово́дство
compds.	*compounds* сло́жные слова́	*hunt.*	*hunting* охо́та
comput.	*computer* компью́терная те́хника	*impers.*	*impersonal (form)* безли́чная фо́рма, безли́чно
contp.	*contemptuously* пренебрежи́тельно	*impf.*	*imperfective (aspect)* несоверше́нный вид
cul.	*culinary term* кулина́рия	*(im)pf.*	*imperfective and perfective (aspect)* несоверше́нный и соверше́нный вид
dat.	*dative (case)* да́тельный паде́ж		
		indecl.	*indeclinable word* несклоня́емое сло́во
dim.	*diminutive* уменьши́тельная фо́рма		
dipl.	*diplomacy* диплома́тия	*inf.*	*infinitive* инфинити́в, неопределённая фо́рма глаго́ла
e.	*endings stressed (throughout)* ударе́ние (сплошь) на оконча́ниях		

instr.	*instrumental (case)* твори́тельный паде́ж
int.	*interjection* междоме́тие
interr.	*interrogative(ly)* вопроси́тельная фо́рма, вопроси́тельно
iro.	*ironically* ирони́чески
irr.	*irregular* непра́вильная фо́рма
iter.	*iterative, frequentative (aspect)* многокра́тный вид
joc.	*jocular* шутли́во
ling.	*linguistics* лингви́стика
lit.	*literary* кни́жное выраже́ние
m	*masculine (gender)* мужско́й род
math.	*mathematics* матема́тика
med.	*medicine* медици́на
mil.	*military term* вое́нный те́рмин
min.	*mineralogy* минерало́гия
mot.	*motoring* автомобили́зм
m/pl.	*masculine plural* мно́жественное число́ мужско́го ро́да
mst.	*mostly* бо́льшей ча́стью
mus.	*musical term* му́зыка
n	*neuter (gender)* сре́дний род
naut.	*nautical term* судохо́дство
no.	*number* но́мер
nom.	*nominative (case)* имени́тельный паде́ж
n/pl.	*neuter plural* мно́жественное число́ сре́днего ро́да
o. a.	*one another* друг дру́га, друг дру́гу
obs.	*obsolete* устаре́вшее сло́во, выраже́ние
once	*semelfactive (aspect)* однокра́тный вид
o. s.	*oneself* себя́, себе́, -ся
P	*popular* просторе́чие
p.	*participle* прича́стие
p.	*person* лицо́
P.	*person* челове́к
paint.	*painting* жи́вопись
part.	1. *particle* части́ца; 2. *particular(ly)* осо́бенно
part. g.	*partitive genitive* роди́тельный раздели́тельный
pej.	*pejorative* пейорати́вно, неодобри́тельно

pers.	*person(al form)* лицо́, ли́чная фо́рма
pf.	*perfective (aspect)* соверше́нный вид
pharm.	*pharmacy* фармаце́втика
philos.	*philosophy* филосо́фия
phot.	*photography* фотогра́фия
phys.	*physics* фи́зика
pl.	*plural* мно́жественное число́
poet.	*poetic* поэти́ческое сло́во, выраже́ние
pol.	*politics* поли́тика
poss.	*possessive (form)* притяжа́тельная фо́рма
p. pr. a. (*p.*)	*present participle active (passive)* действи́тельное (страда́тельное) прича́стие настоя́щего вре́мени
p. pt. a. (*p.*)	*past participle active (passive)* действи́тельное (страда́тельное) прича́стие проше́дшего вре́мени
pr.	*present (tense)* настоя́щее вре́мя
pred.	*predicative usage* предикати́вное употребле́ние (т. е. в ка́честве именно́й ча́сти сказу́емого)
pref.	*prefix* приста́вка
pron.	*pronoun* местоиме́ние
prp.	*preposition* предло́г
pt.	*preterite, past (tense)* проше́дшее вре́мя
rail.	*railway* железнодоро́жное де́ло
refl.	*reflexive (form)* возвра́тная фо́рма
rhet.	*rhetoric* рито́рика
s. b.	*somebody* кто-(кого́-, кому́-)нибудь
s. b.'s	*somebody's* чей-нибудь
sew.	*sewing* швейное де́ло
sg.	*singular* еди́нственное число́
sh.	*short (predicative) form* кра́ткая фо́рма
sl.	*slang* жарго́н
st.	*stem stressed (throughout)* ударе́ние (сплошь) на осно́ве
s. th.	*something* что́-либо
su.	*substantive, noun* и́мя

10

	существи́тельное		
tech.	*technical* техни́ческий те́рмин	*v/aux.*	*auxiliary verb* вспомога́тельный глаго́л
tel.	*telephony* телефо́н	*vb.*	*verb* глаго́л
th.	*thing* вещь, предме́т	*v/i.*	*intransitive verb* непереходный глаго́л
thea.	*theater* теа́тр		
typ.	*typography* типогра́фское де́ло	*v/refl.*	*reflexive verb* возвра́тный глаго́л
univ.	*university* университе́т	*v/t.*	*transitive verb* перехо́дный глаго́л
usu.	*usually* обы́чно	*zo.*	*zoology* зооло́гия

Russian Abbreviations

И	имени́тельный паде́ж nominative (case).	П	предло́жный паде́ж prepositional *or* locative (case).
Р	роди́тельный паде́ж genitive (case).	и т. д.	(и так да́лее) etc. (et cetera).
Д	да́тельный паде́ж dative (case).	и т. п.	(и тому́ подо́бное) and the like.
В	вини́тельный паде́ж accusative (case).	лат.	лати́нский язы́к Latin.
Т	твори́тельный паде́ж instrumental (case).	тж.	та́кже also.

Russian Pronunciation

I. Vowels

1. All vowels in stressed position are half-long in Russian.

2. In unstressed position Russian vowels are very short, except in the first pretonic syllable, where this shortness of articulation is less marked. Some vowel letters (notably о, е, я), when read in unstressed position, not only differ in length (quantity), but also change their timbre, i.e. acoustic quality.

Russian letter		Explanation of its pronunciation	Transcription symbol
a	stressed	= **a** in 'father', but shorter: мáма ['mamə] *mamma*	a
	unstressed	1. = **a** in the above examples, but shorter – in first pretonic syllable: кармáн [kar'man] *pocket*	a
		2. = **a** in 'ago, about' – in post-tonic or second, etc. pretonic syllable(s): атáка [a'takə] *attack* карандáш [kəran'daʃ] *pencil*	ə
		3. = **i** in 'sit' – after ч, щ in first pretonic syllable: часы́ [tʃɪ'si] *watch* щади́ть [ʃtʃɪ'dɪtʲ] *spare*	ɪ
e		Preceding consonant (except ж, ш, ц) is soft.	
	stressed	1. = **ye** in 'yet' – in initial position, i.e. at the beginning of a word, or after a vowel, ъ, ь (if not ё) before a hard consonant: бытиé [bɨtʲi'jɛ] *existence* ел [jɛl] (*I*) *ate* нет [nʲɛt] *no*	jɛ/ɛ
		2. = **e** in 'set' – after consonants, soft or hard (ж, ш, ц), before a hard consonant, as well as in final position, i.e. at the end of a word, after consonants: на лицé [nalʲi'tsɛ] *on the face* шест [ʃɛst] *pole*	ɛ
		3. = **ya** in Yale; before a soft consonant: ель [jelʲ] *fir* петь [pʲetʲ] *to sing*	je/e
	unstressed	1. = **sit**; in initial position and after a vowel preceded by (j) ещё [jɪ'ʃtʃɔ] *still* знáет ['znajɪt] (*he, she, it*) *knows* рекá [rʲɪ'ka] *river*	jɪ/ɪ

Russian letter	Explanation of its pronunciation	Transcription symbol
	2. = **ы** (cf.) after ж, ш, ц: жена́ [ʒɨˈna] *wife* цена́ [tsɨˈna] *price*	ɨ
ё	Preceding consonant (except ж, ш, ц) is soft. only stressed = **yo** in be**yo**nd ёлка [ˈjɔlkə] *fir tree* даёт [daˈjɔt] *(he, she, it) gives* лёд [lʲɔt] *ice*	jɔ/ɔ
и	Preceding consonant (except ж, ш, ц) is soft. 1. stressed = like **ee** in s**ee**n, but shorter – in the instr/sg. of он/оно́ and the oblique forms of они́ initial и- may be pronounced (ji-): и́ва [ˈivə] *willow* юри́ст [juˈr̡ist] *lawyer* их [ix] *or* [jix] *of them (g/pl.)*	i/ji
	2. unstressed = like **ee** in s**ee**n, but shorter – in first pretonic syllable: мину́та [mʲiˈnutə] *minute*	i
	= **i** in s**i**t – in post-tonic or second, etc. pretonic syllable(s): хо́дит [ˈxɔdʲit] *(he, she, it) goes*	ɪ
	3. stressed and unstressed = **ы** (cf.) after ж, ш, ц: ши́на [ˈʃinə] *tire* цили́ндр [tsɨˈlʲindr] *cylinder*	ɨ
о	stressed = **o** in **o**bey: том [tɔm] *volume*	ɔ
	unstressed 1. = **o** in **o**bey; in final position of foreign words кака́о [kaˈkaɔ] *cocoa*	ɔ
	2. = **a** in f**a**ther, but shorter – in first pretonic syllable: Москва́ [masˈkva] *Moscow*	a
	3. = **a** in **a**go, **a**bout – in post-tonic or second, etc. pretonic syllable(s): со́рок [ˈsɔrək] *forty* огоро́д [əgaˈrɔt] *kitchen garden*	ə
у	stressed and unstressed = like **oo** in b**oo**m, but shorter бу́ду [ˈbudu] *(I) will be*	u
ы	stressed and unstressed = a retracted variety of **i**, as in h**i**ll; no English equivalent: вы [vɨ] *you*	
э	stressed and unstressed 1. = **e** in s**e**t э́то [ˈɛtə] *this* эско́рт [ɛsˈkɔrt] *escort*	

Russian letter	Explanation of its pronunciation	Transcription symbol
	2. = resembles the English sound **a** in p**a**le (but without the i-component) – before a soft consonant эти ['etɪ] *these*	e
ю	Preceding consonant is soft.	
	stressed and unstressed = like **yu** in **yu**le, but shorter рабо́таю [ra'bɔtəju] *(I) work* сюда́ [s̬u'da] *here*	ju/u
я	Preceding consonant is soft.	ja/a
	stressed 1. = **ya** in **ya**rd, but shorter – in initial position, after a vowel and before a hard consonant: я́ма ['jamə] *pit* моя́ [ma'ja] *my* мя́со ['m̥asə] *meat*	
	2. = **a** in b**a**d – in interpalatal position, i.e. between soft consonants: пять [pæt̬] *five*	æ
	unstressed 1. = **a** in '**a**go' (preceded by j after vowels) – in final position: со́я [sɔjə] *soya bean* неде́ля [nɪ'd̥elə] *week*	jə/ə
	2. = **i** in '**si**t', but preceded by (j) – in initial position, i.e. also after a vowel and ъ: язы́к [jɪ'zik] *tongue* та́ять ['tajɪt̬] *to thaw* мясни́к [m̥ɪs'ɲik] *butcher*	jɪ/ɪ

II. Semivowel

й	1. = **y** in **y**et – in initial position, i.e. also after a vowel, in loan words: йод [jɔt] *iodine* майо́р [ma'jɔr] *major*	j
	2. = in the formation of diphthongs as their second element:	j
ай	= (i) of (ai) in t**i**me: май [maj] *May*	aj
ой	stressed = **oi** in n**oi**se: бой [bɔj] *fight*	ɔj
	unstressed = **i** in t**i**me: война́ [vaj'na] *war*	aj
уй	= **u** in r**u**le + (j): бу́йвол ['bujvəl] *buffalo*	uj
ый	= ы (cf.) + (j): вы́йти ['vijtɪ] *to go out* кра́сный ['krasnɪj] *red*	ij

Russian letter		Explanation of its pronunciation	Transcription symbol
ий		= и (cf.) + (j):	ij
	stressed	австри́йка [af'strɨjkə] *Austrian woman*	
	unstressed	си́ний ['sɨnɨj] *blue*	
ей	stressed	= (j+) **a** in p**a**le:	jej/ej
		ей [jej] *to her*	
		ле́йка ['lejkə] *watering-can*	
	unstressed	= **ee** in s**ee**n, but shorter + (j):	ɨj
		сейча́с [sɨ(j)'tɕas] *now*	
юй		= ю (cf.) + (j):	juj/uj
		малю́й! [ma'luj] *paint!*	
яй	stressed	= (j+) **a** in b**a**d + (j):	jæj/æj
		я́йца ['jæjtsə] *eggs*	
		лентя́й ['lɪn'tæj] *lazy bones*	
	unstressed	**yi** in **Yi**ddish:	jɪ
		яйцо́ [jɪ(j)'tsɔ] *egg*	

III. Consonants

1. As most Russian consonants may be palatalized (or 'softened') there is, in addition to the series of normal ('hard') consonants, an almost complete set of 'soft' parallel sounds. According to traditional Russian spelling, in writing or printing this 'softness' is marked by a combination of such palatalized consonants with the vowels e, ё, и, ю, я or, either in final position or before a consonant, the so-called 'soft sign' (ь). In phonetic transcription palatalized consonants are indicated by means of a small hook, or comma, attached to them. As a rule a hard consonant before a soft one remains hard; only з, с may be softened before palatalized з, с, д, т, н.

2. The following consonants are always hard: ж, ш, ц.

3. The following consonants are always soft: ч, щ.

4. The voiced consonants б, в, г, д, ж, з are pronounced voicelessly (i. e. = п, ф, к, т, ш, с) in final position.

5. The voiced consonants б, в, г, ж, з, when followed by (one of) their voiceless counterparts п, ф, к, т, ш, с, are pronounced voicelessly (regressive assimilation) and vice versa: voiceless before voiced is voiced (except that there is no assimilation before в).

6. The articulation of doubled consonants, particularly those following a stressed syllable, is marked by their lengthening.

Russian letter		Explanation of its pronunciation	Transcription symbol
б	hard	= **b** in **b**ad: брат [brat] *brother*	b
	soft	= as in al**b**ion:	ḅ
		бе́лка ['ḅelkə] *squirrel*	

Russian letter			Explanation of its pronunciation	Transcription symbol
в	hard		= **w** in **v**ery: вода [va'da] *water*	v
	soft		= as in **v**iew: вёна ['γɛnə] *vein*	γ
г	hard		= **g** in **g**un: газ [gas] *gas*	g
	soft		= as in ar**g**ue: гимн [g̣imn] *anthem*	g̣
	Note:		= (v) in endings -ого, -его: больно́го [baḷ'nɔvə] *of the sick* си́него ['s̨iṇɪvə] *of the blue* ничего́ [ṇɪt̬ʃɪ'vɔ] *nothing*	v
			= (x) in бог *God* and in the combination -гк-, -гч-: мя́гкий ['m̨axḳɪj] *soft* мя́гче ['m̨axt̬ʃɛ] *softer*	x
д	hard		= **d** in **d**oor: да́ма ['damə] *lady*	d
	soft		= as in **d**ew: дю́на ['d̨unə] *dune* In the combination -здн- д is mute: по́здно ['pɔznə] *late*	d̨
ж	hard		= **s** in mea**s**ure, but hard: жа́жда ['ʒaʒdə] *thirst*	ʒ
		жч	= щ: мужчи́на [mu'ʃt̬ʃinə] *man*	ʃt̬ʃ
з	hard		= **z** in **z**oo: зако́н [za'kɔn] *law*	z
	soft		= as in pre**s**ume: зелёный [z̨ɪ'lɔnɨj] *green*	z̨
		зж	= hard or soft doubled ж: по́зже ['pɔʒʒɛ] or ['pɔʒ̨ʒ̨ɛ] *later*	ʒʒ/ʒ̨ʒ̨
		зч	= щ: изво́чик [iz'vɔʃt̬ʃɪk] *coachman*	ʃt̬ʃ
к	hard	=	**c** in **c**ome (unaspirated!): как [kak] *how*	k
	soft		= like **k** in **k**ey: ке́пка ['ḳɛpkə] *cap*	ḳ
л	hard		= **ll** in General American call: ла́мпа ['ɫampə] *lamp*	ɫ
	soft		= **ll** in mi**lli**on: ли́лия ['ḷiḷɪjə] *lily*	ḷ
м	hard	=	**m** in **m**an: мать [mat̨] *mother*	m
	soft		= as in **m**ute: метр [m̨ɛtr] *meter*	m̨
н	hard		= **n** in **n**oise: нос [nɔs] *nose*	n
	soft		= **n** in **n**ew: не́бо ['ṇɛbə] *heaven*	ṇ
п	hard		= **p** in **p**art (unaspirated!): па́па ['papə] *daddy*	p
	soft		= as in scor**p**ion: пить [pit̨] *to drink*	p̨
р	hard		= trilled **r**: рот [rɔt] *mouth*	r
	soft		= as in Ori**e**nt: ряд [r̨at] *row*	r̨

Russian letter			Explanation of its pronunciation	Transcription symbol
с	hard		= **s** in **s**ad: сорт [sɔrt] *sort*	s
	soft		= as in a**ss**ume: сила [ˈşiłə] *force*	ş
		сч	= щ: счастье [ˈʃtʃæstʲjɛ] *happiness*	ʃtʃ
т	hard		= **t** in **t**ent (unaspirated!): такт [takt] *measure*	t
	soft		= as in **t**une: теперь [tʲɪˈpɛrʲ] *now*	tʲ
			= -стн-, -стл- – in these combinations -т- is mute: известно [izˈvʲɛsnə] *known* счастливый [ʃtʃɪsˈlivɨj] *happy*	
ф	hard		= **f** in **f**ar: форма [ˈfɔrmə] *form*	f
	soft		= as in **f**ew: фирма [ˈfʲirmə] *firm*	fʲ
х	hard		= **ch** as in Scottish lo**ch**: ax! [ax] *ah!*	x
	soft		= like **ch** in German i**ch**, no English equivalent: химик [ˈxʲimɪk] *chemist*	xʲ
ц	nur hard		= **ts** in **ts**ar: царь [tsarʲ] *tsar*	ts
ч	nur soft		= **ch** in **ch**eck: час [tʃas] *hour*	tʃ
ш	nur hard		= **sh** in **sh**ip, but hard: шар [ʃar] *ball*	ʃ
щ	nur soft		= **sh** + **ch** in **ch**eck, cf. fre**sh ch**eeks, or = doubled (ʃʃ) as in sure: щи [ʃtʃi] *or* [ʃʃi] *cabbage soup*	ʃtʃ *or* ʃʃ

IV. Surds

ъ	hard sign	= The *jer* or 'hard sign' separates a hard (final) consonant of a prefix and the initial vowel, preceded by (j), of the following root, thus marking both the hardness of the preceding consonant and the distinct utterance of (j) before the vowel: предъявить [prɪdjɪˈvʲit] 'to show, produce' съезд [sjɛst] 'congress'.
ь	soft sign	= The *jer* or 'soft sign' serves to represent the palatal or soft quality of a (preceding) consonant in final position or before another consonant, cf.: брат [brat] 'brother' and брать [bratʲ] 'to take' полка [ˈpɔłkə] 'shelf' and полька [ˈpɔlʲkə] 'polka, Pole (= Polish woman)'.

Russian letter	Explanation of its pronunciation	Transcription symbol
	It is also used before vowels to indicate the softness of a preceding consonant as well as the pronunciation of (j) with the respective vowel, e.g.: семья [sɪm'ja] 'family' – *cf.* сéмя ['semə] 'seed', and in foreign words, such as батальóн [bəta'ljɔn] 'battalion'.	

English Pronunciation

Vowels

[ɑː]	*father*	['fɑːðə]
[æ]	*man*	[mæn]
[e]	*get*	[get]
[ə]	*about*	[ə'baut]
[ɜː]	*first*	[fɜːst]
[ɪ]	*stick*	[stɪk]
[iː]	*need*	[niːd]
[ɒ]	*hot*	[hɒt]
[ɔː]	*law*	[lɔː]
[ʌ]	*mother*	['mʌðə]
[ʊ]	*book*	[bʊk]
[uː]	*fruit*	[fruːt]

Diphthongs

[aɪ]	*time*	[taɪm]
[aʊ]	*cloud*	[klaʊd]
[eɪ]	*name*	[neɪm]
[eə]	*hair*	[heə]
[ɪə]	*here*	[hɪə]
[ɔɪ]	*point*	[pɔɪnt]
[əʊ]	*oath*	[əʊθ]
[ʊə]	*tour*	[tʊə]

Consonants

[b]	*bag*	[bæg]
[d]	*dear*	[dɪə]
[f]	*fall*	[fɔːl]
[g]	*give*	[gɪv]
[h]	*hole*	[həʊl]
[j]	*yes*	[jes]
[k]	*come*	[kʌm]
[l]	*land*	[lænd]
[m]	*mean*	[miːn]
[n]	*night*	[naɪt]
[p]	*pot*	[pɒt]
[r]	*right*	[raɪt]
[s]	*sun*	[sʌn]
[t]	*take*	[teɪk]
[v]	*vain*	[veɪn]
[w]	*wait*	[weɪt]
[z]	*rose*	[rəʊz]
[ŋ]	*bring*	[brɪŋ]
[ʃ]	*she*	[ʃiː]
[tʃ]	*chair*	[tʃeə]
[dʒ]	*join*	[dʒɔɪn]
[ʒ]	*leisure*	['leʒə]
[θ]	*think*	[θɪŋk]
[ð]	*the*	[ðə]
[']	means that the following syllable is stressed: *ability* [ə'bɪlətɪ]

The Russian Alphabet

printed		written		pronounced		printed		written		pronounced	
				transcribed						transcribed		
А	а	𝒜	𝑎	а	a	П	п	𝒫	п	пэ	pɛ
Б	б	𝒷	𝑏	бэ	bɛ	Р	р	𝒫	г	эр	ɛr
В	в	𝒱	𝑣	вэ	vɛ	С	с	𝒞	𝑐	эс	ɛs
Г	г	𝒯	𝑖	гэ	gɛ	Т	т	𝒯	𝑚	тэ	tɛ
Д	д	𝒟	𝑔	дэ	dɛ	У	у	𝒰	𝑦	у	u
Е	е	𝜀	𝑒	е	jɛ	Ф	ф	𝒫	𝜑	эф	ɛf
Ё	ё	𝜀̈	𝑒̈	ё	jɔ	Х	х	𝒳	𝑥	ха	xa
Ж	ж	𝒲	𝑤	жэ	ʒɛ	Ц	ц	𝒰	𝑢	цэ	tsɛ
З	з	𝟹	𝑧	зэ	zɛ	Ч	ч	𝒞	𝑣	че	tʃɛ
И	и	𝒰	𝑢	и	i	Ш	ш	𝒲	𝑤	ша	ʃa
Й	й	𝒰̆	𝑢̆	и[1]		Щ	щ	𝒲̦	𝑤̦	ща	ʃtʃa
К	к	𝒦	𝑘	ка	ka	Ъ	ъ	–	𝑏	[2]	
Л	л	ℒ	𝑙	эль	ɛļ	Ы	ы	–	𝑏𝑙	ы[3]	ɨ
М	м	ℳ	𝑚	эм	ɛm	Ь	ь	–	𝑏	[4]	
Н	н	ℋ	𝑛	эн	ɛn	Э	э	𝟹	𝑒	э[5]	ɛ
О	о	𝒪	𝑜	о	ɔ	Ю	ю	𝒥𝒪	𝑢	ю	iu
						Я	я	𝒜	𝑎	я	ia

[1] и краткое short i
[2] твёрдый знак hard sign
[3] *or* еры́
[4] мягкий знак soft sign
[5] э оборо́тное reversed e

Important English Irregular Verbs

alight	alighted, alit	alighted, alit
arise	arose	arisen
awake	awoke	awoken, awaked
be (am, is, are)	was (were)	been
bear	bore	borne
beat	beat	beaten
become	became	become
begin	began	begun
behold	beheld	beheld
bend	bent	bent
beseech	besought, beseeched	besought, beseeched
bet	bet, betted	bet, betted
bid	bade, bid	bidden, bid
bind	bound	bound
bite	bit	bitten
bleed	bled	bled
blow	blew	blown
break	broke	broken
breed	bred	bred
bring	brought	brought
broadcast	broadcast	broadcast
build	built	built
burn	burnt, burned	burnt, burned
burst	burst	burst
bust	bust(ed)	bust(ed)
buy	bought	bought
cast	cast	cast
catch	caught	caught
choose	chose	chosen
cleave (*cut*)	clove, cleft	cloven, cleft
cling	clung	clung
come	came	come
cost	cost	cost
creep	crept	crept
crow	crowed, crew	crowed
cut	cut	cut
deal	dealt	dealt
dig	dug	dug
do	did	done
draw	drew	drawn
dream	dreamt, dreamed	dreamt, dreamed
drink	drank	drunk
drive	drove	driven
dwell	dwelt, dwelled	dwelt, dwelled
eat	ate	eaten
fall	fell	fallen
feed	fed	fed
feel	felt	felt
fight	fought	fought
find	found	found
flee	fled	fled

fling	flung	flung
fly	flew	flown
forbear	forbore	forborne
forbid	forbad(e)	forbidden
forecast	forecast(ed)	forecast(ed)
forget	forgot	forgotten
forgive	forgave	forgiven
forsake	forsook	forsaken
freeze	froze	frozen
get	got	got, *Am.* gotten
give	gave	given
go	went	gone
grind	ground	ground
grow	grew	grown
hang	hung, (*v/t*) hanged	hung, (*v/t*) hanged
have	had	had
hear	heard	heard
heave	heaved, hove	heaved, hove
hew	hewed	hewed, hewn
hide	hid	hidden
hit	hit	hit
hold	held	held
hurt	hurt	hurt
keep	kept	kept
kneel	knelt, kneeled	knelt, kneeled
know	knew	known
lay	laid	laid
lead	led	led
lean	leaned, leant	leaned, leant
leap	leaped, leapt	leaped, leapt
learn	learned, learnt	learned, learnt
leave	left	left
lend	lent	lent
let	let	let
lie	lay	lain
light	lighted, lit	lighted, lit
lose	lost	lost
make	made	made
mean	meant	meant
meet	met	met
mow	mowed	mowed, mown
pay	paid	paid
plead	pleaded, pled	pleaded, pled
prove	proved	proved, proven
put	put	put
quit	quit(ted)	quit(ted)
read [ri:d]	read [red]	read [red]
rend	rent	rent
rid	rid	rid
ride	rode	ridden
ring	rang	rung
rise	rose	risen
run	ran	run
saw	sawed	sawn, sawed

say	said	said
see	saw	seen
seek	sought	sought
sell	sold	sold
send	sent	sent
set	set	set
sew	sewed	sewed, sewn
shake	shook	shaken
shear	sheared	sheared, shorn
shed	shed	shed
shine	shone	shone
shit	shit(ted), shat	shit(ted), shat
shoe	shod	shod
shoot	shot	shot
show	showed	shown
shrink	shrank	shrunk
shut	shut	shut
sing	sang	sung
sink	sank	sunk
sit	sat	sat
slay	slew	slain
sleep	slept	slept
slide	slid	slid
sling	slung	slung
slink	slunk	slunk
slit	slit	slit
smell	smelt, smelled	smelt, smelled
smite	smote	smitten
sow	sowed	sown, sowed
speak	spoke	spoken
speed	sped, speeded	sped, speeded
spell	spelt, spelled	spelt, spelled
spend	spent	spent
spill	spilt, spilled	spilt, spilled
spin	spun, span	spun
spit	spat	spat
split	split	split
spoil	spoiled, spoilt	spoiled, spoilt
spread	spread	spread
spring	sprang, sprung	sprung
stand	stood	stood
stave	staved, stove	staved, stove
steal	stole	stolen
stick	stuck	stuck
sting	stung	stung
stink	stunk, stank	stunk
strew	strewed	strewed, strewn
stride	strode	stridden
strike	struck	struck
string	strung	strung
strive	strove	striven
swear	swore	sworn
sweep	swept	swept
swell	swelled	swollen

swim	swam	swum
swing	swung	swung
take	took	taken
teach	taught	taught
tear	tore	torn
tell	told	told
think	thought	thought
thrive	throve	thriven
throw	threw	thrown
thrust	thrust	thrust
tread	trod	trodden
understand	understood	understood
wake	woke, waked	woken, waked
wear	wore	worn
weave	wove	woven
wed	wed(ded)	wed(ded)
weep	wept	wept
wet	wet(ted)	wet(ted)
win	won	won
wind	wound	wound
wring	wrung	wrung
write	wrote	written

Russian – English
Dictionary

Russian – English

A

a 1. *cj.* but; **a то** or (else), otherwise; **a что ?** why (so)?; **2.** *int.* ah!; **3.** *part.*, *coll.* eh?

аб|ажу́р *m* [1] lampshade; **~ба́т** *m* [1] abbot; **~ба́тство** *n* [9] abbey; **~за́ц** *m* [1] paragraph; **~онеме́нт** *m* [1] subscription; **~оне́нт** *m* [1] subscriber; **~о́рт** *m* [1] abortion; **~рико́с** *m* [1] apricot; **~солю́тный** [14; -тен, -тна] absolute; **~стра́ктный** [14; -тен, -тна] abstract; **~су́рд** *m* [1] absurdity; **довести́ до ~су́рда** carry to the point of absurdity; **~су́рдный** [14; -ден, -дна] absurd; **~сце́сс** *m* [1] abscess

аван|га́рд *m* [1] avant-garde; **~по́ст** *m* [1] outpost; **~c** *m* [1] advance (of money); **~сом** (payment) in advance; **~тю́ра** *f* [5] adventure, shady enterprise; **~тюри́ст** *m* [1] adventurer; **~тюри́стка** *f* [5; *g/pl.*: -ток] adventuress

авар|и́йный [14] emergency...; **~и́я** *f* [7] accident; *mot.*, *ae.* crash; *tech.* breakdown

а́вгуст *m* [1] August

авиа|ба́за *f* [5] air base; **~биле́т** *m* [1] airline ticket; **~констру́ктор** *m* [1] aircraft designer; **~ли́ния** *f* [7] airline; **~но́сец** *m* [1; -сца] aircraft carrier; **~по́чта** *f* [5] air mail; **~тра́сса** *f* [5] air route; **~цио́нный** [14] air-(craft)...; **~ция** *f* [7] aviation, aircraft *pl.*

аво́сь *part.* *coll.* perhaps, maybe; **на ~** on the off chance

австр|али́ец *m* [1; -и́йца], **~али́йка** *f* [5; *g/pl.*:-и́ек], **~али́йский** [16] Australian; **~и́ец** *m* [1; -и́йца], **~и́йка** *f* [5; *g/pl.*:-и́ек], **~и́йский** [16] Austrian

автобиогра́ф|и́ческий [16], **~афи́чный** [14; -чен, -чна] autobiographic(al); **~а́фия** *f* [7] autobiography

авто́бус *m* [1] (motor) bus

авто|вокза́л *m* [1] bus *or* coach station;

~го́нки *f/pl.* [5; *gen.*: -нок] (car) race; **~гра́ф** *m* [1] autograph; **~заво́д** *m* [1] car factory, automobile plant; **~запра́вочный** [14] **~запра́вочная ста́нция** filling station; **~кра́тия** *f* [7] autocracy; **~магистра́ль** *f* [8] highway; **~ма́т** *m* [1] automaton; *игорный* slot machine; *mil.* submachine gun; *coll.* telephone box *or* booth; **~мати́ческий** [16], **~мати́чный** [14; -чен, -чна] automatic; **~ма́тчик** *m* [1] submachine gunner; **~маши́на** *f* [5] → **~моби́ль**; **~мобили́ст** *m* [1] motorist; **~моби́ль** *m* [4] (motor)-car; *го́ночный* **~моби́ль** racing car, racer; **~но́мия** *f* [7] autonomy; **~отве́тчик** *m* [1] answering machine; **~портре́т** *m* [1] self-portrait

а́втор *m* [1] author; **~изова́ть** [7] (*im*)*pf.* authorize; **~ите́т** *m* [1] authority; **~ский** [16] author's; **~ское пра́во** copyright; **~ство** *n* [9] authorship

авто|ру́чка *f* [5; *g/pl.*:-чек] fountain pen; **~стоя́нка** *f* [5; *g/pl.*: -нок] parking (space); **~стра́да** *f* [5] high-speed, multilane highway

ага́ (*int.*) aha!; (oh,) I see!

аге́нт *m* [1] agent; **~ство** *n* [9] agency

агити́ровать [7], ⟨с-⟩ *pol.* carry on agitation, campaign; *coll.* (*убеждать*) (try to) persuade

агра́рный [14] agrarian

агрега́т *m* [1] *tech.* unit, assembly

агресс|и́вный [14; -вен, -вна] aggressive; **~и́я** *f* [7] aggression

агро|но́м *m* [1] agronomist; **~номи́ческий** [16] agronomic(al); **~но́мия** *f* [7] agronomy

ад *m* [1; в **~у́**] hell

ада́птер (-тєr) *m* [1] *el.* pickup

адвока́т *m* [1] lawyer, attorney (at law), *Brt.* barrister; solicitor; **~у́ра** *f* [5] the legal profession

адеква́тный [14; -тен, -тна] (*совпа-да́ющий*) coincident; adequate

адми|нистрати́вный [14] administrative; **~нистра́ция** *f* [7] administration; **~ра́л** *m* [1] admiral

а́дрес *m* [1; *pl.*: -á, *etc. e.*] address (**не по** Д at wrong); **~а́т** *m* [1] addressee; (*грузополуча́тель*) consignee; **~ова́ть** [7] (*im*)*pf.* address, direct

а́дски *coll.* awfully, terribly

а́дский [16] hellish, infernal

адъюта́нт *m* [1] aide-de-camp

адюльте́р *m* [1] adultery

ажиота́ж *m* [1] hullabaloo; **~ный** [14; -жен, -жна]: **~ный спрос** unusually high demand (for **на** В)

аз *m* [1 *e.*]; **~ы́** *pl.* basics, elements; *coll.* **с ~о́в** from scratch

аза́рт *m* [1] passion, heat, enthusiasm; **войти́ в ~** get excited; **~ный** [14; -тен, -тна] passionate, enthusiastic; **~ные и́гры** games of chance

а́збу|ка *f* [5] alphabet; **~чный** [14] alphabetic(al); **~чная и́стина** truism

азербайджа́|нец *m* [1; -нца], **~нка** *f* [5; *g/pl.*: -нок] Azerbaijani(an); **~нский** [16] Azerbaijani(an)

азиа́т *m* [1], **~ка** *f* [5; *g/pl.*: -ток], **~ский** [16] Asian, Asiatic

азо́т *m* [1] nitrogen; **~ный** [14] nitric

а́ист *m* [1] stork

ай *int.* ah! oh!; *при боли* ouch!

айва́ *f* [5] quince

а́йсберг *m* [1] iceberg

акаде́м|ик *m* [1] academician; **~и́ческий** [16] academic; **~ия** *f* [7] academy; **Акаде́мия нау́к** academy of sciences; **Акаде́мия худо́жеств** academy of arts

ака́ция *f* [7] acacia

аквала́нг *m* [1] aqualung

акваре́ль *f* [8] water colo(u)r

акклиматизи́ровать(ся) [7] (*im*)*pf.* acclimatize

аккомпан|еме́нт *m* [1] *mus.*, *fig.* accompaniment; **~и́ровать** [7] *mus.* accompany

акко́рд *m* [1] *mus.* chord

аккредит|и́в *m* [1] letter of credit; **~ова́ть** [7] (*im*)*pf.* accredit

аккумул|и́ровать [7] (*im*)*pf.* accumulate; **~я́тор** *m* [1] battery

аккура́тный [14; -тен, -тна] (*исполни́тельный*) accurate; punctual; *рабо́та и т. д.* tidy, neat

аксессуа́ры *m* [1] accessories

акт *m* [1] act(ion); *thea.* act; document; *parl.* bill; **~ёр** *m* [1] actor

акти́в *m* [1] *fin.* asset(s); **~ный** [14; -вен, -вна] active

актри́са *f* [5] actress

актуа́льный [14; -лен, -льна] topical, current

аку́ла *f* [5] shark

акусти́|ка *f* [5] acoustics; **~ческий** [16] acoustic(al)

акуше́р|ка *f* [5; *g/pl.*: -рок] midwife; **~ство** *n* [9] obstetrics, midwifery

акце́нт *m* [1] accent; (*ударе́ние*) stress

акци|оне́р *m* [1] stockholder, *Brt.* shareholder; **~оне́рный** [14] jointstock (company); **~они́ровать** [7] turn into a joint-stock company; **~я¹** [7] share; *pl. a.* stock; **~я²** *f* [7] action, démarche

алба́н|ец *m* [1; -ца], **~ка** *f* [5; *g/pl.*: -ок], **~ский** [16] Albanian

а́лгебра *f* [5] algebra

алеба́стр *m* [1] alabaster

але́ть [8] blush, grow red; *заря́ и т. д.* glow

алиме́нты *m/pl.* [1] alimony

алкого́л|ик *m* [1] alcoholic; **~ь** *m* [4] alcohol

аллегори́ческий [16] allegorical

аллерг|е́н *m* [1] allergen; **~ик** *m* [1] one prone to allergy; **~и́ческий** [16] allergic; **~и́я** *f* [7] allergy

алле́я *f* [6; *g/pl.*: -е́й] avenue, lane

алма́з *m* [1], **~ный** [14] *uncut* diamond

алта́рь *m* [4 *e.*] altar

алфави́т *m* [1] alphabet; **~ный** [14] alphabetical

а́лчн|ость *f* [7] greed(iness); **~ый** [14; -чен, -чна] greedy (of, for **к** Д)

а́лый [14 *sh.*] red

альбо́м *m* [1] album; sketchbook

альмана́х *m* [1] literary miscellany

альпини́|зм *m* [1] mountaineering; **~ст** *m* [1], **~стка** *f* [5; *g/pl.*: -ток] mountain climber

альт *m* [1 *e.*] alto; *инструмент* viola

алюми́ний *m* [3] alumin(i)um

амба́р *m* [1] barn; *для хранения зерна* granary

амбулато́рный [14]: ~ **больно́й** outpatient

америка́н|ец *m* [1; -нца], ~**ка** *f* [5; *g/pl.*: -ок], ~**ский** [16] American

ами́нь *part.* amen

амнисти́|ровать [7] (*im*)*pf.*; ~**я** *f* [7] amnesty

амортиза́|тор *m* [1] shock absorber; ~**а́ция** *f* [7] amortization, depreciation

амо́рфный [14; -фен, -фна] amorphous

амплиту́да *f* [5] amplitude

амплуа́ *n* [*indecl.*] *thea.* type, role

а́мпула *f* [5] ampoule

ампут|а́ция *f* [7] amputation; ~**и́ровать** [7] (*im*)*pf.* amputate

амфи́бия *f* [7] amphibian

амфитеа́тр *m* [1] amphitheater (-tre); *thea.* circle

ана́ли|з *m* [1] analysis; ~**зи́ровать** [7] (*im*)*pf.*, ⟨про-⟩ analyze, -se

аналоги́|ческий [14; -чен, -чна] analogous, similar; ~**я** *f* [7] analogy

анана́с *m* [1] pineapple

ана́рхия *f* [7] anarchy

анато́мия *f* [7] anatomy

анга́р *m* [1] hangar

а́нгел *m* [1] angel

анги́на *f* [5] tonsillitis

англи́|йский [16] English; ~**ст** *m* [1] specialist in English studies; ~**ча́нин** *m* [1; *pl.*: -ча́не, -ча́н] Englishman; ~**ча́нка** *f* [5; *g/pl.*: -нок] Englishwoman

анекдо́т *m* [1] anecdote; ~**и́чный** [14; -чен, -чна] anecdotal; (*маловероятный*) improbable

ане|ми́я *f* [7] anemia; ~**стези́я** (-nɛstɛ-) *f* [7] anaesthesia

ани́с *m* [1] anise

анке́та *f* [5] questionnaire; (*бланк*) form

анне́кс|и́ровать [7] (*im*)*pf.* annex; ~**и́я** *f* [7] annexation

аннули́ровать [7] (*im*)*pf.* annul, cancel

анома́лия *f* [7] anomaly

анони́мный [14; -мен, -мна] anonymous

анса́мбль *m* [4] ensemble, *thea.* company

антагони́зм *m* [1] antagonism

антаркти́ческий [16] antarctic

анте́нна (-'tɛn-) *f* [5] aerial, antenna

антибио́тик *m* [1] antibiotic

антиква́р *m* [1] antiquary; dealer in antique goods; ~**иа́т** *m* [1] antiques; ~**ный** [14] antiquarian

антило́па *f* [5] antelope

анти|пати́чный [14; -чен, -чна] antipathetic; ~**па́тия** *f* [7] antipathy; ~**санита́рный** [14] insanitary; ~**семити́зм** *m* [1] anti-Semitism; ~**се́птика** *f* [5] antisepsis, *collect.* antiseptics

анти́чн|ость *f* [8] antiquity; ~**ый** [14] ancient, classical

антоло́гия *f* [7] anthology

антра́кт *m* [1] *thea.* intermission, *Brt.* interval

антропо́л|ог *m* [1] anthropologist; ~**о́гия** *f* [7] anthropology

анчо́ус *m* [1] anchovy

аню́тины [14]: ~ **гла́зки** *m/pl.* [1; *g/pl.*: -зок] pansy

апати́|чный [14; -чен, -чна] apathetic; ~**я** *f* [7] apathy

апелли́|ровать [7] (*im*)*pf.* appeal (to **к** Д); ~**яцио́нный** [14] (*court*) of appeal; ~**яцио́нная жа́лоба** = ~**я́ция** *f* [7] *law* appeal

апельси́н *m* [1] orange

аплоди́|ровать [7], ⟨за-⟩ applaud; ~**сме́нты** *m/pl.* [1] applause

апло́мб *m* [1] self-confidence, aplomb

апоге́й *m* [3] *ast.* apogee; *fig.* climax

апо́стол *m* [1] apostle

апофео́з *m* [1] apotheosis

аппара́т *m* [1] apparatus; *phot.* camera; ~**у́ра** *f collect.* [5] apparatus, gear, *comput.* hardware

аппе́нд|икс *m* [1] *anat.* appendix; ~**ици́т** *m* [1] appendicitis

аппети́т *m* [1] appetite; **прия́тного ~а!** bon appetite!; ~**ный** [14; -йтен, -йтна] appetizing

апре́ль *m* [4] April

апте́ка *f* [5] drugstore, *Brt.* chemist's shop; ~**рь** *m* [4] druggist, *Brt.* (pharmaceutical) chemist

апте́чка *f* [5; *g/pl.*: -чек] first-aid kit

ара́|б *m* [1], ~**бка** *f* [5; *g/pl.*: -бок] Arab;

~бский (**~вийский**)[16] Arabian, Arabic, Arab (*League, etc.*); **~n** *m* [1] *obs.* Moor, Negro

арби́тр *m* [1] arbiter; umpire, referee; **~а́ж** *m* [1] *law* arbitration, arbitrage

арбу́з *m* [1] watermelon

аргенти́н|ец *m* [1; -нца], **~ка** *f* [5; *g/pl.*: -нок], **~ский** [16] Argentine

аргуме́нт *m* [1] argument, reasoning, argumentation; **~а́ция** *f* [7] reasoning, argumentation; **~и́ровать** [7] (*im)pf.* argue

аре́на *f* [5] arena

аре́нд|а *f* [5] lease, rent; **сдава́ть** (**брать**) **в ~у** lease (rent); **~а́тор** *m* [1] lessee, tenant; **~ова́ть** [7] (*im)pf.* rent, lease

аре́ст *m* [1] arrest; **~о́ванный** *su.* [14] prisoner; **~о́вывать** [1], ⟨**~ова́ть**⟩ [7] arrest

аристокра́тия *f* [7] aristocracy

аритми́я *f* [7] *med.* arrhythmia

арифме́т|ика *f* [5] arithmetic; **~и́ческий** [16] arithmetic(al)

а́рия *f* [7] aria

а́рк|а *f* [5; *g/pl.*: -рок] arc; arch

арка́да *f* [5] arcade

аркти́ческий [16] arctic

армату́ра *f* [5] fittings, armature

а́рмия *f* [7] army

армя́н|ин *m* [1; *pl.*: -мя́не, -мя́н], **~ка** *f* [5; *g/pl.*: -нок], **~ский** [16] Armenian

арома́т *m* [1] aroma, perfume, fragrance; **~и́ческий** [16], **~ный** [14; -тен, -тна] aromatic, fragrant

арсена́л *m* [1] arsenal

арте́ль *f* [8] workmen's *or* peasants' cooperative, association

арте́рия *f* [7] artery

арти́кль *m* [4] *gr.* article

артилле́р|ия *f* [7] artillery; **~и́ст** *m* [1] artilleryman; **~и́йский** [16] artillery...

арти́ст *m* [1] artist(e); actor; **~ка** *f* [5; *g/pl.*: -ток] artist(e); actress

артишо́к *m* [1] artichoke

а́рфа *f* [5] harp

архео́лог *m* [1] archeologist; **~и́ческий** [16] archeologic(al); **~ия** *f* [7] archeology

архи́в *m* [1] archives *pl.*

архиепи́скоп *m* [1] archbishop

архипела́г *m* [1] archipelago

архите́кт|ор *m* [1] architect; **~у́ра** *f* [1] architecture; **~у́рный** [14] architectural

арши́н *m* [1; *g/pl.*: арши́н]: **ме́рить на свой ~** measure by one's own yardstick

асбе́ст *m* [1] asbestos

аске́т *m* [1] ascetic; **~и́ческий** [16] ascetic(al)

аспира́нт *m* [1] postgraduate; **~у́ра** *f* [1] postgraduate study

ассамбле́я *f* [6; *g/pl.*: -ле́й]: **Генера́льная** ♀ **Организа́ции Объединённых На́ций** United Nations' General Assembly

ассигнова́|ть [7] (*im)pf.* assign, allocate, allot; **~ние** *n* [12] assignment, allocation, allotment

ассими|ли́ровать [7] (*im)pf.* assimilate, (**-ся** *o.s.*); **~я́ция** *f* [7] assimilation

ассисте́нт *m* [1], **~ка** *f* [5; *g/pl.*: -ток] assistant; *univ.* junior member of research staff

ассортиме́нт *m* [1] assortment, range

ассоци|а́ция *f* [7] association; **~и́ровать** [7] associate

а́стма *f* [5] asthma

а́стра *f* [5] aster

астроно́м *m* [1] astronomer; **~и́ческий** [16] astronomic(al) (*a. fig.*); **~ия** *f* [7] astronomy

асфа́льт *m* [1] asphalt

ата́к|а *f* [5] attack, charge; **~ова́ть** [7] (*im)pf.* attack, charge

атама́н *m* [1] ataman (*Cossack chieftan*)

ателье́ (-тɛ-) *n* [*indecl.*] studio, atelier

атланти́ческий [16] Atlantic...

а́тлас¹ *m* [1] atlas

атла́с² *m* [1] satin

атле́т *m* [1] athlete; **~ика** *f* [5] athletics; **~и́ческий** [16] athletic

атмосфе́р|а *f* [5] atmosphere; **~ный** [16] atmospheric

а́том *m* [1] atom; **~ный** [14] atomic

атрибу́т *m* [1] attribute

аттеста́т *m* [1] certificate; **~ зре́лости** school-leaving certificate

ауди|е́нция *f* [7] audience; **~то́рия** *f* [7] lecture hall; (*слушатели*) audience

аукцио́н *m* [1] auction (**с** Р by)

афе́р|а *f* [5] speculation, fraud, shady

deal; **~ист** m [1], **~истка** f [5; g/pl.: -ток] speculator, swindler

афиш|а f [5] playbill, poster; **~ировать** [7] *impf.* parade, advertise, make known

афори́зм m [1] aphorism

африка́н|ец m [1; -нца], **~ка** f [5; g/pl.: -нок], **~ский** [16] African

ах *int.* ah!; **~ать** [1], *once* ⟨**~нуть**⟩ [20] groan, sigh; (*удиви́ться*) be amazed

ахине́|я f [7] *coll.* nonsense; **нести́ ~ю** talk nonsense

ацетиле́н m [1] acetylene

аэро́|бус m [1] airbus; **~дина́мика** f [5] aerodynamics; **~дро́м** m [1] airdrome (*Brt.* aero-); **~по́рт** m [1] airport; **~сни́мок** m [1; -мка] aerial photograph; **~ста́т** m [1] balloon; **~съёмка** f [5; g/pl.: -мок] aerial survey

Б

б → бы

ба́б|а f [5] married peasant woman; **сне́жная ~а** snowman; **~а-яга́** f old witch (*in Russian folk-tales*), hag; **~ий** [18]: **~ье ле́то** Indian summer; **~ьи ска́зки** f/pl. old wives' tales; **~ка** f [5; g/pl.: -бок] grandmother; **~очка** f [5; g/pl.: -чек] butterfly; **~ушка** f [5; g/pl.: -шек] grandmother, granny

бага́ж m [1 *e.*] baggage, *Brt.* luggage; **ручно́й ~** small baggage; **сдать в ~** check one's baggage, *Brt.* register one's luggage; **~ник** m [1] *mot.* trunk, *Brt.* boot; **~ный** [14]; **~ый ваго́н** baggage car, *Brt.* luggage van

багро́в|еть [8], ⟨по-⟩ turn crimson, purple; **~ый** [14 *sh.*] purple, crimson

бадминто́н m [1] badminton

ба́за f [5] base, basis, foundation; *учреждение* depot, center (-tre)

база́р m [1] market, bazaar; *coll.* uproar, row; **~ный** [14] market...

бази́ровать [7] *impf.* base (**на** П on); **~ся** rest *or* base (**на** П on)

ба́зис m [1] basis

байда́рка f [5; g/pl.: -рок] canoe, kayak

ба́йка f [5] flannelette

байт m [1] *comput.* byte

бак m [1] *naut.* forecastle; container, receptacle; tank, cistern

бакале́йный [14]: **~ейный магази́н** grocery, grocer's store (*Brt.* shop); **~ейные това́ры** m/pl. = **~ея** f [6] groceries pl.

ба́кен m [1] beacon

бак|енба́рды f/pl. [5], **~и** m/pl. [1; *gen.:* бак] side-whiskers

баклажа́н m [1] aubergine

баклу́ши: бить ~ *coll.* idle, dawdle, fritter away one's time

бактерио́лог m [1] bacteriologist; **~и́ческий** [16] bacteriological; **~ия** f [7] bacteriology

бакте́рия f [7] bacterium

бал m [1; на ~у́; *pl. e.*] ball, dance (**на** П at)

балага́н m [1] booth (*at fairs*); *fig.* farce; noise and bustle

балагу́р m [1] *coll.* joker; **~ить** *coll.* [13] jest, crack jokes

балала́йка f [5; g/pl.: балала́ек] balalaika

баламу́тить [15], ⟨вз-⟩ *coll.* stir up, trouble

бала́нс m [1] balance (*a. comm.*); **торго́вый бала́нс** balance of trade; **~и́ровать** [7] balance; **~овый** [14] balance...

балахо́н m [1] *coll.* loose overall; shapeless garment

балбе́с m [1] *coll.* simpleton, booby

балда́ m/f [5] sledgehammer; *coll.* blockhead, dolt

бале́р|ина f [5] (female) ballet dancer; **~т** m [1] ballet

ба́лка¹ f [5; g/pl.: -лок] beam, girder

ба́лка² f [5; g/pl.: -лок] gully, ravine

балка́нский [16] Balkan...

балко́н m [1] balcony

балл *m* [1] grade, mark (*in school*);
point (*sport*)

балла́да *f* [5] ballad

балла́ст *m* [1] ballast

баллисти́ческий [16] ballistic

балло́н *m* [1] balloon (*vessel*); container, cylinder

баллоти́роваться [7] run (**в** B for), be a candidate (**в, на** B for)

ба́лов|анный [14 *sh*.] *coll.* spoiled; **-а́ть** [7] (*a.* **-ся**) be naughty; trifle with; ⟨из-⟩ spoil, coddle; **-ень** *m* [4; -вня] darling, pet; **-ство́** *n* [9] mischievousness; spoiling, pampering

балти́йский [16] Baltic...

бальза́м *m* [1] balsam, balm

балюстра́да *f* [5] balustrade

бамбу́к *m* [1] bamboo

бана́ль|ность *f* [8] banality; commonplace; **-ный** [14; -лен, -льна] banal, trite

бана́н *m* [1] banana

ба́нда *f* [5] band, gang

банда́ж *m* [1 *e*.] bandage; truss

бандеро́ль *f* [8] wrapper for mailing (*newspapers, etc.*); designation for printed matter, book post

банди́т *m* [1] bandit, gangster; **-и́зм** *m* [1] gangsterism

банк *m* [1] bank

ба́нка *f* [5; *g/pl*.: -нок] jar; (**консе́рвная**) **~** can, *Brt.* tin

банке́т *m* [1] banquet

банки́р *m* [1] banker

банкно́т *m* [1] bank note

банкро́т *m* [1] bankrupt; **-иться** [15], ⟨о-⟩ go bankrupt; **-ство** *n* [9] bankruptcy

бант *m* [1] bow

ба́нщик *m* [1] bathhouse attendant

ба́ня *f* [6] (Russian) bath(s)

бапти́ст *m* [1] Baptist

бар *m* [1] (snack) bar; **-мен** *m* [1] barman

бараба́н *m* [1] drum; **-ить** [13], ⟨про-⟩ (beat the) drum; **-ный** [14]: **-ный бой** beat of the drum; **-ная перепо́нка** eardrum; **-щик** *m* [1] drummer

бара́к *m* [1] barracks; hut

бара́н *m* [1] ram; P idiot, ass; **-ий** [18] sheep's; mutton; **согну́ть в -ий рог**

to make s.b. knuckle under; **-ина** *f* [5] mutton

бара́нка *f* [5; *g/pl*.: -нок] ringshaped roll; *coll.* steering wheel

барахло́ *n* [9] old clothes; disused goods and chattels, *Brt.* lumber; trash, junk

бара́хтаться [1] *coll.* flounder

барбари́с *m* [1] barberry

бард *m* [1] bard (*poet and singer*)

барда́к *m* [1] *coll.* complete chaos; P brothel

барелье́ф *m* [1] bas-relief

ба́ржа *f* [5] barge

ба́рий *m* [3] barium

ба́рин *m* [1; *pl*.: ба́ре *or* ба́ры, бар] member of landowning gentry in prerevolutionary Russia; *coll.* refers to s.b. affecting an air of superiority

барито́н *m* [1] baritone

барка́с *m* [1] launch, long boat

баро́кко *n* [*indecl.*] baroque

баро́метр *m* [1] barometer

баррика́да *f* [5] barricade

барс *m* [1] snow leopard

ба́р|ский [16] lordly; **жить на -скую но́гу** live in grand style

барсу́к *m* [1 *e*.] badger

ба́рхат *m* [1] velvet; **-ный** [14] velvet(y)

ба́рыня *f* [6] barin's wife; *coll.* refers to s.b. acting in a haughty manner

бары́ш *m* [1 *e*.] profit, gain(s)

ба́рышня *f* [6; *g/pl*.: -шень] *iro. or joc.* young lady, miss

барье́р *m* [1] barrier

бас *m* [1; *pl. e*.] *mus.* bass

баск *m* [1] Basque

баскетбо́л *m* [1] basketball

басно|пи́сец *m* [1; -сца] fabulist; **-сло́вный** [14; -вен, -вна] legendary; *coll.* fabulous, incredible

ба́сня *f* [6; *g/pl*.: -сен] fable

бассе́йн *m* [1]: **~ реки́** river basin; **пла́вательный ~** swimming pool

ба́ста that will do; no more of this!

бастио́н *m* [1] bastion

бастова́ть [7], ⟨за-⟩ (be *or* go on) strike

батальо́н *m* [1] battalion

батаре́|йка *f* [5; *g/pl*.: -ре́ек] (dry cell) battery; **-я** *f* [6; *g/pl*.: -е́й] *mil., tech.* battery; **-я парово́го отопле́ния** (central heating) radiator

батист m [1] cambric; **~овый** [14] of cambric

батон m [1] long loaf of bread

батюшка m [5; g/pl.: -шек] coll. father; (as mode of address to priest) father

бахвал P m [1] braggart; **~иться** [13] boast, brag; **~ьство** n [9] bragging, vaunting

бахрома f [5] fringe

бахчеводство n [9] melon growing

бациллоноситель m [4] bacilluscarrier

башенка f [5; g/pl.: -нок] turret

башка P f [5] head, noddle

башковитый [14 sh.] coll. brainy

башмак m [1 e.] shoe; **быть под ~ом** be under the thumb of

башня f [6; g/pl.: -шен] tower; mil. turret

баюкать [1], ⟨y-⟩ lull; rock (to sleep)

баян m [1] (kind of) accordion

бдение n [12] vigil, watch

бдительность f [8] vigilance; **~ный** [14; -лен, -льна] vigilant, watchful

бег m [1; на -ý] run(ning); pl. [**бега** etc. e.] race(s); **~ с барьерами** hurdle race; **на короткие дистанции** sprint; **на -ý** while running → **бегом**

бегание n [12] running (a. for s.th., on business)

бегать [1], ⟨по-⟩ run (around); coll. shun (a. p. **от** P); fig. run after (a. p. **за** T); **взапуски** coll. race, vie in a run

бегемот m [1] hippopotamus

беглец m [1 e.] runaway

беглость f [6] речи fluency; cursoriness; **~ый** [14] fluent; cursory

беговой [14] race...; **~ом** on the double; **~отнá** coll. f [6] running about, bustle; **~ство** n [9] flight, escape; **паническое** stampede; **обратить в ~ство** put to flight

бегун m [1 e.] runner, trotter

беда f [5; pl.: бéды] misfortune, disaster, trouble; **что за ~?** what does it matter?; **не беда** that doesn't matter; **там нет беды в том** there's no harm in that; **в тóм-то и ~** that's the trouble; the trouble is (that)...; **на беду** coll. unluckily; **прóсто ~!** it's awful!

бедненький [16] poor, pitiable; **~нéть** [8], ⟨о-⟩ grow (become) poor; **~ность** f [8] poverty; **~нотá** f [5] collect. the poor; **~ный** [14; -ден, -днá, -дно] poor (T in); **~нягá** coll. m/f [5], **~няжка** coll. m/f [5; g/pl.: -жек] poor fellow, wretch; **~няк** m [1 e.] poor man, pauper

бедро n [9; бёдра, -дер, -драм] thigh; hip; loin

бедственный [14 sh.] disastrous, calamitous; **~енное положение** disastrous situation; **~ие** n [12] distress, disaster; **стихийное ~ие** natural calamity; **~овать** [7] suffer want, live in misery

бежевый [14] beige

беженец m [1; -нца], **~ка** f [5; g/pl.: -нок] refugee

без, **~о** (P) without; in the absence of; less; (in designations of time) to: **~ чéтверти час** a quarter to one; **~о всегó** without anything; **без вас** a. in your absence

безаварийный [14; -йен, -ийна] tech. accident-free

безалаберный coll. [14; -рен, -рна] disorderly, slovenly

безалкогольный [14] nonalcoholic

безапелляционный [14; -онен, -óнна] categorical, peremptory

безбéдный [14; -ден, -дна] welloff, comfortable

безбилéтный [14] ticketless; **~ пассажир** на корабле stowaway, passenger traveling without a ticket

безбóжный [14; -жен, -жна] irreligious; coll. shameless, scandalous; **~ые цéны** outrageous prices

безболéзненный [14 sh.] painless

безбородый [14] beardless

безбоязненный [14 sh.] fearless

безбрáчие n [12] celibacy

безбрéжный [14; -жен, -жна] boundless

безвéрие n [12] unbelief

безвéстный [14; -тен, -тна] unknown, obscure

безвéтренный [14 sh.], **~ие** n [12] calm

безви́нный [14; -и́нен, -и́нна] guiltless, innocent

безвку́с|ица f [5] tastelessness, bad taste; ~ный [14; -сен, -сна] tasteless, insipid

безвла́стие n [12] anarchy

безво́дный [14; -ден, -дна] arid

безвозвра́тный [14; -тен, -тна] irrevocable, irretrievable

безвозме́здный (-mezn-) [14] gratuitous; without compensation

безволо́сый [14] hairless, bald

безво́льный [14; -лен, -льна] lacking willpower, weak-willed

безвре́дный [14; -ден, -дна] harmless

безвре́менный [14] premature, untimely

безвы́ездный (-jiznyj) [14] uninterrupted, continuous

безвы́ходный [14; -ден, -дна] 1. permanent; 2. desperate, hopeless

безголо́вый [14] headless; *fig.* stupid, brainless

безгра́мотн|ость f [8] illiteracy, ignorance; ~ый [14; -тен, -тна] illiterate, ignorant

безграни́чный [14; -чен, -чна] boundless, limitless

безда́рный [14; -рен, -рна] untalented, ungifted; (*of a work of art*) feeble, undistinguished

безде́йств|ие n [12] inaction; ~овать [7] be inactive, idle

безде́л|ица f [5]; ~ка f [5; *g/pl.:* -лок] trifle, bagatelle; ~у́шка f [5; *g/pl.:* -шек] knickknack

безде́лье n [12] idleness; ~ник m [1], ~ница f [5] idler; good-for-nothing; ~ничать [1] idle, lounge

безде́нежье n [10] lack of money, impecuniousness

безде́тный [14; -тен, -тна] childless

безде́ятельный [14; -лен, -льна] inactive, sluggish

бе́здна f [5] abyss, chasm; *fig. coll.* lots (of)

бездоказа́тельный [14; -лен, -льна] unsubstantiated

бездо́мный [14; -мен, -мна] homeless

бездо́нный [14; -до́нен, -до́нна] bottomless; *fig.* unfathomable

бездоро́жье n [12] impassability; absence of roads; prohibitive road conditions

бездохо́дный [14; -ден, -дна] unprofitable

безду́мный [14; -мен, -мна] unthinking, thoughtless

безду́шный [14; -шен, -шна] heartless, soulless

безе́ n [*indecl.*] meringue

безжа́лостный (bi33-sn-) [14; -тен, -тна] ruthless, merciless

безжи́зненный (bi33-) [14] lifeless; inanimate; *fig.* dull

беззабо́тный [14; -тен, -тна] carefree, lighthearted; careless

беззаве́тный [14; -тен, -тна] selfless; unreserved

беззако́н|ие n [12] lawlessness; unlawful act; ~ность f [8] illegality; ~ный [14; -о́нен, -о́нна] illegal, unlawful

беззасте́нчивый [14 *sh.*] shameless; impudent; unscrupulous

беззащи́тный [14; -тен, -тна] defenseless; unprotected

беззвёздный (-zn-) [14; -ден, -дна] starless

беззву́чный [14; -чен, -чна] soundless, silent, noiseless

беззло́бный [14; -бен, -бна] good-natured, kind

беззу́бый [14] toothless; *fig.* feeble

безли́кий [16 *sh.*] featureless, faceless

безли́чный [14; -чен, -чна] without personality; impersonal

безлю́дный [14; -ден, -дна] deserted, uninhabited; (*малонаселённый*) sparsely populated

безме́рный [14; -рен, -рна] immeasurable; immense

безмо́зглый [14] *coll.* brainless, stupid

безмо́лв|ие n [12] silence; ~ный [14; -вен, -вна] silent, mute

безмяте́жный [14; -жен, -жна] serene, tranquil, untroubled

безнадёжный [14; -жен, -жна] hopeless

безнадзо́рный [14; -рен, -рна] uncared for; neglected

безнака́занный [14 *sh.*] unpunished

безнали́чный [14] without cash transfer; **~ расчёт** *fin.* clearing

безнра́вственный [14 *sh.*] immoral

безоби́дный [14; -ден, -дна] inoffensive; harmless

безо́блачный [14; -чен, -чна] cloudless; serene

безобра́з|ие *n* [12] ugliness; outrage; disgrace; **~ие!** scandalous! shocking!; **~ничать** [1] behave outrageously; get up to mischief; **~ный** [14; -зен, -зна] ugly; shameful, disgusting

безогово́рочный [14; -чен, -чна] unconditional, unreserved

безопа́с|ность *f* [8] safety; security; **Сове́т 2ности** Security Council; **~ный** [14; -сен, -сна] safe, secure (**от** P from); **~ная бри́тва** safety razor

безору́жный [14; -жен, -жна] unarmed; *fig.* defenseless

безостано́вочный [14; -чен, -чна] unceasing; nonstop...

безотве́тный [14; -тен, -тна] without response; *любовь* unrequited; (*кроткий*) meek

безотве́тственный [14 *sh.*] irresponsible

безотка́зный [14; -зен, -зна] without a hitch; troublefree; *tech.* faultless; reliable

безотлага́тельный [14; -лен, -льна] undelayable, urgent

безотноси́тельно *adv.* irrespective (of **к** Д)

безотра́дный [14; -ден, -дна] cheerless

безотчётный [14; -тен, -тна] not liable to account; not subject to control; inexplicable: *e.g.,* **~ страх** unaccountable fear

безоши́бочный [14; -чен, -чна] faultless; correct; unerring

безрабо́т|ица *f* [5] unemployment; **~ный** [14] unemployed

безра́достный [14; -тен, -тна] joyless; dismal

безразде́льный [14; -лен, -льна] individed; whole-hearted

безразли́ч|ие *n* [12] (**к** Д) indifference; **~ный** [14; -чен, -чна] indifferent; **это мне ~но** it is all the same to me

безрассу́дный [14; -ден, -дна] reckless, rash

безрезульта́тный [14; -тен, -тна] futile, unsuccessful, ineffectual

безро́потный [14; -тен, -тна] uncomplaining humble, meek, submissive

безрука́вка *f* [5; *g/pl.:* -вок] sleeveless jacket *or* blouse

безуда́рный [14; -рен, -рна] unaccented unstressed

безуде́ржный [14; -жен, -жна] unrestrained; impetuous

безукори́зненный [14 *sh.*] irreproachable, impeccable

безу́м|ец *m* [1; -мца] *fig.* madman, lunatic; madcap; **~ие** *n* [12] madness, folly; **~ный** [14; -мен, -мна] crazy, insane; nonsensical, absurd; ill-considered, rash

безумо́лчный [14; -чен, -чна] incessant, uninterrupted

безу́мство *n* [9] madness; foldhardiness

безупре́чный [14; -чен, -чна] blameless, irreproachable

безусло́в|но certainly, surely; **~ный** [14; -вен, -вна] absolute, unconditional; (*несомненный*) indisputable, undoubted

безуспе́шный [14; -шен, -шна] unsuccessful

безуста́нный [14; -а́нен, -а́нна] tireless, indefatigable

безуте́шный [14; -шен, -шна] inconsolable

безуча́стный [14; -тен, -тна] apathetic, unconcerned

безъя́дерный [14] nuclear-free

безымя́нный [14] nameless, anonymous; **~ па́лец** ring finger

безыску́сный [14; -сен, -сна] artless, unaffected, unsophisticated

безысхо́дный [14; -ден, -дна] hopeless, desperate

бейсбо́л *m* [14] baseball

беко́н *m* [1] bacon

беле́сый [14] whitish

беле́ть [8], ⟨по-⟩ grow *or* turn white; *impf.* (*a.* **-ся**) appear *or* show white

белиберда́ *f* [14] *coll.* nonsense, rubbish

белизна́ f [5] whiteness

бели́|ла n/pl. [9]: **свинцо́вые ~** white lead; **ци́нковые ~** zinc white

бели́ть [13; белю́, бели́шь, белённый] **1.** ⟨вы́-⟩ bleach; **2.** ⟨по-⟩ whitewash

бе́лка f [5; g/pl.: -лок] squirrel

белко́вый [14] albuminous

беллетри́стика f [5] fiction

белобры́сый [14] coll. flaxenhaired, tow-haired

белова́тый [14 sh.] whitish

бело|ви́к m [1 e.], **~во́й э́кземпля́р** fair copy; **~гварде́ец** m [1; -е́йца] White Guard (member of troops fighting against the Red Guards and the Red Army in the Civil War 1918-1920)

бело́к m [1; -лка́] albumen, protein; white (of egg or eye)

бело|кро́вие n [12] leukemia; **~ку́рый** [14 sh.] blond, fair; **~ру́с** m [1], **~ру́ска** f [5; g/pl.: -сок], **~ру́сский** [16] Byelorussian; **~сне́жный** [14; -жен, -жна] snowhite

белу́га f [5] white sturgeon

бе́л|ый [14; бел, -а́, -о] white; **~ый свет** (wide) world; **~ые стихи́** m/pl. blank verse; **средь ~а дня** coll. in broad daylight

бель|ги́ец m [1; -ги́йца], **~ги́йка** f [5; g/pl.: -ги́ек], **~ги́йский** [16] Belgian

бельё n [12] linen; **ни́жнее ~** underwear

бельмо́ n [9; pl.: бе́льма, бельм] walleye; **она́ у меня́ как ~ на глазу́** she is an eyesore to me

бельэта́ж m [1] thea. dress circle; second (Brt. first) floor

бемо́ль m [4] flat

бенефи́с m [1] benefit(-night)

бензи́н m [1] gasoline, Brt. petrol

бензо|ба́к m [1] gasoline or petrol tank; **~коло́нка** (a. **запра́вочная ~коло́нка**) [5; g/pl.: -нок] gas or petrol pump, coll. gas or filling station

бенуа́р m [1] thea. parterre box

бе́рег [1; на-гу́; pl.: -ра́, etc. e.] bank, **морско́й**, shore, coast; (suua) land; **вы́йти (вы́ступить) из ~о́в** overflow the banks; **приста́ть к ~у** land; **~ово́й** [14] coast(al), shore…

бережли́вый [14 sh.] economical

бе́режный [14; -жен, -жна] cautious, careful

берёза f [5] birch tree; rod or bundle of twigs for flogging

березня́к m [1 e.] birch grove

берёзовый [14] birch(en)

бере́мен|ная [14] pregnant; **~ность** f [8] pregnancy

бере́т m [1] beret

бере́чь [26 г/ж: берегу́, бережёшь] **1.** ⟨по-⟩ guard, watch (over); **2.** ⟨по-, с-⟩ spare, save, take care of; **3.** ⟨с-⟩ [сбережённый] keep; preserve; **-ся** take care (of o.s.); **береги́сь!** take care! look out!

берло́га f [5] den, lair

берцо́|вый [14]: **~вая кость** shinbone

бес m [1] demon, evil spirit

бесе́д|а f [5] conversation, talk; **~ка** f [5; g/pl.: -док] arbo(u)r, summerhouse; **~овать** [7] converse

бесёнок m [2; -нка; pl.: бесеня́та] imp

беси́ть [15], ⟨вз-⟩ [взбешённый] enrange, madden; **-ся** (fly into a) rage; (резви́ться) romp

бесконе́ч|ность f [8] infinity; **до ~ности** endlessly; **~ный** [14; -чен, -чна] разговор и т. д. endless, infinite; простра́нство, любо́вь unlimited, eternal; **~но ма́лый** infinitesimal

бесконтро́льный [14; -лен, -льна] uncontrolled, unchecked

бескоры́ст|ие n [12] unselfishness; **~ный** [14; -тен, -тна] disinterested

бескра́йний [15; -а́ен, -а́йна] boundless

бескро́вный [14; -вен, -вна] anemic, pale, lacking vitality

бескульту́рье n [10] lack of culture

бесно|ва́ться [7] be possessed, rage, rave

бесо́вщина f [5] devilry

беспа́мятство n [9] unconsciousness, frenzy, delirium

беспарти́йный [14] pol. independent; non-party (man)

бесперебо́йный [14; -бо́ен, -бо́йна] uninterrupted, regular

беспереса́дочный [14] direct (as a train), through…

бесперспекти́вный [14; -вен, -вна]

having no prospects, hopeless

беспе́ч|ность *f* [8] carelessness; **~ный** [14; -чен, -чна] careless

беспла́тный [14; -тен, -тна] free (of charge), gratuitous; **~но** gratis

беспло́д|ие *n* [12] barrenness, sterility; **~ный** [14; -ден, -дна] barren, sterile; *fig.* fruitless, vain

беспово́ро́тный [14; -тен, -тна] unalterable, irrevocable, final

бесподо́бный [14; -бен, -бна] incomparable, matchless

беспозвоно́чный [14] invertebrate

беспоко́|ить [13], ⟨(п)о-⟩ upset, worry; (*меша́ть*) disturb, bother, trouble; **-ся** worry, be anxious (**о** П about); **~о́йный** [14; -ко́ен, -ко́йна] restless; uneasy; **~о́йство** *n* [9] unrest; trouble; anxiety; *прости́те за* **~о́йство** sorry to (have) trouble(d) you

беспол́езный [14; -зен, -зна] useless

беспо́мощный [14; -щен, -щна] helpless

беспоря́до|к *m* [1; -дка] disorder, confusion; *pl.* disturbances, riots; **~чный** [14; -чен, -чна] disorderly, untidy

беспоса́дочный [14]: *перелёт* **~** nonstop flight

беспо́чвенный [14 *sh.*] groundless, unfounded

беспо́шлинный [14] duty-free

беспоща́дный [14; -ден, -дна] pitiless, ruthless, relentless

беспреде́льный [14; -лен, -льна] boundless, infinite, unlimited

беспредме́тный [14; -тен, -тна] aimless

беспрекосло́вный [14; -вен, -вна] absolute, unquestioning, implicit

беспрепя́тственный [14 *sh.*] unhampered, unhindered, free

беспреры́вный [14; -вен, -вна] uninterrupted, continuous

беспреста́нный [14; -а́нен, -а́нна] incessant, continual

беспри́быльный [14; -лен, -льна] unprofitable

беспризо́рный [14; -рен, -рна] homeless, uncared-for

беспримерный [14; -рен, -рна] unprecedented, unparalleled

беспринци́пный [14; -пен, -пна] unprincipled, unscrupulous

беспристра́ст|ие *n* [12] impartiality; **~ный** (-sn-) [14; -тен, -тна] impartial, unprejudiced, unbias(s)ed

беспричи́нный [14; -и́нен, -и́нна] groundless; unfounded

бесприю́тный [14; -тен, -тна] homeless

беспробу́дный [14; -ден, -дна] *сон* deep; *пья́нство* unrestrained

беспросве́тный [14; -тен, -тна] pitch-dark; *fig.* hopeless

беспроце́нтный [14] interest-free; bearing no interest

беспу́тный [14; -тен, -тна] dissolute

бессвя́зный [14; -зен, -зна] incoherent, rambling

бессерде́чный [14; -чен, -чна] heartless, unfeeling, callous

бесси́л|ие *n* [12] debility; impotence; **~ьный** [14; -лен, -льна] weak, powerless, impotent

бессла́вный [14; -вен, -вна] infamous, ignominious, inglorious

бессле́дный [14; -ден, -дна] without leaving a trace, complete

бессловесный [14; -сен, -сна] speechless, dumb; silent

бессме́нный [14; -енен, -е́нна] permanent

бессме́рт|ие *n* [12] immortality; **~ный** [14; -тен, -тна] immortal

бессмы́сл|енный [14 *sh.*] senseless; meaningless; **~ица** *f* [5] nonsense

бессо́вестный [14; -тен, -тна] unscrupulous

бессодержа́тельный [14; -лен, -льна] empty, insipid, dull

бессозна́тельный [14; -лен, -льна] unconscious; (*непроизво́льный*) involuntary

бессо́нн|ица *f* [5] insomnia, **~ый** [14] sleepless

бесспо́рный [14; -рен, -рна] indisputable; doubtless, certain

бессро́чный [14; -чен, -чна] without time-limit; indefinite

бесстра́ст|ие *n* [12] dispassionateness, impassiveness; **~ный** [14; -тен, -тна] dispassionate, impassive

бесстра́ш|ие *n* [12] fearlessness; **~ный**

[14; -шен, -шна] fearless, intrepid

бесстыд|ный [14; -ден, -дна] shameless, impudent; (*непристойный*) indecent; **∼ство** *n* [9] impudence, insolence

бессчётный [14] innumerable

беста́ктн|ость *f* [8] tactlessness; tactless action; **∼ый** [14; -тен, -тна] tactless

бесталанный [14; -а́нен, -а́нна] untalented; ill-starred

бе́стия *f* [7] brute, beast; rogue

бестолко́вый [14 *sh.*] muddleheaded, confused; *человек* slowwitted

бе́столочь *f* [8] *coll.* nitwit

бестре́петный [14; -тен, -тна] intrepid, undaunted

бестсе́ллер *m* [1] bestseller

бесхара́ктерный [14; -рен, -рна] lacking character, weak-willed

бесхи́тростный [14; -тен, -тна] artless, naive, ingenuous, unsophisticated

бесхо́зный [14] *coll.* having no owner

бесхозя́йствен|ность *f* [8] careless and wasteful management; **∼ный** [14] thriftless

бесцве́тный [14; -тен, -тна] colo(u)rless, insipid

бесце́льный [14; -лен, -льна] aimless; *разговор* idle

бесце́н|ный [14; -énен, -éнна] invaluable, priceless; **∼ок** *m* [1; -нка]: *за ∼ок coll.* for a song or a trifling sum

бесцеремо́нный [14; -о́нен, -о́нна] unceremonious, familiar

бесчелове́чн|ость *f* [8] inhumanity; **∼ый** [14; -чен, -чна] inhuman, cruel

бесче́ст|ный [14; -тен, -тна] dishonest; (*непорядочный*) dishono(u)rable; **∼ье** *n* [10] dishono(u)r, disgrace

бесчи́нство [9] excess, outrage; **∼вать** [7] behave outrageously

бесчи́сленный [14 *sh.*] innumerable, countless

бесчу́вств|енный [14 *sh.*] insensible, callous, hard-hearted; **∼ие** *n* [12] insensibility (**к** Д); unconsciousness, swoon

бесшаба́шный [14; -шен, -шна] *coll.* reckless, careless; wanton

бесшу́мный [14; -мен, -мна] noiseless, quiet

бето́н *m* [1] concrete; **∼и́ровать** [7], ⟨за-⟩ concrete; **∼ный** [14] concrete...

бечёвка *f* [5; *g/pl.:* -вок] string

бе́шен|ство *n* [9] **1.** *med.* hydrophobia; **2.** fury, rage; *собака* rabid; **2.** furious, frantic, wild; **3.** *цена* enormous

библе́йский [16] Biblical; Bible...

библиографи́ческий [16] bibliographic(al)

библиоте́|ка *f* [5] library; **∼карь** *m* [4] librarian; **∼чный** [14] library...

би́блия *f* [7] Bible

би́вень *m* [4; -вня] tusk

бигуди́ *n/pl.* [*indecl.*] hair curlers

бидо́н *m* [1] can, churn; milkcan

бие́ние *n* [12] beat, throb

бижуте́рия *f* [7] costume jewel(le)ry

би́знес *m* [1] business; **∼мен** *m* [1] businessman

бизо́н *m* [1] bison

биле́т *m* [1] ticket; card; note, bill; **обра́тный ∼** round-trip ticket, *Brt.* return-ticket

билья́рд *m* [1] billiards

бино́кль *m* [4] binocular(s), **театра́льный ∼** opera glasses; **полево́й ∼** field glasses

бинт *m* [1 *e.*] bandage; **∼ова́ть** [7], ⟨за-⟩ bandage, dress

био́граф *m* [1] biographer; **∼и́ческий** [16] biographic(al); **∼ия** *f* [7] biography

био́лог *m* [1] biologist; **∼и́ческий** [16] biological; **∼ия** *f* [7] biology

биори́тм *m* [1] biorhythm

биохи́мия *f* [7] biochemistry

би́ржа *f* [5] (stock) exchange; **∼ труда́** labor registry office, *Brt.* labour exchange

биржеви́к *m* [1 *e.*] → **бро́кер**

би́рка *f* [5; *g/pl.:* -рок] label-tag, nameplate

бирюза́ *f* [5] turquoise

бис *int.* encore!

би́сер *m* [1] *coll.* (glass) beads *pl.*

бискви́т *m* [1] sponge cake

бит *m* [1] *comput.* bit

би́тва *f* [5] battle

бит|ко́м → **наби́тый**; **∼о́к** *m* [1; -тка́] (mince) meat ball

бить [бью, бьёшь; бей!; би́тый] **1.** ⟨по-⟩ beat; **2.** ⟨про-⟩ [проби́л, -би́ла, проби́-

ло] *часы* strike; **3.** ⟨раз-⟩ [разобью, -бьёшь] break, smash; **4.** ⟨у-⟩ shoot, kill, trump (*card*); **5.** *no pf.* spout; **~ в глаза́** strike the eye; **~ трево́гу** *fig.* raise an alarm; **~ отбо́й** *mst. fig.* beat a retreat; **~ ключо́м 1.** bubble; **2.** boil over; **3.** sparkle; **4.** abound in vitality; *про́бил его́ час* his hour has struck; *би́тый час m* one solid hour; **~ся** *fight;* *се́рдце* beat, struggle, toil (**над** Т); **~ся голово́й о(б) сте́ну** *fig.* beat one's head against a brick wall; **~ся об закла́д** bet; *она́ бьётся как ры́ба об лёд* she exerts herself in vain

бифште́кс *m* [1] (beef) steak
бич *m* [1 *e.*] whip; *fig.* scourge
бла́го *n* [9] good; blessing; *всех благ!* *coll.* all the best; **2веще́ние** *n* [12] Annunciation

благови́дный [14; -ден, -дна] *fig.* seemly, *предлог* specious

благоволи́ть [13] *old use* be favourably disposed (**к** Д); ⟨со-⟩ *iro.* deign

благово́н|**ие** *n* [12] fragrance; **~ный** [14] fragrant

благого|**ве́йный** [14; -ве́ен, -ве́йна] reverent, respectful; **~ве́ние** *n* [12] awe (of), reverence, respect (for) (*пе́ред* Т); **~ве́ть** [8] (*пе́ред* Т) worship, venerate

благодар|**и́ть** [13], ⟨по-, от-⟩ (В *за* В) thank (*a. p. for s.th.*); **~ность** *f* [8] gratitude; thanks; *не сто́ит ~ности* you are welcome, don't mention it; **~ный** [14; -рен, -рна] grateful, thankful (to *a. p. for s.th.* Д / *за* В); **~я́** (Д) thanks *or* owing to

благода́т|**ный** [14; -тен, -тна] *кли́мат* salubrious; *край* rich; **~ь** *f* [8] blessing; *кака́я тут ~ь!* it's heavenly here!

благоде́тель *m* [4] benefactor; **~ница** *f* [5] benefactress

благодея́ние *n* [12] good deed
благоду́ш|**ие** *n* [12] good nature, kindness; **~ный** [14; -шен, -шна] kindhearted, benign

благожела́тель|**ность** *f* [8] benevolence; **~ный** [14; -лен, -льна] benevolent

благозву́ч|**ие** *n* [12], **~ность** *f* [8] eupho-

ny, sonority; **~ный** [14; -чен, -чна] sonorous, harmonious

благ|**о́й** [16] good; **~о́е наме́рение** good intentions

благонадёжный [14; -жен, -жна] reliable, trustworthy

благонаме́ренный [14; *sh.*] well-meaning, well-meant

благополу́ч|**ие** *n* [12] well-being, prosperity, happiness; **~ный** [14; -чен, -чна] happy; safe

благоприя́т|**ный** [14; -тен, -тна] favo(u)rable, propitious; **~ствовать** [7] (Д) favo(u)r, promote

благоразу́м|**ие** *n* [12] prudence, discretion; **~ный** [14; -мен, -мна] prudent, judicious

благоро́д|**ный** [14; -ден, -дна] noble; *иде́и и т. д.* lofty; *мета́лл* precious; **~ство** *n* [9] nobility

благоскло́нный [14; -о́нен, -о́нна] favo(u)rable, well-disposed (to [-ward(s)] а р. **к** Д)

благослов|**е́ние** *n* [12] benediction, blessing; **~ля́ть** [28], ⟨**~ви́ть**⟩ [14 *e.*; -влю, -ви́шь] bless; **~ви́ть свою́ судьбу́** thank one's lucky stars

благосостоя́ние *n* [12] prosperity
благотвори́тельный [14] charitable, charity…

благотво́рный [14; -рен, -рна] beneficial, wholesome, salutary

благоустро́енный [14 *sh.*] well-equipped, comfortable; with all amenities

благоуха́|**ние** *n* [12] fragrance, odo(u)r; **~ть** [1] to be fragrant, smell sweet

благочести́вый [14 *sh.*] pious
блаже́н|**ный** [14 *sh.*] blissful; **~ство** *n* [9] bliss; **~ствовать** [7] enjoy felicity

блажь *f* [2] caprice, whim; *дурь* folly
бланк *m* [1] form; *запо́лнить ~* fill in a form

блат Р *m* [1] profitable connections; *по ~у* on the quiet, illicitly, through good connections; **~но́й** Р [14]: **~но́й язы́к** thieves' slang, cant

бледне́ть [8], ⟨по-⟩ turn pale
бледнова́тый [14 *sh.*] palish
бле́д|**ность** *f* [8] pallor; **~ный** [14; -ден, -дна́, -о] pale, *fig.* colo(u)rless, insipid;

~ный как полотно́ as white as a sheet

блёк|лый [14] faded, withered; ~нуть [21], ⟨по-⟩ fade, wither

блеск m [1] luster, shine, brilliance, glitter; fig. splendo(u)r

блест|е́ть [11; a. бле́щешь], once ⟨блеснýть⟩ shine; glitter; flash; не всё то зо́лото, что ~и́т all is not gold that glitters; блёстки (bloski) f/pl. [5; gen.: -ток] spangle; ~я́щий [17 sh.] shining, bright; fig. brilliant

блеф m [1] bluff

бле́ять [27], ⟨за-⟩ bleat

ближ|а́йший [17] (→ бли́зкий) the nearest, next; ~е nearer; ~ний [15] near(by); su. fellow creature

близ (P) near, close; ~и́ться [15; 3rd p. only], ⟨при-⟩ approach (a p. к Д); ~кий [16; -зок, -зка́, -о; comp.: бли́же], (к Д) near, close; ~кие pl. folk(s), one's family, relatives; ~ко от (P) close to, not far from; ~колежа́щий [17] nearby, neighbo(u)ring

близне́ц m [1 e.] twin

близору́кий [16 sh.] shortsighted

бли́зость f [8] nearness, proximity; об отноше́ниях intimacy

блин m [1 e.] kind of pancake; ~чик m [1] pancake

блиста́тельный [14; -лен, -льна] brilliant, splendid, magnificent

блиста́ть [1] shine

блок m [1] 1. bloc, coalition; 2. tech. pulley; unit

блок|а́да f [5] blockade; ~и́ровать [7] (im)pf. block (up)

блокно́т m [1] notebook, writing pad

блонди́н m [1] blond; ~ка f [5; g/pl.: -нок] blonde

блоха́ f [5; nom/pl.: бло́хи] flea

блуд m [1] coll. fornication; ~ный [14]: ~ный сын prodigal son

блужда́ть [1], ⟨про-⟩ roam, wander

блу́з|а f [5] (working) blouse, smock; ~ка f [5; g/pl.: -зок] (ladies') blouse

блю́дечко n [9; g/pl.: -чек] saucer

блю́до n [9] dish; еда́ course

блю́дце n [11; g/pl.: -дец] saucer

блюсти́ [25], ⟨со-⟩ observe, preserve, maintain; ~тель m [4]: ~тель поря́дка

iro. arm of the law

бля́ха f [5] name plate; number plate

боб m [1 e.] bean; haricot; оста́ться на ~а́х get nothing for one's pains

бобёр [1; -бра] beaver (fur)

бо́би́на f [5] bobbin, spool, reel

бобо́в|ый [14]: ~ые расте́ния n/pl. legumes

бобр m [1 e.], ~о́вый [14] beaver

бо́бсле́й m [3] bobsleigh

бог (bоx) m [1; vocative: бо́же from g/pl. e.] God; god, idol; ~ весть, ~ (его́) зна́ет coll. God knows; Бо́же (мой) oh God!, good gracious!; дай ⚥ God grant, I (let's) hope (so); ра́ди ⚥a for God's (goodness') sake; сла́ва ⚥! I thank God!; сохрани́ (не дай, избави, упаси́) ⚥ (бо́же) God forbid!

богат|е́ть [8], ⟨раз-⟩ grow (become) rich; ~ство n [9] wealth; ~ый [14 sh.; comp.: бога́че] rich, wealthy

богаты́рь m [4 e.] (epic) hero

бога́ч m [1 e.] rich man

боге́ма f [5] (artists leading a) Bohemian life

боги́ня f [6] goddess

Богома́терь f [8] the Blessed Virgin, Mother of God

Богоро́дица f [5] the Blessed Virgin, Our Lady

богосло́в m [1] theologian; ~ие n [12] theology, divinity; ~ский [16] theological

богослуже́ние n [12] divine service; worship, liturgy

боготвори́ть [13] worship, idolize; deify

бода́ть [1], ⟨за-⟩, once ⟨боднýть⟩ [20] (a. ~ся) butt (a. o.a.)

бо́др|ость f [8] vivacity, sprightliness; ~ствовать [20] be awake; ~ый [14; бодр, -а́, -о] sprightly, brisk, vigorous

боеви́к m [1 e.] member of revolutionary fighting group; coll. hit; ~ сезо́на hit of the season

боев|о́й [14] battle..., fighting, war..., military; live (shell etc); pugnacious, militant; ~ые де́йствия operations, hostilities; ~о́й па́рень dashing fellow

бое|головка f [5; g/pl.: -вок] warhead;

~припа́сы *m/pl.*[1] ammunition; **~спосо́бный** [14; -бен, -бна] battleworthy, effective

бое́ц *m* [1; бойца́] soldier, fighter

Бо́же → **бог**; **≈ский** [16] fair, just; **≈ственный** [14 *sh.*] divine, **~ство́** *n* [9] deity, divinity

бо́ж|ий [18] God's, divine; **я́сно как ~ий день** as clear as day

божи́ться [16 *e.*; -жу́сь, -жи́шься], ⟨по-⟩ swear

бо́жья коро́вка *f* [5; *g/pl.:* -вок] ladybird

бой *m* [3; бо́я, в бою́; *pl.:* бои́, боёв, *etc. e.*] battle, combat, fight; **брать** ⟨**взять**⟩ **бо́ем** *or* **с бо́ю** take by assault (storm); **рукопа́шный ~** close fight; **~ часо́в** the striking of a clock; **≈кий** [16; бо́ек, бойка́, бо́йко; *comp.:* бойче́(е)] brisk, lively; *ме́сто* busy; *речь* voluble, glib; **≈кость** *f* [8] liveliness

бойкоти́ровать [7] (*im*)*pf.* boycott

бо́йня *f* [6; *g/pl.:* бо́ен] slaughterhouse; *fig.* massacre, slaughter

бок *m* [1; на боку́; *pl.:* бока́, *etc. e.*] side; **на́ ~, ~ом** sideways; **~ ó ~** side by side; **под бо́ком** *coll.* close by

бока́л *m* [1] wineglass, goblet

боково́й [14] side, lateral

бокс *m* [1] boxing; **~ёр** *m* [1] boxer; **~и́ровать** [7] box

болва́н *m* [1] dolt, blockhead

болга́р|ин *m* [1; *pl.:* -ры, -р] Bulgarian; **~ка** *f* [5; *g/pl.:* -рок], **~ский** [16] Bulgarian

боле́е (→ **бо́льше**) more (than P); **~ высо́кий** higher; **~ и́ли ме́нее** more or less; **~ того́** what is more; **тем ~, что** especially as; **не ~** at (the) most

боле́зненный [14 *sh.*] sickly, ailing; *fig.* morbid; painful (*a. fig.*)

боле́знь *f* [8] sickness, illness; disease; (*mental*) disorder; sick (*leave ... по* Д)

боле́льщик *m* [1] *sport.* fan

боле́ть [8] **1.** be sick, be down (with T); *за́ кого́; о ко́м-то* be anxious (for, about *за* В, *о* П), apprehensive (*sport* support, be a fan of *за* В); **2.** [9; 3*rd p. only*] hurt, ache; *у меня́ боли́т голова́* (*зуб, го́рло*) I have a headache (a toothache, a sore throat)

болеутоля́ющ|ий [17]: **~ее сре́дство** anodyne, analgesic

боло́т|истый [14 *sh.*] boggy, swampy; **~ный** [14] bog..., swamp...; **~о** *n* [9] bog, swamp

болт *m* [1 *e.*] bolt

болта́ть [1] **1.** ⟨вз-⟩ shake up; **2.** (-ся) dangle; **3.** *coll.* ⟨по-⟩ [20] chat(ter); **~ся** *coll.* loaf *or* hang about

болтли́вый [14 *sh.*] talkative

болтовня́ *f* [6] *coll.* idle talk, gossip

болту́н *m* [1; -на́] *coll.*, **~ья** *f* [6] babbler, chatterbox

боль *f* [8] pain, ache

больни́|ца *f* [5] hospital; **вы́писаться из ~цы** be discharged from hospital; **лечь в ~цу** go to hospital; **~чный** [14] hospital...; **~чный лист** medical certificate

бо́льн|о painful(ly); P very; **мне ~о** it hurts me; **глаза́м бо́льно** my eyes smart; **~о́й** [14; бо́лен, больна́] sick, ill, sore; *su.* patient; *fig.* delicate, burning; tender; **стациона́рный ~о́й** inpatient

бо́льше bigger, more; **~ всего́** most of all; above all; **~ не** no more *or* longer; **как мо́жно ~** as much (many) as possible; **~ви́зм** *m* [1] Bolshevism; **~ви́к** *m* [1 *e.*] Bolshevik; **~ви́стский** (-visski-) [16] Bolshevist(ic)

бо́льш|ий [17] bigger, greater; **по ~ей ча́сти** for the most part; **са́мое ~ее** at most; **~инство́** *n* [9] majority; most; **~о́й** [16] big, large, great; *coll.* **взро́слый** grown-up; **~у́щий** [17] *coll.* huge

бо́мб|а *f* [5] bomb; **~арди́рова́ть** [7] bomb, shell; bombard (*a. fig.*); **~арди́ровка** *f* [5; *g/pl.:* -вок] bombardment, bombing; **~арди́ровщик** *m* [1] bomber; **~ёжка** *coll.* *f* [5; *g/pl.:* -жек] → **~арди́ровка**; **~и́ть** [14; *e.*; -блю́, -би́шь (раз-) бомблённый], ⟨раз-⟩ bomb

бомбоубе́жище *n* [11] air-raid *or* bombproof shelter

бор *m* [1; в бору́] pine wood *or* forest; *разгоре́лся сыр ~* passions flared up

бордо́ *n* [*indecl.*] claret; **~вый** [14] dark purplish red

бордю́р *m* [1] border, trimming

боре́ц *m* [1; -рца́] fighter, wrestler; *fig.* champion, partisan

борза́я *f* [14] *su.* borzoi, greyhound

бормота́ть [3], ⟨про-⟩ mutter

бо́ров *m* [1; *from g/pl. e.*] boar

борода́ *f* [5; *ac/sg.*: бо́роду; *pl.* бо́роды, боро́д, -а́м] beard

борода́вка *f* [5; *g/pl.*: -вок] wart

борода́|тый [14 *sh.*] bearded; **~ч** *m* [1 *e.*] bearded man

борозда́ *f* [5; *pl.*: бо́розды, боро́зд, -да́м] furrow; **~и́ть** [15 *e.*; -зжу́, -зди́шь], ⟨вз-⟩ furrow

борон|а́ *f* [5; *ac/sg.*: бо́рону; *pl.*: бо́роны, боро́н, -нам] harrow; **~и́ть** [13], **~ова́ть** [7], ⟨вз-⟩ harrow

боро́ться [17; борю́сь] fight, struggle (for *за* B, against *про́тив* P, wrestle)

борт *m* [1; на -у́; *nom/pl.*: -та́] *naut.* side; board; **на -у́ су́дна** on board a ship; **бро́сить** *за* **~** throw overboard; **челове́к за ~ом!** man overboard!

борщ *m* [1 *e.*] borsch(t), red-beet soup

борьба́ *f* [5] *sport* wrestling; *fig.* fight, struggle

босико́м barefoot

босо́й [14; бос, -а́, -о] barefooted; **на босу́ но́гу** wearing shoes on bare feet

босоно́гий [16] → **босо́й**

босоно́жка *f* [5; *g/pl.*: -жек] sandal

бота́ни|к *m* [1] botanist; **~ка** *f* [5] botany; **~ческий** [16] botanic(al)

ботва́ *f* [5] leafy tops of root vegetables, *esp.* beet leaves

боти́нок *m* [1; *g/pl.*: -нок] shoe, *Brt.* (lace) boot

бо́цман *m* [1] boatswain

бо́чка *f* [5; *g/pl.*: -чек] cask, barrel; **~о́вой** [14]: **~о́вое пи́во** draught beer

бочко́м sideway(s), sidewise

бочо́нок *m* [1; -нка] (small) barrel

боязли́вый [14 *sh.*] timid, timorous

боя́знь *f* [8] fear, dread; **из ~и** for fear of, lest

боя́р|ин *m* [4; *pl.*: -ре, -р], **~ыня** *f* [6] boyar(d) (*member of old nobility in Russia*)

боя́рышник *m* [1] hawthorn

боя́ться [бою́сь, бои́шься; бо́йся, бой-

те́сь], ⟨по-⟩ be afraid (of P); fear; **бою́сь сказа́ть** I don't know exactly, I'm not quite sure

бра *n* [*indecl.*] lampbracket, sconce

бра́во *int.* bravo

бразды́ *f/pl.* [5] *fig.* reins

брази́л|ец *m* [1; -льца] Brazilian; **~ьский** [16], **~ья́нка** *f* [5; *g/pl.*: -нок] Brazilian

брак¹ *m* [1] marriage; matrimony

брак² *m* [1] (*no pl.*) defective articles, rejects, spoilage

бракова́ть [7], ⟨за-⟩ scrap, reject

браконьёр *m* [1] poacher

бракосочета́ние *n* [12] wedding

брани́ть [13], ⟨по-, вы-⟩ scold, rebuke; **~ся** quarrel; swear

бра́нн|ый [14] abusive; **~ое сло́во** swearword

брань *f* [8] abuse, invective

брасле́т *m* [1] bracelet; watchband

брат *m* [1; *pl.*: бра́тья, -тьев, -тьям] brother; (*mode of address*) old boy!; **на ~а** a head, each

бра́тец *m* [1; -тца] *iro.* dear brother

бра́тия *f* [7] *coll. joc.* company, fraternity

бра́т|ский [16; *adv.*: (по-)бра́тски] brotherly, fraternal; **~ская моги́ла** communal grave; **~ство** *n* [9] brotherhood, fraternity, fellowship

брать [беру́, -рёшь; брал, -á, -о; ... бра́нный], ⟨взять⟩ [возьму́, -мёшь; взял, -á, -о; взя́тый (взят, -á, -о)] take; **~ напрока́т** hire; **~ приме́р** (с P) take (a p.) for a model; **~ верх над** (T) be victorious over, conquer; **~ обра́тно** take back; **~ сло́во** take (have) the floor; (с P) **~ сло́во** take (s.o.) promise; **~ свои́ слова́ обра́тно** withdraw one's words; **~ себя́ в ру́ки** *fig.* collect o.s., pull o.s. together; **~ на себя́** assume; **~ за пра́вило** make it a rule; **он взял и уе́хал** he left unexpectedly; **возьми́те напра́во!** turn (to the) right!; → *a.* **взима́ть; с чего́ ты взял?** what makes you think that?; **-ся** [бра́лся, -ла́сь, -ло́сь] ⟨взя́ться⟩ [взя́лся, -ла́сь, взя́ло́сь, взяли́сь] (*за* B) undertake; (*приступи́ть*) set about; (*хвата́ть*) take hold of, seize; **~ся за́ руки** join hands; **~ся за кни́гу (рабо́ту)** set about or start reading a book (working); **отку́да это берётся?** where does that come from?; **отку́да у него́ де́ньги беру́тся?** wherever does he get his money from?; **отку́да ни возьми́сь** all of a sudden

бра́чн|ый [14] matrimonial, conjugal; **~ое свиде́тельство** marriage certificate

бреве́нчатый [14] log...; **~но́** n [9; pl.: брёвна, -вен, -внам] log; beam

бред m [1] delirium; coll. nonsense; **~ить** [15], ⟨за-⟩ be delirious; fig. rave; be crazy, dream (about **о** П); **~ни** f/pl. [6; gen.: -ней] nonsense

брезг|ать [1] (Т) be squeamish, fastidious (about); (гнуша́ться) disdain; **~ли́вость** f [8] squeamishness, disgust; **~ли́вый** [14 sh.] squeamish, fastidious (in **к** Д)

брезе́нт m [1] tarpaulin

бре́зж|ить [16], **~ся** glimmer; (рассвета́ть) dawn

бре́мя n [3; no pl.] load, burden (a. fig.)

бренча́ть [4 e.; -чу́, -чи́шь] clink, jingle; **на гита́ре** strum

брести́ [25], ⟨по-⟩ drag o.s. along; saunter

брете́лька f [5; g/pl.: -лек] shoulder strap

брешь f [8] breach; gap

брига́|да f [5] brigade (a. mil.), team, group of workers; **~ди́р** m [1] foreman

бри́джи pl. [gen.: -жей] breeches

бриллиа́нт m [1], **~овый** [14] brilliant, (cut) diamond

брита́н|ец m [1; -нца] Briton, Britisher; **~ский** [16] British

бри́тва f [5] razor; **безопа́сная ~** safety razor

брить [брею, бре́ешь; брей(те)]; бре́я; брил; бри́тый], ⟨вы-, по-⟩ shave; **~ся** v/i. get shaved, (have a) shave; **~ё** n [10] shaving

бри́финг m [1] pol. briefing

бровь f [8; from g/pl. e.] eyebrow; **хму́рить ~и** frown; **он и ~ью не повёл** coll. he did not turn a hair; **попа́сть не в ~, а в глаз** coll. hit the nail on the head

брод m [1] ford

броди́ть¹ [15], ⟨по-⟩ wander, roam

броди́ть² [15] (impers.) ferment

бродя́|га m [5] tramp, vagabond; **~чий** [17] vagrant; **соба́ка** stray

броже́ние n [12] fermentation; fig. agitation, unrest

бро́кер m [1] broker

бром m [1] bromine

броне|та́нковый [14]: **~та́нковые ча́сти** f/pl. armo(u)red troops; **~транспортёр** m [1] armo(u)red personnel carrier

бро́нз|а f [5] bronze; **~овый** [14] bronze...

брони́ровать [7], ⟨за-⟩ reserve, book

бро́нх|и m/pl. [1] bronchi pl. (sg. **~** bronchus); **~и́т** m [1] bronchitis

броня́ f [6; g/pl.: -не́й] armo(u)r

бро́ня f [6; g/pl.: -ней] reservation

броса́ть [1], ⟨бро́сить⟩ throw, (a. naut.) cast, fling (a. out) (s.th. at **В** or Т/**в** В); (покину́ть) leave, abandon, desert; (прекрати́ть де́лать) give up, quit, leave off; **~ взгляд** cast a glance; **брось(те)...!** coll. (oh) stop...!; **~ся** dash, rush, dart (off **~ся бежа́ть**); fall up(on) (**на** В); go to (**в** В); **~ в глаза́** strike the eye

бро́ский [16] bright, loud

бро́совый [14] catchpenny; under (price)

бро́шка f [5; g/pl.: -шек] brooch

брошю́ра f [5] brochure, pamphlet

брус m [1; pl.: бру́сья, бру́сьев, бру́сьям] (square) beam; bar; pl. **паралле́льные бру́сья** parallel bars

брусни́ка f [5] cowberry

брусо́к m [1; -ска́] **1.** bar, ingot; **2.** (a. **точи́льный ~**) whetstone

бру́тто [indecl.] gross (weight)

брыз|гать [1 or 3], once ⟨~нуть⟩ [20] splash, spatter, sprinkle; gush; **~ги** f/pl. [5] splashes, spray

брык|а́ться [1], once ⟨~ну́ться⟩ [20] kick; fig. rebel

брюзг|а́ m/f [5] coll. grumbler, grouch; **~ли́вый** [14 sh.] peevish, grouchy;

~жа́ть [4 *e.*; -жу́, -жи́шь], ⟨за-⟩ grumble, grouch

брю́ква *f* [5] swede

брю́ки *f/pl.* [5] trousers, pants

брюне́т *m* [1] dark-haired man, brunet; ~ка *f* [5; *g/pl.*: -ток] brunette

брюссе́л|ьский [16]: ~ская капу́ста *f* Brussels sprouts

брю́хо *n* [9] belly, paunch

брюши́на *f* [5] peritoneum; ~но́й [14] abdominal; ~но́й тиф *m* typhoid fever

бря́кать [1], *once* ⟨бря́кнуть⟩ [20] *v/i.* clink, clatter; *v/t. fig. coll.* drop a clanger

бу́бен *m* [1; -бна; *g/pl.*: бу́бен] (*mst. pl.*) tambourine; ~чик *m* [1] jingle, small bell

бу́блик *m* [1] slightly sweetened ring-shaped bread roll

бу́бны *f/pl.* [5; *g/pl.*: бубён, -бнам] (*cards*) diamonds

буго́р *m* [1; -гра́] hill(ock)

бугри́стый [14] hilly; *доро́га* bumpy

бу́дет (→ быть) (*impers.*): ~ тебе́ ворча́ть stop grumbling

буди́льник *m* [1] alarm clock

буди́ть [15] 1. ⟨раз-⟩ (a)wake, waken; 2. ⟨про-⟩ [пробуждённый] *fig.* (a)rouse; ~ мысль set one thinking

бу́дка *f* [5; *g/pl.*: -док] booth, box

бу́дни *m/pl.* [1; *gen.*: -дней] weekdays; *fig.* everyday life, monotony; ~чный [14] everyday; humdrum

будора́жить [16], ⟨вз-⟩ excite

бу́дто as if, as though (*a.* ~ бы, ~ б) that, allegedly

бу́дущ|ее *n* [17] future; *в ближа́йшем* ~ем in the near future; ~ий [17] future (*a. gr.*) *в* ~ем году́ next year; ~ность *f* [8] future

бу́ер *m* [1; *pl.*: -ра, *etc. e.*] iceboat, ice yacht

бузина́ *f* [5] elder

буй *m* [3] buoy

бу́йвол *m* [1] buffalo

бу́йный [14; бу́ен, буйна́, -о] violent, vehement; (*необу́зданный*) unbridled; *расти́тельность* luxuriant

бу́йство *n* [9] rage, violence; ~вать [7] behave violently, rage

бук *m* [1] beech

бу́к|ва *f* [5] letter; *прописна́я (стро́чная)* ~ва upper-(lower)case letter (with *с* P); ~ва́льный [14] literal, verbal; ~ва́рь *m* [4 *e.*] primer; ~вое́д *m* [1] pedant

буке́т *m* [1] bouquet (*a.* of wine), bunch of flowers

букини́ст *m* [1] secondhand bookseller; ~и́ческий [16]: ~и́ческий магази́н secondhand bookshop

бу́ковый [14] beechen, beech...

букси́р *m* [1] tug(boat); *взять на букси́р* take in tow; ~ный [14] tug...; ~ова́ть [7] tow

була́вка *f* [5; *g/pl.*: -вок] pin; *англи́йская* ~ safety pin

була́т *m* [1] Damascus steel *fig.* sword; ~ный [14] steel...; damask...

бу́лка *f* [5; *g/pl.*: -лок] small loaf; roll; white bread

бу́лоч|ка *f* [5; *g/pl.*: -чек] roll; bun; ~ная *f* [14] bakery, baker's shop

булы́жник *m* [1] cobblestone

бульва́р *m* [1] boulevard, avenue; ~ный [14]: ~ный рома́н dime novel, *Brt.* penny dreadful; ~ная пре́сса tabloids; gutter press

булька́ть [1] gurgle

бульо́н *m* [1] broth; stock

бума́|га *f* [5] paper; document; *це́нные* ~ги securities; ~жка *f* [5; *g/pl.*: -жек] slip of paper; ~жник *m* [1] wallet; ~жный [14] paper...

бундеста́г *m* [1] Bundestag

бунт *m* [1] revolt, mutiny, riot; ~а́рь *m* [4 *e.*] → ~овщи́к

бунтова́ть [7] rebel, revolt; ⟨вз-⟩ instigate; ~ско́й [14] rebellious, mutinous; ~щи́к *m* [1 *e.*] mutineer, rebel

бура́в *m* [1 *e.*] gimlet, auger; ~ить [14], ⟨про-⟩ bore, drill

бура́н *m* [1] snowstorm, blizzard

бурда́ *coll. f* [5] slops, wish-wash

буреве́стник *m* [1] (storm) petrel

буре́ние *n* [12] drilling, boring

буржуа́з|ия *f* [7] bourgeoisie; ~ный [14] bourgeois

бури́ть [13], ⟨про-⟩ bore, drill

бу́ркать [1], *once* ⟨-кнуть⟩ mutter

бурли́ть [13] rage; (*кипеть*) seethe

бу́рный [14; -рен, -рна] stormy, storm...; *рост* rapid; boisterous, violent (*a.* fig.)

буру́н *m* [1 *e.*] surf, breaker

бурча́|нье *n* [12] grumbling; *в животе* rumbling; *~ть* [4 *e.*; -чу́, -чи́шь] (*бормотать*) mumble; (*ворчать*) grumble; rumble

бу́рый [14] brown, tawny; *~ медве́дь* brown bear; *~ у́голь* brown coal, lignite

бурья́н *m* [1] tall weeds

бу́ря *f* [6] storm (*a.* fig.); *~ в стака́не воды́* storm in a teacup

бу́сы *f/pl.* [5] *coll.* (glass)beads

бутафо́рия *f* [7] *thea.* properties *pl.*; *в витрине* dummies; *fig.* window dressing

бутербро́д (-тер-) *m* [1] sandwich

буто́н *m* [1] bud

бу́тсы *f/pl.* [5] football boots

буты́л|ка *f* [5; *g/pl.:* -лок] bottle; *~очка f* [5; *g/pl.:* -чек] small bottle; *~ь f* [8] large bottle; *оплетённая* carboy

бу́фер *m* [1; *pl.:* -рá, *etc. e.*] buffer

буфе́т *m* [1] sideboard; bar, lunchroom, refreshment room; *~чик m* [1] counter assistant; barman; *~чица f* [5] counter assistant; barmaid

бух *int.* bounce!, plump!

буха́нка *f* [5; *g/pl.:* -нок] loaf

бу́хать [1], *once* ⟨бу́хнуть⟩ thump, bang

бухга́лтер (bu'ha) *m* [1] bookkeeper; accountant; *~ия f* [7] bookkeeping; *~ский* [16] bookkeeper('s)..., bookkeeping...; *~ский учёт* accounting

бу́хнуть [21] 1. ⟨раз-⟩ swell; 2. → **бу́хать**

бу́хта¹ *f* [5] bay

бу́хта² *f* [5] coil (of rope)

бушева́ть [6; бушую, -уешь] roar, rage, storm

бушла́т *m* [1] (sailor's) peajacket

буя́нить [13] brawl, kick up a row

бы, *short* **б**, *is used to render subjunctive and conditional patterns*: a) *with the preterite, e.g.* **я сказа́л ~, е́сли** ~ **(я) знал** I would say it if I knew it; (*similary*: *should, could, may, might*); b) *with the infinitive, e.g.:* **всё ~ ему́ знать** *iro.* he would like to know everything; **не вам ~ говори́ть!** you had better be qui-

et; c) *to express a wish* **я ~ съел чего́нибудь** I could do with s.th. to eat

быва́лый [14] experienced

быва́|ть [1] **1.** occur, happen; **как ни в чём не** *~ло* as if nothing had happened; **она́** *~ло*, **гуля́ла** she would (*or* used to) go for a walk; **бо́ли как не** *~ло coll.* the pain had (or has) entirely disappeared; **2.** ⟨по-⟩ (*у р*) be (at), visit, stay (with)

бы́вший [17] former, ex-...

бык¹ *m* [1 *e.*] *моста* pier

бык² *m* [1 *e.*] bull

были́на *f* [5] Russian epic

были́нка *f* [5; *g/pl.:* -нок] blade of grass

бы́ло (→ **быть**) (*after verbs*) already; **я уже́ заплати́л** *~* **де́ньги** I had already paid the money, (but)...; almost, nearly, was (were) just going to...; **я чуть ~ не сказа́л** I was on the point of saying, I nearly said

был|о́й [14] bygone, former; *~о́е n* past; *~ь f* [8] true story *or* occurence

быстро|но́гий [16] swift (-footed); *~тá f* [5] quickness, swiftness, rapidity; *~хо́дный* [14; -ден, -дна] fast, high-speed

бы́стрый [14; быстр, -á, -о] quick, fast, swift

быт *m* [1; в быту́] everyday life; **семе́йный** *~* family life; *~ дереве́нской жи́зни* way of life in the country; *~ие́ n* [12] existence, social being; **Кни́га** 2*ия Bibl.* Genesis; *~ность f* [8] **в мою́** *~ность* in my time; *~ово́й* [14] everyday, social, popular, genre; *~овы́е прибо́ры* household appliances

быть [3rd *p.* sg. *pr.:* → **есть**; 3rd *p. pl.:* суть; *ft.:* бу́ду, -дешь; бу́дь[те]!; бу́дучи; был, -á, -о; нé был, -о, -и] be; (→ **бу́дет, быва́ть, бы́ло**); ~ (Д) ... will (inevitably) be or happen; **мне бы́ло (бу́дет) ... (го́да or лет)** I was (I'll be) ... (years old); **как же ~?** what is to be done?; **так и ~!** all right! agreed!; **будь что бу́дет** come what may; **будь пова́шему** have it your own way!; **бу́дьте добры́ (любе́зны)**, ... be so kind as..., would your please...; **у меня́ бы́ло мно́го свобо́дного вре́мени** I had a lot of time

бюдже́т *m* [1], *~ный* [14] budget

бюллете́нь *m* [4] bulletin; ballot paper;

coll. sick-leave certificate

бюро́ *n* [*indecl.*] office, bureau; **спра́-вочное ~** inquiry office; information; **~ путеше́ствий** travel agency *or* bureau

бюрокра́т *m* [1] bureaucrat; **~и́ческий**

[16] bureaucratic; **~и́ческая волоки́та** *f* [5] red tape; **~и́я** *f* [7] bureaucracy

бюст *m* [1] bust; **~га́льтер** (-'haltɛr) *m* [1] bra(ssiere)

бязь *f* [8] calico

В

в, во 1. (B); (*direction*) to, into; for; **в окно́** out of (in through) the window; (*time*) in, at, on, within; **в сре́ду** on Wednesday; **в два часа́** at two o'clock; (*measure, price, etc.*) at, of; **в день** a *or* per day; **длино́й в четы́ре ме́тра** four meters long; **в де́сять раз бо́льше** ten times as much; **2.** (П): *положе́ние* in, at, on; *время* in; **в конце́ (нача́ле) го́да** at the end (beginning) of the year; (*расстояние*) **в пяти́ киломе́трах от** (P) five kilometers from

ва-ба́нк: (*cards*) **идти́ ~** stake everything

ваго́н *m* [1] car(riage *Brt.*); **~ова́тый** [14] (*Brt.* tram) driver; **~-рестора́н** *m* dining car

ва́жн|ичать [1] put on (*or* give *o.s.*) airs; **~ость** *f* [8] importance; conceit; **~ый** [14; ва́жен, -жна́, -о, ва́жны] important, significant; *надменный и т. д.* haughty, pompous; *coll.* **не ~о** rather bad; **э́то не ~о** that doesn't matter *or* is of no importance

ва́за *f* [5] vase, bowl

вазели́н *m* [1] vaseline

вака́н|сия *f* [7] vacancy; **~тный** [14; -тен, -тна] vacant

ва́куум *m* [1] vacuum

вакци́на *f* [5] vaccine

вал *m* [1; на ~у́; *pl. e.*] **1.** *крепостно́й* rampart; *насыпь* bank; **2.** billow, wave; **3.** *tech.* shaft

вале́жник *m* [1] brushwood

вале́нок *m* [1; -нка] felt boot

валерья́н|ка *coll.* *f* [5], **~овый** [14]: **~овые ка́пли** *f/pl.* tincture valerian

валёт *m* [1] (*cards*) knave, jack

ва́лик *m* [1] **1.** *tech.* roller; **2.** bolster

вал|и́ть [13; валю́, ва́лишь; ва́ленный], ⟨по-, с-⟩ **1.** overturn, tumble (down; *v/i.* **-ся**), *лес* fell; **в ку́чу** heap (up) dump; **2.** [3rd *p. only:* -и́т] *о толпе* flock, throng; **снег ~и́т** it is snowing heavily

валово́й [14] gross, total

валто́рна *f* [5] French horn

валу́н *m* [1 *e.*] boulder

ва́льдшнеп *m* [1] woodcock

вальс *m* [1] waltz; **~и́ровать** [7], ⟨про-⟩ waltz

валю́т|а *f* [5] (foreign) currency; **твёрдая ~а** hard currency; **~ный** [14] currency…, exchange…; **~ный курс** *m* rate of exchange

валя́ть [28], ⟨по-⟩ roll, drag; P **валя́й!** OK go ahead!; **валя́й отсю́да!** beat it!; **~ дурака́** idle; play the fool; **-ся** *о человеке* wallow, loll; *о предметах* lie about (in disorder)

вандали́зм *m* [1] vandalism

вани́ль *f* [8] vanilla

ва́нн|а *f* [5] tub; bath; **со́лнечная ~а** sun bath; **приня́ть ~у** take a bath; **~ая** *f* [14] bath(room)

ва́рвар *m* [1] barbarian; **~ский** [16] barbarous; **~ство** *n* [9] barbarity

ва́режка *f* [5; *g/pl.:* -жек] mitten

варе́ние *n* [12] → **ва́рка**; **~ик** *m* [1] (*mst. pl.*) boiled pieces of dough with stuffing; **~ый** [14] cooked, boiled; **~е́нье** *n* [10] jam, confiture

вариа́нт *m* [1] variant, version

вари́ть [13; варю́, ва́ришь; ва́ренный], ⟨с-⟩ cook, boil; brew; *v/i.* **~ся: в со́бственном соку́** stew in one's own juice

ва́рка *f* [5] cooking, boiling

В

варьете́ *n* (-тε) [*indecl.*] variety show

варьи́ровать [7] vary

варя́г *m* [1] *hist.* Varangian; *coll., joc.* alien, stranger

василёк *m* [1; -лька́] cornflower

ва́та *f* [5] absorbent cotton, *Brt.* cotton wool

вата́га *f* [5] gang, band, troop

ватерли́ния (-тε-) *f* [7] water-line

ва́тный [14] quilted; wadded

ватру́шка *f* [5; *g/pl.:* -шек] curd tart, cheese cake

ва́фля *f* [6; *g/pl.:* -фель] waffle, wafer

ва́хт|**а** *f* [5] *naut.* watch; **стоя́ть на ~е** keep watch; **~енный** [14] sailor on duty; **~ёр** *m* [1] janitor, *Brt.* porter

ваш *m*, **~а** *f*, **~е** *n*, *pl.* **~и** [25] your; yours; **по ~ему** in your opinion (*or* language); **(пусть бу́дет) по ~ему** (have it) your own way, (just) as you like; **как по-~ему?** what do you think?; → **наш**

вая́ни|**е** *n* [12] sculpture; **~тель** *m* [4] sculptor; **~ть** [28], ⟨из-⟩ sculpture, cut, model

вбе|**га́ть** [1], ⟨~жа́ть⟩ [4; -гу́, -жи́шь, -гу́т] run *or* rush into

вби|**ва́ть** [1], ⟨~ть⟩ [вобью́, вобьёшь; вбей(те)!; вбил; вби́тый]; drive (*or* hammer) in; **~ть себе́ в го́лову** get/ take into one's head; **~ра́ть** [1], ⟨вобра́ть⟩ [вберу́, -рёшь] absorb, imbibe

вблизи́ nearby; close (to P)

вбок to one side, sideways

вброд: **переходи́ть ~** ford, wade

вва́л|**ивать** [1], ⟨~и́ть⟩ [ввалю́, вва́лишь; вва́ленный] throw, heave (in[-to]), dump; **-ся** fall *or* tumble in; burst in(to); *толпой* flock in

введе́ние *n* [12] introduction

ввезти́ → **ввози́ть**

ввер|**га́ть** [1], ⟨~нуть⟩ [21]: **~а́ть в отча́яние** drive to despair

ввер|**я́ть** [14], ⟨~ить⟩ entrust, commit, give in charge

вве́ртывать [1], ⟨вверте́ть⟩ [11; вверчу́, вве́ртишь] *once* ⟨вверну́ть⟩ [20; ввёрнутый] screw in; *fig.* put in (a word *etc.*)

вверх up(ward[s]); **~ по ле́снице** upstairs; **~ дном** (*or* нога́ми) upside down; **~ торма́шками** head over heels; **ру́ки ~!** hands up!; **~у́** above; overhead

ввести́ → **вводи́ть**

ввиду́ in view (of P), considering; **~ того́, что** as, since, seeing

вви́н|**чивать** [1], ⟨~ти́ть⟩ [15 *e.;* -нчу́, -нти́шь] screw in

ввод *m* [1] *tech.* input

вводи́ть [15], ⟨ввести́⟩ introduce; bring *or* usher (in); **~ть в заблужде́ние** mislead; **~ть в курс де́ла** acquaint with an affair; **~ть в строй** (*or* де́йствие, эксплуата́цию) put into operation; **~ный** [14] introductory; **~ное сло́во** *or* предложе́ние *gr.* parenthesis

ввоз *m* [1] import(s); importation; **~и́ть** [15], ⟨ввезти́⟩ [24] import

вво́лю (P) *coll.* plenty of; to one's heart's content

ввя́з|**ываться** [1], ⟨~а́ться⟩ [3] meddle, interfere (with **в** B); get involved (in)

вглубь deep into, far into

вгля́д|**ываться** [1], ⟨~е́ться⟩ [11] (**в** B) peer (into), look narrowly (at)

вгоня́ть [28], ⟨вогна́ть⟩ [вгоню́, вго́нишь; вогна́л, -а́, -о; во́гнанный (во́гнан, -а́, -о)] drive in (to)

вдава́ться [5], ⟨вда́ться⟩ [вда́мся, вда́шься, *etc.* → **дать**] jut out into; **~ в подро́бности** go (into)

вда́в|**ливать** [1], ⟨~и́ть⟩ [14] press (in)

вдал|**еке́, ~и́** far off, far (from **от** P); **~ь** into the distance

вдви|**га́ть** [1], ⟨~нуть⟩ [20] push in

вдво́|**е** twice (as …, *comp.:* **~е бо́льше** twice as much *or* many); *vb.* + **~е** *a.* double; **~ём** both *or* two (of us, *etc.*, *or* together); **~йне́** twice (as much, *etc.*) doubly

вде|**ва́ть** [1], ⟨~ть⟩ [вде́ну, вде́нешь; вде́тый] (**в** B) put into, thread

вде́л|**ывать** [1], ⟨~ать⟩ [1] set (in[to])

вдоба́вок in addition to; into the bargain, to boot

вдов|**а́** *f* [5; *pl. st.*] widow; **~е́ц** *m* [1; -вца́] widower

вдо́воль *coll.* in abundance; quite enough; plenty of

вдо́вый [14 *sh.*] widowed

B

вдого́нку after, in pursuit of

вдоль (Р, **по** Д) along; lengthwise; **~ и поперёк** in all directions, far and wide

вдох *m* [1] breath, inhalation; **сде́лайте глубо́кий** take a deep breath

вдохнове́|ние *n* [12] inspiration; **~ённый** [14; -вёнен, -ве́нна] inspired; **~ля́ть** [28], ⟨**~и́ть**⟩ [14 e.; -влю, -ви́шь] inspire; **-ся** get inspired (with *or* by T)

вдре́безги to smithereens

вдруг **1.** suddenly, all of a sudden; **2.** what if, suppose

вду|ва́ть [1], ⟨**~ть**⟩ [18] blow into, inflate

вду́м|чивый [14 *sh.*] thoughtful; **~ываться**, ⟨**~аться**⟩ [1] (**в** В) ponder (over), reflect ([up]on)

вдыха́ть [1], ⟨вдохну́ть⟩ [20] inhale; *fig.* inspire (with)

вегета́ри́а́нец *m* [1; -нца] vegetarian; **~тивный** [14] vegetative

ве́д|ать [1] **1.** know; **2.** (Т) be in charge of, manage; **~ение**[1] *n* [12] running, directing; **~е́ние книг** bookkeeping; **~ение**[2] *n* [12]: **в его́ ~ении** in his charge, competence; **~омо** known; **без моего́ ~ома** without my knowledge; **~омость** *f* [8; *from g/pl. e.*] list, roll, register; *периоди́ческое изда́ние* bulletin; **инвента́рная ~омость** inventory; **~омство** *n* [9] department

ведро́ *n* [9; *pl.*: вёдра, -дер, -драм] bucket, pail; **~ для му́сора** garbage can, *Brt.* dustbin

веду́щий *m* [17] leading; basic

ведь indeed, sure(ly); why, well; then; you know, you see; **~ уже́ по́здно** it is late, isn't it?

ве́дьма *f* [5] witch, hag

ве́ер *m* [1; *pl.*: -ра́ *etc. e.*] fan

ве́жлив|ость *f* [8] politeness; **~ый** [14 *sh.*] polite

везде́ everywhere; **~хо́д** *m* [1] allterrain vehicle

везе́ние *n* [12] luck; **како́е ~** what luck!

везти́ [24], ⟨по-, с-⟩ *v/t.* drive (be driving, *etc.*), transport; *са́нки и т. д.* pull; **ему́ (не) везёт** *coll.* he is (un)lucky

век *m* [1; на веку́; *pl.*: века́, *etc. e.*] **1.** century; age; **2.** life (time); **сре́дние ~а́** *pl.* Middle Ages; **на моём ~у́** in my life

(-time); **~ с тобо́й мы не вида́лись** we haven't met for ages

ве́ко *n* [9; *nom/pl.*: -ки] eyelid

в“веково́й [14] ancient, age-old

ве́ксель *m* [4; *pl.*: -ля́, *etc. e.*] bill of exchange, promissory note

веле́ть [9; веле́нный] (*im*)*pf.*; *pt. pf. only* order, tell (p. s.th. Д/В)

велика́н *m* [1] giant

вели́к|ий [16; вели́к, -а́, -о] great; (too) large or big; *only short form*; **от ма́ла до ~а** everybody, young and old; **Пётр ~ий** Peter the Great

велико|ду́шие *n* [12] magnanimity; **~ду́шный** [14; -шен, -шна] magnanimous, generous; **~ле́пие** *n* [12] splendo(u)r, magnificence; **~ле́пный** [14; -пен, -пна] magnificent, splendid

велича́вый [14 *sh.*] majestic, stately

вели́ч|ественный [14 *sh.*] majestic, grand, stately; **~ество** *n* [9] majesty; **~ие** *n* [12] grandeur; greatness; **~ина́** *f* [5; *pl. st.*: -чины́] size; magnitude, quantity; *math.* value; *об учёном и т. д.* celebrity; **~ино́й в** or (**с** В) … big or high

вело|го́нки *f/pl.* [5; *gen.*: -нок] cycle race; **~дро́м** *m* [1] cycling truck

велосипе́д *m* [1] bicycle; **е́здить на ~е** cycle; **~и́ст** *m* [1] cyclist; **~ный** [14] (bi)cycle…, cycling…

вельве́т *m* [1], **~овый** [14] velveteen

ве́на *f* [5] *anat.* vein

венге́р|ка *f* [5; *g/pl.*: -рок], **~ский** [16]; **~р** *m* [1] Hungarian.

венери́ческий [16] venereal

вене́ц *m* [1; -нца] crown; *орео́л* halo; *fig.* consummation

венециа́нский [16] Venetian

ве́нзель *m* [4; *pl.*: -ля́] monogram

ве́ник *m* [1] broom, besom

вено́к *m* [1; -нка́] wreath, garland

вентил|и́ровать [7], ⟨про-⟩ ventilate, air; **~я́тор** *m* [1] ventilator, fan

венча́|льный [14] wedding…, **~ние** *n* [12] wedding (ceremony); **~ть** [1] **1.** ⟨у-⟩ crown; **2.** ⟨об-, по-⟩ marry; **-ся** get married (in church)

ве́ра *f* [5] faith, belief, trust (in **в** В); religion

вера́нда *f* [5] veranda(h)

ве́рба *f* [5] willow

верблю́|д *m* [1] camel; **~жий** [18]: **~жья шерсть** *f* camel's hair

ве́рбн|ый [14]: **Яое воскресе́нье** *n* Palm Sunday

вербов|а́ть [7], ⟨за-, на-⟩ enlist, recruit; **на рабо́ту** engage, hire; **~ка** *f* [5; -вок] recruiting

верёв|ка *f* [5; *g/pl.*: -вок] rope, cord, string; **~очный** [14] rope…

верени́ца *f* [5] row file, line

ве́реск *m* [1] heather

вереща́ть [16 *e.*; -щу́, -щи́шь] chirp; *coll.* squeal

верзи́ла *coll. m* [5] ungracefully tall fellow

ве́рить [13], ⟨по-⟩ believe (in **в** В); believe, trust (acc. Д); **~ на́ сло́во** take on trust; **-ся** (*impers.*): (**мне**) **не ве́рится** one (I) can hardly believe (it)

вермише́ль *f* [8] *coll.* vermicelli

ве́рно *adv.* 1. & 2. → **ве́рный** 1. 2. 3. probably; **-сть** *f* [8] 1. faith(fulness), fidelity, loyalty; 2. correctness, accuracy

верну́ть(ся) [20] *pf.* → **возвраща́ть(ся)**

ве́рн|ый [14; -рен, -рна́, -о] 1. *друг* faithful, true, loyal; 2. (*пра́вильный*) right, correct; (*то́чный*) accurate, exact; 3. (*надёжный*) safe, sure, reliable; 4. (*неизбе́жный*) inevitable, certain; **~ée** (**сказа́ть**) or rather

вероиспове́дание *n* [12] creed; denomination

вероло́м|ный [14; -мен, -мна] perfidious, treacheorus; **~ство** *n* [9] perfidy, treachery

веротерпи́мость *f* [8] toleration

вероя́т|ность *f* [8] probability; **по все́й ~ности** in all probability; **~ный** [14; -тен, -тна] probable, likely

ве́рсия *f* [7] version

верста́к *m* [1 *e.*] workbench

верт|е́л *m* [1; *pl.*: -ла́] spit, skewer; **-е́ть** [11; верчу́, ве́ртишь], ⟨по-⟩ turn, twist; **-ся** 1. turn, revolve; 2. **на сту́ле** fidget; **~е́ться на языке́** be on the tip of one's tongue; **~е́ться под нога́ми** be (or get) in the way; **~ика́льный** [14; -лен, -льна] vertical; **~олёт** *m* [1] helicopter

ве́рующий *m* [17] *su.* believer

верфь *f* [8] shipyard

верх *m* [1; **на верху́**; *pl. e.*] top, upper part; *fig.* height; **взять ~** gain the upper hand, win; **~и́** *pl.* top-rank officials 1. **в ~а́х** summit…; 2. **о зна́ниях** superficial knowledge; **~ний** [15] upper

верхо́в|ный [14] supreme, high; **~ная власть** supreme power; **~ный суд** supreme court; **~о́й** [14] riding…; rider; horseman; **~а́я езда́** *f* riding; **~ье** *n* [10; *g/pl.*: -ьев] upper reaches

верхо́м *adv.* astride, on horseback; **е́здить ~** ride, go on horseback

верху́шка *f* [5; *g/pl.*: -шек] top, apex; high-rank officials

верши́на *f* [5] peak, summit

верши́ть [16 *e.*; -шу́, -ши́шь; -шённый], ⟨за-, с-⟩ 1. manage, control; 2. run (Т); 3. accomplish, decide

вес *m* [1] weight; **на ~** by weight; **уде́льный ~** *phys.* specific gravity; **име́ть ~** *fig.* carry weight; **на ~ зо́лота** worth its weight in gold; **~ом в** (В) weighting…

весел|и́ть [13], ⟨раз-⟩ amuse, divert, (**-ся** enjoy o.s.); **~ёлость** *f* [8] gaiety, mirth; **~ёлый** [14; ве́сел, -а́, -о] gay, merry, cheerful; **как ~ело!** it's such fun!; **ему́ ~ело** he is enjoying himself, is of good cheer; **~е́лье** *n* [10] merriment, merrymaking, fun; **~ельча́к** *m* [1 *e.*] convivial fellow

весе́нний [15] spring…

ве́с|ить [15] *v/i.* weigh; **~кий** [16; ве́сок, -ска] weighty

весло́ *n* [9; *pl.*: вёсла, -сел] oar

весн|а́ *f* [5; *pl.*: вёсны, вёсен] spring (in [the] Т); **~у́шка** *f* [5; *g/pl.*: -шек] freckle

весов|о́й [14] 1. weight…; balance…; 2. sold by weight; **~щи́к** *m* [1 *e.*] weigher

весо́мый [14] *fig.* weighty

вести́¹ *f/pl.* [8] news

вести́² [25], ⟨по-⟩ 1. (be) lead(ing *etc.*), conduct, guide; 2. *разгово́р* carry on; 3. *дневни́к* keep; 4. *маши́ну* drive; **~ (свое́) нача́ло** spring (from **от** Р); **~ себя́** behave (*o.s.*); **и у́хом не ведёт** pays no attention at all; **~сь** be conducted *or* carried on; **так уж у нас пове́ло́сь** that's a custom among us

вестибю́ль m [4] entrance hall

вéст|ник m [1] bulletin; **∼очка** f [5; g/pl.: -чек] coll. news; **∼ь** f [8; from g/pl. e.] news, message; **пропа́сть без ∼и** be missing

весы́ m/pl. [1] scales, balance; ♎ Libra

весь m, **вся** f, **всё** n, pl.: **все** [31] 1. adj. all, the whole; full, life (size; at **в** B); 2. su. n all over; everything, pl. e. everybody; **вот и всё** that's all; **лу́чше всего́ (всех)** best of all, the best; **пре́жде всего́** first and foremost; **при всём том** for all that; **во всём ми́ре** all over the world; **по всей стране́** throughout the country; **всего́ хоро́шего!** good luck!; **во всю → си́ла**; 3. всё adv. always, all the time; only, just; **всё (ещё) не** not yet; **всё бо́льше (и бо́льше)** more and more; **всё же** nevertheless, yet

весьма́ very, extremely, highly; **∼ вероя́тно** most probably

ветв|и́стый [14 sh.] branchy, spreading; **∼ь** f [8; from g/pl. e.] branch (a. fig.), bough

вéтер m [1; -тра] wind; **встре́чный ∼** contrary or head wind; **попу́тный ∼** fair wind; **броса́ть де́ньги (слова́) на ∼** waste money (words); old use **держа́ть нос по ве́тру** be a timeserver

ветера́н m [1] veteran

ветерина́р m [1] veterinary surgeon, coll. vet; **∼ный** [14] veterinary

ветеро́к m [1; -рка́] light wind, breeze, breath

вéтка f [5; g/pl.: -ток] branch(let), twig; rail. branch line

вéто n [indecl.] veto; **наложи́ть ∼** veto

вéтр|еный [14 sh.] windy (a. fig. = flippant); **∼яно́й** [14] wind…; **∼яна́я ме́льница** windmill; **∼яный** [14]: **∼яная о́спа** chicken pox

вéтх|ий [16; ветх, -á, -о; comp.: ве́тше] dom. old, dilapidated; одежда worn out, shabby; decrepit; **∼ость** f [8] decay, dilapidation; **приходи́ть в ∼ость** fall into decay

ветчина́ f [5] ham

ветша́ть [1], ⟨об-⟩ decay, become dilapidated

вéха f [5] landmark, milestone mst. fig.

вéчер m [1; pl.: -pá, etc. e.] 1. evening; 2. **∼ па́мяти** commemoration meeting; **∼ом** in the evening; **сего́дня ∼ом** tonight; **вчера́ ∼ом** last night; **под ∼** toward(s) the evening; **∼éть** [8; impers.] decline (of the day); **∼и́нка** f [5; g/pl.:-нок] (evening) party, soirée; **∼ко́м** coll. = **∼ом**; **∼ний** [15] evening…, night…; **∼я** f [6]: **Тáйная ♀я** the Last Supper

вéчн|ость f [8] eternity; **(це́лую) ∼ость** coll. for ages; **∼ый** [14; -чен, -чна] eternal, everlasting; perpetual

вéша|лка f [5; g/pl.: -лок] (coat) hanger; (пéтля) tab; peg, rack; coll. cloakroom; **∼ть** [1] 1. ⟨пове́сить⟩ [15] hang (up); **-ся** hang o.s. 2. ⟨взве́сить⟩ [15] weigh

веща́ние n [12] → радио∼

вещ|е́ственный [14] material, substantial; **∼ество́** n [9] matter, substance; **∼и́ца** f [8] knickknack; piece; **∼ь** f [8; from g/pl. e.] thing; object; (произведе́ние) work, piece, play; pl. belongings; baggage, Brt. luggage

вéя|ние n [12] fig. trend, tendency, current; **∼ние вре́мени** spirit of the times; **∼ть** [27] v/i. blow, flutter, ⟨по-⟩ smell, breathe of

вжи|ва́ться [1], ⟨∼ться⟩ [-ву́сь, etc. → жить] accustom o.s. (в B to)

взад coll. back(ward[s]); **∼ и вперёд** back and forth, to and fro; up and down

взаи́мн|ость f [8] reciprocity; **∼ый** [14; -мен, -мна] mutual, reciprocal

взаимо|вы́годный [14; -ден, -дна] mutually beneficial; **∼де́йствие** n [12] interaction; сотру́дничество cooperation; **∼де́йствовать** [7] interact, cooperate; **∼отноше́ние** n [12] interrelation; люде́й relationship, relations pl.; **∼по́мощь** f [8] mutual aid; **∼понима́ние** n [12] mutual understanding

взаймы́: брать ∼ borrow (у, от P from); **дава́ть ∼** lend

взаме́н (P) instead of, in exchange for; **∼перти́** locked up, under lock and key

взба́л|мошный coll. [14; -шен, -шна] eccentric, extravagant; **∼тывать**, ⟨взболта́ть⟩ [1] shake or stir up

B

взбе|га́ть [1], ⟨~жа́ть⟩ [4; взбегу́, -жи́шь, -гу́т] run up

взбива́ть [1], ⟨взбить⟩ [взобью́, -бьёшь; взбил, -а; взби́тый] whip, beat up

взбира́ться, ⟨взобра́ться⟩ [взберу́сь, -рёшься; взобрался, -ла́сь, -ло́сь] climb, clamber up (**на** B s.th.)

взби́тый [14]: ~е сли́вки whipped cream

взболта́ть → **взба́лтывать**

взбудора́живать [1] → **будора́жить**

взбунтова́ться → **бунтова́ть**

взбух|а́ть [1], ⟨~нуть⟩ [21] swell

взва́ливать [1], ⟨взвали́ть⟩ [13; взвалю́, -а́лишь; -а́ленный] load, lift, hoist (onto), *обя́занности и т. д.* charge (**на** B with)

взвести́ → **взводи́ть**

взве́|шивать[1], ⟨~сить⟩ [15] weigh; **-ся** weigh o.s.

взви|ва́ть [1], ⟨~ть⟩ [взовью́, -вьёшь; *etc.* → **вить**] whirl up; **-ся** soar up, rise; *fig.* flare up

взви́зг|ивать [1], ⟨~нуть⟩ [20] cry out, squeak, scream; *о соба́ке* yelp

взви́н|чивать [1], ⟨~ти́ть⟩ [15 *e.*; -нчу́, -нти́шь; -и́нченный] excite; *це́ны* raise

взвить → **взвива́ть**

взвод *m* [1] platoon

взводи́ть [15], ⟨взвести́⟩ [25]: ~ куро́к cock (*firearm*)

взволно́|ванный [14 *sh.*] excited; *ис-пы́тывающий беспоко́йство* uneasy; ~ва́ть(ся) → **волнова́ть**

взгляд *m* [1] look; glance; gaze, stare; *fig.* view, opinion; **на мой** ~д in my opinion; **на пе́рвый** ~д at first sight; **с пе́рвого** ~да on the face of it; *любо́вь* at first sight, at once; ~дывать [1], *once* ⟨~ну́ть⟩ [19] (**на** B) (have a) look, glance (at)

взгрустну́ть [20; -ну, -нёшь] *coll.* feel sad

взгромо|зжда́ть [1], ⟨~зди́ть⟩ [15 *e.*; -зжу́, -зди́шь, -мождённый] load, pile up; **-ся** clamber, perch (on **на** B)

вздёр|гивать [1], ⟨~нуть⟩ [20] jerk up; ~нутый нос *m* turned-up nose

вздор *m* [1] nonsense; **нести́** ~ talk nonsense; ~ный [14; -рен, -рна] foolish, absurd; *coll.* (*сварли́вый*) quarrelsome, cantankerous

вздорожа́|ние *n* [12] rise in price(s); ~ть → **дорожа́ть**

вздох *m* [1] sigh; **испусти́ть после́дний** ~ breathe one's last; ~ну́ть → **вздыха́ть**

вздра́гивать[1], *once* ⟨вздро́гнуть⟩[20] start, wince; shudder

вздремну́ть *coll.* [20] *pf.* have a nap, doze

взду|ва́ть[1], ⟨~ть⟩ [18] **1.** *це́ны* run up; **2.** *v/i.* **-ся** swell; **3.** *coll.* give a thrashing; ~тие *n* [12] swelling

взду́ма|ть[1] *pf.* conceive the idea, take it into one's head; **-ся**; **ему́** ~**лось = он** ~**л**; **как** ~**ется** at one's will

взды|ма́ть [1] raise, *клубы́ ды́ма* whirl up; ~ха́ть [1], *once* ⟨вздохну́ть⟩ [20] sigh; ~ха́ть (**по, о** П) long (for); *pf. coll.* pause for breath

взи|ма́ть[1] levy, raise (from **с** P); ~ма́ть штраф collect; ~ра́ть [1] (**на** B) look (at); **невзира́я на** without regard to, notwithstanding

взла́мывать, ⟨взлома́ть⟩ [1] break or force open

взлёт *m* [1] upward flight; *ae.* take off; ~но-поса́дочная полоса́ landing strip, runway

взлет|а́ть[1], ⟨~е́ть⟩[11] fly up, soar; *ae.* take off

взлом *m* [1] breaking in; ~а́ть → **взла́мывать**; ~щик *m* [1] burglar

взмах *m* [1] *руки́ пловца́* stroke; *косы́* sweep; ~ивать [1], *once* ⟨~ну́ть⟩ [20] swing, *руко́й* wave, *кры́льями* flap

взмет|а́ть [3], *once* ⟨~ну́ть⟩ [20] *пыль* whirl or throw up

взмо́рье *n* [10] seashore, seaside

взнос *m* [1] payment; fee; *при поку́пке в рассро́чку* installment

взну́зд|ывать [1], ⟨~а́ть⟩ bridle

взобра́ться → **взбира́ться**

взойти́ → **восходи́ть & всходи́ть**

взор *m* [1] look; gaze; eyes *pl.*

взорва́ть → **взрыва́ть**

взро́слый [14] grown-up, adult

взрыв *m* [1] explosion; *fig.* outburst;

B

~а́тель *m* [4] (detonating) fuse; **~а́ть** [1], **〈взорва́ть〉** [-ву́, -вёшь; взо́рванный] blow up; *fig.* enrage; **-ся** explode; fly into a rage; **~но́й** [14], **~чатый** [14] explosive (*su.:* **~чатое веще́ство**), *coll.* **~ча́тка**

взрыхля́ть [28] → **рыхли́ть**

взъе|зжа́ть [1], **〈~хать〉** [взъе́ду, -дешь; въезжа́й(те)!] ride *or* drive up; **~ро́шивать** [1], **〈~ро́шить〉** [16 *st.*] dishevel, tousle; **-ся** become dishevel(l)ed

взыва́ть [1], **〈воззва́ть〉** [-зову́, -зовёшь; -зва́л, -а́, -о] appeal (to **к** Д); **о по́мощи** call for help

взыска́|ние *n* [12] 1. penalty, exaction, levy; 2. (**вы́говор**) reprimand; **~а́тельный** [14; -лен, -льна] exacting, exigent; **~ивать** [1], **〈~а́ть〉** [3] (**с** P) levy, exact

взя́т|ие *n* [12] seizure, capture; **~ка** *f* [5; *g/pl.:* -ток] 1. bribe; **дать ~ку** bribe; 2. **карты** trick; **~очник** *m* [1] bribe taker, corrupt official; **~очничество** *n* [9] bribery; **~ь** → **брать**

вибр|а́ция *f* [7] vibration; **~и́ровать** [7] vibrate

вид *m* [1] 1. look(s), appearance, air; 2. sight, view; 3. kind, sort; species; 4. *gr.* aspect; **в ~е** (P) in the form of, as, by way of; **в любо́м ~е** in any shape; **под ~ом** under the guise (of P); **при ~е** at the sight of; **на ~у́** (**у** P) in sight; visible (to); **с** (*or* **по**) **~у** by sight; judging from appearance; **ни под каки́м ~ом** on no account; **у него́ хоро́ший ~** he looks well; **де́лать ~** pretend; (не) **теря́ть** *or* **выпуска́ть из ~у** (not) lose sight of (keep in view); **~ы** *pl.* prospects (for **на** B)

вида́ть *coll.* [1], **〈у-, по-〉** see; **его́ давно́ не ~** I *or* we haven't seen him for a long time; **-ся** (*iter.*) meet, see (o.a.; *a p.* **с** T)

виде́ние[1] *n* [12] vision, view; **моё ~ про-бле́мы** the way I see it

виде́ние[2] *n* [12] vision, apparition

ви́део|за́пись *f* [8] video (tape) recording; **~кассе́та** *f* [5] video cassette; **~магнитофо́н** *m* [1] video (tape) recorder

ви́деть [11 *st.*], **〈у-〉** see; catch sight of; **~ во сне** dream (of B); **ви́дишь** (**~ите**)

ли? you see?; **-ся** → **вида́ться** (*but a. once*)

ви́дим|о apparently, evidently; **~о-не-~о** *coll.* lots of, immense quantity; **~ость** *f* [8] 1. visibility; 2. *fig.* appearance; **всё э́то одна́ ~** there is nothing behind this; **~ый** [14 *sh.*] 1. visible; 2. [14] apparent

видне́|ться [8] be visible, be seen; **~о** it can be seen; it appears; apparently; (**мне**) **ничего́ не ~о** I don't *or* can't see anything; **~ый** 1. [14; -ден, -дна́, -дно] visible, conspicuous; 2. [14] distinguished, prominent; *coll. мужчина* portly

видоизмен|е́ние *n* [12] modification, alteration; variety; **~я́ть** [1], **〈~и́ть〉** [13] alter, change

ви́за *f* [5] visa

визави́ [*indecl.*] 1. opposite; 2. person face-to-face with another

византи́йский [16] Byzantine

визг *m* [1] scream, shriek; *животного* yelp; **~гли́вый** [14 *sh.*] shrill; given to screaming; **~жа́ть** [4 *e.*; -жу́, -жи́шь], **〈за-〉** shriek; yelp

визи́ровать [7] (*im*)*pf.* visa

визи́т *m* [1] visit, call; **нанести́ ~** make an official visit; **~ный** [14]: **~ная ка́рточка** *f* calling *or* visiting card

ви́л|ка *f* [5; *g/pl.:* -лок] 1. fork; 2. (**штепсельная**) **~ка** *el.* plug; **~ы** *f/pl.* [5] pitchfork

ви́лла *f* [5] villa

виля́ть [28], **〈за-〉**, *once* **〈вильну́ть〉** [20] wag (one's tail *хвостом*); *о дороге* twist and turn; *fig.* prevaricate; be evasive

вин|а́ *f* [5; *pl. st.*] 1. guilt; fault; blame; 2. (**причина**) reason; **вменя́ть в ~у́** impute (to Д); **сва́ливать ~у́** lay the blame (on **на** B); **э́то не по мое́й ~е́** it's not my fault

винегре́т *m* [1] Russian salad with vinaigrette

вини́т|ельный [14] *gr.* accusative (case); **~ь** [13] blame (**за** B for), accuse (**в** П of)

ви́н|ный [14] wine...; **~о́** *n* [9; *pl. st.*] wine

винова́т|ый [14 *sh.*] guilty (of **в** П); **~!** sorry!, excuse me!; (I beg your) pardon!; **вы в э́том (не) ~ы** it's (not) your fault; **я ~ перед ва́ми** I must apologize to you, (**а. круго́м ~**) it's all my fault

вино́в|ник *m* [1] **1.** culprit; **2. ~ник торжества́** hero; **~ный** [14; -вен, -вна] guilty (of **в** П)

виногра́д *m* [1] **1.** vine; **2.** collect. grapes *pl.*; **~арство** *n* [9] viticulture; **~ник** *m* [1] vineyard; **~ный** [14] (of) grape(s), grape...

виноде́лие *n* [12] winemaking

винт *m* [1 *e.*] screw; **~ик** *m* [1] small screw; **у него́ ~иков не хвата́ет** coll. he has a screw loose; **~о́вка** *f* [5; *g/pl.*: -вок] rifle; **~ово́й** [14] screw...; spiral; **~ова́я ле́стница** spiral (winding) stairs

виньé́тка *f* [5; *g/pl.*: -ток] vignette

виолонче́ль *f* [8] (violon)cello

вира́ж *m* [1 *e.*] bend, curve, turn

виртуо́з *m* [1] virtuoso; **~ный** [14; -зен, -зна] masterly

ви́рус *m* [1] virus

ви́селица *f* [5] gallows

висе́ть [11] hang

ви́ски *n* [indecl.] whisk(e)y

виско́за *f* [5] tech. viscose; *ткань* rayon

ви́снуть coll. [21], ⟨по-⟩ v/i. hang

висо́к *m* [1; -ска́] anat. temple

високо́сный [14]: **~ год** leap year

вися́чий [17] hanging; suspension...; **~ замо́к** padlock

витами́н *m* [1] vitamin; **~ный** [14] vitaminic

вита́|ть [1]: **~а́ть в облака́х** have one's head in the clouds; **~ева́тый** [14] affected, bombastic

вито́к *m* [1; -тка́] coil, spiral

витра́ж *m* [1] stained-glass window

витри́на *f* [5] shopwindow; showcase

вить [вью, вьёшь; вей(те)!; вил, -а́, -о; ви́тый], ⟨с-⟩ [совью́, совьёшь] wind, twist; **~ гнездо́** build a nest; **~ся 1.** wind; *о пыли* spin, whirl; **2.** *о растении* twine, creep; *о волосах* curl; **3.** *о птице* hover

ви́тязь *m* [4] hist. valiant warrior

вихо́р *m* [1; -хра́] forelock

вихрь *m* [4] whirlwind

ви́це-... (in compds.) vice-...

вишнёвый [14] cherry...; **~я** *f* [6; *g/pl.*:

-шен] cherry

вка́пывать [1], ⟨вкопа́ть⟩ dig in; fig. **как вко́панный** stock-still, rooted to the ground

вка́т|ывать [1], ⟨~и́ть⟩ [15] roll in, wheel in

вклад *m* [1] deposit; *капита́ла* investment; fig. contribution (**в** В to); **~ка** *f* [5; *g/pl.*: -док] insert; **~чик** *m* [1] depositor; investor; **~ывать** [1], ⟨вложи́ть⟩ [16] put in, insert, enclose; *де́ньги* invest; deposit

вкле́|ивать [1], ⟨~ить⟩ [13] glue or paste in; **~йка** *f* [5; *g/pl.*: -е́ек] gluing in; sheet, *etc.*, glued in

вкли́ни|вать(ся) [1], ⟨~ть(ся)⟩ [13; a.st.] drive a wedge into

включ|а́ть [1], ⟨~и́ть⟩ [16 *e.*; -чу́, -чи́шь; -чённый] include; insert; el. switch or turn on; **-ся** join (**в** В s.th.); **~а́я** including; **~е́ние** *n* [12] inclusion; insertion; el. switching on, **~и́тельно** included

вкол|а́чивать [1], ⟨~оти́ть⟩ [15] drive or hammer in

вконе́ц coll. completely, altogether

вкопа́ть → **вка́пывать**

вкось askew, aslant, obliquely; **вкривь и ~** pell-mell; amiss

вкра́|дчивый [14 sh.] insinuating, ingratiating; **~дываться** [1], ⟨~сть(ся)⟩ [25] creep or steal in; fig. insinuate o.s.

вкра́тце briefly, in a few words

вкруту́ю: яйцо́ ~ hard-boiled egg

вкус *m* [1] taste (a. fig.), flavo(u)r; **прия́тный на ~** savo(u)ry; **быть (прийти́сь) по вку́су** be to one's taste; relish (or like) s.th.; **име́ть ~** taste (of); **о ~ах не спо́рят** tastes differ; **э́то де́ло ~а** it is a matter of taste; **~ный** [14; -сен, -сна́] tasty; (**э́то**) **~но** it tastes good or nice

вла́га *f* [5] moisture

владе́|лец *m* [1; -льца] owner, proprietor, possessor; **~ние** *n* [12] ownership, possession (of Т); **~ть** [8], ⟨за-, о-⟩ (Т) own, possess; *ситуа́цией* control; *языко́м* have command (Тof); **~ть собо́й** control o.s.

влады́ка *m* [5] eccl. Reverend

вла́жн|ость *f* [8] humidity; **~ый** [14;

-жен, -жна́, -о] humid, damp, moist

вла́мываться [1], ⟨вломи́ться⟩ [14] break in

вла́ст|вовать [7] rule, dominate; **~ели́н** m [1] mst. fig. lord, master; **~и́тель** m [4] sovereign, ruler; **~ный** [14; -тен, -тна] imperious, commanding, masterful; **в э́том я не ~ен** I have no power over it; **~ь** f [8; from g/pl. e.] authority, power; rule, regime; control; pl. authorities

влачи́ть [16 e.; -чу́, -чи́шь; ~ жа́лкое существова́ние** hardly make both ends meet, drag out a miserable existence

вле́во (to the) left

влез|а́ть [1], ⟨~ть⟩ [24 st.] climb or get in(to); climb up

влет|а́ть [1], ⟨~е́ть⟩ [11] fly in; вбежа́ть rush in

влече́|ние n [12] inclination, strong attraction; **к кому́-л.** love; **~ь** [26], ⟨по-у-⟩ drag, pull; fig. attract, draw; **~ь за собо́й** involve, entail

вли|ва́ть [1], ⟨~ть⟩ [волью́, -льёшь; вле́й(те)!; вли́л (-та́, -о)] pour in; **-ся** flow or fall in; **~па́ть** coll. [1], ⟨~снуть⟩ [20] fig. get into trouble; find o.s. in an awkward situation; **~я́ние** n [12] influence; **~я́тельный** [14; -лен, -льна] influential; **~я́ть** [28], ⟨по-⟩ (have) influence

влож|е́ние n [12] investment; fin. invest-ment; **~и́ть** → **вкла́дывать**

вломи́ться → **вла́мываться**

влюб|лённость f [8] (being in) love; **~лённый** enamo(u)red; su. lover; **~ля́ться** [28], ⟨~и́ться⟩ [14] fall in love (**в** B with); **~чивый** [14 sh.] amorous

вмен|я́емый [14 sh.] responsible, accountable; **~я́ть** [28], ⟨~и́ть⟩ [13] consider (**в** B as), impute; **~я́ть в вину́** blame; **~я́ть в обя́занность** impose as duty

вме́сте together, along with; **~ с тем** at the same time

вмести́|мость f [8] capacity; **~тельный** [14; -лен, -льна] capacious, spacious; **~ть** → **вмеща́ть**

вме́сто (P) instead, in place (of)

вмеш|а́тельство n [9] interference, intervention; хирурги́ческое operation;

~ивать [1], ⟨~а́ть⟩ [1] (B/**в** B) (in; with); fig. involve (in); **-ся** interfere, intervene, meddle (**в** B in)

вмеща́|ть [1], ⟨~сти́ть⟩ [15 e.; -ещу́, -ести́шь; -ещённый] **1.** (помести́ть) put, place; **2.** зал и т. д. hold, contain, accommodate; **-ся** find room; hold; go in

вмиг in an instant, in no time

вмя́тина f [5] dent

внача́ле at first, at the beginning

вне (P) out of, outside; beyond; **бы́ть ~ себя́** be beside o.s.; **~ вся́ких сомне́ний** beyond (any) doubt

внебра́чный [14] extramarital; ребёнок illegitimate

внедре́|ние n [12] introduction; **~я́ть** [28], ⟨~и́ть⟩ [13] introduce; **-ся** take root

внеза́пный [14; -пен, -пна] sudden, unexpected

внекла́ссный [14] out-of-class

внеочередно́й [14] out of turn, extra(ordinary)

внесе́|ние n [12] entry; **~ти́** → **вноси́ть**

вне́шн|ий [15] outward, external; pol. foreign; **~ость** f [8] (нару́жность) appearance, exterior

внешта́тный [14] сотру́дник not on permanent staff, freelance

вниз down(ward[s]); **~у́ 1.** (P) beneath, below; **2.** down(stairs)

вник|а́ть [1], ⟨~нуть⟩ [19] (**в** B) get to the bottom (of), fathom

внима́|ние n [12] attention; care; **приня́ть во ~ние** take into consideration; **принима́я во ~ние** taking into account, in view of; **оста́вить без ~ния** disregard; **~тельность** f [8] attentiveness; **~тельный** [14; -лен, -льна] attentive; **~ть** [1], ⟨внять⟩ [inf. & pt. only; внял, -а́, -о] (Д) old use. hear or listen (to)

вничью́: (sport) **сыгра́ть ~** draw

вновь 1. again; **2.** newly

вноси́ть [15], ⟨внести́⟩ [25; -с-: -су́, -сёшь; внёс, внесла́] carry or bring in; **в спи́сок и т. д.** enter, include; де́ньги pay (in); contribute; попра́вки make (correction); предложе́ние submit, put forward

внук *m* [1] grandson; **~и** grandchildren

вну́тренн|ий[15] inner, inside, internal, interior; *мо́ре и т. д.* inland...; (*оте́чественный*) home...; **~ость** *f* [8] interior; (*esp. pl.*) internal organs, entrails

внутр|и́ (P) in(side); within; **~ь** (P) in (-to), inward(s), inside

внуч|а́та *m/f pl.* [2] → **вну́ки**; **~ка** *f* [5; *g/pl.*: -чек] granddaughter

внуш|а́ть [1], ⟨-и́ть⟩ [16 *e.*; -шу́, -ши́шь; -шённый] (Д/В) suggest; *наде́жду, страх* inspire (*a p.* with); *уваже́ние и т. д.* instill; **~е́ние** *n* [12] suggestion; *вы́говор* reprimand; **~и́тельный** [14; -лен, -льна] imposing, impressive; **~и́ть** → **~а́ть**

вня́т|ный [14; -тен, -тна] distinct, intelligible; **~ь** → **внима́ть**

вобра́ть → **вбира́ть**

вовл|ека́ть [1], ⟨-е́чь⟩ [26] draw in; (*впу́тывать*) involve

во́время in *or* on time, timely

во́все: **~ не**(*т*) not (at all)

всю́ *coll.* with all one's might; **стара́ться ~** do one's utmost

во-вторы́х second(ly)

вогна́ть → **вгоня́ть**

во́гнутый [14] concave

вод|а́ *f* [5; *ac/sg.*:во́ду; *pl.*: во́ды, вод, во́дам] water; **в му́тной ~е́ ры́бу лови́ть** fish in troubled waters; **вы́йти сухи́м из ~ы́** come off cleanly; **как в ~у опу́щенный** dejected, downcast; **толо́чь ~у** (**в сту́пе**) beat the air

водвор|я́ть [28], ⟨-и́ть⟩ [13] *поря́док* establish

водеви́ль *m* [4] vaudeville, musical comedy

води́тель *m* [4] driver; **~ский** [16]: **~ские права́** driving licence

вод|и́ть [15], ⟨по-⟩ **1.** lead, conduct, guide; **2.** *маши́ну* drive; **3.** move (T); **-ся** be (found), live; **как ~ится** as usual; **э́то за ним ~ится** *coll.* that's typical of him

во́дка *f* [5; *g/pl.*: -док] vodka

во́дный [14] water...; **~ спорт** aquatic sports

водо|воро́т *m* [1] whirlpool, eddy; **~ём** *m* [1] reservoir; **~измеще́ние** *n* [12] *naut.* displacement, tonnage

водо|ла́з *m* [1] diver; ♌**ле́й** *m* [3] Aquarius; **~лече́ние** *n* [12] hydropathy, water cure; **~напо́рный** [14]: **~напо́рная ба́шня** *f* water tower; **~непроница́емый** [14 *sh.*] watertight, waterproof; **~па́д** *m* [1] waterfall; **~по́й** *m* [3] watering place; watering (*of animals*); **~прово́д** *m* [1] water supply; *в до́ме* running water; **~прово́дчик** *coll. m* [1] plumber; **~разде́л** *m* [1] watershed; **~ро́д** *m* [1] hydrogen; **~ро́дный** [14]: **~ро́дная бо́мба** hydrogen bomb; **~ро́сль** *f*[8] alga, seaweed; **~снабже́ние** *n* [12] water supply; **~сто́к** *m* [1] drain(age), drainpipe; **~сто́чный**[14]: **~сто́чный жёлоб** gutter; **~храни́лище** *n* [11] reservoir

водру|жа́ть [1], ⟨-зи́ть⟩ [15 *e.*; -ужу́, -узи́шь; -ужённый] hoist

вод|яни́стый [14 *sh.*] watery; wishy-washy; **~я́нка** *f* [5] dropsy; **~яно́й** [14] water...

воева́ть [6] wage *or* carry on war, be at war

воеди́но together

военача́льник *m* [1] commander

воениз|а́ция *f* [7] militarization; **~и́ровать** [7] (*im*)*pf.* militarize

вое́нно-возду́шный [14]: **~-возду́шные си́лы** *f/pl.* air force(s); **~-морско́й** [14]: **~-морско́й флот** navy; **~пле́нный** *m* [14] *su.* prisoner of war; **~слу́жащий** [17] serviceman

вое́нн|ый [14] **1.** military, war...; **2.** military man, soldier; **~ый врач** *m* medical officer; **~ый кора́бль** *m* man-of-war, warship; **~ое положе́ние** martial law (under **на** П); **поступи́ть на ~ую слу́жбу** enlist, join; **~ые де́йствия** *n/pl.* hostilities

вож|а́к *m* [1 *e.*] (gang) leader; **~дь** *m* [4 *e.*] chief(tain); leader; **~жи́** *f/pl.* [8; *from g/pl. e.*] reins; **отпусти́ть ~жи** *fig.* slacken the reins

воз *m* [1; на-у́; *pl. e.*] cart(load); *coll. fig.* heaps; **а ~ и ны́не там** nothing has changed

возбу|ди́мый [14 *sh.*] excitable; **~ди́тель** *m* [4] stimulus, agent; **~жда́ть**

В

[1], ⟨∼дить⟩ [15 e.; -ужу́, -уди́шь] excite, stir up; *интере́с, подозре́ние* arouse; incite; *наде́жду* raise; *law* ∼ди́ть де́ло про́тив кого́-л. bring an action against s.o.; ∼жда́ющий [17] stimulating; ∼жде́ние n [12] excitement; ∼ждённый [14] excited

возвести́ → **возводи́ть**

возв|оди́ть [15], ⟨∼ести́⟩ [25] (*в огня́ в*) put up, raise, erect; *в сан* elect; *на престо́л* elevate (to)

возвра́|т m [1] 1. → ∼ще́ние; *1. & 2.*; 2. relapse; ∼ти́ть(ся) → ∼ща́ть(ся); ∼тный [14] back (...); *med.* recurring; *gr.* reflexive; ∼ща́ть [1], ⟨∼ти́ть⟩ [15 e.; -ащу́, -ати́шь; -ащённый] return; give back; *владе́льцу* restore; *долг* reimburse; *здоро́вье* recover; -ся return, come back (*из or c* P from); revert (*к* Д to); ∼ще́ние n [12] 1. return; 2. *об иму́ществе* restitution

возв|ыша́ть [1], ⟨∼ы́сить⟩ [15] raise, elevate; -ся rise; tower (over **над** T); ∼ыше́ние n [12] rise; elevation; ∼ы́шенность f [8] 1. *fig.* loftiness; 2. *geogr.* height; ∼ы́шенный [14] high, elevated, lofty

возгл|авля́ть [28], ⟨∼а́вить⟩ [14] (be at the) head

во́зглас m [1] exclamation, (out)cry

возд|ава́ть [5], ⟨∼а́ть⟩ [-да́м, -да́шь, *etc.* → **дава́ть**] render; (*отплати́ть*) requite; ∼а́ть до́лжное give s.b. his due (Д for)

воздвиг|а́ть [1], ⟨∼нуть⟩ [21] erect, construct, raise

возде́йств|ие n [12] influence, pressure; ∼овать [7] (*im*)*pf.* (**на** В) (*ока́зывать влия́ние*) influence; (*де́йствовать, влия́ть*) act upon, affect

возде́л|ывать, ⟨∼ать⟩ [1] cultivate, till

воздержа́ние n [12] abstinence; abstention

воздер́ж|анный [14 *sh.*] abstemious, temperate; ∼иваться [1], ⟨∼а́ться⟩ [4] abstain (**от** P from); *при двух* ∼а́вшихся *pol.* with two abstentions

во́здух m [1] air; *на откры́том* (*све́жем*) ∼е in the open air, outdoors; ∼оплава́ние n [12] aeronautics

возду́ш|ный [14] air..., aerial 1. ∼ная трево́га f air-raid warning; ∼ное сообще́ние aerial communication; ∼ные за́мки m/pl. castles in the air; 2. [14; -шен, -шна] airy, light

воззва́|ние n [12] appeal; ∼ть → **взыва́ть**

вози́ть [15] carry, transport; *на маши́не* drive; -ся (с Т) busy o.s. with, mess (around) with; (*де́лать ме́дленно*) dawdle; *о де́тях* romp, frolic

возл|ага́ть [1], ⟨∼ожи́ть⟩ [16] (**на** В) lay (on); entrust (with); ∼ага́ть наде́жды на (В) rest one's hopes upon

во́зле (P) by, near, beside

возложи́ть → **возлага́ть**

возлю́блен|ный [14] beloved; m (*su.*) lover; ∼ная f [14] mistress, sweetheart

возме́здие n [12] requital

возме|ща́ть [1], ⟨∼сти́ть⟩ [15 e.: -ещу́, -ести́шь; -ещённый] compensate, make up (for); ∼ще́ние n [12] compensation, indemnity; *law* damages

возмо́жн|о it is possible; possibly; о́чень ∼о very likely; ∼ость f [8] possibility; **по** (**ме́ре**) ∼ости (as far as) possible; ∼ый [14; -жен, -жна] possible; сде́лать всё ∼ое do everything possible

возмужа́лый [14] mature, grown up

возму|ти́тельный [14; -лен, -льна] scandalous, shocking; ∼ща́ть, ⟨∼ти́ть⟩ [15 e.: -щу́, -ути́шь] rouse indignation; -ся be shocked *or* indignant (Tat); ∼ще́ние n [12] indignation; ∼щённый [14] indignant (at)

вознагра|жда́ть [1], ⟨∼ди́ть⟩ [15 e.: -ажу́, -ади́шь; -аждённый] (*награди́ть*) reward; recompense (for); ∼жде́ние n [12] reward, recompense; (*опла́та*) fee

вознаме́ри|ваться [1], ⟨∼ться⟩ [13] form the idea of, intend

Вознесе́ние n [12] Ascension

возник|а́ть [1], ⟨∼нуть⟩ [21] arise, spring up, originate, emerge; *у меня́* ∼ла мысль ... a thought occurred to me ...; ∼нове́ние n [12] rise, origin, beginning

возня́ f [6] 1. fuss; bustle; romp; **мыши́-**

ная ~ petty intrigues; **2.** (*хлопоты*) trouble, bother

возобнов|ле́ние *n* [12] renewal; (*продолже́ние*) resumption; **~ля́ть** [28], ⟨**~и́ть**⟩ [14 *e.*; -влю́, -ви́шь, -влённый] *знако́мство, уси́лия* renew, resume

возра|жа́ть [1], ⟨**~зи́ть**⟩ [15 *e.*; -ажу́, -ази́шь] **1.** object (to *про́тив* P); **2.** return, retort (**я не ~жа́ю** I don't mind); **~же́ние** *n* [12] objection; rejoinder

во́зраст *m* [1] age (**в** П at); **~а́ние** *n* [12] growth, increase; **~а́ть** [1], ⟨**~и́**⟩ [24; -ст-; -расту́; -ро́с, -ла́; -ро́сший] grow, increase, rise

возро|жда́ть [1], ⟨**~ди́ть**⟩ [15 *e.*; -ожу́, -оди́шь; -ождённый] revive (*v/i.* **-ся**); **~жде́ние** *n* [12] rebirth, revival; **эпо́ха Ҩжде́ния** Renaissance

во́ин *m* [1] warrior, soldier; **~ский** [16] military; **~ская обя́занность** service; **~ственный** [14 *sh.*] bellicose

во́истину in truth

вой *m* [3] howl(ing), wail(ing)

во́йло|к *m* [1]: **~чный** [14] felt

войн|а́ *f* [5; *pl. st.*] war (**на** П at); warfare; **идти́ на ~у́** go to war; **объяви́ть ~у́** declare war; **втора́я мирова́я ~а́** World War II

войска́ *n* [9; *pl. e.*] army; *pl.* troops, (land, *etc.*) forces

войти́ → входи́ть

вокза́л *m* [1]: **железнодоро́жный ~** railroad (*Brt.* railway) station; **морско́й ~** port arrival and departure building; **речно́й ~** river-boat station

вокру́г (P) (a)round; (**ходи́ть**) **~ да о́коло** beat about the bush

вол *m* [1 *e.*] ox

волды́рь *m* [4 *e.*] blister; bump

волейбо́л *m* [1] volleyball

во́лей-нево́лей willy-nilly

во́лжский [16] (of the) Volga

волк *m* [1; *from g/pl. e.*] wolf; **смотре́ть ~ом** *coll.* scrowl

волн|а́ *f* [5; *pl. st.*, *from dat. a. e.*] wave; **дли́нные, сре́дние, коро́ткие ~ы** long, medium, short waves; **~е́ние** *n* [12] agitation, excitement; *pl.* disturbances, unrest; **на мо́ре** high seas; **~и́с-**

тый [14 *sh.*] *во́лосы* wavy; *ме́стность* undulating; **~ова́ть** [7], ⟨вз-⟩ **(-ся** be[come]) agitate(d), excite(d); (*трево́житься*) worry; **~у́ющий** [17] disturbing; exciting, thrilling

волоки́та *f* [5] *coll.* red tape; a lot of fuss and trouble

волокн|и́стый [14 *sh.*] fibrous; **~о́** *n* [9; *pl.*: -о́кна, -о́кон, *etc. st.*] fiber, *Brt.* fibre

во́лос *m* [1; *g/pl.*: -ло́с; *from dat. e.*] (*a. pl.*) hair; **~а́тый** [14 *sh.*] hairy; **~о́к** *m* [1; -ска́] hairspring; **быть на ~о́к** (*or* **на ~ке́**) **от сме́рти** *coll.* be on the verge (within a hair's breadth *or* within an ace) of death; **висе́ть на ~ке́** hang by a thread

волосяно́й [14] hair...

волочи́ть [16], ⟨по-⟩ drag, pull, draw; **-ся** drag o.s., crawl along

во́лч|ий [18] wolfish; wolf('s)...; **~и́ца** *f* [5] she-wolf

волчо́к *m* [1; -чка́] top (*toy*)

волчо́нок *m* [2] wolf cub

волше́б|ник *m* [1] magician; **~ница** *f* [5] sorceress; **~ный** [14] magic, fairy...; [-бен, -бна] *fig.* enchanting; **~ство́** *n* [9] magic, wizardry; *fig.* enchantment

волы́нка *f* [5; *g/pl.*: -нок] bagpipe

во́ль|ность *f* [8] liberty; **позволя́ть себе́ ~ости** take liberties; **~ый** [14; -лен, -льна́] free, easy, unrestricted; **~ая пти́ца** one's own master

вольт *m* [1] volt

вольфра́м *m* [1] tungsten

во́л|я *f* [6] **1.** will; **си́ла ~и** willpower; **2.** liberty, freedom; **~я ва́ша** (just) as you like; **не по свое́й ~е** against one's will; **по до́брой ~е** of one's own free will; **отпусти́ть на ~ю** set free; **дать ~ю** give free rein

вон 1. there; **~ там** over there; **2.** **~!** get out!; **пошёл ~!** out *or* away (with you)!; **вы́гнать ~** turn out; **~ (оно́) что!** you don't say!; so that's it!

вонза́ть [1], ⟨**~и́ть**⟩ [15 *e.*; -нжу́, -зи́шь; -зённый] thrust, plunge, stick (into)

вон|ь *f* [8] stench, stink; **~ю́чий** [17 *sh.*] stinking; **~я́ть** [28] stink, reek (of T)

вообра|жа́емый [14 *sh.*] imaginary; fictitious; **~жа́ть** [1], ⟨**~зи́ть**⟩ [15 *e.*; -ажу́,

-азишь; -аженный (*a.* **~жа́ть себе́**) imagine, fancy; **~жа́ть себя́** imagine o.s. (T s.b.); **~жа́ть о себе́** be conceited; **~же́ние** *n* [12] imagination; fancy

вообще́ in general, on the whole; at all

воодушев|ле́ние *n* [12] enthusiasm; **~ля́ть** [28], ⟨**~и́ть**⟩ [14 *e.*: -влю́, -ви́шь; -влённый] (**-ся**) feel inspire(d by T)

вооруж|а́ть [1], ⟨**~и́ть**⟩ [15 *e.*: -жу́, -жи́шь; -жённый] **1.** arm, equip (T with); **2.** stir up (**про́тив** P against); **~е́ние** *n* [12] armament, equipment

вооо́чию with one's own eyes

во-пе́рвых first(ly)

вопи́|ть [14 *e.*: -плю́, -пи́шь], ⟨за-⟩ cry out, bawl; **~ющий** [17] crying, flagrant

воплоща́ть [1], ⟨**~ти́ть**⟩ [15 *e.*: -ощу́, -оти́шь, -ощённый] embody, personify; **~щённый** *a.* incarnate; **~ще́ние** *n* [12] embodiment, incarnation

вопль *m* [4] howl, wail

вопреки́ (Д) contrary to; in spite of

вопро́с *m* [1] question; **под ~ом** questionable, doubtful; **~ не в э́том** that's not the question; **спо́рный ~** moot point; **что за ~!** of course!; **~и́тельный** [14] interrogative; **~и́тельный знак** question mark; **~и́тельный взгляд** inquiring look; **~ни́к** *m* [1] questionnaire

вор *m* [1; *from g/pl. e.*] thief

ворва́ться → **врыва́ться**

воркова́ть [7], ⟨за-⟩ coo; *fig.* bill and coo

воробе́й| *m* [3 *e.*; -бья́] sparrow; **стре́ляный ~ей** *coll.* old hand

ворова́ть [7] steal; **~ка** *f* [5; *g/pl.*: -вок] (female) thief; **~ско́й** [16] thievish; thieves'…; **~ство́** *n* [9] theft; *law* larceny

во́рон *m* [1] raven; **~а** *f* [5] crow; **бе́лая ~а** rara avis; **воро́н счита́ть** *coll.* old use stand about gaping

воро́нка *f* [5; *g/pl.*: -нок] **1.** funnel; **2.** *om бо́мбы, снаря́да* crater

вороно́й [14] black; *su. m* black horse

во́рот *m* [1] **1.** collar; **2.** *tech.* windlass; **~а** *n/pl.* [9] gate; **~и́ть** [15]: **~и́ть нос** turn up one's nose (at); **~ни́к** *m* [1 *e.*] collar; **~ничо́к** *m* [1; -чка́] (small) collar

во́рох *m* [1; *pl.*: -ха́; *etc. e.*] pile, heap; *coll.* lots, heaps

воро́|чать [1] **1.** move, roll, turn; **2.** *coll.* manage, boss (T); **-ся** toss; turn; stir; **~ши́ть** [16 *e.*: -шу́, -ши́шь; -шённый] turn (over)

ворч|а́ние *n* [12] grumbling; *живо́тного* growl; **~а́ть** [4 *e.*: -чу́, -чи́шь], ⟨за-, п(р)о-⟩ grumble; growl; **~ли́вый** [14 *sh.*] grumbling, surly; **~у́н** *m* [1 *e.*], **~у́нья** *f* [6] grumbler

восвоя́си *coll. iro.* home

восемна́дца|тый [14] eighteenth; **~ть** [35] eighteen; → **пять, пя́тый**

во́семь [35; восьми́, *instr.* восемью́] eight; → **пять, пя́тый**; **~деся́т** [35; восьми́десяти] eighty; **~со́т** [36; восьми́сот] eight hundred; **~ю** eight times

воск *m* [1] wax

восклиц|а́ние *n* [12] exclamation; **~а́тельный** [14] exclamatory; **~а́тельный знак** exclamation mark; **~а́ть** [1], ⟨**~и́кнуть**⟩ [20] exclaim

восково́й [14] wax(en)

воскре|са́ть [1], ⟨**~́снуть**⟩ [21] rise (from *из* P); recover; **Христо́с ~с(е́)!** Christ has arisen! (*Easter greeting*); (*reply*:) **вои́стину ~с(е́)!** (He has) truly arisen!; **~се́ние** *n* [12] resurrection; **~се́нье** *n* [10] Sunday (on: **в** B; *pl. по* Д); **~ша́ть** [1], ⟨**~си́ть**⟩ [15 *e.*: -ешу́, -еси́шь; -ешённый] resurrect, revive

воспал|е́ние *n* [12] inflammation; **~е́ние лёгких (по́чек)** pneumonia (nephritis); **~ённый** [14 *sh.*] inflamed; **~и́тельный** [14] inflammatory; **~я́ть** [28], ⟨**~и́ть**⟩ [13] inflame; (**-ся**)

воспе|ва́ть [1], ⟨**~ть**⟩ [-пою́, -поёшь; -пе́тый] sing of, praise

воспит|а́ние *n* [12] education, upbringing; (good) breeding; **~а́нник** *m* [1], **~а́нница** *f* [5] pupil; **~анный** [14 *sh.*] well-bred; **пло́хо ~анный** ill-bred; **~а́тель** *m* [4] educator; (private) tutor; **~а́тельный** [14] educational, pedagogic(al); **~ывать** [1], ⟨**~а́ть**⟩ bring up; educate; **прививать** cultivate, foster

восполн|я́ть [28], ⟨**~и́ть**⟩ [13] fill in; make up (for)

воспо́льзоваться → **по́льзоваться**

воспомина́ние n [12] remembrance, recollection, reminiscence; pl. a. memoirs

воспрепя́тствовать [7] pf. hinder, prevent (from Д)

воспре|**ща́ть** [1], ⟨~ти́ть⟩ [15 e.; -ещу́, -ети́шь; -ещённый] prohibit, forbid; **вход** ~**щён!** no entrance! **кури́ть ~ща́ется!** no smoking!

восприи́мчивый [14 sh.] receptive, impressionable; **к** заболева́нию susceptible (**к** Д to); ~**нима́ть** [1], ⟨~ня́ть⟩ [-приму́, -и́мешь; -и́нял, -á, -о; -и́нятый] take in, understand; ~**я́тие** n [12] perception

воспроиз|**веде́ние** n [12] reproduction; ~**оди́ть** [15], ⟨~ести́⟩ [25] reproduce

воспря́нуть [20] pf. cheer up; ~ **ду́хом** take heart

воссоедин|**е́ние** n [12] reun(ific)at)ion; ~**я́ть** [28], ⟨~и́ть⟩ [13] reunite

восста|**ва́ть** [5], ⟨~ть⟩ [-ста́ну, -ста́нешь] rise, revolt

восстан|**а́вливать** [1], ⟨~ови́ть⟩ [14] **1.** reconstruct, restore; **2.** про́тив antagonize; ~**ие** n [12] insurrection, revolt; ~**ови́ть** → ~**а́вливать**; ~**овле́ние** n [12] reconstruction, restoration

восто́к m [1] east; the East, the Orient; **на** ~ (to[ward]) the east, eastward(s); **на** ~**е** in the east; **с** ~**а** from the east; **к** ~**у от** (P) (to the) east of

восто́р|**г** m [1] delight, rapture; **я в** ~**е** I am delighted (**от** P with); **приводи́ть** (**приходи́ть**) **в** ~**г** = ~**га́ть(ся)** [1] impf. be delight(ed) (T with); ~**женный** [14 sh.] enthusiastic, rapturous

восто́чный [14] east(ern, -erly); oriental

востре́бова|**ние** n [12]: **до** ~**ния** to be called for, poste restante; ~**ть** [7] pf. call for, claim

восхвал|**е́ние** n [12] praise, eulogy; ~**я́ть** [28], ⟨~и́ть⟩ [13; -алю́, -а́лишь] praise, extol

восхи|**ти́тельный** [14; -лен, -льна] delightful; ~**ща́ть** [1], ⟨~ти́ть⟩ [15 e.; -ищу́, -ити́шь; -ищённый] delight, transport; **-ся** (T) be delighted with; admire; ~**ще́ние** n [12] admiration; delight; **приводи́ть** (**приходи́ть**) **в** ~**ще́ние** →

восхо́д m [1] rise; ascent; ~**ди́ть** [15], ⟨взойти́⟩ [взойду́, -дёшь; взошёл] rise, ascend; go back to; **э́тот обы́чай** ~**дит** (**к** Д) this custom goes back (to); ~**жде́ние** n [12] sunrise

восьме́рка f [5; g/pl.: -рок] eight (→ **дво́йка**); ~**еро** [37] eight (→ **дво́е**)

восьми|**деся́тый** [14] eightieth; ~ **пятидеся́тый** [14] -ле́тний [14] eight-year-old; ~**со́тый** [14] eight hundredth

восьмо́й [14] eighth; → **пя́тый**

вот part. here (is); there; now; well; that's ...; ~ **и всё** that's all; ~ (**оно́**) **как** or **что** you don't say!, is that so?; ~ **те**(**бе́**) **раз** or **на́** well I never!; a pretty business this!; ~ **како́й** ... such a ...; ~ **челове́к!** what a man!; ~~! yes, indeed!; ~~ at any moment

воткну́ть → **втыка́ть**

во́тум m [1]: ~ (**не**)**дове́рия** (Д) vote of (no) confidence (in)

воцар|**я́ться** [28], ⟨~и́ться⟩ [13] (fig., third person only) set in; ~**и́лось молча́ние** silence fell

вошь f [8; вши; во́шью] louse

вощи́ть [16 e.], ⟨на-⟩ wax

вою́ющий [17] belligerent

впа|**да́ть** [1], ⟨~сть⟩ [25; впал, -а] (**в** B) fall (flow, run) in(to); ~**де́ние** n [12] flowing into; реки́ mouth, confluence; ~**дина** f [5] cavity; глазна́я socket; geogr. hollow; ~**лый** [14] hollow, sunken; ~**сть** → ~**да́ть**

впервы́е for the first time

вперё|**д** forward; ahead (P of), on(ward); **зара́нее** in advance, beforehand; → a. **взад**

впереди́ in front, ahead (P of); before

вперемёжку alternately

впечатл|**е́ние** n [12] impression; ~**и́тельный** [14; -лен, -льна] impressionable, sensitive; ~**я́ющий** [17 sh.] impressive

впи|**ва́ться** [1], ⟨~ться⟩ [вопью́сь, -пьёшься; впи́лся, -áсь, -óсь] (**в** B) stick (into); уку́сить sting, bite; ~**ва́ться глаза́ми** fix one's eyes (on)

впи́с|**ывать** [1], ⟨~а́ть⟩ [3] enter, insert

впи́т|**ывать** [1], ⟨~а́ть⟩ soak up or in;

fig. imbibe, absorb

впи́х|ивать *coll.* [1], *once* ⟨~ну́ть⟩ [20] stuff *or* cram in(to) (**в** В)

вплавь by swimming

впле|та́ть [1], ⟨~сти́⟩ [25; -т-: вплету́, -тёшь] interlace, braid

вплотну́ю (**к** Д) close, (right) up to; *fig. coll.* seriously; ~ь *fig.* (**до** Р) (right) up to; even (till)

вполго́лоса in a low voice

вполз|а́ть [1], ⟨~ти́⟩ [24] creep *or* crawl in(to), up

вполне́ quite, fully, entirely

впопыха́х → **второпя́х**

впо́ру: **быть** ~ fit

впорхну́ть [20; -ну́, -нёшь] *pf.* flutter *or* flit in(to)

впосле́дствии afterward(s), later

впотьма́х in the dark

впра́вду *coll.* really, indeed

впра́ве: **быть** ~ have a right

вправля́ть [28], ⟨впра́вить⟩ [14] *med.* set; *руба́шку* tuck in; ~ **мозги́** make s.o. behave more sensibly

впра́во (to the) right

впредь henceforth, in future; ~ **до** until

впро́голодь half-starving

впрок **1.** for future use; **2.** to a p.'s benefit; *э́то ему́* ~ *не пойдёт* it will not profit him

впроса́к: *попа́сть* ~ make a fool of o.s.

впро́чем however, but; or rather

впры́г|ивать [1], *once* ⟨~нуть⟩ [20] jump in(to) *or* on; (**в, на** В)

впры́с|кивать [1], *once* ⟨~нуть⟩ [20] *mst. tech.* inject

впря|га́ть [1], ⟨~чь⟩ [26 г/ж; → **напря́чь**] harness, put to (**в** В)

впус|к *m* [1] admission; ~ка́ть [1], ⟨~ти́ть⟩ [15] let in, admit

впусту́ю in vain, to no purpose

впу́т|ывать, ⟨~ать⟩ [1] entangle, involve (**в** В in); -ся become entangled

впя́теро five times (→ **вдво́е**); ~м five (together)

враг *m* [1 *e.*] enemy

враж|да́ *f* [5] enmity; ~де́бность *f* [8] animosity; ~де́бный [14; -бен, -бна] hostile; ~дова́ть [7] be at odds (**с** Т with); ~еский [16], ~ий [18] (the) enemy('s)...

вразбро́д *coll.* separately; without co-ordination

вразре́з: **идти́** ~ be contrary (**с** Т to)

вразум|и́тельный [14; -лен, -льна] intelligible, clear; ~ля́ть [1], ⟨~и́ть⟩ [14] make understand, make listen to reason

враньё *n coll.* [12] lies, fibs *pl.*, idle talk

враспло́х unawares, by surprise; ~сы́пную: *бро́ситься* ~сы́пную scatter in all directions

враст|а́ть [1], ⟨~и́⟩ [24 ст-: -сту́; врос, -ла́] grow in(to)

врата́рь *n* [4 *e.*] goalkeeper

враща́ть [1] (В *or* Т) turn, revolve, rotate; (*v/i.* -ся **в** П associate with); ~а́ющийся revolving; moving; ~е́ние *n* [12] rotation

вред *m* [1 *e.*] harm, damage; **во** ~ (Д) to the detriment (of); ~и́тель *m* [4] *agric.* pest; ~и́ть [15 *e.*; -ежу́, -еди́шь], ⟨по-⟩ (do) harm, (cause) damage (Д to); ~ный [14; -ден, -дна́, -о] harmful, injurious (Д *or* для Р to)

вреза́ть [1], ⟨~ать⟩ [3] (**в** В) cut in(to); set in; -ся run in(to); project into; *в па́мять* impress (on)

вре́менный [14] temporary, transient, provisional

вре́м|я *n* [13] time; *gr.* tense; ~я го́да season; **во** ~я (Р) during; **в настоя́щее** ~я at (the) present (moment); **в пе́рвое** ~я at first; ~я от ~ени, ~ена́ми from time to time, (every) now and then, sometimes; **в ско́ром** ~ени soon; **в то** (**же**) ~я at that (the same) time; **в то** ~я как whereas; *за после́днее* ~я lately, recently; **на** ~я for a (certain) time, temporarily; **со** ~енем, **с тече́нием** ~ени in the course of time, in the long run; *тем* ~енем meanwhile; *ско́лько* ~ени? what's the time?; *ско́лько* ~ени э́то займёт? how long will it take?; *хорошо́ провести́* ~я have a good time; ~яисчисле́ние *n* [12] chronology; ~я(пре)провожде́ние *n* [12] pastime

вро́вень level with, abreast (with **c** T)

вро́де like, such as, kind of

врождённый [14 *sh.*] innate; *med.* congenital

вроз(н)ь separately, apart

врун *coll. m* [1 *e.*], **~ья** *coll. f* [6] liar

вруч|а́ть [1], ⟨~и́ть⟩ [16] hand over; deliver; ⟨*веритъ*⟩ entrust

вры|ва́ть [1], ⟨~ть⟩ [22; -ро́ю, -ро́ешь] dig in(to); -ся, ⟨ворва́ться⟩ [-ву́сь, -вёшься; -ва́лся, -ла́сь] rush in(to); enter (by force)

вряд: **~ ли** hardly, scarcely

вса́дни|к *m* [1] horseman; **~ца** *f* [5] horsewoman

вса́|живать [1], ⟨~ди́ть⟩ [15] thrust or plunge in(to); hit; **~сывать** [1], ⟨всоса́ть⟩ [-су́, -сёшь] suck in or up; absorb

всё, все → **весь**

все|веду́щий [17] omniscient; **~возмо́жный** [14] of all kinds or sorts, various

всегда́ always; **~шний** *coll.* [15] usual, habitual

всего́ (-vɔ) altogether, in all; sum; total; **~** (*то́лько, лишь, на́всего*) only, merely; *пре́жде* **~** above all

вселённая *f* [14] universe; **~я́ть** [28], ⟨~и́ть⟩ [13] settle, move in(to) (*v/i.* **-ся**); *fig.* inspire

все|ме́рный every (or all) … possible; **~ме́рно** in every possible way; **~ми́рный** [14] world…; universal; **~могу́щий** [17 *sh.*] → **~си́льный**; **~наро́дный** [14; -ден, -дна] national, nationwide; *adv.:* **~наро́дно** in public; **~но́щная** *f* [14] vespers *pl.*; **~о́бщий** [17] universal, general; **~объе́млющий** [17 *sh.*] comprehensive, all-embracing; **~ору́жие** *n* [12]: *во* **~ору́жии** fully prepared (for), in full possession of all the facts; **~росси́йский** [16] All-Russian

всерьёз *coll.* in earnest, seriously

все|си́льный [14; -лен, -льна] all-powerful; **~сторо́нний** [15] all-round, thorough

всё-таки for all that, still

всеуслы́шанье: *во* **~** publicly

всеце́ло entirely, wholly

вска́|кивать [1], ⟨вскочи́ть⟩ [16] jump or leap (**на** В up/on); start (**с** P from); *о прыщике, шишке* come up, swell (up); **~пывать**, ⟨вскопа́ть⟩ [1] dig up

вскара́бк|иваться, ⟨~аться⟩ [1] (**на** В) scramble, clamber (up, onto)

вска́рмливать [1], ⟨вскорми́ть⟩ [14] raise, rear or bring up

вскачь at full gallop

вскип|а́ть [1], ⟨~е́ть⟩ [10 *e.*;-плю́, -пи́шь] boil up; *fig.* fly into a rage

вскло́(ко́)чивать [1], ⟨~чить⟩ [16] tousle; **~ченные** or **~чившиеся во́лосы** *m/pl.* dishevel(l)ed hair

всколыхну́ть [20] stir up, rouse

вскользь in passing, cursorily

вскопа́ть → **вска́пывать**

вско́ре soon, before long

вскорми́ть → **вска́рмливать**

вскочи́ть → **вска́кивать**

вскри́|кивать [1], ⟨~ча́ть⟩ [4 *e.*; -чу́, -чи́шь], *once* ⟨~кнуть⟩ [20] cry out, exclaim

вскруж|и́ть [16; -жу́, -у́жи́шь] *pf.;* **~** (Д) *го́лову* turn a p.'s head

вскры|ва́ть [1], ⟨~ть⟩ [-ро́ю] **1.** open; (*обнару́житъ*) *fig.* reveal; **2.** *med.* dissect; **-ся 1.** open; be disclosed; **2.** *med.* burst, break; **~тие** *n* [12] *mst. med.* dissection, autopsy

всласть *coll.* to one's heart's content

вслед (*за* Т, Д) (right) after, behind, following; (Р) in consequence of, owing to; **~ствие э́того** consequently

вслепу́ю *coll.* blindly, at random

вслух aloud

вслу́ш|иваться, ⟨~аться⟩ [1] (**в** В) listen attentively (to)

всма́тр|иваться [1], ⟨всмотре́ться⟩ [9; -отрю́сь, -о́тришься] (**в** В) peer (at); observe closely, scrutinize

всмя́тку: *яйцо́* **~** soft-boiled egg

всо́|вывать [1], ⟨всу́нуть⟩ [20] put, slip (**в** В into); **~са́ть** → **вса́сывать**

вспа́|хивать [1], ⟨~ха́ть⟩ [3] plow (*Brt.* plough) or turn up; **~шка** *f* [5] tillage

всплеск *m* [1] splash; **~ивать** [1], ⟨~нуть⟩ [20] splash; **~ну́ть рука́ми** throw up one's arms

всплы|ва́ть [1], ⟨~ть⟩ [23] rise to the

surface, surface; *fig.* come to light, emerge

всполоши́ть [16 *e.*; -шу́, -ши́шь; -шён-ный] *pf.* alarm; (*v/i.* **-ся**)

вспомина́ть [1], ⟨-снить⟩ [13] (В *or* П) remember, recall; (Д + **-ся** = И + *vb.*); **~ога́тельный** [14] auxiliary

вспорхну́ть [20] *pf.* take wing

вспоте́ть [8] (break out in a sweat)

вспры́гивать [1], *once* ⟨-нуть⟩ [20] jump *or* spring (up/on **на** В)

вспры́скивать [1], ⟨-нуть⟩ [20] sprinkle; wet; *coll. покупку* celebrate

вспуг|ивать [1], *once* ⟨-ну́ть⟩ [20] frighten away

вспух|а́ть [1], ⟨-нуть⟩ [21] swell

вспыл|и́ть [13] *pf.* get angry, flare up; **~ьчивость** *f* [8] irascibility; **~ьчивый** [14 *sh.*] hot-tempered

вспы́хивать [1], ⟨-хнуть⟩ [20] **1.** burst into flames; blaze up; flare up; *огонёк* flash; (*покраснеть*) blush; **2.** *от гне-ва* burst into a rage; *о войне* break out; **~шка** *f* [5; *g/pl.:* -шек] flare, flash; outburst; outbreak

вста|ва́ть [5], ⟨-ть⟩ (вста́ну, -нешь) stand up; get up, rise (from **с** Р); arise; **~вка** *f* [5; *g/pl.:* -вок] insertion; insert; **~вля́ть** [28], ⟨-вить⟩ [14] set *or* put in, insert; **~вно́й** [14] inserted; **~вны́е зу́бы** *m/pl.* false teeth

встрепену́ться [20] *pf.* start; (*ожи-виться*) become animated

встрёпк|а Р *f* [5] reprimand; **зада́ть ~у** (Д) bawl out, scold (a p.)

встре́|тить(ся) → **~ча́ть(ся)**; **~ча** *f* [5] meeting, encounter; *приём* reception; **тёплая ~ча** warm welcome; **~ча́ть** [1], ⟨-тить⟩ [15 *st.*] **1.** meet (*v/t.*, with В) encounter; *случа́йно* come across; **2.** *прибы́вших* meet, receive, welcome **~ча́ть Но́вый год** see the New Year in; celebrate the New Year; *v/i.* **-ся 1.** meet (**с** Т o.a., with); **2.** (*impers.*) occur, happen; there are (were); **~чный** [14] counter…; contrary; head (*wind*); (coming from the) opposite (direction); *маши́на* oncoming; *пе́рвый* **~чный** the first person one meets; anyone; *пе́рвый* **~чный и попере́чный** every Tom, Dick and Harry

встря́|ска *f* [5; *g/pl.:* -сок] shock; **~хивать** [1], *once* ⟨-хну́ть⟩ [20] shake (up); *fig.* stir (up); **-ся** *v/i. coll.* cheer up

вступ|а́ть [1], ⟨-и́ть⟩ [20] *стать чле́ном* (**в** В) enter, join; set foot in, step (into); *в до́лжность* assume; **~и́ть в брак** marry; **~и́ть в де́йствие** come into force; **~и́ть на трон** ascend the throne; **-ся** (*за* В) intercede (for), project; take a p.'s side; **~и́тельный** [14] introductory; opening; *экза́мен и т. д.* entrance…; **~ле́ние** *n* [12] *на пре-сто́л* accession; *в кни́ге и т. д.* introduction

всу́|нуть → **всо́вывать**; **~чивать** *coll.* [1], ⟨-чи́ть⟩ [16] foist (В/Д s.th. on)

всхлип *m* [1], **~ывание** *n* [12] sob(bing); **~ывать** [1], *once* ⟨-нуть⟩ [20 *st.*] sob

всход|и́ть [15], ⟨взойти́⟩ [взойду́, -дёшь; взошёл; *g. pt.:* взойдя́] go *or* climb (**на** В up) on; ascend, rise; *agric.* come up, sprout; **~ы** *m/pl.* [1] standing *or* young crops

всхо́жесть *f* [8] germinating capacity

всхрапну́ть [20] *coll. joc.* have a nap

всыпа́ть [1], ⟨-ать⟩ [2 *st.*] pour *or* put (**в** В into); Р upbraid; give s.b. a thrashing

всю́ду everywhere, all over

вся́|кий [16] **1.** any; every; anyone; everyone; *без* **~кого сомне́ния** beyond any doubt; *во* **~ком слу́чае** at any rate; **2.** = **~ческий** [16] all kinds *or* sorts of, sundry; every possible; **~чески** in every way; **~чески стара́ться** try one's hardest, try all ways; **~чина** *coll. f* [5]: **~кая ~чина** odds and ends

вта́|йне in secret; **~лкивать** [1], ⟨втолкну́ть⟩ [20] push *or* shove in(to); **~пты-вать** [1], ⟨втопта́ть⟩ [3] trample into; **~скивать** [1], ⟨-щи́ть⟩ [16] pull *or* drag in, into, up

вте|ка́ть [1], ⟨-чь⟩ [26] flow in(to)

вти|ра́ть [1], ⟨втере́ть⟩ [12; вотру́, -рёшь; втёр] rub in; **~ра́ть очки́** (Д) throw dust in (p.'s) eyes; **-ся** *coll.* **в до-ве́рие** worm into; **~скивать** [1], ⟨-снуть⟩ [20] squeeze o.s. in(to)

втихомо́лку *coll.* on the sly

втолкну́ть → **вта́лкивать**

втоптать → **втаптывать**

втор|гаться[1], ⟨~гнуться⟩[21] (**в** В) intrude, invade, penetrate; *в чужие дела* meddle (with); **~жение** *n* [12] invasion, incursion; **~ить** [13] *mus.* sing (*or* play) the second part; echo; repeat; **~йчный** [14] second, repeated; *побочный* secondary; **~йчно** once more, for the second time; **~ник** *m* [1] Tuesday (**в** В, *pl.*: **по** Д on); **~ой** [14] second; *из ~ых рук* second-hand; → **первый & пятый**; **~окурсник** *m* [1] sophomore, *Brt.* secondyear student

второпях hurriedly, in haste

второстепенный [14; -енен, -енна] secondary, minor

в-третьих third(ly)

втридорога: *coll.* triple the price; **платить ~** pay through the nose

втро́|е three times (as …, *comp.*: → **вдвое**); *vb.* **~е** *a.* treble; **~ём** three (of us *or* together); **~йне** three times (as much *etc.*), treble

втулка *f* [5; *g/pl.*: -лок] *tech.* sleeve

втыкать[1], ⟨воткнуть⟩[20] put *or* stick in(to)

втя|гивать[1], ⟨~нуть⟩[19] draw *or* pull in(to), on; *вовлечь* involve, engage; **-ся** (**в** В) *fig. в работу* get used (to)

вуаль *f* [8] veil

вуз *m* [1] (**высшее учебное заведение** *n*) institution of higher education

вулкан *m* [1] volcano; **~ический** [16] volcanic

вульгарный [14; -рен, -рна] vulgar

вундеркинд *m* [1] child prodigy

вход *m* [1] entrance; entry; **~а нет** no entry; **плата за ~** entrance *or* admission fee

входи́ть [15], ⟨войти⟩ [войду, -дёшь; вошёл, -шла; вошедший *g. pt.*: войдя] (**в** В) enter, go, come *or* get in(to); (*помещаться*) go in(to), have room for; hold; be a member of; be included in; **~ во вкус** (Р) take a fancy to; **~ в доверие к** (Д) gain a p.'s confidence; **~ в положение** (Р) appreciate a p.'s position; **~ в привычку** (*в поговорку*) become a habit (proverbial); **~ в** (**состав** Р) form part (of), belo (to)

входной [14] entrance…, admission…

вхолостую: **работать ~** run idle

вцеп|ля́ться [28], ⟨~иться⟩ [14] (**в** В) grasp, catch hold of

вчера yesterday; **~шний** [5] yesterday's, of yesterday

вчерне in rough; in draft form

вче́тверо four times (as …, *comp.*: → **вдвое**); **~м** four (of us *etc.*)

вчитываться [1] (**в** В) *impf. only* try to grasp the meaning of

вше́стеро six times (→ **вдвое**)

вши|вать [1], ⟨~ть⟩ [вошью, -шьёшь; **~ши́ть**] sew in(to); **~вый** [14] *mst. coll. fig.* lousy

въе|даться [1], ⟨~сться⟩ [→ **есть**] eat (in[to]); **~дливый** [14 *sh.*] *coll.* corrosive, acid

въе|зд *m* [1] entrance, entry; **~здной** [14]: **~здная виза** entry visa; **~зжать** [1], ⟨~хать⟩ [въеду, -дешь; въезжай(-те)!] enter, ride *or* drive in(to), up, on (**в**, **на** В); move in(to); **~сться** *or* **~даться**

вы [21] you (polite form *a.* Ⓢ); **~ с ним** you and he; **у вас** (**вы** [**были**]) you have (had)

выб|алтывать *coll.* [1], ⟨~олтать⟩ blab *or* let out; **~ега́ть** [1], ⟨~ежать⟩ [4; выбегу, -ежишь] run out; **~ива́ть** [1], ⟨~ить⟩ [выбью, -бьешь, *etc.* → **бить**] beat *or* knock out; *стекло и т. д.* break; smash; (*изгнать*) drive out, *mil.* dislodge; **~ить из колеи** unsettle; **-ся** break out *or* forth; **~ива́ться из сил** be(come) exhausted, fatigued; **~иваться из колеи** go off the beaten track; **~ира́ть** [1], ⟨~рать⟩ [выберу, -решь; -бранный] choose, pick out; (*избирать*) elect; take out; *минутку* find; **-ся** get out; *на концерт и т. д.* find time to go; **~ить** → **~ива́ть**

выбоина *f* [5] dent; *на дороге* pothole; rut

выбор *m* [1] choice, option; *отбор* selection; *pl.* election(s); **на ~** (*or* **по ~у**) at a p.'s discretion; random (*test*); **всеобщие ~ы** *pl.* general election; **дополнительные ~ы** by-election; **~ка** *f* [5; *g/pl.*: -рок] selection; *pl.* excerpts; *statistics* sample; **~ный** [14] electoral; elected

B

выбр|а́сывать [1], ⟨~о́сить⟩ [15] throw (out *or* away); discard; (*исключи́ть*) exclude, omit; ~а́сывать (*зря*) де́ньги waste money; -ся throw o.s. out; ~ать → **выбира́ть**; ~ить [-ею, -еешь; -итый] *pf.* shave clean; (*v*/*i*. -ся); ~о́сить → ~а́сывать

выб|ыва́ть [1], ⟨~ыть⟩ [-буду, -будешь] leave; *из игры́* drop out

выва́|ливать [1], ⟨~алить⟩ [13] discharge, throw out; -ся fall out; ~ривать [1], ⟨~арить⟩ [13] (*экстраги́ровать*) extract; boil (down); ~е́дывать, ⟨~едать⟩ [1] find out, (try to) elicit; ~езти → ~ози́ть

вывё́ртывать [1], ⟨~ернуть⟩ [20] unscrew; *де́рево* tear out; *ру́ку и т. д.* dislocate; *наизна́нку* turn (inside out); *v*/*i*. -ся; slip out; extricate o.s.

вы́вес|ить → выве́шивать; ~ка *f* [5; *g*/*pl*.: -сок] sign(board); *fig.* screen, pretext; ~ти → выводи́ть

выв|е́тривать [1], ⟨~е́трить⟩ [13] (remove by) air(ing); -ся *geol.* weather; disappear ~е́триваться из па́мяти be effaced from memory; ~е́шивать [1], ⟨~есить⟩ [15] hang out *or* put out; ~и́нчивать [1], ⟨~интить⟩ [15] unscrew

вы́вих *m* [1] dislocation; ~нуть [20] *pf.* dislocate, put out of joint

вы́вод *m* [1] 1. *войск* withdrawal; conclusion; **сде́лать ~** draw a conclusion; ~и́ть [15], ⟨вы́вести⟩ [25] 1. take, lead *or* move (out, to); 2. conclude; 3. *птенцо́в* hatch; *сорт расте́ния* cultivate; 4. *пятно́* remove, *насеко́мых* extirpate; 5. *бу́квы* write *or* draw carefully; 6. *о́браз* depict; ~и́ть (В) **из себя́** make s.b. lose his temper; -ся, ⟨-сь⟩ disappear; ~ок *m* [1; -дка] brood

вы́воз *m* [1] export; *му́сора* removal; ~и́ть [15], ⟨вы́везти⟩ [24] remove, take *or* bring out; export

выв|ора́чивать *coll.* [1], ⟨~оротить⟩ [15] → **вывё́ртывать**

выга́|дывать [1], ⟨~адать⟩ [1] gain *or* save (В/на П sth. from)

вы́гиб *m* [1] bend, curve; ~а́ть [1], ⟨вы́гнуть⟩ [20] *о ко́шке* arch; curve, bend

вы́гля|деть [11 *st*.] *impf.* look (s.th. T, like *как*); как она́ ~дит? what does she look like?; он ~дит моло́же свои́х лет he doesn't look his age; ~́дывать [1], *once* ⟨~нуть⟩ [20 *st*.] look *or* peep out (of в В, из Р)

вы́гнать → выгоня́ть

вы́гнуть → выгиба́ть

выгов|а́ривать [1], ⟨~орить⟩ [13] 1. pronounce; utter; 2. *impf. coll.* (Д) tell off; ~ор *m* [1] 1. pronunciation; 2. reproof, reprimand

вы́год|а *f* [5] (*при́быль*) profit; (*преиму́щество*) advantage; (*по́льза*) benefit; ~ный [14: -ден, -дна] profitable; advantageous (Д, **для** Р to)

вы́гон *m* [1] pasture; ~я́ть [28], ⟨вы́гнать⟩ [вы́гоню, -нишь] turn *or* drive out; *coll. с рабо́ты* fire

выгор|а́живать [1], ⟨~одить⟩ [15] fence off; Р shield, absolve from blame; ~а́ть [1], ⟨~еть⟩ [9] 1. burn down; 2. (*вы́цвести*) fade; 3. *coll.* (*получи́ться*) click, come off

выгр|ужа́ть [1], ⟨~узить⟩ [15] unload, discharge; *с су́дна* disembark; (*v*/*i*. -ся); ~узка [5; *g*/*pl*.: -зок] unloading; disembarkation

выдава́ть [5], ⟨вы́дать⟩ [-дам, -дашь, *etc.* → **дать**] 1. give (out), pay (out); 2. *про́пуск* issue; 3. *преда́ть* betray; *друго́му госуда́рству* extradite; ~ (**себя́**) **за** (В) pass (o.s. off) as; ~ (**за́муж**) **за** (В) give (a girl) in marriage to; -ся 1. (*выступа́ть*) stand out; 2. *coll. день и т. д.* happen *or* turn out

выда́|вливать [1], ⟨~авить⟩ [14] press *or* squeeze out (a. *fig.*); ~**авить улы́бку** force a smile; ~а́лбливать [1], ⟨~олбить⟩ [14] hollow out, gouge out

вы́да|ть → ~ва́ть; ~ча *f* [5] 1. (*разда́ча*) distribution; *сда́ча* delivery; *де́нег* payment; 2. issue; 3. disclosure; 4. extradition; **день ~чи зарпла́ты** payday; ~ю́щийся [17: -щегося *etc.*] outstanding, prominent, distinguished

выдви|га́ть [1], ⟨~́нуть⟩ [20] 1. pull out; 2. *предложе́ние* put forward, propose; *на до́лжность* promote; *кандида́та* nominate; -ся 1. slide in and out; 2. *esp. mil.* move forward; 3. *по слу́жбе* advance; **4.** *impf.* → **жно́й** [14] pull-out..., sliding; (*tech.*) telescopic

выде|ле́ние *n* [12] discharge, secretion; **лка** *f* [5; *g/pl.:* -лок] *о качестве* workmanship; *кожи* dressing; **лы-вать**, ⟨**лать**⟩ [1] work, make *кожу*; **ля́ть** [28], ⟨**лить**⟩ [13] **1.** mark out, single out; (*отметить*) emphasize; **2.** *землю и т. д.* allot; satisfy (*co-heirs*); **3.** *med.* secrete; **4.** *chem.* isolate; **-ся** *v/i.* 1, 4; (*отличаться*) stand out, rise above; excel, **ргивать**, ⟨**рнуть**⟩ [20] pull out

выде́рж|ивать [1], ⟨**ать**⟩ [4] stand, bear, endure; *экзамен* pass; *размеры и т. д.* observe; **ать хара́ктер** be firm; **анный** self-possessed; (*последовательный*) consistent; *о вине* mature; **ка** *f* [5; *g/pl.:* -жек] **1.** self-control; **2.** (*отрывок*) excerpt, quotation; **3.** *phot.* exposure

выди|ра́ть *coll.* [1], ⟨**рать**⟩ [-деру, -ерешь] tear out; *зуб* pull; *pf.* thrash; **олбить** → **а́лбливать**; **охнуть** → **ыха́ть**; **ра** *f* [5] otter; **рать** → **ира́ть**; **ра** *f* [5; *g/pl.:* -мок] invention; made-up story, fabrication; **умы-вать**, ⟨**умать**⟩ [1] invent, contrive, devise

выды|ха́ть [1], ⟨**охнуть**⟩ [20] breathe out; **-ся** become stale; *fig.* be played out

вы́езд *m* [1] departure; *из города* town/city gate

выезжа́ть [1], ⟨**вы́ехать**⟩ [вы́еду, -едешь; -езжа́й(те)!] *v/i.* (*из/с* P) **1.** leave, depart; **2.** *на машине, лошади* drive *or* ride out, on(to); **3.** *из кварти-ры* leave *or* move (from)

вы́емка *f* [5; *g/pl.:* -мок] excavation; *ямка* hollow

вы́ехать → **выезжа́ть**

выж|а́ть → **има́ть**; **дать** → **выжи-да́ть**; **ива́ние** *n* [12] survival; **ива́ть** [1], ⟨**ить**⟩ [-иву, -ивешь; -итый] survive; go through; stay; *coll. из дома и т. д.* oust, drive out; **ить из ума́** be in one's dotage; *fig.* take leave of one's senses; **ига́ть** [1], ⟨**ечь**⟩ [26 г/ж: -жгу, -жжешь, -жгут; -жег, -жженный] burn out; burn down; scorch; **ида́ть** [1]

⟨**дать**⟩ [-жду, -ждешь; -жди(те)!] (P *or* B) wait for *or* till (after); **има́ть** [1], ⟨**ать**⟩ [-жму, -жмешь; -жатый] squeeze, press *or о белье* wring out; *sport* lift (weights); **ить** → **има́ть**

вы́звать → **вызыва́ть**

выздор|а́вливать [1], ⟨**оветь**⟩ [10] recover; **а́вливающий** [17] convalescent; **овле́ние** *n* [12] recovery

вы́з|ов *m* [1] call, summons; (*приглашение*) invitation; *mst. fig.* challenge; **убира́ть** → **зубри́ть** 2; **ыва́ть** [1], ⟨**вать**⟩ [-ову, -овешь] **1.** call (to; for *thea.*; up *tel.*); *врача* send for; **2.** summon (**к** Д to; **в суд** before a court); **3.** challenge (to **на** B); **4.** (*приводить*) rouse, cause; *воспоминания* evoke; **-ся** undertake *or* offer; **ыва́ющий** [17] defiant, provoking

выи́гр|ывать, ⟨**ать**⟩ [1] win (from **у** P); (*извлечь выгоду*) gain, benefit; **ыш** *m* [1] win(ning[s]), gain(s), prize; profit; **быть в ыше** have won (profited); **ышный** [14] *положение* advantageous, effective

вы́йти → **выходи́ть**

выка́|лывать [1], ⟨**олоть**⟩ [17] put out; prick out; **а́пывать**, ⟨**опать**⟩ [1] dig out *or* up; **ара́бкиваться**, ⟨**арабкаться**⟩ [1] scramble *or* get out; **а́рмливать** [1], ⟨**ормить**⟩ [14] bring up, rear; **а́тывать** [1], ⟨**атить**⟩ [15] push *or* wheel out; **атить глаза́** P stare

выки́|дывать [1], *once* ⟨**нуть**⟩ [20] **1.** throw out *or* away; discard; (*опустить*) omit; **2.** *белый флаг* hoist (up); **3.** *coll. фокус* play (trick); **дыш** *m* [1] miscarriage

выкла́|дка *f* [5; *g/pl.:* -док] *math.* computation, calculation; *mil.* pack *or* kit; **дывать** [1], ⟨**выложить**⟩ [16] **1.** *день-ги* lay out; tell; **2.** (*отделать*) face with masonry

выключа́|тель *m* [4] *el.* switch; **ть** [1], ⟨**ить**⟩ [16] switch *or* turn off; *двигатель* stop; **ние** *n* [12] switching off, stopping

выко́|вывать [1], ⟨**вать**⟩ [7] forge; *fig.* mo(u)ld; **ола́чивать** [1], ⟨**олотить**⟩ [15] *ковёр* beat *or* knock

B

out; *долги и т. д.* exact; ⟨олоть →
~а́лывать; ⟨опать → **~а́пывать**;
⟨ормить → **~а́рмливать**;
~орчёвывать[1], ⟨орчева́ть⟩ [7] root
up *or* out

вык|ра́ивать [1], ⟨~роить⟩ [13] sew. cut
out; *coll. вре́мя* spare; *де́ньги* find;
~а́шивать [1], ⟨~асить⟩ [15] paint,
dye; **~и́кивать** [1], *once* ⟨~икнуть⟩
[20] cry *or* call (out); ⟨оить → **~а́ивать**;
⟨ойка f [5; *g/pl.:* -оек] pattern

выкр|уты́сы *coll. m/pl.* [1] *о поведении*
vagaries, crotchets; **~у́чивать** [1], ⟨-
⟨уту́ть⟩ [15] twist; *бельё* wring (out);
coll. unscrew; **-ся** *coll. лампо́чку и
т. д.* slip out

вы́куп m [1] redemption; *заложника и
т. д.* ransom; ⟨а́ть⟩[1], ⟨~ить⟩ [14] *вещь*
redeem; ransom; ⟨ать → **купа́ть**

выку́р|ивать [1], ⟨~ить⟩ [13] smoke

выл|а́вливать [1], ⟨~овить⟩ [14] fish
out, draw out; ⟨азка f [5; *g/pl.:* -зок]
mil. sally; **~а́мывать** [1], ⟨омать⟩ [1]
break open

выл|еза́ть[1], ⟨~езть⟩ [24] climb *or* get
out; *о волоса́х* fall out; **~епля́ть** [28],
⟨~епи́ть⟩ [14] model, fashion

вы́лет m [1] *ae.* taking off, flight; ⟨а́ть⟩
[1], ⟨~еть⟩ [11] fly out; *ae.* take off, (*в В*
for); rush out *or* up; (*вы́валиться*) fall
out; slip (a p.'s memory **~еть из голо-
вы́**); **~еть в трубу́** go broke

выл|е́чивать [1], ⟨~ечить⟩ [16] cure,
heal (*v/i.* **-ся**); **~ива́ть** [1], ⟨~ить⟩
[-лью, -льешь; → **лить**] pour out; **~
~и́тый** [14] the image of, just like (*И
s.b.*)

выл|овить → ~а́вливать; **~ожить →
выкла́дывать**; **~ома́ть → ~а́мывать**;
~упля́ться [28], ⟨~иться⟩ [14] hatch

вым|а́зывать [1], ⟨~азать⟩ [3] smear;
daub (**-ся** *o.s.*) (Т with); **~а́ливать** [1],
⟨~олить⟩ [13] get *or* obtain by entrea-
ties; **~а́ливать проще́ние** beg for forgiveness; **~а́нивать** [1], ⟨~анить⟩ [13]
lure (**из** P out of); coax *or* cheat (**у**
P/B a p. out of s.th.); **~а́ривать** [1], ⟨-
⟨орить⟩ [13] exterminate; **~а́чивать**
[1], ⟨~очить⟩ [16] дождём drench; *в
жидкости* soak; **~а́щивать** [1], ⟨-

⟨остить⟩ [15] pave **~е́нивать** [1], ⟨-
⟨еня́ть⟩ [28] exchange (for **на** В);
~ере́ть → ~ира́ть; **~ета́ть** [1], ⟨~ести⟩
[25; -т- *st.:* -ету, -етешь] sweep (out);
~еща́ть [1], ⟨~ести́ть⟩ [15] avenge o.s.
(on Д); *зло́бу* vent (**на** П on p.); **~ира́ть**
[1], ⟨~ереть⟩ [12] die out, become extinct

вымога́т|ельство n [9] blackmail, ex-
tortion; **~ь** [1] extort (B *or* Р/у P s.th.
from)

вым|ока́ть [1], ⟨~окнуть⟩ [21] get wet
through; **~окнуть до ни́тки** get soaked
to the skin; **~олвить** [14] *pf.* utter, say;
~олить → ~а́ливать; **~орить → ~а́ри-
вать**; **~остить → ~а́щивать**; **~очить →
~а́чивать**

вы́мпел m [1] pennant, pennon

вым|ыва́ть [1], ⟨~ыть⟩ [22] wash (out,
up); **~ысел** m [1; -сла] invention; fantasy; *ложь* falsehood; **~ыть → ~ыва́ть**;
~ышля́ть[28], ⟨~ыслить⟩ [15] think up,
invent; **~ышленный** *a.* fictitious

вы́мя n [13] udder

вын|а́шивать [1]: **~а́шивать план** nur-
ture a plan; **~ести → ~оси́ть**

вын|има́ть[1], ⟨~уть⟩ [20] take *or* draw
out, produce

вын|оси́ть [15], ⟨~ести⟩ [24; -с-: -су,
-сешь; -с, -сла -сло] **1.** carry *or* take
out (away), remove; **2.** (*терпе́ть*) endure, bear; **3.** *благода́рность* express;
pass (*a. law*); **~оси́ть сор из избы́** wash
one's dirty linen in public; **~о́сливость**
f[8] endurance; **~о́сливый** [14 *sh.*] sturdy, hardy, tough

вын|ужда́ть [1], ⟨~удить⟩ [15] force,
compel; extort (B/у *or* от P s.th. from);
~ужденный [14 *sh.*] forced; of necessi-
ty; **~ужденная поса́дка** emergency
landing

вы́нырнуть[20] *pf.* come to the surface,
emerge; *coll.* turn up (unexpectedly)

вы́пад m [1] fencing lunge; thrust; *fig.*
attack

выпа|да́ть[1], ⟨~сть⟩[25] **1.** fall *or* drop
(out); (*вы́скользнуть*) slip out; **2.** fall
(Д to, *a.* **на до́лю**) to a p.'s lot); devolve
on

вы́п|а́ливать [1], ⟨~алить⟩ [13] *coll.*

blurt out; shoot (*из* P with); ~а́лывать [1], ⟨о́лоть⟩ [17] weed (out); ~а́ривать [1], ⟨а́рить⟩ [13] steam; clean, disinfect; (*chem.*) evaporate

вып|ека́ть [1], ⟨е́чь⟩ [26] bake; ~ива́ть [1], ~ить⟩ [-пью, -пьешь; → **пить**] drink (up); *coll.* be fond of the bottle; ~ить (**ли́шнее**) *coll.* have one too many; ~ить ча́шку ча́я have a cup of tea; ~ивка *coll.* f [5; g/pl.: -вок] booze

вы́п|иска f [5; g/pl.: -сок] **1.** writing out, copying; **2.** *из те́кста* extract; statement (of account *из счёта*); **3.** order; subscription; **4.** *из больни́цы* discharge; *с ме́ста жи́тельства* notice of departure; ~и́сывать [1], ⟨иса́ть⟩ [3] **1.** write out (*or* down); copy; **2.** → **выводи́ть 6.**; **3.** *журна́л и т. д.* order; subscribe; ~ся sign out; ~и́сываться из больни́цы leave hospital

вы́пла|вка f [5] smelting; ~ка́ть [3] *pf.* cry (one's eyes *глаза́*) out; ~та f [5] payment; ~чивать [1], ~тить⟩ [15] pay (out *or* off)

выпл|ёвывать [1], *once* ⟨ю́нуть⟩ [20] spit out; ~ёскивать [1], ⟨е́скать⟩ [3], *once* ⟨е́снуть⟩ [20] dash *or* splash (out); ~е́снуть с водо́й ребёнка throw the baby out with the bathwater

выпл|ыва́ть [1], ⟨ы́ть⟩ [23] swim out; surface; emerge, appear

выпол|а́скивать [1], ⟨'-оскать⟩ [3] rinse; *го́рло* gargle; ~а́ть [1], ⟨'-зти⟩ [24] creep *or* crawl out; ~не́ние n [12] fulfil(l)ment, execution, realization; ~ня́ть [1], ⟨'-нить⟩ [13] carry out, fulfil(l); execute; '-оть → **выпа́лывать**

выпр|а́вка f [5; g/pl.: -вок]: *вое́нная* ~а́вка soldierly bearing; ~авля́ть [28], ⟨а́вить⟩ [14] set right *or* straighten out; *ру́копись и т. д.* correct; ~а́вить [1], ⟨а́сить⟩ [15] try to get *or* obtain, solicit; ~ова́живать *coll.* [1], ⟨а́воводить⟩ [15] send s.o. packing, turn out; ~ы́гивать [1], ⟨ы́гнуть⟩ [20] jump out; ~яга́ть [1], ⟨ячь⟩ [26 г/ж: -ягу, -яжешь; -яг] unharness; ~ямля́ть [28], ⟨а́мить⟩ [14] straighten; -ся become straight; *спи́ну* straighten

вы́пукл|ость f [8] protuberance; prominence, bulge; ~ый [14] convex; prominent; *fig.* expressive; distinct

вы́пуск m [1] output; issue; publication; (*часть рома́на*) instal(1)ment; *о студе́нтах* graduate class; ~ти́ть⟩ [15] let out; *law* release; *това́ры* produce, issue, publish; (*исключи́ть*) omit, leave out; graduate; ~а́ть в прода́жу put on sale; ~ни́к m [1 *e.*] graduate; ~но́й [14] graduate…, graduation…, final, leaving; *tech.* discharge…; exhaust…

вып|у́тывать, ⟨утать⟩ [1] disentangle *or* extricate (-ся *o.s.*); ~у́чивать [1], ⟨-у́чить⟩ [16] **1.** bulge; P → **тара́щить**

вып|ы́тывать, ⟨ытать⟩ [1] find out, (try to) elicit

выпя́|ливать Р [1], ⟨лить⟩ [13] → **тара́щить**; ~чивать *coll.* [1], ⟨'-тить⟩ [15] stick *or* thrust out; *fig.* emphasize

выраба́|тывать, ⟨отать⟩ [1] manufacture, produce; *план и т. д.* elaborate, work out; develop; '-отка f [15; g/pl.: -ток] manufacture, production; output

выр|а́внивать [1], ⟨овня́ть⟩ [28] **1.** level; smooth out; **2.** align; (*уравни́вать*) equalize; -ся straighten; become even

выра|жа́ть [1], ⟨'-зить⟩ [15] express, show; **жа́ть слова́ми** put into words; ~жа́ться [1], ⟨'-зиться⟩ [15] **1.** express *o.s.*; **2.** manifest itself (*в* П in); ~же́ние n [12] expression; ~зи́тельный [14; -лен, -льна] expressive; *coll.* significant

выр|аста́ть [1], ⟨асти́⟩ [24 -ст-: -асту; → **расти́**] **1.** grow (up); increase; (*преврати́ться*) develop into; **2.** (*появи́ться*) emerge, appear; ~а́щивать [1], ⟨асти́ть⟩ [15] *расте́ние* grow; *живо́тных* breed; *ребёнка* bring up; *fig.* *чемпио́на* train; ~ва́ть **1.** → ~ыва́ть; **2.** → **рвать 3**

вы́рез m [1] notch; cut; **пла́тье с глубо́ким ~ом** low-necked dress; ~а́ть [1], ⟨а́ть⟩ [15] **1.** cut out, clip; **2.** *из де́рева* carve; (*гравирова́ть*) engrave; **3.** slaughter; ~ка f [5; g/pl.: -зок] cutting out, clipping; *cul.* tenderloin; ~но́й [14] carved

вы́ро|док m [1; -дка] *coll.* monster;

B

~жда́ться [1], ⟨~ди́ться⟩ [15] degenerate; **~жде́ние** n [12] degeneration
вы́ронить [13] pf. drop
вы́росший [17] grown
выр|уба́ть [1], ⟨~убить⟩ [14] cut down or fell; **~уча́ть** [1], ⟨~учить⟩ [16] **1.** come to s.o.'s help or rescue; **2.** *за товар* make, net; **~учка** f [5] rescue; assistance, help; *comm.* proceeds; **прийти́ на ~учку** come to the aid (Д of)
выр|ыва́ть [1], ⟨~вать⟩ [-ву, -вешь] **1.** pull out; tear out; **2.** snatch (*из* P, *у* P from); *fig.* extort (В/у P s.th. from a p.); **-ся** break away; tear o.s. away (*из* P from); break loose; escape; **~ыва́ть**, ⟨~ыть⟩ [22] dig out, up
вы́с|адка f [5; *g/pl.:* -док] disembarkation, landing; **~а́живать** [1], ⟨~адить⟩ [15] **1.** land, disembark; **2.** help out; make or let a p. get off; **3.** *растения* transplant; **-ся** *v/i.; a.* get out, off
выс|а́сывать [1], ⟨~осать⟩ [-осу, -осешь] suck out; **~ве́рливать** [1], ⟨~верлить⟩ [13] bore, drill; **~вобожда́ть** [1], ⟨~вободить⟩ [15] free, disentangle
выс|ева́ть [1], ⟨~еять⟩ [27] sow; **~ека́ть** [1], ⟨~ечь⟩ [26] **1.** hew, carve; **2.** → *сечь*; **~еле́ние** n [12] eviction; **~еля́ть** [28], ⟨~елить⟩ [13] evict; **~еять** → *сеять*; **~и́живать** [1], ⟨~идеть⟩ [11] sit out, stay; *яйцо* hatch
выск|а́бливать [1], ⟨~облить⟩ [13] scrape clean; *удалить* erase; **~а́зывать** [1], ⟨~азать⟩ [3] express, tell, state; **~азать предположе́ние** suggest; **-ся** express one's opinion, thoughts, *etc.* (*о* П about); speak (*за* В for; *про́тив* P against); **~а́кивать** [1], ⟨~очить⟩ [16] jump, leap or rush out; **~а́льзывать** [1], ⟨~ользать⟩ [1], ⟨~ользнуть⟩ [20] slip out; **~облить** → **~а́бливать**; **~очить** → **~а́кивать**; **~очка** m/f [5; *g/pl.:* -чек] upstart; **~реба́ть** [1], ⟨~рести⟩ [25 -б-: → **скрести́**] scrape out (off); (*удалить*) scratch out
выс|ла́ть → **~ыла́ть**; **~е́живать** [1], ⟨~едить⟩ [15] track down; **~у́живать** [1], ⟨~ужить⟩ [16] obtain by or for service; **-ся** curry favo(u)r (*перед* T with s.b.); **~у́шивать**, ⟨~ушать⟩ [1] listen

(to), hear (out); *med.* auscultate
высм|е́ивать [1], ⟨~еять⟩ [27] deride, ridicule
выс|о́вывать [1], ⟨~унуть⟩ [20 *st.*] put out; **-ся** lean out
высо́кий [16; высо́к, -а́, -со́ко́; *compr.:* **вы́ше**] high; tall (*a.* **~ ро́стом**); *fig.* lofty
высоко|ка́чественный [14] (of) high-quality; **~квалифици́рованный** [14] highly skilled; **~ме́рие** n [12] haughtiness; **~ме́рный** [14; -рен, -рна] haughty, arrogant; **~па́рный** [14; -рен, -рна] bombastic, high-flown; **~превосходи́тельство** [9] *hist.* Excellency; **~производи́тельный** [14; -лен, -льна] *рабо́та* highly productive; *оборудование* high-efficiency
высосать → **выса́сывать**
высо|та́ f [5; *g/pl.:* -о́ты, *etc. st.*] height; *mus.* pitch; *geogr.* eminence; hill; altitude; *уровень* level; **оказа́ться на ~те́** be equal to the occasion); **высото́й в** (В) ... or ...; **в ~ту́** ... high
вы́сох|нуть → **высыха́ть**; **~ший** [17] dried up, withered
выс|оча́йший [17] highest; *достиже́ние* supreme; **~о́чество** n [9] *hist.* Highness; **~паться** → **высыпа́ться**
вы́спренний [15] bombastic
вы́став|ить → **~ля́ть**; **~ка** f [5; *g/pl.:* -вок] exhibition, show; **~ля́ть** [28], ⟨~ить⟩ [14] **1.** (*выгнать*) put (take) out; **2.** *картину и т. д.* exhibit, display; represent (**себя́** o.s.); **3.** *оценку* give a mark; *mil.* post; *выгнать* turn out; **~ля́ть напока́з** parade; **-ся** exhibit; **~очный** [14] (of the) exhibition, show...
выстр|а́ивать(ся) [1] → **стро́ить(ся)**; **~ел** m [1] shot; (noise) report; **на (расстоя́ние, -ии) ~ел(а)** within gunshot; **~елить** → **стреля́ть**
вы́ступ m [1] projection; **~а́ть** [1], ⟨~ить⟩ [14] **1.** step forth, forward; come or stand out; *слёзы и т. д.* appear; **2.** *в поход* set out; **3.** speak (sing, play) in public; **~а́ть с ре́чью (в пре́ниях)** address an audience, deliver a speech; take the floor; **~ле́ние** n [12] setting out; *pol.* speech; appearance (in public); *thea.*

performance, turn

высунуть(ся) → **высо́вывать(ся)**

высу́ш|ивать [1], ⟨~ить⟩ [16] dry up, *coll.* emaciate

высчи́тывать [1], ⟨~читать⟩ calculate, compute; *coll.* deduct

вы́сш|ий [17] highest, supreme, higher (*a. educ.*), superior; **~ая ме́ра наказа́ния** capital punishment

высыла́ть [1], ⟨~лать⟩ [вы́шлю, -лешь] send, send out; *pol.* exile; *из страны* deport; *из страны* dispatch; exile, expulsion; **~ыпа́ть** [1], ⟨~ыпать⟩ [2] pour out *or* in, on; *v/i. о людях* spill out; **~ыпа́ться** ⟨вы́спаться⟩ [-сплюсь, -спишься] sleep one's fill, have a good night's rest; **~ыха́ть** [1], ⟨~охнуть⟩ [21] dry up, wither; **~ь** *f* [8] height, summit

выт|а́лкивать, *coll.* ⟨~олкать⟩ [1], *once* ⟨~олкнуть⟩ [20 *st.*] throw out; **~а́пливать** [1], ⟨~опить⟩[14] **1.** heat; **2.** *о жире* melt (down); **~а́скивать** [1], ⟨~ащить⟩ [16] drag off *or* out; *coll.* украсть pilfer

выт|ека́ть [1], ⟨~ечь⟩ [26] flow out; *fig.* follow, result; **~ереть** → **~ира́ть**; **~ерпеть** [14] *pf.* endure, bear; **не ~ерпел** couldn't help; **~есня́ть** [28], ⟨~еснить⟩[13] force, push out; *оппонента* supplant; **~ечь** → **~ека́ть**

выт|ира́ть [1], ⟨~ереть⟩ [12] dry, wipe (**-ся** o.s.); wear out

вы́точенный [14] chiseled; *tech.* turned

вы́тр|ебовать [7] *pf.* ask for, demand, order, summon; *добиться требованием* obtain on demand; **~яса́ть** [1], ⟨~ясти⟩ [24 -c-] shake out

выть [22], ⟨вз-⟩ howl

выт|я́гивать [1], ⟨~януть⟩ [20 *st.*] draw, pull *or* stretch (out); elicit; *сведения* endure, bear; **-ся** stretch, extend (o.s.); *вырасти* grow (up); **~яжка** *f chem.* extract

выу́живать [1], ⟨~дить⟩ [15] catch, dig out (*a. fig.*)

выу́ч|ивать [1], ⟨~ить⟩ [16] learn, memorize (В + *inf. or* Д); teach (a p. to … *or* s.th.); **-ся** learn (Д/у Р s.th. from); **~иваться на врача́** become a doctor

вых|а́живать [1], ⟨~одить⟩ [15] *больного* nurse, restore to health; **~ва́тывать** [1], ⟨~ватить⟩ [15] snatch away, from, out; pull out, draw

вы́хлоп *m* [1] exhaust; **~но́й** [14] exhaust…

вы́ход *m* [1] **1.** exit; way out (*a. fig.*); *чувствам* outlet; **2.** departure; withdrawal, *на пенсию* retirement; **3.** *книги* appearance, publication; *thea.* entrance (on stage); **4.** *продукции* yield, output; **~ за́муж** marriage (of woman); **~ в отста́вку** retirement, resignation; **~ец** *m* [1; -дца] immigrant, native of; **быть ~цем из** come from

выходи́ть [15], ⟨вы́йти⟩ [вы́йду, -дешь; вы́шел] **1.** go *or* come out; leave; withdraw; retire; **2.** *о книге* appear, be published *or* issued; **3.** *получиться* come off; turn out, result; happen, arise, originate; **вы́шло!** it's worked!; **вы́йти в отста́вку (на пе́нсию)** retire, resign; **~ за преде́лы** (P) transgress the bounds of; **~ (за́муж) за** (В) marry (*v/t.*; *of woman*); **~ из себя́** be beside o.s.; **~ из терпе́ния** lose one's temper (patience); **окно́ выхо́дит на у́лицу** window facing the street; **~ из стро́я** fail; be out of action; **из него́ вы́шел … ** he has become …; **из э́того ничего́ не вы́йдет** nothing will come of it

выходи́ть → **выха́живать**; **~ка** *f* [5; *g/pl.*: -док] trick, prank; excess; **~но́й** [14] exit…; outlet…; **~но́й день** *m* day off; (have a **быть** Т); **~но́е посо́бие** gratuity

вы́холенный [14] well-groomed

выцве|та́ть [1], ⟨~сти⟩ [25 -т-: -ету] fade

выч|ёркивать [1], ⟨~еркнуть⟩ [20] cross *or* strike out; *из памяти* erase, obliterate; **~ёрпывать** [1], ⟨~ерпать⟩ [1], *once* ⟨~ерпнуть⟩ [20 *st.*] bail, scoop (out); **~есть** → **~ита́ть**; **~ет** *m* [1] deduction; **за ~ом** (Р) less, minus

вычисл|е́ние *n* [12] calculation; **~я́ть** [1], ⟨~ить⟩ [13] calculate, compute

вычи|стить → **~ща́ть**; **~та́емое** *n* [14] subtrahend; **~та́ние** *n* [12] subtraction; **~та́ть** [1], ⟨вы́честь⟩ [25 -т-: -чту, -чел, -чла; *g. pt.*: вы́чтя] deduct; subtract;

~**щáть** [1], ⟨~**стить**⟩ [15] clean, scrub, scour; brush

вы́чурный [14; -рен, -рна] ornate, flowery; fanciful

вы́швырнуть [20 *st.*] *pf.* throw out

вы́ше higher; above; *сил и т. д.* beyond; **онá ~ меня́** she is taller than I (am); **э́то ~ моего́ понима́ния** that's beyond my comprehension

вы́ше... above...

выш|ивáть [1], ⟨~**ить**⟩ [-бу, -бешь; -б, -бла; -бленный] *coll.* (*вы́бить*) knock out; (*вы́гнать*) kick out; ~**ивáние** *n* [12] embroidery; ~**ивáть** [1], ⟨~**ить**⟩ [-шью, -шьешь] embroider; ~**и́вка** *f* [5; *g/pl.*: -вок] embroidery

вышинá *f* [5] height; → **высотá**

вы́шка *f* [5; *g/pl.*: -шек] tower; **буровáя ~** derrick; **диспéтчерская ~** *ae.* control tower

выявля́ть [28], ⟨~**ить**⟩ [14] display, make known; uncover, reveal

выясне́ние *n* [12] clarification; ~**я́ть** [28], ⟨~**ить**⟩ [13] clear up, find out, ascertain; **-ся** turn out; come to light

вью́|га *f* [5] snowstorm; ~**щийся** [17] curly; ~**щееся растéние** *n* creeper, climber

вя́жущий [17] astringent

вяз *m* [1] elm

вязáль|ный [14] knitting...; ~**ый крючóк** crochet hook; ~**ая спи́ца** knitting needle

вязан|ка *f* [5; *g/pl.*: -нок] knitted garment; fag(g)ot; ~**ый** [14] knitted; ~**ье** *n* [10] (*a.* ~**ме** *n* [12]) knitting; **крючкóм** crochet

вязáть [3], ⟨с-⟩ **1.** tie, bind (together); **2.** knit; **крючкóм** crochet; **-ся** *impf.* (*соотвéтствовать*) agree, be in keeping; **разговóр не ~áлся** the conversation flagged; ~**кий** [16; -зок, -зкá, -о] viscous; *о почве* swampy, marshy; ~**нуть** [21], ⟨за-, у-⟩ get stuck in; sink into

вя́лить [13], ⟨про-⟩ dry; dry-cure, jerk (*meat, fish*)

вя́|лый [14 *sh.*] *цветóк* withered, faded; *физически* flabby; *fig.* sluggish; dull (*a. comm.*); ~**нуть** [20], ⟨за-, у-⟩ wither, fade

Г

габари́т *m* [1] *tech.* clearance-related dimension, size

гáвань *f* [8] harbo(u)r

гáга *f* [5] *zo.* eider

гадá|лка *f* [5; *g/pl.*: -лок] fortuneteller; ~**ние** *n* [12] fortune-telling; *догáдка* guessing, conjecture; ~**ть** [1] **1.** ⟨по-⟩ tell fortunes (with cards **на кáртах**); **2.** *impf.* guess, conjecture

гáд|ина *f* [5] *coll.* loathsome person, cur; ~**ить** [15] **1.** ⟨на-, за-⟩ soil; (Д) harm; **2.** ⟨из-⟩ P botch; ~**кий** [16; -док, -дкá, -о; *comp.*: гáже] nasty, ugly, disgusting, repulsive; ~**ли́вый** [14 *sh.*]: ~**ли́вое чу́вство** feeling of disgust; ~**ость** *f* [8] *coll.* filth; low *or* dirty trick; ~**юка** *f* [5] *zo.* viper (*a.* P *fig.*), adder

гáечный ключ *m* [1; *g/pl.*: -ей] spanner; wrench

газ *m* [1] **1.** gas; **дать ~** *mot.* step on the gas; **на пóлном ~у́** at full speed (throttle); *pl. med.* flatulence; **2.** *ткань* gauze

газéль *f* [8] gazelle

газéт|а *f* [5] newspaper; ~**ный** [14] news...; ~**ный кио́ск** *m* newsstand, *Brt.* news stall; ~**чик** *m* [1] *coll.* journalist

газиро́ван|ный [14]: ~**ная водá** soda water

гáз|овый [14] **1.** gas...; ~**овая колóнка** geyser; water heater; ~**овая плитá** gas stove; ~**о́вщик** *m* [1] *coll.* gasman

газóн *m* [1] lawn; ~**окоси́лка** *f* [5; *g/pl.*: -лок] lawnmower

газо|обрáзный [14; -зен, -зна] gaseous; ~**провóд** *m* [1] gas pipeline

га́йка f [5; g/pl.: га́ек] tech. nut

галантере́йный [14]: **~е́йный магази́н** notions store, haberdashery; **~е́йные това́ры** m/pl. = **~ е́я** f [6] notions pl., haberdashery

галд|ёж m [1 e.], row, hubbub; **~е́ть** [11], ⟨за-⟩ clamo(u)r, din

гал|ере́я f [6] gallery; **~ёрка** coll. f [5] thea. gallery, "the gods" (occupants of gallery seats)

галиматья́ f [7] coll. balderdash, nonsense; **сплошна́я ~** sheer nonsense

галифе́ pl. [indecl.] riding breeches pl.

га́лка f [5; g/pl.: -лок] jackdaw

гало́п m [1] gallop; **~ом** at a gallop; **~и́ровать** [7] gallop

га́лочк|а f [5; g/pl.: -чек] tick; **для ~и** for purely formal purposes

гало́ши f/pl. [5] galoshes, rubbers

га́лстук m [1] (neck)tie

галу́н m [1 e.] galloon, braid

гальван|изи́ровать [7] (im)pf. galvanize; **~и́ческий** [16] galvanic

га́лька f [5; g/pl.: -лек] pebble

гам m [1] coll. din, row, rumpus

гама́к m [1 e.] hammock

га́мма f [5] mus. scale; красок range; **~-излуче́ние** gamma rays

гангре́на f [5] gangrene

га́нгстер m [1] gangster

гандбо́л m [1] handball

ганте́ли (-'tɛ-) f/pl. [8] (sport) dumbbells

гара́ж m [1 e.] garage

гарант|и́ровать [7] (im)pf., **~ия** f [7] guarantee

гардеро́б m [1] wardrobe, a. collect.; **~ная** f [14] check-, cloakroom; **~щик** m [1], **~щица** f [5] cloakroom attendant

гарди́на f [5] curtain

гармо́|ника f [5] (kind of) accordion; **губна́я ~** mouth organ, harmonica; **~ни́ровать** [7] harmonize, be in harmony (**с T** with); **~ни́ст** m [1] accordionist; harmonist; **~ни́чный** [14; -чен, -чна] harmonious; **~ня** f [7] harmony; **~нь** f [8], **~шка** f [5; g/pl.: -шек] → **~ника**

гарни|зо́н m [1] garrison; **~р** m [1], **~рова́ть** [7] (im)pf., cul. garnish; **~ту́р** m [1] set; мебели suite

гарпу́н m [1 e.], **~ить** [13] harpoon

гарь f [8] (s.th.) burnt, chared; **па́хнет ~ю** there is a smell of smoke

гаси́ть [15], ⟨по-, за-⟩ extinguish, put or blow out; известь slake; **~ почто́вую ма́рку** frank a postage stamp

га́снуть [21], ⟨по-, у-⟩ grow feeble, die away; fig. fade, wither

гастрол|ёр m [1] guest actor or artiste; coll. casual worker moving from town to town; **~и́ровать** [7] tour; perform on tour; **~и** f/pl. [8] tour

гастроно́м m [1] a. = **~и́ческий магази́н** m grocery store or shop; **~и́ческий** [16] gastronomic(al); **~ия** f [7] provisions; delicacies pl.

гвалт coll. m [1] rumpus, uproar

гварде́|ец m [1; -е́йца] guardsman; **~ия** f [7] Guards pl.

гво́зд|ик dim. → **~ь**; **~и́ка** f [5] carnation, pink; (spice) clove; **~ь** m [4 e.; pl.: гво́зди, -де́й] tack, nail; fig. программы main feature

где where; coll. → **куда́**; **~-~ кое-где́**; → **ни**; **~** = **~-либо**, **~-нибудь**, **~-то** anywhere; somewhere; **~-то здесь** hereabout(s)

гей! int. hi!

гекта́р m [1] hectare

ге́лий m [3] helium

ген m [1] gene

генеало́гия f [7] genealogy

генера́|л m [1] general; **~литет** m [1] collect. generals; coll. top brass; **~льный** [14] general; **~льная репети́ция** f dress rehearsal; **~тор** m [1] generator

гене́ти|ка f [5] genetics; **~ческий** [16] genetic, genic

гени|а́льный [14: -лен, -льна] of genius; ingenious; **~й** m [3] genius

генита́лии m/pl. [3] genitals

геноци́д m [1] genocide

гео́|граф m [1] geographer; **~графи́ческий** [16] geographic(al); **~гра́фия** f [7] geography; **~лог** m [1] geologist; **~ло́гия** f [7] geology; **~ме́трия** f [7] geometry

георги́н (**a** f [5]) m [1] dahlia

гера́нь f [8] geranium

герб m [1 e.] (coat of) arms; emblem;

~овый [14] heraldic; stamp(ed)

геркуле́с m [1] **1.** man of herculean strength; **2.** rolled oats; porridge

герма́нский [16] German, *ling.* Germanic

гермети́ческий [16] airtight

герои́зм m [1] heroism

герои́н m [1] heroin

геро́|иня f [6] heroine; **~и́ческий** [16] heroic; **~й** m [3] hero; **~йский** [16] heroic

гиаци́нт m [1] hyacinth

ги́бель f [8] death; *корабля и т. д.* loss; (*разрушение*) ruin, destruction; **~ный** [14; -лен, -льна] disastrous, fatal

ги́бк|ий [16; -бок, -бка́, -о́; *comp.*: ги́бче] supple, pliant, flexible (*a. fig.*); **~ость** f [8] flexibility

ги́б|лый [14]: **~лое де́ло** hopeless case; **~лое ме́сто** godforsaken place; **~нуть** [21], ⟨по-⟩ perish

гига́нт m [1] giant; **~ский** [16] gigantic, huge

гигие́н|а f [5] hygiene; **~и́ческий** [16], **~и́чный** [14; -чен, -чна] hygienic

гигроскопи́ческий [16; -чен, -чна] hygroscopic

гид m [1] guide

гидравли́ческий [16] hydraulic

гидро|план m [1] seaplane, hydroplane; **~(электро)ста́нция** f [7] hydroelectric (power) station

гие́на f [5] hyena

ги́льза f [5] (cartridge) case; (cylinder) sleeve

гимн m [1] hymn; *госуда́рственный* anthem

гимна́зи|ст m [1] pupil; **~зия** f [7] high school, *Brt.* grammar school; **~ст** m [1] gymnast; **~стёрка** f [5; *g/pl.*: -рок] *mil.* blouse, *Brt.* tunic; **~стика** f [5] gymnastics; **~сти́ческий** [16] gymnastic; **~сти́ческий зал** gymnasium

гипе́рбола¹ f [5] *math.* hyperbola

гипе́рбол|а² f [5] hyperbole; exaggeration; **~и́ческий** [16] hyperbolic, exaggerated

гипертони́я f [7] high blood-pressure, hypertension

гипно́|з m [1] hypnosis; **~тизи́ровать** [7], ⟨за-⟩ hypnotize

гипо́теза f [5] hypothesis

гипс m [1] *min.* gypsum; *tech.* plaster of Paris; **~овый** [14] gypseous, plaster…

гирля́нда f [5] garland

ги́ря f [6] weight

гита́р|а f [5] guitar; **~и́ст** m [1] guitarist

глава́¹ f [5; *pl. st.*] chapter

глав|а́² f [5; *pl. st.*] head; (*быть, стоя́ть*) **во ~е́** (be) at the head; lead (**с** T by); **поста́вить во ~у́ угла́** consider to be of the greatest importance; **~а́рь** m [4 e.] (ring-) leader

гла́венств|о n [9] supremacy; domination; **~овать** [7] command, hold sway (over)

главнокома́ндующий m [17] commander in chief; *Верхо́вный* ~ Commander in Chief; Supreme Commander

гла́вн|ый [14] chief, main, principal, central; head…; … in chief; **~ое (де́ло)** the main thing; above all; **~ым о́браз-ом** mainly, chiefly

глаго́л m [1] *gr.* verb; **~ьный** [14] verbal

глад|и́льный [14] ironing; **~и́льная доска́** ironing board; **~ить** [15] **1.** ⟨вы-⟩ iron, press; **2.** ⟨по-⟩ stroke, caress; *coll.* **~ить по голо́вке** indulge; favo(u)r; **~ить про́тив ше́рсти** rub the wrong way; **~кий** [16; -док, -дка́; *comp.*: гла́же] smooth (*a. fig.*); *во́лосы* lank; *ткань* plain; **~ко** smoothly, successfully; *всё прошло́ ~ко* everything went off smoothly; **~ь** f [8] smoothness; smooth surface; *тишь да ~ь coll.* peace and quiet

глаз m [1; в ~у́; *pl.*: -а́, глаз, -а́м] eye; look; *зре́ние* (eye)sight; *coll.* при-смо́тр heed, care; **в ~а́** (Д) to s.b.'s face; **в мои́х ~а́х** in my view *or* opinion; **за ~а́** in s.b.'s absence, behind one's back; more than enough; **на ~** approximately, by eye; **на ~а́х** (*poss. or* у Р) in s.b.'s presence; **не в бровь, а в ~** *coll.* hit the mark; **с у́ на ~** privately, tête-à-tête; **невооружённым ~ом** with the naked eye; **темно́, хоть ~ вы́коли** *coll.* it is pitch-dark; **~а́стый** *coll.* [14 *sh.*] sharp-sighted; **~е́ть** P [8] stare, gape; **~но́й** [14] eye…, optic; **~но́й врач** m ophthalmologist; **∠ное я́блоко** eyeball; ∠ок *m* [1; -зка́] **1.** [*pl. st.:* -зок] *dim.* → **глаз; аню́тины ∠ки** *pl.* pansy; **2.** [*pl. e.:* -зки́, -зко́в] *bot.* bud; *в две́ри* peephole

глазоме́р *m* [1]: **хоро́ший ∼** good eye

глазу́нья *f* [6] fried eggs *pl.*

глазуро́вать [7] (*im*)*pf.* glaze; **∠ь** *f* [8] glaze, icing

гла́нда *f* [5] tonsil

глас *m* [1]: **∼ вопию́щего в пусты́не** voice of one crying in the wilderness

гла|си́ть [15 *e.*; *3. sg. only*] say, read, run; **∠сность** *f* [8] public(ity), openness; **∠сный** [14] open, public; (*a. su.*) vowel

глетчер *m* [1] glacier

гли́на *f* [5] clay; loam; **∠истый** [14 *sh.*] clayey; loamy; **∠озём** *m* [1] *min.* alumina; **∠яный** [14] clay- *or* earthenware-related

глист *m* [1 *e.*], **∠а́** *f* [5] (intestinal) worm; **(ле́нточный) ∼** tapeworm

глицери́н *m* [1] glycerin(e)

глоб|а́льный [14; -лен, -льна] global, worldwide; **∠ус** *m* [1] globe

глода́ть [3], ⟨об-⟩ gnaw (at, round)

глот|а́ть [1], ⟨про∠и́ть⟩ [15], *once* ⟨∠ну́ть⟩ [20] swallow; *coll.* жа́дно devour; **∠ка** *f* [5; *g/pl.:* -ток] throat; **во всю ∠ку → го́лос; ∠о́к** *m* [1; -тка́] mouthful, gulp (T of)

гло́хнуть [21] **1.** ⟨о-⟩ grow deaf; **2.** ⟨за-⟩ *о зву́ке* fade, die away; *о са́де и т. д.* grow desolate, become wild

глуб|ина́ *f* [5] depth; *веко́в* antiquity *fig.* profundity; *ле́са* heart of the forest; *в* В ..., *or* ... *в* В ... deep; **∠и́нка** *f* [5] remote places; **∠о́кий** [16; -бо́к, -бока́, -бо́ко́; *comp.:* глу́бже] deep; low; remote; *fig.* profound; complete; *ста́рость* extreme old age; **∠о́кой зимо́й (но́чью)** in the dead of winter (late at night)

глубоко|мы́сленный [14 *sh.*] thoughtful, profound; **∠мы́слие** *n* [12] thoughtfulness, profundity; **∠уважа́емый** [14] highly-esteemed; *в письме́* dear

глубь *f* [8] → **глубина́**

глум|и́ться [14 *e.*; -млю́сь, -ми́шься] sneer, mock, scoff (**над** T at); **∠ле́ние**

n [12] mockery

глуп|е́ть [8], ⟨по-⟩ become stupid; **∠е́ц** *m* [1; -пца́] fool, blockhead; **∠и́ть** [14 *e.*; -плю́, -пи́шь] fool; **∠ость** *f* [8] stupidity, foolishness; nonsense; **∠ый** [14; глуп, -а́, -о] foolish, silly, stupid

глух|а́рь *m* [4 *e.*] wood grouse; **∠о́й** [14; глух, -а́, -о; *comp.:* глу́ше] deaf (*a. fig.*; **к** Д to; → **слепо́й**) звук dull, muffled; *ме́сто* desolate; wild; out-of-the-way; *arch.* solid, blind; **∠о́й но́чью** late at night, in the dead of night; **∠онемо́й** [14] deaf-mute; **∠ота́** *f* [5] deafness

глуш|и́тель *m* [4] *tech.* silencer, muffler; **∠и́ть** [16 *e.*; -шу́, -ши́шь, -шённый] **1.** ⟨о-⟩ deafen, stun; **2.** ⟨за-⟩ *о зву́ке* muffler; *боль* mitigate; *подави́ть* smother, suppress (*a. bot.*); *tech.* switch off, throttle; **∠и́ть мото́р** stop the engine; **∠ь** *f* [8] out-of-the-way place

глы́ба *f* [5] lump, clod; block

глюко́за *f* [5] glucose

гля|де́ть [11; гля́дя], ⟨по-⟩, *once* ⟨∠ну́ть⟩ [20] look, glance (**на** В at); peep (*из* Р out of, from); *того́ и ∠ди́* ... it looks as though; *идти́ куда́ глаза́ ∠дя́т* follow one's nose; **на́ ночь ∠дя** late in the evening

гля́н|ец *m* [1; -нца] luster; polish; **∠це-ви́(ы)тый** [14 (*sh.*)] glossy, lustrous; *глазе́д paper*; **∠уть → гляде́ть**

гнать [гоню́, го́нишь; гони́мый; гнал, -а́, -о, ⟨по-⟩ *v/t.* drive; urge on; *из до́ма* turn out; **1.** *hunting* pursue, chase; (*a.* **∠ся за** T; *fig.* strive for); **3.** *coll. v/i.* speed along

гнев *m* [1] anger; **∠а́ться** [1], ⟨раз-, про-⟩ be(come) angry (**на** В with); **∠ный** [14; -вен, -вна́, -о] angry

гнедо́й [14] sorrel, bay

гнезд|и́ться [15] nest; **∠о́** *n* [9; *pl.:* гнёзда, *etc. st.*] nest, aerie; *el.* socket

гнёт *m* [1] *fig.* oppression, yoke

гни|е́ние *n* [12] decay, rot, putrefaction; **∠ло́й** [14; гнил, -а́, -о] rotten, putrid; **∠ль** *f* [8] decay, rot; **∠ть** [гнию́, -ёшь; гнил, -а́, -о], ⟨с-⟩ rot, decay, putrefy

гно|и́ть, (-ся) [13] let rot, fester; **∠й** *m* [3] pus; **∠йный** [14] purulent

гнуса́вить [14] snuffle; twang

гну́сн|ость f [8] vileness; **~ый** [14; -сен, -сна́, -о] vile, foul

гнуть [20], ⟨со-⟩ bend, curve; bow; *coll.* клони́ть drive (**к** Д at)

гнуша́ться [1], ⟨по-⟩ (P *or* T) scorn, despise, disdain

гобеле́н m [1] tapestry

гобо́й m [3] oboe

го́вор m [1] talk; hum; murmur; accent; dialect; **~и́ть** [13], ⟨по-, сказа́ть⟩ [3] speak *or* talk (**о** П, **про** B about, of; **с** T to *or* with p.); say, tell; **~я́т, ~и́тся** they say, it is said; **~и́ть по-ру́сски** speak Russian; **ина́че ~я́** in other words; **не ~я́ уже́ о** (П) let alone; **по пра́вде (со́вести) ~я́** tell the truth; **что вы ~и́те!** you don't say!; **что (как) ни ~и́** whatever you (one) may say; **что и ~и́ть, и не ~и́(те)!** yes, of course!, sure!; **~ли́вый** [14 *sh.*] talkative

говя́|дина f [5], **~жий** [18] beef

го́голь-мо́голь m [4] eggflip

го́гот m [1], **~а́ть** [3], ⟨за-⟩ *гусей* cackle; P roar (with laughter)

год m [1; *pl.*: -ды, -да́, *from g/pl. e.* & лет, *etc. 9 e.*] year (**в** ~ a year, per annum); **в ~а́х** elderly, old; **в ~ы** during; **в те ~ы** in those days; **в э́том (про́шлом) ~у́** this (last) year; **из ~а в ~** year in year out; **~ от ~у** year by year; **кру́глый ~** all (the) year round; **(с) ~а́ми** for years; as years went on; **спустя́ ~** a year later

годи́ться [15 *e.*; гожу́сь, годи́шься], ⟨при-⟩ be of use (**для** Р, **к** Д, **на** B for); do; fit; *pf.* come in handy; **э́то (ни-куда́) не ~ся** that's no good (for anything), that won't do, it's (very) bad

годи́чный [4] annual

го́дный [14; -ден, -дна́, -о, го́дны] fit, suitable; *действу́ющий* valid; *поле́зный* useful, good; **ни на что не ~** good-for-nothing

годова́|лый [14] one-year-old, yearling; **~ой** [14] annual, yearly; **~щина** f [5] anniversary

гол m [1] *sport* goal; **заби́ть ~** score (a goal)

гол|ени́ще n [11] bootleg; **~ень** f [8] shin, shank

голла́нд|ец m [1; -дца] Dutchman; **~ка** f [5; *g/pl.*: -док] Dutchwoman; **~ский** [16] Dutch

голов|а́ f [5; *ac/sg.*: -у; *pl.*: го́ловы, голо́в, -ва́м] head; mind; brain; **как снег на́ ~у** all of a sudden; **лома́ть ~у** rack one's brains; **с ~ до ног** from head to toe; **на свою́ ~у** *coll.* to one's own detriment; **пове́сить ~у** become discouraged *or* despondent; **~а́ идёт кру́гом** (у P s.b.'s) thoughts are in a whirl; **~ка** f [5; *g/pl.*: -вок] small head; *винта́* head; *лу́ка и т. д.* bulb, clove; **~но́й** [14] head...; **~на́я боль** f headache; **~но́й плато́к** head-scarf; **~но́й убо́р** headgear, head-dress

голово|круже́ние n [12] giddiness; **~кружи́тельный** [14] dizzy, giddy; **~ло́мка** f [5; *g/pl.*: -мок] puzzle; **~мо́йка** f [5; *g/pl.*: -мо́ек] *coll.* dressing-down; **~ре́з** *coll. m* [1] daredevil; *банди́т* cutthroat, thug; **~тя́п** *coll. m* [1] booby, bungler

го́лод m [1] hunger; starvation; famine; **~а́ть** [1] hunger, starve; go without food, fast; **~ный** [14; го́лоден, -дна́, -о, го́лодны] hungry, starving; **~о́вка** f [5; *g/pl.*: -вок] hunger strike

гололе́дица f [5] ice-crusted ground

го́лос m [1; *pl.*: -са́, *etc. e.*] voice; *на вы́борах* vote; **пра́во ~а** suffrage; **во весь ~** at the top of one's voice; **в оди́н ~** unanimously; **~а́ за и про́тив** the yeas (ayes) & nays; **~ова́ние** n [12] voting, poll(ing); **та́йное ~ова́ние** secret vote; **~ова́ть** [7], ⟨про-⟩ vote; *coll.* thumb a lift (by raising one's hand); **~ово́й** [14] vocal (cords **свя́зки** f/pl.)

голуб|е́ц m [1; -бца́] cabbage-roll; **~о́й** [14] (sky) blue; **~у́шка** f [5; *g/pl.*: -бо-к(шек)], **~чик** m [1] *often iro.* (my) dear; **~ь** m [4] pigeon; **~я́тня** f [6; *g/pl.*: -тен] dovecote

го́л|ый [14; гол, -а́, -о] naked, nude; bare (*a. fig.*); **~ь** f [8]: **~ь на вы́думки хитра́** necessity is the mother of invention

гомеопа́тия f [7] homeopathy

го́мон *coll. m* [1] din, hubbub

гондо́ла f [5] gondola (*a. ae.*)

гоне́ние n [12] persecution; **~ка** f [5;

г/pl.: -нок] rush; chase; *coll.* haste; *pl.* race(s); *naut.* regatta; **~ка вооружений** arms race

го́нор m [1] *coll.* arrogance, airs *pl.*

гонора́р m [1] honorarium, fee; *а́вторский* royalties

го́ночный [14] race..., racing

гонча́р m [1 *e.*] potter; **~ный** [14] potter's; **~ные изде́лия** *n/pl.* pottery

го́нчая f [17] hound

гоня́ть(ся) [1] drive, etc., → **гнать**

гор|а́ f [5; *ac/sg.:* го́ру, *pl.:* го́ры, гор, гора́м] mountain; *куча* heap, pile; *ката́ться с ~ы́* toboggan; **в ~у** *or* **на ~у** uphill; *fig.* up(ward); *под ~ой* *or* *с ~ы́* downhill; *под ~о́й* at the foot of a hill (*or* mountain); *не за ~а́ми* not far off, soon; *пир ~о́й* sumptuous feast; *стоя́ть ~о́й* (*за* B) defend s.th. *or* s.b. with might & main; *как у меня́ ~а́ с плеч свали́лась* as if a load had been taken off my mind

гора́здо *used with the comp.* much, far

горб m [1 *e.*; на ~у́] hump, hunch; **~а́тый** [14 *sh.*] humpbacked; curved; *нос* aquiline; **~ить** [14], ⟨с-⟩ stoop, bend, curve (*v/i.* **-ся**); **~у́н** m [1 *e.*] hunchback; **~у́ша** f [5] humpback salmon; **~у́шка** f [5; *g/pl.:* -шек] crust (*of a loaf*)

горд|ели́вый [14 *sh.*] haughty, proud; **~е́ц** m [1 *e.*] proud man; **~и́ться** [15 *e.*; горжу́сь, горди́шься], ⟨воз-⟩ (*be*-come) proud (T of); **~ость** f [8] pride; **~ый** [14; горд, -á, -о] proud (T of)

го́р|е n [10] grief, sorrow; misfortune, disaster; *с ~я* out of grief; *ему́ и ~я ма́ло* *coll.* he doesn't care a bit; *с ~ем попола́м* *coll.* hardly, with difficulty; **~ева́ть** [6], ⟨по-⟩ grieve; (*сожалеть*) regret (**о** П s.th.)

горе́л|ка f [5; *g/pl.:* -лок] burner; **~ый** [14] burnt

го́рест|ный [14; -тен, -тна] sorrowful, mournful; **~ь** f [8] → **го́ре**

гор|е́ть [9], ⟨с-⟩ burn (*a. fig.*), be alight, be on fire; (*светиться*) glow, gleam; *не ~и́т* *coll.* there's no hurry; *де́ло ~и́т* *coll.* the matter is very urgent

го́рец m [1; -рца] mountain-dweller; highlander

го́речь f [8] bitter taste; *fig.* bitterness; *утраты* grief

горизо́нт m [1] horizon; skyline; **~а́льный** [14; -лен, -льна] horizontal, level

гори́стый [14 *sh.*] mountainous; hilly

го́рка f [5; *g/pl.:* -рок] *dim.* → **гора́** hillock

горла́нить P [13], ⟨за-, про-⟩ bawl

го́рл|о n [9] throat; gullet; *сосуда* neck (*a.* **~ышко** n [9; *g/pl.:* -шек]); *дел по ~о* *coll.* up to the eyes in work; *я сыт по ~о* *coll.* I've had my fill (*fig.* I'm fed up with [T]); *во всё ~о* → *го́лос*

горн m [1] horn, bugle; **~и́ст** m [1] bugler

го́рничная f [14] (house)maid

горнопромы́шленный [14] mining

горноста́й m [3] ermine

го́рн|ый [14] mountain(ous), hilly; *min.* rock...; mining; **~ое де́ло** n mining; **~я́к** m [1 *e.*] miner; mining engineer

го́род m [1; *pl.:* -дá, *etc. e.*] town; city (large town; *coll.* downtown); *за ~(ом)* go (live) out of town; **~и́ть** P [15], ⟨на-⟩ *вздор etc.* talk nonsense; **~о́к** m [1; -дкá] small town; **~ско́й** [14] town..., city..., urban, municipal; → *горсове́т*

горожа́н|ин m [1; *pl.:* -жáне, -жáн] townsman; *pl.* townspeople; **~ка** f [5; *g/pl.:* -нок] townswoman

горо́|х m [1] *растение* pea; *collect.* peas *pl.*; **~ховый** [14] pea(s)...; **~ховое чу́чело** *n*, *шут ~ховый* m *coll. fig.* scarecrow; buffoon, merryandrew; **~шек** m [1; -шка] *collect.* green peas *pl.*; **~ши́н(-к)а** f [5 (*g/pl.:* -нок)] pea

горсове́т (городско́й сове́т) m [1] city *or* town council

горст|о́чка f [5; *g/pl.:* -чек] very small group of people, *dim. of* **~ь** f [8; *from g/pl. e.*] *о ладони* hollow; *земли и т. д.* handful (*a. fig*)

горта́н|ный [14] guttural; **~ь** f [8] larynx

горчи́|чник m [1] mustard poultice; **~ца** f [5] mustard

горшо́к m [1; -шкá] pot, jug

го́рьк|ий [16; -рек, -рькá, -о; *comp.:* го́рче, го́рше] bitter (*a. fig*); **~ий пья́ница** *coll.* m inveterate drunkard

горю́ч|ее n [17] liquid fuel; gasoline, *Brt.*

petrol; ~ий [17 sh.] combustible; *old use* bitter (tears)

горя́ч|ий [17; горя́ч, -а́] hot (*a. fig.*); (*вспы́льчивый*) fiery, hot-tempered; *любовь, поклонник* ardent, passionate; *спор* heated; *след* warm; *приём* hearty; *время* busy; **~ая то́чка; по ~им следа́м** hot on the trail; *fig.* without delay; ~и́ть [16 *e.*; -чу́, -чи́шь], ⟨раз-⟩ excite, irritate; (*a. fig.*); **-ся** get or be excited; **~ка** f [5] fever (*a. fig.*); **-ро́ть~ку** *coll.* act impetuously; ~ность f [8] zeal, enthusiasm; impulsiveness

гос = госуда́рственный state…

госпитал|изи́ровать [7] hospitalize; **~ь** m [4] *esp. mil.* hospital

господ|и́н m [1; *pl.*: -пода́, -по́д, -да́м] gentleman; Mr.; *pl.* (ladies &) gentlemen; *~и́ть* [16 *e.*; -чу́, -чи́шь], ⟨раз-⟩ excite, irritate *stop* – *господи́н в письме́* Dear Sirs; **~ство** n [9] rule; (*превосходство*) supremacy; (*преоблада́ние*) predominance; **~ствовать** [7] rule, reign; (pre)dominate, prevail (**над** T over); (*возвыша́ться*) command; **~ь** m [Го́спода, -ду; *vocative*: -ди] Lord, God (*a. as int.*, → **Бог**)

госпожа́ f [5] Mrs.; Miss

гостеприи́м|ный [14; -мен, -мна] hospitable; **~ство** n [9] hospitality

гост|и́ная f [14] drawing room, living room; **~и́нец** m [1; -нца] present, gift; **~и́ница** f [5] hotel; inn; **~ить** [15 *e.*; гощу́, гости́шь] be on a visit, stay with (**у** P); **~ь** m [*from g/pl. e.*] guest; visitor (*f* **~ья** [6]); **идти́ (е́хать) в ~и** go to see (**к** Д s.b.); **быть в ~я́х** (у P) → **~**

госуда́рствен|ный [14] state…; public; *изме́на* high (*treason*); **~ый переворо́т** m coup d'état; **~ый строй** m political system, regime; **~ая слу́жба** public or civil service

госуда́р|ство n [9] state; **~ь** m [4] *hist.* sovereign

готова́льня f [6; *g/pl.*: -лен] (case of) drawing utensils *pl.*

готов|ить [14] **1.** ⟨при-⟩ cook; prepare (**-ся к** Д o.s. or get ready for); **2.** ⟨под-⟩ prepare, train; **3.** ⟨за-⟩ store up; lay in (stock); **~ность** f [8] readiness, preparedness, willingness; **~ый** [14 *sh.*]

ready (**к** Д *or inf.* for), on the point of; finished; willing; *оде́жда* ready-made

гофриро́ванн|ый [14]: **~ое желе́зо** corrugated iron

граб m [1] hornbeam

граб|ёж m [1 *e.*] robbery; **~и́тель** m [4] robber; **~и́тельский** [16] *цены* exorbitant; **~ить** [14], ⟨о-⟩ rob, plunder

гра́бли f/pl. [6; *gen.*: -бель, -блей] rake

грав|ёр m [1] engraver; **~и́й** m [3] gravel; **~ирова́ть** [7], ⟨вы́-⟩ engrave; **~иро́вка** f [5; *g/pl.*: -вок] engraving, etching, print, (*a.* **~ю́ра** f [5])

град m [1] hail (*a. fig.* = shower); **вопро́сы посы́пались ~ом** he was showered with questions; **~ идёт** it is hailing; **~ом** thick and fast, profusely

гра́дус m [1] degree (**в** B of); **под ~ом** P under the weather; **~ник** m [1] thermometer

граждан|и́н m [1; *pl.*: гра́ждане, -ан], **~а́нка** f [5; *g/pl.*: -нок] citizen (*address mst. without name*); **~а́нский** [16] civil (*a. war*); civic (*a. right*); **~а́нство** n [9] citizenship; citizens *pl.*: **дать (получи́ть) пра́во ~а́нства** give (or be given) civic rights; (*fig.*) gain general (public) recognition; **приня́ть … ~а́нство** become a … citizen

грамм m [1] gram(me)

грамма́т|ика f [5] grammar; **~и́ческий** [16] grammatical

гра́мот|а f [5] reading & writing; **вери́тельная ~а** credentials; **э́то для меня́ кита́йская ~а** *coll.* it's Greek to me; **~ность** f [8] literacy; **~ный** [14; -тен, -тна] literate; *специали́ст* competent, expert

грана́т m [1] pomegranate; *min.* garnet; **~а** f [5] shell; *ручна́я* grenade

грандио́зный [14; -зен, -зна] grandiose; mighty, vast

гранён|ый [14] facet(t)ed; cut

грани́т m [1] granite

грани́|ца f [5] border, frontier; boundary; *fig.* limit, scope; **за ~цу** (**~цей**) (go, be) abroad; **из-за ~цы** from abroad; **перейти́ все ~цы** pass all bounds; **~чить** [16] border *or* verge (**с** T [up]on)

гра́н|ка f [5; *g/pl.*: -нок] *typ.* galley

Г

(proof); **~ь** f [8] → **грани́ца**; *math.* plane; *драгоценного камня* facet; edge; *fig.* verge

граф m [1] earl (*Brt.*); count

граф|а́ f [5] column; **~ик** m [1] diagram, graph; *временной* schedule; **~ика** f [5] graphic arts; (*произведения*) drawings

графи́н m [1] decanter, carafe

графи́ня f [6] countess

графи́|т m [1] graphite; **~ть** [14 *e.*; -флю́, -фи́шь; -флённый], ⟨раз-⟩ line *or* rule (paper); **~ческий** [16] graphic(al)

граци|о́зный [14; -зен, -зна] graceful; **~я** f [7] grace(fulness)

грач m [1 *e.*] *zo.* rook

греб|ёнка f [5; *g/pl.*: -нок] comb; **стричь всех под одну́ ~ёнку** reduce everyone to the same level; **~ень** m [4; -бня] comb; *волны́, горы́* crest; **~ёц** m [1; -бца́] oarsman; **~ешо́к** m [1; -шка́]; **~ень**; **~ля** f [6] rowing; **~но́й** [14] row(-ing)...

грёза f [5] *rare* (day) dream

грёзить [15] *impf.* dream (**о** П of)

гре́йдер m [1] *tech.* grader; *coll.* earth road

грейпфру́т m [1] grapefruit

грек m [1] Greek

гре́лка f [5; *g/pl.*: -лок] hot-water bottle; **электри́ческая ~** heating pad, electric blanket

грем|е́ть [10 *e.*; гремлю́, -ми́шь], ⟨про-, за-⟩ thunder, peal (*a. о голосе, колоколах, etc.*); *телега, ключи* rattle, clank, tinkle; *посудой* clatter; **~у́чий** [17]: **~у́чая змея́** f rattlesnake

гре́нки m/*pl.* [1 *e.*] toast (*sg.*: -нок)

грести́ [26 -б-: гребу́, греб, гребла́], ⟨по-⟩ row; scull; *граблями* rake

греть [8; ...гре́тый], ⟨со-, на-, разо-, обо-, подо-⟩ warm (**-ся** o.s.) (up); heat; **-ся на со́лнце** sun

грех m [1 *e.*] sin; (*недостаток*) fault; *coll.* → **грешно́**; **с ~о́м попола́м** just manage; → **го́ре**; **есть тако́й ~** *coll.* well, I own it; **как на ~** *coll.* unfortunately

гре́|цкий [16]: **~цкий оре́х** m walnut; **~ча́нка** f [5; *g/pl.*: -нок], **~ческий** [16] Greek

греч|и́ха, **~ка** f [5] buckwheat; **~невый** [14] buckwheat...

греш|и́ть [16 *e.*; -шу́, -ши́шь], ⟨со-⟩ sin (**про́тив** P *a.* against); **~и́ть про́тив и́стины** distort the truth; **~ник** m [1; *e.*], **~ница** f [5] sinner; **~но́** (it's a) shame (on Д); **~ный** [14; -шен, -шна́, -о́] sinful; F *sh.*: sorry

гриб m [1 *e.*] mushroom; **~о́к** m [1; -бка́] *dim.* → **гриб**; fungus

гри́ва f [5] mane

гри́венник *coll.* m [1] ten-kopeck coin

гриль m [4] grill

грим m [1] *thea.* makeup

грима́с|а f [5] grimace; **~ничать** [1] make faces *or* grimaces

гримирова́ть [7], ⟨за-, на-⟩ make up (*v/i.* **-ся**)

грипп m [1] influenza

гриф m [1]: **~ секре́тности** inscription designating the degree of confidentiality

гроб m [1; в -у́ *pl.*: -ы́, -а́, *etc. e.*] coffin; **~ни́ца** f [5] tomb; **~ово́й** [14] coffin...; tomb...; **~ово́е молча́ние** deathly silence

гроза́ f [5; *pl. st.*] (thunder) storm (*a. fig.*); menace; terror

гроздь m [4; *pl.*: -ди, -дей, *etc. e.*, -дья, -дьев] *винограда* bunch; *ягод, цветов* cluster

грози́ть [15 *e.*; грожу́, -зи́шь], ⟨по-⟩ threaten (Д/Т a p. with) (*a.* **-ся**)

гро́з|ный [14; -зен, -зна́, -о] menacing, threatening; *человек* formidable; *coll.* *голос* stern, severe; **~ова́я ту́ча** thundercloud

гром m [1; *from g/pl. e.*] thunder (*a. fig.*); **~ греми́т** it thunders; **как ~ среди́ я́сного не́ба** like a bolt from the blue; **как ~ом поражённый** *fig.* thunderstruck

грома́д|а f [5] bulk, mass of; **~ный** [14; -ден, -дна] vast, huge; *успех и т. д.* tremendous

громи́ть [14 *e.*; -млю́, -ми́шь; -млённый], ⟨раз-⟩ smash, crush; *врага́* rout, smash

гро́мк|ий [16; -мок, -мка́, -о; *compr.*: гро́мче] loud; noisy; *fig.* famous, great, noted; *слова* pompous

громо|вой [14] thunder…; *голос* thunderous; **~гла́сный** [14; -сен, -сна] loud; *mst. adv.* publicly, openly; **~зди́ть(ся)** [15 *e.*; -зжу, -зди́шь] → **взгроможда́ть(ся)**; **~здкий** [16; -док, -дка] bulky, cumbersome; **~отво́д** *m* [1] lightning rod *or* conductor

громыха́ть *coll.* [1] rumble; *посудой* clatter; *о пушках* boom

гроссме́йстер *m* [1] *chess* grand master

грот *m* [1] grotto

гроте́ск *m* [1], **~ный** [14] grotesque

гро́х|нуть *coll.* [20] *pf.* crash, bang down (*v/i.* **-ся** fall with a crash); **~от** *m* [1]; **~ота́ть** [3], ⟨за-⟩ rumble; *пушек* roar

грош *m* [1 *e.*]: **ни ~а́** not a farthing; **~ цена́** *or* **~а́ ло́маного не сто́ит** not worth a pin; **ни в ~ не ста́вить** not care a straw (B for); **~о́вый** [14] *fig.* (dirt-)cheap

гру́да *f* [5] pile, heap

груди́нка *f* [5; *g/pl.*: -нок] brisket; bacon; **~но́й** [14]: **~на́я кле́тка** *f* thorax; **~но́й ребёнок** infant in arms; **~ь** *f* [8; в, на -ди́; *from g/pl.* -е.] breast; chest; **стоя́ть ~ью** (*за* B) champion, defend

груз *m* [1] load (*a. fig.*); *перевозимый* freight; *naut.* cargo

грузи́н *m* [1; *g/pl.*: грузи́н], **~ка** *f* [5; *g/pl.*: -нок] Georgian; **~ский** [16] Georgian

грузи́ть [15 *e.*; -ужу́, -у́зишь], ⟨на-, за-, по-⟩ load, freight

гру́з|ный [14; -зен, -зна́, -о] massive, heavy; **~ови́к** *m* [1 *e.*] truck, *Brt.* lorry; **~ово́й** [14] freight…, goods…; *naut.* cargo; **~ово́й автомоби́ль** *m* → **~ови́к**; **~оподъёмность** *f* [8] carrying capacity; *naut.* tonnage; **~получа́тель** *m* [4] consignee; **~чик** *m* [1] loader; *naut.* docker, stevedore

грунт *m* [1] soil, earth; ground (*a. paint.*); **~ово́й** [14] *о воде* subsoil; *дорога* dirt road

гру́пп|а *f* [5] group; **~ирова́ть(ся)** [7], ⟨с-⟩ (form a) group

грусти́ть [15 *e.*; -ущу́, -сти́шь], ⟨взгрустну́ть⟩ [20] be sad; long for (*по* П); **~ный** [14; -тен, -тна́, -о] sad, sorrowful; grievous, distressing; **мне ~о** I feel sad; **~ь** *f* [8] sadness, grief, melancholy

гру́ша *f* [5] pear (*a. tree*)

гры́жа *f* [5] hernia, rupture

грыз|ня́ *f* [6] squabble; **~ть** [24; *pt. st.*] gnaw (*a. fig.*), nibble; bite; *орехи* crack; **-ся** fight, squabble; **~у́н** *m* [1 *e.*] *zo.* rodent

гряд|а́ *f* [5; *nom/pl. st.*] ridge, range; *agric.* bed (*a.* **~ка** *f* [5; *g/pl.*: -док])

гряду́щий [17] future, coming; **на сон ~** before going to bed

грязе|во́й [14] mud…; **~защи́тный** [14] antisplash; **~елече́бница** *f* [5] therapeutic mud baths; **~и** *f/pl.* [8] (curative) mud; **~ни́ть** [13], ⟨за-⟩ soil (*a. fig.*); **-ся** get dirty; **~нуть** [21], ⟨по-⟩ sink (mud, *etc.*, *fig.*); **~ный** [14; -зен, -зна́, -о, гря́зны] dirty (*a. fig.*); muddy; **~ь** *f* [8; в -зи́] dirt, mud; **в ~и́** dirty; **не уда́рить лицо́м в ~** manage to do s.th. successfully; **смеша́ть с ~ью** sling mud (B at)

гря́нуть [19 *st.*] *pf. гром* burst out; *выстрел* ring, roar; *война* break out; *песня* burst, start

губ|а́ *f* [5; *nom/pl. st.*] lip; *залив, устье* bay; **у него́ ~а́ не ду́ра** his taste isn't bad; he knows which side his bread is buttered on

губерн|а́тор *m* [1] governor; **~ия** *f* [7] *hist.* province

губи́т|ельный [14; -лен, -льна] ruinous; pernicious; **~ь** [14], ⟨по-, с-⟩ destroy, ruin; *время* waste

гу́б|ка *f* [5; *g/pl.*: -бок] **1.** *dim.* → **~а́**; **2.** sponge; **~но́й** [14] labial; **~на́я пома́да** *f* lipstick

гуд|е́ть [11], ⟨за-⟩ buzz; *о гудке* honk, hoot, whistle; *coll. болеть* ache; **~о́к** *m* [1; -дка́] honk, hoot, signal; horn; siren; whistle

гул *m* [1] boom, rumble; *голосов* hum; **~кий** [16; -лок, -лка́, -о] *громкий* booming, loud; resonant

гуля́|нье *n* [10] walk(ing); *массовое*

open-air merrymaking, fête; ~**ть** [28], ⟨по-⟩ [20] go for a walk (*a.* **идти** ~**ть**), stroll; *fig. о ветре и т. д.* sweep; *coll.* carouse, go on a spree

гуля́ш *m* [1; *g/pl.*: -**е́й**] goulash, stew

гуманита́рны|й [14]: ~**е нау́ки** the humanities

гума́нн|ость *f* [8] humanity; ~**ый** [14; -а́нен, -а́нна] humane

гурма́н *m* [1] gourmet

гур|т *m* [1 *e.*] herd, drove (cattle); ~**ба́** *f* [5] crowd (T in)

гу́сеница *f* [5] caterpillar

гуси́ный [14] goose (*a.* gooseflesh *ко-жа*)

густ|е́ть [8], ⟨за-⟩ thicken; ~**о́й** [14; густ -а́, -о; *comp.*: гу́ще] thick, dense; deep, rich (*colo(u)r, sound*)

гусь *m* [4; *from g/pl. e.*] goose; *fig.* **хоро́ш** ~**ь** *b.s.* fine fellow indeed!; **как с ~я вода́** like water off a duck's back, thick-skinned; ~**ько́м** in single file

гу́ща *f* [5] grounds *pl.*; *осадок* sediment; *леса* thicket; *fig.* in the center (-tre) of things

Д

да¹. *part.* yes; oh (yes), indeed (*a. interr.*); (oh) but, now, well; *imperative* do(n't)...!; *tags:* aren't, don't, *etc.*; may, let; **2.** *cj.* (**а.** ~ **и**) and; but; ~ **и то́лько** nothing but; and that's all; ~ **что вы!** you don't say!

да́бы *old use* (in order) that *or* to

да|ва́ть [5], ⟨~**ть**⟩ [дам, дашь, даст, дади́м, дади́те, даду́т ⟨...-⟩ дал, -а́, -о; ⟨...⟩да́нный (дан, -á)] give; (*позволить*) let; (*даровать*) bestow; *клятву* take, pledge; make (way); ~**ва́й|(те)** let's! *with vb.* (*a.* ~**а́й|(те)** let us (me); **ни** ~**ть ни взять** exactly alike; ~**ва́ть ход де́лу** set s.th. going; further s.th., ~**ся** let o.s. be caught, cheated); **с трудо́м и т. д.** (turn out to) be (*e.g.* hard for Д) (can) master (И s.th.)

дави́ть [14] **1.** ⟨на-⟩ press; squeeze (⟨вы́-⟩ out); **2.** ⟨за-, раз-⟩ crush; Р (*сбить машиной*) run over, knock down; **3.** ⟨по-⟩ oppress; suppress; **4.** ⟨при-, с-⟩ press (down *or* together), jam, compress; crush, trample; **5.** ⟨у-⟩ strangle; -**ся** choke; (*повеситься*) hang o.s.

да́в|ка *f* [5] throng, jam; ~**ле́ние** *n* [12] pressure (*a. fig.*)

да́вн|(ишн)ий [15] old; of long standing; ~**о́** long ago; for a long time, long since;

~**опроше́дший** [17] remote, long past; ~**ость** *f* [8] antiquity; *law* prescription; **срок** ~**ости** term of limitation; ~**ым-~о́** very long ago, ages ago

да́же (*а.* ~ **и**) even; ~ **не** not even

да́л|ее → **да́льше**; **и так** ~**ее** and so on (or forth); ~**ёкий** [16; -лёк, -лека́, -леко́ -лёко; *comp.*: да́льше] far (away), distant (**от** Р from); long (way); *fig.* wide (of); strange (to); **он не о́чень ~ёкий челове́к** he is not very clever; ~**еко́**, ~**ёко** far (off, away); a long way (**до** Р to); (Д) ~**еко́ до** P far from, much inferior to; ~**еко́ не** by no means; ~**еко́ за** (В) long after; *о возрасте* well over; ~**еко́ иду́щий** [17] farreaching; ~**ь** *f* [8; в ~**и́**] distance; open space; ~**ьне́йший** [17] further; **в ~ьне́йшем** in future, henceforth; ~**ний** [15] distant (*a. kin*); remote; → *a.* ~**ёкий**; ~**невосто́чный** [14] Far Eastern

дально|бо́йный [14] *mil.* long range; ~**ви́дность** *f* [8] foresight; ~**ви́дный** [14; -ден, -дна] *fig.* farsighted; ~**зо́ркий** [16; -рок, -рка] far-, long-sighted; ~**сть** *f* [8] distance; *mil., tech.* (long-)range

да́льше farther; further (more); then, next; (**чита́йте**) ~**!** go on (reading)

да́м|а *f* [5] lady; (dance) partner; *cards* queen; ~**ба** *f* [5] dam, dike; ~**ка** *f* [5; *g/pl.*: -мок] king (*in draughts*); ~**ский**

[16] ladies', women's

да́нный [16] given, present, in question; ~ные *pl.* data, facts; statistics; *обрабо́тка ~ных* data processing

дань *f* [8] tribute (*a. fig.*); *отдава́ть ~* appreciate, recognize

дар *m* [1; *pl. e.*] gift (*a. fig.*); ~и́ть [13], ⟨по-⟩ give (Д/В a p. s.th.), present (В/Т a p. with); ~мое́д *coll. m* [1] sponger; ~ова́ние *n* [12] donation, giving; talent; ~ови́тый [14 *sh.*] gifted, talented; ~ово́й [14] gratis, free

да́ром *adv.* gratis, for nothing; (*напрасно*) in vain; *пропа́сть ~* be wasted; *э́то ему́ ~ не пройдёт* he will smart for this

да́т|а *f* [5] date; ~ельный [14] *gr.* dative (*case*); ~и́ровать [7] (*im*)*pf.* (*задним число́м* ante)date

да́тский [16] Danish; ~ча́нин *m* [1; *pl.*: -ча́не, -ча́н], ~ча́нка *f* [5; *g/pl.*: -нок] Dane

да́тчик *m* [1] *tech.* sensor

да́ть(ся) → *дава́ть(ся)*

да́ч|а *f* [5] dacha, cottage, summer residence, villa; *на ~е* in a dacha; out of town; in the country; ~ник *m* [1] summer resident; ~ный [14] suburban; country...; garden (suburb *посёлок*)

два *m, n,* **две** *f* [34] two → *пять*, *пя́тый*; *в ~ счёта coll.* in a jiffy

двадцат|**иле́тний** [15] twenty-year; twenty-year-old; ~ый [14] twentieth; → *пя́т(идеся́т)ый*; '~ь [35; -ти́] twenty; → *пять*

два́жды twice; ~ *два math.* two by two; *я́сно как ~ два* (*четы́ре*) plain as day

двена́дцат|и... (*in compds*) twelve...; dodec(a)...; duodecimal, duodenary; ~ый [14] twelfth; → *пя́тый*, ~ь [35] twelve; → *пять*

двер|**но́й** [14] door...; *~но́й проём* doorway; ~ца *f* [5; *g/pl.*: -рец] (*cupboard, etc.*) door; ~ь *f* [8; в -ри́; *from g/pl. e.; instr. a.* -рьми́] door (*a. pl. ~и*)

две́сти [36] two hundred

дви|**га́тель** *m* [4] engine, motor; ~гать [13], ⟨~нуть⟩[20] (В/Т) move, set in motion; stir; -ся move, advance; *отпра́виться* set out; start; ~же́ние *n* [12] movement (*a. pol.*); stir; *phys.* motion;

traffic; *fig.* emotion; *приводи́ть (приходи́ть) в ~же́ние* set going (start [moving]); ~жимый [14 *sh.*] prompted, moved; movable; ~жущий [17]: *~жущая си́ла* driving force; ~нуть → ~гать

дво́е [37] two (in a group, together); *нас бы́ло ~* there were two of us; ~то́чие *n* [12] *gr.* colon

дво́иться [13], ⟨раз-⟩ divide into two; *у меня́ в глаза́х ~ся* I see double

дво́й|ка *f* [5; *g/pl.*: двоёк] two (*a.* boat; team; bus, *etc.*, *no.* 2; cards; *a.* deuce); pair; (*mark*) = *пло́хо*; ~ник *m* [1 *e.*] double; ~но́й [14] double (*a. fig.*); ~ня *f* [6; *g/pl.*: двоён] twins *pl.*; ~ственный [14 *sh.*]; *~ственное отноше́ние* mixed feelings

дво́ичный [14; -чен, -чна] binary

двор *m* [1 *e.*] (court) yard; farm (-stead); *короле́вский* court; *на ~е́* outside, outdoors; ~е́ц *m* [1; -рца́] palace; *⚬ бракосочета́ний* Wedding Palace; *⚬ культу́ры* Palace of Culture; ~ник *m* [1] janitor, (yard and) street cleaner; *mot.* windshield (*Brt.* windscreen) wiper; ~ня́га *coll. f* [5], ~ня́жка *coll. f* [5; *g/pl.*: -жек] mongrel; ~цо́вый [14] court..., palace...; *~цо́вый переворо́т* palace revolution; ~яни́н *m* [1; *pl.*: -я́не, -я́н] nobleman; ~я́нка *f* [5; *g/pl.*: -нок] noblewoman; ~я́нский [16] of the nobility; of noble birth; ~я́нство *n* [9] nobility

двою́родн|ый [14]: *~ый брат m*, *~ая сестра́ f* cousin

двоя́к|ий [16 *sh.*] double, twofold; ~о in two ways

дву|**бо́ртный** [14] double-breasted; ~гла́вый [14] double-headed; ~жи́льный [14] sturdy, tough; *tech.* twin-core; ~кра́тный [14] double; done twice; ~ли́чие *n* [12] duplicity, double-dealing; ~ли́чный [14; -чен, -чна] two-faced; ~смы́сленный [14 *sh.*] ambiguous; ~ство́лка *f* [5; *g/pl.*: -лок] double-barrel(l)ed gun; ~ство́льный [14]: *~ство́льное ружьё n → ~ство́лка*; ~ство́рчатый [14]: *~ство́рчатая дверь f* folding doors; ~сторо́нний

[15] bilateral; *движение* two-way; *ткань* reversible

двух|... (→ *a.* **дву**...): ~**дне́вный** [14] two days; ~**коле́йный** [14] double-track; ~**колёсный** [14] two-wheel(ed); ~**ле́тний** [14] two-years-old; two-years'; ~**ме́стный** [14] two-seat(er); ~**ме́сячный** [14] two months' *or* two-months-old; ~**мото́рный** [14] twin-engine(d); ~**неде́льный** [14] two weeks', *Brt. a.* a fortnight's; ~**со́тый** [14] two hundredth (*Brt.* -reyed); ~**эта́жный** [14] two-storied (*Brt.* -reyed)

двуязы́чный [14; -чен, -чна] bilingual

деба́ты *m/pl.* [1] debate

де́бет *m* [1] *comm.* debit; *занести́ в* ~ = ~**ова́ть** [7] (*im*)*pf.* debit (sum against *or* to a p. В/Д)

дебито́р *m* [1] debtor

дебо́ш *m* [1] shindy, riot

дебр|**и** *f/pl.* [8] thickets; the wilds; *запу́таться в* ~**ях** get bogged down (P in)

дебю́т *m* [1] debut; *chess* opening

де́ва *f* [5]: ♀ *Мари́я* the Virgin; ♀ Virgo; (*ста́рая*) ~ (old) maid

девальва́ция *f* [7] devaluation

дева́ть [1], ⟨**деть**⟩ [де́ну, -нешь] put, leave, mislay; *куда́* ~ *a.* what to do with, how to spend; -ся *go*; *vb.* + И = put, leave + *obj.*; be (*pr.*); *куда́ мне* ~*ся?* where shall I go *or* stay?; *куда́ он де́лся?* what has become of him?

де́верь *m* [4; *pl.:* -рья́, -ре́й, -рья́м] brother-in-law (*husband's brother*)

деви́з *m* [1] motto

деви́ца *f* [5] *iro.* young lady, girl; ~**ичий** [18] maidenly; girlish; ~**очка** *f* [5; *g/pl.:* -чек] (little) girl; ~**ственный** [14 *sh.*] maiden, virgin...; *лес и т. д.* primeval; ~**ушка** *f* [5; *g/pl.:* -шек] young lady, unmarried girl (*a. form of address*); ~**чо́нка** *f* [5; *g/pl.:* -нок] girl

девя|**но́сто** [35] ninety; ~**но́стый** [14] ninetieth; → **пя́т(идеся́т)ый**; ~**тисо́тый** [14] nine hundredth; ~**тка** [5; *g/pl.:* -ток] nine (→ **дво́йка**); ~**тна́дцатый** [14] nineteenth; → **пять**, **пя́тый**; ~**тна́дцать** [35] nineteen; → **пять**; ~**тый** [14] ninth; → **пя́тый**; ~**ть** [35] nine; → **пять**; ~**тьсо́т** [36] nine hun-

dred; ~**тью** nine times

дегенера́т *m* [1] degenerate

деград|**а́ция** *f* [7] degradation; ~**и́ровать** [7] (*im*)*pf.* degrade

дед|(**ушка** *m* [5; *g/pl.:* -шек]) *m* [1] grandfather; old man; *pl.* ~**ы** *a.* forefathers; ~**-моро́з** *m* Santa Claus, Father Christmas

дееприча́стие *n* [12] *gr.* gerund

дежу́р|**ить** [13] be on duty; be on watch; ~**ный** *m* [14] (*p.*) duty..., on duty; ~**ство** *n* [9] duty, (night) watch

дезерти́р *m* [1] deserter; ~**ова́ть** [7] (*im*)*pf.* desert; ~**ство** *n* [9] desertion

дезинф|**е́кция** *f* [7] disinfection; ~**ици́ровать** [7] (*im*)*pf.* disinfect

дезинформ|**а́ция** *f* [7] misinformation; ~**и́ровать** [7] (*im*)*pf.* misinform

дезодора́нт *m* [1] deodorant; air freshener

дезорганизова́ть [7] (*im*)*pf.* disorganize

де́йств|**енный** [14 *sh.*] effective; *сре́дство* efficacious; ~**ие** *n* [12] action; activity; *mil., tech., math.* operation; *thea.* act; *лека́рства и т. д.* effect; (*влия́ние*) influence, impact; **ме́сто** ~**ия** scene; **свобо́да** ~**ий** free play; ~**ительно** really, indeed; ~**и́тельность** *f* [8] reality, (real) life; ~**и́тельный** [14; -лен, -льна] real, actual; *биле́т и т. д.* valid; *mil., gr.* active (*service*; *voice*); ~**овать** [7], ⟨по-⟩ act, work (**на** B on); operate, function; apply; have effect (**на** B on); get (on one's nerves); ~**ующий** [17] active; acting; ~**ующее лицо́** character, personage

декабр|**ь** *m* [4 *e.*] December

дека́да *f* [5] decade

дека́н *m* [1] *acad.* dean; ~**а́т** *m* [1] dean's office

декла|**ми́ровать** [7], ⟨про-⟩ recite, declaim; ~**ма́ция** *f* [7] declamation

декольт|**е́** (de-'te) *n* [*indecl.*] décolleté; ~**и́рованный** [14 *sh.*] lowcut; *thea.*

декора́|**тор** *m* [1] (interior) decorator; *thea.* scene-painter; ~**ция** *f* [7] decoration; *thea.* scenery

декре́т *m* [1] decree, edict; *coll.* maternity leave

де́ла|нный [14 *sh.*] affected, forced; ~ть [1], ⟨с-⟩ make, do; *coll.* ~ть не́чего it can't be helped; ~ся (T) become, grow, turn; happen (**с** T with, to), be going on; **что с ним сде́лалось?** what has become of him?

делега́|т *m* [1] delegate; ~ция *f* [7] delegation

дел|ёж *coll. m* [1 *e.*] distribution, sharing; ~е́ние *n* [12] division (*a. math.*); **на шкале** point, degree (*scale*)

деле́|ц *m* [1; -льца́] *mst. pej.* smart operator; *pers.* on the make

деликате́с *m* [1] *cul.* delicatessen

делика́тн|ость *f* [8] tact(fulness), delicacy; ~ый [14; -тен, -тна] delicate

дели́|мое *n* [14] *math.* dividend; ~тель *m* [4] *math.* divisor; ~ть [13; делю́, де́лишь] 1. ⟨раз-, по-⟩ (**на** B) divide (in[-to]), *a.* by; 2. ⟨по-⟩ share (*a.* -ся [T/с T s.th. with s.b.], exchange; confide [s.th. to], tell; *math.* be divisible)

де́ль|о *n* [9; *pl. e.*] affair, matter, concern; affair(s), work, business (**по** Д on); (*деяние*) deed, act(ion); *law* case, (*a. fig.*) cause; **говори́ть** ~о talk sense; **де́лать** ~о *fig.* do serious work; **то и** ~о continually, time and again; **в чём** ~о? what's the matter?; **в том то и** ~о that's just the point; **како́е вам** ~о?, **э́то не ва́ше** ~о that's no business of yours; **ме́жду** ~ом in between; **на** ~е in practice; **на** (*or* в) **са́мом** ~е in reality, in fact; really, indeed; **пусти́ть в** ~о use; **по** ~а́м on business; **как** ~а́? how are you?; ~о идёт → **идти́**

дело|ви́тый [14 *sh.*], ~во́й [14] businesslike; efficient; *a.* business...; work(ing)

де́льный [14] businesslike; (*разумный*) sensible

де́льта *f* [5] delta

дельфи́н *m* [1] dolphin

демаго́г *m* [1] demagogue; ~ия *f* [7] demagoguery

демаркацио́нный [14] (*adj. of*) demarcation

демилитаризова́ть [7] (*im*)*pf.* demilitarize

демобилизова́ть [7] (*im*)*pf.* demobilize

демокра́т *m* [1] democrat; ~и́ческий [16] democratic; ~ия *f* [7] democracy

демонстр|ати́вный [14; -вен, -вна] demonstrative, done for effect; ~а́ция *f* [7] demonstration; ~и́ровать [7] (*im*)*pf.*, *a.* ⟨про-⟩ demonstrate; **фильм** show

демонта́ж *m* [1] dismantling

де́мпинг *m* [1] *econ.* dumping

де́нежный [14] money..., monetary, pecuniary; currency...; *coll.* moneyed

день *m* [4; дня] day; **в** ~ *a or* per day; **в э́тот** ~ (on) that day; ~ **за днём** day after day; **изо дня́ в** ~ day by day; ~ **ото дня́** with every passing day; **весь** ~ all day (long); **на днях** the other day; in the next few days (*a.* **со дня на** ~); **три часа́ дня** 3 p.m., 3 o'clock in the afternoon; → **днём**; ~ **рожде́ния** birthday

де́ньги *f/pl.* [*gen.*: -нег; *from. dat. e.*] money

департа́мент *m* [1] department

депози́т *m* [1] deposit

депута́т *m* [1] deputy, delegate

дёр|гать [1], *once* ⟨~нуть⟩ [20] pull, tug (*a.* **за** B at), jerk; *о теле* twitch; **отрыва́ть от де́ла** worry, harrass; **чёрт меня́** ~нул why the devil did I do it

дере́в|ене́ть [8], ⟨за-, о-⟩ stiffen; grow numb; ~е́нский [16] village..., country..., rural, rustic; ~е́нский жи́тель *m* villager; ~ня *f* [6; *g/pl.*: -ве́нь, *etc. e.*] village; *не город* country(side); ~о *n* [9; *pl.*: -е́вья, -е́вьев] tree; *sg.* wood; **кра́сное** ~о mahogany; **чёрное** ~о ebony; **резьба́ по** ~у wood carving; ~я́нный [14] wooden (*a. fig.*)

держа́ва *f* [5] *pol.* power

держа́ть [4] hold; keep; support; have (*a. comm.* in stock); ~ **пари́** bet; ~ **в ку́рсе** keep posted; ~ **в неве́дении** in the dark; ~ **себя́ (кого́-либо) в рука́х** (have) control (over) o.s. (*a p.*); ~ **себя́** conduct o.s., behave = ~**ся 1.** ~**ся язы́к за зуба́ми** hold one's tongue; **2.** ⟨у~**ся**⟩ (**за** B, P) hold (on[to]); *fig.* stick (to); keep; (*выдерживать*) hold out, stand

дерз|а́ть [1], ⟨~ну́ть⟩ [20] dare, venture; ~кий [16; -зок, -зка́, -о; *compr.* -зче] impudent, insolent; (*смелый*) bold, daring, audacious; ~ость *f* [8] impudence, cheek; daring, audacity

дёрн *m* [1] turf

дёрнуть → **дёргать**

дес|а́нт *m* [1] landing; troops *pl.* (landed) (**а́вия...** airborne); **~ёрт** *m* [1] dessert; **~на́** *f* [5; *pl.*: дёсна, -сен, *etc. st.*] *anat.* gum; **~ёртный** [14] (*adj. of*) dessert; *вино́* sweet; **~по́т** *m* [1] despot

деся́ти|дне́вный [14] ten days; **~кра́тный** [14] tenfold; **~ле́тие** *n* [12] decade; *годо́вщина* tenth anniversary; **~ле́тний** [15] ten-years; ten-year-old

деся́ти|чный [14] decimal; **~ка** *f* [5; *g/pl.*: -ток] ten (→ **дво́йка**); **~ок** *m* [1; -тка] ten; *pl.* dozens of, many; → **идти́**; *не ро́бкого* **~ка** plucky, not a coward; **~ый** [14] tenth (*a., f.,* part; 3, 2-read: *три це́лых и две* **~ых** = 3. 2); → **пят(и)деся́т)ый**; *с* **~того на** ~ое discursively, in a rambling manner; **~ь** [35 *e.*] ten; → **пять & пя́тый**; **~ю** ten times

дета́л|ь *f* [8] detail; *tech.* part, component; **~но** in detail; **~ный** [14; -лен, -льна] detailed, minute

дет|вора́ *f* [5] *coll.* → **~и**; **~ёныш** *m* [1] young one; cub, *etc.*; **~и** *n/pl.* [-ей, -ям, -ьми́, -ях] children, kids; **дво́е** (**тро́е, че́тверо,** *etc.*) **~ей** two (three, four) children; *sg.*: **дитя́** (*a.* **ребёнок**); **~ский** [16] child(ren)'s; infant(ile); childlike; childish; **~ский дом** children's home; **~ский сад** kindergarten; **~ская** *f* nursery; **~ство** *n* [9] childhood

де́ть(ся) → **дева́ть(ся)**

дефе́кт *m* [1] defect; **~ный** [14] defective, faulty

дефици́т *m* [1] *econ.* deficit; *това́ров* shortage; *това́р* commodity in short supply; **~ный** [14; -тен, -тна] *econ.* showing a loss; in short supply, scarce

деш|еве́ть [8], ⟨по-⟩ fall in price; become cheaper; **~еви́зна, ~ёвка** *f* [5] cheapness, low price(s); *купи́ть по* **~ёвке** buy cheap; **~ёвый** [14; дёшев, дешева́, дёшево; *comp.*: деше́вле] cheap (*a. fig.*)

де́ятель *m* [4]: *госуда́рственный* ~ statesman; *нау́чный* ~ scientist; *обще́ственный* ~ public figure; *полити́ческий* ~ politician; **~ность** *f* [8] activity, -ties *pl.*; work; **~ный** [14; -лен, -льна] active

джин *m* [1] gin

джи́нсы [1] *pl.* jeans

джу́нгли *f/pl.* [*gen.*: -лей] jungle

диабе́т *m* [1] diabetes; **~ик** *m* [1] diabetic

диа́|гноз *m* [1] diagnosis; **~гона́ль** *f* [8] diagonal; **~ле́кт** *m* [1] dialect; **~ле́ктный** [14] dialect..., dialectal; **~ло́г** *m* [1] dialogue; **~метр** *m* [1] diameter; **~пазо́н** *m* [1] range (*a. fig.*); **~позити́в** *m* [1] *phot.* slide; **~фра́гма** *f* [5] diaphragm; *phot.* aperture

дива́н *m* [1] divan, sofa

диве́рсия *f* [7] *mil.* diversion; sabotage

дивиде́нд *m* [1] dividend

диви́зия *f* [7] *mil.* division

ди́вный [14; -вен, -вна] wonderful; amazing

дие́т|а (-'єta) *f* [5] diet; **~и́ческий** [16] dietetic

ди́зель *m* [4] diesel engine; **~ный** [14] diesel...

дизентери́я *f* [7] dysentery

дик|а́рь *m* [4 *e.*] savage (*a. fig.*); *coll.* shy, unsociable person; **~ий** [15; дик, -а́, -о] wild; savage (*a. fig.*); *поведе́ние и т. д.* odd, bizarre, absurd; **~ость** *f* [8] wildness; savagery; absurdity

дикт|а́нт *m* [1] → **~о́вка**; **~а́тор** *m* [1] dictator; **~а́торский** [16] dictatorial; **~ату́ра** *f* [5] dictatorship; **~ова́ть** [7], ⟨про-⟩ dictate; **~о́вка** *f* [5; *g/pl.*: -вок] dictation; **~ор** *m* [1] (radio, TV) announcer

ди́кция *f* [7] articulation, enunciation

диле́мм|а *f* [5] dilemma; *стоя́ть пе́ред* **диле́ммой** face a dilemma

дилета́нт *m* [1] dilettante, dabbler; **~ский** [16] dilettantish

динам|и́зм *m* [1] dynamism; **~ика** *f* [5] dynamics; **~и́т** *m* [1] dynamite; **~и́чный** [14; -чен, -чна] dynamic

дина́стия *f* [7] dynasty

дипло́м *m* [1] diploma; *univ.* degree; *coll.* degree work, research

диплома́т *m* [1] **1.** diplomat; **2.** *coll.* (attaché) case; **~и́ческий** [16] diplomatic; **~и́чный** [14; -чен, -чна] *fig.* diplomatic, tactful; **~ия** *f* [7] diplomacy

дире́к|тор *m* [1; *pl.*: -ра́, *etc. e.*] manager,

director; (*школы*) principal, headmaster; **~ция** *f* [7] management, directorate

дириж|а́бль *m* [4] dirigible, airship; **~ёр** *m* [1] *mus.* conductor; **~и́ровать** [7] (T) conduct

дисгармо́ния *f* [7] *mus. and fig.* disharmony, discord

диск *m* [1] disk

диск|валифици́ровать [7] (*im)pf.* disqualify; **~редити́ровать** [7] (*im)pf.* discredit; **~римина́ция** *f* [7] discrimination

дискуссия *f* [7] discussion

дисп|ансе́р (-'ser) *m* [1] health clinic; **~е́тчер** *m* [1] (traffic) controller; *ae.* flight control officer; **~у́т** *m* [1] dispute, disputation

дис|серта́ция *f* [7] dissertation, thesis; **~сона́нс** *m* [1] *mus. and fig.* dissonance, discord; **~та́нция** *f* [7] distance; **сойти́ с ~та́нции** withdraw; **~тилиро́ванный** [14 *sh.*] distilled; **~циплина** *f* [5] discipline

дитя́ *n* [-я́ти; *pl.* → **де́ти**] child

диф|ира́мб *m* [1] dithyramb; (*fig.*) eulogy; **петь ~ира́мбы** sing praises (to Д); **~тери́т** *m* [1], **~тери́я** *f* [7] diphtheria

дифференц|иа́л *m* [1], **~иа́льный** [14] *math, tech.* differential; **~и́ровать** [7] (*im)pf.* differentiate

дич|а́ть [1], ⟨о-⟩ run wild, grow wild; *fig.* become unsociable; **~и́ться** [16 *e.*; -чу́сь, -чи́шься] be shy *or* unsociable; shun (a p. P); **~ь** *f* [8] game, wild fowl; *coll.* (*чушь*) nonsense, bosh

длин|а́ *f* [5] length; **в ~у́** (at) full length, lengthwise; **~о́й в** (В) … *or* … **в ~у́** long; **~но́…** (*in compds.*) long-…; **~ный** [14; -и́нен, -и́нна, -и́нно] long, too long; *coll.* (*высокий*) tall

дли́т|ельный [14; -лен, -льна] long, protracted, lengthy; **~ься** [13], ⟨про-⟩ last

для (P) for; because of; **~ того́, что́бы** (in order) to, that… may; **~ чего́?** what for; **~ящик ~ пи́сем** mail (*Brt.* letter) box

днев|а́ть [6]: **~а́ть и ночева́ть где-л.** spend all one's time somewhere; **~ни́к** *m* [1 *e.*] journal, diary (*vb.*: **вести́** keep); **~но́й** [14] day('s), daily; day(light

све́т *m*)

днём by day, during the day

дн|о́ *n* [9; *pl.*: **до́нья**, -ньев] bottom; **вверх ~ом** upside down; **золото́е ~о** *fig.* gold mine; **вы́пить до ~а** drain to the dregs; **идти́ ко ~у** *v/i.* (**пусти́ть на ~о** *v/t.*) sink

до (P) *place*: to, as far as, up (*or* down) to; *time*: till, until, to; before; *degree*: to, up to; *age*: under; *quantity*: up to, about; **~ того́** so (much); (Д) **не ~ того́** not be interested in, have no time, *etc.*, for, to

доба́в|ить → **~ля́ть**; **~ле́ние** *n* [12] addition; supplement; **~ля́ть** [28], ⟨~ить⟩ [14] add; **~очный** [14] additional, extra; supplementary, accessory

добе|га́ть [1], ⟨~жа́ть⟩ [-егу́, -ежи́шь, -егу́т] run up to, reach (**до** P)

доб|ива́ть [1], ⟨~и́ть⟩ [-бью, -бьёшь, -бе́й(те)!; -би́тый] deal the final blow, kill, finish off; completely smash; **-ся** (P) (try to) get, obtain *or* reach; (*стреми́ться*) strive for; *правды и т. д.* find out (about); **он ~и́лся своего́** he gained his ends; **~ира́ться** [1], ⟨~ра́ться⟩ [-беру́сь, -рёшься] (**до** P) get to, reach

до́блест|ный [14; -тен, -тна] valiant, brave; **~ь** *f* [8] valo(u)r

добро́ *n* [9] good deed; *coll.* property; **~м** kindly, amicably; **~бы** it would be a different matter if; **~ пожа́ловать!** welcome!; **жела́ть добра́** wish *s.o.* well; **~во́лец** *m* [1; -льца] volunteer; **~во́льный** [14; -лен, -льна] voluntary; **~де́тель** *f* [8] virtue; **~ду́шие** *n* [12] good nature; **~ду́шный** [14; -шен, -шна] good-natured; **~жела́тельный** [14; -лен, -льна] benevolent; **~жела́тельство** *n* [9] benevolence; **~ка́чественный** [14 *sh.*] of good quality; *med.* benign; **~серде́чный** [14; -чен, -чна] good-hearted; **~со́вестный** [14; -тен, -тна] conscientious; **~сосе́дский** [16] friendly, neighbo(u)rly

добр|ота́ *f* [5] kindness; **~о́тный** [14; -тен, -тна] of good *or* high quality; **~ый** [14; добр, -а́, -о, добры́] kind, good; *coll.* solid; **~ых два часа́** two solid hours; **~ое у́тро** (**~ый день, ве́чер**)!

good morning (afternoon, evening); **в ~ый час!**, **всего ~ого!** good luck!; **по ~ой во́ле** of one's own free will; **чего́ ~ого** after all; **бу́дь(те) ~(ы́)!** would you be so kind as to

добы|ва́ть [1], ⟨~ть⟩ -бу́ду, -бу́дешь; добы́л, -á, до́бы́тый (добы́т, добы́та, добы́то)] get, obtain, procure; extract, mine, quarry; **~ча** f[5] procurement; extraction, mining; (*награ́бленное*) booty, spoils; *живо́тного* prey (*a. fig.*); *hunt.* bag, catch

довезти́ → довози́ть

дове́р|енность f[8] (**на** В) power of attorney; → **~ие;~енный** [14] person empowered to act for s.b.; proxy, agent; **~енное де́ло** work entrusted; **~ие** n [12] confidence, trust (**к** Д in); **~и́тельный** [14; -лен, -льна] confidential; **~ → ~я́ть;~чивый** [14 sh.] trusting, trustful; **~ша́ть** [1], ⟨~ши́ть⟩ [16 e.; -шу́, -ши́шь] finish, complete; **~ше́ние** n [12]: **в ~ше́ние всего́** to crown it all, to boot; **~я́ть** [28], ⟨~ить⟩ [13] trust (Д a p.); confide *or* entrust (В/Д s.th. to); entrust (Д/В a p. with); **-ся** (Д) *a.* trust, rely on

дов|ести́ → ~оди́ть; ~од m [1] argument; **~оди́ть** [15], ⟨~ести́⟩ [25] (**до** P) see (a p. to); lead (up [to]); **до конца́** bring (to); **до отча́яния и т. д.** drive, make; **~ести́ до све́дения** inform, bring to the notice (P of)

довое́нный [14] prewar

дов|ози́ть [15], ⟨~езти́⟩ [24] (**до** P) take *or* bring (right up] to)

дово́ль|но enough, sufficient; (*до некото́рой сте́пени*) rather, pretty, fairly; **~ный** [14; -лен, -льна] content(ed), satisfied (with Т);**~ствие** n [12] *mil.* ration, allowance; **~ствоваться** [7] content o.s. (Т with)

дога́д|ываться → ~ываться; ~ка f [5; g/pl.: -док] guess, conjecture **~ливый** [14 sh.] quick-witted; **~ываться**, ⟨~а́ться⟩ [1] (**о** П) guess, surmise

до́гма f[5], **~т** m [1] dogma

догна́ть → догоня́ть

догов|а́ривать [1], ⟨~ори́ть⟩ [13] finish saying *or* telling; **-ся** (**о** П) agree (up-

on), arrange; **~а́ривающиеся сто́роны** f/pl. contracting parties; **~ор** m [1] contract; *pol.* treaty; **~ори́ть(ся) → ~а́ривать(ся); ~о́рный** [14] contract(u-al); **цена́** agreed

дог|оня́ть [28], ⟨~на́ть⟩ [-гоню́, -го́нишь; → **гнать**] catch up (with); **до како́го-л. ме́ста** drive *or* bring to; *impf. a.* pursue, try to catch up, be (on the point of) overtaking; **~ора́ть** [1], ⟨~оре́ть⟩ [9] burn down; *fig.* fade, die out

доде́л|ывать, ⟨~елать⟩ [1] finish, complete; **~у́мываться**, ⟨~у́маться⟩[1] (**до** P) find, reach; hit upon (*s.th.*, by thinking)

доезжа́|ть [1], ⟨дое́хать⟩ [-е́ду, -е́дешь] (**до** P) reach; **не ~я** short of

дожда́|ться → дожида́ться; ~евик m [1 *e.*] raincoat; **~ево́й** [14] rain(y); **~ево́й червь** earthworm; **~ли́вый** [14 sh.] rainy; **~ь** m [4 *e.*] rain (**под** Т, **на** П in); **~ь идёт** it is raining

дож|ива́ть [1], ⟨~и́ть⟩ [-живу́, -вёшь; до́жи́л, -á, -ó (дожи́т, -á, -о)] *impf.* live one's (time, years, *etc.*); (**до** P) *pf.* live (till *or* up to); **до ста́рости** live to see; (*докати́ться*) come to; **~ида́ться** [1], ⟨~да́ться⟩ [-ду́сь, -дёшься; → **ждать**] (P) wait (for, till); *pf. a.* see

до́за f [5] dose

дозвони́ться [13] *pf.* ring s.b. (**до** *or* **к**) by means of telephone *or* doorbell until one gets an answer; get through to s.b. by telephone; gain access to s.b. by doorbell

дои́гр|ываться [1; -а́юсь, -а́ешься], ⟨~а́ться⟩ get o.s. into *or* land o.s. in trouble

доиск|иваться *coll.* [1], ⟨~а́ться⟩ [3] (P) (try to) find (out)

дои́ть(ся) [13], ⟨по-⟩ (give) milk

дойти́ → доходи́ть

док m [1] *naut.* dock

доказ|а́тельство n [9] proof, evidence; **~ывать** [1], ⟨~а́ть⟩ [3] prove; argue

док|а́нчивать [1], ⟨~о́нчить⟩ [16] finish, complete

дока́|тываться [1], ⟨~ти́ться⟩ [15; -ачу́сь, -а́тишься] roll up to; **о зву́ке** reach; **о челове́ке** come to (P)

до́кер *m* [1] docker

докла́д *m* [1] report; lecture (*о* П on); paper; address, talk; **~на́я** [14] (*a.* **запи́ска** *f*) memorandum, report; **~чик** *m* [1] lecturer; speaker; **~ывать** [1], ⟨доложи́ть⟩ [16] report (В s.th. *or* *о* П on); announce (*о* П а р.)

доко́нчить → **дока́нчивать**

до́ктор *m* [1; *pl.*: -рá, *etc. e.*] doctor

доктри́на *f* [5] doctrine

докуме́нт *m* [1] document, paper

долби́ть [14 *e.*; -блю́, -би́шь, -блённый] **1.** ⟨вы́-, про-⟩ hollow (out); chisel; *о птице* peck (*bird*); **2.** Р ⟨в-⟩ *в го́лову* inculcate, cram

долг *m* [1; *pl. e.*] debt; *sg.* duty; (*после́дний*) (last) respects *pl.*; *в* ~ → **взаймы́**; *в* ~у́ indebted (*a. fig.*, *у* Р, *пе́ред* Т to); **~ий** [16; до́лог, долгá, *etc.*; *comp.*: до́льше] long; **~о** long, (for) a long time *or* while

долго|ве́чный [14; -чен, -чна] perennial, lasting; **~во́й** [14]: **~во́е обяза́тельство** *n* promissory note; **~вре́менный** [14 *sh.*] (very) long; **~вя́зый** [14] *coll.* lanky; **~жда́нный** [14] long-awaited; **~ле́тие** *n* [12] longevity; **~ле́тний** [15] longstanding; of several years; **~сро́чный** [14] long-term; **~тá** *f* [5; *pl.*: -го́ты, *etc. st.*] duration; *geogr.* longitude

дол|ета́ть [1], ⟨~ете́ть⟩ [11] (*до* Р) fly (to, as far as), reach; *a.* = **доноси́ться**

до́лж|ен *m*, **~на́** *f*, **~но́** *n* (→ **~но**), **~ны́** *pl.* **1.** must [*pt.*: **~ен был**, **~на́ была́**, *etc.* had to]; **2.** (Д) owe (а р.)

должни́к *m* [1 *e.*] debtor; **~но́** one (it) should *or* ought to (be...); proper(ly); **~но́** = **~но́ быть** probably, apparently; **~ностно́й** [14] official; **~ность** *f* [8] post office; **~ный** [14] due (*a. su.* **~ное** *n*), proper; **~ным о́бразом** duly

доли|ва́ть [1], ⟨~ть⟩ [-лью́, -льёшь; → **лить**] fill (up), add

доли́на *f* [5] valley

до́ллар *m* [1] dollar

доложи́ть → **докла́дывать**

доло́й *coll.* off, down; **~ ...** (В)! down *or* off with ...!; *с глаз* **~ из се́рдца вон** out of sight, out of mind

долото́ *n* [9; *pl. st.*: -ло́та] chisel

до́льше (*comp.* of **до́лгий**) longer

до́ля *f* [6; *from g/pl. e.*] **1.** lot, fate; **2.** part, portion; share; *пра́вды* grain; **льви́ная ~** the lion's share

дом *m* [1; *pl.*: -á, *etc. e.*] house, building; *оча́г* home; (*дома́шние*) household; **вы́йти из ~у** leave (one's home), go out; **на ~** = **~о́й**; **на ~у́** = **~а** at home; **как ~а** at one's ease; (*у* Р) **не все ~а** (be) a bit off (one's head), nutty; **~ о́тдыха** holiday home; **~а́шний** [15] home..., house(hold)..., private; *живо́тное* domestic; *pl. su.* folks; **~а́шняя еда́** home cooking; **~енный** [14]: **~енная печь** *f* → **~на**; **~ик** *m* [1] *dim.* → **дом**

домини́ровать [7] (pre)dominate

домино́ *n* [*indecl.*] dominoes

домкра́т *m* [1] jack

до́мна *f* [5; *g/pl.*: -мен] blast furnace

домовладе́лец *m* [1; -льца] house owner

домога́ться [1] (Р) strive for, solicit

домо́|й home; **~щенный** [14] homespun; crude, primitive; **~се́д** *m* [1] stay-at-home; **~хозя́йка** *f* [5; *g/pl.*: -зя́ек] housewife

домрабо́тница *f* [5] domestic (servant), maid

до́мысел *m* [1; -сла] conjecture

донага́ *adv.*: **разде́ть ~** leave nothing on; *coll. fig.* fleece

доне|се́ние *n* [12] *mst. mil.* dispatch, report; **~сти́(сь)** → **доноси́ть(ся)**

донжуа́н *m* [1] Don Juan, philanderer

до́н|изу to the bottom; **~има́ть** [1], ⟨~я́ть⟩ [дойму́, -мёшь; → **заня́ть**] weary, exhaust (Т with)

до́нор *m* [1] donor (*mst. of blood*)

доно́с *m* [1] *law* denunciation, information (*на* В against); **~и́ть** [15], ⟨донести́⟩ [24; -су́, -сёшь] **1.** carry *or* bring ([up] to); **2.** report (*о* П *s.th.*, about, on); denounce, inform (against *на* В); *a.* **-ся** (*до* Р) waft (to); *о звуке* reach, (re)sound; **~чик** *m* [1] informer

донско́й [16] (*adj. of river* **Дон**) Don...

доня́ть → **донима́ть**

допи|ва́ть [1], ⟨~ть⟩ [-пью́, -пьёшь; → **пить**] drink up

до́пинг *m* [1] stimulant; *fig.* boost, shot in the arm; *sport* use of illicit substances

допла́|**та** *f* [5] additional payment, extra (*or* sur)charge; **~чивать** [1], ⟨**~ти́ть**⟩ [15] pay in addition

допо́длинно for sure

дополн|**е́ние** *n* [12] addition; supplement; *gr.* object; **~и́тельный** [14] additional; supplementary; extra; *adv. a.* in addition; more; **~я́ть** [28], ⟨**~ить**⟩ [13] add to, complete, embellish; *издание* enlarge

допото́пный [14] *joc.* old-fashioned, antediluvian

допра́|**шивать** [1], ⟨**~оси́ть**⟩ [15] *law* interrogate, examine; *impf.* question; **~óс** *m* [1] *law* interrogation, examination; *coll.* questioning; **~оси́ть → ~а́шивать**

до́пу|**ск** *m* [1] access, admittance; *tech.* tolerance; **~ска́ть** [1], ⟨**~сти́ть**⟩ [15] admit (*a.* of), concede; *разрешать* allow; (*терпеть*) tolerate; (*предполагать*) suppose; *ошибку* make; **~сти́мый** [14 *sh.*] admissible, permissible; **~ще́ние** *n* [12] assumption

допы́т|**ываться**, ⟨**~а́ться**⟩ [1] *coll.* (try to) find out

дораб|**а́тывать** [1], ⟨**~о́тать**⟩ [1] complete, finish off; **-ся** exhaust o.s. with work (*до изнеможе́ния*)

дореволюцио́нный [14] prerevolutionary, before the revolution

доро́г|**а** *f* [5] road, way (*a. fig.*); (*путешествие*) passage; trip, journey; **желе́зная ~а** railroad, *Brt.* railway; **по ~е** on the way; **туда́ ему́ и ~а** *coll.* it serves him right; → *a.* **путь**

дорого|**ви́зна** *f* [5] dearness, expensiveness; **~й** [16; до́рог, -á, -о; *comp.*: доро́же] dear (*a. fig.*), expensive

доро́дный [14; -ден, -дна] portly

дорож|**а́ть** [1], ⟨вз-, по-⟩ become dearer, rise in price; **~и́ть** [16 *e.*; -жу́, -жи́шь] (Т) esteem (highly), (set a high) value (on)

доро́ж|**ка** *f* [5; *g/pl.*: -жек] path; *ковровая* runner; *беговáя* **~ка** race track; **~ный** [14] road…, travel…, traffic

доса́да *f* [5] vexation; annoyance; **ка-**

ка́я ~да! how annoying!, what a pity!; **~ди́ть → ~жда́ть**; **~дный** [14; -ден, -дна] annoying, vexatious; (*прискорбный*) deplorable; (**мне**) **~дно** it is annoying (annoys me); **~довать** [7] feel *or* be annoyed *or* vexed (**на** В at, with); **~жда́ть** [1], ⟨**~ди́ть**⟩ [15 *e.*; -ажу́, -ади́шь] vex, annoy (Д/Т a p. with)

доск|**а́** *f* [5; *ac/sg.*: до́ску; *pl.*: до́ски, до́сок, доска́м] board, plank; (*a.* **кла́ссная ~а́**) blackboard; *мемориальная* plate; *ша́хматная* **~а́** chessboard; **поста́вить на одну́ ~у** put on the same level

доскона́льный [14; -лен, -льна] thorough

досло́вный [14] literal, verbatim

досма|**тривать** [1], ⟨**~отре́ть**⟩ [9; -отрю́, -о́тришь] see up to *or* to the end (**до** Р); *на таможне* examine; **~отр** *m* [1] (customs) examination; **~отре́ть → ~а́тривать**

доспе́хи *m/pl.* [1] *hist.* armo(u)r

досро́чный [14] ahead of schedule, early

дост|**ава́ть** [5], ⟨**~а́ть**⟩ [-ста́ну, -ста́нешь] take (out, *etc.*); get; procure; (**до** Р) touch; reach (to); **-ся** (Д) fall to a p.'s lot; (*быть наказанным*) catch it; **~а́вить → ~авля́ть**; **~а́вка** *f* [5; *g/pl.*: -вок] delivery; conveyance; **с ~а́вкой** (**на́ дом**) carriage paid; free to the door; **~авля́ть** [28], ⟨**~а́вить**⟩ [14] deliver, hand; bring; *fig.* cause, give; **~а́ток** *m* [1; -тка] prosperity; sufficiency; **жить в ~а́тке** be comfortably off; **~а́точно** sufficiently; (Р) (be) enough, sufficient; suffice; **~а́точный** [14; -чен, -чна] sufficient

дости|**га́ть** [1], ⟨**~гнуть**⟩, ⟨**~чь**⟩ [21; -г-: -сти́гну, -гнешь] (Р) reach, arrive at, attain (*a. fig.*); *о ценах* amount *or* run up (to); **~же́ние** *n* [12] attainment, achievement; **~жи́мый** [14 *sh.*] attainable

достове́рный [14; -рен, -рна] trustworthy, reliable

досто́|**инство** *n* [9] dignity; (*положительное качество*) merit, virtue;

(*ценность, стоимость*) worth, value; ~йный [14; -бин, -ой-на] worthy (*a.* of P); well-deserved; ~примечательность *f* [8] (*mst. pl.*) place of interest: **осмотр ~примечательностей** sight-seeing; ~яние *n* [12] property (*a. fig.*); **стать ~янием общественности** become public property

доступ *m* [1] access; ~ный [14; -пен, -пна] accessible (*a. fig.*); approachable, affable; (*понятный*) comprehensible; *цена* moderate

досу́г *m* [1] leisure; **на ~е** at leisure, during one's spare time

до́суха (quite) dry; ~сы́та to one's fill

дота́ция *f* [7] state subsidy

дотла́: utterly; **сгоре́ть ~** burn to the ground

дото́шный [14; -шен, -шна] meticulous

дотр|а́гиваться [1], ⟨~о́нуться⟩ [20] (**до** P) touch

до́х|лый [14] *животное* dead; P *о человеке* puny; ~ля́тина *f* [5] carrion; feeble person; ~нуть¹ [21], ⟨из-, по-⟩ (*of animals*) die; P (*of human beings*) coll. croak, kick the bucket; ~нуть² → **дыша́ть**

дохо́д *m* [1] income, revenue; (*выручка*) proceeds *pl.*; ~и́ть [15], ⟨дойти́⟩ [дойду́, -дёшь; → идти́] (**до** P) go or come (to), arrive (at), reach: *hist.* come down to; *о ценах* rise or run up to; ~ный [14; -ден, -дна] profitable

доце́нт *m* [1] senior lecturer, assistant professor, *Brt.* reader

доче́рн|ий [15] daughter's; ~яя компа́ния affiliate

дочи́ста (quite) clean; *coll.* completely

дочи́т|ывать, ⟨~а́ть⟩ finish reading or read up to (**до** P)

до́ч|ка *f* [5; *g/pl.*: -чек] *coll.* = ~ь *f* [до́чери, *etc.* = 8; -чери, -рей, *etc. e.*; *instr.*: -рьми] daughter

дошко́льн|ик *m* [1] child under school age; ~ый *m* [1] preschool

доща́тый [14] of boards, plank...; ~е́чка *f* [5; *g/pl.*: -чек] *dim.* → **доска́**

доя́рка *f* [5; *g/pl.*: -рок] milkmaid

драгоце́нн|ость *f* [8] jewel, gem (*a. fig.*);

precious thing *or* possession; ~ый [14; -це́нен, -це́нна] precious (*a.* stone), costly, valuable

дразни́ть [13; -ню́, дра́знишь] **1.** ⟨по-⟩ tease, mock; **2.** ⟨раз-⟩ excite, tantalize

дра́ка *f* [5] scuffle, fight

драко́н *m* [1] dragon; ~овский [16] draconian, extremely severe

дра́ма *f* [5] drama; *fig.* tragedy; ~ти́ческий [16] dramatic (*a. fig.*); ~ту́рг *m* [1] playwright, dramatist

драп|ирова́ть [7], ⟨за-⟩ drape; ~овый [14] (of thick) woolen cloth (**драп**)

дра|ть [деру́, -рёшь; драл, -á, -о; ...дра́нный], ⟨со-⟩ (→ **сдира́ть**) pull (off); tweak (*p.'s ear* В/**за** В); *coll.* ~ра́ть & раздира́ть; -ся, ⟨по-⟩ scuffle, fight, struggle; ~чли́вый [14 *sh.*] pugnacious

дребе|де́нь *coll. f* [8] trash; ~зг *coll. m* [1] tinkle, jingle, rattle; ~зжа́ть [4; -зжи́т], ⟨за-⟩ tinkle, jingle, rattle

древе|си́на *f* [5] timber; ~е́сный [14]: ~е́сный спирт methyl alcohol; ~е́сный у́голь charcoal; ~ко *n* [9; *pl.*: -ки, -ков] flagpole

дре́вн|ий [15; -вен, -вня] ancient (*a. su.*), antique; aged, (very) old; ~ость *f* [8] antiquity (*a. pl.* – -ties)

дрейф *m* [1] *naut.*, ~ова́ть [7] drift

дрем|а́ть [2], ⟨за-⟩ doze (off), slumber; ~о́та *f* [5] drowsiness, sleepiness; ~у́чий [17] dense (*a. fig.*)

дрессирова́ть [7], ⟨вы́-⟩ train

дроб|и́ть [14 *e.*; -блю́, -би́шь; -блённый], ⟨раз-⟩ break in pieces, crush; (*делить*) divide *or* split up; ~ный [14; -бен, -бна] *math.* fractional; ~ь *f* [8] *coll.* (small) shot; *барабанная math.* [*from g/pl. e.*] fraction; **десяти́чная ~ь** decimal

дрова́ *n pl.* [9] firewood; ~яни́к *m* [1], ~яно́й [14]: ~ сара́й woodshed

дро́|гнуть **1.** [21] (*зябнуть*) shiver *or* shake (with cold); ⟨про-⟩ be chilled to the bone; **2.** [20 *st.*] *pf. голос* quaver; (*заколеба́ться*) waver, falter; flinch; **не ~гнув** without flinching; ~жа́ть [4 *e.*; -жу́, -жи́шь], ⟨за-⟩ tremble, shake, shiver (**от** P with); *о пламени и т. д.* flicker, glimmer; dread (*s.th.* **перед**

T); be anxious (**за** B about); tremble (for s.o.); grudge (**над** T); **~жки** f/pl. [8; *from gen. e.*] yeast; **~жь** f [8] trembling, shiver; vibration

дрозд m [1 *e.*] thrush; **чёрный ~** blackbird

друг m [1; *pl.:* друзья́, -зе́й, -зья́м] friend (*a.* address); **~ ~a** each (one an)other; **~ за ~ом** one after another; **~ с ~ом** with each other; **~ой** [16] (an)other, different; else, next, second; **(н)и тот (н)и ~ой** both (neither); **на ~ой день** the next day

дру́ж|ба f [5] friendship; **~елю́бный** [14; -бен, -бна] amicable, friendly; **~еский** [16], **~ественный** [14 *sh.*] friendly; *comput.* userfriendly; **~ить** [16; -жу́, -у́жишь] be friends, be on friendly terms (**с** T with); **~ище** m [11] old chap *or* boy; **~ный** [14; -жен, -жна́, -о; дру́жны] friendly, on friendly terms; (*совместный*) joint, concerted; *bot., mil., etc.* vigorous; *adv. a.* together; at once

дря́б|лый [14; дрябл, -á, -о] limp, flabby; **~зги** *coll. f/pl.* [5] squabbles; **~нно́й** P [14] wretched, worthless, trashy; **~нь** *coll.* f [8] rubbish, trash (*a. fig.*); P **вещь** rotten thing; *человек* rotter; **~хлый** [14; дряхл, -á, -о] decrepit; *coll. дом и т. д.* dilapidated

дуб m [1; *pl. e.*] oak; **~и́на** f [5] club, cudgel; P boor, dolt; **~и́нка** f [5; *g/pl.:* -нок] (policeman's) club; **~лёр** m [1], **~лика́т** m [1] duplicate; reserve; *thea.* understudy; **~ли́ровать** [7] *impf.* duplicate; *thea.* understudy a part; *cine.* dub; **~о́вый** [14] oak(en)

дуга́ f [5; *pl. st.*] arc (*a. el.*); **согну́ть в ~у́** bring under, compel; **~о́й** arched

ду́дк|а f [5; *g/pl.:* -док] pipe; flute; **~и!** not on your life!; **пляса́ть под чью-л. ~у** dance to s.b.'s tune

ду́ло n [9] muzzle; barrel (gun)

ду́ма f [5] **1.** *old use* thought; meditation; **2.** *pol.* duma, parliament; (*in Russia*) duma = council; elective legislative assembly; **~ть** [1], ⟨по-⟩ think (**о** П about, of); reflect (**над** T, **о** П on); (+ *inf.*) intend to, be going to; care (**о** П about); **как ты ~ешь?** what do you think?;

мно́го о себе́ ~ть be conceited; **не до́лго ~я** without hesitation; **~ся** seem, appear; **~ется, он прав** I think he is right; **мне ~ется, что** I think that ...

дун|ове́ние n [12] waft, breath; **~у́ть → ду́ть**

дупло́ n [9; *pl. st.:* ду́пла, -пел, -плам] *дерева* hollow; *в зубе* cavity (*in tooth*)

дур|а́ f [5] silly woman; **~а́к** m [1 *e.*] fool, simpleton; **~а́к ~ако́м** arrant fool; **сваля́ть ~ака́** do something foolish; **~а́цкий** [16] foolish, silly, idiotic; **~а́чество** *coll.* n [9] tomfoolery; **~а́чить** [16], ⟨о-⟩ fool, hoax; **-ся** play the fool; **~е́ть** *coll.* [8], ⟨о-⟩ become stupefied; **~и́ть** *coll.* [13], ⟨о-⟩ confuse, deceive; **→ ~а́читься**; naughty *or* obstinate

дурма́н m [1] *fig.* narcotic; **~ить** [13], ⟨о-⟩ stupefy

дурн|е́ть [8], ⟨по-⟩ grow plain *or* ugly; **~о́й** [14; ду́рен, -рна́, -о] bad; *о внешности* plain, ugly; **мне ~о** I feel (am) sick *or* unwell; **~ота́** *coll.* f [5] giddiness; nausea

дурь *coll.* f [8] folly, caprice

ду́т|ый [14] *fig. авторите́т* inflated; *ци́фры* distorted; **~ь** [18], ⟨по-⟩, *once* ⟨ду́нуть⟩ [20] blow; **ду́ет** there is a draught (draft); **-ся**, ⟨на-⟩ swell; *coll.* sulk; be angry with (**на** B)

дух m [1] *времени* spirit; *боево́й* courage; (*привиде́ние*) ghost; **здоро́вый ~ в здоро́вом те́ле** a sound mind in a sound body; **(не) в ~е** in a good (bad) temper *or* in high (low) spirits; **в моём ~е** to my taste; **па́дать ~ом** lose heart; **прису́тствие ~а** presence of mind; P **~ом** in a jiffy *or* trice; old use **во весь ~, что есть ~у** at full speed; **~и́** m/pl. [1 *e.*] perfume

духов|е́нство n [9] *coll.* clergy; **~ка** f [5; *g/pl.:* -вок] oven; **~ный** [14] spiritual; *состоя́ние* mental; ecclesiastical, clerical, religious; **~ный мир** inner world; **~о́й** [14] *mus.* wind (*instrument*); **~о́й орке́стр** m brass band

духота́ f [5] sultriness, stuffiness

душ m [1] shower; **приня́ть ~** take a shower

E

душ|а́ f [5; *ac/sg.*: ду́шу; *pl. st.*] soul; *fig.* heart; *hist.* serf; **в ~е́** at heart; **~а́ в ~у** at one; in harmony; **в глубине́ ~и́** in one's heart of hearts; **~и́ не ча́ять** adore; **~а́ о́бщества** life and soul of the party; **не по ~е́** not to like (the idea of) *or* care; **от (всей) ~и́** from (with all) one's heart; **~а́ в пя́тки ушла́** have one's heart in one's mouth

душ|евнобольно́й [14] mentally ill *or* deranged (person); **~е́вный** [14] sincere, heartfelt, cordial; **~ераздира́ющий** [17] heart-rending

души́стый [14 *sh.*] fragrant; *горошек* sweet (*peas*); **~и́ть** [16] 1. ⟨за-⟩ strangle; smother (*a. fig.*); 2. ⟨на-⟩ perfume (**-ся** *o.s.*); **~ный** [14; -шен, -шна́, -о] stuffy, sultry

дуэ́|ль f [8] *hist.* duel (*a. fig.*); **~т** m [1] duet

ды́б|ом (*stand*) on end (*of hair*); **~ы: (встать** *etc.*) **на ~ы́** rear (*a.* up); *fig.* resist, revolt (against)

дым m [1] smoke; **~и́ть** [14 *e.*; -млю́, -ми́шь], ⟨на-⟩ *or* **~и́ться** smoke; **~ка** f [5] haze; **~ный** [14] smoky; **~ово́й** [14]: **~ова́я труба́** chimney; *naut.* funnel; **~о́к** m [1; -мка́] small puff of smoke

дымохо́д m [1] flue

ды́ня f [6] (musk) melon

дыр|а́ f [5; *pl. st.*], **~ка** f [5; *g/pl.*: -рок] hole; **~я́вый** [14 *sh.*] having a hole, full of holes; *coll.* **~я́вая голова́** *coll.* forgetful person

дыха́|ние n [12] breath(ing); **иску́сственное ~ние** artificial respiration; **~тельный** [14] respiratory; **~тельное го́рло** windpipe

дыша́ть [4], ⟨по-⟩, *coll.* (*a.* once) ⟨дохну́ть⟩ [20] breathe (T s.th.); *a.* devote *o.s.* to; **~ све́жим во́здухом** take the air; **е́ле ~** *or* **~ на ла́дан** have one foot in the grave; *о вещах* be completely worn out *or* very old

дья́вол m [1] devil; **~ьский** [16] devilish, diabolical

дья́кон m [1] deacon

дю́жина f [5] dozen

дю́й|м m [1] inch; **~на** f [5] dune

дя́дя m [6; *g/pl.*: -дей] uncle (*a. coll. as mode of address by child to any adult male*)

дя́тел m [1; -тла] woodpecker

Е

Ева́нгелие n [12] *collect.* the Gospels

евре́й m [3] Jew; **~ка** f [5; *g/pl.*: -ре́ек] Jewess; **~ский** [16] Jewish

европ|е́ец m [1; -пе́йца], **~е́йка** f [5; *g/pl.*: -пе́ек], **~е́йский** [16] European; **Ꝗейский Сою́з** European Union

е́герь m [4; *pl.*: *a.* -ря́, *etc.*] hunter, huntsman; chasseur

еги́п|етский [16] Egyptian; **~тя́нин** m [1; *pl.*: -я́не, -я́н], **~тя́нка** f [5; *g/pl.*: -нок] Egyptian

его́ (ji'vɔ) his; its; → **он**

еда́ f [5] food, meal

едва́ (*a.* **~ли**) hardly, scarcely; → *a.* **е́ле**; no sooner; **~ не** almost, nearly; **~ли** perhaps

едине́|ние n [12] unity, union; **~ица** f [5] *math.* one; *часть, величина* unit; *coll.* *оценка* very bad; *pl.* (*a.*) few; **~и́чный** [14; -чен, -чна] single, isolated

еди́но|... (→ *a.* **одно́**): **~бо́рство** n [9] (single) combat; **~вла́стие** n [12] autocracy; **~вре́менный** [14] once only; *пособие* extraordinary; **~гла́сие** n [12] unanimity; **~гла́сный** [14; -сен, -сна] unanimous; **~гла́сно** unanimously; **~ду́шие** n [12] unanimity; **~ду́шный** [14; -шен, -шна] unanimous; **~ли́чный** [14] individual, personal; **~мы́шленник** m [1] like-minded p., associate, confederate; **~обра́зный** [14; -зен, -зна] uniform

еди́нствен|ный [14 *sh.*] only, single, sole; **~ный в своём ро́де** unique;

~ое число́ *gr.* singular

еди́н|ство *n* [9] unity; *взгля́дов и т. д.* unanimity; **~ый** [14 *sh.*] one, single, common; (*то́лько оди́н*) only (one, sole); (*объединённый*) one whole; united; **все до ~ого** all to a man

е́дкий [16; -док, -дка́, -о] caustic

едо́к *m* [1 *e.*] (*coll.* big) eater; **на ка́ждого ~а́** per head; **пять ~о́в в семье́** five mouths to feed

её her; its; → **она́**

ёж *m* [1 *e.*] hedgehog

ежеви́ка *f* [5] blackberry, -ries *pl.*

еже|го́дный [14] annual; **~дне́вный** [14] daily, everyday; **~ме́сячный** [14] monthly; **~мину́тный** [14] (occurring) every minute; (*непреры́вный*) continual; **~неде́льник** *m* [1], **~неде́льный** [14] weekly; **~ча́сный** [14] hourly

ёжиться [16], ⟨съ-⟩ shiver (from cold, fever); shrink (from fear); *от смуще́ния* be shy, hem and haw

ежо́в|ый [14]: **держа́ть в ~ых рукави́цах** rule with a rod of iron

езд|а́ *f* [5] ride, drive; **~ить** [15], go (T by), ride, drive; (*посеща́ть регуля́рно*) come; visit; travel

ей: **~-бо́гу** *int./coll.* really, indeed

е́ле (*a.* **е́ле-е́ле**) hardly, scarcely, barely; *слегка́* slightly; *с трудо́м* with (great) difficulty

еле́йный [14] *fig.* unctuous

ёлка *f* [5; *g/pl.*: ёлок] fir; **рожде́ственская (нового́дняя) ~** Christmas (New Year's) tree *or* (children's) party (**на** B to, for; **на** П at)

ел|о́вый [14] fir; **~ь** *f* [8] fir; **~ьник** *m* [1] fir-grove; *collect.* firwood

ёмк|ий [16; ёмок, ёмка] capacious; **~ость** *f* [8] capacity; **~ость запомина́ющего устро́йства** storage capacity; *comput.* memory capacity

ено́т *m* [1] raccoon

епи́скоп *m* [1] bishop

ерала́ш *m* [1] *coll.* jumble, muddle

е́ре|сь *f* [8] heresy; *fig.* nonsense

ёрзать [1] *coll.* fidget

еро́шить [16] → **взъеро́шивать**

ерунда́ *f* [5] *coll.* nonsense; trifle(s)

ёрш *m* [1 *e.*] **1.** *zo.* ruff; **2.** *coll.* mixture of vodka with beer *or* wine

е́сли if; in case; once (*a.* **~ уж[é]**); **a** *or* **и ~** if ever; whereas; **~ и** *or* (**да**)**же** even though; **ax** *or* **о, ~ б(ы)…** oh, could *or* would…; **~ бы** he but for; **~ то́лько** provided

есте́ств|енно naturally, of course; **~енный** [14 *sh.*] natural; **~енные нау́ки** natural sciences; **~о́** *n* [9] челове́ка nature; essence; **~озна́ние** *n old use* [12] natural science

есть¹ [ем, ешь, ест, еди́м, еди́те, едя́т; е́шь(те)!; ел; …е́денный] **1.** ⟨съ-, по-⟩ eat (*pf. a.* up), have; **2.** ⟨разъ-⟩ eat away (of rust); *chem.* corrode

есть² → **быть** am, is, are; there is (are); **у меня́ ~ …** I have …; **так и ~** I thought as much

ефре́йтор *m* [1] *mil.* private first class, *Brt.* lance-corporal

е́ха|ть [е́ду, е́дешь; поезжа́й!], ⟨по-⟩ (be) go(ing, *etc.*) (by T), drive (T *or* **в, на** П in, on); (**в, на** B) leave (for), go (to); (**за** T) go for, fetch; **по~ли!** → **идти́**

ехи́д|ный [14; -ден, -дна] caustic, spiteful; malicious; **~ство** *n* [9] spite, malice; innuendo

ещё (**не**) (not) yet; (**всё**) **~** still (*a.* with *comp.*); another, more (and more **~ и ~**); **~ раз** once more; again; **кто ~?** who else?; *о вре́мени* as early (late, *etc.*); **~ бы!** (to be) sure! I should think so!, of course!; **пока́ ~** for the time being; **э́то ~ ничего́** it could have been worse; **он ~ мо́лод** he is still young

Ж

ж → же

жа́б|а f [5] toad; **~ра** f [5] gill

жа́воронок m [1; -нка] lark

жа́дничать [1], ⟨по-⟩ be greedy or avaricious; **~ость** f[8] greed(iness), avarice; **~ый** [14; -ден, -дна́, -о] greedy (**на** B, **до** P, **к** Д of), avaricious

жа́жда f [5] thirst (*a. fig.*, P *or inf.* for); **~ть** [-ду, -дешь] thirst, crave (P *or inf.* for)

жаке́т m [1] (lady's) jacket

жале́ть [8], ⟨по-⟩ **1.** pity, feel sorry for; (**о** П) regret; **2.** (P *or* B) spare; (*скупиться*) grudge

жа́лить [13], ⟨у-⟩ sting, bite

жа́лк|ий [16; -лок, -лка́, -о; *compr.*: жа́льче] pitiable; (*несчастный*) pathetic, wretched; **~о** → **жаль**

жа́ло n [9] sting (*a. fig.*)

жа́лоб|а f[5] complaint; **~ный** [14; -бен, -бна] plaintive

жа́лова|нье n [10] *old use* pay, salary; **~ть** [7]: **не ~ть** not like; ⟨по-⟩ *mst. iro.* come (to visit, see a p. **к** Д); **-ся** (**на** B) complain (of, about)

жа́лост|ливый [14 *sh.*] *coll.* compassionate; **~ный** [14; -тен, -тна] mournful; (*соболезнующий*) compassionate; **~ь** f[8] pity, compassion

жаль it is a pity (**как ~** what a pity); (*as adv.*) unfortunately; (Д **~** B): **мне ~ его́** I am sorry for *or* I pity him; *a.* regret; grudge

жанр m [1] genre; **~овый** [14] genre...; **~овая жи́вопись** genrepainting

жар m [1; в ~у́] heat; *med.* fever; *fig.* ardo(u)r; **~á** f [5] heat, hot weather; **~еный** [14] roast, broiled; fried, grilled; → **а. ~ко́е**; **~ить** [13], ⟨за-, из-⟩ roast; fry; *coll. о солнце* burn; **~кий** [16; -рок, -рка́, -о; *compr.*: жа́рче] hot; *fig.* heated, ardent, vehement, intense; **мне ~ко** I am hot; **~ко́е** n [16] roast meat; **~опонижа́ющий** [17] *med.* febrifugal

жасми́н m [1] jasmin(e)

жа́т|ва f [5] harvest(ing); **~венный** [14] reaping

жать¹ [жну, жнёшь; ...жа́тый] ⟨с-⟩ [сожну́], ⟨по-⟩ reap, cut, harvest

жать² [жму, жмёшь, ...жа́тый], ⟨с-⟩, ⟨по-⟩ press, squeeze; **~ ру́ку** shake hands (Д with); *об обуви и т. д.* pinch; **-ся** shrink (**от** P with); crowd, huddle up, snuggle; (*быть в нерешительности*) hesitate, waver

жва́ч|ка f [5] chewing, rumination; *coll.* chewing gum; **~ный** [14]: **~ные (живо́тные)** n/pl. ruminants

жгут m [1 *e.*] *med.* tourniquet

жгу́чий [17 *sh.*] burning; smarting

ждать [жду, ждёшь; ждал, -á, -о], ⟨подо-⟩ wait (for P); (*ожидать*) expect, await; **вре́мя не ждёт** time presses; **~ не дожда́ться** wait impatiently (P for)

же 1. *conj.* but, and; whereas, as to; **2.** → **ведь**; *a. do* + *vb.*: **э́то ~** the (this) very, same *место, время и т. д.*; **э́тот ~ челове́к** this very man; **что ~ ты молча́л?** why on earth didn't you tell me about it?; **скажи́ ~ что-нибудь!** for goodness' sake say something!; **когда́ ~ она́ уйдёт** whenever will she leave?

жева́|ть [7 *e.*; жую́, жуёшь] chew; **~тельный** [14] *движение мышцы* masticatory; *резинка* chewing

жезл m [1 *e.*] *маршальский* staff; rod

жела́|ние n [12] wish, desire; **по (согла́сно) ~нию** at, by (as) request(ed); **~нный** [14] desired; wished for; *гость и т. д.* welcome; (*любимый*) beloved; **~тельный** [14; -лен, -льна] desirable, desired; **мне ~тельно** I am anxious to; **~ть** [1], ⟨по-⟩ wish (Д/P a p. s.th.), desire; **э́то оставля́ет ~ть лу́чшего** it leaves much to be desired; **~ющие** *pl.* [17] those interested in, those wishing to ...

желе́ n [*indecl.*] jelly (*a. fish, meat*)

железа́ f [5; *pl.*: же́лезы, желёз, железа́м] *anat.* gland

желез|нодоро́жник *m* [1] railroad (*Brt.* railway-) man; **~нодоро́жный** [14] railroad…, *Brt.* railway…; **~ный** [14] iron; **~ная доро́га** railway; **~о** *n* [9] iron; **кро́вельное ~о** sheet iron; **куй ~о, пока́ горячо́** strike while the iron is hot; **~обето́н** *m* [1] reinforced concrete

жёлоб *m* [1; *pl.*: -ба́, *etc. e.*] gutter; chute

желте́ть [8], ⟨по-⟩ grow *or* turn yellow; *impf.* (*a.* **-ся**) appear yellow; **~изна́** *f* [5] yellow(ness); **~ова́тый** [14 *sh.*] yellowish; **~о́к** *m* [1; -тка́] yolk; **~у́ха** *f med.* [5] jaundice

жёлтый [14; жёлт, -а́, -о] yellow

желу́док *m* [1; -дка] stomach; **~чный** [14] gastric, stomach

жёлудь *m* [4; *from g/pl. e.*] acorn

жёлч|ный [14] gall…; **~ный пузы́рь** gall bladder; [жёлчен, -а́, -о] *fig.* irritable; **~ь** *f* [8] bile, gall (*a. fig.*)

жема́н|иться [13] *coll.* mince; be prim; behave affectedly; **~ный** [14; -а́нен, -а́нна] affected, mincing, prim; **~ство** *n* [9] primness, prudery, affectedness

жёмчуг *m* [1; *pl.*: -га́, *etc. e.*] *coll.* pearls *pl.*; **~у́жина** *f* [5] pearl; **~у́жный** [14] pearly

жен|а́ *f* [5; *pl. st.*: жёны] wife; **~а́тый** [14 *sh.*] married (*man*; **на** П to a p.); **~и́ть** [13; женю́, же́нишь] (*im*)*pf.* marry (*a man* **на** П to); **-ся** marry (*v/t.* **на** П; *of men*); **~и́тьба** *f* [5] marriage (**на** П to); **~и́х** *m* [1] fiancé; bridegroom; **~оненави́стник** *m* [1] misogynist, woman hater; **~оподо́бный** [14; -бен, -бна] effeminate; **~ский** [16] female, lady's, woman's, women's, girl's; *gr.* feminine; **~ственный** [14 *sh.*] feminine, womanly; **~щина** *f* [5] woman

жердь *f* [8; *from g/pl. e.*] pole

жереб|ёнок *m* [2] foal, colt; **~е́ц** *m* [1; -бца́] stallion

жёрнов *m* [1; *pl. e.*: -ва́] millstone

же́ртв|а *f* [5] victim; sacrifice (*a.* = **приноси́ть в ~у**); **~овать** [7], ⟨по-⟩ (Т) sacrifice (*v/t.*: *o.s.* **собо́й**); (В) give

жест *m* [1] gesture; **~икули́ровать** [7] gesticulate

жёсткий [16; -ток, -тка́, -о; *сотр.*: -тче]

hard; *слова, условия* harsh; *мясо* tough; *материал* stiff, rigid; *критика, меры* severe

жесто́к|ий [16; жесто́к, -а́, -о] cruel; (*ужасный*) terrible, dreadful; *мороз* fierce; *действительность* grim; **~осе́рдие** *n* [12] hard-heartedness; **~ость** *f* [8] cruelty, brutality

жесть *f* [8] tin (plate); **~яно́й** [14] tin…

жето́н *m* [1] counter; token

жечь, ⟨с-⟩ [26; г/ж: (с)жгу́, -жжёшь, -жгу́т; (с)жёг, (со)жгла́; сожжённый] burn (*a. fig.*); torment

живи́т|ельный [14; -лен, -льна] life-giving, vivifying; *воздух* crisp, bracing

жи́вность *f* [8] *coll.* small (domestic) animals, poultry and fowl

жив|о́й [14; жив, -а́, -о] living; alive (*pred.*); (*деятельный*) lively, vivacious; *ум* quick; (*подвижный*) nimble; *воображение* lively, vivid; **в ~ы́х** alive; **как ~о́й** true to life; **и здоро́в** safe and sound; **ни ~ ни мёртв** more dead than alive; petrified with fear *or* astonishment; **заде́ть за ~о́е** cut to the quick; **принима́ть ~о́е уча́стие** take an active part; feel keen sympathy (with); **~опи́сец** *m* [1; -сца] painter; **~опи́сный** [14; -сен, -сна] picturesque; **~о́пись** *f* [8] painting; **~ость** *f* [8] liveliness, vivacity; animation

живо́т *m* [1 *e.*] abdomen, stomach, belly; **~во́рный** [14; -рен, -рна] vivifying; **~ново́дство** *n* [9] cattle breeding; **~ное** *n* [14] animal; **~ный** [14] animal; *fig.* bestial, brutal; **~ный мир** animal kingdom; **~ный страх** blind fear

жив|отрепе́щущий [17] actual, topical, of vital importance; *fig.* burning; **~у́чий** [17 *sh.*] (*выносливый*) hardy, tough; *традиция и т. д.* enduring; **~ьём** alive

жи́дк|ий [16; -док, -дка́, -о; *сотр.*: жи́же] liquid, fluid; (*водянистый*) watery, weak; *каша и т. д.* thin; *волосы и т. д.* sparse, scanty; **~ость** *f* [8] liquid

жи́жа *f* [5] *coll.* liquid; (*грязь*) slush; (*бульон*) broth

жизне|нность *f* [8] viability; vitality; **~нный 1.** [14 *sh.*] (of) life('s), wordly; vivid; **2.** [14] (*жизненно важный*) vital;

~ра́достный [14; -тен, -тна] cheerful, joyful; **~спосо́бный** [14; -бен, -бна] viable

жизн|ь *f* [8] life; (*никогда́*) *в ~и не ...* never (in one's life); *о́браз ~и* way of life; *провести́ в ~ь* put into practice; *при ~и* in a p.'s lifetime; alive; *вопро́сы ~и и сме́рти* vital question

жи́л|а *f* [5] *coll.* sinew, tendon; vein (*a. geol.*); **~е́т** *m* [1], **~е́тка** *f* [5; *g/pl.:* -ток] vest, *Brt.* waistcoat; **~е́ц** *m* [1; -льца́] lodger, roomer; tenant; **~истый** [14 *sh.*] sinewy, wiry; *мясо* stringy; **~и́ще** *n* [11] dwelling, lodging(s); **~и́щный** [14] housing; **~ка** *f* [5; *g/pl.:* -лок] *dim.* → **~**; veinlet; *на листья́х, мра́море* vein (*a. fig.*); **~о́й** [14]: **~о́й дом** dwelling, house; **~пло́щадь** *f* [8] living space; **~ьё** *n* [10] habitation; dwelling; lodging(s)

жир *m* [1; в -у́; *pl. e.*] fat; grease; *ры́бий ~* cod-liver oil; **~е́ть** [8], ⟨о-, раз-⟩ grow fat; **~ный** [14; -рен, -рна́, -о] (of) grease, greasy; *земля́* rich soil; *typ.* bold(faced); **~ово́й** [14] fat(ty)

жит|е́йский [16] wordly, (of) life('s); everyday; **~ель** *m* [4], **~ельница** *f* [5] inhabitant, resident; **~ельство** *n* [9] residence; *вид на ~ельство* residence permit; **~ие́** *n* [12] life, biography (*mst. of a saint*)

жи́тница *f* [5] *fig.* granary

жить [живу́, -вёшь; жил, -а́, -о; не́ жил(и)] live (Т, **на** В [up]on; Т *a.* for); ⟨*прожива́ть*⟩ reside, lodge; *как живёте?*

how are you (getting on)?; *жи́л(и)-бы́л(и) ...* once upon a time there was (were) ...; **~ся** *ей хорошо́ живётся* she is well off; **~ё(-бытьё)** *coll. n* [10] life, living

жмот *m* [1] *coll.* skinflint, miser

жму́рить [13], ⟨за-⟩ screw up, tighten, narrow (one's eyes **-ся**)

жрать Р *coarse* [жру, жрёшь, жрал, -а́, -о], ⟨со-⟩ devour, gorge, gobble

жре́бий *m* [3] lot (*a. fig.* = destiny); *броса́ть* ⟨тяну́ть⟩ ~ cast (draw) lots; ~ *бро́шен* the die is cast

жрец *m* [1 *e.*] (pagan) priest (*a. fig.*)

жужжа́|ние *n* [12], **~ть** [4 *e.*; жужжу́, -и́шь] buzz, hum

жу́к *m* [1 *e.*] beetle; *ма́йский ~к* cockchafer; **~лик** *coll. m* [1] (*моше́нник*) swindler, cheat, trickster; (*вор*) filcher, pilferer; **~льничать** [1], ⟨с-⟩ cheat, trick

жура́вль *m* [4 *e.*] (*zo., well*) crane

жури́ть *coll.* [13], ⟨по-⟩ scold mildly, reprove

журна́л *m* [1] magazine, periodical, journal; diary; *naut.* log(book); **~и́ст** *m* [1] news(paper)man, journalist; **~и́стика** *f* [5] journalism

журча́|ние *n* [12], **~ть** [-чи́т] purl, murmur

жу́т|кий [14; -ток, -тка́, -о] weird, uncanny, sinister; *мне ~ко* I am terrified; *coll.* **~ь** *f* [8] horror; (*меня́*) *пря́мо ~ь берёт* I feel terrified

жюри́ *n* [*indecl.*] jury (prizes)

за 1. (B): (*direction*) behind; over, across, beyond; out of; (*distance*) at; (*time*) after; over, past; before (*a. ~ ...до* P); *ему́ ~ со́рок* he is over forty; (with) in, for, during; (*object*[*ive*], *favo*[*u*]*r, reason, value, substitute*) for; **~то́**, **~ что** because; *~ что?* what for? why?; **2.** (T): (*position*) behind; across, beyond; at, over; after (*time & place*); because of;

with; *~ мной ... a.* I owe ...; *ко́мната ~ мной* I'll take (*or* reserve) the room

заба́в|а *f* [5] amusement, entertainment; **~ля́ть** [28], ⟨(по)~ить⟩ [13] amuse (*-ся* o.s., be amused at Т); **~ный** [14; -вен, -вна] amusing, funny

забасто́в|ка *f* [5; *g/pl.:* -вок] strike, walkout; *всео́бщая ~ка* general strike; **~очный** [14] strike...; **~щик** *m* [1] striker

забве́ние n [12] oblivion

забе́г m [1] *sport* heat, race; **~а́ть** [1], ⟨~жа́ть⟩ [4]; забегу́, -ежи́шь, -егу́т; -еги́!] run in(to), get; *далеко* run off; *coll.* drop in (**к** Д on); **~га́ть вперёд** anticipate, forestall

забере́менеть [8] *pf.* become pregnant

забива́ть [1], ⟨~и́ть⟩ [-бью, -бьёшь; → **бить**] drive in; *гвоздями* nail up; *гол* score; (*засорить*) block (up); *фонтан* spout forth; *тревогу* sound; *coll. голову* stuff; **-ся** *coll.* (*спрятаться*) hide, get; *pf.* begin to beat; get clogged (T with)

заби́|тый [14] browbeaten, cowed, downtrodden; **~ть** → **~ва́ть**; **~я́ка** m/f [5] bully, squabbler

заблаго|вре́менно in good time; in advance; **~вре́менный** [14] done ahead of time; timely; **~рассуди́ться** [15; *impers.* Д with] think fit

заблу|ди́ться [15] *pf.* lose one's way, go astray; **~у́дший** [17] *fig.* gone astray; **~ужда́ться** [1] be mistaken, err; **~уж-де́ние** n [12] error, mistake; (*ложное мнение*) delusion; **ввести́ в ~ужде́ние** mislead

забол|ева́ть [1], ⟨~е́ть⟩ [8] fall sick *or* ill (of T), be taken ill with; *о боли* begin to ache; *su.:* **~ева́ние** n [12] → **боле́знь**

забо́р m [1] fence

забо́т|а f [5] care (**о** П about, of), concern, anxiety, worry, trouble; **без ~** *жизнь* carefree; **~иться** [15], ⟨по-⟩ (**о** П) care (for), take care of, look after; worry, be anxious (about); **~ливый** [14 *sh.*] *хозяин* careful, provident; *по отношению к кому-л.* attentive, thoughtful, solicitous

забр|а́сывать [1] **1.** ⟨~оса́ть⟩ (Т) (*заполнить*) fill up; *вопросами и т. д.* shower (T with); *камнями* pelt; **2.** ⟨~о́сить⟩ [15] throw, fling (*a. fig.*), cast; *дело,*

ребёнка и т. д. neglect; **~а́ть** → **забира́ть**; ⟨~еда́ть⟩ [1], ⟨~ести́⟩ [25] wander or get (in[to], far); **~оса́ть, ~о́сить** → **~а́сывать**; **~о́шенный** [14] neglected; deserted; *ребёнок* unkempt

забры́згать [1] *pf.* splash; *грязью* bespatter

заб|ыва́ть [1], ⟨~ы́ть⟩ [-бу́ду, -бу́дешь] forget (**о** П; **-ся** *перейти границу дозволенного; a.* nap, doze); **~ы́вчивый** [14 *sh.*] forgetful; absent-minded; **~ытьё** n [10; в -ты́] (*беспамятство*) unconsciousness, swoon; (*дремота*) drowsiness; (*лёгкий сон*) slumber

зава́л m [1] obstruction, blockage; **~ивать** [1], ⟨~и́ть⟩ [13; -алю́, -а́лишь] fill or heap (up); cover; *дорогу* block, obstruct, close; *работой* overburden (with T); *экзамен* coll. fail; *дело* ruin; **-ся** fall; *стена* collapse

зава́р|ивать [1], ⟨~и́ть⟩ [13; -арю́, -а́ришь] brew, make (tea); pour boiling water (over); *coll. fig.* **~и́ть ка́шу** stir up trouble

зав|еде́ние n [12] establishment, institution; **вы́сшее уче́бное ~еде́ние** higher education(al) institution; **~е́довать** [7] (Т) be in charge or the head or chief of, manage; **~е́домый** [14] undoubted; **~е́домо зна́я** being fully aware; **дава́ть ~е́домо ло́жные показа́ния** commit perjury; **~е́дующий** m [17] (Т) chief, head; director; **~езти́** → **~ози́ть**

зав|ере́ние n [12] assurance; **~е́рить** → **~еря́ть**; **~ерну́ть** → **~ёртывать**; **~ер-те́ть** [11; -ерчу́, -е́ртишь] *pf.* start turning (*v/i.* **-ся**); **~ёртывать** [1], ⟨~ерну́ть⟩ [20] wrap up; *за угол* turn (*a.* up; *кран и т. д.* off); screw up; (*зайти*) drop in; **~ерша́ть** [1], ⟨~ерши́ть⟩ [16 *e.*; -шу́, -ши́шь, -шённый] finish, complete; **-ся** *успехом* crown; **~ерше́ние** n [12] conclusion, end; completion; **~еря́ть** [28], ⟨~е́рить⟩ [13] assure (В/**в** П a *p.* of); attest, authenticate; *подпись* witness a signature

заве́с|а f [5] *секретности fig.* veil; **ды-мова́я ~са** smoke screen; **~сить** → **~шивать**; **~сти́** → **заводи́ть**

заве́т *m* [1] *Bibl.* (**Ве́тхий** Old, **Но́вый** New) Testament; **~ный** [14]: **~ная мечта́** cherished ambition

заве́|шивать [1], ⟨~сить⟩ [15] cover, hang with, curtain

завеща́|ние *n* [12] testament, will; **~ть** [1] *im(pf.)* leave, bequeath

завзя́тый [14] *coll.* **кури́льщик** inveterate; incorrigible

зав|ива́ть [1], ⟨~и́ть⟩ [-вью́, -вьёшь; → **вить**] *во́лосы* wave, curl; wind round; **~и́вка** *f* [5; *g/pl.:* -вок] wave (*in hair*)

зави́д|ный [14; -ден, -дна] enviable; **~овать** [7], ⟨по-⟩ envy (Д/в П а *p. a th.*), be envious (of)

завин|чивать [1], ⟨~ти́ть⟩ [15 *e.;* -нчу́, -нти́шь] screw up, down *or* tight

зави́с|еть [11] depend (**от** P on); **~имость** *f* [8] dependence; **в ~имости от** (P) depending on; **~имый** [14 *sh.*] dependent

зави́ст|ливый [14 *sh.*] envious; **~ь** *f* [8] envy (**к** Д of, at)

зави|то́й [14] curly; **~то́к** *m* [1; -тка́] curl, ringlet; **~ть** → **~ва́ть**

завлад|ева́ть [1], ⟨~е́ть⟩ [8] (T) take possession *or* hold of, seize, capture (*a. fig.*)

завл|ека́тельный [14; -лен, -льна] enticing, tempting; **~ека́ть** [1], **~е́чь** [26] (al)lure, entice, tempt

заво́д¹ *m* [1] works, factory, plant, mill (**на** П/В at/to); **ко́нский ~** stud farm

заво́д² *m* [1] winding mechanism; **~и́ть** [15], ⟨завести́⟩ [25] **1.** (*приводить*) take, bring, lead; **2.** *дело* establish, set up, found; *привычку, дружбу и т. д.* form, contract; *машину и т. д.* get, procure, acquire; *разговор и т. д.* start (*a. мотор*); begin; *собаку и т. д.* keep; **3.** *часы́* wind up; **-ся**, ⟨завести́сь⟩ appear; (*возбудиться*) become excited; get, have; **~но́й** [14] *tech.* starting; *игрушка* mechanical; *человек* full of beans; **~ский, ~ско́й** [16] works...;

заво|ева́ние *n* [12] conquest; *fig. (mst. pl.)* achievement(s); **~ева́тель** *m* [4] conqueror; **~ёвывать** [1], ⟨~ева́ть⟩ [6] conquer; (*добиться*) win, gain

зав|ози́ть [15], ⟨~езти́⟩ [24] take, bring, drive; *coll.* deliver

завола́|кивать [1], ⟨~о́чь⟩ [26] obscure; *слезами* cloud; get cloudy

завор|а́чивать [1], ⟨~оти́ть⟩ [15] turn (up, down); roll up

завсегда́тай *m* [3] habitué, regular

за́втра tomorrow

за́втрак *m* [1] breakfast (**за** Т at; **на** В, **к** Д for); **~ать** [1], ⟨по-⟩ (have *or* take) breakfast

за́втрашний [15] tomorrow's; **~ день** tomorrow; *fig.* (near) future

за́вуч *m* [1; *g/pl.:* -ей] (= **заве́дующий уче́бной ча́стью**) director of studies (*at school*)

завыва́ть [1], ⟨завы́ть⟩ [22] howl

зав|яза́ть [3], ⟨~язнуть⟩ [21] sink in, stick; *coll. fig.* get involved in; **~язать** → **~я́зывать**; **~я́зка** *f* [5; *g/pl.:* -зок] string, tie; *начало* beginning, starting point; *романа и т. д.* opening; **~я́зывать** [1], ⟨~яза́ть⟩ [3] tie (up), bind, fasten; *fig. разговор и т. д.* begin, start; **~язь** *bot. f* [8] ovary; **~я́нуть** → **вя́нуть**

зага́д|ать → **~а́дывать**; **~а́дить** → **~а́живать**; **~а́дка** *f* [5; *g/pl.:* -док] riddle, enigma; **~а́дочный** [14; -чен, -чна] enigmatic; mysterious; **~а́дывать**, ⟨~ада́ть⟩ [1] *загадку* propose; *coll. замыслить* plan; **~а́живать** [1], ⟨~а́дить⟩ [15] soil, befoul

зага́р *m* [1] sunburn, tan

загво́здка *f* [5; *g/pl.:* -док] hitch; snag

заги́б *m* [1] bend; *страницы* dogear; **~а́ть** [1], ⟨загну́ть⟩ [20] bend, fold (over), turn up; *pf. coll.* exaggerate

загла́в|ие *n* [12] title; **~ный** [14] title...; **~ная бу́ква** capital letter

загла́|живать [1], ⟨~дить⟩ [15] smooth; *утюгом* press, iron; *fig.* make up (*or* amends) for; expiate

загл|о́хнуть → **гло́хнуть 2. ~о́хший** [17] *сад* overgrown; **~уша́ть** [1], ⟨~уши́ть⟩ [16] → **глуши́ть 2.**

загля́|дывать [1], ⟨~ну́ть⟩ [19] glance; peep in; *в книгу* look (through, up); look in; (*навестить*) drop in *or* call (**к** Д on); **~дываться** [1], ⟨~де́ться⟩ [11] (**на** В) gaze, gape *or* stare (at), feast one's eyes *or* gloat (up[on])

заг|на́ть → **~оня́ть; ~ну́ть** → **~иба́ть;
~ова́ривать**, ⟨~овори́ть⟩ [13] **1.**
v/i. begin *or* start to talk *or* speak; **2.**
v/t. tire with one's talk; **3. -ся** *слишком
увлечься разговором* be carried away
by a conversation; ramble, be confused;
~овор *m* [1] conspiracy, plot; **~овори́ть**
→ **~ова́ривать**; **~ово́рщик** *m* [1] conspirator, plotter

загол́овок *m* [1; -вка] heading, headline

заго́н *m* [1] enclosure; **быть в ~е** *fig.* be
kept down, suffer neglect

загоня́ть [28], ⟨загна́ть⟩ [-гоню́, -го́нишь; → **гнать**] drive (in, off); (*измучить*) exhaust, fatigue

загор|а́живать [1], ⟨~оди́ть⟩ [15, 15 *e.*;
-рожу́, -ро́дишь] enclose, fence in; *доро́гу* block (up); **-ся** *от ветра* protect;
~а́ть [1], ⟨~е́ть⟩ [9] sunbathe; become
sunburnt; **-ся** catch fire; begin to burn;
свет light up; *от гнева* blaze up; *щёки*
blush; *спор* break out; **~е́лый** [14] sunburnt; **~оди́ть** → **~а́живать**; **~о́дка**
coll. *f* [5; *g/pl.:* -док] fence, enclosure;
partition; **~о́дный** [14] *дом и т. д.*
country; out-of-town

загот|а́вливать [1] & **~овля́ть** [28],
⟨~о́вить⟩ [14] prepare; *впрок* store
up; lay in; **~о́вка** *f* [5; *g/pl.:* -вок] procurement, storage, laying in

загра|ди́тельный [14] *mil. огонь* barrage; **~жда́ть** [1], ⟨~ди́ть⟩ [15 *e.*;
-ажу́, -ади́шь; -аждённый] block, obstruct; **~жде́ние** *n* [12] block(ing), obstruction; **прово́лочное ~жде́ние**
barbed-wire entanglement

заграни́ц|а *f* [5] *collect.* foreign countries; **жить ~ей** live abroad

заграни́чный [14] foreign, from abroad

загре|ба́ть [1], ⟨~сти́⟩ → **грести́**

загро́бн|ый [14] beyond the grave; *го́лос* sepulchral; **~ый мир** the other
world; **~ая жизнь** the beyond

загромо|жда́ть [1], ⟨~зди́ть⟩ [15 *e.*;
-зжу́, -зди́шь; -можде́нный] block
(up), (en)cumber, crowd; *fig.* cram,
overload

загрубе́лый [14] callous, coarse

загр|ужа́ть [1], ⟨~узи́ть⟩ [15 *e.*; -ужу́,
-узи́шь] (T) load; *coll.* **рабо́той** keep
busy, assign work to; be occupied with
work; **~у́зка** *f* [5] loading; workload;
~ыза́ть [1], ⟨~ы́зть⟩ [24; *pt. st.*: загры́зенный] bite (*fig.* worry) to death

загрязн|е́ние *n* [12] pollution, contamination; **~е́ние окружа́ющей среды́**
environmental pollution; **~я́ть** [28],
⟨~и́ть⟩ [13] (**-ся** become) soil(ed); pollute(d), contaminate(d)

ЗАГС, **загс** *m* [1] (*abbr.* **отде́л за́писей
а́ктов гражда́нского состоя́ния**)
registry office

зад *m* [1; на́-у́; *pl. e.*] back, rear *or* hind
part; buttocks; *животного* rump; *pl.*
things already known *or* learned; **~ом
наперёд** back to front

зад|а́бривать [1], ⟨~о́брить⟩ [13] (B) cajole, coax, wheedle

зада|ва́ть [5], ⟨~а́ть⟩ [-да́м, -да́шь, *etc.*,
→ **дать**] задал, -а́, -о; за́данный (за́дан, -а́, -о)] *зада́ние* set, assign; *вопрос*
ask; **~ва́ть тон** set the tone; *coll.* **я тебе́ ~а́м!** you'll catch it!; **-ся** [*pt.*: -да́лся,
-ла́сь] **це́лью** (**мы́слью**) take it into
one's head to do, set one's mind on doing

зада́|вливать [1], ⟨~и́ть⟩ [14] crush; P
маши́ной run over, knock down; (*задуши́ть*) strangle

зада́ние *n* [12] assignment, task; *ва́жное* mission; **дома́шнее ~** homework

зада́ток *m* [1; -тка] advance, deposit; *pl.*
instincts, inclinations

зада́|ть → **~ва́ть; ~ча** *f* [5] problem (*a.*
math.); task; (*цель*) object(ive), aim,
end; **~чник** *m* [1] book of (mathematical) problems

задви|га́ть [1], ⟨~и́нуть⟩ [20] push (into,
etc.); *ящик* shut; *задви́жку* slide; **~и́жка** *f* [5; *g/pl.:* -жек] bolt; **~ижно́й** [14]
sliding (*door*)

зад|ева́ть [1], ⟨~е́ть⟩ [-е́ну, -е́нешь;
-е́тый] **1.** be caught (**за** B on), brush
against, touch; *fig.* hurt, wound; *med.*
affect; **~е́ть за живо́е** cut to the quick;
2. *coll.* (*подевать*) mislay; **~е́лывать**,
⟨~е́лать⟩ [1] block up, close (up); wall
up

3

задёр|гать [1] *pf. coll.* worry, harrass; **~гивать** [1], ⟨**~нуть**⟩ [20] *занавеску* draw

задержа́ние *n* [12] arrest

задерж|ивать [1], ⟨**~а́ть**⟩ [4] detain, delay; arrest; *выплату и т. д.* withhold, stop; ⟨*замедлить*⟩ slow down; **-ся** stay; be delayed; linger; stop; be late; **~ка** *f* [5; *g/pl.:* -жек] delay; (*a. tech.*) trouble, setback

задёрнуть → **задёргивать**

заде́ть → **задева́ть**

зад|ира́ть [1], ⟨**~ра́ть**⟩ [-деру́, -рёшь; → **драть**] lift or pull (up); *impf.* provoke, pick a quarrel (with); **~(и)ра́ть нос** be haughty, turn up one's nose

за́дний [15] back, hind; *mot.* reverse (*gear*)

задо́лго (**до** P) long before

зад|олжа́ть [1] *pf.* (*наделать долгов*) run into debt; (Д) owe; **~о́лженность** *f* [8] debts *pl.*

за́дом backward(s); → **зад**

задо́р *m* [1] fervo(u)r; *ю́ношеский* ~ youthful enthusiasm; **~ный** [14; -рен, -рна] fervent, ardent

задра́ть → **задира́ть**

заду́|вать [1], ⟨**~ть**⟩ [18] blow out; *ветер* begin to blow; *impf.* blow (in)

заду́|мать → **~мывать**; **~мчивый** [14 *sh.*] thoughtful, pensive; **~мывать**, ⟨**~мать**⟩ conceive; (*решить*) resolve, decide; (*намереваться*) plan, intend; **-ся** think (**о** П about, of); reflect, meditate (**над** Т on); *глубоко́* **~маться** be lost in thought; *coll.* (*колебаться*) hesitate; **~ть** → **~вать**

заду́шевный [14] sincere, intimate

зад|ыха́ться [1], ⟨**~охну́ться**⟩ [21] gasp, pant; choke (*a. fig.* **от** P with)

зае́зд *m* [1] *sport* lap, round

заезжа́ть [1], ⟨**зае́хать**⟩ [-е́ду, -е́дешь; -езжа́й!] call on (*on the way*), drive, go *or* come (**к** Д to [see, *etc.*] *or* **в** В into); pick up, fetch (**за** Т)

заём *m* [1; за́йма] loan

зае́хать → **~езжа́ть**; **~жа́ть** → **~жи-ма́ть**; **~жёчь** → **~жига́ть**

зажи́|ва́ть [1], ⟨**~ть**⟩ [-иву́; -вёшь; за́-жи́л, -а́, -о] **1.** heal, (*затягиваться*)

close up; **2.** begin to live

за́живо alive

зажига́|лка *f* [5; *g/pl.:* -лок] (cigarette) lighter; **~ние** *n* [12] ignition; **~тельный** [14] incendiary; *fig.* stirring, rousing; **~ть** [1], ⟨**зажёчь**⟩ [26 г/ж: -жгу́, -жжёшь; → **жечь**] light, kindle (*a. fig.*); *спичку* strike; *свет* turn on; **-ся** light (up); catch fire; become enthusiastic (T about)

зажи́м *m* [1] clamp; *tech.* terminal; *fig.* suppression; **~а́ть** [1], ⟨**зажа́ть**⟩ [-жму́, -жмёшь; -жа́тый] press, squeeze; clutch; *fig. критику* suppress; *рот* stop; *нос* hold; *уши* close

зажи́|точный [14; -чен, -чна] prosperous; **~точность** *f* [8] prosperity; **~ть** → **~ва́ть**

зевева́ться [1] stand gaping in amazement

зазем|ле́ние *n* [12], **~ля́ть** [28], ⟨**~ли́ть**⟩ [13] *el.* ground, *Brt.* earth

зазна|ва́ться [5], ⟨**~ться**⟩ [1] be(come) conceited; put on airs

зазо́р *m* [1] *tech.* clearance, gap

зазо́рный [14; -рен, -рна] shameful, scandalous; **~рение** *n* [12]: **без ~рения (со́вести)** without remorse *or* shame

зазу́бр|ивать [1] → **зубри́ть**; **~ина** *f* [5] notch

заи́грывать *coll.* [1] (**с** Т) flirt, make advances (to); (*заискивать*) ingratiate o.s. (with)

заи́к|а *m/f* [5] stutterer; **~а́ние** *n* [12] stuttering, stammering; **~а́ться** [1], *once* ⟨**~ну́ться**⟩ [20] stutter; stammer; *coll.* (give a hint) (**о** П at), suggest, mention in passing

заи́мствова|ние *n* [12] borrowing; loan word (*a.* **~нное сло́во**); **~ть** [7] *impf.*, *a.* ⟨**по-**⟩ borrow, adopt

заиндеве́лый [14] frosty, covered with hoar-frost

заинтересо́в|ывать(ся) [1], ⟨**~а́ть(ся)**⟩ [7] (be)come) interest(ed in T), rouse a p.'s interest (**в** П in); *я* **~ан(а)** I am interested (**в** П in)

заи́скивать [1] ingratiate o.s. (**у** P with)

зайти́ → **заходи́ть**

закавка́зский [16] Transcaucasian

закады́чный [14] bosom (friend)

зака́з *m* [1] order; *дать, сде́лать* ~ *(на В/Д)* place an order (for… with); *на* ~ to order; *об оде́жде* (made) to measure; **~а́ть** → **~ывать**; **~но́й** [14]: **~но́е** (*письмо́*) registered (letter); **~чик** *m* [1] customer; **~ывать** [1], ⟨~а́ть⟩ [3] order (*себе́* o.s.)

зака́л|ка *f* [5] tempering; *fig.* hardening; (*выно́сливость*) endurance, hardiness; **~я́ть** [28], ⟨~и́ть⟩ [13] temper; *fig.* harden; **~ённый** *мета́лл* tempered (*metal*); *fig.* hardened

зака́|лывать [1], ⟨~оло́ть⟩ [17] kill, slaughter; *штыко́м и т. д.* stab; *була́вкой* pin (up); *у меня́ ~оло́ло в боку́* I have a stitch in one's side; **~а́нчивать** [1], ⟨~о́нчить⟩ [16] finish, conclude; **~а́пывать** [1], ⟨~опа́ть⟩ [1] bury; *я́му* fill up

зака́т *m* [1] sunset; *fig.* decline; **~ывать** [1] **1.** ⟨~а́ть⟩ roll up; **2.** ⟨~и́ть⟩ [15] roll (*в, под* B into, under, *etc.*); *глаза́* screw up; **~и́ть исте́рику** go into hysterics; *о со́лнце* set (*of sun etc.*); *fig.* end; *сме́хом, слеза́ми* burst (out laughing *or* into tears)

зака́шлять [28] *pf.* start coughing; **-ся** have a fit of coughing

заква́ска *f* [5] ferment; leaven; *fig.* breed

заки́|дывать [1] **1.** ⟨~да́ть⟩ [1] *coll.* *я́му* fill up, cover; *fig.* *вопро́сами* ply; *камня́ми* pelt; **2.** ⟨~нуть⟩ [20] throw (*в, на, за* B in[to], on, over, behind, *etc.*); *сеть* throw out; *го́лову* throw back; fling, cast; **~нуть у́дочку** *fig.* put out feelers

заки|па́ть [1], ⟨~пе́ть⟩ [10; -пи́т] begin to boil; = **кипе́ть**; **~са́ть** [1], ⟨~и́снуть⟩ [21] turn sour

закла́дка *f* [5; *g/pl.*: -док] bookmark; **~ывать** [1], ⟨заложи́ть⟩ [16] put (*a.* in, *etc.*), lay (*a.* out [*сад*]), the foundation [*фунда́мент*] of, found), place; (*заде́ть*) mislay; (*загромозди́ть*) heap, pile (Twith); wall up; *в ломба́рд* pawn; *страни́цу* mark, put in; *impers. нос, у́ши* stuff

заклёвывать [1], ⟨~ева́ть⟩ [6 *e.*; -клюю́, -юёшь] *fig. coll.* bait, hector,

torment; **~ёивать** [1], ⟨~ёить⟩ [13] glue *or* paste up (over); *конве́рт* seal; **~ёпка** *f* [5; *g/pl.*: -пок], **~ёпывать**, ⟨~епа́ть⟩ [1] rivet

заклина́|ние *n* [12] entreaty *mst. pl.*; **~ть** [1] entreat

заключ|а́ть [1], ⟨~и́ть⟩ [16 *e.*; -чу́, -чи́шь; -чённый] enclose, put; *в тюрьму́* confine, imprison; (= finish, with T; = infer, from *из* Р, *по* Д – *что*; *v/t.*: *догово́р* [= make] *мир и т. д.*); *impf.* (*a. в себе́*) contain; ⟨~и́ться⟩ [1] consist (*в* П in); (*зака́нчиваться*) end (T with); **~е́ние** *n* [12] confinement, imprisonment (*a. тюре́мное*); (*вы́вод*) conclusion; **~ённый** [14] prisoner; **~и́тельный** [14] final, concluding

закля́тый [14] sworn; ~ **враг** enemy

зако́л|а́чивать [1], ⟨~оти́ть⟩ [15] drive in; *гвоздя́ми* nail up; *доска́ми* board up; **~до́вывать** [1], ⟨~дова́ть⟩ bewitch, charm; **~до́ванный круг** vicious circle; **~оти́ть** → **~а́чивать**; **~о́ть** → **зака́лывать**

зако́лка *f* [5; *g/pl.*: -лок] hairpin

зако́н *m* [1] law; (*пра́вило*) rule; *нару́шить* ~ break the law; *по* (*вопреки́*) **~у** according (contrary) to law; **~ность** *f* [8] legality, lawfulness; **~ный** [14; -о́нен, -о́нна] legal, lawful, legitimate

законо|да́тель *m* [4] legislator; **~да́тельный** [14] legislative; **~да́тельство** *n* [9] legislation; **~ме́рность** *f* [8] regularity; **~ме́рный** [14; -рен, -рна] regular; normal; **~прое́кт** *m* [1] bill, draft

зако́|нчить → **зака́нчивать**; **~па́ть** → **зака́пывать**; **~пте́лый** [14] sooty; **~ре́не́лый** [14] deeprooted, inveterate, ingrained; (*зло́стный*) hardened; **~рю́чка** *f* [5; *g/pl.*: -чек] *на письме́* flourish; *fig.* hitch; **~у́лок** *m* [1; -лка] alleyway, (*Brt.*) (narrow) lane; *coll. уголо́к* nook; **~чене́лый** [14] numb with cold

закра́|дываться [1], ⟨~сться⟩ [25; *pt. st.*] creep in *mst. fig.*; **~шивать** [1], ⟨~сить⟩ [15] paint over

закрепля́ть [28], ⟨~и́ть⟩ [14 *e.*; -плю́, -пи́шь; -плённый] secure, fasten, (*a. phot.*) fix; *успе́хи* consolidate; assign (*за* T to)

закрепо|ща́ть [1], ⟨∼сти́ть⟩ [15 *e*.; -ощу́, -ости́шь; -ощённый] enserf

закро́|йщик *m* [1], **∼ца** *f* [5] cutter

закругл|е́ние *n* [12] rounding (off); curve; **∼я́ть** [1], ⟨∼и́ть⟩ [13] round (off); **-ся** *coll. joc.* round off

закру́|чивать [1], ⟨∼ти́ть⟩ [15] turn (round, off, up) twist

закрыва́ть [1], ⟨∼бы́ть⟩ [22] shut, close; *на замо́к* lock (up); *кры́шкой и т. д.* cover, hide; *кран* turn off; **∼ыва́ть глаза́ (на** B) shut one's eyes (to); **∼ы́тие** *n* [12] closing, shutting; **вре́мя ∼ы́тия** closing time; **∼ы́ть → ∼ыва́ть; ∼ы́тый** [14] closed; (*та́йный*) secret; *пла́тье* high-necked; **в ∼ы́том помеще́нии** indoor(s)

закули́сный [14] occuring behind the scenes; secret

закуп|а́ть [1], ⟨∼и́ть⟩ [14] buy (*a.* in), purchase; **∼ка** *f* [5; *g/pl.*: -пок] purchase

закупо́р|ивать [1], ⟨∼ить⟩ [13] *буты́лку* cork (up); *бо́чку* bung (up); **∼ка** *f* [5; *g/pl.*: -рок] corking; *med.* embolism

заку́почн|ый [14]: **∼ая цена́** purchase price

заку́пщик *m* [1] purchasing agent, buyer

заку́р|ивать [1], ⟨∼и́ть⟩ [13; -урю́, -у́ришь] light a cigarette *etc.*; **∼и́(те)!** have a cigar(ette)!

заку́с|ка *f* [5; *g/pl.*: -сок] hors d'œuvres; **на ∼ку** *a.* for the last bit; *coll.* as a special treat; **∼очная** *f* [14] snackbar; **∼ывать** [1], ⟨∼и́ть⟩ [15] bite (*a.* one's lip[s]); take *or* have a snack; eat (s.th. [*with, after a drink*] T); **∼и́ть удила́** *fig.* get the bit between one's teeth

заку́т|ывать [1], ⟨∼ать⟩ [1] wrap up

зал *m* [1] hall; room; **спорти́вный ∼** gymnasium

залег|а́ние *n* [12] *geol.* deposit(ion); **∼а́ть** [1], ⟨∼е́чь⟩ [26: -ля́гу, -ля́жешь] *geol.* lie; *в заса́ду* hide; (*заболе́ть*) take to one's bed

заледене́л|ый [14] icy, ice cold; covered with ice

зал|ежа́лый [14] stale, spoiled (by long storage); **∼ёживаться** [1], ⟨∼ежа́ться⟩ [4 *e*.; -жу́сь, -жи́шься] lie (too) long (*a.*

goods, & spoil thus); **∼ежь** *f*[8] *geol.* deposit

зал|еза́ть [1], ⟨∼е́зть⟩ [24 *st.*] climb up, in(to) *etc.*; hide; (*прони́кнуть*) steal *or* get in(to); **∼е́зть в карма́н** pick s.o.'s pocket; **∼е́зть в долги́** run into debt; **∼епля́ть** [28], ⟨∼епи́ть⟩ [14] stop, close; (*закле́ить*) glue *or* paste up; stick over; **∼ета́ть** [1], ⟨∼ете́ть⟩ [11] fly in(to), up, far, off, beyond; **∼ете́ть высоко́** rise in the world

зал|е́чивать [1], ⟨∼чи́ть⟩ [16] heal; *coll.* doctor to death; **∼чь → ∼га́ть**

зал|и́в *m* [1] gulf, bay; **∼ива́ть** [1], ⟨∼и́ть⟩ [-лью́, -льёшь; за́ли́л, -á, -o; за́ли́тый] (T) flood, overflow; pour (all) over, cover; (*влива́ть*) fill; *ого́нь* extinguish; **-ся** break into *or* shed (tears *слеза́ми*), burst out (laughing **сме́хом**); *o пти́це* trill, warble; **∼ивно́е** *n* [14] *su.* fish *or* meat in aspic; **∼ивно́й** [14]: **∼ивно́й луг** water-meadow; **∼и́ть → ∼ива́ть**

зал|о́г *m* [1] pledge (*a. fig.*); security; *gr.* voice; *fig.* guarantee; **отда́ть в ∼о́г** pawn; **под ∼о́г** on the security; **∼ожи́ть → закла́дывать, ∼о́жник** *m* [1], **∼о́жница** *f* [5] hostage

залп *m* [1] volley; salvo; **вы́пить ∼ом** at one draught; *прочита́ть* at one sitting; *произнести́* without pausing for breath

зама́|зка *f* [5] putty; **∼зывать** [1], ⟨∼зать⟩ [3] (*запа́чкать*) smear, soil; *кра́ской* paint over; *ще́ли* putty; *coll. fig.* veil, hush up; **∼лчивать** [1], ⟨замолча́ть⟩ [2 *e.* -чу́, -чи́шь] conceal, keep secret; **∼нивать** [1], ⟨∼ни́ть⟩ [13; -маню́, -ма́нишь] lure, decoy, entice; **∼нчивый** [14 *sh.*] alluring, tempting; **∼хиваться** [1], *once* ⟨∼хну́ться⟩ [20] lift one's arm (*etc.* T/**на** B against), threaten (with); **∼шка** *coll. f* [5; *g/pl.*: -шек] *mst. pl.* habit, manner

замедл|е́ние *n* [12] slowing down, delay; **∼я́ть** [28], ⟨∼ить⟩ [13] slow down, reduce; *ско́рость* decelerate; *разви́тие* retard

заме́|на *f* [5] substitution (T/P of/for), replacement (T by); *law* commutation; substitute; **∼ни́мый** [14 *sh.*] replaceable, exchangeable; **~нитель** *m* [4] substitute; **~нять** [28], ⟨**~нить**⟩ [13]: -меню, -менишь; -менённый] replace (T by), substitute (T/B *p*., *th.* for); *law* commute (for, into)

замере́ть → *замира́ть*

замерза́|ние *n* [12] freezing; **то́чка ~ния** freezing point; **на то́чке ~ния** *fig.* at a standstill; **~ть** [1], ⟨**замёрзнуть**⟩ [21] freeze (up); be frozen (to death, *a. coll.* = feel very cold)

за́мертво (as, if) dead, unconscious

замести́ → *замета́ть*

замести́|тель *m* [4] deputy; vice...; **~ть** → *замеща́ть*

заме|та́ть [1], ⟨**~сти́**⟩ [25; -т-: мету́] sweep (up); *снегом* drift, cover; *дорогу* block up; *следы* wipe out

заме́|тить → **~ча́ть**; **~тка** *f* [5; *g/pl.*:-ток] mark; (*запись*) note; *в газете* paragraph, short article, item; **взять на ~тку** make a note (of); **~тный** [14; -тен, -тна] noticeable, perceptible; marked, appreciable; *успех, человек* outstanding, remarkable; **~тно** *a.* one (it) can (be) see(n), notice(d); **~ча́ние** *n* [12] remark, observation; *pl.* criticism; *выговор* reproof, rebuke; **~ча́тельный** [14; -лен, -льна] remarkable, outstanding; wonderful; noted (T for); **~ча́ть** [1], ⟨**~тить**⟩ [15] notice, mark; (*сказать*) observe, remark

замеша́|тельство *n* [9] confusion, embarrassment; **в ~e** confused, disconcerted, embarrassed; **привести́ в ~o** throw into confusion

зам|е́шивать [1], ⟨**~еша́ть**⟩ [1] involve, entangle; **~е́шан(а)** в (П) *a.* mixed up with; **~е́шкаться** [1] *pf.* linger, tarry; **~еща́ть** [1], ⟨**~ести́ть**⟩ [15 *e.*; -ещу́, -ести́шь; -ещённый] replace; substitute; act for, deputize; *ваканcию* fill; **~еще́ние** *n* [12] substitution (*a. math.*, *chem.*); replacement; deputizing; filling

зам|ина́ть *coll.* [1], ⟨**~я́ть**⟩ [-мну́, -мнёшь; -мя́тый] put a stop to; **~я́ть разгово́р** change the subject; **~ина́ться** [-ся] falter, halt; be(come) confused; **~и́нка** *f* [5; *g/pl.*:-нок] hesitation (*in speech*); hitch; **~ира́ть** [1], ⟨**~ере́ть**⟩ [12; замер,

-рла́, -о] be(come) *or* stand stockstill, transfixed (**от** P with); stop; *о звуках* fade, die away; **у меня́ се́рдце ~ерло** my heart stood still

за́мкнутый [14 *sh.*] exclusive; *жизнь* unsociable; *человек* reserved; → *замыка́ть*

за́м|ок¹ *m* [1; -мка] castle; **возду́шные ~ки** castles in the air

зам|о́к² *m* [1; -мка́] lock; *на ожерелье* clasp; **на ~ке** *or* **под ~ко́м** under lock and key

замо́л|вить [14] *pf.*: **~вить сло́(е́чк)о** *coll.* put in a word (**за** B, **о** П for a *p.*); **~ка́ть** [1], ⟨**~кнуть**⟩ [21] fall silent, stop (speaking *etc.*), cease, break off; *шаги и т. д.* die away *or* off; **~ча́ть** [4 *e.*; -чу́, -чи́шь] *pf.* **1.** *v/i.* → **~ка́ть; 2.** *v/t.* → *зама́лчивать*

замор|а́живать [1], ⟨**~о́зить**⟩ [15] freeze, ice; **~о́зки** *m/pl.* [1] (light morning *or* night) frost; **~ский** [16] oversea(s)

за́муж → выдава́ть & выходи́ть; ~ем married (**за** T for, *of women*); **~ество** *n* [9] marriage (*of women*); **~ний** [15]: **~няя (же́нщина)** married (*of women*)

замуро́в|ывать [1], ⟨**~а́ть**⟩ [7] immure; wall up

замуч|ивать [1], ⟨**~ить**⟩ [16] torment the life out of; bore to death; *измота́ть* fatigue, exhaust

за́мш|а *f* [5], **~евый** [14] chamois, suede

замыка́|ние *n* [12]: **коро́ткое ~ние** *el.* short circuit; **~ть** [1], ⟨**замкну́ть**⟩ [20] (en)close; **-ся** isolate o.s. (**в** B *or* T in); **-ся в себе́** become unsociable

за́м|ысел *m* [1; -сла] project, plan, design; scheme, idea; **~ыслить** → **~ышля́ть; ~ыслова́тый** [14 *sh.*] intricate, ingenious; fanciful; **~ышля́ть** [28], ⟨**~ыслить**⟩ [15] plan, intend; contemplate; *план и т. д.* conceive

замя́ть(ся) → *замина́ть(ся)*

зан|аве́с *m* [1] curtain (*a. thea.*); **~е́сить** → **~е́шивать; ~е́ска** *f* [5; *g/pl.*:-сок] (*window*) curtain; **~е́шивать** [1], ⟨**~е́сить**⟩ [15] curtain

зан|а́шивать [1], ⟨**~оси́ть**⟩ [15] wear out; **~ести́ → ~оси́ть**

занима́|тельный [14; -лен, -льна] interesting, entertaining, amusing; *человек* engaging; **~ть** [1], ⟨**заня́ть**⟩ [займу́, -мёшь; за́нял, -á, -о; заня́вший; за́нятый (за́нят, -á, -о)] **1.** borrow (**у** P from); **2.** (T) occupy, (*a. time*) take; *ме́сто, пост* fill, take up; interest, engross, absorb; *развлека́ть* entertain; **-ся** [заня́лся, -ла́сь] **1.** occupy *or* busy o.s. (with); (*a. sport*) engage in; *кемпо* attend (to); *учи́ться* learn, study; set about, begin to; **2.** *v/i. ого́нь* blaze *or* flare up; *заря́* break, dawn; → *a. заря́*

за́ново anew, afresh

зано́|за *f* [5] splinter; **~зи́ть** [15 *e*.; -ожу́, -ози́шь] *pf.* get a splinter (in)

зано́с *m* [1] drift; **~и́ть** [15] ⟨занести́⟩ [24; -с-: -су́, -сёшь] bring, carry; *в прото́кол и т. д.* note down, enter, register; (*a. impers.*) (be) cast, get; *доро́ги* drift, cover, block up; *ру́ку* lift, raise; *куда́ её занесло́?* where on earth has she got to? **2.** *pf.*, → *зана́шивать*; **~чивый** [14 *sh.*] arrogant, haughty

зану́д|а *coll. m/f* [5] bore; **~ливый** [14 *sh.*] boring, tiresome

заня́т|ие *n* [12] occupation, work, business; excercise (T of); *pl.* studies, lessons; **~ный** [14; -тен, -тна] → *coll.* **занима́тельный**; **~ь(ся)** → **занима́ть(ся)**; **~о́й** [14] busy; **~ый** [14; за́нят, -á, -о] occupied, busy, engaged

заодно́ together; at once; (*попутно*) at the same time, besides, too

заостря́ть [28], ⟨**~и́ть**⟩ [13] sharpen; *fig.* stress; **-ся** become pointed *or* sharp

забо́чн|ик *m univ.* student taking a correspondence course; **~ый** [14] in a *p.'s* absence; **~ое обуче́ние** instruction by correspondence; **~ое реше́ние** *n law* judg(e)ment by default

за́пад *m* [1] west; ♀ the West; → **восто́к**; **~а́ть** [1], ⟨запа́сть⟩ [25; -па́л, -а] fall behind; *в па́мяти и т. д.* impress (*a. на or в* B on); **~ный** [14] west(ern, -erly)

западн|я́ *f* [6; *g/pl.*:-не́й] trap; *попа́сть в ~ю́ fig.* fall into a trap

запа́|здывать [1], ⟨запозда́ть⟩ [1] be late (**на** B for), be slow (**с** T with); **~ивать** [1], ⟨~я́ть⟩ [28] solder (up); **~ко́вывать** [1], ⟨~кова́ть⟩ [7] pack (up), wrap up

запа́л *m* [1] *mil., mining* touchhole, fuse; impulse; fit of passion; **~ьчивый** [14 *sh.*] quick-tempered, irascible

запа́с *m* [1] stock (*a. fig., слов и т. д. =* store, supply, (*a. mil.*) reserve); **у нас два часа́ в ~е** we have two hours in hand; **про ~** in store *or* reserve; **~а́ть** [1], ⟨~ти́⟩ [24 -с-: -су́, -сёшь]; **-ся**, ⟨~ти́сь⟩ provide o.s. (with T); **~ливый** [14 *sh.*] provident; **~но́й**, **~ный** [14] spare (*a. tech.*); reserve… (*a. mil.*); **~ный вы́ход** emergency exit; **~ть** → **запада́ть**

за́п|ах *m* [1] smell, odo(u)r, scent; **~а́хивать** [1] **1.** ⟨~аха́ть⟩ [3] plow (*Brt.* plough) *or* turn up; **2.** ⟨~ахну́ть⟩ [20] wrap (**-ся** o.s.) (**в** B, T in); *дверь* slam; **~а́ть** → **~а́ивать**

запе|ва́ла *m/f* [5] leader (of choir); *coll.* initiator, leader; **~ва́ть** [1], ⟨~ть⟩ [-пою́, -поёшь; -пе́тый] start singing; *impf.*: lead a choir; **~ка́нка** *f* [5; *g/pl.*:-нок] baked pudding; **~ка́ть** [1], ⟨~чь⟩ [-ку́] bake; **-ся** *кровь* clot, coagulate; *губы* crack; **~ре́ть** → **запира́ть**

запеча́т|ать → **~ывать**; **~лева́ть** [1], ⟨~ле́ть⟩ [8] embody, render; *в па́мяти* imprint, impress (**в** П on), retain; **~ывать**, ⟨~ать⟩ [1] seal (up)

запе́чь → **запека́ть**

запи|ва́ть, ⟨~ть⟩ [1 -пью́, -пьёшь; → *пить*] wash down (Twith), drink *or* take (with, after); *pf.* take to drink

зап|ина́ться [1], ⟨~ну́ться⟩ [20] *rare* stumble (**за** *or* **о** B over, against); *о речи* falter, pause, hesitate; **~и́нка** *f* [5]; *без ~и́нки* fluently, smoothly

запира́|тельство *n* [9] disavowal, denial; **~ть** [1], ⟨запере́ть⟩ [12; за́пер, -ла́, -о; за́пертый (за́перт, -á, -о)] lock (up; *a.* **~ть на ключ, замо́к**); **-ся** lock o.s. in

записа́ть → **~ывать**; **~ка** *f* [5; *g/pl.*:-сок] note, short letter; *докладна́я* memorandum; *pl.* воспомина́ния notes, memoirs; *труды́* transactions, proceedings; **~но́й** [14]: **~на́я кни́жка** notebook; **~ывать** [1], ⟨~а́ть⟩ [3] write down, note (down); record (*тж. на плёнку и т. д.*); **в чле́ны и т. д.** enter,

стекле́ misted

enrol(l), register; **-ся** enrol(l), register, enter one's name; make an appointment (**к врачу́** with a doctor); **~ь** f [8] entry; enrol(l)ment; registration; record(ing)

запи́ть → *запива́ть*

запи́х|ивать coll. [1], ⟨**~а́ть**⟩ [1], once ⟨**~ну́ть**⟩ [20] cram, stuff

запла́ка|нный [14 sh.] tearful, in tears, tear-stained; **~ть** [3] pf. begin to cry

запла́та f [5] patch

заплесневе́лый [14] mo(u)ldy

запле|та́ть [1], ⟨**~сти́**⟩ [25 -т-: -плету́, -тёшь] braid, plait; **-ся**: *но́ги* **~та́ются** be unsteady on one's legs; *язы́к* **~та́ется** slur, falter

заплы́|в m [1] *water sports* round, heat; **~ва́ть¹** [1], ⟨**~ть**⟩ [23] swim far out

заплы|ва́ть² [23], ⟨**~ть**⟩ *об отёке* swell, puff up

запну́ться → *запина́ться*

запове́д|ник m [1] reserve, preserve; *госуда́рственный* **~ник** national park; sanctuary; **~ный** [14] prohibited, reserved; *мечта́ и т. д.* secret, precious; **~ь** ('za-) f [8] *Bibl.* commandment

запод|а́зривать [1], ⟨**~о́зрить**⟩ [13] suspect (**в** П of)

запозда́|лый [14] (be) late(d), tardy; **~ть** → *запа́здывать*

запо́|й m [3] periodic hard drinking

заполз|а́ть [1], ⟨**~ти́**⟩ [24] creep into, under

заполн|я́ть [28], ⟨**~ить**⟩ [13] fill (up); *бланк* fill out (Brt. in)

заполя́р|ный [14] polar, transpolar; **~ье** n [10; g/pl.: -ий] polar regions

запомин|а́ть [1], ⟨**~нить**⟩ [13] remember, keep in mind; *стихи́ и т. д.* memorize; **~на́ющий** [17]: **~на́ющее устро́йство** computer memory, storage; **-ся** (Д) remember, stick in one's mind

за́понка f [5; g/pl.: -нок] cuff link; collar button (Brt. stud)

запо́р m [1] bar, bolt; lock; *med.* constipation; **на ~е** bolted, locked

запороши́ть [16 e.; 3ʳᵈ p. only] powder *or* cover (with snow T)

запоте́лый coll. [14] moist, sweaty; *o*

заправ|и́ла m [5] coll. boss, leader; **~ля́ть** [28], ⟨**~ить**⟩ [14] put, tuck (in); *блюдо* (T) dress, season; *горю́чим* tank (up), refuel; **~ка** f [5; g/pl.: -вок] refuel(l)ing; seasoning; condiment; **~очный** [14]: **~очная ста́нция** f filling (gas) station; **~ский** [16] true, real

запра́шивать [1], ⟨**~оси́ть**⟩ [15] ask, inquire (**у** Р/**о** П for/about); (*a.* P) request; coll. *це́ну* charge, ask (**с** Р)

запре́т m [1] → **~ще́ние**; **наложи́ть ~т** place a ban (**на** B on); **~ти́тельный** [14] prohibitive; **~ти́ть** → **~ща́ть**; **~тный** [14] forbidden; **~тная зо́на** *mil.* restricted area; **~ща́ть** [1], ⟨**~ти́ть**⟩ [15 e.; -ещу́, -ети́шь; -ещённый] forbid, prohibit, ban; **~ще́ние** n [12] prohibition; *law* injunction

заприхо́довать [7] pf. enter, book

запроки́|дывать [1], ⟨**~нуть**⟩ [20] throw back

запро́с m [1] inquiry (**о** П about); pl. *потре́бности* needs, interests; **~и́ть** → **запра́шивать**; **~то** without formality

запру́|да f [5] dam, weir; **~живать** [1], ⟨**~ди́ть**⟩ **1.** [15 & 15 e.; -ужу́, -у́ди́шь] dam up; **2.** [15 e.; -ужу́, -уди́шь] coll. block up, crowd

запр|яга́ть [1], ⟨**~я́чь**⟩ [26 г/ж: -ягу́, -я́жешь; → **напря́чь**] harness; **~я́тывать** [1], ⟨**~я́тать**⟩ [3] hide, conceal; put (away); → **запряга́ть**

запу́ск m [1] start; *раке́ты* launching; **~ка́ть** [1], ⟨**~ти́ть**⟩ [15] **1.** neglect; **2.** *tech.* start, set going; *змея* fly; *раке́ту* launch; coll. (*a.* T/**в** B) fling, hurl (s.th. at) put, thrust; **~те́лый** [14] desolate; **~ти́ть** → **~ка́ть**

запу́|тывать, ⟨**~тать**⟩ [1] (**-ся** become, get) tangle(d, etc.); *fig.* confuse, perplex; complicate; coll. **~таться в долга́х** be deep in debt; **~танный** *тж.* intricate; **~танный вопро́с** knotty question; **~щенный** [14] deserted, desolate; neglected, uncared-for, unkempt

запыха́ться coll. [1] pf. pant, be out of breath

3

запя́стье *n* [10] wrist; *poet.* bracelet

запята́я *f* [14] comma; *coll.* snag

зараба́тыва|ть, ⟨~отать⟩ [1] earn; **~атывать на жизнь** earn one's living; **-ся** *coll.* overwork; work late *or* long; **~отный** [14]: **~отная пла́та** wages *pl.*; *служащего* salary; pay; **~оток** [1; -тка] earnings *pl.*

заража́|ть [1], ⟨~зи́ть⟩ [15 *e.*; -ражу́, -рази́шь; -ражённый] infect (*a. fig.*); **-ся** become infected (T with); catch; **~ние** *n* [12] infection; **~же́ние кро́ви** blood poisoning

зара́з *coll.* at once; at one sitting

зара́|за *f* [5] infection; contagion; **~зи́тельный** [14; -лен, -льна] *mst. fig.* infectious; **~зи́ть** → **~жа́ть**; **~зный** [14; -зен, -зна] infectious, contagious

зара́нее beforehand, in advance; **~ ра́доваться** (Д) look forward to

зара|ста́ть [1], ⟨~сти́⟩ [24; -сту́, -стёшь; → **расти́**] be overgrown (with)

за́рево *n* [9] blaze, glow, gleam

заре́з *m* [1] *coll.* disaster; **до́~у, по́~** *coll.* (*need s.th.*) very badly

заре|ка́ться [1], ⟨~чься⟩ [26] forswear, promise to give up; **~комендова́ть** [7]: **~комендова́ть себя́** (T) show o.s., prove o.s. (to be)

заржа́вленный [14] rusty

зарисо́вка *f* 5; *g/pl.*: -вок] drawing, sketch

зарни́ца *f* [5] summer (heat) lightning

зар|оди́ть(ся) → **~ожда́ть(ся)**; **~о́дыш** *m* [1] embryo, f(o)etus, germ (*a. fig.*); **подави́ть в ~о́дыше** nip in the bud; **~ожда́ть** [1], ⟨~оди́ть⟩ [15 *e.*; -ожу́, -оди́шь; -ождённый] generate, engender; **-ся** arise; conception

заро́к *m* [1] vow, pledge, promise

зарони́ть [13; -роню́, -ро́нишь] *pf. fig.* rouse; infuse

за́росль *f* [8] underbrush; thicket

зар|пла́та *f* [5] *coll.* → **~аботный**

заруб|а́ть [1], ⟨~и́ть⟩ [14] kill; **~и́(те) на носу́ (на лбу, в па́мяти)!** mark it well!

зарубе́жный [14] foreign

зар|уби́ть → **~уба́ть**; **~у́бка** *f* [5; *g/pl.*: -бок] incision, notch; **~убцева́ться** [7] *pf.* cicatrize

заруч|а́ться [1], ⟨~и́ться⟩ [16 *e.*; -учу́сь, -учи́шься] (T) secure; **~и́ться согла́сием** obtain consent

зар|ыва́ть [1], ⟨~ы́ть⟩ [22] bury; **~ы́ть тала́нт в зе́млю** bury one's talent

зар|я́ *f* [6; *pl.*: зо́ри, зорь, заря́м, зо́рям] (**у́тренняя**) **~я** (*a. fig.*) dawn; **вече́рняя ~я** evening glow; **на ~е́** at dawn *or* daybreak (*a.* **с ~е́й**); *fig.* at the earliest stage *or* beginning; **от ~и́ до ~и́** from morning to night, all day (night); **~я́ занима́ется** dawn is breaking

заря́|д *m* [1] charge (*mil., el.*); *fig. бо́дрости* store; **~ди́ть** → **~жа́ть**; **~дка** *f*[5] charge, charging; *sport:* gymnastics *pl.*, exercises; **~жа́ть** [1], ⟨~ди́ть⟩ [15 & 15 *e.*; -яжу́, -я́ди́шь; -я́женный & -я́жённый] *mil., phot.* load; *el.* charge; *pl. coll.* set in, go on & on

заса́|да *f* [5] ambush; **попа́сть в ~ду** be ambushed; **~живать** [1], ⟨~ди́ть⟩ [15] plant (T with); *coll. в тюрьму* confine; *за работу и т. д.* compel (*to do s.th.*); **-ся,** *coll.* ⟨засе́сть⟩ [25; -ся́ду, -дешь; -се́л] sit down; *в заса́де* hide, lie in ambush; (**за** B) begin to, bury o.s. in

заса́л|ивать [1], ⟨засоли́ть⟩ [13; -олю́, -о́ли́шь, -о́ленный] salt; *мясо* corn

заса́|ривать [1] & **засоря́ть** [28], ⟨~ори́ть⟩ [13] litter; *трубу и т. д.* clog; *сорняками* become weedy; **~ори́ть глаз(а́)** have (get) s.th. in one's eye(s)

заса́|сывать [1], ⟨~оса́ть⟩ [-су́, -сёшь, -о́санный] suck in; *о болоте* engulf, swallow up

заса́харенный [14] candied, crystallized

засве́т|и́ть(ся) [13; -све́тится] *pf.* light (up); **~ло** by daylight; before dark

засвиде́тельствовать [7] *pf.* testify, attest, authenticate

засе́|в *m* [1] sowing; **~ва́ть** [1], ⟨~я́ть⟩ [27] sow

заседа́|ние *n* [12] *law, parl.* session; meeting; (*prp.*: in, at **на** П); **~тель** *m* [4]: **наро́дный ~тель** approx. juryman; **~ть** [1] **1.** be in session; sit; meet; **2.** ⟨засе́сть⟩ [-ся́ду, -дешь; -се́л] stick

засе|ка́ть [1], ⟨~чь⟩ [26] **1.** [-се́к, -ла́; -сечённый] notch; *время* mark, note;

: чь на ме́сте преступле́ния catch red-handed

засел|е́ние n [12] settlement, colonization; **~я́ть** [28], ⟨**~и́ть**⟩ [13] people, populate; *дом* occupy, inhabit

засе́|сть → **заса́живаться & ~да́ть 2.**; **~чь** → **~ка́ть; ~ять** → **~ва́ть**

заси́|живать [11], ⟨**~де́ть**⟩ [11] **~же́нный** (**му́хами**) flyblow(n); **-ся** sit *or* stay (too) long; sit up late

заскору́злый [14] hardened, calloused

засло́н|ка f [5; *g/pl.*: -нок] (stove) damper; *tech.* slide valve; **~я́ть** [28], ⟨**~и́ть**⟩ [13] shield, screen; *свет* shut off; stand in s.o.'s light; *fig.* put into the background

заслу́|га f [8] merit, desert; **он получи́л по ~гам** (it) serves him right; **~женный** [14] merited, (well-)deserved, just; *челове́к* worthy, hono(u)red (*a. in titles*); **~живать** [1], ⟨**~жи́ть**⟩ [16] merit, deserve (*impf. a.* P); *coll.* earn

заслу́ш|ивать, ⟨**~ать**⟩[1] hear; **-ся** listen (T, P to) with delight

засма́триваться [1], ⟨**~отре́ться**⟩ [9; -отрю́сь, -о́тришься] (**на** В) feast one's eyes ([up]on), look (at) with delight

засме́|ивать [1; -ею, -ёшь], ⟨**~я́ть**⟩ [27 е.] ridicule

засну́ть → **засыпа́ть 2**

зас|о́в m [1] bar, bolt; **~о́вывать** [1], ⟨**~у́нуть**⟩ [20] put, slip, tuck; (*заде́ть куда́-то*) mislay; **~о́ли́ть** → **~а́ливать 2**

засоре́ние n [12] littering, obstruction, clogging up; **~и́ть**, **~я́ть** → **заса́ривать**

засоса́ть → **заса́сывать**

засо́х|ший [17] dry, dried up; *bot.* dead; **~нуть** → **засыха́ть**

заспа́нный *coll.* [14] looking sleepy

заста́|ва f [5]: **пограни́чная ~ва** frontier post; **~ва́ть** [5], ⟨**~ть**⟩ [-а́ну, -а́нешь] *дома и т. д.* find; *неожида́нно* surprise; **~ть на ме́сте преступле́ния** catch red-handed; **~вля́ть** [28], ⟨**~вить**⟩ [14] **1.** compel, force, make; **~вить ждать** keep waiting; **~вить замолча́ть** silence; **2.** (T) block (up); fill; **~ре́лый** [14] inveterate; *med.* chronic; **~ть** → **~ва́ть**

заст|ёгивать [1], ⟨**~егну́ть**⟩ [20; -ёгнутый] button up (*a.* **-ся** o.s. up); *пря́жкой, крючка́ми* buckle, clasp, hook (up); **~ёжка** f [5; *g/pl.*: -жек] fastener; clasp, buckle

застекл|я́ть [28], ⟨**~и́ть**⟩ [13] glaze, fit with glass

засте́нчивый [14 *sh.*] shy, bashful

засти|га́ть [1], ⟨**~гну́ть**⟩, ⟨**~чь**⟩ [21 -г-: -и́гну, -и́гнешь; -и́г, -и́гла; -и́гнутый] surprise, catch; **~гнуть враспло́х** take unawares

засти|ла́ть [1], ⟨**~ла́ть**⟩ [-телю́, -те́лешь; за́стланный] cover; *глаза́, не́бо* cloud

засто́|й m [3] stagnation; *econ.* depression; **~йный** [14] stagnant, chronic; **~льный** [14] table…; drinking; **~я́ться** [-ою́сь, -ои́шься] *pf. пе́ред карти́ной и т. д.* stand *or* stay too long; *о воде́ и т. д.* be(come) stagnant *or* stale

застра́|ивать [1], ⟨**~о́ить**⟩ [13] build on (up, over); **~ахо́вывать** [1], ⟨**~ахова́ть**⟩ [7] insure; *fig.* safeguard; **~ева́ть** [1], ⟨**~я́ть**⟩ [-я́ну, -я́нешь] stick; *coll.* (*задержа́ться*) be delayed; **~е́ливать** [1], ⟨**~ели́ть**⟩ [13: -елю́, -е́лишь; -е́ленный] shoot, kill; **~е́льщик** m [1] skirmisher; *fig.* instigator; initiator; **~о́ить** → **~а́ивать; ~о́йка** f [5; *g/pl.*: -о́ек] building (on); **пра́во на ~о́йку** building permit; **~я́ть** → **~ева́ть**

за́ступ m [1] spade

заступ|а́ться [1], ⟨**~и́ться**⟩ [14] (**за** В) take s.b.'s side; protect; intercede for; **~ник** m [1], **~ница** f [5] defender, protector; **~ничество** n [9] intercession

засты|ва́ть [1], ⟨**~ть**⟩ [-ы́ну, -ы́нешь] cool down; *жир и т. д.* congeal; *на ме́сте* stiffen, stand stockstill; **кровь ~ла у него́ в жи́лах** his blood ran cold

засу́нуть → **засо́вывать**

за́суха f [5] drought

засу́чивать [1], ⟨**~и́ть**⟩ [16] turn *or* roll up

засу́ш|ивать [1], ⟨**~и́ть**⟩ [16] dry (up); **~ливый** [14 *sh.*] dry

засчи́т|ывать, ⟨**~а́ть**⟩ [1] take into account; include, reckon

зас|ыпа́ть [1] **1.** ⟨**~ы́пать**⟩ [2] (T) fill up; (*покры́ть*) cover; *fig.* heap, ply, over-

3

whelm; *цветами и т. д.* strew; **2.**
⟨~ну́ть⟩ [20] fall asleep; **~ыха́ть** [1],
⟨~о́хнуть⟩ [21] dry up; wither

зата́|ивать [1], ⟨~и́ть⟩ [13] conceal, hide;
дыхание hold; *обиду* bear; **~ённый** *a.*
secret

зата́|пливать [1] **~опля́ть** [28],
⟨~опи́ть⟩ [14] **1.** *печь* light; **2.** flood;
судно sink; **~а́птывать** [1], ⟨~опта́ть⟩
[3] trample, tread (down); **~а́скивать**
[1] **1.** ⟨~аска́ть⟩ [1] wear out; **~а́скан-
ный** worn, shabby; *выражение* hackneyed; **2.** ⟨~ащи́ть⟩ [13] drag, pull
(off, away); *(задеть куда-л.)* mislay;
в гости take s.o. to one's *(or* somebody's*)* place

затв|ердева́ть [1], ⟨~ерде́ть⟩ [8] hard-
en

затво́р *m* [1] *винтовки* lock, bolt; *phot.*
shutter; **~я́ть** [28], ⟨~и́ть⟩ [13; -орю́,
-ори́шь; -о́ренный] shut, close; **-ся** shut
o.s. up

зат|ева́ть *coll.* [1], ⟨~е́ять⟩ [27] start, un-
dertake; **что он ~е́ял?** what is he up
to?; **~е́йливый** [14 *sh.*] ingenious, intricate; **~ека́ть** [1], ⟨~е́чь⟩ [26] flow (in,
etc.); *(распухнуть)* swell up; *ноги* be-
(come) numb, be asleep

зате́м then; *по этой причине* for that
reason, that is why; **~ что́бы** in order
to *(or* that)

затемн|е́ние *n* [12] darkening; *mil.*
blackout; *med. в лёгких* dark patch;
~я́ть [28], ⟨~и́ть⟩ [13] darken, overshad-
ow, (*a. fig.*) obscure

затер|е́ть → **затира́ть**; **~я́ть** [28] *pf.* lose;
-ся get *or* be lost; *о вещах* disappear; *се-
ление и т. д.* lost *or* inconspicuous in
the midst of

затеса́ться [3] (в В) worm o.s. into

зате́|чь → **затека́ть**; **~я** *f* [6] plan, under-
taking; escapade; **~ять** → **~ва́ть**

зат|ира́ть *coll.* [1], ⟨~ере́ть⟩ [12] *mst. fig.*
impede, give no chance to get on;
~иха́ть [1], ⟨~и́хнуть⟩ [21] become silent *or* quiet, stop (speaking, *etc.*); *звук*
die away, fade; *(успокоиться)* calm
down, abate; **~и́шье** *n* [10] lull, calm

заткну́ть → **затыка́ть**

затм|ева́ть [1], ⟨~и́ть⟩ [14 *e.*; *no* 1st *p.*

sg.; -ми́шь], **~е́ние** *n* [12] eclipse; **на не-
го́ нашло́ ~е́ние** his mind went blank

зато́ but (then, at the same time), but on
the other hand

затова́ривание *comm.* *n* [12] glut

затоп|и́ть, **~ля́ть** → **зата́пливать**;
~та́ть → **зата́птывать**

зато́р *m* [1] obstruction; **~ у́личного
движе́ния** traffic jam

заточ|а́ть [1], ⟨~и́ть⟩ [16 *e.*; -чу́, -чи́шь,
-чённый] *old use* confine, imprison;
~е́ние *n* [12] confinement, imprisonment

затра́|вливать [1], ⟨~ви́ть⟩ [14] hunt *or*
chase down; *fig.* persecute; bait; **~ги-
вать** [1], ⟨~́гнуть⟩ [20] touch (a.
fig., [up]on); affect; **затро́нуть чьё-л.
самолю́бие** wound s.o.'s pride

затра́|та *f* [5] expense, outlay; **~чивать**
[1], ⟨~ти́ть⟩ [15] spend

затро́нуть → **затра́гивать**

затрудн|е́ние *n* [12] difficulty, trouble;
embarrassment; **в ~е́нии** *a.* at a loss;
~и́тельный [14; -лен, -льна] difficult,
hard; embarrassing; **~и́тельное поло-
же́ние** predicament, ⟨~я́ть⟩ [28], ⟨~и́ть⟩
[13] embarrass, (cause) trouble; *что-л.*
render (more) difficult; *кого-л.* inconve-
nience; *что-л.* aggravate, compli-
cate; **-ся** *a.* at a loss (**в** П, Т for)

зату|ма́нивать(ся) [1], ⟨~ма́нить(ся)⟩
[13] fog, dim, cloud; **~ха́ть** [1], ⟨~́хнуть⟩
[21] die away, fade; *огонь* go out;
~шёвывать [1], ⟨~шева́ть⟩ [6] shade;
fig. coll. veil; gloss over; **~ши́ть** [16]
→ **туши́ть**

за́тхлый [14] musty, fusty

зат|ыка́ть [1], ⟨~кну́ть⟩ [20] stop up,
plug, *(пробкой)* cork; **~кну́ть кого́-л.
за по́яс** *coll.* outdo s.o.; **~ы́лок** *m* [1;
-лка] back of the head

заты́чка *f* [5; *g/pl.*: -чек] stopper, plug

затя́|гивать [1], ⟨~ну́ть⟩ [19] tighten,
draw tight; *(засосать)* draw in, *etc.*;
(покрыть) cover; *рану* close; *время*
protract, delay; **~гивать пе́сню** *coll.*
strike up a song; **~жка** *f* [5; *g/pl.*:
-жек] protraction, delaying; **сде́лать
~жку** draw, inhale, take a whiff; **~жно́й**
[14] long, lengthy, protracted

зау|ны́вный [14; -вен, -вна] doleful, mournful; **~ря́дный** [14; -ден, -дна] common(place), ordinary, mediocre; **~сёница** *f* [5] hangnail

заутреня *f* [6] matins *pl.*

зауч|ивать [1], ⟨**~и́ть**⟩ [16] memorize

захва́т *m* [1] seizure, capture; usurpation; **~ывать** [1], ⟨**~и́ть**⟩ [15] grasp; take (along with one, *a.* **с собо́й**); (*завладе́ть*) seize, capture; usurp; *fig.* absorb, captivate, thrill; (*застигнуть*) catch; *дух* take (away [*breath*], by [*surprise*], *etc.*); **~ни́ческий** [16] aggressive; **~чик** *m* [1] invader, aggressor; **~ывать → ~и́ть**

захвора́ть [1] *pf.* fall sick *or* ill

захл|ёбываться [1], ⟨**~ебну́ться**⟩ [20] choke, stifle (T, **от** P with); *fig. от гне́ва* be beside o.s.; **~ёстывать** [1], ⟨**~естну́ть**⟩ [20; -хлёснутый] swamp, overwhelm; flow over; **~о́пывать(ся)** [1], ⟨**~о́пнуть(ся)**⟩ [20] slam, bang

захо́д *m* [1] (*со́лнца* sun)set; *в порт* call; *ae.* approach; **~и́ть** [5], ⟨зайти́⟩ [зайду́, -дёшь; *g. pt.*: зайдя́; → **идти́**] go *or* come in *or* to (see, *etc.*), call *or* drop in (**к** Д, **в** B on, at); pick up, fetch (**за** T); *naut.* call, enter; *куда́-то* get; *за угол* turn, *ширму и т. д.* go behind (*за* B); *astr.* set; **речь зашла́ о** (П) (we, *etc.*) began (came) to (*or* had a) talk (about)

захолу́ст|ный [14] remote, provincial; **~ье** *n* [10] out-of-the-way place

захуда́лый [14] *coll.* shabby, impoverished

зацеп|ля́ть [28], ⟨**~и́ть**⟩ [14] (*a.* **за** B) catch, hook on, grapple; (*соедини́ть*) fasten; **-ся → задева́ть**

зачаро́в|ывать [1], ⟨**~а́ть**⟩ [7] charm, enchant

зачасти́|ть [15; -щу́, -сти́шь; -и́вший] *pf.* take to doing; begin to visit often (**в го́сти и т. д.**); **~л дождь** it began to rain heavily

зачасту́ю *coll.* often, frequently

зача́|тие *n* [12] conception; **~ток** *m* [1; -тка] embryo; rudiment; **~точный** [14] rudimentary; **~ть → -чну́, -чнёшь; зача́л, -а́, -о; зача́тый (зача́т, -а́, -о)** *pf.* conceive

зачём why, wherefore, what for; **~то** for some reason or other

зачёркивать [1], ⟨черкну́ть⟩ [20; -чёркнутый] cross out, strike out; **~ёрпывать** [1], ⟨черпну́ть⟩ [20; -чёрпнутый] scoop, draw up; *syn* ladle; **~ерстве́лый** [14] stale; **~ёсть → ~и́тывать**; **~ёсывать** [1], ⟨~еса́ть⟩ [3] comb (back); **~ёт** *m* [1] reckoning; *educ.* test; credit; *coll.* **э́то не в ~ёт** this does not count

зачи́нщик *m* [1] instigator; **~исля́ть** [28], ⟨~и́слить⟩ [13] enrol(l), enlist; *в штат* take on the staff; *comm.* enter; **~и́тывать** [1], ⟨~е́сть⟩ [25 -т-: -чту́, -чтёшь; → **проче́сть**] reckon, charge, account; *educ.* credit; **~и́тывать** ⟨~ита́ть⟩ [1] read (to, aloud); *coll.* **взя́тую кни́гу** not return; **-ся** (*увле́чься*) be(come) absorbed (T in); go on reading for too long

заш|ива́ть [1], ⟨~и́ть⟩ [-шью, -шьёшь; → **шить**] sew up; **~нуро́вывать** [1], ⟨~нурова́ть⟩ [7] lace (up); **~то́панный** [14] darned

защёлк|а *f* [5; *g/pl.*: -лок] latch; **~ивать** [1], ⟨~нуть⟩ [20] snap, latch

защем|ля́ть [28], ⟨~и́ть⟩ [14 *e.*; - емлю́, -емишь; -емлённый] pinch, jam; *impers. fig.* ache

защи́|та *f* [5] defense (*Brt.* -nce), protection, cover; *sport, law* the defense (-nce); **~ти́ть → ~ща́ть**; **~тник** *m* [1] defender; protector; *law* advocate (*a. fig.*), counsel for the defense (-nce); *sport* (full)back; **~тный** [14] protective, safety...; *цвет* khaki...; *шлем* crash; **~ща́ть** [1], ⟨~ти́ть⟩ [15; -ищу́, -ити́шь; -ищённый] (**от** P) defend (from, against); *от дождя́ и т. д.* protect (from); uphold, back, stand up for; advocate; *диссерта́цию* maintain, support; *impf. law* defend, plead (for)

заяв|и́ть → ~ля́ть; **~ка** *f* [5; *g/pl.*: -вок] application (for **на** B); claim; request; **~ле́ние** *n* [12] declaration, statement; (*про́сьба*) petition, application (for **о** П); **~ля́ть** [28], ⟨~и́ть⟩ [14] (*a.* **о** П) declare, announce, state; *права́* claim; (*сообщи́ть*) notify, inform

зая́длый coll. [14] → **завзя́тый**

за́яц m [1; за́йца] hare; coll. stowaway; в автобусе и т. д. bilker; **~чий** [18] hare('s)…; **~чья губа́** harelip

зва́ние n [12] mil. rank (тж. академическое); чемпиона и т. д. title; standing; **~ный** [14] invited; **~ть** [зову́, зовёшь; звал, -а́, -о; (…) зва́нный (зван, -а́, -о)] **1.** call; invite (в **~ть в го́сти** к Д, на В to); **2.** (на-) (Т) (be) called; **как Вас зову́т?** what is your (first) name?; **меня́ зову́т Петро́м** or **Пётр** my name is Peter

звезда́ f [5; pl. звёзды, etc. st.] star (a. fig.); **морска́я ~** zo. starfish

звёзд|ный [14] star…, stellar; небо starry; ночь starlit; **~очка** f [5; g/pl.: -чек] starlet; asterisk

звен|е́ть [9], ⟨за-, про-⟩ ring, jingle, clink; **у меня́ ~и́т в уша́х** my ears are ringing

звено́ n [9; pl.: зве́нья, -ьев] link; fig. team, section, производства branch

звери́н|ец m [1; -нца] menagerie; **~ый** [14] animal; fig. savage, brutal; → **зве́рский**

зверово́дство n [9] fur-farming

зве́р|ский [16] → **звери́ный**; fig. brutal; coll. mst. adv. (о́чень) awful(ly), dog(-tired); **~ство** n [9] brutality; pl. atrocities; **~ь** m [4; from g/pl. e.] (wild) animal, beast; fig. brute

звон m [1] ring, jingle, peal, chime; **~а́рь** m [4 e.] bell ringer; rumo(u)rmonger; **~и́ть** [13], ⟨по-⟩ ring (v/t. в В), chime, peal; (Д) telephone, call up; **вы не туда́ звони́те** you've got the wrong number; **~кий** [16; звонок, -нка́, -о; comp.: зво́нче] sonorous, clear; resonant; gr. voiced; **~о́к** m [1; -нка́] bell; (звук)

звук m [1] sound; **пусто́й ~** empty words; **~ово́й** [14] sound…; **~оза́пись** f [8] sound recording; **~онепроница́емый** [14] soundproof; **~ооператор** m [1] cine. sound producer

звуч|а́ние n [12] sounding; **~а́ть** [4 e.; 3rd p. only], ⟨про-⟩ (re)sound; звонок ring; **~ный** [14; -чен, -чна́, -о] sonorous, clear; resonant

звя́к|ать [1], ⟨-нуть⟩ [20] jingle, tinkle

зги: (only in phr.) **ни зги не ви́дно** it is pitch-dark

зда́ние n [12] building

зде|сь (of place) here; (on mail) local; **~сь нет ничего́ удиви́тельного** there is nothing surprising in this; **~шний** [14] local; **я не ~шний** I am a stranger here

здоро́в|аться [1], ⟨по-⟩ (с Т) greet or salute (o.a.); wish good morning, etc.; **~аться за́ руку** shake hands; **~о!**[1] hi!, hello!; **~о²** awfully; well done; **~ый** [14 sh.] com. healthy (a. su.), sound (a. fig.); пища wholesome; климат salubrious; P strong; in good health; **бу́дь(те) ~(ы)!** good-by(e)!, good luck!; (ва́ше здоро́вье!) your health!; **~ье** n [10] health; **как ва́ше ~ье?** how are you?; **за ва́ше ~ье!** your health!, here's to you!; **на ~ье!** good luck (health)!; **е́шь(те) на ~ье!** help yourself, please!

здра́в|ница f [5] health resort, sanatorium; **~омы́слящий** [17] sane, sensible; **~оохране́ние** n [12] public health service; **~ствовать** [7] be in good health; **~ствуй(те)!** hello!, hi!, good morning! (etc.); **при знако́мстве** how do you do?; **~ый** [14 sh.] → **здоро́вый**; fig. sound, sane, sensible; **~ый смысл** common sense; **в ~ом уме́** in one's senses; **~ и невреди́м** safe and sound

зе́бра f [5] zebra

зев m [1] anat. pharynx; **~а́ка** m/f [5] gaper; **~а́ть** [1], once ⟨-ну́ть⟩ [20] yawn; **~а́ть по сторона́м** stand about gaping; **не ~а́й!** look out!; **~о́к** m [1; -вка́] yawn; **~о́та** f [5] yawning

зелен|е́ть [8], ⟨за-, по-⟩ grow, turn or be green; impf. (a. **-ся**) appear or show green; **~ова́тый** [14 sh.] greenish

зелён|ый [14; зёлен, -а́, -о] green (a. fig.), verdant; **~ая у́лица** fig. green light; **~ юнец** coll. greenhorn

зе́л|ень f [8] verdure; green; cul. potherbs, greens pl.; **~ье** n [10] coll. potion, alcoholic drink

земе́льный [14] land…; **~ уча́сток** plot of land

землевладе́|лец m [1; -льца] landowner; **~ние** n [12] land ownership

земледе́л|ец m [1; -льца] farmer; **~ие** n

земле|ме́р *m* [1] (land)surveyor; ~по́-
льзование *n* [12] land tenure;~трясе́-
ние *n* [12] earthquake;~черпа́лка *f* [5;
g/pl.: -лок] dredger, excavator

земли́стый [14 *sh.*] earthy; *цвет лица*
ashy, sallow

земл|я́ *f* [6; *ac/sg.*: зе́млю; *pl.*: зе́мли, зе-
ме́ль, зе́млям] earth (as planet ♁);
land; (*поверхность, почва*) ground,
soil; **на ~ю** to the ground; ~я́к *m* [1
e.] (fellow) countryman; ~яни́ка *f* [5]
(wild) strawberry, -ries *pl.*; ~я́нка *f*
[5; *g/pl.*: -нок] *mil.* dugout; ~яно́й [14]
earth(en); ~ны́е рабо́ты excavations

земново́дный [14] amphibious

земно́й [14] (of the) earth, terrestrial;
earthly; *fig.* earthy, mundane

зени́т *m* [1] zenith (*a. fig.*);~ный [14] *mil.*
anti-aircraft...

зени́ц|а *f* [5]: **бере́чь как ~у о́ка** cherish

зе́ркал|о *n* [9; *pl. e.*] looking glass, mir-
ror (*a. fig.*); ~ьный [14] *fig.* (dead-)-
smooth; ~ьное стекло́ plate glass

зерн|и́стый [14 *sh.*] grainy, granular; ~о́
n [9; *pl.*: зёрна, зёрен, зёрнам] grain (*a.
coll.*), corn (*a. fig.*), seed; ~о́ и́стины
grain of truth; **кофе в зёрнах** coffee
beans; ~ово́й [14] grain...; *su. pl.* cereals

зефи́р *m* [1] sweetmeat (*of egg-white,
sugar and gelatin(e)*)

зигза́г *m* [1], ~ообра́зный [14: -зен,
-зна] zigzag

зим|а́ *f* [5; *ac/sg.*: зи́му; *pl.st.*] winter (T in
[the]; **на** B in); ~ний [14] winter...,
wintry; ~ова́ть [7], ⟨за-, пере-⟩ winter,
hibernate

зия́ть [28] gape

злак *m* [1] *pl.* gramineous plants; **хлеб-
ные ~и** *pl.* cereals

зла́то... *obs.* or *poet.* gold(en)

злить [13], ⟨обо-, разо-⟩ anger, make
angry; (*раздражать*) vex, irritate;
~ся be(come) *or* feel angry (**на** B with);
be in a bad temper

зло *n* [9; *pl. gen.* зол *only*] evil; (*меня*) ~
берёт it annoys me

зло́б|а *f* [5] malice, spite; rage; ~а дня

topic of the day; ~ный [14: -бен,
-бна] spiteful, malicious; ~однев́ный
[14: -вен, -вна] topical, burning;~ство-
вать [7] → **зли́ться**

злов́ещий [17 *sh.*] ominous; ~о́ние *n*
[12] stench; ~о́нный [14; -о́нен, -о́нна]
stinking, fetid; ~ре́дный [14; -ден,
-дна] pernicious, noxious

злоде́|й *m* [3] villian; ~йский [16] *пре-
ступление* vile, outrageous; *замысел
и т. д.* malicious;~йство *n*[9], ~я́ние *n*
[12] outrage, villainy, crime

злой [14; зол, зла, зло] wicked, evil;
язык, действие malicious, spiteful;
angry (with **на** B); *собака* fierce; *нрав*
severe; ~ ге́ний evil genius

зло|ка́чественный [14 *sh.*] *med.* malig-
nant; ~ключе́ние *n* [12] misfortune;
~наме́ренный [14 *sh.*] malevolent;
~па́мятный [14; -тен, -тна] rancorous;
~полу́чный [14; -чен, -чна] unfortunate, ill-fated; ~ра́дный [14; -ден,
-дна] gloating

злосло́ви|е *n* [12], ~ть [14] malicious
gossip, backbiting

злост|ь *f* [14; -тен, -тна] malicious,
spiteful; malevolent; *закоренелый* inveterate; ~ь *f* [8] spite, rage

зло|сча́стный [14; -тен, -тна] → **по-
лу́чный**

злоумы́шленник *m* [1] plotter; male-
factor

злоупотреб|ле́ние *n* [12], ~ля́ть [28],
⟨~и́ть⟩ [14 *e.*; -блю, -би́шь] (Т)
властью, доверием abuse; *спирт-
ным* drink too much

зме|и́ный [14] snake('s), serpent('s), ser-
pentine; ~и́ться [13] meander, wind
(o.s.); ~й *m* [3]: **возду́шный ~й** kite;
~я́ *f* [6; *pl. st.*: зме́и, змей] snake, serpent (*a. fig.*)

знак *m* [1] sign, mark; *дружбы и т. д.*
token; symbol; (*предзнаменование*)
omen; (*значок*) badge; signal; **доро́ж-
ный** ~ road sign; ~и *pl.* препина́ния
punctuation marks; **в** ~ (P) in token
or as a sign of

знако́м|ить [14], ⟨по-⟩ introduce (В/с Т
a *p.* to); *a.* ⟨о-⟩ acquaint (**с** Twith); -ся
(**с** Т) *p.*: meet, make the acquaintance

of, (*a. th.*) become acquainted with; *th.*: familiarize o.s. with, go into; **~ство** *n* [9] acquaintance (-ces *pl.*); **~ый** [14 *sh.*] familiar, acquainted (**с** T with); know; *su.* acquaintance; **~ьтесь, ...**, meet…

знамена́тель *m* [4] denominator; **~ный** [14; -лен, -льна] memorable, remarkable; (*важный*) significant, important

знамен|е *n* [12]: **~ вре́мени** sign of the times; **~и́тость** *f* [8] fame, renown; *p.*: celebrity; **~и́тый** [14 *sh.*] famous, renowned, celebrated (T by, for); **~ова́ть** [7] *impf.* mark, signify

зна́|мя *n* [13; *pl.*: -мёна, -мён] banner, flag; *mil.* standard; colo(u)rs

зна́ние *n* [12] (*a. pl.* **~я**) knowledge; **со ~ем де́ла** capable, competently

зна́т|ный [14; -тен, -тна́, -о] *род и т. д.* noble; **~о́к** *m* [1 *e.*] expert; *ценитель* connoisseur

знать[1] [1] know; **дать ~** (Д) let know; **дать себя́ (о себе́) ~** make itself felt (send news); **кто его́ зна́ет** goodness knows

знать[2] *f* [8] *hist.* nobility, notables *pl.*

значе́ние *n* [12] meaning, sense; *math.* value; significance, importance (*vb.*: **име́ть** be of); **~и́тельный** [14; -лен, -льна] considerable; large; (*важный*) important, significant; **~ить** [16] mean, signify; (*иметь значение*) matter; **~ит** consequently, so; well (then); **-ся** be mentioned, be registered; *impers.* (it) say(s); **~о́к** *m* [1; -чка́] badge; (*помет- ка*) sign

зноби́ть: меня́ ~ I feel shivery

зной *m* [3] heat, sultriness; **~ный** [14; зно́ен, зно́йна] sultry, hot

зоб *m* [1] crop, craw (*of birds*); *med.* goiter (-tre)

зов *m* [1] call

зо́дчество *n* [9] architecture

зола́ *f* [5] ashes *pl.*

золо́вка *f* [5; *g/pl.*: -вок] sister-in-law (*husband's sister*)

золоти́|стый [14 *sh.*] golden; **~ть** [15 *e.*; -очу́, -оти́шь], ⟨по-, вы-⟩ gild

зо́лот|о *n* [9] gold; **на вес ~а** worth its weight in gold; **~о́й** [14] gold(en) (*a. fig.*); **~о́е дно** gold mine; **~о́й запа́с**

econ. gold reserves; **~ы́е ру́ки** golden hands; **~а́я середи́на** golden mean

золочёный [14] gilt, gilded

Зо́лушка *f* [5; *g/pl.*: -шек] Cinderella

зо́н|а *f* [5] zone; **~а́льный** [14] zonal, regional

зонд *m* [1] probe, sound; **~и́ровать** [7] sound; **~и́ровать по́чву** *fig.* explore the ground

зонт, ~ик *m* [1] umbrella; sunshade; **складно́й ~ик** telescopic umbrella

зоо́|лог *m* [1] zoologist; **~логи́ческий** [16] zoological; **~ло́гия** *f* [7] zoology; **~па́рк** *m* [1] zoo(logical garden)

зо́ркий [16; зо́рок, -рка́, -о; *compr.*: зо́рче] sharp-sighted (*a. fig.*); observant, watchful, vigilant

зрачо́к *m* [1; -чка́] *anat.* pupil

зре́л|ище *n* [11] sight; spectacle; show; **~ость** *f* [8] ripeness; *о человеке* maturity; **~ый** [14; зрел, -á, -о] ripe, mature; **по ~ому размышле́нию** on reflection

зре́н|ие *n* [12] (eye)sight; **по́ле ~я** field of vision, eyeshot; *fig.* horizon; **обма́н ~я** optical illusion; **то́чка ~я** point of view; standpoint, angle (*prp.*: **с то́чки ~я = под угло́м ~я** from …)

зреть [8], ⟨со-, вы-⟩ ripen, mature

зри́тель *m* [4] spectator, onlooker, observer; **~ный** [14] visual, optic; **~ный зал** hall, auditorium; **~ная па́мять** visual memory

зря *coll.* in vain, to no purpose, (all) for nothing; **~ ты э́то сде́лал** you should not have done it

зря́чий [17] sighted (*opp. blind*)

зуб *m* [1; *from g/pl. e.*: зу́бья, зу́бьев] tooth; *tech. a.* cog; **до ~о́в** to the teeth; **не по ~а́м** too tough (*a. fig.*); **сквозь ~ы** through clenched teeth; **име́ть ~** (на В) have a grudge against; **~а́стый** [14 *sh.*] *fig.* sharptongued; **~е́ц** *m* [1; -бца́] *tech.* → *зуб*; **~и́ло** *n* [9] chisel; **~но́й** [14] tooth, dental; **~но́й врач** = dentist; **~на́я боль** toothache; **~на́я щётка** toothbrush; **~овраче́бный** [14]: **~овраче́бный кабине́т** dental surgery

зубр *m* [1] European bison; *fig.* diehard; *coll.* pundit

зубр|ёжка *f* [5] cramming; **~и́ть 1.** [13],

⟨за-⟩ notch; *зазу́бренный* jagged; **2.** [13] зубрю́, зубри́шь, ⟨вы-⟩ [зазу́бренный] cram, learn by rote

зу́бчатый [14] *tech.* cog (wheel)..., gear...; jagged

зуд *m* [1], **~е́ть** *coll.* [9] itch; urge; *fig.* complain constantly, talk boringly

зу́ммер *m* [1] buzzer

зы́б|кий [16; зы́бок, -бка́, -о; *compr.*: зы́бче] unsteady, unstable (*a. fig.*) vague; **~ь** *f* [8] ripples *pl.*

зы́чный [14; -чен, -чна; *compr.*: -чнее] loud, shrill

зя́б|нуть [21], ⟨(про)о-⟩ feel chilly; **~ь** *f* [8] winter tillage *or* cold

зять *m* [4; *pl. e.*: зятья́, -ьёв] son- *or* brother-in-law (*daughter's or sister's husband*)

И

и **1.** *cj.* and; and then, and so; but; (even) though, much as; (that's) just (what... is *etc.*), (this) very *or* same; **2.** *part.* oh; too, (n)either; even; *и ... и ...* both ... and ...

и́бо *cj.* for

и́ва *f* [5; *pl. st.*] willow; *плаку́чая* **~** weeping willow

и́волга *f* [5] oriole

игл|а́ *f* [5] needle (*a. tech.*); *bot.* thorn, prickle; *zo.* quill, spine, bristle; **~отерапи́я** *f* [7], **~ука́лывание** *n* [12] acupuncture

игнори́ровать [7] (*im*)*pf.* ignore

и́го *n* [9] *fig.* yoke

иго́л|ка *f* [5; *g/pl.*: -лок] → *игла́*; *как на ~ках* on tenterhooks; *с ~(оч)ки* brand-new, spick-and-span; **~ьный** [14] needle('s)...; **~ьное у́шко** eye of a needle

иго́рный [14] gambling; card...

игр|а́ *f* [5; *pl. st.*] play; game (*в* B of); sparkle; **~ слов** play on words, pun; **~ не сто́ит свеч** it isn't worth while; **~ воображе́ния** pure fantasy; **~льный** [14] *ка́рта* playing; **~ть** [1], ⟨по-, сыгра́ть⟩ play (*в* B, *на* П); *в аза́ртные и́гры* gamble; sparkle (wine, *etc.*); *thea. a.* act; **~ть свое́й жи́знью** risk one's life; **э́то не ~ет ро́ли** it does not matter

игри́|вый [14 *sh.*] playful; **~стый** [14 *sh.*] sparkling

игро́к *m* [1 *e.*] player; gambler

игру́шка *f* [5; *g/pl.*: -шек] toy; *fig.* plaything

идеа́л *m* [1] ideal; **~изи́ровать** [7] (*im*)*pf.* idealize; **~и́зм** *m* [1] idealism; **~и́ст** *m* [1] idealist; **~исти́ческий** [16] idealistic; **~ьный** [14; -лен, -льна] ideal

идентифика́тор *m* [1] *comput.* name

идео́лог *m* [1] ideologist; **~и́ческий** [16] ideologic(al); **~ия** *f* [7] ideology

иде́я *f* [6] idea

иди́лл|ия *f* [7] idyl(l); **~и́ческий** [16] idyllic

идио́ма *f* [5] idiom

идио́т *m* [1] idiot; **~и́зм** *m* [1] idiocy; **~ский** [16] idiotic

и́дол *m* [1] idol (*a. fig.*)

идти́ [иду́, идёшь; шёл, шла; ше́дший; идя́, *coll.* и́дучи], ⟨пойти́⟩ [пойду́, -дёшь; пошёл, -шла́] (be) go(ing, *etc.*); *a. fig.*), walk; come; (*за* Т) follow, *a.* go for, fetch; leave; (*дви́гать[ся]*) move (*a.* chess, T), flow, drift (*в, на* B); *шко́лу и т. д.* enter; *а́рмию и т. д.* join, become; (*происходи́ть*) proceed, be in progress, take place; *thea. фильм* be on; *доро́га* lead (*о ка́рте с* Р); (*на* B) attack; *о това́ре* sell; (*в, на, под* B) be used, spent (for); (*к* Д) suit; (*за* B) marry; **~ в счёт** count; *на вёслах* row; *пойти́ в отца́* take after one's father; *идёт!* all right!, done!; *пошёл (пошли́)!* (let's) go!; *де́ло (речь) идёт о* (П) the question *or* matter is (whether), it is a question *or* matter of; *... is* at stake; *ему́ идёт или пошёл шесто́й год (деся́ток)* he is over five (fifty)

иезуи́т *m* [1] Jesuit (*a. fig.*)

иера́рхия *f* [7] hierarchy

иеро́глиф *m* [1] hieroglyph(ic)

иждиве́н|ец *m* [1; -нца] dependent (-dant); **~ие** *n* [12]: **быть на ~ии** (P) be s.o.'s dependent (-dant)

из., ~о (P) from, out of; of; for, through; with; in; by; **что ж ~ э́того?** what that matter?

изба́ *f* [5; *pl. st.*] (peasant's) house, cottage

избав|и́тель *m* [4] rescuer, deliverer; **~ить → ~ля́ть; ~ле́ние** *n* [12] deliverance, rescue; **~ля́ть** [28], **⟨~ить⟩** [14] **(от** P from) **(**освободи́ть**)** deliver, free; **(**спасти́**)** save; **от боли** relieve; **-ся (от** P) get rid of

избало́ванный [14 *sh.*] spoilt

избе|га́ть [1], **⟨~жа́ть⟩** [4; -егу́, -ежи́шь, -егу́т], **⟨~гну́ть⟩** [21] (P) avoid, shun; *сме́рти* escape; **(**уклони́ться**)** evade; **~жа́ние** *n* [12]: **во ~жа́ние** (P) (in order) to avoid

изб|ива́ть [1], **⟨~и́ть⟩** [изобью́, -бьёшь; **→ бить**] beat unmercifully; **~ие́ние** *n* [12] beating; massacre

избира́тель *m* [4] voter, elector; *pl. a.* electorate; constituency; **~ный** [14] electoral; ballot...; election; **~ный уча́сток** polling station; **~ный о́круг** constituency

изб|ира́ть [1], **⟨~ра́ть⟩** [-беру́, -рёшь; **→ брать**] choose; elect (**B/в** И *pl. or*/Т); **~ранный** *a.* select(ed); **~ранные сочине́ния** selected works

изби́|тый [14 *sh.*] *fig.* hackneyed, trite; **~ть → ~ва́ть**

избра́|ние *n* [12] election; **~нник** *m* [1] (young) man of her choice; **~ть → избира́ть**

избы́т|ок *m* [1; -тка] surplus; abundance, plenty; **в ~ке, с ~ком** in plenty, plentiful(ly); **в ~ке чувств** *fig.* overcome by emotion; **~очный** [14; -чен, -чна] superfluous, surplus...

и́звер|г *m* [1] monster, cruel person; **~же́ние** *n* [12] eruption

изверну́ться → извора́чиваться

извести́ → изводи́ть

изве́ст|ие *n* [12] news *sg.*; information; *pl. a.* bulletin; **после́дние ~ия** *rad.* news(cast), the latest news; **извести́ть**

→ извеща́ть

изве́стк|а *f* [5], **~о́вый** [14] lime

изве́стн|ость *f* [8] reputation, fame; **по́льзоваться (мирово́й) ~остью** be (world-)renowned *or* famous *or* well-known; **ста́вить** (B) **в ~ость** bring s.th. to a p.'s notice **(о** П); **~ый** [14; -тен, -тна] known (for T; as **как, за** B), familiar; well-known, renowned, famous; notorious; **(**не́который**)** certain; **наско́лько мне ~о** as far as I know; **(мне) ~о** it is known (I know); **ему́ э́то хорошо́ ~о** he is well aware of this

изве́ст|ня́к *m* [1 *e.*] limestone; **~ь** *f* [8] lime

изве|ща́ть [1], **⟨~сти́ть⟩** [15 *e.*; -ещу́, -ести́шь; -ещённый] inform **(о** П of); notify; *comm. a.* advise; **~ще́ние** *n* [12] notification, notice; *comm.* advice

изви|ва́ться [1] wind, meander, twist; *о те́ле, зме́е и т. д.* wriggle; **~лина** *f* [5] bend, curve; turn; *мо́зга* convolution; **~листый** [14 *sh.*] winding, tortuous

извин|е́ние *n* [12] apology, excuse; **~и́тельный** [14; -лен, -льна] pardonable; [*no sh.*] apologetic; **~я́ть** [28], **⟨~и́ть⟩** [13] excuse; pardon; forgive (Д/за a p. a th.); **~и́(те)!** excuse me!, I am sorry!; **нет, уж ~и́(те)!** oh no!, on no account!; **-ся** apologize **(пе́ред** Т, **за** B to/for); **~я́юсь** *coll.* **→ ~и́(те)!**

извле|ка́ть [1], **⟨~чь⟩** [26] take *or* draw out; extract **(**a. math.**)**; **вы́году** derive; **~че́ние** *n* [12] extract(ion)

извне́ from outside

изводи́ть *coll.* [15], **⟨извести́⟩** [25] **(**израсхо́довать**)** use up; **(**изму́чить**)** exhaust, torment

изво́л|ить [13] *iro.* please, deign; **~ь(те)** + *inf.* (would you) please + *vb*

извор|а́чиваться [1], **⟨изверну́ться⟩** [20] *coll.* dodge; (try to) wriggle out; **~о́тливый** [14 *sh.*] resourceful; shrewd

извра|ща́ть [1], **⟨~ти́ть⟩** [15 *e.*; -ащу́, -ати́шь; -ащённый] *фа́кты* misconstrue, distort; *о челове́ке* pervert

изги́б *m* [1] bend, curve, turn; *fig.* shade; **~а́ть** [1], **⟨изогну́ть⟩** [20] bend, curve, crook (*v/i.* **-ся**)

изгла|́живать [1], ⟨~дить⟩ [15] (**-ся** be[-come]) efface(d), erase(d); **~дить из па́мяти** blot out of one's memory

изгна́|ние n [12] *old use, lit.* banishment; exile; **~ник** m [1] exile; **~ть** → **изгоня́ть**

изголо́вье n [10] *кровати* head

изг|оня́ть [28], ⟨~на́ть⟩ [-гоню́, -го́нишь; -гна́л, -ла́] drive out; oust; expel; exile, banish

и́згородь f [8] fence; *зелёная* hedge(-row)

изгот|а́вливать [1], **~овля́ть** [28], ⟨~о́вить⟩ [14] make, produce, manufacture; **~овле́ние** n [12] manufacture; making; *mil.* preparation

изда|ва́ть [5], ⟨~ть⟩ [-да́м, -да́шь, *etc.*, → **дать**; и́зданный (и́здан, -а́, -о)] publish; *приказ* issue; *запах* exhale; *звук* utter, emit; *law* promulgate

и́зда|вна for a long time; from time immemorial; **~лека́, ~лёка ~ли** from afar; from a distance

изда́|ние n [12] publication; edition; issue; **~тель** m [4] publisher; **~тельство** n [9] publishing house, publishers *pl.*; **~ть** → **издава́ть**

издева́т|ельство n [9] jeering, scoffing, sneering (**над** T at); **~ься** [1] jeer, sneer, mock (**над** T at); bully

изде́лие n [12] product, article; (needle)work; *pl. a.* goods

издёргать [1] harass, harry; **-ся** overstrain one's nerves; worry one's head off

издерж|а́ться [4] *pf. coll.* spend a lot of (*or* run short of) money; **~ки** f/pl. [5; *gen*: -жек] expenses; *law* costs

издыха́ть [1] → **до́хнуть**

изжи|ва́ть [1], ⟨~́ть⟩ [-живу́, -вёшь; -жи́тый, *coll.* -то́й (изжи́т, -а́, -о)] (gradually) overcome; **~́ть себя́** be(come) outdated, have had one's day; **~́ога** f [5] heartburn

и́з-за (P) from behind; from; because of; over; for (the sake of); **~** *чего́?* why?, for what reason?; **~** *э́того* for that reason

излага́ть [1], ⟨изложи́ть⟩ [16] state, set forth, expound, word

излече́|ние n [12] cure, (medical) treatment; (*выздоровле́ние*) recovery; **~ивать** [1], ⟨~и́ть⟩ [16] cure; **~и́мый** [14 *sh.*] curable

изл|ива́ть [1], ⟨~и́ть⟩ [изолью́, -льёшь; → **лить**]: **~и́ть ду́шу** unbosom o.s.; *гнев* give vent (*to anger*)

изли́ш|ек m [1; -шка] surplus, *a.* **~ество** n [9] excess; **~е** unnecessarily; **~ний** [15; -шен, -шня, -не] superfluous, excessive; (*ненужный*) needless

изл|ия́ние n [12] outpouring, effusion; **~и́ть** [28] → **~ива́ть**

изловч|и́ться *coll.* [16 *e.*; -чу́сь, -чи́шься] *pf.* contrive

излож|е́ние n [12] exposition, account; **~и́ть** → **излага́ть**

изло́манный [14] broken; warped; *жизнь, хара́ктер* spoilt, deformed

излуч|а́ть [1] radiate; **~е́ние** n [12] radiation

излу́чина f [5] *реки* → **изги́б**

излю́бленный [14] favo(u)rite

изме́н|а f [5] treason (Д to); *супружеская* unfaithfulness; **~е́ние** n [12] change, alteration, modification; **~и́ть** → **~я́ть**; **~ник** m [1] traitor; **~чивый** [14 *sh.*] changeable, variable; *о человеке, настрое́нии* fickle; **~я́ть** [28], ⟨~и́ть⟩ [13; -еню́, -е́нишь] **1.** *v/i.* change (*v/i.* **-ся**) alter; modify; vary; **2.** *v/i.* (Д) betray; be(come) unfaithful (to); *кля́тве и т. д.* break, violate; *па́мять* fail

изме́р|ение n [12] measurement; *math.* dimension; **~и́мый** [14 *sh.*] measurable; **~и́тельный** [14]: **~и́тельный прибо́р** measuring instrument, gauge; **~я́ть** [28], ⟨~ить⟩ [13 *st.*] measure; *температу́ру* take; *глубину́* fathom (*a. fig.*)

измождённый [14 *sh.*] *вид* emaciated; (*изнурённый*) exhausted

измо́р: **взять кого́-нибудь ~ом** *fig.* worry s.o. into doing s.th

и́зморозь f [8] rime, hoar-frost

и́морось f [8] drizzle

изму́чи|вать [1], ⟨~ть⟩ [16] (**-ся** be[-come]) fatigue(d), exhaust(ed), wear (worn) out

измышле́ние n [12] fabrication, invention

изна́нка f [5] back, inside; *ткани* wrong side; *fig.* seamy side

изнаси́лов|ание n [12], **~ать** [7] *pf.* rape, assault, violation

изна́ш|ивать [1], ⟨износи́ть⟩ [15] wear out; *v/i.* **-ся**

изне́женный [14] coddled

изнем|ога́ть [1], ⟨~о́чь⟩ [26; г/ж: -огу́, -о́жешь, -о́гут] be(come) exhausted *or* enervated; **~ога́ть от уста́лости** feel dead tired; **~оже́ние** n [12] exhaustion, weariness

изно́с m [1] wear (and tear); **рабо́тать на ~** wear o.s. out with work; **~и́ть →** ***изна́шивать***

изно́шенный [14 *sh.*] worn (out); threadbare

изнур|е́ние n [12] exhaustion, fatigue; **~и́тельный** [14; -лен, -льна] *труд* hard, exhausting; *боле́знь* wasting; **~я́ть** [28], ⟨~и́ть⟩ (**-ся** be[come]) fatigue(d), exhauste(d)

изнутри́ from within; on the inside

изны|ва́ть [1] *impf.* (**от** P); **~ва́ть от жа́жды** be dying of thirst; **~ва́ть от ску́ки** be bored to death

изоби́л|ие n [12] abundance, plenty (P *a.* **в** П of); **~овать** [7] abound (T in); **~ьный** [14; -лен, -льна] rich, abundant (T in)

изоблич|а́ть [1], ⟨~и́ть⟩ [16 *e.*; -чу́, -чи́шь; -чённый] unmask; *impf.* reveal, show

изобра|жа́ть [1], ⟨~зи́ть⟩ [15 *e.*; -ажу́, -ази́шь; -ажённый] represent, portray, depict; describe; express; **~жа́ть из себя́** (B) make o.s. out to be; **~же́ние** n [12] representation; description; *о́браз* image, picture; **~зи́тельный** [14]: **~зи́тельное иску́сство** fine arts

изобре|сти́ → **~та́ть**; **~та́тель** m [4] inventor; **~та́тельный** [14; -лен, -льна] inventive, resourceful; **~та́ть** [1], ⟨~сти́⟩ [25 -т-: -брету́, -тёшь] invent; **~те́ние** n [12] invention

изо́гнут|ый [14 *sh.*] bent, curved; **~ь →** ***изгиба́ть***

изо́дранный [14] *coll.* → ***изо́рванный***

изоли́ровать [7] (*im*)*pf.* isolate; *el. a.* insulate; **~я́тор** m [1] *el.* insulator;

med. isolation ward; *в тюрьме́* cell, jail for imprisonment during investigation; **~я́ция** f [7] isolation; *el.* insulation

изо́рванный [14] torn, tattered

изощр|ённый [14] refine, subtle; **~я́ться**[28], ⟨~и́ться⟩ [13] exert o.s., excel (**в** П *or* T in); **~я́ться в остроу́мии** sparkle with wit

из-под (P) from under; from; from the vicinity of; **буты́лка ~ молока́** milk bottle

изразе́ц m [1; -зца́] (Dutch) tile

и́зредка occasionally; *места́ми* here and there

изре́з|ывать [1], ⟨~ать⟩ [3] cut up

изре|ка́ть [1], ⟨~чь⟩ *iro.* pronounce; **~че́ние** n [12] aphorism, maxim

изруб|а́ть [1], ⟨~и́ть⟩ [14] chop, mince; cut (up)

изря́дный [14; -ден, -дна] *сумма* large, fair; *моро́з* rather severe; *подле́ц* real scoundrel

изуве́ч|ивать [1], ⟨~ить⟩ [16] mutilate

изум|и́тельный [14; -лен, -льна] amazing, wonderful; **~и́ть(ся) → ~ля́ть(ся)**; **~ле́ние** n [12] amazement; **~ля́ть** [28], ⟨~и́ть⟩ [14 *e.*; -млю́, -ми́шь, -млённый] (**-ся** Д be) amaze(d), astonish(ed), surprise(d at)

изумру́д m [1] emerald

изуч|а́ть [1], ⟨~и́ть⟩ [16] study, learn; (*ознако́миться*) familiarize o.s. with; (*овладе́ть*) master; *тща́тельно* scrutinize; **~е́ние** n [12] study

изъе́здить [15] *pf.* travel all over

изъяв|и́тельный [14] *gr.* indicative; **~ля́ть** [28], ⟨~и́ть⟩ [14] express, show; *согла́сие* give

изъя́н m [1] defect, flaw

изыма́ть [1], ⟨изъя́ть⟩ [изыму́, изы́мешь] withdraw, confiscate

изыска́ние n [12] *mst. mining* prospecting

изы́сканный [14 *sh.*] refined, elegant; *еда́ и т. д.* choice, exquisite

изы́ск|ивать [1], ⟨~а́ть⟩ [3] find

изю́м m [1] *coll.* raisins *pl.*; sultanas; **~инка** f [1]: **с ~инкой** piquant

изя́щн|ый [14; -щен, -щна] graceful, elegant

ик|а́ть [1], ⟨~ну́ть⟩ [20] hiccup

ико́н|а f [5] icon; **~опись** f [8] icon painting

ико́та f [5] hiccup

икра́¹ f [5] (hard) roe, spawn, caviar; **зерни́стая ~** soft caviar; **па́юсная ~** pressed caviar

икра́² f [5] *mst. pl.* [*st.*] calf (*of leg*)

ил m [1] silt

и́ли or; or else; **~ ... ~ ...** either... or

иллю́зия f [7] illusion; **~мина́ция** f [7] illumination; **~мини́ровать** [7] (*im*)*pf.* illuminate; otherwise; **~стра́ция** f [7] illustration; **~стри́ровать** [7] (*im*)*pf.* illustrate

имби́рь m [4 *e.*] ginger

име́ние n [12] estate, landed property

имени́н|ы f/pl. [5] name day; nameday party; **~тельный** [14] *gr.* nominative; **~тый** [14 *sh.*] eminent, distinguished

и́менно just, very (*adj.*), exactly, in particular; (*a. a ~, и ~*) namely, to wit, that is to say; (*a.* **вот ~**) *coll.* indeed

именова́ть [7], ⟨на-⟩ call, name

име́ть [8] have, possess; **~ де́ло с** (T) have to do with; **~ ме́сто** take place; **~ в виду́** have in mind, mean, intend; (*не забыва́ть*) remember, bear in mind; **-ся под руко́й** be at, in *or* on hand; (**у** P) there is, are, *etc.*

имита́ция f [7] imitation

иммигра́нт m [1] immigrant

иммунитет m [1] immunity

импера́т|ор m [1] emperor; **~ри́ца** f [5] empress

импе́р|ия f [7] empire; **~ский** [16] imperial

и́мпорт m [1], **~и́ровать** [7] (*im*)*pf.* import; **~ный** [14] imported

импоте́нция f [7] sexual impotence

импровизи́ровать [7] (*im*)*pf.* ⟨сымпровизи́ровать⟩ improvise

и́мпульс m [1] impulse; *el.* pulse; **~и́вный** [14; -вен, -вна] impulsive

иму́щ|ество n [9] property; belongings *pl.*; **недви́жимое ~ество** real estate; **~ий** [17] well-to-do; **власть ~ие** the powers that be

и́мя n [13] (*esp.* first, Christian) name (*a. fig. gr.*; parts of speech = *Lat.* nomen); **и́мени: шко́ла им. Че́хова** Chekhov

school; **во ~ for** the sake of; **от и́мени** in the name of (P); **на ~** addressed to, for; **по и́мени** named; in name (only); (know) by name; **называ́ть ве́щи свои́ми имена́ми** call a spade a spade

и́наче differently; otherwise, (or) else; **так и́ли ~** one way *or* another, anyhow

инвали́д m [1] invalid; **~ труда́ (войны́)** disabled worker (veteran, *Brt.* ex-serviceman)

инвент|ариза́ция f [7] stock-taking; **~а́рь** m [4 *e.*] *список* inventory; stock, equipment; list

инд|е́ец m [1; -е́йца] (American) Indian; **~е́йка** f [5; *g/pl.:* -е́ек] turkey; **~е́йский** [16] (American) Indian; **~иа́нка** f [5; *g/pl.:* -нок] *fem.* of **~е́ец, ~и́ец**

индиви́д m [1] individual; **~уа́льность** f [8] individuality; **~уа́льный** [14; -лен, -льна] individual

инди́|ец m [1; -и́йца] Indian; **~йский** [16] Indian

инду́с m [1], **~ка** f [5; *g/pl.:* -сок], **~ский** [16] Hindu

инд|устриа́льный [14] industrial; **~у́стрия** f [7] industry

индю́к m [1 *e.*] turkey (cock)

и́ней m [3] hoar-frost

ине́рт|ность f [8] inertness, inaction; **~ный** [14; -тен, -тна] inert; **~ция** f [7] inertia; *phys.* **по ~ции** under one's own momentum; *fig.* mechanically

инжене́р m [1] engineer; **~-строи́тель** m [1/4] civil engineer

инициа́|лы m/pl. [1] initials; **~ти́ва** f [5] initiative; **~ти́вный** [14; -вен, -вна] enterprising, full of initiative; **~тор** m [1] initiator, organizer

инкруста́ция f [7] inlay, incrustation

иногда́ sometimes, now and then

иногоро́дний [15] nonresident, person from another town

ино́|й [14] (an)other, different; (*некоторый и т. д.*) some, many a; **~й раз** sometimes; **не кто ~й (не что ~е), как ...** none other than

иноро́дн|ый [14], heterogeneous; **~ое те́ло** *med.* foreign body

иносказа́тельный [14; -лен, -льна] allegorical

иностра́н|ец *m* [1; -нца], **~ка** *f* [5; *g/pl.:* -нок] foreigner; **~ный** [14] foreign; → *a.* **министе́рство**

инсинуа́ция *f* [7] insinuation

инспе́к|тор *m* [1] inspector; **~ция** *f* [7] inspection

инста́нция *f* [7] *pl.* (official) channels; *pol.* level of authority; *law* instance

инсти́нкт *m* [1] instinct; **~ивный** [14; -вен, -вна] instinctive

институ́т *m* [1] institute; **бра́ка и т. д.** institution

инстру́кция *f* [7] instruction, direction; **~ по эксплуата́ции** manual

инструме́нт *m* [1] *mus. etc.* instrument; **рабо́чий** tool

инсу́льт *m* [1] *med.* stroke

инсцени́р|овать [7] *(im)pf.* adapt for the stage *or* screen; *fig.* feign; **~о́вка** *f* [5; *g/pl.:* -вок] dramatization

интегра́ция *f* [7] integration

интелле́кт *m* [1] intellect; **~уа́льный** [14; -лен, -льна] intellectual

интеллиге́н|т *m* [1] intellectual; **~тность** *f* [8] intelligence and good breeding; **~тный** [14; -тен, -тна] cultured, well-educated; **~ция** *f* [7] intelligentsia, intellectuals *pl.*

интенси́вный (-тен-) [14; -вен, -вна] intense, *(a. econ.)* intensive

интерва́л *m* [1] interval; *typ.* space

интервью́ (-тєг-) *n* [*indecl.*], **брать, взять ~, ~и́ровать** (-тєг-) [7] *(im)pf.* interview

интере́с *m* [1] interest (**к** Д in; **име́ть ~ для** P be of/to; **в ~ах** P in the/of); use; **~ный** [14; -сен, -сна] interesting; *о вне́шности* handsome, attractive; **~но, кто э́то сказа́л?** I wonder who said this?; **~ова́ть** [7], ⟨за-⟩ be[-come]) interest(ed), take an interest (T in)

интерна́т *m* [1]: **шко́ла-~** boarding school

интернациона́льный [14; -лен, -льна] international

интерпрета́ция *f* [7] interpretation

интерфе́йс *m* [1] *comput.* interface

интерье́р *m* [1] *art* interior

инти́мн|ость *f* [8] intimacy; **~ый** [14;

-мен, -мна] intimate

интона́ция *f* [7] intonation

интри́г|а *f* [5] intrigue; **~а́н** *m* [1] intriguer; **~а́нка** *f* [5; *g/pl.:* -нок] intrigante; **~ова́ть** [7], ⟨за-⟩ intrigue

интуи́|тивный [14; -вен, -вна] intuitive; **~ция** *f* [7] intuition

интури́ст *m* [1] foreign tourist

инфа́ркт *m* [1] infarction

инфе́кция *f* [7] infection

инфля́ция *f* [7] inflation

информ|а́ция *f* [7] information; **~и́ровать** [7] *(im)pf.*, ⟨про-⟩ inform

инциде́нт *m* [1] *mst. mil., pol.* incident

ипподро́м *m* [1] racetrack (course)

и́рис[1] *m* [1] *bot.* iris

ири́с[2] *m* [1], **~ка** *f* [5; *g/pl.:* -сок] toffee

ирла́нд|ец *m* [1; -дца] Irishman; **~ка** *f* [5; *g/pl.:* -док] Irishwoman; **~ский** [16] Irish

иро́н|изи́ровать [7] speak ironically (about **над** Т); **~и́ческий** [16] ironic(al); **~ия** *f* [7] irony

иск *m* [1] *law* suit, action

иска|жа́ть [1], ⟨~зи́ть⟩ [15 *e.*; -ажу́, -ази́шь; -ажённый] distort, twist; misrepresent; **~же́ние** *n* [12] distortion

иска́ть [3], ⟨по-⟩ (B) look for; (*mst.* P) seek

исключ|а́ть [1], ⟨~и́ть⟩ [15 *e.*; -чу, -чи́шь; -чённый] exclude, leave out; *из шко́лы* expel; **~а́я** (P) except(ing); **~ено́** ruled out; **~е́ние** *n* [12] exclusion; expulsion; exception (**за** T with the; **в ви́де** P as an); **~и́тельный** [14; -лен, -льна] exceptional; **~и́тельная ме́ра наказа́ния** capital punishment; *coll.* excellent; *adv. a.* solely, only; **~и́ть** → **~а́ть**

иско́мый [14] sought-after, looked-for

иско́нный [14] primordial

ископа́ем|ый [14] (*a. fig. su. n*) fossilized; *pl. su.* minerals; **поле́зные ~ые** mineral resources

искорен|я́ть [28], ⟨~и́ть⟩ [13] eradicate, extirpate

и́скоса askance; sideways; **взгляд ~** sidelong glance

и́скра *f* [5] spark(le); flash; **~ наде́жды** glimmer of hope

и́скренн|ий [15; -ренен, -ренна, -е/о,

-и/ы] sincere, frank, candid; **~e Ваш** yours sincerely; **~ость** f [8] sincerity, frankness

искри́стый [14 *sh.*] spark(l)ing; **~иться** [13] sparkle, scintillate

искуп|а́ть [1], ⟨~и́ть⟩ (B) atone for; make up for; **~ле́ние** n [12] atonement

искуси́ть → искуша́ть

искус|ный [14; -сен, -сна] skil(l)ful; expert; skilled; **~ственный** [14 *sh.*] artificial; *зубы и т. д.* false; *жемчуг и т. д.* imitation; **~ство** n [9] fine arts; *мастерство́* skill, trade, craft

иску|ша́ть [1], ⟨~си́ть⟩ [15 *e.*; -ушу́, -уси́шь] tempt; **~ша́ть судьбу́** tempt fate; **~ше́ние** n [12] temptation; **подда́ться ~ше́нию** yield to temptation; **~шённый** [14 *sh.*] experienced

исла́м m [1] Islam

испа́н|ец m [1; -нца], **~ка** f [5; *g/pl.*: -нок] Spaniard; **~ский** [16] Spanish

испар|е́ние n [12] evaporation; *pl. a.* vapo(u)r(s); **~я́ть** [28], ⟨~и́ть⟩ [13] evaporate (*v/i.* **-ся**, *a. fig.*)

испепеля́ть [28], ⟨~пели́ть⟩ [13] *lit.* burn to ashes; **~пеля́ющий взгляд** annihilating look; **~щря́ть** [28], ⟨~щри́ть⟩ [13] mottle, spot (with), cover all over (with)

испи́с|ывать [1], ⟨~а́ть⟩ [3] write on, cover with writing; *тетрадь* fill (up); **~ан** full of notes, *etc.*

испове́доваться [7] (*im*)*pf.* confess (**пе́ред** T to a p.; **в** П *s.th.*)

и́споведь f [8] confession (*eccl.* [*prp.*: **на** В/П to/at] *a. fig.*)

и́спод|воль *coll.* gradually; **~ло́бья** (*недове́рчиво*) distrustfully; (*нахму́рившись*) frowningly; **~тишка́** *coll.* in an underhand way

испоко́н: **~ ве́ку (веко́в) → и́здавна**

исполи́н m [1] giant; **~ский** [16] gigantic

исполн|е́ние n [12] execution; fulfil(l)-ment, performance; *обязанности* discharge; **~и́мый** [14 *sh.*] realizable; practicable; **~и́тель** m [4] executor; *thea.*, *mus.* performer; *law* bailiff; **соста́в ~и́телей** *thea.* cast; **~и́тельный** [14] executive; [-лен, -льна] efficient and reliable; **~я́ть** [28], ⟨~ить⟩[13] carry out, ex-

ecute; *долг* fulfil(l), do; *обещание* keep; *thea.*, *mus.* perform; **-ся** come true; *лет* be: **ей ~илось пять лет** she is five; *прошло* pass (since [**с тех пор**] **как**)

испо́льзова|ние n [12] use, utilization; **~ть** [7] (*im*)*pf.* use, utilize

испо́р|тить → по́ртить; **~ченный** [14 *sh.*] spoilt; (*тж. ребёнок*) broken; *о челове́ке* depraved

исправи́тельно-трудово́й [1]: **~и́тельно-трудова́я коло́ния** *approx.* reformatory; **~ле́ние** n [12] correction; repair; *человека* reform; **~ля́ть** [28], ⟨~ить⟩ [14] correct; improve; reform; repair; **-ся** reform

испра́вн|ость f [8] good (working) order; **в ~ости** = **~ый** [14; -вен, -вна] intact, in good working order

испражн|е́ние n [12] *med.* defecation; *pl.* f(a)eces; **~я́ться** [28], ⟨~и́ться⟩ [13] defecate

испу́г m [1] fright; **~а́ть → пуга́ть**

испус|ка́ть [1], ⟨~ти́ть⟩ [15] *звуки* utter; *запах* emit; **~ти́ть дух** give up the ghost

испыт|а́ние n [12] test, trial; (*a. fig.*) ordeal; examination (**на** П at); **~анный** [14] tried; **~а́тельный** [14] test; *срок* probational; **~у́ющий** [17] *взгляд* searching; **~ывать** [1], ⟨~а́ть⟩ [1] try (*a. fig.*), test; (*подвергнуться*) experience, undergo; *боль и т. д.* feel

иссле́до|вание n [12] investigation, research; *geogr.* exploration; *med.* examination; *chem.* analysis; *научное* treatise, paper, essay (**по** Д on); **~ватель** m [4] research worker, researcher; explorer; **~вательский** [16] research... (*a.* **нау́чно-~вательский**); **~вать** [7] (*im*)*pf.* investigate; explore; do research into; examine (*a. med.*); *chem.* analyze (*Brt.* -yse)

исступл|е́ние n [12] *о слушателях и т. д.* ecstasy, frenzy; (*ярость*) rage; **~ённый** [14] frantic

исс|яка́ть [1], ⟨~я́кнуть⟩ [21] *v/i.* dry (*v/i.* up); *fig. a.* exhaust, wear out (*v/i.* o.s. *or* become ...)

ист|ека́ть [1], ⟨~е́чь⟩ [26] *время* elapse; *срок* expire, become due; **~ека́ть кро́вью** bleed to death; **~е́кший** [17] past, last

истéр|ика f [5] hysterics *pl.*; **~ический** [16], **~ичный** [14; -чен, -чна] hysterical; **~ия** f [7] hysteria

истéц m [1; -тца́] plaintiff; *в бракоразводном процессе* petitioner

истечéни|е n [12] *срока* expiration; *времени* lapse; **по ~и** (P) at the end of

истéчь → **истека́ть**

и́стин|а f [5] truth; **изби́тая ~а** truism; **~ный** [14; -инен, -инна] true, genuine; *правда* plain

истл|ева́ть [1], ⟨**~éть**⟩ [8] rot, decay; *об углях* die away

исто́к m [1] source (*a. fig.*)

истолк|ова́ние n [12] interpretation; commentary; **~о́вывать** [1], ⟨**~ова́ть**⟩ [7] interpret, expound

истóм|а m [5] languor; **~и́ться** [14 *e.*; -млю́сь, -ми́шься] (be[come]) tire(d), weary (-ied)

истопта́ть [3] *pf.* trample; *обувь* wear out

истóр|ик m [1] historian; **~и́ческий** [16] historical; *событие и т. д.* historic; **~ия** f [7] history; *рассказ* story; *coll.* event, affair, thing; **вéчная ~ия!** the same old story!; **~ия болéзни** case history

источ|а́ть [1], ⟨**~и́ть**⟩ [16 *e.*; -чу́, -чи́шь] give off, impart; *запах* emit; **~ник** [1] spring; (*a. fig.*) source

истощ|а́ть [1], ⟨**~и́ть**⟩ [16 *e.*; -щу́, -щи́шь; -щённый] (**-ся** be[come]) exhaust(ed); *запасы* use(d) up; *ресурсы* deplete; **~ённый** [14 *sh.*] *человек* emaciated

истра́чивать [1] → **тра́тить**

истреб|и́тель m [4] destroyer; *ae.* fighter plane; **~и́тельный** [14] *война* de-

structive; fighter...; **~и́ть** → **~ля́ть**; **~лéние** n [12] destruction; *тараканов и т. д.* extermination; **~ля́ть** [28], ⟨**~и́ть**⟩ [14 *e.*; -блю́, -би́шь; -блённый] destroy, annihilate; exterminate

и́стый [14] true, genuine

истяза́|ние n [12], **~ть** [1] torture

исхо́д m [1] end, outcome, result; *Bibl.* Exodus; **быть на ~е** be coming to an end; *о продуктах и т. д.* be running short of; **~и́ть** [15] (*из* P) come, emanate (from); (*происходить*) originate; (*основываться*) proceed (from); **~ный** [14] initial; **~ное положéние** (**~ная тóчка**) point of departure

исхуда́лый [14] emaciated, thin

исцара́пать [1] *pf.* scratch (all over)

исцелéние n [12] healing; (*выздоровлéние*) recovery; **~я́ть** [28], ⟨**~и́ть**⟩ [13] heal, cure; **-ся** recover

исчеза́ть [1], ⟨**~нуть**⟩ [21] disappear, vanish; **~новéние** n [12] disappearance; **~нуть** → **~ать**

исчéрп|ывать, ⟨**~ать**⟩ [1] exhaust, use up; *вопрос и т. д.* settle; **~ывающий** exhaustive

исчисл|éние n [12] calculation; calculus; **~я́ть** [28], ⟨**~ить**⟩ [13] calculate

ита́к thus, so; well, then, now

италья́н|ец m [1; -нца], **~ка** f [5; *g/pl.:* -нок], **~ский** [16] Italian

итóг m [1] sum, total; result; **в ~е** in the end; *подвести* sum up; **~о** (-'vo) altogether; in all; total

их → **они́**, (*a. possessive adj.*) their(s)

ишь *int. coll.* P (just) look!; listen!

ище́йка f [5; *g/pl.:* -еек] bloodhound

ию́|ль m [4] July; **~нь** m [4] June

Й

йог m [1] yogi; **~а** yoga

йод m [1] iodine; **~ный** [14]; **~ный рас-** **тво́р** tincture of iodine

йо́|та f [5]: **ни на ~ту** not a jot

К

к, ко (Д) to, toward(s); *о времени тж.* by; for; **~ тому́ же** besides

-ка *coll.* (*after vb.*) just, will you

каба́к *m* [1 *e.*] *hist.* tavern *fig. coll.* hubbub and disorder

кабала́ *f* [5] *hist.* debt-slavery; *fig.* bondage

каба́н *m* [1 *e.*] (*a.* wild) boar

кабачо́к *m* [1; *g/pl.:* -чко́в] vegetable marrow

ка́бель *m* [4] cable

каби́н|а *f* [5] cabin, booth; *ae.* cockpit; *водителя* cab; **~ét** *m* [1] study, office; *med.* (consulting) room; *pol.* cabinet

каблу́к *m* [1 *e.*] heel (*of shoe*); **быть под ~о́м** *fig.* be under s.o.'s thumb

кабота́ж *m* [1] coastal trade

кавале́р *m* [1] bearer of an order; *old use* boyfriend; *в танце* partner

кавале|ри́йский [16] cavalry…; **~ри́ст** *m* cavalryman; **~рия** *f* [7] cavalry

ка́верзный *coll.* [14] tricky

кавка́з|ец *m* [1; -зца] Caucasian; **~ский** [16] Caucasian

кавы́чк|и *f/pl.* [5; *gen.:* -чек] quotation marks; **в ~ах** *fig. coll.* socalled

ка́дка *f* [5; *g/pl.:* -док] tub, vat

ка́дмий *m* [3] cadmium

кадр *m* [1] *cine.* frame, still; close-up

ка́др|овый [14] *mil.* regular; *рабочий* skilled; **~ы** *pl.* skilled workers; experienced personnel

кады́к *m* [1 *e.*] Adam's apple

каждодне́вный [14] daily

ка́ждый [14] every, each; *su.* everybody, everyone

ка́ж|ется, ~ущийся, → *каза́ться*

каза́к *m* [1 *e.*; *pl. a.* 1] Cossack

каза́рма *f* [5] *mil.* barracks *pl.*

каза́|ться [3], ⟨по-⟩ (Т) seem, appear, look; **мне ка́жется** (**~лось**), **что …** it seems (seemed) to me that; **он, ка́жется, прав** he seems to be right; *тж.* apparently; **ка́жущийся** seeming;

~лось бы one would think; it would seem

каза́х *m* [1], **~ский** [16] Kazak(h)

каза́|цкий [16], **~чий** [18] Cossack('s)…

каза́шка *f* [5; *g/pl.:* -шек] Kazak(h) woman

каз|ённый [14] *подход и т. д.* formal; bureaucratic; *банальный* commonplace; **на ~ённый счёт** at public expense; **~на́** *f* [5] treasury, exchequer; **~наче́й** *m* [3] treasurer

казн|и́ть [13] (*im*)*pf.* execute, put to death; *impf. fig.* **~и́ть себя́, -ся** torment o.s. with remorse; **~ь** *f* [8] execution

кайма́ *f* [5; *g/pl.:* каём] border; hem

как how; as; like; what; since; *coll.* when, if; (+ *su., adv.*) very (much), awfully; (+ *pf., vb.*) suddenly; **я ви́дела, как он шёл …** I saw him going …; **~ бу́дто, ~ бы** as if, as it were; **~ бы мне** (+ *inf.*) how am I to …; **~ ни** however; **~ же!** sure!; **~ (же) так?** you don't say !; **~ …, так и …** both … and …; **~ когда́** *etc.* that depends; **~ не** (+ *inf.*) of course …; **~мо́жно скоре́е** (**лу́чше**) as soon as (in the best way) possible

какао *n* [*indecl.*] cocoa

ка́к-нибудь somehow (or other); anyhow; sometime

како́в [-ва́, -о́] how; what; what sort of; (such) as; **~! **just look (at him)!; **~о́?** what do you say?; **~о́й** [1] which

како́й [16] what, which; *тж.* how; such as; *coll.* any; that; **ещё ~!** and what … (*su.*)**!**; **како́е там!** not at all!; **~-либо, ~-нибудь** any, some; *coll.* no more than, (only) about **~-то** some, a

ка́к-то *adv.* somehow; somewhat; *coll.* (*тж.* **~ раз**) once, one day

каламбу́р *m* [1] pun

каланча́ *f* [5; *g/pl.:* -че́й] watchtower; *fig. coll. о человеке* beanpole

кала́ч *m* [1 *e.*] small (*padlock-shaped*)

white loaf; **тёртый** ~ *fig. coll.* cunning, fellow

кале́ка *m/f* [5] cripple

календа́рь *m* [4 *e.*] calendar

калёный [14] red-hot; *орехи* roasted

кале́чить [16], ⟨ис-⟩ cripple, maim

кали́бр *m* [1] caliber (-bre); *tech.* gauge

ка́лий *m* [3] potassium

кали́на *f* [5] snowball tree

кали́тка *f* [5; *g/pl.*: -ток] wicket-gate

кали́ть [13] **1.** ⟨на-, рас-⟩ heat *орехи*; roast; **2.** ⟨за-⟩ *tech.* temper

кало́рия *f* [7] calorie

ка́лька *f* [5; *g/pl.*: -лек] tracing paper; *fig. ling.* loan translation, calque

калькуля́тор *m* [1] calculator; **-я́ция** *f* [7] calculation

кальсо́ны *f/pl.* [5] long underpants

ка́льций *m* [3] calcium

ка́мбала *f* [5] flounder

камен|е́ть [8], ⟨о-⟩ turn (in)to stone, petrify; **-и́стый** [14 *sh.*] stony; **-ноу́гольный** [14]: **-ноу́гольный бассе́йн** coalfield; **-ный** [14] stone...; *fig.* stony; *соль* rock; **-ный у́голь** coal; **-оло́мня** *f* [6; *g/pl.*: -мен] quarry; **-щик** *m* [1] bricklayer; **-ь** *m* [4; -мня; *from g/pl. e.*] stone; rock; *fig.* weight; **ка́мнем** like a stone; **-ь преткнове́ния** stumbling block

ка́мер|а *f* [5] *тюремная*; cell; *tech.* chamber; *phot.* camera; *mot.* inner tube; **-а хране́ния** left luggage office; **-ный** [14] *mus.* chamber...

ками́н *m* [1] fireplace

камо́рка *f* [5; *g/pl.*: -рок] closet, small room

кампа́ния *f* [7] *mil., pol.* campaign

камфара́ *f* [5] camphor

камы́ш *m* [1 *e.*], **-о́вый** [14] reed

кана́ва *f* [5] ditch; *сточная* gutter

кана́д|ец *m* [1; -дца], **-ка** *f* [5; *g/pl.*: -ок], **-ский** [16] Canadian

кана́л *m* [1] canal; *radio, TV, fig.* channel; **-иза́ция** *f* [7] *городская* sewerage

канаре́йка *f* [5; *g/pl.*: -еек] canary

кана́т *m* [1], **-ный** [14] rope; cable

канва́ *f* [5] canvas; *fig.* basis; outline

кандида́т *m* [1] candidate; kandidat (*in former USSR, holder of postgraduate degree before doctorate*); **-у́ра** *f* [5] candidature

кани́кулы *f/pl.* [5] vacation, *Brt. a.* holidays (**на** П, **в** В during)

кани́те́ль *coll. f* [8] tedious and drawn-out procedure

канона́да *f* [5] cannonade

кано́э *n* [*indecl.*] canoe

кант *m* [1] edging, piping

кану́н *m* [1] eve

ка́нуть [20] *pf.*: **как в во́ду** disappear without trace; **~ в ве́чность (в Ле́ту)** sink into oblivion

канцеля́р|ия *f* [7] office; **-ский** [16] office...; **-ские това́ры** stationery

ка́нцлер *m* [1] chancellor

ка́п|ать [1 & 2], *once* ⟨-нуть⟩ [20] drip, drop, trickle; *дождь* fall; **-елька** [5; *g/pl.*: -лек] droplet; *sg. coll.* bit, grain

капита́л *m* [1] *fin.* capital; *акционе́рный* stock; *оборо́тный* working capital; **-и́зм** *m* [1] capitalism; **-и́ст** *m* [1] capitalist; **-исти́ческий** [16] capitalist(ic); **-овложе́ние** *n* [12] investment; **-ьный** [14] fundamental, main; **-ьный ремо́нт** major repairs

капита́н *m* [1] *naut., mil., sport* captain; *торго́вого су́дна* skipper

капитул|и́ровать [7] (*im*)*pf.* capitulate; **-я́ция** *f* [7] capitulation

капка́н *m* [1] trap (*a. fig.*)

ка́пл|я *f* [6; *g/pl.*: -пель] drop; *sg. coll.* bit, grain; **-ями** drops by; **как две -и воды́** as like as two peas

капо́т *m* [1] *mot.* hood, *Brt.* bonnet

капри́з *m* [1] whim, caprice; **-ничать** *coll.* [1] be capricious; *о ребёнке* play up; **-ный** [14; -зен, -зна] capricious, whimsical; wil(l)ful

ка́псула *f* [5] capsule

капу́ста *f* [5] cabbage; **ки́слая** ~ sauerkraut; **цветна́я** ~ cauliflower

капюшо́н *m* [1] hood

ка́ра *f* [5] punishment

караби́н *m* [1] carbine

кара́бкаться [1], ⟨вс-⟩ climb

карава́й *m* [3] (big) loaf

карава́н *m* [1] caravan; *кораблей и т. д.* convoy

кара́емый [14 *sh.*] *law.* punishable

кара́куля *f* [6] *f* scribble

кара́куль *m* [4], **~евый** [14] astrakhan

караме́ль *f* [8] caramel(s)

каран|да́ш *m* [1 *e.*] pencil; **~ти́н** *m* [1] quarantine

карапу́з *coll. m* [1] chubby tot

кара́сь *m* [4 *e.*] crucian

карате́ *n* [*indecl.*] karate

кара́|тельный [14] punitive; **~ть** [1], ⟨по-⟩ punish

карау́л *m* [1] sentry, guard; **стоя́ть на ~е** be on guard; *int.* **~!** help!; **~ить** [13], ⟨по-⟩ guard, watch (*coll. ...*out, for); **~ьный** [14] sentry... (*a. su.*); **~ьное помеще́ние** guardroom

карбу́нкул *m* [1] carbuncle

карбюра́тор *m* [1] carburet(t)or

каре́л *m* [1] Karelian; **~ка** *f* [5; *g/pl.:* -ок] Karelian

каре́та *f* [5] *hist.* carriage, coach

ка́рий [15] (dark) brown

карикату́р|а *f* [5] caricature, cartoon; **~ный** [14] caricature...; **[-рен, -рна]** comic(al), funny

карка́с *m* [1] frame(work), skeleton

ка́рк|ать [1], *once* ⟨-нуть⟩ [20] croak (*coll., fig.*), caw

ка́рлик *m* [1] dwarf; **~овый** [14] dwarf...; dwarfish

карма́н *m* [1] pocket; **э́то мне не по ~у** *coll.* I can't afford that; **э́то бьёт по ~у** that costs a pretty penny; **держи́ ~ (ши́ре)** that's a vain hope; **она́ за сло́вом в ~е ле́зет** she has a ready tongue; **~ный** [14] pocket...; **~ный вор** pickpocket

карнава́л *m* [1] carnival

карни́з *m* [1] cornice; *для штор* curtain fixture

ка́рт|а *f* [5] map; *naut.* chart; (playing) card; **ста́вить (всё) на ~у** stake (have all one's eggs in one basket); **~а́вить** [14] mispronounce *Russ.* r or l (*esp. as uvular* r or u, v); **~ёжник** *m* [1] gambler (*at cards*)

карти́н|а *f* [5] picture (**на** П in); *cine.* movie; *art* painting; scene (*a. thea.*); **~ка** [5; *g/pl.:* -нок] (small) picture, illustration; **~ный** [14] picture...

карто́н *m* [1] cardboard; **~ка** [5; *g/pl.:* -нок] (cardboard) box

картоте́ка *f* [5] card index

карто́фель *m* [4] *collect.* potatoes *pl.*

ка́рточ|ка *f* [5; *g/pl.:* -чек] card; *coll.* photo; season ticket; **~ный** [14] card(s)...; **~ный до́мик** house of cards

карто́шка *coll. f* [5; *g/pl.:* -шек] potato(es)

карусе́ль *f* [8] merry-go-round

ка́рцер *m* [1] cell, lockup

карье́р *m* [1] full gallop (at T); **с ме́ста в ~** at once; **~а** *f* [5] career; **~и́ст** *m* [1] careerist

каса́|тельная *f* [14] *math.* tangent; **~ться** [1], ⟨косну́ться⟩ [20] touch (*a. fig.*); concern; *coll.* be about, deal *or* be concerned with; **де́ло ~ется = де́ло идёт о → идти́;** что **~ется ...** as regards, as to

ка́ска *f* [5; *g/pl.:* -сок] helmet

каска́д *m* [1] cascade

каспи́йский [16] Caspian

ка́сса *f* [5] pay desk *or* office; *rail.* **биле́тная ~** ticket window, *Brt.* booking office; *thea.* box office; *де́ньги* cash; *в магази́не* cash register; **сберега́тельная ~** savings bank

кассацио́нный [14] → апелляцио́нный; **~ия** *law* [7] cassation

кассе́т|а *f* [5], **~ный** [14] cassette

касси́р *m* [1], **~ша** *f* [5] cashier

ка́ста *f* [5] caste (*a. fig.*)

касто́ровый [14] castor

кастри́ровать [14] (*im*)*pf.* castrate

кастрю́ля *f* [6] saucepan; pot

катакли́зм *m* [1] cataclysm

катализа́тор *m* [1] catalyst

катало́г *m* [1] catalogue

ката́ние *n* [10] driving, riding, skating, *etc.* (→ **ката́ть[ся]**)

катастро́ф|а *f* [5] catastrophe; **~и́ческий** [16] catastrophic

ката́ть [1] roll (*a. tech.*); ⟨по-⟩ (take for a) drive, row, *etc.*; **-ся** (go for a) drive, ride (*a.* **ве́рхом**, *etc.*); row (**на ло́дке**); skate (**на конька́х**); sled(ge) (**на саня́х**), *etc.*; roll

катег|ори́ческий [16], **~ори́чный** [14; -чен, -чна] categorical; **~о́рия** *f* [7] category

ка́тер *m* [1; *pl.*, *etc. e.*] *naut.* cutter; **мо-**

то́рный ~ motor-launch

кати́ть [15], ⟨по-⟩ roll, wheel (*v/i* **-ся**; sweep; *слёзы* flow; *волны* roll; → **ката́ться**)

като́к *m* [1; -тка́] (skating) rink

католи́|к *m* [1], **~чка** *f* [5; *g/pl.*: -чек], **~ческий** [16] (Roman) Catholic

ка́тор|га *f* [5] penal servitude, hard labo(u)r; *fig.* very hard work, drudgery, **~жный** [14] hard, arduous

кату́шка *f* [5; *g/pl.*: -шек] spool; *el.* coil

каучу́к *m* [1] caoutchouc, india rubber

кафе́ *n* [*indecl.*] café

ка́федра *f* [5] *в церкви* pulpit; department (*of English, etc.*); *univ.* chair

ка́фель *m* [4] (Dutch) tile

кача́|лка *f* [5; *g/pl.*: -лок] rocking chair; **~ние** *n* [12] rocking; swing(ing); *нефти, воды* pumping; **~ть** [1] ⟨по-⟩, *once* ⟨качну́ть⟩ [20] rock; swing; shake (*a.* one's head **голово́й**), toss; *naut.* roll, pitch; (**-ся** *v/i.*; stagger, lurch); **2.** ⟨на-⟩ pump

каче́ли *f/pl.* [8] swing; seesaw

ка́честв|енный [14] qualitative; high-quality; **~о** *n* [9] quality; **~е** (Р) in one's capacity as, in the capacity of

ка́ч|ка *f* [5] rolling *naut.* (**бортова́я** or **боковая ~ка**); pitching (**килева́я ~ка**); **~ну́ть(ся)** → **~а́ть(ся)**

ка́ш|а *f* [5] **гре́чневая ~а** buckwheat gruel; **ма́нная ~а** semolina; **овся́ная ~а** porridge; **ри́совая ~а** boiled rice; *coll. fig.* mess, jumble; **завари́ть ~у** stir up trouble

кашало́т *m* [1] sperm whale

ка́ш|ель *m* [4; -шля], **~лять** [28], *once* ⟨~лянуть⟩ [20] cough

кашта́н *m* [1], **~овый** [14] chestnut

каю́та *f* [5] *naut.* cabin, stateroom

ка́яться [27], ⟨по-⟩ (**в** П) repent

квадра́т *m* [1], **~ный** [14] square

ква́к|ать [1], *once* ⟨~нуть⟩ [20] croak

квалифика́ция *f* [7] qualification(s); **~ци́рованный** [14] qualified, competent; *рабочий* skilled, trained

кварта́л *m* [1] quarter (= 3 months); block, *coll.* building (*betw.* 2 cross streets); **~ьный** [14] quarter(ly)

кварти́р|а *f* [5] apartment, *Brt.* flat;

двухко́мнатная ~а two-room apt./flat; **~áнт** *m* [1], **~áнтка** *f* [5; *g/pl.*: -ток] lodger; **~ный** [14] housing, house-…; **~ная пла́та** = **квартпла́та** *f* [5] rent; **~осъёмщик** *m* [1] tenant

квас *m* [1; -а, -у; *pl.* -ы] kvass (*Russ. drink*); **~и́ть** [15], ⟨за-⟩ sour

ква́шеный [14] sour, fermented

кве́рху up, upward(s)

квит|а́нция *f* [7] receipt; **бага́жная ~а́нция** (luggage) ticket; **~(ы)** *coll.* quits, even, square

кво́рум *m* [1] *parl.* quorum

кво́та *f* [5] quota, share

кедр *m* [1] cedar; **сиби́рский ~** Siberian pine; **~овый** [14]; **~овый оре́х** cedar nut

кекс *m* [1] cake

келе́йно privately; in camera

кельт *m* [1] Celt; **~ский** [16] Celtic

ке́лья *f* [6] *eccl.* cell

кем Т → **кто**

ке́мпинг *m* [1] campsite

кенгуру́ *m* [*indecl.*] kangaroo

ке́пка *f* [5; *g/pl.*: -ок] (peaked) cap

кера́м|ика *f* [5] ceramics; **~и́ческий** [16] ceramic

кероси́н *m* [1], **~овый** [14] kerosene

кета́ *f* [5] Siberian salmon

кефа́ль *f* [8] grey mullet

кефи́р *m* [1] kefir

киберне́тика *f* [5] cybernetics

кив|а́ть [1], *once* ⟨~ну́ть⟩ [20] nod; point (to **на** В); **~о́к** [1; -вка́] nod

кида́|ть(ся) [1], *once* ⟨ки́нуть(ся)⟩ [20] → **броса́ть(ся)**; **меня́ ~ет в жар и хо́лод** I'm hot and cold all over

ки́ев|ля́нин *m* [1; *pl.*: -я́не, -я́н], **~ля́нка** *f* [5; *g/pl.*: -нок] person from Kiev; **~ский** [16] Kiev…

кий *m* [3; ки́я; *pl.*: кии́, киёв] cue

кило́ *n* [*indecl.*] → **~гра́мм**; **~ва́тт** (-ча́с) *m* [1; *g/pl.*: -ток] kilowatt(-hour); **~гра́мм** *m* [1] kilogram(me); **~ме́тр** *m* [1] kilometer (*Brt.* -tre)

киль *m* [4] keel; **~ва́тер** (-ter-) *m* [1] wake

ки́лька *f* [5; *g/pl.*: -лек] sprat

кинемато́гр|аф *m* [1], **~а́фия** *f* [7] cinematography

кинеско́п *m* [1] television tube

кинжа́л *m* [1] dagger
кино́ *n* [*indecl.*] movie, motion picture; *Brt.* the pictures, cinema (**в** В/П to/at); *coll.* screen, film; **~актёр** *m* [1] screen (*or* film) actor; **~актри́са** *f* [5] screen (*or* film) actress; **~журна́л** *m* [1] newsreel; **~звезда́** *coll.* *f* [5; *pl.* -звёзды] filmstar; **~карти́на** *f* [5] film; **~ле́нта** *f* [5] reel, film (copy); **~опера́тор** *m* [1] cameraman; **~плёнка** *f* [5; *g/pl.:* -нок] film (strip); **~режиссёр** *m* [1] film director; **~сеа́нс** *m* [1] show, performance; **~сту́дия** *f* [7] film studio; **~сцена́рий** *m* [3] scenario; **~съёмка** *f* [5; *g/pl.:* -мок] shooting (*of a film*), filming; **~теа́тр** *m* [1] movie theater, cinema; **~хро́ника** *f* [5] newsreel
ки́нуть(ся) → **кида́ть(ся)**
кио́ск *m* [1] kiosk, stand; **газе́тый ~** newsstand
ки́па *f* [5] pile, stack; *това́ров* bale, pack
кипари́с *m* [1] cypress
кипе́ние *n* [12] boiling; **то́чка ~ния** boiling point; **~ть** [10 *e.;* -плю́, -пи́шь], ⟨за-, вс-⟩ boil; *от возмуще́ния* seethe; be in full swing (*о рабо́те и т. д.*)
кипу́чий [17 *sh.*] *жизнь* busy, lively, vigorous, exuberant, vehement, seething; *де́ятельность* tireless
кипяти́льник *m* [1] boiler; **~и́ть** [15 *e.;* -ячу́, -яти́шь], ⟨вс-⟩ boil (up; *v/i.* **-ся**); *coll.* be(come) excited; **~о́к** *m* [1; -тка́] boiling (hot) water
кирги́з *m* [1], **~ский** [16] Kirghiz
кири́ллица *f* [5] Cyrillic alphabet
кирка́ *f* [5; *g/pl.:* -рок] pick(ax[e])
кирпи́ч *m* [1 *e.*], **~ный** [14] brick
кисе́ль *m* [4 *e.*] (kind of) blancmange
кисло́|ватый [14 *sh.*] sourish; **~оро́д** [1] oxygen; **~ота́** *f* [5; *pl. st.:* -о́ты] sourness, acidity; **~о́тный** [14] acid; **~ый** [14; -сен, -сла́, -о] sour, acid; **ки́снуть** [21], ⟨с-, про-⟩ turn sour; *coll. fig.* mope
ки́ст|очка *f* [5; *g/pl.:* -чек] brush; *dim. of* **~ь** [8; *from g/pl. e.*] brush; *виногра́да* cluster, bunch; *руки́* hand
кит *m* [1 *e.*] whale
кита́|ец *m* [1; -та́йца] Chinese; **~йский**

[16] Chinese; **~я́нка** *f* [5; *g/pl.:* -нок] Chinese
ки́тель *m* [4; *pl.* -ля́, *etc. e.*] *mil.* jacket
кичи́ться [16 *e.;* -чу́сь, -чи́шься] put on airs; *хва́статься* boast (of T); **~ли́вый** [14 *sh.*] haughty, conceited
кише́ть [кишит] teem, swarm (with T; *тж.* **кишмя́ ~**)
кише́|чник [1] bowels, intestines *pl.;* **~чный** [14] intestinal, enteric; **~ка́** *f* [5; *g/pl.:* -о́к] intestine (small **то́нкая**, large **то́лстая**), gut; *pl. coll.* bowels; *для воды́* hose
клавиату́ра *f* [5] keyboard (*тж. tech.*)
кла́виш *m* [1], **~а** *f* [5] *mus., tech.* key
клад *m* [1] treasure (*a. fig.*); **~бище** *n* [11] cemetery; **~ка** *f* [5] laying, (brick-, *stone*)work; **~ова́я** *f* [14] *в до́ме* pantry, larder; *stock- or* storeroom; **~овщи́к** *m* [1 *e.*] storekeeper
кла́ня|ться [28], ⟨поклони́ться⟩ [13; -оню́сь, -о́нишься] (Д) bow (to); *old use* приве́тствовать greet
кла́пан *m* [1] *tech.* valve; *на оде́жде* flap
класс *m* [1] class; *шко́лы* grade, *Brt.* form; classroom; **~ик** *m* [1] classic; **~ифици́ровать** [7] (*im*)*pf.* class(ify); **~и́ческий** [16] classic(al); **~ный** [14] class; *coll.* classy; **~овый** [14] *pol. soc.* class
класть [кладу́, -дёшь; клал] **1.** ⟨положи́ть⟩ [16] (**в, на,** *etc.,* В) put, lay (down, on, *etc.*); *в банк* deposit; **в осно́ву** (в В take as basis); *положи́ть* **коне́ц** put an end (to Д); *положи́ть* **под сукно́** shelve; **2.** ⟨сложи́ть⟩ [16] *ору́жие* lay (down)
клева́ть [6 *e.;* клюю́, клюёшь], *once* ⟨клю́нуть⟩ [20] peck, pick; *о ры́бе* bite; **~ но́сом** *coll.* nod
кле́вер *m* [1] clover, trefoil
клевет|а́ *f* [5], **~а́ть** [3; -вещу́, -ве́щешь], ⟨о-⟩ *v/t.,* ⟨на-⟩ (**на** В) slander; **~ни́к** *m* [1 *e.*] slanderer; **~ни́ческий** [16] slanderous
кле́нка *f* [5] oilcloth
кле́|ить [13], ⟨с-⟩ glue, paste; **-ся** stick; *coll.* work, get on *or* along; **~й** *m* [3; на клею́] glue, paste; **~йкий** [16; кле́ек, кле́йка] sticky, adhesive

клейм|и́ть [14 *e.*; -млю́, -ми́шь], ⟨за-⟩ brand; *fig. a.* stigmatize; **∠ó** *n* [9; *pl. st.*] brand; *fig.* stigma, stain; **фабри́чное ∠ó** trademark

клён *m* [1] maple

клепа́ть [1], ⟨за-⟩ rivet

клёпка *f* [5; *g/pl.:* -пок] riveting

кле́т|ка *f* [5; *g/pl.:* -ток] cage; square, check; *biol.* (**в ∠очка**) cell; **в ∠(оч)ку** check(er)ed; *Brt.* chequered; **грудна́я ∠ка** thorax; **∠ча́тка** *f* [5] cellulose; **∠чатый** [14] checkered (*Brt.* chequered)

кле|шня́ *f* [6; *g/pl.:* -не́й] claw; **∠щ** *m* [1; *g/pl.:* -ще́й] tick; **∠щи** *f/pl.* [5; *gen.:* -ще́й, *etc. e.*] pincers

клие́нт *m* [1] client; **∠у́ра** *f* [5] *collect.* clientele

кли́зма *f* [5] enema

кли́ка *f* [5] clique

кли́макс *m* [1] climacteric, menopause

кли́мат *m* [1] climate; **∠и́ческий** [16] climatic

клин *m* [3; *pl.:* кли́нья, -ьев] wedge; gusset; **∠ом** (*борода́ и т. д.*) pointed; **свет не ∠ом сошёлся** the world is large; there is always a way out

кли́ника *f* [5] clinic

клино́к *m* [1; -нка́] blade

кли́ренс *m* [1] *tech.* clearance

кли́ринг *m* [1] *fin.* clearing

клич *m* [1] call; **сг|∠ка** *f* [5; *g/pl.:* -чек] *живо́тного* name; (*про́звище*) nickname

клише́ *n* [*indecl.*] cliché (*a. fig.*)

клок *m* [1 *e.*; -о́чья -о́чья, -ьев; клоки́, -ко́в] *во́лос* tuft; shred, rag, tatter

клокота́ть [3] seethe (*тж. fig.*), bubble

клон|и́ть [13; -оню́, -о́нишь] ⟨на-, с-⟩ bend, bow; *fig.* incline; drive (*or* aim) at (**к** Д); **меня́ ∠ит ко сну** I am nodding off; (**-ся** *v/i.*; *a.* decline; approach)

клоп *m* [1 *e.*] bedbug

кло́ун *m* [1] clown

клочо́к *m* [1; -чка́] *бума́ги* scrap; *земли́* patch

клуб[1] *m* [1; *pl. e.*] *ды́ма* cloud, puff; **∠о́к**; **∠**[2] *m* [1] club(house); **∠ень** *m* [4; -бня́] tuber, bulb; **∠и́ться** [14 *e.*; 3rd *p. only*] *дым* wreathe, puff (up); *пыль* whirl

клубни́ка *f* [5] (*cultivated*) strawberry, -ries *pl.*

клубо́к *m* [1; -бка́] *ше́рсти* ball; *противоре́чий* tangle

клу́мба *f* [5] (flower) bed

клык *m* [1 *e.*] *моржа́* tusk; *челове́ка* canine (tooth); *живо́тного* fang

клюв *m* [1] beak, bill

клю́ква *f* [5] cranberry, -ries *pl.*; **разве́систая ∼** *mythology* s.th. improbable, nonsensical

клю́нуть → клева́ть

ключ *m* [1 *e.*] key (*a. fig.*, clue); *tech.* [**га́ечный ∼**] = wrench, spanner; *mus.* clef; (*родни́к*) spring; **∠и́ца** *f* [5] clavicle, collarbone

клю́шка *f* [5; *g/pl.:* -шек] (golf) club; (hockey) stick

клянчить *coll.* [16] beg for

кляп *m* [1] gag

кля|сть [-яну́, -нёшь, -ял, -а́, -о] → **проклина́ть**; **-ся** ⟨покля́сться⟩ swear (**в** П s.th.; Т by); **∠тва** *f* [5] oath; **дать ∠тву** (*or* **∠твенное обеща́ние**) take an oath, swear

кля́уза *f* [5] intrigue; cavil; slander

кля́ча *f* [5] *pej.* (*horse*) jade

кни́г|а *f* [5] book; **∠опеча́тание** *n* [12] (book-)printing, typography; **∠охрани́лище** *n* [11] book depository; library

кни́ж|ка *f* [5; *g/pl.:* -жек] book(let); *записна́я* notebook; *чек* book (*Brt.* cheque)book; **сберега́тельная ∠ка** savings bank book; **∠ный** [14] book...; *о сло́ве* bookish; **∠о́нка** *f* [5; *g/pl.:* -нок] trashy book

кни́зу down, downward(s)

кно́пк|а *f* [5; *g/pl.:* -пок] thumbtack, *Brt.* drawing pin; (*push*) button; (snap), fastener; **нажа́ть на все ∠и** *fig.* pull all wires

кнут *m* [1 *e.*] whip

кня|ги́ня *f* [6] princess (*prince's consort*); **∠жна́** *f* [5; *g/pl.:* -жо́н]) princess (*prince's unmarried daughter*); **∠зь** *m* [4; *pl.:* -зья́, -зе́й] prince; **вели́кий ∠зь** grand duke

коа|лицио́нный [14] coalition...; **∠ли́ция** *f* [7] coalition

кобе́ль *m* [4 *e.*] (male) dog

кобура́ *f* [5] holster

кобы́ла *f* [5] mare; *sport* horse

ко́ваный [14] wrought (*iron.*)

кова́р|ный [14; -рен, -рна] crafty, guileful, insidious; **~ство** *n* [9] craftiness, guile, wile

кова́ть [7 *e.*; кую, куёшь] **1.** ⟨вы-⟩ forge; **2.** ⟨под-⟩ shoe (*horse*)

ковёр *m* [1; -врá] carpet, rug

коверка́ть [1], ⟨ис-⟩ distort; *слова* mispronounce; *жизнь* spoil, ruin

коври́жка *f* [5; *g/pl.:* -жек] gingerbread

ковче́г *m* [1]: **Нóев ~** Noah's Ark

ковш *m* [1 *e.*] scoop; *землечерпалки* bucket

ковы́ль *m* [4 *e.*] feather grass

ковыля́ть [28] hobble; *о ребёнке* toddle

ковыря́ть [28], ⟨по-⟩ pick, poke

когда́ when; while; as; *coll.* if; ever; sometimes; → **ни**; **~ как** it depends; **~либо**, **~нибудь** (at) some time (or other), one day; *interr.* ever; **~то** once, one day, sometime

ко́|готь *m* [-гтя; *from g/pl. e.*] claw

код *m* [1], **~и́ровать** [7], ⟨за-⟩ code

ко́е-где́ here and there, in some places; **~-кáк** anyhow, somehow; with (great) difficulty; **~-какóй** [16] some; any; **~-когдá** off and on; **~-ктó** [23] some(-body); **~-кудá** here and there, (in)to some place(s); somewhere; **~-чтó** [23] something; a little

ко́ж|а *f* [5; *pl. st.*] skin; *материал* leather; **из ~и (вон) лезть** *coll.* do one's utmost; **~а да ко́сти** skin and bone; **~аный** [14] leather…; **~ица** *f* [5] skin, peel; rind; (*a.* **~урá** *f* [5]); cuticle

коз|á *f* [5; *pl. st.*] (she-)goat; **~ёл** [1; -злá] (he-)goat; **~ёл отпуще́ния** scapegoat; **~ий** [18] goat…; **~лёнок** *m* [2] kid; **~лы** *f/pl.* [5; *gen.:* -зел] **для пилки** trestle

ко́зни *f/pl.* [8] intrigues, plots

коз|ырёк *m* [1; -рькá] peak (*of cap*); **~ырь** *m* [2; *from g/pl. e.*] trump; **~ыря́ть** *coll.* [28], *once* ⟨~ырну́ть⟩ [20] (*хвастаться*) boast

ко́йка *f* [5; *g/pl.:* ко́ек] bed, bunkbed;

naut. berth

коке́т|ка *f* [5; *g/pl.:* -ток] coquette; **~ливый** [14 *sh.*] coquettish; **~ничать** [1] flirt (with); **~ство** *n* [9] coquetry

коклю́ш *m* [1] whooping cough

ко́кон *m* [1] cocoon

кок|о́с *m* [1] coco; *плод* coconut; **~о́совый** [14] coco(nut)…

кокс *m* [1] coke

кол 1. [1 *e.*; ко́лья, -ев] stake, picket; **2.** [*pl.* 1 *e.*] **ни ~á ни дворá** neither house nor home

колбаса́ *f* [5; *pl. st.:* -áсы] sausage

колго́тки *f* [5; *g/pl.:* -ток] *pl.* panty hose, *Brt.* tights *pl.*

колдо́бина *f* [5] rut, pothole

колд|ова́ть [7] practice (-ise) witchcraft; conjure; **~овство́** *n* [9] magic, sorcery; **~у́н** *m* [1 *e.*] sorcerer, wizard; **~у́нья** *f* [6] sorceress, witch, enchantress

колеб|а́ние *n* [12] oscillation; vibration; *fig.* (*сомнение*) hesitation; (*a. comm.*) fluctuation; **~а́ть** [2 *st.:* -éблю, *etc.*; -éбли(те); -éбля], ⟨по-⟩, *once* ⟨~ну́ть⟩ [20] shake (*a. fig.*); **~ся** shake; (*a. comm.*) fluctuate; waver, hesitate; oscillate, vibrate

коле́н|о *n* [*sg.:* 9; *pl.:* 4] knee; **стать на ~и** kneel; **по ~и** knee-deep; **ему́ мо́ре по ~о** he doesn't care a damn; [*pl.:* -нья, -ев; *pl. a.* 9] *tech.* bend, crank; **~чатый** [14] *tech.* **вал** crank (shaft)

колес|и́ть *coll.* [15 *e.*; -ешу́, -еси́шь] travel about, rove; **~ни́ца** *f* [5] chariot; **~ó** *n* [9; *pl. st.:* -лёса] wheel; **кружи́ться, как бе́лка в ~é** run round in circles; **вставля́ть кому́-нибудь па́лки в колёса** put a spoke in a p.'s wheel

коле|я́ *f* [6; *g/pl.:* -лей] rut, (*a. rail*) track (*both a. fig.*); **вы́битый из ~и́** unsettled

коли́бри *m/f* [*indecl.*] hummingbird

ко́лики *f/pl.* [5] colic

коли́честв|енный [14] quantitative; *gr.* cardinal (*number*); **~о** *n* [9] quantity; number; amount

ко́лка *f* [5] splitting, chopping

ко́лк|ий [16; ко́лок, колка́, -о] prickly; *fig.* biting; **~ость** *f* [8] sharpness

колле́г|а *m/f* [5] colleague; **~ия** *f* [7] board, collegium; **~ия адвока́тов** the

Bar

коллекти́в m [1] group, body; **~иза́ция** f [7] hist. collectivization; **~ный** [14] collective, joint

коллек|ционе́р m [1] collector; **~ция** [7] collection

коло́да f [5] block; карт pack, deck; **~ец** [1; -дца] well; **~ка** f [5; g/pl.: -док] last; tech. (brake) shoe

ко́лок|ол m [1; pl.: -ла́, etc. e.] bell; **~ольня** f [6; g/pl.: -лен] bell tower, belfry; **~ольчик** m [1] (little) bell; bot. bluebell

коло́ния f [7] colony

коло́н|ка f [5; g/pl.: -нок] typ. column; (apparatus) water heater, Brt. geyser; a. dim. of **~на** f [5] column (arch. a. pillar)

колори́т m [1] colo(u)ring; colo(u)r; **~ный** [14; -тен, -тна] colo(u)rful, picturesque

ко́лос m [pl.: -ло́сья, -ьев], (agric.) ear, spike; **~и́ться** [15 e.; 3ʳᵈ p. only] form ears

колосса́льный [14; -лен, льна] colossal, fantastic

колоти́ть [15] knock (в В, по Д at, on)

коло́ть [17] **1.** ⟨рас-⟩ split, cleave; орехи crack; **2.** ⟨на-⟩ ⟨y-⟩, once ⟨кольну́ть⟩ [20] prick; fig. coll. taunt; **4.** ⟨за-⟩ stab; животное kill, slaughter (animals); impers. have a stitch in one's side

колпа́к m [1 e.] cap; shade; bell glass

колхо́з m [1] collective farm, kolkhoz; **~ный** [14] kolkhoz…; **~ник** m [1], **~ница** f [5] collective farmer

колыбе́ль f [8] cradle; **~ный** [14]: **~ная (пе́сня)** f lullaby

колых|а́ть [3 st.: -ы́шу, etc., or 1], ⟨вс-⟩, once ⟨-ну́ть⟩ [20] sway, swing; листья stir; пламя flicker; **-ся** v/i.

ко́лышек m [1; -шка] peg

кольну́ть → **коло́ть** 3. & impers.

коль|цево́й [14] ring…; circular; **~цо́** n [9; pl. st., gen.: коле́ц] ring; circle; обруча́льное **~цо́** wedding ring; hist. **~чу́га** f [5] shirt of mail

колю́ч|ий [17 sh.] thorny, prickly; проволока barbed; fig. → **ко́лкий**; **~ка** f

[5; g/pl.: -чек] thorn, prickle; barb

коля́ска f [5; g/pl.: -сок] мотоцикла side-car; де́тская baby carriage, Brt. pram; инвали́дная wheelchair

ком m [1; pl.: ко́мья, -ьев] lump, clod

кома́нда f [5] command, order; naut. crew; sport team; **пожа́рная ~** fire brigade

команди́р m [1] commander; **~ова́ть** [7] (im)pf., a. ⟨от-⟩ send (on a mission); **~о́вка** f [5; g/pl.: -вок] business trip; она́ в **~о́вке** she is away on business

кома́нд|ный [14] command(ing); **~ование** n [12] command; **~овать** [7] ⟨над⟩ T) command (a. [give] order[s], ⟨с-⟩); coll. order about **~ующий** [17] (T) commander

кома́р m [1 e.] mosquito, gnat

комба́йн m [1] agric. combine

комбин|а́т m [1] industrial complex; group of complementary enterprises; **~а́т бытово́го обслу́живания** multiple (consumer-)services establishment; **~а́ция** f [7] combination; econ. merger; **~и́ровать** [7], ⟨с-⟩ combine

коме́дия f [7] comedy; farce

коменда́|нт m [1] mil. commandant; superintendent; общежи́тия warden; **~нтский** [16]: **~нтский час** curfew; **~ту́ра** f [7] commandant's office

коме́та f [5] comet

ком|и́зм m [1] comic side; **~ик** m [1] comedian, comic (actor)

комисса́р m [1] commissar; commissioner; **~иа́т** m [1] commissariat

коми́|ссио́нный [14] commission (a. comm.; pl. su. = sum); **~ссия** f [7] commission (a. comm.), committee; **~те́т** m [1] committee

коми́ч|еский [16], **~ный** [14; -чен, -чна] comic(al), funny

ко́мкать [1], ⟨ис-, с-⟩ crumple

комменти́|арий m [3] comment(ary); **~а́тор** m [1] commentator; **~́ровать** [7] (im)pf. comment (on)

коммер|са́нт m [1] merchant; businessman; **~ческий** [16] commercial

комму́н|а f [5] commune; **~а́льный** [14] communal; municipal; **~а́льная кварти́ра** (coll. **~а́лка**) communal flat;

~и́зм *m* [1] communism; ~ика́ция *f* [7] communication (*pl. mil.*); ~и́ст *m* [1], ~и́стка *f* [5; *g/pl.*: -ток], ~исти́ческий [14] communist

коммута́тор *m* [1] *el.* switchboard

ко́мнат|а *f* [5] room; ~ный [14] room...; *bot.* house...

комо́к *m* [1; -мка́] lump, clod

компа́н|ия *f* [7] company (*a. comm*); во-ди́ть ~ию с (T) associate with; ~ьо́н *m* [1] *comm.* partner; companion

компа́ртия *f* [7] Communist Party

ко́мпас *m* [1] compass

компенс|а́ция *f* [7] compensation; ~и́ровать [7] (*im*)*pf.* compensate

компете́н|тный [14; -тен, -тна] competent; ~ция [7] competence; scope

ко́мплек|с *m* [1], ~сный [14] complex; ~т *m* [1] (complete) set; ~тный [14], ~това́ть [7], ⟨у-⟩ complete

комплиме́нт *m* [1] compliment

компози́тор *m* [1] *mus.* composer

компости́ровать [7], ⟨про-⟩ punch

компо́т *m* [1] compote, stewed fruit

компре́сс *m* [1] compress

компром|ети́ровать [7], ⟨с-⟩, ~и́сс *m* [1] compromise (*v/i. a.* идти́ на ~и́сс)

компью́тер *m* [1] computer

комсомо́л *m* [1] *hist.* Komsomol (Young Communist League); ~ец *m* [1; -льца], ~ка *f* [5; *g/pl.*: -лок], ~ьский [16] Komsomol

комфо́рт *m* [1] comfort, convenience; ~а́бельный [14; -лен, -льна] comfortable, convenient

конве́йер *m* [1] (belt) conveyer; assembly line

конве́нция *f* [7] convention, agreement

конве́рсия *f* [7] *econ.* conversion

конве́рт *m* [1] envelope

конв|ои́р *m* [1], ~ои́ровать [7], ~о́й *m* [3], ~о́йный [14] convoy, escort

конгре́сс *m* [1] congress

конденс|а́тор (-дε-) *m* [1] *napa* condenser; *el.* capacitor; ~и́ровать [7] (*im*)*pf.* condense; evaporate (*milk*)

конди́тер|ская *f* [16]: ~ский магази́н confectioner's shop; ~ские изде́лия *pl.* confectionery

кондиционе́р *m* [1] air conditioner

конево́дство *n* [9] horse-breeding

конёк *m* [1; -нька́] skate; *coll.* hobby

кон|е́ц *m* [1; -нца́] end; close; point; *naut.* rope; **без ~ца́** endless(ly); **в ~е́ц (до ~ца́)** completely; **в ~це́ (P)** at the end of; **в ~це́ ~цо́в** at long last; **в оди́н ~е́ц** one way; **в о́ба ~ца́** there and back; **на худо́й ~е́ц** at (the) worst; **под ~е́ц** in the end; **тре́тий с ~ца́** last but two

коне́чно (-∫nə-) of course, certainly

коне́чности *f/pl.* [8] extremities

коне́чн|ый [14; -чен, -чна] *philos., math.* finite; final, terminal; *цель и т. д.* ultimate

конкре́тный [14; -тен, -тна] concrete, specific

конкур|е́нт *m* [1] competitor; rival; ~ентоспосо́бный [14; -бен, -бна] competitive; ~е́нция *coll. f* [7] competition; ~и́ровать [7] compete; ~с *m* [1] competition

ко́нн|ица *f* [5] *hist.* cavalry; ~ый [14] horse...; (of) cavalry

конопл|я́ *f* [6] hemp; ~я́ный [14] hempen

коносаме́нт *m* [1] bill of lading

консерв|ати́вный [14; -вен, -вна] conservative; ~ато́рия *f* [7] conservatory, *Brt.* school of music, conservatoire; ~и́ровать [7] (*im*)*pf. a.* ⟨за-⟩ conserve, preserve; can, *Brt.* tin; ~ный [14], ~ы *m/pl.* [1] canned (*Brt.* tinned) food

ко́нский [16] horse (*hair, etc.*)

консолида́ция *f* [7] consolidation

конспе́кт *m* [1] summary, abstract; synopsis; notes made at a lecture; ~и́ровать [7] make an abstract (of P); make notes at a lecture

конспир|ати́вный [14; -вен, -вна] secret; ~а́ция *f* [7], conspiracy

конст|ати́ровать [7] (*im*)*pf.* establish, ascertain; ~иту́ция *f* [7] constitution

констр|уи́ровать [7] (*im*)*pf. a.* ⟨с-⟩ design; ~укти́вный [14; -вен, -вна] constructive; ~у́ктор *m* [1] designer; constructor; ~у́кция *f* [7] design; construction, structure

ко́нсул *m* [1] consul; ~ьский [16] consular; ~ьство *n* [9] consulate; ~ьта́ция *f* [7] consultation; advice; **юриди́ческая консульта́ция** legal advice office;

~ти́ровать [7], ⟨про-⟩ advise; **-ся** consult (with **с** Т)

конта́кт m [1] contact; **~ный** [14] tech. contact…; [-тен, -тна] coll. sociable

контингéнт m [1] quota, contingent

континéнт m [1] continent

конто́ра f [5] office

контраба́нд|а f [5] contraband, smuggling; **занима́ться ~ой** smuggle; **~и́ст** m [1] smuggler

контр|аге́нт m [1] contractor; **~адмира́л** m [1] rear admiral

контра́кт m [1] contract

контра́льто n [9] contralto

контра́ст m [1], **~и́ровать** [7] contrast

контрата́ка f [5] counterattack

контрибу́ция f [7] contribution

контрол|ёр m [1] inspector (rail. a. ticket collector); **~и́ровать** [7], ⟨про-⟩ control, check; **~ь** m [4] control, checking; **~ьный** [14] control…, check…; **~ьная рабо́та** test (in school, etc.)

контр|разве́дка f [5] counterespionage, counterintelligence; **~револю́ция** f [7] counterrevolution

конту́з|ить [15] pf.; **~ия** f [7] contusion; shell-shock

ко́нтур m [1] contour, outline

конура́ f [5] kennel

ко́нус m [1] cone; **~ообра́зный** [14; -зен, -зна] conic(al)

конфедера|ти́вный [14] confederative; **~ция** f [7] confederation

конфере́нция f [7] conference (at **на** П)

конфе́та f [5] candy, Brt. sweet(s)

конфиде́нциа́льный [14; -лен, -льна] confidential; **~скова́ть** [7] (im)pf. confiscate

конфли́кт m [1] conflict

конфу́з|ить [15], ⟨с-⟩ (**-ся** be[come]) embarrass(ed), confuse(d); **~ливый** coll. [14 sh.] bashful, shy

конц|ентра́т m [1] concentrated product; **~ентрацио́нный** [14] coll., → **~ла́герь**; **~ентри́ровать** [7], ⟨с-⟩ concentrate (**-ся** v/i.); **~е́рт** m [1] concert (**на** П at); mus. concerto; **~ла́герь** m [4] concentration camp

конч|а́ть [1], ⟨~и́ть⟩ [16] finish, end, (**-ся** v/i.); univ., etc. graduate from; **-ся срок**

terminate, expire; **~ено!** enough!; **~ик** m [1] tip; point; **~и́на** f [5] decease

коньюнкту́р|а f [5] comm. state of the market; **~щик** m [1] timeserver

конь m [4 e.; nom/pl. st.] horse; poet. steed; chess knight; **~ки́** m/pl.[6] (**ро́ликовые** roller) skates; **~кобе́жец** m [1; -жца] skater; **~кобе́жный** [14] skating

конья́к m [1 e.; part.g.: -у́] cognac

ко́н|юх m [1] groom; **~юшня** f [6; g/pl.: -шен] stable

коопер|ати́в m [1] cooperative (store, society); **~а́ция** f [7] cooperation; **потреби́тельская ~а́ция** consumers' society

координа́ты f/pl.[5] math. coordinates; coll. particulars for making contact (address, telephone and fax numbers etc.)

координи́ровать [7] (im)pf. coordinate

копа́ть [1], ⟨вы́-⟩ dig (up); **-ся** impf. dig, root; **в веща́х** rummage (about); **в саду́ и т. д.** putter about; (медленно де́лать) dawdle

копе́йка f [5; g/pl.: -éек] kopeck

копи́лка f [5; g/pl.: -лок] money box

копир|ова́льный [14]: **~ова́льная бума́га** f (coll. **~ка**) carbon paper; **~овать** [7], ⟨с-⟩ copy; **~о́вщик** m [1] copyist

копи́ть [14], ⟨на-⟩ accumulate, save; store up

ко́п|ия f [7] copy (vb. **снять ~ию с** Р); **~на́** f [5; pl.: ко́пны, -пён, -пна́м] stack; **во́лос** shock

ко́поть f [8] lampblack; soot

копоши́ться [16 e.; -шу́сь, -ши́шься], ⟨за-⟩ coll. о лю́дях putter about, mess around

копти́ть [15 e.; -пчу́, -пти́шь, -пчённый], ⟨за-⟩ smoke

копы́то n [9] hoof

копьё n [10; pl. st.] spear; lance

кора́ f [5] bark; земли́ и т. д. crust

кораб|лекруше́ние n [12] shipwreck; **~лестрое́ние** n [12] shipbuilding; **~ль** m [4 e.] ship

кора́лл m [1] coral; **~овый** [14] coral…, coralline

Кора́н m [1] Koran

коре́|ец *m* [1; -е́йца], **~йский** [16] Korean

корен|а́стый [14 *sh.*] thickset, stocky; **~и́ться** [13] be rooted in; **~но́й** [14] native; (*основной*) fundamental; *зуб* molar; **~в ко́рне** radically; **пусти́ть ко́рни** take root; **вы́рвать с ко́рнем** pull up by the roots; **~я́** *n/pl.* [*gen.*: -ье́в] roots

корешо́к *m* [1; -шка́] rootlet; *книги* spine; *квитанции* stub, counterfoil

коре́|нка *f* [5; *g/pl.*: -нок] Korean

корзи́н|(к)а *f* [5 (*g/pl.*: -нок)] basket

коридо́р *m* [1] corridor, passage

кори́нка *f* [5; *no pl.*] currant(s)

корифе́й *m* [3] *fig.* luminary

кори́ца *f* [5] cinnamon

кори́чневый [14] brown

ко́рка *f* [5; *g/pl.*: -рок] *хлеба и т. д.* crust; *кожура* rind, peel

корм *m* [1; *pl.*: -ма́ *etc. e.*] fodder

корма́ *f* [5] *naut.* stern

корми́|лец *m* [1; льца] breadwinner; **~ть** [14], ⟨на-, по-⟩ feed; **~ть гру́дью** nurse; ⟨про-⟩ *fig.* maintain, support; **~ся** live on (T); **~ле́ние** *n* [12] feeding; nursing

корнепло́ды *m/pl.* [1] root crops

коро́б|ить [14], ⟨по-⟩ warp (*a. fig.*); jar upon, grate upon; **~ка** *f* [5; *g/pl.*: -бок] box, case

коро́в|а *f* [5] cow; **до́йная ~а** milch cow; **~ий** [18] cow...; **~ка** *f* [5; *g/pl.*: -вок]: *бо́жья ~ка* ladybird; **~ник** *m* [1] cowshed

короле́в|а *f* [5] queen; **~ский** [16] royal, regal; **~ство** *n* [9] kingdom

коро́ль *m* [4 *e.*] king

коромы́сло *n* [9; *g/pl.*: -сел] yoke; (*a. scale*) beam

коро́н|а *f* [5] crown; **~а́ция** coronation; **~ка** *f* [5; *g/pl.*: -нок] (*of tooth*) crown; **~ова́ние** [12] coronation; **~ова́ть** [7] (*im*)*pf.* crown

корот|а́ть *coll.* [1], ⟨с-⟩ while away; **~кий** [16; ко́роток, -тка́, ко́ротко́, ко́ро́тки; *compr.*: коро́че] short, brief; **на ~кой ноге́** on close terms; *коро́че (говоря́)* in a word, in short, in brief; **~ко и я́сно** (quite) plainly; **ру́ки ~ки!** just try!

ко́рпус *m* [1] body; [*pl.*: -са́, *etc. c.*] frame, case; building; (*a. mil., dipl.*) corps; *судна* hull

корректи́в *f* [5] correction; **~и́ровать** [7], ⟨про-⟩ correct; *typ.* proofread; **~ный** [14; -тен, -тна] correct, proper; **~ор** *m* [1] proofreader; **~у́ра** *f* [5] proof(-reading)

корреспонд|е́нт *m* [1] correspondent; **~е́нция** *f* [7] correspondence

корсе́т *m* [1] corset, *Brt. a.* stays *pl.*

корт *m* [1] (tennis) court

корте́ж *f* [5; *g/pl.*: -жей] cortège; motorcade

ко́ртик *m* [1] dagger

ко́рточк|и *f/pl.* [5; *gen.*: -чек]: *сесть (сиде́ть) на ~и (~ах)* squat

корчева́|ние *n* [12] rooting out; **~ть** [7], ⟨вы-, рас-⟩ root out

ко́рчить [16], ⟨с-⟩ *impers.* (**-ся**) writhe (**от бо́ли** with pain); convulse; (*no pf.*) *coll. рожи* make faces; (*a. ~ из себя́*) pose as

ко́ршун *m* [1] kite

коры́ст|ный [14; -тен, -тна] selfish, self-interested; *a.* = **~олюби́вый** [14 *sh.*] greedy, mercenary; **~олю́бие** *n* [12] self-interest, cupidity; **~ь** *f*[8] gain, profit; cupidity

коры́то *n* [9] through

корь *f* [8] measles

ко́рюшка *f* [5; *g/pl.*: -шек] smelt

коря́|вый [14 *sh.*] knotty, gnarled; rugged, rough; *почерк* crooked; *речь* clumsy

коса́ *f* [5; *ac/sg.*: ко́су; *pl. st.*] **1.** plait, braid; **2.** [*ac/sg. a.* косу́] scythe; spit (*of land*)

ко́свенный [14] oblique, indirect (*a. gr.*); *law.* circumstantial

коси́|лка *f* [5; *g/pl.*: -лок] mower machine; **~ть**, ⟨с-⟩ **1.** [15; кошу́, ко́сишь] mow; **2.** [15 *e.*; кошу́, коси́шь] squint; **-ся**, ⟨по-⟩ *v/i.*; *a.* look askance (**на** B at); **~чка** *f* [5; *g/pl.*: -чек] *dim.* → *коса́ 1*

косма́тый [14 *sh.*] shaggy

косме́|тика *f* [5] cosmetics *pl.*: **~ти́ческий** [16] cosmetic; **~и́ческий** [16] cosmic; *корабль* spaceship, spaceкраft; ~она́вт *m* [1] cosmonaut, astronaut

ко́сн|ость *f* [8] sluggishness, inertness, stagnation; ~у́ться [14] → каса́ться; ~ый [14; -сен, -сна] sluggish, inert, stagnant

косо|гла́зый [14 *sh.*] cross- or squint-eyed; ~и́й [14; кос, -а́, -о] slanting, oblique; sloping; *coll. улыбка* wry; ~ла́пый [14 *sh.*] pigeon-toed; *coll.* неуклюжий clumsy

костёр *m* [1; -тра́] (camp)fire, bonfire

кост|и́стый [14 *sh.*] bony; ~ля́вый [14 *sh.*] scrawny, raw-boned; *рыба*; ~очка *f* [5; *g/pl.*: -чек] bone; *bot.* pit, stone; **перемыва́ть ~очки** gossip (Д about)

кость|иль [4 *e.*] crutch

кост|ь *f* [8; в -ти́; *from g/pl. e.*] bone; **промо́кнуть до ~ей** get soaked to the skin

костю́м *m* [1] suit; dress; costume

костя|к *m* [1 *e.*] skeleton; *fig.* backbone; ~но́й [14] bone...

косу́ля *f* [6] roe deer

косы́нка *f* [5; *g/pl.*: -нок] kerchief

коса́к *m* [1 *e.*] (door)post; *птиц* flock; *рыбы* school

кот *m* [1 *e.*] tomcat; → *a.* ко́тик; **купи́ть ~а́ в мешке́** buy a pig in a poke; **~ напла́кал** *coll.* very little

кот|ёл *m* [1; -тла́] boiler, cauldron; ~ело́к *m* [1; -лка́] kettle, pot; *mil.* mess tin; *шляпа* bowler

котёнок *m* [2] kitten

ко́тик *m* [1] *dim.* → кот; fur seal; *mex* sealskin; *adj.*: ~овый [14]

котле́та *f* [5] cutlet; burger; rissole chop

котлови́на *f* [5] *geogr.* hollow, basin

кото́р|ый [14] which; who; that; what; many a; one; ~ый раз how many times; ~ый час? what time is it?; **в ~ом часу́?** (at) what time?

котте́дж *m* [1; *g/pl.* -ей] small detached house

ко́фе *m* [*indecl.*] coffee; **раствори́мый ~** instant coffee; ~ва́рка *f* [5; *g/pl.*: -рок] coffeemaker; ~йник *m* [1] coffeepot; ~мо́лка *f* [5; *g/pl.*: -лок] coffee mill; ~йный [14] coffee...

ко́фт|а *f* [5] (woman's) jacket; (**вя́заная ~а**) jersey, cardigan; ~очка *f* [5; *g/pl.*:

-чек] blouse

коча́н *m* [1 *e.*] head (*of cabbage*)

кочев|а́ть [7] be a nomad; wander, roam; move from place to place; ~ник *m* [1] nomad

коченеть [8], ⟨за-, о-⟩ grow numb (**от** P with), stiffen

кочерга́ *f* [5; *g/pl.*: -рёг] poker

ко́чка *f* [5; *g/pl.*: -ек] hummock; tussock

коша́чий [18] cat('s); feline

кошелёк *m* [1; -лька́] purse

ко́шка *f* [5; *g/pl.*: -шек] cat

кошма́р *m* [1] nightmare; ~ный [14; -рен, -рна] nightmarish; horrible, awful

кощу́нств|енный [14 *sh.*] blasphemous; ~о *n* [9] blasphemy; ~овать [7] blaspheme

коэффицие́нт *m* [1] *math., el.* coefficient; factor; **~ поле́зного де́йствия** efficiency

краб *m* [1] *zo.* crab

кра́деный [14] stolen (*goods n su.*)

краеуго́льный [14] basic; *fig. камень* corner(stone)

кра́жа *f* [5] theft; **~ со взло́мом** burglary

край *m* [3; с кра́ю, в краю́; *pl.*: -ая́, -аёв, *etc. e.*] edge; (b)rim; brink (*a. fig.*: = edge); end; fringe, border, outskirt; region, land, country; ~ний [15] outermost, (*a. fig.*) utmost, extreme; (*a.* utterly, most, very, badly (**~не**); **в ~нем слу́чае** as a last resort; in case of emergency; ~ность *f* [8] extreme; (*о положении*) extremity; **до ~ности = ~не**; **впада́ть в (доходи́ть до) ~ности** go to extremes

крамо́ла *f* [5] *obs.* sedition

кран *m* [1] *tech.* tap; (stop)cock; crane

кра́пать [1 *or* 2 *st.*] drip, trickle

крапи́в|а *f* [5] (stinging) nettle; ~ница *f* [5] nettle rash

кра́пинка *f* [5; *g/pl.*: -нок] speck, spot

крас|а́ *f* [5] → ~ота́; ~а́вец *m* [1; -вца] handsome man; ~а́вица *f* [5] beautiful woman; ~и́вый [14 *sh.*] beautiful; handsome; *a. слова и т. д. iro.* pretty

крас|и́тель *m* [4] dye(stuff); ~ить [15], ⟨(п)о-, вы́-, рас-⟩ paint, colo(u)r, dye; *coll.* ⟨на-⟩ paint, makeup; ~ка *f* [5; *g/pl.*: -сок] colo(u)r, paint, dye

красне́ть [8], ⟨по-⟩ redden, grow *or* turn red; *от стыда́* blush; *impf.* be ashamed; (*a.* **-ся**) appear *or* show red

красно|арме́ец *m* [1; -ме́йца] *hist.* Red Army man; **~ба́й** *m* [3] *coll.* phrasemaker; rhetorician; glib talker; **~ва́тый** [14 *sh.*] reddish; **~речи́вый** [14 *sh.*] eloquent; **~ре́чие** *n* [12] eloquence; **~та́** *f* [5] redness; **~щёкий** [16 *sh.*] ruddy

красну́ха *f* [5] German measles

кра́с|ный [14; -сен, -сна́, -о] red (*a. fig.*); **~ная строка́** *f typ.* (*first line of*) new paragraph, new line; **~ная цена́** *f* outside price; **~ное словцо́** *n coll.* witticism; *проходи́ть* **~ной ни́тью** run through (*of motif, theme, etc.*)

красова́ться [7] stand out *or* impress because of beauty; *coll.* flaunt, show off

красота́ *f* [5; *pl. st.*: -со́ты] beauty

кра́сочный [14; -чен, -чна] colo(u)rful

красть [25 *pt. st.*; кра́денный], ⟨у-⟩ steal (**-ся** *v/i.*, *impf.*; *a.* prowl, slink)

кра́тер *m* [1] crater

кра́т|кий [16; -ток, -тка́, -о; *comp.*: кра́тче] short, brief, concise; *и ~ое* the letter й; → **коро́ткий**; **~овре́менный** [14; -енен, -енна] of short duration; (*преходящий*) transitory; **~осро́чный** [14; -чен, -чна] short; *ссуда и т. д.* shortterm; **~ость** *f* [8] brevity

кра́тный [14; -тен, -тна] divisible without remainder

крах *m* [1] failure, crash, ruin

крахма́л *m* [1], **~ить** [13], ⟨на-⟩ starch; **~ьный** [14] starch(ed)

кра́шеный [14] painted; dyed

креве́тка *f* [5; *g/pl.*: -ток] *zo.* shrimp

креди́т *m* [1] credit; *в* ~ on credit; **~ный** [14], **~овать** [7] (*im*)*pf.* credit; **~о́р** *m* [1] creditor; **~оспосо́бный** [14; -бен, -бна] creditworthy; solvent

кре́йс|ер *m* [1] cruiser; **~и́ровать** [7] cruise; ply

крем *m* [1] cream; ~ *для лица́* face cream; ~ *для о́буви* shoe polish

крем|ато́рий *m* [3] crematorium; **~а́ция** *f* [7] cremation; **~и́ровать** [7] cremate

кремл|ёвский [16], **2ь** *m* [4 *e.*] Kremlin

кре́мний [3] *chem.* silicon

крен *m* [1] *naut.* list, heel; *ae.* bank

кре́ндель *m* [4 *from g/pl. e.*] pretzel

крени́ть [13], ⟨на-⟩ list (**-ся** *v/i.*)

креп *m* [1] crepe, crape

креп|и́ть [14 *e.*; -плю́, -пи́шь] fix, secure; *fig.* strengthen; **-ся** hold out, bear up; **~кий** [16; -пок, -пка́, -о; *comp.*: кре́пче] strong; sturdy; *здоро́вье* sound, robust; **~кий оре́шек** hard nut to crack; **~ко** *a.* strongly, firmly; **~нуть** [21], ⟨о-⟩ grow strong(er)

крепост|но́й [14] *hist. su.* serf; **~но́е пра́во** *n* serfdom; **~ь** *f* [8; *from g/pl. e.*] fortress; → **кре́пкий** strength; firmness, *etc.*

кре́сло *n* [9; *g/pl.*: -сел] armchair

крест *m* [1 *e.*] cross (*a. fig.*); **~-на́-** crosswise; **~и́ны** *f/pl.* [5] baptism, christening; **~и́ть** [15; -щённый] (*im*)*pf.*, ⟨о-⟩ baptize, christen; ⟨пере-⟩ (**-ся** *o.s.*); **~ник** *m* [1] godson; **~ница** *f* [5] goddaughter; **~ный** [14] **1.** (of the) cross; **2.** **~ный (оте́ц)** godfather; **~ная (мать)** godmother

крестья́н|ин *m* [1; *pl.*: -я́не, -я́н] peasant; **~ка** *f* [5; *g/pl.*: -нок] peasant woman; **~ский** [16] farm(er['s]), peasant...; country...; **~ство** *n* [9] *collect.* peasants; peasantry

крети́н *m* [1] cretin; *fig. coll.* idiot

креще́ние *n* [12] baptism, christening; ♀ Epiphany

крив|а́я *f* [14] *math.* curve; **~изна́** *f* [5] crookedness, curvature; **~и́ть** [14 *e.*; -влю́, -ви́шь, -влённый], ⟨по-, с-⟩ (**-ся** be[come]) crook(ed), (bent); ⟨с-⟩ (**-ся**) make a wry face; **~и́ть душо́й** act against one's conscience *or* convictions; **~ля́нье** *n* [12] affectation; **~ля́ться** [18] (make) grimace(s); mince; **~о́й** [14; крив, -а́, -о] crooked (*a. fig*), wry; curve(d); ℙ one-eyed; **~оно́гий** [16 *sh.*] bandy-legged, bowlegged; **~ото́лки** *coll. m/pl.* [1] rumo(u)rs, gossip

кри́зис *m* [1] crisis

крик *m* [1] cry, shout; outcry; *после́дний ~ мо́ды* the latest word in fashion; **~ли́вый** [14 *sh.*] shrill; clamorous; loud; **~нуть** → **крича́ть**

кри|мина́льный [14] criminal; **~ста́лл**

m [1] crystal; **~ста́льный** [14; -лен, -льна] crystalline; *fig.* crystal-clear

крите́рий *m* [3] criterion

кри́ти|к *m* [1] critic; **~ка** *f* [5] criticism; *lit., art* critique, review; **~кова́ть** [7] criticize; **~ческий** [16]; **~чный** [14; -чен, -чна] critical

крича́ть [4 *e*.; -чу́, -чи́шь], ⟨за-⟩, *once* ⟨кри́кнуть⟩ [20] cry (out), shout (**на** В at); scream

кров *m* [1] roof; shelter

крова́|вый [14 *sh*.] bloody; **~ть** *f* [8] bed

кро́вельщик *m* [1] roofer

кровено́сный [14] blood (*vessel*)

кро́вля *f* [6; *g/pl*.: -вель] roof(ing)

кро́вный [14] (*adv.* by) blood; (*жизненно важный*) vital

крово|жа́дный [14; -ден, -дна] bloodthirsty; **~излия́ние** *n* [12] *med.* h(a)emorrhage; **~обраще́ние** *n* [12] circulation of the blood; **~пи́йца** *m/f* [5] bloodsucker; **~подтёк** *m* [1] bruise; **~проли́тие** *n* [12] bloodshed; **~проли́тный** [14; -тен, -тна] → **крова́вый**; **~смеше́ние** *n* [12] incest; **~тече́ние** *n* [12] bleeding; → **~излия́ние**; **~точи́ть** [-чи́т] bleed

кров|ь *f* [8; -ви] blood (*a. fig*.); **~яно́й** [14] blood...

кро|и́ть [13; кро́енный], ⟨вы́-, с-⟩ cut (out); **~йка** *f* [5; *g/pl*.: кро́ек] cutting (out)

крокоди́л *m* [1] crocodile

кро́лик *m* [1] rabbit

кро́ме (P) except, besides (*a.* **~ того́**), apart (*or* aside) from; but

кромса́ть [1], ⟨ис-⟩ hack

кро́на *f* [5] crown (*of tree*); (*unit of currency*) crown, krone, krona

кропи́ть [14 *e*.; -плю́, -пи́шь, -плённый], ⟨о-⟩ sprinkle

кропотли́вый [14 *sh*.] laborious, toilsome; painstaking, assiduous

кроссво́рд *m* [1] crossword puzzle

кроссо́вки *f* [5; *g/pl*.: -вок] running shoes; *Brt.* trainers

крот *m* [1 *e*.] *zo.* mole

кро́ткий [16; -ток, -тка́, -о; *compr*.: кро́тче] gentle, meek

кро́|ха *f* [5; *ac/sg*.: кро́ху; *from dat/pl. e*.] crumb; *о количестве* bit; **~хотный** *coll.* [14; -тен, -тна], **~шечный** *coll.*

[14] tiny; **~ши́ть** [16], ⟨на-, по-, из-⟩ crumb(le); (*мелко руби́ть*) chop; **~шка** *f* [5; *g/pl*.: -шек] crumb; *coll.* little one; *ни* **~шки** not a bit

круг *m* [1; в, на -у́; *pl. e*.] circle (*a. fig.*); *интересов и т. д.* sphere, range; **~ова́тый** [14 *sh*.] roundish; **~лоли́цый** [14 *sh*.] chubbyfaced; **~лый** [14; кругл, -á, -о] round; *coll. дура́к* perfect; **~лая су́мма** round sum; **~лые су́тки** day and night; **~ово́й** [14] circular; *порука* mutual; **~оворо́т** *m* [1] circulation; *событий* succession; **~озо́р** *m* [1] prospect; range of interests; **~óм** round; *вокруг* around, (round) about; **~осве́тный** [14] round-the-world

кру́ж|ево *n* [9; *pl. e*.; *g/pl*.: кру́жев] lace; **~и́ть** [16 & 16 *e*.; кружу́, кру́жишь], ⟨за-, вс-⟩ turn (round), whirl; circle; spin; *плутать* stray about; (*-ся v/i.*); **вскружи́ть го́лову** (Д) turn s.o.'s head; **голова́ ~ится** (*у* P) feel giddy; **~ка** *f* [5; *g/pl*.: -жек] mug; tankard; *пива* glass

кру́жный *coll.* [14] traffic circle, *Brt.* roundabout

кружо́к *m* [1; -жка́] (small) circle; *lit. pol.* study group

круп *m* [1] *лошади* croup

круп|á *f* [5] groats *pl.*; *fig. снег* sleet; **~и́нка** *f* [5; *g/pl*.: -нок] grain (*a. fig.* = **~и́ца** *f* [5])

кру́пный [14; -пен, -пна́, -о] big, large(-scale); great; (*выдаю́щийся*) outstanding; (*важный*) important, serious; *cine.* close (up); *fig.* **~ разгово́р** high words

крутизна́ *f* [5] steep(ness)

крути́ть [15], ⟨за-, с-⟩ twist; twirl; roll (up); turn; whirl; circle; P *impf.* be insincere *or* evasive; trick; *любо́вь* have a love affair (with)

круто́|й [14; крут, -á, -о; *compr*.: кру́че] steep, (*резкий*) sharp, abrupt; (*неожи́данный*) sudden; *яйцо́* hard (*a.* -boiled); *мера и т. д.* harsh; **~сть** *f* [8] harshness

круше́ние *n* [12] wreck; *надежд* ruin; collapse; *a.* rail. derailment

крыжо́вник *m* [1] gooseberry bush; *collect.* gooseberries крыл|а́тый [14 sh.] winged (a. fig.); ~ó n [9; pl.: кры́лья; -льев] wing (a. arch., ae., pol.); ~ьцо́ n [9; pl. кры́льца, -ле́ц, -льца́м] steps pl.; porch

кры́мский [16] Crimean

кры́са f [5] rat

крыть [22], ⟨по-⟩ cover, roof; кра́ской coat; в ка́ртах trump; -ся impf. (в П) lie or be in; be concealed

кры́ш|а f[5] roof; ~ка f[5; g/pl.:-шек] lid, cover; Р (Д p.'s) end

крюк m [1 e.; pl. a.; крю́чья, -ев] hook; coll. detour

крюч|кова́тый [14 sh.] hooked; ~кот-во́рство n [9] chicanery; pettifoggery; ~о́к m [1; -чка́] hook; ~о́к для вяза́-ния crochet hook

кряж m [1] mountain range; chain of hills

кря́к|ать [1], once ⟨~нуть⟩ [20] quack

кряхте́ть [11] groan, grunt

кста́ти to the point (or purpose); oppor-tune(ly), in the nick of time; apropos; besides, too, as well; incidentally, by the way

кто [23] who; ~...,~... some..., others...; ~ бы ни whoever; ~ бы то ни́ был who(so)ever it may be; ~ coll. = ~-либо, ~-нибудь, ~-то [23] anyone; someone

куб m [1] math. cube

ку́барем coll. head over heels

ку́б|ик m [1] (small) cube; игру́шка brick, block (toy); ~и́ческий [16] cubic

ку́бок m [1; -бка] goblet; приз cup

кубоме́тр m [1] cubic meter (-tre)

кувши́н m [1] jug; pitcher

кувши́нка f [5; g/pl.: -нок] water lily

кувырк|а́ться [1], once ⟨~ну́ться⟩ [20] somersault, tumble; ~о́м → ку́барем

куда́ where (... to); what ... for; coll. (a. ~ как[о́й], etc.) very, awfully, how; at all; by far, much; (a. + Д [& inf.]) how can ...; ~ни wherever; (a. ~тут, там) (that's impossible!, certainly not!, what an idea!, (esp. ~ тебе́) rats!; ~ ..., ~ ... to some places ..., to others ...; ~ вы (i. e. идёте)? where are you going?; хоть ~ P fine; couldn't be better; → ни = ~-либо, ~-нибудь, ~-то any-, somewhere

куда́хтать [3] cackle, cluck

куде́сник m [1] magician, sorcerer

ку́др|и f/pl. [-е́й, etc. e.] curls; ~я́вый [14 sh.] curly(-headed); де́рево bushy

кузне́ц m [1 e.] (black)smith; ~е́чик m [1] zo. grasshopper; ~и́ца f [5] smithy

ку́зов m [1; pl.: -ва́, etc. e.] body (of car, etc.)

кукаре́кать [1] crow

ку́киш P m [1] coll. (gesture of derision) fig, fico

ку́к|ла f [5; g/pl.:-кол] doll; ~олка f [5; g/pl.: -лок] 1. dim. → ~ла; 2. zo. chrys-alis; ~ольный [14] doll('s); ~ольный теа́тр puppet show

кукуру́з|а f [5] corn, Brt. maize; ~ный [14] corn...; ~ные хло́пья cornflakes

куку́шка f [5; g/pl.: -шек] cuckoo

кула́к m [1 e.] fist; hist. kulak (prosper-ous farmer or peasant)

кулёк m [1; -лька́] (paper) bag

кули́к m [1 e.] curlew; snipe

кулина́р|ия f[7] cookery; ~ный [14] cul-inary

кули́са f[5] thea. wing, side; за ~ми be-hind the scenes

кули́ч m [1 e.] Easter cake

куло́н m [1] pendant

кулуа́ры m/pl. [1] sg. not used lobbies

куль m [4 e.] sack, bag

культ m [1] cult; ~иви́ровать [7] culti-vate; ~у́ра f [5] culture; standard (зем-леде́лия of farming); зерновы́е ~у́ры cereals; ~у́рный [14; -рен, -рна] cultur-al; cultured, well-bred

культя́ f [7 e.] med. stump

кума́ч m [1 e.] red calico

куми́р m [1] idol

кумовство́ n [9] fig. favo(u)ritism; nep-otism

куни́ца f [5] marten

купа́|льный [14] bathing; ~льный костю́м bathing suit, Brt. bathing cos-tume; ~льщик m [1] bather; ~ть(ся) [1], ⟨вы́-, ис-⟩ (take a) bath; bathe

купе́ n [indecl.] rail. compartment

купе́ц m [1; -пца́] merchant; ~ческий [16] merchant('s); ~чество n [9] collect. merchants

купи́ть → **покупа́ть**
купле́т *m* [1] couplet, stanza; song
ку́пля *f* [6] purchase
ку́пол *m* [1; *pl.*: -ла] cupola, dome
ку́пчая *f* [14] *hist.* deed of purchase
купю́ра *f* [5] bill, banknote; *в тексте* cut, excision
курга́н *m* [1] burial mound, barrow
ку́р|ево *coll. n* [9] tobacco, cigarettes; **~е́ние** *n* [12] smoking; **~и́льщик** *m* [1] smoker
кури́ный [14] chicken…; hen's; *coll.* **па́мять** short; *med.* night (*слепота* blindness)
кури́|тельный [14] smoking; **~ть** [13; курю́, ку́ришь], ⟨по-, вы-⟩ smoke (**-ся** *v/i.*)
ку́рица *f* [5; *pl.*: ку́ры, *etc. st.*] hen; *cul.* chicken
курно́сый [14 *sh.*] snub-nosed
куро́к *m* [1; -рка́] cock (*of weapon*)
куропа́тка *f* [5; *g/pl.*: -ток] partridge
куро́рт *m* [1] health resort
курс *m* [1] course (*naut., ae., med., educ.*); **держа́ть ~ на** (B) head for; *a. univ.* year); *fin.* rate of exchange; *fig.* line, policy; **держа́ть (быть) в ~е** (P) keep (be) (well) posted on; **~а́нт** *m* [1] *mil.* cadet; **~и́в** *m* [1] *typ.* italics; **~и́ровать** [7] ply; **~о́р** *m* [1] *computer* cursor
ку́ртка *f* [5; *g/pl.*: -ток] jacket
курча́вый [14 *sh.*] curly(-headed)
курь|ёз [1] curious; amusing; **~ёр** *m* [1]

messenger; courier
куря́щий *m* [17] smoker
кус|а́ть [1], ⟨укуси́ть⟩ [15] bite (**-ся** *v/i., impf.*), sting; **~о́к** *m* [1; -ска́] piece, bit, morsel; scrap; *мы́ла* cake; *пирога́ и т. д.* slice; **на ~ки́** to pieces; **зараба́тывать на ~о́к хле́ба** earn one's bread and butter; **~о́чек** *m* [1; -чка] *dim.* → **~о́к**
куст *m* [1 *e.*] bush, shrub; **~а́рник** *m* [1] *collect.* bush(es), shrub(s)
куста́р|ный [14] handicraft…; hand(-made); *fig.* primitive, crude; **~ь** *m* [1 *e.*] craftsman
ку́тать(ся) [1], ⟨за-⟩ muffle *or* wrap o.s. (up, in)
кут|ёж *m* [1 *e.*], **~и́ть** [15] carouse
ку́х|ня *f* [6; *g/pl.*: ку́хонь] kitchen; *ру́сская и т. д.* cuisine, cookery; **~онный** [14] kitchen…
ку́цый [14 *sh.*] dock-tailed; short
ку́ч|а *f* [5] heap, pile; a lot of; **~ами** in heaps, in crowds; **вали́ть всё в одну́ ~у** lump everything together; **класть в ~у** pile up; **~ер** *m* [1; *pl.*: -ра, *etc. e.*] coachman; **~ка** *f* [5; *g/pl.*: -чек] *dim.* → **~а**; small group
куша́к *m* [1 *e.*] belt, girdle, sash
ку́ша|нье *n* [10] dish; food; **~ть** [1], ⟨по-⟩ eat (up ⟨с-⟩)
куше́тка *f* [5; *g/pl.*: -ток] couch
кюве́т *m* [1] drainage ditch

Л

лабири́нт *m* [1] labyrinth, maze
лабор|а́нт *m* [1], **~а́нтка** *f* [5; *g/pl.*: -ток] laboratory assistant; **~ато́рия** *f* [7] laboratory
ла́ва *f* [5] lava
лави́на *f* [5] avalanche
лави́ровать [7] *naut.* tack; (*fig.*) maneuver (-noeuvre)
лавр *m* [1] laurel; **~о́вый** [14] (of) laurel(s)
ла́гер|ь 1. [4; *pl.*: -ря́, *etc. e.*] camp (*a., pl.*:

-ри, *etc. st.*, *fig.*); **располага́ться (стоя́ть) ~ем** camp (out), be encamped; **~ный** [14] camp…
лад *m* [1; в ~у́; *pl. e.*]: (не) **в ~у́** (**~а́х**) → (не) **~ить; идти на ~** work (well), get on *or* along; **~ан** *m* [1] incense; **дыша́ть на ~ан** have one foot in the grave; **~ить** *coll.* [15], ⟨по-, с-⟩ get along *or* on (well), *pf. a.* make it up; (*справиться*) manage; **не ~ить** *a.* be at odds *or* variance; **-ся** *coll. impf.* → **идти́ на ~, ~ить; ~но**

coll. all right, O.K.; **~ный** [14; -ден, -дна́, -о] *coll.* fine, excellent

ладо́|нь *f* [8], Р *f* [5] palm; **как на ~ни** spread before the eyes; **бить в ~ши** clap (one's hands)

ладья́ *f* [5] *obs.* boat; *chess*: rook

лазе́|йка *f* [5; *g/pl*.: -е́ек] loophole; **~ить** [15] climb (*v/t.* **на** B); clamber

лазу́р|ный [14; -рен, -рна], **~ь** *f* [8] azure

лай *m* [3] bark(ing), yelp; **~ка** *f* [5; *g/pl*.: ла́ек] **1.** Eskimo dog; **2.** *кожа* kid; **~ковый** [14] kid...

лак *m* [1] varnish, lacquer; **~овый** [14] varnish(ed), lacquer(ed); *кожа* patent leather...

лака́ть [1], ⟨вы́-⟩ lap

лаке́й *m* [3] *fig.* flunk(e)y; **~ский** [16] *fig.* servile

лакирова́ть [7], ⟨от-⟩ lacquer, varnish

ла́ком|иться [14], ⟨по-⟩ (T) enjoy, relish (*a. fig.*), eat with delight; **~ка** *coll. m/f* [5] lover of dainties; **быть ~кой** *a.* have a sweet tooth; **~ство** *n* [9] dainty, delicacy; *pl.* sweetmeats; **~ый** [14 *sh.*] dainty, **~ый кусо́(че)к** *m* tidbit, *Brt.* titbit

лакони́ч|еский [16], **~ный** [14; -чен, -чна] laconic(al)

ла́мп|а *f* [5] lamp; **~а́да** *f* [5 (*g/pl*.:] lamp (*for icon*); **~овый** [14] lamp...; **~очка** *f* [5; *g/pl*.: -чек] bulb

ландша́фт *m* [1] landscape

ла́ндыш *m* [1] lily of the valley

лань *f* [8] fallow deer; hind, doe

ла́па *f* [5] paw; *fig.* clutch

лапша́ *f* [5] noodles *pl.*; noodle soup

ларёк *m* [1; -рька́] kiosk, stand

ласк|а́ *f* [5] caress; **~а́тельный** [14] endearing, pet; *a.* **~овый**, **~а́ть** [1], ⟨при-⟩ caress; pet, fondle; **~ся** endear o.s. (**к** Д to); *о собаке* fawn (*of dog*); **~овый** [14 *sh.*] affectionate, tender; caressing; *ветер* soft

ла́сточка *f* [5; *g/pl*.: -чек] swallow

лата́ть *coll.* [1], ⟨за-⟩ patch, mend

латви́йский [16] Latvian

лати́нский [16] Latin

лату́нь *f* [8] brass

ла́ты *f/pl.* [5] *hist.* armo(u)r

латы́нь *f* [8] Latin

латы́ш *m* [1 *e.*], **~ка** *f* [5; *g/pl*.: -шек] Lett;

~ский [16] Lettish

лауреа́т *m* [1] prizewinner

ла́цкан *m* [1] lapel

лачу́га *f* [5] hovel, shack

ла́ять [27], ⟨за-⟩ bark

лгать [лгу, лжёшь, лгут; лгал, -á, -о], ⟨со-⟩ lie, tell lies

лгун *m* [1 *e.*], **~ья** *f* [6] liar

лебёдка *f* [5; *g/pl*.: -док] winch

лебеди́|ный [14] swan...; **~дь** *m* [4; *from g/pl*.: *e.*] (*poet. a. f*) swan; **~зи́ть** *coll.* [15 *e.*; -бежу́, -бези́шь] fawn (**пе́ред** T upon)

лев *m* [1; льва́] lion; ♌ Leo

лев|ша́ *m/f* [5; *g/pl*.: -ше́й] left-hander; **~ый** [14] left (*a. fig.*), left-hand; *ткани* wrong (*side*; on **с** P)

лега́льный [14; -лен, -льна] legal

леге́нд|а *f* [5] legend; **~а́рный** [14; -рен, -рна] legendary

легио́н *m* [1] legion (*mst. fig* = *a great number of people*)

лёгк|ий (-хк-) [16; -ёгок, легка́; *a.* лёгки; *comp.*: ле́гче] light (*a. fig*); *нетру́дный* easy; *прикоснове́ние* slight; (Д) **легко́** + *inf.* it is very well for ... + *inf.*; **лёгок на поми́не** *coll.* talk of the devil!

легкоатле́т *m* [1] track and field athlete

легко́|ве́рный (-хк-) [14; -рен, -рна] credulous; **~ве́сный** [14; -сен, -сна] lightweight; *fig.* shallow; **~во́й** [14]: **легково́й автомоби́ль** *a.* **~ва́я (á́вто)-маши́на** auto(mobile), car

лёгкое *n* [16] lung

легкомы́сл|енный (-хк-) [14 *sh.*] light--minded, frivolous; thoughtless; **~ие** *n* [12] levity; frivolity; flippancy

лёгкость (-хк-) *f* [8] lightness; easiness; ease

лёд *m* [1; льда́, на льду́] ice

лед|ене́ть [8], ⟨за-, о-⟩ freeze, ice (up, over); grow numb (*with cold*); **~ене́ц** *m* [1; -нца́] (sugar) candy; **~ени́ть** [13], ⟨о(б)-⟩ freeze, ice; *се́рдце* chill; **~ни́к** *m* [1 *e.*] glacier; **~нико́вый** [14] glacial; **~око́л** *m* [1] icebreaker; **~охо́д** *m* [1] pack ice; **~яно́й** [14] ice...; ice-cold; icy (*a. fig.*)

лежа́|ть [4 *e.*; лёжа] lie; (*быть распо-*

ложенным) be (situated); rest, be incumbent; *~ть в осно́ве* (в П form the basis); *~чий* [17] lying; *~чий больно́й* (in)patient

ле́звие *n* [12] edge; razor blade

лезть (28 *st.*: ле́зу; лезь; лез, -ла), ⟨по-⟩ (be) climb(ing, *etc.*; *v/t.*); creep; (*прони́кнуть*) penetrate; *coll.* reach into; (к Д [с Т]) importune, press; *о волоса́х* fall out; (на В) fit (*v/t*); Р не в своё де́ло meddle

лейбори́ст *m* [1] *pol.* Labo(u)rite

ле́й|ка *f* [5; *g/pl.*: ле́ек] watering can; *~копла́стырь* *m* [4] adhesive plaster; *~тена́нт* *m* [1] (second) lieutenant; *~тмоти́в* *m* [1] leitmotif

лека́р|ственный [14] medicinal; *~ство* *n* [9] drug, medicine, remedy (*про́тив* Р for)

ле́ксика *f* [5] vocabulary

ле́к|тор *m* [1] lecturer; *~то́рий* *m* [3] lecture hall; *~ция* *f* [7] lecture (at на П; *vb.*: *слу́шать* [чита́ть] attend [give, deliver]

леле́ять [27] pamper; *fig.* cherish

лён *m* [1; льна] flax

лени́в|ец *m* [1; -вца] → **лентя́й**; *~ица* *f* [5] → **лентя́йка**; *~ый* [14 *sh.*] lazy, idle; вя́лый sluggish

лени́ться [13; леню́сь, ле́нишься], be lazy

ле́нта *f* [5] ribbon; band; *tech.* tape

лентя́й *m* [3], *~ка* *f* [5; *g/pl.*: -я́ек] lazybones; sluggard; *~ничать* *coll.* [1] idle

лень *f* [8] laziness, idleness; *coll.* (мне) ~ I am too lazy to …

леопа́рд *m* [1] leopard

лепе|сто́к *m* [1; -тка́] petal; *~т* *m* [1], *~та́ть* [4], ⟨про-⟩ babble, prattle

лепёшка *f* [5; *g/pl.*: -шек] scone

леп|и́ть [14], ⟨вы́-, с-⟩ sculpture, model, mo(u)ld; *coll.* ⟨на-⟩ stick (на В to); *~ка* model(l)ing; *~но́й* [14] mo(u)lded; *~но́е украше́ние* stucco mo(u)lding

ле́пт|а *f* [5]: *внести́ свою́ ~у* make one's own contribution to s.th

лес *m* [1 (*из* лесу, *из* лесу, в лесу́; в лесу́: *pl.*: леса́, *etc.* е.] wood, forest; *материа́л* lumber, *Brt.* timber; *pl.* scaffolding; *~ом* through a (the) wood

леса́ *f* [5; *pl.*: лёсы, *etc. st.*] (fishing) line

леси́стый [14 *sh.*] woody, wooded

ле́ска *f* [5; *g/pl.*: -сок] → **леса́**

лес|ни́к *m* [1 е.] ranger, forester; *~ни́чество* *n* [9] forest district; *~ни́чий* *m* [17] forest warden; *~но́й* [14] forest…; wood(y); lumber…; timber…

лесо|во́дство *n* [9] forestry; *~насажде́ние* *n* [12] afforestation; wood; *~пи́льный* [14]: *~пи́льный заво́д* = *~пи́льня* *f* [6; *g/pl.*:-лен] sawmill; *~ру́б* *m* [1] lumberman, woodcutter

ле́стн|ица (-sn-) *f* [5] (flight of) stairs *pl.*, staircase; *приста́вная* ladder; *пожа́рная* ~ fire escape

ле́стный [14; -тен, -тна] flattering; *~ь* *f* [8] flattery

лёт *m* [1]: *хвата́ть на лету́* grasp quickly, be quick on the uptake

лета́, лет → **ле́то**; → *а.* **год**

лета́тельный [14] flying

лета́ть [1] fly

лете́ть [1], ⟨по-⟩ (be) fly(ing)

ле́тний [15] summer…

лётный [14] *пого́да* flying; ~ *соста́в* aircrew

ле́т|о *n* [9; *pl.* е.] summer (T in [the]; на В for the); *pl.* years, age (в В at); *ско́лько вам ~?* how old are you? (→ *быть*); в *~ах* elderly, advanced in years; *~опись* *f* [8] chronicle; *~осчисле́ние* *n* [12] chronology; era

летý|чий [17 *sh.*] *chem.* volatile; *~ая мышь* *zo.* bat

лётчи|к *m* [1], *~ца* *f* [5] pilot, aviator, flier, air(wo)man; *лётчик-испыта́тель* test pilot

лече́б|ница *f* [5] clinic, hospital; *~ый* [14] medic(in)al

лече́ние *n* [12] *med.* treatment; *~и́ть* [16] treat; *~ся* undergo treatment, be treated; treat (one's … *от* Р)

лечь → *ложи́ться*; → *а.* **лежа́ть**

ле́ший *m* [17] *Russian mythology* wood goblin; Р Old Nick

лещ *m* [1 е.] *zo.* bream

лже| false; pseudo…; *~ец* *m* [1 е.] mock…; liar; *~и́вость* *f* [8] mendacity; *~и́вый* [14 *sh.*] false, lying; mendacious

ли́, (short, after vowels, а.) **ль 1.** (interr.

part.) **зна́ет ∼ она́ ...?** (= **она́ зна́ет ...?**) does she know...?; **2.** (*cj.*) whether, if; **...,** ∼ **...** ∼ whether ..., or...

либера́л *m* [1], **∼ьный** [14; -лен, -льна] liberal

ли́бо or; ∼ **...,** ∼ **...** either ... or ...

либре́тто *n* [*indecl.*] libretto

ли́вень *m* [4; -вня] downpour, cloud-burst

ливре́я *f* [6; *g/pl.:* -ре́й] livery

ли́га *f* [5] league

ли́дер *m* [1] *pol., sport* leader

лиз|а́ть [3], *once* ⟨∼ну́ть⟩ lick

лик *m* [1] face; countenance; *образ* image; *eccl.* assembly; **причи́слить к ∼у святы́х** canonize

ликвиди́ровать [7] (*im*)*pf.* liquidate

ликёр *m* [1] liqueur

ликова́ть [7], ⟨воз-⟩ exult

ли́лия *f* [7] lily

лило́вый [14] lilac-colo[u]red

лими́т *m* [1] quota, limit; **∼и́ровать** [7] (*im*)*pf.* limit

лимо́н *m* [1] lemon; **∼а́д** *m* [1] lemonade; **∼ный** [14] lemon; **∼ная кислота́** citric acid

ли́мфа *f* [5] lymph

лингви́стика *f* [5] → **языкозна́ние**

лине́й|ка *f* [5; *g/pl.:* -е́ек] line, ruler; **∼ный** [14] linear

ли́н|за *f* [5] lens; **конта́ктные ∼зы** contact lenses; **∼ия** *f* [7] line (*a. fig.*; **по** Д in); **∼ко́р** *m* [1] battleship; **∼ова́ть** [7], ⟨на-⟩ rule; **∼о́леум** *m* [1] linoleum

линчева́ть [7] (*im*)*pf.* lynch

линь *m* [4 *e.*] *zo.* tench

ли́н|ька *f* [5] mo(u)lt(ing); **∼я́лый** *coll.* [14] *о ткани* faded; mo(u)lted; **∼я́ть** [28], ⟨вы-, по-⟩ fade; mo(u)lt

ли́па *f* [5] linden, lime tree

ли́п|кий [16; -пок, -пка́, -о] sticky, adhesive; *пластырь* sticking; **∼нуть** [21], ⟨при-⟩ stick

ли́р|а *f* [5] lyre; **∼ик** *m* [1] lyric poet; **∼ика** *f* [5] lyric poetry; **∼и́ческий** [16], **∼и́чный** [14; -чен, -чна] lyric(al)

лис|(и́ц)а́ *f* [5; *pl. st.*] fox (silver... **черно-бу́рая**); **∼ий** [18] fox...; foxy

лист *m* **1.** [1 *e.*] sheet; (*исполнительный*) writ; **2.** [1 *e.*; *pl. st.*: ли́стья, -ев]

bot. leaf; *coll. a.* → **∼ва́**; **∼а́ть** *coll.* [1] leaf or thumb through; **∼ва́** *f* [5] *collec.* foliage, leaves *pl.*; **∼венница** *f* [5] larch; **∼венный** [14] deciduous; **∼ик** *m* [1] *dim.* → **∼**; **∼о́вка** *f* [5 *g/pl.:*] leaflet; **∼о́к** *m* [1; -тка́] *dim.* → **∼**; slip; **∼ово́й** [14] sheet...; *железо и т. д.*

лите́йный [14]; **∼ цех** foundry

литер|а́тор *m* [1] man of letters; writer; **∼ату́ра** *f* [5] literature; **∼ату́рный** [14; -рен, -рна] literary

лито́в|ец *m* [1; -вца], **∼ка** *f* [5; *g/pl.:* -вок], **∼ский** [16] Lithuanian

лито́й [14] cast

литр *m* [1] liter (*Brt.* -tre)

лить [лью, льёшь; лил, -а, -о; лей(те)! ли́тый (лит, -а́, -о)] pour; *слёзы* shed; *tech.* cast; **дождь льёт как из ведра́** it's raining cats and dogs; **∼ся** flow, pour; *песня* sound; *слёзы и т. д.* stream; **∼ё** *n* [10] founding, cast(ing)

лифт *m* [1] elevator, *Brt.* lift; **∼ёр** *m* [1] lift operator

ли́фчик *m* [1] bra(ssière)

лих|о́й [14; лих, -а́, -о] *coll.* bold, daring; dashing; **∼ора́дка** *f* [5] fever; **∼ора́дочный** [14; -чен, -чна] feverish; **∼ость** *f* [8] *coll.* swagger; spirit; dash

лицев|а́ть [1], ⟨пере-⟩ face; turn; **∼о́й** [14] face...; front...; *сторона* right; **∼о́й счёт** personal account

лицеме́р *m* [1] hypocrite; **∼ие** *n* [12] hypocrisy; **∼ный** [14; -рен, -рна] hypocritical; **∼ить** [13] dissemble

лице́нзия *f* [7] license (*Brt.* -ce) (**В** for **на**)

лицо́ *n* [9; *pl. st.*] face; countenance (*change v/t.* **в** П); front; person, individual(ity); **в ∼о́** by sight; to s.b.'s face; **от ∼а́** (P) in the name of; **∼о́м к ∼у́** face to face; **быть** (Д) **к ∼у́** suit *or* become a p.; **нет ∼а́** be bewildered; **должностно́е ∼о́** official

ли́чинка *f* [5; *g/pl.:* -нок] larva; maggot

ли́чн|ость *f* [8] personality; person, individual; **∼ый** [14] personal; private

лиша́й *m* [3 *e.*] *bot.* lichen (*a.* **∼ник**); *med.* herpes

лиша́|ть [1], ⟨∼и́ть⟩ [16 *e.*; -шу́, -ши́шь, -шённый] deprive; strip (of P); **на-**

следства disinherit; **~а́ть себя́ жи́зни** commit (suicide); **~ённый** *a.* devoid of, lacking; **-ся** (P) lose; **~и́ться чу́вств** faint; **~е́ние** *n* [12] (de)privation; loss; *pl.* privations, hardships; **~е́ние прав** disfranchisement; **~е́ние свобо́ды** imprisonment; **~и́ть(ся)** → **~а́ть(ся)**

ли́шн|ий [15] superfluous, odd, excessive, other...; sur...; *запасно́й* spare; extra; *нену́жный* needless, unnecessary; *su.* outsider; **~ее** undue (*things, etc.*); **вы́пить** (a glass) too much; **... с ~им** over ...; **~ий раз** once again; **не ~е** + *inf.* (p.) had better

лишь (*a.* **+ то́лько**) only; merely; just; as soon as, no sooner ... than, hardly; **~ бы** if only, provided that

лоб *m* [1; лба; во, на лбу] forehead

лови́ть [14], ⟨пойма́ть⟩ [1] catch; *в за́падню* (en)trap; *слу́чай* seize; **~ на сло́ве** take at one's word; *по ра́дио* pick up

ло́вк|ий [16; ло́вок, ловка́, -о; *compr.:* ло́вче] dexterous, adroit, deft; **~ость** *f* [8] adroitness, dexterity

ло́в|ля *f* [6] catching; *ры́бы* fishing; **~у́шка** *f* [5; *g/pl.:* -шек] trap; (*силок*) snare

логари́фм *m* [1] math. logarithm

ло́г|ика *f* [5] logic; **~и́ческий** [16], **~и́чный** [11; -чен, -чна] logical

ло́говище *n* [11], **~о** *n* [9] lair, den

ло́д|ка *f* [5; *g/pl.:* -док] boat; **подво́дная ~ка** submarine

лоды́жка *f* [5; *g/pl.:* -жек] ankle

ло́дырь *coll. m* [4] idler, loafer

ло́жа *f* [5] *thea.* box

ложби́на *f* [5] narrow, shallow gully; *fig. coll.* cleavage

ло́же *n* [11] channel, bed (*a. of river*)

ложи́ться [16 *e.*; -жу́сь, -жи́шься], ⟨лечь⟩ [26] [г/ж: ля́гу, лгут; ляг(те)!; лёг, легла́] lie down; **~ в** (B) go to (bed, *a.* **~ спать**); **~ в больни́цу** go to hospital

ло́жка *f* [5; *g/pl.:* -жек] spoon; **ча́йная ~** teaspoon; **столо́вая ~** tablespoon

ло́ж|ный [14; -жен, -жна] false; **~ный шаг** false step; **~ь** *f* [8; лжи; ло́жью] lie, falsehood

лоза́ *f* [5; *pl. st.*] *виногра́дная* vine

ло́зунг *m* [1] slogan

локализова́ть [7] (*im*)*pf.* localize

локо|моти́в *m* [1] locomotive, railway engine; **~н** *m* [1] curl, lock; **~ть** *m* [4; -ктя́; *from g/pl. e.*] elbow

лом *m* [1; *from g/pl.: e.*] crowbar; *металло́лом* scrap (metal); **~аный** [14] broken; **~а́ть** [1], ⟨по-, с-⟩ break (*a.* up); *дом* pull down; **~а́ть себе́ го́лову** rack one's brains (**над** T over); **-ся** break; ⟨по-⟩ P clown, jest; put on airs

ломба́рд *m* [1] pawnshop

ломи́ть [14] *coll.* → **~а́ть**; *impers.* ache, feel a pain in; **-ся** bend, burst (*в две́рь и т. д.* force (*v/t.* **в** B), break (into); **~а́** *f* [15] breaking (up); **~кий** [16; ло́мок, ломка́, -о] brittle, fragile; **~о́та** *f* [5] rheumatic pain, ache *pl.;* **~о́ть** *m* [4; -мтя́] slice; **~тик** *m* [1] *dim.* → **~о́ть**

ло́н|о *n* [9] *семьи* bosom; **на ~е приро́ды** in the open air

ло́па|сть *f* [8; *from g/pl. e.*] blade; *ae.* vane; **~та** *f* [8] shovel, spade; **~тка** *f* [5; *g/pl.:* -ток] **1.** *dim.* → **~та**; **2.** *anat.* shoulder blade

ло́паться [1], ⟨-нуть⟩ [20] break, burst; split, crack; **чуть не ~ от сме́ха** split one's sides with laughter

лопу́х *m* [1 *e.*] *bot.* burdock; *coll.* fool

лоск *m* [1] luster (-tre), gloss, polish

лоску́т *m* [1 *e.; pl. a.:* -ку́тья, -ьев] rag, shred, scrap

лос|ни́ться [13] be glossy, shine; **~о́сина** *f* [5] *cul.* **~о́сь** *m* [1] salmon

лось *m* [4; *from g/pl. e.*] elk

лотере́я *f* [6] lottery

лото́к *m* [1; -тка́] street vendor's tray *or* stall; **продава́ть с лотка́** sell in the street

лохм|а́тый [14 *sh.*] shaggy, dishevel(l)ed; **~о́тья** *n/pl.* [*gen.:* -ьев] rags

ло́цман *m* [1] *naut.* pilot

лошади́ный [14] horse...; **~ная си́ла** horsepower; **~ь** *f* [8; *from g/pl. e.,* *instr.:* -дьми́ & -дя́ми] horse

лощи́на *f* [5] hollow, depression

лоя́льн|ость *f* [8] loyalty; **~ый** [14; -лен, -льна] loyal

лу|бо́к *m* [1; -бка́] cheap popular print;

~г *m* [1; на -ý; *pl.* -á, *etc. e.*] meadow

лу́ж|а *f* [5] puddle, pool; **сесть в ~у** *coll.* get into a mess

лужа́йка *f* [5; *g/pl.*: -áек] (small) glade

лук *m* [1] **1.** *collect.* onion(s); **2.** bow (*weapon*)

лука́в|ить [14], ⟨с-⟩ dissemble, be cunning; **~ство** *n* [9] cunning, slyness, ruse; **~ый** [14 *sh.*] crafty, wily; (*игривый*) saucy, playful

лу́ковица *f* [5] onion; *bot.* bulb

лун|а́ *f* [5] moon; **~а́тик** *m* [1] sleepwalker, somnambulist; **~ный** [14] moon(lit); *astr.* lunar

лу́па *f* [5] magnifying glass

лупи́ть [14] thrash, flog

лупи́ться [14], ⟨об-⟩ peel, scale (off)

луч *m* [1 *e.*] ray, beam; **~ево́й** [14] radial; radiation (**боле́знь** sickness); **~еза́рный** [14; -рен, -рна] resplendent; **~и́стый** [14 *sh.*] radiant

лу́чш|е *adv.*, *comp.* → **хорошо́**; **~ий** [17] better; best (**в ~ем слу́чае** at …)

лущи́ть [16 *e.*; -щу́, -щи́шь], ⟨вы-⟩ shell, husk

лы́ж|а *f* [5] ski; snowshoe (*vb.*: **ходи́ть**, *etc.*, **на ~ах**); **~ник** *m* [1], **~ница** *f* [5] skier; **~ный** [14] ski…

лы́с|ый [14 *sh.*] bald; **~ина** *f* [5] bald spot, bald patch

ль → **ли**

льви́|ный [14] lion's; **~ный зев** *bot.* snapdragon; **~ца** *f* [5] lioness

льго́т|а *f* [5] privilege; **~ный** [14; -тен, -тна] privileged; (*сниженный*) reduced; preferential; favo(u)rable

льди́на *f* [5] ice floe

льну́ть [20], ⟨при-⟩ cling, stick (to); *fig. coll.* have a weakness (for)

льняно́й [14] flax(en); *ткань* linen…

льст|е́ц *m* [1 *e.*] flatterer; **~и́вый** [14 *sh.*] flattering; **~и́ть** [15], ⟨по-⟩ flatter; delude (o.s. **себя́** with T)

любе́зн|ичать *coll.* [1] (**с** T) pay court (**с** T to), flirt, pay compliments (**с** T to); **~ость** *f* [8] courtesy; kindness; (*услуга*) favo(u)r; *pl.* compliments; **~ый** [14;

-зен, -зна] polite, amiable, kind; obliging

люби́м|ец *m* [1; -мца], **~ица** *f* [5] favo(u)rite, pet; **~ый** [14] beloved, darling; favo(u)rite, pet

люби́тель *m* [4], **~ница** *f* [5] lover, fan; amateur; **~ский** [16] amateur

люби́ть [14] love; like, be (⟨по-⟩ grow) fond of; *pf.* fall in love with

любов|а́ться [7], ⟨по-⟩ (T *or* **на** B) admire, (be) delight(ed) (in); **~ник** *m* [1] lover; **~ница** *f* [5] mistress; **~ный** [14] love…; *отношение* loving, affectionate; **~ная связь** love affair; **~ь** *f* [8; -бви́, -бо́вью] love (**к** Д of, for)

любозна́тельный [14; -лен, -льна] inquisitive, curious; *ум* inquiring; **~ый** [14] either, any(one *su.*); **~пы́тный** [14; -тен, -тна] curious, inquisitive; interesting; **мне ~пы́тно …** I wonder …; **~пы́тство** *n* [9] curiosity; interest; **пра́здное ~пы́тство** idle curiosity

любя́щий [17] loving, affectionate

люд *m* [1] *collect. coll.*, **~и** [-éй, -ям, -ьми́, -ях] people; **вы́йти в ~и** get on in life; **на ~ях** in the presence of others, in company; **~ный** [14; -ден, -дна] crowded; **~ое́д** *m* [1] cannibal; *в сказках* ogre

люк *m* [1] hatch(way); manhole

лю́стра *f* [5] chandelier, luster (*Brt.* -tre)

лютера́н|ин *m* [1; *nom./pl.* -ра́не, g. -ра́н], **~ка** *f* [5; *g/pl.*: -нок], **~ский** [16] Lutheran

лю́тик *m* [1] buttercup

лю́тый [14; лют, -á, -о; *compr.*: -те́е] fierce, cruel

люце́рна *f* [5] alfalfa, lucerne

ляг|а́ть(ся) [1], ⟨~ну́ть⟩ [20] kick

лягуш|а́тник *m* [1] wading pool for children; **~ка** *f* [5; *g/pl.*: -шек] frog

ля́жка *f* [5; *g/pl.*: -жек] *coll.* thigh, haunch

лязг *m* [1], **~ать** [1] clank, clang; *зубами* clack

ля́мк|а *f* [5; *g/pl.*: -мок] strap; **тяну́ть ~у** *fig. coll.* drudge, toil

Л

M

мавзоле́й *m* [3] mausoleum

магази́н *m* [1] store, shop

магистра́ль *f* [8] main; *rail.* main line; *водная* waterway; thoroughfare; trunk (line)

маги́ческий [16] magic(al)

ма́гний *m* [3] *chem.* magnesium

магни́т *m* [1] magnet; **~офо́н** *m* [1] tape recorder

магомета́н|ин *m* [1; *pl.:* -а́не, -а́н], **~ка** *f* [5; *g/pl.:* -нок] Mohammedan

ма́з|ать [3] **1.** ⟨по-, на-⟩ (*пачкать*) smear; *esp. eccl.* anoint; *маслом и т. д.* spread, butter; **2.** ⟨с-⟩ oil, lubricate; **3.** *coll.* ⟨за-⟩ soil; *impf.* daub; **~ня́** *coll. f* [6] daub(ing); **~о́к** *m* [1; -зка́] daub; stroke; *med.* smear; swab; **~у́т** *m* [1] heavy fuel oil; **~ь** *f* [8] ointment

май *m* [3] May

ма́й|ка *f* [5; *g/pl.:* ма́ек] undershirt, T-shirt; sports shirt; **~оне́з** *m* [1] mayonnaise; **~о́р** *m* [1] major; **~ский** [16] May(-Day)…

мак *m* [1] poppy

макаро́ны *m* [1] macaroni

мак|а́ть [1], *once* ⟨~ну́ть⟩ [20] dip

маке́т *m* [1] model; *mil.* dummy

ма́клер *m* [1] *comm.* broker

макну́ть → мака́ть

максим|а́льный [14; -лен, -льна] maximum; **~ум** *m* [1] maximum; at most

маку́шка *f* [5; *g/pl.:* -шек] top; *головы* crown

малева́ть [6], ⟨на-⟩ *coll.* paint, daub

мале́йший [17] least, slightest

ма́ленький [16] little, small; (*низкий*) short; trifling, petty

мали́н|а *f* [5] raspberry, -ries *pl.*; **~овка** *f* [5; *g/pl.:* -вок] robin (в few places); **~овый** [14] raspberry-…; crimson

ма́ло little (*a.* **~ что**); few (*a.* **~ кто**); a little; not enough; less; **~ где** in few places; **~ когда** seldom; *coll.* **~ ли что** much, many things, anything; (*a.*) yes, but …; that doesn't matter, even though; **~ того́** besides, and what is more; **~ того́, что** not only (that)

мало|ва́жный [14; -жен, -жна] insignificant, trifling; **~ва́то** *coll.* little, not (quite) enough; **~вероя́тный** [14; -тен, -тна] unlikely; **~габари́тный** [14; -тен, -тна] small; **~гра́мотный** [14; -тен, -тна] uneducated, ignorant; *подход и т. д.* crude, faulty; **~доказа́тельный** [14; -лен, -льна] unconvincing; **~ду́шный** [14; -шен, -шна] pusillanimous; **~зна́чащий** [17 *sh.*] → **~ва́жный**; **~иму́щий** [17 *sh.*] poor; **~кро́вие** *n* [12] an(a)emia; **~ле́тний** [15] minor, underage; little (one); **~литра́жка** *f* [5; *g/pl.:* -жек] *coll.* compact (car); **~лю́дный** [14; -ден, -дна] poorly populated (*or* attended); **~ма́льски** *coll.* in the slightest degree; at all; **~общи́тельный** [14; -лен, -льна] unsociable; **~о́пытный** [14; -тен, -тна] inexperienced; **~пома́лу** *coll.* gradually, little by little; **~приго́дный** [14; -ден, -дна] of little use; **~ро́слый** [14 *sh.*] undersized; **~содержа́тельный** [14; -лен, -льна] uninteresting, shallow, empty

ма́л|ость *f* [8] *coll.* trifle; a bit; **~оце́нный** [14; -е́нен, -е́нна] of little value, inferior; **~очи́сленный** [14 *sh.*] small (in number), few; **~ый** [14; мал, -а́; *comp.:* ме́ньше] small, little; *ростом* short; → **~енький**; *su.* fellow, guy; **без ~ого** almost, all but; **от ~а до вели́ка** young and old; **с ~ых лет** from childhood; **~ыш** *coll.* [1 *e.*] kid(dy), little boy

ма́льч|ик *m* [1] boy, lad; **~и́шеский** [16] boyish; mischievous; **~и́шка** *coll. m* [5; *g/pl.:* -шек] urchin; greenhorn; **~уга́н** *coll. m* [1] → **ма́лыш**; *a.* → **~и́шка**

малю́тка *m/f* [5; *g/pl.:* -ток] baby, tot

маля́р *m* [1 *e.*] (house) painter

маляри́я *f* [7] *med.* malaria

ма́м|а *f* [5] mam(m)a, mother; **~а́ша** *coll. f* [5], *coll. f* **~очка** *f* [5; *g/pl.:* -чек] mommy, mummy

ма́нго *n* [*indecl.*] mango

мандари́н *m* [1] mandarin(e), tangerine

манда́т *m* [1] mandate

ман|е́вр *m* [1], **~еври́ровать** [7] maneuver, *Brt.* manoeuvre; **~е́ж** *m* [1] riding school; *цирк* arena; **~еке́н** *m* [1] mannequin (*dummy*)

мане́р|а *f* [5] manner; **~ный** [14; -рен, -рна] affected

манже́т(к)а *f* [(5; *g/pl.*: -ток) cuff

манипули́ровать [7] manipulate

мани́|ть [13; маню́, ма́нишь], ⟨по-⟩ (T) beckon; *fig.* entice, tempt

ма́н|ия *f* [7] (**вели́чия** megalo)mania; **~ки́ровать** [7] (*im*)*pf.* (T) neglect

ма́нная [14]: **~ крупа́** semolina

мара́зм *m* [1] *med.* senility; *fig.* nonsense, absurdity

мара́ть *coll.* [1], ⟨за-⟩ soil, stain; ⟨на-⟩ scribble, daub; ⟨вы-⟩ delete

марганцо́вка *f* [5; -вок] *chem.* potassium manganate

маргари́н *m* [1] margarine

маргари́тка *f* [5; *g/pl.*: -ток] daisy

маринова́ть [7], ⟨за-⟩ pickle

ма́рк|а *f* [5; *g/pl.*: -рок] (postage) stamp; make; grade, brand, trademark; **~е́тинг** *m* [1] marketing; **~си́стский** [16] Marxist

ма́рля *f* [6] gauze

мармела́д *m* [1] fruit jelly (*candied*)

ма́рочный [14] *вино* vintage

март *m* [1], **~овский** [16] March

марты́шка *f* [5; *g/pl.*: -шек] marmoset

марш *m* [1], **~ирова́ть** [7] march; **~ру́т** *m* [1] route, itinerary; **~ру́тный** [14]: **~ру́тное такси́** fixedroute taxi

ма́ск|а *f* [5; *g/pl.*: -сок] mask; **~ара́д** *m* [1] (*a.* **бал~ара́д**) masked ball, masquerade; **~ирова́ть** [7], ⟨за-⟩, **~иро́вка** *f* [5; *g/pl.*: -вок] mask; disguise, camouflage

ма́сл|еница *f* [5] Shrovetide; **~ёнка** *f* [5; *g/pl.*: -нок] butter dish; **~еный** [14] → **~яный**; **~и́на** *f* [5] olive; **~и́чный** [14] olive…; oil …; **~о** *n* [9; *pl.*: -сла́, -сел, -слам] (*a.* **сли́вочное ~о**) butter; (*a.* **расти́тельное ~о**) oil; **как по ~у** *fig.* swimmingly; **~озаво́д** creamery; **~яный** [14] oil(y); butter(y); greasy; *fig.* unctuous

ма́сс|а *f* [5] mass; bulk; *люде́й* multitude; *coll.* a lot; **~а́ж** *m* [1], **~и́ровать** [7] (*pt. a. pf.*) massage; **~и́в** *m* [1] *го́рный* massif; **~и́вный** [14; -вен, -вна] massive; **~овый** [14] mass…; popular…

ма́стер *m* [1; *pl.*: -ра́, *etc. e.*] master; (*брига́дир*) foreman; (*уме́лец*) craftsman; (*знато́к*) expert; **~ на все ру́ки** jack-of-all-trades; *coll.* [13], ⟨с-⟩ work; make; **~ска́я** *f* [16] workshop; *худо́жник и т. д.* atelier, studio; **~ско́й** [16] masterly (*adv.* **~ски́**); **~ство́** *n* [9] trade, craft; skill, craftsmanship

масти́тый [14 *sh.*] venerable; eminent

масть *f* [8; *from g/pl. e.*] colo(u)r (*of animal's coat*); *ка́рты* suit

масшта́б *m* [1] scale (on **в** П); *fig.* scope; caliber (-bre); repute

мат *m* [1] **1.** *sport* mat; **2.** *chess* checkmate; **3.** foul language

математи́|к *m* [1] mathematician; **~ка** *f* [5] mathematics; **~ческий** [16] mathematical

материа́л *m* [1] material; **~и́зм** *m* [1] materialism; **~и́ст** *m* [1] materialist; **~исти́ческий** [16] materialistic; **~ьный** [14; -лен, -льна] material; economic; financial

матери́к *m* [1 *e.*] continent

матери́|нский [16] mother('s), motherly, maternal; **~нство** *n* [9] maternity; **~я** *f* [7] matter; *ткань* fabric, material

ма́тка *f* [5; *g/pl.*: -ток] *anat.* uterus

ма́товый [14] dull, dim, mat

матра́с *m* [1] mattress

ма́трица *f* [5] *typ.* matrix; die, mo(u)ld; *math.* array of elements

матро́с *m* [1] sailor, seaman

матч *m* [1] *sport* match

мать *f* [ма́тери, *etc.* = 8; *pl.*: ма́тери, -ре́й, *etc. e.*] mother

мах *m* [1] stroke, swing; **с (одного́) ~у** at one stroke *or* stretch; at once; **дать ~у** miss one's mark, make a blunder; **~а́ть** [3, *coll.* 1], *once* ⟨**~ну́ть**⟩ [20] (T) wave; *хвостом* wag; *крыльями* flap; *pf.* coll. go; **~ну́ть руко́й на** (B) give up; **~ови́к** *m* [1 *e.*], **~ово́й** [14]; **~ово́е колесо́** flywheel

махо́рка *f* [5] coarse tobacco

махро́вый [14] *bot.* double; Turkish *or* terry-cloth (*полоте́нце* towel); *fig.* dyed-in-the-wool

ма́чеха *f* [5] stepmother

ма́чта *f* [5] mast

маши́н|а *f* [5] machine; engine; *coll.* car; **стира́льная ~а** washing machine; **швейна́я ~а** sewing-machine; **~а́льный** [14; -лен, -льна] mechanical, perfunctory; **~и́ст** *m* [1] *rail.* engineer, *Brt.* engine driver; **~и́стка** *f* [5; *g/pl.*: -ток] (girl) typist; **~ка** *f* [5; *g/pl.*: -нок] (*пи́шущая*) typewriter; **~ный** [14] machine..., engine...; **~опись** *f* [8] typewriting; **~остро́ение** *n* [12] mechanical engineering

ма́йк *m* [1 *e.*] lighthouse; beacon; leading light

ма́я|тник *m* [1] pendulum; **~ться** P [27] drudge; *от бо́ли* suffer; **~читься** *coll.* [16] loom

мгла *f* [5] gloom, darkness; heat mist

мгнове́н|ие *n* [12] moment; instant; *в ~ие о́ка* in the twinkling of an eye; **~ный** [14; -ёнен, -ённа] momentary, instantaneous

ме́б|ель *f* [8] furniture; **~лиро́вка** *f* [5] furnishing(s)

мёд *m* [1; *part. g.*: мёду; в меду́; *pl. e.*] honey

меда́ль *f* [8] medal; **~о́н** *m* [1] locket, medallion

медве́|дица *f* [5] she-bear; *astr.* **Ꝺица** Bear; **~дь** *m* [4] bear (*coll. a. fig.*); **~жий** [18] bear('s)...; *услу́га* bad (*service*); **~жо́нок** *m* [2] bear cub

ме́ди|к *m* [1] physician, doctor; medical student; **~кáме́нты** *m/pl.* [1] medication, medical supplies; **~ци́на** *f* [5] medicine; **~ци́нский** [16] medical

ме́дл|енный [14 *sh.*] slow; **~и́тельный** [14; -лен, -льна] sluggish, slow, tardy; **~ить** [14] ⟨про-⟩ delay, linger, be slow, tarry; hesitate

ме́дный [14] copper...

мед|осмо́тр *m* [1] medical examination; **~пу́нкт** *m* [1] first-aid station; **~сестра́** *f* [5; *pl. st.*: -сёстры, -сестёр, -сёстрам] (*medical*) nurse

меду́за *f* [5] jellyfish

медь *f* [8] copper; *coll.* copper (*coin*)

меж, **~ду́**; **~á** *f* [5; *pl.*: ме́жи, меж, межа́м] boundary; **~доме́тие** *n* [12] *gr.* interjection; **~континента́льный** intercontinental

ме́жду (Т) between; among(st); **~ тем** meanwhile, (in the) meantime; **~ тем как** whereas, while; **~городный** [14] *tel.* long-distance....*Brt.* trunk...; interurban; **~наро́дный** [14] international

межплане́тный [14] interplanetary

мексика́н|ец *m* [1; -нца], **~ка** *f* [5; *g/pl.*: -нок], **~ский** [16] Mexican

мел *m* [1; в ~у́] chalk; *для побе́лки* whitewash

меланхо́л|ик *m* [1] melancholic; **~и́ческий** [16], **~и́чный** [14; -чен, -чна] melancholy, melancholic; **~ия** *f* [7] melancholy

меле́ть [8], ⟨об-⟩ grow shallow

ме́лк|ий [16; -лок, -лка́, -о; *compr.*: ме́льче] small, little; *интере́сы* petty; *песо́к* fine; *река́* shallow; *таре́лка* flat; **~ий дождь** drizzle; **~отá** *f* [8] small fry

мелоди|́ческий [16] melodic; melodious; **~чный** [14; -чен, -чна] melodious; **~я** *f* [7] melody

ме́лоч|ность *f* [8] pettiness, smallmindedness, paltriness; **~ный** [14; -чен, -чна] petty, paltry; **~ь** *f* [8; *from g/pl. e.*] trifle; trinket; *coll.* small fry; *де́ньги* (small) change; *pl.* details, particulars

мель *f* [8] shoal, sandbank; **на ~и** aground; *coll.* in a fix

мелькáть [1], ⟨~ну́ть⟩ [20] flash; gleam; flit; fly (past); pass by fleetingly; *~ом* for a brief moment; **взгляну́ть ~ом** cast a cursory glance

ме́льни|к *m* [1] miller; **~ца** *f* [5] mill

мельхио́р *m* [1] cupronickel, German silver

мельчáть [1], ⟨из-⟩ become (**~и́ть** [16 *e.*; -чу́, -чи́шь] make) small(er) *or* shallow(er); become petty

мелюзá *coll.* [5] → **ме́лочь** *coll.*

мемориáл *m* [1], **~ный** [14] memorial; **~ная доска́** memorial plaque

мемуа́ры *m/pl.* [1] memoirs

ме́нее less; **~ всего́** least of all; **тем не ~** nevertheless

ме́ньш|е less; smaller; *a. ме́нее*; **~ий**[17] smaller, lesser; younger; least; **~инство́** *n* [9] minority

меню́ *n* [*indecl.*] menu, bill of fare

меня́ть[28], ⟨по-, об-⟩ exchange, barter (**на** B for); change (→ **пере~**); -**ся** *v/i.* (**Т/с** T s.th. with)

ме́р|а *f* [5] measure; degree, way; *по ~е* (P) *or того́ как* according to (*a. в ~у* P); as far as; while the …, the … (+ *comp.*); *по кра́йней (ме́ньшей) ~е* at least

мере́нга *f* [5] meringue

мере́щиться [16], ⟨по-⟩ (Д) seem (*to hear, etc.*); appear (to), imagine

мерз|а́вец *coll. m* [1; -вца] swine, scoundrel; **~кий** [16; -зок, -зка́, -о] vile, disgusting, loathsome, foul

мёрз|лый [14] frozen; **~нуть** [21], ⟨за-⟩ freeze; feel cold

ме́рзость *f* [8] vileness, loathsomeness

ме́рин *m* [1] gelding; *врать как си́вый ~* lie in one's teeth

ме́р|ить [13], ⟨с-⟩ measure; ⟨при-, по-⟩ *coll.* try on; **~ка** *f* [5; *g/pl.*: -рок]: *снять ~ку* take s.o.'s measure

ме́ркнуть [21], ⟨по-⟩ fade, darken

мерлу́шка *f* [5; *g/pl.*: -шек] lambskin

ме́р|ный [14; -рен, -рна] measured; rhythmical; **~оприя́тие** *n* [12] measure; action

мёртв|енный [14 *sh.*] deathly (pale); **~е́ть** [8], ⟨о-⟩ deaden; *med.* mortify; grow or turn numb (pale, desolate); **~е́ц** *m* [1 *e.*] corpse

мёртв|ый [14; мёртв, мертва́, мёртво; *fig.*: мёртво, мёртвы] dead; *~ая то́чка* dead point, dead center (-tre) *fig.*; *на ~ой то́чке* at a standstill

мерца́|ние *n* [12], **~ть** [1] twinkle

меси́ть [15], ⟨за-, с-⟩ knead

ме́сса *f* [5] *mus.* mass

мести́ [25 -т-; мету́, метёшь; мётший], ⟨под-⟩ sweep, whirl

ме́стн|ость *f* [8] region, district, locality; place; **~ый**[14] local; **~ый жи́тель** local inhabitant

ме́ст|о *n* [9; *pl. e.*] place, site; *сиде́ние* seat; *coll. old use* job, post; *в те́ксте* passage *pl. a.*; → **~ность; о́бщее** (*or из-* **би́тое**) **~о** platitude, commonplace;

(*заде́ть за*) **больно́е ~о** tender spot (touch on the raw); (*не*) **к ~у** in (out of) place; *не на ~е* in the wrong place; **~а́ми** in (some) places, here and there; *спа́льное ~о* berth; **~** [9] residence; **~оиме́ние** *n* [12] *gr.* pronoun; **~онахожде́ние, ~оположе́ние** *n* [12] location, position; **~опребыва́- ние** *n* [12] whereabouts; residence; **~орожде́ние** *n* [12] deposit; *не- фтяно́е* field

месть *f* [8] revenge

ме́ся|ц *m* [1] month; moon; *в ~ц* a month, per month; *медо́вый ~ц* honeymoon; **~чный** [14] month's; monthly

мета́лл *m* [1] metal; **~и́ст** *m* [1] metalworker; **~и́ческий** [16] metal(lic); **~ур- ги́я** *f* [7] metallurgy

метаморфо́за *f* [5] metamorphosis; change in s.o.'s behavio(u)r, outlook, etc.

мет|а́ть [3] 1. ⟨на-, с-⟩ baste, tack; 2. [3], *once* ⟨-ну́ть⟩ [20] throw; **~а́ть икру́** spawn; **-ся** toss (*in bed*); rush about

мете́ль [8] snowstorm, blizzard

метеоро́лог *m* [1] meteorologist; **~и́ческий** [16] meteorological; **~ия** *f* [7] meteorology

ме́т|ить [15], ⟨по-⟩ mark; (*в, на* B) aim, drive at, mean; **~ка** *f* [5; *g/pl.*: -ток] mark(ing); **~кий** [16; -ток, -тка́, -о] well-aimed; *стрело́к* good; keen, accurate, steady; pointed; (*выраже́ние*) apt, to the point

мет|ла́ *f* [5; *pl. st.*: мётлы, мётел; мётлам] broom; **~ну́ть → ~ата́ть**

ме́тод *m* [1] method; **~и́ческий** [16], **~и́чный** [14; -чен, -чна] methodic(al), systematic(al)

метр *m* [1] meter, *Brt.* metre

ме́трика *f* [5] *obs.* birth certificate

метри́ческ|ий[16]: **~ая систе́ма** metric system

метро́ *n* [*indecl.*], **~полите́н** *m* [1] subway, *Brt.* tube, underground

мех *m* [1; *pl.*: -ха́, *etc.*, *e.*] fur; *на ~у́* fur- -lined

механи́зм *m* [1] mechanism; gear; **~ик** *m* [1] mechanic; *naut.* engineer; **~ика** *f* [5] mechanics; **~и́ческий** [16] mechan-

M

ical

мехов|о́й [14] fur...;**~щи́к** *m* [1 *e.*] furrier

меч *m* [1 *e.*] sword; **Дамо́клов~** sword of Damocles

мече́ть *f* [8] mosque

мечта́ *f* [5] dream, daydream, reverie; **~тель** *m* [4] (day)dreamer; **~тельный** [14; -лен, -льна] dreamy; **~ть** [1] dream (**о** П *of*)

меша́|ть [1], ⟨раз-⟩ stir; ⟨с-, пере-⟩ mix; *о чу́вствах* mingle; ⟨по-⟩ disturb; (*препя́тствовать*) hinder, impede, prevent; **вам не ~ет** (**~ло бы**) you'd better; **-ся** meddle, interfere (**в** В *with*); **не ~йтесь не в своё де́ло!** mind your own business!

ме́шк|ать *coll.* [1], ⟨про-⟩ → **ме́длить**; **~ова́тый** [14 *sh.*] (*clothing*) baggy

мешо́к *m* [1; -шка́] sack, bag

меща́н|ин *m* [1; *pl.*: -а́не, -а́н], **~ский** [16] *hist.* (petty) bourgeois, Philistine; narrow-minded

мзда *f* [5] *archaic, now joc.* recompense, payment; *iro.* bribe

миг *m* [1] moment, instant; **~ом** *coll.* in a trice (*or* flash); **~а́ть** [1], *once* ⟨-ну́ть⟩ [20] blink, wink; *звёзды* twinkle; *огоньки́* glimmer

мигре́нь *f* [8] migraine

ми́зерный [14; -рен, -рна] scanty, paltry

мизи́нец [1; -нца] little finger

микро́б *m* [1] microbe

микроско́п *m* [1] microscope

микрофо́н *m* [1] microphone

миксту́ра *f* [5] medicine (*liquid*), mixture

ми́ленький *coll.* [16] lovely; dear; (*as form of address*) darling

милиц|ионе́р *m* [1] policeman; militiaman; **~я** *f* [7] police; militia

милли|а́рд *m* [1] billion; **~ме́тр** *m* [1] millimeter (*Brt.* -tre); **~о́н** *m* [1] million

мило|ви́дный [14; -ден, -дна] nice-looking; **~се́рдие** *n* [12] charity, mercy; **~се́рдный** [14; -ден, -дна] charitable, merciful; **~сты|ня** *f* [6] alms; **~сть** *f* [8] mercy; (*одолже́ние*) favo(u)r; **~сти про́сим!** welcome!; *iro., coll.* **по твое́й** (**ва́шей**) **ми́лости** because

of you

ми́л|ый [14; мил, -а́, -о] nice, lovable, sweet; (my) dear, darling

ми́ля *f* [6] mile

ми́мо (P) past, by; **~ бить** ~ miss; **~лётный** [14; -тен, -тна] fleeting, transient; **~хо́дом** in passing; incidentally

ми́на *f* [5] **1.** *mil.* mine; **2.** mien, expression

минда́|лина *f* [5] almond; *anat.* tonsil; **~ль** *m* [4 *e.*] *collect.* almond(s); **~льничать** *coll.* [1] be too soft (towards **с** Т)

миниатю́р|а *f* [5], **~ный** [14; -рен, -рна] miniature...; *fig.* tiny, diminutive

ми́нимум *m* [1] minimum; **прожи́точный** ~ living wage; *adv.* at the least

министе́рство *n* [9] *pol.* ministry; **~рство иностра́нных** (**вну́тренних**) **дел** Ministry of Foreign (Internal) Affairs; **~р** *m* [1] minister, secretary

мин|ова́ть [7] (*im*)*pf.*, ⟨-у́ть⟩ [20] pass (by); *pf.* be over; escape; (Д) **~у́ло** (*о во́зрасте*) → **испо́лниться**; **~у́вший**; **~у́вшее** *su.* past

мино́рный [14] *mus.* minor; *fig.* gloomy, depressed

ми́нус *m* [1] *math.* minus; *fig.* shortcoming

мину́т|а *f* [5] minute; moment, instant (**в** В at; **на** В for); **сию́ ~у** at once, immediately; at this moment; **с ~ы на ~у** (at) any moment; **~ пя́тый, пять, ~ный** [14] minute('s); moment('s), momentary

мину́ть → **минова́ть**

мир *m* [1] **1.** peace; **2.** [*pl. e.*] world; *fig.* universe, planet; **не от ~а сего́** otherworldly

мир|и́ть [13], ⟨по-, при-⟩ reconcile (to **с** Т); **-ся** make it up, be(come) reconciled; ⟨при-⟩ resign o.s. to; put up with; **~ный** [14; -рен, -рна] peace...; peaceful

мировоззре́ние *n* [12] weltanschauung, world view; ideology

мирово́й [14] world('s); worldwide, universal; *coll.* first-class

миро|люби́вый [14 *sh.*] peaceable; peaceloving; **~тво́рческий** [16] peacemaking

ми́ска f [5; g/pl.: -сок] dish, tureen; bowl

ми́ссия f [7] mission; *dipl.* legation

ми́стика f [5] mysticism

мистифика́ция f [7] mystification; hoax

ми́тинг m [1] *pol.* mass meeting; **~ова́ть** [7] *impf. coll.* hold (*or* take part in) a mass meeting

митрополи́т m [1] *eccl.* metropolitan

миф m [1] myth; **~и́ческий** [16] mythic(al); **~оло́гия** f [7] mythology

ми́чман m [1] warrant officer

мише́нь f [8] target

ми́шка *coll.* m [5; g/pl.:-шек] (*pet name used for*) bear; (**плю́шевый**) teddy bear

мишура́ f [5] tinsel

младе́н|ец m [1; -нца] infant, baby; **~чество** n [9] infancy

мла́дший [17] younger, youngest; junior

млекопита́ющее n [17] *zo.* mammal

мле́чный [14] milk…, milky (*a. ♀, ast.*); **~ сок** latex

мне́ние n [12] opinion (**по** Д in); **обще́ственное ~e** public opinion; **по моему́ ~ю** to my mind

мни́|мый [14 *sh., no m*] imaginary; (*ло́жный*) sham; **~тельный** [14; -лен, -льна] (*подозри́тельный*) hypochondriac(al); suspicious

мно́гие *pl.* [16] many (people, *su.*)

мно́го (P) much, many; a lot (*or* plenty) of; **ни ~ ни ма́ло** *coll.* neither more nor less; **~ва́то** *coll.* rather too much (many); **~вeково́й** [14] centuries-old; **~гра́нный** [14; -а́нен, -а́нна] many-sided; **~де́тный** [14; -тен, -тна] having many children; **~значи́тельный** [14; -лен, -льна] significant; **~кра́тный** [14; -тен, -тна] repeated; *gr.* frequentative; **~ле́тний** [15] longstanding, of many years; *план и т. д.* long-term…; *bot.* perennial **~лю́дный** [14; -ден, -дна] crowded, populous; *ми́тинг mass…*; **~национа́льный** [14; -лен, -льна] multinational; **~обеща́ющий** [17] (very) promising; **~обра́зный** [14; -зен, -зна] varied, manifold; **~сло́вный** [14; -вен, -вна] wordy; **~сторо́нний** [15; -о́нен, -о́нна] many-sided; **~страда́льный** [14; -лен, -льна] long-suffering; **~то́чие** n [12] ellipsis; **~уважа́емый** [14] dear (*address*); **~цве́тный** [14; -тен, -тна] multicolo(u)red; **~чи́сленный** [14 *sh.*] numerous; **~эта́жный** [14] manystoried (*Brt.* -reyed)

мно́ж|ественный [14. *sh.*] *gr.* plural; **~ество** n [9] multitude; a great number; **~имое** n [12] *math.* multiplicand; **~итель** m [4] multiplier, factor, **~ить**, ⟨по-⟩ → **умножа́ть**

мобилизова́ть [7] (*im)pf.* mobilize

моби́льный [14; -лен, -льна] mobile

моги́л|а f [5] grave; **~ьный** [14] tomb…

могу́|чий [17 *sh.*], **~щественный** [14 *sh.*] mighty, powerful; **~щество** n [9] might, power

мо́д|а f [5] fashion, vogue; **~ели́рование** n [12] *tech.* simulation; **~е́ль** (-дэ́л) f [8] model; **~елье́р** m [1] fashion designer; **~е́м** (-дэ-) m [1] *comput.* modem; **~ернизи́ровать** (-дэр-) [7] (*im)pf.* modernize; **~ифици́ровать** [7] (*im)pf.* modify; **~ный** [14; -ден, -дна́, -о] fashionable, stylish; *пе́сня* popular

мо́ж|ет быть perhaps, maybe; **~но** (**мне**, *etc.*) one (I, *etc.*) can *or* may; it is possible; → **как**

можжеве́льник m [1] juniper

моза́ика f [5] mosaic

мозг m [1; -а (-у); в ~у́; *pl.* e.] brain; *ко́стный* marrow; *спинно́й* cord; **шевели́ть ~а́ми** *coll.* use one's brains; **уте́чка ~о́в** brain drain; **~ово́й** [14] cerebral

мозо́|листый [14 *sh.*] horny, calloused; **~лить** [13]: **~лить глаза́** Д *coll.* be an eyesore to; **~ль** f [8] callus; corn

мой m, **~я́** f, **~ё** n, **~и́** pl. [24] my; mine; *pl. su. coll.* my folks; → **ваш**

мо́к|нуть [21], ⟨про-⟩ become wet; soak; **~ро́та** f [5] *med.* phlegm; **~рый** [14; мокр, -а́, -о] wet

мол m [1] jetty, pier, mole

молв|а́ f [5] rumo(u)r; talk; **~ить** [14] (*im)pf. obs.*, ⟨про-⟩ say, utter

молдава́н|ин m [1; *pl.*:-ва́не, -а́н], **~ка** f [5; g/pl.: -нок] Moldavian

моле́бен m [1; -бна] *eccl.* service; public prayer

моле́кул|а f [5] molecule; **~я́рный** [14]

molecular

моли́т|ва f [5] prayer; **~венник** m [1] prayer book; **~ь** [13; молю́, мо́лишь (о П)] implore, entreat, beseech (for); **~ся**, ⟨по-⟩ pray (Д to; о П for); *fig.* idolize (**на** В)

молние|но́сный [14; -сен, сна] instantaneous; **~я** f [7] lightning; (*застёжка*) zipper, zip fastener

молодёжь f [8] *collect.* youth, young people *pl.*; **~е́ть** [8], ⟨по-⟩ grow (look) younger; **~е́ц** *coll.* m [1; -дца́] fine fellow, brick; (*оценка*) *as int.* well done!; **~и́ть** [15 e.; -ложу́, -ло́дишь] make look younger; **~ня́к** m [1 e.] *of животных* offspring; *о лесе* undergrowth; **~ожё́ны** m/pl. [1] newly wedded couple; **~о́й** [14; мо́лод, -а́, -о; *сотр.*: моло́же] young; **картофель**, *месяц* new: *pl. a.* = **~ожё́ны**; **~ость** f [8] youth, adolescence; **~цева́тый** [14 *sh.*] smart; *шаг* sprightly

моложа́вый [14 *sh.*] youthful, young-looking

молок|и́ f/pl. [5] milk, soft roe; **~о́** n [9] milk; **сгущё́нное ~о́** condensed milk; **~осо́с** *coll.* m [1] greenhorn

мо́лот m [1] sledgehammer; **~о́к** m [1; -тка́] hammer; **с ~ка́** by auction; **~ь** [17; мелю́, ме́лешь, меля́], ⟨пере-, с-⟩ grind; *coll.* talk (*вздор* nonsense); **~ьба́** f [5] threshing (time)

молочн|ик m [1] milk jug; **~ый** [14] milk...; dairy...

мо́лча silently, tacitly; in silence; **~ли́вый** [14 *sh.*] taciturn; *согласие* tacit; **~ние** n [12] silence; **~ть** [4 e.; -чу́, -чи́шь], молча́ be (*or* keep) silent; [**за**]**молчи́**! shut up!

моль f [8] (clothes) moth

мольба́ f [5] entreaty; (*молитва*) prayer

моме́нт m [1] moment, instant (**в** В at); (*черта*, *сторона*) feature, aspect; **~а́льный** [14] momentary, instantaneous

мона́рхия f [7] monarchy

мона|сты́рь m [4 e.] monastery; *женский* convent; **~х** m [1] monk; **~хиня** f [6] nun (*a.*, *F*, **~шенка** f [5; *g/pl.*: -нок]); **~шеский** [16] monastic; monk's

монго́льский [16] Mongolian

моне́т|а f [5] coin; **той же ~ой** in a p.'s own coin; **за чи́стую ~у** in good faith; **зво́нкая ~а** hard cash; **~ный** [14] monetary; **~ный двор** mint

монито́р m [1] *tech.* monitor

моно|ло́г m [1] monologue; **~полизи́ровать** [7] (*im*)*pf.* monopolize; **~по́лия** f [7] monopoly; **~то́нный** [14; -то́нен, -то́нна] monotonous

монт|а́ж m [1] assembly, installation, montage; **~ёр** m [1] fitter; electrician; **~и́ровать** [7], ⟨с-⟩ *tech.* assemble, mount, fit; *cine.* arrange

монуме́нт m [1] monument; **~а́льный** [14; -лен, -льна] monumental (*a. fig.*)

мопе́д m [1] moped

мора́ль f [8] morals, ethics *pl.*; morality; moral; **~ чита́ть ~** coll. lecture, moralize; **~ный** [14; -лен, -льна] moral; **~ное состоя́ние** morale

морг m [1] morgue

морг|а́ть [1], ⟨**~ну́ть**⟩ [20] blink (Т); **и гла́зом не ~ну́в** *coll.* without batting an eyelid

мо́рда f [5] muzzle, snout

мо́ре n [10; *pl. e.*] sea; seaside (**на** П at); **~м** by sea; **~пла́вание** n [12] navigation; **~пла́ватель** m [4] navigator, seafarer

морж m [1 e.], **~о́вый** [14] walrus; *coll.* out-of-doors winter bather

мори́ть [13], ⟨за-, у-⟩ exterminate; **~ го́лодом** starve; exhaust

морко́вь f [8], *coll.* **~ка** f [5; *g/pl.*: -вок] carrot(s)

моро́женое n [14] ice cream

моро́з m [1] frost; **~и́льник** m [1] deep-freeze; **~ить** [15], ⟨за-⟩ freeze; **~ный** [14; -зен, -зна] frosty

мороси́ть [15; -си́т] drizzle

моро́чить *coll.* [16] fool, pull the wool over the eyes of

морс m [1]: fruit drink; **клю́квенный ~** cranberry juice

морско́й [14] sea..., maritime; naval; nautical; seaside...; **~ волк** sea dog, old salt

мо́рфий m [3] morphine, morphia

морфоло́гия f [7] morphology

морщи́|на f [5] wrinkle; **~нистый** [14

sh.] wrinkled; **~ть** [16], ⟨на-, с-⟩ wrinkle, frown (*v/i.* **~ться**); *ткань* crease

моря́к *m* [1 *e.*] seaman, sailor

моск|ви́ч *m* [1 *e.*], **~ви́чка** *f* [5; *g/pl.:* -чек] Muscovite; **~о́вский** [16] Moscow...

моски́т *m* [1] mosquito

мост *m* [1 & 1 *e.*; на -у́; *pl. e.*] bridge; **~и́ть** [15 *e.*; мощу́, мости́шь, мощённый], ⟨вы́-⟩ pave; **~и́к** *m/pl.* [1 *e.*] footbridge; **~ова́я** *f* [14] *old use* carriage way

мот *m* [1] spendthrift, prodigal

мот|а́ть [1], ⟨на-, с-⟩ reel, wind; *coll.* ⟨по-⟩, *once* ⟨**~ну́ть**⟩ shake, wag; (*трясти́*) jerk; *coll.* ⟨про-⟩ squander; **~а́й отсю́да!** scram!; **~ся** *impf.* dangle; P knock about

моти́в[1] *m* [1] *mus.* tune; motif

моти́в[2] *m* [1] motive, reason; **~и́ровать** [7] (*im*)*pf.* give a reason (for), justify

мото́к *m* [1; -тка] skein, hank

мото́р *m* [1] motor, engine

мото|ро́ллер *m* [1] motor scooter; **~ци́кл** [1], **~ёт** *m* [1] motorcycle; **~цикли́ст** *m* [1] motorcyclist

мотылёк *m* [1; -лька́] moth

мох *m* [1; мха & мо́ха, во (на) мху́: *pl.:* мхи, мхов] moss

мохна́тый *m* [14 *sh.*] shaggy, hairy

моч|а́ *f* [5] urine; **~а́лка** *f* [5; *g/pl.:* -лок] washing-up mop; loofah; bath sponge; **~ево́й** [14]: **~ево́й пузы́рь** *anat.* bladder; **~и́ть** [16], ⟨на-, за-⟩ wet, moisten; soak, steep (*v/i.* **-ся**; *a.* urinate); **~ка** *f* [5; -чек] lobe (*of the ear*)

мочь[1] *f* [26 г/ж: могу́, мо́жешь, мо́гут; мог, -ла́; могу́щий], ⟨с-⟩ can, be able; may; **я не могу́ не** + *inf.* I can't help ...ing; **мо́жет быть** maybe, perhaps; **не мо́жет быть!** that's impossible!

мочь[2] *f* P [8]: **во всю ~ь, изо всей ~и, что есть ~и** with all one's might; **~и нет** it's unbearable

моше́нни|к *m* [1] swindler, cheat; **~чать** [1], ⟨с-⟩ swindle; **~чество** *n* [9] swindling, cheating

мо́шка *f* [5; *g/pl.:* -шек] midge

мо́щи *f/pl.* [*gen.:* -щéй, *etc.*] relics

мо́щ|ность *f* [8] power; *tech.* capacity; *предприятия* output; **~ный** [14;

мо́щен, -щна́, -о] powerful, mighty; **~ь** *f* [8] power, might; strength

мрак *m* [1] dark(ness); gloom

мра́мор *m* [1] marble

мрачн|е́ть [8], ⟨по-⟩ darken; become gloomy; **~ый** [14; -чен, -чна́, -о] dark; gloomy, somber (*Brt.* -bre)

мсти́|тель *m* [4] avenger; **~тельный** [14; -лен, -льна] revengeful; **~ть** [15], ⟨ото-⟩ revenge o.s., take revenge (Д on); (*за* В) avenge a p.

мудр|ёный [14; -ён, -ена́ -енее] difficult, hard, intricate; (*замыслова́тый*) fanciful; **не ~ено́, что** (it's) no wonder; **~éц** *m* [1 *e.*] sage; **~и́ть** *coll.* [13], ⟨на-⟩ complicate matters unnecessarily; **~ость** *f* [8] wisdom; **зуб ~ости** wisdom tooth; **~ствовать** *coll.* [7] → **~и́ть; ~ый** [14; мудр, -á, -о] wise

муж *m* **1.** [1; *pl.:* -жья́, -жей, -жья́м] husband; **2.** *rare* [1; *pl.:* -жи, -жéй, -жáм] man; **~а́ть** [1], ⟨воз-⟩ mature, grow; **-ся** *impf.* take courage; **~ественный** [14 *sh.*] steadfast; manly; **~ество** *n* [9] courage, fortitude; **~и́к** *m* [1 *e.*] peasant; P man; **~ско́й** [16] male, masculine (*a. gr.*); (gentle)man('s); **~чи́на** *m* [5] man

музе́й *m* [3] museum

му́зы|ка *f* [5] music; **~ка́льный** [14; -лен, -льна] musical; **~а́нт** *m* [1] musician

му́ка[1] *f* [5] pain, torment, suffering, torture(-s); *coll.* trouble

мука́[2] *f* [5] flour

мультфи́льм *m* [1] animated cartoon

му́мия *f* [7] mummy

мунди́р *m* [1] full-dress uniform; **карто́фель в ~е** *coll.* potatoes cooked in their jackets *or* skin

мундшту́к (-нſ-) *m* [1] cigarette holder; *mus.* mouthpiece

муниципалите́т *m* [1] municipality; town council

мураве́й *m* [3; -вья́; *pl.:* -вьи́, -вьёв] ant; **~е́йник** *m* [1] ant hill

мура́шки: ~ (от P) бе́гают по спине́ (у P F) (s.th.) gives (a p.) the creeps

мурлы́кать [3 & 1] purr; *coll. песню* hum

муска́т *m* [1] nutmeg; *вино́* muscat; **~ный** [14]: **~ный оре́х** nutmeg

M

му́скул m [1] muscle; **~ату́ра** f [5] collect. muscles; muscular system; **~истый** [14 sh.] muscular

му́сор m [1] rubbish, refuse; sweepings; **~ить** [13], ⟨за-, на-⟩ coll. litter; **~опро́вод** m [1] refuse chute

муссо́н m [1] monsoon

мусульма́н|ин m [1; pl.: -áне, -áн], **~ка** f [5; g/pl.: -нок] Muslim

мути́ть [15; мучу́, му́тишь], ⟨вз-, по-⟩ make muddy; fig. trouble; fog; **меня́ ~и́т** coll. I feel sick; **-ся** = **~не́ть** [8], ⟨по-⟩ grow turbid; blur; **~ный** [14; -тен, -тна́, -о] muddy (a. fig.); troubled (waters); dull; blurred, foggy; **~о́вка** f [5; g/pl.: -вок] whisk; **~ь** f [8] dregs pl.; murk

му́фта f [5] muff; tech. (**~ сцепле́ния**) clutch sleeve, coupling sleeve

му́фтий m [3] eccl. Mufti

му́х|а f [5] fly; **~омо́р** m [1] fly agaric (mushroom); coll. decrepit old person

муче́|ние n [12] → **му́ка**; **~ник** m [1] martyr; **~и́тель** m [4] tormentor; **~и́тельный** [14; -лен, -льна] painful, agonizing; **~ить** [16], Р **~ать** [1], ⟨за-, из-⟩ torment, torture; fig. vex, worry; **-ся** suffer (pain); fig. suffer torments; **над зада́чей и т. д.** take great pains (over), toil

му́шк|а f [5; g/pl.: -шек] ружья́ (fore)-sight; **взять на ~y** take aim (at)

мчать(ся) [4], ⟨по-⟩ rush or speed (along)

мши́стый [14 sh.] mossy

мще́ние n [12] vengeance

мы [20] we; **~ с ним** he and I

мы́л|ить [13], ⟨на-⟩ soap; **~ить го́лову** (Д) coll. give s.o. a dressing-down, scold; **~о** n [9; pl. e.] soap; **~ьница** f [5] soap dish; **~ьный** [14] soap(y); **~ьная пе́на** lather, suds

мыс m [1] geogr. cape, promontory

мы́сл|енный [14] mental; **~имый** [14 sh.] conceivable; **~итель** m [4] thinker;

~ить [13] think (**о** of, about); reason; (представля́ть) imagine; **~ь** f [8] thought, idea (**о** П of); **за́дняя ~ь** ulterior motive

мыта́рство n [9] hardship, ordeal

мыть(ся) [22], ⟨по-, у-, вы́-⟩ wash (o.s.)

мыча́ть [4 e.; -чу́, -чи́шь] moo, low; coll. mumble

мышело́вка f [5; g/pl.: -вок] mouse-trap

мы́шечный [14] muscular

мы́шк|а f [5; g/pl.: -шек]: **под ~ой** under one's arm

мышле́ние n [12] thinking, thought

мы́шца f [5] muscle

мышь f [8; from g/pl. e.] mouse

мышья́к m [1 e.] chem. arsenic

мэр m [1] mayor

мя́гк|ий (-xк-) [16; -гок, -гка́, -о; compr.: мя́гче] soft; движе́ние smooth; мя́со и. m. д. tender; fig. mild, gentle; lenient; **~ое кре́сло** easy chair; **~ий ваго́н** rail. first-class coach or car(riage); **~осерде́чный** [14; -чен, -чна] soft-hearted; **~ость** f [8] softness; fig. mildness **~оте́лый** [14] fig. flabby, spineless

мя́к|иш m [1] soft part (of loaf); **~нуть** [21], ⟨на-, раз-⟩ become soft; **~оть** f [8] flesh; плода́ pulp

мя́мл|ить Р [13] mumble; **~я** m & f [6] coll. mumbler; irresolute person; milk-sop

мяс|и́стый [14 sh.] fleshy; pulpy; **~ни́к** m [1 e.] butcher; **~но́й** [14] butcher's; **~о** n [9] meat; flesh **~ору́бка** f [5; g/pl.: -бок] mincer

мя́та f [8] mint

мяте́ж m [1 e.] rebellion, mutiny; **~ник** m [1] rebel, mutineer

мять [мну, мнёшь; мя́тый], ⟨с-, по-, из-⟩ [сомну́; изомну́] (c)rumple, press; knead; тра́ву и т. д. trample; **-ся** be easily crumpled; fig. coll. waver, vacillate

мяу́к|ать [1], once ⟨-нуть⟩ mew

мяч m [1 e.] ball; **~ик** [1] dim. → **мяч**

Н

на¹ **1.** (B): (*направление*) on, onto; to, toward(s); into, in; (*длительность, назначение и т. д.*) for; till; *math.* by; **~ что?** what for?; **2.** (П): (*расположение*) on, in, at; with; for; **~ ней ... she has ... on**

на² *int. coll.* there, here (you are); *a.* **вот тебе на!** well, I never!

набав|ля́ть [28], ⟨~ить⟩ [14] raise, add to, increase

наба́т *m* [1]: **бить в ~** *mst. fig.* sound the alarm

набе́г *m* [1] incursion, raid; **~а́ть** [1], ⟨~жа́ть⟩ [4; -егу́, -ежи́шь, -егу́т; -еги́(-те)!] run (into **на** B); (*покрыва́ть*) cover; **~га́ться**[1] *pf.* be exhausted with running about

набекре́нь *coll.* aslant, cocked

на́бережная *f* [14] embankment, quay

наби|ва́ть [1], ⟨~ть⟩ [-бью, -бьёшь; → **бить**] stuff, fill; **~вка** *f* [5; *g/pl.*: -вок] stuffing, padding

набира́ть [1], ⟨набра́ть⟩ [-беру́, -рёшь; → **брать**] gather; **на рабо́ту** recruit; *tel.* dial; *typ.* set; take (*высоту, скорость* gain); **-ся** (*набиться*) become crowded; P (*напиться*) get soused; **-ся сме́лости** pluck up one's courage

наби́|тый [14 *sh.*] (T) packed; P **~тый дура́к** arrant fool; **битко́м ~тый**; *coll.* crammed full; **-ть → ~ва́ть**

наблюд|а́тель *m* [4] observer; **~а́тельный** [14; -лен, -льна] observant, alert; *пост* observation; **~а́ть** [1] (*v/t. & за* T) observe; watch; (*a.* **про-**); see to (it that); **-ся** be observed *or* noted; **~е́ние** *n* [12] observation; supervision

набо́йк|а *f* [5; *g/pl.*: -бо́ек] heel (*of shoe*); **набива́ть** ⟨-би́ть⟩ **~у** put a heel on, heel

на́бок to *or* on one side, awry

наболе́вший [16] sore, painful (*a. fig.*)

набо́р *m* [1] **на ку́рсы и т. д.** enrol(l)-ment; (**компле́кт**) set, kit; typesetting

набр|а́сывать [1] **1.** ⟨~оса́ть⟩ [1] sketch, design, draft; **2.** ⟨~о́сить⟩ [15] throw over *or* on (**на** B); **-ся** fall (up)on

набра́ть → набира́ть

набрести́ [25] *pf. coll.* come across (**на** B); happen upon

набро́сок *m* [1; -ска] sketch, draft

набух|а́ть [1], ⟨~нуть⟩ [21] swell

нава́л|ивать [1], ⟨~и́ть⟩ [13; -алю́ -а́лишь, -а́ленный] heap; *рабо́ту* load (with); **-ся** fall (up)on

нава́лом *adv.* in bulk; *coll.* loads of

наве́д|ываться, ⟨~аться⟩ [1] *coll.* call on (**к** Д)

наве́к, ~и forever, for good

наве́рн|о(е) probably; for certain, definitely; (*a., coll.* **~яка́**) for sure, without fail

наве́рстывать, ⟨наверста́ть⟩ [1] make up for

наве́рх up(ward[s]); *по ле́стнице* upstairs; **~у́** above; upstairs

наве́с *m* [1] awning; annex (*with sloping roof*); shed, carport

навеселе́ *coll.* tipsy, drunk

навести́ → наводи́ть

навести́ → навеща́ть

наве́тренный [14] windward

наве́чно forever, for good

навеща́ть [1], ⟨~сти́ть⟩ [15 *e.*; -ещу́, -ести́шь; -ещённый] call on

на́взничь backwards, on one's back

навзры́д: пла́кать ~ sob

навига́ция *f* [7] navigation

нависа́ть [1], ⟨~нуть⟩ [21] hang (over); *опа́сность и т. д.* impend, threaten

навле|ка́ть [1], ⟨~чь⟩ [26] (**на** B) bring on, incur

наводи́ть[15], ⟨навести́⟩ [25] (**на** B) direct (at); point (at), turn (to); lead (to), bring on *or* about, cause, raise (→ **-на гоня́ть**); make; construct; **~ на мысль** come up with an idea; **~ поря́док** put in order; **~ ску́ку** bore; **~ спра́вки** inquire (**о** П after)

наводн|е́ние *n* [12] flood, inundation; **~я́ть** [28], ⟨~и́ть⟩ [13] flood with (*a. fig.*), inundate with

навóз *m* [1], **~ить** [15], ⟨у-⟩ dung, manure

нáволочка *f* [5; *g/pl.:* -чек] pillowcase

навострúть [13] *pf. уши* prick up

навря́д (ли) hardly, scarcely

навсегдá forever; *раз и ~* once and for all

навстрéчу toward(s); *идтú ~* (Д) go to meet; *fig.* meet halfway

навы́ворот P (*наизнанку*) inside out; *дéлать шúворот~* put the cart before the horse

нáвык *m* [1] experience, skill (*в* П in)

навя́зывать [1], ⟨~áть⟩ [3] *мнéние, вóлю* impose, foist ([up]on; Д *v/i.* -ся); ~чивый [14 *sh.*] obtrusive; ~чивая идéя idée fixe

наг|ибáть [1], ⟨~нýть⟩ [20] bend, bow, stoop (*v/i.* -ся)

нагишóм *coll.* stark naked

наглéть [8], ⟨об-⟩ become impudent; ~éц *m* [1 *e.*] impudent fellow; ~ость *f* [8] impudence, insolence; *верх ~ости* the height of impudence; ~ýхо tightly; ~ый [14; нагл, -á, -о] impudent, insolent, *coll.* cheeky

нагляд|éться [11]: *не ~éться* never get tired of looking (at); ~ный [14; -ден, -дна] clear, graphic; (*очевúдный*) obvious; *пособие* visual; ~ный урóк object lesson

нагнáть → **нагоня́ть**

нагнетáть [1]: *~ страсти* stir up passions

нагноéние *n* [12] suppuration

нагнýть → **нагибáть**

нагов|áривать [1], ⟨~орúть⟩ [13] say, tell, talk ([too] much *or* a lot of …); *coll.* slander (a p. *на* В, *о* П); (*записáть*) record; ~орúться *pf.* talk o.s. out; *не ~орúться* never get tired of talking

нагóй [14; наг, -á, -о] nude, naked, bare

нагон|я́й *coll. m* [3] scolding, upbraiding; ~я́ть [28], ⟨нагнáть⟩ [-гоню́, -гóнишь; → **гнать**] overtake, catch up (with); (*навёрстывать*) make up (for); ~я́ть страх, скýку, *etc. на* (В) frighten, bore, *etc.*

наготá *f* [5] nudity; nakedness

нагот|áвливать [1], ⟨~óвить⟩ [14] prepare; (*запастúсь*) lay in; ~óве in readiness, on call

награбить [14] *pf.* amass by robbery, plunder (a lot of)

нагрáд|а *f* [5] reward (*в* В as a); (*знак отлúчия*) decoration; ~ждáть [1], ⟨~дúть⟩ [15 *e.;* -ажý, -адúшь; -аждённый] (Т) reward; decorate; *fig.* endow with

нагревá|тельный [14] heating; ~ь [1] → **греть**

нагромо|ждáть [1], ⟨~здúть⟩ [15 *e.;* -зжý, здúшь; -ождённый] pile up, heap up

нагрýдник *m* [1] bib, breastplate

нагру|жáть [1], ⟨~зúть⟩ [15 & 15 *e.;* -ужý, -ýзишь; -ýженный] load (with Т); *coll. работой а.* burden, assign; ~зка *f* [5; *g/pl.:* -зок] load(ing); *coll. a.* burden, job, assignment; *преподавáтеля* teaching load

нагрянуть [20] *pf. о гостях* appear unexpectedly, descend (on)

над, **~о** (Т) over, above; *смея́ться; about; трудúться* at, on

надáв|ливать [1], ⟨~úть⟩ [14] (*а. на* В) press; squeeze; *соку* press out

надбáв|ка *f* [5; *g/pl.:* -вок] addition; extra charge; *к зарплáте* increment, rise; ~ля́ть [28], ⟨~ить⟩ [14] *coll.* → **надбавля́ть**

надви|гáть [1], ⟨~нуть⟩ [20] move, push, pull (up to, over); ~гáть шáпку pull one's hat over one's eyes; -ся approach, draw near; (*закры́ть*) cover

нáдвое in two (parts *or* halves); ambiguously; *бáбушка ~ сказáла* it remains to be seen

надгрóбие *n* [12] tombstone

наде|вáть [1], ⟨~ть⟩ [-éну, -éнешь; -éтый] put on (*clothes, etc.*)

надéжд|а *f* [5] hope (*на* В of); *подавáть ~ы* show promise

надёжный [14; -жен, -жна] reliable, dependable; (*прóчный*) firm; (*безопáсный*) safe

надéл|ать [1] *pf.* make (a lot of); (*причиня́ть*) do, cause, inflict; ~я́ть [28], ⟨~úть⟩ [13] *умóм и т. д.* endow with

надéть → **надевáть**

надéяться [27] (*на* В) hope (for); (*по-*

лагаться) rely (on)

надзо́р *m* [1] supervision; *милиции и т. д.* surveillance

надла́|мывать, ⟨**~ома́ть**⟩ [1] *coll.*, ⟨**~оми́ть**⟩ [14] crack; *fig.* overtax, break down

надлежа́|ть [4; *impers. + dat. and inf.*] it is necessary (for Д); (Д) (one) must (*go, etc.*); need; want; **так ему́ и ~** it serves him right; **~бность** *f* [8] need (**в** П for), necessity; affair, matter (**по** Д in); **по ме́ре ~бности** when necessary

надое|да́ть [1], ⟨**~сть**⟩ [-е́м, -е́шь, *etc.*, → **есть¹**] (Д, Т) tire; *вопросами и т. д.* bother, pester; **мне ~е́л...** I'm tired (of) fed up (with); **~дливый** [14 *sh.*] tiresome; *человек* troublesome, annoying

надо́лго for (a) long (time)

надорва́ть → надрыва́ть

надпи́|сывать [1], ⟨**~са́ть**⟩ [3] inscribe; *конверт и т. д.* superscribe; **~сь** *f*[8] inscription

надре́з *m* [1] cut, incision; **~а́ть** *and* **~ывать** [1], ⟨**~ать**⟩ [3] cut, incise

надруга́тельство *n* [9] outrage

надры́в *m* [1] rent, tear; *fig.* strain; **~а́ть** [1], ⟨**надорва́ть**⟩ [-ву́, -вёшь; надорва́л, -á, -о; -о́рванный] tear; undermine; (over)strain (o.s. себя́, **-ся**; be[come] worn out *or* exhausted; let o.s. go; **~а́ть живо́т от сме́ха, ~а́ться** (**со́ смеху**) split one's sides (with laughter)

надстра́|ивать [1], ⟨**~о́ить**⟩ [13] build on; raise the height of; **~о́йка** [5; *g/pl.*: -о́ек] superstructure

наду́|ва́ть [1], ⟨**~ть**⟩ [18] inflate; (*обманывать*) dupe; **~ть гу́бы** pout; *-ся* *v/i. coll.* (*обидеться*) be sulky (**на** В with); **~вно́й** [14] inflatable, air...; **~ть → ~ва́ть**

надум|анный [14] far-fetched, strained; **~ать** *coll.* [1] *pf.* think (of), make up one's mind

наду́тый [1] (*обиженный*) sulky

наеда́ться [1], ⟨**нае́сться**⟩ [-е́мся,

-е́шься, *etc.*, → **есть¹**] eat one's fill

наедине́ alone, in private

нае́зд *m* [1] (**~ом** on) short *or* flying visit(s); **~ник** *m* [1] rider

нае́|зжа́ть [1], ⟨**~хать**⟩ [наеду, -едешь] (**на** В) run into *or* over; *coll.* come (occasionally), call on (**к** Д)

наём *m* [1; на́йма] *работника* hire; *кварти́ры* rent; **~ник** *m* [1] *солдат* mercenary; **~ный** [14] hired

нае́|сться → ~да́ться; **~хать → ~зжа́ть**

нажа́ть → нажима́ть

нажда́|к *m* [1 *e.*], **~чный** [14] emery

нажи́|ва *f* [5] gain, profit; **~ва́ть** [1], ⟨**~ть**⟩ (добро *amass*; со́стояние, *враги́*; *get*; *ревматизм get*; **~вка** *f* [5; *g/pl.*: -вок] bait

нажи́м *m* [1] pressure (*a. fig.*); **~а́ть** [1], ⟨**нажа́ть**⟩ [-жму́, -жмёшь; -жа́тый] (*a.* **на** В) press, push (*a. coll. fig.* = urge, impel; influence)

нажи́ть → нажива́ть

наза́д back(ward[s]); **~!** get back!; **тому́ ~** ago

назва́|ние *n* [12] name; title; **~ть → называ́ть**

назе́мный [14]: **~ тра́нспорт** overland transport

назида́|ние *n* [12] edification (for p.'s **в** В/Д); **~тельный** [14; -лен, -льна] edifying

на́зло́ Д out of spite, to spite (s.b.)

назнача́|ть [1], ⟨**~ить**⟩ [16] appoint (p. s.th. В/Т), designate; *время и т. д.* fix, settle; *лека́рство* prescribe; *день и т. д.* assign; **~е́ние** *n* [12] appointment; assignment; (*цель*) purpose; prescription; (*место ~ения*) destination

назо́йливый [14 *sh.*] importunate

назре|ва́ть [1], ⟨**~ть**⟩ [8] ripen, mature; *fig.* be imminent *or* impending; **~ло вре́мя** the time is ripe

назубо́к *coll.* by heart, thoroughly

называ́|ть [1], ⟨назва́ть⟩ [-зову́, -зовёшь; -зва́л, -á, -о; на́званный (на́зван, -á, -о)] call, name; (*упомянуть*) mention; **~ть себя́** introduce o.s. **~ть ве́щи свои́ми имена́ми** call a spade a spade;

так **~емый** so-called; **-ся** call o.s., be called; *как* **~ется …?** what is (or do you call) …?

наи… in compds. of all, very; **~бо́лее** most, …est of all

найвн|ость f [8] naiveté; **~ый** [14; -вен, -вна] naive, ingenuous

наизна́нку inside out

наизу́сть by heart

наиме́нее least … of all

наименова́ние n [12] name; title

наискосо́к obliquely

найти́|е n [12]: *по ~ю* by intuition

найти́ → **находи́ть**

наказ|а́ние n [12] punishment (*в B* as a) penalty; *coll.* nuisance; **~у́емый** [14 sh.] punishable; **~ывать** [1], ⟨**~а́ть**⟩ [3] punish

нака́л m [1] incandescence; **~ивать** [1], ⟨**~и́ть**⟩ [13] incandesce; *стра́сти* **~и́лись** passions ran high; **~ённый** incandescent, red-hot; *атмосфера* tense

нак|а́лывать [1], ⟨**~оло́ть**⟩ [17] *дров* chop

накану́не the day before; **~** (*P*) on the eve (of)

нака́п|ливать [1] **& ~опла́ть** [28], ⟨**~опи́ть**⟩ [14] accumulate, amass; *де́ньги* save up

наки́|дка f [5; g/pl.: -док] cape, cloak; **~дывать** [1] **1.** ⟨**~да́ть**⟩ [1] throw about; **2.** ⟨**~нуть**⟩ [20] throw on; *coll.* (*наба́вить*) add; raise; **-ся** (*на* B) *coll.* fall (up)on

на́кипь f [8] *пена* scum (a. fig.); *осадок* scale

наклад|на́я f [14] invoice, waybill; **~но́й** [14]: **~ны́е расхо́ды** overhead, expenses, overheads; **~ывать** [1], *and* **налага́ть** [1], ⟨**наложи́ть**⟩ [16] (*на* B) lay (on), apply (to); put (on), set (to); *взыскание, штраф* impose; *отпечаток* leave; (*наполнить*) fill, pack, load

накле́|ивать [1], ⟨**~ить**⟩ [13; -е́ю] glue or paste on; *марку* stick on; **~йка** f [5; g/pl.: -е́ек] label

накло́н m [1] incline; slope; **~е́ние** n [12] *gr.* inclination; mood; **~и́ть** → **~я́ть**; **~ный** [14] inclined, slanting; **~я́ть** [28], ⟨**~и́ть**⟩ [13; -оню́, -о́нишь; -онён-

ный] bend, tilt; bow, stoop; incline; **-ся** v/i.

накова́льня f [6; g/pl.: -лен] anvil

наколо́ть → **нака́лывать**

наконе́ц (**~-то** oh) at last, finally; at length; **~чник** m [1] tip, point

накоп|ле́ние n [12] accumulation; **~ля́ть, ~и́ть** → **нака́пливать**

накрахма́ленный [14] starched

на́крепко fast, tight

накры|ва́ть [1], ⟨**~ть**⟩ [22] cover; *стол* (a. B) lay (the table); *P преступника* catch, trap

накуп|а́ть [1], ⟨**~и́ть**⟩ [14] (P) buy up (a lot)

наку́р|ивать [1], ⟨**~и́ть**⟩ [13; -урю́, -у́ришь; -у́ренный] fill with smoke or fumes

налага́ть → **накла́дывать**

нала́|живать [1], ⟨**~дить**⟩ [15] put right or in order, get straight, fix; *дела* get things going; *отношения* establish

нале́во to or on the left of; → **напра́во**

налега́ть [1], ⟨**~чь**⟩; [26; г/ж: -ля́гу, -ля́жешь, -ля́гут; -лёг, -гла́; -ля́г(те)] (*на* B) lean (on); press (against, down); *fig. на работу и т. д.* apply o.s. (to)

налегке́ *coll.* with no baggage (*Brt.* luggage)

нал|ёт m [1] *mil.*, *ae.* raid, attack; *med. fur; (a. fig.)* touch; **~ета́ть** [1], ⟨**~ете́ть**⟩ [11] (*на* B) fly (at, [a. have, strike] against); swoop down; raid, attack; (*наброситься*) fall ([up]on); *о ветре, буре* spring up; **~ётчик** m [1] bandit

нале́чь → **налега́ть**

нали|ва́ть [1], ⟨**~ть**⟩ [-лью́, -льёшь; -ле́й(те)]; на́лил, -а́, -о; -ли́вший; на́ли-тый (на́лит, -а́, -о)] pour (out); fill; *p. p. (a. ~то́й)* ripe, jucy; *о теле* firm; **-ся** v/i.; *a.* ripen); **~вка** f [5; g/pl.: -вок] (fruit) liqueur; **~м** m [1] burbot

нали́ть, нали́ть → **налива́ть**

налицо́ present, on hand

нали́ч|ие n [12] presence; **~ность** f [8] cash-in-hand; *a* **~ие;** *в* **~ности** → **налицо́; ~ный** [14] (a. pl., su.); *деньги* ready cash (a. down T); (*имеющийся*) present, on hand; *за* **~ные** for cash

нало́г m [1] tax; *на товары* duty;

~оплате́льщик *m* [1] taxpayer

нало́ж|енный [14]: ~енным платежо́м cash (*or* collect) on delivery; ~и́ть → накла́дывать

налюбова́ться [7] *pf.* (T) gaze to one's heart's content; **не** ~ never get tired of admiring (o.s. **собо́й**)

нама́|зывать [1] → *ма́зать*; ~тывать [1] → *мота́ть*

намёк *m* [1] (**на** B) allusion (to), hint (at); ~ека́ть [1], ⟨~екну́ть⟩ [20] (**на** B) allude to, hint (at)

намер|ева́ться [1] intend → (**я** I, *etc.*) ⟨~ен(а)⟩; ~ение *n* [12] intention, design; purpose (**с** T on); ~енный [14] intentional, deliberate

намета́ть → *намётывать*

наме́тить → *намеча́ть*

наме́т|ка *f* [5; *g/pl.*: -ток], ~ётывать [1], ⟨~ета́ть⟩ [3] *sew.* baste, tack

наме|ча́ть [1], ⟨~тить⟩ [15] (*плани́ровать*) plan, have in view; (*отбира́ть*) nominate, select

намно́го much, (by) far

намок|а́ть [1], ⟨~нуть⟩ [21] get wet

намо́рдник *m* [1] muzzle

нанести́ → *наноси́ть*

нани́|зывать [1], ⟨~а́ть⟩ [3] string, thread

нан|има́ть [1], ⟨~я́ть⟩ [наймý, -мёшь; на́нял, -á, -о; -я́вший; на́нятый (на́нят, -á, -о)] rent, hire; *рабо́чего* take on, engage; ~ся *coll.* take a job

на́ново anew, (over) again

наноси́ть [15], ⟨нанести́⟩ [24 -с-: несý, -сёшь; -нёс, -несла́] bring (much, many); *водо́й* carry, waft, deposit, wash ashore; *кра́ску и т. д.* lay on, apply; *на ка́рту и т. д.* plot, draw; (*причиня́ть*) inflict (on Д), cause; *визи́т* pay; *уда́р* deal

наня́ть(ся) → *нанима́ть(ся)*

наоборо́т the other way round, vice versa, conversely; on the contrary

наобу́м *coll.* at random, haphazardly; without thinking

наотре́з bluntly, categorically

напа|да́ть [1], ⟨~сть⟩ [25; *pt. st.*: -па́л, -a; -па́вший] (**на** B) attack, fall (up)on; (*случа́йно обнару́жить*) come across

or upon; hit on; *страх* come over, seize, grip; *спорт* forward; ~де́ние *n* [12] attack, assault; ~да́ющий *m* [17] assailant; *sport* forward; ~дки *f/pl.* [5; *gen.*: -док] accusations; (*приди́рки*) carping, faultfinding *sg.*

напа́ивать [1], ⟨~о́ить⟩ [13] *водо́й и т. д.* give to drink; *спиртны́м* make drunk

напа́|сть **1.** *coll. f* [8] misfortune, bad luck; **2.** → *~да́ть*

напе́в *m* [1] melody, tune; ~а́ть [1] hum, croon

напере|бо́й *coll.* vying with one another; ~го́нки *coll.*: *бежа́ть ~го́нки* racing one another; ~ко́р (Д) in spite *or* defiance (of), counter (to); ~ре́з cutting (across s.b.'s way Д, Р); ~чёт each and every; *as pred.* not many, very few

напёрсток *m* [1; -тка] thimble

напи|ва́ться [1], ⟨~ться⟩ [-пью́сь, -пьёшься; -пи́лся, -пила́сь; пе́йся, -пе́йтесь!] drink, quench one's thirst; (*опьяне́ть*) get drunk

напи́льник *m* [1] (*tool*) file

напи́|ток *m* [1; -тка] drink, beverage; *прохлади́тельные (спиртны́е) ~тки* soft (alcoholic) drinks; ~ться → *~ва́ться*

напи́х|ивать, ⟨~а́ть⟩ [1] cram into, stuff into

наплы́в *m* [1] *покупа́телей и т. д.* influx

напова́л outright, on the spot

наподо́бие (Р) like, resembling

напои́ть → *напа́ивать*

напока́з for show; → *выставля́ть*

наполн|я́ть [28], ⟨~ить⟩ [13] (Т) fill; crowd; *p. pt. p. a.* full

наполови́ну half; (*do*) by halves

напом|ина́ние *n* [12] reminding, reminder; ~ина́ть [1], ⟨~нить⟩ [13] remind (a. p. of Д/**о** П)

напо́р *m* [1] pressure (*a. fig.*); ~истость [8] push, vigo(u)r

напосле́док *coll.* in the end, finally

напра́в|ить(ся) → *~ля́ть(ся)*; ~ле́ние *n* [12] direction (**в** П, **по** Д in); *fig.* trend, tendency; ~ля́ть [28], ⟨~ить⟩ [14] direct, aim; send, refer to; assign, detach; -ся head for; (coll.) get going, get under way; turn (**на** B to)

напра́во (**от** P) to the right, on the right

напра́сн|ый [14; -сен, -сна] vain; (*необоснованный*) groundless, idle; **~о** in vain; (*незаслуженно*) wrongly

напра́шиваться [1], ⟨**~оси́ться**⟩ [15] (**на** B) (pr)offer (o.s. for); solicit; *на оскорбле́ния* provoke; *на комплиме́нты* fish (for); *impf. вы́воды и т. д.* suggest itself

наприме́р for example, for instance

напро|ка́т for hire; **взять** (**дать**) **~ка́т** hire (out); **~лёт** coll. (all)… through(-out); without a break; **~лом** coll.: **идти́ ~ло́м** force one's way; (*act*) regardless of obstacles

напроси́ться → **напра́шиваться**

напро́тив (P) opposite; on the contrary; → a. **наперекор** and **наоборо́т**

напря|га́ть [1], ⟨**~чь**⟩ [26; г/ж: -ягу́, -яжёшь; -пря́г] strain; *му́скулы* tense; **~же́ние** n [12] tension (a. el. voltage), strain, exertion, effort; close attention; **~жённый** [14 sh.] *отноше́ния* strained; *труд и т. д.* (in)tense; *внима́ние* keen, close

напрями́к coll. straight out; outright

напря́чь → **напряга́ть**

напу́ганный [14] scared, frightened

напус|ка́ть [1], ⟨**~ти́ть**⟩ [15] let in, fill; set on (**на** B); coll. (**~ка́ть на себя́**) put on (*airs*); P *стра́ху* cause; **-ся** coll. fly at, go for (**на** B); **~кно́й** [14] affected, assumed, put-on

напу́тств|енный [14] farewell…, parting; **~ие** n [12] parting words

напы́щенный [14 sh.] pompous; *стиль* high-flown

наравне́ (**с** T) on a level with; equally; together (*or along) with

нараспа́шку coll. unbuttoned; (*душа́*) **~** frank, candid

нараспе́в with a singsong voice

нараст|а́ть [1], ⟨**~и́**⟩ [24; -стёт; → **расти́**] grow; *о проце́нтах* accrue; increase; *о зву́ке* swell

нарасхва́т coll. like hot cakes

нареза́|ть [1], ⟨**~ать**⟩ [3] cut; *мя́со* carve; *ло́мтиками* slice; **~ывать** → **~а́ть**

нарека́ние n [12] reprimand, censure

наре́чие[1] n [12] dialect

наре́чие[2] gr. adverb

нарица́тельный [14] econ. nominal; gr. common

нарко́|з m [1] narcosis, an(a)esthesia; **~ма́н** m [1] drug addict; **~тик** m [1] narcotic

наро́д m [1] people, nation; **~ность** f [8] nationality; **~ный** [14] people's, popular, folk…; national; **~ное хозя́йство** national economy

наро́ст m [1] (out)growth

наро́ч|итый [14 sh.] deliberate, intentional; adv. **~но** a. on purpose; coll. in fun; coll. a. **~ на́зло́**; **~ный** [14] courier

на́рты f/pl. [5] sledge (*drawn by dogs or reindeer*)

нару́ж|ность f [8] exterior; outward appearance; **~ный** [14], external; *споко́йствие и т. д.* outward(s); **~у** outside, outward(s); **вы́йти ~у** fig. come to light

наруш|а́ть [1], ⟨**~ить**⟩ [16] disturb; *пра́вило и т. д.* infringe, violate; *тишину́ и т. д.* break; **~е́ние** n [12] violation, transgression, breach; disturbance; **~и́тель** m [4] *грани́цы* trespasser; *споко́йствия* disturber; *зако́на* infringer; **~ить** → **~а́ть**

нарци́сс m [1] daffodil

на́ры f/pl. [5] plank bed

нары́в m [1] abcess; → **гнои́ть**; **~а́ть** [1], ⟨**нарва́ть**⟩ med. come to a head

наря́|д m [1] *оде́жда* attire, dress; **~ди́ть** → **жа́ть**; **~дный** [14; -ден, -дна] well-dressed; elegant; smart

наряду́ (**с** T) together (*or along*) with, side by side; at the same time; a. → **наравне́**

наря|жа́ть [1], ⟨**~ди́ть**⟩ [15 & 15 e.; -яжу́, -я́ди́шь; -я́женный & -яжённый] dress up (as) (v/i. **-ся**)

наса|жда́ть [1], ⟨**~ди́ть**⟩ [15] (im)plant (a. fig.); → a. **~жива́ть**; **~жде́ние** n [12] mst. pl. specially planted trees, bushes; **~жива́ть** [1], ⟨**~жа́ть**⟩, ⟨**~ди́ть**⟩ [15] plant (many); *на ру́чку* haft

насви́стывать [1] whistle

наседа́ть [1] *impf.* press (*of crowds, etc.*)

насеко́мое *n* [14] insect

насел|е́ние *n* [12] population; *города* inhabitants; **‿ённый** [14: -лён, -лена́, -лено́] populated; **‿ённый пункт** (*official designation*) locality, built-up area; **‿я́ть** [28], ⟨**‿и́ть**⟩ [13] people, settle; *impf.* inhabit, live in

наси́женный [14] snug; familiar, comfortable

наси́|лие *n* [12] violence, force; (*принуждение*) coercion; **‿ловать** [7] violate, force; rape; (*a.* **из-**); **‿лу** *coll.* → **е́ле**; **‿льно** by force; forcibly; **‿льственный** [14] forcible; *смерть* violent

наск|а́кивать [1], ⟨**‿очи́ть**⟩ [16] (*на* B) *fig. coll.* fly at, fall (up)on; *камень и т. д.* run *or* strike against; (*столкнуться*) collide (with)

наскво́зь throughout; *coll.* through and through

наско́лько as (far as); how (much); to what extent

на́скоро *coll.* hastily, in a hurry

наскочи́ть → **наска́кивать**

наску́чить *coll.* [16] *pf.*, → **надоеда́ть**

насла|жда́ться [1], ⟨**‿ди́ться**⟩ [15 *e.*: -ажу́сь, -ади́мшься] (*T*) enjoy (o.s.), (be) delight(ed); **‿жде́ние** *n* [12] enjoyment; delight; pleasure

насле́д|ие *n* [12] heritage, legacy; → *a.* **‿ство**; **‿ник** *m* [1] heir; **‿ница** *f* [5] heiress; **‿ный** [14] *принц* crown...; **‿овать** [7] (*im*)*pf.*, ⟨у-⟩ inherit; (*Д*) succeed to; **‿ственность** *f* [8] heredity; **‿ственный** [14] hereditary; *имущество* inherited; **‿ство** *n* [9] inheritance; → *a.* **‿ие**; *vb.* + **в ‿ство** (*or* **по ‿ству**) inherit

наслое́ние *n* [12] stratification

насл|у́шаться [1] *pf.* (*P*) listen to one's heart's content; **не мочь ‿у́шаться** never get tired of listening to; *a.* → **‿ы́шаться** [4] (*P*) hear a lot (of) *or* much; → **понаслы́шке**

насма́рку: **пойти́ ‿** come to nothing

на́смерть to death (*a. fig.*), mortally; **стоя́ть ‿** fight to the last ditch

насме|ха́ться [1] mock, jeer; sneer (at **над** T); **‿шка** *f* [5; *g/pl.*: -шек] mockery,

ridicule; **‿шливый** [14 *sh.*] derisive, mocking; **‿шник** *m* [1], **‿шница** *f* [5] scoffer, mocker

на́сморк *m* [1] cold (*in the head*); **подхвати́ть ‿** catch a cold

насмотре́ться [9: -отрю́сь, -о́тришься] *pf.* → **нагляде́ться**

насо́с *m* [1] pump

на́спех hastily, carelessly

наста|ва́ть [5], ⟨**‿ть**⟩ [-ста́нет] come; **‿вить** → **‿вля́ть**; **‿вле́ние** *n* [12] (*поучение*) admonition, guidance; **‿вля́ть** [28], ⟨**‿вить**⟩ [14] **1.** put, place, set (many P); **2.** (*поучать*) instruct; teach (Д, **в** П s.th.); **‿ивать** [1], ⟨**‿ть**⟩ [-сто́ю, -сто́ишь] insist (**на** П on); *чай и т. д.* draw, extract; **настоя́ть на своём** insist on having it one's own way; **‿ть** → **‿ва́ть**

на́стежь wide open

насти|га́ть [1], ⟨**‿гнуть**⟩ & ⟨**‿чь**⟩ [21; -г-: -и́гну] overtake; catch (up with)

наст|ила́ть [1], ⟨**‿ла́ть**⟩ [-телю́, -те́лешь; на́стланный] lay, spread; *доска́ми* plank; *пол* lay

насто́й *m* [3] infusion, extract; **‿ка** *f* [5; *g/pl.*: -о́ек] liqueur; *a.* → **‿**

насто́йчивый [14 *sh.*] persevering; *требование* urgent, insistent, persistent; (*упорный*) obstinate

насто́ль|ко so (*or as* [much]); **‿ный** [14] table...

настор|а́живаться [1], ⟨**‿ожи́ться**⟩ [16 *e.*; -жу́сь, -жи́шься] prick up one's ears; become suspicious; **‿оже́** on the alert, on one's guard

настоя́|ние *n* [12] insistence, urgent request (**по** Д at); **‿тельный** [14; -лен, -льна] urgent, pressing, insistent; **‿ть** → **наста́ивать**

настоя́щий [17] present (*time*) (**в** B at); *a. gr.* **‿ее время** present tense; true, real, genuine; **по-‿ему** properly

настр|а́ивать [1], ⟨**‿о́ить**⟩ [13] build (many P); *инструмент, оркестр, радио* tune (up, in); *против* set against; *a.* **нала́живать** adjust; **‿о́го** strictly; **‿ое́ние** *n* [12] mood, spirits *pl.*, frame (of mind); **‿о́ить** → **‿а́ивать**; **‿о́йка** *f* [5; *g/pl.*: -о́ек] tuning

Н

наступ|а́тельный [14] offensive; ~а́ть [1], ⟨~и́ть⟩ [14] tread *or* step (**на** B on); (*начаться*) come, set in; *impf. mil.* attack, advance; (*приближаться*) approach; ~ле́ние *n* [12] offensive, attack, advance; coming, approach; *дня* daybreak; *сумерек* nightfall (**с** T at)

насту́рция *f* [7] nasturtium

насу́пить(ся) [14] *pf.* frown

на́сухо dry

насу́щный [14; -щен, -щна] vital; ~ хлеб daily bread

насчёт (P) *coll.* concerning, about

насчи́т|ывать, ⟨~а́ть⟩ [1] number (= *to have or contain*); -ся *impf.* there is (are)

насып|а́ть [1], ⟨~а́ть⟩ [2] pour; fill; ~ь *f* [8] embankment

насы|ща́ть [1], ⟨~тить⟩ [15] satisfy; *влагой* saturate; ~ще́ние *n* [12] satiation; saturation

ната́лкивать [1], ⟨~олкну́ть⟩ [20] (**на** B) push (against, on); *coll.* prompt, suggest; -ся strike against; (*случайно встретить*) run across

натвори́ть *coll.* [13] *pf.* do, get up to

нати́ра́ть [1], ⟨~ере́ть⟩ [12] (T) rub; *мозоль* get; *пол* wax, polish

на́тиск *m* [1] pressure; *mil.* onslaught, charge

наткну́ться → натыка́ться

натолкну́ть(ся) → ната́лкиваться

натоща́к on an empty stomach

натра́в|ливать [1], ⟨~и́ть⟩ [14] set (**на** B on), incite

на́трий *m* [3] *chem.* sodium

нату́г|а *coll. f* [5] strain, effort; ~го *coll.* tight(ly)

нату́р|а *f* [5] (*характер*) nature; (artist's) model (= ~щик *m* [1], ~щица [5]); **с** ~ы from nature *or* life; ~а́льный [14; -лен, -льна] natural

натык|а́ться [1], ⟨~кну́ться⟩ [20] (**на** B) run *or* come across

натя́|гивать [1], ⟨~ну́ть⟩ [19] stretch, draw tight; pull (**на** B on); draw in (*reins*); ~жка *f* [5; *g/pl.:* -жек] forced *or* strained interpretation; **допусти́ть** ~жку stretch a point; **с** ~жкой *a.* at a stretch; ~нутый [14] tight; *отношения*

strained; *улыбка* forced; ~ну́ть → ~гива́ть

науга́д at random, by guessing

нау́ка *f* [5] science; *coll.* lesson

наутёк: *coll.* пусти́ться ~ take to one's heels

нау́тро the next morning

научи́ть [16] teach (В/Д a p. s.th.); -ся learn (Д s.th.)

нау́чный [14; -чен, -чна] scientific

нау́шники *m/pl.* [1] ear- *or* headphones; earmuffs

наха́л *m* [1] impudent fellow; ~льный [14; -лен, -льна] impudent, insolent; ~льство *n* [12] impudence, insolence

нахва́т|ывать ⟨~а́ть⟩ [1] (P) pick up, come by, get hold of; hoard; *a.* -ся

нахлы́нуть [20] *pf.* flow; gush (over, into); *чувства* sweep over

нахму́ривать [1] → хму́рить

наход|и́ть [15], ⟨найти́⟩ [найду́, -дёшь; нашёл, -шла́; -ше́дший; на́йденный; *g. pt.:* найдя́] **1.** find (*a. fig.* = think, consider).; *impf. удово́льствие* take; **2.** come (over **на** B); (*закры́ть*) cover; *тоска и т. д.*) be seized with; (-ся, ⟨найти́сь⟩ be (found, there, [*impf.*] situated, located); (*иметься*) happen to have; (*не растеряться*) not be at a loss; ~ка *f* [5; *g/pl.:* -док] find; *coll.* discovery; *coll. fig.* godsend; **стол** ~ок lost-property office; ~чивый [14 *sh.*] resourceful; quick-witted, smart

наце́нка *f* [5; *g/pl.:* -нок] markup

национал|из(и́р)ова́ть [7] (*im*)*pf.* nationalize; ~и́зм *m* [1] nationalism; ~ьность *f* [5] nationality; ~ьный [14; -лен, -льна] national

на́ция *f* [7] nation

нача́|ло *n* [9] beginning (at a П); (*источник*) source, origin; (*основа*) basis; principle; ~льник *m* [1] head, chief, superior; ~льный [14] initial, first; *строки* opening; ~льство *n* [9] (the) authorities; command(er[s], chief[s], superior[s]); (*администрация*) administration, management; ~тки *m/pl.* [1] elements; ~ть(ся) → начина́ть(ся)

начеку́ on the alert, on the qui vive

на́черно roughly, in draft form

начина́|ние n [12] undertaking; **~ть** [1], ⟨**нача́ть**⟩ [-чну́, -чнёшь; на́чал, -а́, -о; нача́вший; на́чатый (на́чат, -а́, -о) begin, start (**с** P *or* T with); **-ся** v/i.; **~ющий** [17] beginner

начина́я as prep. (**с** P) as (from), beginning (with)

начи́н|ка f [5; g/pl.: -нок] mst. cul. filling, stuffing; **~а́ть** [28] ⟨**~и́ть**⟩ [13] fill, stuff (with T)

начисле́ние n [12] additional sum, extra charge

на́чисто clean; → **на́бело**; (*полностью*) fully

начи́т|анный [14 sh.] well-read; **~а́ться** [1] (P) read (a lot of); *доста́точно* read enough (of); **не мочь ~а́ться** never get tired of reading

наш m, **~а** f, **~е** n, **~и** pl. [25] our; ours; **по ~ему** to our way of thinking; **~а взяла́!** we've won!

нашаты́р|ный [14]: **~ный спирт** m liquid ammonia; coll. a. **~ь** m [4 e.] chem. ammonium chloride

наше́ствие n [12] invasion, inroad

наши|ва́ть [1], ⟨**~ть**⟩ [-шью, -шьёшь; → **шить**] sew on (**на** B *or* П) or many...; **~вка** f [5; g/pl.: -вок] mil. stripe, chevron

нащу́п|ывать, ⟨**~ать**⟩ [1] find by feeling or groping; fig. discover; detect

наяву́ while awake, in reality

не not; no; **~ то** coll. or else, otherwise

неаккура́тный [14; -тен, -тна] (*небрежный*) careless; (*неряшливый*) untidy; **в работе** inaccurate; unpunctual

небе́сный [14] celestial, heavenly; *цвет* sky-blue; (*божественный*) divine; → **небосво́д**

неблаго|ви́дный [14; -ден, -дна] unseemly; **~да́рность** f [8] ingratitude; **~да́рный** [14; -рен, -рна] ungrateful; **~полу́чный** [14; -чен, чна] unfavorable, adverse, bad; adv. not successfully, not favo(u)rably; **~прия́тный** [14; -тен, -тна] unfavo(u)rable, inauspicious; **~разу́мный** [14; -мен, -мна] imprudent; unreasonable; **~ро́дный** [14; -ден, -дна] ignoble, base; **~скло́нный** [14;

-о́нен, -о́нна] unkindly; ill-disposed; **судьба́ ко мне ~скло́нна** fate has not treated me too kindly

не́бо¹ n [9; pl.: небеса́, -е́с] sky (in **на** П); heaven(s); **под откры́тым ~м** in the open air

не́бо² n [9] anat. palate

небога́тый [14 sh.] of modest means; poor

небольш|о́й [17] small; short; **... с ~и́м** ... odd

небо|сво́д m [1] firmament; a. **~скло́н** m [1] horizon; **~скрёб** m [1] skyscraper

небре́жный [14; -жен, -жна] careless, negligent; slipshod

небы|ва́лый [14] unheard-of, unprecedented; **~ли́ца** f [5] fable, invention

нева́жн|ый [14; -жен, -жна, -о] unimportant, trifling; coll. poor, bad; **это ~о** it does not matter

невдалеке́ not far off or from (**от** P)

невдомёк: мне бы́ло ~ it never occurred to me

неве́|дение n [12] ignorance; **~домый** [14 sh.] unknown; **~жа** m/f [5] boor; **~жда** m/f [5] ignoramus; **~жество** n [9] ignorance; **~жливость** f [8] incivility; **~жливый** [14 sh.] impolite, rude

неве́р|ие n [12] в свои силы lack of self-confidence; **~ный** [14; -рен, -рна, -о] incorrect; fig. false; *друг* unfaithful; *походка и т. д.* unsteady; su. infidel; **~оя́тный** [14; -тен, -тна] improbable; incredible

невесо́мый [14 sh.] imponderable; weightless (a. fig.)

неве́ст|а f [5] fiancee, bride; coll. marriageable girl; **~ка** f [5; g/pl.: -ток] daughter-in-law; sister-in-law (*brother's wife*)

невзго́да f [5] adversity, misfortune; **~ира́я** (**на** B) in spite of, despite; without respect (of p.'s); **~нача́й** coll. unexpectedly, by chance; **~ра́чный** [14; -чен, -чна] plain, unattractive; **~ыска́тельный** [14] unpretentious, undemanding

неви́д|анный [14] singular, unprecedented; **~имый** [14 sh.] invisible

неви́нный [14; -и́нен, -и́нна] innocent, virginal

невку́сный [14; -сен, -сна] unpalatable

невме|ня́емый [14 *sh.*] *law* irresponsible; *coll.* beside o.s. **~ша́тельство** *n* [9] nonintervention

невнима́тельный [14; -лен, -льна] inattentive

невня́тный [14; -тен, -тна] indistinct, inarticulate

не́вод *m* [1] seine, sweep-net

невозврати́мый [14 *sh.*], **~вра́тный** [14; -тен, -тна] irretrievable, irreparable, irrevocable; **~мо́жный** [14; -жен, -жна] impossible; **~мути́мый** [14 *sh.*] imperturbable

невол|и́ть [13] force, compel; **~ьный** [14; -лен, -льна] involuntary; (*вынужденный*) forced; **~я** *f* [6] captivity; *coll.* *необходимость* need, necessity; **охо́та пу́ще ~и** where there's a will, there's a way

невоо|брази́мый [14 *sh.*] unimaginable; **~ружённый** [14] unarmed; **~ружённым гла́зом** with the naked eye

невоспи́танный [14 *sh.*] ill-bred

невосполни́мый [14 *sh.*] irreplaceable

невпопа́д *coll.* → **некста́ти**

невреди́мый [14 *sh.*] unharmed, sound

невы́|годный [14; -ден, -дна] unprofitable; *положение* disadvantageous; **~держанный** [14 *sh.*] inconsistent, uneven; *сыр и т. д.* unripe; **~носи́мый** [14 *sh.*] unbearable, intolerable; **~полне́ние** *n* [12] nonfulfil(l)ment; **~полни́мый** → **неисполни́мый**; **~рази́мый** [14 *sh.*] inexpressible, ineffable; **~рази́тельный** [14; -лен, -льна] inexpressive; **~со́кий** [16; -со́к, -а́, -со́ко] low, small; *человек* short; *качество* inferior

не́где there is nowhere (+ *inf.*); **~ сесть** there is nowhere to sit

негла́сный [14; -сен, -сна] secret; *расследование* private

него́д|ный [14; -ден, -дна, -о] unsuitable; unfit; *coll.* worthless; **~ова́ние** *n* [12] indignation; **~ова́ть** [7] be indignant (**на** B with); **~я́й** *m* [3] scoundrel, rascal

негр *m* [1] Negro

негра́мотн|ость → **безгра́мотность**; **~ый** → **безгра́мотный**

негритя́н|ка *f* [5; *g/pl.:* -нок] Negress; **~ский** [16] Negro…

неда́|вний [15] recent; **с ~вних (~вней) пор(ы́)** of late; **~вно** recently; **~лёкий** [16; -ёк, -ека́, -еко́ *and* -ёко] near(by), close; short; not far (off); (*недавний*) recent; (*глуповатый*) dull, stupid; **~льнови́дный** [14] lacking foresight, shortsighted; **~ром** not in vain, not without reason; justly

недви́жимость *f* [8] *law* real estate

неде|йстви́тельный [14; -лен, -льна] invalid, void; **~лимый** [14] indivisible

неде́льный [14] a week's, weekly; **~я** *f* [6] week; **в ~ю** a or per week; **на э́той (про́шлой, бу́дущей) ~е** this (last, next) week; **че́рез ~ю** in a week's time

недобро|жела́тельный [14; -лен, -льна] malevolent, ill-disposed; **~ка́чественный** [14 *sh.*] inferior, low-grade; **~со́вестный** [14; -тен, -тна] *конкуренция* unscrupulous, unfair; *работа* careless

недо́брый [14; -добр, -а́, -о] unkind(ly), hostile; *предзнаменование* evil, bad

недове́р|ие *n* [12] distrust; **~чивый** [14 *sh.*] distrustful (**к** Д of)

недово́ль|ный [14; -лен, -льна] (Т) dissatisfied, discontented; **~ство** *n* [9] discontent, dissatisfaction

недога́дливый [14 *sh.*] slowwitted

недоеда́|ние *n* [12] malnutrition; **~ть** [1] be underfed *or* undernourished

недо́лго not long, short; **~ и** (+ *inf.*) one can easily; **~ ду́мая** without hesitation

недомога́ть [1] be unwell *or* sick

недомо́лвка *f* [5; *g/pl.:* -вок] reservation, innuendo

недооце́н|ивать [1], ⟨**~и́ть**⟩ [13] underestimate, undervalue

недо|пусти́мый [14 *sh.*] inadmisible, intolerable; **~ра́звитый** [14 *sh.*] underdeveloped; **~разуме́ние** *n* [12] misunderstanding (**по** Д through); **~рого́й** [16; -до́рог, -а́, -о] inexpensive

недослы́шать [1] *pf.* fail to hear all of

недосмо́тр *m* [1] oversight, inadvertence (**по** Д through); **~е́ть** [9; -отрю,

-о́тришь; -о́тренный] *pf.* overlook (*s.th.*)

недост|ава́ть [5], ⟨∼а́ть⟩ [-ста́нет] *impers.*: (Д) (be) lack(ing), want(ing), be short *or* in need of (P) *кого́-л.*; miss; *э́того ещё ∼ава́ло*!; and that too!; ∼а́ток *m* [1; -тка] lack, shortage (P, **в** П of); deficiency; defect, shortcoming; *физи́ческий ∼а́ток* [14; -чен, -чна] insufficient, deficient, inadequate; *gr.* defective; ∼а́ть → ∼ава́ть

недо|стижи́мый [14 *sh.*] unattainable; ∼сто́йный [14; -о́ин, -о́йна] unworthy; ∼сту́пный [14; -пен, -пна] inaccessible

недосу́г *coll. m* [1] lack of time (*за* Т, *по* Д for); *мне ∼* I have no time

недосяга́емый [14 *sh.*] unattainable

недоум|ева́ть [1] be puzzled, be perplexed; ∼е́ние *n* [12] bewilderment; **в** ∼е́нии in a quandary

недочёт *m* [1] deficit; *изъя́н* defect

не́дра *n/pl.* [9] *земли́* bowels, depths (*a. fig.*)

не́друг *m* [1] enemy, foe

недружелю́бный [14; -бен, -бна] unfriendly

неду́г *m* [1] ailment

недурно́й [14; -ду́рен & -рён, -рна́, -о] not bad; *собо́й* not bad-looking

недю́жинный [14] out of the ordinary, uncommon

неесте́ственный [14 *sh.*] unnatural; *смех* affected; *улы́бка* forced

нежела́|ние *n* [12] unwillingness; ∼тельный [14; -лен, -льна] undesirable

неже́ли *lit.* → **чем**

нежена́тый [14] single, unmarried

нежило́й [14] not fit for habitation

не́ж|ить [16] luxuriate; ∼ничать *coll.* [1] caress, spoon; ∼ность *f* [8] tenderness; *pl.* display of affection ∼ный [14; -жен, -жна́, -о] tender, affectionate; *о ко́же, вку́се* delicate

незаб|ве́нный [14 *sh.*], ∼ыва́емый [14 *sh.*] unforgettable; ∼у́дка *f* [5; *g/pl.*: -док] *bot.* forget-me-not

незави́сим|ость *f* [8] independence; ∼ый [14 *sh.*] independent

незада́чливый *coll.* [14 *sh.*] unlucky

незадо́лго shortly (**до** P before)

незако́нный [14; -о́нен, -о́нна] illegal, unlawful, illicit; *ребёнок и т. д.* illegitimate

незаме|ни́мый [14 *sh.*] irreplaceable; ∼тный [14; -тен, -тна] imperceptible, inconspicuous; *челове́к* plain, ordinary; ∼ченный [14] unnoticed

неза́|мысловатый *coll.* [14 *sh.*] simple, uncomplicated; ∼па́мятный [14]: **с** ∼па́мятных времён from time immemorial; ∼тейливый [14 *sh.*] plain, simple; ∼уря́дный [14; -ден, -дна] outstanding, exceptional

не́зачем there is no need *or* point

незва́ный [14] uninvited

нездоро́в|иться [14]: *мне ∼ится* I feel (am) unwell; ∼ый [14 *sh.*] sick; morbid (*a. fig.*); *кли́мат и т. д.* unhealthy

незло́бивый [14 *sh.*] forgiving

незнако́м|ец *m* [1; -мца], ∼ка *f* [5; *g/pl.*: -мок] stranger; ∼ый [14] unknown, unfamiliar

незна́|ние *n* [12] ignorance; ∼чи́тельный [14; -лен, -льна] insignificant

незр|е́лый [14 *sh.*] unripe; *fig.* immature; ∼и́мый [14 *sh.*] invisible

незы́блемый [14 *sh.*] firm, stable, unshak(e)able

неиз|бе́жный [14; -жен, -жна] inevitable; ∼ве́стный [14; -тен, -тна] unknown; *su. a.* stranger; ∼глади́мый [14 *sh.*] indelible; ∼лечи́мый [14 *sh.*] incurable; ∼ме́нный [14; -е́нен, -е́нна] invariable; immutable; ∼мери́мый [14 *sh.*] immeasurable, immense; ∼ъясни́мый [14 *sh.*] inexplicable

неим|е́ние *n* [12]: *за* ∼е́нием (P) for want of; ∼ове́рный [14; -рен, -рна] incredible; ∼у́щий [17] poor

неи́с|кренний [15; -енен, -енна] insincere; ∼куше́нный [14; -шён, -шена́] inexperienced, innocent; ∼по́лнение *n* [12] *зако́на* failure to observe (*the law*); ∼полни́мый [14 *sh.*] impracticable

неиспр|ави́мый [14 *sh.*] incorrigible; ∼а́вность *f* [8] disrepair; carelessness; ∼а́вный [14; -вен, -вна] out of order, broken, defective; *плате́льщик* unpunctual

неиссяка́емый [14 sh.] inexhaustible

не́истов|ство n [9] rage, frenzy; **~ствовать** [7] rage; **~ый** [14 sh.] frantic, furious

неис|тощи́мый [14 sh.] inexhaustible; **~треби́мый** [14 sh.] ineradicable; **~цели́мый** [14 sh.] incurable; **~черпа́емый** [14 sh.] → **~тощи́мый**; **~числи́мый** [14 sh.] innumerable

нейло́н m [1], **~овый** [14] nylon (…)

нейтрал|ите́т m [1] neutrality; **~ьный** [14; -лен, -льна] neutral

неказистый coll. [14 sh.] → **невзра́чный**

не́к|ий [24 st.] a certain, some; **~огда** there is (**мне ~когда** I have) no time; once; **~ого** [23] there is (**мне ~кого** I have) nobody or no one (to inf.); **~компете́нтный** [14; -тен, -тна] incompetent; **~корре́ктный** [-тен, -тна] impolite, discourteous; **~который** [14] some (pl. из P of); **~краси́вый** [14 sh.] plain, unattractive; поведе́ние unseemly, indecorous

некроло́г m [1] obituary

некста́ти inopportunely; (неуместно) inappropriately

не́кто somebody, someone; a certain

не́куда there is nowhere (+ inf.); **мне ~ пойти́** I have nowhere to go; coll. **ху́же** u m. д. **~** could not be worse, etc.

некуря́щий [17] nonsmoker, nonsmoking

нел|а́дный coll. [14; -ден, -дна] wrong, bad; **будь он ~а́ден!** blast him!; **~ега́льный** [14; -лен, -льна] illegal; **~е́пый** [14 sh.] absurd

нело́вкий [16; -вок, -вка́, -о] awkward, clumsy; ситуация embarrassing

нело́вко adv. → **нело́вкий**; **чу́вствовать себя́ ~** feel ill at ease

нелоги́чный [14; -чен, -чна] illogical

нельзя́ (it is) impossible, one (**мне** I) cannot or must not; **~!** no!; **как ~ лу́чше** in the best way possible, excellently; **~ не → не (мочь)**

нелюди́мый [14 sh.] unsociable

нема́ло (P) a lot, a great deal (of)

неме́дленный [14] immediate

неме́ть [8], ⟨о-⟩ grow dumb, numb

не́м|ец m [1; -мца], **~е́цкий** [16], **~ка** f [5; g/pl.: -мок] German

неми́лость f [8] disgrace, disfavour

неминуемый [14 sh.] inevitable

немно́|гие pl. [16] (a) few, some; **~го а** little; слегка slightly, somewhat; **~гое** n [16] few things, little; **~гим а** little; **~ж(еч)ко** coll. a (little) bit, a trifle

немо́й [14; нем, -а́, -о] dumb, mute

немо|лодо́й [14; -мо́лод, -а́, -о] elderly; **~та́** f [5] dumbness, muteness

не́мощный [14; -щен, -щна] infirm

немы́слимый [14 sh.] inconceivable, unthinkable

ненави́|деть [11], ⟨воз-⟩ hate; **~стный** [14; -тен, -тна] hateful, odious; **~сть** ('не-) f [8] hatred (**к** Д of)

нена|гля́дный [14] coll. beloved; **~дёжный** [14; -жен, -жна] unreliable; (непрочный) unsafe, insecure; **~до́лго** for a short while; **~ме́ренный** [14] unintentional; **~паде́ние** n [12] nonaggression; **~стный** [14; -тен, -тна] rainy, foul; **~стье** n [10] foul weather; **~сы́тный** [14; -тен, -тна] insatiable

нен|орма́льный [14; -лен, -льна] abnormal; coll. crazy; **~у́жный** [14; -жен, -жна́, -о] unnecessary

необ|ду́манный [14 sh.] rash, hasty; **~ита́емый** [14 sh.] uninhabited; остров desert; **~озри́мый** [14 sh.] immense, boundless; **~осно́ванный** [14 sh.] unfounded; **~рабо́танный** [14] земля́ uncultivated; **~у́зданный** [14 sh.] unbridled, ungovernable

необходи́м|ость f [8] necessity (**по** П of), need (P, **в** П for); **~ый** [14 sh.] necessary (П; **для** P for), essential; → **ну́жный**

необ|щи́тельный [14; -лен, -льна] unsociable, reserved; **~ъясни́мый** [14 sh.] inexplicable; **~ъя́тный** [14; -тен, -тна] immense, unbounded; **~ыкнове́нный** [14; -énен, -énна] unusual, uncommon; **~ы́чный** [14; -ча́(ай)ен, -ч(ай)на] extraordinary, exceptional; **~яза́тельный** [14; -лен, -льна] optional; человек unreliable

неограни́ченный [14 sh.] unrestricted

неод|нокра́тный [14] repeated; ~обре́ние n [12] disapproval; ~обри́тельный [14; -лен, -льна] disapproving; ~оли́мый → **непреодоли́мый**; ~ушевлённый [14] inanimate

неожи́данн|ость f [8] unexpectedness, surprise; ~ый [14 sh.] unexpected, sudden

нео́н m [1] chem. neon; ~овый [14] neon…

неоп|и́суемый [14 sh.] indescribable; ~ла́ченный [14 sh.] unpaid, unsettled; ~ра́вданный [14] unjustified; ~реде-лённый [14; -ёнен, -ённа] indefinite (a. gr.), uncertain, vague; ~рове́ржи-мый [14 sh.] irrefutable; ~ы́тный [14; -тен, -тна] inexperienced

неос|ведомлённый [14; -лён, -лена́, -лены] ill-informed; ~ла́бный [14; -бен, -бна] unremitting, unabated; ~мотри́тельный [14; -лен, -льна] imprudent; ~пори́мый [14 sh.] undisputable; ~торо́жный [14; -жен, -жна] careless, incautious; imprudent; ~уществи́мый [14 sh.] impracticable; ~яза́емый [14 sh.] intangible

неот|врати́мый [14 sh.] inevitable; ~ёсанный [14 sh.] unpolished; coll. челове́к uncouth; ~куда → **не́где**; ~ло́жный [14; -жен, -жна] pressing, urgent; ~лу́чный ever-present → **посто́янный**; ~рази́мый [14 sh.] irresistible; до́вод irrefutable; ~сту́пный [14; -пен, -пна] persistent; importunate; ~чётливый [14 sh.] indistinct, vague; ~ъе́млемый [14 sh.] часть integral; пра́во inalienable

неохо́т|а f [5] reluctance; (мне) ~а coll. I (etc.) am not in the mood; ~но unwillingly

не|оцени́мый [14 sh.] inestimable; invaluable; ~перехо́дный [14] gr. intransitive

неплатёжеспосо́бный [14; -бен, -бна] insolvent

непо|беди́мый [14 sh.] invincible; ~во-ро́тливый [14 sh.] clumsy, slow; ~го́да f [5] foul weather; ~греши́мый [14 sh.] infallible; ~далёку not far (away or off); ~да́тливый [14 sh.] unyielding, in-

tractable

непод|ви́жный [14; -жен, -жна] motionless, fixed, stationary; ~де́льный [14; -лен, -льна] genuine, unfeigned; и́скренний sincere; ~ку́пный [14; -пен, -пна] incorruptible; ~оба́ющий [17] improper, unbecoming; ~ража́емый [14 sh.] inimitable; ~ходя́щий [17] unsuitable; ~чине́ние n [12] insubordination

непо|зволи́тельный [14; -лен, -льна] not permissible; ~колеби́мый [14 sh.] (надёжный) firm, steadfast; (сто́йкий) unflinching; ~ко́рный [14; -рен, -рна] refractory; ~ла́дка coll. f [5; g/pl.: -док] tech. defect, fault; ~лный [14; -лон, -лна́, -о] incomplete; рабо́чий день short; ~ме́рный [14; -рен, -рна] excessive, inordinate

непоня́т|ливый [14 sh.] slow-witted; ~ный [14; -тен, -тна] unintelligible, incomprehensible; явле́ние strange, odd

непо|прави́мый [14 sh.] irreparable, irremediable; ~ря́дочный [14; -чен, -чна] dishono(u)rable; disreputable; ~се́дливый [14 sh.] fidgety; ~си́льный [14; -лен, -льна] beyond one's strength; ~сле́довательный [14; -лен, -льна] inconsistent; ~слу́шный [14; -шен, -шна] disobedient

непо|сре́дственный [14 sh.] immediate, direct; (есте́ственный) spontaneous; ~стижи́мый [14 sh.] inconceivable; ~стоя́нный [14; -янен, -янна] inconstant, changeable, fickle; ~хо́жий [17 sh.] unlike, different (**на** B from)

непра́в|да f [5] untruth, lie; (it is) not true; все́ми пра́вдами и ~дами by hook or by crook; ~доподо́бный [14; -бен, -бна] improbable; implausible; ~ильный [14; -лен, -льна] incorrect, wrong; irregular (a. gr.); improper (a. math); ~ый [14; непра́в, -á, -o] mistaken; (несправедли́вый) unjust

непре|взойдённый [14 sh.] unsurpassed; ~дви́денный [14] unforeseen; ~дубеждённый [14] unbiased; ~кло́нный [14; -о́нен, -о́нна] inflexible; obdurate, inexorable; ~ло́жный [14; -жен, жна] и́стина indisputable; ~ме́нный

[14; -éнен, -éнна] indispensable, necessary; ~мéнно → *обязáтельно*; ~одолúмый [14 *sh.*] insuperable; *стремлéние* irresistible; ~рекáемый [14 *sh.*] indisputable; ~рывный [14; -вен, -вна] uninterrupted, continuous; ~стáнный [14; -áнен, -áнна] incessant

непри|вычный [14; -чен, -чна] unaccustomed; (*необычный*) unusual; ~глáдный [14; -ден, -дна *внешность* homely; unattractive; ungainly; ~гóдный [14; -ден, -дна] unfit; useless; ~éмлемый [14 *sh.*] unacceptable; ~косновéнный [14; -éнен, -éнна] inviolable; *mil. зaпaс* emergency; ~крáшенный [14] unvarnished; ~лúчный [14; -чен, -чна] indecent, unseemly; ~мéтный [14; -тен, -тна] imperceptible; *человек* unremarkable; ~мúримый [14 *sh.*] irreconcilable; ~нуждённый [14 *sh.*] unconstrained; relaxed, laid-back; ~стóйный [14; -óен, -óйна] obscene, indecent; ~ступный [14; -пен, -пна] inaccessible; *крéпость* impregnable; *человек* unapproachable, haughty; ~творный [14; -рен, -рна] genuine, unfeigned; ~тязáтельный [14; -лен, -льна] modest, unassuming

неприя|зненный [14 *sh.*] inimical, unfriendly; ~знь *f* [8] hostility

неприя|тель *m* [4] enemy; ~тельский [16] hostile, enemy('s); ~тность *f* [8] unpleasantness; trouble; ~тный [14; -тен, -тна] disagreeable, unpleasant

непро|глядный [14; -ден, -дна] *тьмa* pitch-dark; ~должúтельный [14; -лен, -льна] short, brief; ~éзжий [17] impassable; ~зрáчный [14; -чен, -чна] opaque; ~изводúтельный [14; -лен, -льна] unproductive; ~извóльный [14; -лен, -льна] involuntary; ~мокáемый [14 *sh.*] waterproof; ~ницáемый [14 *sh.*] impenetrable, impermeable; *улыбкa и т. д.* inscrutable; ~стúтельный [14; -лен, -льна] unpardonable; ~ходúмый [14 *sh.*] impassable; *coll.* complete; ~чный [14; -чен, -чна, -о] flimsy; *мир* unstable

нерабóчий [17] nonworking, free, off (*day*)

нерáв|енство *n* [9] inequality; ~номéрный [14; -рен, -рна] uneven; ~ный [14; -вен, -внá, -о] unequal

нерадúвый [14 *sh.*] careless, negligent

неразбери́ха *coll. f* [5] muddle, confusion; ~бóрчивый [14 *sh.*] illegible; *fig.* undiscriminating; *в срéдствах* unscrupulous; ~витóй [14; -рáзвит, -á, -о] undeveloped; *ребёнок* backward; ~личúмый [14 *sh.*] indistinguishable; ~лучный [14; -чен, -чна] inseparable; ~решúмый [14 *sh.*] insoluble; ~рывный [14; -вен, -вна] indissoluble; ~умный [14; -мен, -мна] injudicious

нерасположéние *n* [12] *к человеку* dislike; disinclination (to, for)

нерационáльный [14; -лен, -льна] unpractical

нерв *m* [1] nerve; ~úровать [7], ~ничать [1] to get on one's nerves; become fidgety *or* irritated; ~(óз)ный [14; -вен, -внá, -о (-зен, -зна)] nervous; high-strung

нереáльный [14; -лен, -льна] unreal; (*невыполнúмый*) impracticable

нерешúтельн|ость *f* [8] indecision; *в ~ости* undecided; ~ый [14; -лен, -льна] indecisive, irresolute

нержавéющ|ий [15] rust-free; ~ая стáль stainless steel

неро|бкий [16; -бок, -бкá, -о] not timid; brave; ~вный [14; -вен, -внá, -о] uneven, rough; *пульс* irregular

неря́|ха *m/f* [5] sloven; ~шливый [14 *sh.*] slovenly; *в рабóте* careless, slipshod

несамостоя́тельный [14; -лен, -льна] not independent

несбы́точный [14; -чен, -чна] unrealizable

не|своевре́менный [14; -енен, -енна] inopportune, untimely; tardy; ~свя́зный [14; зен, зна] incoherent; ~сгора́емый [14] fireproof; ~сде́ржанный [14 *sh.*] unrestrained; ~серьёзный [14; -зен, -зна] not serious, frivolous; ~ска́занный *lit.* [14 *sh., no m*] indescribable; ~скла́дный [14; -ден, -дна] *человек* ungainly; *речь* incoherent; ~склоня́емый [14 *sh.*] *gr.* indeclinable

не́сколько [32] a few; some, several; *adv.* somewhat

не|скро́мный [14; -мен, -мна́, -о] immodest; **∼слы́ханный** [14 *sh.*] unheard-of; (*беспримерный*) unprecedented; **∼сме́тный** [14; -тен, -тна] innumerable, incalculable

несмотря́ (*на* B) in spite of, despite, notwithstanding; (al)though

несно́сный [14; -сен, -сна] intolerable

несо|блюде́ние n [12] nonobservance; **∼верше́нноле́тие** n [12] minority; **∼верше́нный** [14; -ёнен, -ённа] gr. imperfective; **∼верше́нство** n [9] imperfection; **∼вмести́мый** [14 *sh.*] incompatible; **∼гла́сие** n [12] disagreement; **∼измери́мый** [14 *sh.*] incommensurable; **∼круши́мый** [14 *sh.*] indestructible; **∼мне́нный** [14; -ёнен, -ённа] undoubted; **∼мне́нно** a. undoubtedly, without doubt; **∼отве́тствие** n [12] discrepancy; **∼разме́рный** [14; -ерен, -ерна] disproportionate; **∼стоя́тельный** [14; -лен, -льна] *должник* insolvent; (*необоснованный*) groundless, unsupported

несп|око́йный [14; -о́ен, -о́йна] restless, uneasy; **∼осо́бный** [14; -бен, -бна] incapable (*к* Д, *на* B of); **∼раведли́вость** f [8] injustice, unfairness; **∼раведли́вый** [14 *sh.*] unjust, unfair; **∼роста́** coll. → **неда́ром**

несрав|не́нный [14; -ёнен, -ённа] and **∼ни́мый** [14 *sh.*] incomparable, matchless

нестерпи́мый [14 *sh.*] intolerable

нести́ [24; -с-: -су], (по-) (be) carry(ing), etc.); bear; bring; *убытки и т. д.* suffer; *о запахе и т. д.* smell (of T); drift, waft; (**-сь** *v/i.*; a. be heard; spread); ⟨с⟩ lay (eggs **-сь**); talk *чушь*; **несёт** (*сквозит*) there's a draft (*Brt.* draught)

не|стро́йный [14; -о́ен, -о́йна, -о] *звуки* discordant; *ряды* disorderly; **∼сура́зный** coll. [14; -зен, -зна] senseless, absurd; **∼сусве́тный** [14] unimaginable; *чушь* sheer

несча́ст|ный [14; -тен, -тна] unhappy, unfortunate; **∼ный слу́чай** accident; **∼ье** n [12] misfortune; disaster; acci-

dent; **к ∼ью** unfortunately

несчётный [14; -тен, -тна] innumerable

нет 1. part.: no; **∼ ещё** not yet; **2.** *impers.* *vb.* [pt. не́ было, ft. не бу́дет] (P) there is (are) no; **у меня́** (etc.) **∼** I (etc.) have no(ne); **его́** (**её**) **∼** s)he is not (t)here *or* in; **на ∼ и суда́ нет** well, it can't be helped

нета́кти́чный [14; -чен, -чна] tactless

нетвёрдый [14; -вёрд, -верда́] unsteady; shaky (a. fig.)

нетерп|ели́вый [14; -ив] impatient; **∼е́ние** n [12] impatience; **∼и́мый** [14 *sh.*] intolerant; (*невыносимый*) intolerable

не|тле́нный [14; -ёнен, -ённа] imperishable; **∼тре́звый** [14; трезв, -а́, -о] drunk (a. **в ∼тре́звом ви́де**); **∼тро́нутый** [14 *sh.*] untouched; *fig.* chaste, virgin; **∼трудоспосо́бный** [14; -бен, -бна] disabled

нёт|то [indecl.] comm. net; **∼у** coll. → **нет** 2

неу|важе́ние n [12] disrespect (**к** Д for); **∼ве́ренный** [14 *sh.*] uncertain; **∼вяда́емый** [14 *sh.*] *rhet.* unfading; everlasting; **∼вя́зка** [5; g/pl.: -зок] coll. misunderstanding; (*несогласованность*) discrepancy, lack of coordination; *∼гаси́мый* [14 *sh.*] inextinguishable; **∼гомо́нный** [14; -о́нен, -о́нна] restless, untiring

неуда́ч|а f [5] misfortune; failure; **потерпе́ть ∼у** fail; **∼ливый** [14 *sh.*] unlucky; **∼ник** m [1] unlucky person, failure; **∼ный** [14; -чен, -чна] unsuccessful, unfortunate

неуд|ержи́мый [14 *sh.*] irrepressible; **∼иви́тельно** (it is) no wonder

неудо́б|ный [14; -бен, -бна] uncomfortable; *время* inconvenient; *положение* awkward, embarrassing; **∼ство** n [9] inconvenience

неудов|летвори́тельный [14; -лен, -льна] unsatisfactory; **∼летворённость** f [8] dissatisfaction, discontent; **∼о́льствие** n [12] displeasure

неуже́ли interr. part. really?, is it possible?

неу|жи́вчивый [14 *sh.*] unsociable, unaccommodating; **∼кло́нный** [14;

-о́нен, -о́нна] steady; ~клю́жий [17 *sh.*] clumsy, awkward; ~кроти́мый [14 *sh.*] indomitable; ~лови́мый [14 *sh.*] elusive; (*еле заме́тный*) imperceptible; ~ме́лый [14 *sh.*] unskil(l)ful, awkward; ~ме́ние *n* [12] inability; ~ме́ренный [14 *sh.*] intemperate, immoderate; ~ме́стный [14; -тен, -тна] inappropriate; ~моли́мый [14 *sh.*] inexorable; ~мы́шленный [14 *sh.*] unintentional; ~потреби́тельный [14; -лен, -льна] not in use, not current; ~рожа́й *m* [3] bad harvest; ~ста́нный [14; -а́нен, -а́нна] tireless, unwearying; *a.* → ~томи́мый; ~сто́йка [5; *g/pl.*: -оек] forfeit; ~сто́йчивый [14 *sh.*] unstable; unsteady; *пого́да* changeable; ~страши́мый [14 *sh.*] intrepid, dauntless; ~ступчивый [14 *sh.*] unyielding, tenacious; ~толи́мый [14 *sh.*] unquenchable; ~томи́мый [14 *sh.*] tireless, indefatigable

неуч *coll. m* [1] ignoramus

неучти́вый [14 *sh.*] uncivil; ~ю́тный [14; -тен, -тна] comfortless; ~язви́мый [14 *sh.*] invulnerable

нефт|епрово́д *m* [1] pipeline; ~ь *f* [8] (mineral) oil, petroleum; ~яно́й [14] oil…

не|хва́тка *f* [5; *g/pl.*: -ток] shortage; ~хоро́ший [17; -ро́ш, -а́] bad; ~хотя́ unwillingly; ~цензу́рный [14; -рен, -рна] unprintable; ~цензу́рное сло́во swearword; ~ча́янный [14] *встре́ча* unexpected; (*случа́йный*) accidental; (*неумы́шленный*) unintentional

не́чего [23]: (*мне, etc.*) + *inf.* (there is or one can), (I have) nothing to…; (one) need not, (there is) no need; (it is) no use; stop …ing

не|челове́ческий [16] inhuman; *уси́лия* superhuman; ~че́стный [14; -тен, -тна́, -о] dishonest; ~чётный [14] odd (*number*)

нечист|опло́тный [14; -тен, -тна] dirty; *fig.* unscrupulous; ~ота́ *f* [5; *pl. st.*: -о́ты] dirtiness; *pl.* sewage; ~ый [14; -чи́ст, -а́, -о] unclean, dirty; impure; *помыслы и т. д.* evil, vile, bad, foul

не́что something

не|чувстви́тельный [14; -лен, -льна]

insensitive, insensible (к Д to); ~ща́дный [14; -ден, -дна] merciless; ~я́вка *f* [5] nonappearance; ~я́ркий [16; -я́рок, -ярка́, -о] dull, dim; *fig.* mediocre; ~я́сный [14; -сен, -сна́, -о] not clear; *fig.* vague

ни not a (single **оди́н**); ~ …, ~ neither … nor; … ever (*e. g.* **кто [бы]** ~ whoever); **кто (что, когда́, где, куда́) бы то ни́ бы́л(о)** whosoever (what-, when-, wheresoever); **как ~** + *vb. a.* in spite of or for all + *su.*; **как бы (то) ни́ было** anyway, whatever happens; ~ **за что ни про что**, for no apparent reason

нигде́ nowhere

ни́ж|е below, beneath; *ро́стом* shorter; ~еподписа́вшийся *m* [17] (the) undersigned; ~ний [15] lower; under…; *эта́ж* first, *Brt.* ground

низ *m* [1; *pl. e.*] bottom, lower part; ~а́ть [3], ⟨на-⟩ string, thread

низина́ *f* [5] hollow, lowland

ни́зк|ий [16; -зок, -зка́, -о; *compr.*: ни́же] low; *fig.* mean, base; *рост* short; ~оро́слый [14 *sh.*] undersized, stunted; *куста́рник* low; ~осо́ртный [14; -тен, -тна] lowgrade; *това́р* of inferior quality

ни́зменн|ость *f* [8] *geogr.* lowland, plain; ~ый [14 *sh.*] low-lying

низо́|вье *n* [10; *g/pl.*: -вьев] lower reaches (*of a river*); ~сть *f* [8] meanness

ника́к by no means, not at all; ~о́й [16] no … (at all *coll.*)

ни́кель *m* [4] nickel; ~иро́ванный [14 *sh.*] nickel-plated

никогда́ never

ни|ко́й: *now only in* ~ко́им о́бразом by no means *and* ни в ко́ем слу́чае on no account; ~кто́ [23] nobody, no one, none; ~куда́ nowhere; → *a.* **годи́ться, го́дный**; ~кчёмный *coll.* good-for-nothing; ~ма́ло → **ско́лько**; ~отку́да from nowhere; ~почём *coll.* very cheap, easy, *etc.*; ~ско́лько not in the least, not at all

нисходя́щий [17] descending

ни́т|ка *f* [5; *g/pl.*: -ток], ~ь [8] thread; *жемчуга* string; *хлопчатобума́жная* cotton; ~ь *a.* filament; до ~ки *coll.* to the skin; ***ши́то бе́лыми ~ками*** be transparent; ***на живу́ю ~ку*** carelessly, superficially

ничего́ nothing; not bad; so-so; no(t) matter; ***~!*** never mind!, that's all right!; ***~ себе́!*** well (I never)!

ничей m, ***~ья́*** f, ***~ьё*** n, ***~ьи*** pl. [26] nobody's; *su. f в игре́* draw

ничко́м prone

ничто́ [23] nothing → ***ничего́***; ***~же́ство*** n [9] nonentity; ***~жный*** [14: -жен, -жна] insignificant, tiny; *причина* paltry

ничу́ть coll. → ***ниско́лько***; ***~ья́ → ~е́й***

ни́ша f [5] niche

ни́ща|я f [17], ***~енка*** coll. [5; g/pl.: -нок] beggar woman; ***~енский*** [16] beggarly; ***~ета́*** f [5] poverty, destitution; ***~ий 1.*** [17; нищ, -а́, -е] beggarly; **2.** m [17] beggar

но but, yet, still, nevertheless

нова́тор m [1] innovator

нове́лла f [5] short story

но́в|енький [16; -нек] (brand-) new; ***~изна́*** f [5], ***~и́нка*** [5; g/pl.: -нок] novelty; ***~ичо́к*** m [1; -чка́] novice, tyro

ново|бра́чный [14] newly married; ***~введе́ние*** n [12] innovation; ***~го́дний*** [15] New Year's (Eve ***го́дний ве́чер***); ***~лу́ние*** n [12] new moon; ***~рождён-ный*** [14] newborn (child); ***~*** [10] house-warming; **справля́ть** ⟨**спра́вить**⟩ ***~се́лье*** give a house-warming party

но́в|ость f [8] (piece of) news; novelty; ***~шество*** n [9] innovation, novelty; ***~ый*** [14; нов, -а́, -о] new; novel; (*после́дний*) fresh; ***~ый год*** m New Year's Day; **с ~ым го́дом!** Happy New Year!; **что ~ого?** what's (the) new(s)?

ног|а́ f [5; ac/sg.: но́гу; pl.: но́ги, ног, нога́м, etc. e.] foot, leg; **идти́ в ~у со вре́менем** keep abreast of the times; **со всех ~** as fast as one's legs will carry one; **стать на́ ~и выздорове́ть** recover; become independent; **положи́ть ~у на́ ~у** cross one's legs; **ни ~о́й (к Д)** never set foot (in s.o.'s house); (have a narrow) escape; **под ~а́ми** underfoot

но́готь m [4; -гтя; from g/pl.: e.] (finger-, toe-) nail

нож m [1 e.] knife; **на ~а́х** at daggers drawn; ***~ик*** m [1] coll. → ***нож***; ***~ка*** f [5; g/pl.: -жек] dim. → ***нога́***; *сту́ла и m. д.* leg; ***~ницы*** f/pl. [5] (pair of) scissors; *econ.* discrepancy; ***~но́й*** [14] foot…; ***~ны*** f/pl. [5; gen.: -жен] sheath

ноздря́ [6; pl.: но́здри, ноздре́й, etc. e.] nostril

ноль m. = **нуль** m [4] naught; zero

но́мер m [1; pl.: -ра́, etc. e.] number ([with] *за* T); (*разме́р*) size; *в оте́ле* room; *програ́ммы* item, turn; trick; **вы́кинуть ~** do an odd or unexpected thing; (*a., dim.,* ***~о́к*** m [1; -рка́]) cloak-room ticket

номина́льный [14; -лен, -льна] nominal

нора́ f [5; ac/sg.: -ру́; pl. st.] hole, burrow, lair

норве́|жец m [1; -жца], ***~жка*** f [5; g/pl.: -жек], ***~жский*** [16] Norwegian

но́рка f [5; g/pl.: -рок] zo. mink

но́рм|а f [5] norm, standard; *вы́работ-ки и m. д.* rate; ***~ализова́ть*** [7] (*im*)pf. standardize; ***~а́льный*** [14; -лен, -льна] normal

нос m [1; в, на носу́; pl. e.] nose; *птицы* beak; *ло́дки*, bow, prow; **води́ть за ~** lead by the nose; (*вско́ре*) **на ~у́** at hand; **у меня́ идёт кровь из ~** my nose is bleeding; ***~ик*** m [1] dim. → ***нос***; spout

носи́|лки f/pl. [5; -лок] stretcher; ***~льщик*** m [1] porter; ***~тель*** m med. [4] carrier; ***~ть*** [15] carry, bear, etc.; → ***нести́***; wear (v/i. **-ся**); coll. **-ся** run about; (**с** T) a. have one's mind occupied with

носово́й [14] *звук* nasal; *naut.* bow; ***плато́к*** handkerchief

носо́к m [1; -ска́] sock; *боти́нка* toe

носоро́г m [1] rhinoceros

но́т|а f [5] note; *pl. a.* music; **как по ~ам** without a hitch

нота́риус m [1] notary (public)

нота́ция f [7] reprimand, lecture

ноч|ева́ть [7], ⟨**пере-**⟩ pass (or spend) the night; ***~ёвка*** f [5; g/pl.: -вок] overnight stop (or stay or rest); *a. →* ***~лёг***; ***~лёг*** m [1] night's lodging, night quarters; *a. →* ***~ёвка***; ***~но́й*** [14] night(ly); (*a. bot., zo.*) nocturnal; ***~ь*** f [8; в ночи́;

Н

from g|pl. e.] night; **~ью** at (*or* by) night (= *a.* **в ~ь, по ~а́м**); **~ь под ...** (В) ... night

но́ша *f* [5] load, burden

ноя́брь *m* [4 *e.*] November

нрав *m* [1] disposition, temper; *pl.* ways, customs; (**не**) **по ~у** (Д) (not) to one's liking; **~иться** [14], ⟨по-⟩ please (a p. Д); **она́ мне ~ится** I like her; **~оуче́ние** *n* [12] moral admonition; **~ственность** *f* [8] morals *pl.*, morality; **~ственный** [14 *sh.*] moral

ну (*a.* **~ка**) well *or* now (then **же**)! come (on)!, why!, what!; the deuce (take him *or* it **~его́**)!; (*a.* **да ~?**) indeed?, really?, you don't say!; ha?; **~да** of course, sure; **~ так что́ же?** what about it?

ну́дный [14; ну́ден, -á, -о] tedious, boring

нужд|а́ *f* [5; *pl. st.*] need, want (**в** П of); **в слу́чае ~ы́** if necessary; **в э́том нет ~ы́**

there is no need for this; **~а́ться** [1] (**в** П) (be) in need (of); *в деньга́х* be hard up, needy

ну́жн|ый [14; ну́жен, -жна́, -о, ну́жны] necessary (Д for); (Д) **~о** + *inf.* must (→ **на́до**)

нуль → **ноль**

нумер|а́ция *f* [7] numeration; numbering; **~ова́ть** [7], ⟨за-, про-⟩ number

ну́трия *f* [7] *zo.* coypu; *мех* nutria

ны́н|е *obs.* now(adays), today; **~ешний** *coll.* [15] present *coll.* today's; **~че** *coll.* → **~е**

ныр|я́ть [28], *once* ⟨~ну́ть⟩ [20] dive

ныть [22] ache; *coll.* whine, make a fuss

нюх [1], **~ать**, ⟨по-⟩ *о животном* smell, scent

ня́н|чить [16] nurse, tend; **-ся** *coll.* fuss over, busy o.s. (**с** Т with); **~я** *f* [6] (**~ька** [5; -нек]) nurse, *Brt. a.* nanny

о, об, обо 1. (П) about, of; on; **2.** (В) against, (up)on; **бок о́ бок** side by side; **рука́ о́б руку** hand in hand

о! *int.* oh!, o!

о́б|а *m & m, ~е** *f* [37] both

обагр|я́ть [28], ⟨~и́ть⟩ [13]: **~и́ть ру́ки в крови́** steep one's hands in blood

обанкро́титься → **банкро́титься**

обая́|ние *n* [12] spell, charm; **~тельный** [14; -лен, -льна] charming

обва́л *m* [1] collapse; landslide; *снежный* avalanche; **~иваться** [1], ⟨~и́ться⟩ [13; обва́лится] fall in *or* off; **~я́ть** [1] *pf.* roll

обвари́ть [13; -арю́, -а́ришь] scald; pour boiling water over

обве́|сить [15] *coll.* → **~шивать**

обвести́ → **обводи́ть**

обве́тренный [14 *sh.*] weatherbeaten; *губы* chapped

обветша́лый [14] decayed

обве́ш|ивать, ⟨~ать⟩ [1] **1.** hang, cover (Т with); **2.** *pf.* ⟨обве́сить⟩ [1] give short

weight to; cheat

обви|ва́ть [1], ⟨~ть⟩ [обовью́, -вьёшь; → **вить**] wind round; **~ть ше́ю рука́ми** throw one's arms round s.o.'s neck

обвин|е́ние *n* [12] accusation, charge; *law* indictment; the prosecution; **~и́тель** *m* [4] accuser; *law* prosecutor; **~и́тельный** [14] accusatory; *заключе́ние* of 'guilty'; **~я́ть** [28] ⟨~и́ть⟩ [13] (**в** П) accuse (of), charge (with); **~я́емый** accused; (*отве́тчик*) defendant

обви́слый *coll.* [14] flabby

обви́|ть → **~ва́ть**

обводи́ть [13], ⟨обвести́⟩ [25] lead, see *or* look (round, about); enclose, encircle *or* border (Т with); **~ вокру́г па́льца** twist round one's little finger

обвор|а́живать [1], ⟨~ожи́ть⟩ [16 *e.*; -жу́, -жи́шь, -жённый] charm, fascinate; **~ожи́тельный** [14; -лен, -льна] charming, fascinating; **~ожи́ть** → **~а́живать**

обвя́з|ывать [1], ⟨~а́ть⟩ [3] *верёвкой* tie up *or* round

обгоня́ть [28], ⟨обогна́ть⟩ [обогню́, -о́нишь; обо́гнанный] (out) distance, outstrip (*a. fig.*); pass, leave behind

обгрыз|а́ть [1], ⟨~ть⟩ [24; *pt. st.*] gnaw (at, round, away)

обд|ава́ть [5], ⟨~а́ть⟩ [-а́м, -а́шь; → **дать**; обдал, -а́, -о; о́бданный (о́бдан, -а́, -о)] pour over; **~а́ть кипятко́м** scald; **~а́ть гря́зью** bespatter with mud

обдел|я́ть [28], ⟨~и́ть⟩ [13; -елю́, -е́лишь] deprive of one's due share (of T)

обдира́ть [1], ⟨ободра́ть⟩ [обдеру́, -рёшь; ободра́л, -а́, -о; обо́дранный] *кору* bark, *обои и т. д.* tear (off); *тушу* skin; *коле́но* scrape; *fig. coll.* fleece

обду́м|ать → **~ывать**; ~анный [14 *sh.*] well considered; ~ывать, ⟨~ать⟩ consider, think over

обе́д *m* [1] dinner (**за** T at, **на** B, **к** D for), lunch; **до** (*по́сле*) **~а** in the morning (afternoon); ~ать, ⟨по-⟩ have dinner (lunch), dine; ~енный [14] dinner..., lunch...

обедне́вший [17] impoverished

обез|бо́ливание *n* [12] an(a)esthetization; ~вре́живать [1], ⟨~вре́дить⟩ [15] render harmless; neutralize; ~до́ленный [14] unfortunate, hapless; ~зара́живание *n* [12] disinfection; ~лю́деть [8] *pf.* become depopulated, deserted; ~обра́живать [1], ⟨~обра́зить⟩ [15] disfigure; ~опа́сить [15] *pf.* secure (**от** P against); ~ору́живать [1], ⟨~ору́жить⟩ [16] disarm (*a. fig.*); ~у́меть [8] *pf.* lose one's mind, go mad

обезья́н|а *f* [5] monkey; ape; ~ий [18] monkey('s); apish, apelike; ~ичать *coll.* [1] ape

обели́ск *m* [1] obelisk

обер|ега́ть [1], ⟨~е́чь⟩ [26; г/ж: -гу, -жёшь] guard, *v/i.* **-ся**, protect o.s.; (against, from **от** P)

обернуть(ся) → **обёртывать(ся)**

обёрт|ка *f* [5; *g/pl.:* -ток] *кни́ги* cover; ~очный [14] wrapping (*or* brown) paper; ~ывать [1], ⟨оберну́ть⟩ [20] wrap (up); wind; **~ывать лицо́** turn one's face toward(s); **-ся** turn (round, *coll.*

back)

обескура́ж|ивать [1], ⟨~ить⟩ [16] discourage, dishearten

обеспе́ч|ение *n* [12] securing; *о за́йме* (**под** B on) security, guarantee; *поря́дка* maintenance; *социа́льное* security; ~енность *f* [8] (adequate) provision; *зажи́точность* prosperity; ~енный [14] well-to-do; well provided for; ~ивать [1], ⟨~ить⟩ [16] (*снабжа́ть*) provide (for; with T); *мир и т. д.* secure, guarantee; ensure

обесси́л|еть [8] *pf.* become enervated, exhausted; ~ивать [1], ⟨~ить⟩ [13] enervate, weaken

обесцве́|чивать [1], ⟨~тить⟩ discolo(u)r, make colo(u)rless

обесце́н|ивать [1], ⟨~ить⟩ [13] depreciate

обесче́стить [15] *pf.* dishono(u)r; *себя́* disgrace o.s

обе́т *m* [1] vow, promise; ~ова́нный [14]: **~ова́нная земля́** the Promised Land

обеща́|ние *n* [12], ~ть [1] (*im*)*pf.*, *coll. a.* ⟨по-⟩ promise

обжа́лование *n* [12] *law* appeal

обж|ига́ть [1], ⟨~е́чь⟩ [26; г/ж: обожгу́, -жжёшь, обжёг, обожгла́; обожжённый] burn; scorch; *гли́ну* bake; **-ся** burn o.s. (*coll.* one's fingers)

обжо́р|а *coll. m/f* [5] glutton; ~ливый *coll.* [14 *sh.*] gluttonous; ~ство *coll. n* [9] gluttony

обзаво|ди́ться [15], ⟨~ести́сь⟩ [25] provide o.s. (with T), acquire, set up

обзо́р *m* [1] survey; review

обзыва́ть [1], ⟨обозва́ть⟩ [обзову́, -ёшь; обозва́л, -а́, -о; обо́званный] call (*names* T)

оби|ва́ть [1], ⟨~ть⟩ [обобью́, обобьёшь; → **бить**] upholster; ~вка *f* [5] upholstery

оби́д|а *f* [5] insult; **не в ~ду будь ска́зано** no offense (-nce) meant; **не дать в ~ду** let not be offended; ~деть(ся) → **~жа́ть(ся)**; ~ный [14; -ден, -дна] offensive, insulting; **мне ~дно** it is a shame *or* vexing; it offends *or* vexes me; I am sorry (for **за** B); ~дчивый [14 *sh.*] touchy; ~дчик *coll. m* [1] of-

О

fender; ~жа́ть [1], ⟨~де́ть⟩ [11] (~ся be), offend(ed), (*a.* be angry with *or* at на В); wrong; overreach (→ *a.* обиде́лять); ~женный [14 *sh.*] offended (*a.* → ~жа́ть(ся))

оби́лие *n* [12] abundance, plenty

оби́льный [14; -лен, -льна] abundant (Т in), plentiful, rich (in)

обиня́к *m* [1 *e.*] only in phrr. **говори́ть ~а́ми** beat about the bush; **говори́ть без ~о́в** speak plainly

обира́ть coll. [1], ⟨обобра́ть⟩ [оберу́, -ёшь; обобра́л, -á, -о; обо́бранный] rob

обита́|емый [14 *sh.*] inhabited; ~тель *m* [4] inhabitant; ~ть [1] live, dwell, reside

обить → **обива́ть**

обихо́д *m* [1] use, custom, practice; **предме́ты дома́шнего ~а** household articles; ~ный [14; -ден, -дна] everyday; *язык* colloquial

обкла́дывать [1], ⟨обложи́ть⟩ [16] *по-душками* lay round; *тучами* cover; *med.* fur; → **облага́ть**

обкра́дывать [1], ⟨обокра́сть⟩ [25; обкраду́, -дёшь; *pt. st.:* обкра́денный] rob

обла́ва *f* [5] *на охоте* battue; *полиции* raid; roundup

облага́|емый [14 *sh.*] taxable; ~ть [1], ⟨обложи́ть⟩ [16] налогом impose (tax Т)

облагор|а́живать [1], ⟨~о́дить⟩ [15] ennoble, refine

облада́|ние *n* [12] possession (of Т); ~тель *m* [4] possessor; ~ть [1] (Т) possess, have; be in (**хоро́шим здоро́вьем**) good health

о́блак|о *n* [9; *pl.:* -ка́, -ко́в] cloud; **вита́ть в ~áх** be up in the clouds

обл|а́мывать [1], ⟨~ома́ть⟩ [1] & ⟨~оми́ть⟩ [14] break off

обласка́ть [1] *pf.* treat kindly

о́бласт|ной [14] regional; ~ь *f* [8; *from g/pl. e.*] region; *fig.* province, sphere, field

облач|а́ться [1], ⟨~и́ться⟩ [16] *eccl.* put on one's robes; coll. *joc.* array oneself

облачи́ться → **облача́ться**

о́блачный [14; -чен, -чна] cloudy

обле|га́ть [1], ⟨~чь⟩ [26; г/ж: → **лечь**] fit closely

облегч|а́ть [1], ⟨~и́ть⟩ [16 *e.;* -чу́, -чи́шь, -чённый] lighten; (*упрости́ть*) facilitate; *боль* ease, relieve

обледене́лый [14] ice-covered

облез́лый coll. [14] mangy, shabby

обле|ка́ть [1], ⟨~чь⟩ [26] *полномо́чиями* invest (Т with); (*вырази́ть*) put, express

облеп|ля́ть [28], ⟨~и́ть⟩ [14] stick all over (*or* round); (*окружи́ть*) surround; *о мухах и т. д.* cover

облет|а́ть [1], ⟨~е́ть⟩ [11] fly round (*or* all over, past, in); *листья* fall; *о слухах и т. д.* spread

обле́чь [1] → **облега́ть & облека́ть**

обли|ва́ть [1], ⟨~ть⟩ [обо́лью, -льёшь; обле́й!; о́бли́л, -á, -о; о́бли́тый (обли́т, -á, -о)] pour (s.th. Т) over; **~ть гря́зью** coll. fling mud (at); **-ся** [*pf.:* -и́лся, -ила́сь, -ило́сь] (Т) pour over o.s.; *слезами* shed; *потом* be dripping; *or кровью* covered; *сердце* bleed

облига́ция *f* [7] *fin.* bond, debenture

обли́зывать [1], ⟨~а́ть⟩ [3] lick (off); **-ся** lick one's lips (*or* o.s.)

о́блик *m* [1] aspect, look; appearance

обли́|ть(ся) → **~ва́ть(ся)**; ~цо́вывать [1], ⟨~цева́ть⟩ [7] face (with), revet

облич|а́ть [1], ⟨~и́ть⟩ [16 *e.;* -чу́, -чи́шь, -чённый] unmask; (*раскрыва́ть*) reveal; (*обвиня́ть*) accuse (**в** П of); ~и́тельный [14; -лен, -льна] accusatory, incriminating; ~и́ть → ~а́ть

обложе́ние *n* [12] taxation; ~и́ть → **обкла́дывать** and **облага́ть**; ~ка [5; *g/pl.:* -жек] cover; (*супер~ка*) dustcover, folder

обло́к|а́чиваться [1], ⟨~оти́ться⟩ [15 & 15 *e.*] -кочу́сь, -ко́тишься] lean one's elbow (**на** В on)

облом|а́ть, ~и́ть → **обла́мывать**; ~ок *m* [1; -мка] fragment; *pl.* debris, wreckage

облуч|а́ть [1], ⟨~и́ть⟩ [16 *e.;* -чу́, -чи́шь, -чённый] irradiate

облюбова́ть [7] *pf.* take a fancy to, choose

обма́з|ывать [1], ⟨~ать⟩ [3] besmear; plaster, putty, coat, cement

обма́к|ивать [1], ⟨~ну́ть⟩ [20] dip

обма́н *m* [1] deception; deceit, *mst. law* fraud; ~ **зре́ния** optical illusion; ~**ный** [14] deceitful, fraudulent; ~**у́ть(ся)** → ~**ывать(ся)**; ~**чивый** [14 *sh.*] deceptive; ~**щик** *m* [1], ~**щица** *f* [5] cheat, deceiver; ~**ывать** [1], ⟨~**у́ть**⟩ [20] (**-ся** be) deceive(d), cheat; be mistaken (in **в** П)

обма́|тывать, ⟨~**ота́ть**⟩ [1] wind (round); ~**а́хивать** [1], ⟨~**ахну́ть**⟩ [20] *пыль* wipe, dust; *ве́ером* fan

обме́н *m* [1] exchange (in/for **в**/**на** В); interchange (T, P of); ~**ивать** [1], ⟨~**я́ть**⟩ [28] exchange (**на** В for; **-ся** T s.th.)

обме́|ривать → **ме́рить**; ~**ета́ть** [1], ⟨~**ести́**⟩ [25 -т-: обмету́] sweep (off), dust; ~**озго́вывать** [1], ⟨~**озгова́ть**⟩ [7] *coll.* think over

обмо́лв|иться [14] *pf.* make a slip of the tongue; (*упомяну́ть*) mention, say; ~**ка** *f* [5; *g/pl.*: -**вок**] slip of the tongue

обморо́зить [15] *pf.* frostbite

о́бморок *m* [1] fainting spell, swoon

обмот|а́ть → **обма́тывать**; ~**ка** *f* [5; *g/pl.*: -**ток**] *el.* winding

обмундирова́|ние *n* [12], ~**ть** [7] *pf.* fit out with uniform

обмы|ва́ть [1], ⟨~**ть**⟩ [22] bathe, wash (off); *coll. поку́пку и т. д.* celebrate

обнадёж|ивать [1], ⟨~**ить**⟩ [16] (re)assure, encourage, give hope to

обнаж|а́ть [1], ⟨~**и́ть**⟩ [16 *е.*; -жу́, -жи́шь; -жённый] *го́лову* bare, uncover; *fig.* lay bare; *шпа́гу* draw, unsheathe; ~**ённый** [14; -жён, -жена́] naked, bare; nude (*a. su*)

обнаро́довать [7] *pf.* promulgate

обнару́ж|ивать [1], ⟨~**ить**⟩ [16] (*вы́явить*) disclose, show, reveal; (*найти́*) discover, detect; **-ся** appear, show; come to light; be found, discovered

обнести́ → **обноси́ть**

обни|ма́ть [1], ⟨~**я́ть**⟩ (обниму́, обни́мешь; обня́л, -а́, -о; обня́тый (о́бнят, -а́, -о)] embrace, hug, clasp in one's arms

обно́в|(к)а *f* [5; (*g/pl.*: -**вок**)] *coll.* new; article of clothing; ~**и́ть** → ~**ля́ть**; ~**ле́ние** *n* [12] *репертуа́ра и т. д.* renewal; (*ремо́нт и т. д.*) renovation; ~**ля́ть** [28], ⟨~**и́ть**⟩ [14 *е.*; -влю́, -ви́шь;

-влённый] renew; renovate; update; repair

об|носи́ть [15], ⟨~**ести́**⟩ [24; -с-: -су́] pass (round); *coll.* serve; (T) fence in, enclose; **-ся** *coll. impf.* wear out one's clothes

обню́х|ивать, ⟨~**ать**⟩ [1] sniff around

обня́ть → **обнима́ть**

обобра́ть → **обира́ть**

обобщ|а́ть [1], ⟨~**и́ть**⟩ [16 *е.*; -щу́, -щи́шь; -щённый] generalize; ~**и́ть** → ~**а́ть**

обога|ща́ть [1], ⟨~**ти́ть**⟩ [15 *е.*; -ащу́, -ти́шь; -ащённый] enrich; *ру́ду* concentrate

обогна́ть → **обгоня́ть**

обогну́ть → **огиба́ть**

обоготвори́ть [28] → **боготвори́ть**

обогре́ть → **гре́ть**

о́бод *m* [1; *pl.*: обо́дья, -дьев] rim, felloe; ~**о́к** *m* [1; -дка́] rim

обо́др|анный [14 *sh.*] *coll.* ragged, shabby; ~**а́ть** → **обдира́ть**; ~**е́ние** *n* [12] encouragement; ~**я́ть** [28], ⟨~**и́ть**⟩ [13] cheer up, reassure; **-ся** take heart, cheer up

обожа́ть [1] adore, worship

обожеств|ля́ть [28], ⟨~**и́ть**⟩ [14 *е.*; -влю́, -ви́шь; -влённый] deify

обожжённый [14; -ён, -ена́] burnt

обозва́ть → **обзыва́ть**

обознач|а́ть [1], ⟨~**ить**⟩ [16] denote, designate, mark; **-ся** appear; ~**е́ние** *n* [12] designation; *знак* sign, symbol

обозр|ева́ть [1], ⟨~**е́ть**⟩ [9], ~**е́ние** *n* [12] survey; *mst. lit.* revue

обо́|и *m/pl.* [3] wallpaper; ~**йти́(сь)** → **обходи́ть(ся)**; ~**красть** → **обкра́дывать**

оболо́чка *f* [5; *g/pl.*: -**чек**] cover(ing), envelope; *anat.* сли́зистая *и т. д.* membrane; **ра́дужная (рогова́я)** ~ iris (cornea)

оболь|сти́тель *m* [4] seducer; ~**сти́тельный** [14; -лен, -льна] seductive; ~**ща́ть** [1], ⟨~**сти́ть**⟩ [15 *е.*; -льщу́, льсти́шь; -льщённый] seduce; (**-ся** be) delude(d; flatter o.s.)

обомле́ть [8] *pf. coll.* be stupefied

обоня́ние *n* [12] (sense of) smell

обора́чивать(ся) → **обёртывать(ся)**

оборв|а́нец coll. m [1; -нца] ragamuffin; **~анный** [14 sh.] ragged; **~а́ть → обрыва́ть**

обо́рка f [5; g/pl.: -рок] frill, ruffle

оборо́н|а f [5] defense (Brt. defence); **~и́тельный** [14] defensive; **~ный** [14] defense…, armament…; **~ная промы́шленность** defense industry; **~оспосо́бность** f[8] defensive capability; **~я́ть** [28] defend

оборо́т m [1] turn; tech. revolution, rotation; fin. circulation; comm. turnover; сторона́ back, reverse; (см.) **на ~е** please turn over (PTO); **ввести́ в ~** put into circulation; **взять кого́-нибудь в ~** fig. coll. get at s.o.; take s.o. to task; **~и́ть(ся)** P [15] pf. → **оберну́ть(ся)**; **~ливый** [14 sh.] coll. resourceful; **~ный** [14] сторона́ back, reverse; fig. seamy (side); **~ный капита́л** working capital

оборудова|ние n [12] equipment; **вспомога́тельное ~ние** comput. peripherals, add-ons; **~ть** [7] (im)pf. equip, fit out

обосн|ова́ние n [12] substantiation; ground(s); **~о́вывать** [1], ⟨**~ова́ть**⟩ [7] prove, substantiate; **-ся** settle down

обос|обля́ть [28], ⟨**~о́бить**⟩ [14] isolate; **-ся** keep aloof, stand apart

обостр|я́ть [28], ⟨**~и́ть**⟩ [13] (**-ся** become); (ухудшить) aggravate(d), strain(ed); о чу́вствах become keener; med. become acute

обою́дный [14; -ден, -дна] mutual, reciprocal

обраб|а́тывать, ⟨**~о́тать**⟩ [1] work, process; agr. till; текст и т. д. elaborate, finish, polish; chem. treat; coll. work upon, win round кого́-л.; р. p. r. a. промы́шленность manufacturing; **~о́тка** f [5; g/pl.: -ток] processing; agric. cultivation; elaboration; adaptation

о́браз m [1] manner, way (T in), mode; shape, form; lit. figure, character; image; [pl.: -а́, etc. e.] icon; **каки́м (таки́м) ~ом** how (thus); **нико́им ~ом** by no means; **~ жи́зни** way of life; **~е́ц** m [1; -зца́] specimen, sample; (пример)

model, example; материа́ла pattern; **~ный** [14; -зен, -зна] graphic, picturesque, vivid; **~ова́ние** n [12] слова и т. д. formation; education **~о́ванный** [14 sh.] educated; **~ова́тельный** [14] -лен, -льна educational (qualification); **~о́вывать** [1], ⟨**~ова́ть**⟩ [7] form; **-ся** (v/i.) arise; constitute; **~у́мить(ся)** [14] pf. coll. bring (come) to one's senses; **~цо́вый** [14] exemplary, model…; **~чик** m [1] → **~е́ц**

обрам|ля́ть [28], ⟨**~и́ть**⟩ [14 st.], fig. ⟨**~и́ть**⟩ [14 e.; -млю, -ми́шь; -млённый] frame

обраст|а́ть [1], ⟨**~и́**⟩ [24; -ст-: -сту; обро́с, -ла́] мхом и т. д. become overgrown with, covered with

обра|ти́ть → ~ща́ть; **~тный** [14] back, return…; reverse; (a. math. inverse; law retroactive; **~тная связь** tech. feedback (a. fig.); **~тно** back; **~ща́ть** [1], ⟨**~ти́ть**⟩ [15 e.; -ащу́, -ати́шь; -аще́нный] turn; взор direct; eccl. convert; draw or pay or (**на себя́**) attract (attention; to s.th.); **не ~ща́ть внима́ния (на** B) disregard; **-ся** turn (**в** B to); address o.s. (**к** Д to); apply (to; for **за** T); appeal; **~ща́ться в бе́гство** take to flight; impf. (**с** T) treat, handle; двигаться circulate; **~ще́ние** n [12] address, appeal; оборо́т circulation; (**с** T) treatment (of), management; manners

обре́з m [1] edge; **де́нег в ~** just enough money; **~а́ть** [1], ⟨**~ать**⟩ [3] cut (off); cut short; но́гти и т. д. pare; ве́тки prune; coll. (прервать) snub, cut short; **~ок** m [1; -зка] scrap; pl. clippings; **~ывать** [1] → **~а́ть**

обрек|а́ть [1], ⟨**~чь**⟩ [26] condemn, doom (to **на** B, Д)

обремен|и́тельный [14; -лен, -льна] burdensome; **~я́ть** [28], ⟨**~и́ть**⟩ [13] burden

обре|чённый [14] doomed (to **на** B); **~чь → ~ка́ть**

обрисо́в|ывать [1], ⟨**~а́ть**⟩ [7] outline, sketch; **-ся** loom, appear

обро́сший [17] covered with

обруб|а́ть [1], ⟨**~и́ть**⟩ [14] chop (off), lop…; **~ок** m [1; -бка] stump, block

о́бруч *m* [1; *from g/pl.*: *e.*] hoop; **~а́льный** [14] wedding...; **~а́ться** [1], ⟨**~и́ться**⟩ [16 *e.*: -чу́сь, -чи́шься] be(come) engaged (to **to** T); **~е́ние** *n* [12] betrothal

обру́ш|ивать [1], ⟨**~ить**⟩ [16] bring down; **-ся** fall in, collapse; fall (up)on (**на** B)

обры́|в *m* [1] precipice; *tech.* break; **~а́ть** [1], ⟨оборва́ть⟩ [-ву́, -вёшь; -ва́л, -вала́, -о; обо́рванный] tear *or* pluck (off); break off, cut short; **-ся** *a.* fall from **с** P); **~истый** [14 *sh.*] steep; abrupt; **~ок** *m* [1; -вка] scrap, shred; **~очный** [14; -чен, -чна] scrappy

обры́зг|ивать, ⟨**~ать**⟩ [1] sprinkle

обрю́зглый [14] flabby, bloated

обря́д *m* [1] ceremony, rite

обса́живать [1], ⟨обсади́ть⟩ [15] plant round (T with)

обсервато́рия *f* [7] observatory

обсле́дова|ние *n* [12] (P) inspection (of), inquiry (into), investigation (of); medical examination; **~ть** [7] (*im*)*pf.* inspect, examine, investigate

обслу́ж|ивание *n* [12] service; *tech.* servicing, maintenance; operation; **~ивать** [1], ⟨**~и́ть**⟩ [16] serve, attend; *tech.* service

обсо́хнуть → **обсыха́ть**

обста|вля́ть [28], ⟨**~вить**⟩ [14] surround (with); furnish (T with); *coll.* outwit, deceive **~но́вка** *f* [5; *g/pl.*: -вок] furniture; (*обстоятельства*) situation, conditions *pl.*

обстоя́тель|ный [14; -лен, -льна] detailed, circumstantial; *coll. человек и т. д.* thorough; **~ство** *n* [9] circumstance (**при** П, **в** П under, in); **по ~ствам** depending on circumstances

обстоя́ть [-ои́т] be, get on; stand; **как обстои́т де́ло с** (T)? how are things going?

обстре́л *m* [1] bombardment, firing; **~ивать** [1], ⟨**~я́ть**⟩ [28] fire at, on; shell

обстру́кция *f* [7] *pol.* obstruction, filibustering

обступ|а́ть [1], ⟨**~и́ть**⟩ [14] surround

об|сужда́ть [1], ⟨**~суди́ть**⟩ [15; -ждённый] discuss; **~сужде́ние** *n* [12]

discussion; **~суши́ться** [16] *pf.* dry o.s.; **~счита́ть** [1] *pf.* cheat; **-ся** miscalculate

обсып|а́ть [1], ⟨**~ать**⟩ [2] strew, sprinkle

обсыха́ть [1], ⟨**~о́хнуть**⟩ [21] dry

обт|а́чивать [1], ⟨**~очи́ть**⟩ [16] turn; **~ека́емый** [14] streamlined; *ответ* vague; **~ере́ть** *a.* **~ира́ть**; **~ёсывать** [1], ⟨**~еса́ть**⟩ [3] hew; **~ира́ть** [1], ⟨**~ере́ть**⟩ [12; оботру́; обтёр; *g. pt. a.*: -тёрши & -тере́в] rub off *or* down, wipe (off), dry; *coll.* wear thin

обточи́ть → **обта́чивать**

обтрёпанный [14] shabby, *обшлага* frayed

обтя́|гивать [1], ⟨**~ну́ть**⟩ [19] *мебель* cover (T with); *impf.* be closefitting; **~жка** *f* [5]: **в ~жку** closefitting dress

обу|ва́ть [1], ⟨**~ть**⟩ [18] put (**-ся** one's) shoes on; **~вь** *f* [8] footwear, shoes *pl.*

обу́гл|иваться [1], ⟨**~иться**⟩ [13] char; carbonize

обу́за *f* [5] *fig.* burden

обу́зд|ывать [1], ⟨**~а́ть**⟩ [1] bridle, curb

обусло́в|ливать [1], ⟨**~ить**⟩ [14] make conditional (T on); cause

обу́ть(ся) → **обува́ть(ся)**

о́бух *m* [1] *топора* head; **его́ как ~ом по голове́** he was thunderstruck

обуч|а́ть [1], ⟨**~и́ть**⟩ [16] teach (Д s.th.), train; **-ся** (Д) learn, be taught; **~е́ние** *n* [12] instruction, training; education

обхва́т *m* [1] arm's span; circumference; **~ывать** [1], ⟨**~и́ть**⟩ [15] clasp (T in), embrace, enfold

обхо́д *m* [1] round; *полицейского* beat; **де́лать ~** make one's round(s); **пойти́ в ~** make a detour; **~и́тельный** [14; -лен, -льна] affable, amiable; **~и́ть** [15], ⟨обойти́⟩ [обойду́, -дёшь; → **идти́**] go round; visit (all [one's]); (*вопрос*) avoid, evade; *закон* circumvent; pass over (T in); (**-ся**, ⟨-сь⟩) cost (**мне** me); (*справиться*) manage, make, do with(out) (**без** P); there is (*no ... without*); treat (**с** T s.b.); **~ный** [14] roundabout

обш|а́ривать [1], ⟨**~а́рить**⟩ [13] rummage (around); **~ива́ть** [1], ⟨**~и́ть**⟩ [обошью́, -шьёшь; → **шить**] sew round, border (T with); *досками и т. д.* plank, face, *coll.* clothe; **~йвка** *f* [5] trimming, *etc.* (*vb.*)

обши|рный [14; -рен, -рна] vast, extensive; (*многочисленный*) numerous; **~ть →** **~вать**

обща́ться [1] associate (**с** T with)

обще|досту́пный [14; -пен, -пна] popular; *a.* **→ досту́пный**; **~жи́тие** *n* [12] hostel; society, community; communal life; **~изве́стный** [14; -тен, -тна] well-known

обще́ние *n* [12] intercourse; relations

общепри́нятый [14 *sh.*] generally accepted, common

обще́ств|енность *f* [8] community, public; **~енный** [14] social, public; **~енное мне́ние** public opinion; **~о** *n* [9] society; company (*a. econ*); association; community; **акционе́рное ~о** joint-stock company; **~ове́дение** *n* [12] social science

общеупотреби́тельный [14; -лен, -льна] current, in general use

о́бщ|ий [17; общ. -á, -е] general, common (in **~его**); public; total, (**в ~ем** on the whole); **~ина** *f* [5] *eccl. pol.*, *etc.* group, community; **~и́тельный** [14; -лен, -льна] sociable, affable; **~ность** *f* [8] community

объе|да́ть [1], **⟨~сть⟩** [-éм, -ёшь, *etc.* → **есть**] eat *or* gnaw round, away; **-ся** overeat

объедине́ние *n* [12] association, union; *действие* unification; **~я́ть** [28], **⟨~и́ть⟩** [13] unite, join; **-ся** (*v/i.*) join, unite (with)

объе́дки *coll. m/pl.* [1] leftovers

объе́|зд *m* [1] detour, by-pass; *vb.* + **в ~зд = ~зжа́ть** [1] **1.** **⟨~хать⟩** [-éду, -éдешь] go, drive round; travel through *or* over; visit (all [one's]); **2.** **⟨~здить⟩** [15] break in (*horses*); **~кт** *m* [1] object; **~кти́вный** [14; -вен, -вна] objective

объём *m* [1] volume; (*величина*) size; *знаний и т. д.* extent, range; **~истый** [14 *sh.*] *coll.* voluminous, bulky

объе́сть(ся) → объеда́ть(ся)

объе́хать → объезжа́ть *1*

nouncement, notice; *реклама* advertisement; *войны* declaration; **~я́ть** [28], **⟨~и́ть⟩** [14] declare (s.th. *a.* **о** П; s.b. [to be] s.th. B/T), tell, anounce, proclaim; *благода́рность* express

объясн|е́ние *n* [12] explanation; declaration (of love **в любви́**); **~и́мый** [14 *sh.*] explicable, accountable; **~и́тельный** [14] explanatory; **~я́ть** [28], **⟨~и́ть⟩** [13] explain, illustrate; account for; **-ся** explain o.s.; be accounted for; have it out (**с** T with); *impf.* make o.s. understood (T by)

объя́тия *n/pl.* [12] embrace (*vb.*: **заключи́ть в ~**); **с распростёртыми ~ми** with open arms

обыва́тель *m* [4] philistine; **~ский** [16] narrow-minded; philistine…

обы́гр|ывать, **⟨~а́ть⟩** [1] beat (*at a game*); win

обы́денный [14] everyday, ordinary

обыкнове́ние *n* [12] habit; **по ~ю** as usual; **~ный** [14; -éнен, -éнна] ordinary; *действия* usual, habitual

о́быск *m* [1], **~ивать**, **⟨~а́ть⟩** [3] search

обы́ч|ай *m* [3] custom; *coll.* habit; **~ный** [14; -чен, -чна] customary, usual, habitual

обя́занн|ость *f* [8] duty; **во́инская ~ость** military service; *исполня́ющий ~ости* (P) acting; **~ый** [14 *sh.*] obliged; indebted; **он вам обя́зан жи́знью** he owes you his life

обяза́тель|ный [14; -лен, -льна] obligatory, compulsory; **~но** without fail, certainly; **~ство** *n* [9] obligation; *law* liability; engagement; **вы́полнить свои́ ~ства** meet one's obligations

обя́з|ывать [1], **⟨~а́ть⟩** [3] oblige; bind, commit; **-ся** engage, undertake, pledge o.s

овдове́вший [17] widowed

ове́с *m* [1; овса́] oats *pl*

ове́чий [18] sheep('s)

овлад|ева́ть [1], **⟨~е́ть⟩** [8] (T) seize, take possession of; get control over; *зна́ниями* master; **~е́ть собо́й** regain one's self-control

о́вощ|и *m/pl.* [1; *gen.*: -щéй, *etc. e.*] vegetables; **~но́й** [14]: **~но́й магази́н** place selling fresh fruits and vegetables; (*chiefly Brt.*) greengrocer's

овра́г *m* [1] ravine

овся́нка *f* [5; *g/pl.:* -нок] oatmeal

овц|а́ *f* [5; *pl. st.; g/pl.:* ове́ц] sheep; **~ево́дство** *n* [9] sheepbreeding

овча́рка *f* [5; *g/pl.:* -рок] sheepdog; **неме́цкая ~** Alsation (dog)

овчи́на *f* [5] sheepskin

огиба́ть [1], ⟨обогну́ть⟩ [20] turn *or* bend (round)

оглавле́ние *n* [12] table of contents

огла́|ска *f* [5] publicity; **~ша́ть** [1], ⟨~си́ть⟩ [15 *e.;* -ашу́, -аси́шь, -ашённый] announce, make public; **-ся** *криками и т. д.* fill; resound; ring; **~ше́ние** *n* [12] proclamation; publication

оглуша́ть [1], ⟨~и́ть⟩ [16 *e.;* -шу́, -ши́шь, -шённый] deafen; stun; **~и́тельный** [14; -лен, -льна] deafening; stunning

огля́|дка *coll.* *f* [5] looking back; *без* **~дки** without turning one's head; *с* **~дкой** carefully; **~дывать** [1], ⟨~де́ть⟩ [11] examine, look around; **-ся 1.** look round; *fig.* to adapt o.s.; **2.** *pf.:* ⟨~ну́ться⟩ [20] look back (**на** B at)

о́гне|нный [14] fiery; **~опа́сный** [14; -сен, -сна] inflammable; **~сто́йкий** [16; -о́ек, -о́йка] → **~упо́рный**; **~стре́льный** [14] fire (*arm*); **~туши́тель** *m* [4] fire extinguisher; **~упо́рный** [14; -рен, -рна] fireproof

огова́|ривать [1], ⟨~ори́ть⟩ [13] (*оклеве́тать*) slander; *условия* stipulate; **-ся** make a slip of the tongue; → **об-мо́лвиться**; **~о́рка** *f* [5; *g/pl.:* -рок] slip of the tongue; reservation, proviso

оголя́ть [28], ⟨~и́ть⟩ [13] bare

огонёк *m* [1; -нька́] (small) light; *fig.* zest, spirit

ого́нь *m* [4; огня́] fire (*a. fig.*); light; *из* **огня́ да в по́лымя** out of the frying pan into the fire; **пойти́ в ~ и во́ду** through thick and thin; *тако́го днём с огнём не найдёшь* impossible to find another like it

огор|а́живать [1], ⟨~оди́ть⟩ [15 & 15 *e.;* -ожу́, -о́дишь; -оженный] enclose, fence (in); **~о́д** *m* [1] kitchen garden;

~о́дник *m* [1] market *or* kitchen gardener; **~о́дничество** *n* [9] market gardening

огорч|а́ть [1], ⟨~и́ть⟩ [16 *e.;* -чу́, -чи́шь; -чённый] grieve (**-ся** *v/i.*), (be) vex(ed), distress(ed T); **~е́ние** *n* [9] grief, affliction; **~и́тельный** [14; -лен, -льна] grievous; distressing

огра|бле́ние *n* [12] burglary, robbery; **~да** *f* [5] fence; *каменная* wall; **~жда́ть** [1], ⟨~ди́ть⟩ [15 *e.;* -ажу́, -ади́шь; -аждённый] guard, protect; **~жде́ние** *n* [12] barrier; railing

ограни́ч|ение *n* [12] limitation; restriction; **~енный** [14 *sh.*] confined; *средства* limited; *человек* narrow(-minded); **~ивать** [1], ⟨~ить⟩ [16] confine, limit, restrict (o.s. **-ся**; to T); content o.s. with; not go beyond; **~ительный** [14; -лен, -льна] restrictive, limiting

огро́мный [14; -мен, -мна] huge, vast; *интерес и т. д.* enormous, tremendous

огрубе́лый [14] coarse, hardened

огрыз|а́ться *coll.* [1], *once* ⟨~ну́ться⟩ [20] snap (at); **~ок** *m* [1; -зка] bit, end; *карандаша* stump, stub

огу́льный *coll.* [14; -лен, -льна] wholesale, indiscriminate; (*необоснованный*) unfounded

огуре́ц *m* [1; -рца́] cucumber

ода́лживать [1], ⟨одолжи́ть⟩ [16 *e.;* -жу́, -жи́шь] lend (Д/В *a. p. s.th.*); *coll.* **взять** borrow

одар|ённый [14 *sh.*] gifted; talented; **~ивать** [1], ⟨~и́ть⟩ [13] give (presents) to (T); *fig.* (*impf.* **~я́ть** [28]) endow (T with)

оде|ва́ть [1], ⟨~ть⟩ [-е́ну, -е́нешь; -е́тый] dress in; clothe in (**-ся** *v/i.* dress o.s.; clothe o.s.); **~жда** *f* [5] clothes *pl.*, clothing

одеколо́н *m* [1] eau de cologne

одеревене́лый [14] numb

оде́рж|ивать [1], ⟨~а́ть⟩ [4] gain, win; **~а́ть верх над** (T) gain the upper hand (over); **~и́мый** [14 *sh.*] (T) obsessed (by); *страхом* ridden (by)

оде́ть(ся) → **одева́ть(ся)**

одея́ло n [9] blanket, cover(let); *стёганое* quilt

оди́н m, **одна́** f, **одно́** n, **одни́** pl. [33]
one; alone; only; a, a certain; one; ~
мой друг a friend of mine; **одно́** su.
one thing, thought, *etc.*; ~ **на** ~ tête-à-
-tête; **все до одного́** (or все как ~)
all to a (or the last) man

оди́н|а́ковый [14 sh.] identical (with),
the same (as); ~**надцатый** [14] eleventh; → **пя́тый**; ~**надцать** [35] eleven;
→ **пять**; ~**о́кий** [16 sh.] lonely, lone-
some; (*незамужняя и т. д.*) single;
~**о́чество** n [9] solitude, loneliness;
~**о́чка** m/f [5; g/pl.: -чек] lone person;
one-man boat (or coll. cell); ~**о́чкой,
в ~о́чку** alone; ~**о́чный** [14] single; *заключение* solitary; individual; one-
-man...

одио́зный [14; -зен, -зна] odious, offensive

одича́лый [14] (having gone) wild

одна́жды once, one day

одна́ко, (*а.* ~**ж[е]**) however; yet, still; but,
though

одно́|...: ~**бо́кий** [16 sh.] *mst. fig.* one-
-sided; ~**бо́ртный** [14] singlebreasted;
~**вре́менный** [14] simultaneous;
~**зву́чный** [14; -чен, -чна] monotonous; ~**зна́чный** [14; -чен, -чна] synonymous; *math.* simple; ~**имённый** [14;
-ёнен, -ённа] of the same name;
~**кла́ссник** m [1] classmate; ~**коле́й-
ный** [14] single-track; ~**кра́тный** [14;
-тен, -тна] occurring once, single; ~**ле́т-
ний** [15] one-year(-old); *bot.* annual;
~**лето́к** m [1; -тка] of the same age
(as); ~**ме́стный** [14] singleseater; ~**об-
ра́зный** [14; -зен, -зна] monotonous;
~**ро́дный** [14; -ден, -дна] homogeneous; ~**сло́жный** [14; -жен, -жна] mon-
osyllabic; *fig.* terse, abrupt; ~**сторо́н-
ний** [15; -о́нен, -о́ння] one-sided (*a.
fig.*); unilateral; *движение* oneway;
~**фами́лец** m [1; -льца] namesake;
~**цве́тный** [14; -тен, -тна] monochro-
matic; ~**этажный** [14] one-storied
(*Brt.* -reyed)

одобр|е́ние n [12] approval; ~**и́тель-
ный** [14; -лен, -льна] approving; ~**я́ть**

[28], ⟨~**ить**⟩ [13] approve (of)

одол|ева́ть [1], ⟨~**е́ть**⟩ [8] overcome,
defeat; *fig.* master; cope with; *страх
и т. д.* (be) overcome (by)

одолж|е́ние n [12] favo(u)r, service;
~**и́ть** → **ода́лживать**

одува́нчик m [1] dandelion

оду́м|ываться, ⟨~**аться**⟩ [1] change
one's mind

одура́чивать → **дура́чить**

одур|ма́нивать [1], ⟨~**ма́нить**⟩ [13] stu-
pefy

одутлова́тый [14 sh.] puffy

одухотворённый [14 sh.] inspired

одушев|лённый [14] *gr.* animate;
~**ля́ть** [28], ⟨~**и́ть**⟩ [14 *e.*; -влю́, -ви́шь;
-влённый] animate; (*воодушевить*)
inspire

оды́шка f [5] short breath

ожере́лье n [10] necklace

ожесточ|а́ть [1], ⟨~**и́ть**⟩ [16 *e.*; -чу́,
-чи́шь; -чённый] harden; embitter
~**е́ние** n [12] bitterness; ~**ённый** [14 sh.]
a. hardened, fierce, bitter

ожи|ва́ть [1], ⟨~**ть**⟩ [-иву́, -ивёшь; о́жил,
-á, -о] revive; ~**ви́ть(ся)** → ~**вля́ть(ся)**;
~**вле́ние** n [12] animation; ~**влённый**
[14 sh.] animated, lively; ~**вля́ть** [28],
⟨~**ви́ть**⟩ [14 *e.*; -влю́, -ви́шь, -влённый]
revive; enliven, animate; **-ся** quicken,
revive; brighten

ожида́|ние n [12] expectation; *зал* ~**ния**
waiting room; **обману́ть** ~**ния** disappoint; ~**ть** [1] wait (for P); expect; **как
мы и** ~**ли** just as we expected

ожи́ть → **ожива́ть**

ожо́г m [1] burn; *кипятко́м* scald

озабо́|чивать [1], ⟨~**тить**⟩ [15] disquiet,
alarm; ~**ченный** [14 sh.] anxious, wor-
ried (Tabout); (*поглощённый*) preoc-
cupied

озагла́в|ливать [1], ⟨~**ить**⟩ [14] give a
title to; head (*a chapter*)

озада́ч|ивать [1], ⟨~**ить**⟩ [16] puzzle,
perplex

озар|я́ть [28], ⟨~**и́ть**⟩ [13] (**-ся** be[-
come]) illuminate(d), light (lit) up;
brighten, lighten

озвере́ть [8] *pf.* become furious

оздоров|ля́ть [1], ⟨~**и́ть**⟩ [14] *обста-*

новку и т. д. improve

о́зеро *n* [9; *pl.:* озёра, -ёр] lake

ози́мый [14] winter (*crops*)

озира́ться [1] look round

озлоб|ля́ть [28], ⟨**сить**⟩ **(-ся** become) embitter(ed); **сле́ние** *n* [12] bitterness, animosity

ознак|омля́ть [28], ⟨**сóмить**⟩ [14] familiarize **(-ся** o.s., **с** T with)

ознамен|ова́ние *n* [12] marking, commemoration (**в** B in); **сóвывать** [1], ⟨**совáть**⟩ [7] mark, commemorate, celebrate

означа́ть [1] signify, mean

озно́б *m* [1] chill; shivering; **чу́вствовать ~** feel shivery

озор|ни́к *m* [1 *e.*], **~ни́ца** *f* [5] *coll.* → **шалу́н(ья)**; *coll.* **~нича́ть** [1] → **шали́ть**; **~но́й** *coll.* [14] mischievous, naughty; **~ство́** *coll. n* [9] mischief, naughtiness

ой *int.* oh! o dear!

ока́з|ывать [1], ⟨**~а́ть**⟩ [3] show; render, do; *влияние* exert; *предпочтение* give; **-ся** (T) turn out (to be), be found; find o.s

окайм|ля́ть [28], ⟨**~и́ть**⟩ [14 *e.*; -млю́, -ми́шь, -млённый] border

окамене́лый [14] petrified

ока́нчивать [1], ⟨**око́нчить**⟩ [16] finish, end **(-ся** *v/i.*)

ока́пывать [1], ⟨**окопа́ть**⟩ [1] dig round; entrench **(-ся** *v/i.*)

океа́н *m* [1], **~ский** [16] ocean

оки́|дывать [1], ⟨**~нуть**⟩ [20] **(взгля́дом)** take in at a glance

окис|ля́ть [28], ⟨**~ли́ть**⟩ [13] oxidize; **~ь** *f* [8] *chem.* oxide

оккупа|цио́нный [14] occupation…; **~и́ровать** [7] (*im*)*pf.* occupy

окла́д *m* [1] salary; salary scale

окла́дистый [14 *sh.*] (*of a beard*) full

окле́|ивать [1], ⟨**~ить**⟩ [13] paste over (with); *обоями* paper

о́клик *m* [1], **~áть** [1], ⟨**~нуть**⟩ [20] call, hail

окно́ *n* [9; *pl.:* о́кна, о́кон, о́кнам] window (*look through* **в** B); *school sl.* free period

о́ко *n* [9; *pl.:* о́чи, оче́й, *etc. e.*] *mst. poet.* eye

око́вы *f/pl.:* [5] fetters (*mst. fig.*)

околдова́ть [7] *pf.* bewitch

окол|ева́ть [1], ⟨**~е́ть**⟩ [8] die (*of animals*)

о́коло (P) (*приблизительно*) about, around, nearly; (*рядом*) by, at, near; nearby

око́нный [14] window…

оконч|áние *n* [12] end(ing *gr.*) close, termination; *работы* completion ([up]on **по** П); *univ.* graduation; **~áтельный** [14; -лен; -льна] final, definitive; **~ить** → **ока́нчивать**

око́п *m* [1] *mil.* trench; **~а́ть(ся)** → **ока́пывать(ся)**

о́корок *m* [1; *pl.:* -ка, *etc. e.*] ham

око|стене́лый [14] ossified (*a. fig.*); **~чене́лый** [14] numb (with cold)

око́ш|ечко *n* [9; *g/pl.:* -чек], **~ко** [9; *g/pl.:* -шек] *dim.* → **окно́**

окра́ина *f* [5] outskirts *pl.*

окра́с|ка *f* [5] painting; dyeing; colo(u)ring; *fig.* tinge; **~ивать** [1], ⟨**~ить**⟩ [15] paint; dye; stain; tint

окре́ст|ность *f* (*often pl.*) [8] environs *pl.*, ncighbo(u)rhood; **~ый** [14] surrounding; in the vicinity

окрова́вленный [14] bloodstained, bloody

о́круг *m* [1; *pl.:* -rá, *etc. e.*] region, district; circuit

округл|я́ть [28], ⟨**~и́ть**⟩ [13] round (off); **~ый** [14 *sh.*] rounded

окруж|а́ть [1], ⟨**~и́ть**⟩ [16 *e.*; -жу́, -жи́шь, -жённый] surround; **~а́ющий** [17] surrounding; **~е́ние** *n* [12] environment; *mil.* encirclement; *люди* milieu, circle, company; **~и́ть** → **~а́ть**; **~но́й** [14] district…; circular; **~ность** *f* [8] circumference

окрыл|я́ть [28], ⟨**~и́ть**⟩ [13] *fig.* encourage, lend wings, inspire

октя́брь *m* [4 *e.*], **~ский** [16] October; *fig.* Russian revolution of October 1917

окун|а́ть [1], ⟨**~у́ть**⟩ [20] dip, plunge (*v/i.* **-ся**; dive, *a. fig.*)

о́кунь *m* [4; *from g/pl. e.*] perch (*fish*)

окуп|а́ть [1], ⟨**~и́ть**⟩ [14], **(-ся** be) offset, recompense(d), compensate(d)

оку́рок *m* [1; -рка] cigarette end, stub,

butt

окут|ывать, ⟨**ать**⟩ [1] wrap (up); *fig.* shroud, cloak

ола́дья *f* [6; *g/pl.:* -дий] *cul.* fritter

оледене́лый [14] frozen, iced

оле́нь *m* [4] deer; **се́верный ~** reindeer

оли́в|а *f* [5], **~ка** *f* [5; *g/pl.:* -вок], olive (tree); **~ковый** [14] olive…

олимп|иа́да *f* [5] Olympiad, Olympics; **~и́йский** [16] Olympic; **~и́йские и́гры** Olympic Games

олицетворе́ние *n* [12] personification, embodiment; **~я́ть** [28], ⟨**~и́ть**⟩[13] personify, embody

о́лов|о *n* [9], tin; **~я́нный** [14] tin, tin-bearing, stannic

о́лух *m* [1] *coll.* blockhead, dolt

ольх|а́ *f* [5], **~о́вый** [14] alder (tree)

ома́р *m* [1] lobster

оме́ла *f* [5] mistletoe

омерзе́ние *n* [12] loathing; **~и́тельный** [14; -лен, -льна] sickening, loathsome

омертве́лый [14] stiff, numb; *med.* necrotic

омле́т *m* [1] omelet(te)

омоложе́ние *n* [12] rejuvenation

омо́ним *m* [1] *ling.* homonym

омрач|а́ть [1], ⟨**~и́ть**⟩ [16 *e.*; -чу́, -чи́шь; -чённый] darken, sadden (*v/i.* **-ся**)

о́мут *m* [1] whirlpool; deep place (*in river or lake*); **в ти́хом ~е че́рти во́дятся** still waters run deep

омы|ва́ть [1], ⟨**~ть**⟩ [22] wash (*of seas*)

он *m*, **~а́** *f*, **~о́** *n*, **~и́** *pl.* [22] he, she, it, they

онда́тра [5] muskrat; *мех* musquash

онеме́лый [14] dump; numb

опа|да́ть [1], ⟨**~сть**⟩ [25; *pt. st.*] fall (off); (*уменьша́ться*) diminish, subside

опа́зд|ывать, ⟨**опозда́ть**⟩ [1] be late (**на** В, **к** Д for); **на пять мину́т** arrive 5 min, late; **на по́езд** miss; *impf. only* be slow (*of timepieces*)

опал|я́ть [28], ⟨**~и́ть**⟩ [13] singe

опас|а́ться [1] (P) fear, apprehend; beware (of); **~е́ние** *n* [12] fear, apprehension, anxiety; **~ка** *f* [5; *g/pl.:* -сок]: **с ~кой** cautiously, warily; **~ливый** [14 *sh.*] wary; anxious; **~ность** [8] danger, peril; risk (**с** Т/ **для** Р at/of); **с ~ностью для себя́** at a risk to himself;

~ный [14; -сен, -сна] dangerous (**для** Р to); **~сть → опа́сть**

опе́к|а *f* [5] guardianship, (*a. fig.*) tutelage; *над иму́ществом* trusteeship; **~а́ть** [1] be guardian (trustee) of; patronize; **~а́емый** [14] ward; **~у́н** *m* [1 *e.*], **~у́нша** *f* [5] guardian; trustee

о́пера *f* [5] opera

опер|ати́вный [14] *руково́дство* efficient; *med.* surgical; **~а́тор** *m* [1] operator; **~ацио́нный** [14] operating; **~ацио́нная** *su.* operating room; **~а́ция** *f* [7] operation; **перенести́ ~а́цию** be operated on

опере|жа́ть [1], ⟨**~ди́ть**⟩ [15] outstrip (*a. fig.* = outdo, surpass); **~ние** *n* [12] plumage; **~ться → опира́ться**

опери́ровать [7] (*im)pf.* operate

о́перный [14] opera(tic); **~ теа́тр** opera house

опер|и́ться [28], ⟨**~и́ться**⟩ [13] fledge

опеча́т|ка *f* [5; *g/pl.:* -ток] misprint, erratum; **~ывать**, ⟨**~ать**⟩ [1] seal (up)

опе́шить *coll.* [16] *pf.* be taken aback

опи́лки *f/pl.* [5; *gen.:* -лок] sawdust

опира́ться [28], ⟨**опере́ться**⟩ [12; обопру́сь, -рёшься, опёрся, оперла́сь] lean (**на** В against, on), *a. fig.* = rest, rely (up[on])

опис|а́ние *n* [12] description; **~а́тельный** [14] descriptive; **~а́ть → ~ывать**; **~ка** *f* [5; *g/pl.:* -сок] slip of the pen; **~ывать** [1], ⟨**~а́ть**⟩ [3] describe (*a. math.*); list, make an inventory (of); *иму́щество* distrain; **-ся** make a slip of the pen; **~ь** *f* [8] list, inventory; distraint

опла́к|ивать [1], ⟨**~ать**⟩ [3] bewail, mourn (over)

опла́|та *f* [5] pay(ment); (*вознагражде́ние*) remuneration, settlement; **~чивать** [1], ⟨**~ти́ть**⟩ [15] pay (for); *счёт* settle; **~ти́ть убы́тки** pay damages

сплеу́ха *coll. f* [5] slap in the face

оплодотвор|е́ние *n* [12] impregnation; fertilization; **~я́ть** [28], ⟨**~и́ть**⟩ [13] impregnate; fertilize, fecundate

опло́т *m* [1] bulwark, stronghold

опло́шность *f* [8] blunder

опове|ща́ть [1], ⟨**~сти́ть**⟩ [15 *e.*; -ещу́,

-ести́шь; -ещённый] notify; inform

опозда́|ние n [12] lateness; delay; vb. + **с ~нием** = **~ть** → **опа́здывать**

опозн|ава́тельный [14] distinguishing; ~ава́ть [5], ⟨~а́ть⟩ [1] identify

о́ползень m [4; -зня] landslide

ополч|а́ться [1], ⟨~и́ться⟩ [16 е.; -чу́сь, -чи́шься] take up arms (against); *fig.* turn (against)

опо́мниться [13] *pf.* come to *or* recover one's senses

опо́р m [1]: **во весь ~** at full speed, at a gallop

опо́р|а f [5] support, prop, rest; ~ный [14] *tech.* bearing, supporting

опоро́|жнить [13] *pf.* empty; ~чивать [1], ⟨~чить⟩ [16] defile

опошл|я́ть [28], ⟨~и́ть⟩ [13] vulgarize

опоя́с|ывать [1], ⟨~ать⟩ [1] gird

оппозици|о́нный [14], ~я f [7] opposition…

оппон|е́нт m [1] opponent; ~и́ровать [7] (Д) oppose; *univ.* act as opponent at defense of dissertation, *etc.*

опра́ва f [5] камня setting; очков и т. д. rim, frame

оправд|а́ние n [12] justification, excuse; *law* acquittal; ~а́тельный [14] justificatory; ~приговор 'not guilty'; ~ать [1], ⟨~а́ть⟩ [1] justify, excuse; *law* acquit; **~а́ть дове́рие** come up to expectations; ~ся *a.* prove (*or* come) true

оправ|ля́ть [28], ⟨~ить⟩ [14] **ка́мень** set; **-ся** recover (*a. o.s.*)

опра́шивать [1], ⟨опроси́ть⟩ [15] interrogate, cross-examine

определ|е́ние n [12] determination; *ling., etc.* definition; decision; *gr.* attribute; ~ённый [14; -ёнен, -ённа] definite; certain; **в ~ённых слу́чаях** in certain cases; ~я́ть [28], ⟨~и́ть⟩ [13] determine; define; **-ся** take shape; (*проясни́ться*) become clearer

опров|ерга́ть [1], ⟨~е́ргнуть⟩ [21] refute; disprove; ~ерже́ние n [12] refutation; denial

опроки́|дывать [1], ⟨~нуть⟩ [20] overturn, upset, *о лодке* capsize (**-ся** *v/i.*); *пла́ны* upset

опроме́тчивый [14 *sh.*] rash, precipi-

tate; **~метью: вы́бежать ~метью** rush out headlong

опро́с m [1]: interrogation; cross-examination; referendum; **~ обще́ственного мне́ния** opinion poll; ~и́ть → **опра́шивать**; ~ный [14] *adj. of* ~; **~ный лист** questionnaire

опры́с|кивать, ⟨~ать⟩ [1] sprinkle, spray

опря́тный [14; -тен, -тна] tidy

о́птика f [5] optics

опто́|вый [14], ~м *adv.* wholesale

опубликов|а́ние n [12] publication; ~ывать [1] → **публикова́ть**

опуск|а́ть [1], ⟨~ти́ть⟩ [15] lower; let down; *го́лову* hang; *глаза́* look down; (*исключи́ть*) omit; **~ти́ть ру́ки** lose heart; **-ся** sink; *о температу́ре* fall; *о со́лнце, температу́ре* go down; *fig.* come down (in the world); *p. pt. a.* down and out

опусте́|лый [14] deserted; ~ть(ся) → **опуска́ть(ся)**; ~ша́ть [1], ⟨~ши́ть⟩ [16 е.; -шу́, -ши́шь; -шённый] devastate; ~ше́ние n [12] devastation; ~ши́тельный [14; -лен, -льна] devastating

опу́т|ывать, ⟨~ать⟩ [1] entangle (*a. fig.*); ensnare

опух|а́ть [1], ⟨~нуть⟩ [21] swell; ~оль f [8] swelling; tumo(u)r

опу́шка f [5; *g/pl.*:-шек] edge (*of a forest*)

опыл|я́ть [28], ⟨~и́ть⟩ [13] pollinate

о́пыт m [1] *жи́зненный и т. д.* experience; experiment; ~ный [14] [-тен, -тна] experienced; experiment(al); empirical

опьяне́ние n [12] intoxication

опя́ть again; *a. coll.* **~-таки** (and) what is more; but again; however

ора́ва *coll. f* [5] gang, horde, mob

ора́кул m [1] oracle

ора́нже|вый [14] orange…; ~ре́я f [6] greenhouse

ора́ть *coll.* [ору́, орёшь] yell, bawl

орби́т|а f [5] orbit; **вы́вести на ~у** put into orbit

о́рган¹ m [1] *biol., pol.* organ

орга́н² m [1] *mus.* organ

организ|а́тор m [1] organizer; ~м m [1] organism; ~ова́ть [7] (*im*)*pf.* (*impf. a.* ~о́вывать [1]) arrange, organize (*v/i.*

-ся)

органи́ческий [16] organic; **_ный** [14; -чен, -чна]: **_ное це́лое** integral whole

о́ргия *f* [7] orgy

орда́ *f* [5; *pl. st.*] horde

о́рден *m* [1; *pl.*: -на́, *etc. e.*] order, decoration

о́рдер *m* [1; *pl.*: -ра́, *etc. e.*] *law* warrant, writ

орёл *m* [1; орла́] eagle; **_ и́ли ре́шка?** heads or tails?

орео́л *m* [1] halo, aureole

оре́х *m* [1] nut; **гре́цкий _** walnut; **лесно́й _** hazelnut; **муска́тный _** nutmeg; **_овый** [14] nut...; *(wood)* walnut

оригина́льный [14; -лен, -льна] original

ориенти́р|оваться [7] *(im)pf.* orient o.s. **(на** B by), take one's bearings; **_о́вка** *f* [5; *g/pl.*: -вок] orientation, bearings *pl.*; **_о́вочный** [14; -чен, -чна] approximate

орке́стр *m* [1] orchestra; band

орли́ный [14] aquiline

орна́мент *m* [1] ornament, ornamental design

оро|ша́ть [1], ⟨**_си́ть**⟩ [15; -ошу́, -оси́шь; -ошённый] irrigate; **_ше́ние** *n* [12] irrigation

ору́д|ие *n* [12] tool *(a. fig.)*; instrument, implement; *mil.* gun; **_и́йный** [14] gun...; **_овать** *coll.* [7] (T) handle, operate

оруж|е́йный [14] arms...; **_ие** *n* [12] weapon(s), arm(s); **холо́дное** *(cold)* steel

орфогра́ф|ия *f* [7] spelling; **_и́ческий** [16] orthographic(al)

орхиде́я *f* [6] *bot.* orchid

оса́ *f* [5; *pl. st.*] wasp

оса́|да *f* [5] siege; **_ди́ть** → **_жда́ть** and **_жива́ть**; **_док** *m* [1; -дка] precipitation, sediment; *fig.* aftertaste; **_жда́ть** [1], ⟨**_ди́ть**⟩ [15 & 15 *e.*; -ажу́, -а́ди́шь; -аждённый] besiege; **_жда́ть вопро́сами** ply with questions; **_жива́ть** [1], ⟨**_ди́ть**⟩ [15] check, snub

оса́н|истый [14 *sh.*] dignified, stately; **_ка** *f* [5] carriage, bearing

осв|а́ивать [1], ⟨**_о́ить**⟩ [13] *(овладе-*

вать) assimilate, master; *новые земли и т. д.* open up; **-ся** accustom o.s. **(в** П to); familiarize o.s. **(с** T with)

осведом|ля́ть [28], ⟨**_ить**⟩ [14] inform **(о** П of); **-ся** inquire **(о** П after; for; about); **_лённый** [14] informed; versed (in)

освеж|а́ть [1], ⟨**_и́ть**⟩ [16 *e.*; -жу́, -жи́шь; -жённый] refresh; freshen *or* touch up; *fig.* brush up; **_а́ющий** [17 *sh.*] refreshing

осве|ща́ть [1], ⟨**_ти́ть**⟩ [15 *e.*; -ещу́, -ети́шь; -ещённый] light (up), illuminate; *fig.* elucidate, cast light on; cover, report on *(in the press)*

освиде́тельство|вание *n* [12] examination; **_ть** [7] *pf.* examine

освист|ывать [1], ⟨**_а́ть**⟩ [3] hiss (off)

освобо|ди́тель *m* [4] liberator; **_ди́тельный** [14] emancipatory, liberation; **_жда́ть** [1], ⟨**_ди́ть**⟩ [15 *e.*; -ожу́, -оди́шь; -ождённый] (set) free, release; liberate; *рабов и т. д.* emancipate; *от уплаты* exempt; *место* clear; **_ди́ть от до́лжности** relieve of one's post; **_жде́ние** *n* [12] liberation; release, emancipation; exemption

осво|е́ние *n* [12] assimilation; mastering; *земель* opening up; **_ить(ся)** → **осва́ивать(ся)**

освя|ща́ть [1], ⟨**_ти́ть**⟩ [15 *e.*; -ящу́, -яти́шь; -ящённый] *eccl.* consecrate

осе|да́ть [1], ⟨**_сть**⟩ [25; оса́дет; осёл; → **сесть**] subside, settle; **_длый** [14] settled

осёл *m* [1; осла́] donkey, ass *(a. fig.)*

осени́ть → **осеня́ть**

осе́н|ний [15] autumnal, fall...; **_ь** *f* [8] fall, autumn (in [the] T)

осен|я́ть [28], ⟨**_и́ть**⟩ [13] overshadow; **_и́ть кресто́м** make the sign of the cross; **меня́ _и́ла мысль** it dawned on me, it occurred to me

осе́сть → **оседа́ть**

осётр *m* [1 *e.*] sturgeon

осетри́на *f* [5] *cul.* sturgeon

осе́чка *f* [5; *g/pl.*: -чек] misfire

оси́ли|вать [1], ⟨**_ть**⟩ [13] → **одолева́ть**

оси́н|а *f* [5] asp; **_овый** [14] asp

оси́пнуть [21] *pf.* grow hoarse

осироте́лый [14] orphan(ed); *fig.* deserted

оска́ли|вать [1], ⟨~ть⟩ [13]: ~ть зу́бы bare one's teeth

оскандáли|ваться [1], ⟨~иться⟩ [13] *coll.* disgrace o.s.; make a mess of s. th.

оскверн|я́ть [28], ⟨~и́ть⟩ [13] profane, desecrate, defile

оско́лок *m* [1; -лка] splinter, fragment

оскорб|и́тельный [14; -лен, -льна] offensive, insulting; ~ле́ние *n* [12] insult, offence; ~**я́ть** [28], ⟨~и́ть⟩ [14 *e.*; -блю́, -би́шь; -блённый] (**-ся** feel) offend(ed), insult(ed)

оскуд|ева́ть [1], ⟨~е́ть⟩ [8] grow scarce

ослаб|ева́ть [1], ⟨~е́ть⟩ [8] grow weak *or* feeble; *натяже́ние* slacken; *ве́тер и т. д.* abate; ~**ть** → ~**ля́ть**; ~**ле́ние** *n* [12] weakening; slackening; relaxation; ~**ля́ть** [28], ⟨~и́ть⟩ [14] weaken, slacken; *внима́ние и т. д.* relax, loosen

ослеп|и́тельный [14; -лен, -льна] dazzling; ~**ля́ть** [28], ⟨~и́ть⟩ [14 *e.*; -плю́, -пи́шь; -плённый] blind; dazzle; ~**ну́ть** [21] *pf.* go blind

осложне́ние *n* [12] complication; ~**я́ть** [28], ⟨~и́ть⟩ [13] (**-ся** be[come]) complicate(d)

ослу́ш|иваться, ⟨~аться⟩ [1] disobey

ослы́шаться [4] *pf.* mishear

осма́тривать [1], ⟨~отре́ть⟩ [9; -отрю́, -о́тришь; -о́тренный] view, look around; examine, inspect; see; **-ся** look round; *fig.* take one's bearings; see how the land lies

осме́|ивать [1], ⟨~я́ть⟩ [27 *e.*; -ею́, -еёшь; -е́янный] mock, ridicule, deride

осме́ли|ваться [1], ⟨~ться⟩ [13] dare, take the liberty (of), venture

осмея́|ние *n* [12] ridicule, derision; ~**ть** → **осме́ивать**

осмо́тр *m* [1] examination; inspection; *достопримеча́тельностей* sightseeing; ~**е́ть(ся)** → **осма́тривать(ся)**; ~**и́тельность** *f* [8] circumspection; ~**и́тельный** [14; -лен, -льна] circumspect

осмы́сл|енный [14 *sh.*] sensible; intelligent; ~**ивать** [1] *and* ~**я́ть** [28], ⟨~ить⟩ [13] comprehend, grasp, make sense of

осна́|стка *f* [5] *naut.* rigging (out, up); ~**ща́ть** [1], ⟨~сти́ть⟩ [15 *e.*; -ащу́, -асти́шь; -ащённый] rig; equip; ~**ще́ние** *n* [12] rigging, fitting out; equipment

осно́в|а *f* [5] basis, foundation, fundamentals; *gr.* stem; ~**а́ние** *n* [12] foundation, basis; *math., chem.* base; (*причи́на*) ground(s), reason; argument; ~**а́тель** *m* [4] founder; ~**а́тельный** [14; -лен, -льна] wellfounded, sound, solid; (*тща́тельный*) thorough; ~**а́ть** → ~**ывать**; ~**но́й** [14] fundamental, basic, principal, primary; **в ~но́м** on the whole; ~**оположник** *m* [1] founder; ~**ывать**, ⟨~а́ть⟩ [7] found; establish; **-ся** be based, rest (on)

осо́ба *f* [5] person; personage; **ва́жная ~** bigwig

осо́бенн|ость *f* [8] peculiarity; feature; ~**ый** [14] (e)special, particular, peculiar

особня́к *m* [1 *e.*] private residence, detached house

особняко́м by o.s., separate(ly); **держа́ться ~** keep aloof

осо́б|ый [14] → ~**енный**

осозн|ава́ть [5], ⟨~а́ть⟩ [1] realize

осо́ка *f* [5] *bot.* sedge

о́сп|а *f* [5] smallpox; **ветряна́я ~а** chickenpox

осп|а́ривать [1], ⟨~о́рить⟩ [13] contest, dispute; *зва́ние чемпио́на и т. д.* contend (for)

остава́ться [5], ⟨оста́ться⟩ [-а́нусь, -а́нешься] (T) remain, stay; be left; keep, stick (to); be(come); have to go, get off; (**за** T) get, win; *пра́во и т. д.* reserve; *долг* owe; **~ без** (P) lose, have no (left); **~ с но́сом** *coll.* get nothing

остав|ля́ть [28], ⟨~ить⟩ [14] leave; abandon; (*отказа́ться*) give up; drop, stop; *в поко́е* leave (*alone*); keep; ~**ля́ть за собо́й** reserve

остально́|й [14] remaining; *pl. a.* the others; *n & pl. a. su.* the rest (**в ~м** in other respects; *as for the rest*)

остан|а́вливать [1], ⟨~ови́ть⟩ [14] stop, bring to a stop; *взгляд* rest, fix; **-ся** stop; *в оте́ле и т. д.* put up (**в** П at); *в ре́чи* dwell (**на** П on); ~**ки**

m/pl. [1] remains; ~ови́ть(ся) → **~а́вли-вать(ся)**; ~о́вка *f* [5; *g/p.*: -вок] stop(-page); *авто́бусная* bus stop; **~о́вка за … (T)** (*only*) … is holding up

оста́|ток *m* [1; -тка] remainder (*a. math*), rest; *тка́ни* remnant; *pl.* remains; ~ться → **~ва́ться**

остекл|я́ть [28], ⟨~и́ть⟩ [13] glaze

остервене́лый [14] frenzied

остере|га́ться [1], ⟨~е́чься⟩ [26 г/ж: -егу́сь, -ежёшься, -егу́тся] (P) beware of, be careful of

о́стов *m* [1] frame, framework; *anat.* skeleton

остолбене́лый *coll.* [14] dumbfounded

осторо́жн|ость *f* [8] care; caution; **об-ра́щаться с ~остью!** handle with care!; ~ый [14; -жен, -жна] cautious, careful; (*благоразумный*) prudent; **~o!** look out!

остри|га́ть [1], ⟨~чь⟩ [26; г/ж: -игу́, -ижёшь, -игу́т] cut; *овец* shear; *ногти* pare; ~ё; *n* [12; *g/pl.*:-иёв] point; spike; ~ть [13], ⟨за-⟩ sharpen; ⟨с-⟩ joke; be witty; ~чь → **~га́ть**

о́стров *m* [1; *pl.*: -ва́, *etc. e.*] island; isle; ~итя́нин *m* [1; -я́не, -я́н] islander; ~о́к *m* [1; -вка́] islet

остро|гла́зый *coll.* [14 *sh.*] sharp-sight-ed; ~коне́чный [14; -чен, -чна] pointed; ~та́¹ *f* [5; *pl. st*; -о́ты] sharpness, keenness, acuteness; ~та́² *f* [5] witti-cism; joke; ~у́мие *n* [12] wit; ~у́мный [14; -мен, -мна] witty; *реше́ние* ingen-ious

о́стр|ый [14; остр, (*coll. a.* остёр), -а́, -о] sharp, pointed; *интере́с* keen; *у́гол и т. д.* acute; critical; ~я́к *m* [1 *e.*] wit(ty fellow)

оступ|а́ться [1], ⟨~и́ться⟩ [14] stumble

остыва́ть [1] → **сты́нуть**

осу|жда́ть [1], ⟨~ди́ть⟩ [15; -уждённый] censure, condemn; *law* convict; ~жде́-ние *n* [12] condemnation; *law* convic-tion

осу́нуться [20] *pf.* grow thin

осуш|а́ть [1], ⟨~и́ть⟩ [16] drain; dry (up); (*опоро́жнить*) empty

осуществ|и́мый [14 *sh.*] feasible; prac-ticable; ~ля́ть [28], ⟨~и́ть⟩ [14 *e.*; -влю́,

-ви́шь; -влённый] bring about, realize; ~ся be realized, fulfilled, implemented; *мечта́* come true; ~ле́ние *n* [12] real-ization

осчастли́вить [14] *pf.* make happy

осып|а́ть [1], ⟨~а́ть⟩ [2] strew (with); shower (on); *звёздами* stud (with); *fig.* heap (on); ~ся crumble; fall

ось *f* [8; *from g/pl. e.*] axis; axle

осяза́|емый [14 *sh.*] tangible; ~ние *n* [12] sense of touch; ~тельный [14] tactile; [-лен, -льна] palpable; ~ть [1] touch, feel

от, **ото** (P) from; of; off; against; for, with; in; *имени* on behalf of

ота́пливать [1], ⟨отопи́ть⟩ [14] heat

отбав|ля́ть [28], ⟨~ить⟩ [14]: *coll.* **хоть ~ля́й** more than enough, in plenty

отбе|га́ть [1], ⟨~жа́ть⟩ [4; -бегу́, -бе-жи́шь, -бегу́т] run off

отби|ва́ть [1], ⟨~ть⟩ [отобью́, -бьёшь; → **бить**] beat, strike (*or* kick) off; *mil.* re-pel; *coll. де́вушку* take away (**у** P from;) *край* break away; *охоту* discourage s.o. from sth.; ~ся ward off (**от** P); *от гру́ппы* get lost; drop behind; break off; *coll.*; (*избавиться*) get rid of

отбивна́я *f* [14]: *cul.* ~ **котле́та** *su.* chop

отби|ра́ть [1], ⟨отобра́ть⟩ [отберу́, -рёшь; отобра́л, -а́, -о; отобранный] (*забра́ть*) take (away); seize; (*вы-бра́ть*) select, pick out; *биле́ты* col-lect

отби́ть(ся) → **отбива́ть(ся)**

о́тблеск *m* [1] reflection, gleam

отбо́й *m* [3]: **нет отбо́ю от** (P) have very many

отбо́р *m* [1] selection, choice; ~ный [14] select, choice; ~очный [14]: **~очное со-ревнова́ние** *sport* knock-out competi-tion

отбра́|сывать [1], ⟨~осить⟩ [15] throw off *or* away; *mil.* throw back; *идею* re-ject; *тень* cast; ~осы *m/pl.* [1] refuse, waste

отбы|ва́ть [1], ⟨~ть⟩ [-бу́ду, -бу́дешь; от-бы́л, -а́, -о] **1.** *v/i.* leave, depart (**в** B for); **2.** *v/t. срок и т. д.* serve, do (time); ~тие *n* [12] departure

отва́|га *f* [5] bravery, courage; ~жи-

ваться [1], ⟨**~житься**⟩ [16] have the courage to, venture to, dare to; **~жный** [14; -жен, -жна] valiant, brave

отвал: **до ~а** coll. one's fill; **~ивать(ся)** [1], ⟨**~и́ться**⟩ [13]: **-али́ться** fall off; slip

отварно́й [14] cul. boiled

отвезти́ → **отвози́ть**

отверга́ть [1], ⟨**~нуть**⟩ [21] reject, turn down; repudiate; spurn

отвердева́ть [1] → **тверде́ть**

отверну́ть(ся) → **отвёртывать** and **отвора́чивать(ся)**

отвёрт|ка [5; g/pl.: -ток] screwdriver; **~ывать** [1], ⟨**отверну́ть**⟩ [20; отвёрнутый], ⟨**отверте́ть**⟩ coll. [11] unscrew

отве́с|ный [14; -сен, -сна] precipitous, steep, sheer; **~ти́** → **отводи́ть**

отве́т m [1] answer, reply (**в ~ на** B in reply to); **быть в ~е** be answerable (**за** for)

ответвл|е́ние n [12] branch, offshoot; **~и́ться** [28] branch off

отве́|тить → **~ча́ть**; **~тственность** f [8] responsibility; **~тственный** [14 sh.] responsible (to **пе́ред** T); **~тчик** m [1] defendant; **~ча́ть** [1], ⟨**~тить**⟩ [15] (**на** B) answer, reply (to); (**за** B) answer, account (for); (**соотве́тствовать**) (Д) answer, suit, meet

отви́н|чивать [1], ⟨**~ти́ть**⟩ [15 e.; -нчу́, -нти́шь; -и́нченный] unscrew

отвис|а́ть [1], ⟨**~нуть**⟩ [21] hang down, flop, sag; **~лый** [14] loose, flopping, sagging

отвле|ка́ть [1], ⟨**~чь**⟩ [26] divert, distract; **~чённый** [14 sh.] abstract

отво|ди́ть [15], ⟨**отвести́**⟩ [25] lead, take; **глаза́** avert; **уда́р** parry; **кандидату́ру** reject; **зе́млю** allot; **~ди́ть ду́шу** coll. unburden one's heart

отво|ёвывать [1], ⟨**~ева́ть**⟩ [6] (re)conquer, win back; **~зи́ть** [15], ⟨**отвезти́**⟩ [24] take, drive away

отвора́чивать [1], ⟨**отверну́ть**⟩ [20] turn off; **-ся** turn away

отвори́ть(ся) → **отворя́ть(ся)**

отворо́т m [1] lapel

отворя́ть [28], ⟨**~и́ть**⟩ [13; -орю́, -о́ришь; -о́ренный] open (v/i. **-ся**)

отврати́тельный [14; -лен, -льна] dis-

gusting, abominable; **~ща́ть** [1], ⟨**~ти́ть**⟩ [15 e.; -ащу́, -ати́шь; -ащённый] avert; **~ще́ние** n [12] aversion, disgust (**к** Д for, at)

отвык|а́ть [1], ⟨**~нуть**⟩ [21] (**от** P) get out of the habit of, grow out of, give up

отвя́з|ывать [1], ⟨**~а́ть**⟩ [3] (**-ся** [be]come) untie(d), undo(ne); coll. (**отде́лываться**) get rid of (**от** P); **отвяжи́сь!** leave me alone!

отга́д|ывать [1], ⟨**~а́ть**⟩ guess; **~ка** f [5; g/pl.: -док] solution (to a riddle)

отгиба́ть [1], ⟨**отогну́ть**⟩ [20] unbend; turn up (or back)

отгов|а́ривать [1], ⟨**~ори́ть**⟩ [13] dissuade (**от** P from); **~о́рка** f [5; g/pl.: -рок] excuse, pretext

отголо́сок m [1; -ска] → **о́тзвук**

отгоня́ть [28], ⟨**отогна́ть**⟩ [отгоню́, -о́нишь; отгнанный; → гнать] drive (or frighten) away; fig. **мысль** banish, suppress

отгор|а́живать [1], ⟨**~оди́ть**⟩ [15 & 15 e.; -ожу́, -о́дишь; -о́женный] fence in; **в до́ме** partition off

отгру|жа́ть [1], ⟨**~зи́ть**⟩ [15 & 15; e.;-ужу́, -у́зишь; -у́женный & -ужённый] ship, dispatch

отгрыза́ть [1], ⟨**~ть**⟩ [24; pt. st.] bite off, gnaw off

отда|ва́ть [5], ⟨**~ть**⟩ [-да́м, -да́шь, etc., → **дать**; о́тдал, -а́, -о] give back, return; give (away); **в шко́лу** send (**в** B to); **долг** pay; **~ва́ть честь** (Д) mil. salute; coll. sell; **~ва́ть до́лжное** give s.o. his due; **~ва́ть прика́з** give an order; impf. smell or taste (T of); **-ся** devote o.s. to; **чу́вство** surrender, give o.s. to; **о зву́ке** resound

отда́в|ливать [1], ⟨**~и́ть**⟩ [14] crush; (**наступи́ть**) tread on

отдал|е́ние n [12]: **в ~е́нии** in the distance; **~ённый** [14 sh.] remote; **~я́ть** [28], ⟨**~и́ть**⟩ [13] move away; **встре́чу** put off, postpone; fig. alienate; **-ся** move away (**от** P from); fig. become estranged; digress

отда́|ть(ся) → **отдава́ть(ся)**; **~ча** f [5] return; mil. recoil; tech. output, efficiency

отде́л m [1] department; **в газе́те** sec-

O

tion; ~ **ка́дров** personnel department; ~**ать(ся)** → ~**ывать(ся)**; ~**е́ние** n [12] separation; department, division; branch (office); *mil.* squad; *в столе и т. д.* compartment; *в больнице* ward; *концерта* part; *coll.* (police) station; ~**е́ние свя́зи** post office; ~**и́мый** [14 *sh.*] separable; ~**и́ть(ся)** → ~**я́ть(ся)**; ~**ка** f [5; *g/pl.*: -лок] finishing; *одежды* trimming; ~**ывать**, ⟨~**ать**⟩ [1] finish, put the final touches to; decorate; **-ся** get rid of (**от** P); get off, escape (T with); ~**ьность** f [8]: **в ~ьности** individually; ~**ьный** [14] separate; individual; ~**я́ть** [28], ⟨~**и́ть**⟩ [13; -елю́, -е́лишь] separate (*v/i.* **-ся от** P from; come off)

отдёр|гивать [1], ⟨~**нуть**⟩ [20] draw back; pull aside

отдира́ть [1], ⟨**отодра́ть**⟩ [отдеру́, -рёшь; отодра́л, -á, -о; ото́дранный] tear *or* rip (off); *pf. coll.* thrash

отдохну́ть → **отдыха́ть**

отду́шина f [5] (air) vent (*a. fig.*)

о́тдых m [1] rest, relaxation; holiday; ~**а́ть** [1], ⟨**отдохну́ть**⟩ [20] rest, relax

отдыша́ться [1] *pf.* get one's breath back

отёк m [1] swelling, edema

оте|ка́ть [1], ⟨~**чь**⟩ [26] swell

оте́ль m [4] hotel

оте́ц m [1; отца́] father

оте́че|ский [16] fatherly; paternal; ~**ственный** [14] native, home...; *война* patriotic; ~**ство** n [9] motherland, fatherland, one's (native) country

оте́чь → **отека́ть**

отжи|ва́ть [1], ⟨~**ть**⟩ [-живу́, -вёшь; о́тжил, -á, -о; о́тжи́тый (о́тжи́т, -á, -о)] (have) live(d, had) (one's time *or* day); *о традиции и т. д.* become obsolete, outmoded; die out

о́тзвук m [1] echo, repercussion; *чувство* response

о́тзыв m [1] opinion, judg(e)ment (**по** Д on *or* about); reference; comment, review; *дипломата* recall; ~**а́ть** [1], ⟨**отозва́ть**⟩ [отзову́, -вёшь; ото́званный] take aside; recall; **-ся** respond, answer; speak (**о** П of *or* to); (re)sound; (*вызвать*) call forth (Ts.th.); (*влиять*) af-

fect (**на** В s.th.); ~**чивый** [14 *sh.*] responsive

отка́з m [1] refusal, denial, rejection (**в** П, Р of); renunciation (**от** P of); *tech.* failure; **без** ~**а** smoothly; **по́лный до** ~**а** cram-full; **получи́ть** ~ be refused; ~**ывать** [1], ⟨~**а́ть**⟩ [3] refuse, deny (a p. s.th. Д/в P); *tech.* fail; **-ся** (**от** P) refuse, decline, reject; renounce, give up; (**я**) **не откажу́сь** *coll.* I wouldn't mind

отка́|лывать [1], ⟨**отколо́ть**⟩ [17] break *or* chop off; *булавку* unpin, unfasten; **-ся** break off; come undone; *fig.* break away; ~**пывать**, ⟨**откопа́ть**⟩ [1] dig up, unearth; ~**рмливать** [1], ⟨**откорми́ть**⟩ [14] fatten up; ~**тывать**, ⟨~**ти́ть**⟩ [15] roll, haul (away) (**-ся** *v/i.*; ~**чивать**, ⟨~**ча́ть**⟩ [1] pump out; resuscitate; ~**шливаться** [1], ⟨~**шляться**⟩ [28] clear one's throat

отки|дно́й [14] *сидение* tip-up; ~**дывать** [1], ⟨~**нуть**⟩ [20] throw away; turn back, fold back; **-ся** lean back recline

откла́|дывать [1], ⟨**отложи́ть**⟩ [16] lay aside; *деньги* save; (*отсрочить*) put off, defer, postpone

откле́|ивать [1], ⟨~**ить**⟩ [13] unstick; **-ся** come unstuck

о́тклик m [1] response; comment; → *а.* **о́тзвук**; ~**а́ться** [1], ⟨~**нуться**⟩ [20] (**на** В) respond (to), answer; comment (on)

отклон|е́ние n [12] deviation; *от темы* digression; *предложения* rejection; ~**я́ть** [28], ⟨~**и́ть**⟩ [13; -оню́, -о́нишь] decline, reject; **-ся** deviate; digress

отключа́|ть [4], ⟨~**чи́ть**⟩ [16] *el.* cut off, disconnect; *p. p. p.* dead

отк|оло́ть → ~**а́лывать**, ~**опа́ть** → ~**а́пывать**; ~**орми́ть** → ~**а́рмливать**

отко́с m [1] slope, scarp, escarp

открове́н|ие n [12] revelation; ~**ный** [14; -éнен, -éнна] frank, candid, blunt, outspoken

откры|ва́ть [1], ⟨~**ть**⟩ [22] open; *кран* turn on; *новую планету* discover; *тайну* disclose, reveal; *памятник* unveil; *учреждение* inaugurate; **-ся** open; *кому-л.* unbosom o.s.; ~**тие** n [12] opening; discovery; revelation; inauguration; unveiling; **∠тка** f [5; g/pl.: -ток] (*с ви́дом* picture) post card; **∠тый** [14] open; *слу́шания и т. д.* public; **∠ть(ся)** → **∠ва́ться**

откуда where from?; whence; ~ **вы?** where do you come from? → **вы зна́ете?** how do you know …?; **∠-нибудь**, **∠-то** (from) somewhere or other

откупа́|ться [1], ⟨∠иться⟩ [14] pay off

откупо́ри|вать [1], ⟨∠ть⟩ [13] uncork; open

отку́с|ывать [1], ⟨∠и́ть⟩ [15] bite off

отлага́тельство n [9]: *де́ло не те́рпит* **∠а** the matter is urgent

отлага́ться [1], ⟨отложи́ться⟩ [16] *geol.* be deposited

отла́мывать, ⟨отлома́ть⟩ [1], ⟨отломи́ть⟩ [14] break of (*v/i.* **-ся**)

отлёт m [1] *пти́ц* flying away; **∠ета́ть** [1], ⟨∠ете́ть⟩ [11] fly away *or* off; *coll.* come off

отли́в¹ m [1] ebb (tide)

отли́в² m [1] play of colo(u)rs, shimmer

отли|ва́ть¹ [1], ⟨∠ть⟩ [отолью́, -льёшь; о́тли́л, -á, -о; ∠тый] pour off, in, out (some… P); *tech.* found, cast

отлива́ть² *impf.* (T) shimmer, play

отлича́|ть [1], ⟨∠и́ть⟩ [16 *е.*; -чу́, -чи́шь; -чённый] distinguish (**от** P from); **-ся** *a. impf.* differ; be noted (T for); **∠ие** n [12] distinction, difference; **в ∠ие от** (P) as against; **зна́ки ∠ия** decorations; **∠и́тельный** [14] distinctive; **∠ник** m [1], **∠ница** f [5] excellent pupil, *etc.*; **∠ный** [14; -чен, -чна] excellent, perfect; *om чего́-л.* different; *adv. a.* very good (*as su. a mark* → **пятёрка**)

отло́гий [16 *sh.*] sloping

отлож|е́ние n [12] deposit; **∠и́ть(ся)** → **откла́дывать & отлага́ться**; **∠но́й** [14] *воротни́к* turndown

отлома́|ть ⟨∠и́ть⟩ → **отла́мывать**

отлуча́|ться [1], ⟨∠и́ться⟩ [16 *е.*; -чу́сь, -чи́шься] (**из** P) leave, absent o.s. (from); **∠ка** f [5] absence

отма́лчиваться [1] keep silent

отма́|тывать [1], ⟨отмота́ть⟩ [1] wind *or* reel off, unwind; **∠хиваться** [1], ⟨∠хну́ться⟩ [20] disregard, brush aside

о́тмель f [8] shoal, sandbank

отме́н|а f [5] *зако́на* abolition; *спекта́кля* cancellation; *прика́за* countermand; **∠ный** [14; -е́нен, -е́нна] → **отли́чный**; **∠я́ть** [28], ⟨∠и́ть⟩ [14; -ню́, -е́нишь] abolish; cancel; countermand

отмер|е́ть → **отмира́ть**; **∠а́ть** [1], ⟨отмёрнуть⟩ [21] be frostbitten

отме́р|ивать [1] & **∠я́ть** [28], ⟨∠ить⟩ [13] measure (off)

отме́стк|а *coll.* f [5]: **в ∠у** in revenge

отме́|тка f [5; g/pl.: -ток] mark, *шко́льная* тж. grade; **∠ча́ть** [1], ⟨∠тить⟩ [15] mark, note

отмира́ть [1], ⟨отмере́ть⟩ [12; отомрёт; о́тмер, -рла́, -о; отме́рший] *об обы́чае* die away *or* out

отмор|а́живать [1], ⟨∠о́зить⟩ [15] frostbite

отмота́ть → **отма́тывать**

отмы|ва́ть [1], ⟨∠ть⟩ [22] clean; wash (off); **∠ка́ть** [1], ⟨∠ и́ть⟩ [20] unlock, open; **∠чка** f [5; g/pl.: -чек] master key; picklock

отне́киваться *coll.* [1] deny, disavow

отнести́(сь) → **относи́ть(ся)**

отнима́|ть [1], ⟨отня́ть⟩ [-ниму́, -ни́мешь; о́тнял, -á, -о; о́тнятый (о́тнят, -á, -о)] take away (**у** P from); *вре́мя* take; amputate; ~ **от гру́ди** wean; *coll.* be paralyzed

относи́тельный [14; -лен, -льна] relative; **∠о** (P) concerning, about

отно|си́ть [15], ⟨отнести́⟩ [24: -с-, -есу́; -ёс, -есла́] take (Д в В, **к** Д to); *ве́тром и т.п.* carry (off, away); *на ме́сто* put; *fig.* refer to; ascribe; **-ся**, ⟨отнести́сь⟩ (**к** Д) treat, be; *impf.* concern; refer; belong; date from; be relevant; **э́то к де́лу не ∠сится** that's irrelevant; **∠ше́ние** n [12] attitude (toward[s] **к** Д); treatment; relation; *math.* ratio; respect (**в** П, **по** Д in, with); **по ∠ше́нию (к** Д) as regards, to(ward[s]); **име́ть ∠ше́ние (к** Д) concern, bear a relation to

отны́не *old use* henceforth

отню́дь: ~ **не** by no means

отня́ть(ся) → **отнима́ть(ся)**

отобра|жа́ть [1], ⟨∠зи́ть⟩ [15 *е.*; -ажу́, -ази́шь; -ажённый] represent; reflect

ото|бра́ть → **отбира́ть**; ~всю́ду from everywhere; ~гна́ть → **отгоня́ть**; ~гну́ть → **отгиба́ть**; ~грева́ть [1], ⟨~гре́ть⟩ [8]; -гре́тый warm (up); ~дви́га́ть [1], ⟨~дви́нуть⟩ [20 *st.*] move aside, away (*v/i.* **-ся**)

отодра́ть → **отдира́ть**

отож(д)еств|ля́ть [28], ⟨~и́ть⟩ [14; -влю́, -ви́шь; -влённый] identify

ото|зва́ть(ся) → **отзыва́ть(ся)**; ~йти́ → **отходи́ть**; ~мкну́ть → **отмыка́ть**; ~мсти́ть (*минова́ть*) mst'; -ся spite

отоп|и́ть [28] → **ота́пливать**; ~ле́ние *n* [12] heating

оторва́ть(ся) → **отрыва́ть(ся)**

оторопе́ть [8] *pf.* coll. be struck dumb

отосла́ть → **отсыла́ть**

отпа|да́ть [1], ⟨~сть⟩ [25; *pt. st.*] (**от** P) fall off *or* away; *fig.* (*минова́ть*) pass

отпе|ва́ние *n* [12] funeral service; ~тый [14] *coll.* inveterate, out-and-out; ~ре́ть(ся) → **отпира́ть(ся)**

отпеча́т|ок *m* [1; -тка] (im)print; impress; *a. fig.* ~ок па́льца fingerprint; ~ывать, ⟨~ать⟩ [1] print; type; -ся imprint, stamp

отпи|ва́ть [1], ⟨~ть⟩ [отопью́, -пьёшь; о́тпил, -á, -о; -пе́й(те)!] drink (some… P); ~ли́вать [1], ⟨~ли́ть⟩ [13] saw off

отпира́ть [1], ⟨отпере́ть⟩ [12; отопру́, -прёшь; о́тпер, -прлá, -о; отпе́рший; о́тпертый (-ерт, -á, -о)] unlock, unbar, open; -ся¹ open

отпира́ться² deny; disown

отпи́ть → **отпива́ть**

отпи́х|ивать *coll.* [1], *once* ⟨~ну́ть⟩ [20] push off; shove aside

отпла́|та *f* [5] repayment, requital; ~чивать [1], ⟨~ти́ть⟩ [15] (re)pay, requite

отплы|ва́ть [1], ⟨~ть⟩ [23] sail, leave; swim (off); ~тие *n* [12] sailing off, departure

о́тповедь *f* [8] rebuff, rebuke

отпо́р *m* [1] repulse, rebuff

отпоро́ть [17] *pf.* rip (off)

отправ|и́тель *m* [4] sender; ~и́ть(ся) → ~ля́ть(ся); ~ка *coll. f* [5] sending off, dispatch; ~ле́ние *n* [12] dispatch; departure; ~ля́ть [28], ⟨~ить⟩ [14] send, dis-

patch, forward; mail; *impf. only* exercise, perform (*duties, functions, etc.*); -ся set out; go; leave, depart (**в, на** B for); ~но́й [14] starting…

отпра́шиваться [1], ⟨отпроси́ться⟩ [15] ask for leave; *pf.* ask for and obtain leave

отпры́г|ивать [1], *once* ⟨~нуть⟩ [20] jump, spring back (*or* aside)

о́тпрыск *m* [1] *bot. and fig.* offshoot, scion

отпря́нуть [20 *st.*] *pf.* recoil

отпу́г|ивать [1], ⟨~ну́ть⟩ [20] scare away

о́тпуск *m* [1; *pl.* -ка́, *etc. e.*] holiday(s), leave (*a.* mil.), vacation (on: *go* **в** B; *be* **в** П); ~ **по боле́зни** sick leave; ~а́ть [1], ⟨отпусти́ть⟩ [15] **1.** let go; release, set free; dismiss; slacken; *бо́роду* grow; *coll.* шу́тку crack; **2.** *това́р* serve; ~ни́к *m* [1 *e.*] vacationer, holiday maker; ~но́й [14] **1.** vacation…, holiday…; **2.** *econ.* цена́ selling

отпуще́н|ие *n* [12] **козёл** ~ия scapegoat

отраба́тывать [1], ⟨~отать⟩ [1] долг и т. д. work off; finish work; *p. pt. p. a.* tech. waste, exhaust

отрав|а́ *f* [5] poison; *fig.* bane; ~ле́ние *n* [12] poisoning; ~ля́ть [28], ⟨~и́ть⟩ [14] poison; *fig.* spoil

отра́д|а *f* [5] comfort, joy, pleasure; ~ный [14; -ден, -дна] pleasant, gratifying, comforting

отра|жа́ть [1], ⟨~зи́ть⟩ [15 *e.*; -ажу́, -ази́шь; -ажённый] repel, ward off; *в зе́ркале, о́бразе* reflect, mirror; -ся (*v/i.*) (**на** П) affect; show

о́трасль *f* [8] branch

отра|ста́ть [1], ⟨~сти́⟩ [24; -ст-: -сту́; → **расти́**] grow; ~щивать [1], ⟨~сти́ть⟩ [15 *e.*; -ащу́, -асти́шь; -ащённый] (let) grow

отре́бье *n* [10] *obs.* waste; *fig.* rabble

отре́з *m* [1] length (*of cloth*); ~ать, ~ывать [1], ⟨~ать⟩ [3] cut off; *coll.* give a curt answer

отрезвля́ть [28], ⟨~и́ть⟩ [14 *e.*; -влю́, -ви́шь; -влённый] sober

отре́з|ок *m* [1; -зка] piece; *доро́ги* stretch; *вре́мени* space; *math.* segment; ~ывать → ~а́ть

отре|ка́ться [1], ⟨~чься⟩ [26] (**от** P) disown, disavow; *от убежде́ний и т. д.* renounce; **~чься от престо́ла** abdicate

отре|че́ние *n* [12] renunciation; abdication; **~чься → ~ка́ться**; **~шённый** [14] estranged, aloof

отрица́|ние *n* [12] negation, denial; **~тельный** [14; -лен, -льна] negative; **~ть** [1] deny; (*law*) **~ть вино́вность** plead not guilty

отро́|г *m* [1] *geogr.* spur; **~ду** *coll.* in age; from birth; in one's life; **~чье** *n* [10] *coll. pej.* spawn; **~сток** *m* [1; -тка] *bot.* shoot; *anat.* appendix; **~чество** *n* [9] boyhood; adolescence

отруб|а́ть [1], ⟨~и́ть⟩ [14] chop off

о́труби *f/pl.* [8; *from g/pl. e.*] bran

отры́в *m* [1]: **в ~е** (**от** P) out of touch (with); **~а́ть** [1] 1. ⟨оторва́ть⟩ [-рву́, -вёшь, -ва́л, -а́, -о; ото́рванный] tear off; *от рабо́ты* tear away; separate; **-ся** (**от** P) come off; tear o.s. away; *от друзе́й* lose contact (with); **не ~я́сь** without rest; 2. ⟨отры́ть⟩ [22] dig up, unearth; **~истый** [14 *sh.*] abrupt; **~но́й** [14] perforated; tearoff (*sheet, block, calendar etc.*); **~ок** *m* [1; -вка] fragment; extract, passage; **~очный** [14; -чен, -чна] fragmentary, scrappy

отры́жка *f* [5; *g/pl.*: -жек] belch(ing), eructation

отры́ть → отрыва́ть

отря́|д *m* [1] detachment; *biol.* class; **~хивать** [1], *once* ⟨~хну́ть⟩ [20] shake off

отсве́чивать [1] be reflected; shine (with T)

отсе́|ивать [1], ⟨~ять⟩ [27] sift, screen; *fig.* eliminate; **~ка́ть** [1], ⟨~чь⟩ [26; *pt.*: -се́к, -секла́ -сечённый] sever; cut off; **~че́ние** *n* [12]: **дава́ть го́лову на ~че́ние** *coll.* stake one's life

отси́|живать [1], ⟨~де́ть⟩ [11; -жу́, -ди́шь] sit out; *в тюрьме́* serve; *но́гу* have pins and needles (in one's leg)

отска́|кивать [1], ⟨~очи́ть⟩ [16] jump aside, away; *мяч* rebound; *coll.* break off, come off

отслу́|живать [1], ⟨~и́ть⟩ [16] *в а́рмии* serve (one's time); *оде́жда и т. д.* be

worn out

отсове́товать [7] *pf.* dissuade (from)

отсо́хнуть → отсыха́ть

отсро́ч|ивать [1], ⟨~ить⟩ [16] postpone; **~ка** *f* [5; *g/pl.*: -чек] postponement, delay; *law* adjourn

отста|ва́ть [5], ⟨~ть⟩ [-а́ну, -а́нешь] (**от** P) lag *or* fall behind; be slow (**на пять мину́т** 5 min.); *обои и т. д.* come off; *coll. pf.* leave alone

отста́в|ка *f* [5] resignation; retirement; (*увольне́ние*) dismissal; **в ~е** = **~но́й**; **~ля́ть** [28], ⟨~ить⟩ [14] remove, set aside; **~но́й** [14] *mil.* retired

отст|а́ивать¹ [1], ⟨~оя́ть⟩ [-ою́, -ои́шь] defend; *права́ и т. д.* uphold, maintain; stand up for

отста́ивать² [1], ⟨~оя́ть⟩ stand (through), remain standing

отста́|лость *f* [8] backwardness; **~лый** [14] backward; **~ть → ~ва́ть**

отстёг|ивать [1], ⟨отстегну́ть⟩ [20; -ёгнутый] unbutton, unfasten

отстоя́ть [1] *pf.* be at a distance (of P)

отстоя́ть(ся) → отста́ивать(ся)

отстр|а́ивать [1], ⟨~о́ить⟩ [13] finish building; build (up); **~аня́ть** [28], ⟨~ани́ть⟩ [13] push aside, remove; *от до́лжности* dismiss; **-ся** (**от** P) dodge; shirk; keep aloof; **~о́ить → ~а́ивать**

отступ|а́ть [1], ⟨~и́ть⟩ [14] step back; *mil.* retreat, fall back; *в у́жасе* recoil; *fig.* back down; go back on; *от пра́вила* deviate; **~ле́ние** *n* [12] retreat; deviation; *в изложе́нии* digression

отсу́тств|ие *n* [12] absence; **в её ~ие** in her absence; **за ~ием** for lack of; **находи́ться в ~ии** be absent; **~овать** [7] be absent; be lacking

отсчи́т|ывать [1], ⟨~а́ть⟩ [1] count (out); count (off)

отсыл|а́ть [1], ⟨отосла́ть⟩ [-ошлю́, -шлёшь; ото́сланный] send (off, back); refer (**к** Д to); **~ка** *f* [5; *g/pl.*: -лок] → **ссы́лка**

отсып|а́ть [1], ⟨~а́ть⟩ [2] pour (out); measure (out)

отсы|ре́лый [14] damp; **~ха́ть** [1], ⟨отсо́хнуть⟩ [21] dry up; wither

отсю́да from here; (*сле́довательно*)

hence; (*fig.*) from this

отта́|ивать [1], ⟨~ять⟩ [27] thaw out; ~лкивать [1], ⟨оттолкну́ть⟩ [20] push away, aside; *fig.* antagonize; *друзе́й* alienate; ~лкивающий [17] repulsive, repellent; ~скивать [1], ⟨~щи́ть⟩ [16] drag away, aside; ~чивать [1], ⟨отточи́ть⟩ [16] whet, sharpen; *стиль и т. д.* perfect; ~ять → ~ивать

отте́н|ок *m* [1; -нка] shade, nuance (*a. fig.*); tinge; ~я́ть [28], ⟨~и́ть⟩ [13] shade; (*подчеркну́ть*) set off, emphasize

о́ттепель *f* [8] thaw

оттесн|я́ть [28], ⟨~и́ть⟩ [13] push back, aside; *mil.* drive back

о́ттиск *m* [1] impression, offprint

отто|го́ therefore, (*a.* ~го́ и) that's why; ~го́ что because; ~лкну́ть → **отта́лкивать**; ~пы́рить *coll.* [13] pf. bulge, protrude, stick out (*v/i.* -ся); ~чи́ть → **отта́чивать**

отту́да from there

оття́|гивать [1], ⟨~ну́ть⟩ [20; -я́нутый] draw out, pull away (*mil.*) draw off (back); *coll. реше́ние* delay; **он хо́чет ~ну́ть вре́мя** he wants to gain time

отуча́|ть [1], ⟨~и́ть⟩ [16] break (**от** P of), cure (**от** P); wean; **-ся** break o.s. (of)

отхлы́нуть [20] *pf.* flood back, rush back

отхо́д *m* [1] departure; withdrawal; *fig.* deviation; ~и́ть [15], ⟨отойти́⟩ [-ойду́, -дёшь; отошёл, -шла́; отойдя́] move (away, off); leave, depart; deviate; *mil.* withdraw; (*успоко́иться*) recover; ~ы *m/pl.* [1] waste

отцве|та́ть [1], ⟨~сти́⟩ [25; -т-: -ету́] finish blooming, fade (*a. fig.*)

отцеп|ля́ть [28], ⟨~и́ть⟩ [14] unhook; uncouple; *coll.* ~и́сь! leave me alone!

отцо́в|ский [16] paternal; fatherly; ~ство *n* [9] paternity

отча́|иваться [1], ⟨~я́ться⟩ [27] despair (of **в** П); be despondent

отча́ли|вать [1], ⟨~ть⟩ [13] cast off, push off; *coll.* ~вай! beat it!; scram!

отча́сти partly, in part

отча́я|ние *n* [12] despair; ~нный [14 *sh.*] desperate; ~ться → **отча́иваться**

о́тче: 2 наш Our Father; Lord's Prayer

отчего́ why; ~-то that's why

отчека́н|ивать [1], ⟨~ить⟩ [13] mint, coin; say distinctly

о́тчество *n* [9] patronymic

отчёт *m* [1] account (**o**, **в** П of), report (on); (**от**)дава́ть себе́ ~ **в** (П) realize *v/t.*; ~ливый [14 *sh.*] distinct, clear; ~ность *f* [8] accounting

отчи́|зна *f* [5] fatherland; ~й [17]: ~й дом family home; ~м *m* [1] stepfather

отчисл|е́ние *n* [12] (*вы́чет де́нег*) deduction; *студе́нта* expulsion; ~я́ть [28], ⟨~ить⟩ [13] deduct; dismiss

отчи́т|ывать *coll.*, ⟨~а́ть⟩ [1] *coll.* read a lecture to; tell off; **-ся** give *or* render an account (to **пе́ред** Т)

от|чужда́ть [1] *law.* alienate; estrange; ~шатну́ться [20] *pf.* start *or* shrink back; recoil; ~швы́рнуть *coll.* [20] *pf.* fling (away); throw off; ~ше́льник *m* [1] hermit; *fig.* recluse

отъе́зд *m* [1] departure; ~зжа́ть [1], ⟨~хать⟩ [-е́ду, -е́дешь] drive (off), depart

отъя́вленный [14] inveterate, thorough, out-and-out

оты́гр|ывать [1], ⟨~а́ть⟩ [1] win back, regain; **-ся** regain one's lost money

оты́ск|ивать [1], ⟨~а́ть⟩ [3] find; track down; **-ся** turn up; appear

отяго|ща́ть [1], ⟨~ти́ть⟩ [15 *e.*; -щу́, -ти́шь; -ощённый] burden

отягч|а́ть [4], ⟨~и́ть⟩ [16] make worse, aggravate

офице́р *m* [1] officer; ~ский [16] office(r's, -s'); ~иа́льный [14; -лен, -льна] official; ~иа́нт *m* [1] waiter; ~иа́нтка *f* [5] waitress

оформ|ля́ть [28], ⟨~ить⟩ [14] *кни́гу* design; *докуме́нты* draw up; *витри́ну* dress; *брак* register; ~ить на рабо́ту take on the staff

офо́рт *m* [1] etching

ох *int.* oh!, ah!; ~анье *n* [10] *col.* moaning, groaning

оха́пка *f* [5; *g/pl.:* -пок] armful

о́х|ать [1], *once* ⟨~ну́ть⟩ [20] groan

охва́т|ывать [1], ⟨~и́ть⟩ [15] enclose; *о чу́встве* seize, grip; *вопро́сы* embrace; *пла́менем* envelop; *fig.* comprehend

охла|дева́ть, ⟨**~де́ть**⟩ [8] grow cold (toward); *a. fig.* lose interest in; **~жда́ть** [1], ⟨**~ди́ть**⟩ [15 *e.*; -ажу́, -ади́шь; -аждённый] cool; **~жде́ние** *n* [12] cooling

охмеле́ть [8] *coll.* get tipsy

о́хнуть → **о́хать**

охо́та¹ *f* [5] *coll.* desire (for), mind (to)

охо́т|а² *f* [5] (**на** В, **за** Т) hunt(ing) (of, for); chase (after); **~иться** [15] (**на** В, **за** Т) hunt; chase (after); **~ник**¹ *m* [1] hunter

охо́тник² *m* [1] volunteer; lover (of **до** P)

охо́тн|о willingly, gladly, with pleasure; **~ее** rather; **~ее всего́** best of all

охра́н|а *f* [5] guard(s); *прав* protection; **ли́чная ~а** bodyguard; **~я́ть** [28], ⟨**~и́ть**⟩ [13] guard, protect (**от** P from, against)

охри́п|лый *coll.* [14], **~ший** [17] hoarse

оце́н|ивать [1], ⟨**~и́ть**⟩ [13; -еню́, -е́нишь] value (**в** В at); estimate; *ситуа́цию* appraise; (*по достоинству*) appreciate; **~ка** *f* [5; *g/pl.:* -нок] evaluation, estimation; appraisal; appreciation; *шко́льная* mark

оцепене́|лый [14] torpid, benumbed; *fig.* petrified, stupefied; **~ние** *n* [12]: **в ~нии** petrified

оцеп|ля́ть [28], ⟨**~и́ть**⟩ [14] encircle, cordon off

оча́г *m* [1 *e.*] hearth (*a. fig.*); *fig.* center (-tre), seat

очаро́в|а́ние *n* [12] charm, fascination; **~а́тельный** [14; -лен, -льна] charming; **~ывать** [1], ⟨**~а́ть**⟩ [7] charm, fascinate, enchant

очеви́д|ец *m* [1; -дца] eyewitness; **~ный** [14; -ден, -дна] evident, obvious

о́чень very; (very) much

очередно́й [14] next (in turn); yet another; latest

о́черед|ь *f* [8; *from g/pl. e.*] turn (**по ~и** in turns); order, succession; line (*Brt.* queue); *mil.* volley; **ва́ша ~ь** *or* **~ за ва́ми** it is your turn; **на ~и** next; **в свою́ ~ь** in (for) my, *etc.*, turn (part)

о́черк *m* [1] sketch; essay

черня́ть [28] → **черни́ть**

очерстве́лый [14] hardened, callous

очер|та́ние *n* [12] outline, contour, **~чивать** [1], ⟨**~ти́ть**⟩ [15] outline, sketch; **~тя́ го́лову** *coll.* headlong

очи́|стка *f* [5; *g/pl.:* -ток] clean(s)ing; *tech.* refinement; *pl.* peelings; **для ~стки со́вести** clear one's conscience; **~ща́ть** [1], ⟨**~стить**⟩ [15] clean(se); clear; peel; purify; *tech.* refine

очки́ *n/pl.* [1] spectacles, eyeglasses; **защи́тные ~й** protective goggles; **~о́** *n* [9; *pl.:* -ки́, -ко́в] *sport:* point; *cards:* pip, *Brt.* pip; **~овти́ра́тельство** *coll. n* [9] eyewash, deception

очну́ться [20] *pf.* → **опо́мниться**

очути́ться [15; *1 st. p. sg. not used*] find o.s.; come to oneself

ошале́лый *coll.* [14] crazy, mad

оше́йник *m* [1] collar (*on a dog only*)

ошеломля́ть [28], ⟨**~и́ть**⟩ [14 *e.*; -млю́, -ми́шь; -млённый] stun, stupefy

ошиб|а́ться [1], ⟨**~и́ться**⟩ [-бу́сь, -бёшься; -и́бся, -и́блась] be mistaken, make a mistake, err; be wrong *or* at fault; **~ка** *f* [5; *g/pl.:* -бок] mistake (**по** Д by), error, fault; **~очный** [14; -чен, -чна] erroneous, mistaken

ошпа́р|ивать [1], ⟨**~ить**⟩ [13] scald

ощу́п|ывать, ⟨**~ать**⟩ [1] feel, grope about; touch; **~ь** *f* [8]: **на ~ь** to the touch; **дви́гаться на ~ь** grope one's way; **~ью** *adv.* gropingly; *fig.* blindly

ощут|и́мый [14 *sh.*], **~и́тельный** [14; -лен, -льна] palpable, tangible; felt; (*заме́тный*) appreciable; **~ща́ть** [1], ⟨**~и́ть**⟩ [15 *e.*; -ущу́, -ути́шь; -ущённый] feel, sense; experience; **~ся** be felt; **~ще́ние** *n* [12] sensation; feeling

П

павиа́н *m* [1] baboon
павильо́н *m* [1] pavilion; exhibition hall
павли́н *m* [1], **~ий** [18] peacock
па́водок *m* [1; -дка] flood, freshet
па́|губный [14; -бен, -бна] ruinous, pernicious; **~даль** *f* [8] carrion
па́да|ть [1] **1.** ⟨упа́сть⟩ [25; *pt. st.*] fall; *цена́* drop; **2.** ⟨пасть⟩ [15] *fig.* fall; **~ть ду́хом** lose heart
паде́ж¹ *m* [1 *e.*] *gr.* case; **~ёж²** *m* [1 *e.*] *скота́* murrain; epizootic; **~е́ние** *n* [12] fall; *fig.* downfall; **~кий** [16; -док, -дка] (**на** B) greedy (for), having a weakness (for)
па́дчерица *f* [5] stepdaughter
паёк *m* [1; пайка́] ration
па́зух|а *f* [5] bosom (**за** B, **за** T in); *anat.* sinus; **держа́ть ка́мень за ~ой** harbo(u)r a grudge (against)
пай *m* [3; *pl. е.*: пай, паёв] share; **~щик** *m* [1] shareholder
паке́т *m* [1] parcel, package, packet; paper bag
па́кля *f* [6] (*material*) tow, oakum
накова́ть [7], ⟨у-, за-⟩ pack
па́кость *f* [8] filth, smut; dirty trick; **пакт** *m* [1] pact, treaty
пала́т|а *f* [5] chamber (*often used in names of state institutions*); *parl.* house; *больничная* ward; **оруже́йная ~а** armo(u)ry; **~ка** *f* [5; *g/pl.*: -ток] tent; **в ~ках** under canvas
пала́ч *m* [1 *e.*] hangman, executioner; *fig.* butcher
па́л|ец *m* [1; -льца] finger; *ноги* toe; **смотре́ть сквозь па́льцы** connive (**на** B at); **знать как свои́ пять ~ьцев** have at one's fingertips; **~иса́дник** *m* [1] (small) front garden
пали́тра *f* [5] palette
пали́ть [13] **1.** ⟨с-⟩ burn, scorch; **2.** ⟨о-⟩ singe; **3.** ⟨вы-⟩ fire, shoot
па́л|ка *f* [5; *g/pl.*: -лок] stick; *трость* cane; **из-под ~ки** *coll.* under constraint; **э́то ~ка о двух конца́х** it cuts both ways; **~очка** *f* [5; *g/pl.*: -чек]

(small) stick; *mus.* baton; *волше́бная* wand; *med.* bacillus
пало́мни|к *m* [1] pilgrim; **~чество** *n* [9] pilgrimage
па́лтус *m* [1] halibut
па́луба *f* [5] deck
пальба́ *f* [5] firing; fire
па́льма *f* [5] palm (tree)
пальто́ *n* [*indecl.*] (over)coat
па́мят|ник *m* [1] monument, memorial; **~ный** [14; -тен, -тна] memorable, unforgettable; **~ь** *f* [8] memory (**на, о** П in/of); remembrance; recollection (**о** П of); **на ~ь** *a.* by heart; **без ~и** *coll.* mad (**от** P about s.o.)
пане́ль *f* [8] panel; panel(l)ing
па́ника *f* [5] panic
панихи́да *f* [5] funeral service; **гражда́нская ~** civil funeral
пансиона́т *m* [1] boardinghouse
панте́ра *f* [5] panther
па́нты *f/pl.* [5] antlers of young Siberian stag
па́нцирь *m* [4] coat of mail
па́па¹ *coll. m* [5] papa, dad(dy)
па́па² *m* [5] pope
па́перть *f* [8] porch (*of a church*)
папиро́са *f* [5] Russian cigarette
па́пка *f* [5; *g/pl.*: -пок] folder; file
па́поротник *m* [1] fern
пар [1; в -у; *pl. е.*] **1.** steam; **2.** fallow
па́ра *f* [5] pair, couple
пара́граф *m* [1] *текста* section; *догово́ра и т. д.* article
пара́д *m* [1] parade; **~ный** [14] *фо́рма* full; *дверь* front
парадо́кс *m* [1] paradox; **~а́льный** [14; -лен, -льна] paradoxical
парали|зова́ть [7] (*im*)*pf.* paralyze (*a. fig.*); **~ч** *m* [1] paralysis
паралле́ль *f* [8] parallel; **провести́ ~** draw a parallel; (*между*) between
парашю́т (-'ʃut) *m* [1] parachute; **~и́ст** [1] parachutist
паре́ние *n* [12] soar(ing), hover(ing)
па́рень *m* [4; -рня; *from g/pl. е.*] lad, boy;

пари́ *n* [*indecl.*] bet, wager (*vb.*: **держа́ть ~**)

парижа́нин *m* [1; *pl.*: -а́не, -а́н], **~а́нка** *f* [5; *g/pl.*: -нок] Parisian

пари́к *m* [1 *e.*] wig; **~ма́хер** *m* [1] hairdresser, barber; **~ма́херская** *f* [16] hairdressing salon, barber's (shop)

пари́|ровать [7] (*im*)*pf.*, *a.* ⟨от-⟩ parry; **~ть**[1] [13] soar, hover

па́рить[2] [13] steam (*in a bath*: **-ся**)

парке́т *m* [1], **~ный** [14] parquet

парла́мент *m* [1] parliament; **~а́рий** *m* [3] parliamentarian; **~ский** [16] parliamentary

парни́к *m* [1 *e.*], **~о́вый** [14] hotbed; **~о́вый эффе́кт** greenhouse effect

парни́шка *m* [5; *g/pl.*: -шек] *coll.* boy, lad, youngster

па́рный [14] paired; twin…

паро|во́з *m* [1] steam locomotive; **~во́й** [14] steam…; **~ди́ровать** [7] (*im*)*pf.*, **~дия** *f* [7] parody

паро́ль *m* [4] password, parole

паро́м *m* [1] ferry(boat); **переправля́ть на ~е** ferry; **~щик** *m* [1] ferryman

парохо́д *m* [1] steamer; **~ный** [14] steamship…; **~ство** *n* [9] steamship line

па́рта *f* [5] school desk; **~ёр** *m* (-'tεr) [1] *thea.* stalls; **~иза́н** *m* [1] guerilla, partisan; **~иту́ра** *f* [5] *mus.* score; **~ия** *f* [7] party; *comm.* lot, consignment, batch; *sport* game; set; match; *mus.* part; **~нёр** *m* [1], **~нёрша** *f* [5] partner

па́рус *m* [1; *pl.*: -са́, *etc. e.*] sail; **на всех ~а́х** under full sail; **~и́на** *f* [5] sailcloth, canvas, duck; **~и́новый** [14] canvas…; **~ник** *m* [1] = **~ное су́дно** *n* [14/9] sailing ship

парфюме́рия *f* [7] perfumery

парча́ *f* [5], **~о́вый** [14] brocade

парши́вый [14 *sh.*] mangy; *coll.* **на-**строе́ние bad

пас *m* [1] pass (*sport, cards*); **я ~** count me out

па́сека *f* [5] apiary

па́сквиль *m* [4] lampoon

па́смурный [14; -рен, -рна] dull, cloudy; *вид* gloomy

пасова́ть[7] pass (*sport, cards*; ⟨с-⟩); *coll.*

give in, yield (**пе́ред** T to)

па́спорт *m* [1; *pl.*: -та́, *etc. e.*], **~ный** [14] passport

пассажи́р *m* [1], **~ка** *f* [5; *g/pl.*: -рок], **~ский** [16] passenger

пасси́в *m* [1] *comm.* liabilities *pl.*; **~ный** [14; -вен, -вна] passive

па́ста *f* [5] paste; **зубна́я ~** toothpaste

па́ст|бище *n* [11] pasture; **~ва** *f* [5] *eccl.* flock; **~и́** [24 -с-] graze (*v/i.* **-сь**), pasture; **~у́х** *m* [1 *e.*] herdsman, shepherd; **~ь 1.** → **па́дать**; **2.** *f* [8] jaws *pl.*, mouth

Па́сха *f* [5] Easter (**на** B for); Easter pudding (*sweet dish of cottage cheese*); **~льный** [14] Easter…

па́сынок *m* [1; -нка] stepson

пате́нт *m* [1], **~ова́ть** [7] (*im*)*pf.*, *a.* ⟨за-⟩ patent

па́тока *f* [5] molasses, *Brt. a.* treacle

патри́от *m* [1] patriot; **~оти́ческий** [16] patriotic; **~о́н** *m* [1] cartridge, shell; (*lamp*) socket; **~онта́ш** *m* [1] cartridge belt, pouch; **~ули́ровать**[7], **~у́ль** *m* [4 *e.*] *mil.* patrol

па́уза *f* [5] pause

пау́к *m* [1 *e.*] spider

паути́на *f* [5] cobweb

па́фос *m* [1] pathos; enthusiasm, zeal (for)

пах *m* [1; в -у́] *anat.* groin

паха́ть [3], ⟨вс-⟩ plow (*Brt.* plough), till

пахн|у́ть[1] [20] smell (Tof); **~у́ть**[2] [20] *pf.* *coll.* puff, blow

па́хот|а *f* [5] tillage; **~ный** [14] arable

паху́чий [17 *sh.*] odorous, strongsmelling

пацие́нт *m* [1], **~ка** *f* [5; *g/pl.*: -ток] patient

па́чка *f* [5; *g/pl.*: -чек] pack(et), package; *писем* batch

па́чкать [1], ⟨за-, ис-, вы-⟩ soil

па́шня *f* [6; *g/pl.*: -шен] tillage, field

паште́т *m* [1] pâté

пая́льник *m* [1] soldering iron

пая́ть [28], ⟨за-⟩ solder

певе́|ц *m* [1 -вца], **~и́ца** *f* [5] singer; **~у́чий** [17 *sh.*] melodious; **~чий** [17] singing; **~чая пти́ца** songbird; *su. eccl.* choirboy

педаго́г *m* [1] pedagogue, teacher; **~ика**

f [5] pedagogics; **~и́ческий** [16]: **~и́ческий институ́т** teachers' training college; **~и́чный** [14; -чен, -чна] sensible

педа́ль *f* [8] treadle, pedal

педа́нт *m* [1] pedant; **~и́чный** [14; -чен, -чна] pedantic

педиа́тр *m* [1] p(a)ediatrician

пейза́ж *m* [1] landscape

пека́р|ня *f* [6; *g/pl.*: -рен] bakery; **~ь** *m* [4; *a.* -ря́, *etc. e.*] baker

пелена́ *f* [5] shroud; **~а́ть** [1], ⟨за-, с-⟩ swaddle

пелён|ка *f* [5; *g/pl.*: -нок] diaper, *Brt. a.* nappy; **~** *coll. fig.* from the cradle

пельме́ни *m/pl.* [-ней] *cul.* kind of ravioli

пе́на *f* [5] foam, froth; *мы́льная* lather, soapsuds

пе́ние *n* [12] singing; *петуха́* crow

пе́н|истый [14 *sh.*] foamy, frothy; **~иться** [13], ⟨вс-⟩ foam, froth; **~ка** *f* [5; *g/pl.*: -нок] *на молоке и т. д.* skin; **снять ~ки** skim (**с** Р); *fig.* take the pickings (of)

пенсио|не́р *m* [1] pensioner; **~о́нный** [14], **~я** *f* [7] pension

пень *m* [4; пня] stump

пенька́ *f* [5] hemp; **~о́вый** [14] hemp(en)

пе́ня *f* [6; *g/pl.*: -ней] fine (*penalty*)

пеня́|ть *coll.* [28] blame; **~й на себя́!** it's your own fault!

пе́пел [1; -пла] ashes *pl.*; **~ище** *n* [11] site of a fire; **~ьница** *f* [5] ashtray; **~ьный** [14] ashy; *цвет* ashgrey

пе́рвен|ец *m* [1; -нца] first-born; **~ство** *n* [9] first place; *sport* championship

перви́чный [14; -чен, -чна] primary

перво|бы́тный [14; -тен, -тна] primitive, primeval; **~исто́чник** *m* [1] primary source; origin; **~кла́ссный** [14] first-rate *or* -class; **~ку́рсник** *m* [1] freshman; **~ на́перво** Р *coll.* first of all; **~нача́льный** [14; -лен, -льна] original; primary; **~очередно́й** [14] first and foremost; immediate; **~со́ртный** → **~кла́ссный**, **~степе́нный** [14; -ёнен, -ённа] paramount, of the first order

пе́рв|ый [14] first; former; earliest; **~ый эта́ж** first (*Brt.* ground) floor; **~ое**

вре́мя at first; **~ая по́мощь** first aid; **~ый рейс** maiden voyage; *из ~ых рук* firsthand; *на ~ый взгляд* at first sight; **~ое** *n* first course (*meal*; *на* В for); **~ым де́лом (до́лгом)** *or* **в пе́рвую о́чередь** first of all, first thing; *coll.* **~éйший** the very first; → **пя́тый**

перга́мент *m* [1] parchment

переб|ега́ть [1], ⟨~ежа́ть⟩ [4; -егу́, -ежи́шь, -егу́т] run over (*or* across); **~е́жчик** *m* [1] traitor, turncoat; **~ива́ть** [1], ⟨~и́ть⟩ [-бью, -бьёшь, → *би́ть*] interrupt

переб|ива́ться ⟨~и́ться⟩ *coll.* make ends meet

переб|ира́ть [1], ⟨~ра́ть⟩ [-беру́, -рёшь; -бра́л, -а́, -о; -ёбранный] look through; sort out (*a. fig.*); turn over, think over; *impf. mus.* finger; **-ся** move (**на, в** В into); cross (*v/t. че́рез* В)

переб|и́ть 1. → **~ива́ть; 2.** *pf.* kill, slay; *посу́ду* break; **~о́й** *m* [3] interruption, intermission; **~оро́ть** [17] *pf.* overcome, master

пребра́нка F *f* [5; *g/pl.*: -нок] wrangle; **~а́сывать** [1], ⟨~о́сить⟩ [15] throw over; *mil., comm.* transfer, shift; **-ся**: *слова́ми* exchange (*v/t.* Т); **~а́ть(ся)** → **переби-ра́ть(ся)**; **~о́ска** *f* [5; *g/pl.*: -сок] transfer

перева́л *m* [1] pass; **~ивать** [1], ⟨~и́ть⟩ [13; -алю́, -алишь; -а́ленный] transfer, shift (*v/i.* **-ся**; *impf.* waddle); *coll.* cross, pass; *impers.* **ему́ ~и́ло за 40** he is past 40

перева́р|ивать [1], ⟨~и́ть⟩ [13; -арю́, -аришь; -а́ренный] digest; *coll. fig.* **она́ его́ не ~ивает** she can't stand him

переве́з|ти́ → **~во́зить**, **~вёртывать** [1], ⟨~верну́ть⟩ [20; -вёрнутый] turn over (*v/i.* **-ся**); **~вéс** *m* [1] preponderance; *superiority* → **переводи́ть(ся)**; **~вéшивать** [1], ⟨~вéсить⟩ [15] hang (elsewhere); reweigh; *fig.* outweigh; **-ся** lean over; **~вира́ть** [1], ⟨~вра́ть⟩ [-вру́, -врёшь; -ёвранный] *coll.* garble, misquote; misinterpret

перево́д *m* [1] transfer; translation (*с* Р/*на* В from/into); *де́нег* remittance; *почто́вый* (money *or* postal) order;

~и́ть [15], ⟨перевести́⟩ [25] lead; transfer; translate (с/**на** B from/into) interpret; remit; set (*watch, clock*; *usu.* **стре́лку**); **~и́ть дух** take a breath; **-ся**, ⟨-сь⟩ be transferred, move; **~ный** [14] translated (*a. comm.*) transfer…; **~чик** *m* [1], **~чица** *f* [5] translator; interpreter

перевози́ть [15], ⟨перевезти́⟩ [24] transport, convey; *мебель* remove; *через реку и т. д.* ferry (over); **~ка** *f* [5; *g/pl.*: -зок] transportation, conveyance, ferrying, *etc.*

пере|вооруже́ние *n* [12] rearmament; **~вора́чивать** [1] → **~верну́ть**; **~воро́т** *m* [1] revolution; *государственный coup d'état*; **~воспита́ние** *n* [12] reeducation; **~вра́ть** → **~вира́ть**; **~вы́боры** *m/pl.* [1] reelection

перевя́з|ка *f* [5; *g/pl.*: -зок] dressing, bandage; **~очный** [14] dressing…; **~ывать** [1], ⟨~а́ть⟩ [3] tie up; *рану и т. д.* dress, bandage

переги́б *m* [1] bend, fold; *fig.* exaggeration; **~а́ть** [1], ⟨перегну́ть⟩ [20] bend; **~а́ть па́лку** too far; **-ся** lean over

перегля́|дываться [1], *once* ⟨~ну́ться⟩ [19] exchange glances

перегн|а́ть → **~оня́ть**; **~ной** *m* [3] humus; **~у́ть(ся)** → **~иба́ть(ся)**

перегова́ривать [1], ⟨~ори́ть⟩ [13] talk (s. th.) over (**о** T), discuss; **~о́ры** *m/pl.* [1] negotiations; *вести* **~о́ры** (**с** T) negotiate (with)

перег|о́нка *f* [5] distillation; **~оня́ть** [28], ⟨~на́ть⟩ [гоню́, го́нишь; г-на́л, -а́, -о́; -ей́ганный] **1.** outdistance, leave behind; *fig.* overtake, outstrip, surpass, outdo; **2.** *chem.* distil

перегор|а́живать [1], ⟨~оди́ть⟩ [15 & 15 e.; -рожу́, -роди́шь] partition (off); **~а́ть** [1], ⟨~е́ть⟩ [9] *лампочка, пробка* burn out; **~о́дка** *f* [5; *g/pl.*: -док] partition

перегр|ева́ть [1], ⟨~е́ть⟩ [8; -е́тый] overheat; **~ужа́ть** [1], ⟨~узи́ть⟩ [15 & 15 e.; -ужу́, -у́зишь], overload; **~у́зка** *f* [5; *g/pl.*: -зок] *двигателя* overload; *о работе* overwork; **~уппирова́ть** [7] *pf.* regroup; **~уппиро́вка** *f* [5; -вок] regrouping; **~ыза́ть** [1], ⟨~ы́зть⟩ [24; *pt.*

st.: -ы́зенный] gnaw through

пе́ред¹, **~о** (T) before; in front of; *извини́ться* **~ кем-л.** apologize to s.o.

пе́ред² *m* [1; пе́реда; *pl.*: -да́, *etc. e.*] front

перед|ава́ть [5], ⟨~а́ть⟩ [-да́м, -да́шь, *etc.* → **да́ть**] *pt.* пе́редал, -а́, -о] pass, hand (over); deliver; give (*a. привет*); *radio, TV* broadcast, transmit; *содержание* render; tell; *по телефону* take a message (for Д, *on the phone*); **-ся** *med.* be transmitted, communicated; **~а́тчик** *m* [1] transmitter; **~а́ть(ся)** → **~ава́ть(ся)**; **~а́ча** *f* [5] delivery, handing over; transfer; broadcast, (*a. tech.*) transmission; *mot.* gear

передв|ига́ть [1], ⟨~и́нуть⟩ [20] move, shift; **~иже́ние** *n* [12] movement; *грузов* transportation; **~ижно́й** [14] travel(l)ing, mobile

переде́л|ка *f* [5; *g/pl.*: -лок] alteration; *coll.* **попа́сть в ~ку** get into a pretty mess; **~ывать** [1], ⟨~ать⟩ [1] do again; alter; **~ать мно́го дел** do a lot

пере́дн|ий [15] front…, fore…; **~ик** *m* [1] apron; **~яя** *f* [15] (entrance) hall, lobby

передов|и́ца *f* [5] leading article, editorial; **~о́й** [14] foremost; *mil.* frontline; **~а́я статья́** → **передови́ца**

пере|дохну́ть [20] *pf.* pause for breath or a rest; **~дра́знивать** [1], ⟨~дразни́ть⟩ [13; -азню́, -а́знишь] mimic; **~дря́га** *coll.* *f* [5] fix, scrape; **~ду́мывать**, ⟨~ду́мать⟩ [1] change one's mind; *coll.* → **обду́мать**; **~ды́шка** *f* [5; *g/pl.*: -шек] breathing space, respite

пере|е́зд *m* [1] *rail., etc.* crossing; *в другое место* move (**в, на** B [in]to); **~езжа́ть** [1], ⟨~е́хать⟩ [-е́ду, -е́дешь; -е́зжай!] **1.** *v/i.* cross (*v/t.* **че́рез** B); move (**в, на** B [in]to); **2.** *v/t.* *машиной* run over

пережид|а́ть → **~ида́ть**; **~ёвывать** [1], ⟨~ева́ть⟩ [7 e.; -жую́, -жуёшь] masticate, chew; *fig.* repeat over and over again; **~ива́ние** *n* [12] emotional experience; worry *etc.*; **~ива́ть**, ⟨~и́ть⟩ [-живу́, -вёшь; пе́режил, -а́, -о; пе́режитый (пе́режи́т, -а́, -о)] experience; live

П

through, endure; *жить дольше* survive, outlive; ~ида́ть [1], ⟨~да́ть⟩ [-жду́, -ждёшь; -жда́л, -á, -о] wait (till s.th. is over); ~йток *m* [1; -тка] survival

перезаключа́ть [1], ⟨~чи́ть⟩ [16 *е.*; -чу́, -чи́шь; -чённый] ~чи́ть догово́р (**контра́кт**) renew a contract

перезре́лый [14] overripe; *fig.* past one's prime

переизбира́ть [1], ⟨~бра́ть⟩ [-беру́, -рёшь; -бра́л, -á, -о; -и́збранный] re-elect; ~бра́ние *n* [12] reelection; ~дава́ть [5], ⟨~да́ть⟩ [-да́м, -да́шь, *etc.* → **дать**]; -да́л, -á, -о] reprint, republish; ~да́ние *n* [12] republication; new edition, reprint; ~да́ть → **дава́ть**

переименова́ть [7] *pf.* rename

переина́чи|вать *coll.* [1], ⟨~ть⟩ [16] alter, modify; ⟨*исказить*⟩ distort

перейти́ → **переходи́ть**

переки́|дывать [1], ⟨~нуть⟩ [20] throw over (**че́рез** В); -ся exchange (*v/t.* Т); *огонь* spread

переки|па́ть [1], ⟨~пе́ть⟩ [10 *е.*; *3rd p. only*] boil over

переки́сь *f* [8] *chem.* peroxide; ~ **водоро́да** hydrogen peroxide

перекла́д|ина *f* [5] crossbar, crossbeam; ~ывать [1], ⟨переложи́ть⟩ [16] put, lay (elsewhere); move, shift; interlay (Т with); → **перелага́ть**

перекл|ика́ться [1], ⟨~и́кнуться⟩ [20] call to o.a.; have s.th. in common (**с** Т with); reecho (*v/i.* **с** Т)

переключа́|тель *m* [4] switch; ~ть [1], ⟨~и́ть⟩ [16; -чу́, -чи́шь; -чённый] switch over (*v/i.* **-ся**); *внимание* switch; ~ние *n* [12] switching over; ~и́ть → **~а́ть**

переко́шенный [14] twisted, distorted; *дверь и т. д.* warped; wry

перекрёст|ный [14] cross...; **~ный ого́нь** cross-fire; **~ный допро́с** cross-examination; ~ок *m* [1; -тка] crossroads, crossing

перекры́|вать [1], ⟨~ть⟩ [22] cover *идл т рекорд и т. д.* exceed, surpass; *закрыть блок, реку* dam; ~тие *n* [12] *arch.* ceiling; floot

перекус|ывать [1], ⟨~и́ть⟩ [15] *bit* through; *coll.* have a bite *or* snack

перелага́ть [1], ⟨~ожи́ть⟩ [16]: **~ожи́ть на му́зыку** set to music

перела́|мывать [1] **1.** ⟨~оми́ть⟩ [14] break in two; *fig.* overcome; change; **2.** ⟨~ома́ть⟩ [1] break

переле|за́ть [1], ⟨~е́зть⟩ [24 *st.*; -ле́з] climb over, get over (**че́рез** В)

переле́т *m* [1] *птиц* passage; *ae.* flight; ~та́ть [1], ⟨~те́ть⟩ [15] fly over (across); migrate; overshoot; ~тный [14]: **~тная пти́ца** bird of passage *a. fig.*, migratory bird

перели́в *m* [1] *голоса* modulation; *цвета* play; ~а́ние *n* [12] *med.* transfusion; ~а́ть [1], ⟨~ть⟩ [-лью́, -льёшь, *etc.* → **лить**] decant, pour from one vessel into another; *med.* transfuse; ~**ва́ть из пусто́го в поро́жнее** mill the wind; -ся overflow; *impf. о цвете* play, shimmer

перели́ст|ывать, ⟨~а́ть⟩ [1] *страницы* turn over; *книгу* look *or* leaf through

перели́ть → **перелива́ть**

перелицева́ть [7] *pf.* turn, make over

переложе́ние *n* [12] transposition; arrangement; *на музыку* setting to music; ~и́ть → **перекла́дывать**, **перелага́ть**

перело́м *m* [1] break, fracture; *fig.* crisis, turning point; ~а́ть, ~и́ть → **перела́мывать**

перема́л|ывать [1], ⟨~оло́ть⟩ [17; -мелю́, -ме́лешь; -меля́] grind, mill; ~ежа́ть(ся) [1] alternate

переме́н|а *f* [5] change; *в школе* break; ~и́ть(ся) → ~**я́ть(ся)**; ~ный [14] variable; *el.* alternating; ~чивый *coll.* [14] changeable; ~я́ть [28], ⟨~и́ть⟩ [13; -еню́, -е́нишь] change (*v/i.* -ся)

переме|сти́ть(ся) → ~**ща́ть(ся)**; ~шивать, ⟨~ша́ть⟩ [1] intermingle, intermix; *coll.* mix (up); -ся: **у меня́ в голове́ всё ~ша́лось** I feel confused; ~ща́ть [1], ⟨~сти́ть⟩ [15 *е.*; -ещу́, -ести́шь; -ещённый] move, shift (*v/i.* -ся)

переми́рие *n* [12] armistice, truce

перемоло́ть → **перема́лывать**

перенаселе́ние *n* [12] overpopulation

пере́но́ти́ → **переноси́ть**

перен|има́ть [1], ⟨∼я́ть⟩ [-ейму́, -мёшь; переня́л, -á, -о; пере́нятый (пе́ренят, -á, -о)] adopt; *манеру и т. д.* imitate

перено́с *m* [1] *typ.* word division; **знак ∼a** hyphen; ∼и́ть, ⟨перенести́⟩ [24 -с-] transfer, carry over; (*испыта́ть*) bear, endure, stand; (*отложи́ть*) postpone, put off (till **на** B); ∼и́ца *f* [5] bridge (*of nose*)

перено́с|ка *f* [5; *g/pl.:* -сок] carrying over; ∼ный [14] portable; figurative

переня́ть → **перенима́ть**

переобору́дова|ть [7] (*im*)*pf*; refit, reequip; ∼ние *n* [12] reequipment

переоде́ва|ться [1], ⟨∼е́ться⟩ [-éнусь, -нешься] change (one's clothes); ∼тый [14 *sh.*] *a.* disguised

переоце́н|ивать [1], ⟨∼и́ть⟩ [13; -еню́, -е́нишь] overestimate, overrate; (*оцени́ть заново*) revalue; ∼ка *f* [5; *g/pl.:* -нок] overestimation; revaluation

пе́репел *m* [1; *pl.:* -лá, *etc. e.*] *zo.* quail

перепеча́т|ка *f* [5; *g/pl.:* -ток] reprint; ∼ывать, ⟨∼ать⟩ [1] reprint; *на маши́нке* type

перепи́с|ка *f* [5; *g/pl.:* -сок] correspondence; ∼ывать [1], ⟨∼а́ть⟩ [3] rewrite, copy; ∼а́ть на́бело make a fair copy; -ся *impf.* correspond (**с** T with); ∼ь ('ре-) *f* [8] census

перепла́|чивать [1], ⟨∼ти́ть⟩ [15] overpay

перепл|ета́ть [1], ⟨∼ести́⟩ [25 -т-] *книгу* bind; interlace, intertwine (*v/i.* **-ся** ⟨-сь⟩); ∼ёт *m* [1] binding, book cover; ∼ётчик *m* [1] bookbinder; ∼ыва́ть [1], ⟨∼ы́ть⟩ [23] swim *or* sail (**че́рез** B across)

переполз|а́ть [1], ⟨∼ти́⟩ [24] creep, crawl

перепо́лн|енный [14 *sh.*] overcrowded; *жи́дкостью* overflowing; overfull; ∼я́ть [28], ⟨∼ить⟩ [13] overfill; -ся (*v/i.*) be overcrowded

переполо́|х *m* [1] commotion, alarm, flurry; ∼ши́ть *coll.* [16 *e.*; -шу́, -ши́шь; -шённый] *pf.* (**-ся** get) alarm(ed)

перепо́нка [5; *g/pl.* -нок] membrane; *пти́цы* web; **бараба́нная ∼** eardrum

перепра́в|а *f* [5] crossing, passage; *брод* ford; temporary bridge; ∼ля́ть [28], ⟨∼ить⟩ [14] carry (over), convey, take across; transport (to); *mail* forward; -ся cross, get across

перепрод|ава́ть [5], ⟨∼а́ть⟩ [-да́м, -да́шь, *etc.* → **дать**]; *pt.*: -о́дал, -дá, -о] resell; ∼а́жа *f* [5] resale

перепры́г|ивать [1], ⟨∼нуть⟩ [20] jump (over)

перепу́г *coll. m* [1] fright (*of* **с ∼у**); ∼а́ть [1] *pf.* (**-ся** get) frighten(ed)

перепу́тывать [1] → **пу́тать**

перепу́тье *n* [10] *fig.* crossroad(s)

перераб|а́тывать, ⟨∼о́тать⟩ [1] work into; remake; *кни́гу* revise; ∼о́тка *f* [5; *g/pl.:* -ток] processing; remaking; revision; ∼о́тка втори́чного сырья́ recycling

перерас|та́ть [1], ⟨∼ти́⟩ [24; -ст-; -ро́с, -слá] (*видоизмени́ться*) grow, develop; *о ро́сте* outstrip; ∼хо́д *m* [1] excess expenditure

перере́з|ать *and* ∼ыва́ть [1], ⟨∼а́ть⟩ [3] cut (through); cut off, intercept; kill (all *or* many of)

переро|жда́ться [1], ⟨∼ди́ться⟩ [15 *e.*; -ожу́сь, -оди́шься; -ождённый] *coll.* be reborn; *fig.* regenerate; *biol.* degenerate

переруб|а́ть [1], ⟨∼и́ть⟩ [14] hew *or* cut through

переры́в *m* [1] interruption; break; interval; **∼ на обе́д** lunch time

переса́|дка *f* [5; *g/pl.:* -док] *bot.*, *med.* transplanting; *med.* grafting; *rail.* change; ∼живать [1], ⟨∼ди́ть⟩ [15] transplant; graft; make change seats; -ся, ⟨пересе́сть⟩ [25; -ся́ду, -ся́дешь; -се́л] take another seat, change seats; *rail.* change (*trains*)

пересд|ава́ть [5], ⟨∼а́ть⟩ [-да́м, -да́шь, *etc.*, → **дать**] repeat (*exam.*)

пересе|ка́ть [1], ⟨∼чь⟩ [26; *pt.* -сéк, -секлá] traverse; intersect, cross (*v/i.* **-ся**)

пересел|е́нец *m* [1; -нца] migrant; (re)settler; *fig.* (e)migration; ∼я́ть [28], ⟨∼и́ть⟩ [13] (re)move (*v/i.* **-ся**; [e]migrate)

пересе́сть → **переса́живаться**

пересе|че́ние *n* [12] crossing; intersection; **∼чь** → **∼ка́ть**

переси́ли|вать [1], ⟨∼ть⟩ [13] overpower; *fig.* master, subdue

переска́з *m* [1] retelling; **∼ывать** [1], ⟨∼а́ть⟩ [3] retell

переск|а́кивать [1], ⟨∼очи́ть⟩ [16] jump (over **че́рез** B); *при чтении* skip over

пересла́ть → **пересыла́ть**

пересма́|тривать [1], ⟨∼отре́ть⟩ [9; -отрю́, -о́тришь; -о́тренный] reconsider, *планы* revise; *law* review; **∼отр** *m* [1] reconsideration, revision; *law* review

пересо́л|и́ть [13; -солю́, -о́лишь] *pf.* put too much salt (**в** B in); *coll. fig.* go too far; **∼хнуть** → **пересыха́ть**

переспа́ть → **спать**; oversleep; *coll.* spend the night; sleep with s.o.

переспр|а́шивать [1], ⟨∼оси́ть⟩ [15] repeat one's question

пересо́риться [13] *pf.* quarrel (*mst. with everybody*)

перест|ава́ть [5], ⟨∼а́ть⟩ [-а́ну, -а́нешь] stop, cease, quit; **∼авля́ть** [28], ⟨∼а́вить⟩ [14] put (elsewhere), (*тж. часы*) set, move; *мебель* rearrange; **∼ано́вка** *f* [5; *g/pl.*: -вок] transposition; rearrangement; *math.* permutation; **∼а́ть** → **∼ава́ть**

перестр|а́ивать [1], ⟨∼о́ить⟩ [13] rebuild, reconstruct; *работу* reorganize; *силы* regroup; **-ся** (*v/i.*) adapt, change one's views; **∼е́ливаться** [1], **∼е́лка** *f* [5; *g/pl.*: -лок] firing; skirmish; **∼о́ить** → **∼а́ивать**; **∼о́йка** *f* [5; *g/pl.*: -о́ек] rebuilding, reconstruction; reorganization; perestroika

переступ|а́ть [1], ⟨∼и́ть⟩ [14] step over, cross; *fig.* transgress

пересчи́т|ывать [1], ⟨∼а́ть⟩ [1] (re)count; count up

пересы|ла́ть [1], ⟨∼ла́ть⟩ [-ешлю́, -шлёшь; -есланный] send (over), *деньги* remit; *письмо* send forward; **∼лка** *f* [5; *g/pl.*: -лок] remittance; **сто́имость ∼лки** postage; carriage; **∼ха́ть** [1], ⟨∼о́хнуть⟩ [21] dry up; *горло* be parched

перетá|скивать [1], ⟨∼щи́ть⟩ [16] drag *or* carry (**че́рез** B over, across)

перетя́|гивать [1], ⟨∼ну́ть⟩ [19] draw

(*fig.* **на свою сто́рону** win) over; **верёвкой** cord

переубе|жда́ть [1], ⟨∼ди́ть⟩ [15 *e.*; *no 1st. p. sg.*; -ди́шь, -еждённый] make s.o. change his mind

переу́лок *m* [1; -лка] lane, alleyway; side street

переутомл|е́ние *n* [12] overstrain; overwork; **∼ённый** [14 *sh.*] overtired

переучёт *m* [1] stock-taking

перехва́т|ывать [1], ⟨∼и́ть⟩ [15] intercept, catch; *coll.* money borrow; **перекуси́ть** have a quick snack

перехитри́ть [13] *pf.* outwit

перехо́д *m* [1] passage; crossing; *fig.* transition; **∼и́ть** [15], ⟨перейти́⟩ [-йду́, -дёшь; -шёл, -шла́; → **идти́**] cross, go over; pass (on), proceed; (**к** Д to); turn (**в** B [in]to); *границы* exceed, transgress; **∼ный** [14] transitional; *gr.* transitive; intermittent; **∼я́щий** [17] *sport* challenge (*cup, etc.*)

пе́рец *m* [1; -рца] pepper; **стручко́вый ∼** paprika

пе́речень *m* [4; -чня] list; enumeration

пере|чёркивать [1], ⟨∼черкну́ть⟩ [20] cross out; **∼че́сть** → **∼счи́тывать** & **∼чи́тывать**; **∼числя́ть** [28], ⟨∼чи́слить⟩ [13] enumerate; *деньги* transfer; **∼чи́тывать**, ⟨∼чита́ть⟩ [1] & ⟨∼че́сть⟩ [-чту́, -чтёшь, -чёл, -чла́] reread; read (many, all …); **∼чить** *coll.* [16] contradict; oppose; **∼чница** *f* [5] pepper-pot; **∼шагну́ть** [20] *pf.* step over; cross; **∼шéек** *m* [1; -шéйка] isthmus; **∼шёптываться** [1] whisper (to one another); **∼шива́ть** [1], ⟨∼ши́ть⟩ [-шью́, -шьёшь, *etc.* → **шить**] sew alter; **∼щеголя́ть** *coll.* [28] *pf.* outdo

пери́ла *n/pl.* [9] railing; banisters

пери́на *f* [5] feather bed

перио́д *m* [1] period; *geol.* age; **∼ика** *f* [5] *collect.* periodicals; **∼и́ческий** [16] periodic(al); *math.* recurring

перифери́я *f* [7] periphery; outskirts *pl.* (**на** П in); the provinces

перламу́тр *m* [1] mother-of-pearl

перло́вый [14] pearl (*крупа* barley)

перна́тые *pl.* [14] *su.* feathered, feathery (*birds*)

перо́ n [9; pl.: пе́рья, -ьев] feather, plume; pen; **ни пу́ха ни пера́!** good-luck!; **~чи́нный** [14]: **~чи́нный но́ж(ик)** penknife

перро́н m [1] rail. platform

перс|и́дский [16] Persian; **~ик** m [1] peach; **~о́на** f [5] person; **~она́л** m [1] personnel; staff; **~пекти́ва** f [5] perspective; fig. prospect, outlook; **~пекти́вный** [14; -вен, -вна] with prospects; forward-looking, promising

пе́рстень m [4; -тня] ring (with a precious stone, etc.)

пе́рхоть f [8] dandruff

перча́тка f [5; g/pl.: -ток] glove

пёс m [1; пса] dog

пе́сенка f [5; g/pl.: -нок] song

песе́ц m [1; песца́] Arctic fox; **бе́лый (голубо́й) ~** white (blue) fox (fur)

пе́сн|ь f [8] (poet., eccl.), **~я** f [6; g/pl.: -сен] song; coll. **до́лгая ~я** long story; **ста́рая ~я** it's the same old story

песо́|к m [1; -ска́] sand; **са́харный** granulated sugar; **~чный** [14] sand(y); **~чное пече́нье** shortbread

пессимисти́ч|еский [16], **~ный** [14; -чен, -чна] pessimistic

пестр|е́ть [8] оши́бками be full (of); **~и́ть** [13], **~ый** [14; пёстр, пестра́, пёстро & пестро́] variegated, parti-colo(u)red, motley (a. fig.); gay

песч|а́ный [14] sand(y); **~и́нка** f [5; g/pl.: -нок] grain of sand

петли́ца f [5] buttonhole; tab

пе́тля f [6; g/pl.: -тель] loop (a., ae., **мёртвая ~**); для крючка́ eye; stitch; дверна́я hinge; **спусти́ть пе́тлю** drop a stitch

петру́шка f [5] parsley

пету́|х m [1 e.] rooster, cock; **~ши́ный** [14] cock(s)…

петь [пою́, поёшь; пе́тый] **1.** ⟨с-, про-⟩ sing; **2.** ⟨про-⟩ nemyx crow

пехо́т|а f [5], **~ный** [14] infantry; **~и́нец** m [1; -нца] infantryman

печа́л|ить [13], ⟨о-⟩ grieve (v/i. **-ся**); **~ь** f [8] grief, sorrow; **~ьный** [14; -лен, -льна] sad, mournful, sorrowful

печа́т|ать [1], ⟨на-⟩ print; **на маши́нке** type; **-ся** impf. be in the press; appear in

(в П); **~ник** m [1] printer; **~ный** [14] printed; printing; **~ь** f [8] seal, stamp (a. fig.); пресса press; ме́лкая, чёткая print, type; **вы́йти из ~и** be published

печён|ка f [5; g/pl.: -нок] cul. liver; **~ый** [14] baked

пе́чень f [8] anat. liver

пече́нье n [10] cookie, biscuit

пе́чка f [5; g/pl.: -чек] → **печь¹**

печь¹ f [8; в -чи́; from g/pl. e.] stove; oven; tech. furnace; kiln

печь² [26], ⟨ис-⟩ bake; со́лнце scorch

пеш|ехо́д m [1], **~ехо́дный** [14] pedestrian; **~ка** f [5; g/pl.: -шек] in chess pawn (a. fig.); **~ко́м** on foot

пеще́ра f [5] cave

пиан|и́но n [indecl.] upright (piano); **~и́ст** m [1] pianist

пивна́я f [14] pub, saloon

пи́во n [9] beer; **све́тлое ~** pale ale; **~ва́р** m [1] brewer; **~ва́ренный** [14]: **~ва́ренный заво́д** brewery

пигме́нт m [1] pigment

пиджа́к m [1 e.] coat, jacket

пижа́ма f [5] pajamas (Brt. py-) pl.

пик m [1] peak; **часы́ ~** rush hour

пика́нтный [14; -тен, -тна] piquant, spicy (a. fig.)

пика́п m [1] pickup (van)

пике́т m [1], **~и́ровать** [7] (im)pf. picket

пи́ки f/pl. [5] spades (cards)

пики́ровать ae. [7] (im)pf. dive

пи́кнуть [20] pf. peep; **он и ~ не успе́л** before he could say knife; **то́лько пи́кни!** (threat implied) just one peep out of you!

пил|а́ f [5; pl. st.], **~и́ть** [13; пилю́, пи́лишь] saw; **~о́т** m [1] pilot

пилю́ля f [6] pill

пингви́н m [1] penguin

пино́к m [1; -нка́] coll. kick

пинце́т m [1] pincers, tweezers pl.

пио́н m [1] peony

пионе́р m [1] pioneer

пипе́тка [5; g/pl.: -ток] med. dropper

пир [1; в ~у́; g/pl. e.] feast

пирами́да f [5] pyramid

пира́т m [1] pirate

пиро́|г m [1 e.] pie; **~жное** n [14] pastry; (fancy) cake; **~жо́к** m [1; -жка́] pastry;

patty

пиру́шка *f* [5; *g/pl.*: -шек] carousal, binge, revelry; **~шество** *n* [9] feast, banquet

писа́|ние *n* [12] writing; (*свяще́нное*) Holy Scripture; **~тель** *m* [4] writer, author; **~тельница** *f* [5] authoress; **~ть** [3], ⟨на-⟩ write; *карти́ну* paint

писк *m* [1] chirp, squeak; **~ли́вый** [14 *sh.*] squeaky; **~нуть** → **пища́ть**

пистоле́т *m* [1] pistol

пи́счий [17]: **~ая бума́га** writing paper, note paper

пи́сьмен|ность *f* [8] *collect.* literary texts; written language; **~ный** [14] written; in writing; *стол и т. д.* writing

письмо́ *n* [9; *pl. st., gen.*: пи́сем] letter; writing (*на* П in); **делово́е ~** business letter; **заказно́е ~** registered letter

пита́|ние *n* [12] nutrition; nourishment; feeding; **~тельный** [14; -лен, -льна] nutritious, nourishing; **~ть** [1] nourish (*a. fig.*), feed (*a. tech.*); *наде́жду и т. д.* cherish; *не́нависть* bear against (*к* Д); **~ться** feed *or* live (T on)

пито́м|ец *m* [1; -мца], **~ица** *f* [5] foster child; charge; pupil; alumnus; **~ник** *m* [1] nursery

пить [пью, пьёшь; пил, -á, -о; пе́й(те)!; пи́тый; пит, пита́, пи́то], ⟨вы-⟩ drink (*pf. a.* up; *за* B to); have, take; *мне хо́чется ~* I feel thirsty; **~ён** *n* [10] drink(-ing); **~ево́й** [14] *вода́* drinking

пи́хта *f* [5] fir tree

пи́цца *f* [5] pizza; **~ери́я** *f* [5] pizzeria

пи́чкать *coll.* [1], ⟨на-⟩ *coll.* stuff, cram (with T)

пи́шущий [17]: **~ая маши́нка** typewriter

пи́ща *f* [5] food (*a. fig.*)

пища́ть [4 *e.*; -щу́, -щи́шь], ⟨за-⟩, *once* ⟨пи́скнуть⟩ [20] peep, squeak, cheep

пищева́р|е́ние *n* [12] digestion; **~во́д** *m* [1] *anat.* (o)esophagus, gullet; **~во́й** [14]: **~вы́е проду́кты** foodstuffs

пия́вка *f* [5; *g/pl.*: -вок] leech

пла́ва|ние *n* [12] swimming; *naut.* navigation; (*путеше́ствие*) voyage, trip; **~ть** [1] swim; float; sail, navigate

пла́в|ить [14], ⟨рас-⟩ smelt; **~ки** *pl.* [5;

g/pl.: -вок] swimming trunks; **~кий** [16]; **~кий предохрани́тель** fuse; **~ник** *m* [1 *e.*] fin, flipper

пла́вный [14; -вен, -вна] *речь и т. д.* fluent; *движе́ние и т. д.* smooth

плаву́ч|есть *f* [8] buoyancy; **~ий** [17] *док* floating

плагиа́т *m* [1] plagiarism

плака́т *m* [1] poster

пла́к|ать [3] weep, cry (*от* P for; *о* П); **-ся** *coll.* complain (*на* B of); **~са** *coll.* *m/f* [5] crybaby; **~си́вый** *coll.* [14 *sh.*] *го́лос* whining

пламе|не́ть [8] blaze, flame; **~нный** [14] flaming, fiery; *fig. a.* ardent; **~я** *n* [13] flame; blaze

план [1] plan; scheme; plane; *уче́бный ~* curriculum; **пере́дний ~** foreground; **за́дний ~** background

планёр, пла́нер *ae. m* [1] *ae.* glider

плане́та *f* [5] planet

плани́р|овать [7] **1.** ⟨за-⟩ plan; **2.** ⟨с-⟩ *ae.* glide; **~ка** *f* [5; *g/pl.*: -вок] planning; *па́рка и т. д.* lay(ing)-out

пла́нка *f* [5; *g/pl.*: -нок] plank; *sport* (cross)bar

пла́но|вый [14] planned; plan(ning); **~ме́рный** [14; -рен, -рна] systematic, planned

планта́ция *f* [7] plantation

пласт *m* [1 *e.*] layer, stratum

пла́ст|ика *f* [5] plastic arts *pl.*; eurhythmics; **~и́нка** *f* [5; *g/pl.*: -нок] plate; record, disc; **~и́ческий** [16]: **~и́ческая хиру́ргия** plastic surgery; **~ма́сса** *f* [5] plastic; **~ырь** *m* [4] plaster

пла́т|а *f* [5] pay(ment); fee; wages *pl.*; *за прое́зд* fare; *за кварти́ру* rent; **~ёж** *m* [1 *e.*] payment; **~ёжеспосо́бный** [14; -бен, -бна] solvent; **~ёжный** [14] of payment; **~ина** *f* [5] platinum; **~и́ть** [15], ⟨за-, у-⟩ pay (T in; *за* B for); settle (*account по* Д); **-ся**, ⟨по-⟩ *fig.* pay (T with, *за* B for); **~ный** [14] paid; be paid for

плато́к *m* [1; -тка́] handkerchief

платфо́рма *f* [5] platform (*a. fig.*)

пла́т|ье *n* [10; *g/pl.*: -ьев] dress, gown; **~яно́й** [14] clothes...; **~яно́й шкаф** wardrobe

пла́ха *f* [5] (*hist.* executioner's) block

плац|да́рм m [1] base; *mil.* bridgehead; **~ка́рта** *f* [5] ticket for a reserved seat *or* berth

пла́|ч m [1] weeping; **~че́вный** [14; -вен, -вна] deplorable, pitiable, lamentable; **~шмя́** flat, prone

плащ m [1 *e.*] raincoat; cloak

плебисци́т m [1] plebiscite

плева́|ть [6 *e.*; плюю́, плюёшь], *once* ⟨плю́нуть⟩ [20] spit (out); not care (**на** B for)

плево́к [1; -вка] spit(tle)

плеври́т m [1] pleurisy

плед m [1] plaid, blanket

плем|енно́й [14] tribal; **~енны́е** *лоша́дь* stud...; **~я́** *n* [13] tribe; breed; *coll.* brood; **на ~я** for breeding

племя́нни|к m [1] nephew; **~ца** *f* [5] niece

плен m [1; в **~у́**] captivity; **взять (по-па́сть) в ~** (be) take(n) prisoner

плен|а́рный [14] plenary; **~и́тельный** [14; -лен, -льна] captivating, fascinating; **~и́ть(ся)** → **~я́ть(ся)**

плёнка *f* [5; *g/pl.*: -нок] film; *для записи* tape

пле́н|ник m [1], **~ный** m [14] captive, prisoner; **~я́ть** [28], ⟨**~и́ть**⟩ [13] (**-ся** be) captivate(d)

пле́нум m [1] plenary session

пле́сень *f* [8] mo(u)ld

плеск m [1], **~а́ть** [3], *once* ⟨плесну́ть⟩ [20], **-а́ться** *impf.* splash

пле́сневеть [8], ⟨за-⟩ grow mo(u)ldy, musty

пле|сти́ [25 -т-: плету́], ⟨с-, за-⟩ braid, plait; weave; *coll.* **~сти́ небыли́цы** spin yarns; **~сти́ интри́ги** intrigue (against); *coll.* **что ты ~тёшь?** what on earth are you talking about?; **-сь** drag, lag; **~тёный** [14] wattled; wicker...; **~те́нь** *m* [4; -тня] wattle fence

плётка *f* [5; *g/pl.*: -ток], **плеть** *f* [8; *from g/pl. e.*] lash

плеч|о́ *n* [9; *pl.*: пле́чи, плеч, -ча́м] shoulder; *tech.* arm; **с(о всего́) ~а́** with all one's might; (И) **не по ~у́** (Д) not be equal to a th.; → *a.* **гора́** *coll.*

плешь *f* [8] bald patch

плит|а́ *f* [5; *pl. st.*] slab, (flag-, grave-) stone; *металли́ческая* plate; (*kitchen*) range; (*gas*) cooker, stove; **~ка** *f* [5; *g/pl.*: -ток] tile; *шокола́да* bar; cooker, stove; electric hotplate

пло́в|е́ц m [1; -вца́] swimmer

плод m [1 *e.*] fruit; **~и́ть** [15 *e.*; пложу́, -ди́шь], ⟨рас-⟩ propagate, multiply (*v/i.*-**ся**); **~ови́тый** [14 *sh.*] fruitful, prolific (*a. fig.*); **~ово́дство** *n* [9] fruit growing; **~о́вый** [14] fruit...; **~о́вый сад** orchard; **~оно́сный** [14; -сен, -сна] fruit-bearing; **~оро́дие** *n* [12] fertility; **~оро́дный** [14; -ден, -дна] fertile; **~отво́рный** [14; -рен, -рна] fruitful, productive; *влия́ние* good, positive

пло́мб|а *f* [5] (lead) seal; *зубна́я filling*; **~и́ровать** [7], ⟨о-⟩ seal; ⟨за-⟩ fill, stop

пло́ск|ий [16; -сок, -ска́, -о; *compr.*: пло́ще] flat (*a. fig.* = stale, trite), level; **~огор** *n* [10] plateau, tableland; **~огу́бцы** *pl.* [1; *g/pl.*: -цев] pliers; **~ость** *f* [8; *from g/pl. e.*] flatness; plane (*a. math.*); platitude

плот m [1 *e.*] raft; **~и́на** *f* [5] dam, dike; **~ник** m [1] carpenter

пло́тн|ость *f* [8] density (*a. fig.*); solidity; **~ый** [14; -тен, -тна́, -о] compact, solid; *ткань* dense, close, thick; *о сложе́нии* thickset

пло́т|ои́дный [14; -ден, -дна] carnivorous; *взгляд* lascivious; **~ский** [16] carnal; **~ь** *f* [8] flesh

плох|о́й [16; плох, -а́, -о; *compr.*: ху́же] bad; **~о** bad(ly); *coll.* bad mark; → **дво́йка & едини́ца**

пло́ща|дка *f* [5; *g/pl. e.*: -док] ground, area; *де́тская* playground; *sport* court; platform; *ле́стничная* landing; **пускова́я ~ка** launching pad; **строи́тельная ~ка** building site; **~ь** *f* [8; *from g/pl. e.*] square; area (*a. math*); space; *жила́я ~ь* → **жилпло́щадь**

плуг m [1; *pl. e.*] plow, *Brt.* plough

плут m [1 *e.*] rogue; trickster, cheat; **~а́ть** [1] *coll.* stray; **~ова́ть** [7], ⟨с-⟩ trick, cheat; **~овство́** *n* [9] trickery, cheating

плыть [23] (be) swim(ming); float(ing); *на корабле́* sail(ing); **~ по тече́нию** *fig.* swim with the tide; → **пла́вать**

плю́нуть → **плева́ть**

плюс (*su. m* [1]) plus; *coll.* advantage
плюш *m* [1] plush
плющ *m* [1 *e.*] ivy
пляж *m* [1] beach
пляс|а́ть [3], ⟨с-⟩ dance; **~ка** *f* [5; *g/pl.*: -сок] (folk) dance; dancing
пневмати́ческий [16] pneumatic
пневмони́я *f* [7] pneumonia
по 1. (Д); on, along; through; all over; in; by; according to, after; through; owing to; for; over; across; upon; each, at a time (*2, 3, 4, with* **по два**); **2.** (В) to, up to; till, through; for; **3.** (П) (up)on; **~ мне** for all I care; **~ ча́су в день** an hour a day
по- (in *compds.*); → **ру́сский, ваш**
поба́иваться [1] be a little afraid of (P)
побе́г *m* [1] escape, flight; *bot.* shoot, sprout
побег|у́шки: быть на ~у́шках *coll.* run errands (**у** P for)
побе́|да *f* [5] victory; **~ди́тель** *m* [4] victor; winner; **~ди́ть** → **~жда́ть**; **~дный** [14], **~доно́сный** [14; -сен, -сна] victorious; **~жда́ть** [1], ⟨~ди́ть⟩ [15 *e.*; *1st p. sg. not used*] -дишь, -еждённый] be victorious (В over), win (*a.* victory), conquer, defeat; beat; *страх, сомнения* overcome
побере́жье *n* [10] coast, seaboard, littoral
побла́жка *coll. f* [5; *g/pl.*: -жек] indulgence
поблизости close by; (**от** P) near
побо́и *m/pl.* [3] beating; **~ще** *n* [11] bloody battle
побо́р|ник *m* [1] advocate; **~о́ть** [17] *pf.* conquer; overcome; beat
побо́чный [14] *эффект* side; *продукт* by-(*product*); *old use сын, дочь* illegitimate
побу|ди́тельный [14]: **~ди́тельная причи́на** motive; **~жда́ть** [1], ⟨~ди́ть⟩ [15 *e.*; -ужу́, -уди́шь; -уждённый] induce, prompt, impel; **~жде́ние** *n* [12] motive, impulse, incentive
пова́д|иться *coll.* [15] *pf.* fall into the habit (of [visiting] *inf.*); **~ка** [5; *g/pl.*: -док] *coll.* habit
пова́льный [14] indiscriminate; *ув-*

лече́ние general
по́вар *m* [1; *pl.*: -рá, *etc. e.*] culinary; cook; **~енный** [14] *кни́га* cook (*book, Brt.* cookery book); *соль* (*salt*) table
пове|де́ние *n* [12] behavio(u)r, conduct; **~ли́тельный** [14; -лен, -льна] *тон* peremptory; *gr.* imperative
поверг|а́ть [1], ⟨~нуть⟩ [21] *в отчая́ние* plunge into (**в** В)
пове́р|енный [14]: **~енный в дела́х** chargé d'affaires; **~ить** → **ве́рить**; **~ну́ть(ся)** → **повора́чивать(ся)**
пове́рх (P) over, above; **~ностный** [14; -тен, -тна] *fig.* superficial; surface...; **~ность** *f* [8] superficiality
пове́рье *n* [10] popular belief, superstition
пове́сить(ся) → **ве́шать(ся)**
повествова́|ние *n* [12] narration, narrative; **~тельный** [14] *стиль* narrative; **~тельное предложе́ние** *gr.* sentence; **~ть** [7] narrate (*v/t.* **о** П)
пове́ст|ка *f* [5; *g/pl.*: -ток] *law* summons; (*уведомле́ние*) notice; **~ка дня** agenda; **~ь** *f* [8; *from g/pl. e.*] story, tale
по-ви́димому apparently
пови́дло *n* [9] jam
пови́н|ность *f* [8] duty; **~ный** [14; -и́нен, -и́нна] guilty; **~ова́ться** [7] (*pt. a. pf.*) (Д) obey; comply with; **~ове́ние** *n* [12] obedience
по́вод *m* **1.** [1] ground, cause; occasion (on **по** Д); **по ~у** (P) as regards, concerning; **2.** [1; в -ду́: *pl.*: -о́дья, -о́дьев] rein; **на ~у́** (**у** P) be under s.b.'s thumb; **~о́к** *m* [1; -дка́ *и т. д.*; *pl.* -дки́ *и т. д.*] (dog's) lead
пово́зка *f* [5; *g/pl.*: -зок] vehicle, conveyance; (*not equipped with springs*) carriage; cart
повор|а́чивать [1], ⟨поверну́ть⟩ [20] turn (*v/i.* -ся; **~а́чивайся!** come on!); **~о́т** *m* [1] turn; **~отли́вый** [14 *sh.*] nimble, agile; **~о́тный** [14] turning (*a. fig.*)
повре|жда́ть [1], ⟨~ди́ть⟩ [15 *e.*; -ежу́, -еди́шь; -еждённый] damage; *ногу и т. д.* injure, hurt; **~жде́ние** *n* [12] damage; injury
повре|мени́ть [13] *pf.* wait a little; **~ённый** [14] *опла́та* payment on time ba-

sis (*by the hour, etc.*)

повсе|дне́вный [14; -вен, -вна] everyday, daily; ~ме́стный [14; -тен, -тна] general, universal; ~ме́стно everywhere

повста́н|ец *m* [1; -нца] rebel, insurgent; ~ческий [16] rebel(lious)

повсю́ду everywhere

повторе́ние *n* [12] repetition; *материала* review; *событий* recurrence; ~ный [14] repeated, recurring; ~я́ть [28], ⟨~и́ть⟩ [13] repeat (-ся o.s.); review

повы|ша́ть [1], ⟨~сить⟩ [15] raise, increase; *по службе* promote; -ся rise; *в звании* advance; ~ше́ние *n* [12] rise; promotion; ~шенный [14] increased, higher; *температура* high

повя́з|ка *f* [5; *g/pl.:* -зок] *med.* bandage; band, armlet

пога|ша́ть [1], ⟨~си́ть⟩ [15] put out, extinguish; *долг* pay; *марку* cancel

погиб|а́ть [1], ⟨~нуть⟩ [21] perish; be killed, fall; ~ший [17] lost, killed

погло|ща́ть [1], ⟨~ти́ть⟩ [15; -ощу́, -ощённый] swallow up, devour; (*впитывать*) absorb (*a. fig.*)

погля́дывать [1] cast looks (**на** В at)

погов|а́ривать [1]; ~а́ривают there is talk (о П of); ~о́рка *f* [5; *g/pl.:* -рок] saying, proverb

пого́|да *f* [5] weather (**в** В, *при* П in); *э́то ~ды не де́лает* this does not change anything; ~ди́ть *coll.* [15 *e.;* -гожу́, -годи́шь] *pf.* wait a little; ~дя́ later; ~́вный [14] general, universal; ~́вно without exception; ~́вье *n* [10] livestock

пого́н *m* [1] *mil.* shoulder strap

пого́н|я *f* [6] pursuit (**за** Т of); pursuers *pl.;* ~я́ть [28] drive *or* urge (on); drive (*for a certain time*)

пограни́ч|ный [14] border...; ~ик *m* [1] border guard

по́гре|б [1; *pl.:* -ба́, *etc. e.*] cellar; ~ба́льный [14] funeral; ~бе́ние *n* [12] burial; funeral; ~мушка *f* [5; *g/pl.:* -шек] rattle; ~шность *f* [8] error, mistake

погру|жа́ть [1], ⟨~зи́ть⟩ [15 & 15 *e.;* -ужу́, -у́зишь; -у́женный & -ужённый] immerse; sink, plunge, submerge (*v/i.*

-ся); ~жённый *a.* absorbed, lost (**в** В in); load, ship; ~зно́й [14] *подводно* diving; *аппарата* submersion; ~зка [5; *g/pl.:* -зок] loading, shipment

погряз|а́ть [1], ⟨~нуть⟩ [21] get stuck (**в** Т in)

под, ~о 1. (В) (*направление*) under; toward(s), to; (*возраст, время*) about; on the eve of; for, suitable as; 2. (Т) (*расположение*) under, below, beneath; near, by; *сраже́ние*; *для* (used) for; *по́ле* ~ **ро́жью** rye field

пода|ва́ть [5], ⟨~ть⟩ [-да́м, -да́шь, *etc.*, → **дать**] give; serve (*a. sport*); *заявле́ние* hand (*or* send) in; *жалобу* lodge; *пример* set; *руку помощи* render; ~ть **в суд** (**на** В) bring an action against; *не* ~*ва́ть ви́ду* give no sign; -ся move; yield

подав|и́ть → ~ля́ть; ~и́ться *pf.* [14] choke; ~ле́ние *n* [12] suppression; ~ля́ть [28], ⟨~и́ть⟩ [14] suppress; repress; depress; crush; ~ля́ющий *a.* overwhelming

пода́|вно *coll.* so much *or* all the more

пода́|гра *f* [5] gout; podagra

пода́|льше *coll.* a little farther

пода́|рок *m* [1; -рка] present, gift; ~тливый [14 *sh.*] (com)pliant; ~ть(ся) → ~ва́ть(ся); ~ча *f* [5] serve; *sport* service; *материала* presentation; *воды, газа* supply; *tech.* feed(ing); ~чка *f* [5; *g/pl.:* -чек] sop; *fig.* tip

подбе|га́ть [1], ⟨~жа́ть⟩ [4; -бегу́, -бежишь, -бегу́т] run up (**к** Д to)

подби|ва́ть [1], ⟨~ть⟩ (подобью́, -бьёшь, *etc.*, → **бить**) line (Т with); *подмётку* (re)sole; hit, injure; *coll.* instigate, incite; ~тый *coll. глаз* black

под|бира́ть [1], ⟨~обра́ть⟩ [подберу́, -рёшь; подобра́л, -á, -о; подобранный] pick up; *юбку* tuck up; *живот* draw in; (*отбирать*) pick out, select; -ся sneak up (**к** Д to); ~би́ть → ~бива́ть; ~бо́р *m* [1] selection; assortment; **на** ~бо́р choice, well-matched, select

подборо́док *m* [1; -дка] chin

подбра́|сывать [1], ⟨~о́сить⟩ [15] throw *or* toss (up); jolt; *в огонь* add; (*подвез-*

П

ти) give a lift

подва́л *m* [1] basement; cellar

подвезти́ → **подвози́ть**

подвер|га́ть [1], ⟨*≈гнуть*⟩ [21] subject, expose; *≈гнуть испыта́нию* put to the test; *≈гнуть сомне́нию* call into question; *-ся* undergo; *≈женный* [14 *sh.*] subject to

подве́с|ить → **подве́шивать**; *≈но́й* [14] hanging, pendant; *мост* suspension; *мотор* outboard

подвести́ → **подводи́ть**

подве́тренный [14] *naut.* leeward; sheltered side

подве́|шивать [1], ⟨*≈сить*⟩ [15] hang (under; on); suspend (from)

по́двиг *m* [1] feat, exploit, deed

подви|га́ть [1], ⟨*≈нуть*⟩ [20] move little (*v/i. -ся*); *≈жной* [14] *mil.* mobile; *rail.* rolling; *≈жность* *f* [8] mobility; *человека* agility; *≈нуть(ся)* → *≈га́ть(ся)*

подвла́стный [14; -тен, -тна] subject to, dependent on

подво́|дить [15], ⟨*подвести́*⟩ [25] lead ([up] to); *фундамент* lay; build; *coll.* let a p. down (*обмануть и т. д.*); *≈ито́ги* sum up

подво́дный [14] underwater; submarine; *≈ая ло́дка* submarine; *≈ый ка́мень* reef; *fig.* unexpected obstacle

подво́з *m* [1] supply; *≈и́ть* [15], ⟨*подвезти́*⟩ [24] bring; transport; *кого-л.* give a p. a lift

подвы́пивший *coll.* [17] tipsy, slightly drunk

подвя́зывать [1], ⟨*≈а́ть*⟩ [3] tie (up)

под|гиба́ть [1], ⟨*≈огну́ть*⟩ [20] tuck (under); bend (*a. -ся*); *но́ги ≈гиба́ются от уста́лости* I am barely able to stand (*with tiredness*)

подгля́д|ывать [1], ⟨*≈е́ть*⟩ [11] peep at, spy on

подгово́р|ивать [1], ⟨*≈и́ть*⟩ [13] instigate, put a p. up to

под|гоня́ть [1], ⟨*≈огна́ть*⟩ [подгоню́, -го́нишь, → **гнать**] drive to *or* urge on, hurry; *к фигуре и т. д.* fit, adapt (to)

подгора́ть [1], ⟨*≈е́ть*⟩ [9] burn slightly

подгото́в|ительный [14] preparatory; *рабо́та* spadework; *≈ка* *f* [5; *g/pl.*: -вок] preparation, training (*к* Д for); *≈ля́ть* [28], ⟨*≈ить*⟩ [14] prepare; *≈ить по́чву* *fig.* pave the way

подда|ва́ться [5], ⟨*≈ться*⟩ [-да́мся, -да́шься, *etc.*, → **дать**] yield; *не ≈ва́ться описа́нию* defy *or* beggar description

поддаќ|ивать [1], ⟨*≈нуть*⟩ [20] say yes (to everything), consent

по́дда|нный *m* [14] subject; *≈нство* *n* [9] nationality; citizenship; *≈ться* → *≈ва́ться*

подде́л|ка [5; *g/pl.*: -лок] *бумаг*, *подписи*, *денег и т. д.* forgery, counterfeit; *≈ывать*, ⟨*≈ать*⟩ [1] forge; *≈ьный* [14] counterfeit...; sham...

подде́рж|ивать [1], ⟨*≈а́ть*⟩ [4] support; back (up); *поря́док* maintain; *разгово́р и т. д.* keep up; *≈ка* *f* [5; *g/pl.*: -жек] support; backing

поде́л|ать *coll.* [1] *pf.* do; *ничего́ не ≈аешь* there's nothing to be done; → *а. де́лать*; *coll.* *≈ом*: *≈ом ему́* it serves him right

поде́ржанный [14] secondhand; worn, used

поджа́р|ивать [1], ⟨*≈ить*⟩ [13] fry, roast, grill slightly; brown; *хлеб* toast

поджа́рый [14 *sh.*] lean

поджа́ть → **поджима́ть**

под|же́чь → *≈жига́ть*; *≈жига́ть* [1], ⟨*≈же́чь*⟩ [26: подожгу́; -ожжёшь; поджёг, подожгла́; подожжённый] set on fire (*or* fire to)

под|жида́ть [1], ⟨*≈ожда́ть*⟩ [-ду́, -дёшь; -а́л, -а́, -о] wait (for P, B)

под|жима́ть [1], ⟨*≈жа́ть*⟩ [подожму́, -мёшь; поджа́тый] draw in; *но́ги* cross (one's legs); *гу́бы* purse (one's lips); *≈жа́ть хвост* have one's tail between one's legs; *вре́мя ≈жима́ет* time is pressing

поджо́г *m* [1] arson

подзаголо́вок *m* [1; -вка] subtitle

подзадо́р|ивать *coll.* [1], ⟨*≈ить*⟩ [13] egg on, incite (*на* B, *к* Д to)

подза́ты́льник *m* [1] cuff on the back of the head; *≈щи́тный* *m* [14] *law* client

подзе́мный [14] underground, subterranean; **~ толчо́к** tremor

под|зыва́ть [1], ⟨~озва́ть⟩ [подзову́, -ёшь; подозва́л, -á, -o; подо́званный] call, beckon

под|кара́уливать coll. [1], ⟨~карау́лить⟩ [13] → **подстерега́ть**; **~ка́рмли-вать** [1], ⟨~корми́ть⟩ [14] *скот* feed up, fatten; *растения* give extra fertilizer; **~ка́тывать** [1], ⟨~кати́ть⟩ [15] roll *or* drive up; **~ка́шиваться** [1], ⟨~коси́ться⟩ [15] give way

подки́|дывать [1], ⟨~нуть⟩ [20] → **под-бра́сывать**; **~дыш** *m* [1] foundling

подкла́д|ка [5; *g/pl.*: -док] lining; **~ывать** [1], ⟨~ложи́ть⟩ [16] lay (under); (*добавить*) add; **подложи́ть свинью́** *approx.* play a dirty trick on s.o

подкле́|ивать [1], ⟨~ить⟩ [13] glue, paste

подключа́|ть [4], ⟨~и́ть⟩ [16] *tech.* connect, link up; *fig.* include, attach

подко́в|а *f* [5] horseshoe; **~ывать** [1], ⟨~áть⟩ [7 *e.*; -кую́, -куёшь] shoe; give a grounding in; **~анный** [14] *a.* versed in

подко́жный [14] hypodermic

подкоси́ть|ся → **подка́шиваться**

подкра́|дываться [1], ⟨~сться⟩ [25] steal *or* sneak up (**к** Д to); **~шивать** [1], ⟨~сить⟩ [15] touch up one's make-up (*a.* **-ся**)

подкреп|ля́ть [28], ⟨~и́ть⟩ [14 *e.*; -плю́, -пи́шь, -плённый] reinforce, support; *fig.* corroborate; **-ся** fortify o.s.; **~ле́ние** *n* [12] *mil.* reinforcement

по́дкуп *m* [1], **~а́ть** [1], ⟨~и́ть⟩ [14] suborn; bribe; *улыбкой и т. д.* win over, charm

подла́|живаться [1], ⟨~диться⟩ [15] adapt o.s. to, fit in with; humo(u)r, make up to

по́дле (P) beside, by (the side of); nearby

подлежа́ть [4 *e.*; -жу́, -жи́шь] be subject to; be liable to; (И) **не ~и́т сомне́нию** there can be no doubt (about); **~áщий** [17] subject (Д to); liable to; **~áщее** *n gr.* subject

подле|за́ть [1], ⟨~зть⟩ [24 *st.*] creep (under; up); **~со́к** *m* [1; -ска и т. д.] under-

growth; **~та́ть** [1], ⟨~те́ть⟩ [11] fly up (to)

подле́ц *m* [1 *e.*] scoundrel, rascal

подли|ва́ть [1], ⟨~ть⟩ [подолью́, -льёшь; подле́й! подли́л, -а, -o; подли́-тый (-ли́т, -á, -o)] add to, pour on; **~вка** *f* [5; *g/pl.*: -вок] gravy; sauce

подли́|за coll. *m/f* [5/pl.]; **~зываться** coll. [1], ⟨~áться⟩ [3] flatter, insinuate o.s. (**к** Д with), toady (to)

по́длинн|ик *m* [1] original; **~ый** [14; -инен, -инна] original; authentic, genuine; true, real

подли́ть → **подлива́ть**

подло́|г *m* [1] forgery; **~жи́ть** → **под-кла́дывать**; **~жный** [14; -жен, -жна] spurious, false

по́дл|ость *f* [8] meanness; baseness; low-down trick; **~ый** [14; подл, -á, -o] mean, base, contemptible

подма́з|ывать [1], ⟨~ать⟩ [3] grease (*a.*, coll. *fig.*); **-ся** coll. insinuate o.s., curry favo(u)r (**к** Д with)

подма́н|ивать [1], ⟨~и́ть⟩ [13; -аню́, -áнишь] beckon, call to

подме́н|а *f* [5] substitution (*of s.th. false for s.th. real*), exchange; **~ивать** [1], ⟨~и́ть⟩ [13; -еню́, -е́нишь] substitute (Т/Д s.th./for), (ex)change

подме|та́ть [1], ⟨~сти́⟩ [25; -т-: -мету́] sweep; **~ти́ть** → **подмеча́ть**

подме́тка *f* [5; *g/pl.*: -ток] sole

подме|ча́ть [1], ⟨~ти́ть⟩ [15] notice, observe, perceive

подме́ш|ивать, ⟨~áть⟩ [1] mix *or* stir (into), add

подми́г|ивать [1], ⟨~ну́ть⟩ [20] wink (Д at)

подмо́га coll. *f* [5] help, assistance

подмок|а́ть [1], ⟨~нуть⟩ get slightly wet

подмо́стки *m/pl.* [1] *thea.* stage

подмо́ченный [14] slightly wet; coll. *fig.* tarnished

подмы|ва́ть [1], ⟨~ть⟩ [22] wash (*a.* out, away); undermine; *impf.* coll. (*impers.*) **меня́ так и ~ва́ет…** I can hardly keep myself from…

поднести́ → **подноси́ть**

поднима́ть [1], ⟨подня́ть⟩ [-ниму́, -ни-мешь; по́днятый (-нят, -á, -o)] lift; pick up (с P from); hoist; *тревогу, плату* raise; *оружие* take up; *флаг* hoist; *якорь* weigh; *паруса* set; *шум* make; ~ **нос** put on airs; ~ **на́ ноги** rouse; ~ **на́ смех** ridicule; **-ся** [*pt.*: -ня́лся, -ла́сь] (с P from) rise; go up (stairs **по ле́стнице**); *coll.* climb (hill **на холм**); *спор и т. д.* arise; develop

подного́тная *coll. f* [14] all there is to know; the ins and outs *pl.*

подно́ж|ие *n* [12] foot, bottom (*of a hill, etc.*; at **у** P); pedestal; **-ка** *f* [5; *g/pl.*: -жек] footboard; *mot.* running board; (*wrestling*) tripping up one's opponent

подно́с *m* [1] tray; **-и́ть**, ⟨-сти́⟩ [15; подне́сти⟩ [24 -с-] bring, carry, take; present (Д); **-ше́ние** *n* [12] gift, present

подня́т|ие *n* [12] lifting; raising, hoisting, *etc.*, →; **поднима́ть(ся); -ь(ся)** → **поднима́ть(ся)**

подоб|а́ть: *impf.* (*impers.*) **-а́ет** it becomes; befits; **-ие** *n* [12] resemblance; image (*a. eccl.*); *math.* similarity; **-ный** [14; -бен, -бна] similar (Д to); such; **и тому́ -ное** and the like; **ничего́ -ного** nothing of the kind; **-но тому́ как** just as; **-остра́стный** [14; -тен, -тна] servile

подо|бра́ть(ся) → **подбира́ть(ся); -гна́ть** → **подгоня́ть; -гну́ть(ся)** → **подгиба́ть(ся); -грева́ть**, ⟨-гре́ть⟩ [8; -гре́тый] warm up, heat up; rouse; **-двига́ть** [1], ⟨-дви́нуть⟩ [20] move (**к** Д [up] to) (*v/i.* **-ся**); **-жда́ть** → **поджида́ть** & **жда́ть; -зыва́ть** → **подзыва́ть**

подозр|ева́ть [1], ⟨заподо́зрить⟩ [13] suspect (**в** П of); **-е́ние** *n* [12] suspicion; **-и́тельный** [14; -лен, -льна] suspicious

подойти́ → **подходи́ть**

подоко́нник *m* [1] window sill

подо́л *m* [1] hem (*of skirt*)

подо́лгу (for a) long (time)

подо́нки *pl.* [*sg.*1; -нка] dregs; *fig.* scum, riffraff

подо́пытный [14; -тен, -тна] experimental; ~ **кро́лик** *fig.* guineapig

подорва́ть → **подрыва́ть**

подоро́жник *m* [1] *bot.* plantain

подо|сла́ть → **подсыла́ть; -спе́ть** [8] *pf.* come (in time); **-стла́ть** → **подсти-**

-ла́ть

подотчётный [14; -тен, -тна] accountable to

подохо́дный [14]; ~ **нало́г** income tax

подо́шва *f* [5] sole (*of foot or boot*); *холма́ и т. д.* foot, bottom

подпа|да́ть [1], ⟨-сть⟩ [25; *pt. st.*] fall (under); **-ли́ть** [13] *pf. coll.* → **поджёчь**; singe; *coll.* **-сть** → **-да́ть**

подпира́ть [1], ⟨подпере́ть⟩ [12; подопру́, -прёшь] support, prop up

подпи́с|ать(ся) → **-ывать(ся); -ка** *f* [5; *g/pl.*: -сок] subscription (**на** B to; for); signed statement; **-но́й** [14] subscription...; **-чик** *m* [1] subscriber; **-ывать(ся)** [1], ⟨-а́ть(ся)⟩ [3] sign; subscribe (**на** B to; for); **-ь** *f* [8] signature (for **на** B); **за -ью** (P) signed by

подплы|ва́ть [1], ⟨-ть⟩ [23] swim up to; sail up to (**к** Д)

подпо́|лза́ть [1], ⟨-лзти́⟩ [24] creep or crawl (**под** B under; **к** Д up to); **-лко́вник** *m* [1] lieutenant colonel; **-лье** [10; *g/pl.*: -ьев] cellar; (*fig.*) underground work or organization; underground...; **-р(к)а** *f* [5 (*g/pl.*: -рок)] prop; **-чва** *f* [5] subsoil; **-я́сывать** [1], ⟨-я́сать⟩ [3] belt; gird

подпр|ы́гивать [1], *once* ⟨-ы́гнуть⟩ [20] jump up

подпус|ка́ть [1], ⟨-ти́ть⟩ [15] allow to approach

подра|ба́тывать [1], ⟨-бо́тать⟩ [1] earn additionally; put the finishing touches to

подр|а́внивать [1], ⟨-овня́ть⟩ [28] straighten; level; *изгородь* clip; *во́лосы* trim

подража́|ние *n* [12] imitation (in/of **в** В/Д); **-тель** *m* [4] imitator (of Д); **-ть** [1] imitate, copy (*v/t.* Д)

подразделе́|ние *n* [12] subdivision; subunit; **-я́ть** [28], ⟨-и́ть⟩ [13] (**-ся** be) subdivide(d) (into **на** B)

подра|зумева́ть [1] mean (**под** T by), imply; **-ся** be implied; be meant, be understood; **-ста́ть** [1], ⟨-сти́⟩ [24 -ст-; -ро́с, -ла́] grow (up); grow a little older; **-ста́ющее поколе́ние** the rising generation

подрез|а́ть &; **~ывать** [1], ⟨~а́ть⟩ [3] cut; clip, trim

подро́бн|ость f [8] detail; **вдава́ться в ~ости** go into details; **~ый** [14; -бен, -бна] detailed, minute; **~о** in detail, in full

подровня́ть → **подра́внивать**

подро́сток m [1; -стка] juvenile, teenager; youth; young girl

подруба́ть [1], ⟨~и́ть⟩ [14] **1.** cut; **2.** sew. hem

подру́га [5] (girl) friend

по-дру́жески (in a) friendly (way)

подружи́ться [16 e.; -жу́сь, -жи́шься] pf. make friends (**с** T with)

подрумя́ниться [13] pf. rouge; cul. brown

подру́чный [14] improvised; su. assistant; mate

подры́|в m [1] undermining; blowing up; **~ва́ть** [1] **1.** ⟨~ть⟩ [22] здоровье и т. д. sap, undermine; **2.** ⟨подорва́ть⟩ [-рву́, -рвёшь; -рва́л, -а́, -о; подо́рванный] blow up, blast, fig. undermine; **~вно́й** деятельность subversive; **~вно́й заря́д** charge

подря́д 1. adv. successive(ly), running; one after another; **2.** m [1] contract; **~чик** m [1], contractor

подс|а́живать [1], ⟨~ади́ть⟩ [15] help sit down; растения plant additionally; **-ся**, ⟨~е́сть⟩ [25; -ся́ду, -ся́дешь; -сел] sit down (**к** Д near, next to)

подсве́чник m [1] candlestick

подсе́сть → **подса́живаться**

подска́з|ывать [1], ⟨~а́ть⟩ [3] prompt; **~ка** coll. f [5] prompting

подскак|а́ть [3] pf. gallop (**к** Д up to); **~ивать** [1], ⟨подскочи́ть⟩ [16] run (**к** Д [up] to); jump up

под|сла́щивать [1], ⟨~сласти́ть⟩ [15 e.; -ащу́, -асти́шь; -ащённый] sweeten; **~сле́дственный** m [14] take under investigation; **~слепова́тый** [14 sh.] weak-sighted; **~слу́шивать**, ⟨~слу́шать⟩ [1] eavesdrop, overhear; **~сма́тривать** [1], ⟨~смотре́ть⟩ [9; -отрю́, -о́тришь] spy, peep; **~сме́иваться** [1] laugh (**над** T at); **~смотре́ть** → **сма́тривать**

подсне́жник m [1] bot. snowdrop

подсо́|бный [14] subsidiary, by-..., side...; рабочий auxiliary; **~вывать** [1], ⟨подсу́нуть⟩ [20] shove under; coll. palm (Д [off] on); **~зна́тельный** [14; -лен, -льна] subconscious; **~лнечник** m [1] sunflower; **~хнуть** → **подсыха́ть**

подспо́рье coll. n [1] help, support; **быть хоро́шим ~м** be a great help

подста́в|ить → **~ля́ть; ~ка** f [5; g/pl.: -вок] support, prop, stand; **~ля́ть** [28], ⟨~ить⟩ [14] put, place, set (**под** B under); math. substitute; (подвести) coll. let down; **~ля́ть но́гу** or (**но́жку**) (Д) trip (a p.) up; **~но́й** false; substitute; **~но́е лицо́** figurehead

подстан|о́вка f [5; g/pl.: -вок] math. substitution; **~ция** f [7] el. substation

подстер|ега́ть [1], ⟨~е́чь⟩ [26 г/ж: -регу́, -режёшь; -рёг, -регла́] lie in wait for, be on the watch for; **его́ ~ега́ла опа́сность** he was in danger

подстил|а́ть [1], ⟨подостла́ть⟩ [подстелю́, -е́лешь; подо́стланный & подсте́ленный] spread (**под** B under)

подстра́|ивать [1], ⟨~о́ить⟩ [13] build on to; coll. fig. bring about by secret plotting; connive against

подстрек|а́тель m [4] instigator; **~а́тельство** n [9] instigation; **~а́ть** [1], ⟨~ну́ть⟩ [20] incite (**на** B to); stir up, provoke

подстре́|ливать [1], ⟨~ели́ть⟩ [13; -елю́, -е́лишь] hit, wound; **~ига́ть** [1], ⟨~и́чь⟩ [26 г/ж: -игу́, -ижёшь; -и́г, -и́гла; -иженный] cut, crop, clip; trim, lop; **~бить** → **подстра́ивать; ~о́чный** [14] interlinear; foot(note)

по́дступ m [1] approach (a. mil.); **~а́ть** [1], ⟨~и́ть⟩ [14] approach (v/t. **к** Д); rise; press

подсуди́|мый m [14] defendant; **~ность** f [8] jurisdiction

подсу́нуть → **подсо́вывать**

подсчёт m [1] calculation, computation, cast; **~и́тывать**, ⟨~ита́ть⟩ [1] count (up), compute

подсы|ла́ть [1], ⟨подосла́ть⟩ [-шлю́, -шлёшь; -о́сланный] send (secretly); **~па́ть** [1], ⟨~пать⟩ [2] add, pour; **~ха́ть**

[1], ⟨подсо́хнуть⟩ [21] dry (up)

подта́лкивать [1], ⟨подтолкну́ть⟩ [20] push; nudge; **~со́вывать** [1], ⟨~сова́ть⟩ [7] shuffle garble; **~чивать** [1], ⟨под-точи́ть⟩ [16] eat (away); wash (out); sharpen; *fig.* undermine

подтвер|жда́ть [1], ⟨~ди́ть⟩ [15 *e.*; -ржу́, рди́шь; -рждённый] confirm, corroborate; acknowledge; **-ся** prove (to be) true; **~жде́ние** [12] confirmation; acknowledg(e)ment

под|тере́ть → **~тира́ть**; **~тёк** *m* [1] bloodshot spot; **~тира́ть** [1], ⟨~тере́ть⟩ [12; подотру́; подтёр] wipe (*up*); **~тол-кну́ть** → **~та́лкивать**; **~точи́ть** → **~та́чивать**

подтру́н|ивать [1], ⟨~и́ть⟩ [13] tease, banter, chaff (*v/t.* **над** Т)

подтя́|гивать [1], ⟨~ну́ть⟩ [19] pull (up); draw (in *reins*); tighten; raise (*wages*) wind *or* key up; egg on; join in (*song*); **-ся** sing; brace up; improve, pick up; **~жки** *f/pl.* [5; *gen.:* -жек] suspenders, *Brt.* braces

поду́м|ывать [1] think (*o* П about)

подуч|а́ть [1], ⟨~и́ть⟩ [16] → **учи́ть**

поду́шка *f* [5; *g/pl.:* -шек] pillow; cushion, pad

подхали́м *m* [1] toady, lickspittle

подхва́т|ывать [1], ⟨~и́ть⟩ [15] catch; pick up; take up; join in

подхо́д *m* [1] approach (*a. fig.*); **~и́ть** [15], ⟨подойти́⟩ [-ойду́, -дёшь; -ошёл; -шла́; *g. pt.*-ойдя́] (**к** Д) approach, go (up to); arrive, come; (Д) suit, fit; **~я́щий** [17] suitable, fit(ting), appropriate; convenient

подцеп|ля́ть [28], ⟨~и́ть⟩ [14] hook on; couple; *fig.* pick up; *насморк* catch (a cold)

подча́с at times, sometimes

подчёрк|ивать [1], ⟨~еркну́ть⟩ [20; -ёркнутый] underline; stress

подчин|е́ние *n* [12] subordination (*a. gr.*); submission; subjection; **~ённый** [14] subordinate; **~я́ть** [28], ⟨~и́ть⟩ [13] subject, submit; put under (Д s.b.'s) command; **-ся** (Д) submit (to); *прика́зу* obey

под|шива́ть [1], ⟨~ши́ть⟩ [подошью́,

-шьёшь; → **шить**] sew on (**к** Д to); hem; file (*papers*); **~ши́пник** *m* [1] *tech.* bearing; **~ши́ть** → **~шива́ть**; **~шу́чивать** [1], ⟨~шути́ть⟩ [15] play a trick (**над** Т on); chaff, mock (**над** Т at)

подъе́|зд *m* [1] entrance, porch; *доро́га* drive; approach; **~зжа́ть** [1], ⟨~хать⟩ [-е́ду, -е́дешь] (**к** Д) drive or ride up (to); approach; *coll.* drop in (on); *fig.* get round s.o., make up to s.o.

подъём *m* [1] lift(ing); ascent, rise (*a. fig.*); enthusiasm; *ноги* instep; **лёгок (тяжёл) на ~** nimble (slow); **~ник** *m* [1] elevator, lift, hoist; **~ный** [14]: **~ный мост** drawbridge

подъе́|хать → **~зжа́ть**

подыма́ть(ся) → **~нима́ть(ся)**

подыск|ивать [1], ⟨~а́ть⟩ [3] *impf.* seek, look for; *pf.* seek out, find; (*выбрать*) choose

подыто́ж|ивать [1], ⟨~ить⟩ [16] sum up

поеда́ть [1], ⟨пое́сть⟩ → **есть¹**

поеди́нок *m* [1; -нка] duel (with weapons **на** П) (*mst. fig.*)

пое́зд *m* [1; *pl.:* -да́, *etc. e.*] train; **~ка** *f* [5; *g/pl.:* -док] trip, journey; tour

пожа́луй maybe, perhaps; I suppose; **~ста** please; certainly, by all means; *в ответ на благода́рность* don't mention it; → *a.* (**не́ за**) **что**

пожа́р *m* [1] fire (**на** В/П to/at); conflagration; **~ище** *n* [11] scene of a fire; *coll.* big fire; **~ник** *m* [1] fireman; **~ный** [14] fire...; *su.* → **~ник**; → **кома́нда**

пожа́ть → **пожима́ть** & **пожина́ть**

пожела́ни|е *n* [12] wish, desire; **наи-лу́чшие ~я** best wishes

пожелте́лый [14] yellowed

поже́ртвование *n* [12] donation

пожи|ва́ть [1]: **как (вы) ~ва́ете?** how are you (getting on)?; **~ви́ться** [14 *e.*; -влю́сь, -ви́шься] *pf. coll.* get s.th. at another's expense; **~зненный** [14] life...; **~ло́й** [14] elderly

пожи|ма́ть [1], ⟨пожа́ть⟩ [-жму́, -жмёшь; -жа́тый] → **жать¹**; press, squeeze; **~ма́ть ру́ку** shake hands; **~ма́ть плеча́ми** shrug one's shoulders; **~на́ть** [1], ⟨пожа́ть⟩ [-жну́, -жнёшь; -жа́тый] → **жать²**; **~ра́ть** Р [1], ⟨пожра́ть⟩ [-жру́, -рёшь; -а́л, -á, -о] eat up, devour; ⟨тки *coll. m/pl.* [1] belongings, (one's) things

по́за *f* [5] pose, posture, attitude

позавчера́ the day before yesterday; ⟨ди́ (P) behind; past; ⟨про́шлый [14] the ... before last

позвол|е́ние *n* [12] permission (с P with), leave (by); ⟨и́тельный [14; -лен, -льна] permissible; ⟨я́ть [28], ⟨ли́ть⟩ [13] allow (*a.* of), permit (Д); ⟨я́ть себе́ allow o.s.; venture; *расходы* afford; ⟨ь(те) may I? let me

позвоно́|к *m* [1; -нка́] *anat.* vertebra; ⟨чник *m* [1] spinal (*or* vertebral) column, spine, backbone; ⟨чный [14] vertebral; vertebrate

по́здн|ий [15] (-zn-) (⟨о *a.* it is) late

поздоро́виться *coll. pf.*: *ему́ не ⟨ся* it won't do him much good

поздрав|и́тель *m* [4] congratulator; ⟨и́тельный [14] congratulatory; ⟨и́ть → ⟨ля́ть; ⟨ле́ние [12] congratulation; *pl.* compliments of ... (с Т); ⟨ля́ть [28], ⟨и́ть⟩ [14] (с Т) congratulate (on), wish many happy returns of ... (*the day, occasion, event, etc.*); send (*or* give) one's compliments (of the season)

по́зже later; *не ~* (P) ... at the latest

пози́ти́вный [14; -вен, -вна] positive

пози́ция *f* [7] *fig.* stand, position, attitude (*по* Д on); *заня́ть твёрдую ⟨ю* take a firm stand

позна|ва́ть [5], ⟨ть⟩ [1] perceive; (come to) know; ⟨ние *n* [12] perception; *pl.* knowledge; *philos.* cognition

позоло́та *f* [5] gilding

позо́р *m* [1] shame, disgrace, infamy; ⟨ить [13], ⟨о-⟩ dishono(u)r, disgrace; ⟨ный [14; -рен, -рна] shameful, disgraceful, infamous, ignominious

поимённый [14] of names; nominal; by (roll) call

по́ис|ки *m/pl.* [1] search (*в* П in), quest; ⟨тине truly, really

по́й|ти [13], ⟨на-⟩ *скот* water; give to drink (s.th. Д)

пойма́ть → *лови́ть*; ⟨ти́ → *идти́*

пока́ for the time being (*a.* → *что*); meanwhile; *cj.* while; *~* (*не*) until; *~!* *coll.* so

long!, (I'll) see you later!

пока́з *m* [1] demonstration; showing; ⟨а́ние (*usu. pl.*) *n* [12] evidence; *law* deposition; *techn.* reading (*on a meter, etc.*); ⟨а́тель *m* [4] *math.* exponent; index; *выпуска проду́кции и т. д.* figure; ⟨а́тельный [14; -лен, -льна] significant; revealing; ⟨а́ть(ся) → ⟨ывать(ся); ⟨но́й [14] ostentatious; for show; ⟨ывать [1], ⟨~а́ть⟩ [3] *фильм и т. д.* show; demonstrate; point; (*на* В at); *tech.* indicate, read; ⟨а́ть себя́ (Т) prove o.s. *or* one's worth; *и ви́ду не ⟨ывать* seem to know nothing; look unconcerned; -ся appear, seem (Т); come in sight; ⟨ываться врачу́ see a doctor

пока́т|ость *f* [8] declivity; slope, incline; ⟨ый [14 *sh.*] slanting, sloping; *лоб* retreating

покая́ние *n* [12] confession; repentance

покида́ть [1], ⟨~нуть⟩ [20] leave, quit; (*бросить*) abandon, desert

покла|да́я: *не ⟨дая́ рук* indefatigably; ⟨дистый [14 *sh.*] complaisant; accommodating; *суда́ и т. д.* load; luggage

покло́н *m* [1] bow (*in greeting*); *fig.* *посла́ть ⟨ы* send regards *pl.*; ⟨е́ние *n* [12] (Д) worship; ⟨и́ться → *кла́няться*; ⟨ник *m* [1] admirer; ⟨я́ться [28] (Д) worship

поко́иться [13] rest, lie on; (*осно́вываться*) be based on

поко́|й *m* [3] rest, peace; calm; *оста́вить в ⟨е* leave alone; *приёмный ⟨й* casualty ward; ⟨йник *m* [1], ⟨йница *f* [5] the deceased; ⟨йный [14; -о́ен, -о́йна] the late; *su.* → *⟨йник*, *⟨йница*

поколе́ние [12] generation

поко́нчить [16] *pf.* ([с] Т) finish; (с Т) do away with; *дурно́й привы́чкой* give up; *~ с собо́й* commit suicide

покоре́|ние [12] *природы* subjugation; ⟨и́тель *m* [4] subjugator; ⟨и́ть (ся) → *⟨я́ть(ся)*; ⟨ность *f* [8] submissiveness, obedience; ⟨ный [14; -рен, -рна] obedient, submissive; ⟨я́ть [28], ⟨и́ть⟩ [13] subjugate; subdue; *се́рдце* win; -ся submit; *необходи́мости и т. д.* resign o.s.

покос *m* [1] (hay)mowing; meadow (-land)

покрикивать coll. [1] shout (**на** B at)

покров *m* [1] cover

покровитель *m* [4] patron, protector; **~ница** *f* [5] patroness, protectress; **~ственный** [14] protective; patronizing; *тон* condescending; **~ство** *n* [9] protection (of Д); patronage; **~ствовать** [7] (Д) protect; patronize

покрой *m* [3] одежды cut

покры|вало *n* [9] coverlet; **~вать** [1], ⟨**~ть**⟩ [22] (T) cover (*a.* = defray); *краской* coat; *cards* beat, trump; **-ся** cover o.s.; *сыпью* be(come) covered; **~тие** *n* [12] cover(ing); coat(ing); defrayal; **~шка** *f* [5; -шек] *mot.* tire (*Brt.* tyre)

покупа|тель *m* [4], **~тельница** *f* [5] buyer; customer; **~ательный** [14] purchasing; **~ать** [1], ⟨**купить**⟩ [14] buy, purchase (from **у** P); **~ка** *f* [5; *g/pl.*: -пок] purchase; *идти́ за ~ками* go shopping; **~ной** [14] bought, purchased

поку|шаться [1], ⟨**~си́ться**⟩ [15 *e.*; -ушусь, -уси́шься] attempt (*v/t.* **на** B); *на чьи-л. права* encroach ([up]on; **~шение** *n* [12] attempt (**на** B [up]on)

пол¹ *m* [1; на́ ~; на ~у́; *pl. e.*] floor

пол² *m* [1; *from g/pl. e.*] sex

пол³(...) [*g/sg., etc.*: ~(у)...] half (...)

полага́|ть, ⟨**положи́ть**⟩ [16] think, suppose, guess; *на́до ~ть* probably; *поло́жим, что ...* suppose, let's assume that; **-ся** rely (**на** B); (Д) **~ется** must be due *or* proper; *как ~ется* properly

пол|день *m* [*gen.*: -(у́)дня: *g/pl.*: -дён] noon (**в** B at); → **обе́д**; *после ~удня* in the afternoon; **~доро́ги** → **~пути́**; **~дюжины** [*gen.*: -удюжины] half (a) dozen

по́ле *n* [10; *pl. e.*] field (*a. fig.*: **на**, **в** П in, **по** Д across); ground; (*край листа*) *mst. pl.* margin; **~во́й** [14] field...; *цветы* wild

поле́зный [14; -зен, -зна] useful, of use; *совет и т. д.* helpful; *для здоровья* wholesome, healthy

полем|изи́ровать [7] engage in polemics; **~ика** *f* [5], **~и́ческий** [16] polemic

поле́но *n* [9; *pl.*: -нья, -ньев] log

полёт *m* [1] flight; **бре́ющий ~** lowlevel flight

по́лз|ать [1], **~ти́** [24] creep, crawl; **~ко́м** on all fours; **~у́чий** [17]: **~у́чее расте́ние** creeper, climber

поли|ва́ть [1], ⟨**~ть**⟩ [-лью, -льёшь, → **лить**] water; *pf.* start raining (*or* pouring); **~вка** *f* [5] watering

полиго́н *m* [1] *mil.* firing range

поликли́ника *f* [5] polyclinic; *больничная* outpatient's department

полиня́лый [14] faded

поли|рова́ть [7], ⟨**от-**⟩ polish; **~ро́вка** *f* [5; *g/pl.*: -вок] polish(ing)

по́лис *m* [1]: **страхово́й ~** insurance policy

политехни́ческий [16]: **~ институ́т** polytechnic

политзаключённый *m* [14] political prisoner

поли́т|ик *m* [1] politician; **~ика** *f* [5] policy; politics *pl.*; **~и́ческий** [16] political

поли́ть → **полива́ть**

полиц|е́йский [16] police(man *su.*); **~ия** *f* [7] police

поли́чн|ое *n* [14]: **пойма́ть с ~ым** catch red-handed

полиэтиле́н *m* [1], **~овый** [14] polyethylene (*Brt.* polythene)

полк *m* [1 *e.*: в ~у́] regiment

по́лка *f* [5; *g/pl.*: -лок] shelf

полко́в|ник *m* [1] colonel; **~ец** *m* [1; -дца] (*not a designation of military rank*) commander, military leader, warlord; one who leads and supervises; **~о́й** [14] regimental

полне́йший [17] utter, sheer

полне́ть [8], ⟨**по-**⟩ grow stout

полно|ве́сный [14; -сен, -сна] of full weight; weighty; **~вла́стный** [14; -тен, -тна] sovereign; **~во́дный** [14; -ден, -дна] deep; **~кро́вный** [14; -вен, -вна] fullblooded; **~лу́ние** *n* [12] full moon; **~мо́чие** *n* [12] authority, (full) power; **~мо́чный** [14; -чен, -чна] plenipotentiary; → **полпре́д**; **~пра́вный** [14; -вен, -вна]: **~пра́вный член** full member; **~стью** completely, entirely; **~та́** *f* [5] fullness; *информации* completeness; (*тучность*) corpulence;

для ~ты́ карти́ны to complete the picture; **~це́нный** [14; -е́нен, -е́нна] full (value)...; *fig.* специали́ст fullfledged

по́лночь *f* [8; -(у́)ночи] midnight

по́лн|ый [14; по́лон, полна́, по́лно́; полне́е] full (of P *or* T); (*наби́тый*) packed; complete, absolute; perfect (*a. right*); (*ту́чный*) stout; **~ое собра́ние сочине́ний** complete works; **~ым** *coll.* chock-full, packed (with P); lots of

полови́к *m* [1 *e.*] mat

полови́н|а *f* [5] half (**на** B by); **~a** (**в ~**) **пя́того** (at) half past four; **два с ~ой** two and a half; **~ка** *f* [5; *g/pl.:* -нок] half; **~чатый** [14] *fig.* determinate

полови́ца *f* [5] floor; board

полово́дье *n* [10] high tide (*in spring*)

полово́й[1] [14] floor...; **~áя тря́пка** floor cloth; **~о́й**[2] [14] sexual; **~áя зре́лость** puberty; **~ие о́рганы** *m/pl.* genitals

поло́гий [16; *comp.:* поло́же] gently sloping

положе́ние *n* [12] position, location; situation; (*состоя́ние*) state, condition; *социа́льное* standing; (*пра́вила*) regulations *pl.*; thesis; **семе́йное ~е́ние** marital status; **~и́тельный** [14; -лен, -льна] positive; *отве́т* affirmative; **~и́ть(ся)** → **класть 1. & полага́ть(ся)**

поло́мка *f* [5; *g/pl.:* -мок] breakage; breakdown

полоса́ *f* [5; *ac/sg.:* полосу́; *pl.:* по́лосы, поло́с, -са́м] stripe, streak; strip; belt, zone; field; period; **~ неуда́ч** a run of bad luck; **~тый** [14 *sh.*] striped

полоска́ть [3], ⟨про-⟩ rinse; gargle; **-ся** paddle; *о фла́ге* flap

по́лость *f* [8; *from g/pl. e.*] *anat.* cavity; **брюшна́я ~** abdominal cavity

полоте́нце *n* [11; *g/pl.:* -нец] towel (T on); **ку́хонное ~** dish towel; **махро́вое ~** Turkish towel

полотн|и́ще *n* [11] width; **~о́** *n* [9; *pl.:* -о́тна, -о́тен, -о́тнам], **~я́ный** [14] linen(...)

поло́ть [17], ⟨вы-, про-⟩ weed

пол|пре́д *m* [1] plenipotentiary; **~пути́** halfway (*a.* **на ~пути́**); **~сло́ва** [9; *gen.:* -(у)сло́ва] **ни ~сло́ва** not a word;

(a few) word(s); **останови́ться на ~(у)сло́ве** stop short; **~со́тни** [6; *g/sg.:* -(у)со́тни; *g/pl.:* -лусо́тен] fifty

полто́р|а *m & n*, **~ы́** *f* [*gen.:* -у́тора, -ры (f)] *or* **~á** [14]; **~а́ста** [*obl. cases:* -у́тораста] a hundred and fifty

полу|боти́нки *old use m/pl.* [1; *g/pl.:* -нок] (low) shoes; **~го́дие** *n* [12] half year, six months; **~годи́чный** [14], **~годово́й** [14] half-yearly; **~гра́мотный** [14; -тен, -тна] semiliterate; **~де́нный** [14] midday...; **~живо́й** [14; -жи́в, -á, -о] half dead; **~защи́тник** *m* [1] *sport* halfback; **~кру́г** *m* [1] semicircle; **~ме́сяц** *m* [1] half moon, crescent; **~мра́к** *m* [1] twilight, semidarkness; **~но́чный** [14] midnight...; **~оборо́т** *m* [1] half-turn; **~о́стров** *m* [1; *pl.:* -вá, *etc. e.*] peninsula; **~проводни́к** *m* [1] semiconductor, transistor; **~стано́к** *m* [1; -нка] *rail.* stop; **~тьма́** *f* [5] → **~мра́к**; **~фабрика́т** *m* [1] semifinished product *or* foodstuff

получ|а́тель *m* [4] addressee, recipient; **~а́ть** [1], ⟨~и́ть⟩ [16] receive; get; *разреше́ние и т. д.* obtain; *удово́льствие* derive; **-ся** (*оказа́ться*) result; prove, turn out; **~е́ние** *n* [12] receipt; **~ка** *coll. f* [5; *g/pl.:* -чек] pay(day)

полу|ша́рие *n* [12] hemisphere; **~шу́бок** *m* [1; -бка] knee-length sheepskin coat

пол|цены́: за ~цены́ at half price; **~часá** *m* [1; *g/sg.:* -уча́са] half (an) hour

по́лчище *n* [11] horde; *fig.* mass

по́лый [14] hollow

полы́нь *f* [8] wormwood

полынья́ *f* [6] polnya, patch of open water in sea ice

по́льз|а *f* [5] use; benefit (**на, в** B, **для** P for), profit, advantage; **в ~у** (P) in favo(u)r of; **~ователь** *m* [4] user; **~оваться** [7], ⟨вос~оваться⟩ (T) use, make use of; avail o.s. of; *репута́цией и т. д.* enjoy, have; *слу́чаем* take

по́ль|ка *f* [5; *g/pl.:* -лек] **1.** Pole, Polish woman; **2.** polka; **~ский** [16] Polish

полюбо́вный [14] amicable

по́люс *m* [1] pole (*a. el*)

поля́|к *m* [1] Pole; **~на** *f* [5] *лесна́я* glade; clearing; **~рный** [14] polar

пома́да *f* [5] pomade; **губна́я ~** lipstick

помале́ньку *coll.* so-so; in a small way; (постепе́нно) little by little

пома́лкивать *coll.* [1] keep silent *or* mum

пома́|рка [5; *g/pl.*: -рок] blot; correction

помести́ть(ся) → **помеща́ть(ся)**

поме́стье *n* [10] *hist.* estate

по́месь *f* [8] crossbreed, mongrel

помёт *m* [1] dung; (*приплод*) litter, brood

поме́|тить → ~ча́ть; ~тка *f* [5; *g/pl.*: -ток] mark, note; ~ха *f* [5] hindrance; obstacle; *pl. only radio* interference; ~ча́ть [1], ⟨~тить⟩ [15] mark, note

поме́ш|анный *coll.* [14 *sh.*] crazy; mad (about на П); ~а́тельство *n* [9] insanity; ~а́ть → **меша́ть**; -ся *pf.* go mad; be mad (на П about)

помеща́|ть [1], ⟨~сти́ть⟩ [15 *e.*; -ещу́, -ести́шь; -ещённый] place; (*поселить*) lodge, accommodate; *капитал* invest; insert, publish; -ся locate; lodge, find room; (*вмещать*) hold; be placed *or* invested; *impf.* be (located); ~е́ние *n* [12] premise(s), room; investment; ~щик *m* [1] *hist.* landowner, landlord

помидо́р *m* [1] tomato

поми́л|ование *n* [12], ~ова́ть [7] *pf. law* pardon; forgiveness; ~уй бог! God forbid!

поми́мо (Р) besides, apart from

помин |*m* [1]: лёгок на ~е talk of the devil; ~а́ть [1], ⟨помяну́ть⟩ [19] speak about, mention; commemorate; **не ~а́ть лихом** bear no ill will (toward[s] a p. В); ~ки *f/pl.* [5; *gen.*: -нок] commemoration (for the dead); ~у́тно every minute; constantly

по́мнить [13], ⟨вс-⟩ remember (о П); **мне ~ся** (as far as) I remember; **не ~ь себя́ от ра́дости** be beside o.s. with joy

помога́ть [1], ⟨~чь⟩ [26; г/ж: -огу́, -о́жешь, -о́гут, -о́г, -огла́] (Д) help; aid, assist; *о лекарстве* relieve, bring relief

помо́|и *m/pl.* [3] slops; *coll.* ~йка *f* [5; *g/pl.*: -о́ек] rubbish heap

помо́л *m* [1] grind(ing)

помо́лвка *f* [5; *g/pl.*: -вок] betrothal, engagement

помо́ст *m* [1] dais; rostrum; scaffold

помо́чь → **помога́ть**

помо́щ|ник *m* [1], ~ница *f* [5] assistant; helper, aide; ~ь *f* [8] help, aid, assistance (с Т, *при* П with, на В/Д to one's); relief; **маши́на ско́рой ~и** ambulance; **пе́рвая ~ь** first aid

по́мпа *f* [5] pomp

помутне́ние *n* [12] dimness; turbidity

по́мы|сел *m* [1; -сла] thought; (*намерение*) design; ~шля́ть [28], ⟨~слить⟩ [13], think (о П of), contemplate

помяну́ть → **помина́ть**

помя́тый [14] (c)rumpled; *трава* trodden

пона́|добиться [14] *pf.* (Д) be, become necessary; ~слы́шке *coll.* by hearsay

понево́ле *coll.* willy-nilly; against one's will; ~де́льник *m* [1] Monday (**в** В, *pl.* **по** Д on)

понемно́|гу, *coll.* ~жку (a) little; little by little, gradually; *coll. a.* (*так себе*) so-so

пони|жа́ть [1], ⟨~зить⟩ [15] lower; (*ослабить, уменьшить*) reduce (*v/i.* -ся; fall, sink); ~же́ние *n* [12] fall; reduction; drop

поник|а́ть [1], ⟨~нуть⟩ [21] droop, hang (one's head головой); *цветы* wilt

понима́|ние *n* [12] comprehension, understanding; conception; **в моём ~нии** as I see it; ~ть [1], ⟨поня́ть⟩ [пойму́, -мёшь; по́нял, -á, -о; по́нятый (по́нят, -á, -о)] understand, comprehend; realize; (*ценить*) appreciate; ~ю (~ешь, ~ете [ли]) I (you) see

поно́с *m* [1] diarrh(o)ea

поноси́ть [15] revile, abuse

поно́шенный [14 *sh.*] worn, shabby

понто́н *m* [1], ~ный [14] pontoon

пону|жда́ть [1], ⟨~ди́ть⟩ [15; -у-, -жде́нный] force, compel

понука́ть [1] *coll.* urge on, spur

пону́р|ить [13] hang; ~ый [14 *sh.*] downcast

по́нчик *m* [1] doughnut

поны́не *obs.* until now

поня́т|ие *n* [12] idea, notion; concept(ion); (**я**) **не име́ю ни мале́йшего ~ия** I haven't the faintest idea; ~ливый

[14 *sh.*] quick-witted; **~ный** [14; -тен, -тна] understandable; intelligible; clear, plain; **~ь** → **понима́ть**

поо́|даль at some distance; **~ди́ночке** one by one; **~черёдный** [14] taken in turns

поощр|е́ние *n* [12] encouragement; **материа́льное ~е́ние** bonus; **~я́ть** [28], ⟨**~и́ть**⟩ [13] encourage

попа|да́ние *n* [12] hit; **~да́ть** [1], ⟨**~сть**⟩ [25; *pt. st.*] (**в**, **на** В) (*оказа́ться*) get; fall; find o.s.; **в цель** hit; **на по́езд** catch; *coll.* (Д *impers.*) catch it; **не ~сть** miss; **как ~ло** anyhow, at random, haphazard; **кому́ ~ло** to the first comer (= **пе́рвому ~вше́муся**); **-ся** (**в** В) be caught; fall (into a trap **на у́дочку**); *coll.* (Д + *vb.* = статья и *m. д.*) come across, chance (up)on, meet; (**быва́ть**) occur, there is (are); strike (Д **на глаза́** a p.'s eye); **вам не ~да́лась моя́ кни́га?** did you happen to see my book?

попа́рно in pairs, two by two

попа́сть → **попада́ть(ся)**

попере́|к (P) across, crosswise; *доро́ги* in (*a p. 's way*); **~ме́нно** in turns; **~чный** [14] transverse; diametrical

попечи́тел|е *n* [12] care, charge (in **на** П); **~итель** *m* [4] guardian, trustee

попла́в|ок *m* [1; -вка́] float (*a. tech*)

попло́йка *coll.* *f* [5; *g/pl.*: -о́ек] booze

попол|а́м in half; half-and-half; fifty-fifty; **~знове́ние** *n* [12]: **у меня́ бы́ло ~знове́ние** I had half a mind to ...; **~ня́ть** [28], ⟨**~нить**⟩ [13] replenish, supplement; **зна́ния** enrich

пополу́дни in the afternoon, p. m.

поправ|и́ть(ся) → **~ля́ть(ся)**; **~ка** *f* [5; *g/pl.*: -вок] correction; *parl.* amendment; (*улучше́ние*) improvement; recovery; **~ля́ть** [28], ⟨**~ить**⟩ [14] adjust; correct, (a)mend; improve; *здоро́вье* recover (*v/i.* **-ся**); put on weight

по-пре́жнему as before

попрек|а́ть [1], ⟨**~ну́ть**⟩ [20] reproach (with Т)

по́прище *n* [11] field (**на** П in); walk of life, profession

попро́|сту plainly, unceremoniously;

~сту говоря́ to put it plainly; **~ша́йка** *coll.* *m/f* [5; *g/pl.*: -а́ек] beggar; cadger

попуга́й *m* [3] parrot

популя́р|ность *f* [8] popularity; **~ый** [14; -рен, -рна] popular

попус|ти́тельство *n* [9] tolerance; connivance; **~ту** *coll.* in vain, to no avail

попу́т|ный [14] accompanying; *ве́тер* fair, favo(u)rable; (**~но** in) passing, incidental(ly); **~чик** *m* [1] travel(l)ing companion; *fig. pol.* fellow-travel(l)er

попы́т|а́ть [1] *pf.* try (one's luck **сча́стья**); **~ка** [5; *g/pl.*: -ток] attempt

пор|а́¹ *f* [5; *ac/sg.*: по́ру; *pl. st.*] time; season; **в зи́мнюю ~у** in winter (time); (**давно́**) **~á** it's (high) time (for Д); **до ~ы, до вре́мени** for the time being; not forever; **до ~ы́ каки́х ~?** how long (since when)?; **до сих ~** so far, up to now (here); **до тех ~** (, **пока́**) so (or as) long (as); **с тех ~** since then (since); **на пе́рвых ~а́х** at first, in the beginning; **~о́й** at times; **вече́рней ~о́й** → **ве́чером**

по́ра² *f* [5] pore

пора|боща́ть [1], ⟨**~ти́ть**⟩ [15 *e.*; -ощу́, -оти́шь; -още́нный] enslave, enthrall

поравня́ться [28] *pf.* draw level (**с** Т with), come up (to), come alongside (of)

пора|жа́ть [1], ⟨**~зи́ть**⟩ [15 *e.*; -ажу́, -ази́шь; -ажённый] strike (*a. fig.* = amaze; *med.* affect; defeat; **~же́ние** *n* [12] defeat; *law* disenfranchisement; **~зи́тельный** [14; -лен, -льна] striking; **~зи́ть** → **~жа́ть**; **~ни́ть** [13] *pf.* wound, injure

порва́ть(ся) → **порыва́ть(ся)**

поре́з [1], **~ать** [3] *pf.* cut

поре́й *m* [3] leek

по́ристый [14 *sh.*] porous

порица́|ние [12], **~ть** [1] blame, censure

по́ровну in equal parts, equally

поро́г *m* [1] threshold; *pl.* rapids

поро́|да *f* [5] breed, species, race; *о чело́веке* stock; *geol.* rock; **~дистый** [14 *sh.*] thoroughbred; **~жда́ть** [1], ⟨**~ди́ть**⟩ [15 *e.*; -ожу́, -оди́шь; -ожде́нный] engender, give rise to, entail

поро́жний *coll.* [15] empty; idling

по́рознь *coll.* separately; one by one

поро́к *m* [1] vice; *речи* defect; *сердца* disease

пороло́н *m* [1] foam rubber

поросёнок *m* [2] piglet

поро́|ть [17] **1.** ⟨рас-⟩ undo, unpick; *impf. coll.* talk (**вздор** nonsense); **2.** *coll.*⟨вы-⟩ whip, flog; ʼ∼**м**[1] gunpowder; ∼**ховой** [14] gunpowder

поро́ч|ить [16], ⟨о-⟩ discredit; *репута́цию* blacken, defame; ∼**ный** [14; -чен, -чна] *круг* vicious; *идеи и т. д.* faulty; *человек* depraved

порошо́к *m* [1; -шка́] powder

порт *m* [1; в ∼у́; *from* g/pl. *e.*] port; harbo(u)r

порта́тивный [14; -вен, -вна] portable; ∼**ить** [15], ⟨ис-⟩ spoil; -**ся** (*v/i.*) break down

порт|ни́ха *f* [5] dressmaker; ∼**ной** *m* [14] tailor

порто́в|ый [14] port..., dock...; ∼**ый го́род** seaport

портре́т *m* [1] portrait; (*похо́жесть*) likeness

портсига́р *m* [1] cigar(ette) case

португа́л|ец *m* [1; -льца] Portuguese; ∼**ка** *f* [5; g/pl.:-лок], ∼**ьский** [16] Portuguese

порт|упе́я *f* [6] *mil.* sword belt; shoulder belt; ∼**фе́ль** *m* [4] brief case; *мини́стра* (*functions and office*) portfolio

пору́|ка *f* [5] bail (**на** В *pl.* on), security, guarantee; *кругова́я* ∼**ка** collective guarantee; ∼**ча́ть** [1], ⟨∼**чи́ть**⟩ [16] charge (Д/В a p. with); commission, bid, instruct (+ *inf.*); entrust; ∼**че́ние** *n* [12] commission; instruction; (*a. comm.*) order (**по** Д by, on behalf of); ∼**чик** *m* [1] *obs.* (first) lieutenant; ∼**чи́тель** *m* [4] guarantor; ∼**чи́тельство** *n* [9] (*зало́г*) bail, surety, guarantee; ∼**чи́ть** → ∼**ча́ть**

порх|а́ть [1], *once* ⟨∼**ну́ть**⟩ [20] flit

по́рция *f* [7] (*of food*) portion, helping

по́р|ча *f* [5] spoiling; damage; ∼**шень** *m* [4; -шня] (*tech.*) piston

поры́в *m* [1] gust, squall; *гнева и т. д.* fit, outburst; *благоро́дный* impulse; ∼**а́ть** [1], ⟨порва́ть⟩ [-ву́, -вёшь; -а́л, -á, -о; по́рванный] tear; break off (**с** T with); -**ся** *v/i.*; *impf.* strive; *a.* → **рва́ть(ся)**; ∼**истый** [14 *sh.*] gusty; *fig.* impetuous, fitful

поря́дко|вый [14] *gr.* ordinal; ∼**м** *coll.* rather

поря́д|ок *m* [1; -дка] order; (*после́довательность*) sequence; *pl.* conditions; ∼**ок дня** agenda; **в** ∼**ке исключе́ния** by way of an exception; **это в** ∼**ке веще́й** it's quite natural; **по** ∼**ку** one after another; ∼**очный** [14; -чен, -чна] *человек* decent; fair(ly large *or* great)

поса́д|ка → **сажа́ть & сади́ть**; ∼**ка** *f* [5; g/pl.:-док] planting; *naut.* embarkation, (*a. rail.*) boarding; *ae.* landing; **вы́нужденная** ∼**ка** forced landing; ∼**очный** [14] landing...

по-сво́ему in one's own way

посвя|ща́ть [1], ⟨∼**ти́ть**⟩ [15 *e.*; -ящу́, -яти́шь; -ящённый] devote ([o.s.] to [**себя́**] Д); *кому́-л.* dedicate; *в та́йну* let, initiate (**в** В into); ∼**ще́ние** *n* [12] initiation; dedication

посе́в *m* [1] sowing; crop; ∼**но́й** [14] sowing; ∼**на́я пло́щадь** area under crops

посед́е́вший [14] (turned) gray, *Brt.* grey

посел|е́нец [1; -нца] settler

посёл|ок *m* [1; -лка] urban settlement; ∼**я́ть** [28], ⟨∼**и́ть**⟩ [13] settle; -**ся** (*v/i.*) put up (**в** П at)

посереди́не in the middle *or* midst of

посе|ти́тель [4], ∼**ти́тельница** *f* [5] visitor, caller; ∼**ти́ть** → ∼**ща́ть**; ∼**ща́емость** *f* [8] attendance; ∼**ща́ть** [1], ⟨∼**ти́ть**⟩ [15 *e.*; -ещу́, -ети́шь; -ещённый] visit, call on; *impf. заня́тия и т. д.* attend; ∼**ще́ние** *n* [12] visit (P to), call

поси́льный [14; -лен, -льна] one's strength *or* possibilities; feasible

поскользну́ться [20] *pf.* slip

поско́льку so far as, as far as

посла́|ние *n* [12] message; lit. epistle; ∼**ть** → **посыла́ть**; ᛰ**ния** *Bibl.* the Epistles; ∼**нник** *m* [1] *dipl.* envoy; ∼**ть** → **посыла́ть**

по́сле 1. (P) after (*a.* ∼ **того́ как** + *vb.*); ∼ **чего́** whereupon; **2.** *adv.* after(ward[s]), later (on); ∼**вое́нный** [14] postwar после́дний [15] last; *известия, мода* latest; (*окончательный*) last, final; *из двух* latter; worst

после́д|ователь *m* [4] follower; ~ова́тельный [14: -лен, -льна] consistent; successive; ~ствие *n* [12] consequence; ~ующий [17] subsequent, succeeding, following

после|за́втра the day after tomorrow; ~сло́вие *n* [12] epilogue

посло́вица *f* [5] proverb

послуш|а́ние *n* [12] obedience; ~ник *m* [1] novice; ~ный [14: -шен, -шна] obedient

посма́тривать [1] look (at) from time to time; ~е́иваться [1] chuckle; laugh (**над** T at); ~е́ртный [14] posthumous; ~е́шище *n* [11] laughingstock, butt; ~е́яние *n* [12] ridicule

посо́б|ие *n* [12] relief, benefit; textbook, manual; *нагля́дные ~ия* visual aids; ~ие *по безрабо́тице* unemployment benefit

посо́л *m* [1; -сла́] ambassador; ~ство *n* [9] embassy

поспа́ть [-сплю́, -спи́шь; -спа́л, -а́, -о] *pf.* (have a) nap

поспе|ва́ть [1], ⟨~ть⟩ [8] (*созревать*) ripen; (*of food being cooked or prepared*) be done; *coll.* → *успева́ть*

поспе́шн|ость *f* [8] haste; ~ый [14: -шен, -шна] hasty, hurried; (*необдуманный*) rash

посред|и́(не) (P) amid(st), in the middle (of); ~ник *m* [1] mediator, intermediary, *comm.* middleman; ~ничество *n* [9] mediation; ~ственность *f* [8] mediocrity; ~ственный [14 *sh.*] middling; mediocre; ~ственно *a.* fair, so-so, satisfactory, C (mark; → *тро́йка*); ~ством (P) by means of

пост¹ *m* [1 *e.*] post; ~ *управле́ния tech.* control station

пост² *m* [1 *e.*] fasting; *eccl.* Вели́кий ~ Lent

поста́в|ить → ~ля́ть & *ста́вить*; ~ка *f* [5; *g/pl.*: -вок] delivery (on при); supply; ~ля́ть [28], ⟨~ить⟩ [14] deliver (*v/t.*; Д р.); supply, furnish; ~щик *m* [1 *e.*] supplier

постан|ови́ть → ~овля́ть; ~о́вка *f* [5; *g/pl.*: -вок] *thea.* staging, production; *дела* organization; ~о́вка *вопро́са* the way a question is put; ~овле́ние *n* [12] resolution, decision; *parl., etc.* decree; ~овля́ть [28], ⟨~ови́ть⟩ [14] decide; decree; ~о́вщик *m* [1] stage manager; director (of film); producer (of play)

посте|ли́ть → *стла́ть*; ~ль *f* [8] bed; ~пе́нный [14: -е́нен, -е́нна] gradual

пости|га́ть [1], ⟨~гнуть⟩ & ⟨~чь⟩ [21] comprehend, grasp; *несчастье* befall; ~жи́мый [14 *sh.*] understandable; conceivable

пост|ила́ть [1] → *стла́ть*; ~и́ться [15 *e.*; пощу́сь, пости́шься] fast; ~и́чь → ~ига́ть; ~ный [14: -тен, -тна, -о] *coll. мясо* lean; *fig.* sour; (*ханжеский*) sanctimonious

посто́льку: ~ поско́льку to that extent, insofar as

посторо́нн|ий [15] strange(r *su.*), outside(r), foreign (*тж. предмет*); unauthorized; ~*м вход воспрещён* unauthorized persons not admitted

постоя́н|ный [14: -я́нен, -я́нна] constant, permanent; (*непрерывный*) continual, continuous; *работа* steady; *el.* direct; ~ство *n* [9] constancy

пострада́вший [17] victim; *при аварии* injured

постре́л *coll. m* [1] little imp, rascal

постри|га́ть [1], ⟨~чь⟩ [26 г/ж: -игу́, -ижёшь, -игу́т] (*-ся* have one's hair) cut; become a monk *or* nun

постро́йка *f* [5; *g/pl.*: -о́ек] construction; *здание* building; building site

поступ|а́тельный [14] forward, progressive; ~а́ть [1], ⟨~и́ть⟩ [14] act; (*с* Т) treat, deal (with), handle; (*в, на* В) enter, join; *univ.* matriculate; *заявление* come in, be received (**на** В for); ~и́ть *в прода́жу* be on sale; -ся (Т) waive; ~ле́ние *n* [12] entry; matriculation; receipt; ~ле́ние дохо́дов revenue return; ~о́к *m* [1; -пка] act; (*поведение*) behavio(u)r, conduct; ~ь *f* [8] gait, step

посты́|дный [14: -ден, -дна] shameful;

~лый [14 sh.] coll. hateful; repellent

посу́да f [5] crockery; plates and dishes; **фая́нсовая (фарфо́ровая)** ~ earthenware (china)

посчастли́ви|ться [14; impers.] pf.: **ей ~лось** she succeeded (in inf.) or was lucky enough (to)

посыл|а́ть [1], ⟨посла́ть⟩ [пошлю́, -шлёшь; по́сланный send (for **за** T); dispatch; **~ка**¹ f [5; g/pl.: -лок] package, parcel

посы́лка² f [5; g/pl.: -лок] philos. premise

посып|а́ть [1], ⟨~а́ть⟩ [2] (be-) strew (T over; with); sprinkle (with); ~а́ться pf. begin to fall; fig. rain; coll. **о вопросах** shower (with)

посяг|а́тельство n [9] encroachment; infringement; ~а́ть [1], ⟨~ну́ть⟩ [20] encroach, infringe (**на** B on); attempt

пот m [1] sweat; **весь в ~у́** sweating all over

пота|йно́й [14] secret; ~ка́ть coll. [1] indulge; ~со́вка coll. f [5; g/pl.: -вок] scuffle

по-тво́ему in your opinion; as you wish; **пусть бу́дет** ~ have it your own way

потво́рство n [9] indulgence, connivance; ~вать [7] indulge, connive (Д at)

потёмки f/pl. [5; gen.: -мок] darkness

потенциа́л m [1] potential

потерпе́вший [17] victim

потёртый [14 sh.] shabby, threadbare, worn

поте́ря f [6] loss; **вре́мени, де́нег** waste

потесни́ть → тесни́ть; -ся squeeze up (to make room for others)

поте́ть [8], ⟨вс-⟩ sweat, coll. toil; **стекло́** ⟨за-⟩ mist over

поте́|ха f [5] fun, coll. lark; ~шный [14; -шен, -шна] funny, amusing

потира́ть coll. [1] rub; ~ху́ньку coll. slowly; silently; secretly, on the sly

по́тный [14; -тен, -тна; -о] sweaty

пото́к m [1] stream; torrent; flow

пото|ло́к m [1; -лка́] ceiling; **взять что́-л. с ~лка́** spin s.th. out of thin air

пото́м afterward(s); then; ~ок m [1; -мка] descendant, offspring; ~ственный [14] hereditary; ~ство n [9] poster-

ity, descendants pl.

потому́ that is why; ~ **что** because

пото́п m [1] flood, deluge

потреб|и́тель m [4] consumer; ~и́ть → ~ля́ть; ~ле́ние n [12] consumption; use; ~ля́ть [28], ⟨~и́ть⟩ [14 e.; -блю́, -би́шь; -блённый] consume; use; ~ность f [8] need, want (**в** П of); requirement

потрёпанный coll. [14] shabby, tattered, worn

потро|ха́ m/pl. [1] pluck; giblets; ~ши́ть [16 e.; -шу́, -ши́шь; -шённый], ⟨вы-⟩ draw, disembowel

потряс|а́ть [1], ⟨~ти́⟩ [24; -с-] shake (a. fig.); ~а́ющий [17] tremendous; ~е́ние n [12] shock; ~ти́ → ~а́ть

поту́|ги f/pl. [5] fig. (vain) attempt; ~пля́ть [28], ⟨~пи́ть⟩ [14] взгляд cast down; **го́лову** hang; ~ха́ть [1] → **ту́хнуть**

потя́гивать(ся) → тяну́ть(ся)

поуч|а́ть [1] coll. preach at, lecture; ~и́тельный [14; -лен, -льна] instructive

поха́бный P [14; -бен, -бна] coll. obscene, smutty

похвал|а́ f [5] praise; commendation; ~ьный [14; -лен, -льна] commendable, praiseworthy

похи|ща́ть [1], ⟨~тить⟩ [15; -и́щу; -и́щенный] purloin; **челове́ка** kidnap; ~ще́ние n [12] theft; kidnap(p)ing, abduction

похлёбка f [5; g/pl.: -бок] soup

похме́лье n [10] hangover

похо́д m [1] march; mil. fig., campaign; **тури́стский** hike; **кресто́вый** ~ crusade

походи́ть [15] (**на** B) be like, resemble

похо́д|ка f [5] gait; ~ный [14] **пе́сня** marching

похожде́ние n [12] adventure

похо́ж|ий [17 sh.] (**на** B) like, resembling; similar (to); **быть ~им** look like; **ни на что́ не ~е** coll. like nothing else; unheard of

по-хозя́йски thriftily; wisely

похо|ро́нный [14] funeral...; **ма́рш** dead; **~ро́нное бюро́** undertaker's office; **~роны** f/pl. [5; -о́н, -она́м] funeral,

burial (**на** П at); **~тли́вый** [14 *sh.*] lust-
ful, lewd; **~ть** f [8] lust

поцелу́й *m* [3] kiss (**в** B on)

по́чва f [5] soil, (*a. fig.*) ground

почём coll. how much (is/are)…; (*only
used with parts of verb* знать) **~ я
зна́ю, что …** how should I know that

почему́ why; **~то** for some reason

по́черк *m* [1] handwriting

почерпну́ть [20; -е́рпнутый] get, obtain

по́честь f [8] hono(u)r

почёт *m* [1] hono(u)r, esteem; hono(u)r-
able; (*карау́л* guard) of hono(u)r

почи́н *m* [1] initiative; **по со́бственно-
му ~у** on his own initiative

почи́н|ка f [5; *g/pl.*: -нок] repair; **отда-
ва́ть в ~ку** have s.th. repaired; **~я́ть**
[28] → **чини́ть** *1a*

почита́ть¹ [1], ⟨**~ти́ть**⟩ [-чту́, -ти́шь;
-чтённый] esteem, respect, hono(u)r;
~ти́ть па́мять встава́нием stand in
s.o.'s memory; **~ита́ть**² [1] *pf.* read (a
while)

по́чка f [5; *g/pl.*: -чек] **1.** *bot.* bud; **2.** *anat.*
kidney

по́чт|а f [5] mail, *Brt.* post (**по** Д by); **~а-
льо́н** *m* [1] mailman, *Brt.* postman;
~а́мт *m* [1] main post office (**на** П at)

почте́ние *n* [12] respect (**к** Д for), esteem; **~ный** [14; -е́нен, -е́нна] respect-
able; *во́зраст* venerable

почти́ almost, nearly, all but; **~тель-
ность** f [8] respect; **~тельный** [14;
-лен, -льна] respectful; *coll. о рас-
стоя́нии и т. д.* considerable; **~ть**
→ **почита́ть**

почто́в|ый [14] post(al), mail…; post-of-
fice; **~ый я́щик** mail (*Brt.* letter) box;
~ый и́ндекс zip (*Brt.* post) code; **~ое
отделе́ние** post office

по́шл|ина f [5] customs, duty; **~ость** [8]
vulgarity; **~ый** [14; -пошл, -а́, -о] vulgar

поштучный [14] by the piece

поща́да f [5] mercy

поэ́|зия f [7] poetry; **~т** *m* [1] poet;
~ти́ческий [16] poetic(al)

поэ́тому therefore, and so

появ|и́ться → **~ля́ться**; **~ле́ние** *n* [12]
appearance; **~ля́ться** [28], ⟨**~и́ться**⟩
[14] appear; emerge

по́яс *m* [1; *pl.*: -са́, *etc. e.*] belt; zone

пояснé|ниеn [12] explanation; **~и́тель-
ный** [14] explanatory; **~и́ть** → **~я́ть**;
~и́ца f [5] small of the back; **~о́й** [14]
waist…; zonal; *портрет* half-length;
~я́ть [28], ⟨**~и́ть**⟩ [13] explain

прабáбушка f [5; *g/pl.*: -шек] great-
-grandmother

прáвд|а f [5] truth; (*это*) **~а** it is true;
вáша ~а you are right; **не ~а ли?** isn't
it, (s)he?, aren't you, they?, do(es)n't …
(*etc.*)?; **~и́вый** [14 *sh.*] true, truthful;
~оподо́бный [14; -бен, -бна] (*ве-
роя́тный*) likely, probable; (*похо́жий
на пра́вду*) probable, likely

прáведн|ик *m* [1] righteous person;
~ый [14; -ден, -дна] just, righteous, upright

прáвил|оn [9] rule; principle; *pl.* regula-
tions; **как ~о** as a rule; **~а у́личного
движе́ния** traffic regulations; **~ьный**
[14; -лен, -льна] correct, right; *черты́
лица́ и т. д.* regular

прави́тель *m* [4] ruler; **~ственный** [14]
governmental; **~ство** *n* [9] government

прáв|ить [14] (T) govern, rule; *mot.*
drive; *гра́нки* (proof) read; **~ка** f [5]
proofreading; **~ле́ние** *n* [12] governing;
board of directors; managing *or* governing body

прáвнук *m* [1] great-grandson

прáво¹*n* [9; *pl. e.*] right (**на** B to; **по** Д of,
by); law; *води́тельские права́* driving
license (*Brt.* licence); **~**² *adv.* coll. indeed, really; **~во́й** [14] legal; **~мо́чный**
[14; -чен, -чна] competent; authorized;
(*опра́вданный*) justifiable; **~наруши́-
тель** *m* [1] offender; **~писа́ние** *n* [12]
orthography, spelling; **~сла́вие** *n* [12]
Orthodoxy; **~сла́вный** [14] Orthodox;
~су́дие *n* [12] administration of the
law; **~тá** f [5] rightness

прáвый [14; *fig.* прав, -á, -о] right, correct (*a. fig.*; *a. side*; on a. **с** P), right-hand

прáвящий [17] ruling

прáдед *m* [1] great-grandfather

прáздн|ик *m* [1] (public) holiday; (reli-
gious) feast; festival; **с ~иком!** compliments *pl.* (of the season)!; **~ичный** [14]
festive, holiday…; **~ование** *n* [12] cele-

bration; ~овать [7], ⟨от⟩ celebrate; ~ость *f* [8] idleness; ~ый [14; -ден, -дна] idle, inactive

пра́кти|к *m* [1] practical worker *or* person; ~ка *f*[5] practice (**на** П in); войти́ в ~ку become customary; ~кова́ть [7] practice (-ise) -ся (*v/i.*); be in use *or* used; ~ческий [16], ~чный [14; чен, -чна] practical

пра́порщик *m* [1] (*in tsarist army*) ensign; (*in Russian army*) warrant officer

прах *m* [1; *no pl.*] *obs. rhet.* dust; ashes *pl.* (*fig.*); всё пошло́ ∠ом our efforts were in vain

пра́чечная *f* [14] laundry

пребыва́|ние *n* [12], ~ть [1] stay

превзойти́ → превосходи́ть

превоз|мога́ть [1], ⟨~мо́чь⟩ [26; г/ж: -огу́, -о́жешь, -о́гут; -о́г, -гла́] overcome, surmount; ~носи́ть [15], ⟨~нести́⟩ [24 -с-] extol, exalt

превосх|оди́тельство *n* [9] *hist.* Excellency; ~оди́ть [15], ⟨превзойти́⟩ [-йду́, -йдёшь, *etc.*, → идти́; -йдённый] excel (in), surpass (in); ~о́дный [14; -ден, -дна] superb, outstanding; *качество* superior; superlative *a. gr.*; ~о́дство *n* [9] superiority

превра|ти́ть(ся) → ~ща́ть(ся); ~тность *f* [8] vicissitude; *судьбы* reverses; ~тный [14; -тен, тна] неве́рный wrong, mis-...; ~ща́ть [1], ⟨~ти́ть⟩ [15 *e.*; -ащу́, -ати́шь; -ащённый] change, convert, turn, transform (**в** В into) (*v/i.* -ся); ~ще́ние *n* [12] change; transformation

превы|ша́ть [1], ⟨~сить⟩ [15] exceed; ~ше́ние *n* [12] excess, exceeding

прегра́|да *f*[5] barrier; obstacle; ~жда́ть [1], ⟨~ди́ть⟩ [15 *e.*; -ажу́, -ади́шь; -аждённый] bar, block, obstruct

пред → пе́ред

преда|ва́ть [1], ⟨~ть⟩ [-да́м, -да́шь, *etc.*, → да́ть] пре́дал, -а́, -о; -да́й(те)!; пре́данный (-ан, -а́, -о)] betray; ~ть гла́сности make public; ~ть забве́нию consign to oblivion; ~ть суду́ bring to trial; -ся (Д) indulge (in) devote o.s., give o.s. up (to); *отчаянию* give way to (despair); ~ние *n* [12] legend; tradition; ~нный [14 *sh.*] devoted, faithful, true;

→ и́скренний; ~тель *m* [4] traitor; ~тельский [16] treacherous; ~тельство *n* [9] *pol.* betrayal, perfidy, treachery; ~ть(ся) → ~ва́ть(ся)

предвар|и́тельно as a preliminary, before(hand); ~и́тельный [14] preliminary; ~я́ть [28], ⟨~и́ть⟩ [13] (В) forestall; anticipate; *выступление и т. д.* preface

предве́|стие → предзнаменова́ние; ~стник *m* [1] precursor, herald; ~ща́ть [1] portend, presage

предвзя́тый [14 *sh.*] preconceived

предви́деть [11] foresee

предвку|ша́ть [1], ⟨~си́ть⟩[15] look forward (to); ~ше́ние *n* [12] (pleasurable) anticipation

предводи́тель *m* [4] leader; *hist.* marshal of the nobility; ringleader; ~ство *n* [9] leadership

предвосх|ища́ть [1], ⟨~и́тить⟩ [15; -ищу́] anticipate, forestall

предвы́борный [14] (pre)election...

преде́л *m* [1] limit, bound(ary) (**в** П within); *страны* border; *pl.* precincts; положи́ть ~ put an end (to); ~ьный [14] maximum..., utmost, extreme

предзнаменова́|ние *n* [12] omen, augury, portent; ~ть[7]*pf.* portend, augur, bode

предисло́вие *n* [12] preface

предл|ага́ть [1], ⟨~ожи́ть⟩ [16] offer (a p. s.th. Д/В); *идею и т. д.* propose, suggest; (*веле́ть*) order

предло́г *m* [1] pretext (on, under **под** Т), pretense (under); *gr.* preposition; ~же́ние *n* [12] offer; proposal, proposition, suggestion; *parl.* motion; *comm.* supply; *gr.* sentence, clause; ~жи́ть → предлага́ть; ~жный [14] *gr.* prepositional (*case*)

предме́стие *n* [10] suburb

предме́т *m* [1] object; subject (matter); *comm.* article; **на** ~ (P) with the object of; ~ный [14]; ~ный указа́тель index

предназн|ача́ть [1], ⟨~а́чить⟩ [16] (-ся be) intend(ed) for, destine(d) for

преднаме́ренный [14 *sh.*] premeditated, deliberate

пре́док *m* [1; -дка] ancestor

предопредел|е́ние *n* [12] predestination; **~я́ть** [28], ⟨**~и́ть**⟩ [13] predetermine

предост|авля́ть [28], ⟨**~а́вить**⟩ [14] (Д) let (a p.) leave (to); give; *кредит, пра́во* grant; *в распоряже́ние* place (at a p.'s disposal)

предостер|ега́ть [1], ⟨**~е́чь**⟩ [26; г/ж] warn (**от** P of, against); **~еже́ние** *n* [12] warning, caution

предосторо́жност|ь *f* [8] precaution(-ary measure *ме́ра ~и*)

предосуди́тельный [14; -лен, льна] reprehensible, blameworthy

предотвра|ща́ть [1], ⟨**~ти́ть**⟩ [15 *e.*; -ащу́, -ати́шь; -ащённый] avert, prevent; **~ще́ние** *n* [12] prevention

предохран|е́ние *n* [12] protection (**от** P from, against); **~и́тельный** [14] precautionary; *med.* preventive; *tech.* safety...; **~я́ть** [28], ⟨**~и́ть**⟩ [13] guard, preserve (**от** P from, against)

предпис|а́ние *n* [12] order, injunction; instructions, directions; **~ывать** [1], ⟨**~а́ть**⟩ [3] order, prescribe

предпол|ага́ть [1], ⟨**~ожи́ть**⟩ [16] suppose, assume; *impf.* (*намерева́ться*) intend, plan; (*быть усло́вием*) presuppose; **~ожи́тельный** [14; -лен, -льна] conjectural; hypothetical; *да́та* estimated; **~ожи́ть** → **~ага́ть**

предпо|сла́ть → **~сыла́ть**; **~сле́дний** [15] penultimate, last but one; **~сыла́ть** [1], ⟨**~сла́ть**⟩ [-шлю, -шлёшь; → **слать**] preface (*T* with); **~сы́лка** *f* [5; *g/pl.*: -лок] (pre)condition, prerequiste

предпоч|ита́ть [1], ⟨**~е́сть**⟩ [25; -т-: -чту́, -чтёшь; -чёл, -чла́; -чтённый] prefer; *pt.* + **бы** would rather; **~е́ние** *n* [12] preference; predilection; **отда́ть ~те́ние** (Д) show a preference for; give preference to; **~ти́тельный** [14; -лен, -льна] preferable

предприи́мчивость *f* [8] enterprise; **~и́мчивый** [14 *sh.*] enterprising; **~има́тель** *m* [4] entrepreneur; employer; **~нима́ть** [1], ⟨**~ня́ть**⟩ [-иму́, -и́мешь; -и́нял, -а́, -о; -и́нятый (-и́нят, -а́, -о)] undertake; **~я́тие** *n* [12] undertaking, enterprise; *заво́д и т. д.* plant, works,

factory (**на** П at); *риско́ванное ~я́тие* risky undertaking

предраспол|ага́ть [1], ⟨**~ожи́ть**⟩ [16] predispose; **~оже́ние** *n* [12] predisposition (**to**)

предрассу́док *m* [1; -дка] prejudice

предрешённый [14; -шён, -шена́] predetermined, already decided

председа́тель *m* [4] chairman; president; **~ство** *n* [9] chairmanship; presidency; **~ствовать** [7] preside (**на** П over); be in the chair

предсказ|а́ние *n* [12] prediction; *пого́ды* forecast; (*проро́чище*) prophecy; **~ывать** [1], ⟨**~а́ть**⟩ [3] foretell, predict; forecast; prophesy

предсме́ртный [14] occurring before death

представи́тель *m* [4] representative; → *a.* **полпре́д**; **~ный** [14; -лен, -льна] representative; *о вне́шности* stately, imposing; **~ство** *n* [9] representation; → *a.* **полпре́дство**

предста́в|ить(ся) → **~ля́ть(ся)**; **~ле́ние** *n* [12] книги *и т. д.* presentation; *thea.* performance; *при знако́мстве* introduction; idea, notion; **~ля́ть** [28], ⟨**~ить**⟩ [14] present; represent o.s., occur, offer; (*предъявля́ть*) produce; introduce (o.s.) (*a.* **собо́й**) represent, be; act (*a.* = feign **~ля́ться** [T]); (*esp.* **~ля́ть себе́**) imagine; (*к зва́нию*) propose (**к** Д for); *refl. a.* appear; seem

предст|ава́ть [5], ⟨**~а́ть**⟩ [-а́ну, -а́нешь] appear (before); **~оя́ть**, [-ои́т] be in store (Д for); lie ahead; (will) have to; **~оя́щий** [17] (forth)coming

преду|бежде́ние *n* [12] prejudice, bias; **~га́дывать** [1], ⟨**~гада́ть**⟩ [1] guess; foresee; **~мы́шленный** [14] → **преднаме́ренный**

предупре|ди́тельный [14; -лен, -льна] preventive; *челове́к* obliging; **~жда́ть** [1], ⟨**~ди́ть**⟩ [15 *e.*; -ежу́, -еди́шь; -еждённый] forestall; anticipate (*p.*); (*предотвраща́ть*) prevent (*th.*); *об опа́сности и т. д* warn (**о** П of); *об ухо́де* give notice (of); **~жде́ние** *n* [12] warning; notice, notification; prevention

П

предусм|а́тривать [1], ⟨∠отре́ть⟩ [9]; -отрю́, -о́тришь foresee; (*обеспечивать*) provide (for), stipulate; ∼отри́тельный [14; -лен, -льна] prudent, far-sighted

предчу́вств|ие n [12] presentiment; foreboding; ∼овать[7] have a presentiment (of)

предше́ств|енник m [1] predecessor; ∼овать[7] (Д) precede

предъяв|и́тель m [4] bearer; ∼ля́ть [28], ⟨∼и́ть⟩[14] present, produce, show; law ∼ля́ть иск bring a suit *or* an action (*про́тив* Д against); ∼ля́ть пра́во на (В) raise a claim to

пре|дыду́щий[17] preceding, previous; ∼е́мник m [1] successor

пре́ж|де formerly; (at) first; (P) before (*a.* ∼де чем); ∼девре́менный [14; -енен, -енна] premature, early; ∼ний [15] former, previous

президе́нт m [1] president; ∠иум m [1] presidium

през|ира́ть [1] despise; ⟨∼ре́ть⟩ [9] scorn, disdain; ∼ре́ние n [12] contempt (к Д for); ∼ре́ть → ∼ира́ть; ∼ри́тельный [14; -лен, -льна] contemptuous, scornful, disdainful

преиму́ществ|енно chiefly, principally, mainly; ∼о n [9] advantage; preference; privilege; по ∼у → ∼енно

прейскура́нт m [1] price list

преклон|е́ние n [12] admiration (*пе́ред* Т of); ∼и́ться → ∼я́ться; ∠ный [14] old; advanced; ∼я́ться [28], ⟨∼и́ться⟩ [13] revere, worship

прекосло́вить[14] contradict

прекра́сный [14; -сен, -сна] beautiful; fine; splendid, excellent; ∼ пол the fair sex; *adv. a.* perfectly well

прекра|ща́ть [1], ⟨∼ти́ть⟩ [15 e.; -ащу́, -ати́шь; -ащённый] stop, cease, end (*v/i.* -ся); (*прерывать*) break off; ∼ще́ние n [12] cessation, discontinuance

преле́ст|ный [14; -тен, -тна] lovely, charming, delightful; ∼ь f [8] charm; coll. → ∼ный

прелом|ле́ние n [12] *phys.* refraction; *fig.* interpretation; ∼ля́ть [28], ⟨∼и́ть⟩

[14; -млённый] (-ся be) refract(ed)

пре́лый [14 *sh.*] rotten; musty

прель|ща́ть [1], ⟨∼сти́ть⟩ [15 e.; -льщу́, -льсти́шь; -льщённый] (-ся be) charm(ed), tempt(ed), attract(ed)

прелю́дия f [7] prelude

преми́нуть [19] *pf.* fail (*used only with* не + *inf.:*) not fail to

пре́мия f [7] prize; bonus; *страхова́я* premium

премье́р m [1] premier, (*usu.* ∼-мини́стр) prime minister; ∼а f [5] *thea.* première, first night

пренебр|ега́ть [1], ⟨∼е́чь⟩ [26 г/ж]; ∼еже́ние n [12] (*невнимание*) neglect, disregard; (*презрение*) disdain, scorn, slight; ∼ежи́тельный [14; -лен, -льна] slighting; scornful, disdainful; ∼е́чь → ∼ега́ть

пре́ния n/pl. [12] debate, discussion

преоблада́|ние n [12] predominance; ∼ть[1] prevail; *численно* predominate

преобра|жа́ть[1], ⟨∼зи́ть⟩ [15 e.; -ажу́, -ази́шь, -ажённый] change, (*vi.* -ся); ∼же́ние n [12] transformation; ∠же́ние *eccl.* Transfiguration; ∼зи́ть(ся) → ∼жа́ть(ся); ∼зова́ние n [12] transformation; reorganization; reform; ∼зо́вывать[1], ⟨∼зова́ть⟩ [7] reform, reorganize; transform

преодол|ева́ть [1], ⟨∼е́ть⟩ [8] overcome, surmount

препара́т m [1] *chem.*, *pharm.* preparation

препира́тельство n [9] altercation, wrangling

преподава́|ние n [12] teaching, instruction; ∼тель m [4], ∼тельница f [5] teacher; lecturer; instructor; ∼ть teach

препод|носи́ть [15], ⟨∼нести́⟩ [24 -с-] present with, make a present of; *∼нести́ сюрпри́з* give s.o. a surprise

препрово|жда́ть [1], ⟨∼ди́ть⟩ [15 e.; -ожу́, -оди́шь; -ождённый] *докуме́нты* forward, send, dispatch

препя́тств|ие n [12] obstacle, hindrance; *ска́чки с ∼иями* steeplechase; *бег с ∼иями* hurdles (race); ∼овать[7], ⟨вос-⟩ hinder, prevent (Д/в П a p. from) прер|ва́ть(ся) → ~ыва́ть(ся); ~ание *n* [12] squabble, argument; ~ыва́ть[1], ⟨~ва́ть⟩ [~у, -вёшь; -а́л, -а́, -о; прёрванный (-ан, -а́, -о)] interrupt; break (off), *v/i.* **-ся**; ~ывистый [14 *sh.*] broken, faltering

пересе|ка́ть[1], ⟨~чь⟩ [26] cut short; *попытки* suppress; *~чь в ко́рне* nip in the bud; **-ся** break; stop

пресле́дова|ние *n* [12] pursuit; (*притеснение*) persecution; *law* prosecution; ~ть [7] pursue; persecute; *law* prosecute

пресло́вутый [14] notorious

пресмыка́|ться [1] creep, crawl; *fig.* grovel, cringe (*пе́ред* T to); ~ющиеся *n/pl.* [17] reptiles

пре́сный [14; -сен, -сна́, -о] *вода* fresh, *fig.* insipid, stale

пресс *m* [1] the press; ~а *f* [5] the press; ~-конфере́нция *f* [7] press conference

престаре́лый [14] aged, advanced in years

престо́л *m* [1] throne; *eccl.* altar

преступ|а́ть [1], ⟨~и́ть⟩ [14] break, infringe; ~ле́ние *n* [12] crime; **на ме́сте ~ле́ния** red-handed; ~ник *m* [1] criminal, offender; ~ность *f* [8] criminality; crime

пресы́|ща́ться[1], ⟨~титься⟩ [15], ~ще́ние *n* [12] satiety

претвор|я́ть [28], ⟨~и́ть⟩ [13]: *~я́ть в жизнь* put into practice, realize

прете|нде́нт *m* [1] claimant (to); candidate (for); *на престо́л* pretender; ~дова́ть[7] (**на** В) (lay) claim (to); ~зия *f* [7] claim, pretension (**на** В, **к** Д to); *быть в ~зии* (**на** В [**за** В]) have a grudge against s.o.

претерп|ева́ть [1], ⟨~е́ть⟩ [10] suffer, endure; (*подве́ргнуться*) undergo

преувел|иче́ние *n* [12] exaggeration; ~и́чивать[1], ⟨~и́чить⟩ [16] exaggerate

преусп|ева́ть [1], ⟨~е́ть⟩ [8] succeed; (*процвета́ть*) thrive, prosper

при (П) by, at, near; (*битва*) of; under, in the time of; (a p.'s possession): by, with, on; about (one *~ себе́*); with; in (*пого́де и т. д.*); for (all that *~ всём том*) when; on (-ing); at that; *~ э́том* at that;

быть ни ~ чём coll. have nothing to do with (it *тут*), not be a p.'s fault

приба́в|ить(ся) → *~ля́ть(ся)*; ~ка [5; *g/pl.*: -вок] augmentation, supplement; *семе́йства* addition; ~ле́ние *n* [12] augmentation, supplement; ~ля́ть [28], ⟨~ить⟩ [14] (В *or* Р) add; augment; put on (*weight* **в** П); *~ля́ть ша́гу* quicken one's steps; **-ся** increase; be added; (a)rise; grow longer; *~очный* [14] additional; *сто́имость* surplus…

прибалти́йский [16] Baltic

прибе|га́ть [1] **1.** ⟨~жа́ть⟩ [4; -егу́, -ежи́шь, -егу́т] come running; **2.** ⟨~гнуть⟩ [20] resort, have recourse (**к** Д to); ~га́ть[1], ⟨~гнуть⟩ [26 г/ж] save up, reserve

приби|ва́ть [1], ⟨~ть⟩ [-бью, -бьёшь, *etc.*, → бить] nail; *пыль и т. д.* lay, flatten; *к бе́регу* throw *or* wash ashore (*mst. impers.*); ~ра́ть [1], ⟨прибра́ть⟩ [-беру́, -рёшь; -бра́л -а́, -о; при́бранный] tidy *or* clean (up); *прибра́ть к рука́м* lay one's hands on s.th.; take s.o. in hand; ~ть → *~ва́ть*

прибли|жа́ть [1], ⟨~зить⟩ [15] approach, draw near (**к** Д; *v/i.* **-ся**); *собы́тие* hasten; *о величина́х* approximate; ~же́ние *n* [12] approach(ing); approximation; ~зи́тельный [14; -лен, -льна] approximate; ~зить(ся) → *~жа́ть(-ся)*

прибо́й *m* [3] surf

прибо́р *m* [1] apparatus; instrument

прибра́ть → *прибира́ть*

прибре́жный [14] coastal, littoral

прибы|ва́ть [1], ⟨~ть⟩ [-бу́ду, -де́шь; при́был, -а́, -о] arrive (**в** В in, at); *о воде́* rise; ~ль *f* [8] profit, gains *pl.*; ~льный [14; -лен, -льна] profitable; ~тие *n* [12] arrival (**в** В in, at; *по* Д upon); ~ть → *~ва́ть*

прива́л *m* [1] halt, rest

привезти́ → *привози́ть*

привере́дливый [14 *sh.*] fastidious; squeamish

приве́рже|нец *m* [1; -нца] adherent; ~ность *f* [8] devotion; ~ный [14 *sh.*] devoted

привести́ → *приводи́ть*

приве́т *m* [1] greeting(s); regards, compliments *pl.*; coll. hello!, hi!; ~ливый

[14 *sh.*] affable; **~ственный** [14] salutatory, welcoming; **~ствие** *n* [12] greeting, welcome; **~ствовать** [7; *pt.a.pf.*] greet, salute; (*одобрять*) welcome

приви|ва́ть [1], ⟨~ть⟩ [-вью́, -вьёшь, *etc.*, → вить] inoculate, vaccinate; *bot.* graft; *привычки и т. д. fig.* cultivate, inculcate; **-ся** **~вка** *f* [5; *g/pl.:* -вок] inoculation, vaccination; grafting; **~де́ние** *n* [12] ghost; **~легиро́ванный** [14] privileged; **~акции** preferred; **~ле́гия** *f* [7] privilege; **~нчивать** [1], ⟨~нти́ть⟩ [15 *e.*; -нчу́, -нти́шь] screw on; **~ть(ся)** → **~ва́ть(ся)**

при́вкус *m* [1] aftertaste; smack (of) (*a. fig.*)

привле|ка́тельный [14; -лен, -льна] attractive; **~ка́ть** [1], ⟨~чь⟩ [26] draw, attract; **к работе** recruit (**к** Д); call (**к ответственности** to account); bring (**к суду** to trial)

приво́д *m* [1] *tech.* drive, driving gear; **~и́ть** [15], ⟨привести́⟩ [25] bring; lead; result (**к** Д in); (*цитировать*) adduce, cite; **~** reduce; *в порядок* put, set; *в отча́яние* drive; **~но́й** [14] driving (*ремень и т. д.* belt, *etc.*)

привози́ть [15], ⟨привезти́⟩ [24] bring (*other than on foot*); import; **~но́й** [14] imported

приво́лье *n* [10] open space, vast expanse; freedom

привы|ка́ть [1], ⟨~кнуть⟩ [21] get or be(come) accustomed *or* used (**к** Д to); **~чка** *f* [5; *g/pl.:* -чек] habit; custom; **~чный** [14; -чен, -чна] habitual, usual

привя́з|анность *f* [8] attachment (to); **~ать(ся)** → **~ывать(ся)**; **~чивый** [14 *sh.*] *coll.* affectionate; (*надоедливый*) obtrusive; **~ывать** [1], ⟨~а́ть⟩ [3] (**к** Д) tie, attach (to); **-ся** become attached; *coll.* pester; **~ь** [8] leash, tether

пригла|си́тельный [14] invitation…; **~ша́ть** [1], ⟨~си́ть⟩ [15 *e.*; -ашу́, -аси́шь; -ашённый] invite (to *mst* **на** В), ask; *врача* call; **~ше́ние** *n* [12] invitation

пригна́ть → пригоня́ть

пригова́|ривать [1], ⟨~ори́ть⟩ [13] sentence; condemn; *impf. coll.* keep saying; **~о́р** *m* [1] sentence; verdict (*a.*

fig.); **~ори́ть** → **~а́ривать**

приго́дный [14; -ден, -дна] → го́дный

пригоня́ть [28], ⟨пригна́ть⟩ [-гоню́, -го́нишь; -гна́л, -а́, -о; при́гнанный] fit, adjust

пригор|а́ть [1], ⟨~е́ть⟩ [9] be burnt; **~од** *m* [1] suburb; **~одный** [14] suburban; *поезд и т. д.* local; **~шня** *f* [6; *g/pl.:* -ней & -шен] hand(ful)

пригото|вливать(ся) [1] → **~овля́ть(ся)**; ⟨~о́вить(ся)⟩ → **~овля́ть(ся)**; **~овле́ние** *n* [12] preparation (**к** Д for); **~овля́ть** [28], ⟨~о́вить⟩ [14] prepare; **-ся** (*v/i.*) prepare o.s. (**к** Д for)

прида|ва́ть [5], ⟨~ть⟩ [-да́м, -да́шь, *etc.*, → дать; при́дал, -а́, -о; при́данный (-ан, -а́, -о)] add; give; *значение* attach; **~ное** *n* [14] dowry; **~точный** [14] supplementary; *gr.* subordinate (*clause*); **~ть** → **~ва́ть**; **~ча** *f* [5]: **в ~чу** in addition

придви|га́ть [1], ⟨~нуть⟩ [20] move up (*v/i.* **-ся**; draw near)

придво́рный [14] court (*of a sovereign or similar dignitary*); courtier (*su. m*)

приде́л|ывать [1], ⟨~ать⟩ [1] fasten, fix (**к** Д to)

приде́рж|ивать [1], ⟨~а́ть⟩ [4] hold (back); **-ся** *impf.* (P) hold, adhere (to)

придир|а́ться [1], ⟨придра́ться⟩ [-ру́сь, -рёшься; -дра́лся, -ала́сь, -а́лось] (**к** Д) find fault (with), carp *or* cavil (at); **~ка** *f* [5; *g/pl.:* -рок] faultfinding, carping; **~чивый** [14 *sh.*] captious, faultfinding

придра́ться → придра́ться

приду́м|ывать, ⟨~ать⟩ [1] think up, devise, invent

прие́з|д *m* [1] arrival (**в** В in); **по ~е** on arrival (in, at); **~жа́ть** [1], ⟨прие́хать⟩ [-е́ду, -е́дешь] arrive (*other than on foot* **в** В in, at); **~жий** [17] newly arrived; guest…

прие́м *m* [1] reception; *в университет и т. д.* admission; *лекарства* taking; (*способ действия*) way, mode; device, trick; method; **в оди́н ~ём** at one go; **~лемый** [14 *sh.*] acceptable; *допустимый* admissible; **~ная** *f* [14] *su.* reception room; waiting room;

~ёмник m [1] *tech.* receiver; *для детей* reception center, *Brt.* -tre; → **радио-приёмник**; **~ёмный часы** office; *экзамен* entrance; *отец, сын* foster

при|éхать → **~езжáть**; **~жáть(ся)** → **~жимáть(ся)**; **~жигáть** [1], ⟨**~жéчь**⟩ [26 г/ж: -жгу, -жжёшь, → **жечь**] cauterize; **~жимáть** [1], ⟨**~жáть**⟩ [-жму, -жмёшь; -áтый] press, clasp (**к** Д to, on); **-ся** press o.s. (to, against); nestle, cuddle up (to); **~жúмистый** [14 *sh.*] tightfisted, stingy; **~з** m [1] prize

призвá|ние n [12] vocation, calling; **~ть** → **призывáть**

приземл|я́ться [28], ⟨**~и́ться**⟩ [13] *ae.* land; **~éние** n [12] landing, touchdown

призёр m [1] prizewinner

при́зма f [5] prism

призна|вáть [5], ⟨**~ть**⟩ [Т; *a.* **за** В] recognize, acknowledge (as); (*сознавать*) see, admit, own; (*считать*) find, consider; **-ся** confess (**в** П s.th., admit); **~ться** *or* **~юсь** tell the truth, frankly speaking; **~к** m [1] sign; indication; **~ние** n [12] acknowledge(e)ment, recognition; **~ние в преступлéнии** confession; declaration (**в любви́** of love); **~тельность** f [8] gratitude; **~тельный** [14; -лен, -льна] grateful, thankful (for **за** В); **~ть(ся)** → **~вáть(ся)**

при́зра|к m [1] phantom, specter (*Brt.* -tre); **~чный** [14; -чен, -чна] spectral, ghostly; *надежда* illusory

призыв m [1] appeal, call (**на** В for); *mil.* draft, conscription; **~áть** [1], ⟨**призвáть**⟩ [-зову́, -вёшь; -звáл, -á, -о; при́званный] call, move dawn appeal (**на** В for); *mil.* draft, call up (**на** В to); **~ник** m [1 *e.*] draftee, conscript; **~нóй** [14]: **~нóй вóзраст** call-up age

при́иск m [1] mine (*for precious metals*); **золотóй** ~ gold field

прийти́(сь) → **приходи́ть(ся)**

прикáз m [1] order, command; **~áть** → **~ывать**; **~ывать** [1], ⟨**~áть**⟩ [3] order, command; give orders

при|кáлывать [1], ⟨**колóть**⟩ [17] pin, fasten; **~касáться** [1], ⟨**коснýться**⟩ [20] (**к** Д) touch (lightly); **~кúдывать**,

⟨**~кúнуть**⟩ [20] weigh; estimate (approximately); **~кúнуть в умé** *fig.* ponder, weigh up; **-ся** pretend *or* feign to be, act (the Т)

приклáд m [1] *винтовки* butt

приклáд|нóй [14] applied; **~ывать** [1], ⟨**приложи́ть**⟩ [16] (**к** Д) apply (to), put (on); *к письму́ и т. д.* enclose (with); *печать* affix a seal

приклéи|вать [1], ⟨**~ть**⟩ [13] paste

приключá|ться *coll.* [1], ⟨**~и́ться**⟩ [16 *e.*; 3rd *p. only*] happen, occur; **~éние** n [12] (**~éнческий** [16] of) adventure(…)

прико́|вывать [1], ⟨**~вáть**⟩ [7 *e.*; -кую́, -куёшь] chain; *внимание и т. д.* arrest; **~лáчивать** [1], ⟨**~лоти́ть**⟩ [15] nail (on, **к** к), fasten with nails; **~лóть** → **прикáлывать**; **~мандирóвать** [7] *pf.* attach; **~сновéние** n [12] touch, contact; **~снýться** → **прикасáться**

прикрáс|а f [5] *coll.* embellishment; **без** ~ unvarnished

прикреп|и́ть(ся) → **~ля́ть(ся)**; **~ля́ть** [28], ⟨**~и́ть**⟩ [14 *e.*; -плю́, пи́шь; -плённый] fasten; attach; **-ся** register (at, with **к** Д)

прикри́к|ивать [1], ⟨**~нуть**⟩ [20] shout (at **на** В)

прикры|вáть [1], ⟨**~ть**⟩ [22] cover; (*защищать*) protect; **~тие** n [12] cover, escort (*a. mil*); *fig.* cloak

прилáвок m [1; -вка] (*shop*) counter

прилагá|тельное n [14] *gr.* adjective (*a.* **и́мя ~тельное**); **~ть** [1], ⟨**приложи́ть**⟩ [16] (**к** Д) enclose; apply (to); *усилия* take, make (*efforts*); **~емый** enclosed

прила́|живать [1], ⟨**~дить**⟩ [15] fit to, adjust to

приле|гáть [1] **1.** (**к** Д) (ad)join, border; **2.** ⟨**~чь**⟩ [26 г/ж: -ля́гу, -ля́жешь, -ля́гут; -лёг, легла́, -ля́г(те)!] lie down (for a while); **3.** *об одежде* fit (closely); **~жá-ние** n [12] diligence; **~жный** [14; -жен, -жна] industrious; **~пля́ть** [28], ⟨**~пи́ть**⟩ [14] stick to top, **~тáть** [1], ⟨**~тéть**⟩ [11] arrive by air, fly in; **~чь** → **~гáть 2**

прили́в m [1] flood, flow; *fig. крови́* rush; **~в энéргии** surge of energy; **~вáть** [1], ⟨**~ть**⟩ [-лью́, -льёшь; → **лить**]

П

flow; rush to; ~**па́ть**[1], ⟨~пнуть⟩ [21] stick; ~**ть** → ~**ва́ть**

прили́ч|ие *n* [12] decency, decorum; ~**ный** [14; -чен, -чна] decent, proper; *coll.* sum and *m. д.* decent, fair

приложе́н|ие *n* [12] enclosure (*document with a letter etc.*); *журнальное* supplement; *сил и т. д.* application (putting to use); *в книге* appendix, addendum; *gr.* apposition; ~**и́ть** → **прикла́дывать** & **прилага́ть**

прима́нка *f* [5; *g/pl.:* -нок] bait, lure; (*fig.*) enticement

примен|е́ние *n* [12] application; use; ~**и́мый** [14 *sh.*] applicable; ~**и́тельно** in conformity with; ~**я́ть** [28], ⟨~и́ть⟩ [13; -еню́, -е́нишь; -енённый] apply (**к** Д to); use, employ

приме́р *m* [1] example; **привести́ в** ~ cite as an example; **не в** ~ *coll.* unlike; **к** ~**у** *coll.* → **наприме́р**; ~**ивать** [1], ⟨~**и́ть**⟩ [13] try on; fit; ~**ка** *f* [5; *g/pl.:* -рок] trying on; fitting; ~**ный** [14; -рен, -рна] exemplary; (*приблизи́тельный*) approximate; ~**я́ть** [28] → ~**ива́ть**

при́месь *f* [8] admixture; *fig.* touch

приме́|та *f* [5] mark, sign; *дурная* omen; **на** ~**те** in view; ~**тный** → **заме́тный**; ~**ча́ние** *n* [12] (foot)note; ~**ча́тельный** [14; -лен, -льна] notable, remarkable

примире́н|ие *n* [12] reconciliation; ~**и́тельный** [14; -лен, -льна] conciliatory; ~**я́ть(ся)** [28] → **мири́ть(ся)**

примити́вный [14; -вен, -вна] primitive, crude

прим|кну́ть → ~**ыка́ть**; ~**о́рский** [16] coastal, seaside…; ~**о́чка** *f* [5; *g/pl.:* -чек] lotion; ~**ула** *f* [5] primrose; ~**ус** *m* [1] *trademark* Primus (stove); ~**ча́ться** [4 *e.;* -мчу́сь, -чи́шься] *pf.* come in a great hurry; ~**ыка́ть** [1], ⟨~кну́ть⟩ [20] join (*v/t.* **к** Д); *о здании и т. д. impf.* adjoin

принадл|ежа́ть [4 *e.;* -жу́, -жи́шь] belong (**[к]** Д to); ~**е́жность** *f* [8] belonging (**к** P to); *pl.* accessories

принести́ → **приноси́ть**

принима́ть [1], ⟨приня́ть⟩ [приму́, -и́мешь; при́нял, -а́, -о; при́нятый -ят,

á, -о)] take (*a.* over; *за* B for; *measures*); *предложение* accept; *гостей* receive; *в школу и т. д.* admit (**в, на** B [in] to); *закон и т. д.* pass, adopt; *обязанности* assume; ~ **на себя́** take (up)on o.s., undertake; ~ **на свой счёт** take as referring to o.s.; -**ся** [-ня́лся, -ла́сь] (*за* B) start; begin; set to, get down to; *coll.* take in hand; *bot., med.* take effect (injections)

приноро́виться [14 *e.;* -влю́сь, -ви́шься] *pf. coll.* adapt o.s. to

прин|оси́ть [15], ⟨~ести́⟩ [24 -с-: -есу́; -ёс, -есла́] bring (*a.* forth, in), *плоды* yield; make (sacrifice **в** B); ~**оси́ть по́льзу** be of use *or* of benefit

прину|ди́тельный [14; -лен, -льна] forced, compulsory, coercive; ~**жда́ть** [1], ⟨~ди́ть⟩ [15] force, compel, constrain; ~**жде́ние** *n* [12] compulsion, coercion, constraint (**по** Д under)

при́нцип *m* [1] principle; **в** ~**е** in principle; **из** ~**а** on principle; ~**иа́льный** [14; -лен, -льна] of principle; guided by principle

приня́|тие *n* [12] taking, taking up; acceptance; admission (**в, на** B to); *закона и т. д.* passing, adoption; ~**тый** [14] customary; ~**ть(ся)** → **принима́ть(ся)**

приобре|та́ть [1], ⟨~сти́⟩ [25 -т-] acquire, obtain, get; buy; ~**те́ние** *n* [12] acquisition

приоб|ща́ть [1], ⟨~щи́ть⟩ [16 *e.;* -щу́, -щи́шь; -щённый] (**к** Д) *документ* file; introduce (to); **-ся** join (in); consort with

приостан|а́вливать [1], ⟨~ови́ть⟩ [14] call a halt to (*v/i.* **-ся**); *law* suspend

припа́док *m* [1; -дка] fit, attack

припа́сы *m/pl.* [1] supplies, stores; **съестны́е** ~ provisions

припа́ть[1] *pf.* solder (**к** Д to)

припе́|в *m* [1] refrain; ~**ка́ть** [1], ⟨~чь⟩ [26] *coll.* (*of the sun*) burn, be hot

припи́с|ка*f*[5; *g/pl.:*-сок] postscript; addition; ~**ывать** [1], ⟨~а́ть⟩ [3] ascribe, attribute (**к** Д to)

припла́та *f* [5] extra payment

припло́д *m* [1] increase (*in number of animals*)

приплы|ва́ть[1], ⟨∠ть⟩ [23] swim; sail (**к** Д up to)

приплю́снутый [14] flat (*nose*)

приподн|има́ть [1], ⟨∠я́ть⟩ [-ниму́, -ни́мешь; -по́днял, -á, -о; -по́днятый -ят, -á, -о] lift *or* raise (**-ся** rise) (a little); ∠я́тый [14] *настрое́ние* elated; animated

приполз|а́ть[1], ⟨∠ти́⟩ [24] creep up, in

припом|ина́ть[1], ⟨∠нить⟩ [13] remember, recollect; **он тебе́ э́то ∠нит** he'll get even with you for this

приправ|а f [5] seasoning; dressing; ∠ля́ть [28], ⟨∠ить⟩ [14] season; dress

припух|а́ть[1], ⟨∠нуть⟩ [21] swell (a little)

прира|ба́тывать[1], ⟨∠бо́тать⟩ [1] earn in addition

прира́вн|ивать[1], ⟨∠я́ть⟩ [28] equate (with); place on the same footing (as)

прира|ста́ть [1], ⟨∠сти́⟩ [24 -ст-: -стёт; -рóс, -слá] take; grow (**к** Д to); increase (**на** В by); ∠ще́ние n [12] increment

приро́|да f [5] nature; **от ∠ды** by nature, congenitally; **по ∠де** by nature, naturally; ∠дный [14] natural; *a.* **∼ жждённый** [14] (in)born, innate; ∠ст m [1] increase, growth

прируч|а́ть[1], ⟨∠и́ть⟩ [16 е.; -чу́, -чи́шь; -чённый] tame

при|са́живаться [1], ⟨∠се́сть⟩ [25; -ся́ду; -сéл] sit down (for a while), take a seat

присв|а́ивать [1], ⟨∠о́ить⟩ [13] appropriate; *сте́пень и т. д.* confer ([up] on Д); **∠о́ить зва́ние** promote to the rank (of); **∠о́ить и́мя** name; ∠ое́ние n [12] appropriation

присе|да́ть [1], ⟨∠сть⟩ [25; -ся́ду, -сéл] sit down; squat; ∠ст m [1]: **в оди́н ∠ст** at one sitting; ∠сть → **∠да́ть & при∠са́живаться**

приско́рб|ие n [12] sorrow; regret; ∠ный [14; -бен, -бна] regrettable, deplorable

присла́ть → **присыла́ть**

прислон|я́ть[28], ⟨∠и́ть⟩ [13] lean (*v/i.* **-ся; к** Д against)

прислу́|га[5] maid; servant; ∠живать[1] wait (up)on (Д), serve; ∠живаться

⟨∠шаться⟩ [1] listen, pay attention (**к** Д to)

присм|а́тривать [1], ⟨∠отре́ть⟩ [9; -отрю́, -о́тришь; -о́тренный] look after (**за** Т); *coll.новый дом и т. д.* find; **-ся** (**к** Д) peer, look narrowly (at); examine (closely); *к кому-л.* size s.o. up; *к рабо-те и т. д.* familiarize o.s., get acquainted (with); ∠о́тр m [1] care, supervision; surveillance; ∠отре́ть(ся) → **∠а́тривать(ся)**

присоедин|е́ние n [12] addition; *pol.* annexation; ∠я́ть [28], ⟨∠и́ть⟩ [13] (**к** Д) join (*a.* **-ся**); connect, attach (to); annex, incorporate

приспосо́б|ить(ся) → **∠ля́ть(ся); ∠ле́-ние** n [12] adaptation; (*устройство*) device; ∠ля́ть[28], ⟨∠ить⟩ [14] fit, adapt (**-ся** o.s.; **к** Д, **под** В to, for)

приста|ва́ть [5], ⟨∠ть⟩ [-а́ну, -а́нешь] (**к** Д) stick (to); *к кому-л.* bother, pester; *о лодке* put in; *о судне* tie up; ∠вить → **∼вля́ть; ∠вка** f [5; *g/pl.*: -вок] *gr.* prefix; ∼вля́ть[28], ⟨∠вить⟩ [14] (**к** Д) set, put (to), lean (against); (*приделать*) add on; ∠льный [14; -лен, -льна] steadfast, intent; ∠нь f [8; *from g/pl. e.*] landing stage; quay, wharf, pier; ∠ть → **∼ва́ть**

пристёг|ивать [1], ⟨пристегну́ть⟩ [20] button (up), fasten

пристра́|ивать [1], ⟨∠о́ить⟩ [13] (**к** Д) add *or* attach (to); settle; place; provide; **-ся** *coll.* → **устра́иваться**; join

пристра́ст|ие n [12] predilection, weakness (**к** Д for); bias; ∠ный [14; -тен, -тна] bias(s)ed, partial (**к** Д to)

пристре́ли|вать[1], ⟨∠ть⟩ [13; -стрелю́, -éлишь] shoot down

пристр|о́ить(ся) → **∼а́ивать(ся)**; ∠о́й-ка f [5; *g/pl.*: -óек] annex(e); out-house

при́ступ m [1] *mil.* assault, onslaught, storm (by Т); *med.* fit, attack; *боли* pang; *болезни* bout; ∠а́ть [1], ⟨∠и́ть⟩ [14] set about, start, begin

присужда́ть [1], ⟨∠ди́ть⟩ [15; -уждён-ный] (**к** Д) *law* sentence to; condemn to; *приз и т. д.* award; ∠жде́ние n [12] awarding; adjudication

прису́тств|ие n [12] presence (in **в** П; of mind **ду́ха**); ∠овать[7] be present (**на,**

в, при П at); **~ующий** [17] present

прис|ущий [17 *sh.*] inherent (in Д)

прис|ыла́ть [1], ⟨~ла́ть⟩ [-шлю́, -шлёшь; при́сланный] send (**за** Т for)

прися|га f [5] oath (**под** Т on); **~га́ть** [1], ⟨~гну́ть⟩ [20] swear (to); **~жный** [14] juror; **суд ~жных** jury; *coll.* born, inveterate

прита|и́ться [13] *pf.* hide; keep quiet; **~́скивать** [1], ⟨~щи́ть⟩ [16] drag, haul (**-ся** *coll.* o.s.; **к** Д [up] to); *coll.* bring (come)

притвор|и́ть(ся) → **~я́ть(ся)**; **~ный** [14; -рен, -рна] feigned, pretended, sham; **~ство** n [9] pretense, -nce; **~я́ть** [28], ⟨~и́ть⟩ [13; -орю́, -о́ришь; -о́ренный] leave ajar; **-ся** [13] feign, pretend (to be Т); be ajar

притесн|е́ние n [12] oppression; **~и́тель** m [4] oppressor; **~я́ть** [28], ⟨~и́ть⟩ [13] oppress

притих|а́ть [1], ⟨~нуть⟩ [21] become silent, grow quiet; *ветер* abate

прито́к m [1] tributary; influx (*a. fig.*)

прито́м (and) besides

прито́н m [1] den

при́торный [14; -рен, -рна] too sweet, cloying (*a. fig.*)

притр|а́гиваться [1], ⟨~о́нуться⟩ [20] touch (*v/t.* **к** Д)

притуп|ля́ть [1], ⟨~и́ть⟩ [14] (**-ся** become) blunt; *fig.* dull

при́тча f [5] parable

притя́|гивать [1], ⟨~ну́ть⟩ [19] drag, pull; *о магните* attract; *coll.* → **привлека́ть**; **~жа́тельный** [14] *gr.* possessive; **~же́ние** n [12] (*phys.*) attraction; **~за́ние** n [12] claim, pretension (**на** В to); **~ну́ть** → **~гивать**

приу|ро́чить [16] *pf.* time, date (for *or* to coincide with **к** Д); **~са́дебный** [14]: **~са́дебный уча́сток** plot adjoining the (farm)house; **~ча́ть** [1], ⟨~чи́ть⟩ [16] accustom; train

при|хва́рывать *coll.* [1], ⟨~хворну́ть⟩ [20] be(come *pf.*) unwell

прихо́д m [1] **1.** arrival, coming; **2.** *comm.* receipt(s); **3.** *eccl.* parish; **~и́ть** [15], ⟨прийти́⟩ [приду́, -дёшь; пришёл, -шла́, -ше́дший; *g. pt.*: придя́] come

(to), arrive (**в, на** В in, at, **за** Т for); **~и́ть в упа́док** fall into decay; **~и́ть в я́рость** fly into a rage; **~и́ть в го́лову, на ум**, *etc.* think of, cross one's mind, take into one's head; **~и́ть в себя́** (*or* **чу́вство**) come to (o.s.);**-ся** *родственником* be; *праздник* fall (**в** В on, **на** В to); **мне ~ится** I have to, must; **~ский** [16] parish...

прихож|а́нин m [1; *pl.* -а́не, -а́н] parishioner; **~ая** f [17] → **пере́дняя**

прихот|ли́вый [14 *sh.*] *узор* fanciful; **~ь** f [8] whim

прихра́мывать [1] limp slightly

прице́|л m [1] sight; **~ливаться** [1], ⟨~литься⟩ [13] (take) aim (at **в** В)

прице́п m [1] trailer; **~ля́ть** [28], ⟨~и́ть⟩ [14] hook on (**к** Д to); couple; **-ся** stick, cling; → **a. приста́(ва́)ть**

прича́л m [1] mooring; **~ивать** [1], ⟨~и́ть⟩ [13] moor

прича́|стие n [12] *gr.* participle; *eccl.* Communion; the Eucharist; **~стный** [14; -тен, -тна] participating *or* involved (**к** Д in); **~ща́ть** [1], ⟨~сти́ть⟩ [15 *e.*: -ащу́, -асти́шь; -ащённый] administer (**-ся** receive) Communion; **~ще́ние** n [12] receiving Communion

причём moreover; in spite of the fact that; while

причёс|ка f [5; *g/pl.*: -сок] haircut; hairdo, coiffure; **~ывать** [1], ⟨причеса́ть⟩ [3] do, brush, comb (**-ся** one's hair)

причи́н|а f [5] cause; reason (**по** Д for); **по ~е** because of; **по той и́ли ино́й ~е** for some reason or other; **~я́ть** [28], ⟨~и́ть⟩ [13] cause, do

причисля́ть [28], ⟨~сли́ть⟩ [13] rank, number (**к** Д among); **~та́ние** n [12] (ritual) lamentation; **~та́ть** [1] lament; **~та́ться** [1] be due, (p.: **с** Р) have to pay

причу́д|а f [5] whim, caprice; *хара́ктера* oddity; **~ливый** [14 *sh.*] odd; quaint; *coll.* whimsical, fanciful

при|ше́лец m [1; -льца] newcomer, stranger; a being from space; **~ши́бленный** *coll.* [14] dejected; **~шива́ть** [1], ⟨~ши́ть⟩ [-шью, -шьёшь, *etc.* → **шить**] (**к** Д) sew ([on] to); **~щемля́ть** [28], ⟨~щеми́ть⟩ [14 *e.*: -млю́, ми́шь;

-млённый pinch, squeeze; **~щёпка** f [5; g/pl.: -пок] clothes-peg; **~щу́ривать** [1], ⟨**~щу́рить**⟩ [13] → **жму́рить**

прию́т m [1] refuge, shelter; **~и́ть** [15 e.; -ючу́, -юти́шь] pf. give shelter (v/i. **-ся**)

прия́|тель m [4], **~тельница** f [5] friend; **~тельский** [16] friendly; **~тный** [14; -тен, -тна] pleasant, pleasing, agreeable

про coll. (В) about, for, of; **~ себя́** to o.s., (read) silently

про́ба f [5] *для анализа* sample; *о золоте* standard; *на изделии* hallmark

пробе́|г m [1] *sport* run, race; **~га́ть** [1], ⟨**~жа́ть**⟩ [4 e.; -егу́, -ежи́шь, -гу́т] run (through, over), pass (by); *расстояние* cover; *глазами* skim

пробе́л m [1] blank, gap (a. fig.)

проби|ва́ть [1], ⟨**~ть**⟩ [-бью́, -бьёшь; -бей(те)!; пробил, -а, -о] break through; pierce, punch; **-ся** fight (or make) one's way (**сквозь** B through); *bot* come up; *солнце* shine through; pass (by), ⟨**про-бра́ть**⟩ [-беру́, -рёшь, → **брать**] coll. scold; *до костей* chill (to the bone); **-ся** -бра́лся, -ла́сь, -ло́сь force one's way (**сквозь** B through); steal, slip; **~ка** f [5; g/pl.: -рок] test tube; **~ть(ся)** → **~ва́ть(ся)**

про́бк|а f [5; g/pl.:-бок] cork (*material of bottle*); stopper, plug; *el.* fuse; *fig.* traffic jam; **~овый** [14] cork…

пробле́ма f [5] problem; **~ти́чный** [14; -чен, -чна] problematic(al)

про́блеск m [1] gleam; flash; **~ наде́жды** ray of hope

про́бный [14] trial…, test…; **экземпля́р** specimen…, sample…; **~ный ка́мень** touchstone (a. *fig.*); **~овать** [5], ⟨по-⟩ try; *на вкус* taste

пробо́ина f [5] hole; *naut.* leak

пробо́р m [1] parting (*of the hair*)

пробра́ться → **пробира́ть(ся)**

пробу|жда́ть [1], ⟨**~ди́ть**⟩ [15; -уждён-ный] waken, rouse; **-ся** awake, wake up; **~жде́ние** n [12] awakening

пробы́ть [-бу́ду, -бу́дешь; пробы́л, -á, -о] pf. stay

прова́л m [1] collapse; *fig.* failure; **~ивать** [1], ⟨**~и́ть**⟩ [13; -алю́ -а́лишь; -а́ленный] *на экзамене* fail; **~ивай(те)!**

coll. beat it!; **-ся**; collapse, fall in; fail, flunk; (*исчезнуть*) coll. disappear, vanish

прове́|дать coll. [1] pf. visit; (*узнать*) find out; **~де́ние** n [12] carrying out, implementation; **~зти́** → **провози́ть**; **~рить** → **~ря́ть**; **~рка** f [5; g/pl.: -рок] inspection, examination, check, control; **~ря́ть** [28], ⟨**~рить**⟩ [13] inspect, examine, check (up on), control; **~сти́** → **проводи́ть**; **~тривать** [1], ⟨**~трить**⟩ [13] air, ventilate

провини́ться [13] pf. commit an offense (-nce), be guilty (**в** П of), offend (**пе́ред** Т p.; **в** П with); **~нциа́льный** [14; -лен, -льна] mst. *fig.* provincial; **~нция** f [7] province(s)

про́вод m [1; pl.: -да́, etc. e.] wire, line; *el.* lead; **~ди́мость** f [8] conductivity; **~ди́ть** [15] **1.** ⟨**провести́**⟩ [25] lead, a. *el. impf.* conduct, guide; (*осуществлять*) carry out (or through), realize, put (*into practice*); put or get through; pass; spend (*время*; **за** Т); *линию и т. д.* draw; *водопро-вод и т. д.* lay; *политику* pursue; *со-брание* hold; coll. trick, cheat; **2.** → **~жа́ть**; **~дка** f [5; g/pl.: -док] installation; *el.* wiring; *tel.* line, wire(s); **~дни́к** m [1 e.] guide; *rail., el.* conductor (*Brt. rail.* guard); **~жа́ть** [1], ⟨**~ди́ть**⟩ [15] see (off), accompany; *глазами* follow with one's eyes; **~з** m [1] conveyance; transport(ation)

провозгла|ша́ть [1] ⟨**~си́ть**⟩ [15 e.;-ашу́, -аси́шь; -ашённый] proclaim; **~шать** propose

провози́ть [15], ⟨**провезти́**⟩ [24] convey, transport, bring (with one)

провока́|тор m [1] agent provocateur; instigator; **~ция** f [7] provocation

проволо́ка f [5] wire; **~о́чка** coll. f [5; g/pl.:-чек] delay (**с** Т in), protraction

прово́р|ный [14; -рен, -рна] quick, nimble, deft; **~ство** n [9] quickness, nimbleness, deftness

провоци́ровать [7] ⟨*im*⟩pf., a. ⟨с-⟩ provoke (**на** В to)

прогада́ть [1] pf. coll. miscalculate (**на** П by)

П

прога́лина f [5] glade

прогл|а́тывать [1], ⟨~оти́ть⟩ [15] swallow, gulp; *coll.* **~а́тывать язы́к** lose one's tongue; **~а́дывать**[1]**1.**⟨~яде́ть⟩ [11] overlook; (*просма́тривать*) look over (*or* through); **2.** ⟨~яну́ть⟩ [19] peep out, appear

прогн|а́ть → **прогоня́ть**; ~о́з*m* [1] (**пого́ды**) (weather) forecast; *med.* prognosis

прого|ва́ривать[1], ⟨~вори́ть⟩ [13] say; talk; **-ся** blab (out) (*v/t.* **о** П); **~ло-да́ться**[1]*pf.* eat *or* feel hungry; **~ня́ть** [28], ⟨прогна́ть⟩ [-гоню́, -го́нишь; -гна́л, -á, -о; про́гнанный] drive (away); *coll.* **рабо́ты** fire; **~ра́ть** [1], ⟨~ре́ть⟩ [9] burn through; *coll.* (*обанкро́титься*) go bust

прого́рклый [14] rancid

програ́мм|а f [5] program(me *Brt.*); **~и́ровать** [1] program(me); **~и́ст** *m* [1] (computer) program(m)er

прогре́сс *m* [1] progress; **~и́вный** [14; -вен, -вна] progressive; **~и́ровать** [1] (make) progress; *о боле́зни* get progressively worse

прогрыз|а́ть [1], ⟨~ть⟩ [24; *pt. st.*] gnaw *or* bite through

прогу́л *m* [1] truancy; absence from work; **~ивать** [1], ⟨~я́ть⟩ [28] shirk (work); play truant; **-ся** take (*or* go for a) walk; **~ка** f [5; *g/pl.*:-лок] walk (**на** В for), stroll, *верхо́м* ride; **~ьщик** *m* [1] shirker; truant; **~я́ть(ся)** → **~ивать(ся)**

прода|ва́ть [5], ⟨~ть⟩ [-да́м, -да́шь, *etc.*, → **дать**]; про́дал, -á, -о; про́данный (про́дан, -á, -о)] sell; **-ся** (*v/i.*) be for *or* on sale; **~ве́ц** *m* [1; -вца́], **~вщи́ца** f [5] seller, sales(wo)man, (store) clerk, *Brt.* shop assistant; **~жа** f [5] sale (**в** П on; **в** В for); **~жный** [14] for sale; *цена́* sale; [-жен, -жна] venal, corrupt; **~ть(ся)** → **~ва́ть(ся)**

продви|га́ть [1], ⟨~нуть⟩ [20] move, push (ahead); **-ся** advance; **~же́ние** *n* [12] advance(ment)

проде́л|ать → **~ывать**; **~ка** f [5; *g/pl.*: -лок] trick, prank; **~ывать**, ⟨~ать⟩ [1] *отве́рстие* break through, make; *ра-*

бо́ту и т. д. carry through *or* out, do

проде́ть [-де́ну, -де́нешь; -де́нь (-те)]!; -де́тый] *pf.* pass, run through; *ни́тку* thread

продл|ева́ть [1], ⟨~и́ть⟩ [13] extend, prolong; **~е́ние** *n* [12] extension, prolongation

продово́льств|енный[14] food…; grocery…; **~ие** *n* [12] food(stuffs), provisions *pl.*

продол|гова́тый [14 *sh.*] oblong; **~ка-тель** *m* [4] continuer; **~жа́ть** [1], ⟨~жить⟩ [16] continue, go on; lengthen; prolong; **-ся** last; **~же́ние** *n* [12] continuation; *рома́на* sequel; **~же́ние сле́-дует** to be continued; **~жи́тельность** f [8] duration; **~жи́тельный** [14; -лен, -льна] long; protracted; **~жить(ся)** → **~жа́ть(ся)**; **~ьный** [14] longitudinal

продро́гнуть [21] *pf.* be chilled to the marrow

проду́к|т *m* [1] product; *pl. a.* foodstuffs; **~ти́вный** [14; -вен, -вна] productive; fruitful; **~то́вый** [14] grocery (*store*); **~ция** f [7] production, output

проду́м|ывать, ⟨~ать⟩ [1] think over, think out

про|еда́ть[1], ⟨~е́сть⟩ [-е́м, -е́шь, *etc.*, → **есть¹**] eat through, corrode; *coll.* spend on food

прое́з|д *m* [1] passage, thoroughfare; **~да нет!** "no thoroughfare!"; **~дом** on the way, en route; **пла́та за ~д** fare; **~дить** → **~жа́ть**; **~дно́й**[14]: **~дно́й биле́т** season ticket; **~жа́ть** [1], ⟨про-е́хать⟩ [-е́ду, -е́дешь; -езжа́й(те)!] pass, drive *or* ride through (*or* past, by); travel; **-ся** *coll.* take a drive *or* ride; **~жий** [17] (through) travel(l)er; passerby transient; **~жая доро́га** thoroughfare

прое́к|т *m* [1] project, plan, scheme; *до-ку́мента* draft; **~ти́ровать** [7], ⟨с-⟩ project, plan; design; **~ция** f [7] *math.* projection; view

прое́|сть → **~да́ть**; **~хать** → **~зжа́ть**

проже́ктор *m* [1] searchlight

прожи|ва́ть [1], ⟨~ть⟩ [-иву́, -ивёшь; про́жил, -á, -о; про́житый (про́жит, -á, -о)] live; *pf.* spend; **~га́ть**[1], ⟨проже́чь⟩ [26 г/ж: -жгу́, -жжёшь] burn (through);

~гáть жизнь *coll.* live fast; ~точный [14]: ~точный мúнимум *m* living *or* subsistence wage; ~ть → ~вáть

прожóрлив|ость *f* [8] gluttony, voracity; ~ый [14 *sh.*] gluttonous

прóза *f* [5] prose; ~ик *m* [1] prose writer; ~úческий [16] prosaic; prose…

прó|звище *n* [11] nickname: **по** ~звищу nicknamed; ~зевáть → ~зевáть & зевáть *coll.* [1] *pf.* miss; let slip; ~зóрливый [14 *sh.*] perspicacious; ~зрáчный [14; -чен, -чна] transparent; *a. fig.* limpid; ~зрéть [9] *pf.* recover one's sight; begin to see clearly; perceive; ~зывáть [1], ⟨~звáть⟩ [-зовý, -вёшь; -звáл, -á, -о; прóзванный] (T) nickname; ~зябáть [1] vegetate; ~зя́бнуть[21] *coll.* → продрóгнуть

проúгр|ывать [1], ⟨~áть⟩ [1] lose (at play); *coll.* play; -ся lose all one's money; ~ыш *m* [1] loss (**в** П)

произве|дéние *n* [12] work, product(ion); ~вестú → ~одúть; ~одúтель *m* [4] producer; (*animal*) male parent, sire; ~одúтельность *f* [8] productivity; *завóда* output; ~одúтельный [14; -лен, -льна] productive; ~одúть [15], ⟨~естú⟩ [25] (-ся *impf.* be) make (made), carry (-ried) out, execute(d), effect(ed); (*tech. usu. impf.*) produce(d); *на свет* bring forth; *impf.* derive (d; **от** P from); ~óдный [14] *слово* derivative (*a. su. f math.*); ~óдственный[14] production…; manufacturing, works…; ~óдство *n* [9] production, manufacture; *coll.* plant, works, factory (**на** П at)

произв|óл *m* [1] arbitrariness; *судьбы* mercy; tyranny; ~óльный [14; -лен, -льна] arbitrary; ~носúть [15], ⟨~нестú⟩ [24 -с] pronounce; *речь* deliver, make; utter; ~ношéние *n* [12] pronunciation; ~ойтú → произходúть

прóис|ки *m/pl.* [1] intrigues; ~ходúть [15], ⟨произойтú⟩ [-зойдёт; -зошёл, -шла; *g. pt.*: -зошедшá] take place, happen; (*возникать*) arise, result (**от** P from); *о человеке* descend (**от, из** P from); ~хождéние *n* [12] origin (by [= birth] **по** Д); descent; ~шéствие

n [12] incident, occurrence, event

пройтú(сь) → ~ходúть & ~хáживаться

прок *coll. m* [1] → пóльза

прокáз|а *f* [5] **1.** prank, mischief; **2.** *med.* leprosy; ~ник *m* [1], ~ница *f* [5] → *coll.* шалýн(ья); ~ничать [1] *coll.* → шалúть

прокá|лывать [1], ⟨проколóть⟩ [17] pierce; perforate; *шину* puncture; ~пывать[1], ⟨прокопáть⟩ [1] dig (through); ~рмливать[1], ⟨прокормúть⟩ [14] support, nourish; feed

прокáт *m* [1] hire (**на** B for); *фильма* distribution; ~úть(ся) [15] *pf.* take (take) a drive *or* ride; ~ывать, ⟨~áть⟩ [1] mangle; ride; -ся *coll.* ~úться

проклáд|ка *f* [5; *g/pl.*: -док] трубопровóда construction; *tech.* gasket, packing; ~ывать [1], ⟨проложúть⟩ [16] lay (*a.* = build); *fig.* pave; force (one's *way* through); *между* interlay

прокл|инáть[1], ⟨~я́сть⟩ [-яну́, -янёшь; прóклял, -á, -о; прóклятый (прóклят, -á, -о)] curse, damn; ~я́тие *n* [12] damnation; ~я́тый[14] cursed, damned

прокóл *m* [1] perforation; *mot.* puncture; ~лóть → прокáлывать; ~пáть → прокáпывать; ~рмúть → прокáрмливать

прокрá|дываться[1], ⟨~сться⟩ [25; *pt. st.*] steal, go stealthily

прокурóр *m* [1] public prosecutor; *на судé* counsel for the prosecution

про|лагáть → ~клáдывать; ~лáмывать[1], ⟨~ломáть⟩ [1] & ⟨~ломúть⟩ [14] break (through); *v/i.* -ся); fracture; ~легáть[1] lie; run; ~лезáть[1], ⟨~лéзть⟩ [24 *st.*] climb *or* get (in[to], through); ~лёт*m*[1] flight; *мóста* span; *лéстницы* well; ~летариáт *m* [1] proletariat; ~летáрий *m* [3], ~летáрский [16] proletarian; ~летáть [1], ⟨~летéть⟩ [15] fly (covering a certain distance); fly (past, by, over); *fig.* flash, flit

проли́|в *m* [1] strait (*e.g.* ~**в Паде-Калé** Strait of Dover *the Pas de Calais*); ~вáть[1], ⟨~ть⟩ [-лью, -льёшь; лéй(те)!; прóлило; прóлитый (прóлит, -á, -о) spill; (*v/i.* -ся); *слёзы, свет* shed;

~вной [14]: **~вно́й до́ждь** pouring rain, pelting rain; **~ть** → **~ва́ть**

проло́|г *m* [1] prologue; **~жи́ть** → **прокла́дывать**; **~м** *m* [1] breach; **~ма́ть**, **~мить** → **прола́мывать**

про́мах *m* [1] miss; blunder (make **дать** or **сде́лать** a. slip, fail); *coll.* **он па́рень не** ~ he is no fool; **~иваться** [1], ⟨~ну́ться⟩ [20] miss

промедле́ние *n* [12] delay; procrastination

промежу́то|к *m* [1; -тка] interval (**в** П at; **в** В of); period; **~чный** [14] intermediate

проме́|лькну́ть → **мелькну́ть**; **~нивать** [1], ⟨~ня́ть⟩ [28] exchange (**на** В for); **~рза́ть** [1], ⟨промёрзнуть⟩ [21] freeze (through); *coll.* → **продро́гнуть**

промо|ка́ть [1], ⟨~кнуть⟩ [21] get soaked *or* drenched; *impf. only* let water through; not be water proof; **~лча́ть** [4 *e.*; -чу́, -чи́шь] *pf.* keep silent; **~** [16] *pf.* get soaked *or* drenched

промтова́ры *m/pl.* [1] manufactured goods (*other than food stuffs*)

промча́ться [4] *pf.* dart, tear *or* fly (past)

промы|ва́ть [1], ⟨~ть⟩ [22] wash (out, away); *med.* bathe, irrigate

про́мы|сел *m* [1; -сла]: **наро́дные ~слы** folk crafts; **~сло́вый** [14]: **~словый сезо́н** fishing (hunting, *etc.*) season; **~ть** → **~ва́ть**

промы́шлен|ник *m* [1] manufacturer, industrialist; **~ность** *f* [8] industry; **~ный** [14] industrial

пронести́(сь) → **проноси́ть(ся)**

прон|за́ть [1], ⟨~зи́ть⟩ [15 *e.*; -нжу́, -нзи́шь; -нзённый] pierce, stab; **~зи́тельный** [14; -лен, -льна] shrill, piercing; *взгляд* penetrating; **~за́ивать** [1], ⟨~иза́ть⟩ [3] penetrate; pierce

прони|ка́ть [1], ⟨~кнуть⟩ [21] penetrate; permeate (**че́рез** through); get (in); **-ся** be imbued (T with); **~кнове́ние** *n* [12] penetration; *fig.* fervo(u)r; **~кнове́нный** [14; -е́нен, -е́нна] heartfelt; **~ца́емый** [14 *sh.*] permeable; **~ца́тельный** [14; -лен, -льна] penetrating, searching;

челове́к acute, shrewd

про|носи́ть [15] **1.** ⟨~нести́⟩ [24 -с-: -есу́; -ёс, -есла́] carry (through), by, away); **-ся**, ⟨-сь⟩ *о пу́ле, ка́мне* fly (past, by); pass *or слухи* spread (swiftly); **2.** *pf.* *coll.* wear out; **~ны́рливый** [14 *sh.*] crafty; pushy; **~ню́хать** [1] *coll.* get wind of

прообраз *m* [1] prototype

пропага́нда *f* [5] propaganda

пропа|да́ть [1], ⟨~сть⟩ [25; *pt. st.*] get *or* be lost; *да́ром* go to waste; be missing; *a.* **~сть без ве́сти**); *интере́с* lose, vanish; **~жа** *f* [5] loss; **~сть¹** → **~да́ть**; **~сть²** *f* [8] precipice, abyss; **на краю́ ~сти** on the verge of disaster; *coll.* **~мно́го** lots *or* a lot (of)

пропи|ва́ть [1], ⟨~ть⟩ [-пью, -пьёшь; -пе́й(те)!; про́пил, -а́, -о; про́питый (пропи́т, -а́, -о)] spend on drink

пропис|а́ть(ся) → **~ывать(ся)**; **~ка** *f* [5; *g/pl.*: -сок] registration; **~но́й** [14] capital, → **бу́ква**; **~на́я и́стина** truism; **~ывать** [1], ⟨~а́ть⟩ [3] *med.* prescribe (Д for); register (*v/i.* **-ся**); **~ью** (*write*) in full

пропи́|тывать, ⟨~та́ть⟩ [1] (**-ся** be[come]) steeped in, saturate(d; T with); **~ть** → **~ва́ть**

проплы|ва́ть [1], ⟨~ть⟩ [23] swim *or* sail (by); float, drift (by, past); *fig. joc.* sail (by, past)

пропове́д|ник *m* [1] preacher; **~овать** [1] preach; *fig.* advocate; **~ь** ('про-) *f* [8] *eccl.* sermon

пропол|за́ть [1], ⟨~зти́⟩ [24] creep, crawl (by, through, under); **~ка** *f* [5] weeding

пропорциона́льный [14; -лен, -льна] proportional, proportionate

про́пус|к *m* [1] **1.** [*pl.*: -ки] omission, blank; (*отсу́тствие*) absence; **2.** [*pl.*: -ка́, *etc.e.*] pass, permit; admission; **~ка́ть** [1], ⟨~ти́ть⟩ [15] let pass (*or* through), admit; (*опусти́ть*) omit; *заня́тие и т. д.* miss; let slip; *impf.* (*течь*) leak

прора|ба́тывать, ⟨~бо́тать⟩ *coll.* [1] study; **~ста́ть** [1], ⟨~сти́⟩ [24 -ст-: -стёт; -ро́с, -росла́] germinate; sprout;

shoot (*of plant*)

прорва́ть(ся) → **прорыва́ть(ся)**

проре́з|ать [1], ⟨~а́ть⟩ [3] cut through; **-ся** *о зубах* cut (*teeth*)

проре́ха *f* [5] slit, tear

проро́|к *m* [1] prophet; **~и́ть** [13: -ою́, -о́ишь; -о́ненный] *pf.* utter; **~ческий** [16] prophetic; **~чество** *n* [9] prophecy; **~чить** [16] prophesy

проруб|а́ть [1], ⟨~и́ть⟩ [14] cut (through); **~ь** *f* [8] hole cut in ice

прор|ы́в *m* [1] break; breach; **~ыва́ть** [1] **1.** ⟨~ва́ть⟩ [-ву́, -вёшь; -ва́л, -а́, -о; про́рванный (-ан, -а́, -о)] break through; **-ся** (*v/i.*) break through; burst open; force one's way; **2.** ⟨~ы́ть⟩ [22] dig (through)

про|са́чиваться [1], ⟨~сочи́ться⟩ [16 *е.*; *3rd p. only*] ooze (out), percolate; **~сверли́ть** [13] *pf.* drill, bore (through)

просве́|т *m* [1] *в облаках* gap; (*щель*) chink; *fig.* ray of hope; **~ти́ть** → **~ща́ть & ~чива́ть 2.**; **~тле́ть** [8] *pf.* clear up, brighten up; **~чивать** [1] **1.** shine through, be seen; **2.** ⟨~ти́ть⟩ [15] *med.* X-ray; **~ща́ть** [1], ⟨~ти́ть⟩ [15 *е.*; -ещу́, -ети́шь; -ещённый] enlighten, educate, instruct; **~ще́ние** *n* [12] education; 2**ще́-ние** Enlightenment

про́|седь *f* [8] streaks of gray (*Brt.* grey), grizzly hair; **~се́ивать** [1], ⟨~се́ять⟩ [27] sift; **~се́ка** *f* [5] cutting, opening (*in a forest*); **~сёлочный** [14]: **~сёлочная доро́га** country road, cart track, un-metalled road; **~се́ять** → **~се́ивать**

проси́|живать [1], ⟨~де́ть⟩ [11] sit (up); stay, remain (*for a certain time*); *над чем-л.* spend; **~ть** [15], ⟨по-⟩ ask (В/о П; *у* P/P p. for), beg, request; (*приглаша́ть*) invite; intercede (*за* B for); **прошу́, про́сят** *a.* please; **прошу́!** please come in!; **-ся** (*в, на* B) ask (for; leave [to enter, go]); **~я́ть** [28] *pf.* begin to shine; light up with

проск|ользну́ть [20] *pf.* slip, creep (*в* B in); **~очи́ть** [16] *pf.* rush by, tear by; slip through; fall between *or* through

просл|авля́ть [28], ⟨~а́вить⟩ [14] glorify, make (**-ся** become) famous; **~еди́ть** [15 *е.*; -ежу́, -еди́шь; -еженный] *pf.*

track down; trace; **~ези́ться** [15 *е.*; -ежу́сь, -ези́шься] *pf.* shed (a few) tears

просло́йка *f* [5; *g/pl.*: -оек] layer

про|слу́шать [1] *pf.* hear; (*through*); *med.* auscultate; coll. miss, not catch (*what is said e.g.*); **~сма́тривать** [1], ⟨~смотре́ть⟩ [9; -отрю́, -о́тришь; -о́тренный] survey; view; look through or over; (*не заме́тить*) overlook; **~смо́тр** *m* [1] документов examination, survey; review (*о фильме тж.* preview); **~сну́ться** → **~сыпа́ться**; **~со** *n* [9] millet; **~со́вывать** [1], ⟨~су́нуть⟩ [20] pass or push (through); **~со́х-нуть** → **~сыха́ть**; **~сочи́ться** → **~са́чиваться**; **~спа́ть** → **~сыпа́ть**

проспе́кт[1] *m* [1] avenue

проспе́кт[2] *m* [1] prospectus

просро́ч|ивать [1], ⟨~ить⟩ [16] let lapse *or* expire; exceed the time limit; **~ка** *f* [5; *g/pl.*: -чек] expiration; (*превыше́-ние сро́ка*) exceeding

прост|а́ивать [1], ⟨~оя́ть⟩ [-ою́, -ои́шь] stand stay (*for a certain time*); *tech.* stand idle; **~а́к** *m* [1 *е.*] simpleton

прост|ира́ть [1], ⟨~ере́ть⟩ [12] stretch (*v/i.* **-ся**), extend

прости́тельный [14; -лен, -льна] pardonable, excusable

проститу́тка *f* [5; *g/pl.*: -ток] prostitute

прости́ть(ся) → **проща́ть(ся)**

простоду́ш|ие *n* [12] naïveté; **~ный** [14; -шен, -шна] ingenuous; artless; simple-minded

прост|о́й[1] [14; прост, -а́, -о; *comp.*: про́ще] simple, plain; easy; *мане́ры и т. д.* unaffected, unpretentious; *о лю́дях* ordinary, common; *math.* prime

прост|о́й[2] *m* [3] stoppage, standstill

простоква́ша *f* [5] sour milk, yog(h)urt

просто́|р *m* [1] open (space); freedom (*на* П in); *fig.* scope; **~ре́чие** *n* [12] popular speech; common parlance; **~рный** [14; -рен, -рна] spacious, roomy; **~рта́** *f* [5] simplicity; naïveté; **~я́ть** → **простаива́ть**

простра́н|ный [14; -а́нен, -а́нна] vast; *о ре́чи, письме́* long-winded, verbose; **~ство** *n* [9] space; expanse

простра́ция *f* [7] prostration, complete

physical *or* mental exhaustion

простре́л *m* [1] *coll.* lumbago; **~ивать** [1], ⟨**~и́ть**⟩ [13: -елю́, -е́лишь; -елённый] shoot (through)

просту́|да *f* [5] common cold; **~жа́ть** [1], ⟨**~ди́ть**⟩ [15] chill; **-ся** catch a cold

просту́пок *m* [1; -пка] misdeed; offense (-ce); *law* misdemeano(u)r

простыня́ *f* [6; *pl.:* про́стыни, -ы́нь, *etc.* e.] (bed) sheet

просу́|нуть → **просо́вывать**; **~шивать** [1], ⟨**~ши́ть**⟩ [16] dry thoroughly

просчита́ться [1] *pf.* miscalculate

просыпа́ть [1], ⟨**~проспа́ть**⟩ [-плю́, -пишь; -спа́л, -á, o] oversleep; sleep; *coll.* miss (by sleeping); **-ся**, ⟨про-сну́ться⟩ [20] awake, wake up

просых|а́ть [1], ⟨**~о́хнуть**⟩ [21] get dry, dry out

про́сьба *f* [5] request (*по* П at; *о* П for); please (don't *не* + *inf.*) *у меня́ к вам* ~ I have a favo(u)r to ask you

про|та́лкивать [1], *once* ⟨**~толкну́ть**⟩ [20], *coll.* ⟨**~толка́ть**⟩ [1] push (through); **-ся** force one's way (through); **~та́птывать** [1], ⟨**~топта́ть**⟩ [3] *доро́жку* tread; **~та́скивать** [1], ⟨**~тащи́ть**⟩ [16] carry *or* drag (past, by); *coll.* smuggle in

проте́з ('tes) *m* [1] prosthetic appliance; artificial limb; *зубно́й* ~ false teeth, dentures

проте|ка́ть [1], ⟨**~чь**⟩ [26] *impf. only* (of a river *or* stream) flow, run (by); *ло́дка* leak; *pf.* время pass, elapse; take its course; **~кция** *f* [7] patronage; **~ре́ть** → **протира́ть**; **~ст** *m* [1], **~стова́ть** [7], *v/t.* (*im*)*pf.* & ⟨о-⟩ protest; **~чь** → **~ка́ть**

про́тив (P) against; opposite; *быть* или *име́ть* ~ (have) object(ion; to), mind; **~иться** [14], ⟨вос-⟩ (Д) oppose, object; **~ник** *m* [1] opponent, adversary; enemy; **~ный**¹ [14: -вен, -вна] repugnant, disgusting, offensive, nasty; **~ный**² opposite, contrary; opposing, opposed; *мне* **~но** *a.* I hate; *в* **~ном слу́чае** otherwise

противо|ве́с *m* [1] counterbalance; **~возду́шный** [14] antiaircraft...; **~воз-**

~ду́шная оборо́на air defense (-ce); **~де́йствие** *n* [12] counteraction; (*со-противле́ние*) resistance; **~де́йство-вать** [7] counteract; resist; **~есте́ствен-ный** [14 *sh.*] unnatural; **~зако́нный** [14; -о́нен, -о́нна] unlawful, illegal; **~за-ча́точный** [14] contraceptive; **~пока-за́ние** *n* [12] *med.* contra-indication; **~положность** *f*[8] contrast, opposition (*в* B in); antithesis; **~поло́жный** [14; -жен, -жна] opposite; contrary, op-posed; **~поставля́ть** [28], ⟨-поста́вить⟩ [14] oppose; **~поставле́ние** *n* [12] op-position; **~раке́тный** [14] antimissile; **~речи́вый** [14 *sh.*] contradictory; **~ре́чие** *n* [12] contradiction; **~ре́чить** [16] (Д) contradict; **~стоя́ть** [-ою́, -ои́шь] (Д) withstand; stand against; **~я́дие** *n* [12] antidote

про|тира́ть [1], ⟨**~тере́ть**⟩ [12] wear (through); *стекло́* wipe; **~ткну́ть** → **~тыка́ть**; **~ток** *m* [1] (-токоли́ро-вать** [7] [*im*]*pf.*, *a.*, ⟨за-⟩ take down (the) minutes *pl.*, record; *su. a.* protocol; **~толка́ть**, **~толкну́ть** → **~та́лкивать**; **~топта́ть** → **~та́птывать**; **~торённый** [14] *доро́га* beaten well-trodden; **~то-ти́п** *m* [1] prototype; **~то́чный** [14] flow-ing, running; **~трезви́ться** [28], ⟨-трезви́ться⟩ [5 *e*.: -влюсь, -ви́шься, -влённый] sober up; **~тыка́ть** [1], *once* ⟨-ткну́ть⟩ [20] pierce, skewer; transfix

протя́|гивать [1], ⟨**~ну́ть**⟩ [19] stretch (out), extend, hold out; (*переда́ть*) pass; **~же́ние** *n* [12] extent, stretch (*на* П over, along); (*of time*) space (*на* П for, during); **~жный** [14: -жен, -жна] *звук* drawn-out; **~ну́ть** → **~гивать**

проучи́ть *coll.* [16] *pf.* teach a lesson

профессиона́льный [14] professional; trade... (*e.g.* trade union → **проф-сою́з**); **~ия** *f* [7] profession, trade (*по* Д by); **~ор** *m* [1; *pl.:* -ра́, *etc.* e.] profes-sor; **~ура** *f* [5] professorship; *collect.* the professors

про́филь *m* [4] **1.** profile; **2.** ~ *учи́лища* type of school or college

профо́рма *coll. f* [5] form, formality

профсою́з *m* [1], **~ный** [14] trade union

про|ха́живаться [1], ⟨∼йти́сь⟩ [-йду́сь, -йдёшься; -шёлся, -шла́сь] (go for a walk, stroll; *coll.* have a go at s.o. (**на чей-либо счёт**); ∼хво́ст *coll. m* [1] scoundrel

прохла́д|а *f* [5] coolness; ∼и́тельный [14; -лен, льна́] *∼и́тельные напи́тки* soft drinks; ∼ный [14; -ден, -дна] cool (*a. fig.*), fresh

прохо́д *m* [1] passage; pass; *anat.* duct (**за́дний ∼д** anus); ∼и́мец *m* [1; -мца] rogue, scoundrel; ∼и́мость *f* [8] *доро́ги* passability; *anat.* permeability; ∼ди́ть [15], ⟨пройти́⟩ [пройду́, -дёшь; -шёл; шёдший; про́йденный; *g. pt.*: пройдя́] pass, go (by, through, over, along); take a … course, be; ∼дно́й [14] *двор* (with a) through passage; ∼жде́ние *n* [12] passage, passing; ∼жий *m* [17] passerby

процвета́ть [1] prosper, thrive

проце|ду́ра *f* [5] procedure; ∼жива́ть [1], ⟨∼ди́ть⟩ [15] filter, strain; ∼нт *m* [1] percent(age) (**на** В by); (*usu. pl.*) interest; *ста́вка ∼нта* rate of interest; ∼сс *m* [1] process; *law* trial (**на** П at); ∼ссия [7] procession

прочесть → **прочи́тывать**

про́ч|ий [17] other; *n & a. su.* the rest; **и ∼ее** and so on *or* forth, *etc.*; **ме́жду ∼им** by the way, incidentally; **поми́мо всего́ ∼его** in addition

прочи|сти́ть → ∼ща́ть; ∼тывать, ⟨∼та́ть⟩ [1] & ⟨прочесть⟩ [25 -т-: -чту́, -тёшь; -чёл, -чла́; *g. pt.*: -чтя́, -чтённый] read (through); ∼ть [16] intend (for), have s.o. in mind (**в** В as); *успех* destine (for); ∼ща́ть [1], ⟨∼стить⟩ [15] clean

про́чн|ость *f* [8] durability, firmness; ∼ый [14; -чен, -чна́; -о] firm, solid, strong; *мир* lasting; *зна́ния* sound

прочте́ние *n* [12] reading; perusal; *fig.* interpretation

прочь away → **доло́й; я не ∼** + *inf. coll.* I wouldn't mind …ing

проше́дший [17] past, last (*a. su.* ∼**е́дшее** the past); *gr.* past (tense); ∼**ствие** *n* [12] → *истече́ние*; ∼**лого́дний** [15] last year's; ∼**лый** [14] past (*a. su. n* ∼**лое**), bygone; ∼**мыгну́ть** *coll.* [20]

pf. slip, whisk (by, past)

проща́й(те)! farewell!, goodby(e)!, adieu!; ∼**а́льный** [14] farewell…; *слова́* parting; ∼**а́ние** *n* [12] parting (**при** П, **на** В when, at), leavetaking, farewell; ∼**а́ть** [1], ⟨прости́ть⟩ [15 *е.*; -ощу́, -ости́шь; -ощённый] forgive (*p.* Д), excuse, pardon; **-ся** (**с** Т) take leave of (*p.*), say goodby (to); ∼**е́ние** *n* [12] forgiveness, pardon

прояви́тель *m* [4] *phot.* developer; ∼**и́ть(ся)** → ∼**ля́ть(ся)**; ∼**ле́ние** *n* [12] manifestation, display, demonstration; *phot.* development; ∼**ля́ть** [28], ⟨∼**и́ть**⟩ [14] show, display, manifest; *phot.* develop

проясня́|ться [28], ⟨∼**и́ться**⟩ [13] (*of weather*) clear up (*a. fig.*); brighten

пруд *m* [1 *е.*; в ∼у́] pond

пружи́на *f* [5] spring; **скры́тая ∼** motive

прут *m* [1; *a. е.*; *pl.*: -ья, -ьев] twig; *желе́зный rod*

пры́га|ть [1], *once* ⟨∼**нуть**⟩ [20] jump, spring, leap; ∼**гу́н** *m* [1 *е.*] (*sport*) jumper; ∼**жо́к** *m* [1; -жка́] jump, leap, bound; *в во́ду* dive; ∼**ткий** [16; -ток, -тка, -о] nimble, quick; ∼**ть** *coll. f* [8] agility; speed (**во всю** at full); ∼**щ** *m* [1 *е.*]; ∼**щик** *m* [1] pimple

пряди́льный [14] spinning

пря́|дь *f* [8] lock, tress, strand; ∼**жа** *f* [5] yarn; ∼**жка** *f* [5; *g/pl.*: -жек] buckle

прям|изна́ *f* [5] straightness; ∼**о́й** [14; прям, -а́, -о] straight (*a.* = bee) line (∼**а́я** *su. f*); direct (*a. gr.*); *railroad*…; *у́гол* right; *fig.* straight (-forward), downright, outspoken, frank; ∼**а́я кишка́** rectum; ∼**олине́йный** [14; -е́ен, -е́йна] rectilinear; *fig.*; → ∼**о́й** *fig.*; ∼**ота́** *f* [5] straightforwardness, frankness; ∼**оуго́льник** *m* [1] rectangle; ∼**оуго́льный** [14] rectangular

пря́|ник *m* [1] *имби́рный* gingerbread; **медо́вый ∼ик** honeycake; ∼**ость** *f* [8] spice; ∼**ый** [14 *sh.*] spicy, *fig.* piquant

прясть [25; -ял, -á, -о], ⟨с-⟩ spin

пря́т|ать [3], ⟨с-⟩ hide (*v/i.* **-ся**), conceal; ∼**ки** *f/pl.* [5; *gen.*: -ток] hide-and-seek

псал|о́м *m* [1; -лма́] psalm; ∼**ты́рь** *f* [8] Psalter

П

…евдони́м m [1] pseudonym

…сихиа́тр m [1] psychiatrist; **∠ика** f [5] state of mind; psyche; mentality; **∠и́ческий** [16] mental, psychic(al); **∠и́ческое заболева́ние** mental illness; **∠о́лог** m [1] psychologist; **∠оло́гия** f [7] psychology

птене́ц m [1; -нца́] nestling, fledgling

пти́|ца f [5] bird; **дома́шняя ∠ца** collect. poultry; **∠цево́дство** n [9] poultry farming; **∠чий** [18] bird('s); poultry…; **вид с ∠чьего полёта** bird's-eye view; **∠чка** f [5; g/pl.: -чек] (*галочка*) tick

пу́бли|ка f [5] audience; public; **∠ка́ция** f [7] publication; **∠кова́ть** [7], ⟨о-⟩ publish; **∠ци́ст** m [1] publicist; **∠чный** [14] public; **∠чный дом** brothel

пуга́|ло n [9] scarecrow; **∠а́ть** [1], ⟨ис-, на-⟩, *once* ⟨-ну́ть⟩ [20] (**-ся** be) frighten(ed; of P), scare(d); **∠ли́вый** [14 sh.] timid, fearful

пу́говица f [5] button

пу́дель m [4; pl. a. etc. e.] poodle

пу́др|а f [5] powder; **са́харная ∠а** powdered (*Brt.* caster) sugar; **∠еница** f [5] powder compact; **∠ить** [13], ⟨на-⟩ powder

пуза́тый P [14 sh.] paunchy; **∠о** P n [9] paunch, potbelly

пузыр|ёк m [1; -рька́] vial; a. dim. → **∠ь** m [4 e.] bubble; *anat.* bladder; *coll.* **на ко́же** blister

пулемёт m [1] machine gun

пуль|веризáтор m [1] spray(er); **∠с** m [1] pulse; *coll.* **щу́пать ∠с** feel the pulse; **∠си́ровать** [7] puls(at)e; **∠т** m [1] conductor's stand; *tech.* control panel or desk

пу́ля f [6] bullet

пункт m [1] point, station; place, spot; *докуме́нта* item, clause, article; **по ∠ам** point by point; **∠и́р** m [1] dotted line; **∠уа́льность** f [8] punctuality; accuracy; **∠уа́льный** [14; -лен, -льна] punctual; accurate; **∠уа́ция** f [7] punctuation

пунцо́вый [1] crimson

пунш m [1] punch (*drink*)

пуп|о́к m [1; -пка́], *coll.* **∠** m [1 e.] navel

пурга́ f [5] blizzard, snowstorm

пу́рпур m [1], **∠ный**, **∠овый** [14] purple

пуск m [1] (a. **∠ в ход**) start(ing), setting in operation; **∠а́й** → *coll.* **пусть**; **∠а́ть** [1], ⟨пусти́ть⟩ [15] let (go; in[to]), set going, in motion or operation [a. **∠ в ход**]; start; (*бро́сить*) throw; *ко́рни* take root; *fig.* begin; **в прода́жу** offer (*for sale*); **∠а́ть под отко́с** derail; **-ся** (+ *inf.*) **в путь** start (…ing; v/ct. **в** B), set out (**в** B on); begin, undertake; enter upon

пусте́ть [8], ⟨о-, за-⟩ become empty or deserted; **∠и́ть** → **пуска́ть**

пуст|о́й [14; пуст, -о́, -о] empty; *наде́жда, разгово́р* vain, idle (talk **∠о́е**; n su. → a. **∠я́к**); *ме́сто* vacant; *взгляд* blank; *geol. поро́да* barren rock; (*по́лый*) hollow; **∠ота́** f [5; pl. st.: -о́ты] emptiness; void; *phys.* vacuum

пусты́|нный [14; -ы́нен, -ы́нна] uninhabited, deserted; **∠ня** f [6] desert, wilderness; **∠рь** m [4 e.] waste land; **∠шка** f [5; g/pl.: -шек] *coll.* baby's dummy; *fig.* hollow man

пусть let (him, *etc.* + *vb.*); **∠ [он]** + *vb.* 3rd *p.*); even (if)

пустя́|к *coll.* m [1 e.] trifle; *pl* (it's) nothing; **па́ра ∠ко́в** child's play; **∠ко́вый**, **∠чный** *coll.* [14] trifling, trivial

пу́та|ница f [5] confusion, muddle, mess; **∠ть** [1], ⟨за-, с-, пере-⟩ (**-ся** get) confuse(d), muddle(d), mix up; entangle(d), **-ся под нога́ми** get in the way

путёвка f [5; g/pl.: -вок] pass, authorization (*for a place on a tour, in a holiday home, etc.*)

путе|води́тель m [4] guide(book) (**по** Д to); **∠во́дный** [14] *звезда́* lodestar; **∠во́й** [14] travel(l)ing; **∠вы́е заме́тки** travel notes

путеше́ств|енник m [1] travel(l)er; **∠ие** n [12] journey, trip; voyage, **мо́рем** cruise; **∠овать** [7] travel (**по** Д through)

пу́т|ник m [1] travel(l)er, wayfarer; **∠ный** *coll.* [14] → **де́льный**

путч m [1] *pol.* coup, putsch

путь m [8 e.; instr/sg.: -тём] way (a. fig.: [in] *that* way **∠ём**, a. by means of P); road, path; *rail* track, line; (*спо́соб*) means; (*пое́здка*) trip, journey (**в** B *or* П on); route; **в** *or* **по ~й** on the way; in passing; **нам по ~й** I (we) am (are) going the same way (**с** Tas); **быть на ло́жном ~й** be on the wrong track

пух *m* [1; в -ху́] down, fluff; **в ~ (и прах)** (*defeat*) utterly, totally; **~ленький** *coll.* [16], **~лый** [14; пухл, -á, -o] chubby, plump; **~нуть** [21], ⟨рас-⟩ swell; **~о́вый** [14] downy

пучи́на *f* [5] gulf, abyss (*a. fig.*)

пучо́к *m* [1; -чка́] bunch; *coll.* bun (hairdo)

пу́ш|ечный [14] gun…, cannon…; **~и́нка** *f* [5; *g/pl.*: -нок] down, fluff; **~и́стый** [14 *sh.*] downy, fluffy; **~ка** *f* [5; *g/pl.*: -шек] gun, cannon; **~ни́на** *f* [5] *collect.* furs, pelts *pl.*; **~но́й** [14] fur…; **~о́к** *coll. m* [1; -шка́] fluff

пчел|á *f* [5; *pl. st.*: пчёлы] bee; **~ово́д** *m* [1] beekeeper; **~ово́дство** *n* [9] beekeeping

пшен|и́ца *f* [5] wheat; **~и́чный** [14] wheaten; **пшённый** ('рʃо-) [14] millet…; **~ó** *n* [9] millet

пыл *m* [1] *fig.* ardo(u)r, zeal; **в ~у́ сраже́ния** in the heat of the battle; **~а́ть** [1], ⟨за-⟩ blaze, flame, *o лице* glow, burn; rage; (T) *гневом*; **~есо́с** *m* [1] vacuum cleaner; **~и́нка** *f* [5; *g/pl.*: -нок] mote, speck of dust; **~и́ть** [13], ⟨за-⟩ get dusty; **-ся** be(come) dusty; **~кий** [16; -лок, -лка, -o] ardent, passionate

пыль *f* [8; в пыли́] dust; **~ный** [14; -лен, -льна́, -o] dusty (*a.* = **в ~и́**); **~ца́** *f* [5] pollen

пыт|а́ть [1] torture; **~а́ться** [1], ⟨по-⟩ try, attempt; **~ка** *f* [5; *g/pl.*: -ток] torture; **~ли́вый** [14 *sh.*] inquisitive, searching

пыхте́ть [11] puff, pant; *coll.* **~ над че́м-либо** sweat over something

пы́шн|ость *f* [8] splendo(u)r, pomp; **~ый** [14; -шен, -шна́, -o] magnificent,

splendid, sumptuous; *волосы, расти́тельность* luxuriant, rich

пьедеста́л *m* [1] pedestal

пье́са *f* [5] *thea.* play; *mus.* piece

пьян|е́ть [8], ⟨o-⟩ get drunk (*a. fig.*; from, on **oт** P); **~и́ца** *m/f* [5] drunkard; **~ство** *n* [9] drunkenness; **~ствовать** [7] drink heavily; *coll.* booze; **~ый** [14; пьян, -á, -o] drunk(en), *a. fig.* (**oт** P with)

пюре́ (-'re) *n* [*indecl.*] purée; **карто́фельное ~** mashed potatoes *pl.*

пята́ *f* [5; *nom/pl. st.*] heel; **ходи́ть за ке́м-л. по ~м** follow on s.o.'s heels

пят|а́к *coll. m* [1 *e.*], **~ачо́к** *coll. m* [1; -чка́] five-kopeck (*Brt.* -copeck) coin; **~ёрка** *f* [5; *g/pl.*: -рок] five (→ **дво́йка**); *coll.* → **отли́чно**; five-ruble (*Brt.* -rouble) note; **~еро** [36] five (→ **дво́е**)

пяти|деся́тый [14] fiftieth; **~деся́тые го́ды** *pl.* the fifties; → **пя́тый**; **~ле́тний** [15] five-year (old), of five; **~со́тый** [14] five hundredth

пя́титься [15], ⟨по-⟩ (move) back

пя́тк|а *f* [5; *g/pl.*: -ток] heel (take to one's heels **показа́ть ~и**)

пятна́дцат|ый [14] fifteenth; → **пя́тый**; **~ь** [35] fifteen; → **пять**

пятни́стый [14 *sh.*] spotted, dappled

пя́тн|ица *f* [5] Friday (on: **в** B; *pl.*: **по** Д); **~ó** *n* [9; *pl. st.*; *g/pl.*: -тен] spot, stain (*a. fig.*), blot(ch) (*pl.* **в** B with); **роди́мое ~ó** birthmark

пя́т|ый [14] fifth; (*page, chapter, etc.*) five; **~ая** *f su. math.* a fifth (*part*); **~ое** *n su.* the fifth (*date*; on P: **~ого**; → **число́**); **~ь мину́т ~ого** five (minutes) past four; **~ь** [35] five; **без ~и́ (мину́т) час** (**два**, *etc.*, [часá]), five (minutes) to one (two, *etc.* [o'clock]); **~ь**, *etc.* (**часо́в**) five, *etc.* (o'clock); **~ьдеся́т** [35] fifty; **~ьсо́т** [36] five hundred; **~ью** five times

П

Р

раб m [1 e.], **~á** f [5] slave

рабо́т|**а** f [5] work (**за** T; **на** П at); job; labo(u)r, toil; *качество* workmanship; **~ать** [1] work (**над** Top; **на** B for; Tas); labo(u)r, toil; *tech.* run, operate; *магазин и т. д.* be open; **~ник** m [1], **~ница** f [5] worker, working (wo)man; day labo(u)rer, (farm)hand; official; functionary; employee; *научный* scientist; **~ода́тель** m [4] employer, *coll.* boss; **~оспосо́бный** [14; -бен, -бна] able-bodied; hard-working; **~ящий** [17 *sh.*] industrious

рабо́чий m [17] (*esp. industrial*) worker; *adj.*: working, work (*a.* day); workers', labo(u)r…; **~ая си́ла** manpower; work force; labo(u)r

ра́б|**ский** [5] slave…; slavish, servile; **~ство** n [9] slavery, servitude; **~ыня** f [6] → **~á**

ра́в|**енство** n [9] equality; **~ни́на** f [5] *geog.* plain; **~но́** alike; as well as; **всё ~но́** it's all the same, it doesn't matter; anyway, in any case; **не всё ли ~но́?** what's the difference?

равно|**ве́сие** n [12] balance (*a. fig.*), equilibrium; **~ду́шие** n [12] indifference (**к** Д to); **~ду́шный** [14; -шен, -шна] indifferent (**к** Д to); **~ме́рный** [14; -рен, -рна] uniform, even; **~пра́вие** n [12] equality of (rights); **~пра́вный** [14; -вен, -вна] (enjoying) equal (rights); **~си́льный** [14; -лен, -льна] of equal strength; tantamount to; equivalent; **~це́нный** [14; -е́нен, -е́нна] equal (in value)

ра́вн|**ый** [14; ра́вен, -вна́] equal (*a. su.*); **~ым о́бразом** → **~о́**; **ему́ нет ~ого** he is unrivalled; **~я́ть** [28], ⟨с-⟩ equalize; *coll.* compare with, treat as equal to; (*v/i.* **-ся**; *a.* be [equal to Д])

рад [14; ра́да] (be) glad (Д at, of; *a.* to see p.), pleased, delighted; **не ~** (be) sorry; regret

рада́р m [1] radar

ра́ди (P) for the sake of; for (…'s) sake; for

радиа́тор m [1] radiator

радика́л [1], **~ьный** [14; -лен, -льна] radical

ра́дио n [*indecl.*] radio (**по** Д on); **~акти́вность** f [8] radioactivity; **~акти́вный** [14; -вен, -вна] radioactive; **~акти́вное загрязне́ние (оса́дки)** radioactive contamination (fallout); **~веща́ние** n [12] broadcasting (system); **~люби́тель** m [4] radio amateur; **~переда́ча** f [5] (radio) broadcast, transmission; **~приёмник** m [1] radio set; receiver; **~слу́шатель** m [4] listener; **~ста́нция** f [7] radio station; **~телефо́н** m [1] radiotelephone

ради́ст m [1] radio operator

ра́диус m [1] radius

ра́до|**вать** [7], ⟨об-, по-⟩ (B) gladden, please; **-ся** (Д) rejoice (at), be glad *or* pleased (at, of; at); **~стный** [14; -тен, -тна] joyful, glad; merry; **~сть** f [8] joy, gladness; pleasure

ра́ду|**га** f [5] rainbow; **~жный** [14] iridescent, rainbow…; *fig.* rosy; **~жная оболо́чка** *anat.* iris

раду́шие n [12] cordiality; kindness; (*гостеприимство*) hospitality; **~ный** [14; -шен, -шна] kindly, hearty; hospitable

раз m [1; *pl. e., gen.* раз] time ([**в**] B this, *etc.*); one; **оди́н ~** once; **два ~а** twice; **ни ~у** not once, never; **не ~** repeatedly; **как ~** just (in time *coll.* **в са́мый** → *a.* **впо́ру**), the very; **вот тебе́ ~** → **на²**

разба|**вля́ть** [28], ⟨~вить⟩ [14] dilute; **~лтывать** *coll.*, ⟨разболта́ть⟩ [1] blab out, give away

разбе́|**г** m [1] running start, run (with, at **с** P); **~га́ться** [1], ⟨~жа́ться⟩ [4; -егу́сь, -ежи́шься, -егу́тся] take a run; *в ра́зные сто́роны* scatter; **у меня́ глаза́ ~жа́лись** I was dazzled

разби|**ва́ть** [1], ⟨~ть⟩ [разобью́, -бьёшь; разбе́й(те)!; -и́тый] break (to pieces), crash, crush; defeat (*a. mil.*); (*разде-*

лить) divide up (into **на** В); *парк* lay out; *палатку* pitch; *колено и т. д.* hurt badly; *доводы и т. д.* smash; -ся break; get broken; *на группы* break up, divide; hurt o.s. badly; **~ра́тельство** *n* [9] examination, investigation; **~ра́ть** [1], ⟨разобра́ть⟩ [разберу́, -рёшь; разобра́л, -а́, -о; -о́бранный] take to pieces, dismantle; *дом* pull down; *дело* investigate, inquire into; (*различать*) make out, decipher, understand; sort out; (*раскупать*) buy up; -ся (*в* П) grasp, understand; **~тый** [14 *sh.*] broken; *coll.* (*усталый*) jaded; **~ть(ся) → ~ва́ть(ся)**

разбо́й *m* [3] robbery; **~ник** *m* [1] robber; *joc.* (little) rogue; scamp

разболта́ть → разба́лтывать

разбо́р *m* [1] analysis; *произведения* review, critique; *дела* investigation, inquiry (into); *без ~а, ~у coll.* indiscriminately; **~ка** *f* [5] taking to pieces, dismantling; (*сортировка*) sorting (out); **~ный** [14] collapsible; **~чивость** *f* [8] *почерка* legibility; *о человеке* scrupulousness; **~чивый** [14 *sh.*] scrupulous, fastidious; legible

разбра́сывать, ⟨~оса́ть⟩ [1] scatter, throw about, strew; **~еда́ться** [1], ⟨~ести́сь⟩ [25] disperse; **~о́д** [1] disorder; **~о́санный** [14] sparse; scattered; **~оса́ть → ~а́сывать**

разбух|а́ть [1], ⟨~нуть⟩ [21] swell

разва́л *m* [1] collapse, breakdown; disintegration; **~ивать** [1], ⟨~и́ть⟩ [13; -алю́, -а́лишь] pull (*or* break) down; disorganize; **-ся** fall to pieces, collapse; *coll. в кресле* collapse, sprawl; **~ины** *f pl.* [5] ruins (*coll. a. sg.* = *p.*)

ра́зве really; perhaps; only; except that

развева́ться [1] fly, flutter, flap

разве́д|ать → ~ывать; **~ение** *n* [12] breeding; *растений* cultivation; **~ённый** [14] divorced; divorcé(e) *su.*; **~ка** *f* [5; *g/pl.:* -док] *mil.* reconnaissance; intelligence service; *geol.* prospecting; **~чик** *m* [1] scout; intelligence officer; reconnaissance aircraft; **~ывательный** [14] reconnaissance...; **~ывать**, ⟨~ать⟩ [1] reconnoiter (*Brt.*

-tre); *geol.* prospect; *coll.* find out

разве|зти́ → ~вози́ть; **~нча́ть** [1] *pf. fig.* debunk

развёр|нутый [14] (*широкомасшта́бный*) large-scale; detailed; **~тывать** [1], ⟨разверну́ть⟩ [20] unfold, unroll, unwrap; *mil.* deploy; *fig.* develop; (**-ся** *v/i.*)

разве|сно́й [14] sold by weight; **~сить → ~шивать**; **~сти́(сь) → разводи́ть(ся)**; **~твле́ние** *n* [12] ramification, branching; **~твля́ться** [28], ⟨~тви́ться⟩ [14 *e.*; *3rd p. only*] ramify; branch; **~шивать** [1], ⟨~сить⟩ [15] weigh (out); *бельё* hang (up); **~ять** [27] *pf.* disperse; *сомнения* dispel

разви|ва́ть [1], ⟨~ть⟩ [разовью́, -вьёшь; разве́й(те)!; разви́л, -а́, -о; -ви́тый (ра́звит, -á, -о)] develop (*v/i.* -ся); evolve; **~нчивать** [1], ⟨~нти́ть⟩ [15 *e.*; -нчу́, -нти́шь; -и́нченный] unscrew; **~тие** *n* [12] development, evolution; **~то́й** [14; ра́звит, -á, -о] developed; *ребёнок* advanced, well-developed; **~ть(ся) → ~ва́ть(ся)**

развле|ка́ть [1], ⟨~чь⟩ [26] entertain, amuse (**-ся** o.s.); (*развлечь отвлекая*) divert; **~че́ние** *n* [12] entertainment, amusement; diversion

разво́д *m* [1] divorce; *быть в ~е* be divorced; **~и́ть** [15], ⟨развести́⟩ [25] take (along); bring; divorce (**с** T from); (*растворить*) dilute; *животных* rear, breed; *agric.* plant, cultivate; *огонь* light, make; *мост* raise; **-ся, -сь**) get *or* be divorced (**с** T from); *coll.* multiply, grow *or* increase in number

раз|вози́ть [15], ⟨~везти́⟩ [24] *товары* deliver; *гостей* drive; **~вора́чивать** *coll.* → **~вёртывать**

развра́т *m* [1] debauchery; depravity; **~ти́ть(ся) → ~ща́ть(ся)**; **~тник** *m* [1] profligate; debauchee, rake; **~тный** [14; -тен, -тна] depraved, corrupt; **~ща́ть** [1], ⟨~ти́ть⟩ [15 *e.*; -ащу́, -ати́шь; -ащённый] (**-ся** become) deprave(d), debauch(ed); corrupt; **~щённость** *f* [8] depravity

развяз|а́ть → ~ывать; **~ка** *f* [5; *g/pl.:* -зок] *lit.* denouement; outcome; upshot; **де́ло идёт к ке** things are coming to a head; **ный** [14; -зен, -зна] forward, (overly) familiar; **вывать** [1], ⟨**а́ть**⟩ [3] untie, undo; *fig.* **войну́** unleash; *coll.* **язы́к** loosen; **-ся** come untied; *coll.* (**освободи́ться**) be through (**с T** with)

разгада́|ть → **вывать**; **жа́ка** [5; *g/pl.:* -док] solution; **вывать**, ⟨**а́ть**⟩ [1] guess; **зага́дку** solve

разга́р *m* [1] (**в П** *or* **В**) **в же спо́ра** in the heat of; **в же ле́та** at the height of; **в по́лном же** in full swing

раз|гиба́ть [1], ⟨**жогну́ть**⟩ [20] unbend, straighten (**-ся** o.s.)

разгла́|живать [1], ⟨**жди́ть**⟩ [15] smooth out; **швы** и т. д. iron, press; **жша́ть** [1], ⟨**жси́ть**⟩ [15 *е.;* -ашу́, -аси́шь; -ашённый] divulge, give away, let out

разгляд|е́ть [11] *pf.* make out; discern; **вывать** [1] examine, scrutinize

разгне́ванный [14] angry

разгов|а́ривать [1] talk (**с T** to, with; **о П** about, of), converse, speak; **жор** *m* [1] talk, conversation; **же речь**; **перемени́ть те́му жора** change the subject; **жо́рный** [14] colloquial; **жо́рчивый** [14 *sh.*] talkative, loquacious

разго́н *m* [1] *mil.*, *etc.* dispersal; *a.* → **разбе́г**; **жа́ть** [28], ⟨**разогна́ть**⟩ [разгоню́, -о́нишь; разгна́л, -а́, -о; разо́гнанный] drive away, disperse; **тоску́** и т. д. dispel; *coll.* drive at high speed; **-ся** gather speed; gather momentum

разгора́|ться [1], ⟨**же́ться**⟩ [9] flare up; **щёки** flush

разгра|бля́ть [28], ⟨**жби́ть**⟩ [14], **жбле́ние** *n* [12] plunder, pillage, loot; **жниче́ние** *n* [12] delimitation, differentiation; **жни́чивать** [1], ⟨**жни́чить**⟩ [16] demarcate, delimit; **обя́занности** divide

разгро́м *m* [1] *mil.*, *etc.* crushing defeat, rout; *coll.* (**по́лный беспоря́док**) havoc, devastation, chaos

разгру|жа́ть [1], ⟨**жзи́ть**⟩ [15 & 15 *е.;* -ужу́, -у́зишь; -у́женный *or* -ужённый] (**-ся** be) unload(ed); **жзка** *f* [5; *g/pl.:* -зок] unloading

разгу́л *m* [1] (**кутёж**) revelry, carousal; **шовини́зма** outburst of; **живать** F [1]

stroll, saunter; **-ся**, ⟨**жя́ться**⟩ [28] *о пого́де* clear up; **жьный** *coll.* [14; -лен, -льна]: **жьный о́браз жи́зни** life of dissipation

разда|ва́ть [5], ⟨**жть**⟩ [-да́м, -да́шь, *etc.* → **дать**; ро́здал, раздала́, ро́здало; ро́зданный, (-ан, раздана́, ро́здано)] distribute; dispense; give (*cards:* deal); **-ся** (re)sound, ring out, be heard; **жвля́ть** → **дави́ть 2.**; **жть(ся)** → **жва́ть(ся)**; **жча** *f* [5] distribution

раздва́иваться → **двои́ться**

раздви|га́ть [1], ⟨**жнуть**⟩ [20] part, move apart; **занаве́ски** draw back; **жжно́й** [14] **стол** expanding; **дверь** sliding

раздвое́ние *n* [12] division into two, bifurcation; **~ ли́чности** *med.* split personality

раздева́|лка *coll. f* [5; *g/pl.:* -лок] checkroom, cloakroom; **жть** [1], ⟨**разде́ть**⟩ [-де́ну, -де́нешь; -де́тый] undress (*v/i.* **-ся**) strip (of)

разде́л *m* [1] division; **кни́ги** section; **жа́ться** *coll.* [1] *pf.* get rid *or* be quit (**с То**); **же́ние** *n* [12] division (**на В** into); **жи́тельный** [14] dividing; *gr.* disjunctive; **жи́ть(ся)** → **жа́ть(ся)** & **дели́ть(ся)**; **жьный** [14] separate; (*отчётливый*) distinct; **жя́ть** [28], ⟨**жи́ть**⟩ [13; -елю́, -е́лишь; -елённый] divide (**на В** into; *a.* [-ed] by); separate; **го́ре** и т. д. share; **-ся** (be) divide(d)

разде́ть(ся) → **раздева́ть(ся)**

раз|дира́ть *coll.* [1], ⟨**жодра́ть**⟩ [раздеру́, -рёшь; разодра́л, -а́, -о; -о́дранный] *impf.* rend; *pf. coll.* tear up; **ждобы́ть** *coll.* [-бу́ду, -бу́дешь] *pf.* get, procure, come by

раздо́лье *n* [10] → **приво́лье**

раздо́р *m* [1] discord, contention; **я́блоко жа** bone of contention

раздоса́дованный *coll.* [14] angry

раздраж|а́ть [1], ⟨**жи́ть**⟩ [16 *е.;* -жу́, -жи́шь; -жённый] irritate, provoke; vex, annoy; **-ся** become irritated; **же́ние** *n* [12] irritation; **жи́тельный** [14; -лен, -льна] irritable, short-tempered; **жи́ть(ся)** → **жа́ть(ся)**

раздробл|е́ние *n* [12] breaking, smashing to pieces; **жя́ть** [28] → **дроби́ть**

разду|ва́ть [1], ⟨‹-ть›⟩ [18] fan; blow about; (*распухнуть*) swell; (*преувели́вать*) inflate; exaggerate; **-ся** swell
разду́м|ывать, ⟨‹-ать›⟩ [1] (*переду́мать*) change one's mind; *impf.* deliberate, consider; **не ‹-ывая** without a moment's thought; **‹-ье** *n* [10] thought(s), meditation; (*сомнение*) doubt(s)
разду́ть(ся) → *раздува́ть(ся)*
разева́ть coll. [1], ⟨‹-йнуть›⟩ [20] open wide; **‹-ева́ть рот** gape; **‹-жа́лобить** [14] *pf.* move to pity; **‹-жа́ть** → **‹-жима́ть**; **‹-жёвывать** [1], ⟨‹-жева́ть›⟩ [7 *e.*; -жую́, -жуёшь] chew; **‹-жига́ть** [1], ⟨‹-жéчь›⟩ [г/ж: -зожгу́, -зожжёшь; -жгут; разжёг, -зожгла́; разожжённый] kindle (*a. fig.*); *страсти* rouse; *вражду́* stir up; **‹-жима́ть** [1], ⟨‹-жа́ть›⟩ [разожму́, -мёшь; разжа́тый] unclasp, undo; **‹-йнуть** → **‹-ева́ть**; **‹-йня** coll. m/f [6] scatterbrain; **‹-йтельный** [14; -лен, -льна] striking; **‹-йть** [13] reek (T of)
раз|лага́ть [1], ⟨‹-ложи́ть›⟩ [16] break down, decompose; (*v/i.* **-ся**); (become) demoralize(d), corrupt(ed); go to pieces; **‹-ла́д** *m* [1] discord; **‹-ла́живаться** [1], ⟨‹-ла́диться›⟩ [1] get out of order; coll. go wrong; **‹-ла́мывать** [1], ⟨‹-лома́ть›⟩ [14] break (in pieces); **‹-лета́ться** [1], ⟨‹-лете́ться›⟩ [11] fly (away, asunder); coll. shatter (to pieces); *наде́жды* come to naught (*о новостях и т. д.* spread quickly
разли́|в *m* [1] flood; **‹-ва́ть** [1], ⟨‹-ть›⟩ [разолью́, -льёшь; -ле́й(те); -ли́, -á, -о; -и́тый (-и́т, -á, -о)] spill; pour out; bottle; *суп и т. д.* ladle; **-ся** (*v/i.*) flood, overflow
различа́|ть [1], ⟨‹-йть›⟩ [16 *e.*; -чу́, -чи́шь; -чённый] (*отлича́ть*) distinguish; (*разгляде́ть*) discern; *impf.* differ (T, *по* Д in); **‹-ие** *n* [12] distinction, difference; **‹-йтельный** [14] distinctive; **‹-йть** → **‹-áть**; **‹-ный** [14; -чен, -чна] different, various, diverse
разложе́ние *n* [12] decomposition, decay; *fig.* corruption; **‹-йть(ся)** → *разлага́ть (-ся) & раскла́дывать*
разлом|а́ть, **‹-и́ть** → *разла́мывать*

разлу́|ка *f* [5] separation (**с** T from), parting; **‹-ча́ть** [1], ⟨‹-чи́ть›⟩ [16 *e.*; -чу́, -чи́шь] **‹-чённый** separate (*v/i.* **-ся**; **с** T from), part
разма́з|ывать [1], ⟨‹-ать›⟩ [3] smear, spread; **‹-ывать** [1], ⟨‹-мота́ть›⟩ unwind, uncoil; **‹-х** *m* [1] swing; span (*ae. & fig.*); sweep; *ма́ятника* amplitude; *fig.* scope; **‹-хивать** [1], *once* ⟨‹-хну́ть›⟩ [20] (T) swing, sway; *саблей и т. д.* brandish; gesticulate; **-ся** lift (one's hand T); *fig.* do things in a big way; **‹-шистый** coll. [14 *sh.*] *шаг, жест* wide; *почерк* bold
разме|жева́ть [7] *pf.* delimit, demarcate; **‹-льча́ть** [1], ⟨‹-льчи́ть›⟩ [16 *e.*; -чу́, -чи́шь; -чённый] pulverize
размéн [1], **‹-ивать** [1], ⟨‹-ть›⟩ [28] (ex)change (**на** B for); **‹-ный** [14]: **‹-ная монéта** small change
размéр *m* [1] size, dimension(s); rate (**в** П at); amount; scale; extent; **в широ́ких ‹-ах** on a large scale; *доска́* **‹-ом 0.2 x 2 мéтра** board measuring 0.2 x 2 meters, *Brt.* -tres; **‹-енный** [14 *sh.*] measured; **‹-ить** [28], ⟨‹-ить›⟩ [13] measure (off)
разме|сти́ть → **‹-ща́ть**; **‹-ча́ть** [1], ⟨‹-тить›⟩ [15] mark (out); **‹-ши́вать** [1], ⟨‹-ша́ть›⟩ [1] stir (up); **‹-ща́ть** [1], ⟨‹-сти́ть›⟩ [15 *e.*; -ещу́, -ести́шь; -ещённый] place; lodge, accommodate (**в** П, *по* Д in, at, with); (*распредели́ть*) distribute; stow; **‹-щéние** *n* [12] distribution; accommodation; arrangement, order; *груза* stowage; *mil.* stationing, quartering; *fin.* placing, investment
разми|на́ть [1], ⟨‹-размя́ть›⟩ [разомну́, -нёшь; размя́тый] knead; coll. *ноги* stretch (one's legs); **‹-ну́ться** coll. *pf.* [20] *о письмах* cross; miss o.a.
размнож|а́ть [1], ⟨‹-ить›⟩ [16] multiply; duplicate; (*v/i.* **-ся**); reproduce; breed; **‹-éние** *n* [12] multiplication; mimeographing; *biol.* propagation, reproduction; **‹-ить(ся)** → **‹-а́ть(ся)**
размо|зжи́ть [16 *e.*; -жу́, -жи́шь; -жённый] *pf.* smash; **‹-ка́ть** [1], ⟨‹-кнуть›⟩ [21] get soaked; **‹-лвка** *f* [5; *g/pl.*: -вок] tiff, quarrel; **‹-ло́ть** [17;

-мелю́, -ме́лешь] grind; ~та́ть → **разма́тывать**; ~чи́ть [16] *pf.* soak; steep
размы|ва́ть [1], ⟨~́ть⟩ [22] *geol.* wash away; erode; ~ка́ть [1], ⟨разомкну́ть⟩ [20] open (*mil.* order, ranks); disconnect, break (*el.* circuit); ~ть → **~ва́ть**
размышл|е́ние *n* [12] reflection (**o** П on), thought; *по зре́лому ~е́нию* on second thoughts; ~я́ть [28] reflect, meditate (**o** П on)
размягч|а́ть [1], ⟨~и́ть⟩ [16 *e.*; -чу́, -чи́шь; -чённый] soften; *fig.* mollify
раз|мя́ть → ~мина́ть, ~на́шивать, ⟨~носи́ть⟩ [15] *туфли* wear in; *~нести́* → **~носи́ть 1.**; ~нима́ть [1], ⟨~ня́ть⟩ [-ниму́, -нимешь; -ня́л & ро́знял, -á, -о; -ня́тый (-ня́т, -á, -о)] *деру́щихся* separate, part
ра́зница *f* [5; *sg. only*; -цей] difference
разбо́й *m* [3] disagreement; *в де́йствиях* lack of coordination
разно|ви́дность *f* [8] variety; ~гла́сие *n* [12] discord, disagreement; difference; (*расхожде́ние*) discrepancy; ~кали́берный *coll.* [14]; ~ма́стный [14; -тен, -тна] → **~шёрстный**; ~обра́зие *n* [12] variety, diversity, multiplicity; ~обра́зный [14; -зен, -зна] varied, various; ~реч... → **противоре́ч...**; ~ро́дный [14; -ден, -дна] heterogeneous
разно́с *m* [1] *почты́* delivery; *coll.* **устро́ить** ~ give s.o. a dressingdown; ~и́ть [15] 1. ⟨разнести́⟩ [25 -с-] deliver (**по** Д to, at); carry; *слухи и т. д.* spread; (*разби́ть*) smash, destroy; *ветром* scatter; *coll.* (*распу́хнуть*) swell; 2. → **разна́шивать**
разно|сторо́нний [15; -о́нен, -о́нна] many-sided; *fig.* versatile; *math.* scalene; ~сть *f* [8] difference; ~счик *m* [1] peddler (*Brt.* pedlar); *газе́т* delivery boy; ~счик телегра́мм one delivering telegrams; ~цве́тный [14; -тен, -тна] of different colo(u)rs; multicolo(u)red; ~шёрстный [14; -тен, -тна] *coll.* motley, mixed
разну́зданный [14 *sh.*] unbridled
ра́зн|ый [14] various, different, diverse; ~́ть → **~има́ть**
разо|блача́ть [1], ⟨~блачи́ть⟩ [16 *e.*; -чу́,

-чи́шь; -чённый] *eccl.* disrobe, divest; *fig.* expose, unmask; ~блаче́ние *n* [12] exposure, unmasking; ~бра́ть(ся) → **разбира́ть(ся)**; ~гна́ть(ся) → **разгоня́ть(ся)**; ~греба́ть [1], ⟨~гре́ть⟩ [8; -е́тый] warm (up); ~де́тый *coll.* [14 *sh.*] dressed up; ~дра́ть → **раздира́ть**; ~йти́сь → **расходи́ться**; ~мкну́ть → **размыка́ть**; ~рва́ть(ся) → **разрыва́ть(ся)**
разоре́|ние *n* [12] *fig.* ruin; *в результа́те войны́* devastation; ~и́тельный [14; -лен, -льна] ruinous; ~и́ть(ся) → **~я́ть(ся)**; ~жу́, ~жи́шь; -жённый] disarm (*v/i.* **-ся**); ~же́ние *n* [12] disarmament; ~я́ть [28], ⟨~и́ть⟩ [13] ruin; devastate; (**-ся** be ruined, bankrupt)
разосла́ть → рассыла́ть
разостла́ть → расстила́ть
разочаро́|вание *n* [12] disappointment; ~о́вывать [1], ⟨~ова́ть⟩ [7] (**-ся** be) disappoint(ed) (**в** П in)
разра|ба́тывать [1], ⟨~бо́тать⟩ [1] *agric.* cultivate; work out, develop, elaborate; *mining* exploit; ~бо́тка *f* [5; *g/pl.*: -ток] *agric.* cultivation; working (out), elaboration; exploitation; ~жа́ться [1], ⟨~зи́ться⟩ [15 *e.*; -ажу́сь, -ази́шься] *о шторме, войне́* break out; *смехом* burst out laughing; ~ста́ться [1], ⟨~сти́сь⟩ [24; *3rd p. only*:-тётся, -ро́сся, -сла́сь] grow (*a. fig.*); *расте́ния* spread
разрежённый [14] *phys.* rarefied; rare
разре́з *m* [1] cut; (*сече́ние*) section; *глаз* shape of the eyes; ~а́ть [1], ⟨~ать⟩ [3] cut (up), slit; ~ыва́ть [1] → **~а́ть**
разреш|а́ть [1], ⟨~и́ть⟩ [16 *e.*; -шу́, -ши́шь; -шённый] permit, allow; *пробле́му* (re)solve; (*ула́живать*) settle; **-ся** be (re)solved; permit(ted); ~е́ние *n* [12] permission (**с** Р with); permit; authorization (**на** В for); *пробле́мы* (re)solution; *конфли́ктов и т. д.* settlement; ~и́ть(ся) → **~а́ть(ся)**
раз|рисова́ть [7] *pf.* cover with drawings; ornament; ~ро́зненный [14] broken up (as, e.g., a set); left over *or* apart (from, e.g., a set); odd; ~руба́ть [1],

⟨-руби́ть⟩ [14] chop; **~руби́ть го́рдиев у́зел** cut the Gordian knot

разру́|ха *f* [5] ruin; **экономи́ческая ~ха** dislocation; **~ша́ть** [1], ⟨~шить⟩ [16] destroy, demolish; *здоро́вье* ruin; (*расстро́ить*) frustrate; **-ся** fall to ruin; **~ше́ние** *n* [12] destruction, devastation; **~шить(ся)** → **~ша́ть(ся)**

разры́|в *m* [1] breach, break, rupture; (*взрыв*) explosion; (*промежу́ток*) gap; **~ва́ть** [1] **1.** ⟨разорва́ть⟩ [-ву́, -вёшь; -ва́л, -а́, -о; -о́рванный] tear (to *pieces* **на** В); break (off); **(-ся** *v/i.*, *a.* explode); **2.** ⟨~ть⟩ [22] dig up; **~да́ться** [1] *pf.* break into sobs; **~ть** → **~ва́ть 2.**; **~хлы́ть** [28] → **рыхли́ть**

разря́|д *m* [1] **1.** category, class; *sport* rating; **2.** *el.* discharge; **~ди́ть** → **~жа́ть**; **~дка** *f* [5; *g/pl.*: -док] **1.** *typ.* letterspacing; **2.** discharging; unloading; *pol.* détente; **~жа́ть** [1], ⟨~ди́ть⟩ [15 *e.* & 15; -я́жу, -я́дишь; -я́женный & -я́женный] discharge; *typ.* space out; **~ди́ть атмосфе́ру** relieve tension

разу|бежда́ть [1], ⟨~беди́ть⟩ [15 *e.*; -ежу́, -еди́шь; -еждённый] **(в** П) dissuade (from); **-ся** change one's mind about; **~ва́ться** [1], ⟨~ться⟩ [18] take off one's shoes; **~вери́ться** [28], ⟨~ве́риться⟩ [13] **(в** П) lose faith in); **~знава́ть** *coll.* [5], ⟨~зна́ть⟩ [1] find out **(о** П, B about); *impf.* make inquiries about; **~кра́шивать** [1], ⟨~кра́сить⟩ decorate, embellish; **~крупня́ть** [28], ⟨~крупни́ть⟩ [14] break up into smaller units

ра́зум *m* [1] reason; intellect; **~е́ть** [8] understand; know; mean, imply **(под** Т by); **~е́ться** [8]: **само́ собо́й ~е́ется** it goes without saying; **разуме́ется** of course; **~ный** [14; -мен, -мна] rational; reasonable, sensible; wise

разу́|чить → **~ва́ться**; **~чивать** [1], ⟨~чи́ть⟩ [16] learn, study, *стихи́ и т. д.* learn; **-ся** forget

разъе|да́ть [1] → **есть** 1 2.; **~дина́ть** [28], ⟨~дини́ть⟩ [13] separate; *el.* disconnect; **~зжа́ть** [1] drive, ride, go about; be on a journey *or* trip; **-ся** ⟨~хаться⟩ [-е́дусь, -е́дешься; -езжа́йтесь!] leave **(по** П for); *о супру́гах* separate; *о маши́нах*

pass o.a. **(с** Т)

разъярённый [14] enraged, furious

разъясн|е́ние *n* [12] explanation; clarification; **~я́ть** [28], ⟨~и́ть⟩ [13] explain, elucidate

разы́|грывать, ⟨~гра́ть⟩ [1] play; *в лоте́рее* raffle; (*подшути́ть*) play a trick (on); **-ся** *о бу́ре* break out; *о страстя́х* run high; happen; **~ски́вать** [1], ⟨~ска́ть⟩ [3] seek, search (for; *pf.* out = find)

рай *m* [3; в раю́] paradise

рай|о́н *m* [1] district; region, area; **~о́нный** [14] district...; regional; **~сове́т** *m* [1] (**райо́нный сове́т**) district soviet (*or* council)

рак *m* [1] crayfish; *med.* cancer; *astron.* Cancer; **кра́сный как ~** red as a lobster

раке́т|а *f* [5] rocket; missile; **~ка** *f* [5; *g/pl.*: -ток] *sport* racket; **~ный** [14] rocket-powered; missile...; **~чик** *m* [1] missile specialist

ра́ковина *f* [5] shell; *на ку́хне* sink; **ушна́я ~** helix

ра́м|(к)а *f* [5; (*g/pl.*: -мок) frame (-work, *a. fig.* = limits; **в** П within); **~па** *f* [5] footlights

ра́н|а *f* [5] wound; **~г** *m* [1] rank; **~е́ние** *n* [12] wound(ing); **~еный** [14] wounded (*a. su.*); **~ец** *m* [1; -нца] *шко́льный* schoolbag, satchel; **~ить** [13] (*im*)*pf.* wound, injure **(в** В in)

ра́н|ний [15] early (*adv.* **~о**); **~о и́ли по́здно** sooner *or* late; **~ова́то** *coll.* rather early; **~ьше** earlier; formerly; (*сперва́*) first; (**P**) before; **как мо́жно ~ьше** as soon as possible

рап|и́ра *f* [5] foil; **~орт** [1], **~ортова́ть** [7] (*im*)*pf.* report; **~со́дия** *f* [7] *mus.* rhapsody

ра́са *f* [5] race

раска́|иваться [1], ⟨~яться⟩ [27] repent (*v/t.*; **в** П of); **~лённый** [14], **~ли́ть(ся)** → **~ля́ть(ся)**; **~лывать** [1], ⟨расколо́ть⟩ [17] split, cleave; crack; (*v/i.* **-ся**); **~пать** [28], ⟨~па́ть⟩ [1] make (**-ся** become) red-hot, white-hot; **~пывать** [1], ⟨раскопа́ть⟩ [1] dig out *or* up; **~т** *m* [1] roll, peal; **~тистый** [14 *sh.*] rolling; **~тывать**, ⟨~та́ть⟩ [1] (un)roll; *v/i.*

-ся; **~чивать**, ⟨~ча́ть⟩ [1] swing; shake;
-ся coll. bestir o.s.; **~яние** n [12] repentance (**в** П of); **~яться** → **~ивáться**

раски́дистый [14 sh.] spreading

раски́|дывать [1], ⟨~нуть⟩ [20] spread
(out); stretch (out); шатёр pitch, set up

раскла|дно́й [14] folding, collapsible;
~ду́шка coll. f [5; g/pl.: -шек] folding
or folding bed; **~дывать** [1], ⟨разло-
жи́ть⟩ [16] lay or spread out, distribute;
костёр make, light; (распределить)
apportion

раско́л m [1] hist. schism, dissent; pol.
division, split; **~ло́ть(ся)** → **раскáлы-
вать(ся)**; **~пáть** → **раскáпывать**;
~пка f [5; g/pl.: -пок] excavation

раскрá|шивать [1], → **крáсить**;
~пощáть [1], ⟨~пости́ть⟩ [15 e.:
-ощу́, -ости́шь; -ощённый] emancipate,
liberate; **~пощéние** n [12] emancipation,
liberation; **~итикова́ть** [7] pf. se-
verely criticize; **~ичáться** [4 e.; -чу́сь,
-чи́шься] pf. shout, bellow (**на** В at);
~ывáть [1], ⟨~ы́ть⟩ [22] open wide
(v/i. **-ся**); uncover, disclose, reveal;
~ы́ть свои́ ка́рты show one's cards
or one's hand

раску́|пать [1], ⟨~пи́ть⟩ [14] buy up;
~по́ривать [1], ⟨~по́рить⟩ [13] uncork;
open; **~сывать** [1], ⟨~си́ть⟩ [15] bite
through; pf. only get to the heart of; coll.
кого-л. see through; что-л. understand; **~тывать**, ⟨~тать⟩ [1] unwrap

рáсовый [14] racial

распáд m [1] disintegration; радиоак-
тивный decay

распа|да́ться [1], ⟨~сться⟩ [25; -па́лся,
-лась; -па́вшийся] fall to pieces; disintegrate; break up (**на** В into); collapse;
chem. decompose; **~ко́вывать** [1],
⟨~кова́ть⟩ [7] unpack; **~рывать** [1] →
поро́ть; **~сться** → **~да́ться**; **~хивать**
[1] **1.** ⟨~ха́ть⟩ plow (Brt. plough)
up; **2.** ⟨~хну́ть⟩ [20] throw or fling open
(v/i. **-ся**); **~шо́нка** f [5; g/pl.: -нок]
baby's undershirt (Brt. vest)

распе|ва́ть [1] sing for a time; **~ка́ть**
coll. [1], ⟨~чь⟩ [26] scold; **~ча́тка** f [5;
g/pl.: -ток] tech. hard copy; comput.
printout; **~ча́тывать**, ⟨~ча́тать⟩ [1] **1.**

unseal; open; **2.** print out

распи́|ливать [1], ⟨~ли́ть⟩ [13; -илю́,
-и́лишь; -и́ленный] saw up; **~на́ть** [1],
⟨распя́ть⟩ [-пну́, -пнёшь; -пя́тый] cruci-
fy

распис|а́ние n [12] timetable (rail.)
~а́ние поездо́в; **~а́ние уро́ков** schedule (**по** Д of, for); **~а́ть(ся)** →
~ывать(ся); **~ка** f [5; g/pl.: -сок] receipt
(**под** В against); **~ывать** [1], ⟨~а́ть⟩ [3]
write, enter; art paint; ornament; **-ся**
sign (one's name); (acknowledge) receipt (**в** П); coll. register one's marriage

распла́|вля́ть [28] → **пла́вить**;
~каться [3] pf. burst into tears; **~та**
f [5] payment; (возмездие) reckoning;
~чиваться, ⟨~ти́ться⟩ [15] (**с** Т)
pay off, settle accounts (with); pay
(**за** В for); **~ска́ть** [3] pf. spill

распле|та́ть [1], ⟨~сти́⟩ [25 -т-] (**-ся**,
⟨-сь⟩ come) unbraid(ed); untwist(ed),
undo(ne)

распл|ыва́ться, ⟨~ться⟩ [23] spread;
чернила и т. д. run; на воде swim
about; очертания blur; **~ться в улы́б-
ке** break into a smile; **~вчатый** [14 sh.]
blurred, vague

расплю́щить [16] pf. flatten out, hammer out

распозн|ава́ть [5], ⟨~а́ть⟩ [1] recognize,
identify; болезнь diagnose

распол|ага́ть [1], ⟨~ожи́ть⟩ [16] ar-
range; войск dispose; impf. (Т) dispose
(of), have (at one's disposal); **-ся** settle;
encamp; pf. be situated; **~ага́ющий** [17]
prepossessing; **~зáться** → **~зти́сь**
[24] creep or crawl away; слухи spread;
~ожéние n [12] arrangement; (dis)posi-
tion (**к** Д toward[s]); location, situation;
(влечение, доброе отношение) inclination, propensity; **~ожéние ду́ха**
mood; **~о́женный** [14] a. situated;
(well-)disposed (**к** Д toward[s]); inclined; **~ожи́ть(ся)** → **~ага́ть(ся)**

распор|яди́тельность f [8] good man-
agement; **~яди́тельный** [14; -лен,
-льна] capable; efficient; **~яди́ться**
→ **~яжа́ться**; **~я́док** [1; -дка] order;
в больнице и т. д. regulations pl.;
~яжа́ться [1], ⟨~яди́ться⟩ [15 e.:

-яжу́сь, -яди́шься] order; (T) dispose (of); see to, take care of; *impf.* (*управля́ть*) be the boss; manage; **~яже́ние** *n* [12] order(s), instruction(s); disposal (**в** B; **в** П at; **име́ть в своём ~яже́нии** have at one's disposal

распра́в|а *f* [5] violence; reprisal; *крова́вая* massacre; **~ля́ть** [28], ⟨~ить⟩ [14] straighten; smooth; *кры́лья* spread; *но́ги* stretch; **-ся** (**с** T) deal with; make short work of

распределе́|ние *n* [12] distribution; **~и́тельный** [14] distributing; *el. щит* switch…; **~я́ть** [28], ⟨~и́ть⟩ [13] distribute; *зада́ния и т. д.* allot; (*напра́вить*) assign (**по** Д to)

распрод|ава́ть [5], ⟨~а́ть⟩ [-да́м, -да́шь; *etc.*, → **дать**]: -про́дал, -á, -о; -про́данный] sell out (*or* off); **~а́жа** *f* [5] (clearance) sale

распрост|ира́ть [1], ⟨~ере́ть⟩ [12] stretch out; *влия́ние* extend (*v/i.* **-ся**); **~ёртый** *a.* open (arms *объя́тия pl*); outstretched; prostrate, prone; **~и́ться** [15 *e.*; -ощу́сь, -ости́шься] (**с** T) bid farewell (to); (*отказа́ться*) give up, abandon

распростране́|ние *n* [12] *слу́хов и т. д.* spread(ing); *зна́ний* dissemination, propagation; **получи́ть широ́кое ~е́ние** become popular; be widely practiced; **~ённый** [14] widespread; **~я́ть** [28], ⟨~и́ть⟩ [13] spread, diffuse (*v/i.* **-ся**); propagate, disseminate; extend; *за́пах* give off; **~я́ться** *coll.* enlarge upon

распроща́ться [1] *coll.* → **~сти́ться**

ра́спря *f* [6; *g/pl.*: -рей] strife, conflict; **~га́ть** [1], ⟨~чь⟩ [26 г/ж: -яг у́, -яжёшь] unharness

распу́|скать [1], ⟨~сти́ть⟩ [15] dismiss, disband; *parl.* dissolve; *на кани́кулы* dismiss for; *знамя* unfurl; *вяза́ние* undo; *во́лосы* loosen; *слу́хи* spread; *ма́сло* melt; *fig.* spoil; *-ся цвето́к* open; (*раствори́ться*) dissolve; *coll.* become intractable; let o.s. go; **~ста́ть** → **~тыва́ть**; **~ти́ца** *f* [5] season of bad roads; **~тыва́ть**, ⟨~тать⟩ [1] untangle; **~тье** *n* [10] crossroad(s); **~ха́ть** [1], ⟨-

~хну́ть⟩ [21] swell; **~хший** [17] swollen; **~щенный** [14 *sh.*] spoiled, undisciplined; dissolute

распыл|и́тель *m* [4] spray(er), atomizer; **~я́ть** [28], ⟨~и́ть⟩ [13] spray, atomize; *fig.* dissipate

распя́|тие *n* [12] crucifixion; crucifix; **~ть** → **распина́ть**

расса́|да *f* [5] seedlings; **~ди́ть** → **~живать**; **~дник** *m* [1] seedbed; *a. fig.* hotbed; **~живать** [1], ⟨~ди́ть⟩ [15] transplant; *люде́й* seat; **-ся**, ⟨рассе́сться⟩ [расся́дусь, -де́шься; -се́лся, -се́лась] sit down, take one's seat; *fig.* sprawl

рассве́|т *m* [1] dawn (**на** П at), daybreak; **~та́ть** [1], ⟨~сти́⟩ [25 -т-: -светёт; -свело́] dawn

рассе́|дла́ть [1] *pf.* unsaddle; **~ивать** [1], ⟨~ять⟩ [27] sow; *толпу* scatter; *тучи* disperse (*v/i.* **-ся**); *сомне́ния* dispel; **~ка́ть** [1], ⟨~чь⟩ [26] cut through, cleave; (*of a cane, etc.*) swish; **~ля́ть** [28], ⟨~ли́ть⟩ [13] settle in a new location (*v/i.* **-ся**); **~сться** → **расса́живаться**; **~янность** *f* [8] absent-mindedness; **~янный** [14 *sh.*] absent-minded; scattered; *phys.* diffused; **~ять(ся)** → **~ивать(ся)**

расска́з *m* [1] account, narrative; tale, story; **~а́ть** → **~ывать**; **~чик** *m* [1] narrator; storyteller; **~ывать** [1], ⟨~а́ть⟩ [3] tell; recount, narrate

расслаб|ля́ть [28], ⟨~и́ть⟩ [14] weaken, enervate (*v/i.* **~е́ть** [8] *pf.*)

рассле́|дование *n* [12] investigation, inquiry; **~довать** [7] (*im)pf.* investigate, inquire into; **~е́ние** *n* [12] stratification; **~ышать** [16] *pf.* catch (*what a p. is saying*); **не ~ышать** not (quite) catch

рассма́|тривать [1], ⟨~отре́ть⟩ [-отрю́, -о́тришь; -о́тренный] examine, view; consider; (*различи́ть*) discern, distinguish; **~е́ться** [27 *e.*; -ею́сь, -ее́шься] *pf.* burst out laughing; **~отре́ние** *n* [12] examination (**при** П at); consideration; **~отре́ть** → **~а́тривать**

рассо́л *m* [1] brine

расспра́|шивать [1], ⟨~оси́ть⟩ [15] inquire, ask; **~о́сы** *pl.* [1] inquiries

рассро́чка f [5] (payment by) instal(l)-ments (**в** B sg. by)

расста|ва́ние → **проща́ние** [5], ⟨~ться⟩ [-аю́сь, -а́нешься] part (**с** T with); leave; *с мечтой и т. д.* give up; ~**вля́ть** [28], ⟨~вить⟩ [14] place; arrange; set up; (*раздвигать*) move apart; ~**но́вка** f [5; *g/pl.*: -вок] arrangement; punctuation; *персонал* placing; ~**но́вка полити́ческих сил** political scene; ~**ться** → ~**ва́ться**

расст|ёгивать, ⟨~егну́ть⟩ [20] unbutton; unfasten (*v/i.* -**ся**); ~**ила́ть** [1], ⟨разостла́ть⟩ [расстелю́, -е́лешь; разо́стланный] spread out; lay (*v/i.* -**ся**); ~**оя́ние** n [12] distance (at a **на** П); **держа́ться на ~оя́нии** keep aloof

расстра́|ивать, ⟨~о́ить⟩ [13] upset; disorganize; disturb, spoil; shatter; *планы* frustrate; *mus.* put out of tune; -**ся** be(come) upset, illhumo(u)red, *etc.*

расстре́л m [1] execution by shooting; ~**ивать** [1], ⟨~я́ть⟩ [28] shoot

расстро́|ить(ся) → **расстра́ивать(ся)**; ~**йство** n [9] disorder, confusion; derangement; frustration; *желудка* stomach disorder; *coll.* diarrh(o)ea

расступа́|ться, ⟨~и́ться⟩ [14] make way; *о толпе* part

рассу|ди́тельность f [8] judiciousness; ~**ди́тельный** [14; -лен, -льна] judicious, reasonable; ~**ди́ть** [15] *pf.* judge; arbitrate; think, consider; decide; ~**до́к** m [1; -дка́] reason; common sense; ~**до́чный** [14; -чен, -чна] rational; ~**жда́ть** [1] argue, reason; discourse (on); argue (about); discuss; ~**жде́ние** n [12] reasoning, argument, debate, discussion

рассчи́т|ывать, ⟨~а́ть⟩ [1] calculate, estimate; *с работы* dismiss, sack; *impf.* count *or* reckon (**на** B on); (*ожидать*) expect; (*намереваться*) intend; -**ся** settle accounts, *fig.* get even (**с** T with); (*расплатиться*) pay off

рассыл|а́ть [1], ⟨разосла́ть⟩ [-ошлю́, -ошлёшь; -о́сланный] send out (*or* round); ~**ка** f [5] distribution; dispatch

рассып|а́ть [1], ⟨~ать⟩ [2] scatter, spill; *v/i.* -**ся** crumble, fall to pieces; break up;

~**а́ться в комплиме́нтах** shower compliments (on Д)

раста́|лкивать, ⟨растолка́ть⟩ [1] push asunder, apart; (*будить*) shake; ~**пливать** [1], ⟨растопи́ть⟩ [14] light, kindle; *жир* melt; (*v/i.* -**ся**); ~**птывать** [1], ⟨растопта́ть⟩ [3] trample, stamp (on); crush; ~**скивать** [1], ⟨~щи́ть⟩ [16], *coll.* ⟨~ска́ть⟩ [1] (*раскрасть*) pilfer; *на части* take away, remove little by little; *дерущихся* separate

раство́р m [1] *chem.* solution; *цемента* mortar; ~**и́мый** [14 *sh.*] soluble; ~**я́ть** [28], ⟨~и́ть⟩ **1.** [13] dissolve; **2.** [13; -орю́, -о́ришь; -о́ренный] open

расте́|ние n [12] plant; ~**ре́ть** → **растира́ть**; ~**рза́ть** [1] *pf.* tear to pieces; ~**рянный** [14 *sh.*] confused, perplexed, bewildered; ~**ря́ть** [28] *pf.* lose (little by little); (-**ся** get lost, lose one's head; be[come] perplexed *or* puzzled)

расти́ [24 -ст-: -сту́, -стёшь; рос, -сла́; ро́сший] ⟨вы́-⟩ grow; grow up; (*увеличиваться*) increase

расти|ра́ть [1], ⟨~ере́ть⟩ [12; разотру́, -трёшь] grind, pulverize; rub in; rub, massage

расти́тельн|ость f [8] vegetation; verdure; *на лице* hair; ~**ый** [14] vegetable; **вести́ ~ый о́браз жи́зни** vegetate

расти́ть [15 *e.*; ращу́, расти́шь] rear; grow, cultivate

расто|лка́ть → **раста́лкивать**; ~**лкова́ть** [7] *pf.* expound, explain; ~**пи́ть** → **раста́пливать**; ~**пта́ть** → **раста́птывать**; ~**пы́рить** [13] *pf.* spread wide; ~**рга́ть** [1], ⟨~ргну́ть⟩ [21] *договор* cancel, annul; *брак* dissolve; ~**рже́ние** n [12] cancellation; annulment; dissolution; ~**ро́пный** [14; -пен, -пна] *coll.* smart, deft, quick; ~**ча́ть** [1], ⟨~чи́ть⟩ [16 *e.*; -чу́, -чи́шь; -чённый] squander, waste, dissipate; *похвалы* lavish (Д on); ~**чи́тель** m [4], squanderer, spendthrift; ~**чи́тельный** [14; -лен, -лен] wasteful, extravagant

растра́|вля́ть [28], ⟨~ви́ть⟩ [14] irritate; *душу* aggravate; ~**ви́ть ра́ну** *fig.* rub salt in the wound; ~**та** f [5] squandering; embezzlement; ~**тчик** m [1] embezzler;

~чивать [1], ⟨~тить⟩ [15] spend, waste; embezzle

растр|епа́ть [2] *pf.* (**-ся** be[come]) tousle(d, **~ёпанный** [14]), dishevel([l]ed); **в ~ёпанных чу́вствах** confused, mixed up

растро́гать [1] *pf.* move, touch

растя́|гивать [1], ⟨~ну́ть⟩ [19] stretch (*v*/*i.* **-ся**; *coll.* fall flat); *med.* sprain, strain; *слова* drawl; *во вре́мени* drag out, prolong; **~же́ние** *n* [12] stretching; strain(ing); **~жи́мый** [14 *sh.*] extensible, elastic; *fig.* vague; **~нутый** [14] long-winded, prolix; **~ну́ться** → **~ги́ваться**

рас|формирова́ть [8] *pf.* disband; **~ха́живать** [1] walk about, pace up and down; **~хва́ливать** [1], ⟨~хвали́ть⟩ [13; -алю́, -а́лишь; -а́ленный] shower praise on; **~хва́тывать**, *coll.* ⟨~хвата́ть⟩ [1] snatch away; (*раскупить*) buy up (quickly)

расхи|ща́ть [1], ⟨~тить⟩ [15] plunder; misappropriate; **~ще́ние** *n* [12] theft; misappropriation

расхо́д *m* [1] expenditure (**на** B for), expense(s); *то́плива и т. д.* consumption; **~ди́ться** [15], ⟨разойти́сь⟩ [-ойду́сь, -ойдёшься; -оше́дшийся; *pf.*-ойдя́сь] go away; disperse; break up; *во мне́ниях* differ (**с** T from); *т. ж. о ли́ниях* diverge; (*расста́ться*) part, separate; *pass* (*without meeting*) (*letters*) cross; *това́р* be sold out, sell; *де́ньги* be spent, (**у** P) run out of; **~довать** [7], ⟨из-⟩ spend, expend; *pf. a.* use up; **~жде́ние** *n* [12] divergence, difference (**в** П of)

расцара́п|ывать [1], ⟨~ать⟩ [1] scratch (all over)

расцве́|т *m* [1] bloom, blossoming; *fig.* flowering; heyday, prime; *иску́сства и т. д.* flourishing; **в ~те лет** in his prime; **~та́ть** [1], ⟨~сти́⟩ [25; -т] blos(s)om; flourish, thrive; **~тка** *f* [5; *g*/*pl.*: -ток] colo(u)ring, colo(u)rs

расце́|нивать [1], ⟨~ни́ть⟩ [13; -еню́, -е́нишь; -енённый] estimate, value, rate; (*счита́ть*) consider, think; **~нка** *f* [5; *g*/*pl.*: -нок] valuation; *цена́*

price; *об опла́те* rate; **~пла́ть** [28], ⟨~пи́ть⟩ [14] uncouple, unhook; disengage

рас|чеса́ть → **~чёсывать**; **~чёска** *f* [5; *g*/*pl.*: -сок] comb; **~че́сть** → **рассчита́ть**; **~чёсывать** [1], ⟨~чеса́ть⟩ [3] comb (one's hair **-ся** *coll.*)

расчёт *m* [1] calculation; estimate; settlement (of accounts); payment; (*увольне́ние*) dismissal, sack; account, consideration; **принима́ть в ~** take into account; **из ~а** on the basis (of); **в ~е** quits with; **безнали́чный ~** payment by written order; by check (*Brt.* cheque); **~ нали́чными** cash payment; **~ливый** [14 *sh.*] provident, thrifty; circumspect

рас|чища́ть [1], ⟨~чи́стить⟩ [15] clear; **~члене́ть** [28], ⟨~члени́ть⟩ [13] dismember; divide; **~ша́тывать**, ⟨~шата́ть⟩ [1] loosen (*v*/*i.* **-ся** become lose; *о не́рвах, здоро́вье* be[come]) impair(ed); shatter(ed); **~шевели́ть** *coll.* [13] *pf.* stir (up)

расши|ба́ть → **ушиба́ть**; **~ва́ть** [1], ⟨~ть⟩ [разошью́, -шьёшь; → **шить**] embroider; **~ре́ние** *n* [12] widening, enlargement; expansion; **~ря́ть** [28], ⟨~рить⟩ [13] widen, enlarge; extend, expand; *med.* dilate; **~рить кругозо́р** broaden one's mind; **~ть** → **~ва́ть**; **~фро́вывать** [1], ⟨~фрова́ть⟩ [7] decipher, decode

рас|шнуро́вывать [7] *pf.* unlace; **~ще́лина** *f* [5] crevice, cleft, crack; **~щепле́ние** *n* [12] splitting; *phys.* fission; **~щепля́ть** [28], ⟨~щепи́ть⟩ [14 *e.*; -плю́, -пи́шь; -плённый] split

ратифи|ка́ция *f* [7] ratification; **~ци́ровать** [7] (*im*)*pf.* ratify

ра́товать [7] *за что-л.* fight for, stand up for; *про́тив* inveigh against, declaim against

рахи́т *m* [1] rickets

рацион|ализи́ровать [7] (*im*)*pf.* rationalize, improve; **~а́льный** [14; -лен, -льна] rational (*a. math.*, *no sh.*); efficient

рвану́ть [20] *pf.* jerk; tug (**за** B at); **-ся** dart

рвать [рву, рвёшь; рвал, -á, -о] **1.** ⟨разо-, изо-⟩ [-óрванный] tear (**на, в** B to *pieces*), *v/i.* **-ся; 2.** ⟨со-⟩ pluck; **3.** ⟨вы-⟩ pull out; *impers.* (B) vomit, spew; **4.** ⟨пре-⟩ break off; **5.** ⟨взо-⟩ blow up; **~ и метáть** *coll.* be in a rage; **-ся** break; (*стремиться*) be spoiling for

рвéние *n* [12] zeal; eagerness

рвóт|а *f* [5] vomit(ing); **~ный** [14] emetic (*a. n, su.*)

реа|билитировать [7] (*im*)*pf.* rehabilitate; **~гировать** [7] (**на** B) react (to); respond (to); **~ктивный** [14] *chem.* reactive; *tech. ae.* jet-propelled; **~ктор** *m* [1] *tech.* reactor, pile; **~кционер** *m* [1], **~кционный** [14] reactionary; **~кция** *f* [7] reaction

реал|изм *m* [1] realism; **~изовáть** [7] realize; *comm. a.* sell; **~истический** [16] realistic; **~ьность** *f* [8] reality; **~ьный** [14; -лен, -льна] real; (*осуществимый*) realizable

ребёнок *m* [2; *pl. a.* дéти] child, *coll.* kid; baby; **грудной** **~** suckling

ребр|ó *n* [9; *pl.*: рёбра, рёбер, рёбрам] rib; edge (on **~м**); **постáвить вопрóс ~м** *fig.* put a question point-blank

ребя́|та *pl. of* **ребёнок;** *coll.* children; (*of adults*) boys and lads; **~ческий** [16], **~чий** *coll.* [18] childish; **~чество** *n* [9] *coll.* childishness; **~читься** *coll.* [16] behave childishly

рёв *m* [1] roar; bellow; howl

рев|áнш *m* [1] revenge; *sport* return match; **~éнь** *m* [4 *e.*] rhubarb; **~éть** [-вý, -вёшь] roar; bellow; howl; *coll.* cry

реви́з|ия *f* [7] inspection; *fin.* audit; *наличия товаров и т. д.* revision; **~óр** *m* [1] inspector; auditor

ревмати́|зм *m* [1] rheumatism; **~ческий** [16] rheumatic

ревн|и́вый [14 *sh.*] jealous; **~овáть** [7], ⟨при-⟩ be jealous (**к** Д [B] of [p.'s]); **~ость** *f* [8] jealousy; **~остный** [14; -тен, -тна] zealous, fervent

револь|вéр *m* [1] revolver; **~юционéр** *m* [1], **~юцио́нный** [14] revolutionary; **~юция** *f* [7] revolution

реги́стр *m* [1], **~и́ровать** [7], *pf. and impf., pf. also* ⟨за-⟩ register, record;

(*v/i.* **~и́роваться**); register (o.s.); register one's marriage

рег|лáмент *m* [1] order, regulation *pl.*; **~рéсс** *m* [1] regression

регул|и́ровать [7], ⟨у-⟩ regulate; adjust; (*esp. pf.*) settle; **~иро́вщик** *m* [1] traffic controller; **~я́рный** [14; -рен, -рна] regular; **~я́тор** *m* [1] regulator

редак|ти́ровать [7], ⟨от-⟩ edit; **~тор** *m* [1] editor; **~ция** *f* [7] editorial staff; editorial office; wording; **под ~цией** edited by

редéть [8], ⟨по-⟩ thin, thin out; **~и́ска** *f* [5; *g/pl.*: -сок] (*red*) radish

рéд|кий [16; -док, -дкá, -о; *comp.*: рéже] uncommon; *волосы* thin, sparse; *кни́га и т. д.* rare; *adv. a.* seldom; **~ость** *f* [8] rarity, curiosity; uncommon (thing); **на ~ость** *coll.* exceptionally

рéдька *f* [5; *g/pl.*: -дек] radish

режи́м *m* [1] regime(n); routine; (*усло́вия рабо́ты*) conditions

режиссёр *m* [1] *cine.* director; *thea.* producer

рéз|ать [3] **1.** ⟨раз-⟩ cut (up, open); slice; *мя́со* carve; **2.** ⟨за-⟩ slaughter, kill; **3.** ⟨вы-⟩ carve, cut (**по** B, **на** П in *wood*); **4.** ⟨с-⟩ *coll. на экзамене* fail; **5. -ся** *coll.* cut (*one's teeth*)

резв|и́ться [14 *e.*; -влю́сь, -ви́шься] frolic, frisk, gambol; **~ый** [14; -резв, -á, -о] frisky, sportive, frolicsome; quick; *ребёнок* lively

резéрв *m* [1] *mil., etc.* reserve(s); **~и́ст** *m* [1] reservist; **~ный** [14] reserve

резéц *m* [1; -зцá] *зуб* incisor; *tech.* cutter; cutting tool

рези́н|а *f* [5] rubber; **~овый** [14] rubber...; **~ка** *f* [5; *g/pl.*: -нок] eraser; rubber band, (*piece of*) elastic

рéз|кий [16; -зок, -зкá, -о; *comp.*: рéзче] sharp, keen; *ветер* biting, piercing; *боль* acute; *звук* harsh; shrill; *свет* glaring; *манера* rough, abrupt; **~кость** *f* [8] sharpness, *etc.*, → **~кий;** harsh word; **~ной** [14] carved; **~ня́** *f* [6] slaughter; **~олюция** *f* [7] resolution; instruction; **~óн** *m* [1] reason; **~онáнс** *m* [1] resonance; (*о́тклик*) response; **~óнный** *coll.* [14; -о́нен, -о́нна] reasonable;

~ультáт *m* [1] result (as a **в** П); ~ьбá*f* [5] carving, fretwork

резюмé *n* [*indecl.*] summary; ~и́ровать [7] (*im*)*pf.* summarize

рейд¹ *m* [1] *naut.* road(stead)

рейд² *m* [1] *mil.* raid

рейс *m* [1] trip; voyage; flight

рекá*f* [5; *ac/sg a. st.*; *pl. st.*; *from dat/pl. a. e.*] river

рéквием *m* [1] requiem

реклáм|а *f* [5] advertising; advertisement; publicity; ~и́ровать [7] (*im*)*pf.* advertise; publicize; boost; ~ный [14] publicity

реко|мендáтельный [14] of recommendation; ~мендáция *f* [7] (*совет*) advice, recommendation; (*документ*) reference; ~мендовáть [7] (*im*)*pf., a.,* ⟨по-⟩ recommend, advise; ~нструи́ровать [7] (*im*)*pf.* reconstruct; ~рд *m* [1] record; **установи́ть ~рд** set a record; ~рдный [14] record...; record-breaking; ~рдсмéн *m* [1], ~рдсмéнка *f* [5; *g/pl.*: -нок] record-holder

рéктор *m* [1] president, (*Brt.* vice-) chancellor of a university

рели|гиóзный [14; -зен, -зна] religious; ~гия *f* [7] religion; ~квия [7] relic

рельс *m* [1] *rail.* rail; track

ремéнь *m* [4; -мня́] strap, belt

ремéсл|енник *m* [1] craftsman, artisan; *fig.* bungler; ~енный [14] trade...; handicraft...; ~ó *n* [9; -мёсла, -мёсел, -мёслам] trade; (handi)craft; occupation

ремóнт *m* [1] repair(s); maintenance; *капитáльный* overhaul; ~и́ровать [7] (*im*)*pf.,* ~ный [14] repair...

рентáбельный [14; -лен, -льна] profitable, cost effective

рентгéновск|ий [16]: ~ий **сни́мок** X-ray photograph

реорганизовáть [7] (*im*)*pf.* reorganize

рéп|а *f* [5] turnip; *прóще пáреной ~ы* (as) easy as ABC

репа|трáция *f* [7] reparation; ~три́ровать [7] (*im*)*pf.* repatriate

репéйник *m* [1] burdock

репертуáр *m* [1] repertoire, repertory

репети́|ровать [7], ⟨про-⟩ rehearse;

~тор *m* [1] coach (*teacher*); ~ция *f* [7] rehearsal

рéплика*f* [5] rejoinder, retort; *thea.* cue

репортáж *m* [1] report(ing)

репортёр *m* [1] reporter

репресс|и́рованный *m* [14] *su.* one subjected to repression; ~ия *f* [7] *mst. pl.* repressions *pl.*

ресни́ца *f* [5] eyelash

респýблик|а *f* [5] republic; ~áнец *m* [1; -нца], ~áнский [16] republican

рессóра *f* [5] *tech.* spring

ресторáн *m* [1] restaurant (**в** П at)

ресýрсы *m/pl.* [5] resources

реферáт *m* [1] synopsis; essay

референдум *m* [1] referendum

реформ|а *f* [5], ~и́ровать [7] (*im*)*pf.* reform; ~áтор *m* [1] reformer

рефрижерáтор *m* [1] *tech.* refrigerator; *rail.* refrigerator car, *Brt.* van

рецензéнт *m* [1] reviewer; ~и́ровать [7], ⟨про-⟩, ~ия *f* [7] review

рецéпт *m* [1] *cul.* recipe; *med.* prescription

рецид|и́в *m* [1] *med.* relapse; recurrence; *law* repeat offence

рéчка *f* [5; *g/pl.*: -чек] (small) river; ~нóй [14] river...

речь *f* [8; *from g/pl. e.*] speech; (*выступлéние*) address, speech; **об э́том не мóжет быть и ~и** that is out of the question; → **идти́**

реш|áть [1], ⟨~и́ть⟩ [16 *e.*; -шý, -ши́шь; -шённый] *проблéму* solve; (*приня́ть решéние*) decide, resolve (*a.* **-ся** [на В on, to], make up one's mind); (*осмéлиться*) dare, risk; **не ~áться** hesitate; ~áющий [17] decisive; ~éние *n* [12] decision; (re)solution; ~ётка *f* [5; -ток] grating; lattice; trellis; fender; ~етó *n* [9; *pl. st.*: -шёта] sieve; ~и́мость*f* [8] resoluteness; determination; ~и́тельный [14; -лен, -льна] *человéк* resolute, firm; decisive; definite; ~и́ть(ся) → ~áть(ся)

ржа|вéть [8], ⟨за-⟩, ~вчина *f* [5] rust; ~вый [14] rusty; ~нóй [14] rye...; ~ть [ржёт], ⟨за-⟩ neigh

ри́м|ский [14] Roman; ~ская ци́фра Roman numeral

ри́нуться [20] *pf.* dash; rush; dart

рис *m* [1] rice

риск *m* [1] risk; **на свой (страх и)** ~ at one's own risk; **с** ~ом at the risk (**для** P of); ~ова́ть [7], ⟨~ну́ть⟩ [20] (*usu.* T) risk, venture

рисова́|**ние** *n* [12] drawing; ~ть, ⟨на-⟩ draw; *fig.* depict, paint; ~ся act, pose

ри́совый [14] rice...

рису́нок *m* [1; -нка] drawing; design; picture, illustration; figure

ритм *m* [1] rhythm; ~**и́чный** [14; -чен, -чна] rhythmical

ритуа́л *m* [1], ~**ьный** [14; -лен, -льна] ritual

риф *m* [1] reef

ри́фма *f* [5] rhyme

роб|**е́ть** [8], ⟨о-⟩ be timid, quail; **не** ~**е́й!** don't be afraid!; ~**кий** [16; -бок, -бка́, -о; *comp.*: ро́бче] shy, timid; ~**ость** *f* [8] shyness, timidity

ро́бот *m* [1] robot

ров *m* [1; рва; во рву] ditch

рове́сник *m* [1] of the same age

ро́вн|**ый** [14; -вен, -вна́, -о] even, level, flat; straight; equal; *хара́ктер* equable; ~**о** precisely, exactly; *о времени тж.* sharp; *coll.* absolutely; ~**я** *f* [5] equal, match

рог *m* [1; *pl. e.*: -а́] horn; antler; ~ **изоби́лия** horn of plenty; ~**а́тый** [14 *sh.*] horned; *кру́пный* ~**а́тый скот** cattle; ~**ови́ца** *f* [5] cornea; ~**ово́й** [14] horn...

род *m* [1; в, на -у́; *pl. e.*] *biol.* genus; *челове́ческий* ~ human race; (*поколе́ние*) generation; family; (*сорт*) kind; *gr.* gender; (*происхожде́ние*) birth (T by); **в своём** ~**е** in one's own way; ~**ом из, с** P come *or* be from; **от** ~**у** (Д) be ... old; **с** ~**у** in one's life

роди́льный [14] maternity (hospital **дом** *m*); ~**мый** [14] → ~**'нка**; ~**на** *f* [5] native land, home(land) (**на** П in); ~**нка** *f* [5; *g/pl.*: -нок] birthmark; mole; ~**тели** *m/pl.* [4] parents; ~**тельный** [14] *gr.* genitive; ~**тельский** [16] parental, parent's

роди́ть [15 *e.*; рожу́, роди́шь; -ил, -а (*pf.*: -а́), -о; рождённый] (*im*)*pf.* (*impf. a.*

рожда́ть, *coll.* **рожа́ть** [1]) bear, give birth to; *fig.* give rise to; ~**ся** [*pf.*: -и́лся] be born; come into being

родн|**и́к** *m* [1 *e.*] (*source of water*) spring; ~**о́й** [14] own (*by blood relationship*); *го́род и т. д.* native; (*my*) dear; *pl.* = ~**я́** *f* [6] relative(s), relation(s)

родо|**нача́льник** *m* [1] ancestor, (*a. fig.*) father; ~**сло́вный** [14] genealogical; ~**сло́вная** *f* family tree

ро́дствен|**ник** *m* [1], ~**ница** *f* [5] relative, relation; ~**ный** [14 *sh.*] related, kindred; *языки́* cognate; of blood

родств|**о́** *n* [9] relationship; **в** ~**е́** related (**с** T to)

ро́ды *pl.* [1] (child)birth

ро́жа *f* [5] 1. *med.* erysipelas; 2. P mug

рожда́|**емость** *f* [8] birthrate; ~**ть(ся)** → **роди́ть(ся)**; ~**ние** *n* [12] birth (**от** P by); **день** ~**ния** birthday (**в** B on); ~**е́ственский** [16] Christmas...; ~**ество́** *n* [9] (*a.* **Рⁿество́** [христо́во]) Christmas (**на** B at); **поздра́вить с Рⁿество́м христо́вым** wish a Merry Christmas; **до (по́сле) Р.хр.** B.C. (A.D.)

рож|**о́к** *m* [1; -жка́] feeding bottle; *для обу́ви* shoehorn; ~**ь** *f* [8; ржи; *instr./sg.*: ро́жью] rye

ро́за *f* [5] rose

розе́тка *f* [5; *g/pl.*: -ток] 1. jam-dish; 2. *el.* socket, wall plug

ро́зн|**ица** *f* [5]: **в** ~**ицу** retail; ~**ичный** [14] retail...

ро́зовый [14 *sh.*] pink, rosy

ро́зыгрыш *m* [1] (*жеребьёвка*) draw; drawing in a lottery; (*шу́тка*) (practical) joke; ~ **ку́бка** play-off

ро́зыск *m* [1] search; *law* inquiry; **уголо́вный** ~ criminal investigation department

ро|**и́ться** [13] swarm (*of bees*); crowd (*of thoughts*); ~**й** [3; в рою́; *pl. e.*: рои́, роёв] swarm

рок *m* [1] 1. fate; 2. *mus.* rock; ~**ер** *m* [1] rocker; ~**ово́й** [14] fatal; ~**от** *m* [1], ~**ота́ть** [3] roar, rumble

роль *f* [8; *from g/pl. e.*] *thea.* part, role; **э́то не игра́ет ро́ли** it is of no importance

ром *m* [1] rum

рома́н *m* [1] novel; *coll.* (love) affair; **~и́ст** *m* [1 *e.*] novelist; **~с** *m* [1] *mus.* romance; **~ти́зм** *m* [1] romanticism; **~ти́ка** *f* [5] romance; **~ти́ческий** [16], **~ти́чный** [14; -чен, -чна] romantic

рома́шка *f* [5; *g/pl.*: -шек] *bot.* camomile; **~б** *m* [1] *math.* rhombus

роня́ть [28], ⟨урони́ть⟩ [13; -оню́, -о́нишь; -о́ненный] drop; *листья* shed; *fig.* disparage, discredit

ро́пот *m* [1], **~та́ть** [3; -пщу́, ро́пщешь] murmur, grumble, complain (about *на* B)

роса́ *f* [5; *pl. st.*] dew

роско́шный [14; -шен, -шна] luxurious; sumptuous, luxuriant; **~ь** *f* [8] luxury; luxuriance

ро́слый [14] big, tall

ро́спись *f* [8] *art* fresco, mural

ро́спуск *m* [1] *parl.* dissolution; *на каникулы* breaking up

рост *m* [1] growth; *цен и т. д.* increase, rise; *человека* stature, height; **высо́кого ~а** tall

росто́к *m* [1; -тка́] sprout, shoot; **~черк** *m* [1] flourish; **одни́м ~черком пера́** with a stroke of the pen

рот *m* [1; рта, во рту́] mouth

ро́та *f* [5] *mil.* company

ро́ща *f* [5] grove

роя́ль *m* [4] (grand) piano

ртуть *f* [8] mercury, quicksilver

руба́|нок *m* [1; -нка] plane; **~шка** *f* [5; *g/pl.*: -шек] shirt; **ни́жняя ~шка** undershirt (*Brt.* vest); **ночна́я ~шка** nightshirt; *женская* nightgown

рубе́ж *m* [1 *e.*] boundary; border(line), frontier; **за ~о́м** abroad

руберо́ид *m* [1] ruberoid

рубе́ц *m* [1; -бца́] *шов* hem; *на теле* scar

руби́н *m* [1] ruby

руби́ть [14] 1. ⟨на-⟩ chop, cut, hew, hack; **2.** ⟨с-⟩ fell

ру́бка¹ *f* [5] *леса* felling

ру́бка² *f* [5] *naut.* wheelhouse

ру́бленый [14] minced, chopped

рубль *m* [4 *e.*] ruble (*Brt.* rouble)

ру́брика *f* [5] heading

ру́га|нь *f* [8] abuse; **~тельный** [14] abu-

sive; **~тельство** *n* [9] swearword, oath; **~ть** [1], ⟨вы-⟩ abuse, swear at; attack verbally; **-ся** swear, curse; abuse o.a.

руд|а́ *f* [5; *pl. st.*] ore; **~ни́к** *m* [1 *e.*] mine, pit; **~око́п** *m* [1] miner

руж|е́йный [14] gun…; **~ьё** *n* [10; *pl. st.*; *g/pl.*: -жей] (hand)gun, rifle

руи́на *f* [5] ruin (*mst. pl.*)

рук|а́ *f* [5; *ac/sg.*: ру́ку; *pl.*: ру́ки, рук, -ка́м] hand; arm; **~а́ о́б ~у** hand in hand (arm in arm); **по́д ~у** arm in arm; with s.o. on one's arm; **из ~ вон** (пло́хо) *coll.* wretchedly; **быть на́ ~у** (Д) suit (well); **махну́ть ~о́й** give up as a bad job; **на́ ~ нечи́ст** light-fingered; **от ~и́** handwritten; **пожа́ть ~у** shake hands (Д with); **по ~а́м!** it's a bargain!; **под ~о́й** at hand, within reach; **~о́й пода́ть** it's no distance (a stone's throw); **(у Р) ~и ко́ротки́** P not in one's power; **из пе́рвых ~** at first hand; **приложи́ть ~у** take part in s.th. bad

рука́в *m* [1 *e.*; *pl.*: -ва́, -во́в] sleeve; *реки* branch; *tech.* hose; **~и́ца** *f* [5] mitten; gauntlet

руковод|и́тель *m* [4] leader; head, manager; **нау́чный ~и́тель** supervisor (of studies); **~и́ть** [15] (Т) lead, direct, manage; **~ство** *n* [9] leadership; guidance; *mst. tech.* instruction(s); handbook, guide, manual; **~ствовать(ся)** [7] manual; follow; be guided (by Т); **~я́щий** [17] leading

руко|де́лие *n* [12] needlework; **~мо́йник** *m* [1] washstand; **~па́шный** [14] hand-to-hand; **~пись** *f* [8] manuscript; **~плеска́ние** *n* [12] (*mst. pl.*) applause; **~пожа́тие** *n* [12] handshake; **~я́тка** *f* [5; *g/pl.*: -ток] handle, grip; hilt

рул|ево́й [14] steering; *su. naut.* helmsman; **~о́н** *m* [1] roll; **~ь** *m* [4 *e.*] *судна* rudder, helm; *mot.* steering wheel; *велосипеда* handlebars

румы́н *m* [1], **~ка** *f* [5; *g/pl.*: -нок], **~ский** [16] Romanian

румя́н|ец *m* [1; -нца] ruddiness; blush; **~ить** [13] **1.** ⟨за-⟩ redden; **2.** ⟨на-⟩ rouge; **~ый** [14 *sh.*] ruddy, rosy; *яблоко* red

ру́пор *m* [1] megaphone; *fig.* mouthpiece

руса́лка f [5; g/pl.: -лок] mermaid

ру́сло n [9] (river)bed, (a. fig.) channel

ру́сский [16] Russian (a. su.); adv. по-ру́сски (in) Russian

ру́сый [14 sh.] light brown

рути́н|а f [5], ~ный [14] routine

ру́хлядь coll. f [8] lumber, junk

ру́хнуть [20] pf. crash down; fig. fail

руча́ться [1], ⟨поручи́ться⟩ [16] (за B) warrant, guarantee, vouch for

руче́й m [3; -чья́] brook, stream

ру́чка f [5; -чек] dim. → рука́; две́ри handle, knob; кре́сла arm; ша́риковая ~ ballpoint pen

ручно́й [14] hand...; труд manual; ~ рабо́ты handmade; small; живо́тное tame

ру́шить [16] (im)pf. pull down; -ся collapse

ры́б|а f [5] fish; ~а́к m [1 e.] fisherman; ~ий [18] fish...; жир cod-liver oil; ~ный [14] fish(y); ~ная ло́вля fishing

рыболо́в m [1] fisherman; angler; ~ный [14] fishing; fish...; ~ные принадле́жности fishing tackle; ~ство n [9] fishery

рыво́к m [1; -вка́] jerk; sport spurt, dash

рыг|а́ть [1], ⟨~ну́ть⟩ [20] belch

рыда́|ние n [12] sob(bing); ~ть [1] sob

ры́жий [17; рыж, -а́, -о] red (haired), ginger

ры́ло n [9] snout; P mug

ры́н|ок m [1; -нка] market (на П in); ~чный [14] market...

рыс|а́к m [1 e.] trotter; ~ка́ть [3] rove, run about; ~ь f [8] 1. trot (at T); 2. zo. lynx

ры́твина f [5] rut, groove; hole

рыть [22], ⟨вы-⟩ dig; burrow; ~ся rummage

рыхл|и́ть [13], ⟨вз-, раз-⟩ loosen (soil); ~ый [14; рыхл, -а́, -о] friable, loose; те́ло flabby; podgy

ры́цар|ский [16] knightly, chivalrous; knight's; ~ь m [4] knight

рыча́г m [1 e.] lever

рыча́ть [4; -чу́, -чи́шь] growl, snarl

рья́ный [14 sh.] zealous

рюкза́к m [1] rucksack, knapsack

рю́мка f [5; g/pl.: -мок] (wine)glass

ряби́на f [5] mountain ash

ряб|и́ть [14; -и́т] ripple; impers. flicker (в глаза́х у P before one's eyes)

ряб|чик m [1] zo. hazelhen; ~ь f ripples pl.; в глаза́х dazzle

ря́вк|ать coll. [1], once ⟨~нуть⟩ [20] bellow, roar (на B at)

ряд m [1; в -ý; pl. e.; after 2, 3, 4, ряда́] row; line; series; в ~е слу́чаев in a number of cases; pl. ranks; thea. tier; ~а́ми in rows; из ~а вон выходя́щий remarkable, extraordinary; ~ово́й [14] ordinary; su. mil. private; ~ом side by side; (c T) beside, next to; next door; close by; сплошь и ~ом more often than not

ря́са f [5] cassock

С

с, со 1. (P) from; since; with; for; 2. (B) about; 3. (T) with; of; to; мы ~ ва́ми you and I; ско́лько ~ меня́? how much do I owe you?

са́бля f [6; g/pl.: -бель] saber (Brt. -bre)

сабот|а́ж m [1], ~и́ровать [7] (im)pf. sabotage

сад m [1; в -ý; pl. e.] garden; фрукто́вый ~ orchard

сади́ть [15], ⟨по-⟩ → сажа́ть; ~ся, ⟨сесть⟩ [25; ся́ду, -дешь; сел, -а; се́в-

ший] (на, в B) sit down; в маши́ну и т. д. get in(to) or on, board a. rail.; naut. embark; на ло́шадь mount; о пти́це alight; ae. land; со́лнце set, sink; ткань shrink; set (за B to work); run (around на мель)

садо́в|ник m [1] gardener; ~о́дство n [9] gardening, horticulture

са́ж|а f [5] soot; в ~е sooty

сажа́ть [1] (iter. of сади́ть) seat; в тюрьму́ put into; расте́ния plant

са́женец m [1; -нца и т. д.] seedling; sapling

са́йра f [5] saury

сала́т m [1] salad; *bot.* lettuce

са́ло n [9] fat, lard

сало́н m [1] lounge; showroom; saloon; *ae.* passenger cabin; **косме́тический ~** beauty salon

салфе́тка f [5; g/pl.: -ток] (table) napkin

са́льдо n [*indecl.*] *comm.* balance

са́льный [14; -лен, -льна] greasy; *анекдот* bawdy

салю́т m [1], **~ова́ть** [7] (*im*)*pf.* salute

сам m, **~а́** f, **~о́** n, **~и** pl. [30] -self: **я ~(а́)** I … myself; **мы ~и** we … ourselves; **~о́ собо́й разуме́ется** it goes without saying; **~е́ц** m [1; -мца́] *zo.* male; **~ка** f [5; g/pl.: -мок] *zo.* female

само|бы́тный [14; -тен, -тна] original; **~ва́р** m [1] samovar; **~во́льный** [14; -лен, -льна] unauthorized; **~го́н** m [1] home-brew, moonshine; **~де́льный** [14] homemade

самодержа́вие n [12] autocracy

само|де́ятельность f [8] independent action or activity; *художественная* amateur performances (*theatricals, musicals, etc.*); **~дово́льный** [14; -лен, -льна] self-satisfied, self-complacent; **~защи́та** f [5] self-defense (-nce); **~кри́тика** f [5] self-criticism

самолёт m [14; airplane (*Brt.* aeroplane), aircraft; **пассажи́рский ~** airliner

само|люби́вый [14 *sh.*] proud, touchy; **~лю́бие** n [12] pride, self-esteem; **~мне́ние** n [12] conceit; **~надея́нный** [14 *sh.*] self-confident, presumptuous; **~облада́ние** n [12] self-control; **~обма́н** m [1] self-deception; **~оборо́на** f [5] self-defense (-nce); **~обслу́живание** n [12] self-service; **~определе́ние** n [12] self-determination; **~отве́рженный** [14 *sh.*] selfless; **~отво́д** m [1] *кандидату́ры* withdrawal; **~поже́ртвование** n [12] self-sacrifice; **~сва́л** m [1] dump truck; **~сохране́ние** n [12] self-preservation

самостоя́тельн|ость f [8] independence; **~ый** [14; -лен, -льна] independent

само|су́д m [1] lynch or mob law; **~уби́йство** n [9], **~уби́йца** m/f [5] suicide; **~уве́ренный** [14 *sh.*] self-confident; **~управле́ние** n [12] self-government; **~у́чка** m/f [5; g/pl.: -чек] self-taught pers.; **~хо́дный** [14] self-propelled; **~цветы́** m/pl. [1] semiprecious stones; **~це́ль** f [8] end in itself; **~чу́вствие** n [12] (state of) health

са́м|ый [14] the most, …est; the very; the (self)same; just, right; early or late; **~ое большо́е (ма́лое)** *coll.* at (the) most (least)

сан m [1] dignity, office

санато́рий m [3] sanatorium

санда́лии f/pl. [7] sandals

са́ни f/pl. [8; *from gen. e.*] sled(ge), sleigh

санита́р m [1], **~ка** f [5; g/pl.: -рок] hospital attendant, orderly; **~ный** [14] sanitary

сан|кциони́ровать [7] (*im*)*pf.* sanction; **~те́хник** m [1] plumber

сантиме́тр m [1] centimeter (*Brt.* -tre)

сану́зел m [1] lavatory

сапёр m [1] engineer

сапо́г m [1 *e*; g/pl.: сапо́г] boot

сапо́жник m [1] shoemaker

сапфи́р m [1] sapphire

сара́й m [3] shed

саранча́ f [5; g/pl.: -че́й] locust

сарафа́н m [1] sarafan (*Russian peasant women's dress*)

кард|е́лька f [5; g/pl.: -лек] (*sausage*) saveloy, polony.; **~и́на** f [5] sardine

сарка́зм m [1] sarcasm

сатана́ m [5] Satan

сати́н m [1] sateen, glazed cotton

сати́р|а f [5] satire; **~ик** m [1] satirist; **~и́ческий** [16] satirical

са́хар m [1; *part.g.*: -у] sugar; **~истый** [14 *sh.*] sugary; **~ница** f [5] sugar bowl; **~ный** [14] sugar…; **~ная боле́знь** diabetes

сачо́к m [1; -чка́] butterfly net

сбав|ля́ть [28], ⟨**~ить**⟩ [14] reduce

сбе|га́ть¹ [1], ⟨**~жа́ть**⟩ [4; -егу́, -ежи́шь, -егу́т] run down (from); *pf.* run away, escape, flee; **-ся** come running; **~га́ть²** [1] *pf.* run for, run to fetch (**за** T)

сбере|га́тельный [14] savings

(bank)...;~**га́ть**[1], ⟨~**чь**⟩ [26 г/ж: -регу́, -реже́шь, -регу́т⟩ save; preserve; ~**же́-ние** n [12] economy; savings pl.

сберка́сса f [5] savings bank

сби|ва́ть [1], ⟨~**ть**⟩ [собью́, -бьёшь; сбей; сби́тый] knock down (or off, *a.* **с ног**); *ae.* shoot down; *сли́вки* whip; *яйца́* beat up; *ма́сло* churn; ⟨*сколо-ти́ть*⟩ knock together; lead (astray **с пути́**; **-ся** lose one's way); ~**ть с то́лку** confuse; *refl. a.* run o.s. off (one's legs **с ноги́**); flock, huddle (together **в ку́чу**); ~**вчивый** [14 *sh.*] confused; inconsistent; ~**ть(ся)** → ~**ва́ть(ся)**

сбли|жа́ть [1], ⟨~**зить**⟩ [15] bring *or* draw together; **-ся** become friends (**с** T with) *or* lovers; ~**же́ние** n [12] (*a. pol.*) rapprochement; approach(es)

сбо́ку from one side; on one side; (*рядом*) next to

сбор m [1] collection; gathering; ~ *уро-жа́я* harvest; ~ *нало́гов* tax collection; *порто́вый* ~ harbo(u)r dues; *тамо́-женный* ~ customs duty; *pl.* preparations; **в** ~**е** assembled; ~**ище** n [11] mob, crowd; ~**ка** f [5; *g/pl.:* -рок] sew. gather; *tech.* assembly, assembling; ~**ник** m [1] collection; ~**ный** [14] *sport* combined team; ~**очный** [14] assembly

сбра́|сывать [1], ⟨~**осить**⟩ [15] throw down; drop; *оде́жду и т. д.* shed; ~**од** m [1] rabble, riff-raff; ~**осить** → ~**а́сывать**; ~**у́я** f [6] harness

сбы|ва́ть [1], ⟨~**ть**⟩ [сбу́ду, -дешь; сбыл, -а́, -о] sell, market; get rid of (*a.* **с рук**); **-ся** come true; ~**т** m [1] sale; ~**ть(ся)** → ~**ва́ть(ся)**

сва́д|ебный [14], ~**ьба** f [5; *g/pl.:* -деб] wedding

сва́л|ивать [1], ⟨~**и́ть**⟩ [13; -алю́, -а́лишь] bring down; *де́рево* fell; *в ку́чу* dump; heap up; *вину́* shift (**на** В to); **-ся** fall down; ~**ка** f [5; *g/pl.:* -лок] dump; (*дра́ка*) brawl

сва́р|ивать [1], ⟨~**и́ть**⟩ [13; сварю́, сва́ришь, сва́ренный] weld; ~**ка** f [5], ~**очный** [14] welding

сварли́вый [14 *sh.*] quarrelsome

сва́я f [6; *g/pl.*: свай] pile

све́д|ение n [12] information; *приня́ть*

к ~ению note; ~**ущий** [17 *sh.*] well-informed, knowledgable

све́ж|есть f[8] freshness; coolness; ~**е́ть** [8], ⟨по-⟩ freshen, become cooler; *pf. a.* look healthy; ~**ий** [15; свеж, -á, -ó, све́-жи́] fresh; cool; *но́вости* latest; *хлеб* new

свезти́ → **свози́ть**

свёкла f [5; *g/pl.:* -кол] red beet

свёк|ор m [1; -кра́] father-in-law (*husband's father*); ~**ро́вь** f [8] mother-in--law (*husband' mother*)

сверга́ть [1], ⟨све́ргнуть⟩ [21] overthrow; dethrone (*с престо́ла*); ~**же́ние** n [12] overthrow; ~**ть** → ~**а́ть**

сверк|а́ть [1], *once* ⟨~**ну́ть**⟩ [20] sparkle, glitter; *мо́лнии* flash

сверл|е́ние n [12], ~**и́льный** [14] drilling; ~**и́ть** [13], ⟨про-⟩, ~**о́** n [9; *pl. st.:* свёрла] drill

свер|ну́ть(ся) → **свёртывать(ся)** & **свора́чивать**; ~**стник** → **рове́сник**

свёрт|ок m [1; -тка] roll; parcel; bundle; ~**ывать**[1], ⟨сверну́ть⟩ [20] roll (up); *за угол* turn; ⟨*сократи́ть*⟩ curtail; *строи́тельство* stop; twist; **-ся** coil up; *молоко́* curdle; *кровь* coagulate

сверх (P) above, beyond; over; besides; ~ *вся́ких ожида́ний* beyond (all) expectations; ~ *того́* moreover; ~**звуко-во́й**[14] supersonic; ~**при́быль** f[8] excess profit; ~**у** from above; ~**уро́чный** [14] overtime; ~**ъесте́ственный** [14 *sh.*] supernatural

сверчо́к m [1; -чка́] *zo.* cricket

свер|я́ть [28], ⟨~**ить**⟩ [13] compare, collate

све́сить → **све́шивать**

свести́(сь) → **своди́ть(ся)**

свет m [1] light; world (**на** П in); *вы́пу-стить в* ~ publish; *чуть* ~ at dawn; ~**а́ть** [1] dawn; ~**и́ло** n [9] *poet.* the sun; luminary (*a. fig.*); ~**и́ть(ся)** [15] shine

светл|е́ть [8], ⟨по-⟩ brighten; grow light(er); ~**о́**... light...; ~**ый** [14; -тел, -тла́, -о] light; bright; lucid; *све́тлая голова́* good head; ~**я́к** m [1 *e.*; -чка́] glowworm

свето|во́й[14] light...; ~**фо́р** m [1] traffic light

све́тский [16] worldly

светя́щийся [17] luminous

свеча́ f [5; pl.: све́чи, -е́й, -а́м] candle; el. spark(ing) plug; candlepower

све́шивать [1], ⟨~сить⟩ [15] let down; dangle; hang over; pf. lean over

свива́ть [1], ⟨~ть⟩ [совью, -вьёшь; → **вить**] wind, twist; *гнездо* build

свида́ни|е [12] appointment, meeting, date; *до ~я* good-by(e)

свиде́тель m [4], **~ница** f [5] witness; **~ство** n [9] evidence; testimony; certificate; **~ство о рожде́нии** birth certificate; **~ствовать** [7], ⟨за-⟩ testify; attest *тж. подпись*; *impf.* (о П) show

свине́ц m [1; -нца́] metal lead

свин|и́на f [5] pork; **~ка** f [5; g/pl.: -нок] *med.* mumps; **морска́я ~ка** guinea pig; **~о́й** [14] pig..., pork...; **~ство** n [9] dirty or rotten act

сви́н|чивать [1], ⟨~ти́ть⟩ [15 e.; -нчу́, -нти́шь; свинченный] screw together, fasten with screws; unscrew

свинья́ f [6; pl. st., gen.: -не́й; a. -нья́м] pig, sow; *fig.* swine; **подложи́ть ~ю́ кому́-л.** play a mean trick (on)

свире́п|ствовать [7] rage; **~ый** [14 sh.] fierce, ferocious

свиста́ть [1] hang down, droop

свист m [1] whistle; hiss; **~а́ть** [13] & **~е́ть** [11], *once* ⟨~ну́ть⟩ [20] whistle; pf. P (*стянуть*) pilfer; **~о́к** m [1; -тка́] whistle

свистопля́ска f [5; g/pl.: -сок] turmoil and confusion

сви́т|а f [5] retinue, suite; **~ер** (-тɛr) m [1] sweater; **~ок** m [1; -тка] scroll; **~ь → свива́ть**

свихну́ть coll. [20] pf. sprain; **-ся** go mad

свищ m [1 e.] *med.* fistula

свобо́д|а f [5] freedom, liberty; **вы́пустить на ~у** set free; **~ный** [14; -ден, -дна] free (**от** P from, of); *место и т. д.* vacant; *время и т. д.* spare; *доступ* easy; *одежда* loose; *владение* fluent; exempt (**от** P from); **~омысля́щий** [17] freethinking; *su.* freethinker, liberal

свод m [1] *arch.* arch, vault

сводить [15], ⟨свести́⟩ [25] lead; take

down (from, off); bring (together); reduce (**к** Д to); *счёты* square; *ногу* cramp; drive (mad **с ума́**); **~ на нет** bring to nought; **-ся**, ⟨-сь⟩ (**к** Д) come or amount to; result (in)

сво́д|ка f [5; g/pl.: -док] report, communiqué; **~ный** [14] *таблица* summary; *брат* step...; **~чатый** [14] vaulted

своево́льный [14; -лен, -льна] self-willed, wil(l)ful; **~временный** [14; -менен, -менна] timely; **~нра́вный** [14; -вен, -вна] capricious; **~обра́зный** [14; -зен, -зна] original, peculiar, distinctive

свози́ть [15], ⟨свезти́⟩ [24] take, convey

сво|й m, **~я́** f, **~ё** n, **~и́** pl. [24] my, his, her, its, our, your, their (*refl.*); one's own; peculiar; **в ~ё вре́мя** at one time; in due course; *su. pl.* one's people, folks, relations; **не ~й** frantic (*voice* in T); **~йственный** [14 sh.] peculiar (Д to); (Д p.'s) usual; **~йство** n [9] property, quality, characteristic

сво́|лочь f [8] scum, swine; **~ра** f [5] pack; **~ра́чивать** [1], ⟨сверну́ть⟩ [20] turn (**с** P off); roll (up); **~ченица** f [5] sister-in-law (*wife's sister*)

свы́|ка́ться [1], ⟨~кнуться⟩ [21] get used (**с** T to); **~со́ка** haughtily; **~ше** from above; (P) over, more than

связ|а́ть(ся) → ~ывать(ся); **~и́ст** m [1] signalman; **~ка** f [5; g/pl.: -зок] bunch; *anat.* ligament; *anat.* (vocal) cord; *gr.* copula; **~ный** [14; -зен, -зна] coherent; **~ывать** [1], ⟨~а́ть⟩ [3] tie (together); bind; connect, join; unite; associate; *eleph.* put through, connect; **-ся** get in touch (with), contact; get involved with (**с** T); **~ь** f [8; в -зи́] tie, bond; connection; relation; contact; *половая* liaison; communication (radio, telephone, post, *etc.*)

свят|и́ть [15 e.; -ячу́, -яти́шь], ⟨о-⟩ consecrate, hallow; **~ки** f/pl. [5; gen.: -ток] Christmas (**на** П at); **~о́й** [14; свят, -á, -о] holy; sacred (a. fig.); *su.* saint; **~ость** f [8] holiness; **~ота́тство** n [9] sacrilege; **~ы́ня** f [6] eccl. sacred place; (fig.) sacred object

свяще́нн|ик m [1] priest; **~ый** [14 sh.]

holy; sacred

сгиб *m* [1], **~а́ть**, ⟨согну́ть⟩ [20] bend, fold; *v/i.* **-а́ться**

сгла́|живать, ⟨~дить⟩ [15] smooth out; **-ся** become smooth

сгнива́ть → **гнить**

сго́вор *m* [1] *usu. pej* agreement; collusion; **~и́ться** [13] *pf.* agree; come to terms; **~чивый** [14 *sh.*] compliant, amenable

сго|ня́ть [28], ⟨согна́ть⟩ [сгоню́, сго́нишь; со́гнанный] drive (off); **~ра́ние** *n* [12] combustion; **~ра́ть** [1], ⟨~ре́ть⟩ [9] burn down; **~ра́ть от стыда́** burn with shame; **~ряча́** in a fit of temper

сгр|еба́ть [1], ⟨~ести́⟩ [24 -б-: сгребу́; сгрёб, сгребла́] rake up; shovel off; from; **~ужа́ть** [1], ⟨~узи́ть⟩ [15 & 15 *e.*; -ужу́, -у́зишь; -у́женный & -ужённый] unload

сгу|сти́ть → **~ща́ть**; **~сток** *m* [1; -тка] clot; **~ща́ть** [1], ⟨~сти́ть⟩ [15 *e.*; -ущу́, -усти́шь; -ущённый] thicken; condense; **~ща́ть кра́ски** lay it on thick, exaggerate; **~щёнка** *f* [5; *g/pl.*: -нок] condensed milk

сда|ва́ть [5], ⟨~ть⟩ [сдам, сдашь *etc.* → **дать**] deliver, hand in (*or* over); *багаж* check, register; *дом и т. д.* rent, let (out); *карты* deal; *экзамен* pass; *mil.* surrender; **-ся** surrender; **~ётся...** for rent (*Brt.* to let); **~вливать** [1], ⟨~ви́ть⟩ [14] squeeze; **~ть(ся)** → **~ва́ть(ся)**; **~ча** *f* [5] *mil.* surrender; (*передача*) handing over; *деньги* change

сдвиг *m* [1] shift; *geol.* fault; *fig.* change (for the better), improvement; **~а́ть** [1], ⟨сдви́нуть⟩ [20] move, shift (*v/i.* **-ся**); *брови* knit; push together

сде́л|ка *f* [5; *g/pl.*: -лок] bargain, transaction, deal; **~ьный** [14] piecework

сде́рж|анный [14 *sh.*] reserved, (self-)-restrained; **~ивать** [1], ⟨~а́ть⟩ [4] check, restrain; *гнев и т. д.* suppress; *слово и т. д.* keep; **-ся** control o.s.

сдира́ть [1], ⟨содра́ть⟩ [сдеру́, -рёшь; содра́л, -а́, -о; со́дранный] tear off (*or* down), strip; *шкуру* flay (*a. fig.*)

сдо́бн|ый [14] *cul.* rich, short; **~ая бу́л(оч)ка** bun

сдружи́ться → **подружи́ться**

сду|ва́ть [1], ⟨~ть⟩ [16], *once* ⟨~нуть⟩ [20] blow off (*or* away); **~ру** *coll.* foolishly

сеа́нс *m* [1] sitting; *cine.* show

себесто́имость *f* [8] cost; cost price

себ|я́ [21] myself, yourself, himself, herself, itself, ourselves, yourselves, themselves (*refl.*); oneself; **к ~е́** home; into one's room; **мне не по ~е́** I don't feel quite myself, I don't feel too well; **та́к ~е́** so-so

сев *m* [1] sowing

се́вер *m* [1] north; → **восто́к**; **~ный** [14] north(ern); northern; arctic; **~о-восто́к** *m* [1] northeast; **~о-восто́чный** [14] northeast...; **~о-за́пад** *m* [1] northwest; **~о-за́падный** [14] northwest...; **~я́нин** *m* [1; *pl.* -я́не, -я́н и т. д.] northerner

севрю́га *f* [5] stellate sturgeon

сего́дня (sɪv'o-) today; **~ у́тром** this morning; **~шний** [15] today's

сед|е́ть [8], ⟨по-⟩ turn gray (*Brt.* grey); **~ина́** *f* [5] gray hair

седл|а́ть [1], ⟨о-⟩ *n* [9; *pl. st.*: сёдла, сёдел, сёдлам] saddle

седо|воло́сый [14 *sh.*], **~й** [14; сед, -а́, -о] gray-haired (*Brt.* grey)

седо́к *m* [1 *e.*] horseman, rider; *(passenger)*

седьмо́й [14] seventh; → **пя́тый**

сезо́н *m* [1] season; **~ный** [14] seasonal

сей *m*, **сия́** *f*, **сие́** *n*, **сий** *pl. obs.* [29] this; **по ~ день** till now; **на ~ раз** this time; **сию́ мину́ту** at once; right now; **сего́ го́да (ме́сяца)** of this year (month)

сейф *m* [1] safe

сейча́с now, at present; (*очень ско́ро*) presently, (*a.* **~ же**) immediately, at once; (*то́лько что*) just (now)

сека́тор *m* [1] secateurs, pruning shears

секре́т *m* [1] secret (**по** Д, **под** Т in); **~ариа́т** *m* [1] secretariat; **~а́рь** *m* [*e.*] secretary; **~ничать** *coll.* [1] be secretive; **~ный** [14; -тен, -тна] secret; confidential

сек|суа́льный [14; -лен, -льна] sexual; **~та** *f* [5] sect; **~тор** *m* [1] sector

секу́нд|а *f* [5] (*of time*) second; **~ный**

[14] second…; **~ная стре́лка** (*of time-piece*) second hand; **~оме́р** *m* [1] stop-watch

селёдка *f* [5; *g/pl.*: -док] herring

селезёнка *f* [5; *g/pl.*: -нок] *anat.* spleen; **~ень** *m* [4; -зня] drake

селе́кция *f* [7] *agric.* selection, breeding

сели́ть(ся) [13] → **поселя́ть(ся)**

село́ *n* [9; *pl. st.*: сёла] village (**в** *or* **на П** in); **ни к у́ ни к го́роду** *coll.* for no reason at all; neither here nor there

сельдере́й *m* [3] celery; **~ь** *f* [8; *from g/pl. e.*] herring

се́ль|ский [16] rural, country…, village…; **~ское хозя́йство** agriculture; **~скохозя́йственный** [14] agricultural; **~сове́т** *m* [1] village soviet

сёмга *f* [5] salmon

семе́й|ный [14] family…; having a family; **~ство** *n* [9] family

семена́ → **се́мя**

семени́ть *coll.* [13] (*when walking*) mince; **~но́й** [14] seed…; *biol.* seminal

семёрка *f* [5; *g/pl.*:-рок] seven; → **дво́йка**

се́меро [37] seven; → **дво́е**

семе́стр *m* [1] term, semester

сёмечко *n* [9; *pl.*:-чки, -чек, -чкам] *dim. of* **се́мя**; (*pl.*) sunflower seeds

семи|деся́тый [14] seventieth; → **пя́(ти)деся́т**; **~ле́тний** [15] seventy-year-old; of seventy

семина́р *m* [1] seminar; **~ия** *f* [7] seminary; **духо́вная ~ия** theological college

семисо́тый [14] seven hundredth

семна́дцатый [14] seventeenth; → **пя́тый**; **~ь** [35] seventeen; → **пять**

семь [35] seven; → **пять & пя́тый**; **~деся́т** [35] seventy; **~со́т** [36] seven hundred; **~ю** seven times

семья́ *f* [6; *pl.*: се́мьи, семе́й, се́мьям] family; **~нин** *m* [1] family man

се́мя *n* [13; *pl.*:-мена́, -мя́н, -мена́м] seed (*a. fig.*); *biol.* semen

сена́т *m* [1] senate; **~ор** *m* [1] senator

се́ни *f/pl.* [8; *from gen. e.*] entryway (*in a Russian village house*)

се́но *n* [9] hay; **~ва́л** *m* [1] hayloft; **~ко́с** *m* [1] haymaking; → **коси́лка**

сенсацио́нный [14; -о́нен, -о́нна] sen-sational; **~тимента́льный** [14; -лен, -льна] sentimental

сентя́брь *m* [4 *e.*] September

сень *f* [8; в -ни] *obs. or poet.* canopy, shade; *fig.* protection

сепарати́ст *m* [1] separatist; **~ный** [14] separate

се́п|сис *m* [1] *med.* sepsis

се́ра *f* [5] sulfur; *coll.* earwax

серб *m* [1], **~(ия́н)ка** *f* [5; *g/pl.*:-б(ия́н)ок] Serb(ian); **~ский** [16] Serbian

серви́з *m* [1] service, set; **~рова́ть** [7] (*im*)*pf.* serve

се́рвис *m* [1] (*consumer*) service

серде́чный [14; -чен, -чна] of the heart; *прие́м* hearty, cordial; *челове́к* warm-hearted; *благода́рность* heartfelt; **~ при́ступ** heart attack

серди́|тый [14 *sh.*] angry, mad (**на В** with; at); **~ть** [15], ⟨рас-⟩ annoy, vex, anger; **-ся** be(come) angry, cross (**на В** with)

се́рдц|е *n* [11; *pl. e.*:-дца́, -де́ц, -дца́м] heart; **в ~а́х** in a fit of temper; **принима́ть бли́зко к ~у** take to heart; **от всего́ ~а** wholeheartedly; **по́ ~у** (Д) to one's liking; **положа́ ру́ку на́ сердце** *coll.* (quite) frankly; **~ебие́ние** *n* [12] palpitation; **~еви́на** *f* [5] core, pith, heart

серебр|и́стый [14 *sh.*] silvery; **~и́ть** [13], ⟨по-, вы-⟩ silver; **-ся** become silvery; **~о́** *n* [9] silver; **~яный** [14] silver(y)

середи́на *f* [5] middle; midst; mean

серёжка *f* [5; *g/pl.*:-жек] earring; *bot.* catkin

сере́ть [8], ⟨по-⟩ turn (*impf.* show) gray (*Brt.* grey)

сержа́нт *m* [1] sergeant

сери́йный [14] serial; **~я** *f* [7] series

се́рна *f* [5] *zo.* chamois

се́р|ный [14] sulfuric; sulfur…; **~ова́тый** [14 *sh.*] grayish, *Brt.* greyish

серп *m* [1 *e.*] sickle; *луны́* crescent

серпанти́н *m* [1] paper streamer; road with sharp, U-shaped curves

сертифика́т *m* [1] *ка́чества и т. д.* certificate

се́рфинг *m* [1] surfing

се́рый [14; сер, -á, -о] gray, *Brt.* grey;

dull, dim

се́рьги f/pl. [5; серёг, серьга́м; sg. e.] earrings

серьёзн|ый [14; -зен, -зна] serious, grave; earnest; **~о** a. indeed, really

се́ссия f [7] session (**на** П in)

сестра́ f [5; pl.: сёстры, сестёр, сёстрам] sister; (first) cousin; nurse

сесть → **сади́ться**

се́т|ка f [5; g/pl.: -ток] net; тарифов и т. д.; **~овать** [1] complain (**на** B about); **~ча́тка** f [5; g/pl.: -ток] anat. retina; **~ь** f [8; в сети́; from g/pl. e.] net; (система) network

сече́ние n [12] section; cutting; **ке́сарево ~** cesarean birth

сечь¹ [26; pt. e.; сек, секла́] cut (up); **-ся** split; **~²** [26; pt. st.; сек, се́кла], ⟨вы-⟩ whip

се́ялка f [5; g/pl.: -лок] drill

се́ять [27], ⟨по-⟩ sow (a. fig.)

сжа́литься [13] pf. (**над** T) have or take pity (on)

сжа́т|ие n [12] pressure; compression; **~ый** [14] (воздух и т. д.) compressed; fig. compact, concise, terse; **~ь(ся)** → **сжима́ть(ся)** & **жать¹, жать²**

сжига́ть [1], ⟨сжечь⟩ → **жечь**

сжима́ть [1], ⟨сжать⟩ [сожму́, -мёшь; сжа́тый] (com)press, squeeze; (кулаки) clench; **-ся** contract; shrink; become clenched

сза́ди (from) behind (as prp.: P)

сзыва́ть → **созыва́ть**

сиби́р|ский [16], **~я́к** m [1 e.], **~я́чка** f [5; g/pl.: -чек] Siberian

сига́р(ет)а f [5] cigar(ette)

сигна́л [1], **~изи́ровать** [7] (im)pf., **~ьный** [14] signal, alarm

сиде́лка f [5; g/pl.: -лок] nurse

сиде́|нье n [10] seat; **~ть** [11; сидя́] sit (**за** Tat, over); дома be, stay; об одежде fit (**на** П a p.); на корточках squat; **-ся**: **ему́ не сиди́тся на ме́сте** he can't sit still

сидр m [1] cider

сидя́чий [17] образ жизни sedentary; sitting

си́зый [14; сиз, -á, -о] blue-gray, Brt. -grey; dove-colo(u)red

си́л|а f [5] strength; force (тж. привы́чки); power, might; vigo(u)r; intensity; energy; звука volume; **свои́ми ~ами** unaided, by o.s.; **в ~у** (P) by virtue of; **не в ~ах** unable; **не по ~ам, свы́ше чьи́х-л. сил** beyond one's power; **изо всех сил** coll. with all one's might; **~á́ч** m [1 e.] strong man; **~и́ться** [13] try, endeavo(u)r; **~ово́й** [14] power…

силуэ́т m [1] silhouette

си́льн|ый [14; си́лен & силён, -льна́, -о, си́льны] strong; powerful, mighty; intense; дождь heavy; насморк bad; **~о** a. very much; strongly; badly

си́мвол m [1] symbol; **~и́ческий** [16], **~и́чный** [14; -чен, -чна] symbolic

симметри́|чный [14; -чен, -чна] symmetrical; **~я** f [7] symmetry

симпат|изи́ровать [7] sympathize (with Д); **~и́чный** [14; -чен, -чна] nice, attractive; **он мне ~и́чен** I like him; **~ия** f [7] liking (**к** Д for)

симпто́м m [1] symptom

симули́ровать [7] (im)pf. feign, sham; simulate; **~я́нт** m [1], **~я́нтка** f [5; g/pl.: -ток] simulator; malingerer

симфони́|ческий [16] symphonic, symphony…; **~я** f [7] symphony

син|ева́ f [5] blue; **~ева́тый** [14 sh.] bluish; **~е́ть** [8], ⟨по-⟩ turn (impf. show) blue; **~ий** [15; синь, синя́, си́не] blue; **~и́ть** [13], ⟨под-⟩ blue; apply blueing to; **~и́ца** f [5] titmouse

син|о́д m [1] eccl. synod; **~о́ним** m [1] synonym; **~та́ксис** m [1] syntax; **~тез** m [1] synthesis; **~те́тика** f [5] synthetic material; **~тети́ческий** [16] synthetic; **~хронизи́ровать** [7] (im)pf. synchronize; **~хро́нный** [14] synchronous; **~хро́нный перево́д** interpretation

синь f [8] blue colo(u)r; **~ка** f [5; g/pl.: -нек] blue; blueing; blueprint

синя́к m [1 e.] bruise

си́плый [14; сипл, -á, -о] hoarse

сире́на f [5] siren

сире́н|евый [14], **~ь** f [8] lilac (colo[u]r)

сиро́п m [1] syrup

сирота́ m/f [5; pl. st.: сиро́ты] orphan

систе́ма f [5] system; **~ управле́ния** control system; **~ти́ческий** [16],

~ти́чный [14; -чен, -чна] systematic

си́тец *m* [1; -тца] chintz, cotton

си́то *n* [9] sieve

ситуа́ция *f* [7] situation

сия́|ние *n* [12] radiance; (*нимб*) halo; **се́верное ~ние** northern lights; **~ть** [28] shine; *от ра́дости* beam; *от сча́стья* radiate

сказа́|ние *n* [12] legend; story; tale; **~ть** → **говори́ть**; **~ка** *f* [5; *g/pl.:* -зок] fairy tale; *coll.* tall tale, fib; **~очный** [14; -чен, -чна] fabulous; fantastic; fairy (tale)…

сказу́емое *n* [14] *gr.* predicate

скак|а́ть [3] skip, hop, jump; gallop; race; **~ово́й** [14] race…; racing

скал|а́ *f* [5; *pl. st.*] rock face, crag; cliff; reef; **~и́стый** [14 *sh.*] rocky, craggy; **~и́ть** [13], ⟨о-⟩ show, bare; *coll.* **~и́ть зу́бы** *impf.* grin; jeer; **~ка** *f* [5; *g/pl.:* -лок] rolling pin; **~ывать** [1], ⟨сколо́ть⟩ [17] pin together; (*отка́лывать*) break (off)

скам|е́ечка *f* [5; -чек] footstool; *a. dim. of* **~е́йка** *f* [5; *g/pl.:* -е́ек] bench; **~ья́** *f* [6; *nom/pl. a. st.*] bench; **~ья́ подсуди́мых** law dock

сканда́л *m* [1] scandal; disgrace; *coll.* shame; **~ить** [13], ⟨на-⟩ row, brawl; **~ьный** [14; -лен, -льна] scandalous

скандина́вский [16] Scandinavian

ска́пливать(ся) [1] → **скопля́ть(ся)**

скар|б *coll.* [1] belongings; goods and chattels; **~лати́на** *f* [5] scarlet fever

скат *m* [1] slope, pitch

скат|а́ть → **ска́тывать** 2; **~ерть** *f* [8; *from g/pl. e.*] tablecloth; **~ертью доро́га** good riddance!

ска́т|ывать [1]. **1.** ⟨~и́ть⟩ [15] roll (*or* slide) down (*v/i.* **-ся**); **2.** ⟨~а́ть⟩ [1] roll (up)

ска́ч|ка *f* [5; *g/pl.:* -чек] galloping; *pl.* horse race(s); **~о́к** → **прыжо́к**

ска́шивать [1], ⟨скоси́ть⟩ [15] mow

сква́жина *f* [5] slit, hole; **замо́чная ~** keyhole; **нефтяна́я ~** oil well

сквер *m* [1] public garden; **~носло́вить** [14] use foul language; **~ный** [14; -рен, -рна́, -о] *ка́чество* bad, poor; *челове́к, посту́пок* nasty, foul

сквоз|и́ть [15 *e.*; -и́т] *о све́те* shine through; **~и́т** there is a draft, *Brt.* draught; **~но́й** [14] through…; **~ня́к** *m* [1 *e.*] draft, *Brt.* draught; **~ь** (B) *prp.* through

скворе́|ц *m* [1; -рца́] starling; **~чница** *f* (-ʃn-) [5] nesting box

скеле́т *m* [1] skeleton

скепти́ческий [16] skeptical (*Brt.* sceptical)

ски́|дка *f* [5; *g/pl.:* -док] discount, rebate; **де́лать ~дку** make allowances (**на** for); **~дывать** [1], ⟨~нуть⟩ [20] throw off *or* down; *оде́жду* take *or* throw off; *coll. це́ну* knock off (from); **~петр** *m* [1] scepter, *Brt.* -tre; **~пида́р** *m* [1] turpentine; **~рда́** *f* [5] stack, rick

скис|а́ть [1], ⟨~нуть⟩ [21] turn sour

скита́ться [1] wander, rove

склад *m* [1] **1.** warehouse, storehouse (**на** П in); *mil.* depot; **2.** (*нрав*) disposition, turn of mind; **~ка** *f* [5; *g/pl.:* -док] pleat, fold; *на брю́ках и т. д.* crease; *на лбу* wrinkle; **~но́й** [14] fold(-ing), collapsible; camp…; **~ный** [14; -ден, -дна] *речь* coherent, smooth; Р well-made (*or* -built); **~чина** *f* [5]: **в ~чину** by clubbing together; **~ывать** [1], ⟨сложи́ть⟩ [16] lay *or* put (together); pile up; pack (up); fold; *числа́* add up; *пе́сню* compose; *ору́жие, жизнь* lay down; *сложа́ ру́ки* idle; (*be*) form(ed), develop; *coll.* club together

скле́и|вать [1], ⟨~ть⟩ [13; -е́ю] stick together, glue together (*v/i.* **-ся**)

склеп *m* [1] crypt, vault

скло́ка *f* [5] squabble

склон *m* [1] slope; **~е́ние** *n* [12] *gr.* declension; *astr.* declination; **~и́ть(ся)** → **~я́ть(ся)**; **~ность** *f* [8] inclination (*fig.*; **к** Д to, for), disposition; **~ный** [14; -о́нен, -о́нна, -о] inclined (**к** Д to), disposed; **~я́ть** [28] **1.** ⟨~и́ть⟩ [13; -оню́, -о́нишь, -онённый] bend, incline (*a. fig.*; *v/i.* **-ся**; *о со́лнце* sink); (*убеди́ть*) persuade; **2.** ⟨просклоня́ть⟩ *gr.* (**-ся** be) decline(d)

скоб|а́ *f* [5; *pl.:* ско́бы, скоб, скоба́м] cramp (iron), clamp; **~ка** *f* [5; *g/pl.:* -бок] cramp; *gr., typ.* bracket, parenthe-

sis; ~ли́ть [13]; -облю́, -обли́шь, -обле́н-
ный] scrape; plane

скова́ть → ско́вывать

сковорода́ f [5; pl.: ско́вороды, -ро́д,
-да́м] frying pan

ско́вывать [1], ⟨~а́ть⟩ [7 e.; скую́,
скуёшь] forge (together); weld; fig. fetter; bind; arrest

сколо́ть → ска́лывать

скользи́ть [15 e.;-льжу́, -льзи́шь], once
⟨~ну́ть⟩ [20] slide, glide, slip; ~кий [16;
-зок, -зка́, -о] slippery

ско́лько [32] how (or as) much, many;
coll. ~ лет, ~ зим → ве́чность coll.

сконча́ться [1] pf. die, expire

скоп|ля́ть[28], ⟨~и́ть⟩ [14] accumulate,
gather (v/i. -ся), amass; save; ~ле́ние n
[12] accumulation; люде́й gathering,
crowd

скорб|е́ть [10 e.;-блю́, -би́шь] grieve (о
П over); ~ный [14; -бен, -бна] mourn-
ful, sorrowful; ~ь f [8] grief, sorrow

скорлупа́ f [5; pl. st.-лу́пы] shell

скорня́к m [1 e.] furrier

скоро|гово́рка f [5; g/pl.:-рок] tongue
twister; речь patter; ~пали́тельный
[14 sh.] hasty, rash; ~пости́жный [14;
-жен, -жна] sudden; ~спе́лый [14 sh.]
early; fig. hasty; ~стно́й [14] (high-)
speed...; ~сть f [8; from g/pl. e.] speed;
све́та и т. д. velocity; mot. gear; со
~стью at the rate of; груз ма́лой
~стью slow freight

ско́р|ый [14; скор, -а́, -о] quick, fast, rap-
id, swift; по́мощь first (aid); будущем
near; ~о a. soon; ~ее всего́ coll. most
probably; на ~ую ру́ку coll. in haste, anyhow

скоси́ть → ска́шивать

скот m [1 e.] cattle, livestock; ~и́на f [5]
coll. cattle; P beast, brute; ~ный [14]:
~ный двор cattle yard; ~обо́йня f [6;
g/pl.:-о́ен] slaughterhouse; ~ово́дство
n [9] cattle breeding; ~ский [16] brutish,
bestial

скра́|шивать [1], ⟨~сить⟩ [15] fig. re-
lieve, lighten, smooth over

скребо́к m [1; -бка́] scraper

скре́жет [1], ~а́ть [3] (T) gnash

скреп|и́ть → ~ля́ть; ~ка f [5; g/pl.:-пок]

(paper) clip; ~ле́ние n [12] fastening;
~ля́ть[28], ⟨~и́ть⟩ [14 e.; -плю́, -пи́шь,
-плённый] fasten together; clamp;
make fast; по́дписью countersign; ~я́
се́рдце reluctantly

скрести́ [24 -б-: скребу́; скрёб] scrape;
scratch

скре́щива|ть [1], ⟨скрести́ть⟩ [15 e.;
-ещу́, -ести́шь; -ещённый] cross; clash
(v/i. -ся); ~ние n [12] crossing; inter-
section

скрип m [1] creak, squeak; снега́
crunch; ~а́ч m [1 e.] violinist; ~е́ть
[10 e.; -плю́, -пи́шь], ⟨про-⟩, once ⟨-
ну́ть⟩ [20] creak, squeak; crunch; зу-
ба́ми grit, gnash; ~ка f [5; g/pl.:-пок]
violin

скро́мн|ость f [8] modesty; ~ый [14;
-мен, -мна́, -о] modest; обе́д frugal

скру́|чивать[1], ⟨~ти́ть⟩ [15] twist; roll;
bind

скры|ва́ть [1], ⟨~ть⟩ [22] hide, conceal
(от P from); -ся disappear;
(пря́таться) hide; ~тность f [8] reserve; ~тный [14; -тен, -тна] reserved,
reticent; ~тый [14] concealed; latent
(a. phys.); secret; смысл hidden;
~ть(ся) → ~ва́ть(ся)

скря́га m/f [5] miser, skinflint

ску́дный [14; -ден, -дна] scanty, poor

ску́ка f [5] boredom, ennui

скула́ f [5; pl. st.] cheekbone; ~стый [14
sh.] with high or prominent cheek-
-bones

скули́ть [13] whimper

ску́льпт|ор m [1] sculptor; ~у́ра f [5]
sculpture

ску́мбрия f [7] mackerel

скуп|а́ть [1], ⟨~и́ть⟩ buy up, corner

скуп|и́ться[14], ⟨по-⟩ be stingy (or spar-
ing), stint (на B in, of); ~о́й[14; скуп, -а́,
-о] stingy; sparing (на B in); inadequate;
taciturn (на слова); su. miser; ~ость f
[8] stinginess, miserliness

скуч|а́ть [1] be bored (о П, по Д) long
(for), miss; ~ный [14; -чен,
-чна́, -о] boring, tedious, dull; (Д)
~но feel bored

слаб|е́ть[8], ⟨о-⟩ weaken; о ветре и т.
д. slacken; ~и́тельный [14] laxative (n

a. su.); **~ово́льный** [14; -лен, -льна] weak-willed; **~ость** *f* [8] weakness, *a. fig.* = foible (**к** Д for); infirmity; **~оу́мный** [14; -мен, -мна] feeble-minded; **~охара́ктерный** [14; -рен, -рна] characterless; of weak character; **~ый** [14; слаб, -á, -о] weak (*a. el.*); feeble; *звук, сходство* faint; *здоровье* delicate; *характер* flabby; *зрение* poor

сла́в|а *f* [5] glory; fame, renown; reputation, repute; **~а бо́гу!** thank goodness!; **на ~у** *coll.* first-rate, wonderful, right-on; **~ить** [14], ⟨про-⟩ glorify; praise, extol; **-ся** be famous (Т for); **~ный** [14; -вен, -вна, -о] famous, glorious; *coll.* nice; splendid

славян|и́н *m* [1; *pl.*: -я́не, -я́н], **~ка** *f* [5; *g/pl.*: -нок] Slav; **~ский** [16] Slavic, Slavonic

слага́ть [1], ⟨сложи́ть⟩ [16] *песню* compose; *оружие* lay down; *полномочия* resign (from); *обязанности* relieve o.s. (of); → **скла́дывать(ся)**

сла́д|кий [16; -док, -дкá, -о; *compr.*: -сла́ще] sweet; sugary; **~кое** *su.* dessert (**на** В for); **~остный** [14; -тен, -тна] sweet, delightful; **~остра́стие** *n* [12] voluptuousness; **~остра́стный** [14] voluptuous; **~ость** *f* [8] sweetness, delight; → **сла́сти**

сла́женный [14 *sh.*] harmonious; *действия* coordinated

слайд *m* [1] slide, transparency

сла́нец *m* [1; -нца] shale, slate

сла́сти *f/pl.* [8; *from gen. e.*] candy *sg.*, *Brt. a.* sweets

слать [шлю, шлёшь], ⟨по-⟩ send

слаща́вый [14 *sh.*] sugary, sickly sweet

сле́ва on, to (*or* from) the left

слегка́ slightly; somewhat; *прикосну́ться* lightly, gently

след *m* [1; *g/sg. e.* & -ду; на -ду́; *pl. e.*] trace (*a. fig.*); track; footprint; (*запах*) scent; **~ом** (right) behind; **его́ и ~ просты́л** *coll.* he vanished into thin air; **~и́ть** [15 *e.*; -ежу́, -еди́шь] ⟨за Т⟩ watch, follow; (*присма́тривать*) look after; *тайно* shadow; *за собы́тиями* keep up (**за** Т with)

сле́доват|ель *m* [4] investigator; **~ель-**

но consequently, therefore; so; **~ь** [7] ⟨за Т; Д⟩ follow; result (**из** Р from); be bound for; (Д) *impers.* should, ought to; **как сле́дует** properly, as it should be; **кому́** *or* **куда́ сле́дует** to the proper person *or* quarter

сле́дствие *n* [12] **1.** consequence; **2.** investigation

сле́дующий [17] following, next

слёжка *f* [5; *g/pl.*: -жек] shadowing

слез|á *f* [5; *pl.*: слёзы, слёз, слеза́м] tear; **~а́ть** [1], ⟨-ть⟩ [24 *st.*] come or get down (from); *с ло́шади* dismount; *coll. о коже, краске* come off; **~и́ться** [15; -и́тся] water; **~ли́вый** [14 *sh.*] prone to crying; tearful, lachrymose; **~ото-чи́вый** [14] *глаза́* running; *газ* tear; **~ть** → **~а́ть**

слеп|éнь *m* [4; -пня́] gadfly; **~éц** *m* [1; -пца́] blind man; *fig.* one who fails to notice the obvious; **~и́ть 1.** [14 *e.*; -плю́, -пи́шь], ⟨о-⟩ [ослеплённый] *я́рким све́том* dazzle; **2.** [14] *pf.*; *impf.* **~ля́ть** [28] stick together (*v/i.* **-ся**) → *a.* **лепи́ть**; **~нуть** [21], ⟨о-⟩ go (*or* become) blind; **~о́й** [14; слеп, -á, -о] blind (*a. fig.*); *текст* indistinct; *su.* blind man; **~о́к** *m* [1; -пка] mo(u)ld, cast; **~отá** *f* [5] blindness

сле́сар|ь *m* [4; *pl.*: -ря́, *etc. e.*, & -ри] metalworker; fitter; locksmith

слет|а́ть [1], ⟨-éть⟩ [11] fly down, (from); *coll.* fall down, off); **-ся** fly together

слечь *coll.* [26 г/ж: сля́гу, сля́жешь; сля́г(те)!] *pf.* fall ill; take to one's bed

сли́ва *f* [5] plum

сли|ва́ть [1], ⟨-ть⟩ [солью́, -льёшь; → **лить**] pour (off, out, together); *о фирмах и т. д.* merge, amalgamate (*v/i.* **-ся**)

сли́в|ки *f/pl.* [5; *gen.*: -вок] cream (*a. fig.* = elite); **~очный** [14] creamy; **~очное ма́сло** butter; **~очное моро́женое** ice cream

слизистый [14 *sh.*] mucous; slimy; **~истая оболо́чка** mucous membrane; **~ь** *f* [8] slime; mucus, phlegm

слипа́ться [1] stick together; *о глаза́х* close

С

сли́т|ный [14] joined; united; **~ное написа́ние слов** omission of hyphen from words; **~но** *a.* together; **~ок** *m* [1; -тка] ingot; **~ь(ся)** → **слива́ться**

слича́ть [1], ⟨~и́ть⟩ [16 *e.*; -чу́, -чи́шь; -чённый] compare, collate

сли́шком too; too much; **э́то (уж) ~** *coll.* that beats everything

слия́ние *n* [12] *рек* confluence; *фирм* amalgamation, merger

слова́к *m* [1] Slovak

слова́р|ный [14]: **~ный соста́в** stock of words; **~ь** *m* [4 *e.*] dictionary; vocabulary, glossary; lexicon

слова́цкий [16]; **~а́чка** *f* [5; *g/pl.*: -чек] Slovak; **~е́нец** *m* [1; -нца], **~е́нка** *f* [5; *g/pl.*: -нок], **~е́нский** [16] Slovene

слове́с|ость *f* [8] literature; *obs.* philology; **~ый** [14] verbal, oral

сло́вно as if; like; *coll.* as it were

сло́в|о *n* [9; *pl. e.*] word; **~ом** in a word; **~о за ~о** word for word; speech; **к ~у сказа́ть** by the way; **по слова́м** according to; **проси́ть (предоста́вить** Д**) ~** ask (give p.) permission to speak; **~оизмене́ние** *n* [12] inflection (*Brt.* -xion); **~оохо́тливый** [14 *sh.*] talkative

слог *m* [1; *from g/pl. e.*] syllable; style

слоёный [14] *тесто* puff pastry

сложе́ние *n* [12] *math.* addition; *человека* constitution, build; *полномочий* laying down; **~и́ть(ся)** → **скла́дывать(ся), слага́ть(ся)** & **класть 2.**; **~ность** *f* [8] complexity; **в о́бщей ~ности** all in all; **~ный** [14; -жен, -жна́, -о] complicated, complex, intricate; *слово* compound

сло́|истый [14 *sh.*] stratiform; flaky; **~й** *m* [3; *pl. e.*: слои́, слоёв] layer, stratum (in Т *pl.*); *краски* coat(ing)

слом *m* [1] demolition, pulling down; **~и́ть** [14] *pf.* break, smash; *fig.* overcome; **~я́ го́лову** *coll.* headlong, at breakneck speed

слон *m* [1 *e.*] elephant; bishop (*chess*); **~о́вый** [14] *~о́вая кость* ivory

слоня́ться *coll.* [28] loiter about

слуга́ *m* [5; *pl. st.*] servant; **~жащий** [17] employee; **~жба** *f* [5] service; work; employment; **~жебный** [14] office…; official; **~же́ние** *n* [12] service; **~жи́ть** [16], ⟨по-⟩ serve (a p./th. Д); be in use

слух *m* [1] hearing; ear (**на** В by; **по** Д); rumo(u)r, hearsay; **~обо́й** [14] of hearing; acoustic; ear…

слу́ча|й *m* [3] case; occurrence, event; occasion (**по** Д on; **при** П), opportunity, chance; (*a.* **несча́стный ~й**) accident; **во вся́ком ~е** in any case; **в проти́вном ~е** otherwise; **на вся́кий ~й** to be on the safe side; **по ~ю** on the occasion (of P); **~йность** *f* [8] chance; **~йный** [14; -аен, -айна] accidental, fortuitous; casual; chance (**~йно** by chance); **~ться** [1], ⟨случи́ться⟩ [16 *e.*; 3 rd *p. or impers.*] happen (**с** Т to); come about; take place; **что бы ни случи́лось** come what may

слу́ша|тель *m* [4] listener, hearer; student; *pl. collect.* audience; **~ть** [1], ⟨по-⟩ listen (В to); *лекции* attend; **~ю!** (*on telephone*) hello!; **-ся** obey (Р р.); *совета* take

слыть [23], ⟨про-⟩ (Т) have a reputation for

слы́|шать [4], ⟨у-⟩ hear (of, about **о** П); **~шаться** [4] be heard; **~шимость** *f* [8] audibility; **~шно** one can hear; **мне ~шно** I can hear; **что ~шно?** what's new?; **~шный** [14; -шен, -шна, -о] audible

слюда́ *f* [5] mica

слюн|а́ *f* [5], **~и** *coll. pl.* [8; *from gen. e.*] saliva, spittle; **~и** *coll. fl/pl.*: (**у** Р) **от э́того ~и теку́т** makes one's mouth water

сля́коть *f* [8] slush

сма́з|ать → **~ывать**; **~ка** *f* [5; *g/pl.*: -зок] greasing, oiling, lubrication; lubricant; **~очный** [14] lubricating; **~ывать** [1], ⟨~ать⟩ [3] grease, oil, lubricate; *coll. очертания* slur; blur

сма́|нивать [1], ⟨~ни́ть⟩ [13; сманю́, -а́нишь; -а́ненный & -анённый] lure, entice; **~тывать**, ⟨смота́ть⟩ [1] wind, reel; **~хивать** [1], ⟨~хну́ть⟩ [20] brush off (*or* aside); *impf. coll.* (*походить*) have a likeness (**на** В to); **~чивать** [1], ⟨смочи́ть⟩ [16] moisten

сме́жный [14; -жен, -жна́] adjacent

смéл|ость *f* [8] boldness; courage; **~ый** [14; смел, -á, -о] courageous; bold; **~о** *a. coll.* easily; **могу́ ~о сказа́ть** I can safely say

смéн|а *f* [5] shift (**в** B in); change; changing; replacement; successors *pl.*; **прийти́ на ~у** → **~я́ться**; **~я́ть** [28], ⟨**~и́ть**⟩ [13; -еню́, -éнишь; -енённый] (**-ся** be) supersede(d; o.a.), relieve(d), replace(d by T), substitut(ed; for); give way to

смерк|а́ться [1], ⟨**~ну́ться**⟩ [20] grow dusky *or* dark

смерт|éльный [14; -лен, -льна] mortal; *исхо́д* fatal; *яд* deadly; **~ность** *f* [8] mortality, death rate; **~ный** [14; -тен, -тна] mortal (*a. su.*); *грех* deadly; *law* death…; *казнь* capital; **~ь** *f* [8; *from g/pl. e.*] death; *coll.* **надоéсть до́ ~и** bore to death; **при ~и** at death's door

смерч *m* [1] waterspout; tornado

смести́ → **смета́ть**; **~ть** → **смеща́ть**

смéс|ь *f* [8] mixture; blend, compound; **~та** *f* [5] *fin.* estimate

смета́на *f* [5] sour cream

смета́ть [1], ⟨**~сти́**⟩ [25 -т-] sweep *or* away; sweep into; **~ с лица́ земли́** wipe off the face of the earth

смéтливый [14 *sh.*] sharp, quick on the uptake

сметь [8], ⟨**по-**⟩ dare, venture

смех *m* [1] laughter; **со́ ~у** with laughter; **~а ра́ди** for a joke, for fun, in jest; **подня́ть на́ ~** ridicule; → **шу́тка**

смéш|анный [14] mixed; **~а́ть(ся)** → **~ивать(ся)**; **~ивать**, ⟨**~а́ть**⟩ [1] mix with, blend with (*v/i.* **-ся**; get *or* be[come]) confuse(d); *с толпо́й* mingle with

смеши́ть [16 *e.*; -шу́, -ши́шь], ⟨**рас-**⟩ [-шённый] make laugh; **~но́й** [14; -шóн, -шнá] laughable, ludicrous; ridiculous; funny; **мне не ~но́** I don't see anything funny in it

сме|ща́ть [1], ⟨**~сти́ть**⟩ [15 *e.*; -ещу́, -ести́шь; -ещённый] displace, shift, remove; **~ще́ние** *n* [12] displacement, removal

смея́ться [27 *e.*; -еюсь, -еёшься], ⟨**за-**⟩ laugh (*impf.* **над** T at); mock (at); de-

ride; *coll.* **шути́ть** joke

смире́|ние *n* [12], **~нность** *f* [8] humility; meekness; **~и́ть(ся)** → **~я́ть(ся)**; **~ный** [14; -рен (*coll.* -рён), -рнá, -о] meek, gentle; (*поко́рный*) submissive; **~я́ть** [28], ⟨**~и́ть**⟩ [13] restrain, check; **-ся** resign o.s. (**с** T to)

смо́кинг *m* [1] tuxedo, dinner jacket

смол|á *f* [5; *pl. st.*] resin; pitch; tar; **~и́стый** [14 *sh.*] resinous; **~и́ть** [13], ⟨**вы-**, **за-**⟩ pitch, tar; **~ка́ть** [1], ⟨**~кнуть**⟩ [21] grow silent; *звук* cease; **~оду** *coll.* from *or* in one's youth; **~яно́й** [14] pitch…, tar…

сморка́ться [1], ⟨**вы-**⟩ blow one's nose

сморо́дина *f* [5] currant(s *pl.*)

смота́ть → **сма́тывать**

смотр|éть [9; -отрю́, -о́тришь; -о́тренный], ⟨**по-**⟩ look (**на** B at); gaze; view, see, watch; *больно́го и т. д.* examine, inspect; **~я́** depending (**по** Д on), according (to); **~éть в о́ба** keep one's eyes open, be on guard; **~й не опозда́й!** mind you are not late!; **~и́тель** *m* [4] supervisor; *музе́я* custodian, keeper

смочи́ть → **сма́чивать**

смрад *m* [1] stench; **~ный** [14; -ден, -дна] stinking

сму́глый [14; смугл, -á, -о] swarthy

смут|и́ть(ся) → **смуща́ть(ся)**; **~ный** [14; -тен, -тна] vague, dim; *на душе́* restless, uneasy

смуща́ть [1], ⟨**смути́ть**⟩ [15 *e.*; -ущу́, -ути́шь; -ущённый] (**-ся** be[come]) embarrass(ed), confuse(d), perplex(ed); **~éние** *n* [12] embarrassment, confusion; **~ённый** [14] embarrassed, confused

смы|ва́ть [1], ⟨**~ть**⟩ [22] wash off (*or* away); **~ка́ть** [1], ⟨**сомкну́ть**⟩ [20] close (*v/i.* **-ся**); **~сл** *m* [1] sense, meaning; **в э́том ~сле** in this respect; *coll.* **како́й ~сл?** what's the point?; **~слить** *coll.* [13] understand; **~ть** → **~ва́ть**; **~чко́вый** [14] *mus.* stringed; **~чо́к** *m* [1; -чкá] *mus.* bow; **~шлёный** *coll.* [14] clever, bright

смягч|а́ть (-xtʃ-) [1], ⟨**~и́ть**⟩ [16 *e.*; -чу́, -чи́шь; -чённый] soften (*v/i.* **-ся**); *наказа́ние, боль* mitigate, alleviate; **-ся** *a.*

relent; **~а́ющий** *law* extenuating; **~е́ние** *n* [12] mitigation; **~и́ть(ся)** → **~а́ть(ся)**

смяте́ние *n* [12] confusion

снаб|жа́ть [1], ⟨**~ди́ть**⟩ [15 *e.*; -бжу́, -бди́шь; -бжённый] supply, furnish, provide (with P); **~же́ние** *n* [12] supply, provision

снайпер *m* [1] sharpshooter, sniper

снаружи on the outside; from (the) outside

снаря́д projectile, missile, shell; *гимнасти́ческий* apparatus; **~жа́ть** [1], ⟨**~ди́ть**⟩ [15 *e.*; -яжу́, -яди́шь; -яжённый] equip, fit out (T with); **~же́ние** *n* [12] equipment; outfit; *mil.* munitions *pl.*

снасть *f* [8; *from g/pl. e.*] tackle; *usu. pl.* rigging

снача́ла at first; first; (*снова*) all over again

снег *m* [1; в-у; *pl. e.*: -á] snow; **~ идёт** it is snowing; **~и́рь** *m* [4 *e.*] bullfinch; **~опа́д** *m* [1] snowfall

снеж|и́нка *f* [5; *g/pl.*: -нок] snowflake; **~ный** [14; -жен, -жна] snow(y); **~о́к** *m* [1; -жка́] *dim.* → **снег**; light snow; snowball

сни|жа́ть [1], ⟨**~зить**⟩ [15] lower; (*уменьши́ть*) reduce, decrease; (**-ся** *v/i.*; *a.* fall) (*себесто́имости*) cut production costs; **~же́ние** *n* [12] lowering, reduction, decrease; fall; **~зойти́** → **~сходи́ть**; **~зу** from below

сним|а́ть [1], ⟨**снять**⟩ [сниму́, сни́мешь; снял, -á, -о; сня́тый (снят, -á, -о)] take (off *or* down); remove, discard; *с рабо́ты* sack, dismiss; *кандидату́ру* withdraw; *фильм* shoot; *ко́мнату* rent; (take a) photograph (of); *урожа́й* reap, gather; *оса́ду* raise; *ко́пию* make; **~а́ть сли́вки** skim; **-ся** weigh (**с я́коря** anchor); have a picture of o.s. taken; *с уче́та* be struck off; **~о́к** *m* [1; -мка] photograph, photo, print (**на** П in)

сниска́ть [3] get, win

снисхо|ди́тельный [14; -лен, -льна] condescending; indulgent; **~ди́ть** [15], ⟨**снизойти́**⟩ [-ойду́, -ойдёшь; → **идти́**] condescend; **~жде́ние** *n* [12] indul-

gence, leniency; condescension

сни́ться [13], ⟨при-⟩ *impers.* (Д) dream (of И)

сно́ва (over) again, anew

сно|ва́ть [7 *e.*] scurry about, dash about; **~виде́ние** *n* [12] dream

сноп *m* [1 *e.*] sheaf

сноро́вка *f* [5] knack, skill

сно|си́ть [15], ⟨**снести́**⟩ [24 -с-: снесу́, снёс] carry (down, away *or* off); take; *зда́ние* pull down, demolish; (*терпе́ть*) endure, bear, tolerate; → *a.* **нести́**; **~ска** *f* [5; *g/pl.*:-сок] footnote; **~ный** [14; -сен, -сна] tolerable

снотво́рное *n* [14] *su.* soporific

сноха́ *f* [5; *pl. st.*] daughter-in-law

сня́т|ой [14]: **~ое молоко́** skimmed milk; **~ь(ся)** → **снима́ть(ся)**

соба́|ка *f* [5] dog; hound; **~чий** [18] dog('s), canine

собесе́дник *m* [1] interlocutor

собира́т|ель *m* [4] collector; **~ельный** [14] *gr.* collective; **~ь**[1], ⟨собра́ть⟩ [-беру́, -рёшь; -ал, -á, -о; со́бранный (-ан, -á, -о)] gather, collect; *tech.* assemble; prepare; **-ся** gather, assemble; prepare for, make o.s. (*or* be) ready to start (*or* set out *or* go; **в путь** on a journey); (*намерева́ться*) be going to, intend to; collect (**с мы́слями** one's thoughts); (*с си́лами*) brace up

собла́зн *m* [1] temptation; **~и́тель** *m* [4] tempter; seducer; **~и́тельный** [14; -лен, -льна] tempting, seductive; **~я́ть** [28], ⟨**~и́ть**⟩ [13] (**-ся** be) tempt(ed); allured, enticed

соблю|да́ть [1], ⟨**~сти́**⟩ [25] observe, obey, adhere (to); *поря́док* maintain; **~де́ние** *n* [12] observance; maintenance; **~сти́** → **~да́ть**

соболе́знова|ние *n* [12] sympathy, condolences; **~ть** [7] sympathize (Д with)

собо́|ль *m* [4; *pl. a.* -ля́, *etc. e.*] sable; **~р** *m* [1] cathedral

собра́|ние *n* [12] meeting (**на** В at, in), assembly; collection; **~ть(ся)** → **собира́ть(ся)**

со́бственн|ик *m* [1] owner, proprietor; **~ость** *f* [8] property; possession, ownership; **~ый** [14] own; *и́мя* proper; personal

собы́тие n [12] event, occurrence

сова́ f [5; pl. st.] owl

сова́ть [7 e.; сую́, суёшь, ⟨су́нуть⟩ [20] shove, thrust; coll. slip; butt in, poke one's nose into

соверш|а́ть [1], ⟨~и́ть⟩ [16 e.; -шу́, -ши́шь; -шённый] accomplish; преступление и т. д. commit; поездку и т. д. make; сде́лку strike; **-ся** happen, take place; **~енноле́тие** n [12] majority, full age; **~еннолетний** [15] ⟨стать T come) of age; **~ённый** [14; -ёнен, -ённа] perfect(ive gr); coll. absolute, complete; adv. a. quite; **~е́нство** n [9] perfection; в ~é**нстве** a. perfectly; **~е́нствовать** [7], ⟨у-⟩ perfect (**-ся** o.s.), improve, develop; **~и́ть(ся)** → **соверша́ть(ся)**

со́вест|ливый [14 sh.] conscientious; **~но** (p. Д) ashamed; **~ь** f [8] conscience; по ~и honestly, to be honest

сове́т m [1] advice; law opinion; board; soviet; ♀ **Безопа́сности** Security Council; **~ник** m [1] adviser; (as title of office or post) councillor; **~овать** [7], ⟨по-⟩ advise (Д p.); **-ся** ask advice, consult (о П on); **~ский** [16] soviet (of local bodies); **~чик** m [1] adviser

совеща́|ние n [12] conference (at **на** П), meeting (a. in); (обсужде́ние) deliberation; **~тельный** [14] deliberative, consultative; **~ться** [1] confer, consult, deliberate

совме|сти́мый [14 sh.] compatible; **~сти́ть** → **~ща́ть**; **~стный** [14] joint, combined; **~стно** common; **~ща́ть** [1], ⟨~сти́ть⟩ [15 e.; -ещу́, -ести́шь; -ещён-ный] combine; tech. match

сово́к m [1; -вка́] shovel; scoop; для му́сора dustpan

совоку́пн|ость f [8] total(ity), aggregate, whole; **~ый** [14] join(t)

совпа|да́ть [1], ⟨~сть⟩ [25; pt. st.] coincide with; agree with; **~де́ние** n [12] coincidence, etc. → vb.

совреме́нн|ик m [1] contemporary; **~ый** [14; -е́нен, -е́нна] contemporaneous; of the time (of); present-day; up-to-date; → a. **~ик** contemporary

совсе́м quite, entirely; at all; **я его́ ~ не зна́ю** I don't know him at all

совхо́з m [1] (**сове́тское хозя́йство**) state farm; → **колхо́з**

согла́|сие n [12] consent (**на** B to; **с** P with); agreement (**по** Д by); harmony, concord; **~си́ться** → **~ша́ться**; **~сно** (Д) according to, in accordance with; **~сный** [14; -сен, -сна] agreeable; harmonious; **я ~сен** (f ~сна) I agree (**с** T with; **на** B to); (a. su.) consonant; **~сова́ние** n [12] coordination; gr. agreement; **~сова́ть** → **~со́вывать**; **~сова́ться** [7] (im)pf. (**с** T) conform (to); agree (with); **~со́вывать** [1], ⟨~сова́ть⟩ [7] coordinate; come to an agreement (**с** T with); (a. gr.) make agree; **~ша́ться** [1], ⟨~си́ться⟩ [15 e.; -ашу́сь, -аси́шься] agree (**с** T with; **на** B to), consent (to); coll. (признава́ть) admit; **~ше́ние** n [12] agreement, understanding; covenant

согна́ть → **сгоня́ть**

согну́ть(ся) → **сгиба́ть(ся)**

согре|ва́ть [1], ⟨~ть⟩ [28] warm, heat

соде́йств|ие n [12] assistance, help; **~овать** [7] (im)pf., a. ⟨по-⟩ (Д) assist, help; успе́ху, согла́сию contribute (to), further, promote

содерж|а́ние n [12] content(s); семьи́ и т. д. maintenance, support, upkeep; **~а́тельный** [14; -лен, -льна] pithy, having substance and point; **~а́ть** [4] contain, hold; maintain, support; keep; **-ся** be contained, etc.; **~и́мое** [14] contents pl.

содра́ть → **сдира́ть**

содрог|а́ние n [12], **~а́ться** [1], once ⟨~ну́ться⟩ [20] shudder

содру́жеств|о n [9] community; concord; **Брита́нское ~о на́ций** the British Commonwealth; **в те́сном ~е** in close cooperation (**с** T with)

соедине́ние n [12] joining; conjunction; (at a. **на** П), connection; combination; chem. compound; tech. joint; **~и́тельный** [14] connective; a. gr. copulative; **~я́ть** [28], ⟨~и́ть⟩ [13] unite, join; connect; link (by telephone, etc.); (v/i. **-ся**) → **США**

C

сожал|ение n [12] regret (**о** П for); **к ~ению** unfortunately, to (p.'s) regret; **~еть** [8] (**о** П) regret

сожжение n [12] burning; cremation

сожительство n [9] cohabitation

созв|ать → **созывать**; **~ездие** n [12] constellation; **~ониться** coll. [13] pf. (**с** Т) speak on the phone; arrange s.th. on the phone; phone; **~учный** [14; -чен, -чна] in keeping with, consonant with

созда|вать [5], ⟨~ть⟩ [-дам, -дашь etc., → **дать**]; создал, -á, -о; созданный (-ан, -á, -о)] create; produce; found; establish; **~ся** arise, form; **у меня ~лось впечатление** I have gained the impression that ...; **~ние** n [12] creation; (существо) creature; **~тель** m [4] creator; founder; **~ть(ся)** → **~вать(ся)**

созерца|тельный [14; -лен, -льна] contemplative; **~ть** [1] contemplate

созида́тельный [14; -лен, -льна] creative

созна|вать [5], ⟨~ть⟩ [1] realize, be conscious of, see; **-ся** (**в** П) confess; **~ние** n [12] consciousness; **без ~ния** unconscious; **~тельный** [14; -лен, -льна] conscious; отношение и т. д. conscientious; **~ть(ся)** → **~вать(ся)**

созы́в m [1] convocation; **~ать** [1], ⟨созвать⟩ [созову, -вёшь; -звал, -á, -о; созванный] гостей invite; собрание call, convene; parl. convoke

соизмери́мый [14 sh.] commensurable

сойти́(сь) → **сходи́ть(ся)**

сок m [1; в -ý] juice; берёзовый и т. д. sap; **~овыжима́лка** f [5; -лок] juice extractor

со́кол m [1] falcon

сокра|ща́ть [1], ⟨~ти́ть⟩ [15 e.; -ащу, -ати́шь; -ащённый] shorten; abbreviate; abridge; расходы reduce, curtail; p. pt. p. a. short, brief; **-ся** grow shorter; decrease; о мышцах и т. д. contract; **~ще́ние** n [12] shortening, abbreviation, reduction, curtailment; текста abridgement; contraction

сокрове́нный [14 sh.] innermost; secret; concealed; **~ище** n [11] treasure; **~ищница** f [5] treasury

сокруш|а́ть [1], ⟨~и́ть⟩ [16 e.; -шу, -ши́шь; -шённый] shatter, smash; **~и́ть врага́** rout the enemy; **-ся** impf. grieve, be distressed; **~и́тельный** [14; -лен, -льна] shattering; **~и́ть** → **~а́ть**

солда́т m [1; g/pl.: солда́т] soldier; **~ский** [16] soldier's

сол|е́ние n [12] salting; **~ёный** [14; со́лон, -á, -о] salt(y); corned; pickled; fig. spicy; (short forms only) hot

солида́рн|ость f [8] solidarity; **~ый** [14; -рен, -рна] in sympathy with, at one with; law jointly liable

соли́дн|ость f [8] solidity; **~ый** [14; -ден, -дна] solid, strong, sound; фирма reputable, respectable; coll. sizable

соли́ст m [1], **~ка** f [5; g/pl.: -ток] soloist

соли́ть [13; солю́, со́лишь; со́ленный] **1.** ⟨по-⟩ salt; **2.** ⟨за-⟩ corn; pickle; ⟨на-⟩ coll. spite; cause annoyance; do s.o. a bad turn

со́лн|ечный [14; -чен, -чна] sun(ny); solar; **~це** ('son-) n [11] sun (**на** П lie in); **~цепёк** m [1]: **на ~цепёке** in the blazing sun

солове́й m [3; -вья́] nightingale

со́лод m [1]. **~овый** [14] malt

соло́м|а f [5] straw; thatch; **~енный** [14] straw...; thatched; грязь (widow); **~инка** f [5; g/pl.: -нок] straw; **хвата́ться за ~инку** clutch at straws

соло́нка f [5; g/pl.: -нок] saltcellar

соль f [8; from g/pl. e.] salt (a. fig.); coll. **вот в чём вся ~ь** that's the whole point; **~яно́й** [14] salt...; saline

сом m [1 e.] catfish

сомкну́ть(ся) → **смыка́ть(ся)**

сомн|ева́ться [1], ⟨усомни́ться⟩ [13] (**в** П) doubt; **~е́ние** n [12] doubt (**в** П about); question (**под** Т in); **~и́тельный** [14; -лен, -льна] doubtful; questionable, dubious

сон m [1; сна] sleep; dream (in **в** П); **~ли́вый** [14 sh.] sleepy; **~ный** [14] sleeping (a. med.); sleepy, drowsy; **~я** coll. m/f [6; g/pl.: -ней] sleepyhead

сообра|жа́ть [1], ⟨~зи́ть⟩ [15 e.; -ажу́, -ази́шь; -ажённый] consider, weigh, think (over); (поня́ть) grasp, understand; **~же́ние** n [12] consideration;

(*причина*) reason; ~зи́тельный [14; -лен, -льна] sharp, quick-witted; ~зи́ть → ~жа́ть; ~зный [14; -зен, -зна] conformable (**с** T to); *adv. a.* in conformity (with); ~зова́ть [7] (*im*)*pf.* (make) conform, adapt (to) (**с** T); -**ся** conform, adapt (**с** T to)

сообща́ together, jointly

сообща́|ть [1], ⟨~и́ть⟩ [16 *e.*; -щу́, -щи́шь; -щённый] communicate (*v/i.* -**ся** *impf.*), report; inform (Д/**о** П *p. of*); impart; ~éние *n* [12] communication, report; statement; announcement; information; ~éство *n* [9] association, fellowship; community; ~и́ть → ~а́ть; ~ник *m* [1], ~ница *f* [5] accomplice

сооруж|а́ть [1], ⟨~и́ть⟩ [15 *e.*; -ужу́, -уди́шь; -ужённый] build, construct, erect, raise; ~éние *n* [12] construction, building, structure

соотве́тств|енный [14 *sh.*] corresponding; *adv. a.* according(ly) (Д to), in accordance (with); ~ие *n* [12] conformity, accordance; ~овать [7] (Д) correspond, conform (to), agree; ~ующий [17] corresponding, appropriate

соотéчественни|к *m* [1], ~ца *f* [5] compatriot, fellow country (wo)man

соотноше́ние *n* [12] correlation

сопе́рни|к *m* [1] rival; ~чать [1] compete, vie (with); rival; be a match (for **с** T); ~чество *n* [9] rivalry

соп|е́ть [10 *e.*; соплю́, сопи́шь] breathe heavily through the nose; wheeze; ~ка *f* [5; *g/pl.*: -пок] hill; volcano; ~ли *P pl.* [6; *gen.*: -лей, *etc. e.*] snot

сопоставл|е́ние *n* [12] comparison; confrontation; ~я́ть [28], ⟨~я́вить⟩ [14] compared

соприкаса́ться [1], ⟨~косну́ться⟩ [20] (**с** T) (*примыка́ть*) adjoin; (*каса́ться*) touch; **с** людьми́ deal with; ~коснове́ние *n* [12] contact

сопрово|ди́тельный [14] covering (*letter*); ~жда́ть [1] **1.** accompany; escort; **2.** ⟨~ди́ть⟩ [15 *e.*; -ожу́, -оди́шь; -ождённый] *примеча́нием и т. д.* provide (T with); -**ся** *impf.* be accompanied (T by); entail; ~жде́ние *n* [12] accompaniment; **в** ~жде́нии (P) accompanied

(by)

сопротивл|е́ние *n* [12] resistance; opposition; ~я́ться [28] (Д) resist; oppose

сопряжённый [14; -жён, -жена́] connected with; entailing

сопу́тствовать [14] (Д) accompany

сор *m* [1] dust; litter

соразме́рно in proportion (Д to)

сорв|ане́ц *coll. m* [1; -нца́] madcap; (*of a child*) a terror; ~а́ть(ся) → **срыва́ть(ся)**; ~иголова́ *coll. m/f* [5; *ac/ sg.*: сорвиголову́; *pl.* → **голова́**] daredevil

соревнова́|ние *n* [12] competition; contest; **отбо́рочные** ~ния heats, qualifying rounds; ~ться [7] (**с** T) compete (with)

сор|и́ть [13], ⟨на-⟩ litter; *fig. деньга́ми* squander; ~ный [14]; ~ная трава́ = ~ня́к *m* [1 *e.*] weed

со́рок [35] forty; ~а *f* [5] magpie

сороко|во́й [14] fortieth; → **пятт(идеся́т)ый**; ~но́жка *f* [5; *g/pl.*: -жек] centipede

соро́чка *f* [5; -чек] shirt; undershirt; chemise

сорт *m* [1; *pl.*: -та́, *etc. e.*] sort, brand, variety, quality; ~ирова́ть [7], ⟨рас-⟩ sort out; *по разме́ру* grade; ~иро́вка *f* [5] sorting

соса́ть [-су́, -сёшь; со́санный] suck

сосе́д *m* [*sg.*: 1; *pl.*: 4], ~ка *f* [5; *g/pl.*: -док] neighbo(u)r; ~ний [15] neighbo(u)ring, adjoining; ~ский [16] neighbo(u)r's; ~ство *n* [9] neighbo(u)rhood

соси́ска *f* [5; *g/pl.*: -сок] sausage; frankfurter

со́ска *f* [5; *g/pl.*: -сок] (*baby's*) dummy, pacifier

соск|а́кивать [1], ⟨~очи́ть⟩ [16] jump *or* spring (off, down); come off; ~а́льзывать [1], ⟨~ользну́ть⟩ [20] slide (down, off); slip (off); ~у́читься [16] *pf.* become bored; miss (**по** Д); → **скуча́ть**

сосл|ага́тельный [14] *gr.* subjunctive; ~а́ть(ся) → **ссыла́ться**; ~у́живец *m* [1; -вца] colleague

сосна́ *f* [5; *pl. st.*: со́сны, со́сен, со́снам] pine tree

сосо́к *m* [1; -ска́] nipple, teat

сосредото́ч|ение *n* [12] concentration; **~ивать**[1], ⟨**~ить**⟩[16] concentrate (*v/i.* **-ся**); *p. pt. p. a.* intent

соста́в *m* [1] composition (*a. chem.*); structure; *студентов и т. д.* body; *thea.* cast; *rail.train*; **подвижно́й** rolling stock; **в ~е** (P) *a.* consisting of; **~и́тель** *m* [4] compiler; author; **~ить → ~ля́ть**; **~ле́ние** *n* [12] *словаря и т. д.* compilation; *документа и т. д.* drawing up; **~ля́ть** [28], ⟨**~ить**⟩ [14] compose, make (up; put together; *план и т. д.* draw up, work out; compile; (*образовывать*) form, constitute; (*равняться*) amount (*or* come to); **~но́й** [14]: composite; **~на́я часть** constituent part; component

состоя́|ние *n* [12] state, condition; position; (*богатство*) fortune; **быть в ~нии ...** *a.* be able to ...; **я не в ~нии** I am not in a position ...; **~тельный** [14; -лен, -льна] well-to-do, well-off; (*обоснованный*) sound, well-founded; **~ть** [-ою, -ойшь] consist (*из* P of; **в** П in); членом *и т. д.* be (*a.* T); **-ся** *pf.* take place

сострада́ние *n* [12] compassion, sympathy

состяза́|ние *n* [12] contest, competition; match; **~ться** [1] compete, vie, contend (with)

сосу́д *m* [1] vessel

сосу́лька *f* [5; *g/pl.:* -лек] icicle

сосуществова́|ние *n* [12] coexistence; **~ть** [7] coexist

сотворе́ние *n* [12] creation

со́тня *f* [6; *g/pl.:* -тен] a hundred

сотру́дни|к *m* [1] employee; *pl.* staff; *газеты* contributor; colleague; **~чать** [1] collaborate with; contribute to; **~чество** *n* [9] collaboration, cooperation

сотрясе́ние *n* [12] shaking; *мозга* concussion

со́ты *m/pl.* [1] honeycomb(s); **~й** [14] hundredth; → **пя́тый**; **две це́лых и два́дцать пять ~х** 2.25

со́ус *m* [1] sauce; gravy

соуча́ст|ие *n* [12] complicity; **~ник** *m* [1] accomplice

со́хнуть [21] **1.** ⟨**вы-**⟩ dry; **2.** ⟨**за-**⟩ *coll.* wither; **3.** *coll. impf.* pine away

сохран|е́ние *n* [12] preservation; conservation; **~и́ть(ся)** → **~я́ть(ся)**; **~ность** *f* [8] safety; undamaged state; **в ~ности** *a.* safe; **~я́ть** [28], ⟨**~и́ть**⟩ [13] keep; preserve; retain; maintain; reserve (for o.s. *за собо́й*); **Бо́же сохрани́!** God forbid!; **-ся** be preserved; *в па́мяти и т. д.* remain

социа́л|-демокра́т *m* [1] social democrat; **~-демократи́ческий** [16] social democrat(ic); **~и́зм** *m* [1] socialism; **~и́ст** *m* [1] socialist; **~исти́ческий** [16] socialist(ic); **~ьный** [14] social

соцстра́х *m* [1] social insurance

соче́льник *m* [1] Christmas Eve

сочета́|ние *n* [12] combination; **~ть** (*v/i.* **-ся**) combine

сочин|е́ние *n* [12] composition; writing, work; *научное* thesis; *gr.* coordination; **~я́ть** [28], ⟨**~и́ть**⟩ [13] compose (*a lit. or mus. work*); write; (*выдумать*) invent, make up

сочи́ться [16 *e.*; 3 *rd P. only*] exude; ooze (out); *о крови* bleed; **~** [14; -чен, -чна] juicy; *fig.* succulent; rich

сочу́вств|енный [14 *sh.*] sympathetic, sympathizing; **~овать**[7] (Д) sympathize (**к** Д with, for); **~овать**[7] (Д) sympathize with, feel for; **~ующий**[17] sympathizer

сою́з *m* [1] union; alliance; confederation; league; *gr.* conjunction; **~ник** *m* [1] ally; **~ный** [14] allied

со́я *f* [6] soya bean

спад *m* [1] *econ.* recession; slump; **~а́ть** [1], ⟨**~сть**⟩ [25; *pt. st.*] fall; **~ива́ть 1.** ⟨**~я́ть**⟩ [28] solder; **2.** *coll.* (*споить*) [13] accustom to drinking; **~йка** *f* [5] *fig.* union

спа́льн|ый[14] sleeping; bed...; **~ое ме́сто** bunk, berth; **~я***f*[6; *g/pl.:*-лен] bedroom

спа́ржа *f* [5] asparagus

спаса́|тель *m* [4] one of a rescue team; (*at seaside*) lifeguard; **~тельный** [14] rescue...; life-saving; **~ть** [1], ⟨**~ти́**⟩ [24 -с-] save, rescue; **~ти́ положе́ние** save the situation; **-ся**, ⟨**-сь**⟩ save o.s.; *a.* escape (*v/i.* **от** P); **~е́ние**[12] rescue;

escape; salvation

спаси́бо (**вам**) thank you (very much **большо́е** ~), thanks (**за** B, **на** П for)

спаси́тель m [4], ♀ the Savio(u)r; rescuer; ~**ный** [14] saving

спас|ти́ → ~**а́ть**; ~**ть** → **спада́ть**

спать [сплю, спишь; спал, -á, -o] sleep; be asleep; (a. **идти́, ложи́ться** ~) go to bed; coll. **мне не спи́тся** I can't (get to) sleep

спая́ть → **спа́ивать 1**

спека́ться [1] coll. → **запека́ться**

спекта́кль m [4] thea. performance; show

спекул|и́ровать [7] speculate (T in); ~**я́нт** m [1] speculator, profiteer; ~**я́ция** f [7] speculation (in); profiteering; philos. speculation

спе́лый [14; спел, -á, -o] ripe

сперва́ coll. (at) first

спе́реди in front (of); at the front, from the front (as prp.: P)

спёртый coll. [14 sh.] stuffy, close

спеть [8], ⟨по-⟩ ripen; → a. **петь**

спех coll. m [1]: **не к** ~**у** there is no hurry

специ|ализи́роваться [7] (im)pf. specialize (**в** П, **по** Д in); ~**али́ст** m [1] specialist, expert (**по** Д in); ~**а́льность** f [8] speciality, special interest, profession (**по** Д by); ~**а́льный** [14; -лен, -льна] special; ~**фи́ческий** [16] specific

спе́ция f [7] mst.pl. spice

спецоде́жда f [5] working clothes; overalls pl.

спеш|и́ть [16 e.; -шу́, -ши́шь] hurry (up); hasten; of clock be fast (**на пять мину́т** 5 min.); ~**ка** coll. f [5] haste, hurry; ~**ный** [14; -шен, -шна] urgent, pressing; **в** ~**ном поря́дке** quickly

спин|а́ f [5; ac. sg.: спи́ну; pl. st.] back; ~**ка** f [5; g/pl.: -нок] of piece of clothing or furniture back; ~**но́й** [14] spinal (**мозг** cord); vertebral (**хребе́т** column), back (**bone**)

спи́ннинг m [1] (method of fishing) spinning

спира́ль f [8], ~**ный** [14] spiral

спирт m [1; a. в -ý; pl. e.] alcohol, spirit(s pl.); ~**но́й** [14] alcoholic; **напи́ток** тж. strong

спис|а́ть → ~**ывать**; ~**о́к** m [1; -ска] list, register; ~**ывать** [1], ⟨~а́ть⟩ [3] copy; **долг** и т. д. write (off); plagiarize, crib; naut. transfer, post (out of)

спи́х|ивать [1], once ⟨~ну́ть⟩ coll. [20] push (down, aside)

спи́ца f [5] spoke; knitting needle

спи́чка f [5; g/pl.: -чек] match

сплав m [1] **1.** alloy; **2.** леса float(ing); ~**ля́ть** [28], ⟨~ить⟩ [14] **1.** alloy; **2.** float

спла́чивать [1], ⟨сплоти́ть⟩ [15 e.; -очу́, -оти́шь; -очённый] rally (v/i. -**ся**)

сплет|а́ть [1], ⟨сплести́⟩ [25 -т-] plait, braid; (inter)lace; ~**е́ние** n [12] interlacing; **со́лнечное** ~**е́ние** solar plexus; ~**ник** m [1], ~**ница** f [5] scandalmonger; ~**ничать** [1], ⟨на-⟩ gossip; ~**ня** f [6; g/pl.: -тен] gossip

спло|ти́ть(ся) → **спла́чивать(ся)**; ~**хова́ть** coll. [7] pf. blunder; ~**че́ние** n [12] rallying; ~**шно́й** [14] масса и т. д. solid, compact; (непреры́вный) continuous; coll. sheer, utter; ~**шь** throughout, entirely, all over; ~**шь и ря́дом** quite often

сплю́щить [16] pf. flatten, laminate

споить... → **спа́ивать 2**

споко́й|ный [14; -о́ен, -о́йна] calm, quiet, tranquil; (сде́ржанный) composed; ~**но** coll. → **сме́ло** coll.; ~**ной но́чи!** good night!; **бу́дьте** ~**ны!** don't worry!; ~**ствие** n [12] calm(ness), tranquillity; composure; **в о́бществе** и т. д. peace, order

сполз|а́ть [1], ⟨~ти́⟩ [24] climb down (from); fig. coll. slip (into)

сполна́... wholly, in full

сполосну́ть [20] pf. rinse (out)

спо́нсор m [1] sponsor

спор m [1] dispute, controversy, argument; ~**у нет** undoubtedly; ~**ить** [13], ⟨по-⟩ dispute, argue, debate; coll. **держа́ть пари́** bet (on); ~**иться** coll. [13] **рабо́та** go well; ~**ный** [14; -рен, -рна] disputable, questionable

спорт m [1] sport; **лы́жный** ~ skiing; ~**и́вный** [14] sporting, athletic; sport(s)...; ~**и́вный зал** gymnasium; ~**сме́н** m [1] sportsman; ~**сме́нка** f [5; g/pl.: -нок] sportswoman

спо́соб m [1] method, means; way, mode

(T in); *употребления* directions *pl.* (for *use* P); **~ность** *f* [8] (cap)ability (**к** Д for); talent; *к языкам и т. д.* faculty, capacity; power; **покупа́тельная ~ность** purchasing power; **~ный** [14; -бен, -бна] (**к** Д) able, talented, clever (at); capable (of; *a.* **на** В); **~ствовать** [7], ⟨по-⟩ (Д) promote, further, contribute to

спот|ыка́ться [1], ⟨~кну́ться⟩ [20] stumble (**о** В against, over)

спохва́т|ываться [1], ⟨~и́ться⟩ [15] suddenly remember

спра́ва to the right (of)

справедли́в|ость *f* [8] justice, fairness; **~ый** [14 *sh.*] just, fair; (*правильный*) true, right

спра́в|иться → **~ля́ться**; **~ка** *f* [5; *g/pl.*: -вок] inquiry (make **наво́дить**); information; certificate; **~ля́ться** inquiry (**о** П about); consult (*v/t.* **в** П); (**с** Т) manage, cope with; **~очник** *m* [1] reference book; *телефонный* directory; *путеводитель* guide; **~очный** [14] (of) *бюро* inquiries…; *книга* reference…

спра́шива|ть [1], ⟨спроси́ть⟩ [15] ask (p. *a.* **у** Р; for s.th. *a.* Р), inquire; (**с** Р) make answer for, call to account; **~ется** one may ask

спрос *m* [1] *econ.* demand (**на** В for); **без ~а** *or* **~у** *coll.* without permission; **~ и предложе́ние** supply and demand

спросо́нок *coll.* half asleep

спроста́: *coll.* **не ~** it's not by chance

спры́|гивать [1], *once* ⟨~гнуть⟩ [20] jump down (from); **~скивать** [1], ⟨~снуть⟩ [20] sprinkle

спря|га́ть [1], ⟨про-⟩ *gr.* (**-ся** *impf.* be) conjugate(d); **~же́ние** *n* [12] *gr.* conjugation

спу́г|ивать [1], ⟨~ну́ть⟩ [20; -ну́, -нёшь] frighten off

спуск *m* [1] lowering; descent; *склон* slope; *корабля* launch(ing); *воды* drain(ing); **не дава́ть ~ку** (Д) *coll.* give no quarter; **~ка́ть** [1], ⟨~ти́ть⟩ [15] lower, let down; launch; drain; *собаку* unchain, set free; *курок* pull; *о шине* go down; **-ся** go (*or* come) down (*stairs по лестнице*), descend; **~тя́** (В) later, after

спу́тни|к *m* [1], **~ца** *f* [5] travelling companion; *жизни* companion; **~к** *astr.* satellite; *искусственный тж.* sputnik

спя́чка *f* [5] hibernation

сравне́|ние *n* [12] comparison (**по** Д/**с** Т in/with); *lit.* simile; **~ивать** [1] **1.** ⟨~и́ть⟩ [13] compare (**с** Т; *v/i.* **-ся** to, with); **2.** ⟨~я́ть⟩ [28] level, equalize; **~и́тельный** [14] comparative; **~я́ть(ся)** → **~ивать 2**

сра|жа́ть [1], ⟨~зи́ть⟩ [15 *e.*; -ажу́, -ази́шь; -ажённый] smite; overwhelm; **-ся** fight, battle; *coll.* contend, play; **~же́ние** *n* [12] battle; **~зи́ть(ся)** → **~жа́ть(ся)**

сра́зу at once, straight away

срам *m* [1] shame, disgrace; **~и́ть** [14 *e.*; -млю́, -ми́шь], ⟨о-⟩ [осрамлённый] disgrace, shame, compromise; **-ся** bring shame upon o.s

сраст|а́ться [1], ⟨~и́сь⟩ [24 -ст-; сро́сся, сросла́сь] *med.* grow together, knit

среда́ *f* **1.** [5; *ac/sg.*: **сре́ду**; *nom/pl. st.*] Wednesday (on: **в** В, *pl.*: **по** Д); **2.** [5; *ac/sg.*: -ду́; *pl. st.*] environment, surroundings *pl.*, milieu; *phys.* medium; midst; **в на́шей ~е** in our midst; **~и́** (Р) among, in the middle (of), amid(st); **~изе́мный** [14], **~иземномо́рский** [16] Mediterranean; **~неве́ковый** [14] medieval; **~ний** [15] middle; medium…; central; (*посредственный*) middling; average… (**в** П on); *math.* mean; *gr.* neuter; *школа* secondary

средото́чие *n* [12] focus, center (*Brt.* -tre)

сре́дство *n* [9] means ([**не**]**по** Д *pl.* within [beyond] one's); (*лекарство*) remedy; *pl. a.* facilities

сре́з|ать, **~ывать** [1], ⟨~ать⟩ [3] cut off; *coll.* **на экза́мене** fail (*v/i.* **~аться**)

сровня́ть → **сра́внивать 2**

сро|к *m* [1] term (Т/**на** В for/of), date, deadline; time (**в** В; **к** Д in, on), period; **продли́ть ~к ви́зы** extend a visa; **~чный** [14; -чен, -чна́, -о] urgent, pressing; at a fixed date

сруб|а́ть [1], ⟨~и́ть⟩ [14] cut down, fell; *дом* build of logs

сры|в *m* [1] frustration; derangement; *переговоров* breakdown; **~ва́ть** [1], ⟨сорва́ть⟩ [-ву, -вёшь; сорва́л, -а́, -о; со́рванный] tear off; *цветы и т. д.* pluck, pick; *планы и т. д.* disrupt, frustrate; *злость* vent; **-ся (с Р)** come off; break away (*or* loose); fall down; *coll. с места* dart off; *о планах* fail, miscarry

сса́ди|на *f* [5] scratch, abrasion; **~ть** [15] *pf.* graze

сса́живать [1], ⟨ссади́ть⟩ [15; -жу́, -дишь] help down; help alight; make get off (*public transport*)

ссо́р|а *f* [5] quarrel; **~иться** [13], ⟨по-⟩ quarrel, falling-out

ссу́д|а *f* [5] loan; **~и́ть** [15] *pf.* lend, loan

ссыл|а́ть [1], ⟨сосла́ть⟩ [сошлю́, -лёшь; со́сланный] exile, deport, banish; **-ся (на** В**)** refer to, cite; **~ка** *f* [5; *g/pl.*: -лок] **1.** exile; **2.** reference (**на** В to)

ссыпа́|ть [1], ⟨~ть⟩ [2] pour

стабил|изи́(ир)овать [7] (*im*)*pf.* stabilize; **~ьный** [14; -лен, -льна] stable, firm

ста́вень *m* [4; -вня] shutter (*for window*)

ста́в|ить [14], ⟨по-⟩ put, place, set, stand; *часы и т. д.* set; *памятник и т. д.* put (*or* set) up; *на лошадь* stake, (**на** В) back; *thea.* stage; *условия* make; *в известность* inform, bring to the notice of; **~ить в тупи́к** nonplus; **~ка** *f* [5; *g/pl.*: -вок] (*учётная и т. д.*) rate; (*зарплата*) wage, salary; **сде́лать ~ку** gamble (on **на** В); **~ленник** *m* [1] protegé; **~ленный** [-вен] → **~ень**

стадио́н *m* [1] stadium (**на** П in)

ста́дия *f* [7] stage

ста́до *n* [9; *pl. e.*] herd, flock

стаж *m* [1] length of service

стажёр *m* [1] probationer; student in special course not leading to degree

стака́н *m* [1] glass

ста́лкивать [1], ⟨столкну́ть⟩ [20] push (off, away); **-ся (с** Т**)** come into collision with; *a. fig.* conflict with; *с кем-л.* come across; run into

сталь *f* [8] steel; **нержаве́ющая ~** stainless steel; **~но́й** [14] steel…

стаме́ска *f* [5; *g/pl.*: -сок] chisel

станда́рт *m* [1] standard; **~ный** [14; -тен, -тна] standard…

стани́ца *f* [5] Cossack village

станови́ться [14], ⟨стать⟩ [ста́ну, -нешь] *impf.* (T) become, grow, get; stand; stop; **~ в о́чередь** get in line, *Brt.* queue up; *pf.* begin to; start; *лучше* feel; **во что бы то ни ста́ло** at all costs, at any cost

стано́к *m* [1; -нка] machine; *тока́рный* lathe; *печа́тный* press; **тка́цкий ~** loom

ста́нция *f* [7] station (**на** П at); *tel.* exchange

ста́птывать [1], ⟨стопта́ть⟩ [3] trample; (*сноси́ть*) wear out

стара́|ние *n* [12] pains *pl.*, care; endeavo(u)r; **~тельный** [14; -лен, -льна] assiduous, diligent; painstaking; **-ться** [1], ⟨по-⟩ endeavo(u)r, try (hard)

стар|е́ть [21] **1.** ⟨по-⟩ grow old, age; **2.** ⟨у-⟩ grow obsolete; **~и́к** *m* [1 *e.*] old man; **~ина́** *f* [5] olden times, days of yore (**в** В in); *coll.* old man *or* chap; **~и́нный** [14] ancient, antique; old; *обычай* time-hono(u)red; **~ить** [13], ⟨со-⟩ make (**-ся** grow) old

старо|мо́дный [14; -ден, -дна] old-fashioned, out-of-date; **~ста** *m класса* prefect, monitor; **~сть** *f* [8] old age (in one's **на** П *лет*)

стартова́ть [7] (*im*)*pf. sport* start; *ae.* take off

стар|у́ха *f* [5] old woman; **~ческий** [16] old man's; senile; **~ший** [17] elder, older, senior; eldest, oldest; *по должности* senior, superior; head, chief; *лейтена́нт* first; **~шина́** *m* [5] *mil.* first sergeant (*naut.* mate); **~шинство́** *n* [9] seniority

ста́р|ый [14; стар, -а́, -о; *comp.*: ста́рше *or* -ре́е] old; *времена* olden; **~ьё** *n* [10] *coll.* old clothes *pl.*; junk, *Brt.* lumber

ста́|скивать [1], ⟨~щи́ть⟩ [16] drag off, pull off; drag down; take, bring; *coll.* filch

стати́ст *m* [1], **~ка** *f* [5; *g/pl.*: -ток] *thea.* supernumerary; *film* extra; **~ика** *f* [5] statistics; **~и́ческий** [16] statistical

ста́т|ный [14; -тен, -тна, -о] wellbuilt;

С

~у́я f [6; g/pl.: -у́й] statue; ~ь¹ f [8]: **с како́й ~и?** coll. why (should I, etc.)?

стать² → станови́ться; ~ся coll. (impers.) happen (to с T); **мо́жет ~ся** it may be, perhaps

статья́ f [6; g/pl.: -те́й] article; *догово́ра u m. ∂.* clause, item, entry; coll. matter (another *осо́бая*)

стациона́р m [1] permanent establishment; *лече́бный* hospital; ~ный [14] permanent, fixed; ~ный **больно́й** in-patient

ста́чка f [5; g/pl.: -чек] strike

стащи́ть → ста́скивать

ста́я f [6; g/pl.: стай] flight, flock; *волко́в* pack

ста́ять [27] pf. thaw, melt

ствол m [1 e.] trunk; *ружья́* barrel

сте́бель m [4; -бля; from g/pl. e.] stalk, stem

стёганый [14] quilted

стека́ть [1], ⟨~чь⟩ [26] flow (down); -ся flow together; (*собира́ться*) gather, throng

стек|ло́ [9; pl.: стёкла, стёкол, стёклам] glass; *око́нное* pane; **пере́днее ~ло́** windshield (Brt. windscreen); ~ля́нный [14] glass...; glassy; ~о́льщик m [1] glazier

стел|и́ть(ся) coll. → стла́ть(ся); ~лаж m [1 e.] shelf; ~ька f [5; g/pl.: -лек] inner sole

стен|а́ f [5; as/sg.: сте́ну; pl.: сте́ны, стен, стена́м] wall; ~газе́та f [5] (**стенна́я газе́та**) wall newspaper; ~д m [1] stand; ~ка f [5; g/pl.: -нок] wall; **как об ~ку горо́хом** like talking to a brick wall; ~но́й [14] wall...

стеногра́|мма f [5] shorthand (verbatim) report or notes pl.; ~фи́стка f [5; g/pl.: -ток] stenographer; ~фия f [7] shorthand

сте́пень f [8; from g/pl. e.] degree (to **до** P), extent; *math.* power

степ|но́й [14] steppe...; ~ь f [8; в -пи́; from g/pl. e.] steppe

сте́рва P f [5] (*as term of abuse*) bitch

сте́рео- *combining form* stereo-; стереоти́п m [1], **стереоти́пный** [14; -пен, -пна] stereotype

стере́ть → стира́ть

стере́чь [26 г/ж: -егу́, -ежёшь; -ёг, -егла́] guard, watch (over)

сте́ржень m [4; -жня] tech. rod, pivot

стерил|изова́ть [7] (im)pf. sterilize; ~ьный [14; -лен, -льна] sterile, free of germs

стерпе́ть [10] pf. endure, bear

стесн|е́ние n [12] constraint; ~и́тельный [14; -лен, -льна] shy; ~я́ть [28], ⟨~и́ть⟩ [13] constrain, restrain; (*смуща́ть*) embarrass; (*меша́ть*) hamper; ~я́ться, ⟨по-⟩ feel (or be) shy, self-conscious or embarrassed; (P) be ashamed of; (*колеба́ться*) hesitate

стеч|е́ние n [12] confluence; *обстоя́тельств* coincidence; *наро́да* concourse; ~ь(ся) → стека́ть(ся)

стиль m [4] style; **но́вый ~** New Style (*according to the Gregorian calendar*); **ста́рый ~** Old Style (*according to the Julian calendar*)

сти́мул m [1] stimulus, incentive

стипе́ндия f [7] scholarship, grant

стира́|льный [14] washing; ~ть [1] **1.** ⟨стере́ть⟩ [12; сотру́, -трёшь; стёр(ла́); стёрши & стере́в] wipe or rub off; efface, efface, blot out; *но́гу* rub sore; **2.** ⟨вы-⟩ wash, launder; ~ка f [5] wash(-ing), laundering; **отда́ть в ~ку** send to the wash

сти́с|кивать [1], ⟨~нуть⟩ [20] squeeze, clench; *в объя́тиях* hug

стих (*a.* -и́ *pl.*) m [1 e.] verse; *pl. a.* poem(s); ~а́ть [1], ⟨~нуть⟩ [21] *ве́тер u m. ∂.* abate; subside; (*успоко́иться*) calm down, become quiet; ~и́йный [14; -и́ен, -и́йна] elemental; *fig.* spontaneous; *бе́дствие* natural; ~я f [7] element(s); ~нуть → ~а́ть

стихотворе́ние n [12] poem

стла́ть & coll. стели́ть [стелю́, сте́лешь], ⟨по-⟩ [по́стланный] spread, lay; *посте́ль* make; -ся impf. (be) spread; drift; bot. creep

сто [35] hundred

стог m [1; в сто́ге & в стогу́; pl.: -а́, etc. e.] agric. stack, rick

сто́и|мость f [8] cost; value, worth (...

Т/**в** В); **~ть** [13] cost; be worth; (*заслуживать*) deserve; **не ~т** coll. → **нé за что**

стой! stop!, halt!

стóй|ка *f* [5; *g/pl.:* стóек] stand; *tech.* support; *в бáнке* counter; *в ресторáне* bar; **~кий** [16; стóек, стойкá, -о; *compr.* стóйче] firm, stable, steady; (*in compounds*) … proof; **~кость** *f* [8] firmness; steadfastness

сток *m* [1] flowing (off); drainage, drain

стол *m* [1 *e.*] table (**за** Т at); (*питание*) board, fare; diet; **~ нахóдок** lost property office

столб *m* [1 *e.*] post, pole; *дыма* pillar; **~éц** *m* [1; -бцá], **~ик** *m* [1] column (*in newspaper, etc.*); **~нáк** *m* [1 *e.*] *med.* tetanus

столéтие *n* [12] century; (*годовщина*) centenary

стóлик *m* [1] *dim.* → **стол**; small table

столи|ца *f* [5] capital; **~чный** [14] capital…; metropolitan

столкн|овéние *n* [12] collision; *fig. mil.* clash; **~ýть(ся)** → **стáлкивать(ся)**

столóв|ая *f* [14] dining room; café, restaurant; *на предприятии* canteen; **~ый** [14]: **~ая лóжка** table spoon; **~ый сервиз** dinner service

столп *m* [1 *e.*] *arch.* pillar, column

стóль| so; **~ко** [32] so much, so many; **~ко же** as much *or* many

столя́р *m* [1 *e.*] joiner, cabinetmaker; **~ный** [14] joiner's

стон *m* [1], **~áть** [-нý, стóнешь; стоня́], ⟨про-⟩ groan, moan

стоп! stop!; **~ сигнáл** *mot.* stoplight; **~á 1.** [5 *e.*] foot; **идти́ по чьи́м-л. стопáм** follow in s.o.'s footsteps; **~ка** *f* [5; *g/pl.:* -пок] pile, heap; **~орить** [13], ⟨за-⟩ stop; bring to a standstill; **~тáть** → **стáптывать**

стóрож *m* [1; *pl.:* -á; *etc. e.*] guard, watchman; **~евóй** [14] watch…; on duty; *naut.* escort…; patrol…; **~ить** [16 *e.*; -жý, -жи́шь] guard, watch (over)

сторон|á *f* [5; *ac/sg.:* сторону; *pl.:* стóроны, сторóн, -нáм] side (*on a.* **по** Д; **с** Р); (*направление*) direction; part (**с** Р on); (*местность*) place, region, country; *в*

суде и т. д. party; distance (**в** П at; **с** Р from); **в ~у** aside, apart (*a.* joking **шу́тки**); **в ~é от** at some distance (from); **с однóй ~ы** on the one hand; **… с вáшей ~ы** *a.* … of you; **со своéй ~ы** on my part; **~и́ться** [13; -онюсь, -óнишься], ⟨по-⟩ make way, step aside; (*избегáть*) (Р) avoid, shun; **~ник** *m* [1] adherent, follower; supporter

стóчный [14] waste…; *вóды* sewage

стоя́нка *f* [5; *g/pl.:* -нок] stop (**на** П at); **автомоби́льная ~** parking place *or* lot; *naut.* anchorage; **~ такси́** taxi stand (*Brt.* rank)

стоя́ть [стою́, -ои́шь; стóй] stand; be; stop; stand up (**за** В for), defend, insist (**на** П on); **стóйте!** stop!; *coll.* wait!; **~чий** [17] *положéние* upright; *вода* stagnant; *воротни́к* stand-up

стоя́щий [17] worthwhile; *человéк* worthy, deserving

страда́|лец *m* [1; -льца] sufferer; *iro.* martyr; **~ние** *n* [12] suffering; **~тельный** [14] *gr.* passive; **~ть** [1], ⟨по-⟩ suffer (**от** Р, Т from); **он ~ет забы́вчивостью** he has a poor memory

стрáжа *f* [5] guard, watch; **~ поря́дка** *mst. pl.* the militia

стран|á *f* [5; *pl. st.*] country; **~и́ца** *f* [5] page (→ **пя́тый**); **~ность** *f* [8] strangeness, oddity; **~ный** [14; -áнен, -áнна, -о] strange, odd; **~ствовать** [7] wander, travel

страст|нóй [14] *недéля* Holy; *пя́тница* Good; **~ный** (-sn-) [14; -тен, -тнá, -о] passionate, fervent; **он ~ный люби́тель джáза** he's mad about jazz; **~ь** *f* [8; *from g/pl. e.*] passion (**к** Д for)

стратéг|ический [16] strategic; **~ия** *f* [7] strategy

стрáус *m* [1] ostrich

страх *m* [1] fear (**от, со** Р for); risk, terror (**на** В at); **~овáние** *n* [12] insurance (*fire…* **от** Р); **~овáть** [7], ⟨за-⟩ insure (**от** Р against); *fig.* safeguard o.s. (against); **~óвка** *f* [5; *g/pl.:* -вок] insurance (rate); **~овóй** [14] insurance…

страши́ть [16 *e.*; -шý, -ши́шь], ⟨у-⟩ [-шённый] (**-ся** be) frighten(ed; at P; fear, dread, be afraid of); **~ный** [14;

-шен, -шна́, -о] terrible, frightful, dreadful; *coll.* awful; **∠ный суд** the Day of Judg(e)ment; **мне ∠но** I'm afraid, I fear

стрекоза́ *f* [5; *pl. st.*: -о́зы, -о́з, -о́зам] dragonfly

стрел|а́ *f* [5; *pl. st.*] arrow; *a. fig.* shaft, dart; **∠ка** *f* [5; *g/pl.*: -лок] (*of a clock or watch*) hand; *компаса и т. п.* needle; *на рисунке* arrow; **∠ко́вый** [14] shooting...; (*of*) rifles *pl.*; **∠о́к** *m* [1; -лка́] marksman, shot; **∠ьба́** *f* [5; *pl. st.*] shooting, fire; **∠я́ть** [28], ⟨вы́стрелить⟩ [13] shoot, fire (**в** В, **по** Д at; *gun* из Р)

стрем|гла́в headlong; **∠и́тельный** [14; -лен, -льна] impetuous, headlong, swift; **∠и́ться** [14 *e.*; -млю́сь, -ми́шься] (**к** Д) aspire (to), strive (for); **∠ле́ние** *n* [12] aspiration (to), striving (for), urge, desire (to)

стремя́нка *f* [5; *g/pl.*: -нок] stepladder

стресс *m* [1] *psych.* stress

стриж *m* [1 *e.*] sand martin

стри́|жка *f* [5] haircut(ting); *овец* shearing; *ногтей* clipping; **∠чь** [26; -игу́, -ижёшь; *pl. st.*], ⟨по-, о-(об-)⟩ cut; shear; clip, (*подровня́ть*) level, trim; **-ся** have one's hair cut

строга́ть [1], ⟨вы́-⟩ plane

стро́г|ий [16; строг, -а́, -о; *comp.*: стро́же] severe; strict; *стиль и т. п.* austere; *взгляд* stern; **∠о говоря́** strictly speaking; **∠ость** *f* [8] severity; austerity; strictness

строе|во́й [14] building...; **∠во́й лес** timber; **∠ние** *n* [12] construction, building; structure

строи́тель *m* [4] builder, constructor; **∠ный** [14] building...; **∠ная площа́дка** building *or* construction site; **∠ство** *n* [9] construction

стро́ить [13], ⟨по-⟩ build (up), construct; *пла́ны и т. д.* make, scheme; play *fig.* (*из* Р); **-ся** ⟨вы́-, по-⟩ be built; build (*a house, etc.*); *в о́чередь* form

строй *m* **1.** [3; в строю́; *pl. e.*: строй, строёв] order, array; line; **2.** [3] system, order, regime; **ввести́ в** ∠ put into operation; **∠ка** *f* [5; *g/pl.*: -о́ек] construc-

tion; building site; **∠ность** *f* [8] proportion; *mus.* harmony; *о сложе́нии* slenderness; **∠ный** [14; -о́ен, -о́йна́, -о] slender, slim; well-shaped; *mus.*, *etc.* harmonious, well-balanced

строка́ *f* [5; *ac/sg.*: стро́ку; *pl.* стро́ки, строк, стро́кам] line; **кра́сная ∼** *typ.* indent

стропи́ло *n* [9] rafter, beam

стропти́вый [14 *sh.*] obstinate, refractory

строфа́ *f* [5; *nom/pl. st.*] stanza

строч|и́ть [16 & 16 *e.*; -очу́, -о́чи́шь; -о́ченный & -очёный] stitch, sew; *coll.* (*писа́ть*) scribble, dash off; **∠ка** *f* [5; *g/pl.*: -чек] line; *sew.* stitch

стру́|жка *f* [5; *g/pl.*: -жек] shavings *pl.*; **∠и́ться** [13] stream, flow; **∠йка** *f* [5; *g/pl.*: -йек] *dim.* → **∼я́**

структу́ра *f* [5] structure

стру́н|а́ *f* [5; *pl. st.*] *mus.*, **∠ный** [14] string

стрючко́вый → **бобо́вый**; **∠о́к** *m* [1; -чка́] pod

струя́ *f* [6; *pl. st.*: -у́й] stream (Т in); jet; *во́здуха* current; **бить струёй** spurt

стря́|пать *coll.* [1], ⟨со-⟩ cook; concoct; **∠хивать** [1], ⟨∠хну́ть⟩ [20] shake off

студе́н|т *m* [1], **∠тка** *f* [5; *g/pl.*: -ток] student, undergraduate; **∠ческий** [16] students'...

сту́день *m* [4; -дня] aspic

сту́дия *f* [7] studio, atelier

сту́жа *f* [7] hard frost

стук *m* [1] *в дверь* knock, rattle, clatter, noise; **∠нуть** → **стуча́ть**

стул *m* [1; *pl.*: сту́лья, -льев] chair; seat; *med.* stool

ступ|а́ть [1], ⟨∠и́ть⟩ [14] step, tread, go; **∠е́нь** *f* **1.** [8; *pl.* ступе́ни, ступе́ней] step (*of stairs*); rung (*of ladder*). **2.** [8; *pl.*: ступе́ни, -не́й, *etc. e.*] stage, grade; *раке́ты* rocket stage; **∠е́нька** *f* [5; *g/pl.*: -нек] = **2.**; **∠и́ть** → **∠а́ть**; **∠ка** *f* [5; *g/pl.*: -пок] (small) mortar; **∠ня́** *f* [6; *g/pl.*: -не́й] foot, sole (*of foot*)

стуча́ть [4 *e.*; -чу́, -чи́шь], ⟨по-⟩, *once* ⟨∠кнуть⟩ [20] knock (*door* в В at; *a.* **-ся**); rap, tap; *о се́рдце и т. д.* throb; (*зуба́ми*) chatter; clatter, rattle; **∠ча́т** there's a knock at the door; **∠кнуть** → **испол**-

ниться

стыд *m* [1 *e.*] shame; **~и́ть** [15 *e.*; -ыжу́, -ыди́шь], ⟨при-⟩ [пристыжённый] shame, make ashamed; **-ся**, ⟨по-⟩ be ashamed (P of); **~ли́вый** [14 *sh.*] shy, bashful; *~но!* (for) shame!; **мне ~но** I am ashamed (*за* B of p.)

стык *m* [1] joint, juncture (**на** П at); **~о́в-ка** *f* [5; *g/pl.:* -вок] docking (*of space vehicles*), rendezvous

сты́|(ну)ть [21], ⟨о-⟩ (become) cool

сты́чка *f* [5; *g/pl.:* -чек] skirmish, scuffle

стюарде́сса *f* [5] stewardess, air hostess

стя́|гивать [1], ⟨**~ну́ть**⟩ [19] tighten; pull together; *mil.* gather, assemble; pull off; *coll.* pilfer

суб|бо́та *f* [5] Saturday (on: **в** B *pl.*: **по** Д); **~си́дия** *f* [7] subsidy

субтропи́ческий [16] subtropical

субъе́кт *m* [1] subject; *coll.* fellow; **~и́в-ный** [14; -вен, -вна] subjective

сувени́р *m* [1] souvenir

суверен|ите́т *m* [1] sovereignty; **~ный** [14; -ёнен, -ённа] sovereign

суг|ро́б *m* [1] snowdrift; **~у́бо** *adv.* especially; *э́то ~у́бо ча́стный вопро́с* this is a purely private matter

суд *m* [1 *e.*] (*суждение*) judg(e)ment; court (of law); trial (*отда́ть под ~* put on trial; *преда́ть ~у́* bring to trial, prosecute; (*правосу́дие*) justice

суда́к *m* [1 *e.*] pike perch

суда́р|ыня *f* [6] *obs.* (*mode of address*) madam; **~ь** *m* [4] *obs.* (*mode of address*) sir

суде́|бный [14] judicial, legal; forensic; law…; (of the) court; **~и́ть** [15; суждён-ный] **1.** ⟨по-⟩ judge (*по* Д by); *fig.* form an opinion (**о** П of); **2.** (*im*)*pf.* try, judge; **~я́ по** (Д) judging by

суд|но́ *n* [9; *pl.:* суда́, -о́в] *naut.* ship, vessel; **~но на возду́шной поду́шке** hovercraft; **~но на возду́шных кры́льях** hydrofoil

судопроизво́дство *n* [9] legal proceedings

су́доро|га *f* [5] cramp, convulsion, spasm; **~жный** [14; -жен, -жна] convulsive, spasmodic

судо|строе́ние *n* [12] shipbuilding;

~строи́тельный [14] shipbuilding…; ship(yard); **~хо́дный** [14; -ден, -дна] navigable; **~хо́дство** *n* [9] navigation

судьб|а́ *f* [5; *pl.:* су́дьбы, су́деб, су́дьбам] destiny, fate; *благодари́ть ~у́* thank one's lucky stars

судья́ *m* [6; *pl.:* су́дьи, суде́й, су́дьям] judge; *sport* referee, umpire

суеве́р|ие *n* [12] superstition; **~ный** [14; -рен, -рна] superstitious

суе|та́ *f* [5], **~ти́ться** [15 *e.*; суечу́сь, суети́шься] bustle, fuss; **~тли́вый** [14 *sh.*] bustling, fussy

сужде́ние *n* [12] opinion, judg(e)ment; **~е́ние** *n* [12] narrowing; **~ивать** [1], ⟨су́-зить⟩ [15] narrow (*v/i.:* **-ся**; taper); *пла́тье* take in

сук *m* [1 *e.*; на ~у́; *pl.:* су́чья, -ьев & -й, -о́в] bough; *в дре́весине* knot

су́к|а *f* [5] bitch (*also as term of abuse*); **~ин** [19]: **~ин сын** son of a bitch

сукно́ *n* [9; *pl. sg.:* су́кна, су́кон, су́кнам] broadcloth; heavy, coarse cloth; *поло-жи́ть под ~* *fig.* shelve

сули́ть [13], ⟨по-⟩ promise

султа́н *m* [1] sultan

сумасбро́д|ный [14; -ден, -дна] wild, extravagant; **~ство** *n* [9] madcap *or* extravagant behavio(u)r

сумасше́|дший [17] mad, insane; *su.* madman; **~дший дом** *fig.* madhouse; **~ствие** *n* [12] madness, lunacy

сумато́ха *f* [5] turmoil, confusion, hurly-burly

сум|бу́р *m* [1] → *пу́таница*; **~е́рки** *f/pl.* [5; *gen.:* -рек] dusk, twilight; **~ка** *f* [5; *g/pl.:* -мок] (hand)bag; *biol.* pouch; **~ма** *f* [5] sum (**на** B/**в** B for/of), amount; **~ма́рный** [14; -рен, -рна] total; **~ми́ро-вать** [7] (*im*)*pf.* sum up

су́мочка *f* [5; *g/pl.:* -чек] handbag

су́мра|к *m* [1] twilight, dusk; gloom; **~чный** [14; -чен, -чна] gloomy

сунду́к *m* [1 *e.*] trunk, chest

су́нуть(ся) → *сова́ть(ся)*

суп *m* [1; *pl. e.*], **~о́вой** [14] soup(…)

суперобло́жка *f* [5; *g/pl.:* -жек] dust jacket

супру́|г *m* [1] husband; **~га** *f* [5] wife; **~жеский** [16] matrimonial, conjugal;

С

жизнь married; **~жество** *n* [9] matrimony, wedlock

сургу́ч *m* [1 *e.*] sealing wax

суро́в|ость *f* [8] severity; **~ый** [14 *sh.*] harsh, rough; *климат и т. д.* severe; stern; *дисциплина* rigorous

суррога́т *m* [1] substitute

суста́в *m* [1] *anat.* joint

су́тки *f/pl.* [5; *gen.*: -ток] twentyfour-hour period; *кру́глые* ~ round the clock

су́точный [14] day's, daily; twentyfour-hour, round-the-clock; *pl. su.* daily allowance

суту́лый [14 *sh.*] round-shouldered

суть *f* [8] essence, crux, heart; *по ~и де́ла* as a matter of fact

суфле́ *n* [*indecl.*] soufflé

суха́рь *m* [4 *e.*] *сдобный* rusk, zwieback; dried piece of bread; **~ожи́лие** *n* [12] sinew; **~о́й** [14; сух, -á, -о; *comp.*: су́ше] dry; *климат и др.* dry; *дерево* dead; *fig.* cool, cold; *доклад* boring, dull; **~о́е молоко́** dried milk; **~опу́тный** [14] land...; **~ость** *f* [8] dryness, etc. → **~о́й**; **~ощ́авый** [14 *sh.*] lean; skinny; **~офру́кты** *pl.* [1] dried fruit

сучо́к *m* [1; -чка́] *dim.* → **сук**

су́ш|а *f* [5] (dry) land, dry; **~ёный** [14] dried; **~и́лка** *m* [5; *g/pl.*: -лок] *coll.* dish drainer; **~и́ть** [16], ⟨вы-⟩ dry; **~ка** *f* [5; *g/pl.*: -шек] drying; dry, ring-shaped cracker

суще́ств|енный [14 *sh.*] essential, substantial; **~и́тельное** [14] noun, substantive (*a.* **и́мя ~и́тельное**); **~о́** *n* [9] creature, being; *суть* essence; **по ~у́** at bottom; to the point; **~ова́ние** *n* [12] existence, being; *сре́дства к ~ова́нию* livelihood; **~ова́ть** [7] exist, be; live, subsist

су́щ|ий [17] *coll. правда* plain; *вздор* absolute, sheer, downright; **~ность** *f* [8] essence, substance; *в ~ности* in fact; really and truly

сфе́ра *f* [5] sphere; field, realm

схват|и́ть(ся) → **~ывать(ся)**; **~ка** *f* [5; *g/pl.*: -ток] skirmish, fight, combat; scuffle; *a. pl.* contractions, labo(u)r, birth pangs; **~ывать** [1], ⟨~и́ть⟩ [15] seize (*за* B by), grasp (*a. fig.*), grab; snatch; (*поймать*) catch (*a cold,*

etc.); **-ся** seize; *coll.* grapple (with)

схе́ма *f* [5] diagram, chart (in *на* П), plan, outline; **~ти́ческий** [16] schematic; *fig.* sketchy

сходи́ть [15], ⟨сойти́⟩ [сойду́, -дёшь; сошёл, -шла́; *g. pt.*: сойдя́] go (*or* come) down, descend (from *с* P); *о коже и т. д.* come off; *о снеге* melt; *coll.* pass (*за* B for); P do; pass off; *ей всё ~ит с рук* she can get away with anything; **~и́ть** *pf.* go (& get *or* fetch *за* T); → **ум**; **-ся**, ⟨-сь⟩ meet; gather; become friends; agree (*в* П upon); (*совпасть*) coincide; *coll.* click; **~ни** *f/pl.* [6; *gen.*: -ней] gangplank, gangway; **~ный** [14; -ден, -дна, -о] similar (*с* T to), like; *coll. цена* reasonable; **~ство** *n* [9] similarity (*с* T to), likeness

сце́ди́ть [15] *pf.* pour off; draw off

сце́н|а *f* [5] stage; scene (*a. fig.*); **~а́рий** [3] scenario, script; **~и́ческий** [16] stage..., scenic

сцеп|и́ть(ся) → **~ля́ть(ся)**; **~ка** *f* [5; *g/pl.*: -пок] coupling; **~ле́ние** *n* [12] *phys.* adhesion; cohesion; *tech.* clutch, coupling; **~ля́ть** [28], ⟨~и́ть⟩ [14] link; couple (*v/i.* **-ся**: *coll.* quarrel, grapple)

счаст|ли́вец *m* [1; -вца] lucky man; **~ли́вый** [14; сча́стли́в, -а, -о] happy; fortunate; lucky; **~ли́вого пути́!** bon voyage!; **~ли́во** good luck!; **~ли́во отде́латься** have a narrow escape; **~ье** *n* [10] happiness; luck; good fortune; **к ~ью** fortunately

счесть(ся) → **счита́ть(ся)**

счёт *m* [1; на ~е & счету́; *pl.*: счета́, *etc. e.*] count, calculation; *в ба́нке* account (*в* B; *на* B on); *счёт к оплате* bill; *sport* score; *в два ~а* in a jiffy, in a trice; *в коне́чном ~е* ultimately; *за* ~ (P) at the expense (of); *на э́тот* ~ on this score, in this respect; *ска́зано на мой* ~ aimed at me; *быть на хоро́шем счету́* (*у* P) be in good repute

счёт|чик *m* [1] meter; counter; **~ы** *pl.* [1] abacus *sg.*; *свести́ ~ы* square accounts, settle a score (with)

счита́|ть [1], ⟨со-⟩ & ⟨счесть⟩ [25; сочту́, -тёшь; счёл, сочла́; сочтённый; *g. pt.*: сочта́] count; (*pf.* счесть) (T, *за* B) consider, regard (*a.* as), hold, think;

~я *a.* including; ~**нные** *pl.* very few; ~**ться** (Т) be considered (*or* reputed) to be; (**с** Т) consider, respect

сши|ва́ть [1], ⟨~ть⟩ [сошью́, -шьёшь; сше́й(те)!; сши́тый] sew (together)

съеда́|ть [1], ⟨съесть⟩ → **есть** *1*; ~**бный** [14; -бен, -бна] edible

съезд *m* [1] congress (**на** П at); ~**дить** [15] *pf.* go; (**за** Т) fetch; (**к** Д) visit; ~**жа́ть** [1], ⟨съе́хать⟩ [съе́ду, -дешь] go *or* drive (*or* slide) down; **-ся** meet; gather

съёмка *f* [5; *g/pl.*: -мок] survey; *фи́льма* shooting

съёмный [14] detachable

съестно́й [14] food...

съе́хать(ся) → **съезжа́ть(ся)**

сы́|воротка *f* [5; *g/pl.*: -ток] whey; *med.* serum; ~**гра́ть** → **игра́ть**

сы́знова *coll.* anew, (once) again

сын *m* [1; *pl.*: сыновья́, -ве́й, -вья́м; *fig. pl.* сыны́) son; *fig. a.* child; ~**о́вний** [15] filial; ~**о́к** *coll.* *m* [1; -нка́] (*as mode of address*) sonny

сы́п|ать [2], ⟨по-⟩ strew, scatter; pour; **-ся** pour; *уда́ры, град* hail; *дождь, град* pelt; ~**но́й** [14]: ~**но́й тиф** typhus; spotted fever; ~**у́чий** [17 *sh.*] *те́ло* dry; ~**ь** *f* [8] rash

сыр *m* [1; *pl. e.*] cheese; **ката́ться как ~ в ма́сле** live off the fat of the land; ~**е́ть** [8], ⟨от-⟩ become damp; ~**е́ц** *m* [1; -рца́] **шёлк-~е́ц** raw silk; ~**ник** *m* [1] curd fritter; ~**ный** [14] cheese...; ~**ова́тый** [14 *sh.*] dampish; rare, undercooked; ~**о́й** [14; сыр, -á, -о] damp; moist; (*не варё́ный*) raw; *нефть* crude; *хлеб* sodden; ~**ость** *f* [8] dampness; humidity; ~**ьё** [10] *collect.* raw material

сы́т|ный [14; сы́тен, -тна́, -о] substantial, copious; ~**ый** [14; сыт, -á, -о] satisfied, full

сыч *m* [1 *e.*] little owl

сы́щик *m* [1] detective

сюда́ here; hither

сюже́т *m* [1] subject; plot

сюи́та *f* [5] *mus.* suite

сюрпри́з *m* [1] surprise

Т

та → **тот**

таба́|к *m* [1 *e.*; *part.g.*: -ý] tobacco; ~**чный** [14] tobacco...

та́б|ель *m* [1] table; time-keeping *or* attendance record (*in a factory, school, etc.*); ~**ле́тка** *f* [5; *g/pl.*: -ток] pill, tablet; ~**ли́ца** *f* [5] table; ~**ли́ца умноже́ния** multiplication table; **электро́нная ~ли́ца** *comput.* spreadsheet; ~**ло́** *n* [*indecl.*] indicator *or* score board; ~**ор** *m* [1 *e.*] camp; Gypsy encampment

табу́н *m* [1 *e.*] herd, drove

табуре́тка *f* [5; *g/pl.*: -ток] stool

таджи́к *m* [1], ~**ский** [16] Tajik

таз *m* [1; в -ý; *pl. e.*] basin; *anat.* pelvis

таи́нст|венный [14 *sh.*] mysterious; secret(ive); ~**о** *n* [9] sacrament

таи́ть[13] hide, conceal; **-ся** be in hiding; *fig.* lurk

тайга́ *f* [5] *geog.* taiga

тай|ко́м secretly; behind (one's back) (**от** Р); ~**м** *m* [1] *sport* half, period; ~**мер** *m* [1] timer; ~**на** *f* [5] secret; mystery; ~**ни́к** *m* [1] hiding (place); ~**ный** [14] secret; stealthy

так so, thus; like that; (~ **же** just) as; so much; just so; then; well; yes; one way...; → *a.* **пра́вда**; *coll.* properly; **не** ~ wrong(ly); ~ **и** (*both*...) and; ~ **как** as, since; **и** ~ even so; without that; ~**же** also, too; ~**же не** neither, nor; **а** ~**же** as well as; ~**и** *coll.* all the same; indeed; ~**называемый** so called; alleged; ~**ово́й** [14; -ко́в, -кова́] such; (a)like; same; **был(á) ~ов(á)** disappeared, vanished; ~**о́й** [16] such; so; ~**о́е** *su.* such things; ~**о́й же** the same; as...; ~**о́й-то** such-and-such; so-and-so; **что (э́то) ~о́е?** *coll.* what's that?; what did you say?, what's on?; **кто вы ~о́й (~а́я)?**

= **кто вы?**

та́кса[1] *f* [5] statutory price; tariff

та́кса[2] *f* [5] dachshund

такси́ *n* [*indecl.*] taxi(cab); **~ст** *m* [1] taxi driver

такт *m* [1] *mus.* time, measure, bar; *fig.* tact; **~ика** *f* [5] tactics *pl.* & *sg.*; **~и́ческий** [16] tactical; **~и́чность** *f* [8] tactfulness; **~и́чный** [14; -чен, -чна] tactful

тала́нт *m* [1] talent, gift (**к** Д for); man of talent; gifted person; **~ливый** [14 *sh.*] talented, gifted

та́лия *f* [7] waist

тало́н *m* [1] coupon

та́лый [14] thawed; melted

там there; when; **~ же** in the same place; ibid.; **~ ви́дно бу́дет** we shall see; **~ и ся́м** here, there, and everywhere; **как бы ~ ни́ было** at any rate

та́мбур *m* [1] *rail.* vestibule

тамо́ж|енный [14] customs…; **~ня** [6; *g/pl.*: -жен] customs house

та́мошний [15] *coll.* of that place

та́н|ец *m* [1; -нца] dance (*go dancing* **на** В; *pl.*); **~к** *m* [1] tank; **~кер** *m* [1] tanker; **~ковый** [14] tank…

танц|ева́льный [14] dancing…; **~ева́ть** [7], ⟨с-⟩ dance; **~о́вщик** *m* [1], **~о́вщица** *f* [5] (ballet) dancer; **~о́р** *m* [1] dancer

та́почка *f* [5; *g/pl.*: -чек] *coll.* slipper; *sport* sneaker, *Brt.* trainer

та́ра *f* [5] packing, packaging

тарака́н *m* [1] cockroach

тарахте́ть *coll.* [11] rumble, rattle

тара́|щить [16], ⟨вы́-⟩: **~ глаза́** goggle (at **на** В; with *suprise* **от** Р)

таре́л|ка *f* [5; *g/pl.*: -лок] plate; *глубо́кая* soup plate; *лета́ющая* **~ка** flying saucer; *чу́вствовать себя́ не в свое́й* **~ке** feel out of place; feel ill at ease

тари́ф *m* [1] tariff; **~ный** [14] tariff…; standard (*wages*)

таска́ть [1] carry; drag; pull; *coll.* steal; P wear; **-ся** wander, gad about

тасова́ть [7], ⟨с-⟩ shuffle (cards)

тата́р|ин *m* [1; *pl.*: -ры, -р, -рам], **~ка** *f* [5; *g/pl.*: -рок], **~ский** [16] Ta(r)tar

тахта́ *f* [5] ottoman

та́чка *f* [5] wheelbarrow

тащи́ть [16] **1.** ⟨по-⟩ drag, pull, carry; ⟨при-⟩ bring; **2.** *coll.* ⟨с-⟩ steal, pilfer; **-ся** *coll.* trudge, drag o.s. along

та́ять [27], ⟨рас-⟩ thaw, melt; *fig.* fade, wane, languish (**от** Р with)

тварь *f* [8] creature; *collect.* creatures (*a. pej.* miscreant)

тверде́ть [8], ⟨за-⟩ harden

твёрд|ость *f* [8] firmness, hardness; **~ый** [14; твёрд, тверда́, -о] hard; solid; firm; (*a. fig.*) stable, steadfast; *зна́ния* sound, good; *це́ны* fixed, *coll.* sure; **~о** *a.* well, for sure; **~о обеща́ть** make a firm promise

тво|й *m*, **~я́** *f*, **~ё** *n*, **~и́** *pl.* [24] your; yours; *pl. su. coll.* your folks; → **ваш**

твор|е́ние *n* [12] creation; work; (*существо́*) creature; being; **~е́ц** *m* [1; -рца́] creator, author; **~и́тельный** [14] *gr.* instrumental (case); **~и́ть** [13], ⟨со-⟩ create, do; **-ся** *coll.* be (going) on; **~о́г** *m* [1 *e.*] curd(s); **~о́жник** curd pancake

тво́рче|ский [16] creative; **~ство** *n* [9] creation; creative work(s)

теа́тр *m* [1] theater (*Brt.* -tre; **в** П at); the stage; **~а́льный** [14; -лен, -льна] theatrical; theater…, drama…

тёзка *f* [5; *g/pl.*: -зок] namesake

текст *m* [1] text; words, libretto

тексти́ль *m* [4] *collect.* textiles *pl.*; **~ный** [14] textile; *комбина́т* weaving

теку́|щий [17] current; *ме́сяц* the present; *ремо́нт* routine; **~щие собы́тия** current affairs

телеви́|дение *n* [12] television, TV; *по* **~дению** on TV; **~зио́нный** [14] TV; **~зор** *m* [1] TV set

теле́га *f* [5] cart

телегра́мма *f* [5] telegram

телегра́ф *m* [1] telegraph (office); **~и́ровать** [7] (*im*)*pf.* (Д) telegraph, wire, cable; **~ный** [14] telegraph(ic); telegram…; by wire

теле́|жка *f* [5; *g/pl.*: -жек] handcart

~лекс *m* [1] telex

телёнок *m* [2] calf

телепереда́ча *f* [5] telecast

телеско́п *m* [1] telescope

теле́сный [14] *наказа́ние* corporal; *по-*

вреждения physical; fleshcolo(u)red

телефо́н *m* [1] telephone (**по** Д by); **звони́ть по** ~**у** call, phone, ring up; ~-**автома́т** *m* [1] telephone booth, *Brt.* telephone box; ~**и́ст** *m* [1], ~**и́стка** *f* [5; *g/pl.*: -ток] telephone operator; ~**ный** [14] tele(phone)…

Теле́ц *m* [1] *astr.* Taurus

те́ло *n* [9; *pl. e.*] body; **иноро́дное** ~ foreign body; **всем** ~**м** all over; ~**сложе́ние** *n* [12] build; ~**храни́тель** *m* [4] bodyguard

теля́тина *f* [5], ~**чий** [18] veal

тем → **тот**

те́м(**а́тик**)**а** *f* [5] subject, topic, theme(s)

тембр ('te-) *m* [1] timbre

темн|**е́ть** [8] **1.** ⟨по-⟩ darken; **2.** ⟨с-⟩ grow *or* get dark; **3.** (*a.* -**ся**) appear dark; loom

тёмно… (*in compds.*) dark…

темнота́ *f* [5] darkness; dark

тёмный [14; тёмен, темна́] dark; *fig.* obscure; gloomy; (*подозрительный*) shady, dubious; (*силы*) evil; (*невежественный*) ignorant

темп (te-) *m* [1] tempo; rate, pace, speed

темпера́мент *m* [1] temperament; spirit; ~**ный** [14; -тен, -тна] energetic; vigorous; spirited

температу́ра *f* [5] temperature

те́мя *n* [13] crown, top of the head

тенденци|**о́зный** (-tende-) [-зен, -зна] biased; ~**я** (ten'de-) *f* [7] tendency

те́ндер *fin.* ('tender) *m* [1] *naut. rail.* tender

тени́стый [14 *sh.*] shady

те́ннис *m* [1] tennis; **насто́льный** ~ table tennis; ~**и́ст** *m* [1] tennis player

те́нор *m* [1; *pl.*: -ра́, *etc. e.*] *mus.* tenor

тень *f* [8; в тени́; *pl.*: те́ни, тене́й; *etc. e.*] shade; shadow; **ни те́ни сомне́ния** not a shadow of doubt

теор|**е́тик** *m* [1] theorist; ~**ети́ческий** [16] theoretical; ~**ия** *f* [7] theory

тепе́р|**ешний** [1] *coll.* present; ~**ь** now, nowadays, today

тепл|**е́ть** [8; *3rd p. only*] ⟨по-⟩ grow warm; ~**иться** [13] *mst. fig.* gleam, flicker, glimmer; ~**и́ца** *f* [5], ~**и́чный** [14] greenhouse, hothouse; ~**о́ 1.** *n* [9]

warmth; *phys.* heat; warm weather; **2.** *adv.* → **тёплый**; ~**ово́з** *m* [1] diesel locomotive; ~**ово́й** [14] (of) heat, thermal; ~**ота́** *f* [5] warmth; *phys.* heat; ~**охо́д** *m* [1] motor ship

тёплый [14; тёпел, тепла́, -о́ & тепло́] warm (*a. fig.*); (**мне**) **тепло́** it is (I am) warm

терапи́я *f* [7] therapy

тере|**би́ть** [14 *e.*; -блю́, -би́шь] pull (at); pick (at); tousle; *coll.* (*надоедать*) pester; ~**ть** [12] rub; на тёрке grate

терза́|**ние** *n* [12] *lit.* torment, agony; ~**ть** [1] **1.** ⟨ис-⟩ torment, torture; **2.** ⟨рас-⟩ tear to pieces

тёрка *f* [5; *g/pl.*: -рок] grater

те́рмин *m* [1] term

термо́|**метр** *m* [1] thermometer; ~**с** ('te-) *m* [1] vacuum flask; ~**я́дерный** [14] thermonuclear

тёрн *m* [1] *bot.* blackthorn, sloe

терни́стый [14 *sh.*] thorny

терп|**ели́вый** [14 *sh.*] patient; ~**е́ние** *n* [12] patience; ~**е́ть** [10], ⟨по-⟩ suffer, endure; (*мириться*) tolerate, bear, stand; **вре́мя** ~**и́т** there is no time to be lost; (Д) **не** -**ся** *impf.* be impatient *or* eager; ~**и́мость** *f* [8] tolerance (**к** Д toward[s]); ~**и́мый** [14 *sh.*] tolerant; *условия и т. д.* tolerable, bearable

те́рпкий [16; -пок, -пка́, -о; *compr.*: те́рпче] tart, astringent

терра́са *f* [5] terrace

террит|**ориа́льный** [14] territorial; ~**о́рия** *f* [7] territory

терро́р *m* [1] terror; ~**изи́ровать** &; ~**изова́ть** [7] *im(pf.)* terrorize

тёртый [14] ground, grated

теря́ть [28], ⟨по-⟩ lose; *время* waste; *листву* shed; *надежду* give up; **не** ~ **из ви́ду** keep in sight; *fig.* bear in mind; -**ся** get lost; disappear, vanish; (*смущаться*) become flustered; be at a loss

теса́ть [3], ⟨об-⟩ hew, cut

тесни́ть [13], ⟨с-⟩ press, crowd; -**ся** crowd, throng; jostle; ~**ота́** *f* [5] crowded state; narrowness; crush; ~**ый** [14; -се́н, тесна́, -о] crowded; cramped; narrow; *fig.* tight; close; *отношения* intimate; **мир те́сен** it's a small world

те́ст|о n [9] dough, pastry; **~ь** m [4] father-in-law (*wife's father*)

тесьма́ f [5; g/pl.: -сём] tape; ribbon

те́терев m [1; pl.: -á, etc. e.] zo. black grouse, blackcock

тетива́ f [5] bowstring

тётка f [5; g/pl.: -ток] aunt; (*as term of address to any older woman*) ma'am, lady

тетра́д|ь f [8], **~ка** f [5; g/pl.: -док] exercise book, notebook, copybook

тётя coll. f [6; g/pl.: -тей] aunt

те́хн|ик m [1] technician; **~ика** f [5] engineering; *исполнения и т. д.* technique; equipment; **~икум** m [1] technical college; **~и́ческий** [16] technical; engineering...; **~и́ческое обслу́живание** maintenance; **~и́ческие усло́вия** specifications; **~ологи́ческий** [16] technological; **~оло́гия** f [7] technology

тече́ние n [12] current; stream **[вверх [вниз] по** Д up[down]); course (**в** В in; **с** T/P in/of *time*) *fig.* trend; tendency; **~ь** [8] flow, run; stream; *время* pass; (*протека́ть*) leak; **2.** f [8] leak (spring **дать**)

тёща f [5] mother-in-law (*wife's mother*)

тибе́тец m [1; -тца] Tibetan

тигр m [1] tiger; **~и́ца** f [5] tigress

ти́ка|нье [10], **~ть** [1] of clock tick

ти́на f [5] slime, mud, ooze

тип m [1] type; *coll.* character; **~и́чный** [14; -чен, -чна] typical; **~огра́фия** f [7] printing office

тир m [1] shooting gallery

тира́да f [5] tirade

тира́ж m [1 e.] circulation; edition; *лоте́реи* drawing; **~о́м в 2000** edition of 2,000 copies

тира́н m [1] tyrant; **~ить** [13] tyranize; **~и́я** f [7], **~ство** f [9] tyranny

тире́ n [indecl.] dash

ти́с|кать [1], **⟨~нуть⟩** [20] squeeze, press; **~ки́** m/pl. [1 e.] vise, Brt. vice; grip; **в ~ка́х** in the grip of (P); **~нёный** [14] printed

титр m [1] cine. caption, subtitle, credit

ти́тул m [1] title; **~ьный лист** [14] title page

тиф m [1] typhus

ти́|хий [16; тих, -á, -о; comp.: ти́ше] quiet, still; calm; soft, gentle; *ход* slow; **~ше!** be quiet!, silence!; **~шина́** f [5] silence, stillness, calm; **~шь** [8; в тиши́] quiet, silence

тка|нь f [8] fabric, cloth; *anat.* tissue; **~ть** [тку, ткёшь; ткал, ткала́, -о], **⟨со-⟩ ⟨со́тканный⟩** weave; **~цкий** [16] weaver's; weaving; **~ч** m [1 e.], **~чи́ха** f [5] weaver

ткну́ть(ся) → **ты́кать(ся)**

тле́|ние n [12] decay, putrefaction; *угле́й* smo(u)ldering; **~ть** [8], **⟨ис-⟩** smo(u)lder; decay, rot, putrefy; *о надежде* glimmer

то 1. [28] that; **~ же** the same; **к ~му́** (же) in addition (to that), moreover; add to this; **ни ~ ни сё** coll. neither fish nor flesh; **ни с ~го́ ни с сего́** coll. all of a sudden, without any visible reason; **до ~го́** so; **она́ до ~го́ разозли́лась** she was so angry; **до ~го́ вре́мени** before (that); **2.** (cj.) then; **~ ... ~** now ... now; **не ~ ... не ~ ...** or **~ ли ... ~ ли ...** either ... or ..., half ... half ...; **не ~, что́бы** not that; **а не ~** (or) else; **3. ~~** just, exactly; **в то́м и де́ло** that's just it

това́р m [1] commodity, article; *pl.* goods, wares; **~ы широ́кого потребле́ния** consumer goods

това́рищ m [1] comrade, friend; mate, companion (*по* Д in *arms*); colleague; **~ по шко́ле** schoolmate; **~ по университе́ту** fellow student; **~еский** [16] friendly; **~ество** n [9] comradeship, fellowship; *comm.* association, company

това́р|ный [14] goods...; **~ный склад** warehouse; *rail.* freight...; **~ообме́н** m [1] barter; **~ооборо́т** m [1] commodity circulation

тогда́ then, at that time; **~ как** whereas, while; **~шний** [15] of that (*or* the) time, then

то́ есть that is (to say), i.e

тожде́ств|енный [14 sh.] identical; **~о** n [9] identity

то́же also, too, as well; → **та́кже**

ток m [1] current

тока́р|ный [14] turner's; *стано́к* turning; **~ь** *m* [4] turner, lathe operator

токси́чный [14; -чен, -чна] toxic

толк *m* [1; *бе́з* ~y] sense; use; understanding; *знать* ~ *(в* П*)* know what one is talking about; *бе́з* ~y senselessly; **сбить с ~y** muddle; **~а́ть** [1], *once* ⟨~ну́ть⟩ [20] push, shove, jog; *fig.* induce, prompt; *coll.* urge on, spur; **-ся** push (o.a.); **~ова́ть**[7] 1. ⟨ис-⟩ interpret, expound, explain; comment; 2. ⟨по-⟩ talk (**с** T to); **~о́вый** [14] explanatory; [*sh.*] smart, sensible; **~о́м** plainly; **я ~о́м не зна́ю …** I don't really know …; **~отня́** *coll.* f [6] crush, crowding

толо|кно́ *n* [9] oat meal; **~кно́й** [14; -лку, -лчёшь, -лку́т; -ло́к, -лкла́; -лчённый], ⟨рас-, ис-⟩ pound, crush

толп|а́ f [5; *pl. st.*], **~и́ться** [14 *e.*; *no 1st. & 2 p. sg.*], ⟨с-⟩ crowd, throng

толст|е́ть[8], ⟨по-, рас-⟩ grow fat; grow stout; **~око́жий** [17 *sh.*] thick-skinned; **~ый** [14; толст, -á, -о; *compr.*: -то́лще] thick; heavy; (*тучный*) stout; fat; **~я́к** *coll. m* [1 *e.*] fat man

толч|ёный [14] pounded; **~ея́** *coll.* f [6] crush, crowd; **~о́к** *m* [1; -чка́] push; shove; jolt; *при землетрясе́нии* shock, tremor; *fig.* impulse, spur

толщин|а́f[5] fatness; corpulence; thickness; **~о́й в** (В), **… в ~у́** …thick

толь *m* [4] roofing felt

то́лько only, but; *как ~* as soon as; *лишь (or едва́)* ~ no sooner … than; *~ бы* if only; ~ *что* just now, **~~** *coll.* barely

том *m* [1; *pl.*: -á; *etc. e.*] volume

тома́т *m* [1], **~ный** [14] tomato; **~ный сок** tomato juice

том|и́тельный [14; -лен, -льна] wearisome; trying; *ожида́ние* tedious; *жара́* oppressive; **~но́сть** f [8] languor; **~ный** [14; -мен, -мна́, -о] languid, languorous

тон *m* [1; *pl.*:-á; *etc. e.*] *mus.* and *fig.* tone

то́нк|ий [16; -нок, -нка́, -о; *compr.*: то́ньше] thin; *та́лия и т. д.* slim, slender; *шёлк и т. д.* fine; *вопро́с и т. д.* delicate, subtle; *слух* keen; *го́лос* high; *поли́тик* clever, cunning; **~ость**f[8] thinness, *etc.* → **~ий**; delicacy, subtlety; *pl.* details (go into **вдава́ться в** B; *coll.* split hairs

то́нна f [5] ton; **~ж** *m* [1] (*metric*) ton

тонне́ль (-'nɛ́-) *m* [4] tunnel

то́нус *m* [1] *med.* tone

тону́ть [19] *v/i.* 1. ⟨по-, за-⟩ sink; 2. ⟨у-⟩ drown

то́п|ать [1], *once* ⟨~нуть⟩ [20] stamp; **~ить** [14] *v/t.* 1. ⟨за-, по-⟩ sink; *водо́й* flood; 2. ⟨за-, по-⟩ stoke (*a stove, etc.*); heat up; 3. ⟨рас-⟩ melt; 4. ⟨у-⟩ drown; **~кий** [16; -пок, -пка́, -о] boggy, marshy; **~лёный** [14] melted; *молоко́* baked; **~ливо** *n* [9] fuel; *жи́дкое ~ливо* fuel oil; **~нуть → ~ать**

топогра́|фия f [7] topography

то́поль *m* [4; *pl.*: -ля́; *etc. e.*] poplar

топо́р *m* [1 *e.*] ax(e); **~ный** [14; -рен, -рна] clumsy; coarse; uncouth

то́пот *m* [1] stamp(ing); tramp(ing)

топта́ть [3], ⟨по-, за-⟩ trample, tread; ⟨вы-⟩ trample down; ⟨с-⟩ wear out; **-ся** tramp(le); *coll.* hang about; mark time (*на ме́сте*)

топь f [8] marsh, bog, swamp

торг *m* [1; на -ý; *pl.*: -и́; *etc. e.*] trading; bargaining, haggling; *pl.* auction (**с** P by; *на* П at); **~а́ш** *m* [1 *e.*] *pej.* (petty) tradesman; mercenaryminded person; **~ова́ть** [8] trade, deal (in T) sell; **-ся**, ⟨с-⟩ (strike a) bargain (**о** П for); **~о́вец** *m* [1; -вца] dealer, trader, merchant; **~о́вка** f [5; *g/pl.*: -вок] market woman; **~о́вля** f [6] trade, commerce; *нарко́тиками* traffic; **~о́вый** [14] trade…, trading, commercial, of commerce; *naut.* merchant…; **~пре́д** *m* [1] trade representative; **~пре́дство** *n* [9] trade delegation

торже́ств|енностьf[8] solemnity; **~енный** [14 *sh.*] solemn; festive; **~о** *n* [9] triumph; (*пра́зднество*) festivity, celebration; **~ова́ть** [7], ⟨вос-⟩ triumph (*над* T); *impf.* celebrate

тормо|зm 1. [1; *pl.*: -á, *etc. e.*] brake; 2. [1] *fig.* drag; **~зи́ть** [15 *e.*; -ожу́, -ози́шь; -ожённый], ⟨за-⟩ (put the) brake(s on); *fig.* hamper; *psych.* inhibit; **~ши́ть** *coll.* [16; -шу́, -ши́шь] → **тереби́ть**

торо́п|ить [14], ⟨по-⟩ hasten, hurry up (*v/i.* **-ся**; *a.* be in hurry); **~ли́вый** [14 *sh.*] hasty, hurried

торпе́д|а f [5], **~и́ровать** [7] (im)pf. torpedo (a. fig.); **~ный** [14] torpedo..

торт m [1] cake

торф m [1] peat; **~яно́й** [14] peat...

торча́ть [4 e.; -чу́, -чи́шь] stick up, stick out; coll. hang about

торше́р m [1] standard lamp

тоск|а́ f [5] melancholy; (томление) yearning; (скука) boredom, ennui; **~а́ по ро́дине** homesickness; **~ли́вый** [14] melancholy; погода dull, dreary; **~ова́ть** [7] grieve, feel sad (or lonely); feel bored; yearn or long (for **по** П or Д); be homesick (по родине)

тост m [1] toast; **предложи́ть ~** propose a toast (**за** В to)

тот m, **та** f, **то** n, **те** pl. [28] that, pl. those; the one; the other; **не ~** wrong; **(н)и тот (н)и друго́й** both (neither); **тот же (са́мый)** the same; **тем бо́лее** the more so; **тем лу́чше** so much the better; **тем са́мым** thereby; **~ a. то**

тоталитар|и́зм m [1] totalitarianism; **~ный** [14] totalitarian

то́тчас (же) immediately, at once

точёный [14] sharpened; черты лица chisel(l)ed; фигура shapely

точи́|льный [14]: **~льный брусо́к** whetstone; **~ть 1.** ⟨на-⟩ whet, grind; sharpen; **2.** ⟨вы-⟩ turn; **3.** ⟨ис-⟩ eat (or gnaw) away

то́чк|а f [5; g/pl.: -чек] point; dot; gr. period, full stop; **вы́сшая ~а** zenith, climax (**на** П at); **~а с запято́й** gr. semicolon; **~а зре́ния** point of view; **попа́сть в са́мую ~у** hit the nail on the head; **дойти́ до ~и** coll. come to the end of one's tether

то́чн|о adv. **~ый;** a. **~ сло́вно;** indeed; **~ость** f [8] accuracy, exactness, precision; **в ~ости →~о; ~ый** [14; -чен, -чна́, -o] exact, precise, accurate; punctual; прибор (of) precision

точь: ~ в ~ coll. exactly

тошн|и́ть [13]: **меня́ ~и́т** I feel sick; I loathe; **~ота́** f [5] nausea

то́щий [17; тощ, -а́, -o] lean, lank, gaunt; coll. empty; растительность scanty, poor

трава́ f [5; pl. st.] grass; med. pl. herbs;

сорная weed

трав|и́ть [14 sh.] **1.** ⟨за-⟩ fig. persecute; **2.** ⟨вы-⟩ exterminate; **~ля** f [6; g/pl.: -лей] persecution

трав|яни́стый [14 sh.], **~я́ной** [14] grass(y)

траг|е́дия f [7] tragedy; **~ик** m [1] tragic actor, tragedian; **~и́ческий** [16], **~и́чный** [14; -чен, -чна] tragic

традици|о́нный [14; -о́нен, -о́нна] traditional; **~я** f [7] tradition, custom

тракт m [1]: high road, highway; anat. **желу́дочно-кише́чный ~** alimentary canal; **~ова́ть** [7] treat; discuss; interpret; **~о́вка** [5; g/pl.: -вок] treatment; interpretation; **~ори́ст** m [1] tractor driver; **~орный** [14] tractor...

тра́льщик m [1] trawler; mil. mine sweeper

трамбова́ть [7], ⟨у-⟩ ram

трамва́й m [3] streetcar, Brt. tram(car) (Т, **на** П by)

трампли́н m [1] sport springboard (a. fig.); **лы́жный ~** ski-jump

транзи́стор m [1] el. (component) transistor

транзи́т m [1], **~ный** [14] transit

транс|криби́ровать [7] (im)pf. transcribe; **~ли́ровать** [7] (im)pf. broadcast, transmit (by radio); relay; **~ля́ция** f [7] transmission; **~пара́нт** m [1] transparency; banner

тра́нспорт m [1] transport; transport(ation; a. system [of]); **~и́ровать** [7] (im)pf. transport, convey; **~ный** [14] (of) transport(ation)...

трансформа́тор m [1] el. transformer

транше́я f [6; g/pl.: -е́й] trench

трап m [1] naut. ladder; ae. gangway

тра́сса f [5] route, line

тра́т|а f [5] expenditure; waste; **пуста́я ~а вре́мени** a waste of time; **~ить** [15], ⟨ис-, по-⟩ spend, expend; use up; waste

тра́ур m [1] mourning; **~ный** [14 mourning...; марш и т. д. funeral...

трафаре́т m [1] stencil; stereotype; cliché (a. fig.)

трах int. bang!

тре́бова|ние n [12] demand (**по** Д on); request, requirement; (претензия) claim; *судьи* order; **~тельный** [14; -лен, -льна] exacting; (*разборчивый*) particular; **~ть** [7], ⟨по-⟩ (P) demand; require; claim; summon, call for; **-ся** be required (*or* wanted); be necessary

трево́|га *f* [5] alarm, anxiety; *mil. etc.* warning, alert; **~жить** [16] **1.** ⟨вс-, рас-⟩ alarm, disquiet; **2.** ⟨по-⟩ disturb, trouble; **-ся** be anxious; worry; **~жный** [14; -жен, -жна] worried, anxious, uneasy; *известия и т. д.* alarm(ing), disturbing

тре́зв|ость *f* [8] sobriety; **~ый** [14; трезв, -á, -о] sober (*a. fig.*)

тре́нер *m* [1] trainer, coach

тре́ние *n* [12] friction (*a. fig.*)

трениро́в|ать [12], ⟨на-⟩ train, coach; *v/i.* **-ся**; **~ка** *f* [7] training, coaching

трепа́ть [2], ⟨по-⟩ *ветром* tousle; dishevel; blow about; **~ кому́-л. не́рвы** get on s.o.'s nerves

тре́пет *m* [1] trembling, quivering; **~а́ть** [3], ⟨за-⟩ tremble (**от** P with); quiver, shiver; *о пламени* flicker; *от ужаса* palpitate; **~ный** [14; -тен, -тна] quivering; flickering

треск *m* [1] crack, crackle

треска́ *f* [5] cod

тре́ск|аться [1], ⟨по-, тре́снуть⟩ [20] crack, split; *о коже и т. д.* chap; **~отня́** *f* [6] *о речи* chatter, prattle; **~у́чий** [17 *sh.*] *мороз* hard, ringing; *fig.* bombastic

тре́снуть → **тре́скаться & треща́ть**

трест *m* [1] *econ.* trust

тре́т|ий [18] third; **~и́ровать** [7] slight; **~ь** *f* [8; *from g/pl.*] (one) third

треуго́льн|ик *m* [1] triangle; **~ый** [14] triangular

тре́фы *f/pl.* [5] clubs (*cards*)

трёх|годи́чный [14] three-year; **~дне́вный** [14] three-day; **~колёсный** [14] three-wheeled; **~ле́тний** [15] three-year; threeyear-old; **~со́тый** [14] three hundredth; **~цве́тный** [14] tricolo(u)r; **~эта́жный** [14] threestoried (*Brt.* -reyed)

треща́ть [4 *е.*; -щу́, -щи́шь] **1.** ⟨за-⟩ crack; crackle; *о мебели* creak; *coll.* prattle; **голова́ ~и́т** have a splitting headache; **2.** ⟨тре́снуть⟩ [20] burst; **~и́на** *f* [5] split

(*a. fig.*), crack, cleft, crevice, fissure; *на коже* chap

три [34] three; → **пять**

трибу́н|а *f* [5] platform; rostrum; tribune; (*at sports stadium*) stand; **~а́л** *m* [1] tribunal

тривиа́льный [14; -лен, -льна] trivial; trite

тригономе́трия *f* [7] trigonometry

тридца́|тый [14] thirtieth; → **пятидеся́тый**; **~ть** [35 *е.*] thirty

три́жды three times

трикота́ж *m* [1] knitted fabric; *collect.* knitwear

трило́гия *f* [7] trilogy

трина́дца|тый [14] thirteenth; → **пя́тый**; **~ть** [35] thirteen; → **пять**

три́ста [36] three hundred

триу́мф *m* [1] triumph; **~а́льный** [14] *арка* triumphal; triumphant

тро́га|тельный [14; -лен, -льна] touching, moving; **~ть** [1], *once* ⟨тро́нуть⟩ [20] touch (*a. fig.* = affect, move); *coll.* pester; **не тронь её!** leave her alone!; **-ся** start; set out (**в путь** on a journey)

тро́е [37] three (**в дво́е**); **~кра́тный** [14; -тен, -тна] thrice-repeated

Тро́ица *f* [5] Trinity; Whitsun(day); 2 *coll.* trio

тро́й|ка *f* [5; *g/pl.*: тро́ек] three (→ **дво́йка**); troika (*team of three horses abreast* [+ *vehicle*]); *coll.* (*of school mark* =) **посре́дственно**; **~но́й** [14] threefold, triple, treble; **~ня** *f* [6; *g/pl.*: тро́ен] triplets *pl.*

тролле́йбус *m* [1] trolley bus

трон *m* [1] throne; **~ный** [14] *речь* King's, Queen's

тро́нуть(ся) → **тро́гать(ся)**

троп|а́ *f* [5; *pl.*: тро́пы, троп, -па́м] path, track; **~и́нка** [5; *g/pl.*: -нок] (small) path

тропи́ческий [16] tropical

трос *m* [1] *naut.* line; cable, hawser

тростни́к *m* [1 *е.*] reed; *сахарный* cane; **~нико́вый** [14] reed...; cane...; **~ь** *f* [8; *from g/pl.*] cane, walking stick

тротуа́р *m* [1] sidewalk, *Brt.* pavement

трофе́й *m* [3] trophy (*a. fig.*); *pl.* spoils of war; booty; **~ный** [14] *mil.* captured

тро|ю́родный [14] second (*cousin* **брат**

m, **сестра́** *f*); **~я́кий** [16 *sh.*] threefold, triple

труб|а́ *f* [5; *pl. st.*] pipe; *печная* chimney; *naut.* funnel; *mus.* trumpet; **вы́лететь в ~у́** go bust; **~а́ч** *m* [1 *e.*] trumpeter; **~и́ть** [14; -блю́, -би́шь], ⟨про-⟩ blow (the **в** В); **~ка́** [5; *g/pl.*: -бок] tube; *для курения* pipe; *teleph.* receiver; **~опрово́д** *m* [1] pipeline; **~очный** [14] *таба́к* pipe

труд *m* [1 *e.*] labo(u)r, work; pains *pl.*, trouble; difficulty (**c T** with*a.* hard[ly]); scholarly work; *pl. (in published records of scholarly meetings, etc.)* transactions; *coll.* (*услуга*) service; **взять на себя́ ~** take the trouble (to); **~и́ться** [15], ⟨по-⟩ work; toil; **~ность** *f* [8] difficulty; **~ный** [14; -ден, -дна́, -о] difficult, hard; *coll.* heavy; **де́ло оказа́лось ~ным** it was heavy going; **~ово́й** [14] labo(u)r…; *день* working; *дохо́д* earned; *стаж* service…; **~олюби́вый** [14 *sh.*] industrious; **~оспосо́бный** [14; -бен, -бна] able-bodied, capable of working; **~я́щийся** [17] working; *su. mst. pl.* working people

тру́женик *m* [1] toiler, worker

труп *m* [1] corpse, dead body

тру́ппа *f* [5] company, troupe

трус *m* [1] coward

тру́сики *no sg.* [1] shorts, swimming trunks, undershorts

тру́с|ить [15], be a coward; ⟨c-⟩ be afraid (of Р); **~и́ха** *coll.* / *f* [5] *f* → *трус*; **~ли́вый** [14 *sh.*] cowardly; **~ость** *f* [8] cowardice

тру́сы *no sg.* = *тру́сики*

трущо́ба *f* [5] thicket; *fig.* out-of-the-way place; slum

трюк *m* [1] feat, stunt; *fig.* gimmick; *pej.* trick

трюм *m* [1] *naut.* hold

трюмо́ *n* [*indecl.*] pier glass

тря́п|ка *f* [5; *g/pl.*: -пок] rag; *для пыли* duster; *pl. coll.* finery; *о человеке* milksop; **~ьё** *n* [10] rag(s)

тря́с|ка *f* [5] jolting; **~ти́** [24; -с-], *once* ⟨тряхну́ть⟩ [20] shake (a *p.'s* Д hand, head, *etc.* T; *a. fig.*); (*impers.*) jolt; **~ти́сь** shake; shiver (with **от** Р)

тряхну́ть → *трясти́*

тсс! *int.* hush!; ssh!

туале́т *m* [1] toilet, lavatory; dress, dressing

туберкулёз *m* [1] tuberculosis; **~ный** [14] *больно́й* tubercular

туго́|й [14; туг, -а́, -о *сотр.*: ту́же] tight, taut; *замо́к* stiff; (*туго наби́тый*) crammed; hard (*a.* starting **на у́хо**); *adv. a.* **открыва́ться** hard; with difficulty; **у него́ ~ с деньга́ми** he is short of money

туда́ there, thither; that way

туз *m* [1 *e.*] cards ace

тузе́м|ец *m* [1; -мца] native; **~ный** [14] native

ту́ловище *n* [11] trunk, torso

тулу́п *m* [1] sheepskin coat

тума́н *m* [1] fog, mist; *ды́мка* haze (*a. fig.*); **~ный** [14; -а́нен, -а́нна] foggy, misty; *fig.* hazy, vague

ту́мбочка *f* [5; *g/pl.*: -чек] bedside table

ту́ндра *f* [5] *geog.* tundra

туне́ц *m* [1; -нца́ и т. д.] tuna *or* tunny fish

тунне́ль → *тонне́ль*

туп|е́ть [8], ⟨по-⟩ *fig.* grow blunt; **~и́к** *m* [1 *e.*] blind alley, cul-de-sac; *fig.* deadlock, impasse; **ста́вить в ~и́к** reach a deadlock; **стать в ~и́к** be at a loss, be nonplussed; **~о́й** [14; туп, -а́, -о] blunt; *math.* obtuse; *fig.* dull, stupid; **~ость** *f* [8] bluntness; dullness; **~оу́мный** [14; -мен, -мна] dull, obtuse

тур *m* [1] *переговоров* round; tour; turn (*at a dance*); *zo.* aurochs

турба́за *f* [5] hostel

турби́на *f* [5] turbine

туре́цкий [16] Turkish

тури́|зм *m* [1] tourism; **~ст** *m* [1] tourist

туркме́н *m* [1] Turkmen; **~ский** [16] Turkmen

турне́ (-'nε) *n* [*indecl.*] tour (*esp. of performers or sports competitors*)

турни́к *m* [1 *e.*] *sport* horizontal bar

турнике́т [1] turnstile; *med.* tourniquet

турни́р *m* [1] tournament (**на** П in)

тур|о́к *m* [1; -рка; *g/pl.*: ту́рок], **~ча́нка** [5; *g/pl.*: -нок] Turk

ту́ск|лый [14; тускл, -а́, -о] *свет* dim; dull; **~не́ть** [8], ⟨по-⟩ & **~нуть** [20] grow dim *or* dull; lose luster (-tre); pale (*пе*-

ред Т before)

тут here; there; then; ~! present!, here!; ~ **же** there and then, on the spot; ~ **как** ~ coll. there he is; there they are; that's that

ту́тов|ый [14]: ~**ое де́рево** mulberry tree

ту́фля f [6; g/pl.: -фель] shoe; до-ма́шняя slipper

тух|лый [14; тухл, -á, -о] яйцо́ bad, rotten; ~**нуть**[21] **1.** 〈по-〉 о све́те go out; о костре́ go or die out; **2.** 〈про-〉 go bad

ту́ч|а f [5] cloud; rain or storm cloud на-ро́да crowd; мух swarm; dim. ~**ка** f [5; g/pl.:-чек], ~**ный** [14; -чен, -чна́, -о] corpulent, stout

туш m [1] mus. flourish

ту́ша f [5] carcass

туш|ёнка f [5] coll. corned beef or pork; ~**ёный** [14] stewed; ~**и́ть** [16], 〈по-〉 **1.** switch off, put out, extinguish; сканда́л quell; **2.** impf. stew

тушь f [8] Indian ink; mascara

тща́тель|ость f [8] thoroughness; care(fulness); ~**ый** [14; -лен, -льна] painstaking; careful

тще|ду́шный [14; -шен, -шна] sickly; ~**сла́вие** n [12] vanity; ~**сла́вный** [14; -вен, -вна] vain (-glorious); ~**тный** [14; -тен, -тна] vain, futile; ~**тно** in vain

ты [21] you; obs. thou; **быть на** ~ (с Т) be on familiar terms with s.o.

ты́кать [3], 〈ткнуть〉 [20] poke, jab, thrust; (v/i. -**ся**) knock (**в** В against, into)

ты́ква f [5] pumpkin

тыл m [1; в -ý; pl. e.] rear, back

ты́сяч|а f [5] thousand; ~**еле́тие** n [12] millenium; ~**ный** [14] thousandth; of thousand(s)

тьма f [5] dark(ness); coll. a host of, a multitude of

тьфу! coll. fie!, for shame!

тю́бик m [1] tube (of toothpaste, etc.)

тюк m [1 e.] bale, pack

тюле́нь m [4] zo. seal

тюль m [4] tulle

тюльпа́н m [1] tulip

тюр|е́мный [14] prison...; ~**е́мный контролёр** jailer, Brt. gaoler, warder; ~**ьма́** f [5; pl.: тюрьмы, -рем, -рьмам] prison, jail, Brt. gaol

тюфя́к m [1 e.] mattress (filled with straw, etc.)

тя́вкать coll. [1] yap, yelp

тя́г|а f [5] в печи́ draft, Brt. draught; си-ла traction; fig. bent (**к** Д for); craving (for); ~**аться** coll. [1] (**с** Т) be a match (for), vie (with); ~**остный** [14; -тен, -тна] (обремени́тельный) burden-some; (неприя́тный) painful; ~**ость** f [8] burden (be... to **в** В/Д); ~**оте́ние** n [12] земно́е gravitation; a. → ~**а** fig.; gravitate (toward[s] **к** Д); weigh (upon **над** Т); ~**оте́ть** [15 e.; -ощу́, -оти́шь] weigh upon, be a burden to; -**ся** feel a burden (Т of); ~**у́чий** [17 sh.] жи́дкость viscous; речь drawling

тяж|елове́с m [1] sport heavyweight; ~**елове́сный** [14; -сен, -сна] heavy, ponderous; ~**ёлый** [14; -жел, -жела́] heavy, difficult, hard; стиль laborious; ране́ние и т. д. serious; уда́р, положе́ние severe, grave; обстоя́тельства и т. д. grievous, sad, oppressive, painful; во́здух close; (Д) ~**ело́** feel miserable; ~**есть** f [8] heaviness; weight; load; burden; gravity; seriousness; ~**кий** [16; тя́жек, тяжка́, -о] heavy (fig.), etc., → ~**ёлый**

тяну́ть [19] pull, draw; naut. tow; мед-лить protract; слова́ drawl (out); (влечь) attract; long; have a mind to; would like; о за́пахе waft; ~**ет** there is a draft (Brt. draught) (Т of); coll. красть steal; take (**с** Р from); -**ся** stretch (a. = extend); last; drag; draw on; reach out (**к** Д for)

У

у (Р) at, by, near; with; (at) ...'s; at ...'s place; **у меня (был, -á ...)** I have (had); my; **взять, узнать** и т. д. from, of; **берега** и т. д. off; in; **у себя** in (at) one's home or room or office

убавл|я́ть [28], ⟨~ить⟩ [14] reduce, diminish, decrease; **~ить в ве́се** lose weight; v/i. **-ся**

убе|га́ть [1], ⟨~жа́ть⟩ [4; -егу́, -жи́шь, -гу́т] run away; **та́йком** escape

убеди́тельный [14; -лен, -льна] convincing; **про́сьба** urgent; ⟨~жда́ть⟩ [1], ⟨~ди́ть⟩ [15 e.; no 1st p. sg.; -еди́шь, -еждённый] convince (**в** П of); (**угово-ри́ть**) persuade (impf. a. try to…); ~жде́ние n [12] persuasion; conviction; belief

убеж|а́ть → убега́ть; ~и́ще n [11] shelter, refuge; **полити́ческое** asylum

убер|ега́ть [1], ⟨~е́чь⟩ [26 г/ж] keep safe, safeguard

уби|ва́ть [1], ⟨~ть⟩ [убью, -ьёшь; уби́тый] kill, murder; assassinate; fig. drive to despair; **~ва́ть вре́мя** kill or waste time

уби́й|ственный [14 sh.] killing; **взгляд** murderous; ~ство n [9] murder; **полити́ческое** assassination; **покуше́ние на ~ство** murderous assault; ~ца m/f [5] murderer; assassin

убира́|ть [1], ⟨убра́ть⟩ [уберу́, -рёшь; убра́л, -á, -о; у́бранный] take (or put, clear) away (in); gather, harvest; tidy up; (**украша́ть**) decorate, adorn, trim; **-ся** clear off; **~йся (вон)!** get out of here!, beat it!

уби́ть → убива́ть

убо́гий [16 sh.] (**бе́дный**) needy, poor; **жили́ще** miserable; ~жество n [9] poverty; mediocrity

убо́й m [3] slaughter (of livestock) (**for на** В)

убо́р m [1]: **головно́й ~** headgear; ~истый [14 sh.] close; ~ка f [5; g/pl.: -рок] harvest, gathering; **ко́мнаты** и т. д. tidying up; ~ная f [14] lavatory, toilet;

thea. dressing room; ~очный [14] harvest(ing); ~щица f [5] cleaner (in offices, etc.); charwoman

убра́|нство n [9] furniture, appointments; interior decor; ~ть(ся) → **убира́ть(ся)**

убы|ва́ть [1], ⟨~ть⟩ [убу́ду, -убу́дешь; убы́л, -á, -о] о воде́ subside, fall; (**уменьша́ться**) decrease; ~ль f [8] diminution, fall; ~ток m [1; -тка] loss, damage; ~точный [14; -чен, -чна] unprofitable; ~ть → **убыва́ть**

уваж|а́емый [14] respected; dear (as salutation in letter); ~а́ть [1], ~е́ние n [12] respect, esteem (su. **к** Д for); ~и́тельный [14; -лен, -льна] **причи́на** valid; **отноше́ние** respectful

уведом|ля́ть [28], ⟨~ить⟩ [14] inform, notify, advise (**о** П of); ~ле́ние n [12] notification, information

увезти́ → увози́ть

увекове́чи|вать [1], ⟨~ть⟩ [16] immortalize, perpetuate

увеличе́ние n [12] increase; phot. enlargement; ~ивать [1], ⟨~ить⟩ [16] increase; enlarge; extend; v/i. **-ся**; ~и́тельный [14] magnifying

увенча́ться [1] pf. (Т) be crowned

увер|е́ние n [12] assurance (of **в** П); ~енность f [8] assurance; certainty; confidence (**в** П in); ~енный [14 sh.] confident, sure, certain (**в** П of); **бу́дь-те ~ены** you may be sure, you may depend on it; ~ить → **~я́ть**

уве́рт|ка coll. f [5; g/pl.: -ток] subterfuge, dodge, evasion; ~ливый [14 sh.] evasive, shifty

увертю́ра f [5] overture

увер|я́ть [28], ⟨~ить⟩ [13] assure (**в** П of); убеди́ть(ся) make believe (sure **-ся**), persuade

уве́систый [14 sh.] rather heavy; coll. weighty

увести́ → уводи́ть

уве́ч|ить [16], ⟨из-⟩ maim, mutilate; ~ный [14] maimed, mutilated, crippled;

~ье *n* [10] mutilation

уве**щ(ев)а́ние** *n* [12] admonition; ~**ть** [1] admonish

уви́л|ивать [1], ⟨~ьну́ть⟩ [20] shirk

увлажн|я́ть[28], ⟨~и́ть⟩[13] wet, dampen, moisten

увле|ка́тельный [14; -лен, -льна] fascinating, absorbing; ~**ка́ть** [1], ⟨~чь⟩ [26] carry (away; *a. fig.* = transport, captivate); -**ся** (T) be carried away (by), be(come) enthusiastic (about); (*погрузиться*) be(come) absorbed (in); (*влюбиться*) fall (*or* be) in love (with); ~**че́ние** *n* [12] enthusiasm, passion (for T)

уво|ди́ть [15], ⟨увести́⟩ [25] take, lead (away, off); *coll.* (*украсть*) steal; ~зи́ть [15], ⟨увезти́⟩ [24] take, carry, drive (away, off); abduct, kidnap

уво́л|ить → ~**ня́ть**; ~**не́ние** *n* [12] dismissal (**с** P from); ~**ня́ть** [28], ⟨~**ить**⟩ [13] dismiss (**с** P from)

увы́! *int.* alas!

увя|да́ние *n* [12] withering; *о человеке* signs of aging; ~**да́ть** [21], ⟨~**нуть**⟩ [20] wither, fade (*or* fade away); ~**дший** [17] withered

увяз|а́ть [1] **1.** ⟨~**нуть**⟩ [21] get stuck (in); *fig.* get bogged down (in); **2.** → ~**ывать(ся)**; ~**ка** *f* [5] coordination; ~**ывать** (away, off); [3] tie up; (*согласовывать*) coordinate (*v/i.* -**ся**)

уга́д|ывать [1], ⟨~**а́ть**⟩ [1] guess

уга́р *m* [1] charcoal fumes; *fig.* ecstasy, intoxication

угас|а́ть [1], ⟨~**нуть**⟩ [21] *об огне* die down; *о звуке* die (*or* fade) away; *надежда* die; *силы* fail; *о человеке* fade away

угле|ки́слый [14] *chem.* carbonate (of); (~**ки́слый газ** carbon dioxide); ~**ро́д** *m* [1] carbon

углово́й [14] *дом* corner...; angle...; angular

углуб|и́ть(ся) → ~**ля́ть(ся)**; ~**ле́ние** *n* [12] deepening; (*впадина*) hollow, cavity, hole; *знаний* extension; ~**лённый** [14 *sh.*] profound; *a. p. pt. p. of* ~**и́ть(ся)**; ~**ля́ть** [28], ⟨~**и́ть**⟩ [14 *e.*; -блю́, -би́шь; -блённый] deepen (*v/i.* -**ся**); make (become) more profound, extend; -**ся** *a.* go deep (**в** B into), be(come) absorbed (in)

угна́ть → **угоня́ть**

угнет|а́тель *m* [4] oppressor; ~**а́ть** [1] oppress; (*мучить*) depress; ~**е́ние** *n* [12] oppression; (*a.* ~**ённость** *f*[8]) depression; ~**ённый** [14; -тён, -тена́] oppressed; depressed

угов|а́ривать [1], ⟨~**ори́ть**⟩ [13] (B) (*impf.* try to) persuade; -**ся** arrange, agree; ~**о́р** *m* [1] agreement; *pl.* persuasion; ~**ори́ть(ся)** → ~**а́ривать(ся)**

уго́д|а *f*[5]: **в** ~**у** (Д) for the benefit of, to please; ~**и́ть** → ~**жда́ть**; ~**ливый** [14 *sh.*] fawning, ingratiating, toadyish; ~**ник** *m* [1]: **свято́й** ~**ник** saint; ~**но** please; **как (что) вам** ~**но** just as (whatever) you like; **(что) вам** ~**но?** what can I do for you?; **ско́лько (душе́)** ~**но** → **вдо́воль & всла́сть**

уго|жда́ть [1], ⟨~**ди́ть**⟩ [15 *e.*; -ожу́, -оди́шь] (Д, **на** В) please; *pf. coll.* (into) в я́му fall (into); *в беду́* get; *в глаз и т. д.* hit

у́гол *m* [1; угла́; в, на углу́] corner (**на** П at); *math.* angle

уголо́вный [14] criminal; ~ **ко́декс** criminal law

уголо́к *m* [1; -лка́] nook, corner

у́голь *m* [4; у́гля] coal; **как на** ~**я́х** *coll.* on tenterhooks; ~**ный** [14] coal...; carbonic

угомони́ть(ся)[13]*pf. coll.* calm (down)

угоня́ть [28], ⟨угна́ть⟩ [угоню́, уго́нишь; угна́л] drive (away, off); *машину* steal; *самолёт* hijack; -**ся**coll. catch up (**за** T with)

угор|а́ть [1], ⟨~**е́ть**⟩ [9] be poisoned by carbon monoxide fumes

у́горь¹ *m* [4 *e.*; угря́] eel

у́горь² *m* [4 *e.*; угря́] *med.* blackhead

уго|ща́ть [1], ⟨~**сти́ть**⟩ [15 *e.*; -ощу́, -ости́шь; -още́нный] treat (T), entertain; ~**ще́ние** *n* [12] entertaining; treating (to); refreshments; food, drinks *pl.*

угро|жа́ть[1]threaten (p. with Д/T); ~**за** *f* [5] threat, menace

угрызе́ние| *n* [12]: ~**я** *pl.* **со́вести** pangs of conscience; remorse

угрю́мый [14 *sh.*] morose, gloomy

уда́в *m* [1] boa, boa constrictor

удава́ться [5], ⟨~ться⟩ [уда́стся, -аду́тся; удался́, -ала́сь] succeed; **мне ~ётся (~ло́сь)** (+ *inf.*) I succeed(ed) (in …ing)

удале́ние *n* [12] removal; *зуба* extraction; sending away (*sport* off); **на ~е́нии** at a distance; ~и́ть(ся)→ **~я́ть(ся)**; **~о́й** [14; удал, -а, -о] bold, daring; ~ь *f* [8], *coll.* **~ьство́** *n* [9] boldness, daring; ~я́ть [28], ⟨~и́ть⟩ [13] remove; *зуб* extract; **-ся** retire, withdraw; move away

уда́р *m* [1] blow (*a. fig.*); (*a. med.*) stroke; *el.* shock (*a. fig.*); (*столкнове́ние*) impact; *ножо́м* slash; *гро́ма* clap, peal; *form.* **он в ~е** he's in good form; **~е́ние** *n* [12] stress, accent; ~и́ться→ **~я́ться**; **~ный** [14]: **~ные инструме́нты** percussion instruments; ~я́ть [28], ⟨~ить⟩ [13] strike (**по** Д on), hit; knock; beat; sound (*трево́гу*); punch (*кулако́м*); butt (*голово́й*); kick (*ного́й*); *моро́зы* set in; **-ся** strike *or* knock (Т/о В with/against); hit (**в** В); **~я́ться в кра́йности** go to extremes

уда́ться → удава́ться

уда́ч|а *f* [5] success, (good) luck; **~ник** *coll.* *m* [1] lucky person; **~ный** [14; -чен, -чна] successful; good

удв|а́ивать [1], ⟨~о́ить⟩ [13] double (*v/i.* **-ся**)

уде́л *m* [1] lot, destiny; **~и́ть → ~я́ть**; **~ьный** [14] *phys.* specific; ~я́ть [28], ⟨~и́ть⟩ [13] devote, spare; allot

уде́рж|ивать [1], ⟨~а́ть⟩ [withhold, restrain; *в па́мяти* keep, retain; *де́ньги* deduct; **-ся** hold (*за* В on; to; *a.* out); refrain (from **от** Р)

удешев|ля́ть [28], ⟨~и́ть⟩ [14 *e.*; -влю́, -ви́шь, -влённый] become cheaper

удив|и́тельный [14; -лен, -льна] astonishing, surprising; (*необы́чный*) amazing, strange; (**не**) **~и́тельно** it is a (no) wonder; ~и́ть(ся)→ **~ля́ть(ся)**; **~ле́ние** *n* [12] astonishment, surprise; ~ля́ть [28], ⟨~и́ть⟩ [14 *e.*; -влю́, -ви́шь, -влённый] (**-ся**) astonish(ed *or* at Д), surprise(d, wonder)

удила́ *n/pl.* [9; -и́л, -ила́м]: **закуси́ть ~** get (*or* take) the bit between one's teeth

уди́ть [15] angle (for *v/t.*), fish

удира́ть *coll.* [1], ⟨удра́ть⟩ [удеру́, -рёшь; удра́л, -а́, -о] make off; run away

удлин|е́ние *n* [12] lengthening; ~я́ть [28], ⟨~и́ть⟩ [13] lengthen, prolong

удо́б|ный [14; -бен, -бна] (*подходя́щий*) convenient; *ме́бель и т. д.* comfortable; **воспо́льзоваться ~ным слу́чаем** take an opportunity; **~о…** easily…; **~ре́ние** *n* [12] fertilizer; fertilization; ~ря́ть[28], ⟨~рить⟩ [13] fertilize, manure; **~ство** *n* [9] convenience; comfort

удовлетвор|е́ние *n* [12] satisfaction; **~и́тельный** [14; -лен, -льна] satisfactory; *adv. a.* "fair" (*as school mark*); ~я́ть [28], ⟨~и́ть⟩ [13] satisfy; *про́сьбу* grant; (Д) meet; **-ся** content o.s. (Т with)

удо|во́льствие *n* [12] pleasure; **~рожа́ть**[1], ⟨~рожи́ть⟩ [16] raise the price of

удост|а́ивать [1], ⟨~о́ить⟩ [13] (**-ся** be award(ed)); deign (*взгля́да*, **-ом** В to look at p.); **~овере́ние** *n* [12] certificate, certification; **~овере́ние ли́чности** identity card; ~оверя́ть [28], ⟨~ове́рить⟩ [13] certify, attest; *ли́чность* prove; *по́дпись* witness; convince (**в** П of; **-ся** o.s.; *a.* make sure); ~о́ить(ся) → **~а́ивать(ся)**

удосу́житься *coll.* [16] find time

у́дочк|а *f* [5; *g/pl.*: -чек] fishing rod; **заки́нуть ~у** *fig.* cast a line, put a line out; **попа́сться на ~у** swallow the bait

удра́ть → удира́ть

удружи́ть [16 *e.*; -жу́, -жи́шь] *coll.* do a service *or* good turn; *iro.* unwittingly do a disservice

удруч|а́ть [1], ⟨~и́ть⟩ [16 *e.*; -чу́, -чи́шь; -чённый] deject, depress

удуш|е́ние *n* [12] suffocation; **~ли́вый** [14 *sh.*] stifling, suffocating; **~ье** *n* [10] asthma; asphyxia

едине́ние *n* [12] solitude; **~ённый** [14 *sh.*] secluded, lonely, solitary; ~я́ться [28], ⟨~и́ть(ся)⟩ [13] withdraw, go off (by o.s.); seclude o.s.

уе́зд *m* [1] *hist.*, **~ный** [14] district

уезжа́ть [1], ⟨уе́хать⟩ [уе́ду, -де́шь] (**в** В) leave (for), go (away; to)

уж 1. *m* [1 *e.*] grass snake; **2.** → **уже́;** indeed, well; *do, be* (+ *vb.*)

у́жас *m* [1] horror; terror, fright; *coll.* → **~ный, ~но; ~а́ть** [1], ⟨~ну́ть⟩ [20] horrify; **-ся** be horrified *or* terrified (P, Д at); **~а́ющий** [17] horrifying; **~ный** [14; -сен, -сна] terrible, horrible, dreadful; awful

уже́ already; by this time; by now; **~ не** not… any more; (**вот**) **~** for; **~ пора́** it's time (to + *inf.*)

уже́ние *n* [12] angling, fishing

ужи|ва́ться [1], ⟨~ться⟩ [14; -иву́сь, -вёшься; -и́лся, -ила́сь] get accustomed (**в** П to); get along (**с** T with); **~вчивый** [14 *sh.*] easy to get on with

у́жин *m* [1] supper (**за** T at; **на** В, **к** Д for); **~ать** [1], ⟨по-⟩ have supper

ужи́ться → **ужива́ться**

узако́н|ивать [1], ⟨~ить⟩ [13] legalize

узбе́к *m* [1], **~ский** [16] Uzbek

узда́ *f* [5; *pl. st.*], **~е́чка** *f* [5; *g/pl.:* -чек] bridle

у́зел *m* [1; узла́] knot; *rail.* junction; *tech.* assembly; *вещей* bundle; **-лка́**] knot; small bundle

у́зк|ий [16; у́зок, узка́, -о; *сотр.:* у́же] narrow (*a. fig.*); (*тесный*) tight; **~ое ме́сто** bottleneck; weak point; **~око-ле́йный** [14] narrowgauge

узлов|а́тый [14 *sh.*] knotty; **~о́й** [14] (*основной*) central, chief

узна|ва́ть [5], ⟨~ть⟩ [1] recognize (by **по** Д); learn (**от** P from: p.; **из** P th.), find out, (get to) know

у́зник *m* [1] prisoner

узо́р *m* [1] pattern, design; **с ~ами =** **~чатый** [14 *sh.*] figured; decorated with a pattern

у́зость *f* [8] narrow(-minded)ness

у́зы *f/pl.* [5] bonds, ties

у́йма *coll. f* [5] lots of, heaps of

уйти́ → **уходи́ть**

ука́з *m* [1] decree, edict; **~а́ние** *n* [12] instruction (**по** Д by), direction; indication (P, на В of); **~а́тель** *m* [4] в книге index; indicator (*a. mot.*); **~а́тельный** [14] indicating; (*палец*) index finger; *gr.* demonstrative; **~а́ть** → **~ывать;** **~ка** *f* [5] pointer; *coll.* orders *pl.*, bidding

(*of s.o. else*) (**по** Д by); **~ывать** [1], ⟨~а́ть⟩ [3] point out; point (**на** В to); *путь и т. д.* show; indicate

ука́ч|ивать ⟨~а́ть⟩ [1] rock to sleep, lull; *impers.* make (sea)sick

укла́д *m* [1] structure; mode, way (*жизни*); **~ка** *f* [5] packing; *рельсов и т. д.* laying; *волос* set(ting); ⟨уложи́ть⟩ [16] put (to bed); lay; stack, pack (up *coll.* **-ся**); place; cover; **-ся** *a.* go into; fit; *coll.* manage; **~ываться в голове́** sink in

укло́н *m* [1] slope, incline; slant (*a. fig.* = bias, bent, tendency); *pol.* deviation; **~е́ние** *n* [12] evasion; **~и́ться** → **~я́ться; ~чивый** [14 *sh.*] evasive; **~я́ться** [28], ⟨~и́ться⟩ [13; -оню́сь, -о́нишься] *от темы и т. д.* digress, deviate; evade (*v/t.* **от** P)

уклю́чина *f* [5] oarlock (*Brt.* row-)

уко́л *m* [1] prick; jab; *med.* injection

укомплекто́в|ывать [1], ⟨~а́ть⟩ [7] complete, bring up to (full) strength; supply (fully; with T)

уко́р *m* [1] reproach

укор|а́чивать [1], ⟨~оти́ть⟩ [15 *e.*; -очу́, -оти́шь; -о́ченный] shorten; **~еня́ться** [28], ⟨~ени́ться⟩ [13] take root; **~и́зна** *f* [5] → **~;** **~и́зненный** [14] reproachful; **~и́ть** → **~я́ть; ~оти́ть** → **~а́чивать; ~я́ть** [28], ⟨~и́ть⟩ [13] reproach (with), blame (for) (**в** П, **за** В)

укра́дкой furtively

украи́н|ец *m* [1; -нца], **~ка** *f* [5; *g/pl.:* -нок], **~ский** [16] Ukranian

укра|ша́ть [1], ⟨~сить⟩ [15] adorn; (**-ся** be) decorat(ed); trim; embellish, **~ше́ние** *n* [12] adornment; decoration; ornament; embellishment

укреп|и́ть(ся) → **~ля́ть(ся); ~ле́ние** *n* [12] strengthening; (*положения*) reinforcing; *mil.* fortification; **~ля́ть** [28], ⟨~и́ть⟩ [14 *e.*; -плю́, -пи́шь; -плённый] strengthen; make fast; consolidate; *mil.* fortify; **-ся** strengthen, become stronger

укро́|мный [14; -мен, -мна] secluded; **~п** *m* [1] dill fennel

укроти́тель *m* [4], **~ти́тельница** *f* [5] (animal) tamer; **~ща́ть** [1], ⟨~ти́ть⟩

[15 *е.*; -ощу, -отишь; -ощённый] tame; (*умерить*) subdue, restrain; **~щение** *n* [12] taming

укрупн|я́ть [28], **⟨~и́ть⟩** [13] enlarge, extend; amalgamate

укры|ва́ть [1], **⟨~ть⟩** [22] cover; give shelter; (*прятать*) conceal, harbo(u)r; **-ся** cover o.s.; hide; take shelter or cover; **~тие** *n* [12] cover, shelter

у́ксус *m* [1] vinegar

уку́с *m* [1] bite; **~ить →** *куса́ть*

уку́тывать, ⟨~ать⟩ [1] wrap up (in)

ула́|вливать [1], **⟨уловить⟩** [14] catch; perceive, detect; *coll.* seize (*an opportunity, etc.*); (*понять*) grasp; **~живать** [1], **⟨~дить⟩** [15] settle, arrange, resolve

у́лей *m* [3; у́лья] beehive

улет|а́ть [1], **⟨~е́ть⟩** [11] fly (away)

улету́чи|ваться [1], **⟨~ться⟩** [16] evaporate, volatilize; *coll.* disappear, vanish

уле́чься [26 г/ж; уля́гусь, уля́жешься, уля́гутся; улёгся *pf.*] lie down, go (to bed); *о пыли и т. д.* settle; (*утихнуть*) calm down, abate

ули́ка *f* [5] evidence

ули́тка *f* [5; *g/pl.*: -ток] snail

у́лиц|а *f* [5] street (in, on **на** П); **на ~е** *a.* outside, outdoors

улич|а́ть [1], **⟨~и́ть⟩** [16 *е.*: -чу́, -чи́шь, -чённый] (*в* П) catch out in lying; establish the guilt (of); **~и́ть во лжи** give s.o. the lie

у́личн|ый [14] street...; **~ое движе́ние** road traffic

уло́в *m* [1] catch; **~и́мый** [14 *sh.*] perceptible; **~и́ть →** *ула́вливать*; **~ка** *f* [5; *g/pl.*: -вок] trick, ruse

уложи́ть(ся) → *укла́дывать(ся)*

улучша́ть *coll.* [1], **⟨~и́ть⟩** [16 *е.*: -чу́, -чи́шь; -чённый] find, seize, catch

улучш|а́ть [1], **⟨~и́ть⟩** [16] improve; *v/i.* **-ся**; **~е́ние** *n* [12] improvement; **~и́ть(ся) →** *~а́ть(ся)*

улыб|а́ться [1], **⟨~ну́ться⟩** [20], **~ка** *f* [5; *g/pl.*: -бок] smile (at П)

ультимати́вный [14; -вен, -вна] categorical, express; **~ум** *m* [1] ultimatum

ультра|звуково́й [14] ultrasonic; **~коро́ткий** [16] ultra-short (frequency)

ум *m* [1 *е.*] intellect; mind; sense(s); **без**

~á mad (about **от** P); **за́дним ~о́м кре́пок** wise after the event; **быть на ~е́** (у P) be on one's mind; **э́то не его́ ~а́ де́ло** it's not his business; **сойти́ с ~а́** go mad; **сходи́ть с ~а́** *coll. a.* be mad (about **по** П); *coll.* **~ за ра́зум захо́дит** I'm at my wits end

умал|е́ние *n* [12] belittling; **~я́ть →** **~я́ть**; **~чивать** [1], **⟨умолча́ть⟩** [4 *е.*: -чу́, -чи́шь] (**о** П) pass over in silence; **~я́ть** [28], **⟨~и́ть⟩** [13] belittle, derogate, disparage

уме́|лый [14] able, capable, skilled; **~ние** *n* [12] skill, ability, know-how

уменьш|а́ть [1], **⟨~и́ть⟩** [16 & 16 *е.*; -еньшу́, -е́ньши́шь; -е́ньшенный & -шённый] reduce, diminish, decrease (*v/i.* **-ся**); **~и́ть расхо́ды** cut down expenditures; **~е́ние** *n* [12] decrease, reduction; **~и́тельный** [14] diminishing; *gr.* diminutive; **~и́ть(ся) →** **~а́ть(ся)**

уме́ренн|ость *f* [12] moderation; **~ый** [14 *sh.*] moderate, (*a. geogr.* [*no sh.*]) temperate

умер|е́ть → *умира́ть*; **~и́ть →** **~я́ть**; **~тви́ть →** **~щвля́ть**; **~ший** [17] dead; **~щвля́ть** [28], **⟨~тви́ть⟩** [14; -рщвлю́, -ртви́шь; -рщвлённый] kill; **~я́ть** [28], **⟨~и́ть⟩** [13] become moderate

уме|сти́ть(ся) → **~ща́ть(ся)**; **~стный** (-'mesn) [14; -тен, -тна] appropriate; **~сть** [8], **⟨с-⟩** be able to; know how to; **~ща́ть** [1], **⟨~сти́ть⟩** [15 *е.*: -ещу́, -ести́шь; -ещённый] fit, get (into **в** B); **-ся** find room

умил|е́ние *n* [12] emotion, tenderness; **~ённый** [14] touched, moved; **~я́ть** [28], **⟨~и́ть⟩** [13] (**-ся** be) move(d), touch(ed)

умира́ть [1], **⟨умере́ть⟩** [12; *pt.*: у́мер, умерла́, -о; уме́рший] die (of, from **от**); **~ со ску́ки** be bored to death

умиротворённый [14; -ена, -ён] tranquil; contented

умн|е́ть [8], **⟨по-⟩** grow wiser; **~и́к** *coll. m* [1], **~и́ца** *m/f* [5] clever person; **~ича́ть** *coll.* [1] → *мудри́ть*

умнож|а́ть [1], **⟨~и́ть⟩** [16] multiply (by **на** B); (*увеличивать*) increase; *v/i.* **-ся**; **~е́ние** *n* [12] multiplication

ýм|ный [14; умён, умна́, умно́] clever, smart, wise, intelligent; **~озаключе́ние** *n* [12] conclusion; **~озри́тельный** [14; -лен, -льна] speculative

умол|и́ть [28], ⟨**~я́ть**; **~ж**: *без* **~ку** incessantly; **~ка́ть** [1], ⟨**~кнуть**⟩ [21] *шум* stop; lapse into silence, become silent; **~ча́ть → ума́лчивать**; **~я́ть** [28], ⟨**~и́ть**⟩ [13; -олю́, -о́лишь] implore (*v*/*t*.), beseech, entreat (for *о* П)

умопомрача́тельный [14; -лен, -льна] *coll.* fantastic

умо́р|а *coll. f* [5], **~и́тельный** *coll.* [14; -лен, -льна] side-splitting, hilarious; **~и́ть** *coll.* [13] *pf.* kill; exhaust, fatigue (*a.* with laughing **со́ смеху**)

ýмственный [14] intellectual, mental; *рабо́та* brainwork

умудря́ть [28], ⟨**~и́ть**⟩ [13] teach; make wiser; **-ся** *coll.* contrive, manage

умыва́льник *m* [1] washbowl, *Brt.* wash-basin; **~ние** *n* [12] washing; wash; **~ть** [1], ⟨умы́ть⟩ [22] (**-ся**) wash (*a.* o.s.)

ýмы|сел *m* [1; -сла] design, intent(ion); **с ~слом** (*без ~сла*) (un-) intentionally; **~ть(ся) → ~ва́ть** (**-ся**); **~шленный** [14] deliberate; intentional

унести́(сь) → уноси́ть(ся)

универ|ма́г *m* [1] (*~са́льный магази́н*) department store; **~са́льный** [14; -лен, -льна] universal; **~са́м** *m* [1] supermarket; **~ситет** *m* [1] university (at, in *в* П)

уни|жа́ть [1], ⟨**~зить**⟩ [15] humiliate; **~же́ние** *n* [12] humiliation; **~жённый** [14 *sh.*] humble; **~зи́тельный** [14; -лен, -льна] humiliating; **~зить → ~жа́ть**

унима́ть [1], ⟨уня́ть⟩ [уйму́, уймёшь; уня́л, -á, -о; -я́тый (-я́т, -á, -о)] appease, soothe; *боль* still; **-ся** calm *or* quiet down; *ве́тер и т. д.* subside

уничт|ожа́ть [1], ⟨**~о́жить**⟩ [16] annihilate, destroy; **~оже́ние** *n* [12] annihilation; **~о́жить → ~ожа́ть**

уноси́ть [15], ⟨унести́⟩ [24 -с-] carry, take (away, off); **-ся** (сь-) speed away

уны|ва́ть [1] be depressed, be dejected; **~лый** [14 *sh.*] depressed; dejected; **~ние** *n* [12] despondency; depression; dejection

уня́ть(ся) → унима́ть(ся)

упа́до|к *m* [1; -дка] decay, decline; **~к ду́ха** depression; **~к сил** breakdown

упако́в|а́ть → ~ывать; **~ка** *f* [5; *g*/*pl.*: -вок] packing; wrapping; **~щик** *m* [1] packer; **~ывать** [1] ⟨**~а́ть**⟩ [7] pack (up), wrap up

упа́сть → па́дать

упира́ть [1], ⟨упере́ть⟩ [12] rest, prop (against *в* В); **-ся** lean, prop (s.th. Т; against *в* В); *в сте́нку и т. д.* knock *or* run against; (*наста́ивать*) insist on; be obstinate

упи́танный [14 *sh.*] well-fed, fattened

упла́|та *f* [5] payment (in *в* В); **~чивать** [1], ⟨**~ти́ть**⟩ [15] pay; *по счёту* pay, settle

уплотн|е́ние *n* [12] compression; packing; **~я́ть** [28], ⟨**~и́ть**⟩ [13] condense, make compact; fill up (with work); *tech.* seal

уплы|ва́ть [1], ⟨**~ть**⟩ [23] swim or sail (away, off); pass (away), vanish

упова́ть [1] (*на* В) trust (in), hope (for)

упод|обля́ть [28], ⟨**~о́бить**⟩ [14] liken, become like (*v*/*i.* **-ся**)

упо́ение *n* [12] rapture, ecstasy; **~ённый** [14; -ён, -ена́] enraptured; **~и́тельный** [14; -лен, -льна] rapturous, intoxicating

уползти́ [24] *pf.* creep away

уполномо́ч|енный [14 *sh.*] authorized; **~ивать** [1], ⟨**~ить**⟩ [16] authorize, empower (to *на* В)

упомина́|ние *n* [12] mention (of *о* П); **~ть** [1], ⟨упомяну́ть⟩ [19] mention (*v*/*i.* В, *о* П)

упо́р *m* [1] rest; support, prop; stop; *де́лать ~* lay stress *or* emphasis (on *на* В); *в ~* point-blank, straightforward; *смотре́ть в ~ на кого-л.* look full in the face of s.o.; **~ный** [14; -рен, -рна] persistent, persevering; (*упря́мый*) stubborn, obstinate; **~ство** *n* [9] persistence, perseverance; obstinacy; **~ствовать** [7] be stubborn; persevere, persist (in *в* П)

употреби́тельный [14; -лен, -льна] common, customary; *сло́во* in current use; **~и́ть → ~ля́ть**; **~ле́ние** *n* [12] use; usage; **~ля́ть** [28], ⟨**~и́ть**⟩ [14 *e.*; -блю́,

-би́шь; -блённый (*impf.* -**ся** be) use(d), employ(ed); **~йть все сре́дства** make every effort; **~йть во зло** abuse

упра́в|иться → ~ля́ться; **~ле́ние** n [12] administration (of P; T), management; *tech.* control; *gr.* government; *маши́ной* driving; **орке́стр под ~ле́нием** orchestra conducted by (P); **~ля́ть** (T) manage, operate; rule; govern (*a. gr.*); drive; *naut.* steer; *tech.* control; *mus.* conduct; **-ся** <~иться> manage/finish; [14] (с T) manage/finish; **~ля́ющий** [17] manager

упражн|е́ние n [12] exercise; practice; **~я́ть** [28] exercise (*v/i., v/refl.* -**ся в** II): practice (-ise) s/th.)

упраздн|е́ние n [12] abolition; liquidation; **~я́ть** [28], <~и́ть> [13] abolish; liquidate

упра́шивать [1], <упроси́ть> [15] (*impf.*) beg, entreat; (*pf*) prevail upon

упрёк m [1] reproach

упрек|а́ть [1], <~ну́ть> [20] reproach (with **в** П)

упро|си́ть → упра́шивать; **~сти́ть → ~ща́ть**; **~че́ние** n [12] consolidation; **~чивать** [1], <~чить> [16] consolidate (*v/i.* -**ся**), stabilize; **~ща́ть** [1], <~сти́ть> [15 *e.*; -ощу́, -ости́шь; -ощённый] simplify; **~ще́ние** n [12] simplification

упру́г|ий [16 *sh.*] elastic, resilient; **~ость** f [8] elasticity

упря́м|иться [14] be obstinate; persist in; **~ство** n [9] obstinacy, stubbornness; **~ый** [14 *sh.*] obstinate, stubborn

упря́т|ывать [1], <~ать> [3] hide

упу|ска́ть [1], <~сти́ть> [15] let go; let slip; let fall; *возмо́жность* miss; **~ще́ние** n [12] neglect, ommission

ура́! *int.* hurrah!

уравн|е́ние n [12] equalization; *math.* equation; **~ивать** [1] **1.** <уровня́ть> [28] level; **2.** <~я́ть> [28] level, equalize *fig.*; **~и́ловка** f [5; *g/pl.:* -вок] *pej.* egalitarianism (*esp.* with respect to economic rights and wage level[l]ing); **~ове́шивать** [1], <~ове́сить> [15] balance; *p. pt. p. a.* well-balanced, composed, calm; **~я́ть → ~ивать 2**

урага́н m [1] hurricane

ура́льский [16] Ural(s)

ура́н m [1], **~овый** [14] uranium

урегули́рование n [12] settlement; regulation; *vb.* → **регули́ровать**

урез|а́ть & ~ывать *coll.* [1], <~ать> [3] cut down, curtail; axe; **~о́нить** *coll.* [13] *pf.* bring to reason

у́рна f [5] ballot box; refuse bin

у́ров|ень m [4; -вня] level (at, on **на** П; **в** В); standard; *tech.* gauge; (*показа-тель*) rate; **жи́зненный ~ень** standard of living; **~ня́ть → ура́внивать 1**

уро́д m [1] monster; *coll.* ugly creature; **~ливый** [14 *sh.*] deformed; ugly; abnormal; **~овать** [7], <из-> deform, disfigure; (*кале́чить*) mutilate; maim; **~ство** n [9] deformity; ugliness; *fig.* abnormality

урож|а́й m [3] harvest, (abundant) crop; **~а́йность** f [8] yield (heavy **высо́кая**), productivity; **~а́йный** [14] productive; *год* good year for crops; **~е́нец** m [1; -нца], **~е́нка** f [5; *g/pl.:*-нок] native (of)

уро́|к m [1] lesson; *m* [1] (*уще́рб*) loss(es); *репута́ции* injury; **~ни́ть → роня́ть**

урча́ть [4 *e.*; -чу́, -чи́шь] *в желу́дке* rumble; *пёс* growl

урывка́ми *coll.* by fits and starts; in snatches; at odd moments

ус m [1; *pl. e.*] (*mst. pl.*) m(o)ustache

уса́д|ить → ~живать; ~ьба́ f [5; *g/pl.:* -деб] farmstead, farm center (-tre); *hist.* country estate, country seat; **~живать** [1], <~ди́ть> [15] seat; set; *дере́вьями и т. д.* plant (with T); **-ся** <усе́сться> [25; усяду́сь, -дешься; усядься!; усе́лся, -лась] sit down, take a seat; settle down (to **за** В)

уса́тый [14] with a m(o)ustache; (*of animals*) with whiskers

усв|а́ивать [1], <~о́ить> [13] *привы́чку* adopt; *зна́ния* acquire, assimilate; *язы́к и т. д.* master, learn; **~о́ение** n [12] adoption; acquirement; assimilation; mastering, learning

усе́|ивать [1], <~ять> [27] sow, cover litter, strew (with); **звёздами** stud

усе́рд|ие n [12] zeal; (*приле́жание*) diligence, assiduity; **~ный** [14; -ден, -дна] zealous; diligent, assiduous

усе́сться → **уса́живаться**

усея́ть → **усе́ивать**

усиде́ть [11] *pf.* remain sitting; keep one's place; sit still; *coll.* (*вы́держать*) hold out, keep a job; **~чивый** [14 *sh.*] assiduous, persevering

усиле́ние *n* [12] strengthening, *звука* intensification; *el.* amplification; **~енный** [14] intensified; *пита́ние* high-caloric; **~ивать** [1], ⟨**~ить**⟩ [13] strengthen, reinforce; intensify; *звук* amplify; *боль и т. д.* aggravate; *el.* **~-**in-crease; **~ие** *n* [12] effort, exertion; **приложи́ть все ~ия** make every effort; **~и́тель** *m* [4] *el.* amplifier; *tech.* booster; **~иваться** → **~ивать(ся)**

ускольза́ть [1], ⟨**~ну́ть**⟩ [20] slip (off, away), escape (from **от** P)

ускоре́ние *n* [12] acceleration; **~я́ть** [28], ⟨**~ить**⟩ [13] quicken; speed up, accelerate; *v/i.* **-ся**

усла́вливаться [1], ⟨**усло́виться**⟩ [14] arrange; settle, agree (up on **о** П); **~ть** → **усыла́ть**

усло́вие *n* [12] condition (on **с** Т, **при** II; under **на** П), term; stipulation; proviso; *pl.* circumstances; **~иться** → **усла́вливаться**; **~ленный** [14 *sh.*] agreed, fixed; **~ность** *f* [8] conditionality; convention; **~ный** [14; -вен, -вна] *рефлекс* conditional; (*относи́тельный*) relative; **~ный пригово́р** suspended, sentence; **~ный знак** conventional sign

усложня́ть [28], ⟨**~и́ть**⟩ [13] (**-ся** become) complicate(d)

услу́га *f* [5] service (at **к** Д *pl.*), favo(u)r; **~живать** [1], ⟨**~жи́ть**⟩ [16] do (p. Д) a service or favo(u)r; → *iro.* **удружи́ть**; **~жливый** [14 *sh.*] obliging

усма́тривать [1], ⟨**~отре́ть**⟩ [9; -отрю́, -о́тришь; -о́тренный] see (in **в** П); **~еха́ться** [1], ⟨**~ехну́ться**⟩ [20], **~е́шка** *f* [5; *g/pl.*: -шек] smile, grin; **~ире́ние** *n* [12] suppression; **~иря́ть** [28], ⟨**~ири́ть**⟩ [13] pacify; *си́лой* suppress; **~отре́ние** *n* [12] discretion (at **по** Д; to **на** В), judg(e)ment; **~отре́ть** → **~а́тривать**

усну́ть [20] *pf.* go to sleep, fall asleep

усоверше́нствован|ие *n* [12] improve-ment, refinement; **~ный** [14] improved, perfected

усомни́ться → **сомнева́ться**

усо́пший [17] *lit.* deceased

успе|ва́емость *f* [8] progress (*in studies*); **~ва́ть** [1], ⟨**~ть**⟩ [8] have (*or* find) time, manage, succeed; arrive, be in time (for **к** Д, **на** В); catch (*train* **на по́-езд**); *impf.* get on, make progress, learn; **не ~л(а́)** (+ *inf.*), **как** no sooner + *pt.* than; **~ется** *pf. impers.* there is no hurry; **~х** *m* [1] success; *pl. a.* progress; **с тем же ~хом** with the same result; **~шный** [14; -шен, -шна] successful; **~шно** *a.* with success

успок|а́ивать [1], ⟨**~о́ить**⟩ [13] calm, soothe; reassure; **-ся** calm down; *ве́тер, боль* subside; become quiet; content o.s. (with **на** П); **~ое́ние** *n* [12] peace; calm; **~о́ительный** [14: -лен, -льна] soothing, reassuring; **~о́ить(ся)** → **~а́ивать(ся)**

уст|а́ *n/pl.* [9] *obs. or poet.* mouth, lips *pl.*; **узна́ть из пе́рвых ~** learn at first hand; **у всех на ~а́х** everybody is talking about it

уста́в *m* [1] statute(s); regulations *pl.*; **~ ООН и т. д.** charter

уста|ва́ть [5], ⟨**~ть**⟩ [-а́ну, -а́нешь] get tired; **~вля́ть** [28], ⟨**~вить**⟩ [14] place; cover (with Т), fill; *взгляд* direct, fix (eyes on **на** В); **-ся** stare (at **на** *or* **в** В); **~лость** *f* [8] weariness, fatigue; **~лый** [14] tired, weary; **~на́вливать** [1], ⟨**~нови́ть**⟩ [14] set *or* put up; *tech.* mount; arrange; fix; *поря́док* establish; (*узна́ть*) find out, ascertain; adjust (to **на** В); **-ся** be established; form; *пого́да* set in; **~но́вка** *f* [5; *g/pl.*: -вок] *tech.* mounting, installation; *силова́я* plant; *fig.* orientation (toward[s] **на** В); **~новле́ние** *n* [12] establishment; **~ре́лый** [14] obsolete, out-of-date; **~ть** → **~ва́ть**

устила́ть [1], ⟨**устла́ть**⟩ [-телю́, -те́лешь; у́стланный] cover, pave (with Т)

у́стный [14] oral, verbal

усто|й *m/pl.* [9] foundation; **~йчивость** *f* [8] stability; **~йчивый** [14 *sh.*] stable; **~я́ть** [-ою́, -ои́шь] keep one's balance; stand one's ground; resist (*v/t.* **про́тив**

Р; **перед** Т)

устр|а́ивать [1], ⟨~о́ить⟩ [13] arrange, organize; (*создавать*) set up, establish; *сце́ну* make; provide (*job* **на** В; place in **в** В); *coll. impers.* (*подходить*) suit; **-ся** be settled; settle; get a job (*a.* **на рабо́ту**); **~ане́ние** *n* [12] removal; elimination; **~аня́ть** [28], ⟨~ани́ть⟩ [13] remove; eliminate, clear; **~аша́ть** [1] (**-ся**) → **страши́ться**; **~емля́ть** [28], ⟨~еми́ть⟩ [14 *e.*; -млю́, -ми́шь; -млённый] (**на** В) direct (to, at), fix (on); **-ся** rush; be directed; **~ица** *f* [5] oyster; **~о́ить(ся)** → **~а́ивать(ся)**; **~о́йство** *n* [9] arrangement; organization; *общественное* structure, system; device; mechanism

усту́п *m* [1] *скалы́* ledge; projection; terrace; **~а́ть** [1], ⟨~и́ть⟩ [14] cede, let (р. Д) have; *в спо́ре* yield; (*быть хуже*) be inferior to (Д); (*продать*) sell; **~а́ть доро́гу** [1] let pass, give way; **~а́ть ме́сто** give up one's place; **~ка** *f* [5; *g/pl.*: -пок] concession; cession; **~чивый** [14 *sh.*] compliant, pliant

устыди́ть [15 *e.*; -ыжу́, -ыди́шь; -ыжённый] (**-ся**) be ashame(d; of Р)

у́стье *n* [10; *g/pl.*: -ьев] (*of a river*) mouth, estuary (at **в** П)

усугуб|ля́ть [28], ⟨~и́ть⟩ [14 & 14 *e.*; -гублю́, -гу́би́шь; -гу́бленный & -гублённый] increase, intensify; aggravate

усы́ → **ус; ~ла́ть** [1], ⟨усла́ть⟩ [ушлю́, ушлёшь; у́сланный] send (away); **~новля́ть** [28], ⟨~нови́ть⟩ [14 *e.*; -влю́, -ви́шь; -влённый] adopt; **~па́ть** [1], ⟨~па́ть⟩ [2] (be)strew (with Р); **~пля́ть** [28], ⟨~пи́ть⟩ [14 *e.*; -плю́, -пи́шь; -плённый] put to sleep (*by means of narcotics, etc.*) lull to sleep; *живо́тное* put to sleep; *fig.* lull, weaken, neutralize

ута́|ивать [1], ⟨~и́ть⟩ [13] conceal, keep to o.s.; appropriate; **~йка** *coll.*: **без ~йки** frankly; **~птывать** [1], ⟨утопта́ть⟩ [3] tread *or* trample (down); **~скивать** [1], ⟨~щи́ть⟩ [16] carry, drag *or* take (off, away); *coll.* walk off with, pilfer

у́тварь *f* [8] *collect.* equipment; utensils

pl.; **церко́вная ~** church plate

утверди́тельный [14; -лен, -льна] affirmative; **~ди́тельно** in the affirmative; **~жда́ть** [1], ⟨~ди́ть⟩ [15 *e.*; -ржу́, -рди́шь; -рждённый] confirm; (*укреплять*) consolidate (*v/i.* **-ся**); *impf.* affirm, assert, maintain; **~жде́ние** *n* [12] confirmation; affirmation, assertion; consolidation

уте|ка́ть [1], ⟨~чь⟩ [26] flow (away); leak; (*of gas, etc.*) escape; *coll.* run away; **~ре́ть** → **утира́ть; ~рпе́ть** [10] *pf.* restrain o.s.; **не ~рпе́л, что́бы не** (+ *inf. pf.*) could not help ...ing

утёс *m* [1] cliff, crag

утё|чка *f* [5] leakage (*a. fig.*); *га́за* escape; **~чка мозго́в** brain drain; **~чь** → **~ка́ть; ~ша́ть** [1], ⟨~шить⟩ [16] console, comfort; **-ся** *a.* take comfort in (Т); **~ше́ние** *n* [12] comfort, consolation; **~ши́тельный** [14; -лен, -льна] comforting, consoling

ути́|ль *m* [4] *collect.* salvage, waste, scrap; **~ра́ть** [1], ⟨утере́ть⟩ [12] wipe; **~ха́ть** [1], ⟨~хнуть⟩ [21] subside, abate; *зву́ки* cease; (*успокоиться*) calm down

у́тка *f* [5; *g/pl.*: у́ток] duck; *газе́тная* canard; false *or esp.* fabricated report

уткну́ть(ся) *coll.* [20] *pf. лицо́м* bury, hide; *в кни́гу* be(come) engrossed; (*наткнуться*) run up against

утол|и́ть → **~я́ть; ~ща́ть** [1], ⟨~сти́ть⟩ [15 *e.*; -щу́, -лсти́шь; -лщённый] become thicker; **~ще́ние** *n* [12] thickening; **~я́ть** [28], ⟨~и́ть⟩ [13] *жа́жду* slake, quench; *го́лод* appease; *жела́ние* satisfy

утоми́тельный [14; -лен, -льна] wearisome, tiring; tedious, tiresome; **~и́ть(ся)** → **~ля́ть(ся); ~ле́ние** *n* [12] fatigue, exhaustion; **~лённый** [14; -лён, -ена́] tired, weary; **~ля́ть** [28], ⟨~и́ть⟩ [14 *e.*; -млю́, -ми́шь; -млённый] tire, weary (*v/i.* **-ся**; *a.* get tired)

утонча́ть [1], ⟨~и́ть⟩ [16 *e.*; -чу́, -чи́шь; -чённый] make thinner; *p. pt. p.* thin; *fig.* refine; make refined (*v/i.* **-ся**)

утоп|а́ть [1] **1.** ⟨утону́ть⟩ → **тону́ть 2.**; **2.** drown; **~ленник** *m* [1] drowned man;

~ленница *f* [5] drowned woman; ~та́ть → ута́птывать

уточн|е́ние *n* [12] expressing *or* defining more precisely; amplification; elaboration; ~я́ть [28], ⟨~и́ть⟩ [13] amplify; elaborate

утра́|ивать [1], ⟨утро́ить⟩ [13] treble; *v/i.* -ся; ~мбова́ть [7] *pf.* ram, tamp; ~та *f* [5] loss; ~чивать [1], ⟨~тить⟩ [15] lose

у́тренний [15] morning

утри́ровать [7] exaggerate

у́тро *n* [9; с, до -á; к -ý] morning (in the ~ом; *по* ~а́м) ...а́ а... A.M. → день; ~о́ба *f* [5] womb; ~о́ить(ся) → у́а́ивать(ся); ~ужда́ть [1], ⟨~уди́ть⟩ [15 *e.*; ~ужý, ~уди́шь; ~уждённый] trouble, bother

утря|са́ть [3; -сти́, -сý, -сёшь], ⟨~сти́⟩ [25] *fig.* settle

утю́|г *m* [1] (flat)iron; ~жить [16], ⟨вы-, от-⟩ iron

уха́ *f* [5] fish soup; ~б *m* [1] pothole; ~бистый [14 *sh.*] bumpy

уха́живать [1] (*за* Т) nurse, look after; *за же́нщиной* court, woo

ухва́т|ывать [1], ⟨~и́ть⟩ [15] (*за* В) seize, grasp; -ся snatch; cling to; *fig.* seize, jump at

ухи|тря́ться [28], ⟨~три́ться⟩ [13] contrive, manage; ~щре́ние *n* [12] contrivance; ~щря́ться [28] contrive

ухмыл|я́ться *coll.* [28], ⟨~ьну́ться⟩ [20] grin, smirk

у́хо *n* [9; *pl.*: у́ши, ушей, *etc. e.*] ear (in *на* В); *влюби́ться по́ уши* be head over heels in love; *пропуска́ть ми́мо уше́й* turn a deaf ear (to В); *держа́ть ~ востро́* → *насторо́же*

ухо́д *m* [1] going away, leaving, departure; (*за* Т) care, tending, nursing; ~и́ть [15], ⟨уйти́⟩ [уйдý, уйдёшь; ушёл, ушла́; уше́дший; *g. pl.*: уйдя́] leave (*v/t. из, от* Р) go away; (*миновать*) pass; *от наказа́ния* escape; *от отве́та* evade, *в отста́вку* resign; *на пе́нсию* retire; *coll.* be worn out, spent (for *на* В); *уйти́ в себя́* shrink into o.s.

ухудш|а́ть [1], ⟨~ить⟩ [16] deteriorate (*v.i.* -ся); ~е́ние *n* [12] deteriorating;

worsening

уцеле́ть [8] *pf.* come through alive; survive; escape

уцепи́ться [14] *coll.* → ухвати́ться

уча́ст|вовать [7] participate, take part (in *в* П); ~вующий [17] → ~ник; ~ие *n* [12] (*в* П) participation (in); (*сочу́вствие*) interest (in), sympathy (with); ~и́ть(ся) *or* уча́ща́ть(ся) → ~ли́вый [14 *sh.*] sympathizing, sympathetic; ~ник *m* [1], ~ница *f* [5] participant, participator; competitor (*sports*); *член* member; ~ок *m* [1; -тка] *земли́* plot; (*часть*) part, section; *избира́тельный* ~о́к electoral district; polling station; ~ь [8] fate, lot

уча|ща́ть [1], ⟨~сти́ть⟩ [15 *e.*; -ащý, -асти́шь; -ащённый] make (-ся become) more frequent

уча́щийся *m* [17] schoolchild, pupil, student; ~е́ба *f* [5] studies *pl.*, study; (*подгото́вка*) training; ~е́бник *m* [1] textbook; ~е́бный [14] school...; educational; (*посо́бие*) text (*book*), exercise...; ~е́бный план curriculum

уче́н|ие *n* [12] learning; instruction apprenticeship; *mil.* training, practice; teaching, doctrine; ~и́к *m* [1 *e.*] *and* ~и́ца *f* [5] pupil; student; *слесаря́ и т. д.* apprentice; (*после́довать*) disciple; ~и́ческий [16] crude, immature

учён|ость *f* [8] learning; erudition; ~ый [14 *sh.*] learned; ~ая сте́пень (university) degree; *su.* scholar, scientist

уч|е́сть → учи́тывать; ~ёт *m* [1] calculation; registration; *това́ров* stock-taking; *с ~ётом* taking into consideration

учи́лище *n* [11] school, college (at *в* П)

учиня́ть [28] → чини́ть 2

учи́тель *m* [4; *pl.*: -ля́, *etc. e.*; *fig. st.*], ~ница *f* [5] teacher, instructor; ~ский [16] (of) teachers'); ~ская *as. su.* teachers' common room

учи́тывать [1], ⟨уче́сть⟩ [25; учтý, -тёшь; учёл, учла́; *g. pt.*: учтя́; учтённый] take into account, consider; register; *ве́ксель* discount

учи́ть [16] **1.** ⟨на-, об-, вы-⟩ teach (p. s.th. В/Д), instruct; train; (*a.* -ся Д); **2.** ⟨вы-⟩ learn, study

учреди́тель *m* [4] founder; **~ный** [14] constituent

учре|жда́ть [1], ⟨**~ди́ть**⟩ [15 *e*.; -ежу́, -еди́шь; -ежде́нный] found, establish, set up; **~жде́ние** *n* [12] founding, setting up, establishment; (*заведение*) institution

учти́вый [14 *sh*.] polite, courteous

уша́нка *f* [5; *g/pl*.: -нок] cap with earflaps

уши́б *m* [1] bruise; injury; **~а́ть** [1], ⟨**~и́ть**⟩ [-бу́, -бёшь; -и́б(ла); уши́бленный] hurt, bruise (*o.s.* **-ся**)

ушко́ *n* [9; *pl*.: -ки́, -ко́в] *tech*. eye, lug; (*of a needle*) eye

ушно́й [14] ear...; aural

уще́лье *n* [10] gorge, ravine

ущем|ля́ть [28], ⟨**~и́ть**⟩ [14 *e*.; -млю́, -ми́шь; -млённый] *права* infringe

ущерб *m* [1] damage; loss; **в ~** to the detriment

ущипну́ть → **щипа́ть**

ую́т *m* [1] coziness (*Brt*. cosiness); **~ный** [14; -тен, -тна] snug, cozy (*Brt*. cosy), comfortable

язв|и́мый [14 *sh*.] vulnerable; **~ля́ть** [28], ⟨**~и́ть**⟩ [14 *e*.; -влю́, -ви́шь; -влённый] *fig*. hurt

уясн|я́ть [28], ⟨**~и́ть**⟩ [13] *себе* understand

Ф

фа́бри|ка *f* [5] factory (in **на** П); mill; **~кова́ть** [7], *pf.* ⟨с-⟩ *fig. coll*. fabricate

фа́була *f* [5] plot, story

фа́за *f* [5] phase

фаза́н *m* [1] pheasant

файл *m* [1] *comput*. file

фа́кел *m* [1] torch

факс *m* [1] fax

факт *m* [1] fact; **~ тот, что** the fact is that; **~и́ческий** [16] (f)actual, real; *adv. a.* in fact; **~ура** *f* [5] *lit*. style, texture

факульте́т *m* [1] faculty (in **на** П); department

фаль|сифици́ровать [7] (*im*)*pf.* falsify; forge; **~ши́вить** [14], ⟨с-⟩ sing out of tune, play falsely; *coll*. act incinerely, be false; **~ши́вка** *f* [5; *g/pl*.: -вок] forged document; false information; **~ши́вый** [14 *sh*.] false, forged, counterfeit; *монета* base; **~шь** *f* [8] falseness; *лицемерие* hypocrisy, insincerity

фами́л|ия *f* [7] surname; **как ва́ша ~ия?** what is your name?; **~ья́рный** [14; -рен, -рна] familiar

фанати́|зм *m* [1] fanaticism; **~чный** [14; -чен, -чна] fanatical

фане́ра *f* [5] plywood; veneer

фанта|зёр *m* [1] dreamer, visionary; **~зи́ровать** [7] *impf. only* indulge in fancies, dream; ⟨с-⟩ invent; **~зия** *f* [7] imagination; fancy; (*выдумка*) invention, fib; *mus*. fantasia; *coll*. (*прихоть*) whim; **~стика** *f* [5] *lit*. fantasy, fiction; **нау́чная ~стика** science fiction; *collect*. the fantastic, the unbelievable; **~сти́ческий** [16], **~сти́чный** [14; -чен, -чна] fantastic

фар|а *f* [5] headlight; **~ва́тер** *m* [1] *naut*. fairway; **~маце́вт** *m* [1] pharmacist; **~тук** *m* [1] apron; **~фо́р** [1], **~фо́ровый** [14] china, porcelain; **~ш** *m* [1] stuffing; minced meat; **~широва́ть** [7] *cul*. stuff

фаса́д *m* [1] facade, front

фасо́в|ать [7] *impf.*; **~ка** *f* [5; *g/pl*.: -вок] prepackage

фасо́ль *f* [8] string (*Brt*. runner) bean(s); **~н** *m* [1] cut, style

фата́льный [14; -лен, -льна] fatal

фаши|зм *m* [1] fascism; **~ст** *m* [1] fascist; **~стский** [16] fascist...

фая́нс *m* [1], **~овый** [14] faience

февра́ль *m* [4 *e*.] February

федера́|льный [14] federal; **~ти́вный** [14] federative, federal; **~ция** *f* [7] federation

фейерве́рк *m* [1] firework(s)

фельд|ма́ршал *m* [1] *hist*. field marshal; **~шер** *m* [1] doctor's assistant, medical attendant

фельето́н *m* [1] satirical article

фен *m* [1] hairdryer

фено́мен *m* [1] phenomenon

феода́льный [14] feudal

ферзь *m* [4 *e.*] queen (*chess*)

фе́рм|а *f* [5] farm; **~ер** *m* [1] farmer

фестива́ль *m* [4] festival

фетр *m* [1] felt; **~овый** [14] felt...

фехтова́|льщик *m* [1] fencer; **~ние** *n* [12] fencing; **~ть** [7] fence

фиа́лка *f* [5; *g/pl.*: -лок] violet

фи́г|а *f* [5], **~овый** [14] fig

фигу́р|а *f* [5] figure; chess piece (*excluding pawns*); **~а́льный** [14; -лен, -льна] figurative; **~и́ровать** [7] figure, appear; **~ный** [14] figured; **~ное ката́ние** figure skating

фи́зи|к *m* [1] physicist; **~ка** *f* [5] physics; **~оло́гия** *f* [7] physiology; **~оно́мия** [7] physiognomy; **~ческий** [14] physical; *труд* manual

физкульту́р|а *f* [5] physical training; gymnastics; **~ник** *m* [1] sportsman; **~ни́ца** *f* [5] sportswoman

фик|си́ровать [7], ⟨за-⟩ record in writing; fix; **~ти́вный** [14; -вен, -вна] fictitious; **~ция** *f* [7] fiction; invention, untruth

фила|нтро́п *m* [1] philanthropist; **~рмони́ческий** [16] philharmonic; **~рмо́ния** *f* [7] philharmonic society, the philharmonic

филе́ *n* [*indecl.*] tenderloin, fil(l)et

филиа́л *m* [1] branch (*of an institution*)

фи́лин *m* [1] eagle owl

фило́л|ог *m* [1] philologist; **~оги́ческий** [16] philological; **~о́гия** *f* [7] philology

филосо́|ф *m* [1] philosopher; **~фия** *f* [7] philosophy; **~фский** [16] philosophical; **~фствовать** [7] philosophize

фильм *m* [1] film (*vb.* снима́ть **~**); **документа́льный ~** documentary (film); **мультипликацио́нный ~** cartoon; **худо́жественный ~** feature film

фильтр *m* [1], **~ова́ть** [7] filter

фина́л *m* [1] final; *mus.* finale

финанс|и́ровать [7] (*im*)*pf.* finance; **~овый** [14] financial; **~ы** *m/pl.* [1] finance(s)

фи́ник *m* [1] date (*fruit*)

финифть *f* [8] *art* enamel

фи́ниш *m* [1] *sport* finish; **~ная пряма́я** last lap

финн *m* [1], **~ка** *f* [5; *g/pl.*: -ок], **~ский** [16] Finnish

фиоле́товый [14] violet

фи́рма *f* [5] firm

фиска́льный [14] fiscal

фити́ль *m* [4 *e.*] wick; (*igniting device*) fuse; (*detonating device*) *usu.* fuze

флаг *m* [1], flag, colo(u)rs *pl.*

фланг *m* [1], **~овый** [14] *mil.* flank

фланел|евый [14], **~ь** *f* [8] flannel

флегмати́чный [14; -чен, -чна] phlegmatic

фле́йта *f* [5] flute

фли|гель *arch. m* [4; *pl.*: -ля, *etc. e.*] wing; outbuilding; **~рт** *m* [1] flirtation; **~ртова́ть** [7] flirt

флома́стер *m* [1] felt-tip pen

флот *m* [1] fleet; **вое́нно-морско́й ~** navy; **вое́нно-возду́шный ~** (air) force; **~ский** [16] naval

флю́|гер *m* [1] weather vane; weathercock; **~с** *m* [1] gumboil

фля́|га *f* [5], **~жка** *f* [5; *g/pl.*: -жек] flask; *mil.* canteen

фойе́ *n* [*indecl.*] lobby, foyer

фо́кус *m* [1] (juggler's *or* conjurer's) trick, sleight of hand; *coll.* caprice; whim; **~ник** *m* [1] juggler, conjurer; **~ничать** *coll.* [1] play tricks; *о ребёнке* play up; behave capriciously

фольга́ *f* [5] foil

фолькло́р *m* [1], **~ный** [14] folklore

фон *m* [1] background (against на П)

фона́р|ик *m* [1] flashlight, *Brt.* torch; **~ь** *m* [4 *e.*] lantern; (street) lamp; *coll.* black eye

фонд *m* [1] fund; *pl.* reserves, stock(s); **~овый** [14] stock...

фоне́тика *f* [5] phonetics; **~и́ческий** [16] phonetic(al)

фонта́н *m* [1] fountain

форе́ль *f* [8] trout

фо́рм|а *f* [5] form, shape; *tech.* mo(u)ld; cast; *mil.* uniform; dress (*sports*); **~а́льность** *f* [8] formality; **~а́льный** [14;

Ф

-лен, -льна] formal; ~а́т m [1] size, format (a. tech.); ~енный [14] uniform; coll. proper; regular; ~енная оде́жда uniform; ~ирова́ть [7], ⟨с-⟩ (-ся be) form(ed); ~ули́ровать [7] (im)pf. & ⟨с-⟩ formulate; ~улиро́вка [5; g/pl.: -вок] formulation

форпо́ст m [1] mil. advanced post; outpost (a. fig.)

форси́ровать [7] (im)pf. force

фо́сфорточка f [5; g/pl.: -чек] window leaf; ~рум m [1] forum; ~сфор m [1] phosphorus

фото|аппара́т m [1] camera; ~граф m [1] photographer; ~графи́ровать [7], ⟨с-⟩ photograph; ~графи́ческий [16] photographic; → ~аппара́т; ~гра́фия f [7] photograph; photography; photographer's studio

фрагмента́рный [14; -рен, -рна] fragmentary

фра́за f [5] phrase

фрак m [1] tailcoat, full-dress coat

фра́кция f [7] pol. faction; (chem.) fraction

франт m [1] dandy, fop

франц|у́женка f [5; g/pl.: -нок] Frenchwoman; ~у́з m [1] Frenchman; ~у́зский [16] French

фрахт m [1], ~ова́ть [7] freight

фре́ска f [5] fresco

фронт m [1] mil. front; ~ово́й [14] front...; front-line

фрукт m [1] (mst. pl.) fruit; ~о́вый [14] fruit...; ~о́вый сад orchard

фу! int. (expressing revulsion) ugh!; (expressing surprise) oh!; ooh!

фунда́мент m [1] foundation; основа basis; ~а́льный [14; -лен, -льна] fundamental

функциони́ровать [7] function

фунт m [1] pound

фур|а́ж m [1 e.] fodder; ~а́жка f [5; g/pl.: -жек] mil. service cap; ~го́н m [1] van; ~о́р m [1] furor(e); ~у́нкул m [1] furuncle, boil

футбо́л m [1] football, soccer (Brt. a. association football); ~и́ст m [1] soccer player; ~ьный [14] soccer..., football...

футля́р m [1] case, container

фы́рк|ать [1], ⟨~нуть⟩ [20] snort; coll. grouse

Х

ха́ки [indecl.] khaki

хала́т m [1] dressing gown, bathrobe; врача́ smock; ~ный coll. [14; -тен, -тна] careless, negligent

халту́ра coll. f [5] potboiler; hackwork; extra work (usu. inferior) chiefly for profit

хам m [1] cad, boor, lout

хандр|а́ f [5] depression, blues pl.; ~и́ть [13] be depressed or in the dumps

ханж|а́ m/f [5; g/pl.: -жей] hypocrite; ~ество́ n [9] hypocrisy

хао́|с m [1] chaos; ~ти́ческий [16], ~ти́чный [14; -чен, -чна] chaotic

хара́ктер m [1] character, nature; человека temper, disposition; ~изова́ть [7] (im)pf. & ⟨о-⟩ characterize; (описывать) describe; ~и́стика f [5]

character(istic); characterization; (документ) reference; ~ный [14; -рен, -рна] characteristic (для Р of)

ха́риус m [1] zo. grayling

ха́ря coll. f [6] mug (= face)

ха́та f [5] peasant house

хвал|а́ f [5] praise; ~ебный [14; -бен, -бна] laudatory; ~ёный [14] iro. much-vaunted; ~и́ть [13; хвалю́, хва́лишь] praise; -ся boast (Т of)

хваст|аться & coll. ~а́ть [1], ⟨по-⟩ boast, brag (Т of); ~ли́вый [14 sh.] boastful; ~овство́ n [9] boasting; ~у́н m [1 e.] coll. boaster, braggart

хват|а́ть [1] 1. ⟨(с)хвати́ть⟩ [15] (за В) snatch (at); grasp, seize (by); a., coll., (-ся за В to; lay hold of); 2. ⟨~и́ть⟩ (impers.) (Р) suffice, be sufficient; (р. Д,

у P) have enough; last (v/t. **на** B); (*этого мне*) **~ит** (that's) enough (for me)

хво́йный [14] coniferous

хвора́ть coll. [1] be sick or ill

хво́рост m [1] brushwood

хвост m [1 e.] tail; coll. (*очередь*) line, Brt. queue; **в ~é** get behind, lag behind; **поджа́ть ~** coll. become more cautious

хвоя́ f [6] (pine) needle(s or branches pl.)

хе́рес m [1] sherry

хи́жина f [5] hut, cabin

хи́лый [14; хил, -á, -о] weak, sickly, puny

хи́ми|к m [1] chemist; **~ческий** [16] chemical; **~я** f [7] chemistry

химчи́стка f [5; g/pl.:-ток] dry cleaning; dry cleaner's

хини́н m [1] quinine

хире́ть [8] weaken, grow sickly; *растение* wither; fig. decay

хиру́рг m [1] surgeon; **~и́ческий** [16] surgical; **~и́я** f [7] surgery

хитр|е́ц m [1 e.] cunning person; **~и́ть** [13], ⟨с-⟩ use guile; → **му́дри́ть**; **~ость** f [8] craft(iness), cunning; (*приём*) artifice, ruse, trick; stratagem; **~ый** [14; -тёр, -тра́, хи́тро] cunning, crafty, sly, wily; coll. artful; (*изобрета́тельный*) ingenious

хихи́кать [1] giggle, titter

хище́ние n [12] theft; embezzlement

хи́щн|ик m [1] beast (or bird) of prey; **~ический** [14] predatory; fig. injurious (to nature); **~ый** [16: -щен, -щна] rapacious, predatory; of prey

хладнокро́в|ие n [12] composure; **~ный** [14; -вен, -вна] cool(headed), calm

хлам m [1] trash, rubbish

хлеб m [1] **1.** bread; **2.** [1; pl.:-бá, etc. e.] grain, Brt. corn; (*пропита́ние*) livelihood; pl. cereals; **~ный** [14] grain..., corn..., cereal...; bread...; **~опека́рня** f [6; g/pl.:-рен] bakery; **~осо́льный** [14; -лен, -льна] hospitable

хлев m [1; в -é & -ý; pl.:-á, etc. e.] cattle shed; fig. pigsty

хлест|а́ть [1], once, ⟨**~ну́ть**⟩ [20] lash, whip, beat; *о воде* gush, spurt; *о дожде* pour

хлоп|! int. bang! crack!, plop!; → a. **~а́ть**

[1], ⟨по-⟩, once ⟨**~ну́ть**⟩ [20] по спине slap; в ладо́ши clap; две́рью и т. д. bang, slam (v/t. T)

хло́пок m [1; -пка] cotton

хлопо́к m [1; -ка́ и т. д.] clap; bang

хлопот|а́ть [3], ⟨по-⟩ (о П) busy or exert o.s. (**о** П, **за** В on behalf of); impf. по хозяйству toil, bustle (about); **~ли́вый** [14 sh.] о человеке busy, fussy; **~ный** [14] troublesome; exacting; **~ы** f/pl. [5; g/pl.: -по́т] trouble(s), efforts (on behalf of; for); cares

хлопчатобума́жный [14] cotton...

хло́пья n/pl. [10; gen.:-ьев] flakes; **кукуру́зные ~** corn flakes

хлор m [1] chlorine; **~истый** [14] chlorine...; chloride...

хлы́нуть [20] pf. gush (forth); rush; *дождь* (begin to) pour in torrents

хлыст m [1 e.] whip; switch

хлю́пать coll. [1] squelch

хмель¹ m [4] hop(s)

хмель² m [4] intoxication

хму́р|ить [13], ⟨на-⟩ frown, knit one's brows; **-ся** frown, scowl; *погода* be(come) overcast; **~ый** [14; хмур, -á, -о] gloomy, sullen; *день* cloudy

хны́кать coll. [3] whimper, snivel; fig. whine

хо́бби n [indecl.] hobby

хо́бот m [1] zo. trunk

ход m [1; в (на) -ý & -е; pl.: хо́ды] motion; (*ско́рость*) speed (**на** П at), pace; *исто́рии и т. д.* course; *подзе́мный* passage; *поршня* stroke; *чёрный* entrance; lead (cards); move (chess, etc.); **на ~ý** in transit; *o. while walking, etc.*; **пусти́ть в ~** start; motion; *оружие* use; **знать все ~ы и вы́ходы** know all the ins and outs; **по́лным ~ом** in full swing; **~ мы́слей** train of thought

хода́тай|ство n [9] intercession; petition; **~ствовать** [7], ⟨по-⟩ intercede (у P, **за** B with/for); petition (**о** П for)

ходи́ть [15] go (**в**, **на** B to); walk; *под парусом* sail; *поезд и т. д.* run, ply; *в ша́шках и т. д.* move; visit, attend (v/t. **в**, **на** B; p. к Д); *о слу́хах* circulate; (*носить*) (**в** П) wear; **~кий** [16; хо́док, -дка́, -о; сотр.: хо́дче] coll. fast; *товар*

marketable, saleable; in great demand; **~ульный** [14; -лен, -льна] stilted; **~ьбá** f [5] walking; walk; **~я́чий** [17] popular; current; *coll. больнóй* ambulant

хожде́ние n [12] going, walking; (*распространение*) circulation

хозя́ин m [1; *pl.*: хозя́ева, хозя́ев] owner; boss, master; *домовладелец* landlord; *принимающий гостей* host; **~ева** [-я & -ин & ~йка; **~йка** f [5; g/pl.: -я́ек] mistress; landlady; hostess; housewife; **~йничать** [1] keep house; manage (at will); be o.s. at home; **~йственный** [14 *sh.*] economic(al), thrifty; **~йственные товáры** household goods; **~йство** n [9] economy; household; farm

хоккей m [3] hockey; **~ с ша́йбой** ice hockey

холера f [5] cholera

хóлить [13] tend, care for

холл m [1] vestibule, foyer

холм m [1 e.] hill; **~и́стый** [14 *sh.*] hilly

хóлод m [1] cold (**на** П in); chill (*a. fig.*); pl. [-á, *etc.*] cold (weather) (**в** В in); **~éть** [8], ⟨по-⟩ grow cold, chill; **~и́льник** m [1] refrigerator; **~ность** f [8] coldness; **~ный** [14; хóлоден, -днá, -о] cold (*a. fig.*); *geogr. & fig.* frigid; (**мне**) **~но** it is (I am) cold

холостóй [14; хóлост] single, unmarried; bachelor('s); *патрóн* blank; *tech. ход* idle; **~я́к** m [1 e.] bachelor

холст m [1 e.] canvas

хомя́к m [1 e.] hamster

хор m [1] choir; **~ом** all together

хорвáт m [1], **~ка** f [5; g/pl.: -ток] Croat; **~ский** [16] Croatian

хорёк m [1; -рькá] polecat, ferret

хореогрáфия f [7] choreography

хоровóд m [1] round dance

хорони́ть [13; -оню́, -óнишь], ⟨по-⟩ bury

хорóшенький *coll.* **~енько** *coll.* properly, throughly; **~éть** [8], ⟨по-⟩ grow prettier; **~ий** [17; хорóш, -á; *compr.*: лу́чше] good; fine, nice; (*a.* **собóй**) pretty, goodlooking, handsome; **~ó** well; *отметка* good, В (→ **четвёрка**); all right!, OK!, good!; **~ó, что вы** it's a good thing you…; **~ó**

вам (+ *inf.*) it is all very well for you to…

хоте́ть [хочý, хóчешь, хóчет, хоти́м, хоти́те, хотя́т], ⟨за-⟩ (P) want, desire; **я ~л**(**а**) **бы** I would (*Brt.* should) like; **я хочý, чтóбы вы** + *pt.* I want you to…; **хóчешь не хóчешь** willy-nilly; **-ся** (*impers.*): **мне хóчется** I'd like; *a.* **→ ~ть**

хоть (*a.* **~ бы**) at least; even; even (if even (if though); if only; **~ … ~** whether … whether, (either) or; *coll.* **~ бы и так** even if it be so; **~ убéй** for the life of me; *a.* **хотя́**

хотя́ although, though (*a.* **~ и**); **~ бы** even though; if; → *a.* **хоть**

хóхот m [1] guffaw; loud laugh; **~áть** [-ачý, -óчешь], ⟨за-⟩ roar (with laughter)

храбре́ц m [1 e.] brave person; **~ость** f [8] valo(u)r, bravery; **~ый** [14; храбр, -а, -о] brave, valiant

храм m [1] *eccl.* temple, church

хране́ние n [12] keeping; *товáров* storage; **кáмера ~éния** *rail., ae., etc.*; cloakroom, *Brt.* left-luggage office; *автомати́ческая* left-luggage locker; **~и́лище** n [11] storehouse; depository; **~и́тель** m [4] keeper, custodian; *музéя* curator; **~и́ть** [13], ⟨со-⟩ keep; maintain; store *tech. a.* of computer; *пáмяти* preserve; (*соблюдáть*) observe

храп m [1], **~éть** [10 *e.*; -плю́, -пи́шь] snore; snorting

хребе́т m [1; -бтá] *anat.* spine; spinal column; (*mountain*) range

хрен m [1] horseradish

хрип m [1], **~éние** n [12] wheeze; wheezing; **~éть** [10; -плю́, -пи́шь] wheeze; be hoarse; *coll.* speak hoarsely; **~лый** [14; хрипл, -á, -о] hoarse, husky; **~нуть** [21], ⟨о-⟩ become hoarse; **~отá** [5] hoarseness; husky voice

христиани́н m [1; *pl.*: -áне, -áн], **~и́анка** f [5; g/pl.: -нок], **~иáнский** [16] Christian; **~иáнство** n [9] Christianity; **2óс** m [Христá] Christ

хром m [1] chromium; chrome

хромáть [1] limp; be lame; **~óй** [1] *coll.* хром, -á, -о] lame

хрóника f [5] chronicle; current events; newsreel; **~и́ческий** [16] chronic(al);

~ологи́ческий [16] chronological; **~оло́гия** *f* [7] chronology

хру́п|кий [16; -пок, -пка́, -о; *compr.:* хру́пче] brittle, fragile, frail, infirm; **~ста́ль** *m* [4 *e.*] crystal; **~сте́ть** [11] crunch; **~щ** *m* [1 *e.*] cockchafer

худо́ж|ественный [14 *sh.*] artistic; art(s)…; of art; belles(-*lettres*); applied (*arts*); **~ество** *n* [9] (applied) art; **~ник** *m* [1] artist; painter

худо́й [14; худ, -а́, -о; *compr.:* худе́е] thin, lean, scrawny; [*compr.:* ху́же] bad, evil; **~ший** [16] worse, worst; → **лу́чший**

ху́же worse; → **лу́чше & тот**

хулига́н *m* [1] rowdy, hooligan

Ц

ца́п|ать *coll.* [1], *once* ⟨~нуть⟩ [20] snatch, grab; scratch

ца́пля *f* [6; *g/pl.:* -пель] heron

цара́п|ать [1], ⟨(п)о-⟩, *once* ⟨~нуть⟩ [20], **~ина** *f* [5] scratch

царе́вич *m* [1] czarevitch; prince; **~евна** *f* [5; *g/pl.:* -вен] princess; **~ить** [13] *fig.* reign; **~и́ца** *f* [5] czarina, (Russian) empress; *fig.* queen; **~ский** [16] of the czar(s), czarist; royal; **~ство** *n* [9] realm; kingdom (*a. fig.*); rule; *a.* → **~ствование** *n* [12] reign (**в** B in); **~ствовать** [7] reign, rule; **~ь** *m* [4 *e.*] czar, (Russian) emperor; *fig.* king; **без ~я́ в голове́** stupid

цвести́ [25 -т-] bloom, blossom

цвет *m* [1] **1.** [*pl.:* -а́, *etc. e.*] colo(u)r; *fig.* cream, pick; *лица́* complexion; *защи́тного* **~а** khaki; **2.** [*only pl.:* -ы́, *etc. e.*] flowers; **3.** [*no pl.:* **в -у́**] in bloom; blossom, bloom; **~е́ние** *n* [12] flowering; **~и́стый** [14 *sh.*] multicolo(u)red, florid; **~ни́к** [1 *e.*] flower bed, garden; **~но́й** [14] colo(u)red; colo(u)r; *мета́ллы* nonferrous; **~на́я капу́ста** cauliflower; **~о́к** *m* [1; -тка́; *pl. usu.* = 2] flower; **~о́чный** [14] flower…; **~о́чный магази́н** florist's; **~у́щий** [17 *sh.*] flowering; *fig.* flourishing; *во́зраст* prime (of life)

целе́|бный [14; -бен, -бна] curative, medicinal; **~во́й** [14] special, having a special purpose; **~сообра́зный** [14; -зен, -зна] expedient; **~устремлённый** [14 *sh.*] purposeful

цели́|ко́м entirely, wholly; **~на́** *f* [5] virgin lands; virgin soil; **~тельный** [14; -лен, -льна] salutary, curative; **~ть(ся)** [13], ⟨при-⟩ aim (**в** B at)

целлюло́за *f* [5] cellulose

целова́ть(ся) [7], ⟨по-⟩ kiss

це́л|ое [14] whole (**в** П on the); **~омудренный** [14 *sh.*] chaste; **~омудрие** *n* [12] chastity; **~остность** *f* [8] integrity; **~ость** *f* [8]: safety; **в ~ости** intact; **~ый** [14; цел, -а́, -о] whole, entire, intact; **~ый и невреди́мый** safe and sound; **~ое число́** whole number, integer; → **деся́тый & со́тый**

цель *f* [8] aim, end, goal, object; (*мише́нь*) target; purpose (**с** T, **в** П *pl.* for); **име́ть ~ю** aim at; **~ность** *f* [8] integrity; **~ный** [14; це́лен, -льна, -о] of one piece; entire, whole; *челове́к* self-contained; *молоко́* [*no sh.*] unskimmed

цеме́нт *m* [1] cement; **~и́ровать** [7] *tech.* cement, case-harden

цен|а́ *f* [5; *ac/sg.:* це́ну; *pl. st.*] price (P of; **по** Д/**в** B at/of), cost; value (Д of *or* one's); **знать себе́ ~у** know one's worth; **~ы́ нет** (Д) be invaluable; **любо́й ~о́й** at any price; **~зу́ра** *f* [5] censorship

цени́тель *m* [4] judge, connoisseur; **~и́ть** [13; ценю́, це́нишь], ⟨о-⟩ estimate; value, appreciate; **~ность** *f* [8] value; *pl.* valuables; **~ный** [14; -е́нен, -е́нна] valuable; *fig.* precious, important; **~ные бума́ги** *pl.* securities

це́нтнер *m* [1] centner

центр *m* [1] center, *Brt.* centre; **~ализо-**

ва́ть [7] (*im*)*pf.* centralize; **~а́льный** [14] central; **~а́льная газе́та** national newspaper; **~обе́жный** [14] centrifugal

цеп|ене́ть [8], ⟨о-⟩ become rigid, freeze; be rooted to the spot; *fig.* be transfixed; **~кий** [16; -пок, -пка́, -о] tenacious (*a. fig.*); **~ля́ться** [28] cling (to **за** В); **~но́й** [14] chain(ed); **~о́чка** *f* [5; *g/pl.*: -чек] chain; **~ь** *f* [8; в, на -и́; *from* *g/pl.e.*] chain (*a. fig.*); *mil.* line; *el.* circuit

церемо́н|иться [13], ⟨по-⟩ stand on ceremony; **~ия** *f* [7] ceremony; **~ный** [14] ceremonious

церко́в|ный [14] church…; ecclesiastical; **~ь** *f* [8; -кви; *instr./sg.*: -ковью; *pl.*: -кви, -ве́й, -ва́м] church (*building and organization*)

цех *m* [1] shop (*section of factory*)

цивилиз|а́ция *f* [7] civilization; **~о́ванный** [14] civilized

цикл *m* [1] cycle; **~лекций** course; **~о́н** *m* [1] cyclone

цико́рий *m* [3] chicory

цили́ндр *m* [1] cylinder; **~и́ческий** [16] cylindrical

цинга́ *f* [5] *med.* scurvy

цини́|зм *m* [1] cynicism; **~к** *m* [1] cynic; **~чный** [14; -чен, -чна] cynical

цинк *m* [1] zinc; **~о́вый** [14] zinc…

цино́вка *f* [5; *g/pl.*: -вок] mat

цирк *m* [1], **~ово́й** [14] circus

циркул|и́ровать [7] circulate; **~ь** *m* [4] (a pair of) compasses *pl.*; **~я́р** *m* [1] (official) instruction

цисте́рна *f* [5] cistern, tank

цитаде́ль (-'дэ-) *f* [8] citadel; *fig.* bulwark; stronghold

цита́та *f* [5] quotation

цити́ровать [7], ⟨про-⟩ quote

ци́трусовые [14] citrus (trees)

цифербла́т *m* [1] dial; *часо́в* face; **~ра** *f* [5] figure; number

цо́коль *m* [4] *arch.* socle; *el.* screw base (*of light bulb*)

цыга́н *m* [1; *nom./pl.*: -е & -ы; *gen.*: цыга́н], **~ка** *f* [5; *g/pl.*: -нок], **~ский** [16] Gypsy, *Brt.* Gipsy

цыплёнок *m* [2] chicken

цы́почк|и: **на ~ах** (**~и**) on tiptoe

Ч

чад *m* [1; в -ý] fume(s); *fig.* daze; intoxication; **~и́ть** [15 *e.*; чажу́, чади́шь], ⟨на-⟩ smoke

ча́до *n* [9] *obs. or joc.* child

чаевы́е *pl.* [14] tip, gratuity

чай *m* [3; *part. g.*: -ю; в -е & -ю́; *pl. e.*: чаи́, чаёв] tea; **дать на ~** tip

ча́йка *f* [5; *g/pl.*: ча́ек] (sea) gull

ча́й|ник *m* [1] для заварки teapot; tea-kettle; **~ный** [14] *ло́жка и т. д.* tea

чалма́ *f* [5] turban

чан *m* [1; в -é] tub, vat

ча́р|ка *f* [5; *g/pl.*: -рок] *old use* cup, goblet; **~ова́ть** [20] charm; **~оде́й** *m* [3] magician, wizard (*a. fig.*)

час *m* [1; в -е & -ý; *after* 2, 3, 4: -á; *pl. e.*] hour (for *pl.* **~а́ми**); (one) o'clock (at **в** В); time, moment (at **в** В); an hour's…; **второ́й ~** (it is) past one; **в пя́том ~ý**

between four and five; (→ **пять & пя́тый**); **кото́рый ~?** what's the time?; **с ~у на ~** soon; **~ от ~у не ле́гче** things are getting worse and worse; **~о́вня** *f* [6; *g/pl.*: -вен] chapel; **~ово́й** [14] hour's; watch…, clock…; *su.* sentry, guard; **~ово́й по́яс** time zone; **~ово́й ма́стер** = **~овщи́к** *m* [1 *e.*] watchmaker

части́|ца *f* [5] particle; **~и́чный** [14; -чен, -чна] partial; **~ик** *coll.* private trader; owner of a small business; **~ое** *n* [14] *math.* quotient; **~ность** *f* [8] detail; **~ный** [14] private; particular, individual; **~ная со́бственность** private property; **~ота́** *f* [5; *pl. st.*: -о́ты] frequency; **~у́шка** *f* [5; *g/pl.*: -шек] humorous or topical two- or four-lined verse; **~ый** [14; част, -á, -о; *comp.*: ча́ще] frequent (*adv. a.* often); *густо́й* thick, dense;

стежки и т. д. close; *пульс и т. д.* quick, rapid; **~ь** *f* [8; *from g/pl. e.*] part (in T; *pl. а.* **по** Д); (*доля*) share; piece; section; *mil.* unit; **бо́льшей ~ью, по бо́льшей ~и** for the most part, mostly; **разобра́ть на ~и** take to pieces

час|ы́ *no sg.* [1] *ручны́е* watch; clock; **по мои́м ~а́м** by my watch

ча́х|лый [14 *sh.*] sickly; *расти́тельность* stunted; **~нуть** [21], ⟨за-⟩ wither away; *о челове́ке* become weak, waste away

ча́ш|а *f* [5] cup, bowl; *eccl.* chalice; **~ечка** *f* [5] *dim.* → **ча́шка: коле́нная ~ечка** kneecap; **~ка** *f* [5; *g/pl.:* -шек] cup; *весо́в* pan

ча́ща *f* [5] thicket

ча́ще more (**~ всего́** most) often

ча́я|ние *n* [12] expectation, aspiration

чей *m,* **чья** *f,* **чьё** *n,* **чьи** *pl.* [26] whose; **~ э́то дом?** whose house is this?

чек *m* [1 *e.*] check, *Brt.* cheque; *для опла́ты* chit, bill; *опла́ченный* receipt; **~а́нить** [13], ⟨вы́-⟩ mint, coin; *узо́р* chase; **~а́нка** *f* [5; *g/pl.:* -нок] minting, coinage; chasing; **~и́ст** *m* [1] (state) security officer; *hist.* member of the cheka; **~овый** [14] check...

челно́|к *m* [1 *e.*], **~чный** [14] shuttle

чело́ *n* [9; *pl. st.*] *obs.* brow

челове́|к *m* [1; *pl.:* лю́ди; 5, 8, *etc.* -е́к] man, human being; person, individual; **ру́сский ~к** Russian; **~колю́бие** *n* [12] philanthropy; **~ческий** [16] human(e); **~чество** *n* [9] mankind, humanity; **~чный** [14; -чен, -чна] humane

че́люсть *f* [8] jaw; (full) denture

чем than; rather than, instead of; **~ ..., тем ...** the more ... the more ...; **~ скоре́е, тем лу́чше** the sooner, the better; **~ода́н** *m* [1] suitcase

чемпио́н *m* [1] champion; **~а́т** *m* [1] championship

чепуха́ *f* [5] *coll.* nonsense; (*ме́лочь*) trifle

чепчик *m* [1] baby's bonnet

че́рв|и *f/pl.* [4; *from gen. e.*] & **~ы** *f/pl.* [5] hearts (*cards*)

черви́вый [14 *sh.*] worm-eaten

черво́нец *m* [1; -нца] *hist.* (*gold coin*)

chervonets; (*ten-r(o)uble bank note in circulation 1922-47*)

червь [4; *e.; nom/pl. st.:* че́рви, черве́й], **~я́к** *m* [1 *e.*] worm

черда́к *m* [1 *e.*] garret, attic, loft

черёд *coll. m* [1 *e.*] (*о́чередь*) turn; (*поря́док*) course

чередова́|ние *n* [12] alternation; **~ть(ся)** [7] alternate (with)

че́рез (В) through; *у́лицу* across, over; *вре́мя* in, after; *е́хать* via; **~ день** *a.* every other day

черёмуха *f* [5] bird cherry

че́реп *m* [1; *pl.:* -á, *etc. e.*] skull

черепа́|ха *f* [5] tortoise; *морска́я* turtle; **~ховый** [14] tortoise(shell)...; **~ший** [18] tortoise's, snail's

черепи́ца *f* [5] tile (*of roof*); **~чный** [14] tiled; **~о́к** *m* [1; -пка́] fragment, piece

чере|счу́р too, too much; **~шня** *f* [6; *g/pl.:* -шен] (sweet) cherry, cherry tree

черкну́ть *coll.* [20] *pf.:* scribble; dash off; **~ па́ру** (or **не́сколько**) **слов** drop a line

черн|е́ть [8], ⟨по-⟩ blacken, grow black; *impf.* show up black; **~и́ка** *f* [5] bilberry, -ries *pl.*; **~и́ла** *n/pl.* [9] ink; **~и́ть** [13], ⟨o-⟩ *fig.* blacken, denigrate, slander

черно|ви́к *m* [1 *e.*] rough copy; draft; **~во́й** [14] draft...; rough; **~воло́сый** [14 *sh.*] black-haired; **~гла́зый** [14 *sh.*] black-eyed; **~зём** *m* [1] chernozem, black earth; **~ко́жий** [17 *sh.*] black; *as su.* [-его́] *m* black (man); negro; **~мо́рский** [16] Black Sea...; **~сли́в** *m* [1] prune(s); **~та́** *f* [5] blackness

чёрн|ый [14; чёрен, черна́] black (*a. fig.*); *хлеб* brown; *мета́лл* ferrous; *рабо́та* rough; *ход* back; **на ~ый день** for a rainy day; **~ым по бе́лому** in black and white

чернь *f* [8] *art* niello

че́рп|ать [1], ⟨~ну́ть⟩ [20] scoop, ladle; *зна́ния, си́лы* derive, draw (from **из** Р, **в** П)

черстве́ть [8], ⟨за-, по-⟩ grow stale; *fig.* harden

чёрствый [14; чёрств, -á, -о] stale; hard; *fig.* callous

чёрт *m* [1; *pl.* 4: че́рти, -те́й, *etc. e.*] devil;

Ч

coll. **~побери** the devil take it; **на кой** *coll.* what the deuce; **ни черта́** *coll.* nothing at all; **~а с два!** like hell!

черт|а́ *f* [5] line; trait, feature (*a.* **~ы́ ли- ца́**); **в ~е́ го́рода** within the city boundary

чертёж *m* [1 *e.*] drawing, draft (*Brt.* draught), design; **~ник** *m* [1] draftsman, *Brt.* draughtsman; **~ный** [14] *доска́ и т. д.* drawing (*board, etc.*)

черт|и́ть [15], ⟨на-⟩ draw, design; **~о́в- ский** [16] *coll.* devilish

чёрточка *f* [5; *g/pl.*: -чек] hyphen

черче́ние *n* [12] drawing

чеса́ть [3] 1. ⟨по-⟩ scratch; 2. ⟨при-⟩ comb; **-ся** itch

чесно́к *m* [1 *e.*] garlic

чесо́тка *f* [5] scab, rash, mange

чест|вование *n* [12] celebration; **~во- вать** [7] celebrate, hono(u)r; **~ность** *f* [8] honesty; **~ный** [14; че́стен, -тна́, -о] honest, upright; (*справедливый*) fair; **~олюби́вый** [14 *sh.*] ambitious; **~олюбие** *n* [12] ambition; **~ь** *f* [8] hon- o(u)r (*in* **в** *P*); credit; **э́то де́лает вам ~ь** it does you credit; *coll.* **~ь ~ью** prop- erly, well

чета́ *f* [5] couple, pair; match; **она́ ему́ не ~** she is no match for him

четвёр|г *m* [1 *e.*] Thursday (on **в** *B, pl.*: **по** *Д*); **~еньки** *coll. f/pl.* [5] all fours (on **на** *B, П*); **четвёрка** *f* [5; *g/pl.*: -рок] four (→ **тро́йка**); *coll.* (*mark*) → **хорошо́**; **~о** [37] four (→ **дво́е**); **четвёртый** (-'vэr-) [14] fourth → **пя́тый**; **~ь** *f* [8; *from g/pl. e.*] (one) fourth; *шко́ль- ная* (school-)term; quarter (*to* **без** *P*; past one **второ́го**)

чёткий [16; чёток, четка́, -о] precise; clear; *почерк* legible; (*точный*) exact, accurate

чётный [14] even (*of numbers*)

четы́ре [34] four; → **пять**; **~жды** four times; **~ста** [36] four hundred

четырёх|ле́тний [15] of four years; four- year; **~ме́стный** [14] fourseater; **~со́- тый** [14] four hundredth; **~уго́льник** *m* [1] quadrangle; **~уго́льный** [14] quadrangular

четы́рнадца|тый [14] fourteenth; →

пя́тый; **~ть** [35] fourteen; → **пять**

чех *m* [1] Czech

чехарда́ *f* [5] leapfrog; **министе́рская ~** frequent changes in personnel (*esp. in government appointments*)

чехо́л *m* [1; -хла́] case, cover

чечеви́ца *f* [5] lentil(s)

че́ш|ка *f* [5; *g/pl.*: -шек] Czech (woman); **~ский** [16] Czech

чешуя́ *f* [6] *zo.* scales *pl.*

чи́бис *m* [1] *zo.* lapwing

чиж *m* [1 *e.*], **~ик** *m* [1] *zo.* siskin

чин *m* [1; *pl. e.*] *mil.* rank

чин|и́ть [13; чиню́, чи́нишь] a) ⟨по-⟩ mend, repair; b) ⟨о-⟩ *каранда́ш* sharp- en, point; **~и́ть препя́тствие** (*Д*) ob- struct, impede; **~ный** [14; чи́нен, чинна́, чи́нно] proper; sedate; **~о́вник** *m* [1] offi- cial, functionary

чири́к|ать [1], ⟨~нуть⟩ [20] chirp

чи́рк|ать [1], ⟨~нуть⟩ [20] strike

чи́сл|енность *f* [8] number; **~енный** [14] numerical; **~и́тель** *m* [4] *math.* numer- ator; **~и́тельное** *n* [14] *gr.* numeral (*a.* **и́мя ~и́тельное**); **~и́ться** [13] be *or* be reckoned (**в** *П or* **по** *Д/Р*); **~о́** *n* [9; *pl. st.*: чи́сла, чи́сел, чи́слам] num- ber; date, day; **како́е сего́дня ~о́?** what is the date today? (→ **пя́тый**); **в том ~е́** including

чи́ст|ить [15] 1. ⟨по-, вы́-⟩ clean(se); brush; *обувь* polish; 2. ⟨о-⟩ peel; **~ка** *f* [5; *g/pl.*: -ток] clean(s)ing; *pol.* purge; **~окро́вный** [14; -вен, -вна] thorough- bred; **~опло́тный** [14; -тен, -тна] clean- ly; *fig.* clean, decent; **~осерде́чный** [14; -чен, -чна] openhearted, frank, sin- cere; **~ота́** *f* [5] clean(li)ness; purity; **~ый** [14; чист, -а́, -о; *compr.*: чи́ще] clean; *зо́лото и т. д.* pure; *спирт* neat; *небо* clear; *вес* net; *лист* blank; *рабо́та* fine, faultless; *пра́вда* plain; *случа́йность* mere

чита́|льный [14]: **~льный зал** reading room; **~тель** *m* [4] reader; **~ть** [1], ⟨про-⟩ & *coll.* ⟨проче́сть⟩ [25; -чту́, -чтёшь; чёл, -чла́; -чтённый] read, re- cite; give (*lecture on* **о** *П*), deliver; **~ть мора́ль** lecture

чи́тка *f* [5; *g/pl.*: -ток] reading (*usu. by a*

group)

чих|а́ть [1], *once* ⟨∼ну́ть⟩ [20] sneeze

член *m* [1] member; (*конечности*) limb; part; **∼ораздéльный** [14: -лен, -льна] articulate; **∼ский** [16] member(-ship)…; **∼ство** *n* [9] membership

чмо́к|ать *coll.* [1], *once* ⟨∼нуть⟩ [20] smack; (*поцеловать*) give s.o. a smacking kiss

чо́к|аться [1], *once* ⟨∼нуться⟩ [20] clink (glasses T) (with **с** T)

чо́|порный [14; -рен, -рна] prim, stiff; **∼рт → чёрт**

чрева́тый [14 *sh.*] fraught (with T); **∼о** [9] womb

чрез → че́рез

чрезвыча́йный [14; -áен, -áйна] extraordinary; extreme; special; **∼вычáйное положéние** state of emergency; **∼мéрный** [14; -рен, -рна] excessive

чте́|ние *n* [12] reading; *художéственное* recital; **∼ц** *m* [1 *e.*] reader

чтить → почита́ть[1]

что [23] **1.** *pron.* what (*a.* **∼ за**); that, which; how; (*a.* **а ∼?**) why (so?); (*a.* **а ∼**) what about; what's the matter; *coll.* **а ∼?** well?; **вот ∼** the following; listen; that's it; **∼ до меня́** as for me; **∼ вы (ты)!** you don't say!, what next!; **нé за ∼** (you are) welcome, *Brt.* don't mention it; **ни за ∼** not for the world; **ну и ∼?** what of that; (**уж**) **на ∼** *coll.* however; **с чего́ бы э́то?** *coll.* why? why …?; **∼ и говори́ть** *coll.* sure; → **ни**; *coll.* → **∼-нибудь, ∼-то; 2.** *cj.* that; like, as if; **∼ (ни)** …, **то** … every … (a) …

что́б(ы) (in order) that *or* to (*a.* **с тем, ∼**); **∼ не** lest, for fear that; **вмéсто того́ ∼** + *inf.* instead of …ing; **скажи́ ему́, ∼ он** + *pt.* tell him to *inf.*

что́|-либо, ∼-нибудь, ∼-то [23] something; anything; *coll.* somehow, for some reason or other

чу́вств|енный [14 *sh.*] sensuous; (*плотский*) sensual; **∼и́тельность** *f* [8] sensibility; **∼и́тельный** [14: -лен, -льна] sensitive; sentimental; sensible (*a.* = considerable, great, strong); **∼о** *n* [9] sense; feeling; sensation; *coll.* love; **о́рганы ∼** organs of sense; **∼овать** [7], ⟨по-⟩ feel (*a.* **себя́** [T *s.th.*]); **-ся** be felt

чугу́н *m* [1 *e.*] cast iron; **∼ный** [14] cast-iron…

чуд|а́к *m* [1 *e.*] crank, eccentric; **∼а́чество** *n* [9] eccentricity; **∼éсный** [14; -сен, -сна] wonderful, marvel(l)ous; *спасéние* miraculous; **∼и́ть** [15 *e.*] *coll.* → **дури́ть; ∼и́ться** [15] *coll.* → **мерéщиться; ∼ный** [14; -ден, -дна] wonderful, marvel(l)ous; **∼о** *n* [9; *pl.*: чудеса́, -éс, -есáм] miracle, marvel; wonder; *a.* → **∼но; ∼о́вище** *n* [11] monster; **∼о́вищный** [14; -щен, -щна] monstrous; *потéри и т. д.* enormous

чуж|би́на *f* [5] foreign country (in **на** П; *a.* abroad); **∼да́ться** [1] (P) shun, avoid; **∼дый** [14; чужд, -á, -о] foreign; alien; free (from P); **∼о́й** [14] someone else's, others'; alien; strange, foreign; *su. a.* stranger, outsider

чула́н *m* [1] storeroom, larder; **∼о́к** *m* [1; -лка́; *g/pl.*: -ло́к] stocking

чума́ *f* [5] plague

чурба́н *m* [1] block; *fig.* blockhead

чу́тк|ий [16; -ток, -ткá, -о; *compr.*: чу́тче] sensitive (to **на** B), keen; *coll.* light; *слух* quick (of hearing); *человéк* sympathetic; **∼ость** *f* [8] keenness; delicacy (of feeling)

чу́точку *coll.* a wee bit

чуть hardly, scarcely; a little; **∼ не** nearly, almost; **∼ ли не** *coll.* almost, all but; **∼ что** *coll.* on the slightest pretext; **чуть-чуть → чуть**

чутьё *n* [10] instinct (for **на** B); flair

чу́чело *n* [9] stuffed animal; **∼ горо́ховое** scarecrow; *coll.* dolt

чушь *coll. f* [8] bosh, twaddle

чу́ять [27], ⟨по-⟩ scent, *fig.* feel

Ш

шаба́шник *m* [1] coll. pej. moonlighter

шабло́н *m* [1] stencil, pattern, cliché; **~ный** [14] trite, hackneyed

шаг *m* [1; *after* 2, 3, 4: -á; в -ý; *pl. e.*] step (by step → **за** T) (*a. fig.*); *большо́й* stride; *звук* footsteps; *tech.* pitch; **приба́вить ~у** quicken one's pace; **ни ~у** (*да́льше*) not a step further; **на ка́ждом ~ý** everywhere, at every turn, continually; **~áть** [1], *once* ⟨~ну́ть⟩ [20] step, stride; walk; pace; (*через*) cross; *pf.* take a step; **далеко́ ~ну́ть** *fig.* make great progress; **~áть взад и вперёд** pace back and forth

ша́йба *f* [5] *tech.* washer; *sport* puck

ша́йка *f* [5; *g/pl.*: ша́ек] gang

шака́л *m* [1] jackal

шала́ш *m* [1] hut

шал|и́ть [13] be naughty, frolic, romp; fool (about), play (pranks); **~и́шь!** coll. (rebuke) don't try that on me!; none of your tricks!; **~овли́вый** [14 sh.] mischievous, playful; **~опа́й** coll. *m* [3] loafer; **~ость** *f* [8] prank; **~у́н** *m* [1 e.] naughty boy; **~у́нья** *f* [6; *g/pl.*: -ний] naughty girl

шалфе́й *m* [3] *bot.* sage

шаль *f* [8] shawl

шальн|о́й [14] mad, crazy; *пуля* stray...; **~ые де́ньги** easy money

ша́мкать [1] mumble

шампа́нское *n* [16] champagne

шампиньо́н *m* [1] field mushroom

шампу́нь *m* [4] shampoo

шанс *m* [1] chance, prospect (of **на** B)

шанта́ж *m* [1], **~и́ровать** [7] blackmail

ша́пка *f* [5; *g/pl.*: -пок] cap; *typ.* banner headlines

шар *m* [1; *after* 2, 3, 4: -á; *pl. e.*] sphere; ball; **возду́шный ~** balloon; **земно́й ~** globe

шара́х|аться coll. [1], ⟨~ну́ться⟩ [20] dash, jump (aside), recoil; *о лошади* shy

шарж *m* [1] cartoon, caricature; **дру́жеский ~** harmless, wellmeant caricature

ша́рик *m* [1] dim. → **шар**; **~овый** [14] → **ру́чка**; **~оподши́пник** *m* [1] ball bearing

ша́рить [13], ⟨по-⟩ **в чём-л.** rummage; grope about, feel

ша́р|кать [1], *once* ⟨~кнуть⟩ [20] shuffle

шарни́р *m* [1] *tech.* hinge, joint

шаро|ва́ры *f/pl.* [5] baggy trousers; **~ви́дный** [14; -ден, -дна] **~обра́зный** [14; -зен, -зна] spherical, globe-shaped

шарф *m* [1] scarf, neckerchief

шасси́ *n* [*indecl.*] chassis; *ae.* undercarriage

шат|а́ть [1], *once* ⟨(по)шатну́ть⟩ [20] shake; rock; **-ся** *о зубе и т. д.* be loose; *о человеке* stagger, reel, totter; *coll. без дела* lounge *or* loaf, gad about

шатёр *m* [1; -трá] tent, marquee

ша́т|кий [16; -ток, -тка] shaky, unsteady (*a. fig.*); *мебель* rickety; *fig. friend, etc.* unreliable; fickle; **~ну́ть(ся)** → **~а́ть(ся)**

шах *m* [1] shah; check (*chess*)

шахмат|и́ст *m* [1] chess player; **~ный** [14] chess...; **~ы** *f/pl.* [5] chess; **игра́ть в ~ы** play chess; chessmen

ша́хт|а *f* [5] mine, pit; *tech.* shaft; **~ёр** *m* [1] miner; **~ёрский** [16] miner's

ша́шка¹ *f* [5; *g/pl.*: -шек] saber, *Brt.* sabre

ша́шка² *f* [5; *g/pl.*: -шек] checker, draughtsman; *pl.* checkers, *Brt.* draughts

шашлы́к *m* [1] shashlik, kebab

швартова́ться [7], ⟨при-⟩ *naut.* moor, make fast

швед *m* [1], **~ка** *f* [5; *g/pl.*: -док] Swede; **~ский** [16] Swedish

швейн|ый [14] sewing; **~ая маши́на** sewing machine

швейца́р *m* [1] doorman, doorkeeper, porter

швейца́р|ец *m* [1; -рца], **~ка** *f* [5; *g/pl.*: -рок] Swiss; **Ⴑия** [7] Switzerland; **~ский** [16] Swiss

швыр|я́ть [28], *once* ⟨~ну́ть⟩ [20] hurl, fling (*a.* T)

шеве|ли́ть [13; -елю́, -е́ли́шь], ⟨по-⟩, *once* ⟨(по)льну́ть⟩ [20] stir, move (*v/i.* **-ся**); **~ли́ть мозга́ми** *coll.* use one's wits

шевелю́ра *f* [5] (head of) hair

шеде́вр (-'dɛvr) *m* [1] masterpiece, chef d'œuvre

ше́йка *f* [5; *g/pl.*: ше́ек] neck

ше́лест *m* [1], **~е́ть** [11] rustle

шёлк *m* [1; *g/sg. a.* -у; в шелку́; *pl.*: шелка́, *etc. e.*] silk

шелкови́|стый [14 *sh.*] silky; **~ца** *f* [5] mulberry (tree)

шёлковый [14] silk(en); **как ~** meek as a lamb

шел|охну́ться [20] *pf.* stir; **~уха́** *f* [5], **~ушить** [16 *e.*] -шу́, -ши́шь] peel, husk; **~уши́ться** *о коже* peel

шельмова́|ть [7], ⟨о-⟩ *hist.* punish publicly; *coll.* defame, charge falsely

шепеля́в|ить [14] lisp; **~ый** [14 *sh.*] lisping

шёпот *m* [1] whisper (in a T)

шеп|та́ть [3], ⟨про-⟩, *once* ⟨~ну́ть⟩ [20] whisper (*v/i. a.* **-ся**)

шере́нга *f* [5] file, rank

шерохова́тый [14 *sh.*] rough, *fig.* uneven, rugged

шерсть *f* [8; *from g/pl. e.*] wool; *животного* coat; *овцы* fleece; **~яно́й** [14] wool([l])en

шерша́вый [14 *sh.*] rough

шест *m* [1 *e.*] pole

ше́ств|ие *n* [12] procession; **~овать** [7] stride, walk (*as in a procession*)

шестёрка *f* [5; *g/pl.*: -рок] six (→ **тро́йка**); six-oar boat; **~ерня́** *f* [5; *g/pl.* -рён] *tech.* pinion; cogwheel; **~еро** [37] six (→ **двое**); **~идеся́тый** [14] sixtieth → **пят(идеся́т)ый**; **~име́сячный** [14] of six months; six-month; **~исо́тый** [14] six hundredth; **~иуго́льник** *m* [1] hexagon; **~на́дцатый** [14] sixteenth; → **пя́тый**; **~на́дцать** [35] sixteen; → **пять**; **~о́й** [14] sixth; → **пя́тый**; **~ь** [35 *e.*] six; → **пять**; **~ьдеся́т** [35] sixty; **~ьсо́т** [36] six hundred; **~ью** six times

шеф *m* [1] chief, head; *coll.* boss

ше́я *f* [6; *g/pl.*: -шей] neck

ши́ворот: взять за ~ seize by the collar

шик|а́рный [14; -рен, -рна] chic, smart; **~ать** *coll.* [1], *once* ⟨~нуть⟩ [20] shush, hush, urge to be quiet

ши́ло *n* [1; *pl.*: -лья, -льев] awl

ши́на *f* [5] tire, *Brt.* tyre; *med.* splint

шине́ль *f* [8] greatcoat

шинкова́ть [7] chop, shred

шип *m* [1 *e.*] thorn; *на обуви* spike

шипе́|ние *n* [12] hiss(ing); **~ть** [10], ⟨про-⟩ hiss; *о кошке* spit; *на сковороде* sizzle

шипо́вник *m* [1] *bot.* dogrose

шип|у́чий [17 *sh.*] sparkling, fizzy; **~у́чка** *f* [5; *g/pl.*: -чек] *coll.* fizzy drink; **~я́щий** [17] sibilant

ширина́ *f* [5] width, breadth; **~но́й в** (B) *or* **... в ~у́** ... wide; **~ть** [13] (**-ся**) widen, expand

ши́ринка *f* [5; *g/pl.*: -нок] fly (of trousers)

ши́рма *f* [5] (*mst. pl.*) screen

широ́к|ий [16; широ́к, -ока́, -о́ко́; *compr.*: ши́ре] broad; wide; vast; great; mass...; *наступление и т. д.* large-scale; **на ~ую но́гу** in grand style; **~омасшта́бный** [14; -бен, -бна] large-scale; **~опле́чий** [17 *sh.*] broad-shouldered

шир|ота́ *f* [5; *pl. st.*: -о́ты] breadth; *geogr.* latitude; **~потре́б** *coll. m* [1] consumer goods; **~ь** *f* [8] expanse width; extent

шить [шью, шьёшь, шей(те)!; ши́тый], ⟨с-⟩ [сошью, -ьёшь, сши́тый] sew (*pf. a.* together); (*вышить*) embroider; **себе́** *have made*; **~ё** *n* [10] sewing; needlework; embroidery

ши́фер *m* [1] (roofing) slate

шифр *m* [1] cipher, code; *библиотечный* pressmark (*chiefly Brt.*); **~ова́ть** [7], ⟨за-⟩ encipher, encode

шиш *m* [1 *e.*]: **ни ~а́** damn all

ши́шка *f* [5; *g/pl.*: -шек] *на голове* bump, lump; *bot.* cone; *coll.* bigwig

шка|ла́ *f* [5; *pl. st.*] scale; **~ту́лка** *f* [5; *g/pl.*: -лок] casket; **~ф** *m* [1; в ~у́; *pl. e.*] cupboard; *платяной* wardrobe; **кни́жный ~ф** bookcase

шквал *m* [1] squall, gust

шкив *m* [1] *tech.* pulley

шко́л|а *f* [5] school (*go to* **в** B; *be at, in* **в** П); **вы́сшая ~а** higher education establishment(s); **~а-интерна́т** boarding school;~ьник *m* [1] schoolboy;~ница *f* [5] schoolgirl;~ьный [14] school…

шкýр|а *f* [5] skin (*a.* ~ка *f* [5; *g/pl.:* -рок]), hide

шлагбáум *m* [1] barrier (*at road or rail crossing*)

шлак *m* [1] slag

шланг *m* [1] hose

шлем *m* [1] helmet

шлёпать [1], *once* ⟨~нуть⟩ [20] slap, spank (*v/i. coll.* -ся fall with a plop); plump down

шлифовáть [7], ⟨от-⟩ grind; (*полировáть*) polish

шлю|з *m* [1] sluice, lock;~пка *f* [5; *g/pl.:* -пок] launch, boat; *спасáтельная* lifeboat

шля́п|а *f* [5] hat;~ка *f* [5; *g/pl.:* -пок] *dim.* → ~а hat; *гвоздя́* head

шля́ться *coll.* [1] → шатáться

шмель *m* [4 *e.*] bumblebee

шмы́г|ать *coll.* [1], *once* ⟨~нýть⟩ [20] whisk, scurry, dart; *носом* sniff

шни́цель *m* [4] cutlet, schnitzel

шнур *m* [1 *e.*] cord;~овáть [7], ⟨за-⟩ lace up;~óк *m* [1; -ркá] shoestring, (shoe) lace

шныря́ть *coll.* [28] dart about

шов *m* [1; шва] seam; *tech.* joint; *в вы́шивке* stitch (*a. med.*)

шок *m* [1], ~и́ровать [7] shock

шоколáд *m* [1] chocolate

шóрох *m* [1] rustle

шóрты *no sg.* [1] shorts

шоссé *n* [*indecl.*] highway

шотлáнд|ец *m* [1; -дца] Scotsman, *pl.* the Scots; ~ка *f* [5; *g/pl.:*-док] Scotswoman; ~ский [16] Scottish

шофёр *m* [1] driver, chauffeur

шпáга *f* [5] *sport* épée; sword

шпагáт *m* [1] cord, string; *gymnastics* split(s)

шпáл|а *f* rail. *f* [5] cross tie, *Brt.* sleeper; ~éра *f* [5] *для виногрáда и т. д.* trellis

шпаргáлка *coll. f* [5; *g/pl.:* -лок] pony, *Brt.* crib (*in school*)

шпиговáть [7], ⟨на-⟩ lard

шпик *m* [1] lard; fatback; *coll.* secret agent

шпиль *m* [4] spire, steeple

шпи́|лька *f* [5; *g/pl.:* -лек] hairpin; hat pin; tack; *fig.* taunt, caustic remark, (*v/b.:* **подпусти́ть** В);~нáт *m* [1] spinach

шпио́н *m* [1], ~ка *f* [5; *g/pl.:* -нок] spy; ~áж *m* [1] espionage; ~ить [13] spy

шприц *m* [1] syringe

шпрóты *m/pl.* [1] sprats

шпýлька *f* [5; *g/pl.:* -лек] spool, bobbin

шрам *m* [1] scar

шрифт *m* [1] type, typeface; script

штаб *m* [1] *mil.* staff; headquarters

штáбель *m* [4; *pl.:* -ля́, *etc. e.*] pile

штамп *m* [1], ~овáть [7], ⟨от-⟩ stamp, impress

штáнга *f* [5] *sport:* weight; (*переклади́на*) crossbar

штаны́ *coll. m/pl.* [1 *e.*] trousers

штат¹ *m* [1] state (*administrative unit*)

штат² *m* [1] staff; ~ный [14] (on the) staff; ~ский [16] civilian; *одéжда* plain

штемпел|евáть ('ʃtɛ-) [6], ~ь *m* [4; *pl.:* -ля́, *etc. e.*] stamp; postmark

штéпсель ('ʃtɛ-) *m* [4; *pl.:* -ля́, *etc. e.*] plug; ~ный [14]: ~ная розéтка socket

штиль *m* [4] *naut.* calm

штифт *m* [1 *e.*] *tech.* joining pin, dowel

штóп|ать [1], ⟨за-⟩ darn, mend; ~ка *f* [5] darning, mending

штóпор *m* [1] corkscrew; *ae.* spin

штóра *f* [5] blind; curtain

шторм *m* [1] *naut.* gale; storm

штраф *m* [1] fine; **наложи́ть** ~ impose a fine; ~нóй [14] *sport* penalty…; ~овáть [7], ⟨о-⟩ fine

штрейкбрéхер *m* [1] strikebreaker

штрих *m* [1 *e.*] stroke (*in drawing*), hachure; *fig.* trait; **добáвить нéсколько** ~ов add a few touches; ~овáть [7], ⟨за-⟩ shade, hatch

штуди́ровать [7], ⟨про-⟩ study

штýка *f* [5] item; piece; *coll.* thing; (*вы́ходка*) trick

штукатýр|ить [13], ⟨о-⟩, ~ка *f* [5] plaster

штурвáл *m* [1] *naut.* steering wheel

штурм *m* [1] storm, onslaught

штýрм|ан *m* [1] navigator; ~овáть [7] storm, assail; ~ови́к *m* [1 *e.*] combat aircraft

штýчный [14] (by the) piece (*not by*

weight)

штык *m* [1 *e.*] bayonet

шу́ба *f* [5] fur (coat)

шум *m* [1] noise; din; *воды* rush; *листьев* rustle; *машины, в ушах* buzz; *coll.* hubbub, row, ado; **~ и гам** hullabaloo; **наде́лать ~у** cause a sensation; **~е́ть** [10 *e.*; шумлю́, шуми́шь] make a noise; rustle; rush; roar, buzz; **~и́ха** *coll. f* [5] sensation, clamo(u)r; **~ный** [14; -мен, -мна́, -о] noisy, loud; sensational; **~о́вка** *f* [5; *g/pl.*: -вок] skimmer; **~о́к** [1; -мка́]: **под ~о́к** *coll.* on the sly

шу́р|ин *m* [1] brother-in-law (*wife's brother*); **~а́ть** [4 *e.*; -шу́, -ши́шь], ⟨за-⟩ rustle

шу́стрый *coll.* [14; -тёр, -тра́, -o] nimble

шут *m* [1 *e.*] fool, jester; *горо́ховый* clown, buffoon; *coll.* **~ его́ зна́ет** deuce knews; **~и́ть** [15], ⟨по-⟩ joke, jest; make fun (of **над** T); **~ка** *f* [5; *g/pl.*: -ток] joke, jest (in **в** B); fun (for **ра́ди** P); *coll.* trifle (it's no **~ка ли**); **кро́ме ~ок** joking apart; are you in earnest?; **не на ~ку** serious(ly); (Д) **не до ~ок** be in no laughing mood; **~ли́вый** *coll.* [14 *sh.*] jocose, playful; **~ни́к** *m* [1 *e.*] joker, wag; **~о́чный** [14] joking, sportive, comic; *де́ло* laughing; **~я́** jokingly (**не** in earnest)

шушу́кать(ся) *coll.* [1] whisper

шху́на *f* [5] schooner

ш-ш shush!

Щ

щаве́ль *m* [4 *e.*] *bot.* sorrel

щади́ть [15 *e.*; щажу́, щади́шь], ⟨по-⟩ [щажённый] spare; have mercy (on)

щебень *m* [4; -бня] broken stone or cinders; road metal

щебета́ть [3] chirp, twitter

щего́л *m* [1; -гла́] goldfinch

щегол|ева́тый [14 *sh.*] foppish, dandified; **~ь** *m* [4] dandy, fop; **~я́ть** [28] overdress; give exaggerated attention to fashion; *coll.* flaunt, parade, show off

ще́др|ость *f* [8] generosity; **~ый** [14; щедр, -á, -o] liberal, generous

щека́ [5; *ac/sg.*: щёку; *pl.*: щёки, щёк, щека́м, *etc. e.*] cheek

щеко́лда *f* [5] latch

щекот|а́ть [3], ⟨по-⟩, **~ка** *f* [5] tickle; **~ли́вый** [14 *sh.*] ticklish, delicate

щёлк|ать [1], *once* ⟨~нуть⟩ [20] **1.** языком и т. д. *v/i.* click (T), *пальцами* snap; *кнутом* crack; *зубами* chatter; *птица* warble, sing; **2.** *v/t.* flick, fillip (on *по лбу*); **~о́вый** [14] alkaline

щёло|чь *f* [8; *from g/pl. e.*] alkali; **~чно́й** [14] alkaline

щелчо́к *m* [1; -чка́] flick, fillip; crack

щель *f* [8; *from g/pl. e.*] chink, crack,

crevice; slit

щеми́ть [14 *e.*; *3rd p. only, a. impers.*] *о сердце* ache

щено́к *m* [1; -нка́; *pl.*: -нки́ & (2) -ня́та] puppy; *дикого животного* whelp

щеп|ети́льный [14; -лен, -льна] scrupulous, punctilious; fussy, finicky; **~а** *f* [5; *g/pl.*: -пок] chip; **худо́й как ~ка** thin as a rake

щепо́тка *f* [5; *g/pl.*: -ток] pinch (*of salt, ect.*)

щети́н|а *f* [5] bristle(s); *coll.* stubble; **~иться** [13], ⟨о-⟩ bristle

щётка *f* [5; *g/pl.*: -ток] brush

щи *f/pl.* [5; *gen.*: -щей] shchi (cabbage soup)

щи́колотка *f* [5; *g/pl.*: -ток] ankle

щип|а́ть [2], *once* ⟨(у)ну́ть⟩ [20], pinch, tweak (*v/t.* **за** B), (*тж. от мороза*) nip, bite; ⟨об-⟩ pluck; *траву* browse; **~цы́** *m/pl.* [1 *e.*] tongs, pliers, pincers, nippers; *med.* forceps; (nut)crackers; **~чики** *m/pl.* [1] tweezers

щит *m* [1 *e.*] shield; *распредели́тельный* ~ switchboard

щитови́дный [14] *железа* thyroid

щу́ка *f* [5] *zo.* pike (fish)

щу́п|альце *n* [11; *g/pl.*: -лец] feeler, tentacle; ~áть [1], ⟨по-⟩ feel; probe; touch; ⟨про-⟩ *fig.* sound; ~лый *coll.* [14; щупл, -á, -о] puny, frail

щу́рить [13] screw up (one's eyes **-ся**)

Э

эваку|áция *f* [7] evacuation; **~и́ровать** [7] (*im*)*pf.* evacuate

эволюцио́нный [14] evolutionary

эги́д|а *f* [5]: **под ~ой** under the aegis (of P)

эгои́|зм [1] ego(t)ism, selfishness; **~ст** *m* [1], **~стка** *f* [5; *g/pl.:* -ток] egoist; **~сти́ческий** [16], **~сти́чный** [14; -чен, -чна] selfish

эй! *int.* hi!, hey!

эквивале́нт [1], **~ный** [14; -тен, -тна] equivalent

экзáм|ен *m* [1] examination (in **по** Д); **~ена́тор** *m* [1] examiner; **~ено-вáть** [7], ⟨про-⟩ examine; **-ся** be examined (by **у** P), have one's examination (with); *p. pr. p.* examine

экземпля́р *m* [1] copy; (*образец*) specimen

экзоти́ческий [16] exotic

экип|áж *m* [1] *naut.*, *ae.* crew; **~ирова́ть** [7] (*im*)*pf.* fit out, equip; **~иро́вка** *f* [5; *g/pl.:* -вок] equipping; equipment

эколо́ги|я *f* [7] ecology; **~ческий** [16] ecologic(al)

эконо́м|ика *f* [5] economy; *наука* economics; **~ить** [14], ⟨с-⟩ save; economize; **~и́ческий** [16] economic; **~ия** *f* [7] economy; saving (of P, **в** П); **~ный** [14; -мен, -мна] economical, thrifty

экра́н *m* [1] *cine.* screen; *fig.* film industry; shield, shade

экскавáтор *m* [1] excavator

экскурс|áнт *m* [1] tourist, excursionist; **~ия** *f* [7] excursion, outing, trip; **~ово́д** *m* [1] guide

экспеди́|тор *m* [1] forwarding agent; **~ция** *f* [7] dispatch, forwarding; expedition

экспер|имента́льный [14] experimental; **~т** *m* [1] expert (in **по** Д); **~ти́за** *f* [5] examination; (expert) opinion

эксплуа|тáтор *m* [1] exploiter; **~тáция** *f* [7] exploitation; *tech.* operation; **сдать в ~тáцию** comission, put into operation; **~ти́ровать** [7] exploit; *tech.* operate, run

экспон|áт *m* [1] exhibit; **~и́ровать** [7] (*im*)*pf.* exhibit; *phot.* expose

э́кспорт *m* [1], **~и́ровать** [7] (*im*)*pf.* export; **~ный** [14] export…

экс|про́мт *m* [1] impromptu, improvisation; **~про́мтом** *a.* extempore; **~тáз** *m* [1] ecstasy; **~трáкт** *m* [1] extract; **~тренный** [14 *sh.*] *выпуск* special; urgent; **в ~тренных слу́чаях** in case of emergency; **~центри́чный** [14; -чен, -чна] eccentric

эласти́чн|ость *f* [8] elasticity; **~ый** [14; -чен, -чна] elastic

элегáнтн|ость *f* [8] elegance; **~ый** [14; -тен, -тна] elegant, stylish

электр|ик *m* [1] electrician; **~и́ческий** [16] electric(al); **~и́чество** *n* [9] electricity; **~и́чка** *f* [5; *g/pl.:* -чек] *coll.* suburban electric train; **~ово́з** *m* [1] electric locomotive; **~омонтёр → ~ик**; **~о́н** *m* [1] electron; **~о́ника** *f* [5] electronics; **~опрово́дка** *f* [5; *g/pl.:* -док] electric wiring; **~останция** *f* [7] electric power station; **~оте́хник** *m* [1] → **эле́ктрик**; **~оте́хника** *f* [5] electrical engineering

элеме́нт *m* [1] element; *comput.* pixel; *el.* cell, battery; *coll.* type, character; **~áрный** [14; -рен, -рна] elementary

эмáл|евый [14], **~ирова́ть** [7], **~ь** *f* [8] enamel

эмбáрго *n* [*indecl.*] embargo; **наложи́ть ~** place an embargo (on **на** В)

эмбле́ма *f* [5] emblem; *mil.* insignia

эмигр|áнт *m* [1], **~áнтка** *f* [5; *g/pl.:* -ток], **~áнтский** [16] emigrant; émigré; **~и́ровать** [7] (*im*)*pf.* emigrate

эми́ссия *f* [7] *денег* emission

эмоциона́льный [14; -лен, -льна] emotional

энерге́тика f [5] power engineering

энерг|и́чный [14; -чен, -чна] energetic; forceful, drastic; *~ия* f [7] energy; *fig. a.* vigo(u)r; *~оёмкий* [16; -мок, -мка] power-consuming

энтузиа́зм m [1] enthusiasm

энциклопе́д|ия f [7] (*a. ~и́ческий слова́рь* m) encyclop(a)edia

эпи|гра́мма f [5] epigram; *~де́мический* [16], *~де́мия* f [7] epidemic; *~зо́д* m [1] episode; *~ле́псия* f [7] epilepsy; *~ло́г* m [1] epilogue; *~тет* m [1] epithet; *~це́нтр* m [1] epicenter, *Brt.* -tre

э́по|с m [1] epic (literature), epos; *~ха* f [5] epoch, era, period (in *в* В)

эроти́ческий [16] erotic

эруди́ция f [5] erudition

эска́др|а f [5] *naut.* squadron; *~и́лья* f [6; *g/pl.:* -лий] *ae.* squadron

эс|кала́тор m [1] escalator; *~ки́з* m [1] sketch; *~кимо́с* m [1] Eskimo, Inuit; *~корти́ровать* [7] escort; *~ми́нец* m [1; -нца] *naut.* destroyer; *~се́нция* f [7] essence; *~тафе́та* f [5] relay race;

~тети́ческий [16] aesthetic

эсто́н|ец m [1; -нца], *~ка* f [5; *g/pl.:* -нок], *~ский* [16] Estonian

эстра́да f [5] stage, platform; → *варьете́*

эта́ж m [1 *e.*] floor, stor(e)y; *дом в три ~а́* three-storied (*Brt.* -reyed) house

э́так(ий) *coll.* → *так(о́й)*

эта́п m [1] stage, phase; *sport* lap

э́тика f [5] ethics (*a. pl.*)

этике́тка f [5; *g/pl.:* -ток] label

этимоло́гия f [7] etymology

этногра́фия f [7] ethnography

э́т|от m, *~а* f, *~о* n, *~и* pl. [27] this, pl. these; *su.* this one; the latter; that; it; there

этю́д m [1] *mus.* étude, exercise; *art lit.* study, sketch; *chess* problem

эфе́с m [1] (*sword*) hilt; *~и́р* m [1] ether; *fig.* air; *переда́ть в ~и́р* broadcast; *~и́рный* [14; -рен, -рна] ethereal

эффект|и́вность f [8] effectiveness, efficacy; *~и́вный* [14; -вен, -вна] efficacious; *~ный* [14; -тен, -тна] effective, striking

эх! *int.* eh!; oh!; ah!

эшело́н m [1] echelon; train

Ю

юбил|е́й m [3] jubilee, anniversary; *~е́йный* [14] jubilee...; *~я́р* m [1] pers. (*or* institution) whose anniversary is being marked

ю́бка f [5; *g/pl.:* ю́бок] culotte, split skirt

ювели́р m [1] jewel(l)er; *~ный* [14)] jewel(l)er's

юг m [1] south; *е́хать на* ~ travel south; → *восто́к; ~о-восто́к* m [1] southeast; *~о-восто́чный* [14] southeast...; *~о-за́пад* m [1] southwest; *~о-за́падный* [14] southwest

ю́жный [14] south(ern); southerly

ю́зом *adv.* skidding

ю́мор m [1] humo(u)r; *~исти́ческий* [16] humorous; comic

ю́нга m [5] sea cadet

ю́ность f [8] youth (*age*)

ю́нош|а m [5; *g/pl.:* -шей] youth (*person*); *~ество* n [9] youth

ю́ный [14; юн, -а́, -о] young, youthful

юри́ди́ческий [16] juridical, legal; of the law; *~ди́ческая консульта́ция* legal advice office; *~сконсульт* m [1] legal adviser

юри́ст m [1] lawyer; legal expert

ю́рк|ий [16; ю́рок, юрка́, -о] nimble, quick; *~нуть* [20] *pf.* scamper, dart (away)

ю́рта f [5] yurt, nomad's tent

юсти́ция f [7] justice

юти́ться [15 *e.*; ючу́сь, юти́шься] huddle together; take shelter

Я

я [20] I; **э́то я** it's me

я́бед|а coll. f [5] tell-tale;**~ничать** [1] tell tales; inform on

я́бло|ко n [9; pl.: -ки, -к] apple; *глазно́е* eyeball;**~ня** f [6] apple tree

яв|и́ть(ся) → **~ля́ть(ся)**;**~ка** f [5] appearance; attendance; rendezvous; *ме́сто* place of (secret) meeting;**~ле́ние** n [12] phenomenon; occurrence; event; *thea.* scene;**~ля́ть** [28], ⟨**~и́ть**⟩ [14] present; display, show;**~ся** appear, turn up; come; (T) be;**~ный** [14; я́вен, я́вна] obvious, evident; *вздор* sheer;**~ствовать** [7] follow (*logically*); be clear

ягнёнок m [2] lamb

я́год|а f [5], **~ный** [14] berry

я́годица f [5] buttock

яд m [1] poison; *fig. a.* venom

я́дерный [14] nuclear

ядови́тый [14 sh.] poisonous; *fig.* venomous

ядрёный coll. [14 sh.] *здоро́вый* strong, stalwart, *моро́з* severe; **~о́** n [9; pl. st.; g/pl.: я́дер] kernel; *phys.*, nucleus; *fig.* core, pith

я́зв|а f [5] ulcer, sore; *fig.* plague;**~и́тельный** [14; -лен, -льна] sarcastic, caustic

язы́к m [1 e.] tongue; language (in **на** П); speech; **на ру́сском ~е́** (*speak, write, etc.*) in Russian; **держа́ть ~ за зуба́ми** hold one's tongue; **~ово́й** [14] language…; linguistic;**~озна́ние** n [12] linguistics

язы́|ческий [16] pagan;**~ество** n [9] paganism;**~ник** m [1] pagan

язычо́к m [1; -чка́] *anat.* uvula

яи́чн|ица f [5] (*a.* **~ица-глазу́нья**) fried eggs pl.;**~ый** [14] egg-…

яйцо́ n [9; pl.: я́йца, яи́ц, я́йцам] egg; **~ вкруту́ю (всмя́тку)** hard-boiled (soft-boiled) egg

я́кобы allegedly; as it were

я́кор|ь m [4; pl.: -ря́, etc.] anchor (at **на** П); **стоя́ть на ~е** ride at anchor

я́м|а f [5] hole, pit; **~(оч)ка** [5; g/pl.: я́мо(че)к] dimple

ямщи́к m [1 e.] *hist.* coachman

янва́рь m [4 e.] January

янта́рь m [4 e.] amber

япо́н|ец m [1; -нца], **~ка** f [5; g/pl.: -нок], **~ский** [16] Japanese

я́ркий [16; я́рок, ярка́, -о; *comp.*: я́рче] *свет* bright; *цвет* vivid, rich; *пла́мя* blazing; *fig.* striking, outstanding

яр|лы́к m [1 e.] label;**~марка** f [5; g/pl.: -рок] fair (at **на** П)

яров|о́й [14] *agric.* spring; *as su.* **~о́е** spring crop

я́рост|ный [14; -тен, -тна] furious, fierce; **~ь** f [8] fury, rage

я́рус m [1] *thea.* circle; *geol.* layer

я́рый [14 sh.] ardent; vehement

я́сень m [4] ash tree

я́сли m/pl. [4; gen.: я́слей] day nursery, Brt. crèche

ясн|ови́дец m [1; -дца] clairvoyant; **~ость** f [8] clarity;**~ый** [14; я́сен, ясна́, -о] clear; bright; *пого́да* fine; (*отчётливый*) distinct; (*очеви́дный*) evident; *отве́т* plain

я́стреб m [1; pl.: -ба́ & -бы] hawk

я́хта f [5] yacht

яче́|йка f [5; g/pl.: -е́ек] *biol. pol.* cell; **~йка па́мяти** *computer* storage cell; **~я́** f [6; g/pl.: ячéй] mesh

ячме́нь m [4 e.] barley; *med.* sty

я́щерица f [5] lizard

я́щик m [1] box, case, chest; *выдвига́ющийся* drawer; **почто́вый ~** mailbox (Brt. letter-box); **откла́дывать в до́лгий ~** shelve, put off

я́щур m [1] foot-and-mouth disease

English – Russian
Dictionary

English – Russian

A

a [eɪ, ə] *неопределённый артикль; как правило, не переводится;* ~ *table* стол; *ten r(o)ubles a dozen* де́сять рубле́й дю́жина

A [eɪ] *su.: from ~ to Z* от "А" до "Я"

aback [ə'bæk] *adv.: taken* ~ поражён, озада́чен

abandon [ə'bændən] **1.** (*give up*) отка́зываться [-за́ться] от (P); (*desert*) оставля́ть [-а́вить], покида́ть [-и́нуть]; ~ *o.s.* преда́(ва́)ться (*to* Д); **2.** непринуждённость *f*; ~**ed** поки́нутый

abase [ə'beɪs] унижа́ть [уни́зить]; ~**ment** [-mənt] униже́ние

abash [ə'bæʃ] смуща́ть [смути́ть]

abate [əb'eɪt] *v/t.* уменьша́ть [-е́ньшить]; *of wind, etc. v/i.* утиха́ть [ути́хнуть]

abb|ess ['æbɪs] настоя́тельница монастыря́; ~**ey** ['æbɪ] монасты́рь *m*; ~**ot** ['æbət] абба́т, настоя́тель *m*

abbreviat|e [ə'bri:vɪeɪt] сокраща́ть [-рати́ть]; ~**ion** [əbri:vɪ'eɪʃn] сокраще́ние

ABC [eibi:'si:] а́збука, алфави́т; (*as*) *easy as* ~ ле́гче лёгкого

abdicat|e ['æbdɪkeɪt] отрека́ться от престо́ла; *of rights, office* отка́зываться [-за́ться] от (P); ~**ion** [æbdɪ'keɪʃn] отрече́ние от престо́ла

abdomen ['æbdəmən] брюшна́я по́лость *f*, *coll.* живо́т

aberration [æbə'reɪʃn] *judg(e)ment or conduct* заблужде́ние; *mental* помраче́ние ума́; *deviation* отклоне́ние от но́рмы; *astr.* аберра́ция

abeyance [ə'beɪəns] состоя́ние неизве́стности; *in ~ law* вре́менно отменённый

abhor [əb'hɔ:] ненави́деть; (*feel disgust*) пита́ть отвраще́ние (к Д); ~**rence** [əb'hɔrəns] отвраще́ние; ~**rent**

[-ənt] □ отврати́тельный

abide [ə'baɪd] [*irr.*]: ~ *by* приде́рживаться (P); *v/t. not* ~ не терпе́ть

ability [ə'bɪlətɪ] спосо́бность *f*

abject ['æbdʒekt] □ жа́лкий; ~ *poverty* кра́йняя нищета́

ablaze [ə'bleɪz]: *be* ~ пыла́ть; ~ *with anger of eyes, cheeks* пыла́ть гне́вом; ~ *with light* я́рко освещён(ный)

able ['eɪbl] □ спосо́бный; *be* ~ мочь, быть в состоя́нии; ~**-bodied** [-bɔdɪd] здоро́вый; го́дный

abnormal [æb'nɔ:məl] ненорма́льный; анома́льный; *med.* ~ *psychology* психопатоло́гия

aboard [ə'bɔ:d] *naut.* на су́дне, на борту́; *go* ~ сади́ться на су́дно (в самолёт; в авто́бус, на по́езд)

abolish [ə'bɔlɪʃ] отменя́ть [-ни́ть]; *of custom, etc.* упраздня́ть [-ни́ть]

A-bomb ['eɪbɔm] а́томная бо́мба

abomina|ble [ə'bɔmɪnəbl] □ отврати́тельный; ~ *snowman* сне́жный челове́к; ~**tion** [əbɔmɪ'neɪʃn] отвраще́ние; *coll.* како́й-то *or* про́сто у́жас

aboriginal [æbə'rɪdʒənl] = **aborigine** [-'rɪdʒɪnɪ] *as su.* коренно́й жи́тель, тузе́мец *m*, -мка *f*, абориге́н; *as adj.* коренно́й, тузе́мный

abortion [ə'bɔ:ʃn] або́рт

abound [ə'baʊnd] быть в изоби́лии; изоби́ловать (*in* T)

about [ə'baʊt] **1.** *prp.* вокру́г (P); о́коло (P); о (П), об (П), насчёт (P); у (P); про (B); **2.** *adv.* вокру́г, везде́; приблизи́тельно; *be* ~ *to* собира́ться

above [ə'bʌv] **1.** *prp.* над (T); вы́ше (P); свы́ше (P); ~ *all* пре́жде всего́; **2.** *adv.* наверху́, наве́рх; вы́ше; **3.** *adj.* вышеска́занный; ~**-board**

[-'bɔːd] *adv. & adj.* че́стный, откры́тый; **~-mentioned** [-'menʃənd] вышеупомя́нутый

abrasion [ə'breɪʒn] *of skin* сса́дина

abreast [ə'brest] в ряд; **keep ~ of** *fig.* быть в ку́рсе; **keep ~ of the times** идти́ в но́гу со вре́менем

abridg|e [ə'brɪdʒ] сокраща́ть [-рати́ть]; **~(e)ment** [-mənt] сокраще́ние

abroad [ə'brɔːd] за грани́цей, за грани́цу; **there is a rumo(u)r ~** хо́дит слух

abrogate [ə'brəgeɪt] *v/t.* отменя́ть [-ни́ть]; аннули́ровать *(im)pf.*

abrupt [ə'brʌpt] *(steep)* круто́й; *(sudden)* внеза́пный; *(blunt)* ре́зкий

abscess [ˈæbsɪs] нары́в, абсце́сс

abscond [əb'skɒnd] *v/i.* скры(ва́)ться, укры́(ва́)ться

absence [ˈæbsəns] отсу́тствие; **~ of mind** рассе́янность *f*

absent 1. [ˈæbsənt] ☐ отсу́тствующий *(a. fig.)*; **2.** [æb'sent] **~ o.s.** отлуча́ться [-чи́ться]; **~-minded** рассе́янный

absolute [ˈæbsəluːt] ☐ абсолю́тный; *coll.* по́лный, соверше́нный

absorb [əb'sɔːb] впи́тывать [впита́ть], поглоща́ть [-лоти́ть] *(a. fig.)*; *of gas, etc.* абсорби́ровать *(im)pf.*; **~ing** [-ɪŋ] *fig.* увлека́тельный

abstain [əb'steɪn] возде́рживаться [-жа́ться] **(from** от Р**)**

abstention [əb'stenʃən] воздержа́ние

abstinence [ˈæbstɪnəns] уме́ренность *f*; *from drink* тре́звость *f*

abstract 1. [ˈæbstrækt] отвлечённый, абстра́ктный *(a. gr.)*; **2.** резюме́, кра́ткий обзо́р; **in the ~** теорети́чески; **3.** [æb'strækt] *(take out)* извлека́ть [-ле́чь]; *(purloin)* похища́ть [-хи́тить]; резюми́ровать *(im)pf.*; **~ed** [-ɪd] *of person* погружённый в свои́ мы́сли; **~ion** [-kʃn] абстра́кция

abstruse [æb'struːs] ☐ *fig.* непоня́тный, тёмный, мудрёный

abundan|ce [ə'bʌndəns] изоби́лие; **~t** [-dənt] ☐ оби́льный, бога́тый

abus|e [ə'bjuːs] **1.** *(misuse)* злоупотребле́ние; *(insult)* оскорбле́ние; *(curse)* брань *f*; **2.** [ə'bjuːz] злоупотребля́ть [-би́ть] (Т); [вы́]руга́ть; **~ive** [ə'bjuː-

sɪv] ☐ оскорби́тельный

abyss [ə'bɪs] бе́здна

acacia [ə'keɪʃə] ака́ция

academic|(al ☐) [ækə'demɪk(əl)] акаде́мический; **~ian** [əkædə'mɪʃn] акаде́мик

accede [æk'siːd] **~ to** *(assent)* соглаша́ться [-аси́ться] (с Т); *of office* вступа́ть [-пи́ть] (в В)

accelerat|e [ək'seləreɪt] ускоря́ть [-о́рить]; **~or** [ək'seləreɪtə] *mot.* педа́ль *f* га́за

accent [ˈæksənt] *(stress)* ударе́ние; *(mode of utterance)* произноше́ние, акце́нт; **~uate** [æk'sentjʊeɪt] де́лать и́ли ста́вить ударе́ние на (П); *fig.* подчёркивать [-черкну́ть]

accept [ək'sept] принима́ть [-ня́ть], соглаша́ться [-гласи́ться] (с Т); **~able** [ək'septəbl] ☐ прие́млемый; *of a gift* прия́тный; **~ance** [ək'septəns] приня́тие; *(approval)* одобре́ние; *comm.* акце́пт

access [ˈækses] до́ступ; *(way)* прохо́д, прое́зд; **easy of ~** досту́пный; **access code** *comput.* код до́ступа; **~ory** [æk'sesərɪ] соуча́стник (-ица); **~ible** [æk'sesəbl] ☐ досту́пный, достижи́мый; **~ion** [æk'seʃn]; **~ to the throne** вступле́ние на престо́л

accessory [æk'sesərɪ] ☐ **1.** дополни́тельный, второстепе́нный; **2.** *pl.* принадле́жности *f/pl.*; *gloves, etc.* аксессуа́ры

accident [ˈæksɪdənt] *(chance)* случа́йность *f*; *(mishap)* несча́стный слу́чай; *mot., tech.* ава́рия; *rail.* круше́ние; **~al** [æksɪ'dentl] случа́йный

acclaim [ə'kleɪm] **1.** аплоди́ровать; приве́тствовать; **2.** приве́тствие; ова́ция

acclimatize [ə'klaɪmətaɪz] акклиматизи́ровать(ся) *(im)pf.*

accommodat|e [ə'kɒmədeɪt] *(adapt)* приспособля́ть [-собить]; предоста́вить жильё (Д); *(hold)* вмеща́ть [вмести́ть]; *comm.* вы́да(ва́)ть ссу́ду; **~ion** [əkɒmə'deɪʃn] жильё, помеще́ние

accompan|iment [ə'kʌmpənɪmənt] сопровожде́ние; аккомпанеме́нт; **~y** [-pənɪ] v/t. (escort) сопровожда́ть [-води́ть]; mus. аккомпани́ровать (Д)

accomplice [ə'kʌmplɪs] соуча́стник (-ица) (in crime)

accomplish [ə'kʌmplɪʃ] (fulfill) выполня́ть [вы́полнить]; (achieve) достига́ть [-и́гнуть] (Р); (complete) заверша́ть [-и́ть]; **~ment** [-mənt] выполне́ние; достиже́ние

accord [ə'kɔːd] 1. (agreement) согла́сие; соглаше́ние; **of one's own** по со́бственному жела́нию; **with one** ~ единоду́шно; 2. v/i. согласо́вываться [-сова́ться] (с Т), гармони́ровать (с Т); v/t. предоставля́ть [-ста́вить]; **~ance** [-əns] согла́сие; **in ~ with** в соотве́тствии с (Т); **~ing** [-ɪŋ]: **~ to** согла́сно (Д); **~ingly** [-ɪŋlɪ] adv. соотве́тственно; таки́м о́бразом

accost [ə'kɒst] загова́ривать [-вори́ть] с (Т)

account [ə'kaʊnt] 1. comm. счёт; (report) отчёт; (description) сообще́ние, описа́ние; **by all ~s** су́дя по всему́; **on no ~** ни в ко́ем слу́чае; **on ~ of** из-за (Р); **take into ~, take ~ of** принима́ть во внима́ние; **turn to (good) ~** испо́льзовать (с вы́годой) (im)pf.; **call to ~** призыва́ть к отве́ту; **~ number** но́мер счёта; 2. v/i. **~ for** отвеча́ть [-е́тить] за (В); (explain) объясня́ть [-ни́ть]; v/t. (consider) счита́ть [счесть] (В/Т); **~able** [ə'kaʊntəbl] □ (responsible) отве́тственный (**to** пе́ред Т, **for** за В); **~ant** [-ənt] квалифици́рованный бухга́лтер

accredit [ə'kredɪt] of ambassador, etc. аккредитова́ть (im)pf.; (attribute) припи́сывать [-са́ть]; credit выдава́ть [-дать] креди́т

accrue [ə'kruː]: **~d interest** наро́сшие проце́нты

accumulat|e [ə'kjuːmjʊleɪt] нака́пливать(ся) [-копи́ть(ся)]; скопля́ть(ся) [-пи́ть(ся)]; **~ion** [əkjuːmjuːˈleɪʃn] накопле́ние; скопле́ние

accura|cy ['ækjʊrəsɪ] то́чность f; **in shooting** ме́ткость f; **~te** [-rɪt]

то́чный; of aim or shot ме́ткий

accurs|ed [ə'kɜːsɪd], **~t** [-st] про́кля́тый

accus|ation [ækjuːˈzeɪʃn] обвине́ние; **~e** [ə'kjuːz] обвиня́ть [-ни́ть]; **~er** [-ə] обвини́тель m, -ница f

accustom [ə'kʌstəm] приуча́ть [-чи́ть] (**to** к Д); **get ~ed** привыка́ть [-вы́кнуть] (**to** к Д); **~ed** [-d] привы́чный; (inured) приу́ченный; (usual) обы́чный

ace [eɪs] туз; fig. первокла́ссный лётчик, ас; **be within an ~ of** быть на волосо́к от (Р)

acerbity [ə'sɜːbətɪ] те́рпкость f

acet|ic [ə'siːtɪk] у́ксусный

ache [eɪk] 1. боль f; 2. v/i. боле́ть

achieve [ə'tʃiːv] достига́ть [-и́гнуть] (Р); **~ment** [-mənt] достиже́ние

acid ['æsɪd] 1. кислота́; 2. ки́слый; fig. е́дкий; **~ rain** кисло́тный дождь

acknowledg|e [ək'nɒlɪdʒ] v/t. подтвержда́ть [-ерди́ть]; confess призна́(ва́)ть; **~(e)ment** [-mənt] призна́ние; подтвержде́ние

acorn ['eɪkɔːn] bot. жёлудь m

acoustics [ə'kaʊstɪks] аку́стика

acquaint [ə'kweɪnt] v/t. [по]знако́мить; **~ o.s. with** ознако́миться с (Т); **be ~ed with** быть знако́мым с (Т); **~ance** [-əns] знако́мство; pers. знако́мый; **make s.o.'s ~** познако́миться с ке́м-л.

acquire [ə'kwaɪə] v/t. приобрета́ть [-ести́]

acquisition [ækwɪˈzɪʃn] приобрете́ние

acquit [ə'kwɪt] law v/t. опра́вдывать [-да́ть]; **~ o.s. well** хорошо́ прояви́ть себя́; **~tal** [-l] оправда́ние

acrid ['ækrɪd] о́стрый, е́дкий (a. fig.)

across [ə'krɒs] 1. adv. поперёк; на ту сто́рону; **two miles ~** ширино́й в две ми́ли; 2. prp. че́рез (В)

act [ækt] 1. v/i. де́йствовать; поступа́ть [-пи́ть]; thea. игра́ть [сыгра́ть]; 2. посту́пок; постановле́ние, зако́н; thea. де́йствие, акт; **~ing** [-ɪŋ] 1. исполня́ющий обя́занности; 2. thea. игра́

action ['ækʃn] (*conduct*) посту́пок; (*acting*) де́йствие; (*activity*) де́ятельность *f*, *mil.* бой; *law* иск; *take* ~ принима́ть ме́ры

activ|e ['æktɪv] □ акти́вный; энерги́чный; де́ятельный; ~ity [æk'tɪvətɪ] де́ятельность *f*, рабо́та; акти́вность *f*; эне́ргия

act|or ['æktə] актёр; ~ress [-trɪs] актри́са

actual ['æktʃʊəl] □ действи́тельный; факти́ческий; ~ly факти́чески, на са́мом де́ле

acute [ə'kjuːt] □ си́льный, о́стрый; (*penetrating*) проница́тельный

adamant ['ædəmənt] *fig.* непрекло́нный

adapt [ə'dæpt] приспособля́ть [-посо́бить] (*to*, *for* к Д); *text* адапти́ровать; ~ *o.s.* адапти́роваться; ~ation [ædæp'teɪʃn] приспособле́ние; *of text* обрабо́тка; *of organism* адапта́ция

add [æd] *v/t.* прибавля́ть [-а́вить]; *math.* скла́дывать [сложи́ть]; *v/i.* увели́чи(ва)ть (*to* В)

addict ['ædɪkt]: *drug* ~ нарком́ан; ~ed [ə'dɪktɪd] скло́нный (*to* к Д)

addition [ə'dɪʃn] *math.* сложе́ние; прибавле́ние; *in* ~ кро́ме того́, к тому́ же; *in* ~ *to* вдоба́вок к (Д); ~al [-əl] доба́вочный, дополни́тельный

address [ə'dres] *v/t.* **1.** *a letter* адресова́ть (*im*)*pf*.; (*speak to*) обраща́ться [обрати́ться] к (Д); **2.** а́дрес; обраще́ние; речь *f*; ~ee [ædre'siː] адреса́т

adept ['ædept] иску́сный; уме́лый

adequa|cy ['ædɪkwəsɪ] соотве́тствие; доста́точность *f*, адеква́тность; ~te [-kwɪt] (*sufficient*) доста́точный; (*suitable*) соотве́тствующий, адеква́тный

adhere [əd'hɪə] прилипа́ть [-ли́пнуть] (*to* к Д), *fig.* приде́рживаться (*to* Р); ~nce [-rəns] приве́рженность *f*; ~nt [-rənt] приве́рженец (-нка)

adhesive [əd'hiːsɪv] ли́пкий, кле́йкий; ~ *plaster* лейкопла́стырь *m*; ~ *tape* ли́пкая ле́нта

adjacent [ə'dʒeɪsənt] □ сме́жный (*to* с Т), сосе́дний

adjoin [ə'dʒɔɪn] примыка́ть [-мкну́ть] к (Д); прилега́ть *pf.* к (Д)

adjourn [ə'dʒɜːn] *v/t.* (*suspend proceedings*) закрыва́ть [-ы́ть]; (*carry over*) переноси́ть [-нести́]; (*postpone*) отсро́чи(ва)ть; *parl.* дел́ать переры́в; ~ment [-mənt] отсро́чка; переры́в

administ|er [əd'mɪnɪstə] руководи́ть, управля́ть (Т); ~ *justice* отправля́ть правосу́дие; ~ration [ədmɪnɪ'streɪʃn] администра́ция; ~rative [əd'mɪnɪstrətɪv] администрати́вный; исполни́тельный; ~rator [əd'mɪnɪstreɪtə] администра́тор

admir|able ['ædmərəbl] превосхо́дный; замеча́тельный; ~ation [ædmɪ'reɪʃən] восхище́ние; ~e [əd'maɪə] восхища́ться [-и́ться] (Т); [по]любова́ться (Т *or* на В)

admiss|ible [əd'mɪsəbl] □ допусти́мый, прие́млемый; ~ion [əd'mɪʃən] (*access*) вход; (*confession*) призна́ние; ~ *fee* пла́та за вход

admit [əd'mɪt] *v/t.* (*let in*) впуска́ть [-сти́ть]; (*allow*) допуска́ть [-сти́ть]; (*confess*) призна́(ва́)ть(ся); ~tance [-əns] до́ступ, вход

admixture [əd'mɪkstʃə] при́месь *f*

admon|ish [əd'mɒnɪʃ] (*exhort*) увеще(ва)́ть *impf.*; (*warn*) предостерега́ть [-ре́чь] (*of* от Р); ~ition [ædmə'nɪʃn] увеща́ние; предостереже́ние

ado [ə'duː] суета́; хло́поты *f/pl.*; *without much* ~ без вся́ких церемо́ний

adolescen|ce [ædə'lesəns] о́трочество; ~t [-snt] **1.** подростко́вый; **2.** *person* подро́сток

adopt [ə'dɒpt] *v/t.* усыновля́ть [-ви́ть]; *girl* удочеря́ть [-ри́ть]; *resolution, etc.* принима́ть [-ня́ть]; ~ion [ə'dɒpʃn] усыновле́ние; удочере́ние; приня́тие

ador|able [ə'dɔːrəbl] обожа́емый, преле́стный; ~ation [ædə'reɪʃn] обожа́ние; ~e [ə'dɔː] *v/t.* обожа́ть

adorn [ə'dɔːn] украша́ть [укра́сить]; ~ment [-mənt] украше́ние

adroit [ə'drɔɪt] □ ло́вкий, иску́сный

adult ['ædʌlt] взрослый, совершеннолетний

adulter|ate [ə'dʌltəreɪt] (debase) [ис]портить; (dilute) разбавлять [-а́вить]; фальсифицировать (im)pf.; **~y** [-гɪ] нарушение супружеской верности, адюльтер

advance [əd'vɑ:ns] 1. v/i. mil. наступать; (move forward) продвигаться [продвинуться]; (a. fig.) делать успехи; v/t. продвигать [-инуть]; idea, etc. выдвигать [выдвинуть]; платить авансом; 2. mil. наступление; in studies успех; прогресс; of salary аванс; **~d** [əd'vɑ:nst] передовой; in years престарелый, пожилой; **~ment** [-mənt] успех; продвижение

advantage [əd'vɑ:ntɪdʒ] преимущество; (benefit) выгода; **take ~ of** [вос]пользоваться (Т); **~ous** [ædvən'teɪdʒəs, ædvən~] выгодный, полезный, благоприятный

adventur|e [əd'ventʃə] приключение; **~er** [-гə] искатель приключений; авантюрист; **~ous** [-гəs] предприимчивый; авантюрный

advers|ary ['ædvəsərɪ] (antagonist) противник (-ица); (opponent) соперник (-ица); **~e** ['ædvɜːs] неблагоприятный; **~ity** [əd'vɜːsɪtɪ] несчастье, беда

advertis|e ['ædvətaɪz] рекламировать (im)pf.; in newspaper помещать [-естить] объявление; **~ement** [əd'vɜːtɪsmənt] объявление; реклама; **~ing** [ædvə'taɪzɪŋ] рекламный

advice [əd'vaɪs] совет

advis|able [əd'vaɪzəbl] □ желательный, целесообразный; **~e** [əd'vaɪz] v/t. [по]советовать (Д), [по]рекомендовать; (inform) сообщать [-щить]; **~er** [-ə] official советник, professional консультант

advocate 1. ['ædvəkət] сторонник (-ица); law адвокат, защитник; 2. [-keɪt] поддерживать; speak in favo(u)r of выступить [выступить] (за В)

aerial ['eərɪəl] антенна; **outdoor ~** наружная антенна

aero... [eərə] а́эро...; **~bics** [-bɪks] аэробика; **~drome** ['eərədrəum] аэродром; **~naut** [-nɔːt] аэронавт; **~nautics** [-nɔːtɪks] аэронавтика; **~plane** [-pleɪn] самолёт; **~sol** [-səl] аэрозоль m; **~stat** [-stæt] аэростат

aesthetic [iːs'θetɪk] эстетический; **~s** [-s] эстетика

afar [ə'fɑː] adv.: вдалеке; **from ~** издалека

affable ['æfəbl] приветливый

affair [ə'feə] business дело; love любовная связь f, роман

affect [ə'fekt] v/t. [по]влиять на (В); зад(ев)а́ть; med. поражать [-разить]; (pretend) притворяться [-риться]; **~ation** [æfek'teɪʃən] жеманство; **~ed** [ə'fektɪd] □ притворный; манерный; **~ion** [ə'fekʃn] привязанность f, любовь f; **~ionate** [ə'fekʃnət] □ нежный, ласковый, любящий

affiliate [ə'fɪlɪeɪt] 1. v/t. join, attach присоединять [-нить] (как филиал); 2. дочерняя компания; компания-филиал

affinity [ə'fɪnɪtɪ] closeness близость f, relationship родство; attraction влечение

affirm [ə'fɜːm] утверждать [-рдить], **~ation** [æfə'meɪʃn] утверждение; **~ative** [ə'fɜːmətɪv] □ утвердительный

affix [ə'fɪks] прикреплять [-пить] (**to** к Д)

afflict [ə'flɪkt]: **be ~ed** страдать (**with** Т, от Р); постигать [-ичь or -игнуть]; **~ion** [ə'flɪkʃn] го́ре; недуг

affluen|ce ['æfluəns] изобилие, богатство; **~t** [-ənt] □ обильный, богатый

afford [ə'fɔːd] позволять [-волить] себе; **I can ~ it** я могу себе это позволить; yield, give (пре-)доставлять [-а́вить]

affront [ə'frʌnt] 1. оскорблять [-бить]; 2. оскорбление

afield [ə'fiːld] adv. вдалеке; **far ~** далеко

afloat [ə'fləut] на воде, на плаву (a. fig.)

afraid [ə'freɪd] испу́ганный; *be ~ of* боя́ться (P)

afresh [ə'freʃ] *adv.* сно́ва, сы́знова

African ['æfrɪkən] **1.** африка́нец (-нка); **2.** африка́нский

after ['ɑːftə] **1.** *adv.* пото́м, по́сле, зате́м; позади́; *shortly ~* вско́ре; **2.** *prp.* за (T), позади́ (P); че́рез (B); по́сле (P); *time~time* оди́н раз; *~all* в конце́ концо́в; всё же; **3.** *cj.* с тех пор, как; по́сле того́, как; **4.** *adj.* после́дующий; ~**math** ['ɑːftəmæθ] отава; *fig.* после́дствия *n/pl.;* ~**noon** [-'nuːn] вре́мя по́сле полу́дня; ~**taste** (остаю́щийся) при́вкус; ~**thought** мысль, прише́дшая по́здно; ~**wards** [-wədz] *adv.* впосле́дствии, пото́м

again [ə'gen] *adv.* сно́ва, опя́ть; *~ and ~, time and ~* неоднокра́тно; сно́ва и сно́ва; *as much ~* ещё сто́лько же

against [ə'genst] *prp.* про́тив (P); о, об (B); на (B); *as ~* по сравне́нию с (T); *~ the wall* у стены́, к стене́

age [eɪdʒ] **1.** век, во́зраст; года́ *m/pl.;* век, эпо́ха; *of ~* совершенноле́тний; *under ~* несовершенноле́тний; **2.** *v/t.* [co]ста́рить; *v/i.* [по]ста́рить; ~**d** ['eɪdʒɪd] престаре́лый

agency ['eɪdʒənsɪ] аге́нтство

agenda [ə'dʒendə] пове́стка дня

agent ['eɪdʒənt] аге́нт; дове́ренное лицо́; *chem.* сре́дство

aggravate ['ægrəveɪt] (*make worse*) усугубля́ть [-би́ть]; ухудша́ть [уху́дшить]; (*irritate*) раздража́ть [-жи́ть]

aggregate ['ægrɪgət] совоку́пность; о́бщее число́; *in the ~* в це́лом

aggress|ion [ə'greʃn] агре́ссия; ~**or** [ə'gresə] агре́ссор

aghast [ə'gɑːst] ошеломлённый, поражённый у́жасом

agil|e ['ædʒaɪl] □ прово́рный, подви́жный, живо́й; *~ity* [ə'dʒɪlɪtɪ] прово́рство; жи́вость *f*

agitat|e ['ædʒɪteɪt] *v/t.* [вз]волнова́ть, возбужда́ть [-уди́ть]; *v/i.* агити́ровать (*for* за B); ~**ion** [ædʒɪ'teɪʃn] волне́ние; агита́ция

agnail ['ægneɪl] заусе́ница

ago [ə'gəu]: *a year ~* год тому́ наза́д;

long ~ давно́; *not long ~* неда́вно

agonizing ['ægənaɪzɪŋ] мучи́тельный

agony ['ægənɪ] аго́ния; муче́ние

agree [ə'griː] *v/i.* (*consent, accept*) соглаша́ться [-ласи́ться] (*to* с T, на B); *~ (up)on* (*settle, arrange*) усла́вливаться [усло́виться] о (P)); (*reach a common decision*) догова́риваться [-вори́ться]; (*pleasing*) ~**able** [-əbl] прия́тный; (*consenting*) согла́сный (*to* с T, на B); ~**ment** [~mənt] согла́сие; (*contract, etc.*) соглаше́ние, догово́р

agricultur|al [ægrɪ'kʌltʃərəl] сельскохозя́йственный; ~**e** ['ægrɪkʌltʃə] се́льское хозя́йство; земледе́лие; ~**ist** [ægrɪ'kʌltʃərɪst] агроно́м

ahead [ə'hed] вперёд, впереди́; *straight ~* пря́мо, вперёд

aid [eɪd] **1.** по́мощь *f;* по́мощник (-ица); *pl.* (*financial, etc.*) посо́бия; **2.** помога́ть [помо́чь] (Д)

AIDS [eɪdz] *med.* СПИД (синдро́м приобретённого иммунодефици́та); ~**infected** инфици́рованный СПИДом

ail|ing ['eɪlɪŋ] больно́й, нездоро́вый; ~**ment** ['eɪlmənt] недомога́ние, боле́знь *f*

aim [eɪm] **1.** *v/i.* прице́ли(ва)ться (*at* в B); *fig.* ~ *at* име́ть в виду́; *v/t.* направля́ть [-ра́вить] (*at* на B); **2.** цель *f,* наме́рение; ~**less** [eɪmlɪs] □ бесце́льный

air¹ [eə] **1.** во́здух; *by ~* самолётом; авиапо́чтой; *go on the ~ of person* выступа́ть [вы́ступить] по ра́дио; *in the ~* (*uncertain*) висе́ть в во́здухе; *of rumour, etc.* носи́ться в во́здухе; *clear the ~* разряжа́ть [-яди́ть] атмосфе́ру. **2.** (*ventilate*) прове́три(ва)ть(ся) (*a. fig.*)

air² [-] вид; *give o.s. ~s* ва́жничать

air³ [-] *mus.* мело́дия; пе́сня

air|bag поду́шка безопа́сности; ~**base** авиаба́за; ~**conditioned** с кондициони́рованным во́здухом; ~**craft** самолёт; ~**field** аэродро́м; ~**force** вое́нно-возду́шные си́лы; ~ *hostess* стюарде́сса; ~**lift** возду́шная перево́зка; ~**line** авиали́ния; ~**liner** (авиа)ла́йнер; ~**mail** авиапо́чта; ~**man** лётчик, авиа́тор; ~**plane** *Am.* самолёт; ~**port** аэропо́рт; ~**raid** возду́шный налёт; ~**shelter** бомбоубе́жище; ~**strip** взлётнопоса́дочная полоса́; ~**tight** гермети́ческий

airy ['eəri] □ по́лный во́здуха; *of plans, etc.* беспе́чный, легкомы́сленный

aisle [ail] *thea.* прохо́д (ме́жду ряда́ми)

ajar [ə'dʒɑː] приоткры́тый

akin [ə'kın] ро́дственный, сро́дный (**to** Д)

alacrity [ə'lækrıtı] гото́вность *f*; рве́ние

alarm [ə'lɑːm] **1.** трево́га; (*fear*) страх; *tech.* трево́жно-предупреди́тельная сигнализа́ция; **2.** [вс]трево́жить, [вз]волнова́ть; ~ **clock** буди́льник; ~**ing** [-ıŋ] *adj.*: ~ **news** трево́жные изве́стия *n/pl.*

album ['ælbəm] альбо́м

alcohol ['ælkəhɒl] алкого́ль *m*; спирт; ~**ic** [ælkə'hɒlık] **1.** алкого́льный; **2.** алкого́лик; ~**ism** ['ælkəhɒlızəm] алкоголи́зм

alcove ['ælkəʊv] алько́в, ни́ша

alder ['ɔːldə] ольха́

ale [eıl] пи́во, эль *m*

alert [ə'lɜːt] **1.** □ (*lively*) живо́й, прово́рный; (*watchful*) бди́тельный; насторо́женный; **2.** сигна́л трево́ги; **on the** ~ насторо́же

algorithm ['ælgərıðəm] алгори́тм

alien ['eılıən] **1.** иностра́нный; чу́ждый; **2.** иностра́нец *m*, -ка *f*; ~**ate** [-eıt] *law* отчужда́ть; (*estrange*) отдаля́ть [-ли́ть]; (*turn away*) отта́лкивать [-толкну́ть]

alight¹ [ə'laıt] сходи́ть [сойти́] (с Р)

alight² [-] *pred. adj.* (*on fire*) зажжённый; в огне́; (*lit up*) освещённый

align [ə'laın] выра́внивать(ся) [вы́ровнять(ся)]; ~**ment** [-mənt] выра́внивание; (*arrangement*) расста́новка

alike [ə'laık] **1.** *pred. adj.* (*similar*) подо́бный, похо́жий; (*as one*) одина́ковый; **2.** *adv.* то́чно так же; подо́бно

alimentary [ælı'mentərı]: ~ **canal** пищевари́тельный тракт

alimony ['ælımənı] алиме́нты *m/pl.*

alive [ə'laıv] (*living*) живо́й; (*alert, keen*) чу́ткий (**to** к Д); (*infested*) киша́щий (**with** Т); **be** ~ **to** я́сно понима́ть

all [ɔːl] **1.** *adj.* весь *m*, вся *f*, всё *n*, все *pl*; вся́кий; всевозмо́жный; **for** ~ **that** несмотря́ на то; **2.** всё, все; **at** ~ вообще́; **not at** ~ во́все не; **not at** ~**!** не́ за что!; **for** ~ (**that**) *I care* мне безразли́чно; **for** ~ **I know** наско́лько я зна́ю; **3.** *adv.* вполне́, всеце́ло, соверше́нно; ~ **at once** сра́зу; ~ **the better** тем лу́чше; ~ **but** почти́; ~ **right** хорошо́, ла́дно

allay [ə'leı] успока́ивать [-ко́ить]

allegation [ælı'geıʃn] голосло́вное утвержде́ние

allege [ə'ledʒ] утвержда́ть (без основа́ния)

allegiance [ə'liːdʒəns] ве́рность *f*, пре́данность *f*

allergic [ə'lɜːdʒık] аллерги́ческий; ~**y** ['ælədʒı] аллерги́я

alleviate [ə'liːvıeıt] облегча́ть [-чи́ть]

alley ['ælı] переу́лок; **blind** ~ тупи́к

alliance [ə'laıəns] сою́з

allocate ['æləkeıt] *money* ассигнова́ть; *land, money* выделя́ть [вы́делить] (*distribute*); распределя́ть [-ли́ть]; ~**ion** [ælə'keıʃn] распределе́ние

allot [ə'lɒt] *v/t.* распределя́ть [-ли́ть]; разда(ва́)ть; ~**ment** [-mənt] распределе́ние; до́ля, часть *f*; *Brt.* (*plot of land*) земе́льный уча́сток

allow [ə'laʊ] позволя́ть [-о́лить]; допуска́ть [-сти́ть]; *Am.* утвержда́ть; ~**able** [-əbl] □ позволи́тельный; ~**ance** [-əns] посо́бие, пе́нсия; *fin.* ски́дка; **make** ~ **for** принима́ть во внима́ние

alloy ['ælɔı] сплав

all-purpose многоцелево́й, универса́льный

all-round всесторо́нний

allude [ə'luːd] ссыла́ться [сосла́ться] (**to** на В); (*hint at*) намека́ть [-кну́ть] (**to** на В)

allure [ə'ljʊə] (*charm*) привлека́ть

[-лечь]; (*lure*) завлека́ть [-ле́чь]; ~ing привлека́тельный, зама́нчивый

allusion [ə'lu:ʒn] намёк, ссы́лка

ally [ə'laɪ] **1.** соединя́ть [-ни́ть] (*to, with* с Т); **2.** сою́зник

almighty [ɔ:l'maɪtɪ] всемогу́щий

almond [ɑːmənd] минда́ль *m*

almost ['ɔ:lməʊst] почти́, едва́ не

alone [ə'ləʊn] оди́н *m*, одна́ *f*, одно́ *n*, одни́ *pl.*; одино́кий (-кая); *let* (*или* *leave*) ~ оста́вить *pf.* в поко́е; *let* ~ ... не говоря́ уже́ о ... (П)

along [ə'lɒŋ] **1.** *adv.* вперёд; *all* ~ всё вре́мя; ~ *with* вме́сте с (Т); *coll. get* ~ *with you!* убира́йтесь; **2.** *prp.* вдоль (Р), по (Д); ~**side** [-saɪd] бок о́ бок, ря́дом

aloof [ə'lu:f]: *stand* ~ держа́ться в стороне́ *or* особняко́м

aloud [ə'laʊd] гро́мко, вслух

alpha|bet ['ælfəbet] алфави́т; ~**betic** [,-'etɪk] азбучный, алфави́тный; ~**numeric** *comput.* алфави́тно- *or* бу́квенно-цифрово́й

already [ɔ:l'redɪ] уже́

also ['ɔ:lsəʊ] та́кже, то́же

altar ['ɔ:ltə] алта́рь *m*

alter ['ɔ:ltə] *v/t. & v/i.* меня́т(ся) (*impf.*); изменя́ть(ся) [-ни́ть(ся)]; ~**ation** [ɔ:ltə'reɪʃn] измене́ние, переде́лка (*to* Р)

alternat|e 1. ['ɔ:ltəneɪt] чередова́ть(ся); **2.** [ɔ:l'tɜ:nɪt] □ переме́нный; *alternating current* переме́нный ток; ~**ion** [ɔ:ltə'neɪʃn] чередова́ние; ~**ive** [ɔ:l'tɜ:nətɪv] **1.** альтернати́вный; переме́нно де́йствующий; **2.** альтернати́ва; вы́бор

although [ɔ:l'ðəʊ] хотя́

altitude ['æltɪtju:d] высота́

altogether [ɔ:ltə'ɡeðə] (*entirely*) вполне́, соверше́нно; (*in general*; *as a whole*) в це́лом, в о́бщем

alumin(i)um [æljʊ'mɪnɪəm, *Am:* ə'lu:mɪnəm] алюми́ний

always ['ɔ:lweɪz] всегда́

Alzheimer's disease ['æltshaɪməz] боле́знь Альцге́ймера

am [æm; *в предложении:* əm] [*irr.*] *1st pers. sg. pr. om* **be**

A.M. (*abbr. of* **ante meridiem**) утра́, у́тром

amalgamate [ə'mælɡəmeɪt] *v/t.* объединя́ть [-ни́ть]; *v/i.* объединя́ться [-ни́ться] (*with* с Т)

amass [ə'mæs] соб(и)ра́ть; (*accumulate*) накопля́ть [-пи́ть]

amateur ['æmətə] люби́тель *m*, -ница *f*; дилета́нт *m*, -ка *f*, *attr.* люби́тельский

amaz|e [ə'meɪz] изумля́ть [-ми́ть], пора́жа́ть [порази́ть]; ~**ement** [-mənt] изумле́ние; ~**ing** [ə'meɪzɪŋ] удиви́тельный, порази́тельный

ambassador [æm'bæsədə] посо́л

amber ['æmbə] янта́рь *m*

ambigu|ity [æmbɪ'ɡju:ətɪ] двусмы́сленность *f*; ~**ous** [æm'bɪɡjʊəs] □ двусмы́сленный

ambitio|n [æm'bɪʃn] честолю́бие; (*aim*) мечта́, стремле́ние; ~**us** [-ʃəs] честолюби́вый

amble ['æmbl] идти́ лёгкой похо́дкой, прогу́ливаться

ambulance ['æmbjʊləns] маши́на ско́рой по́мощи

ambush ['æmbʊʃ] заса́да

amenable [ə'mi:nəbl] (*tractable*) □ пода́тливый; (*obedient*) послу́шный; (*complaisant*) сгово́рчивый

amend [ə'mend] исправля́ть(ся) [-а́вить(ся)]; вноси́ть [внести́] попра́вки в (В); ~**ment** [-mənt] исправле́ние; попра́вка; ~**s** [ə'mendz]: *make* ~ *for* компенси́ровать (В)

amenity [ə'mi:nətɪ] *mst. pl.* удо́бства; *in town* места́ о́тдыха и развлече́ний; *of family life* пре́лести

American [ə'merɪkən] **1.** америка́нец *m*, -нка *f*; **2.** америка́нский

amiable ['eɪmjəbl] □ доброду́шный; (*sweet*) ми́лый

amicable ['æmɪkəbl] □ дружелю́бный, дру́жественный

amid(st) [ə'mɪd(st)] среди́ (Р), посреди́ (Р), ме́жду (Т)

amiss [ə'mɪs] *adv.* непра́вильно; *take* ~ обижа́ться [оби́деться]

amity ['æmɪtɪ] дру́жба

ammonia [ə'məʊnɪə] аммиа́к; *liquid* ~

нашатырный спирт

ammunition [æmju'nɪʃn] боеприпасы *m/pl.*

amnesty ['æmnəstɪ] **1.** амнистия; **2.** амнистировать (*im*)*pf.*

among(st) [ə'mʌŋ(st)] среди (P), между (T *sometimes* P)

amoral [eɪ'mɒrəl] □ аморальный

amorous ['æmərəs] □ (*in love*) влюблённый (**of** в B); (*inclined to love*) влюбчивый

amount [ə'maunt] **1.** ~ **to** равняться (Д); *fig.* быть равносильным; **it** ~**s to this** дело сводиться к следующему; **2.** сумма, количество

ample ['æmpl] (*sufficient*) достаточный, (*abundant*) обильный; (*spacious*) просторный

amplifier ['æmplɪfaɪə] *el.* усилитель *m*; ~**fy** [-faɪ] усили(ва)ть; (*expand*) расширять [-ирить]; ~**tude** [-tju:d] широта, размах; амплитуда

ampoule ['æmpu:l] ампула

amputate ['æmpjuteɪt] ампутировать (*im*)*pf.*

amuse [ə'mju:z] забавлять, позабавить *pf.*, развлекать [-éчь]; ~**ment** [-mənt] развлечение, забава; ~ **park** площадка с аттракционами

an [æn, ən] *неопределённый артикль*

an(a)emi|a [ə'ni:mɪə] анемия; ~**c** [-mɪk] анемичный

an(a)esthetic [ænɪs'θetɪk] обезболивающее средство; *general* ~ общий наркоз; *local* ~ местный наркоз

analog|ous [ə'næləgəs] □ аналогичный, сходный; ~**y** [ə'nælədʒɪ] аналогия, сходство

analysis [ə'næləsɪs] анализ

analyze, *Brit.* -**yse** ['ænəlaɪz] анализировать (*im*)*pf.*, *pf. a.* [про-]

anarchy ['ænəkɪ] анархия

anatomy [ə'nætəmɪ] (*science*) анатомия; (*dissection*) анатомирование; (*analysis*) разбор; (*human body*) тело

ancestor ['ænsɪstə] *mst.* предок; ~**ral** [æn'sestrəl] родовой; ~**ry** ['ænsestrɪ] (*lineage*) происхождение; (*ancestors*) предки *m/pl.*

anchor ['æŋkə] **1.** якорь *m*; **at** ~ на якоре; **2.** *come to* ~ станови́ться [стать, на якорь

anchovy ['æntʃəvɪ] анчоус

ancient [eɪnʃənt] древний; античный

and [ənd, ən, ænd] и

anew [ə'nju:] (*again*) снова; (*in a different way*) по-новому, заново

angel ['eɪndʒəl] ангел, ~**ic(al** □) [æn'dʒelɪk(l)] ангельский

anger ['æŋgə] **1.** гнев; **2.** [рас]сердить

angle[1] ['æŋgl] угол; (*viewpoint*) точка зрения

angle[2] [-] удить рыбу; *fig.* напрашиваться (**for** на В); ~**r** [-ə] рыболов

Anglican ['æŋglɪkən] **1.** член англиканской церкви; **2.** англиканский

angry ['æŋgrɪ] сердитый (**with** на В)

anguish ['æŋgwɪʃ] страдание, мука

angular ['æŋgjulə] *mst. fig.* угловатый; (*awkward*) неловкий

animal ['ænɪml] **1.** животное; *pack* ~ вьючное животное; **2.** животный; ~ *kingdom* животное царство

animat|e ['ænɪmeɪt] оживлять [-вить]; ~**ion** [ænɪ'meɪʃn] живость *f*; оживление

animosity [ænɪ'mɒsətɪ] враждебность *f*

ankle ['æŋkl] лодыжка

annals ['ænlz] *pl.* летопись *f*

annex [ə'neks] аннексировать (*im*)*pf.*; присоединять [-нить]; ~**ation** [ænek-'seɪʃn] аннексия

annex(e) ['æneks] (*to a building*) пристройка; крыло; (*to document, etc.*) приложение

annihilate [ə'naɪəleɪt] уничтожать [-ожить], истреблять [-бить]

anniversary [ænɪ'vɜːsərɪ] годовщина

annotat|e ['ænəteɪt] аннотировать (*im*)*pf.*; снабжать примечаниями; ~**ion** [ænə'teɪʃn] аннотация; примечание

announce [ə'nauns] объявлять [-вить]; заявлять [-вить]; ~**ment** [-mənt] объявление, заявление; *on the radio, etc.* сообщение; ~**r** [-ə] *radio* диктор

annoy [ə'nɔɪ] надоедать [-есть] (Д); досаждать [досадить] (Д); раздражать; **~ance** [-əns] доса́да; раздраже́ние; неприя́тность *f*

annual ['ænjʊəl] **1.** *publication* □ ежего́дный; годово́й; **2.** *plant* ежего́дник; одноле́тнее расте́ние

annul [ə'nʌl] аннули́ровать (*im*)*pf*.; отменя́ть [-ни́ть]; *contract* расторга́ть [-о́ргнуть]; **~ment** [-mənt] отме́на, аннули́рование

anodyne ['ænədaɪn] болеутоля́ющее сре́дство; успока́ивающее сре́дство

anomalous [ə'nɒmələs] □ *adj.* анома́льный

anonymous [ə'nɒnɪməs] □ анони́мный

another [ə'nʌðə] друго́й, ещё; **one after ~** оди́н за други́м; **quite~ thing** совсе́м друго́е де́ло

answer ['ɑ:nsə] **1.** *v/t.* отвеча́ть [-е́тить] (Д); (*fulfil*) удовлетворя́ть [-ри́ть]; **~ back** дерзи́ть; **~ the bell or door** откры́ть дверь на звоно́к; **~ the telephone** взять *or* снять тру́бку; *v/i.* отвеча́ть [-е́тить] (**to a p.** Д, **to a question** на вопро́с); **~ for** отвеча́ть [-е́тить] за (В); отвеча́ть за (В); реше́ние *a. math.*; **~able** ['ɑ:nsərəbl] □ отве́тственный; **~ing machine** автоотве́тчик

ant [ænt] мураве́й

antagonism [æn'tægənɪzəm] антагони́зм, вражда́

antagonize [æn'tægənaɪz] настра́ивать [-ро́ить] (**against** про́тив Р)

antenatal [ænti'neɪtl]: **~ clinic** *approx.* же́нская консульта́ция

antenna [æn'tenə] *Am.* → **aerial**

anterior [æn'tɪərɪə] *of time* предше́ствующий (**to** Д); *of place* пере́дний

anthem ['ænθəm] хора́л, гимн; **national ~** госуда́рственный гимн

anti… [ænti…] противо…, анти…

antiaircraft [ænti'eəkrɑ:ft] противовозду́шный; **~ defence** противовозду́шная оборо́на (ПВО)

antibiotic [-baɪ'ɒtɪk] антибио́тик

anticipate [æn'tɪsɪpeɪt] (*foresee*) предви́деть, предчу́вствовать; (*expect*) ожида́ть; предвкуша́ть [-уси́ть]; (*forestall*) предупрежда́ть [-реди́ть];

~ion [æntɪsɪ'peɪʃn] ожида́ние; предчу́вствие; **in ~** в ожида́нии, в предви́дении

antics ['æntɪks] ша́лости *f/pl.*, прока́зы *f/pl.*, прода́елки *f/pl.*

antidote ['æntɪdəʊt] противоя́дие

antipathy [æn'tɪpəθɪ] антипа́тия

antiqua|ry ['æntɪkwərɪ] антиква́р; **~ted** [-kweɪtɪd] устаре́лый; (*old-fashioned*) старомо́дный

antiqu|e [æn'ti:k] **1.** анти́чный; стари́нный; **2. the ~** (*art*) анти́чное иску́сство; **~ity** [æn'tɪkwətɪ] дре́вность *f*; старина́; анти́чность *f*

antiseptic [æntɪ'septɪk] антисепти́ческое сре́дство

antlers ['æntləz] *pl.* оле́ньи рога́ *m/pl.*

anvil ['ænvɪl] накова́льня

anxiety [æŋ'zaɪətɪ] беспоко́йство, (*alarm*) трево́га; (*keen desire*) стра́стное жела́ние; (*apprehension*) опасе́ние

anxious ['æŋkʃəs] озабо́ченный; беспоко́ящийся (**about, for** о П); *of news, warning signals, etc.* трево́жный

any ['enɪ] **1.** *pron.* & *adj.* како́йнибудь; вся́кий, любо́й; **at ~ rate** во вся́ком слу́чае; **not ~** никако́й; **2.** *adv.* ско́лько-нибудь, ниско́лько; **~body, ~one** кто́-нибудь; вся́кий; **~how** ка́к-нибудь; так и́ли ина́че, всё же; **~thing** что́-нибудь; **~ but** то́лько не…; **~where** где́-нибудь, куда́-нибудь

apart [ə'pɑ:t] отде́льно; по́рознь; **~ from** кро́ме (Р); **~ment** [-mənt] → **flat** *Brt.; mst. pl.* апартаме́нты *m/pl.; Am.* кварти́ра; **~ house** многокварти́рный дом

ape [eɪp] **1.** обезья́на; **2.** подража́ть (Д), [с]обезья́нничать

aperient [ə'pɪərɪənt] слаби́тельное

aperitif [ə'perɪtɪf] аперити́в

aperture ['æpətʃə] отве́рстие; *phot.* диафра́гма

apex ['eɪpeks] верши́на

apiece [ə'pi:s] за шту́ку; за ка́ждого, за челове́ка

apolog|etic [əpɒlə'dʒetɪk] (**~ally**): **be ~** извиня́ться [-ни́ться] (**about, for** в В); **~ air** винова́тый вид; **~ize**

[ə'pɒlədʒaɪz] извиня́ться [-ни́ться] (*for* за В; *to* пе́ред Т); ~y [-dʒɪ] извине́ние

apoplectic [æpə'plektɪk]: ~ **stroke** уда́р, инсу́льт

apostle [ə'pɒsl] апо́стол

apostrophe [ə'pɒstrəfɪ] *gr.* апостро́ф

appall *or* Brt. **appal** [ə'pɔ:l] ужаса́ть [-сну́ть]

apparatus [æpə'reɪtəs] прибо́р; аппара́тура, аппара́т; *sport* снаря́ды *m/pl.*

appar|ent [ə'pærənt] (*obvious*) очеви́дный; (*visible, evident*) ви́димый; *for no ~ reason* без ви́димой причи́ны; ~ently по-ви́димому; ~ition [æpə'rɪʃən] при́зрак

appeal [ə'pi:l] 1. апелли́ровать (*im*)*pf.*; обраща́ться [обрати́ться] (*to* к Д); (*attract*) привлека́ть [-е́чь] (*to* В); *law* обжа́ловать; 2. воззва́ние, призы́в; привлека́тельность *f*; обжа́лование; ~ing [-ɪŋ] (*moving*) тро́гательный; (*attractive*) привлека́тельный

appear [ə'pɪə] появля́ться [-ви́ться]; (*seem*) пока́зываться [-за́ться]; *on stage etc.* выступа́ть [вы́ступить]; *it ~s to me* мне ка́жется; ~ance [ə'pɪərəns] появле́ние; вне́шний вид; *person's* нару́жность *f*; ~ances *pl.* приличия *n/pl.*; *keep up~* соблюда́ть приличия

appease [ə'pi:z] умиротворя́ть [-ри́ть]; успока́ивать [-ко́ить]

append [ə'pend] прилага́ть [-ложи́ть] (к Д); ~icitis [əpendɪ'saɪtɪs] аппендици́т; ~ix [ə'pendɪks] *of a book, etc.* приложе́ние; *anat.* аппе́ндикс

appetite ['æpɪtaɪt] аппети́т (*for* на В); *fig.* влече́ние, скло́нность *f* (*for* к Д)

appetizing ['æpɪtaɪzɪŋ] аппети́тный

applaud [ə'plɔ:d] *v/t.* аплоди́ровать (Д); (*approve*) одобря́ть [одо́брить]

applause [ə'plɔ:z] аплодисме́нты *m/pl*; *fig.* (*approval*) одобре́ние

apple [æpl] я́блоко; ~ *of discord* я́блоко раздо́ра; ~ *tree* я́блоня

appliance [ə'plaɪəns] устро́йство, приспособле́ние, прибо́р

applica|ble ['æplɪkəbl] примени́мый, (*appropriate*) подходя́щий (*to* к Д);

delete where ~ зачеркни́те, где необходи́мо; ~nt [-kənt] кандида́т (*for* на В); *not* ~ не отно́сится (*to* к Д); ~tion [æplɪ'keɪʃn] примене́ние; заявле́ние; про́сьба (*for* о П); *send in an* ~ пода́ть заявле́ние, зая́вку

apply [ə'plaɪ] *v/t.* (*bring into action*) прилага́ть [-ложи́ть] (*to* к Д); (*lay or spread on*) прикла́дывать [приложи́ть]; (*use*) применя́ть [-ни́ть] (*to* к Д); ~ *o.s. to* занима́ться [заня́ться] (Т); *v/i.* (*approach, request*) обраща́ться [обрати́ться] (*for* за Т; *to* к Д); (*concern, relate to*) относи́ться

appoint [ə'pɔɪnt] назнача́ть [-на́чить]; ~ment [-mənt] назначе́ние; (*meeting*) встре́ча; (*agreement*) договорённость *f*; *by* ~ по предвари́тельной договорённости, по за́писи

apportion [ə'pɔ:ʃn] разделя́ть [-ли́ть]

apprais|al [ə'preɪzl] оце́нка; ~e [ə-'preɪz] оце́нивать [-ни́ть], расце́нивать [-ни́ть]

apprecia|ble [ə'pri:ʃəbl] □ заме́тный, ощути́мый; ~te [-ɪeɪt] *v/t.* оце́нивать [-ни́ть]; [о]цени́ть; (*understand*) понима́ть [-ня́ть]; *v/i.* повыша́ться [-вы́ситься] в цене́; ~tion [əpri:ʃɪ'eɪʃn] (*gratitude*) призна́тельность *f*; оце́нка, понима́ние

apprehen|d [æprɪ'hend] (*foresee*) предчу́вствовать; (*fear*) опаса́ться; (*seize, arrest*) заде́рживать [-жа́ть], аресто́вывать [-ова́ть]; ~sion [-'henʃn] опасе́ние, предчу́вствие; аре́ст; ~sive [-'hensɪv] □ озабо́ченный, по́лный трево́ги

apprentice [ə'prentɪs] учени́к; ~ship [-ʃɪp] уче́ние, учени́чество

approach [ə'prəʊtʃ] 1. приближа́ться [-бли́зиться] к (Д); (*speak to*) обраща́ться [обрати́ться] к (Д); 2. приближе́ние; по́дступ; *fig.* подхо́д; ~ing [-ɪŋ] приближа́ющийся; ~ *traffic* встре́чное движе́ние

approbation [æprə'beɪʃn] одобре́ние; са́нкция, согла́сие

appropriate 1. [ə'prəuprɪeɪt] (*take possession of*) присва́ивать [-сво́ить]; 2. [-ət] (*suitable*) подходя́щий, соотве́тствующий

approv|al [ə'pru:vl] одобре́ние; утвержде́ние; **~e** [ə'pru:v] одобря́ть [одо́брить]; утвержда́ть [-ди́ть]; санкциони́ровать (*im*)*pf*.

approximate 1. [ə'prɒksɪmeɪt] приближа́ть(ся) [-бли́зить(ся)] к (Д); **2.** [-mət] приблизи́тельный

apricot ['eɪprɪkɒt] абрико́с

April ['eɪprəl] апре́ль *m*

apron ['eɪprən] пере́дник, фа́ртук

apt [æpt] □ (*suitable*) подходя́щий, (*pertinent*) уме́стный; (*gifted*) спосо́бный; **~ to** скло́нный к (Д); **~itude** ['æptɪtju:d], **~ness** [-nɪs] спосо́бность *f*; скло́нность *f* (**for, to** к Д); уме́стность *f*

aqualung ['ækwəlʌŋ] аквала́нг

aquarium [ə'kweərɪəm] аква́риум

Aquarius [ə'kweərɪəs] Водоле́й

aquatic [ə'kwætɪk] **1.** водяно́й, во́дный; **2. ~s** *pl.* во́дный спорт

aqueduct ['ækwɪdʌkt] акведу́к

Arab ['æræb] ара́б *m*, -ка *f*; **~ic** ['ærəbɪk] **1.** ара́бский язы́к; **2.** ара́бский

arable ['ærəbl] па́хотный

arbit|er ['a:bɪtə] (*judge*) арби́тр; (*third party*) трете́йский судья́; **~rariness** ['a:bɪtrərɪnɪs] произво́л; **~rary** [ɪ_trərɪ] произво́льный; **~rate** ['a:bɪtreɪt] выступа́ть в ка́честве арби́тра; **~ration** [a:bɪ'treɪʃn] арбитра́ж; **~rator** ['a:bɪtreɪtə] трете́йский судья́, арби́тр

arbo(u)r ['a:bə] бесе́дка

arc [a:k] дуга́; **~ade** [a:'keɪd] (*covered passageway*) арка́да; *with shops* пасса́ж

arch[1] [a:tʃ] **1.** а́рка, свод; дуга́; **2.** придава́ть фо́рму а́рки; выгиба́ться

arch[2] [~] **1.** хи́трый, лука́вый; **2.** *pref.* архи…; гла́вный

archaic [a:'keɪk] (**~ally**) устаре́лый, устаре́вший; дре́вний

archbishop [a:tʃ'bɪʃəp] архиепи́скоп

archery ['a:tʃərɪ] стрельба́ из лу́ка

architect ['a:kɪtekt] архите́ктор; **~ural** [a:kɪ'tektʃərəl] архитекту́рный; **~ure** ['a:kɪtektʃə] архитекту́ра

archway ['a:tʃweɪ] сво́дчатый прохо́д

arctic ['a:ktɪk] аркти́ческий; **the Arc-** tic А́рктика

ardent ['a:dənt] □ *mst. fig.* горя́чий, пы́лкий; я́рый

ardo(u)r ['a:də] рве́ние, пыл

arduous ['a:djʊəs] □ тру́дный

are [a:; *в предложении:* ə] → **be**

area ['eərɪə] (*measurement*) пло́щадь *f*; **~ of a triangle** пло́щадь треуго́льника; (*region*) райо́н, край, зо́на; (*sphere*) о́бласть

Argentine ['a:dʒəntaɪn] **1.** аргенти́нский; **2.** аргенти́нец *m*, -нка *f*

argue ['a:gju:] *v/t.* обсужда́ть [-уди́ть]; дока́зывать [-за́ть]; **~ a p. into** убежда́ть [убеди́ть] в (П); *v/i.* [по]спо́рить (с Т); **~ against** приводи́ть до́воды про́тив (Р)

argument ['a:gjʊmənt] до́вод, аргуме́нт; (*discussion, debate*) спор; **~ation** [a:gjʊmen'teɪʃn] аргумента́ция

arid ['ærɪd] сухо́й (*a. fig.*); засу́шливый

Aries ['eəri:z] Овен

arise [ə'raɪz] (*get up, stand up*) встава́ть [встать]; (*fig., come into being*) возника́ть [-ни́кнуть] (**from** из Р); явля́ться [яви́ться] результа́том (**from** из Р); **~n** [ə'rɪzn] *p. pt. om* **arise**

aristocra|cy [ærɪ'stɒkrəsɪ] аристокра́тия; **~t** ['ærɪstəkræt] аристокра́т; **~tic** [ærɪstə'krætɪk] аристократи́ческий

arithmetic [ə'rɪθmətɪk] арифме́тика

ark [a:k]: **Noah's ~** Но́ев ковче́г

arm[1] [a:m] рука́; (*sleeve*) рука́в

arm[2] [~] вооружа́ть(ся) [-жи́ть(ся)]; **~ed forces** вооружённые си́лы

armament ['a:məmənt] вооруже́ние

armchair кре́сло

armful ['a:mfʊl] оха́пка

armistice ['a:mɪstɪs] переми́рие

armo(u)r ['a:mə] *hist.* доспе́хи *m/pl.*; броня́; **~y** [-rɪ] арсена́л; оруже́йная пала́та

armpit ['a:mpɪt] подмы́шка

arms [a:mz] ору́жие

army ['a:mɪ] а́рмия; *fig.* мно́жество

arose [ə'rəʊz] *pt. om* **arise**

around [ə'raʊnd] **1.** *adv.* всю́ду, круго́м; **2.** *prp.* вокру́г (Р)

arouse [ə'raʊz] [раз]буди́ть (*a. fig.*);

fig. возбуждать [-удить]; *interest, envy etc.* вызывать [вызвать]

arrange [ə'reɪndʒ] приводить в порядок; *a party etc.* устраивать [-роить]; (*agree in advance*) уславливаться [условиться] (*im*)*pf.*; **~ment** [-mənt] устройство; расположение; соглашение, мероприятие; *mus.* аранжировка

array [ə'reɪ] *fig. assemblage* множество, *display* коллекция; целый ряд

arrear(s) [ə'rɪə] *mst. pl.* отставание; задолженность *f*

arrest [ə'rest] **1.** арест, задержание; **2.** арестовывать [-овать], задерживать [-жать]

arriv|al [ə'raɪvl] прибытие, приезд; **~als** *pl.* прибывшие *pl.*; **~e** [ə'raɪv] прибы(ва́)ть; приезжать [-ехать] (*at* в, на В)

arroga|nce ['ærəgəns] надменность *f*, высокомерие; **~nt** [-nt] надменный, высокомерный

arrow ['ærəʊ] стрела; *as symbol on road sign, etc.* стрелка

arsenal ['ɑːsənl] арсенал

arsenic ['ɑːsnɪk] мышьяк

arson ['ɑːsn] *law* поджог

art [ɑːt] искусство; *fine* **~s** изящные *or* изобразительные искусства

arter|ial [ɑː'tɪərɪəl]: **~ road** магистраль *f*; **~y** ['ɑːtərɪ] *anat.* артерия

artful ['ɑːtfəl] ловкий; хитрый

article ['ɑːtɪkl] (*object*) предмет, вещь *f*; (*piece of writing*) статья; (*clause*) пункт, параграф; *gr.* артикль *m*

articulat|e [ɑː'tɪkjʊleɪt] **1.** отчётливо, ясно произносить; **2.** [-lət] отчётливый; членораздельный; **~ion** [ɑːtɪkjʊ'leɪʃn] артикуляция

artificial [ɑːtɪ'fɪʃl] искусственный

artillery [ɑː'tɪlərɪ] артиллерия; **~man** [-mən] артиллерист

artisan [ɑːtɪ'zæn] ремесленник

artist ['ɑːtɪst] художник (-ица); (*actor*) актёр, актриса; **~e** [ɑː'tiːst] артист(-ка); **~ic(al** □) [ɑː'tɪstɪk(l)] артистический, художественный

artless ['ɑːtlɪs] естественный; (*ingenuous*) простодушный; (*unskilled*) неискусный

as [əz, æz] *cj. a. adv.* когда; в то время как; так как; хотя; **~ far ... I know** насколько мне известно; **~ it were** так сказать; как бы ...; **~ well** также; в такой же мере; **such ~** такой как; как например; **~ well ~** и ... и ... ...; *prp.* **~ for, ~ to** что касается (Р); **~ from** с (Р)

ascend [ə'send] подниматься [-няться]; восходить [взойти]

ascension [ə'senʃn]: **☉ (Day)** Вознесение

ascent [ə'sent] восхождение; (*upward slope*) подъём

ascertain [æsə'teɪn] удостоверяться [-вериться] в (П); устанавливать [-новить]

ascribe [ə'skraɪb] приписывать [-сать] (Д/В)

aseptic [eɪ'septɪk] *med.* асептический, стерильный

ash¹ [æʃ] *bot.* ясень *m*; **mountain ~** рябина

ash² [-] *mst. pl.* **~es** ['æʃɪz] зола, пепел

ashamed [ə'ʃeɪmd] пристыжённый; **I'm ~ of you** мне стыдно за тебя; **feel ~ of o.s.** стыдиться

ash can *Am.* ведро для мусора

ashen ['æʃən] пепельного цвета; (*pale*) бледный

ashore [ə'ʃɔː] на берег, на берегу

ashtray ['æʃtreɪ] пепельница

ashy ['æʃɪ] *of or relating to ashes* пепельный

Asian ['eɪʃn] **1.** азиатский; **2.** азиат *m*, -ка *f*

aside [ə'saɪd] в сторону, в стороне

ask [ɑːsk] *v/t.* (*request*) [по]просить (*a th. of, from a p.* что-нибудь у кого-нибудь); **~ that** просить, чтобы ...; (*inquire*) спрашивать [спросить]; **~ (a p.) a question** задавать вопрос (Д); *v/i.* **~ for** [по]просить (В *or* Р *or* о П)

askance [ə'skæns]: **look ~** косо посмотреть (*at* на В)

askew [ə'skjuː] криво

asleep [ə'sliːp] спящий; **be ~** спать

asparagus [ə'spærəgəs] спаржа

aspect ['æspekt] вид (*a. gr.*); аспект, сторона

aspen ['æspən] оси́на

asperity [æ'sperəti] (sharpness) ре́зкость f; with ~ ре́зко; (severity) суро́вость f

asphalt ['æsfælt] 1. асфа́льт; 2. покрыва́ть асфа́льтом

aspir|ation [æspə'reɪʃn] стремле́ние; ~e [ə'spaɪə] стреми́ться (to, after, at к Д)

aspirin ['æsprɪn] аспири́н

ass [æs] осёл (a. fig.); make an ~ of o.s. поста́вить себя́ в глу́пое положе́ние; coll. сваля́ть дурака́

assail [ə'seɪl] (attack) напада́ть [-па́сть] на (В); fig. энерги́чно бра́ться за; with questions засыпа́ть [засы́пать] вопро́сами; ~ant [-ənt] напада́ющий

assassin [ə'sæsɪn] уби́йца m/f; ~ate [-ɪneɪt] уби(ва́)ть; ~ation [əsæsɪ'neɪʃn] уби́йство

assault [ə'sɔːlt] 1. нападе́ние; mil. ата́ка, штурм; 2. напада́ть [напа́сть], набра́сываться [-ро́ситься] на (В)

assemble [ə'sembl] (gather) собира́ть(ся) [-бра́ться]; tech. [c]монти́ровать, собира́ть [-бра́ть]; ~y [-i] собра́ние; ассамбле́я; tech. сбо́рка

assent [ə'sent] 1. согла́сие; 2. соглаша́ться [-ласи́ться] (to на В; с Т)

assert [ə'sɜːt] утвержда́ть [-рди́ть]; ~ion [ə'sɜːʃn] утвержде́ние

assess [ə'ses] оце́нивать [-ни́ть] (a. fig.); taxes etc. определя́ть [-ли́ть], устана́вливать [-нови́ть]; ~ment [-mənt] for taxation обложе́ние; valuation оце́нка

asset ['æset] це́нное ка́чество; fin. статья́ дохо́да; ~s pl. fin. акти́в(ы); ~ and liabilities акти́в и пасси́в

assiduous [ə'sɪdjʊəs] приле́жный

assign [ə'saɪn] (appoint) назнача́ть [-на́чить]; (allot) ассигно́вывать, ассигнова́ть (im)pf.; (charge) поруча́ть [-чи́ть]; room, etc. отводи́ть [-вести́]; ~ment [-mənt] назначе́ние; зада́ние, поруче́ние

assimilat|e [ə'sɪmɪleɪt] ассимили́ровать(ся) (im)pf.; (absorb) усва́ивать [-во́ить]; ~ion [əsɪmɪ'leɪʃn] ассими-

ля́ция; усвое́ние

assist [ə'sɪst] помога́ть [-мо́чь] (Д); [по]соде́йствовать (im)pf. (Д); ~ance [-əns] по́мощь f; ~ant [-ənt] ассисте́нт(ка); помо́щник (-ица); ~ professor univ. Am. ассисте́нт; shop ~ Brt. продаве́ц

associa|te [ə'səʊʃɪeɪt] 1. обща́ться (with с Т); (connect) ассоции́ровать(ся) (im)pf.; 2. [-ʃɪət] колле́га m; соуча́стник; comm. компаньо́н; ~tion [əsəʊsɪ'eɪʃn] ассоциа́ция; объедине́ние, о́бщество

assort|ed [ə'sɔːtɪd] разнообра́зный; ~ chocolates шокола́д ассорти́ indecl.; ~ment [-mənt] ассортиме́нт

assume [ə'sjuːm] (suppose) предполага́ть [-ложи́ть]; (take up) вступа́ть [-пи́ть]; ~ption [ə'sʌmpʃn] предположе́ние; eccl. Ꝺption Успе́ние

assur|ance [ə'ʃʊərəns] (promise) увере́ние; (confidence) уве́ренность f; (insurance) страхо́вка; ~e [ə'ʃʊə] уверя́ть [уве́рить]; ~edly [-rɪdlɪ] adv. коне́чно, несомне́нно

aster ['æstə] bot. а́стра

astir [əs'tɜː] в движе́нии; на нога́х

astonish [ə'stɒnɪʃ] удивля́ть [-ви́ть], изумля́ть [-ми́ть]; be ~ed удивля́ться [-ви́ться] (at Д); ~ing [-ɪʃɪŋ] удиви́тельный, порази́тельный; ~ment [-mənt] удивле́ние, изумле́ние

astound [ə'staʊnd] поража́ть [порази́ть]

astrakhan [æstrə'kæn] (lambskin) кара́куль m

astray [ə'streɪ]: go ~ заблуди́ться, сби́ться с пути́ (a. fig.); lead s.o. ~ сбить с пути́ (и́стинного)

astride [ə'straɪd] верхо́м (of на П)

astringent [ə'strɪndʒənt] med. вя́жущее сре́дство

astro|logy [ə'strɒlədʒɪ] астроло́гия; ~nomer [ə'strɒnəmə] астроно́м; ~nomy [ə'strɒnəmɪ] астроно́мия

astute [ə'stjuːt] □ (cunning) хи́трый; (shrewd) проница́тельный; ~ness [-nɪs] хи́трость f; проница́тельность f

asylum [ə'saɪləm] (place of refuge) убе́жище; (shelter) прию́т; (mental in-

stitution) сумасше́дший дом

at [æt, ət] *prp.* в (П, В); при (П); на (П, В); о́коло (Р); за (Т); ~ *school* в шко́ле; ~ *the age of* в во́зрасте (Р); ~ *first* снача́ла; ~ *first sight* с пе́рвого взгля́да; на пе́рвый взгляд; ~ *last* наконе́ц

ate [et, eɪt] *pt. om* eat

atheism ['eɪθɪɪzəm] атеи́зм

athlet|e ['æθliːt] спортсме́н, атле́т; ~**ic(al** □) [æθ'letɪk(əl)] атлети́ческий; ~**ics** [æθ'letɪks] *pl.* (лёгкая) атле́тика

atmospher|e ['ætməsfɪə] атмосфе́ра (*a. fig.*); ~**ic(al** □) [ætməs'ferɪk(əl)] атмосфе́рный

atom ['ætəm] а́том; *not an* ~ *of truth* нет и до́ли и́стины; ~**ic** [ə'tɒmɪk] а́томный; ~ *pile* а́томный реа́ктор; ~ *power plant* а́томная электроста́нция; ~ *waste* отхо́ды а́томной промы́шленности

atone [ə'təʊn]: ~ *for* загла́живать [-ла́дить], искупа́ть [-пи́ть]

atroci|ous [ə'trəʊʃəs] □ зве́рский, *coll.* ужа́сный; ~**ty** [ə'trɒsətɪ] зве́рство

attach [ə'tætʃ] *v/t. com.* прикрепля́ть [-пи́ть]; *document* прилага́ть [-ложи́ть]; *importance, etc.* прид(ав)а́ть; *law* налага́ть аре́ст на (В); ~ *o.s.* to привя́зываться [-за́ться] к (Д); ~**ment** [-mənt] (*affection*) привя́занность f, (*devotion*) пре́данность f

attack [ə'tæk] **1.** *mil.* ата́ка; нападе́ние (*a. mil.*); *in press, etc.* ре́зкая кри́тика; *med.* при́ступ; **2.** *v/t.* атакова́ть (*im*)*pf.*; напада́ть [напа́сть] на (В), набра́сываться [-ро́ситься] на (В); подверга́ть [-ве́ргнуть] ре́зкой кри́тике

attain [ə'teɪn] *v/t.* достига́ть [-и́гнуть] (Р), доби(ва́)ться (Р); ~**ment** [-mənt] достиже́ние

attempt [ə'tempt] **1.** попы́тка; *on s.o.'s life* покуше́ние; **2.** [по]пыта́ться, [по]про́бовать

attend [ə'tend] *v/t.* (*wait, serve*) обслу́живать [-жи́ть]; (*go to*) посеща́ть [-ети́ть]; *med.* уха́живать за (Т); *be present* прису́тствовать (*at* на П); (*accompany*) сопровожда́ть *mst. impf.*;

~**ance** [ə'tendəns] прису́тствие (*at* на П); наплы́в пу́блики; посеща́емость f; *med.* ухо́д (за Т); ~**ant** [-ənt] **1.**: ~ *nurse* дежу́рная медсестра́; **2.** *in elevator* (*Brt. lift*) лифтёр

attent|ion [ə'tenʃn] внима́ние [-tɪv] внима́тельный

attest [ə'test] (*certify*) удостоверя́ть [-ве́рить]; (*bear witness to*) [за]свиде́тельствовать

attic ['ætɪk] черда́к; манса́рда

attire [ə'taɪə] наря́д

attitude ['ætɪtjuːd] отноше́ние, пози́ция; (*pose*) по́за

attorney [ə'tɜːnɪ] уполномо́ченный, дове́ренный; *at law* пове́ренный в суде́, адвока́т; *power of* ~ дове́ренность f; *attorney general Am.* мини́стр юсти́ции

attract [ə'trækt] *v/t.* привлека́ть [-вле́чь] (*a. fig.*); *magnet* притя́гивать [-яну́ть]; *fig.* прельща́ть [-льсти́ть]; ~**ion** [ə'trækʃn] притяже́ние; *fig.* привлека́тельность f; *the town has many* ~**s** в го́роде мно́го достопримеча́тельностей; ~**ive** [-tɪv] привлека́тельный, зама́нчивый; ~**iveness** [-tɪvnɪs] привлека́тельность f

attribute 1. [ə'trɪbjuːt] припи́сывать [-са́ть] (Д/В); (*explain*) объясня́ть [-сни́ть]; **2.** ['ætrɪbjuːt] сво́йство, при́знак; *gr.* определе́ние

aubergine ['əʊbəʒiːn] баклажа́н

auction ['ɔːkʃn] **1.** аукцио́н, торги́ *m/pl.*; *sell by* ~, *put up for* ~ продава́ть с аукцио́на; **2.** продава́ть с аукцио́на (*mst.* ~ *off*); ~**eer** [ɔːkʃə'nɪə] аукциони́ст

audaci|ous [ɔː'deɪʃəs] (*daring*) отва́жный, де́рзкий; (*impudent*) на́глый; ~**ty** [ɔː'dæsətɪ] отва́га; де́рзость f; на́глость f

audible ['ɔːdəbl] вня́тный, слы́шный

audience ['ɔːdɪəns] слу́шатели *m/pl.*, зри́тели *m/pl.*, пу́блика; (*interview*) аудие́нция (*of, with* у Р)

audiovisual [ɔːdɪəʊ'vɪʃʊəl] аудиовизуа́льный

audit ['ɔːdɪt] **1.** прове́рка фина́нсовой

отчётности, ауди́т; **2.** проверя́ть [-е́рить] отчётность *f*; **~or** [ˈɒdɪtə] бухга́лтер-ревизо́р, контролёр

auditorium [ɔːdɪˈtɔːrɪəm] аудито́рия; зри́тельный зал

augment [ɔːgˈment] увели́чи(ва)ть

August [ˈɔːgəst] а́вгуст

aunt [ɑːnt] тётя, тётка

auspices [ˈɔːspɪsɪz] *pl.*: *under the ~* под эги́дой

auster|**e** [ɒˈstɪə] □ стро́гий, суро́вый; **~ity** [ɒˈsterətɪ] стро́гость *f*, суро́вость *f*

Australian [ɒˈstreɪlɪən] **1.** австрали́ец *m*, -и́йка *f*; **2.** австрали́йский

Austrian [ˈɒstrɪən] **1.** австри́ец *m*, -и́йка *f*; **2.** австри́йский

authentic [ɔːˈθentɪk] (**~ally**) по́длинный, достове́рный

author [ˈɔːθə] а́втор, **~itative** [ɔːˈθɒrɪtətɪv] □ авторите́тный; **~ity** [ɔːˈθɒrɪtɪ] авторите́т; (*right*) полномо́чие; власть *f* (**over** над Т); *on the ~ of* на основа́нии (Р); по утвержде́нию (Р); **~ize** [ˈɔːθəraɪz] уполномо́чи(ва)ть; (*sanction*) санкциони́ровать (*im*)*pf.*; **~ship** [-ʃɪp] а́вторство

autobiography [ɔːtəbaɪˈɒgrəfɪ] автобиогра́фия

autogenic [ɔːtəˈdʒenɪk]: *~ training* аутоге́нная трениро́вка

autograph [ˈɔːtəgrɑːf] авто́граф

automatic [ɔːtəˈmætɪk] (**~ally**) автомати́ческий; *fig.* машина́льный; *~ machine* автома́т

automobile [ˈɔːtəməbiːl] автомаши́на, автомоби́ль *m.*; *attr.* автомоби́льный

autonomy [ɔːˈtɒnəmɪ] автоно́мия

autumn [ˈɔːtəm] о́сень *f*; **~al** [ɔːˈtʌmnəl] осе́нний

auxiliary [ɔːgˈzɪlɪərɪ] вспомога́тельный; (*additional*) дополни́тельный

avail [əˈveɪl] **1.** помога́ть [помо́чь] (Д); *~ o.s. of* [вос]по́льзоваться (Т); **2.** по́льза, вы́года; *of no ~* напра́сно; *to no ~* напра́сно; **~able** [əˈveɪləbl] (*accessible*) досту́пный; (*on hand*) име́ющийся (в нали́чии)

avalanche [ˈævəlɑːnʃ] лави́на

avaric|**e** [ˈævərɪs] ску́пость *f*; жа́дность *f*; (*greed*) жа́дный; **~ious** [əvəˈrɪʃəs] скупо́й; жа́дный

aveng|**e** [əˈvendʒ] [ото]мсти́ть (Д за В); **~er** [-ə] мсти́тель *m*, -ница *f*

avenue [ˈævənjuː] алле́я; *Am.* широ́кая у́лица, проспе́кт; *fig.* (*approach, way*) путь *m*

aver [əˈvɜː] утвержда́ть [-ди́ть]

average [ˈævərɪdʒ] **1.**: *on an (the) ~* в сре́днем; **2.** сре́дний; **3.** (в сре́днем) составля́ть [-а́вить]

avers|**e** [əˈvɜːs] □ нерасполо́женный (*to, from* к Д); *I'm not ~ to* я не прочь, я люблю́; **~ion** [əˈvɜːʃn] отвраще́ние, антипа́тия

avert [əˈvɜːt] отвраща́ть [-рати́ть]; *eyes* отводи́ть [-вести́] (*a. fig.*); *head* отвора́чивать [-верну́ть]

aviation [eɪvɪˈeɪʃn] авиа́ция

avocado [ævəˈkɑːdəʊ], *~ pear* авока́до *indecl.*

avoid [əˈvɔɪd] избега́ть [-ежа́ть]

await [əˈweɪt] ожида́ть (Р)

awake [əˈweɪk] **1.** бо́дрствующий; *be ~ to* всё понима́ть; *v/t. (mst. ~n* [əˈweɪkən]) [раз]буди́ть; *interest, etc.* пробужда́ть [-уди́ть] (к Д); *v/i.* просыпа́ться [проснýться]; *~ to a th.* осозн(ав)а́ть (В)

award [əˈwɔːd] **1.** награ́да; *univ.* стипе́ндия; **2.** присужда́ть [-уди́ть]

aware [əˈweə]: *be ~ of* знать (В *o* Ð П), сознава́ть (В); *become ~ of* почу́вствовать

away [əˈweɪ] прочь; далеко́

awe [ɔː] благогове́ние, тре́пет (*of* пе́ред Т)

awful [ˈɔːfʊl] □ стра́шный, ужа́сный (*a. coll.*)

awhile [əˈwaɪl] на не́которое вре́мя; *wait ~* подожди́ немно́го

awkward [ˈɔːkwəd] (*clumsy*) неуклю́жий, нело́вкий (*a. fig.*); (*inconvenient, uncomfortable*) неудо́бный

awl [ɔːl] ши́ло

awning [ˈɔːnɪŋ] наве́с, тент

awoke [əˈwəʊk] *pt.* и *pt. p. от* **awake**

awry [əˈraɪ] ко́со, на́бок; *everything went ~* всё пошло́ скве́рно

ax(e) [æks] топо́р, колу́н
axis ['æksɪs], *pl.* **axes** [~si:z] ось *f*
axle ['æksl] *tech.* ось *f*

ay(e) [aɪ] *affirmative vote* го́лос "за"
azure ['æʒə] **1.** лазу́рь *f*; **2.** лазу́рный

B

babble ['bæbl] **1.** ле́пет; болтовня́; **2.** [по]болта́ть; [за]лепета́ть
baboon [bə'bu:n] *zo.* бабуи́н
baby ['beɪbɪ] **1.** младе́нец, ребёнок, дитя́ *n*; **2.** небольшо́й; ма́лый; ~ *carriage* де́тская коля́ска; ~ *grand* каби-
не́тный роя́ль; ~*hood* ['beɪbɪhud] младе́нчество
bachelor ['bætʃələ] холостя́к; *univ.* бакала́вр
back [bæk] **1.** спина́; *of chair, dress, etc.* спи́нка; *of cloth* изна́нка; *sport* **full~** защи́тник; *of head* заты́лок; *of coin, etc.* обра́тная сторона́; **2.** *adj.* за́дний; обра́тный; отдалённый; **3.** *adv.* наза́д, обра́тно; тому́ наза́д; **4.** *v/t.* подде́рживать [-жа́ть]; подкрепля́ть [-пи́ть]; *fin.* субсиди́ровать, финанси́ровать; гаранти́ровать; *v/i.* отступа́ть [-пи́ть]; [по]пя́титься; ~**bone** позвоно́чник, спинно́й хребе́т; *fig.* опо́ра; ~**er** ['bækə] *fin.* субсиди́рующий; гара́нт; ~**ground** за́дний план, фон; ~**ing** подде́ржка; ~**side** (*coll. buttocks*) зад; за́дница; ~**stairs** та́йный, закули́сный; ~**stroke** пла́вание на спине́; ~ **talk** *Am.* де́рзкий отве́т; ~**up 1.** подде́рж-ка, *comput.* резе́рвная ко́пия; **2.** созда-ва́ть [созда́ть] резе́рвную ко́пию; ~**ward** ['bækwəd] **1.** *adj.* обра́тный; отста́лый; **2.** *adv.* (*a.* ~**ward[s]** [-z]) наза́д; за́дом; наоборо́т; обра́тно
bacon ['beɪkən] беко́н
bacteri|ologist [bæktɪərɪ'ɒlədʒɪst] бактерио́лог; ~**um** [bæk'tɪərɪəm], *pl.* ~**a** [-rɪə] бакте́рия
bad [bæd] □ плохо́й, дурно́й, скве́р-ный; (*harmful*) вре́дный; ~ *cold* си́ль-ный на́сморк; ~ *mistake* серьёзная (гру́бая оши́бка); *he is* ~*ly off* он в не-вы́годном положе́нии; ~*ly wounded*

тяжелора́неный; *coll. want* ~*ly* о́чень хоте́ть
bade [beɪd, bæd] *pt. om* **bid**
badge [bædʒ] значо́к
badger ['bædʒə] **1.** *zo.* барсу́к; **2.** изво-ди́ть [извести́]
baffle ['bæfl] (*confuse*) сбива́ть с то́л-ку
bag [bæg] **1.** *large* мешо́к; су́мка, *small, hand*~ су́мочка; **2.** класть [положи́ть] в мешо́к
baggage ['bægɪdʒ] бага́ж; ~ *check Am.* бага́жная квита́нция
bagpipe ['bægpaɪp] волы́нка
bail [beɪl] **1.** зало́г; (*guarantee*) по-ручи́тельство; **2.** поруча́ться [-чи́ться]
bait [beɪt] **1.** нажи́вка, прима́нка (*a. fig.*); *fig.* искуше́ние; **2.** прима́нивать [-ни́ть]; *fig.* пресле́довать, изводи́ть [-вести́]
bak|e [beɪk] [ис]пе́чь(ся); ~**er** ['beɪkə] пе́карь *m*; ~'*s* (*shop*) бу́лочная; ~**ery** [-rɪ] пека́рня; ~**ing soda** со́да (питье-ва́я)
balance ['bæləns] **1.** (*scales*) весы́ *m/pl.*; (*equilibrium*) равнове́сие, *fin.* бала́нс; са́льдо *n indecl.*; *coll.* (*remainder*) оста́ток; ~ *of power* полити́ческое равнове́сие; ~ *of trade* тор-го́вый бала́нс; **2.** [с]баланси́ровать (В); сохраня́ть равнове́сие; *fin.* подводи́ть бала́нс; *mentally* взве́шивать [-е́сить]; быть в равнове́сии
balcony ['bælkənɪ] балко́н
bald [bɔ:ld] лы́сый, плеши́вый, *fig.* (*unadorned*) неприкра́шенный; ~*ly: to put it* ~ говоря́ пря́мо
bale [beɪl] ки́па, тюк
balk [bɔ:k] *v/t.* (*hinder*) [вос]препя́тст-вовать (Д), [по]меша́ть (Д)

ball[1] [bɔːl] мяч; шар; *of wool* клубо́к; **keep the ~ rolling** *of a conversation* подде́рживать разгово́р

ball[2] [-] бал, танцева́льный ве́чер

ballad ['bæləd] балла́да

ballast ['bæləst] балла́ст

ballbearing (**s** *pl.*) шарикоподши́пник

ballet ['bæleɪ] бале́т

balloon [bə'luːn] возду́шный шар, аэроста́т

ballot ['bælət] 1. голосова́ние; 2. [про]голосова́ть; **~ box** избира́тельная у́рна; **~ paper** избира́тельный бюллете́нь *m*

ballpoint → pen

ballroom танцева́льный зал

ballyhoo [bælɪ'huː] шуми́ха

balm [baːm] бальза́м; *fig.* утеше́ние

balmy ['baːmɪ] □ арома́тный; успокои́тельный; *air* благоуха́нный

baloney [bə'ləʊnɪ] *Am. sl.* вздор

balsam ['bɔːlsəm] бальза́м; *bot.* бальзами́н

balustrade [bælə'streɪd] балюстра́да

bamboo [bæm'buː] бамбу́к

bamboozle *coll.* [bæm'buːzl] наду́(ва́)ть, обма́нывать [-ну́ть]

ban [bæn] 1. запре́т; **be under a ~** быть под запре́том; **raise the ~** снять запре́т; 2. налага́ть запре́т на (В)

banana [bə'naːnə] бана́н

band [bænd] 1. ле́нта; *of robbers, etc.* ша́йка, ба́нда; гру́ппа, отря́д; *mus.* орке́стр; 2.: **~ together** объединя́ться [-ни́ться] (**against** про́тив Р)

bandage ['bændɪdʒ] 1. бинт, повя́зка; 2. [за]бинтова́ть, перевя́зывать [-за́ть]

bandit ['bændɪt] банди́т

bandmaster ['bændmaːstə] капельме́йстер

bandy ['bændɪ] обме́ниваться [-ня́ться] (*словами, мячом и т.п.*) *coll.* перебра́ниваться

bane [beɪn] *fig.* поги́бель, беда́; прокля́тие

bang [bæŋ] 1. уда́р, стук; 2. (*hit*) ударя́ть(ся) [уда́рить(ся)]; стуча́ть; *once* [сту́кнуть(ся)]; *door* хло́пать, *once* [-пнуть]

banish ['bænɪʃ] *from country* высыла́ть [вы́слать]; *from one's mind* гнать

banisters ['bænɪstəz] *pl.* пери́ла *n/pl.*

bank[1] [bæŋk] бе́рег

bank[2] [-] 1. банк; **~ of issue** эмиссио́нный банк; 2. *fin.* класть (де́ньги) в банк; *v/i.* **~ on** полага́ться [-ложи́ться] на (В); **~ account** счёт в ба́нке; **~er** ['bæŋkə] банки́р; **~ing** ['bæŋ-kɪŋ] ба́нковое де́ло; **~ rate** учётная ста́вка; **~rupt** ['bæŋkrʌpt] 1. банкро́т; 2. обанкро́тившийся; неплатёжеспосо́бный; 3. де́лать банкро́том; **~ruptcy** ['bæŋkrʌptsɪ] банкро́тство

banner ['bænə] зна́мя *n*, *poet.* стяг, флаг

banquet ['bæŋkwɪt] пир; *formal* банке́т

banter ['bæntə] подшу́чивать [-ути́ть], поддра́знивать [-ни́ть]

baptism ['bæptɪzəm] креще́ние

Baptist ['bæptɪst] бапти́ст

baptize [bæp'taɪz] [о]крести́ть

bar [baː] 1. брусо́к, *of chocolate* пли́тка; *across door* засо́в; *отмель f*; *in pub* бар; *mus.* такт; *fig.* прегра́да, препя́тствие; *law* адвокату́ра; 2. запира́ть на засо́в; (*obstruct*) прегражда́ть [-ради́ть]; (*exclude*) исключа́ть [-чи́ть]

barbed [baːbd]: **~ wire** колю́чая про́волока

barbar|ian [baː'beərɪən] 1. ва́рвар; 2. ва́рварский; **~ous** ['baːbərəs] □ ди́кий; (*cruel*) жесто́кий

barbecue ['baːbɪkjuː] гриль для жа́рки мя́са на откры́том во́здухе

barber ['baːbə] (мужско́й) парикма́хер; **~shop** парикма́херская

bare [beə] 1. го́лый, обнажённый; (*empty*) пусто́й; **the ~ thought** да́же мысль (о П); 2. обнажа́ть [-жи́ть], откры́(ва́)ть; **~faced** ['beəfeɪst] бессты́дный; **~foot** босико́м; **~footed** босо́й; **~headed** с непокры́той голово́й; **~ly** ['beəlɪ] едва́, е́ле-е́ле

bargain ['baːgɪn] 1. сде́лка; (*sth. bought*) вы́годная поку́пка; **into the ~** в прида́чу; 2. [по]торгова́ться (о

П, с T)

barge [bɑ:dʒ] **1.** ба́ржа; **2.:** (**~ into**) coll. ната́лкиваться [-толкну́ться]; влеза́ть [влезть]; **~ in** вва́ливаться [-и́ться]

bark¹ [bɑ:k] **1.** кора́; **2.** strip сдира́ть кору́ с (P)

bark² [-] **1.** of dog лай; **2.** [за]ла́ять

barley [ˈbɑ:lɪ] ячме́нь m

bar|maid [ˈbɑ:meɪd] официа́нтка в ба́ре; **~man** [-mən] ба́рмен

barn [bɑ:n] амба́р, сара́й

baron [ˈbærən] баро́н; **~ess** [-ɪs] бароне́сса

baroque [bəˈrɒk, bəˈrəʊk] **1.** баро́чный; **2.** баро́кко n indecl.

barrack (**s** pl.) [ˈbærək(s)] бара́к; каза́рма

barrel [ˈbærəl] (cask) бо́чка, (keg) бочо́нок; of gun ствол

barren [ˈbærən] □ неплодоро́дный, беспло́дный

barricade [bærɪˈkeɪd] **1.** баррика́да; **2.** [за]баррикади́ровать

barrier [ˈbærɪə] барье́р; rail. шлагба́ум; fig. препя́тствие, поме́ха

barring [ˈbɑ:rɪŋ] prp. кро́ме; за исключе́нием

barrister [ˈbærɪstə] адвока́т

barrow [ˈbærəʊ] та́чка; ручна́я теле́жка

barter [ˈbɑ:tə] **1.** ба́ртер, обме́н; ба́ртерная сде́лка; **2.** [по]меня́ть, обме́нивать [-ня́ть] (**for** на B)

base¹ [beɪs] □ по́длый, ни́зкий

base² [-] **1.** осно́ва, ба́зис, фунда́мент; **2.** осно́вывать [-ова́ть] (В на П), бази́ровать

base|ball [ˈbeɪsbɔ:l] бейсбо́л; **~less** [-lɪs] необосно́ванный; **~ment** [-mənt] подва́л, подва́льный эта́ж

bashful [ˈbæʃfəl] □ засте́нчивый, ро́бкий

basic [ˈbeɪsɪk] основно́й; **~ally** в основно́м

basin [beɪsn] таз, ми́ска; (sink) ра́ковина; geogr. бассе́йн

bas|is [ˈbeɪsɪs], pl. **~es** [-i:z] основа́ние, осно́ва

bask [bɑ:sk]: **~ in the sun** гре́ться на со́лнце

basket [ˈbɑ:skɪt] корзи́на; **~ball** баскетбо́л

bass [beɪs] mus. **1.** бас; **2.** басо́вый

bassoon [bəˈsu:n] фаго́т

bastard [ˈbæstəd] внебра́чный ребё-нок

baste [beɪst] sew. смётывать [смета́ть]

bat¹ [bæt] zo. лету́чая мышь

bat² [-] **1.** at games бита́ (в крике́те); **2.** [за]лая́ть

bat³ [-]: **without ~ting an eyelid** и гла́зом не моргну́в

batch [bætʃ] па́ртия; of letters, etc. па́чка

bath [bɑ:θ] **1.** ва́нна; **2.** [вы-, по]мы́ть; [вы]купа́ть

bathe [beɪð] [вы]купа́ться

bathing [ˈbeɪðɪŋ] купа́ние

bath|robe [ˈbɑ:θrəʊb] (купа́льный) хала́т; **~room** ва́нная (ко́мната); **~ towel** купа́льное полоте́нце

batiste [bæˈti:st] бати́ст

baton [ˈbætən] mus. дирижёрская па́лочка

battalion [bəˈtæljən] батальо́н

batter [ˈbætə] **1.** взби́тое те́сто; **2.** си́льно бить, [по]колоти́ть, изби́ть pf.; **~ down** взла́мывать [взлома́ть]; **~y** [-rɪ] батаре́я; mot. аккумуля́тор; for clock, etc. батаре́йка

battle [ˈbætl] **1.** би́тва, сраже́ние (**of** под T); **2.** сража́ться [срази́ться]; боро́ться

battle|field поле сраже́ния; **~ship** лине́йный кора́бль, линко́р

bawdy [ˈbɔ:dɪ] непристо́йный

bawl [bɔ:l] крича́ть [кри́кнуть], [за]ора́ть; **~ out** выкри́кивать [вы́крикнуть]

bay¹ [beɪ] зали́в, бу́хта

bay² [-] лавро́вое де́рево

bay³ [-] **1.** (bark) лай; **2.** [за]ла́ять; **bring to ~** fig. припере́ть pf. к стене́; **keep at ~** не подпуска́ть [-сти́ть]

bayonet [ˈbeɪənɪt] mil. штык

bay window [beɪ ˈwɪndəʊ] arch. э́ркер

bazaar [bəˈzɑ:] база́р

be [bi:, bɪ] [irr.]: **a)** быть, быва́ть; (be

situated) находи́ться; *of position* лежа́ть, стоя́ть; *there is, are* есть; ~ *about to* соб(и)ра́ться (+ *inf.*); ~ *away* отсу́тствовать; ~ *at s.th.* де́лать, быть за́нятым (Т); ~ *off* уходи́ть [уйти́], отправля́ться [-а́виться]; ~ *on* идти́ *of a film, etc.*; ~ *going on* происходи́ть; *how are you?* как вы пожива́ете?, как вы себя́ чу́вствуете? b) *v/aux.* *(для образования дли́тельной фо́рмы)* ~ *reading* чита́ть; c) *v/aux.* *(для образова́ния пасси́ва)*: ~ *read* чита́ться, быть чи́танным (чита́емым)

beach [bi:tʃ] **1.** пляж, взмо́рье; **2.** *(pull ashore)* вы́тащить *pf.* на бе́рег

beacon ['bi:kən] сигна́льный ого́нь; мая́к; ба́кен

bead [bi:d] бу́сина, би́серина; *of sweat* ка́пля

beads [bi:dz] *pl.* бу́сы *f/pl.*

beak [bi:k] клюв

beam [bi:m] **1.** ба́лка, брус; *(ray)* луч; **2.** сия́ть; излуча́ть [-чи́ть]

bean [bi:n] боб; *full of* ~s экспанси́вный, живо́й; *spill the* ~s проболта́ться *pf.*

bear[1] [beə] медве́дь *m* (-ве́дица *f*)

bear[2] [-] *[irr.]* *v/t.* носи́ть, нести́; *(endure)* [вы́]терпе́ть, выде́рживать [вы́держать]; *(give birth)* рожда́ть [роди́ть]; ~ *down* преодолева́ть [-ле́ть]; ~ *out* подтвержда́ть [-рди́ть]; ~ *o.s.* держа́ться, вести́ себя́; ~ *up* подде́рживать [-жа́ть]; ~ *(up)on* каса́ться (косну́ться) (Р); име́ть отноше́ние (к Д); *bring to* ~ употребля́ть [-би́ть]

beard [biəd] борода́; ~ed [-ɪd] борода́тый

bearer ['beərə] челове́к, несу́щий груз; *in expedition, etc.* носи́льщик; *of letter* предъяви́тель(ница *f*) *m*

bearing ['beərɪŋ] *(way of behaving)* мане́ра держа́ть себя́; *(relation)* отноше́ние; *beyond* (all) ~ невыноси́мо; *find one's* ~s [с]ориенти́роваться (a. *fig.*); *lose one's* ~s заблуди́ться, *fig.* растеря́ться

beast [bi:st] зверь *m*; скоти́на; ~ly [-lɪ] *coll.* ужа́сный

beat [bi:t] **1.** *[irr.]* *v/t.* [по]би́ть; *(one blow)* ударя́ть [уда́рить]; ~ *a retreat* отступа́ть [-пи́ть]; ~ *up* изби(ва́)ть; *eggs, etc.* взби(ва́)ть; ~ *about the bush* ходи́ть вокру́г да о́коло; *v/i. drums* бить; *heart* би́ться; *on door* колоти́ть; **2.** уда́р; бой; бие́ние; ритм; ~en ['bi:tn] **1.** *p. pt. от* beat; **2.** би́тый, побеждённый; *track* проторённый

beautician [bju:'tɪʃn] космето́лог

beautiful ['bju:tɪfl] □ краси́вый, прекра́сный, *day, etc.* чу́дный

beautify ['bju:tɪfaɪ] украша́ть [укра́сить]

beauty ['bju:tɪ] красота́, краса́вица; ~ *parlo(u)r*, *Brt.* ~ *salon* космети́ческий кабине́т

beaver ['bi:və] бобр

became [bɪ'keɪm] *pt. от* become

because [bɪ'kɒz] потому́ что, так как; ~ *of* и́з-за (Р)

beckon ['bekən] [по]мани́ть

become [bɪ'kʌm] *[irr. (come)]* *v/i.* [с]де́латься; станови́ться [стать]; *of clothes* *v/t.* быть к лицу́, идти́ (Д); подоба́ть (Д); ~ing [-ɪŋ] подоба́ющий; *of dress, etc.* (иду́щий) к лицу́

bed [bed] **1.** посте́ль *f*; крова́ть *f*; *agric.* гря́дка, клу́мба; *of river* ру́сло; **2.** *(plant)* выса́живать [вы́садить]

bedclothes *pl.* посте́льное бельё

bedding ['bedɪŋ] посте́льные принадле́жности *f/pl.*

bed|ridden ['bedrɪdn] прико́ванный к посте́ли; ~room спа́льня; ~spread покрыва́ло; ~time вре́мя ложи́ться спать

bee [bi:] пчела́; *have a* ~ *in one's bonnet coll.* быть поме́шанным на чём-л.

beech [bi:tʃ] бук, бу́ковое де́рево

beef [bi:f] говя́дина; ~steak бифште́кс; ~ tea кре́пкий бульо́н; ~y [bi:fɪ] мускули́стый

bee|hive у́лей; ~keeping пчелово́дство; ~line: *make a* ~ пойти́ напряму́ю, стрело́й помча́ться

been [bi:n, bɪn] *pt. p. от* be

beer [bɪə] пи́во; *small* ~ сла́бое пи́во, *fig.* ме́лкая со́шка

beet [biːt] свёкла (*chiefly Brt.: beetroot*)

beetle [biːtl] жук

before [bɪˈfɔː] 1. *adv.* впереди, вперёд; раньше; ~ **long** вскоре; **long** ~ задолго; 2. *cj.* прежде чем; пока не; перед тем как; скорее чем; 3. *prp.* перед (Т); впереди (Р); до (Р); **~hand** заранее, заблаговременно

befriend [bɪˈfrend] относиться подружески к (Д)

beg [beg] *v.t.* [по]просить (Р); умолять [-лить] (*for* о П); выпрашивать [выпросить] (*of* у Р); *v/i.* нищенствовать

began [bɪˈɡæn] *pt. om* **begin**

beggar [ˈbeɡə] 1. нищий, нищенка; **lucky** ~ счастливчик; **poor** ~ бедняга; 2. разорить [-рить], доводить [-вести] до нищеты; **it ~s all description** не поддаётся описанию

begin [bɪˈɡɪn] [*irr.*] нач(ин)ать (**with** с Р); **to** ~ **with** во-первых; сначала, для начала; **~ner** [-ə] начинающий, новичок; **~ning** [-ɪŋ] начало; **in or at the** ~ вначале

begrudge [bɪˈɡrʌdʒ] (*envy*) [по]завидовать (Д в П); жалеть, скупиться

begun [bɪˈɡʌn] *p. pt. om* **begin**

behalf [bɪˈhɑːf]: *on or in* ~ *of* для (Р), ради (Р); от имени (Р)

behav|e [bɪˈheɪv] вести себя; держаться; поступать [-пить]; **~iour** [-jə] поведение

behind [bɪˈhaɪnd] 1. *adv.* позади, сзади; **look** ~ оглянуться *pf.*; **be** ~ **s.o.** отставать [-стать] от кого-л. (**in** в П); 2. *prp.* за (Т); позади (Р), сзади (Р); после (Р)

beige [beɪʒ] бежевый

being [ˈbiːɪŋ] бытие, существование; (*creature*) живое существо; **for the time** ~ в настоящее время; на некоторое время, пока

belated [bɪˈleɪtɪd] запоздалый

belch [beltʃ] 1. отрыжка; 2. рыгать [рыгнуть]

belfry [ˈbelfrɪ] колокольня

Belgian [ˈbeldʒən] 1. бельгиец *m*, -ийка *f*; 2. бельгийский

belief [bɪˈliːf] вера (**in** в В); убеждение;

beyond ~ (просто) невероятно; **to the best of my** ~ по моему убеждению; насколько мне известно

believe [bɪˈliːv] [по]верить (**in** в В); **~r** [-ə] верующий

belittle [bɪˈlɪtl] *fig.* умалять [-лить], принижать [-низить]

bell [bel] колокол; звонок

belles-lettres [belˈletrə] *pl.* художественная литература, беллетристика

bellicose [ˈbelɪkəus] □ воинственный, агрессивный

belligerent [bɪˈlɪdʒərənt] 1. воюющая сторона; 2. воюющий

bellow [ˈbeləu] 1. *of animal* мычание; *of wind, storm* рёв; 2. реветь; орать

belly [ˈbelɪ] 1. *coll.* живот, *coll.* брюхо; 2. наду(ва)ть(ся); **~ful** [-ful]: **have had a** ~ *coll.*, *fig.* быть сытым по горло (*of* Т)

belong [bɪˈlɒŋ] принадлежать (Д); относиться (к Д); **~ings** [-ɪŋz] *pl.* вещи *f/pl.*, пожитки

beloved [bɪˈlʌvɪd, *pred.* bɪˈlʌvd] возлюбленный, любимый

below [bɪˈləu] 1. *adv.* внизу; ниже; 2. *prp.* ниже (Р); под (В, Р)

belt [belt] 1. пояс, *of leather* ремень; зона; *tech.* приводной ремень; *mil.* портупея; **safety** ~ *mot.* ремень безопасности; *ae.* привязной ремень; 2. подпояс(ыв)ать; (*thrash*) пороть ремнём

bemoan [bɪˈməun] оплак(ив)ать

bench [bentʃ] скамья; (*work*~) верстак

bend [bend] 1. сгиб, изгиб; *of road* поворот, изгиб; *of river* излучина; 2. [*irr.*] *v/t.* [по-, со]гнуть; *head, etc.* наклонять [-нить]; *v/i.* наклоняться [-ниться]; сгибаться [согнуться]

beneath [bɪˈniːθ] → **below**

benediction [benɪˈdɪkʃn] благословение

benefactor [ˈbenɪfæktə] благодетель; (*donor*) благотворитель

beneficial [benɪˈfɪʃl] □ благотворный, полезный

benefit [ˈbenɪfɪt] 1. выгода, польза; (*allowance*) пособие; *thea.* бенефис; 2. приносить пользу; извлекать пользу

benevolen|ce [bɪˈnevələns] благожела́тельность *f*; **~t** [-ənt] □ благожела́тельный

benign [bɪˈnaɪn] □ доброcерде́чный; *climate* благотво́рный; *med.* доброка́чественный

bent [bent] **1.** *pt. и p. pt. от* **bend**; **~ on** поме́шанный на (П); **2.** скло́нность *f*, спосо́бность *f*; **follow one's ~** сле́довать свои́м накло́нностям

bequeath [bɪˈkwiːð] завеща́ть *(im)pf.*

bequest [bɪˈkwest] насле́дство

bereave [bɪˈriːv] *[irr.]* лиша́ть [-ши́ть] (Р); отнима́ть [-ня́ть]

beret [ˈbereɪ] бере́т

berry [ˈberɪ] я́года

berth [bɜːθ] *naut.* я́корная стоя́нка; *(cabin)* каю́та; *(sleeping place)* ко́йка; *rail.* спа́льное ме́сто, по́лка; *fig. (выгодная)* до́лжность *f*

beseech [bɪˈsiːtʃ] *[irr.]* умоля́ть [-ли́ть], упра́шивать [упроси́ть] (+ *inf.*)

beset [bɪˈset] *[irr. (set)]* окружа́ть [-жи́ть]; *with questions, etc.* осажда́ть [осади́ть]; *I was ~ by doubts* меня́ одолева́ли сомне́ния

beside [bɪˈsaɪd] *prp.* ря́дом с (Т), о́коло (Р), близ (Р); *mi* **~o.s.** вне себя́ *(with* от Р); **~ the point** не по существу́; не отно́сится к де́лу; **~s** [-z] **1.** *adv.* кро́ме того́, сверх того́; **2.** *prp.* кро́ме (Р)

besiege [bɪˈsiːdʒ] осажда́ть [осади́ть]

besought [bɪˈsɔːt] *pt. от* **beseech**

bespatter [bɪˈspætə] забры́з(ив)ать

best [best] **1.** *adj.* лу́чший; **~ man at a wedding** ша́фер; **the ~ part** бо́льшая часть; **2.** *adv.* лу́чше всего́, всех; **3.** са́мое лу́чшее; **to the ~ of ...** наско́лько ...; **make the ~ of** испо́льзовать наилу́чшим о́бразом; **at ~** в лу́чшем слу́чае; **all the ~!** всего́ са́мого лу́чшего!

bestial [ˈbestɪəl, ˈbestʃəl] □ *(behaviour)* cко́тский; *cruelty, etc.* зве́рский

bestow [bɪˈstəʊ] ода́ривать [-ри́ть]; награжда́ть [-гради́ть] (В/Т); *title* присва́ивать [-во́ить]

bet [bet] **1.** пари́ *n indecl.*; **2.** *[irr.]* держа́ть пари́; би́ться об закла́д; **~ on horses** игра́ть на ска́чках

betray [bɪˈtreɪ] преда(ва́)ть; *(show)* выда(ва́)ть; **~al** [-əl] преда́тельство; **~er** [-ə] преда́тель *m*, -ница *f*

betrothal [bɪˈtrəʊðl] помо́лвка

better [ˈbetə] **1.** *adj.* лу́чший; **he is ~** ему́ лу́чше; **2.:** *change for the ~* переме́на к лу́чшему; *get the ~ of* взять верх над (Т); [пре]одоле́ть; **3.** *adv.* лу́чше; бо́льше; **so much the ~** тем лу́чше; **you had ~ go** вам бы лу́чше уйти́; **think ~ of it** переду́мать *pf.*; **4.** *v/t.* улучша́ть [улу́чшить]

between [bɪˈtwiːn] **1.** *adv.* ме́жду; **2.** *prp.* ме́жду (Т); **~ you and me** ме́жду на́ми (говоря́)

beverage [ˈbevərɪdʒ] напи́ток

beware [bɪˈweə] бере́чься, остерега́ться (Р) *impf.*; **~ of the dog!** осторо́жно, зла́я соба́ка!

bewilder [bɪˈwɪldə] смуща́ть [смути́ть]; ста́вить в тупи́к; *(confuse)* сбива́ть с то́лку; **~ment** [-mənt] смуще́ние, замеша́тельство; пу́таница

bewitch [bɪˈwɪtʃ] околдо́вывать [-дова́ть], очаро́вывать [-рова́ть]

beyond [bɪˈjɒnd] **1.** *adv.* вдали́, на рассто́янии; **this is ~ me** э́то вы́ше моего́ понима́ния; **2.** *prp.* за (В, Т); вне (Р); сверх (Р); по ту сто́рону (Р)

bias [ˈbaɪəs] **1.** *(prejudice)* предубежде́ние (про́тив Р); *(tendency of mind)* скло́нность *f*; склоня́ть [-ни́ть]; **~ed opinion** предвзя́тое мне́ние

bib [bɪb] де́тский нагру́дник

Bible [ˈbaɪbl] Би́блия

biblical [ˈbɪblɪkl] □ библе́йский

bicarbonate [baɪˈkɑːbənət]: **~ of soda** питьева́я со́да

bicker [ˈbɪkə] пререка́ться (с Т)

bicycle [ˈbaɪsɪkl] **1.** велосипе́д; **2.** е́здить на велосипе́де

bid [bɪd] **1.** *[irr.]* *price* предлага́ть [-ложи́ть]; **2.** предложе́ние, *(at sale)* зая́вка; *final* ~ оконча́тельная цена́; **~den** [bɪdn] *p. pt. от* **bid**

biennial [baɪˈenɪəl] двухле́тний

bifocal [baɪˈfəʊkl] бифока́льный

big [bɪg] большо́й, кру́пный; *(tall)* высокий; *of clothes* вели́к; *coll. fig.* ва́жный; *coll. fig.* **~ shot** ши́шка; **talk ~** [по]хва́статься

bigamy ['bɪgəmɪ] двоебра́чие

bigot ['bɪgət] слепо́й приве́рженец, фана́тик

bigwig ['bɪgwɪg] *coll.* ши́шка

bike [baɪk] *coll.* велосипе́д

bilateral [baɪ'lætərəl] двусторо́нний

bilberry ['bɪlbərɪ] черни́ка

bile [baɪl] жёлчь *f*; *fig.* жёлчность *f*

bilious ['bɪlɪəs]: **~ attack** при́ступ тошноты́; рво́та

bill¹ [bɪl] *of a bird* клюв

bill² [-] законопрое́кт, билль *m*; счёт; *(poster)* афи́ша; *fin.* ве́ксель *m*; **~ of credit** аккредити́в; **~ of fare** меню́; **that will fill the ~** э́то подойдёт; **foot the ~** оплати́ть счёт *pf.*

billiards ['bɪljədz] *pl.* билья́рд

billion ['bɪljən] биллио́н; *Am.* милли́а́рд

billow ['bɪləʊ] **1.** вал, больша́я волна́; **2.** *of sea* вздыма́ться; *sails* надува́ть [-ду́ть]

bin [bɪn] *rubbish* ~ му́сорное ведро́

bind [baɪnd] *v/t.* [c]вяза́ть; свя́зывать [-за́ть]; *(oblige)* обя́зывать [-за́ть]; *book* переплета́ть [-плести́]; **~er** ['baɪndə] переплётчик; **~ing** [-ɪŋ] *(book cover)* переплёт

binoculars [bɪ'nɒkjʊləz] бино́кль *m*

biography [baɪ'ɒgrəfɪ] биогра́фия

biology [baɪ'ɒlədʒɪ] биоло́гия

biosphere ['baɪəsfɪə] биосфе́ра

birch [bɜːtʃ] *(~ tree)* берёза

bird [bɜːd] *zo.* пти́ца; **early ~** ра́нняя пта́шка *(о человеке)*; **~'s-eye** ['bɜːdzaɪ]: **~ view** вид с пти́чьего полёта

Biro ['baɪərəʊ] *Brt. trademark* ша́риковая ру́чка

birth [bɜːθ] рожде́ние; *(origin)* происхожде́ние; **give ~** рожда́ть [роди́ть]; **~day** день рожде́ния; **~place** ме́сто рожде́ния; **~rate** рожда́емость *f*

biscuit ['bɪskɪt] пече́нье

bishop ['bɪʃəp] *eccl.* епи́скоп; *chess* слон; **~ric** [-rɪk] епа́рхия

bison ['baɪsn] *zo.* бизо́н, зубр

bit¹ [bɪt] кусо́чек, части́ца; немно́го

bit² [-] *comput.* бит, двои́чная ци́фра

bit³ [-] *pt. om* **~e**

bitch [bɪtʃ] су́ка

bit|e [baɪt] **1.** уку́с; *of fish* клёв; кусо́к; **have a ~** перекуси́ть *pf.*; **2.** *[irr.]* куса́ть [укуси́ть]; клева́ть [клю́нуть]; *of pepper, etc.* жечь; *of frost* щипа́ть; **~ing** *wind* прони́зывающий; *remark, etc.* язви́тельный

bitten ['bɪtn] *p. pt. om* **bite**

bitter ['bɪtə] □ го́рький, ре́зкий; *fig.* го́рький, мучи́тельный; *struggle, person* ожесточённый

blab [blæb] *coll.* разба́лтывать [-болта́ть]

black [blæk] **1.** чёрный; тёмный; ~ **eye** синя́к под гла́зом; **in ~ and white** чёрным по бе́лому; **give s.o. a ~ look** мра́чно посмотре́ть на (В); **2.** *fig.* очерни́ть; **~ out** потеря́ть созна́ние; **3.** чёрный цвет; *(Negro)* чернокожий; **~berry** ежеви́ка; **~bird** чёрный дрозд; **~board** кла́ссная доска́; **~en** ['blækn] *v/t.* [за]черни́ть; *fig.* [о]черни́ть; *v/i.* [по]черне́ть; **~guard** ['blɑːgɑːd] негодя́й, подле́ц; **~head** *med.* угри́ *m/pl.*; **~letter day** несча́стливый день; **~mail 1.** вымога́тельство, шанта́ж; **2.** вымога́ть *(pf.)* де́ньги у (Р); **~out** затемне́ние; *med.* поте́ря созна́ния; **~smith** кузне́ц

bladder ['blædə] *anat.* пузы́рь *m*

blade [bleɪd] ло́пасть *f*; *of knife* ле́звие; **~ of grass** трави́нка

blame [bleɪm] **1.** вина́; **2.** вини́ть, обвиня́ть [-ни́ть]; **he has only himself to ~** он сам во всём винова́т; **~less** ['bleɪmləs] безупре́чный

blanch [blɑːntʃ] *(grow pale)* побледне́ть *pf.*; *cul.* бланши́ровать

blank [blæŋk] **1.** □ *(empty)* пусто́й; *(expressionless)* невырази́тельный; *of form, etc.* незапо́лненный; **~ cartridge** холосто́й патро́н; **2.** *(empty space)* пробе́л; **my mind was a ~** у меня́ в голове́ не́ было ни одно́й мы́сли

blanket ['blæŋkɪt] шерстяно́е одея́ло; *fig.* покро́в

blare [bleə] *radio* труби́ть, реве́ть

blasphemy ['blæsfəmɪ] богохульство

blast [blɑːst] 1. сильный порыв ветра; *of explosion* взрыв; **at full ~** на полную мощность; 2. взрывать [взорвать]; *mus.* трубить; **~ed** [-ɪd] *coll.* проклятый; **~ furnace** доменная печь *f*

blatant ['bleɪtənt] наглый, вопиющий

blaze [bleɪz] 1. пламя *n*; *of flame, passion* вспышка; 2. *v/i.* гореть, пылать (*a. fig.*); сверкать [-кнуть]; **~r** ['bleɪzə] спортивная куртка

bleach [bliːtʃ] белить

bleak [bliːk] унылый, безрадостный; *prospects etc.* мрачный

bleary ['blɪərɪ] затуманенный, неясный; **~-eyed** ['blɪərɪaɪd] с мутными глазами

bleat [bliːt] 1. блеяние; 2. [за]блеять

bled [bled] *pt. и pt. p. от* **bleed**

bleed [bliːd] [*irr.*] *v/i.* кровоточить; истекать [-течь] кровью; **~ing** ['bliːdɪŋ] кровотечение

blemish ['blemɪʃ] недостаток; пятно (*a. fig.*)

blend [blend] 1. смешивать(ся) [-шать(ся)]; (*harmonize*) сочетать(ся) (*im*)*pf.*; 2. смесь *f*

bless [bles] благословлять [-вить]; одарять [-рить]; **~ed** ['blesɪd] *adj.* счастливый, блаженный; **~ing** ['blesɪŋ] *eccl.* благословение; благо, счастье

blew [bluː] *pt. от* **blow**

blight [blaɪt] 1. *disease* головня; ржавчина; мучнистая роса *и т.д.*; то, что разрушает (*планы*), отравляет (*жизнь и т.д.*); 2. *hopes, etc.* разби(ва)ть

blind [blaɪnd] 1. □ слепой (*fig.* **~ to** к Д); *handwriting* нечёткий, неясный; **~ alley** тупик; **turn a ~ eye** закрывать [закрыть] глаза (**to** на В); **~ly** *fig.* наугад, наобум; 2. штора; жалюзи *n indecl.*; 3. ослеплять [-пить]; **~fold** ['blaɪndfəʊld] завязывать глаза (Д); **~ness** слепота

blink [blɪŋk] 1. (*of eye*) моргание, *of light* мерцание; 2. *v/i.* моргать [-гнуть]; мигать [мигнуть]

bliss [blɪs] блаженство

blister ['blɪstə] 1. волдырь *m*; 2. покрываться волдырями

blizzard ['blɪzəd] буран, сильная метель *f*

bloat [bləʊt] распухать [-пухнуть]; разду(ва)ться

block [blɒk] 1. *of wood* колода, чурбан; *of stone, etc.* глыба; *between streets* квартал; **~ of apartments** (*Brt.* **flats**) многоэтажный дом; 2. (*obstruct*) преграждать [-адить]; **~ in** набрасывать вчерне; (*mst.* **~ up**) блокировать (*im*)*pf.*; *of pipe* засоряться [-риться]

blockade [blɒ'keɪd] 1. блокада; 2. блокировать (*im*)*pf.*

blockhead ['blɒkhed] болван

blond(e) [blɒnd] блондин *m*, -ка *f*; белокурый

blood [blʌd] кровь *f*; **in cold ~** хладнокровно; **~shed** кровопролитие; **~thirsty** кровожадный; **~ vessel** кровеносный сосуд; **~y** ['blʌdɪ] окровавленный, кровавый

bloom [bluːm] 1. цветок, цветение; *fig.* расцвет; **in ~** в цвету; 2. цвести, быть в цвету

blossom ['blɒsəm] 1. цветок (фруктового дерева). 2. цвести, расцветать [-ести]

blot [blɒt, blɑːt] 1. пятно (*a. fig.*); 2. *fig.* запятнать *pf.*

blotch [blɒtʃ] клякса, пятно

blouse [blaʊz] блуза, блузка

blow[1] [bləʊ] удар (*a. fig.*)

blow[2] [-] [*irr.*] 1. [по]дуть; **~ up** взрывать(ся) [взорвать(ся)]; **~ one's nose** [вы]сморкаться; 2. дуновение; **~n** [-n] *pt. p. от* **blow**

blue [bluː] 1. голубой; лазурный; (*dark ~*) синий; *coll.* (*be sad, depressed*) унылый, подавленный; 2. голубой цвет; синий цвет; 3. окрашивать в синий, голубой цвет; *of washing* [под]синить; **~bell** колокольчик

blues [bluːz] *pl.* меланхолия, хандра

bluff[1] [blʌf] (*abrupt*) резкий; (*rough*) грубоватый; *of headlands, etc.* обрывистый

bluff[2] [-] **1.** обма́н, блеф; **2.** v/t. обма́-
нывать[-ну́ть]; v/i. блефова́ть

blunder ['blʌndə] **1.** гру́бая оши́бка; **2.**
де́лать гру́бую оши́бку

blunt [blʌnt] **1.** □ тупо́й; *remark, etc.*
ре́зкий; **2.** [за]тупи́ть; *fig.* притупля́ть
[-пи́ть]

blur [blɜ:] **1.** (*indistinct outline*) не-
я́сное очерта́ние; пятно́; **2.** v/t. сде́-
лать нея́сным *pf.*; сма́зывать [-зать];
tears, etc. затума́нить *pf.*

blush [blʌʃ] **1.** кра́ска от смуще́ния
или стыда́; **2.** [по]красне́ть

boar [bɔ:] бо́ров, *hunt.* каба́н

board [bɔ:d] **1.** доска́; (*food*) стол; *of
ship* борт; *thea.* сце́на; *of* подмо́стки
m/pl.; council правле́ние; **~ of directors** правле́ние директоро́в; **2.** v/t. на-
ст(и)ла́ть; v/i. столова́ться; *train,
plane, etc.* сади́ться [сесть] на, в (B);
~er ['bɔ:dər] жиле́ц, опла́чивающий
ко́мнату и пита́ние; *ing house* пан-
сио́н; *ing school* шко́ла-интерна́т

boast [bəʊst] **1.** хвастовство́; **2.** гор-
ди́ться (T); (*of, about*) [по]хва́статься
(T); **~ful** ['bəʊstfʊl] хвастли́вый

boat [bəʊt] *small* ло́дка, *vessel* су́дно,
~ing ['bəʊtɪŋ] ката́ние на ло́дке под-
пры́гивать [-гнуть]

bobbin ['bɒbɪn] кату́шка; шпу́лька

bode [bəʊd]: (*portend*) **~ well** быть хо-
ро́шим зна́ком

bodice ['bɒdɪs] лиф

bodily ['bɒdɪlɪ] теле́сный, фи-
зи́ческий

body ['bɒdɪ, 'bɑ:dɪ] те́ло; (*corpse*)
труп; *mot.* ку́зов; **~ building** бо́диби-
лдинг, культури́зм

bog [bɒg] **1.** боло́то, тряси́на; **2. get
~ged down** увяза́ть [увя́знуть]

boggle ['bɒgl] отша́тываться
[-тну́ться] отпря́нуть (*out of surprise,
fear, or doubt*); **the mind ~s** уму́ непо-
стижи́мо

bogus ['bəʊgəs] подде́льный

boil[1] [bɔɪl] *med.* фуру́нкул

boil[2] [-] **1.** кипе́ние; **2.** [с]вари́ть(ся);
[вс]кипяти́ть(ся); кипе́ть; **~er** ['bɔɪlə]
tech. котёл

boisterous ['bɔɪstərəs] □ бу́рный,

шу́мный; *child* ре́звый

bold [bəʊld] □ (*daring*) сме́лый; *b.s.*
на́глый; *typ.* жи́рный; **~ness** ['bəʊld-
nɪs] сме́лость f; на́глость f

bolster ['bəʊlstə] **1.** ва́лик; опо́ра; **2.**
(*prop*) подде́рживать [-жа́ть]; подпи-
ра́ть [-пере́ть]

bolt [bəʊlt] **1.** болт; *on door* засо́в, за-
ди́жка; (*thunder~*) уда́р гро́ма; **a ~
from the blue** гром среди́ я́сного не́ба;
2. v/t. запира́ть на засо́в; v/i. нести́сь
стрело́й; (*run away*) убега́ть [убе-
жа́ть]

bomb [bɒm] **1.** бо́мба; **2.** бомби́ть

bombard [bɒm'bɑ:d]: **~ with questions**
бомбардирова́ть, забра́сывать [-ро-
са́ть] вопро́сами

bombastic [bɒm'bæstɪk] напы́щен-
ный

bond [bɒnd] *pl. fig.:* **~s** у́зы *f/pl.; fin.* об-
лига́ции *f/pl.*

bone [bəʊn] **1.** кость f; **~ of contention**
я́блоко раздо́ра; **make no ~s about**
coll. не [по]стесня́ться; не церемо́-
ниться с (T); **2.** вынима́ть, выреза́ть
ко́сти

bonfire ['bɒnfaɪə] костёр

bonnet ['bɒnɪt] *baby's* че́пчик; *mot.*
капо́т

bonus ['bəʊnəs] *fin.* пре́мия, возна-
гражде́ние

bony ['bəʊnɪ] костля́вый

book [bʊk] **1.** кни́га; **2.** (*tickets*) зака́-
зывать, заброни́ровать (*a. room in
a hotel*); **~case** кни́жный шкаф;
~ing clerk ['bʊkɪŋklɑ:k] *rail.* касси́р;
~ing office биле́тная ка́сса; **~keeping**
бухгалте́рия; **~let** брошю́ра, букле́т;
~seller продаве́ц книг; **second-hand
~** букини́ст

boom[1] [bu:m] **1.** *econ.* бум; **2.** *of business* процвета́ть *impf.*

boom[2] [-] **1.** *of gun, thunder, etc.* гул;
ро́кот; **2.** бу́хать, рокота́ть

boon [bu:n] бла́го

boor [bʊə] гру́бый, невоспи́танный
челове́к; **~ish** ['bʊərɪʃ] гру́бый, не-
воспи́танный

boost [bu:st] *trade* стимули́ровать
(разви́тие); *tech.* уси́ливать [-лить];

it ~ed his morale это его подбодрило; (*advertise*) рекламировать

boot¹ [bu:t]: *to ~* в придачу, вдобавок *adv.*

boot² [-] сапог, ботинок; *mot.* багажник; **~lace** ['-leɪs] шнурок для ботинок

booth [bu:ð] киоск; *telephone ~* телефонная будка; *polling ~* кабина для голосования

booty ['bu:tɪ] добыча

border ['bɔ:də] **1.** граница; (*edge*) край; *on tablecloth, etc.* кайма; **2.** граничить (*upon* с Т)

bore¹ [bɔ:] **1.** расточенное отверстие; *of gun* калибр; *fig.* зануда; **2.** [про]сверлить; *fig.* надоедать [-есть] (Д); наводить скуку на (В)²

bore² [-] *pt. om bear²*

boredom ['bɔ:dəm] скука

born [bɔ:n] рождённый; *fig.* прирождённый; **~e** [-] *pt. p. om bear²*

borough ['bʌrə] (*town*) город; (*section of a town*) район

borrow ['bɔrəʊ] *money* брать [взять] взаймы; занимать [-нять] (*from* у Р); *book* взять почитать

Bosnian ['bɒznɪən] **1.** босниец *m*, -ийка *f*; **2.** боснийский

bosom ['bʊzəm] грудь *f*; *fig.* лоно; *~ friend* закадычный друг

boss [bɒs] *coll.* **1.** шеф, босс, начальник; **2.** командовать (Т); **~y** ['bɒsɪ] любящий командовать

botany ['bɒtənɪ] ботаника

botch [bɒtʃ] портить; сделать *pf.* плохо или кое-как

both [bəʊθ] оба, обе; и тот и другой; *~ ... and ...* как ... так и ...; и ... и ...

bother ['bɒðə] *coll.* **1.** беспокойство; *oh ~!* какая досада!; **2.** возиться; надоедать [-есть] (Д); [по]беспокоить

bottle ['bɒtl] **1.** бутылка; *baby's ~* рожок; *hotwater ~* грелка; **2.** разливать по бутылкам; *~-opener* ключ, открывалка

bottom ['bɒtəm] **1.** дно; *of boat* днище; нижняя часть *f*; *of hill* подножье; *coll.* зад; *fig.* основа, суть *f*; *at the ~* внизу; *be at the ~ of sth.* быть причиной или

зачинщиком (Р); *get to the ~ of sth.* добраться до сути (Р); **2.** самый нижний

bough [baʊ] сук; ветка, ветвь *f*

bought [bɔ:t] *pt. и pt. p. om buy*

boulder ['bəʊldə] валун

bounce [baʊns] **1.** прыжок, скачок; *full of ~* полный энергии; **2.** подпрыгивать [-гнуть]; *of ball* отскакивать [отскочить]

bound¹ [baʊnd] **1.** граница; предел (*a. fig.*); ограничивать; (*be the boundary of*) граничить (с Т)

bound² [-]: *be ~* направляться (*for* в В)

bound³ [-] **1.** прыжок, скачок; **2.** прыгать [-гнуть]; [по]скакать; (*run*) бежать скачками

bound⁴ [-] **1.** *pt. и pt. p. om bind*; **2.** связанный; (*obliged*) обязанный; *of book* переплетённый

boundary ['baʊndərɪ] граница; *between fields* межа; *fig.* предел

boundless ['baʊndlɪs] безграничный

bouquet [bʊ'keɪ] букет (*a. of wine*)

bout [baʊt] *of illness* приступ; *in sports* встреча

bow¹ [baʊ] **1.** поклон; **2.** *v/i.* [со]гнуться; кланяться [поклониться]; (*submit*) подчиняться [-ниться] (Д); *v/t.* [со]гнуть

bow² [bəʊ] лук; (*curve*) дуга; (*knot*) бант; *mus.* смычок

bow³ [baʊ] *naut.* нос

bowels ['baʊəlz] *pl.* кишки *f/pl.*; *of the earth* недра *n/pl.*

bowl¹ [bəʊl] миска; ваза

bowl² [-] **1.** шар; *pl.* игра в шары; **2.** *v/t.* [по]катить; *v/i.* играть в шары; *be ~ed over* быть покорённым или ошеломлённым (*by* Т)

box¹ [bɒks] **1.** коробка; ящик; *thea.* ложа; **2.** укладывать в ящик

box² [-] *sport* **1.** боксировать; **2.** *on the ear* пощёчина; *~er* ['-ə] *sportsman, dog* боксёр; *~ing* ['-ɪŋ] *sport* бокс

box office театральная касса

boy [bɔɪ] мальчик; юноша; *~friend* ['-frend] друг (*девушки*); *~hood* ['-hʊd] отрочество; *~ish* ['bɔɪʃ] □

мальчи́шеский

brace [breɪs] **1.** *tech.* коловоро́т, скоба́; **~ and bit** дрель; **2.** (*support*) подпира́ть [-пере́ть]; **~ up** подбодря́ть [-бодри́ть]; **~ o.s.** собра́ться с ду́хом

bracelet ['breɪslɪt] брасле́т

braces [breɪsɪz] *pl.* **suspenders** подтя́жки *f/pl.*

bracket ['brækɪt] **1.** *tech.* кронште́йн; (*income* **~**) катего́рия, гру́ппа; *typ.* ско́бка; **2.** заключа́ть [-чи́ть] в ско́бки; *fig.* ста́вить на одну́ до́ску с (T)

brag [bræg] [по]хва́статься

braggart ['brægət] хвасту́н

braid [breɪd] **1.** *of hair* коса́; (*band*) тесьма́; *on uniform* галу́н; **2.** заплета́ть [-ести́]; обшива́ть тесьмо́й

brain [breɪn] мозг; (*fig. mst.* **~s**) рассу́док, ум; у́мственные спосо́бности *f/pl.* **rack one's ~s** лома́ть себе́ го́лову (над T); **use your ~s!** шевели́ мозга́ми!; **~wave** блестя́щая иде́я; **~y** ['-ɪ] *coll.* башкови́тый

brake [breɪk] **1.** *mot.* то́рмоз; **2.** [за]тормози́ть

branch [brɑːntʃ] **1.** ветвь *f*, ве́тка (*a. rail*); сук (*pl.:* су́чья); *of science* о́трасль *f*; *of bank, etc.* отделе́ние, филиа́л; **2.** развётвля́ть(ся) [-етви́ть(ся)]; расширя́ться [-ши́риться]

brand [brænd] **1.** клеймо́; сорт; торго́вая ма́рка; **2.** *fig.* (*stigmatize*) [за]клейми́ть, [о]позо́рить

brandish ['brændɪʃ] разма́хивать [-хну́ть] (T)

brand-new [brænd'njuː] *coll.* совсе́м но́вый, с иго́лочки

brandy ['brændɪ] конья́к

brass [brɑːs] лату́нь; *coll.* (*impudence*) на́глость *f*, наха́льство; **~ band** духово́й орке́стр

brassière ['bræsɪə] ли́фчик, бюстга́льтер

brave [breɪv] **1.** хра́брый, сме́лый; **2.** хра́бро встреча́ть; **~ry** ['breɪvərɪ] хра́брость *f*, сме́лость *f*

brawl [brɔːl] **1.** шу́мная ссо́ра, пота́совка; **2.** [по]сканда́лить, [по]дра́ться

brawny ['brɔːnɪ] си́льный; му́скули-

стый

brazen ['breɪzn] ме́дный, бро́нзовый; бессты́дный, на́глый (*a.* **~faced**)

Brazilian [brə'zɪlɪən] **1.** брази́льский; **2.** брази́лец *m*, брази́ля́нка *f*

breach [briːtʃ] **1.** проло́м; *fig.* (*breaking*) разры́в; *of rule, etc.* наруше́ние; (*gap*) брешь *f*; **2.** пробива́ть брешь в (П)

bread [bred] хлеб

breadth [bredθ] ширина́; *fig.* широта́ (кругозо́ра); широ́кий разма́х

break [breɪk] **1.** (*interval*) переры́в; па́уза; (*crack*) тре́щина; разры́в; *coll.* шанс; **a bad ~** неуда́ча; **2.** [*irr.*] *v/t.* [с]лома́ть; разби́(ва́)ть; разруша́ть [-ру́шить]; (*interrupt*) прер(ы)ва́ть; (*a lock, etc.*) взла́мывать [взлома́ть]; **~ up** разла́мывать [-лома́ть]; разби́(ва́)ть; *v/i.* пор(ы)ва́ть (с T); [по]лома́ться, разби́(ва́)ться; **~ away** отделя́ться [-ли́ться] (от P); **~ down** техн. потерпе́ть *pf.* ава́рию, вы́йти *pf.* из стро́я; **~ out** вспы́хивать [-хнуть]; **~able** ['breɪkəbl] ло́мкий, хру́пкий; **~age** ['breɪkɪdʒ] поло́мка; **~down** *of talks, etc.* прекраще́ние; *tech.* поло́мка; **nervous ~** не́рвное расстро́йство

breakfast ['brekfəst] **1.** за́втрак; **2.** [по]за́втракать

breakup распа́д, разва́л

breast [brest] грудь *f*; **make a clean ~ of sth.** чистосерде́чно сознава́ться в чём-л.; **~stroke** *sport* брасс

breath [breθ] дыха́ние; вздох; **take a ~** перевести́ *pf.* дух; **with bated ~** затаи́в дыха́ние; **~e** [briːð] *v/i.* дыша́ть [дохну́ть]; **~er** [briːðə] *pause* переды́шка; **~less** ['breθlɪs] запыха́вшийся; *of a day* безве́тренный

bred [bred] *pt. u pt. p. om* **breed**

breeches ['brɪtʃɪz] *pl.* бри́джи *pl.*

breed [briːd] **1.** [*irr.*] *v/t.* выводи́ть [вы́вести]; разводи́ть *v/i.* [-вести́], размножа́ться [-о́житься]; [рас]плоди́ться; **~er** ['briːdə] *of animal* производи́тель *m*; ското́вод; **~ing** [-dɪŋ] разведе́ние (живо́тных); *of person* воспита́ние; **good ~** воспи́танность *f*

breez|e [briːz] лёгкий ветеро́к, бриз; **~y** ['briːzɪ] ве́тренный; *person* живо́й, весёлый

brevity ['brevɪtɪ] кра́ткость f

brew [bruː] *v/t. beer* [с]вари́ть; *tea* зава́ривать [-ри́ть]; *fig.* затева́ть [зате́ять]; **~ery** ['bruːərɪ] пивова́ренный заво́д

brib|e [braɪb] **1.** взя́тка; по́дкуп; **2.** подкупа́ть [-пи́ть]; дава́ть взя́тку (Д); **~ery** ['braɪbərɪ] взя́точничество

brick [brɪk] кирпи́ч; *fig.* молодчи́на; сла́вный па́рень *m*; **drop a ~** сморо́зить *pf.* глу́пость; (*say*) ля́пнуть *pf.*; **~layer** ка́менщик

bridal ['braɪdl] □ сва́дебный

bride [braɪd] неве́ста; *just married* новобра́чная; **~groom** жени́х; *just married* новобра́чный; **~smaid** подру́жка неве́сты

bridge [brɪdʒ] **1.** мост; **~ of the nose** перено́сица; **2.** соединя́ть мо́стом; стро́ить мост че́рез (В); (*overcome*) *fig.* преодоле(ва́)ть

bridle ['braɪdl] **1.** узда́; **2.** *v/t.* взну́здывать [-да́ть]

brief [briːf] **1.** коро́ткий, кра́ткий, сжа́тый; **2.** [про]инструкти́ровать; **~case** портфе́ль *m*

brigade [brɪ'geɪd] *mil.* брига́да

bright [braɪt] □ я́ркий; све́тлый, я́сный; (*intelligent*) смышлёный; **~en** ['braɪtn] *v/t.* оживля́ть [-ви́ть]; *v/i. weather* проясня́ться [-ни́ться]; *person:* оживля́ться [-ви́ться]; **~ness** ['-nɪs] я́ркость f; блеск

brillian|ce, ~cy ['brɪljəns, -sɪ] я́ркость f; блеск; (*splendo[u]r*) великоле́пие; (*intelligence*) блестя́щий ум; **~t** [-jənt] **1.** □ блестя́щий (*a. fig.*); сверка́ющий; **2.** бриллиа́нт

brim [brɪm] **1.** край; *of hat* поля́ *n/pl.*; **2.** наполня́ть(ся) до краёв; **~over** *fig.* перелива́ться [-ли́ться] че́рез край

brine [braɪn] *cul.* рассо́л

bring [brɪŋ] [*irr.*] приноси́ть [-нести́]; доставля́ть [-а́вить]; *in car, etc.* привози́ть [-везти́]; (*lead*) приводи́ть [-вести́]; **~ about** осуществля́ть [-ви́ть]; **~ down prices** снижа́ть [сни-

зить]; **~ down the house** вы́звать *pf.* бу́рю аплодисме́нтов; **~ home to** довести́ что́-нибудь до чьего́-нибудь созна́ния; **~ round** приводи́ть [-вести́] в созна́ние; **~ up** воспи́тывать [-та́ть]

brink [brɪŋk] (*edge*) край (*a. fig.*); (круто́й) бе́рег; **on the ~ of war** на грани́ войны́

brisk [brɪsk] ско́рый, оживлённый

bristl|e ['brɪsl] **1.** щети́на; **2.** [о]щети́ниться; **~ with anger** [рас]серди́ться; **~ with** изоби́ловать (Т); **~y** [-ɪ] щети́нистый, колю́чий

British ['brɪtɪʃ] брита́нский; **the~** брита́нцы *m/pl.*

brittle ['brɪtl] хру́пкий, ло́мкий

broach [brəʊtʃ] *question* поднима́ть [-ня́ть]; (*begin*) нач(ин)а́ть

broad [brɔːd] □ широ́кий, обши́рный; *of humour* грубова́тый; **in ~ daylight** средь бе́ла дня; **~cast** [*irr.* (*cast*)] **1.** *rumour, etc.* распространя́ть [-ни́ть]; передава́ть по ра́дио, трансли́ровать; **2.** радиопереда́ча, трансля́ция; радиовеща́ние

brocade [brə'keɪd] парча́

broil [brɔɪl] жа́рить(ся) на огне́; *coll.* жа́риться на со́лнце

broke [brəʊk] *pt. om break*; **be ~** быть без гроша́; **go ~** обанкро́титься *pf.*

broken ['brəʊkən] **1.** *pt. p. om break*; **2.** разби́тый, раско́лотый; **~ health** надло́мленное здоро́вье

broker ['brəʊkə] бро́кер, ма́клер

bronchitis [brɒŋ'kaɪtɪs] бронхи́т

bronze [brɒnz] **1.** бро́нза; **2.** бро́нзовый; **3.** загора́ть [-ре́ть]

brooch [brəʊtʃ] брошь, бро́шка

brood [bruːd] **1.** вы́водок; *fig.* ора́ва; **2.** *fig.* гру́стно размышля́ть

brook [brʊk] ручей

broom [bruːm] метла́, ве́ник

broth [brɒθ] бульо́н

brothel ['brɒθl] публи́чный дом

brother ['brʌðə] брат; собра́т; **~hood** [-hud] бра́тство; **~in-law** [-rɪnlɔː] (*wife's brother*) шу́рин; (*sister's husband*) зять *m*; (*husband's brother*) де́верь *m*; **~ly** [-lɪ] бра́тский

brought [brɔːt] *pt. и pt. p. om bring*

brow [braʊ] лоб; (eye~) бровь f; of hill вершина; ~beat [irr. (beat)] запугивать [-гать]

brown [braʊn] **1.** коричневый цвет; **2.** коричневый; смуглый; загорелый; **3.** загорать [-реть]

browse [braʊz] пастись; fig. читать беспорядочно, просматривать

bruise [bruːz] **1.** синяк, кровоподтёк; **2.** ушибать [-бить]; поставить pf. (себе) синяки

brunt [brʌnt]: **bear the ~ of sth.** fig. выносить всю тяжесть чего-л.

brush [brʌʃ] **1.** for sweeping, brushing, etc. щётка; for painting кисть f; **2.** v/t. чистить щёткой; причёсывать щёткой; **~ aside** отмахиваться [-хнуться] (от Р); **~ up** приводить в порядок; fig. освежать в памяти; v/i. **~ by** прошмыгивать [-гнуть]; **~ against s.o.** слегка задеть кого-либо; **~wood** ['brʌʃwʊd] хворост, валежник

brusque [brʊsk] □ грубый; (abrupt) резкий

brussels sprouts [brʌsəls'spraʊts] брюссельская капуста

brut|al ['bruːtl] □ грубый; (cruel) жестокий; **~ality** [bruː'tæləti] грубость f; жестокость f; **~e** [bruːt] **1.** жестокий; by ~ **force** грубой силой; **2.** animal животное; pers. скотина

bubble ['bʌbl] пузырь m, dim. пузырёк; **2.** пузыриться; (boil) кипеть; of spring бить ключом (a. fig.)

buck [bʌk] **1.** zo. самец (оленя, зайца и др.); **2.** становиться на дыбы; **~ up** coll. встряхнуться pf.; оживляться [-виться]

bucket ['bʌkɪt] ведро; of dredging machine ковш

buckle ['bʌkl] **1.** пряжка; **2.** v/t. застёгивать [-тегнуть]; v/i. of metal, etc. [по]коробиться; **~ down to** приниматься за дело

buckwheat ['bʌkwiːt] гречиха; cul. гречневая крупа

bud [bʌd] **1.** почка, бутон; fig. зародыш; **nip in the ~** подавить pf. в зародыше; **2.** v/i. bot. давать почки; fig. разви(ва)ться

budge ['bʌdʒ] mst. v/i. сдвигаться [-инуться]; шевелить(ся) [-льнуть(ся)]; fig. уступать [-пить]

budget ['bʌdʒɪt] **1.** бюджет; финансовая смета; **2.** ~ for ассигновать определённую сумму на что-то; предусматривать [-смотреть]

buff [bʌf] тёмно-жёлтый

buffalo ['bʌfələʊ] zo. буйвол

buffer ['bʌfə] rail. буфер

buffet¹ ['bʌfɪt] ударять [-арить]; ~ **about** бросать из стороны в сторону

buffet² **1.** [~] буфет; **2.** ['bʊfeɪ] буфетная стойка; ~ **supper** ужин "аля-фуршет"

buffoon [bə'fuːn] шут

bug [bʌg] клоп; Am. насекомое; hidden microphone подслушивающее устройство

build [bɪld] **1.** [irr.] [по]строить; сооружать [-рудить]; nest [с]вить; ~ **on** полагаться [положиться], возлагать надежды на (В); **2.** (тело) сложение; ~er ['bɪldə] строитель m; ~ing ['-ɪŋ] здание; строительство

built [bɪlt] pt. и pt. p. от **build**

bulb [bʌlb] bot. луковица; el. лампочка

bulge [bʌldʒ] **1.** выпуклость f; выпячиваться [выпятиться], выдаваться [выдаться]

bulk [bʌlk] объём; основная часть f; in ~ навалом; ~y ['bʌlkɪ] громоздкий; person тучный

bull [bʊl] бык; **take the ~ by the horns** взять pf. быка за рога; ~ **in a china shop** слон в посудной лавке

bulldog ['bʊldɒg] бульдог

bulldozer ['bʊldəʊzə] бульдозер

bullet ['bʊlɪt] пуля

bulletin ['bʊlətɪn] бюллетень m

bull's-eye ['bʊlzaɪ] яблочко мишени; **hit the ~** попасть pf. в цель (a. fig.)

bully ['bʊlɪ] **1.** задира m; **2.** задирать, запугивать [-гать]

bum [bʌm] coll. зад(ница); Am. sl. лодырь m; бродяга m

bumblebee ['bʌmblbiː] шмель m

bump [bʌmp] **1.** глухой удар; (swelling) шишка; **2.** ударять(ся) [ударить(ся)]; ~ *into* наталкиваться [-толкнуться] (*a. fig*); *of cars, etc.* сталкиваться [столкнуться]; ~ *against* стукаться [-кнуться]

bumper ['bʌmpə] *mot.* буфер

bumpy ['bʌmpɪ] ухабистый, неровный

bun [bʌn] булочка

bunch [bʌntʃ] *of grapes* гроздь, кисть; *of keys* связка; *of flowers* букет; *of people* группа

bundle ['bʌndl] **1.** узел; **2.** *v/t.* (*put together*) собирать вместе, связывать в узел (*a.* ~ *up*)

bungalow ['bʌŋgələʊ] одноэтажный коттедж

bungle ['bʌŋgl] неумело, небрежно работать; [на]портить; *coll.* завалить

bunk[1] [bʌŋk] вздор

bunk[2] [-] койка (*a. naut.*); *rail.* спальное место, полка

buoy [bɔɪ] *naut.* бакен, буй; ~**ant** ['bɔɪənt] □ плавучий; (*cheerful*) жизнерадостный; бодрый

burden ['bɜːdn] **1.** ноша; *fig.* бремя *n*, груз; **2.** нагружать [-рузить]; обременять [-нить]; ~**some** [-səm] обременительный

bureau ['bjʊərəʊ] контора; бюро *n indecl.*; *information* ~ справочное бюро; ~**cracy** [bjʊə'rɒkrəsɪ] бюрократия

burglar ['bɜːglə] взломщик; ~**y** [-rɪ] кража со взломом

burial ['berɪəl] похороны *f/pl.*; ~ *service* заупокойная служба

burly ['bɜːlɪ] здоровенный, дюжий

burn [bɜːn] **1.** ожог; **2.** [*irr.*] *v/i.* гореть; *of food* подгорать [-реть]; *sting* жечь; *v/t.* [с]жечь; сжигать [сжечь]; ~**er** ['bɜːnə] горелка

burnt [bɜːnt] *pt. и pt. p. от* **burn**

burrow ['bʌrəʊ] **1.** нора; **2.** [вы́]рыть нору

burst [bɜːst] **1.** (*explosion*) взрыв *a. fig.; of anger, etc.* вспышка; **2.** [*irr.*] *v/i.* взрываться [взорваться]; *dam* прор(ы)ваться; *pipe, etc.* лопаться [лопнуть]; ~ *into the room* врываться [ворваться] в комнату; ~ *into tears*

разрыдаться; *v/t.* взрывать [взорвать]

bury ['berɪ] [по]хоронить; *a bone, etc. in earth* зары(ва)ть

bus [bʌs] автобус

bush [bʊʃ] куст, кустарник; *beat about or around the* ~ ходить вокруг да около

business ['bɪznɪs] дело; бизнес; торговое предприятие; *have no* ~ *to* inf. не иметь права (+ inf.); ~**like** [-laɪk] деловой; практичный; ~**man** бизнесмен, предприниматель; ~**trip** деловая поездка

bus station автовокзал; ~ *stop* автобусная остановка

bust [bʌst] бюст; женская грудь *f*

bustle ['bʌsl] **1.** суматоха; суета; **2.** *v/i.* [по]торопиться, [за]суетиться; *v/t.* [по]торопить

busy ['bɪzɪ] **1.** □ занятой (*at* T); занятый (*a. tel.*); **2.** (*mst.* ~ *o.s.*) заниматься [заняться] (*with* T)

but [bʌt, bət] **1.** *cj.* но, а; однако; тем не менее; *если бы не;* **2.** *prp.* кроме (P), за исключением (P); *the last* ~ *one* предпоследний; ~ *for* без (P); **3.** *adv.* только, лишь; ~ *now* только что; *all* ~ едва не ...; *nothing* ~ ничего кроме, только; *I cannot help* ~ inf. не могу не (+ inf.)

butcher ['bʊtʃə] **1.** мясник; *fig.* убийца *m;* *cattle* забивать; *people* уби(ва)ть; ~**y** [-rɪ] бойня, резня

butler ['bʌtlə] дворецкий

butt [bʌt] **1.** (*blow*) удар; *of rifle* приклад; (*of cigarette*) окурок; *fig. of person* мишень для насмешек; **2.** ударять головой; (*run into*) натыкаться [наткнуться]; ~ *in* перебивать [-бить]

butter ['bʌtə] **1.** (сливочное) масло; **2.** намазывать маслом; ~**cup** *bot.* лютик; ~**fly** бабочка

buttocks ['bʌtəks] *pl.* ягодицы *f/pl.*

button ['bʌtn] **1.** пуговица; *of bell, etc.* (*knob*) кнопка; **2.** застёгивать [-тегнуть]; ~**hole** петля

buxom ['bʌksəm] пышная, полногрудая

buy [baɪ] [*irr.*] *v/t.* покупать [купить]

(*from* у Р); **~er** ['baɪə] покупа́тель *m*, -ница *f*

buzz [bʌz] **1.** жужжа́ние; *of crowd* гул; **2.** *v/i.* [за]жужжа́ть

by [baɪ] **1.** *prp.* у (Р), при (П), о́коло (Р); к (Д); вдоль (Р); **~ the dozen** дю́жинами; **~ o.s.** оди́н *m*, одна́ *f*; **~ land** назе́мным тра́нспортом; **~ rail** по желе́зной доро́ге; **day ~ day** день за днём; **2.** *adv.* бли́зко, ря́дом; ми́мо; **~ and ~** вско́ре; **~ the way** ме́жду про-

чим; **~ and large** в це́лом; **~-election** ['baɪlekʃn] дополни́тельные вы́боры *m/pl.*; **~gone** про́шлый; **~pass** объе́зд, объездна́я доро́га; **~-product** побо́чный проду́кт; **~stander** ['-stændə] очеви́дец (-дица); **~street** у́лочка

byte [baɪt] *comput.* байт

by|way глуха́я доро́га; **~word** при́тча во язы́цех

C

cab [kæb] такси́ *n indecl.*; *mot., rail.* каби́на

cabbage ['kæbɪdʒ] капу́ста

cabin ['kæbɪn] (*hut*) хи́жина; *ae.* каби́на; *naut.* каю́та

cabinet ['kæbɪnɪt] *pol.* кабине́т; *of TV, radio, etc.* ко́рпус

cable ['keɪbl] **1.** ка́бель *m*; (*rope*) кана́т; телегра́мма; **~ television** ка́бельное телеви́дение; **2.** *tel.* телеграфи́ровать (*im*)*pf.*

cackle ['kækl] **1.** куда́хтанье; гого́танье; **2.** [за]куда́хтать; *of geese and man* [за]гогота́ть

cad [kæd] негодя́й

cadaverous [kə'dævərəs] исхуда́вший как скеле́т

caddish ['kædɪʃ] по́длый

cadet [kə'det] каде́т, курса́нт

cadge [kædʒ] *v/t.* кля́нчить; *v/i.* попроша́йничать; **~r** ['kædʒə] попроша́йка

café ['kæfeɪ] кафе́ *n indecl.*

cafeteria [kæfɪ'tɪərɪə] кафете́рий; *at factory, univ.* столо́вая

cage [keɪdʒ] *for animals* кле́тка; (*of elevator*) каби́на ли́фта

cajole [kə'dʒəʊl] угова́ривать [-вори́ть]; *coll.* обха́живать; доби́ться *pf.* чего́-л. ле́стью и́ли обма́ном

cake [keɪk] кекс, торт; *fancy* пиро́жное; *of soap* кусо́к

calamity [kə'læmətɪ] бе́дствие

calcium ['kælsɪəm] ка́льций

calculat|e ['kælkjʊleɪt] *v/t.* вычисля́ть [вы́числить]; *cost, etc.* подсчи́тывать [-ита́ть]; *v/i.* рассчи́тывать (**on** на В); **~ion** [kælkjʊ'leɪʃn] вычисле́ние; расчёт; **~or** ['kælkjʊleɪtə] калькуля́тор

calendar ['kælɪndə] календа́рь *m*

calf[1] [kɑːf], *pl.* **calves** [kɑːvz] телёнок (*pl.*: теля́та); (*a.* **~skin**) теля́чья ко́жа, опо́ек

calf[2] [-], *pl.* **calves** *of the leg(s)* [-] икра́

caliber *or* **calibre** ['kælɪbə] кали́бр (*a. fig.*)

calico ['kælɪkəʊ] си́тец

call [kɔːl] **1.** крик, зов, о́клик; *tel.* звоно́к; (*summon*) вы́зов; (*appeal*) призы́в; визи́т, посеще́ние; **on** ~ *of nurse, doctor* дежу́рство на дому́; **2.** *v/t.* [по]зва́ть; оклика́ть [-и́кнуть]; (*summon*) соз(ы)ва́ть; вызыва́ть [вы́звать]; [раз]буди́ть; призыва́ть; **~ off** отменя́ть [-ни́ть] (Р); **~ up** призыва́ть на вое́нную слу́жбу; **~ s.o.'s attention to** привле́чь *pf.* чьё-л. внима́ние (к Д); *v/i.* крича́ть [кри́кнуть]; *tel.* [по]звони́ть; (*visit*) заходи́ть [зайти́] (**at** в В; **on** *a p.* к Д); **~ for** [по]тре́бовать; **~ for** *a p.* заходи́ть [зайти́] за (Т); **~ in** *coll.* забега́ть [-ежа́ть] (к Д); **on** наве́щать [-ести́ть] (В); приз(ы)ва́ть (**to do** *etc.* сде́лать *и т.д.*); **~box** ['kɔːlbɒks] *Am.* телефо́н-автома́т, телефо́нная бу́дка; **~er** ['kɔːlə] гость(я

C

f) m

calling ['kɔːlɪŋ] (*vocation*) призва́ние; профе́ссия

call|ous ['kæləs] □ огрубе́лый; мозо́листый; *fig.* бессерде́чный; **~us** ['kæləs] мозо́ль

calm [kɑːm] **1.** □ споко́йный; безве́тренный; **2.** тишина́; *of sea* штиль *m.*; споко́йствие; **3. ~ down** успока́ивать(ся) [-ко́ить(ся)]; *of wind, etc.* стиха́ть [-и́хнуть]

calorie ['kælərɪ] *phys.* кало́рия

calve [kɑːv] [о]тели́ться; **~s** *pl. om* **calf**

cambric ['keɪmbrɪk] бати́ст

came [keɪm] *pt. om* **come**

camera ['kæmərə] фотоаппара́т; *cine.* киноаппара́т; **in ~** при закры́тых дверя́х

camomile ['kæməmaɪl] рома́шка

camouflage ['kæmʊflɑːʒ] **1.** камуфля́ж, маскиро́вка (*a. mil.*); **2.** [за]маскирова́ть(ся)

camp [kæmp] **1.** ла́герь *m*; **~ bed** похо́дная крова́ть; **2.** стать ла́герем; **~ out** расположи́ться *pf.* и́ли ночева́ть на откры́том во́здухе

campaign [kæm'peɪn] **1.** *pol., etc.* кампа́ния; **2.** проводи́ть кампа́нию; агити́ровать (**for** за В, **against** про́тив Р)

camphor ['kæmfə] камфара́

camping ['kæmpɪŋ] ке́мпинг (= *a.* **~ site**)

campus ['kæmpəs] *Am. university grounds and buildings* университе́тский городо́к

can¹ [kæn] *v/aux.* [c]мочь, быть в состоя́нии [c]уме́ть

can² [-] **1.** *for milk* бидо́н; (*tin*) ба́нка; *for petrol* кани́стра; **2.** консерви́ровать (*im*)*pf.*, *pf. a.* [за-]; **~ opener** консе́рвный нож

canal [kə'næl] кана́л

canary [kə'neərɪ] канаре́йка

cancel ['kænsl] (*call off*) отменя́ть [-ни́ть]; (*cross out*) вычёркивать [вы́черкнуть]; *agreement, etc.* аннули́ровать (*im*)*pf.*; *stamp* погаша́ть [погаси́ть]; *math.* (*a.* **~ out**) сокраща́ть [-рати́ть]

cancer ['kænsə] *astr.* созве́здие Ра́ка;

med. рак; **~ous** [-rəs] ра́ковый

candid ['kændɪd] □ и́скренний, прямо́й; **~ camera** скры́тая ка́мера

candidate ['kændɪdət] кандида́т (**for** на В)

candied ['kændɪd] заса́харенный

candle ['kændl] свеча́; **the game is (not) worth the ~** игра́ (не) сто́ит свеч; **~stick** [-stɪk] подсве́чник

cando(u)r ['kændə] открове́нность *f*; и́скренность *f*

candy ['kændɪ] ледене́ц; *Am.* конфе́ты *f/pl.*, сла́сти *f/pl.*

cane [keɪn] *bot.* тростни́к; *for walking* трость *f*

canned [kænd] консерви́рованный

cannon ['kænən] пу́шка; ору́дие

cannot ['kænɒt] не в состоя́нии, → **can¹**

canoe [kə'nuː] кано́э

canon ['kænən] *eccl.* кано́н; пра́вило

cant [kænt] пусты́е слова́; ханжество́

can't [kɑːnt] = **cannot**

canteen [kæn'tiːn] *eating place* буфе́т; столо́вая

canvas ['kænvəs] *cloth* холст; *for embroidery* канва́; *fig.* карти́на; паруси́на

canvass [-] *v/t.:* **~ opinions** иссле́довать обще́ственное мне́ние; собира́ть голоса́ перед вы́борами

caoutchouc ['kaʊtʃʊk] каучу́к

cap [kæp] **1.** *with peak* ке́пка, *mil.* фура́жка; *without peak* ша́пка; *tech.* колпачо́к; *of mushroom* шля́пка; **~ in hand** в ро́ли проси́теля; **2.** накрыва́ть [-ры́ть] кры́шкой; *coll.* перещеголя́ть *pf.*; **to~it all** в доверше́ние всего́

capab|ility [keɪpə'bɪlətɪ] спосо́бность *f*; **~le** ['keɪpəbl] □ спосо́бный (**of** на В); (*gifted*) одарённый

capaci|ous [kə'peɪʃəs] □ вмести́тельный; **~ty** [kə'pæsətɪ] объём, вмести́мость *f*; (*ability*) спосо́бность *f*, *tech.* производи́тельность *f*; *of engine* мо́щность *f*; *el.* ёмкость *f*; **in the ~ of** в ка́честве (Р)

cape¹ [keɪp] плащ

cape² [-] *geogr.* мыс

C

caper ['keɪpə] прыжо́к, ша́лость; *cut ~s* выде́лывать антраша́; дура́читься

capital ['kæpɪtl] **1.** □ (*crime*) карае́мый сме́ртью; (*sentence, punishment*) сме́ртный; **2.** столи́ца; (*wealth*) капита́л; (*a. ~ letter*) загла́вная бу́ква; **~ism** ['kæpɪtəlɪzəm] капитали́зм; **~ize** ['kæpɪtəlaɪz]: **~ on** обраща́ть в свою́ по́льзу

capitulate [kə'pɪtʃʊleɪt] капитули́ровать, сд(ав)а́ться (**to** Д) (*a. fig.*)

capric|e [kə'priːs] капри́з, причу́да; **~ious** [kə'prɪʃəs] □ капри́зный

capsize [kæp'saɪz] *v/i. naut.* опроки́дываться [-ки́нуться]; *v/t.* опроки́дывать [-ки́нуть]

capsule ['kæpsjuːl] *med.* ка́псула

captain ['kæptɪn] *mil., naut., sport* капита́н

caption ['kæpʃn] *title, words accompanying picture* по́дпись к карти́нке; заголо́вок; *cine.* ти́тры *m/pl.*

captiv|ate ['kæptɪveɪt] пленя́ть [-ни́ть], очаро́вывать [-ова́ть]; **~e** ['kæptɪv] пле́нный; *fig.* пле́нник; **~ity** [kæp'tɪvətɪ] плен; нево́ля

capture ['kæptʃə] **1.** пойма́ть, захва́тывать [-ти́ть]; брать в плен; **2.** пои́мка; захва́т

car [kaː] *rail vehicle* ваго́н; *motor vehicle* автомоби́ль, маши́на; *by ~* маши́ной

caramel ['kærəmel] караме́ль *f*

caravan ['kærəvæn] карава́н; дома́в-топри́цеп

caraway ['kærəweɪ] тмин

carbohydrate [ˌkaːbəʊ'haɪdreɪt] углево́д

carbon ['kaːbən] углеро́д; **~ paper** ко́пи́рка

carburet(t)or [kaːbjʊ'retə] *mot.* карбюра́тор

carcase ['kaːkəs] ту́ша

card [kaːd] ка́рта, ка́рточка; **~board** ['kaːdbɔːd] карто́н

cardigan ['kaːdɪɡən] кардига́н

cardinal ['kaːdənəl] **1.** □ (*chief*) гла́вный, основно́й; (*most important*) кардина́льный; **~ number** ко-

ли́чественное числи́тельное; **2.** *eccl.* кардина́л

card|index ['kaːdɪndeks] картоте́ка; **~phone** ка́рточный телефо́н

care [keə] **1.** забо́та; (*charge*) попече́ние; (*attention*) внима́ние; (*tending*) присмо́тр (за Т); (*nursing*) ухо́д (за Т); **~ of** (*abbr. c/o*) по а́дресу (Р); *take ~ of* [с]бере́чь (В); присмотре́ть за (Т); *handle with ~!* осторо́жно!; име́ть жела́ние, [за]хоте́ть (**to:** + *inf.*); **~ for: a)** [по]забо́титься о (П); **b)** люби́ть (В); *coll. I don't ~!* мне всё равно́!; *well ~d for* ухо́женный

career [kə'rɪə] **1.** *fig.* карье́ра; **2.** нести́сь, мча́ться

carefree ['keəfriː] беззабо́тный

careful ['keəfl] □ (*cautious*) осторо́жный; (*done with care*) аккура́тный, тща́тельный; внима́тельный (к Д); *be ~ (of, about, with)* забо́титься (о П); стара́ться (+ *inf.*); **~ness** [-nɪs] осторо́жность *f*; тща́тельность *f*

careless ['keəlɪs] □ *work, etc.* небре́жный; *driving, etc.* неосторо́жный; **~ness** [-nɪs] небре́жность *f*

caress [kə'res] **1.** ла́ска; **2.** ласка́ть

caretaker ['keəteɪkə] сто́рож

carfare ['kaːfeə] *Am.* пла́та за прое́зд

cargo ['kaːɡəʊ] *naut., ae.* груз

caricature ['kærɪkətʃʊə] **1.** карикату́ра; **2.** изобража́ть в карикату́рном ви́де

car jack ['kaːdʒæk] *lifting device* домкра́т

carnal ['kaːnl] □ *sensual* чу́вственный, пло́тский; *sexual* полово́й

carnation [kaː'neɪʃn] гвозди́ка

carnival ['kaːnɪvl] карнава́л

carol ['kærəl] рожде́ственский гимн

carp¹ [kaːp] *zo.* карп

carp² [-] придира́ться

carpent|er ['kaːpəntə] пло́тник; **~ry** [-trɪ] пло́тничество

carpet ['kaːpɪt] **1.** ковёр; **2.** устила́ть ковро́м

carriage ['kærɪdʒ] *rail.* ваго́н; перево́зка, транспортиро́вка; *of body* оса́нка; **~ free, ~ paid** опла́ченная доста́вка

carrier ['kærɪə] (*porter*) носи́льщик; *med.* носи́тель инфе́кции; ~s тра́нспортное аге́нтство; ~ **bag** су́мка

carrot ['kærət] морко́вь; *collect.* морко́вь *f*

carry ['kærɪ] 1. *v/t.* носи́ть, [по]нести́; *in train, etc.* вози́ть, [по]везти́; ~ **o.s.** держа́ться, вести́ себя́; *of law, etc.* **be carried** быть при́нятым; ~ **s.th. too far** заходи́ть сли́шком далеко́; ~ **on** продолжа́ть [-до́лжить]; ~ **out** *или* **through** доводи́ть до конца́; выполня́ть [вы́полнить]; *v/i. of sound* доноси́ться [донести́сь]

cart [kɑːt] теле́га, пово́зка

cartilage ['kɑːtɪlɪdʒ] хрящ

carton ['kɑːtn] *container* карто́нка; *for milk, etc.* паке́т

cartoon [kɑːˈtuːn] карикату́ра, шарж; *animated* мультфи́льм, *coll.* му́льтик

cartridge ['kɑːtrɪdʒ] патро́н

carve [kɑːv] *on wood* ре́зать; *meat* наре́зать [наре́зать]

carving ['kɑːvɪŋ] *object* резьба́

case¹ [keɪs] я́щик; *for spectacles, etc.* футля́р; (*suit~*) чемода́н; (*attaché ~*) (портфе́ль-)диплома́т

case² [-] слу́чай; (*state of affairs*) положе́ние; (*circumstances*) обстоя́тельство; *law* суде́бное де́ло; *in any* ~ в любо́м слу́чае; *in ~ of need* в слу́чае необходи́мости; *in no* ~ ни в ко́ем слу́чае

cash [kæʃ] 1. де́ньги, нали́чные де́ньги *f/pl.*; *on a ~ basis* за нали́чный расчёт; ~ **on delivery** нало́женным платежо́м; 2. получа́ть де́ньги по (Д); ~ *in on* воспо́льзоваться; ~**ier** [kæˈʃɪə] касси́р(ша)

cask [kɑːsk] бо́чка, бочо́нок

casket ['kɑːskɪt] шкату́лка; *Am. a.* = *coffin* гроб

casserole ['kæsərəʊl] гли́няная кастрю́ля; запека́нка

cassette [kəˈset] кассе́та

cassock ['kæsək] ря́са, сута́на

cast [kɑːst] 1. (*act of throwing*) бросо́к, мета́ние; *thea.* (*actors*) соста́в исполни́телей; 2. [*irr.*] *v/t.* броса́ть [бро-

сить] (*a. fig.*); *shadow* отбра́сывать; *tech. metals* отли(ва́)ть; *thea. roles* распределя́ть [-ли́ть]; ~ *light on* пролива́ть [-ли́ть] свет на (В); ~ *lots* броса́ть жре́бий; *be ~ down* быть в уны́нии; *v/i.* ~ *about for* разы́скивать

caste [kɑːst] ка́ста

castigate ['kæstɪɡeɪt] нака́зывать [-за́ть]; *fig.* жесто́ко критикова́ть

cast iron чугу́н; *attr.* чугу́нный

castle ['kɑːsl] за́мок; *chess* ладья́

castor ['kɑːstə]: ~ *oil* касто́ровое ма́сло

castrate [kæˈstreɪt] кастри́ровать (*im*)*pf.*

casual ['kæʒjʊl] □ (*chance*) случа́йный; (*careless*) небре́жный; ~**ty** [-tɪ] несча́стный слу́чай; *person* пострада́вший, же́ртва; *pl. mil.* поте́ри

cat [kæt] ко́шка; (*male*) кот

catalog(ue) ['kætəlɒɡ] 1. катало́г; 2. составля́ть [-вить] катало́г, вноси́ть в катало́г

cataract ['kætərækt] (*waterfall*) водопа́д; *med.* катара́кта

catarrh [kəˈtɑː] ката́р

catastrophe [kəˈtæstrəfɪ] катастро́фа; *natural* стихи́йное бе́дствие

catch [kætʃ] 1. *of fish* уло́в; (*trick*) подво́х; *on door* задви́жка; 2. [*irr.*] *v/t.* лови́ть [пойма́ть]; (*take hold of*) схва́тывать [схвати́ть]; *disease* заража́ться [зарази́ться] (Т); *train, etc.* поспе(ва́)ть к (Д); ~ *cold* просту́живаться [-уди́ться]; ~ *s.o.'s eye* пойма́ть взгляд (Р); ~ *up* догоня́ть [догна́ть]; 3. *v/i.* заце́пля́ться [-пи́ться]; *coll.* ~ *on* станови́ться мо́дным; ~ *up with* догоня́ть [догна́ть] (В); ~**ing** ['kætʃɪŋ] *fig.* зарази́тельный; *med.* зара́зный; ~**word** (*popular phrase*) мо́дное слове́чко

categor|ical [kætɪˈɡɒrɪkl] □ категори́ческий; ~**y** ['kætɪɡərɪ] катего́рия, разря́д

cater ['keɪtə]: ~ *for* обслу́живать (В)

caterpillar *zo.* ['kætəpɪlə] гу́сеница

catgut ['kætɡʌt] струна́; *med.* ке́тгут

cathedral [kəˈθiːdrəl] собо́р

Catholic ['kæθəlɪk] 1. като́лик; 2. католи́ческий

catkin ['kætkɪn] *bot.* серёжка

cattle ['kætl] кру́пный рога́тый скот; ~ **breeding** скотово́дство

caught [kɔːt] *pt. и pt. p. от* **catch**

cauliflower ['kɒlɪflaʊə] цветна́я капу́ста

cause ['kɔːz] **1.** причи́на, основа́ние; (*motive*) по́вод; **2.** причиня́ть [-ни́ть]; (*make happen*) вызыва́ть [вы́звать]; ~**less** ['kɔːzlɪs] □ беспричи́нный, необосно́ванный

caution ['kɔːʃn] **1.** (*prudence*) осторо́жность *f*; (*warning*) предостереже́ние; **2.** предостерега́ть [-ре́чь] (**against** от Р)

cautious ['kɔːʃəs] □ осторо́жный, осмотри́тельный; ~**ness** [-nɪs] осторо́жность *f*, осмотри́тельность *f*

cavalry ['kævlrɪ] кавале́рия

cave [keɪv] **1.** пеще́ра; **2.** ~ **in:** *v/i.* оседа́ть [осе́сть]; *fig., coll.* сда́ться *pf.*

caviar(e) ['kævɪɑː] икра́

cavil ['kævl] **1.** приди́рка; **2.** приди(ра́)ться (**at, about** к Д, за В)

cavity ['kævɪtɪ] впа́дина; по́лость *f*; *in tooth, tree* дупло́

cease [siːs] *v/i.* перест(ав)а́ть; *v/t.* прекраща́ть [-крати́ть]; остана́вливать [-нови́ть]; ~**-fire** прекраще́ние огня́; переми́рие; ~**less** ['siːsləs] □ непреры́вный, непреста́нный

cedar ['siːdə] кедр

cede [siːd] уступа́ть [-пи́ть] (В)

ceiling ['siːlɪŋ] потоло́к; *attr.* макси-ма́льный; **price** ~ преде́льная цена́

celebrat|e ['selɪbreɪt] [от]пра́здновать; ~**ed** [-ɪd] знамени́тый; ~**ion** [selɪ'breɪʃn] торжества́ *n/pl.*; пра́зднование

celebrity [sɪ'lebrɪtɪ] *pers. and state of being* знамени́тость *f*

celery ['selərɪ] сельдере́й

celestial [sɪ'lestɪəl] □ небе́сный

cell [sel] *pol.* ячейка; *in prison* ка́мера; *eccl.* ке́лья; *biol.* кле́тка; *el.* элеме́нт

cellar ['selə] подва́л; **wine** ~ ви́нный по́греб

cello ['tʃeləʊ] виолонче́ль

Cellophane® ['seləfeɪn] целлофа́н

cement [sɪ'ment] **1.** цеме́нт; **2.** цементи́ровать (*im*)*pf.*; *fig.* ~ **relations** укрепля́ть [-пи́ть] свя́зи

cemetery ['semɪtrɪ] кла́дбище

censor ['sensə] **1.** це́нзор; **2.** подверга́ть цензу́ре; ~**ship** ['sensəʃɪp] цензу́ра

censure ['senʃə] **1.** осужде́ние, порица́ние; **2.** осужда́ть [осуди́ть], порица́ть

census ['sensəs] пе́репись *f*

cent [sent] *Am. coin* цент

centenary [sen'tiːnərɪ] столе́тняя годовщи́на, столе́тие

center (*Brt.* -**tre**) ['sentə] **1.** центр; (*focus*) средото́чие; **in the~** в середи́не; **2.** [c]концентри́ровать(ся); сосредото́чи(ва)ть(ся)

centi|grade ['sentɪɡreɪd]: ... **degrees** ~ ... гра́дусов по Це́льсию; ~**meter** (*Brt.* -**tre**) [-miːtə] сантиме́тр; ~**pede** [-piːd] *zo.* соро́коно́жка

central ['sentrəl] □ центра́льный; гла́вный; ~ **office** управле́ние; ~**ize** [-laɪz] централизова́ть (*im*)*pf.*

centre → **center**

century ['sentʃərɪ] столе́тие, век

ceramics [sɪ'ræmɪks] кера́мика

cereal ['sɪərɪəl] хле́бный злак

cerebral ['serɪbrəl] мозгово́й, церебра́льный

ceremon|ial [serɪ'məʊnɪəl] □ торже́ственный; ~**ious** [-nɪəs] церемо́нный; ~**y** ['serɪmənɪ] церемо́ния

certain ['sɜːtn] □ (*definite*) определённый; (*confident*) уве́ренный; (*undoubted*) несомне́нный; не́кий, не́который; **a** ~ **Mr. Jones** не́кий г-н Джо́унз; **to a** ~ **extent** до не́которой сте́пени; ~**ty** [-tɪ] уве́ренность *f*; определённость *f*

certi|ficate 1. [sə'tɪfɪkət] свиде́тельство; спра́вка; **birth** ~ свиде́тельство о рожде́нии; **2.** [-keɪt] вы́дать удостовере́ние (Д); ~**fy** ['sɜːtɪfaɪ] удостоверя́ть [-е́рить]; ~**tude** [-tjuːd] уве́ренность *f*

cessation [se'seɪʃn] прекраще́ние

CFC chlorofluorocarbon фрео́н

chafe [tʃeɪf] *v/t. make sore* натира́ть

[натере́ть]; *v/i.* раздража́ться [-жи́ться]

chaff [tʃɑːf] подшу́чивать [-шути́ть] над (Т), подтру́нивать [-ни́ть]

chagrin ['ʃægrɪn] **1.** доса́да, огорче́ние; **2.** досажда́ть [досади́ть] (Д); огорча́ть [-чи́ть]

chain [tʃeɪn] **1.** цепь *f* (*a. fig.*); *dim.* цепо́чка; ~*s pl. fig.* око́вы *f/pl.*; у́зы *f/pl.*; ~ **reaction** цепна́я реа́кция; **2.** *dog.* держа́ть на цепи́

chair [tʃeə] *be in the* ~ председа́тельствовать; ~**man** ['tʃeəmən] председа́тель *m*; ~**woman** [-womən] (же́нщина-)председа́тель, председа́тельница

chalk [tʃɔːk] **1.** мел; **2.** писа́ть, рисова́ть ме́лом; ~ *up* (*register*) отмеча́ть [е́тить]

challenge ['tʃælɪndʒ] **1.** вы́зов; **2.** вызыва́ть [вы́звать]; *s.o.'s right, etc.* оспа́ривать [оспо́рить]

chamber ['tʃeɪmbə] (*room*) ко́мната; (*official body*) ~ *of commerce* торго́вая пала́та; ~**maid** го́рничная; ~**music** ка́мерная му́зыка

chamois ['ʃæmwɑː] за́мша

champagne [ʃæm'peɪn] шампа́нское

champion ['tʃæmpɪən] **1.** чемпио́н *m*, -ка *f*; защи́тник *m*, -ница *f*; **2.** защища́ть [-ити́ть]; боро́ться за (В); ~**ship** пе́рвенство, чемпиона́т

chance [tʃɑːns] **1.** случа́йность *f*; риск; (*opportunity*) удо́бный слу́чай; шанс (*of* на В); *by* ~ случа́йно; *take a* ~ рискова́ть [-кну́ть]; **2.** случа́йный; **3.** *v/i.* случа́ться [-чи́ться]

chancellor ['tʃɑːnsələ] ка́нцлер

chancy ['tʃɑːnsɪ] *coll.* риско́ванный

chandelier [ʃændə'lɪə] лю́стра

change [tʃeɪndʒ] **1.** переме́на, измене́ние; *of linen* сме́на; *small ~ money* сда́ча; *for a* ~ для разнообра́зия; **2.** *v/t.* [по]меня́ть; изменя́ть [-ни́ть]; *money* разме́нивать [-ня́ть]; *v/i.* [по]меня́ться, изменя́ться [-ни́ться]; *into different clothes* переоде́(ва́)ться; обме́ниваться [-ня́ть]; *rail.* переса́живаться [-се́сть]; ~**able** ['tʃeɪndʒəbl] □ непостоя́нный, изме́нчивый

channel ['tʃænl] *river* ру́сло; (*naut. fairway*) фарва́тер; *geogr.* проли́в; *fig.* (*source*) исто́чник; *through official* ~*s* по официа́льным кана́лам

chaos ['keɪɒs] ха́ос, беспоря́док

chap[1] [tʃæp] **1.** (*split, crack of skin*) тре́щина; **2.** [по]тре́скаться

chap[2] [-] *coll.* па́рень *m*

chapel ['tʃæpl] часо́вня

chapter ['tʃæptə] глава́

char [tʃɑː] (*burn*) обугли(ва)ть(ся)

character ['kærəktə] хара́ктер; (*individual*) ли́чность *f*; *thea.* де́йствующее лицо́; *lit.* геро́й, персона́ж; (*letter*) бу́ква; ~**istic** [kærəktə'rɪstɪk] **1.** (~*ally*) характе́рный; типи́чный (*of* для Р); **2.** характе́рная черта́; сво́йство; ~**ize** ['kærəktəraɪz] характеризова́ть (*im*)*pf.*

charcoal ['tʃɑːkəʊl] древе́сный у́голь *m*

charge [tʃɑːdʒ] **1.** пла́та; *el.* заря́д; (*order*) поруче́ние; *law* обвине́ние; *mil.* ата́ка; *fig.* попече́ние, забо́та; ~*s pl. comm.* расхо́ды *m/pl.*; изде́ржки *f/pl.*; *be in* ~ *of* руководи́ть (Т); быть отве́тственным (за В); **2.** *v/t. battery* заряжа́ть [-яди́ть]; поруча́ть [-чи́ть] (Д); обвиня́ть [-ни́ть] (*with* в П); *price* проси́ть (*for* за В); (*rush*) броса́ться ['-ситься]

charisma [kə'rɪzmə] ли́чное обая́ние

charitable ['tʃærətəbl] □ благотвори́тельный; (*kind*) милосе́рдный

charity ['tʃærətɪ] милосе́рдие; благотвори́тельность *f*

charm [tʃɑːm] **1.** (*trinket*) амуле́т; *fig.* ча́ры *f/pl.*; обая́ние, очарова́ние; **2.** заколдо́вывать [-дова́ть]; *fig.* очаро́вывать [-ова́ть]; ~**ing** ['tʃɑːmɪŋ] □ очарова́тельный, обая́тельный

chart [tʃɑːt] *naut.* морска́я ка́рта; диагра́мма; *pl.* спи́сок шля́геров, бестсе́ллеров

charter ['tʃɑːtə] **1.** *hist.* ха́ртия; ~ *of the UN* Уста́в ООН; **2.** *naut.* [за]фрахтова́ть (*судно*)

charwoman ['tʃɑːwʊmən] убо́рщица, приходя́щая домрабо́тница

chase [tʃeɪs] **1.** пого́ня *f*; *hunt.* охо́та; **2.**

охо́титься за (T); пресле́довать; ~
away прогоня́ть [-гна́ть]

chasm [kæzəm] бе́здна, про́пасть f

chaste [tʃeɪst] целому́дренный

chastity ['tʃæstətɪ] целому́дрие;
де́вственность f

chat [tʃæt] 1. бесе́да; 2. [по]болта́ть,
[по]бесе́довать

chattels ['tʃætlz] pl. (*mst.* **goods and
~**) иму́щество, ве́щи f/pl.

chatter ['tʃætə] 1. болтовня́ f; щебета́-
ние; 2. [по]болта́ть; **~box**, **~er** [-rə]
болту́н m, -нья f

chatty ['tʃætɪ] разгово́рчивый

chauffeur ['ʃəʊfə] води́тель m;
шофёр

cheap [tʃiːp] деше́вый; *fig.* плохо́й;
~en ['tʃiːpən] [по]деше́веть; *fig.* уни-
жа́ть [уни́зить]

cheat [tʃiːt] 1. *pers.* обма́нщик, плут;
(*fraud*) обма́н; 2. обма́нывать [-ну́ть]

check [tʃek] 1. *chess* шах; (*restraint*)
препя́тствие; остано́вка; (*verification,
examination*) контро́ль m (**on**
над T); прове́рка (**on** P); *luggage/bag-
gage ticket* бага́жная квита́нция; *bank
draft* (Brt. **cheque**), *receipt or bill in
restaurant, etc.* чек; 2. проверя́ть [-ве́-
рить]; [про]контроли́ровать; при-
остана́вливать [-нови́ть]; препя́т-
ствовать; **~book** че́ковая кни́жка;
~er ['tʃekə] контролёр; **~s** ['tʃekəz]
pl. Am. ша́шки f/pl.; **~mate** 1. шах и
мат; 2. де́лать мат; **~up** прове́рка;
med. осмо́тр

cheek [tʃiːk] щека́ (pl.: щёки); *coll.* на́г-
лость f, де́рзость f

cheer [tʃɪə] 1. весе́лье; одобри́тель-
ные во́згласы m/pl.; 2. v/t. подба́дри-
вать [-бодри́ть]; приве́тствовать во́з-
гласами; v/i. **~ up** приободри́ться; **~ful**
['tʃɪəfl] бо́дрый, весёлый; **~less**
[-ləs] уны́лый, мра́чный; **~y** [-rɪ]
живо́й, весёлый, ра́достный

cheese [tʃiːz] сыр

chemical ['kemɪkl] 1. хими́ческий;
2. **~s** [-s] pl. хими́ческие препара́ты
m/pl., химика́лии f/pl.

chemist ['kemɪst] *scientist* хи́мик;
pharmacist апте́карь m; **~ry** ['kemɪs-

tri] хи́мия; **~'s** Brt. апте́ка

cherish ['tʃerɪʃ] *hope* леле́ять; *in
memory* храни́ть; (*love*) не́жно
люби́ть

cherry ['tʃerɪ] ви́шня

chess [tʃes] ша́хматы f/pl.; **~board**
ша́хматная доска́; **~man** ша́хматная
фигу́ра

chest [tʃest] я́щик, сунду́к; *anat.* груд-
на́я кле́тка; ~ **of drawers** комо́д; *get
s.th. off one's* ~ облегчи́ть ду́шу

chestnut ['tʃesnʌt] 1. кашта́н; 2. каш-
та́новый

chew [tʃuː] жева́ть; ~ **over** (*think
about*) размышля́ть; **~ing gum**
['tʃuːɪŋgʌm] жева́тельная рези́нка,
coll. жва́чка

chic [ʃiːk] элега́нтный

chick [tʃɪk] цыплёнок; **~en** ['tʃɪkɪn]
ку́рица; *cul.* куря́тина; **~enpox** ветря́-
на́я о́спа

chief [tʃiːf] 1. гла́вный; 2. глава́, ру-
ководи́тель, нача́льник, *coll.* шеф;
~ly гла́вным о́бразом

child [tʃaɪld] ребёнок, дитя́ n (pl.: де́-
ти); ~ *prodigy* ['prɒdɪdʒɪ] вундерки́нд;
~birth ро́ды m/pl.; **~hood** ['-hʊd]
де́тство; *from~* с де́тства; **~ish** ['tʃaɪl-
dɪʃ] ребя́ческий; **~like** [-laɪk] как
ребёнок; **~ren** ['tʃɪldrən] pl. от **child**

chill [tʃɪl] 1. хо́лод; *fig.* хо́лодность f;
med. просту́да; 2. охлажда́ть; *fig.* рас-
холаживающий; 3. v/t. охлажда́ть
[-лади́ть]; [о]студи́ть; v/i. охлаж-
да́ться [-лади́ться]; **~y** ['tʃɪlɪ] холо́д-
ный, прохла́дный (*both a. fig.*)

chime [tʃaɪm] 1. звон колоколо́в; бой
часо́в; 2. [за]звони́ть; *of clock* про-
би́ть pf.; ~ *in* вме́шиваться [-ша́ться];
fig. ~ (*in*) *with* гармонизи́ровать; соот-
ве́тствовать

chimney ['tʃɪmnɪ] дымова́я труба́

chin [tʃɪn] подборо́док

china ['tʃaɪnə] фарфо́р

Chinese [tʃaɪ'niːz] 1. кита́ец m, -ая́нка
f; 2. кита́йский

chink [tʃɪŋk] *crevice* щель f, тре́щина

chip [tʃɪp] 1. *of wood* ще́пка; *of glass*
оско́лок; *on plate, etc.* щерби́нка; **~s**
Brt. карто́фель-чи́псы; 2. v/t. отби́ть

C

pf. край; *v/i.* отла́мываться [отло-
ма́ться]

chirp [tʃɜ:p] **1.** чири́канье; щебета́ние;
2. чири́кать [-кнуть]; [за]щебета́ть

chisel ['tʃɪzl] **1.** долото́, стаме́ска;
sculptor's резе́ц; **2.** рабо́тать до-
лото́м, резцо́м; **~led features** точёные
черты́ лица́

chitchat ['tʃɪt tʃæt] болтовня́

chivalrous ['ʃɪvəlrəs] □ *mst. fig.* ры́-
царский

chlor|inate ['klɔ:rɪneɪt] хлори́ровать;
~oform ['klɒrəfɔ:m] хлорофо́рм

chocolate ['tʃɒklɪt] шокола́д; *pl.* шоко-
ла́дные конфе́ты *f/pl.*

choice ['tʃɔɪs] **1.** вы́бор; альтернати́-
ва; **2.** □ отбо́рный

choir ['kwaɪə] хор

choke [tʃəʊk] *v/t.* [за]души́ть; (*mst.* ~
down) глота́ть с трудо́м; *laughter* да-
ви́ться (**with** от P); *v/i.* (*suffocate*) за-
дыха́ться [-дохну́ться]; [по]дави́ться
(**on** T)

choose [tʃu:z] (*irr.*) выбира́ть [вы́-
брать]; (*decide*) предпочита́ть
[-че́сть]; **~ to** *inf.* хоте́ть (+ *inf.*)

chop [tʃɒp] **1.** отбивна́я (котле́та); **2.**
v/t. wood, etc. [на]руби́ть; *parsley,
etc.* [на]кроши́ть; **~ down** сруба́ть
[-би́ть]; **~ and change** бесконе́чно
меня́ть свои́ взгля́ды, пла́ны *и т.д.*;
~per (*decide*) *tool* топо́р; *sl. helicopter*
вертолёт; **~py** *sea* неспоко́й-
ный

choral ['kɔ:rəl] □ хорово́й; **~(e)**
[kɒ'rɑːl] хора́л

chord [kɔːd] струна́; *mus.* акко́рд

chore [tʃɔː] ну́дная рабо́та; повсе-
дне́вные дела́

chorus ['kɔːrəs] хор; му́зыка для хо́-
ра; *of song* припе́в, рефре́н; **in~** хо́ром

chose [tʃəʊz] *pt. om* **choose**; **~n** [-n] **1.**
pt. p. om **choose**; **2.** и́збранный

Christ [kraɪst] Христо́с

christen ['krɪsn] [о]крести́ть; **~ing**
[-ɪŋ] крести́ны *f/pl.*; креще́ние

Christian ['krɪstʃən] **1.** христиа́нский;
~ name и́мя (*в отли́чие от фами́-
лии*); **2.** христиа́нин *m*, -а́нка *f*; **~ity**
[krɪstɪ'ænəti] христиа́нство

Christmas ['krɪsməs] Рождество́

chromium ['krəʊmɪəm] хром; **~-plated**
хроми́рованный

chronic ['krɒnɪk] (**~ally**) хрони́ческий
(*a. med.*); **~le** [-l] хро́ника, ле́топись *f*

chronolog|ical [ˌkrɒnə'lɒdʒɪkl] □ хро-
ноло́гический; **~y** [krə'nɒlədʒɪ] хроно-
ло́гия

chubby ['tʃʌbɪ] *coll.* по́лный; *child*
пу́хленький

chuck [tʃʌk] броса́ть [бро́сить]; *coll.*
швыря́ть [-рну́ть]; **~ out** выбра́сы-
вать [вы́бросить]; *from work* вышвы́-
ривать [вы́швырнуть]

chuckle ['tʃʌkl] посме́иваться

chum [tʃʌm] *coll.* **1.** прия́тель; **2.** быть
в дру́жбе

chump [tʃʌmp] коло́да, чурба́н; *sl.*
(*fool*) болва́н

chunk [tʃʌŋk] *coll. of bread* ло́моть *m*;
of meat, etc. то́лстый кусо́к

church [tʃɜːtʃ] це́рковь *f.*; **~ service** бо-
гослуже́ние; **~yard** пого́ст, кла́дбище

churlish ['tʃɜːlɪʃ] □ (*ill-bred*) гру́бый;
(*bad-tempered*) раздражи́тельный

churn [tʃɜːn]: масло́бойка; бидо́н

chute [ʃuːt] *slide, slope* спуск; (*rubbish
~*) мусоропрово́д; *for children* го́рка

cider ['saɪdə] сидр

cigar [sɪ'gɑː] сига́ра

cigarette [sɪgə'ret] сигаре́та; (*of Russian type*) папиро́са; **~ holder** мунд-
шту́к

cinch [sɪntʃ] *coll.* не́что надёжное,
ве́рное

cinder ['sɪndə]: **~s** *pl.* у́гли; **~ track** *sport*
га́ревая доро́жка

cinema ['sɪnɪmə] кинематогра́фия,
кино́ *n indecl.*

cinnamon ['sɪnəmən] кори́ца

cipher ['saɪfə] **1.** шифр; (*zero*) нуль *m*
or ноль *m*; **2.** зашифро́вывать
[-ова́ть]

circle ['sɜːkl] **1.** круг (*a. fig.*); (*ring*)
кольцо́; *thea.* я́рус; **business ~s** дело-
вы́е круги́; **2.** враща́ться вокру́г (P);
соверша́ть круги́, кружи́ть(ся)

circuit ['sɜːkɪt] (*route*) маршру́т; объ-
е́зд; *el.* цепь *f*, схе́ма

circular ['sɜːkjʊlə] **1.** □ кру́глый; *road*

круговой; ~ **letter** циркуля́рное письмо́; **2.** циркуля́р; (*advertisement*) проспе́кт

circulat|e ['sɜːkjʊleɪt] *v/i.* rumo(u)r распространя́ться [-ни́ться]; циркули́ровать (*a. fig.*); ~**ing** [-ɪŋ]: ~ **library** библиоте́ка с вы́дачей книг на́ дом; ~**ion** [sɜːkjʊ'leɪʃn] кровообраще́ние; циркуля́ция; *of newspapers etc.* тира́ж; *fig.* распростране́ние

circum... ['sɜːkəm] *pref.* (*в сложных словах*) вокру́г, круго́м

circum|ference [sə'kʌmfərəns] окру́жность *f*; перифери́я *f*; ~**spect** ['sɜːkəmspekt] □ осмотри́тельный, осторо́жный; ~**stance** ['sɜːkəmstəns] обстоя́тельство; ~**stantial** [sɜːkəm'stænʃl] □ обстоя́тельный, подро́бный; ~**vent** [-'vent] (*law, etc.*) обходи́ть [обойти́]

circus ['sɜːkəs] цирк; *attr.* цирково́й

cistern ['sɪstən] бак; *in toilet* бачо́к

cit|ation [saɪ'teɪʃn] цита́та, ссы́лка, цити́рование; ~**e** [saɪt] ссыла́ться [сосла́ться] на (В)

citizen ['sɪtɪzn] граждани́н *m*, -да́нка *f*; ~**ship** [-ʃɪp] гражда́нство

citrus ['sɪtrəs]: ~ **fruit** цитру́совые

city ['sɪtɪ] го́род; *attr.* городско́й; **the** ♀ Си́ти (*деловой центр в Лондоне*)

civic ['sɪvɪk] гражда́нский; *of town* городско́й

civil ['sɪvl] □ *of a community* гражда́нский (*a. law*); шта́тский; (*polite*) ве́жливый; ~ **servant** госуда́рственный служа́щий, *contr.* чино́вник; ~ **service** госуда́рственная слу́жба; ~**ian** [sɪ'vɪljən] шта́тский; ~**ity** [sɪ'vɪlətɪ] ве́жливость *f*; ~**ization** [sɪvəlaɪ'zeɪʃn] цивилиза́ция

clad [klæd] *pt. u pt. p. om* **clothe**

claim [kleɪm] **1.** претендова́ть, (*demand*) на (В); [по]тре́бовать; (*assert*) утвержда́ть [-рди́ть]; предъявля́ть права́ на (В); **2.** тре́бование; прете́нзия; *law* иск; ~ **for damages** иск за причине́нный уще́рб; ~ **to be** выдава́ть себя́ за (В); ~**ant** ['kleɪmənt] претенде́нт; *law* исте́ц

clairvoyant [kleə'vɔɪənt] яснови́дец

clamber ['klæmbə] [вс]кара́бкаться

clammy ['klæmɪ] □ (*sticky*) ли́пкий; *hands* холо́дный и вла́жный; *weather* сыро́й и холо́дный

clamo(u)r ['klæmə] **1.** шум, кри́ки *m/pl.*; шу́мные проте́сты *m/pl.*; **2.** шу́мно тре́бовать (Р)

clamp [klæmp] **1.** *tech.* скоба́; зажи́м; **2.** скрепля́ть [-пи́ть]; заж(им)а́ть

clandestine [klæn'destɪn] □ та́йный

clang [klæŋ] **1.** лязг; *of bell* звон; **2.** ля́згать [-гнуть]

clank [klæŋk] **1.** звон, лязг, бряца́ние; **2.** бряца́ть, [за]греме́ть

clap [klæp] **1.** хлопо́к; хло́панье; *of thunder* уда́р; **2.** хло́пать, аплоди́ровать; ~**trap** пуста́я болтовня́; (*nonsense*) чепуха́

clarify ['klærɪfaɪ] *v/t. liquid, etc.* очища́ть [очи́стить]; (*make transparent*) де́лать прозра́чным; *fig.* выясня́ть [вы́яснить]; *v/i.* де́латься прозра́чным, я́сным

clarity ['klærətɪ] я́сность *f*

clash [klæʃ] **1.** столкнове́ние; (*contradiction*) противоре́чие; конфли́кт; **2.** ста́лкиваться [столкну́ться]; *of opinions, etc.* расходи́ться [разойти́сь]

clasp [klɑːsp] **1.** пря́жка, застёжка; *fig.* (*embrace*) объя́тия *n/pl.*; *v/t.* (*fasten*) застёгивать [застегну́ть]; (*hold tightly*) сж(им)а́ть; *fig.* заключа́ть в объя́тия; *hand* пож(им)а́ть

class [klɑːs] **1.** *school* класс; *social* обще́ственный класс; (*evening*) ~**es** (вече́рние) ку́рсы; **2.** классифици́ровать (*im*)*pf.*

classic ['klæsɪk] **1.** кла́ссик; **2.** ~**(al** □) [-(ə)l] класси́ческий

classi|fication [klæsɪfɪ'keɪʃn] классифика́ция; ~**fy** ['klæsɪfaɪ] классифици́ровать (*im*)*pf.*

clatter ['klætə] **1.** *of dishes* звон; *of metal* гро́хот (маши́н); (*talk*) болтовня́; *of hoofs, etc.* то́пот; **2.** [за]греме́ть; [за]то́пать; *fig.* [по]болта́ть

clause [klɔːz] *of agreement, etc.* пункт, статья́; *gr.* **principal/subordinate** ~ гла́вное/прида́точное предложе́ние

claw [klɔː] **1.** *of animal* ко́готь *m*; *of*

C

crustacean клешня́; 2. разрыва́ть, терза́ть когтя́ми

clay [kleɪ] гли́на

clean [kliːn] 1. *adj.* □ чи́стый; (*tidy*) опря́тный; 2. *adv.* на́чисто; соверше́нно, по́лностью; 3. [по]чи́стить; **~ up** уб(и)ра́ть; приводи́ть в поря́док; **~er** ['kliːnə] убо́рщик *m*, -ица *f*; **~er's** химчи́стка; **~ing** ['kliːnɪŋ] чи́стка; *of room* убо́рка, **~liness** ['klenlɪnɪs] чистопло́тность *f*, **~ly** 1. *adv.* ['kliːnlɪ] чи́сто; 2. *adj.* ['klenlɪ] чистопло́тный; **~se** [klenz] очища́ть [очи́стить]

clear [klɪər] 1. □ све́тлый, я́сный (*a. fig.*); (*transparent*) прозра́чный; *fig.* свобо́дный (**from, of** от Р); *profit, etc.* чи́стый; (*distinct*) отчётливый; (*plain*) я́сный, поня́тный; 2. *v/t.* убра́ть [-бра́ть]; очища́ть [очи́стить] (**from, of** от Р); расчища́ть [-и́стить] (*free from blame*) опра́вдывать [-да́ть]; **~ the air** разряди́ть атмосфе́ру; *v/i.* (*a.* **~ up**) *of mist* рассе́яться [-е́яться]; *of sky* проясня́ться [-ни́ться]; **~ance** ['klɪərəns] разреше́ние (на прово́з, на вы́воз, *naut.* на вы́ход); **~ing** ['klɪərɪŋ] *tech.* зазо́р; *mot.* кли́ренс; *in forest* про́сека, поля́на; *fin.* кли́ринг; **~ly** я́сно; (*obviously*) очеви́дно

cleave [kliːv] [*irr.*] *split* раска́лывать(ся) [-коло́ть(ся)]; рассека́ть [-е́чь]; *adhere* прилипа́ть [-ли́пнуть]

clef [klef] *mus.* ключ

cleft [kleft] рассели́на

clemen|cy ['klemənsɪ] милосе́рдие; снисхожде́ние; **~t** ['klemənt] милосе́рдный; *weather* мя́гкий

clench [klentʃ] заж(им)а́ть; *fists* сж(и)-м)а́ть; *teeth* сти́скивать [сти́снуть]; → **clinch**

clergy ['klɜːdʒɪ] духове́нство; **~man** [-mən] свяще́нник

clerical ['klerɪkl] □ *eccl.* духо́вный; *of clerks* канцеля́рский

clerk [klɑːk] кле́рк, конто́рский слу́жащий; *Am.* **sales ~** продаве́ц

clever ['klevə] □ у́мный; (*skilled*) уме́лый; *mst. b.s.* ло́вкий

click [klɪk] 1. щёлканье; 2. *lock* щёл-

кать [-кнуть]; *tongue* прищёлкивать [-кнуть]; *fig.* идти́ гла́дко; **~ on** *comput.* щёлкнуть мы́шью

client ['klaɪənt] клие́нт; покупа́тель *m*, **~ele** [kliːɑːn'tel] клиенту́ра

cliff [klɪf] утёс, скала́

climate ['klaɪmɪt] кли́мат

climax ['klaɪmæks] 1. кульмина́ция, достига́ть [-и́гнуть] кульмина́ции

climb [klaɪm] [*irr.*] влеза́(а)ть на (В); *mountain* поднима́ться [-ня́ться] (на В); **~er** ['klaɪmə] альпини́ст; *fig.* карьери́ст; *bot.* вью́щееся расте́ние

clinch [klɪntʃ] *fig.* оконча́тельно догова́риваться *pf.*, реши́ть *pf.*; **that ~ed the matter** э́тим вопро́с был оконча́тельно решён

cling [klɪŋ] [*irr.*] (**to**) [при]льну́ть к (Д); **~ together** держа́ться вме́сте

clinic ['klɪnɪk] кли́ника; поликли́ника; **~al** [-ɪkl] клини́ческий

clink [klɪŋk] 1. звон; 2. [за]звене́ть; **~ glasses** чо́каться [-кнуться]

clip¹ [klɪp] 1. *newspaper* вы́резка; *TV* клип; 2. выреза́ть [вы́резать]; (*cut*) [о-, под]стри́чь

clip² [-] 1. скре́пка; 2.: **~ together** скрепля́ть [-пи́ть]

clipp|er ['klɪpə]: (*a pair of*) (*nail-*) **~ers** *pl.* маникю́рные но́жницы *f/pl.*; *hort.* сека́тор; **~ings** [-ɪŋz] *pl.* газе́тные вы́резки *f/pl.*; обре́зки *m/pl.*

cloak [kləʊk] 1. плащ; *of darkness* покро́в; *fig.* (*pretext*) предло́г; 2. покры́(ва́)ть; *fig.* прикры(ва́)ть; **~room** гардеро́б, *coll.* раздева́лка; *euph.*, *mst. Brt.* туале́т; **~room attendant** гардеро́бщик *m*, -щица *f*

clock [klɒk] часы́ *m/pl.* (*стенные и т.д.*); **~wise** по часово́й стре́лке

clod [klɒd] ком; (*fool*) ду́рень *m*, о́лух

clog [klɒg] засоря́ть(ся) [-ри́ть(ся)], забива́ться [-би́ться]

cloister ['klɔɪstə] монасты́рь *m*; *arch.* кры́тая арка́да

close [kləʊs] 1. □ (*restricted*) закры́-тый; (*near*) бли́зкий; (*tight*) те́сный; *air* ду́шный, спёртый; (*stingy*) скупо́й; *study, etc.* внима́тельный, тща́тель-ный; **~ by** *adv.* ря́дом, побли́зости;

C

to о́коло (Р); **2.** [kləuz] коне́ц; (*conclusion*) заверше́ние; **come to a ~** зако́нчиться, заверши́ться; **3.** [kləuz] *v/t.* закры́(ва́)ть; зака́нчивать [-ко́нчить]; конча́ть [ко́нчить]; заключа́ть [-чи́ть] (речь); *v/i.* закры́(ва́)ться; конча́ться [ко́нчиться]; **~ in** приближа́ться [-ли́зиться]; наступа́ть [-пи́ть]; **~ness** [ˈkləusnis] бли́зость *f*; скупость *f*

closet [ˈklɒzit] *Am.* чула́н; стенно́й шкаф

close-up: **take a ~** снима́ть [снять] кру́пным пла́ном

closure [ˈkləuʒə] закры́тие

clot [klɒt] **1.** *of blood* сгу́сток; комо́к; **2.** *mst. of blood* свёртываться [сверну́ться]

cloth [klɒθ], *pl.* **~s** [klɒθs] ткань *f*, материа́л; **length of ~** отре́з

clothe [kləuð] [*a. irr.*] оде́(ва́)ть; *fig.* облека́ть [обле́чь]

clothes [kləuðz] *pl.* оде́жда; **change one's ~** переоде́ться; **~line** верёвка для су́шки белья́; **~ peg** прище́пка

clothing [ˈkləuðiŋ] оде́жда; **ready-made ~** гото́вая оде́жда

cloud [klaud] **1.** о́блако, ту́ча; **have one's head in the ~s** вита́ть в облака́х; **2.** покрыва́ть(ся) ту́чами, облака́ми; *fig.* омрача́ть(ся) [-чи́ть(ся)]; **~burst** ли́вень *m*; **~less** [ˈklaudlis] □ безо́блачный; **~y** [-i] □ о́блачный; *liquid* му́тный; *ideas* тума́нный

clove[1] [kləuv] гвозди́ка (пря́ность)

clove[2] [-] *pt. om* **cleave**

clover [ˈkləuvə] кле́вер; **in ~** жить припева́ючи

clown [klaun] кло́ун

club [klʌb] **1.** *society* клуб; (*heavy stick*) дуби́на; *Am.* дуби́нка (полице́йского); **~s** *pl. at cards* тре́фы *f/pl.*; **2.** *v/t.* [по]би́ть; *v/i.* собира́ться вме́сте; **~ together** сложи́ться [скла́дываться]; (*share expense*) устра́ивать скла́дчину

clue [kluː] ключ к разга́дке; **I haven't a ~** поня́тия не име́ю

clump [klʌmp] **1.** *of bushes* куста́рник; *of trees* ку́па, гру́ппа; **2.** *tread heavily*

тяжело́ ступа́ть

clumsy [ˈklʌmzi] □ неуклю́жий; нело́вкий (*a. fig.*); (*tactless*) беста́ктный

clung [klʌŋ] *pt. и pt. p. om* **cling**

cluster [ˈklʌstə] **1.** кисть *f*; гроздь *f*; **2.** расти́ гро́здьями; **~ round** окружа́ть [-жи́ть]

clutch [klʌtʃ] **1.** *of car* сцепле́ние; **fall into s.o.'s ~s** попа́сться pf. в чьи́-л. ла́пы; **2.** (*seize*) схва́тывать [-ти́ть]; ухвати́ться pf. (**at** за В)

clutter [ˈklʌtə] **1.** беспоря́док; **2.** завали́ть, загромозди́ть

coach [kəutʃ] **1.** *Brt.* междугоро́дный автобус; (*trainer*) тре́нер; (*tutor*) репети́тор; *rail.* пассажи́рский ваго́н; **2.** [на]трениро́вать; ната́скивать к экза́мену

coagulate [kəuˈægjuleit] свёртываться, коагули́роваться

coal [kəul] (ка́менный) у́голь *m*

coalition [kəuəˈliʃn] коали́ция

coal|mine, **~ pit** у́гольная ша́хта

coarse [kɔːs] □ *material* грубый; *sugar, etc.* кру́пный; *fig.* неотёсанный; *joke* непристо́йный

coast [kəust] морско́й бе́рег, побере́жье; **~al**: **~ waters** прибре́жные во́ды; **~er** [ˈkəustə] *naut.* су́дно кабота́жного пла́вания

coat [kəut] **1.** (*man's jacket*) пиджа́к; (*over~*) пальто́ *n indecl.*; (*fur*) мех, шерсть *f*; (*layer of paint, etc.*) слой; **~ of arms** герб; **2.** (*cover*) покры́(ва́)ть; **~ hanger** ве́шалка; **~ing** [ˈkəutiŋ] слой

coax [kəuks] угова́ривать [уговори́ть]

cob [kɒb] *of maize* поча́ток

cobbler [ˈkɒblə] сапо́жник

cobblestone [ˈkɒblstəun] булы́жник; *attr.* булы́жный

cobweb [ˈkɒbweb] паути́на

cock [kɒk] **1.** (*rooster*) пету́х; (*tap*) кран; *in gun* куро́к; **2.** *ears* настора́живать [-рожи́ть]

cockatoo [kɒkəˈtuː] какаду́ *m indecl.*

cockchafer [ˈkɒktʃeifə] ма́йский жук

cock-eyed [ˈkɒkaid] *sl.* косогла́зый; косо́й; *Am.* пья́ный

cockpit [ˈkɒkpit] *ae.* каби́на

cockroach [ˈkɒkrəutʃ] *zo.* тарака́н

cock|sure [kɒk'ʃʊə] coll. самоуве́ренный; **~tail** [-'teɪl] коктейль m; **~y** ['kɒkɪ] □ coll. наха́льный, де́рзкий

cocoa ['kəʊkəʊ] powder or drink кака́о n indecl.

coconut ['kəʊkənʌt] коко́с, коко́совый оре́х

cocoon [kə'ku:n] ко́кон

cod [kɒd] треска́

coddle ['kɒdl] [из]ба́ловать, [из]не́жить

code [kəʊd] 1. of conduct, laws ко́декс; of symbols, ciphers код; 2. коди́ровать (im)pf.

cod-liver: ~ oil ры́бий жир

coerc|e [kəʊ'ɜ:s] принужда́ть [-ну́дить]; **~ion** [-ʃn] принужде́ние

coexist [kəʊɪɡ'zɪst] сосуществова́ть (с T)

coffee ['kɒfɪ] ко́фе m indecl.; **instant** ~ раствори́мый ко́фе; ~ **grinder** кофемо́лка; ~ **set** кофе́йный серви́з; **~pot** кофе́йник

coffin ['kɒfɪn] гроб

cog [kɒɡ] зубе́ц

cogent ['kəʊdʒənt] □ (convincing) убеди́тельный

cognac ['kɒnjæk] конья́к

cohabit [kəʊ'hæbɪt] сожи́тельствовать, жить вме́сте

coheren|ce [kəʊ'hɪərəns] связь f; согласо́ванность f; **~t** [-rənt] □ story, etc. свя́зный; поня́тный; согласо́ванный

cohesion [kəʊ'hi:ʒn] сцепле́ние; сплочённость f

coiffure [kwa:'fjʊə] причёска

coil [kɔɪl] 1. кольцо́; el. кату́шка; 2. (a. ~ **up**) свёртываться кольцо́м (спира́лью)

coin [kɔɪn] 1. моне́та; **pay s.o. back in his own** ~ отплати́ть pf. кому́-л. той же моне́той; 2. (mint) чека́нить; **~age** ['kɔɪnɪdʒ] чека́нка

coincide [kəʊɪn'saɪd] совпада́ть [-па́сть]; **~nce** [kəʊ'ɪnsɪdəns] совпаде́ние; fig. случа́йное стече́ние обстоя́тельств; **by sheer** ~ по чи́стой случа́йности

coke[1] [kəʊk] кокс

coke[2] [-] coll. ко́ка-ко́ла

colander ['kʌləndə] дуршла́г

cold [kəʊld] 1. □ холо́дный; fig. непривет́ливый; 2. хо́лод; просту́да; **catch (a)** ~ простуди́ться; **~ness** ['kəʊldnɪs] of temperature хо́лод; of character, etc. хо́лодность f

colic ['kɒlɪk] med. ко́лики f/pl.

collaborat|e [kə'læbəreɪt] сотру́дничать; **~ion** [kəlæbə'reɪʃn] сотру́дничество; **in** ~ **with** в сотру́дничестве (с T)

collapse [kə'læps] 1. (caving in) обва́л; разруше́ние; of plans, etc. круше́ние; med. по́лный упа́док сил, колла́пс; 2. of a structure обру́ши(ва)ться, ру́хнуть; of person упа́сть без созна́ния

collar ['kɒlər] 1. воротни́к; dog's оше́йник; 2. sl. a criminal схвати́ть pf.; **~bone** anat. ключи́ца

collateral [kə'lætərəl] побо́чный; evidence ко́свенный

colleague ['kɒli:ɡ] колле́га f/m, сослужи́вец m, -вица f

collect [kə'lekt] v/t. (get together) соб(ир)а́ть; stamps etc. коллекциони́ровать; (call for) заходи́ть [зайти́] за (T); o.s. (control o.s.) овладева́ть собо́й; v/i. (gather) соб(и)ра́ться (a. fig.); ~ **on delivery** Am. нало́женным платежо́м; **~ed** [kə'lektɪd] □ fig. споко́йный; ~ **works** собра́ние сочине́ний; **~ion** [kə'lekʃn] колле́кция, собра́ние; **~ive** [-tɪv] □ коллекти́вный; совоку́пный; **~or** [-tə] коллекционе́р; of tickets, etc. контролёр

college ['kɒlɪdʒ] колле́дж; институ́т, университе́т

collide [kə'laɪd] ста́лкиваться [столкну́ться]

collie ['kɒlɪ] ко́лли m/f indecl.

collier ['kɒlɪər] углеко́п, шахтёр; **~y** ['kɒljərɪ] каменноу́гольная ша́хта

collision ['kəlɪʒn] столкнове́ние

colloquial [kə'ləʊkwɪəl] □ разгово́рный

colon ['kəʊlən] typ. двоето́чие

colonel ['kɜ:nl] полко́вник

colonial [kə'ləʊnɪəl] колониа́льный

colony ['kɒlənɪ] коло́ния

colo(u)r ['kʌlə] **1.** цвет; (*paint*) кра́ска; *on face* румя́нец; *fig.* колори́т; **~s** *pl.* госуда́рственный флаг; **be off ~** нева́жно себя́ чу́вствовать; **2.** *v/t.* [по]кра́сить; окра́шивать [окра́сить]; *fig.* приукра́шивать [-кра́сить]; *v/i.* [по]красне́ть; **~-blind:** **be ~** быть дальто́ником; **~ed** [-d] окра́шенный; цветно́й; **~ful** [-fʊl] я́ркий; **~ing** [-rɪŋ] окра́ска, раскра́ска; *fig.* приукра́шивание; **~less** [-ləs] □ бесцве́тный (*a. fig.*)

colt [kəʊlt] жеребёнок (*pl.:* жеребя́та); *fig.* птене́ц

column ['kɒləm] *arch., mil.* коло́нна; *of smoke, etc.* столб; *of figures* столбе́ц

comb [kəʊm] **1.** гре́бень *m*, гребёнка; **2.** *v/t.* расчёсывать [-чеса́ть], причёсывать [-чеса́ть]

combat ['kɒmbæt] **1.** бой, сраже́ние; **2.** сража́ться [срази́ться]; боро́ться (*a. fig.*); **~ant** ['kɒmbətənt] бое́ц

combin|ation [kɒmbɪ'neɪʃn] сочета́ние; **~e** [kəm'baɪn] объединя́ть(ся) [объедини́ть(ся)]; сочета́ть(ся) (*impf.*); **~ business with pleasure** сочета́ть прия́тное с поле́зным

combusti|ble [kəm'bʌstəbl] горю́чий, воспламеня́емый; **~on** [-tʃən] горе́ние, сгора́ние; **internal ~ engine** дви́гатель вну́треннего сгора́ния

come [kʌm] [*irr.*] приходи́ть [прийти́]; *by car, etc.* приезжа́ть [прие́хать]; **to ~** бу́дущий; **~ about** случа́ться [-чи́ться], происходи́ть [произойти́]; **~ across** встреча́ться [-ре́титься] с (Т), ната́лкиваться [наткну́ться] на (В); **~ back** возвраща́ться [-ти́ться]; **~ by** дост(ав)а́ть (случа́йно); **~ from** быть ро́дом из (Р); **~ off**; (*be successful*) удава́ться *pf.*; *of skin, etc.* сходи́ть [сойти́]; **~ round** приходи́ть в себя́; *coll.* заходи́ть [зайти́] к (Д); *fig.* идти́ на усту́пки; **~ to** доходи́ть [дойти́] до (Р); (*equal*) равня́ться (Д), сто́ить (В *or* Р); **~ up to** соотве́тствовать (Д); **~ to know s.o. (sth.)** познако́миться *pf.* с (Т) (узнава́ть [-на́ть] В); **~ what may** что бы ни случи́лось

comedian [kə'miːdɪən] ко́мик

comedy ['kɒmədɪ] коме́дия

comeliness ['kʌmlɪnɪs] милови́дность *f*

comfort ['kʌmfət] **1.** комфо́рт, удо́бство; *fig.* (*consolation*) утеше́ние; (*support*) подде́ржка; **2.** утеша́ть [уте́шить]; успока́ивать [-ко́ить]; **~able** [-əbl] удо́бный, комфорта́бельный; *income, life* вполне́ прили́чный; **~less** [-lɪs] □ неую́тный

comic ['kɒmɪk] **1.** коми́ческий, смешно́й; юмористи́ческий; **2.** ко́мик; **the ~s** ко́миксы

coming ['kʌmɪŋ] **1.** прие́зд, прибы́тие; **2.** бу́дущий; наступа́ющий

comma ['kɒmə] запята́я

command [kə'mɑːnd] **1.** кома́нда, прика́з; (*authority*) кома́ндование; **have at one's ~** име́ть в своём распоряже́нии; **2.** прика́зывать [-за́ть] (Д); владе́ть (Т); *mil.* кома́ндовать; **~er** [kə'mɑːndə] *mil.* команди́р; *navy* капита́н; **~er-in-chief** [-rɪn'tʃiːf] главноко́мандующий; **~ment** [-mənt] *eccl.* за́поведь *f*

commemora|te [kə'meməreɪt] *anniversary* ознаменова́ть; *event* отмеча́ть [отме́тить]; **~tion** [kəmemə'reɪʃn] ознаменова́ние

commence [kə'mens] нач(ин)а́ть(-ся); **~ment** [-mənt] нача́ло, торже́ственное вруче́ние дипло́мов

commend [kə'mend] отмеча́ть [-е́тить], [по]хвали́ть (*for* за В); рекомендова́ть (*impf.*)

comment ['kɒment] **1.** (*remark*) замеча́ние; *on text, etc.* коммента́рий; **no ~!** коммента́рии изли́шни!; **2.** (*on*) коммента́ровать (*impf.*); отзыва́ться [отозва́ться]; [с]де́лать замеча́ние; **~ary** ['kɒmənntrɪ] коммента́рий; **~ator** ['kɒmenteɪtə] коммента́тор

commerce ['kɒmɜːs] торго́вля, комме́рция; **~ial** [kə'mɜːʃl] □ торго́вый, комме́рческий; *su. radio, TV* рекла́ма

commiseration [kəmɪzə'reɪʃn] сочу́вствие, соболе́знование

commission [kə'mɪʃn] **1.** (*body of per-*

sons) коми́ссия; *(authority)* полномо́чие; *(errand)* поруче́ние; *(order)* зака́з; *comm.* комиссио́нные; **2.** зака́зывать [-за́ть]; поруча́ть [-чи́ть]; **~er** [-ʃənə] уполномо́ченный; член коми́ссии

commit [kə'mɪt] *(entrust)* поруча́ть [-чи́ть]; вверя́ть [вве́рить]; *for trial, etc.* преда(ва́)ть; *crime* соверша́ть [-ши́ть]; **~** *(o.s.)* обя́зывать(ся) [-за́ть(ся)]; **~** *(to prison)* заключа́ть [-чи́ть] в тюрьму́); **~ment** [-mənt] *(promise)* обяза́тельство; **~tee** [-ɪ] коми́ссия; комите́т; *be on a ~* быть чле́ном коми́ссии

commodity [kə'mɒdətɪ] това́р, предме́т потребле́ния

common ['kɒmən] □ о́бщий; *(ordinary)* просто́й, обыкнове́нный; *(mediocre)* заура́дный; *(widespread)* распространённый; *it is ~ knowledge that* ... общеизве́стно, что ...; **~** незаура́дный; **~ sense** здра́вый смысл; *we have nothing in ~* у нас нет ничего́ о́бщего; **~place** **1.** бана́льность *f;* **2.** бана́льный, *coll.* изби́тый; **~s** [-z] *pl.* простонаро́дье; *(mst. House of)* ♀ Пала́та общи́н; **~wealth** [-welθ] госуда́рство, соду́жество; *the British* ♀ *of Nations* Брита́нское Содру́жество На́ций

commotion [kə'məʊʃn] волне́ние, смяте́ние, возня́

communal ['kɒmjʊnl] *(pertaining to community)* обще́ственный, коммуна́льный; **~** *apartment or flat* коммуна́льная кварти́ра

communicat|e [kə'mju:nɪkeɪt] *v.t.* сообща́ть [-щи́ть]; перед(ав)а́ть; *v/i.* сообща́ться [-щи́ться]; **~ion** [kəmju:nɪ'keɪʃn] сообще́ние; коммуника́ция; связь *f;* **~** *satellite* спу́тник свя́зи; **~ive** [kə'mju:nɪkətɪv] □ общи́тельный, разгово́рчивый

communion [kə'mju:njən] обще́ние; *sacrament* прича́стие

communiqué [kə'mju:nɪkeɪ] коммюнике́ *n indecl.*

communis|m ['kɒmjʊnɪzəm] коммуни́зм; **~t** **1.** коммуни́ст *m,* -ка *f;* **2.** коммунисти́ческий

community [kə'mju:nətɪ] о́бщество; *local ~* ме́стные жи́тели

commute [kə'mju:t] *law* смягчи́ть наказа́ние; *travel back and forth regularly* е́здить на рабо́ту *(напр. из при́города в го́род)*

compact [kəm'pækt] *adj.* компа́ктный; *(closely packed)* пло́тный; *style* сжа́тый; *v/t.* сж(им)а́ть; уплотня́ть [-ни́ть]; **~** *disc* компа́ктдиск

companion [kəm'pænjən] това́рищ, подру́га; *(travel[l]ing ~)* спу́тник; **~ship** [-ʃɪp] компа́ния; дру́жеские отноше́ния *n/pl.*

company ['kʌmpənɪ] о́бщество; *comm.* компа́ния; акционе́рное о́бщество, фи́рма; *(guests)* го́сти *pl.;* *thea.* тру́ппа; *have ~* принима́ть госте́й

compar|able ['kɒmpərəbl] □ сравни́мый; **~ative** [kəm'pærətɪv] сравни́тельный; **~e** [kəm'peər] **1.** *beyond ~* вне вся́кого сравне́ния; **2.** *v/t.* сра́внивать [-ни́ть], слич́ать [-чи́ть], *(to c* T); *v/i.* сра́вниваться [-ни́ться]; **~ favo(u)rably with** вы́годно отлича́ться от P; **~ison** [kəm'pærɪsn] сравне́ние; *by ~* по сравне́нию (с T)

compartment [kəm'pɑ:tmənt] отделе́ние; *rail.* купе́ *n indecl.*

compass ['kʌmpəs] ко́мпас; *(extent)* преде́л; *(a pair of)* **~es** *pl.* ци́ркуль *m*

compassion [kəm'pæʃn] сострада́ние, жа́лость *f;* **~ate** [-ʃənət] □ сострада́тельный, сочу́вственный

compatible [kəm'pætəbl] □ совмести́мый *(a. comput.)*

compatriot [kəm'pætrɪət] сооте́чественник *m,* -ница *f*

compel [kəm'pel] заставля́ть [-а́вить]; принужда́ть [-нуди́ть]

compensat|e ['kɒmpənseɪt] *v/t.* компенси́ровать; *losses* возмеща́ть [-ести́ть]; **~ion** [kɒmpən'seɪʃn] возмеще́ние, компенса́ция

compete [kəm'pi:t] соревнова́ться, состяза́ться; конкури́ровать *(with* с T, *for* за B)

competen|ce, ~cy ['kɒmpɪtəns, -ɪ]

способность f; компетентность f; ~t [-tənt] □ компетентный

competit|ion [kɒmpə'tɪʃn] состязание, соревнование; *comm.* конкуренция; *of pianists, etc.* конкурс; ~**ive** [kəm'petətɪv] конкурентоспособный; ~**or** [kəm'petɪtə] конкурент *m*, -ка *f*; (*rival*) соперник *m*, -ица *f*; участник конкурса

compile [kəm'paɪl] составлять [-а́вить]

complacen|ce, ~cy [kəm'pleɪsəns, -ɪ] самодовольство

complain [kəm'pleɪn] [по]жаловаться (*of* на в); *law* обжаловать; ~**t** [-t] жалоба; *med.* болезнь f; *comm.* рекламация

complement ['kɒmplɪmənt] 1. дополнение; комплект; 2. дополнять [дополнить]; [у]комплектовать

complet|e [kəm'pli:t] 1. □ (*whole*) полный; (*finished*) законченный; *coll.* fool круглый; ~ **stranger** совершенно незнакомый человек; 2. заканчивать [закончить], а. [-'pliʃn] окончание

complex ['kɒmpleks] 1. □ (*intricate*) сложный; (*composed of parts*) комплексный, составной; *fig.* сложный, запутанный; 2. комплекс; ~**ion** [kəm'plekʃn] цвет лица; ~**ity** [-sɪtɪ] сложность f

compliance [kəm'plaɪəns] уступчивость f; согласие; *in ~ with* в соответствии с (Т)

complicat|e ['kɒmplɪkeɪt] усложнять(ся) [-нить(ся)]; ~**ion** [-'keɪʃn] сложность f, трудность f; *pl.* осложнения n/pl., a. med.

compliment 1. ['kɒmplɪmənt] комплимент; (*greeting*) привет; 2. [-ment] v/t. говорить комплименты (Д); поздравлять [-авить] (*on* с Т)

comply [kəm'plaɪ] уступать [-ить], соглашаться [-ласиться] (*with* с Т); (*yield*) подчиняться [-ниться] (*with* Д)

component [kəm'pəʊnənt] 1. компонент; составная часть f; 2. составной

compos|e [kəm'pəʊz] (*put together*) составлять [-авить]; (*create*) сочинять [-нить]; *compose o.s.* успо-

каиваться [-коиться]; ~**ed** [-d] □ спокойный, сдержанный; ~**er** [-ə] композитор; ~**ition** [kɒmpə'zɪʃn] *art* композиция; (*structure*) *lit., mus.* сочинение; ~**ure** [kəm'pəʊʒə] самообладание, спокойствие

compound 1. ['kɒmpaʊnd] *chem.* состав, соединение; *gr.* сложное слово; **2.** сложный; ~ *interest* сложные проценты *m/pl.*

comprehend [kɒmprɪ'hend] постигать [постигнуть], понимать [-нять]; (*include*) охватывать [охватить]

comprehen|sible [kɒmprɪ'hensəbl] понятный, постижимый; ~**sion** [-ʃn] понимание; понятливость f; ~**sive** [-sɪv] □ (*inclusive*) (все)объемлющий; исчерпывающий; *study* всесторонний

compress [kəm'pres] сж(им)ать; ~**ed air** сжатый воздух

comprise [kəm'praɪz] состоять; заключать в себе

compromise ['kɒmprəmaɪz] **1.** компромисс; **2.** v/t. [с]компрометировать; v/i. пойти pf. на компромисс

compuls|ion [kəm'pʌlʃn] принуждение; ~**ory** [-'pʌlsərɪ] *education, etc.* обязательный; принудительный

comput|e [kəm'pju:t] вычислять [вычислить]; ~**er** [-ə] компьютер

comrade ['kɒmreɪd] товарищ

con [kɒn] = *contra* против; *the pros and ~s* (голоса) за и против

conceal [kən'si:l] скры(ва)ть; утаивать [-ить], умалчивать [умолчать]

concede [kən'si:d] уступать [-пить]; (*allow*) допускать [-стить]

conceit [kən'si:t] самонадеянность, самомнение; ~**ed** [-ɪd] самонадеянный

conceiv|able [kən'si:vəbl] мыслимый; постижимый; *it's hardly ~* вряд ли; ~**e** [kən'si:v] v/i. представлять себе; v/t. задум(ыв)ать

concentrate ['kɒnsəntreɪt] сосредоточи(ва)ть(ся)

conception [kən'sepʃn] концепция; замысел; *biol.* зачатие

concern [kən'sɜːn] **1.** дело; (*anxiety*)

C

беспокойство; интерес; *comm.* предприятие; **what ~ is it of yours?** какое вам до этого дело?; **2.** касаться [коснуться] (Р); иметь отношение к (Д); **~ o.s. about, with** [за]интересоваться, заниматься [заняться] (Т); **~ed** [-d] □ заинтересованный; имеющий отношение; озабоченный; **~ing** [-ɪŋ] *prp.* относительно (Р)

concert ['kɒnsət] концерт; **act in ~** действовать согласованно

concerto [kən'tʃeətəu] концерт

concession [kən'seʃn] уступка; *econ.* концессия; **in price** скидка

conciliate [kən'sɪlɪeɪt] примирять [-рить]; **~or** [-ə] посредник

concise [kən'saɪs] □ сжатый, краткий; **~ness** [-nɪs] сжатость *f*, краткость *f*

conclude [kən'klu:d] *agreement, etc.* заключать [-чить]; *(finish)* закончить [закончить]; **to be ~d** окончание следует

conclusi|on [kən'klu:ʒn] окончание; *(inference)* заключение; вывод; **draw a ~** сделать *pf.* вывод; **~ve** [-sɪv] □ *(final)* заключительный; *(convincing)* убедительный

concoct [kən'kɒkt] [co]стряпать *(a. fig.)*; *fig.* придум(ыв)ать

concord ['kɒŋkɔ:d] *(agreement)* согласие

concrete ['kɒŋkri:t] **1.** конкретный; **2.** бетон; **3.** [за]бетонировать

concur [kən'kɜ:] *(agree)* соглашаться [-ласиться]; *(coincide)* совпадать [-пасть]

concussion [kən'kʌʃn] сотрясение мозга

condemn [kən'dem] осуждать [осудить]; *(blame)* порицать; приговаривать [-ворить] (к Д); [за]браковать; **~ation** [kɒndəm'neɪʃn] осуждение

condens|ation [kɒnden'seɪʃn] конденсация, сгущение; **~e** [kən'dens] сгущать(ся); *fig.* сокращать [-ратить]

condescen|d [kɒndɪ'send] снисходить [снизойти]; **~sion** [-'senʃn] снисхождение; снисходительность *f*

condiment ['kɒndɪmənt] приправа

condition [kən'dɪʃn] **1.** условие; *(state)* состояние; **~s** *pl. (circumstances)* обстоятельства *n/pl.*; условия *n/pl.*; **on ~ that** при условии, что; **2.** ставить условия; обусловливать [-овить]; **~al** [-əl] □ условный

condol|e [kən'dəul] соболезновать (**with** Д); **~ence** [-əns] соболезнование

condom ['kɒndəm] презерватив, кондом

condone [kən'dəun] прощать; *(overlook)* смотреть сквозь пальцы

conduct 1. ['kɒndʌkt] поведение; **2.** [kən'dʌkt] вести себя; *affairs* руководить; *mus.* дирижировать; **~or** [kən'dʌktə] *mus.* дирижёр; *el.* проводник

cone [kəun] конус; *bot.* шишка

confectionery [kən'fekʃənərɪ] кондитерские изделия *n/pl.*

confedera|te 1. [kən'fedərət] федеративный; **2.** [-] член конфедерации; союзник; *(accomplice)* соучастник, сообщник; **3.** [-reɪt] объединяться в союз; **~tion** [kənfedə'reɪʃn] конфедерация

confer [kənfɜ:] *v/t. (award)* присуждать [-удить]; *v/i. (consult)* совещаться; **~ence** ['kɒnfərəns] конференция; совещание

confess [kən'fes] призн(ав)аться, созн(ав)аться в (П); **~ion** [-'feʃn] признание; **to a priest** исповедь *f*; *creed, denomination* вероисповедание

confide [kən'faɪd] доверять (**in** Д); *(entrust)* вверять [вверить]; *(trust)* полагаться [положиться] (**in** на В); **~nce** ['kɒnfɪdəns] доверие; *(firm belief)* уверенность *f*; **~nt** ['kɒnfɪdənt] □ уверенный; **~ntial** [kɒnfɪ'denʃəl] конфиденциальный; секретный

configure [kən'fɪɡə] *comput.* конфигурировать

confine [kən'faɪn] ограничи(ва)ть; **to prison** заключать [-чить]; **be ~d of** *pregnant woman* рожать [родить]; **~ment** [-mənt] ограничение; заключение; роды *m/pl.*

confirm [kən'fɜ:m] подтверждать

[-рди́ть]; **~ed bachelor** убеждённый холостя́к; **~ation** [kɒnfəˈmeɪʃn] подтвержде́ние

confiscat|e [ˈkɒnfɪskeɪt] конфискова́ть *(im)pf.*; **~ion** [ˌkɒnfɪˈskeɪʃn] конфиска́ция

conflagration [kɒnfləˈgreɪʃn] бушу́ющий пожа́р

conflict 1. [ˈkɒnflɪkt] конфли́кт, столкнове́ние; 2. [kənˈflɪkt] быть в конфли́кте; *v/i.* противоре́чить

confluence [ˈkɒnfluəns] *of rivers* слия́ние

conform [kənˈfɔːm] согласо́вывать [-сова́ть] **(to** с Т); *(obey)* подчини́ться [-ни́ться] **(to** Д); *to standards etc.* удовлетворя́ть [-ри́ть], соотве́тствовать; **~ity** [-ɪtɪ] соотве́тствие; подчине́ние; **in** ~ **with** в соотве́тствии с (Т)

confound [kənˈfaʊnd] *(amaze)* поража́ть [порази́ть]; *(stump)* [по]ста́вить в тупи́к; *(confuse)* [с]пу́тать; ~ **it!** чёрт побери́!

confront [kənˈfrʌnt] стоя́ть лицо́м к лицу́ с (Т)

confus|e [kənˈfjuːz] [с]пу́тать; *(embarrass)* смуща́ть [-ути́ть]; **~ion** [kənˈfjuːʒən] смуще́ние; *(disorder)* беспоря́док; **throw into** ~ привести́ в замеша́тельство

congeal [kənˈdʒiːl] засты́(ва́)ть

congenial [kənˈdʒiːnɪəl] □ бли́зкий по ду́ху, прия́тный; *climate* благоприя́тный

congenital [kənˈdʒenɪtl] врождённый

congestion [kənˈdʒestʃən] *traffic* перегру́женность *f*; перенаселённость *f*

conglomeration [kənɡlɒməˈreɪʃn] скопле́ние, конгломера́т

congratulat|e [kənˈɡrætʃuleɪt] поздравля́ть [-а́вить] **(on** с Т); **~ion** [kənɡrætʃʊˈleɪʃn] поздравле́ние

congregat|e [ˈkɒnɡrɪɡeɪt] соб(и)ра́ть(ся); **~ion** [kɒnɡrɪˈɡeɪʃn] *in Bitte church* собра́ние прихожа́н

congress [ˈkɒnɡres] конгре́сс; съезд; **~man** *Am.* конгрессме́н

congruous [ˈkɒnɡruəs] □ *(fitting)* соотве́тствующий; гармони-

рующий **(to** с Т)

conifer [ˈkɒnɪfə] де́рево хво́йной поро́ды

conjecture [kənˈdʒektʃə] 1. дога́дка, предположе́ние; 2. предполага́ть [-ложи́ть]

conjugal [ˈkɒndʒʊɡl] супру́жеский

conjunction [kənˈdʒʌŋkʃn] соедине́ние; *gr.* сою́з; связь *f*; **in** ~ **with** совме́стно (с Т)

conjunctivitis [kəndʒʌŋktɪˈvaɪtɪs] конъюнктиви́т

conjur|e [ˈkʌndʒə] ~ **up** *fig.* вызыва́ть в воображе́нии; *v/i.* пока́зывать фо́кусы; **~er**, **~or** [-rə] фо́кусник

connect [kəˈnekt] соединя́ть(ся) [-ни́ть(ся)]; *(link)* свя́зывать(ся) [-за́ть(ся)]; *tel.* соединя́ть [-ни́ть]; **~ed** [-ɪd] □ свя́занный; *be ~ with* име́ть свя́зи (с Т); **~ion** [kəˈnekʃn] связь *f*; соедине́ние; **~s** свя́зи; *(family)* ро́дственники

connive [kəˈnaɪv]: ~ **at** потво́рствовать (Д), попусти́тельствовать

connoisseur [kɒnəˈsɜː] знато́к

conquer [ˈkɒŋkə] *country* завоёвывать [-ева́ть]; *(defeat)* побежда́ть [победи́ть]; **~or** [-rə] победи́тель(-ница *f*) *m*; завоева́тель *m*, -ница *f*

conquest [ˈkɒŋkwest] завоева́ние; побе́да

conscience [ˈkɒnʃəns] со́весть *f*; *have a guilty* ~ чу́вствовать угрызе́ния со́вести

conscientious [kɒnʃɪˈenʃəs] □ добросо́вестный

conscious [ˈkɒnʃəs] □ *effort, etc.* созна́тельный; *(aware)* сознаю́щий; **~ness** [-nɪs] созна́ние

conscript [kənˈskrɪpt] призывни́к; **~ion** [kənˈskrɪpʃn] во́инская пови́нность *f*

consecrate [ˈkɒnsɪkreɪt] *a church, etc.* освяща́ть [-яти́ть]

consecutive [kənˈsekjʊtɪv] □ после́довательный

consent [kənˈsent] 1. согла́сие; 2. соглаша́ться [-ласи́ться]

consequen|ce [ˈkɒnsɪkwens] (по)сле́дствие; *(importance)* ва́жность *f*;

C

∼t [-kwənt] обусло́вленный; (*subsequent*) после́дующий; **∼tly** [-kwəntlı] сле́довательно; поэ́тому

conserv|ation [kɒnsə'veıʃn] сохране́ние; *nature* ∼ охра́на приро́ды; **∼ative** [kən'sɜ:vətıv] **1.** □ консервати́вный; **2.** *pol.* консерва́тор; **∼atory** [-trı] оранжере́я; *mus.* консервато́рия; **∼e** [kən'sɜ:v] сохраня́ть [-ни́ть]

consider [kən'sıdə] *v/t.* обсужда́ть [-уди́ть]; (*think over*) обду́м(ыв)ать; (*regard*) полага́ть, счита́ть; (*take into account*) счита́ться с (Т); **∼able** [-rəbl] □ значи́тельный; большо́й; **∼ate** [-rət] внима́тельный (к Д); **∼ation** [kənsıdə'reıʃn] обсужде́ние; факт; соображе́ние; внима́ние; *take into* ∼ принима́ть во внима́ние, учи́тывать; **∼ing** [kən'sıdərıŋ] *prp.* учи́тывая (В), принима́я во внима́ние (В)

consign [kən'saın] перед(ав)а́ть; поруча́ть [-чи́ть]; *comm.* пос(ы)ла́ть (груз) по а́дресу; **∼ee** [kɒnsaı'ni:] грузополуча́тель, адреса́т гру́за; **∼ment** [-mənt] груз, па́ртия това́ров

consist [kən'sıst] состоя́ть (*of* из Р); заключа́ться (*in* в П); **∼ence**, **∼ency** [-əns, -ənsı] логи́чность *f*; консисте́нция *f*; **∼ent** [-ənt] □ после́довательный; согласу́ющийся (*with* с Т)

consol|ation [kɒnsə'leıʃn] утеше́ние; **∼e** [kən'səʊl] утеша́ть [уте́шить]

consolidate [kən'sɒlıdeıt] *position, etc.* укрепля́ть [-пи́ть]; (*unite*) объединя́ть(ся) [-ни́ть(ся)]; *comm.* слива́ться [-и́ться]

consonant ['kɒnsənənt] □ (*in accord*) согла́сный, созву́чный

conspicuous [kən'spıkjʊəs] □ заме́тный, броса́ющийся в глаза́

conspir|acy [kən'spırəsı] за́говор; **∼ator** [-tə] загово́рщик *m*, -ица *f*; **∼e** [kən'spaıə] устра́ивать за́говор, сгова́риваться [сговори́ться]

constable ['kʌnstəbl] *hist.* консте́бль *m*; (*policeman*) полице́йский

constan|cy ['kɒnstənsı] постоя́нство; (*faithfulness*) ве́рность *f*; **∼t** [-stənt] □ постоя́нный; ве́рный

consternation [kɒnstə'neıʃn] смяте́ние; замеша́тельство (*от стра́ха*)

constipation [kɒnstı'peıʃn] запо́р

constituen|cy [kən'stıtjʊənsı] избира́тельный о́круг; (*voters*) избира́тели *m/pl.*; **∼t** [-ənt] **1.** (*part*) составно́й; *pol.* учреди́тельный; **2.** избира́тель *m*; составна́я часть *f*

constitut|e ['kɒnstıtju:t] (*make up*) составля́ть [-а́вить]; (*establish*) осно́вывать [-нова́ть]; **∼ion** [kɒnstı'tju:ʃn] (*makeup*) строе́ние; конститу́ция; учрежде́ние; физи́ческое *or* душе́вное здоро́вье; **∼ional** [-ʃənl] □ конституцио́нный; *of body* органи́ческий

constrain [kən'streın] принужда́ть [-нуди́ть]; вынужда́ть [вы́нудить]; (*limit*) сде́рживать [-жа́ть]; **∼t** [-t] принужде́ние; вы́нужденность *f*; *of feelings* ско́ванность *f*

constrict [kən'strıkt] стя́гивать [стяну́ть]; сж(им)а́ть; **∼ion** [-kʃn] сжа́тие; стя́гивание

construct [kən'strʌkt] [по]стро́ить; сооружа́ть [-уди́ть]; *fig.* созд(ав)а́ть; **∼ion** [-kʃn] строи́тельство, стро́йка; (*building, etc.*) строе́ние; ∼ *site* стро́йка; **∼ive** [-tıv] конструкти́вный

construe [kən'stru:] истолко́вывать [-кова́ть]

consul ['kɒnsl] ко́нсул; ∼ *general* генера́льный ко́нсул; **∼ate** ['kɒnsjʊlət] ко́нсульство

consult [kən'sʌlt] *v/t.* спра́шивать сове́та у (Р); *v/i.* [про]консульти́роваться, совеща́ться; ∼ *a doctor* пойти́ на консульта́цию к врачу́; **∼ant** [-ənt] консульта́нт; **∼ation** [kɒnsl'teıʃn] *specialist advice and advice bureau* консульта́ция, конси́лиум (враче́й)

consum|e [kən'sju:m] *v/t.* съеда́ть [съесть]; (*use*) потребля́ть [-би́ть]; [из]расхо́довать; **∼er** [-ə] потреби́тель *m*; ∼ *goods* потреби́тельские това́ры

consummate [kən'sʌmıt] □ соверше́нный, зако́нченный

consumption [kən'sʌmpʃn] потребле́ние, расхо́д; *med.* туберкулёз лёгких

contact ['kɒntækt] конта́кт (*a. fig.*);

business ~s деловы́е свя́зи

contagious [kən'teɪdʒəs] □ зара́зный, инфекцио́нный

contain [kən'teɪn] содержа́ть (в себе́), вмеща́ть [-ести́ть]; ~ **o.s.** сде́рживаться [-жа́ться]; ~**er** [-ə] конте́йнер

contaminat|e [kən'tæmɪneɪt] *water, etc.* загрязня́ть [-ни́ть]; заража́ть [зарази́ть]; *fig.* ока́зывать [-за́ть] па́губное влия́ние; ~**ion** [kəntæmɪ'neɪʃn]: **radioactive** ~ радиоакти́вное загрязне́ние

contemplat|e ['kɒntəmpleɪt] обду́м(ыв)ать; ~**ion** [kɒntem'pleɪʃn] созерца́ние; размышле́ние

contempora|neous [kəntempə'reɪnɪəs] □ совпада́ющий по вре́мени, одновреме́нный; ~**ry** [kən'tempərərɪ] **1.** совреме́нный; **2.** совреме́нник *m*, -ица *f*

contempt [kən'tempt] презре́ние (**for** к Д); ~**ible** [-əbl] □ презре́нный; ~**uous** [-ʃuəs] □ презри́тельный

contend [kən'tend] *v/i.* боро́ться; сопе́рничать; *v/t.* утвержда́ть

content 1. [kən'tent] **1.** дово́льный; **2.** удовлетворя́ть [-ри́ть]; **3.** удовлетворе́ние; **to one's heart's** ~ вво́лю; **4.** ['kɒntent] содержа́ние; **table of** ~**s** оглавле́ние; ~**ed** [kən'tentɪd] □ дово́льный, удовлетворённый

contention [kən'tenʃn] *dissension* спор, ссо́ра; *assertion* утвержде́ние

contentment [kən'tentmənt] удовлетворённость *f*

contest 1. ['kɒntest] ко́нкурс; *sport* соревнова́ние; **2.** [kən'test] оспа́ривать [оспо́рить]; *one's rights, etc.* отста́ивать [отстоя́ть]; (*struggle*) боро́ться (**за** В); ~**ant** уча́стник (-ица) состяза́ния

context ['kɒntekst] конте́кст

continent ['kɒntɪnənt] матери́к, контине́нт; **the** Ω *Brt.* (материко́вая) Евро́па

contingen|cy [kən'tɪndʒənsɪ] случа́йность *f*; непредви́денное обстоя́тельство; **be prepared for every** ~ быть гото́вым ко вся́ким случа́йностям; ~**t** [-dʒənt] □ **1.**

случа́йный, непредви́денный; **2.** гру́ппа; *mil.* континге́нт

continu|al [kən'tɪnjuəl] □ непреры́вный, беспреста́нный; ~**ation** [kəntɪnju'eɪʃn] продолже́ние; ~**e** [kən'tɪnjuː] *v/t.* продолжа́ть [-до́лжить]; **to be** ~**d** продолже́ние сле́дует; *v/i.* продолжа́ться [-до́лжиться]; *of forest, road, etc.* простира́ться, тяну́ться; ~**ity** [kɒntɪ'njuːəti] непреры́вность *f*; ~**ous** [kən'tɪnjuəs] □ непреры́вный; (*unbroken*) сплошно́й

contort [kən'tɔːt] *of face* искажа́ть [искази́ть]

contour ['kɒntuə] ко́нтур, очерта́ние

contraband ['kɒntrəbænd] контраба́нда

contraceptive [kɒntrə'septɪv] противозача́точное сре́дство

contract 1. [kən'trækt] *v/t. muscle* сокраща́ть [-рати́ть]; *alliance* заключа́ть [-чи́ть]; *v/i.* сокраща́ться [-рати́ться]; *of metal* сж(им)а́ть(ся); **2.** ['kɒntrækt] контра́кт, догово́р; ~**ion** [-ʃən] сжа́тие; сокраще́ние; ~**or** [-tə] подря́дчик

contradict [kɒntrə'dɪkt] противоре́чить (Д); ~**ion** [-kʃn] противоре́чие; ~**ory** [-tərɪ] □ противоречи́вый

contrary ['kɒntrərɪ] **1.** противополо́жный; *person* упря́мый; ~ **to** *prp.* вопреки́ (Д); **2.** обра́тное; **on the** ~ наоборо́т

contrast 1. ['kɒntrɑːst] противополо́жность *f*; контра́ст; **2.** [kən'trɑːst] *v/t.* сопоставля́ть [-а́вить], сра́внивать [-ни́ть]; *v/i.* отлича́ться от (Р); контрасти́ровать с (Т)

contribut|e [kən'trɪbjuːt] (*donate*) [по]же́ртвовать; *to a newspaper, etc.* сотру́дничать (**to** в П); *share* [kɒntrɪ'bjuːʃn] вклад; взнос; ~**or** [kən'trɪbjutə] а́втор; же́ртвователь

contriv|ance [kən'traɪvəns] вы́думка; *mechanism, etc.* приспособле́ние; ~**e** [kən'traɪv] *v/t.* (*invent*) приду́м(ыв)ать; (*scheme*) затева́ть [-е́ять]; *v/i.* ухитря́ться [-ри́ться]; умудря́ться [-ри́ться]

C

control [kən'trəʊl] 1. управле́ние (*a. tech.*), регули́рование; контро́ль *m*; **~ desk** пульт управле́ния; **lose ~ of o.s.** потеря́ть самооблада́ние; **under ~** в поря́дке; 2. управля́ть (Т); [про]контроли́ровать (*im*)*pf.*; *feelings, etc.* сде́рживать [-жа́ть]; **~ler** [-ə] контролёр, инспе́ктор; *ae.*, *rail.* диспе́тчер

controver|sial [kɒntrə'vɜːʃl] □ спо́рный; **~sy** ['kɒntrəvɜːsɪ] спор, поле́мика

convalesce [kɒnvə'les] выздора́вливать *impf.*; **~nce** [-ns] выздоровле́ние; **~nt** [-nt] выздора́вливающий

convene [kən'viːn] *meeting, etc.* соз(ы)ва́ть; (*come together*) соб(и)ра́ть(ся)

convenien|ce [kən'viːnɪəns] удо́бство; **at your earliest ~** как то́лько вы смо́жете; **public ~** *euph.* убо́рная; **~t** [-ɪənt] □ удо́бный

convent ['kɒnvənt] монасты́рь *m*; **~ion** [kən'venʃn] съезд; (*agreement*) конве́нция, соглаше́ние; (*custom*) обы́чай, усло́вность *f*

converge [kən'vɜːdʒ] сходи́ться [сойти́сь] (в одну́ то́чку)

convers|ation [kɒnvə'seɪʃn] разгово́р, бесе́да; **~ational** [-ʃənl] разгово́рный; **~e** [kən'vɜːs] разгова́ривать, бесе́довать; **~ion** [kən'vɜːʃn] превраще́ние; *eccl., etc.* обраще́ние; *el.* преобразова́ние; *stocks, etc.* конве́рсия

convert [kən'vɜːt] превраща́ть [-ати́ть]; *el.* преобразо́вывать [-ва́ть]; *fin.* конверти́ровать; *eccl., etc.* обраща́ть [-рати́ть] (в другу́ю ве́ру); **~ible** [-əbl]: **~ currency** конверти́руемая валю́та

convey [kən'veɪ] *goods* перевози́ть [-везти́], переправля́ть [-пра́вить]; *greetings, electricity, etc.* перед(ав)а́ть; **~ance** [-əns] перево́зка; доста́вка; тра́нспортное сре́дство; **~or** [-ə] (**~ belt**)

convict 1. ['kɒnvɪkt] осуждённый; 2. [kən'vɪkt] признава́ть вино́вным; **~ion** [kən'vɪkʃn] *law* осужде́ние; (*firm belief*) убежде́ние

convinc|e [kən'vɪns] убежда́ть [убеди́ть]; (**of** в П); **~ing** [-ɪŋ] убеди́тельный

convoy ['kɒnvɔɪ] *naut.* конво́й; сопровожде́ние

convuls|e [kən'vʌls] содрога́ться [-гну́ться]; **be ~d with laughter** смея́ться до упа́ду; **her face was ~d with pain** её лицо́ искази́лось от бо́ли; **~ion** [-ʃn] *of ground* колеба́ние; *of muscles* су́дорога; **~ive** [-sɪv] су́дорожный

coo [kuː] воркова́ть

cook [kʊk] 1. по́вар; 2. [при]гото́вить еду́; **~ery** ['kʊkərɪ] кулина́рия; приготовле́ние еды́; **~ie**, **~y** ['kʊkɪ] *Am.* пече́нье

cool [kuːl] 1. прохла́дный; *fig.* хладнокро́вный; (*imperturbable*) невозмути́мый; *pej.* де́рзкий, наха́льный; **keep ~!** не горячи́сь!; 2. прохла́да; 3. охлажда́ть(ся) [охлади́ть(ся)]; осты́(ва́)ть; **~headed** [kuːl'hedɪd] □ хладнокро́вный

coolness ['kuːlnɪs] холодо́к; прохла́да; хладнокро́вие

coop [kuːp] **~ up** или **in** держа́ть взаперти́

cooperat|e [kəʊ'ɒpəreɪt] сотру́дничать; **~ion** [kəʊɒpə'reɪʃn] сотру́дничество; **~ive** [kəʊ'ɒpərətɪv] коопера́тивный; **~ society** кооперати́в

coordinat|e [kəʊ'ɔːdɪneɪt] координи́ровать (*im*)*pf.*; согласо́вывать [-ова́ть]; **~ion** [kəʊɔːdɪ'neɪʃn] координа́ция

cope [kəʊp]: **~ with** справля́ться [-а́виться] с (Т)

copier ['kɒpɪə] копирова́льный аппара́т

copious ['kəʊpɪəs] □ оби́льный

copper ['kɒpə] 1. медь *f*; (*coin*) ме́дная моне́та; 2. ме́дный

copy ['kɒpɪ] 1. ко́пия; (*single example*) экземпля́р; 2. перепи́сывать [-са́ть]; снима́ть [снять] ко́пию с (Р); **~book** тетра́дь *f*; **~right** а́вторское пра́во

coral ['kɒrəl] кора́лл

cord [kɔːd] 1. верёвка, шнур; **vocal ~s** голосовы́е свя́зки; 2. свя́зывать

[-за́ть] верёвкой

cordial ['kɔ:dɪəl] **1.** □ серде́чный, и́скренний; **2.** стимули́рующий напи́ток; **~ity** [kɔ:dɪˈælətɪ] серде́чность *f*; раду́шие

cordon ['kɔ:dn] **1.** кордо́н; **2.** **~ off** отгора́живать [-роди́ть]

corduroy ['kɔ:dərɔɪ] вельве́т в ру́бчик; **~s** *pl.* вельве́товые брю́ки *m/pl.*

core [kɔ:] сердцеви́на; *fig.* суть *f*; **to the ~** *fig.* до мо́зга косте́й

cork [kɔ:k] **1.** про́бка; **2.** затыка́ть про́бкой; **~screw** што́пор

corn¹ [kɔ:n] зерно́; хлеба́ *m/pl.*; *Am.*, *maize* кукуру́за

corn² [-] *on a toe* мозо́ль

corner ['kɔ:nə] **1.** у́гол; **2.** *fig.* загна́ть *pf.* в у́гол; припере́ть *pf.* к стене́

cornflakes корнфле́кс; кукуру́зные хло́пья

cornice ['kɔ:nɪs] *arch.* карни́з

coronary ['kɒrənərɪ] корона́рный; *su. coll.* инфа́ркт

coronation [kɒrəˈneɪʃn] корона́ция

corpor|al ['kɔ:pərəl] **1.** □ теле́сный; **2.** *mil. approx.* ефре́йтор; **~ation** [kɔ:pəˈreɪʃn] корпора́ция

corps [kɔ:]: *diplomatic* **~** дипломати́ческий ко́рпус

corpse [kɔ:ps] труп

corpulen|ce ['kɔ:pjʊləns] ту́чность *f*; **~t** [-lənt] ту́чный

correct [kəˈrekt] **1.** □ пра́вильный, ве́рный, то́чный; (*proper*) корре́ктный; **2.** *v/t.* исправля́ть [-а́вить], корректи́ровать; *manuscript* пра́вить; **~ion** [kəˈrekʃn] (*act of correcting*) исправле́ние; (*the correction made*) попра́вка

correlat|e ['kɒrəleɪt] устана́вливать соотноше́ние; **~ion** [kɒrəˈleɪʃn] соотноше́ние, взаимосвя́зь *f*

correspond [kɒrɪˈspɒnd] соотве́тствовать (*with, to* Д); *by letter* перепи́сываться (с Т); **~ence** [-əns] соотве́тствие, перепи́ска; **~ent** [-ənt] **1.** соотве́тствующий; **2.** корреспонде́нт *m*, -ка *f*; **~ing** [-ɪŋ] □ соотве́тствующий (Д)

corridor ['kɒrɪdɔ:] коридо́р

corroborate [kəˈrɒbəreɪt] подтвержда́ть [-рди́ть]

corro|de [kəˈrəʊd] разъеда́ть [-е́сть]; [за]ржаве́ть; **~sion** [kəˈrəʊʒn] корро́зия, ржа́вчина; **~sive** [-sɪv] **1.** корро́зийный; **2.** разъеда́ющее вещество́

corrugated ['kɒrəgeɪtɪd]: **~ iron** рифлёное желе́зо

corrupt [kəˈrʌpt] **1.** □ коррумпи́рованный, прода́жный; (*containing mistakes*) искажённый; (*depraved*) развращённый; **2.** *v/t.* искажа́ть [-зи́ть]; развраща́ть [-рати́ть]; подкупа́ть [-пи́ть]; *v/i.* [ис]по́ртиться, искажа́ться [-зи́ться]; **~ion** [-pʃn] искаже́ние; корру́пция, прода́жность *f*; развращённость *f*

corset ['kɔ:sɪt] корсе́т

cosmetic [kɒzˈmetɪk] **1.** космети́ческий; **2.** *pl.* косме́тика

cosmic ['kɒzmɪk] косми́ческий

cosmonaut ['kɒzmənɔ:t] космона́вт

cosmos ['kɒzmɒs] ко́смос

cost [kɒst] **1.** цена́, сто́имость *f*; *pl.* расхо́ды, изде́ржки; **~ effectiveness** рента́бельность *f*; **2.** [*irr.*] сто́ить

costly ['kɒstlɪ] дорого́й, це́нный

costume ['kɒstju:m] костю́м; **~ jewel(-le)ry** бижуте́рия

cosy ['kəʊzɪ] □ ую́тный

cot [kɒt] де́тская крова́ть

cottage ['kɒtɪdʒ] котте́дж, небольшо́й дом (*обычно в деревне*); *Am.* ле́тняя да́ча; **~ cheese** творо́г

cotton ['kɒtn] **1.** хло́пок; (*thread*) ни́тки; **2.** хлопчатобума́жный; **~ wool** ва́та; **3.**: **~ on** *coll.* понима́ть [-ня́ть]

couch [kaʊtʃ] дива́н; *Brt.* куше́тка

cough [kɒf] **1.** ка́шель *m*; *a bad* **~** си́льный ка́шель; **2.** ка́шлять [ка́шлянуть]

could [kəd; *strong* kʊd] *pt. om* **can**

council ['kaʊnsl] сове́т; *Security* 2 Сове́т Безопа́сности; *town* **~** городско́й сове́т, муниципалите́т; **~(l)or** [-sələ] член сове́та

counsel ['kaʊnsl] **1.** сове́т, совеща́ние; *law* адвока́т; **~ for the prosecution** обви́нитель *m*; **2.** дава́ть сове́т (Д); ~(l)or [-ələ] *dipl.*, *pol.* сове́тник

count¹ [kaʊnt] **1.** счёт; (*counting up*) подсчёт; **2.** *v/t.* [co]счита́ть; подсчи́тывать [-ита́ть]; (*include*) включа́ть [-чи́ть]; *v/i.* счита́ться; (*be of account*) име́ть значе́ние

count² [-] граф

countenance ['kaʊntənəns] **1.** лицо́; выраже́ние лица́; (*support*) подде́ржка; *lose* ~ потеря́ть самооблада́ние; **2.** подде́рживать [-жа́ть], поощря́ть [-ри́ть]

counter¹ ['kaʊntə] прила́вок; *in bar, bank* сто́йка; *tech.* счётчик

counter² [-] **1.** противополо́жный (*to* Д); встре́чный; **2.** *adv.* обра́тно; напро́тив; **3.** [вос]проти́виться (Д); *a blow* наноси́ть встре́чный уда́р

counteract [kaʊntər'ækt] противоде́йствовать (Д); нейтрализова́ть (*im*)*pf*.

counterbalance 1. ['kaʊntəbæləns] *mst.* *fig.* противове́с; **2.** [kaʊntə'bæləns] уравнове́шивать [-ве́сить]; служи́ть противове́сом (Д)

counterespionage [kaʊntər'espɪə-nɑːʒ] контрразве́дка

counterfeit ['kaʊntəfɪt] **1.** подде́льный; **2.** подде́лка; **3.** подде́л(ыв)ать

counterfoil ['kaʊntəfɔɪl] корешо́к (биле́та, квита́нции)

countermand [kaʊntə'mɑːnd] *order* отменя́ть [-ни́ть]

countermove ['kaʊntəmuːv] *fig.* отве́тная ме́ра, контруда́р

counterpane ['kaʊntəpeɪn] покрыва́ло

counterpart ['kaʊntəpɑːt] представи́тель друго́й стороны́ (*занима́ющий тот же пост, до́лжность и т.д.*); *the English MPs met their Russian ~s* англи́йские парламента́рии встре́тились со свои́ми ру́сскими колле́гами

countersign ['kaʊntəsaɪn] *v/t.* [по]ста́вить втору́ю по́дпись (на П)

countess ['kaʊntɪs] графи́ня

countless ['kaʊntlɪs] бесчи́сленный, несчётный

country ['kʌntrɪ] **1.** страна́; ме́стность *f*; *go to the* ~ пое́хать за́ город; *live in the* ~ жить в се́льской ме́стности; **2.** дереве́нский; ~man [-mən] се́льский жи́тель; земля́к, соотече́ственник; ~side [-saɪd] се́льская ме́стность *f*

county ['kaʊntɪ] гра́фство; *Am.* о́круг

coup [kuː] уда́чный ход (*уда́р и т.п.*)

couple ['kʌpl] **1.** па́ра; **2.** соединя́ть [-ни́ть]; *zo.* спа́риваться

coupling ['kʌplɪŋ] *tech.* му́фта сцепле́ния

coupon ['kuːpɒn] купо́н, тало́н

courage ['kʌrɪdʒ] му́жество, сме́лость *f*, хра́брость *f*, отва́га; *pluck up one's* ~ набра́ться *pf.* хра́брости; ~ous [kə'reɪdʒəs] □ му́жественный, сме́лый, хра́брый

courier ['kʊrɪə] курье́р, наро́чный

course [kɔːs] (*direction*) направле́ние, курс; *of events* ход; *of river* тече́ние; (*food*) блю́до; *of* ~ коне́чно; *in the* ~ *of* в тече́ние

court [kɔːt] **1.** двор (*a. fig.*); (*law* ~) суд; *sport* площа́дка; *tennis* ~ те́ннисный корт; **2.** (*woo*) уха́живать за (Т); (*seek favo[u]r of*) иска́ть расположе́ния (Р); ~eous ['kɜːtɪəs] □ ве́жливый, учти́вый; ~esy ['kɜːtəsɪ] учти́вость *f*, ве́жливость *f*; ~ martial *mil.* **1.** вое́нный трибуна́л; **2.** суди́ть вое́нным трибуна́лом; ~ship ['-ʃɪp] уха́живание; ~yard двор

cousin ['kʌzn] *male* кузе́н, двою́родный брат; *female* кузи́на, двою́родная сестра́

cove [kəʊv] (ма́ленькая) бу́хта

cover ['kʌvə] **1.** (*lid, top*) кры́шка; *for bed, etc.* покрыва́ло; *of book* обло́жка; (*shelter*) укры́тие; *fig.* покро́в; *send under separate* ~ посла́ть в отде́льном письме́, паке́те; **2.** покры́(ва́)ть (*a. comm.*); прикры́(ва́)ть; (*a. up*) скры́(ва́)ть; ~ing [-rɪŋ]: ~ *letter* сопроводи́тельное письмо́

coverage ['kʌvərɪdʒ] репорта́ж; охва́т

covert ['kʌvət] □ скры́тый, та́йный

covet ['kʌvɪt] жа́ждать (Р); ~ous [-əs] □ жа́дный, а́лчный; скупо́й

cow[1] [kaʊ] коро́ва

cow[2] [-] запу́гивать [-га́ть]; терроризова́ть (*im*)*pf*.

coward ['kaʊəd] трус *m*, -и́ха *f*; **~ice** [-ɪs] трýсость *f*; малодýшие; **~ly** [-lɪ] трусли́вый

cowboy ['kaʊbɔɪ] *Am*. ковбо́й

cower ['kaʊə] съёжи(ва)ться

cowl [kaʊl] капюшо́н

coy [kɔɪ] □ засте́нчивый

cozy ['kəʊzɪ] ую́тный

crab[1] [kræb] *zo*. краб

crab[2] [-] *bot*. ди́кая я́блоня; *coll*. ворчу́н

crack [kræk] **1.** (*noise*) треск; тре́щина; щель *f*; рассе́лина; *coll*. (*blow*) уда́р; *Am*. саркасти́ческое замеча́ние; **at the ~ of dawn** на заре́; **2.** *coll*. первокла́ссный; **3.** *v/t*. раска́лывать [-коло́ть], коло́ть; **~ a joke** отпусти́ть шýтку; *v/i*. производи́ть треск, шум; [по]тре́скаться; раска́лываться [-коло́ться]; *of voice* лома́ться; **~ed** [-t] тре́снувший; *coll*. вы́живший из ума́; **~er** ['-ə] хлопýшка; *Am*. кре́кер; **~le** ['-l] потре́скивание, треск

cradle ['kreɪdl] **1.** колыбе́ль *f*; *fig*. нача́ло; младе́нчество; **2.** бе́режно держа́ть в рука́х (как ребёнка)

craft [krɑːft] (*skill*) ло́вкость *f*, сноро́вка; (*trade*) ремесло́; (*boat*) су́дно (*pl*. суда́); **~sman** ['-smən] ма́стер; **~y** ['-ɪ] ло́вкий, хи́трый

crag [kræg] скала́, утёс; **~gy** ['-ɪ] скали́стый

cram [kræm] набива́ть [-би́ть]; впи́хивать [-хнýть]; [на]пи́чкать; *coll*. [за]зубри́ть

cramp [kræmp] **1.** су́дорога; **2.** (*hamper*) стесня́ть [-ни́ть]; (*limit*) сýживать [сýзить]

cranberry ['krænbərɪ] клю́ква

crane [kreɪn] **1.** *bird* жура́вль *m*; *tech*. подъёмный кран; **2.** поднима́ть кра́ном; *neck* вытя́гивать [вы́тянуть] ше́ю

crank [kræŋk] **1.** *mot*. заводна́я рýчка; *coll. person* челове́к с причýдами; **2.** заводи́ть [-вести́] рýчкой (автомаши́ну); **~shaft** *tech*. коле́нчатый вал; **~y**

['-ɪ] капри́зный; эксцентри́чный

cranny ['krænɪ] щель *f*; тре́щина

crape [kreɪp] креп

crash [kræʃ] **1.** гро́хот, гром; *ae*. ава́рия; *rail*. круше́ние; *fin*. крах; **2.** па́дать, рýшиться с тре́ском; разби́(ва́)ться (*a. ae*.); *ae*. потерпе́ть *pf*. ава́рию; **~ helmet** защи́тный шлем; **~ landing** авари́йная поса́дка

crater ['kreɪtə] кра́тер; *mil*. воро́нка

crave [kreɪv] стра́стно жела́ть, жа́ждать (**for** P)

crawl [krɔːl] **1.** по́лзание; *swimming* кроль; **2.** по́лзать, [по]ползти́; *fig*. пресмыка́ться

crayfish ['kreɪfɪʃ] рак

crayon ['kreɪən] цветно́й каранда́ш; пасте́ль *f*, рису́нок пасте́лью *или* цветны́м каранда́шом

craz|e [kreɪz] **1.** *coll*. ма́ния, пова́льное увлече́ние; **be the ~** быть в мо́де; **2.** своди́ть с ума́; **~y** ['kreɪzɪ] □ поме́шанный; *plan, etc*. безýмный; **be ~ about** быть поме́шанным (на П)

creak [kriːk] **1.** скрип; **2.** [за]скрипе́ть

cream [kriːm] **1.** сли́вки *f/pl*.; крем; (*the best part*) са́мое лýчшее; **shoe ~** крем для о́буви; **sour ~** смета́на; **whipped ~** взби́тые сли́вки; **2.** снима́ть сли́вки с (P); **~y** ['kriːmɪ] □ (*containing cream*) сли́вочный

crease [kriːs] скла́дка; (*on paper*) сгиб; **2.** [по]мя́ть(ся); загиба́ть [загнýть]; **~-proof** немнýщийся

creat|e [kriː'eɪt] [со]тво́рить; созд(а́)в)а́ть; **~ion** [-'eɪʃn] созда́ние; (со)творе́ние; **~ive** [-ɪv] тво́рческий; **~or** [-ə] созда́тель *m*, творе́ц; **~ure** ['kriːtʃə] созда́ние, существо́

creden|ce ['kriːdns] ве́ра, дове́рие; **~tials** [krɪ'denʃlz] *pl. dipl*. вери́тельные гра́моты *f/pl*.; удостовере́ние

credible ['kredəbl] □ заслýживающий дове́рия; *story* правдоподо́бный; **it's hardly ~ that** малове́ройтно, что

credit ['kredɪt] **1.** дове́рие; хоро́шая репута́ция; *fin*. креди́т; **2.** ве́рить, доверя́ть (Д); *fin*. кредитова́ть (*im*)*pf*.; **~ s.o. with s.th.** счита́ть, что; **~able**

['-əbl] □ похва́льный; ~ **card** креди́тная ка́рточка; **~or** [-ə] кредито́р; **~worthy** кредитоспосо́бный

credulous ['kredjʊləs] □ легкове́рный, дове́рчивый

creek [kriːk] бу́хта, небольшо́й зали́в; *Am.* руче́й

creep [kriːp] [*irr.*] по́лзать, [по]ползти́; *of plants* стла́ться, ви́ться; (*stealthily*) кра́сться; *fig.* **in** вкра́дываться [вкра́сться]; **~er** ['-ə] вью́щееся расте́ние

cremate [krə'meɪt] креми́ровать

crept [krept] *pt. и pt. p. om* **creep**

crescent ['kresnt] полуме́сяц

crest [krest] *of wave, hill* гре́бень *m*; **~fallen** ['krestfɔːlən] упа́вший ду́хом, уны́лый

crevasse [krɪ'væs] рассе́лина

crevice ['krevɪs] шель *f*, расще́лина, тре́щина

crew[1] [kruː] *of train* брига́да; *naut., ae.* экипа́ж, *mil.* кома́нда

crew[2] [-] *chiefly Brt. pt. om* **crow**

crib [krɪb] *Am.* де́тская крова́тка; *educ.* шпарга́лка

cricket[1] ['krɪkɪt] *zo.* сверчо́к

cricket[2] [-] *game* крике́т; *coll.* **not** ~ не по пра́вилам, нече́стно

crime [kraɪm] преступле́ние

criminal ['krɪmɪnl] **1.** престу́пник; **2.** престу́пный; крими́нальный, уголо́вный; ~ **code** уголо́вный ко́декс

crimson ['krɪmzn] **1.** багро́вый, мали́новый; **2.** [по]красне́ть

cringe [krɪndʒ] пресмыка́ться

crinkle ['krɪŋkl] **1.** скла́дка; морщи́на; **2.** [с]мо́рщиться; [по]мя́ться

cripple ['krɪpl] **1.** кале́ка *m/f*, инвали́д; **2.** [ис]кале́чить, [из]уро́довать; *fig.* парализова́ть (*im*)*pf.*

crisis ['kraɪsɪs] кри́зис

crisp [krɪsp] **1.** *having curls* кудря́вый; *snow, etc.* хрустя́щий; *air* бодря́щий; **2. potato** ~**s** хрустя́щий карто́фель

crisscross ['krɪskrɒs] **1.** *adv.* крестна́крест, вкось; **2.** перечёркивать крест-на́крест; **~ed with roads** покры́тый се́тью доро́г

criteri|on [kraɪ'tɪərɪən], *pl.* ~**a** [-rɪə]

крите́рий, мери́ло

criti|c ['krɪtɪk] кри́тик; **~cal** ['krɪtɪkl] крити́ческий; **~cism** [-sɪzəm], **~que** ['krɪtiːk] кри́тика, реце́нзия; **~cize** ['krɪtɪsaɪz] [рас]критикова́ть; (*judge severely*) осужда́ть [осуди́ть]

croak [krəʊk] [за]ка́ркать; [за]ква́кать

Croat ['krəʊæt] хорва́т, хорва́тка; **~ian** [krəʊ'eɪʃən] хорва́тский

crochet ['krəʊʃeɪ] **1.** вяза́ние (крючко́м); **2.** вяза́ть

crock [krɒk] гли́няный горшо́к; **~ery** ['krɒkərɪ] гли́няная/фая́нсовая посу́да

crony ['krəʊnɪ] *coll.* закады́чный друг

crook [krʊk] **1.** (*bend*) поворо́т; изги́б; *sl.* моше́нник; **2.** сгиба́ть(ся) [согну́ть(ся)]; **~ed** ['krʊkɪd] изо́гнутый; криво́й; *coll.* нече́стный

croon [kruːn] напева́ть вполго́лоса

crop [krɒp] **1.** урожа́й; посе́вы *m/pl.*; ~ **failure** неурожа́й; **2.** (*bear a crop*) уроди́ться; *hair* подстрига́ть [-ри́чь]; ~ **up** возника́ть [-и́кнуть]; обнару́житься

cross [krɒs] **1.** крест; **2.** □ (*transverse*) попере́чный; *fig.* серди́тый; **3.** *v/t. arms, etc.* скре́щивать [-ести́ть]; (*go across*) переходи́ть [перейти́], переезжа́ть [перее́хать]; *fig.* противоде́йствовать (Д); пере́чить; ~ **o.s.** [пере]крести́ться; *v/i. of mail* размину́ться *pf.*; **~bar** попере́чина; **~breed** по́месь *f*; (*plant*) гибри́д; **~eyed** косогла́зый; **~ing** ['krɒsɪŋ] перекрёсток; перепра́ва; перехо́д; **~roads** *pl. или sg.* перекрёсток; ~ **section** попере́чное сече́ние; **~wise** поперёк; крестна́крест; **~word puzzle** кроссво́рд

crotchet ['krɒtʃɪt] *mus.* четвертна́я но́та; *caprice* фанта́зия

crouch [kraʊtʃ] нагиба́ться [нагну́ться]

crow [krəʊ] **1.** воро́на; пе́ние петуха́; **2.** кукаре́кать; **~bar** лом

crowd [kraʊd] **1.** толпа́; ма́сса; *coll.* толкотня́, да́вка; *coll.* компа́ния; **2.** собира́ться толпо́й, толпи́ться; набива́ться битко́м

crown [kraʊn] 1. коро́на; *fig.* вене́ц; *of tree* кро́на; *of head* маку́шка; 2. коронова́ть (*im*)*pf.*; *fig.* увенча́ть(ся); **to~ it all** в доверше́ние всего́

cruci|al ['kruːʃl] □ крити́ческий; реша́ющий; **~fixion** [kruːsɪˈfɪkʃn] распя́тие; **~fy** ['kruːsɪfaɪ] распина́ть [-пя́ть]

crude [kruːd] □ (*raw*) сыро́й; (*unrefined*) неочи́щенный; *statistics* гру́бый

cruel ['kruːəl] □ жесто́кий; *fig.* мучи́тельный; **~ty** [-tɪ] жесто́кость *f*

cruise [kruːz] 1. *naut.* круи́з; 2. крейси́ровать; соверша́ть ре́йсы; **~r** ['kruːzə] *naut.* кре́йсер

crumb [krʌm] кро́шка; **~le** ['krʌmbl] [рас-, ис]кроши́ть(ся)

crumple ['krʌmpl] [из-, по-, с]мя́ть(ся); [с]ко́мкать(ся)

crunch [krʌntʃ] жева́ть с хру́стом; хрусте́ть [хрустну́ть]

crusade [kruːˈseɪd] кресто́вый похо́д; кампа́ния; **~r** [-ə] крестоно́сец; *fig.* боре́ц

crush [krʌʃ] 1. да́вка; толкотня́; 2. *v/t.* [раз]дави́ть; (*~ out*) выжима́ть [вы́жать]; *enemy* разбива́ть [-би́ть]

crust [krʌst] *of bread* ко́рка; *of earth* кора́; покрыва́ть(ся) ко́ркой; **~y** ['krʌstɪ] □ покры́тый ко́ркой

crutch [krʌtʃ] косты́ль *m*

crux [krʌks]: **the ~ of the matter** суть де́ла

cry [kraɪ] 1. крик; вопль; плач; 2. [за]пла́кать; (*exclaim*) воскликну́ть [-и́кнуть]; (*shout*) крича́ть [кри́кнуть]; **~ for** [по]тре́бовать (P)

cryptic ['krɪptɪk] (*mysterious*) таи́нственный; (*secret*) сокрове́нный

crystal ['krɪstl] *cut glass or rock* хруста́ль *m*; *tech.* криста́лл; *attr.* хруста́льный; **~lize** [-təlaɪz] кристаллизова́ть(ся) (*im*)*pf.*

cub [kʌb] детёныш

cub|e [kjuːb] *math.* 1. куб; **~ root** куби́ческий ко́рень *m*; 2. возводи́ть в куб; **~ic(al)** ['kjuːbɪk(l)] куби́ческий

cubicle ['kjuːbɪkl] каби́нка

cuckoo ['kʊkuː] куку́шка

cucumber ['kjuːkʌmbə] огуре́ц

cuddle ['kʌdl] *v/t.* прижима́ть к себе́; *v/i.* приж(им)а́ться (друг к дру́гу)

cue [kjuː] (*billiárdный*) кий; (*hint*) намёк; *thea.* ре́плика

cuff [kʌf] 1. манже́та, обшла́г; 2. (*blow*) шлепо́к; дать затре́щину; **~links** за́понки

culminat|e ['kʌlmɪneɪt] достига́ть [-ти́гнуть] вы́сшей то́чки (*или* сте́пени); **~ion** [kʌlmɪˈneɪʃn] кульмина́ция

culprit ['kʌlprɪt] (*offender*) престу́пник; вино́вник

cultivat|e ['kʌltɪveɪt] обраба́тывать [-бо́тать], возде́л(ыв)ать; *plants* культиви́ровать; *friendship* стреми́ться завяза́ть дру́жеские отноше́ния; **~ion** [kʌltɪˈveɪʃn] *of soil* обрабо́тка, возде́лывание; *of plants* разведе́ние

cultural ['kʌltʃərəl] □ культу́рный

cultur|e ['kʌltʃə] культу́ра (*a. agric.*); **~ed** [-d] культу́рный; интеллиге́нтный

cumbersome ['kʌmbəsəm] громо́здкий; *fig.* обремени́тельный

cumulative ['kjuːmjʊlətɪv] □ совоку́пный, накопи́вшийся

cunning ['kʌnɪŋ] 1. ло́вкий; хи́трый; кова́рный; *Am. a.* привлека́тельный; 2. ло́вкость *f*; хи́трость *f*; кова́рство

cup [kʌp] ча́шка; ча́ша; *as prize* ку́бок; **~board** ['kʌbəd] шкаф(чик); **~ final** фина́л ро́зыгрыша ку́бка

cupola ['kjuːpələ] ку́пол

curable ['kjʊərəbl] излечи́мый

curb [kɜːb] 1. узда́ (*a. fig.*); подгу́бный реме́нь; обу́здывать [-да́ть] (*a. fig.*)

curd [kɜːd] простоква́ша; *pl.* творо́г; **~le** ['kɜːdl] свёртываться [сверну́ться]

cure [kjʊə] 1. лече́ние; сре́дство; 2. [вы́]лечи́ть, изле́чивать [-чи́ть]; *meat* [за]копти́ть

curfew ['kɜːfjuː] коменда́нтский час

curio ['kjʊərɪəʊ] ре́дкая антиква́рная вещь *f*; **~sity** [kjʊərɪˈɒsɪtɪ] любопы́тство; ре́дкая вещь; *f*, **~us** ['kjʊərɪəs] любопы́тный; пытли́вый;

стра́нный; **~ly enough** как э́то ни стра́нно

curl [kɜːl] **1.** ло́кон, завито́к; *pl.* ку́дри *f/pl.*; **2.** ви́ться; *of smoke* клуби́ться; **~y** ['kɜːlɪ] кудря́вый, вью́щийся

currant ['kʌrənt] сморо́дина; кори́нка

curren|cy ['kʌrənsɪ] *fin.* де́ньги *f/pl.*, валю́та; **hard**~ конверти́руемая (неконверти́руемая) валю́та; **~t** [-ənt] **1.** □ теку́щий; *opinion, etc.* ходя́чий; **2.** пото́к; *in sea* тече́ние; *el.* ток

curriculum [kə'rɪkjələm] уче́бный план

curry[1] ['kʌrɪ] ка́рри *n*

curry[2] [-]: **~ favo(u)r with** заи́скивать пе́ред (Т)

curse [kɜːs] **1.** прокля́тие; руга́тельство; *fig.* бич, бе́дствие; **2.** проклина́ть [-кля́сть]; руга́ться; **~d** ['kɜːsɪd] □ прокля́тый

cursory ['kɜːsərɪ] бе́глый, бы́стрый; **give a ~ glance** пробежа́ть глаза́ми

curt [kɜːt] *answer* ре́зкий

curtail [kɜː'teɪl] укора́чивать [-роти́ть]; уре́з(ыв)ать; *fig.* сокраща́ть [сократи́ть]

curtain ['kɜːtn] **1.** занаве́ска; *thea.* за́навес; **2.** занаве́шивать [-ве́сить]

curv|ature ['kɜːvətʃə] кривизна́; **~e** [kɜːv] **1.** *math.* крива́я; *of road, etc.* изги́б; **2.** повора́чивать [-верну́ть]; изгиба́ть(ся) [изогну́ть(ся)]; *of path, etc.* ви́ться

cushion ['kʊʃn] **1.** поду́шка; **2.** *on falling* смягча́ть [-чи́ть] уда́р

custody ['kʌstədɪ] опе́ка, попече́ние; **take into ~** задержа́ть, аресто́вать

custom ['kʌstəm] обы́чай; (*habit*) привы́чка; клиенту́ра; **~s** *pl.* тамо́жня; (*duties*) тамо́женные по́шлины *f/pl.*; **~ary** [-ərɪ] □ обы́чный; **~er** [-ə] покупа́тель *m*, -ница *f*; клие́нт

m, -ка *f*; **~s examination** тамо́женный досмо́тр; **~s house** тамо́жня

cut [kʌt] **1.** разре́з, поре́з; *of clothes* покро́й; **short ~** коро́ткий путь *m*; **2.** [*irr.*] *v/t.* [от]ре́зать; разре́зать [-ре́зать]; *hair* [по]стри́чь; *precious stone* [от]шлифова́ть; *grass* [с]коси́ть; *teeth* проре́з(ыв)а́ться; **~ short** обрыва́ть [обрыва́ть]; **~ down** сокраща́ть [-рати́ть]; **~ out** выреза́ть [вы́резать]; *dress* [с]крои́ть; *fig.* вытесня́ть [вы́теснить]; **be ~ out for** быть сло́вно со́зданным для (P); *v/i.* ре́зать; **~ in** вме́шиваться [-ша́ться]; **it ~s both ways** па́лка о двух конца́х

cute [kjuːt] □ *coll.* хи́трый; *Am.* ми́лый, привлека́тельный

cutlery ['kʌtlərɪ] нож, ножевы́е изде́лия; столо́вые прибо́ры

cutlet ['kʌtlɪt] отбивна́я (котле́та)

cut|out *el.* автомати́ческий выключа́тель *m*, предохрани́тель *m*; **~ter** ['kʌtər] *cutting tool* резе́ц; *chopping knife* реза́к; *naut.* ка́тер; **~ting** ['kʌtɪŋ] **1.** □ о́стрый, ре́зкий; язви́тельный; **2.** *ре́зание*; *of clothes* кро́йка; *bot.* черено́к

cyber|netics [saɪbə'netɪks] киберне́тика; **~space** ['saɪbəspeɪs] виртуа́льная реа́льность

cycl|e ['saɪkl] **1.** цикл (*a. tech.*); круг; (*bicycle*) велосипе́д; **2.** е́здить на велосипе́де; **~ist** [-ɪst] велосипеди́ст *m*, -ка *f*

cyclone ['saɪkləʊn] цикло́н

cylinder ['sɪlɪndə] *geometry* цили́ндр

cymbal ['sɪmbl] *mus.* таре́лки *f/pl.*

cynic ['sɪnɪk] ци́ник; **~al** [-l] цини́чный

cypress ['saɪprəs] *bot.* кипари́с

czar [zɑː] царь

Czech [tʃək] **1.** чех *m*, че́шка *f*; **2.** че́шский

D

dab [dæb] **1.** *with brush* мазо́к; *of colour* пятно́; **2.** слегка́ прикаса́ться, прикла́дывать (В); де́лать лёгкие мазки́ на (П)

dabble ['dæbl] плеска́ть(ся); *hands, feet etc.* болта́ть нога́ми *и т.* в воде́; занима́ться чем-л. пове́рхностно

dad [dæd], **~dy** ['dædɪ] *coll.* па́па

daffodil ['dæfədɪl] жёлтый нарци́сс

dagger ['dægə] кинжа́л; *be at ~s drawn* быть на ножа́х (с Т)

dahlia ['deɪlɪə] георги́н

daily ['deɪlɪ] **1.** *adv.* ежедне́вно; **2.** ежедне́вный; *cares etc.* повседне́вный; **3.** ежедне́вная газе́та

dainty ['deɪntɪ] **1.** □ ла́комый; изя́щный; изы́сканный; **2.** ла́комство, делика́те́с

dairy ['deərɪ] *shop* магази́н моло́чных проду́ктов

daisy ['deɪzɪ] маргари́тка

dale [deɪl] доли́на, дол

dally ['dælɪ] зря теря́ть вре́мя

dam [dæm] **1.** да́мба, плоти́на; **2.** запру́живать [-уди́ть]

damage ['dæmɪdʒ] **1.** вред; повреждéние; (*loss*) уще́рб; **~s** *pl. law* уще́рб; компенса́ция (за причинённый уще́рб); **2.** повреди́ть [-еди́ть], [ис]по́ртить

damn [dæm] проклина́ть [-ля́сть]; (*censure*) осужда́ть [осуди́ть]; (*swear at*) руга́ться

damnation [dæm'neɪʃn] *int.* прокля́тие; осужде́ние

damp [dæmp] **1.** сы́рость *f*, вла́жность *f*; **2.** вла́жный, сыро́й; **~en** ['dæmpən] [на]мочи́ть; *fig.* обескура́жи(ва)ть

danc|e [dɑːns] **1.** та́нец; та́нцы *m/pl.*; **2.** танцева́ть; **~er** [-ə] танцо́р, танцо́вщик *m*, -и́ца *f*; **~ing** [-ɪŋ] та́нцы *m/pl.*; пля́ска; *attr.* танцева́льный; **~ partner** партнёр, да́ма

dandelion ['dændɪlaɪən] одува́нчик

dandle ['dændl] [по]кача́ть (на рука́х)

dandruff ['dændrʌf] пе́рхоть *f*

dandy ['dændɪ] **1.** щёголь *m*; **2.** *Am. sl.* первокла́ссный

Dane [deɪn] датча́нин *m*, -ча́нка *f*

danger ['deɪndʒə] опа́сность *f*; **~ous** ['deɪndʒrəs] □ опа́сный

dangle ['dæŋgl] висе́ть, свиса́ть [сви́снуть]; *legs* болта́ть (Т)

Danish ['deɪnɪʃ] да́тский

dar|e [deə] *v/i.* [по]сме́ть; отва́жи(ва)ться; *v/t.* пыта́ться подби́ть; **~edevil** смельча́к, сорвиголова́ *m*; **~ing** ['deərɪŋ] **1.** □ сме́лый, отва́жный; **2.** сме́лость *f*, отва́га

dark [dɑːk] **1.** тёмный; *skin* сму́глый; (*hidden*) та́йный; *look etc.* мра́чный; **~ horse** тёмная лоша́дка; **2.** темнота́, тьма; неве́дение; *keep s.o. in the ~* держа́ть кого́-л. в неве́дении; *keep s.th. ~* держа́ть в та́йне; **~en** ['dɑːkən] [с]темне́ть; [по]мрачне́ть; **~ness** ['dɑːknɪs] темнота́, тьма

darling ['dɑːlɪŋ] **1.** люби́мец (-мица); **2.** ми́лый, люби́мый

darn [dɑːn] [за]што́пать

dart [dɑːt] **1.** *in game* стрела́; (*sudden movement*) прыжо́к, рыво́к; **2.** *v/i. fig.* мча́ться стрело́й

dash [dæʃ] **1.** *of wave etc.* уда́р; (*rush*) стреми́тельное движе́ние; (*dart*) рыво́к; *fig.* при́месь *f*, чу́точка; *typ.* тире́ *n indecl.*; **2.** *v/t.* броса́ть [бро́сить]; разби́(ва́)ть в неве́дении; *v/i.* броса́ться [бро́ситься]; *I'll have to ~* мне ну́жно бежа́ть; **~board** *mot.* прибо́рная доска́; **~ing** ['dæʃɪŋ] □ лихо́й

data ['deɪtə] *pl.*, *Am. a. sg.* да́нные *n/pl.*; фа́кты *m/pl.*; **~ bank** банк да́нных; **~ processing** обрабо́тка да́нных

date[1] [deɪt] **1.** да́та, число́; *coll.* свида́ние; *out of ~* устаре́лый; *up to ~* нове́йший; совреме́нный; **2.** дати́ровать (*im*)*pf.*; *Am. coll.* усла́вливаться [-о́виться] (с Т) (о встре́че); име́ть свида́ние

date[2] [-] *bot.* фи́ник

daub [dɔːb] **1.** [вы́-, из-, на]ма́зать;

[на]малевать; 2. мазня

daughter ['dɔːtə] дочь f; **~-in-law** [-rɪnlɔː] невестка, сноха

daunt [dɔːnt] устрашать [-шить], запугивать [-гать]; **~less** ['dɔːntlɪs] неустрашимый, бесстрашный

dawdle ['dɔːdl] *coll.* бездельничать

dawn [dɔːn] 1. рассвет, утренняя заря; *fig.* заря; 2. светать

day [deɪ] день m; (*mst.* **~s** *pl.*) жизнь f; **~ off** выходной день m; **every other ~** через день; **the ~ after tomorrow** послезавтра; **the other ~** на днях; недавно; **~break** рассвет; **~dream** мечтать, грезить наяву

daze [deɪz] ошеломлять [-мить]

dazzle ['dæzl] ослеплять [-пить]

dead [ded] 1. мёртвый; *flowers* увядший; (*numbed*) онемевший; *silence etc.* полный; **come to a ~ stop** резко остановиться; **~ end** тупик; 2. *adv.* полно, совершенно; **~ against** решительно против; 3. **the ~** мёртвые *m/pl.*; **in the ~ of night** глубокой ночью; **~en** ['dedn] лишать(ся) силы; *sound* заглушать [-шить]; **~lock** *fig.* тупик; **~ly** [-lɪ] смертельный; *weapon* смертоносный

deaf [def] □ глухой; **~en** [defn] оглушать [-шить]

deal [diːl] 1. (*agreement*) соглашение; (*business agreement*) сделка; **a good ~** много; **a great ~** очень много; 2. [*irr.*] *v/t.* (*distribute*) разд(ав)ать; распределять [-лить]; *at cards* сдавать [сдать]; *v/i.* торговать; **~ with** обходиться [обойтись] *or* поступать [-пить] с (Т); иметь дело с (Т); **~er** ['diːlə] дилер, торговец; **~ing** ['diːlɪŋ] (*mst.* **~s** *pl.*): **have~s with** вести дела (с Т); **~t** [delt] *pt. и pt. p. om* **~**

dean [diːn] настоятель собора; *univ.* декан

dear [dɪə] 1. дорогой (*a. = costly*), милый; (*in business letter*) (глубоко)уважаемый; 2. прекрасный человек f; 3. *coll.* **oh ~!**, **~ me!** Господи!

death [deθ] смерть f; **~ duty** налог на наследство; **~ly** [-lɪ]: **~ pale** бледный как смерть; **~ rate** смертность f; **~ trap** опасное место

debar [dɪˈbɑː] (вос)препятствовать; не допускать [-стить]; (*exclude*) исключать [-чить]; *from voting etc.* лишать права

debase [dɪˈbeɪs] унижать [-изить]; снижать качество (P), курс (валюты)

debat|able [dɪˈbeɪtəbl] □ спорный; дискуссионный; **~e** [dɪˈbeɪt] 1. дискуссия; прения *n/pl.*, дебаты *m/pl.*; 2. обсуждать [-удить]; [по]спорить; (*ponder*) обдум(ыв)ать

debauch [dɪˈbɔːtʃ] 1. разврат; (*carouse*) попойка; 2. развращать [-ратить]

debilitate [dɪˈbɪlɪteɪt] (*weaken*) ослаблять [-абить]

debit ['debɪt] *fin.* 1. дебет; 2. дебетовать (*im*)*pf.*, вносить в дебет

debris ['debriː] развалины *f/pl.*; обломки *m/pl.*

debt [det] долг; **~or** ['detə] должник *m*, -ица f

decade [deˈkeɪd] десятилетие; *of one's age* десяток

decadence ['dekədəns] упадок; *in art* декадентство

decant [dɪˈkænt] сцеживать [сцедить]; **~er** [-ə] графин

decay [dɪˈkeɪ] 1. гниение; разложение; *of teeth* разрушение; *кариес; **fall into~** *of building* [об] ветшать; *fig.* приходить [прийти] в упадок; 2. [с]гнить; разлагаться [-ложиться]

decease [dɪˈsiːs] *part. law* смерть f, кончина; **~d** [-t] покойный

deceit [dɪˈsiːt] обман; **~ful** [-fʊl] лживый; (*deceptive*) обманчивый

deceive [dɪˈsiːv] обманывать [-нуть]; **~er** [-ə] обманщик (-ица)

December [dɪˈsembə] декабрь *m*

decen|cy ['diːsnsɪ] приличие; **~t** [-nt] □ приличный; *kind, well-behaved coll.* порядочный; *coll.* славный; **it's very ~ of you** очень любезно с вашей стороны

deception [dɪˈsepʃn] обман; ложь f

decide [dɪˈsaɪd] решать(ся) [решить(ся)]; принимать решение;

~d [-ɪd] *(clear-cut)* □ определённый; *(unmistakable)* бесспо́рный

decimal ['desɪml] **1.** десяти́чный; **2.** десяти́чная дробь *f*

decipher [dɪ'saɪfə] расшифро́вывать [-ова́ть]; *poor handwriting* разбира́ть [разобра́ть]

decisi|on [dɪ'sɪʒn] реше́ние *(a. law)*; **~ve** [dɪ'saɪsɪv] *conclusive* реша́ющий; *resolute* реши́тельный; **~veness** реши́тельность *f*

deck [dek] *naut.* па́луба; *Am. cards* коло́да; **~chair** шезло́нг

declar|able [dɪ'kleərəbl] подлежа́щий деклара́ции; **~ation** [deklə'reɪʃn] заявле́ние; деклара́ция *(a. fin.)*; *customs ~* тамо́женная деклара́ция; **~e** [dɪ'kleər] объявля́ть [-ви́ть]; заявля́ть [-ви́ть]; выска́зываться [вы́сказаться] *(for* за В, *against* про́тив Р); *to customs officials* предъявля́ть [-ви́ть]

decline [dɪ'klaɪn] **1.** *(fall)* паде́ние; *of strength* упа́док; *in prices* сниже́ние; *of health* ухудше́ние; *of life* зака́т; **2.** *v/t. an offer* отклоня́ть [-ни́ть]; *gr.* [про]склоня́ть; *v/i.* приходи́ть в упа́док; *of health etc.* ухудша́ться [ухýдшиться]

decode [diː'kəʊd] расшифро́вывать [-рова́ть]

decompose [diːkəm'pəʊz] разлага́ть(ся) [-ложи́ть(ся)]; [с]гнить

decorate ['dekəreɪt] украша́ть [укра́сить]; *(confer medal, etc. on)* награжда́ть [-ди́ть]; **~ion** [dekə'reɪʃn] украше́ние; о́рден, знак отли́чия; **~ive** ['dekərətɪv] декорати́вный

decor|ous ['dekərəs] □ присто́йный; **~um** [dɪ'kɔːrəm] этике́т

decoy [dɪ'kɔɪ] прима́нка *(a. fig.)*

decrease 1. ['diːkriːs] уменьше́ние, пониже́ние; **2.** [diː'kriːs] уменьша́ть(ся) [уме́ньшить(ся)], сниж́ать [-изить]

decree [dɪ'kriː] **1.** *pol.* ука́з, декре́т, постановле́ние; *law* реше́ние; **2.** постановля́ть [-ви́ть]

decrepit [dɪ'krepɪt] дря́хлый

dedicate ['dedɪkeɪt] посвяща́ть

[-яти́ть]; **~ion** [dedɪ'keɪʃn] *(devotion)* пре́данность *f*; *(inscription)* посвяще́ние; *work with ~* по́лностью отдава́ть себя́ рабо́те

deduce [dɪ'djuːs] [с]де́лать вы́вод, заключа́ть [-чи́ть]

deduct [dɪ'dʌkt] вычита́ть [вы́честь]; **~ion** [dɪ'dʌkʃn] вы́чет; *(conclusion)* вы́вод, заключе́ние; *comm.* ски́дка

deed [diːd] **1.** де́йствие; посту́пок; *law* акт; *~ of purchase* догово́р ку́пли/прода́жи; **2.** *Am.* передава́ть по а́кту

deem [diːm] *v/t.* счита́ть [счесть]; *v/i.* полага́ть

deep [diːp] **1.** глубо́кий; *colo(u)r* стой́; **2.** *poet.* мо́ре, океа́н; **~en** ['diːpən] углубля́ть(ся) [-би́ть(ся)]; уси́ливать(ся) [уси́лить(ся)]; **~freeze** → *freezer*; **~ness** [-nɪs] глубина́; **~rooted** глубоко́ укорени́вшийся

deer [dɪə] оле́нь *m*

deface [dɪ'feɪs] обезобра́живать [-а́зить]

defam|ation [defə'meɪʃn] клевета́; **~e** [dɪ'feɪm] [о]клевета́ть

default [dɪ'fɔːlt] **1.** невыполне́ние обяза́тельств; нея́вка; *comput.* автомати́ческий вы́бор; **2.** не выполня́ть обяза́тельств

defeat [dɪ'fiːt] **1.** пораже́ние; *of plans* расстро́йство; **2.** *mil., sport etc.* побежда́ть [-еди́ть]; расстра́ивать [-ро́ить]

defect [dɪ'fekt] недоста́ток; *(fault)* неиспра́вность *f*; дефе́кт, изъя́н; **~ive** [-tɪv] несоверше́нный, □ повреждённый; *~ goods* брако́ванные това́ры; *mentally ~* у́мственно отста́лый

defence → *defense*

defend [dɪ'fend] обороня́ть(ся), [-ни́ть(ся)], защища́ть на суде́; **~ant** [-ənt] *law* подсуди́мый; *civil* отве́тчик; **~er** [-ə] защи́тник

defense [dɪ'fens] оборо́на, защи́та; **~less** [-lɪs] беззащи́тный

defensive [dɪ'fensɪv] **1.** оборо́на; **2.** оборо́нный, оборони́тельный

defer [dɪ'fɜː] откла́дывать [отложи́ть]; отсро́чи(ва)ть

defian|ce [dɪˈfaɪəns] (*challenge*) вы́зов; (*disobedience*) неповинове́ние; (*scorn*) пренебреже́ние; ∼t [-ənt] □ вызыва́ющий

deficien|cy [dɪˈfɪʃənsɪ] недоста́ток, нехва́тка; ∼t [-ənt] недоста́точный; несоверше́нный

deficit [ˈdefɪsɪt] недочёт; недоста́ча; дефици́т

defile [dɪˈfaɪl] загрязня́ть [-ни́ть]

defin|e [dɪˈfaɪn] определя́ть [-ли́ть]; дава́ть характери́стику; (*show limits of*) оче́рчивать [-рти́ть], обознача́ть; ∼ite [ˈdefɪnɪt] □ определённый; (*exact*) то́чный; ∼ition [defɪˈnɪʃn] определе́ние; ∼itive [dɪˈfɪnɪtɪv] □ (*final*) оконча́тельный

deflect [dɪˈflekt] отклоня́ть(ся) [-ни́ть(ся)]

deform|ed [dɪˈfɔːmd] изуро́дованный, иска́жённый; ∼ity [dɪˈfɔːmətɪ] уро́дство

defraud [dɪˈfrɔːd] обма́нывать [-ну́ть]; выма́нивать (*of* В)

defray [dɪˈfreɪ] опла́чивать [оплати́ть]

defrost [diːˈfrɒst] отта́ивать [-а́ять]; размора́живать [-ро́зить]

deft [deft] □ ло́вкий, иску́сный

defy [dɪˈfaɪ] вызыва́ть [вы́звать]; броса́ть [бро́сить] вы́зов; вести́ себя́ вызыва́юще; (*flout*) пренебрега́ть [-бре́чь] (Т)

degenerate [dɪˈdʒenəreɪt] вырожда́ться [вы́родиться]

degrad|ation [degrəˈdeɪʃn] деграда́ция; ∼e [dɪˈgreɪd] *v/t.* (*lower in rank*) понижа́ть [пони́зить]; (*abase*) унижа́ть [уни́зить]

degree [dɪˈgriː] (*unit of measurement*) гра́дус; (*step or stage in a process*) у́ровень *m*; сте́пень *f*; (*a. univ.*) зва́ние; **honorary** ∼ почётное зва́ние; **by** ∼**s** постепе́нно; **in no** ∼ ничу́ть, ниско́лько; **to some** ∼ в изве́стной сте́пени

deign [deɪn] снисходи́ть [снизойти́]; соизволя́ть [-о́лить]; *usu. iron.* удоста́ивать [-сто́ить]

deity [ˈdiːɪtɪ] божество́

deject|ed [dɪˈdʒektɪd] □ удручённый; угнетённый; ∼ion [dɪˈdʒekʃn] уны́ние

delay [dɪˈleɪ] **1.** заде́ржка; отсро́чка; **2.** *v/t.* заде́рживать [-жа́ть]; откла́дывать [отложи́ть]; ме́длить с (Т); *v/i.* ме́длить, ме́шкать

delega|te 1. [ˈdelɪgət] делега́т, представи́тель(ница *f*) *m*; **2.** [-geɪt] делеги́ровать (*im*)*pf.*, поруча́ть [-чи́ть]; ∼tion [delɪˈgeɪʃn] делега́ция

deliberat|e 1. [dɪˈlɪbəreɪt] *v/t.* обду́м(ыв)ать; взве́шивать [взве́сить]; обсужда́ть [обсуди́ть]; *v/i.* совеща́ться; **2.** [-rət] □ преднаме́ренный, умы́шленный; ∼ion [dɪlɪbəˈreɪʃn] размышле́ние; обсужде́ние; осмотри́тельность *f*; *act with* ∼ де́йствовать с осмотри́тельностью

delica|cy [ˈdelɪkəsɪ] делика́тность *f*; *food* ла́комство; утончённость *f*; не́жность *f*; ∼te [-kɪt] □ делика́тный; (*fragile*) хру́пкий; изя́щный; чу́вки иску́сный; чувстви́тельный; щепети́льный; ∼tessen [delɪkəˈtesn] магази́н деликате́сов, гастроно́м

delicious [dɪˈlɪʃəs] восхити́тельный; о́чень вку́сный

delight [dɪˈlaɪt] **1.** удово́льствие; восто́рг; наслажде́ние; **2.** восхища́ть [-ити́ть]; наслажда́ться [-ди́ться] дости́вить удово́льствие (*in* Т): **be** ∼**ed with** быть в восто́рге (от Р); **be** ∼**ed** *inf.* име́ть удово́льствие (+ *inf.*); ∼**ful** [-fʊl] □ *girl etc.* очарова́тельный; восхити́тельный

delinquent [dɪˈlɪŋkwənt]: **juvenile** ∼ несовершенноле́тний престу́пник

deliri|ous [dɪˈlɪrɪəs] находя́щийся в бреду́, вне себя́, в исступле́нии; **with joy** вне себя́ от ра́дости; ∼**um** [-əm] бред

deliver [dɪˈlɪvə] *newspapers etc.* доставля́ть [-а́вить]; *a speech* произноси́ть [-нести́]; *order* сда(ва́)ть; *a blow* наноси́ть [нанести́] (*уáр*); **be** ∼**ed** *med.* роди́ть(ся); (*rescue*) спасе́ние; ∼**ance** [-rəns] освобожде́ние; (*rescue*) спасе́ние

delude [dɪˈluːd] вводи́ть в заблужде́ние; (*deceive*) обма́нывать [-ну́ть]

deluge [ˈdeljuːdʒ] **1.** наводне́ние;

(rain) ли́вень; *fig.* пото́к; **2.** затопля́ть [-пи́ть]; наводня́ть [-ни́ть] *a. fig.*

delus|ion [dɪ'luːʒn] заблужде́ние; иллю́зия; **~ive** [-sɪv] □ обма́нчивый; иллюзо́рный

demand [dɪ'mɑːnd] **1.** тре́бование; потре́бность *f; comm.* спрос; **be in great ~** по́льзоваться больши́м спро́сом; **2.** [по]тре́бовать (P)

demilitarize [diː'mɪlɪtəraɪz] демилитаризова́ть *(im)pf.*

demobilize [diː'məʊbɪlaɪz] демобилизова́ть *(im)pf.*

democra|cy [dɪ'mɒkrəsɪ] демокра́тия; **~tic(al □)** [demə'krætɪk(əl)] демократи́ческий

demolish [dɪ'mɒlɪʃ] разруша́ть [-ру́шить]; *(pull down)* сноси́ть [снести́]

demon ['diːmən] де́мон, дья́вол

demonstrat|e ['demənstreɪt] [про]демонстри́ровать; *(prove)* дока́зывать [-за́ть]; **~ion** [demən'streɪʃn] демонстра́ция; доказа́тельство; **~ive** [dɪ'mɒnstrətɪv] □ *person, behaviour* экспанси́вный; *gr.* указа́тельный

demoralize [dɪ'mɒrəlaɪz] деморализова́ть

demure [dɪ'mjʊə] □ скро́мный; *smile* засте́нчивый

den [den] ло́говище; берло́га; прито́н

denial [dɪ'naɪəl] отрица́ние; *official* опроверже́ние; *(refusal)* отка́з

denomination [dɪnɒmɪ'neɪʃn] *eccl.* вероисповеда́ние; се́кта

denote [dɪ'nəʊt] означа́ть *impf.*, обознача́ть [-на́чить]

denounce [dɪ'naʊns] *(expose)* разоблача́ть [-чи́ть]; *to police* доноси́ть; *termination of a treaty, etc.* денонси́ровать *(im)pf.*

dens|e [dens] □ густо́й; пло́тный *(a. phys.)*; *fig.* глу́пый, тупо́й; **~ity** ['densətɪ] густота́; пло́тность *f*

dent [dent] **1.** вмя́тина; **2.** вда́вливать [вдави́ть]; *v/i.* [по]гну́ться

dentist ['dentɪst] зубно́й врач

denture ['dentʃə] *mst. pl.* зубно́й проте́з

denunciation [dɪnʌnsɪ'eɪʃn] доно́с;

обличе́ние, обвине́ние

deny [dɪ'naɪ] отрица́ть; отка́зываться [-за́ться] от (P); *(refuse to give, allow)* отка́зывать [-за́ть] в (П); **there is no ~ing** сле́дует призна́ть

deodorant [diː'əʊdərənt] дезодора́нт

depart [dɪ'pɑːt] *v/i.* уходи́ть [уйти́], уезжа́ть [уе́хать], отбы(ва́)ть, отправля́ться [-а́виться]; отступа́ть [-пи́ть] *(from* от P); **~ment** [-mənt] *univ.* отделе́ние, факульте́т; *of science* о́бласть *f,* о́трасль; *in shop* отде́л; *Am.* министе́рство; **State 2** министе́рство иностра́нных дел; **~ store** универма́г; **~ure** [dɪ'pɑːtʃə] отъе́зд; ухо́д; *rail.* отправле́ние; *(deviation)* отклоне́ние

depend [dɪ'pend]: **~ (up)on** зави́сеть от (P); *coll.* **~s** смотря́ по обстоя́тельствам; **you can ~ on him** на него́ мо́жно положи́ться; **~able** [-əbl] надёжный; **~ant** [-ənt] иждиве́нец *m,* -нка *f;* **~ence** [-əns] зави́симость *f; (trust)* дове́рие; **~ent** [-ənt] □ *(on)* зави́сящий (от P)

depict [dɪ'pɪkt] изобража́ть [-рази́ть]; *fig.* опи́сывать [-са́ть]

deplete [dɪ'pliːt] истоща́ть [-щи́ть]

deplor|able [dɪ'plɔːrəbl] □ приско́рбный, заслу́живающий сожале́ния; *state* плаче́вный; **~e** [dɪ'plɔː] *(disapprove of)* порица́ть; сожале́ть о (П)

deport [dɪ'pɔːt] депорти́ровать

depose [dɪ'pəʊz] *from office* смеща́ть [смести́ть]; *(dethrone)* сверга́ть [све́ргнуть]

deposit [dɪ'pɒzɪt] **1.** *geol.* отложе́ние; за́лежь *f; fin.* вклад; депози́т; зада́ток; **~ account** депози́тный счёт; **2.** класть [положи́ть]; депони́ровать *(im)pf.;* дава́ть [дать] зада́ток; **~or** [dɪ'pɒzɪtə] вкла́дчик *m,* -ица *f,* депози́тор

depot 1. ['depəʊ] *rail.* депо́ *n indecl.; storage place* склад; **2.** ['diːpəʊ] *Am. rail.* железнодоро́жная ста́нция

deprave [dɪ'preɪv] развраща́ть [-рати́ть]

depreciat|e [dɪ'priːʃɪeɪt] обесце́ни(ва)ть; **~ion** [dɪpriːʃɪ'eɪʃn] сниже́ние сто́имости; обесце́нение; амортиза́-

ция

depress [dɪ'pres] угнетать *impf.*; подавлять [-вить]; **~ed** [-t] *fig.* унылый; **~ion** [dɪ'preʃn] угнетённое состояние; *geogr.* впадина; *econ.* депрессия

deprive [dɪ'praɪv] лишать [лишить] (*of* P)

depth [depθ] глубина; *be out of one's* **~** быть не под силу, быть недоступным пониманию

deputation [depjʊ'teɪʃn] делегация; **~y** ['depjʊtɪ] делегат; депутат; заместитель(ница *f*) *m*

derange [dɪ'reɪndʒ] *plans etc.* расстраивать [-роить]; (*put out of order*) приводить в беспорядок

derelict ['derɪlɪkt] *ship* покинутый; *house* (за)брошенный

deride [dɪ'raɪd] осмеивать [-еять], высмеивать [высмеять]; **~sion** [dɪ'rɪʒn] высмеивание; **~sive** [dɪ'raɪsɪv] □ издевательский; *scornful* насмешливый

derive [dɪ'raɪv] (*originate*) происходить [-изойти]; *benefit* извлекать [-влечь] (*from* от P)

derogatory [dɪ'rɒgətrɪ] пренебрежительный

descend [dɪ'send] спускаться [спуститься]; сходить [сойти]; *ae.* снижаться [снизиться]; *from a person* происходить [-изойти] (*from* из P); **~** (*up*)*on* обруши(ва)ться на (В); **~ant** [-ənt] потомок

descent [dɪ'sent] спуск; снижение; (*slope*) склон, происхождение

describe [dɪ'skraɪb] описывать [-сать]

description [dɪ'skrɪpʃn] описание; *of every* **~** самые разные

desert[1] [dɪ'zɜːt]: *get one's* **~s** получить по заслугам

desert[2] **1.** ['dezət] пустыня; **2.** [dɪ'zɜːt] *v/t.* (*leave*) бросать [бросить]; (*go away*) покидать [покинуть]; *v/i.* дезертировать (*im*)*pf.*; **~ed** [-ɪd] *street* пустынный; (*neglected*) заброшенный; (*abandoned*) покинутый; **~er** [-ə] дезертир; **~ion** [-ʃn] дезертирство; *spouse's* уход

deserve [dɪ'zɜːv] заслуживать [-жить]; **~edly** [-ɪdlɪ] заслуженно; **~ing** [-ɪŋ] заслуживающий, достойный (*of* P)

design [dɪ'zaɪn] **1.** (*intention*) замысел, намерение, план; *arch.* проект; *tech.* дизайн; (*pattern*) узор; **2.** предназначать [-значить]; задум(ыв)ать; [с]проектировать; *machinery* [с]конструировать

designate ['dezɪgneɪt] определять [-лить]; (*mark out*) обозначать [-значить]; (*appoint*) назначать [-значить]

designer [dɪ'zaɪnə] (*engineer*) конструктор; дизайнер; *dress* **~** модельер

desirable [dɪ'zaɪərəbl] □ желательный; **~e** [dɪ'zaɪə] **1.** желание; требование; **2.** [по]желать (P); [по]требовать (P); *leave much to be* **~d** оставлять желать лучшего; **~ous** [-rəs] желающий (*of* P); *be* **~ of knowing** стремиться/желать узнать

desk [desk] письменный стол; **~** *diary* настольный календарь; **~top** *publishing* настольное издательство

desolate 1. ['desəleɪt] опустошать [-шить]; разорять [-рить]; **2.** [-lət] □ опустошённый; несчастный; одинокий; **~ion** [desə'leɪʃn] опустошение; одиночество

despair [dɪ'speə] **1.** отчаяние; *drive s.o. to* **~** доводить [-вести] кого-л. до отчаяния; **2.** отчаиваться [-чаяться]; терять надежду (*of* на В); **~ing** [-rɪŋ] □ отчаивающийся

despatch → **dispatch**

desperate ['despərət] □ *effort etc.* отчаянный; *state* безнадёжный; *adv.* отчаянно, страшно; **~ion** [despə'reɪʃn] отчаяние

despise [dɪ'spaɪz] презирать

despite [dɪ'spaɪt] *prp.* несмотря на (В)

despondent [dɪ'spɒndənt] □ подавленный, удручённый

dessert [dɪ'zɜːt] десерт; *attr.* десертный

destination [destɪ'neɪʃn] (*purpose*, *end*) назначение; место назначения;

~e ['destɪn] предназнача́ть [-зна́-чить]; **be ~d** (be fated) предопределя́ть [-ли́ть]; **~y** [-tɪnɪ] судьба́

destitute ['destɪtjuːt] нужда́ющийся; лишённый (**of** P)

destroy [dɪ'strɔɪ] уничтожа́ть [-о́жить]; истребля́ть [-би́ть]; buildings, etc. разруша́ть [-ру́шить]; **~er** [-ə] warship эсми́нец

destruct|ion [dɪ'strʌkʃn] разруше́ние; уничтоже́ние; **~ive** [-tɪv] □ разруши́тельный; па́губный; вре́дный

detach [dɪ'tætʃ] отделя́ть [-ли́ть]; разъединя́ть [-ни́ть]; (tear off) отрыва́ть [оторва́ть]; **~ed** [-t] отде́льный; fig. беспристра́стный; **~ment** [-mənt] mil. отря́д; fig. беспристра́стность f

detail ['diːteɪl] подро́бность f, дета́ль f; **in ~** дета́льно, подро́бно; **go into ~s** вника́ть (вдава́ться) в подро́бности

detain [dɪ'teɪn] заде́рживать [-жа́ть] (a. by the police); **he was ~ed at work** он задержа́лся на рабо́те

detect [dɪ'tekt] обнару́жи(ва)ть; (notice) замеча́ть [-е́тить]; **~ion** [dɪ'tekʃn] обнаруже́ние; of crime рассле́дование; **~ive** [-tɪv] **1.** детекти́в, операти́вник; **2.** детекти́вный

detention [dɪ'tenʃn] (holding) задержа́ние; (custody) содержа́ние под аре́стом; (confinement) заключе́ние

deter [dɪ'tɜː] уде́рживать [-жа́ть] (**from** от P)

deteriorat|e [dɪ'tɪərɪəreɪt] ухудша́ть(ся) [уху́дшить(ся)]; [ис]по́ртить(ся); **~ion** [dɪtɪərɪə'reɪʃn] ухудше́ние

determin|ation [dɪtɜːmɪ'neɪʃn] определе́ние; (firmness) реши́тельность f, **~e** [dɪ'tɜːmɪn] v/t. определя́ть [-ли́ть]; реша́ть [реши́ть]; v/i. реша́ться [реши́ться]; **~ed** [-d] реши́тельный

detest [dɪ'test] ненави́деть; пита́ть отвраще́ние к (Д); **~able** [-əbl] отврати́тельный

detonate ['detəneɪt] детони́ровать; взрыва́ть(ся) [взорва́ть(ся)]

detour ['diːtʊə] око́льный путь m; объе́зд; **make a ~** сде́лать pf. крюк

detract [dɪ'trækt] умаля́ть [-ли́ть], уменьша́ть [уме́ньшить]

detriment [dɪ'trɪmənt] уще́рб, вред

devalue [diː'væljuː] обесце́ни(ва)ть

devastat|e ['devəsteɪt] опустоша́ть [-ши́ть]; разоря́ть [-ри́ть]; **~ion** [devə'steɪʃn] опустоше́ние

develop [dɪ'veləp] разви(ва́)ть(ся); mineral resources разраба́тывать [-бо́тать]; phot. проявля́ть [-ви́ть]; **~ment** [-mənt] разви́тие; разрабо́тка; (event) собы́тие

deviat|e ['diːvɪeɪt] отклоня́ться [-ни́ться]; **~ion** [diːvɪ'eɪʃn] отклоне́ние

device [dɪ'vaɪs] tech. приспособле́ние, устро́йство; (way, method, trick) приём; **leave a p. to his own ~s** предоставля́ть челове́ка самому́ себе́

devil ['devl] дья́вол, чёрт, бес; **~ish** [-əlɪʃ] □ дья́вольский; coll. чёрто́вский; **~ry** [-vlrɪ] чертовщи́на

devious ['diːvɪəs] □ **by ~ means** нече́стным путём

devise [dɪ'vaɪz] приду́м(ыв)ать; изобрета́ть [-рести́]

devoid [dɪ'vɔɪd] (**of**) лишённый (P)

devot|e [dɪ'vəʊt] посвяща́ть [-яти́ть] (В/Д); **~ed** [-ɪd] □ пре́данный, лю́бящий; **~ion** [dɪ'vəʊʃn] пре́данность f, привя́занность f

devour [dɪ'vaʊə] пож(и)ра́ть; **be ~ed with curiosity** сгора́ть от любопы́тства

devout [dɪ'vaʊt] □ supporter, etc. пре́данный; relig. благочести́вый

dew [djuː] роса́; **~y** [-ɪ] роси́стый, покры́тый росо́й

dexter|ity [dek'sterətɪ] ло́вкость f; **~ous** ['dekstrəs] ло́вкий

diabolic|al [daɪə'bɒlɪk(əl)] дья́вольский; phot. жесто́кий, злой

diagnosis [daɪəg'nəʊsɪs] диа́гноз

diagram ['daɪəgræm] диагра́мма; схе́ма

dial ['daɪəl] **1.** of clock, etc. цифербла́т; tech. шкала́ (цифербла́того ти́па); tel. диск; **2.** tel. набира́ть [-бра́ть] номер; позвони́ть *pf.*

dialect ['daɪəlekt] диале́кт, наре́чие

dialogue ['daɪəlɒg] диало́г; разгово́р

diameter [daɪ'æmɪtə] диа́метр

diamond ['daɪəmənd] алма́з; *precious stone* бриллиа́нт; ромб; *~s* [-s] *pl. cards:* бу́бны *f/pl.*

diaper ['daɪəpər] (*Brt.: nappy*) пелёнка

diaphragm ['daɪəfræm] *anat.* диафра́гма *a. optics*

diarrh(o)ea [daɪə'rɪə] поно́с

diary ['daɪərɪ] дневни́к

dice [daɪs] (*pl. om die²*) игра́льные ко́сти *f/pl.*

dictat|e 1. ['dɪkteɪt] (*order*) предписа́ние; *of conscience* веле́ние; *pol.* дикта́т; 2. [dɪk'teɪt] [про]диктова́ть (*a. fig.*); предпи́сывать [-са́ть]; *~ion* [dɪk'teɪʃn] *educ.* дикто́вка, дикта́нт; предписа́ние; *~orship* [dɪk'teɪtəʃɪp] диктату́ра

diction ['dɪkʃn] ди́кция; *~ary* [-rɪ] слова́рь *m*

did [dɪd] *pt. om do*

die¹ [daɪ] умира́ть [умере́ть], сконча́ться *pf.; coll.* стра́стно жела́ть; *~ away, ~ down of sound* замира́ть [-мере́ть]; *of wind* затиха́ть [-и́хнуть]; *of flowers* увяда́ть [-я́нуть]; *of fire* угаса́ть [уга́снуть]

die² [-] (*pl. dice*) игра́льная кость *f; the ~ is cast* жре́бий бро́шен

diet ['daɪət] 1. *customary* пи́ща; *med.* дие́та; 2. *v/t.* держа́ть на дие́те; *v/i.* быть на дие́те

differ ['dɪfə] различа́ться, отлича́ться; (*disagree*) не соглаша́ться [-ласи́ться], расходи́ться [разойти́сь] (*from* с Т, *in* в П); *tastes ~* о вку́сах не спо́рят; *~ence* ['dɪfrəns] ра́зница; разли́чие; разногла́сие; *math.* ра́зность *f; it makes no ~ to me* мне всё равно́; *~ent* [-nt] □ ра́зный; друго́й, не тако́й (*from* как), ино́й; *~entiate* [dɪfə'renʃɪeɪt] различа́ть(ся) [-чи́ть(ся)], отлича́ть [-чи́ть(ся)]

difficult ['dɪfɪkəlt] □ тру́дный; *~y* [-ɪ] тру́дность *f;* затрудне́ние

diffiden|ce ['dɪfɪdəns] (*lack of confidence*) неуве́ренность *f;* (*shyness*) засте́нчивость *f; ~t* [-dənt] неуве́ренный; засте́нчивый

diffus|e 1. [dɪ'fju:z] *fig.* распростра́нять [-ни́ть]; 2. [dɪ'fju:s] распространённый; *light* рассе́янный; *~ion* [dɪ'fju:ʒn] распростране́ние; рассе́ивание; *of gas, liquids* диффу́зия

dig [dɪg] 1. [*irr.*] копа́ть(ся) [вы́]копать; ры́ться; [вы́]рыть; 2. *coll.* (*a. cutting remark*) толчо́к

digest 1. [dɪ'dʒest] *food* перева́ривать [-ри́ть]; *information, etc.* усва́ивать [усво́ить] (*a. fig.*); *v/i.* перева́риваться [-ри́ться]; усва́иваться [усво́иться]; 2. ['daɪdʒest] (*literary*) дайдже́ст; *~ible* [dɪ'dʒestəbl] *fig.* удобовари́мый; легко́ усва́иваемый (*a. fig.*); *~ion* [-tʃən] *of food* пищеваре́ние; *of knowledge* усвое́ние

digital ['dɪdʒɪtl] цифрово́й

dignif|ied ['dɪgnɪfaɪd] преиспо́лненный досто́инства; *~y* [-faɪ] *fig.* облагора́живать [-ро́дить]

dign|itary ['dɪgnɪtərɪ] сано́вник; лицо́, занима́ющее высо́кий пост; *eccl.* иера́рх; *~y* [-ɪ] досто́инство

digress [daɪ'gres] отклоня́ться [-ни́ться]

dike [daɪk] да́мба; плоти́на; (*ditch*) кана́ва

dilapidated [dɪ'læpɪdeɪtɪd] ве́тхий, ста́рый

dilate [daɪ'leɪt] расширя́ть(ся) [-шири́ть(ся)]

diligen|ce ['dɪlɪdʒəns] прилежа́ние, усе́рдие; *~t* □ приле́жный, усе́рдный

dill [dɪl] укро́п

dilute [daɪ'lju:t] разбавля́ть [-ба́вить]; разводи́ть [-вести́]

dim [dɪm] 1. □ *light* ту́склый; *outlines, details* нея́сный; *eyesight* сла́бый; *recollections* сму́тный; *coll.* (*stupid*) тупо́й; 2. [по]тускне́ть; [за]тума́нить(ся); *~ one's headlights* включи́ть ближний свет

dime [daɪm] *Am.* моне́та в де́сять це́нтов

dimension [dɪ'menʃn] разме́р; объём; измере́ние

dimin|ish [dɪ'mɪnɪʃ] уменьша́ть(ся) [уме́ньшить(ся)]; убы́(ва́)ть; **~utive** [dɪ'mɪnjutɪv] □ миниатю́рный

dimple ['dɪmpl] я́мочка (на щеке́)

din [dɪn] шум; гро́хот

dine [daɪn] [по]обе́дать; [по]у́жинать; **~r** ['daɪnə] обе́дающий; *rail.* (*part. Am.*) ваго́н-рестора́н

dinghy ['dɪŋgɪ] ма́ленькая ло́дка

dingy ['dɪndʒɪ] □ гря́зный

dining|car *rail.* ваго́н-рестора́н; **~ room** столо́вая

dinner ['dɪnər] обе́д; *at* **~** за обе́дом; *formal* **~** официа́льный обе́д

dint [dɪnt]: *by* **~** *of* посре́дством (P)

dip [dɪp] **1.** *v/t.* погружа́ть [-узи́ть], окуна́ть [-ну́ть]; *brush* обма́кивать [-кну́ть]; *into pocket* су́нуть; *v/i.* погружа́ться [-узи́ться], окуна́ться [-ну́ться]; *of flag* приспуска́ть [-сти́ть]; *of road* спуска́ться [-сти́ться]; **2.** (*slope*) укло́н; купа́ние; *have a* **~** искупа́ться

diploma [dɪ'pləʊmə] дипло́м; **~cy** [-sɪ] дипломати́я; **~t** ['dɪpləmæt] диплома́т; **~tic(al** □) [dɪplə'mætɪk(əl)] дипломати́ческий

dire ['daɪə] ужа́сный

direct [dɪ'rekt, daɪ-] **1.** □ прямо́й; (*immediate*) непосре́дственный; (*straightforward*) я́сный; откры́тый; **~ current** *el.* постоя́нный ток; **~ train** прямо́й по́езд; **2.** *adv.* = **~ly; 3.** руководи́ть (Т); управля́ть (Т); направля́ть [-а́вить]; ука́зывать доро́гу (Д); **~ion** [dɪ'rekʃən, daɪ-] направле́ние; руково́дство; указа́ние, инстру́кция; **~ive** [dɪ'rektɪv] директи́ва; **~ly** [-lɪ] **1.** *adv.* пря́мо, непосре́дственно; неме́дленно; **2.** *cj.* как то́лько

director [dɪ'rektər, daɪ-] дире́ктор; *cine.* режиссёр; *board of* **~s** сове́т директоро́в; **~ate** [-rɪt] дире́кция; правле́ние; **~y** [-rɪ] (телефо́нный) спра́вочник

dirt [dɜːt] грязь *f*; **~ cheap** *coll.* о́чень дешёвый; *adv.* по дешёвке; **~y** ['dɜːtɪ] **1.** □ гря́зный; *joke* неприли́чный; *weather* нена́стный; **~ trick** по́длый посту́пок; **2.** [за]па́чкать

disability [dɪsə'bɪlətɪ] нетрудоспосо́бность *f*; бесси́лие; физи́ческий недоста́ток; **~ pension** пе́нсия по нетрудоспосо́бности

disabled [dɪs'eɪbld] искале́ченный; (*unable to work*) нетрудоспосо́бный; **~ veteran** инвали́д войны́

disadvantage [dɪsəd'vɑːntɪdʒ] недоста́ток; невы́годное положе́ние; уще́рб; неудо́бство

disagree [dɪsə'griː] расходи́ться во взгля́дах; противоре́чить друг дру́гу; (*quarrel*) [по]спо́рить; быть вре́дным (*with* для P); **~able** [-əbl] □ неприя́тный; **~ment** [-mənt] разногла́сие; несогла́сие

disappear [dɪsə'pɪə] исчеза́ть [-е́знуть]; пропада́ть [-па́сть]; *from sight* скры(ва́)ться; **~ance** [-rəns] исчезнове́ние

disappoint [dɪsə'pɔɪnt] разочаро́вывать [-рова́ть]; *hopes etc.* обма́нывать [-ну́ть]; **~ment** [-mənt] разочарова́ние

disapprov|al [dɪsə'pruːvl] неодобре́ние; **~e** [dɪsə'pruːv] не одобря́ть [одо́брить] (P); неодобри́тельно относи́ться (*of* к Д)

disarm [dɪs'ɑːm] *v/t. mst. fig.* обезору́жи(ва)ть; разоружа́ть [-жи́ть]; *v/i.* разоружа́ться [-жи́ться]; **~ament** [dɪs'ɑːməmənt] разоруже́ние

disarrange [dɪsə'reɪndʒ] (*upset*) расстра́ивать [-ро́ить]; (*put into disorder*) приводи́ть в беспоря́док

disast|er [dɪ'zɑːstə] бе́дствие; катастро́фа; **~rous** [-trəs] □ бе́дственный; катастрофи́ческий

disband [dɪs'bænd] распуска́ть [-усти́ть]

disbelieve [dɪsbɪ'liːv] не [по]ве́рить; не доверя́ть (Д)

disc [dɪsk] диск

discard [dɪs'kɑːd] (*throw away*) выбра́сывать [-росить]; *hypothesis* отверга́ть [-е́ргнуть]

discern [dɪ'sɜːn] различа́ть [-чи́ть]; распозн(ав)а́ть *pf.*; отлича́ть [-чи́ть]; **~ing** [-ɪŋ] □ *person* проница́тельный

discharge [dɪs'tʃɑːdʒ] **1.** *v/t.* (*unload*)

разгружа́ть [-узи́ть]; *prisoner* освобожда́ть [-боди́ть]; *from work* увольня́ть [уво́лить]; *duties* выполня́ть [вы́полнить]; *gun, etc.* разряжа́ть [-яди́ть]; *from hospital* выпи́сывать [вы́писать]; *v/i. of wound* гнои́ться; **2.** разгру́зка; *(shot)* вы́стрел; освобожде́ние; увольне́ние; *el.* разря́д; выполне́ние

disciple [dɪ'saɪpl] после́дователь (-ница *f*) *m*; *Bibl.* апо́стол

discipline ['dɪsɪplɪn] **1.** дисципли́на, поря́док; **2.** дисциплини́ровать *(im)pf.*

disclose [dɪs'kləʊz] обнару́жи(ва)ть; раскры́(ва́)ть

disco ['dɪskəʊ] *coll.* дискоте́ка

discolo(u)r [dɪs'kʌlə] обесцве́чивать(ся) [-е́тить(ся)]

discomfort [dɪs'kʌmfət] **1.** неудо́бство; дискомфо́рт; *(uneasiness of mind)* беспоко́йство; **2.** причиня́ть [-ни́ть] неудо́бство (Д)

disconsert [dɪskən'sɜːt] [вз]волнова́ть; смуща́ть [смути́ть]; приводи́ть в замеша́тельство

disconnect [dɪskə'nekt] разъединя́ть [-ни́ть] (*a. el.*); разобща́ть [-щи́ть]; *(uncouple)* расцепля́ть [-пи́ть]; **~ed** [-ɪd] □ *thoughts, etc.* бессвя́зный

disconsolate [dɪs'kɒnsələt] □ неуте́шный

discontent [dɪskən'tent] недово́льство; неудовлетворённость *f*; **~ed** [-ɪd] □ недово́льный; неудовлетворённый

discontinue [dɪskən'tɪnjuː] прер(ы)ва́ть; прекраща́ть [-рати́ть]

discord ['dɪskɔːd] разногла́сие; разла́д

discotheque ['dɪskətek] → *disco*

discount **1.** ['dɪskaunt] *comm.* ди́сконт, учёт векселе́й; ски́дка; *at a* **~** со ски́дкой; **2.** [dɪs'kaunt] дисконти́ровать *(im)pf.*, учи́тывать [уче́сть] (ве́ксель); де́лать ски́дку

discourage [dɪs'kʌrɪdʒ] обескура́жи(ва)ть; отбива́ть охо́ту (Д; *from* к Д)

discourse 1. [dɪs'kɔːs] рассужде́ние;

речь *f*; бесе́да; **2.** ['dɪskɔːs] вести́ бесе́ду

discourte|ous [dɪs'kɜːtɪəs] □ неве́жливый, неучти́вый; **~sy** [-tɪs] неве́жливость *f*, неучти́вость *f*

discover [dɪs'kʌvə] де́лать откры́тие (Р); обнару́жи(ва́)ть; **~y** [-ɪ] откры́тие

discredit [dɪs'kredɪt] **1.** дискредита́ция; **2.** дискредити́ровать *(im)pf.*; [о]позо́рить

discreet [dɪ'skriːt] □ *(careful)* осторо́жный, осмотри́тельный; такти́чный

discrepancy [dɪs'krepənsɪ] *(lack of correspondence)* расхожде́ние; противоречи́вость *f*; *(difference)* несхо́дство

discretion [dɪ'skreʃn] благоразу́мие; осторо́жность *f*; усмотре́ние; *at your* **~** на ва́ше усмотре́ние

discriminat|e [dɪ'skrɪmɪneɪt] относи́ться по-ра́зному; **~** *between* отлича́ть, различа́ть; **~** *against* дискримини́ровать; относи́ться предвзя́то (к Д); **~ing** [-ɪŋ] □ дискриминацио́нный; *taste, etc.* разбо́рчивый; **~ion** [-'neɪʃn] *(judgment, etc.)* проница́тельность *f*; *(bias)* дискримина́ция

discuss [dɪ'skʌs] обсужда́ть [-уди́ть], дискути́ровать; **~ion** [-ʌʃən] обсужде́ние, диску́ссия; *public* пре́ния *n/pl.*

disdain [dɪs'deɪn] **1.** *(scorn)* презира́ть [-зре́ть]; *(think unworthy)* счита́ть ни́же своего́ досто́инства; **2.** презре́ние; пренебреже́ние

disease [dɪ'ziːz] боле́знь *f*; **~d** [-d] больно́й

disembark [dɪsɪm'bɑːk] выса́живать(ся) [вы́садить(ся)]; сходи́ть на бе́рег; *goods* выгружа́ть [вы́грузить]

disengage [dɪsɪn'geɪdʒ] *(make free)* высвобожда́ть(ся) [вы́свободить(ся)]; *tech. (detach)* разъединя́ть [-ни́ть]

disentangle [dɪsɪn'tæŋgl] распу́т(ыв)ать(ся); *fig.* выпу́тываться [вы́путать(ся)]

disfavo(u)r [dɪs'feɪvə] **1.** неми́лость *f*; *regard with* **~** относи́ться отрица́-

тельно; **2.** не одобря́ть [одо́брить]

disfigure [dɪs'fɪgə] обезобра́живать [-ра́зить], [из]уро́довать

disgrace [dɪs'greɪs] **1.** (*loss of respect*) бесче́стье; (*disfavour*) неми́лость *f*; (*cause of shame*) позо́р; **2.** [о]позо́рить; **~ful** [-ful] □ посты́дный, позо́рный

disguise [dɪs'gaɪz] **1.** маскиро́вка; переодева́ние; обма́нчивая вне́шность *f*; ма́ска; **in ~** переоде́тый; **2.** [за]маскирова́ть(ся); переоде(ва́)ть(ся); (*hide*) скры(ва́)ть

disgust [dɪs'gʌst] **1.** отвраще́ние; **2.** внуша́ть [-ши́ть] отвраще́ние (Д); (*make indignant*) возмуща́ть [-ути́ть]; **~ing** [-ɪŋ] □ отврати́тельный

dish [dɪʃ] **1.** блю́до, таре́лка, ми́ска; **the ~es** *pl.* посу́да; (*food*) блю́до; **2.**: **~ out** раскла́дывать на таре́лки

dishearten [dɪs'hɑːtn] приводи́ть [-вести́] в уны́ние

dishevel(l)ed [dɪ'ʃevld] растрёпанный, взъеро́шенный

dishonest [dɪs'ɒnɪst] □ нече́стный; недобросо́вестный; **~y** [-ɪ] нече́стность *f*; недобросо́вестность *f*; обма́н

dishono(u)r [dɪs'ɒnə] **1.** бесче́стье, позо́р; **2.** [о]позо́рить; *young girl* [о]бесче́стить; **~able** [-rəbl] □ бесче́стный, ни́зкий

disillusion [dɪsɪ'luːʒn] **1.** разочарова́ние; **2.** разруша́ть [-у́шить] иллю́зии (Р); **~ed** [-d] разочаро́ванный

disinclined [dɪsɪn'klaɪnd] нерасположе́нный

disinfect [dɪsɪn'fekt] дезинфици́ровать (*im*)*pf.*; **~ant** [-ənt] дезинфици́рующее сре́дство

disintegrate [dɪs'ɪntɪgreɪt] распада́ться [-па́сться]; разруша́ться [-у́шиться]

disinterested [dɪs'ɪntrəstɪd] □ (*without self-interest*) бескоры́стный; (*without prejudice*) беспристра́стный

disk [dɪsk] диск; **~ drive** дисково́д

diskette [dɪ'sket] *comput.* диске́та

dislike [dɪs'laɪk] **1.** не люби́ть; **2.** не-

любо́вь *f* (*of* к Д); антипа́тия; *take a ~ to* невзлюби́ть (В)

dislocate ['dɪsləkeɪt] *med.* вывихивать [вы́вихнуть]; (*put out of order*) наруша́ть [нару́шить]

dislodge [dɪs'lɒdʒ] (*move*) смеща́ть [смести́ть]; *mil.* выбива́ть [вы́бить]

disloyal [dɪs'lɔɪəl] □ *to state, etc.* нелоя́льный; *friend* неве́рный

dismal ['dɪzməl] □ (*gloomy*) мра́чный, уны́лый; гнету́щий

dismantle [dɪs'mæntl] *tech.* разбира́ть [разобра́ть]; демонти́ровать (*im*.)*pf.*; **~ing** [-ɪŋ] демонта́ж

dismay [dɪs'meɪ] **1.** смяте́ние, потрясе́ние; **2.** *v/t.* приводи́ть [-вести́] в смяте́ние

dismiss [dɪs'mɪs] *v/t.* (*allow to go*) отпуска́ть [-сти́ть]; *from work, service, etc.* увольня́ть [уво́лить]; **~ all thoughts of** отбро́сить да́же мысль (о П); **~al** [-l] увольне́ние; отстране́ние

dismount [dɪs'maunt] *v/i.* слеза́ть с ло́шади, с велосипе́да

disobedien|ce [dɪsə'biːdɪəns] непослуша́ние, неповинове́ние; **~t** [-t] □ непослу́шный

disobey [dɪsə'beɪ] не [по]слу́шаться (Р); *order* не подчиня́ться [-ни́ться] (Д)

disorder [dɪs'ɔːdə] беспоря́док; *med.* расстро́йство; **~s** *pl.* (*riots*) беспоря́дки *m*/*pl.*; *throw into ~* переверну́ть всё вверх дном; **~ly** [-lɪ] беспоря́дочный; неорганизо́ванный; бу́йный

disorganize [dɪs'ɔːɡənaɪz] дезорганизова́ть (*im*)*pf.*, расстра́ивать [-ро́ить]

disown [dɪs'əun] не призн(ав)а́ть; отка́зываться [-за́ться] от (Р)

dispassionate [dɪ'spæʃənət] □ (*impartial*) беспристра́стный; (*cool*) бесстра́стный

dispatch [dɪ'spætʃ] **1.** отпра́вка; отправле́ние; (*message*) сообще́ние; **2.** пос(ы)ла́ть; отправля́ть [-а́вить]

dispel [dɪ'spel] рассе́ивать [-се́ять]; *crowd etc.* разгоня́ть [разогна́ть]

dispensary [dɪ'spensərɪ] больни́чная

апте́ка; *in drugstore* рецепту́рный отде́л

dispense [dɪ'spens] *v/t. prescription* приготовля́ть; (*deal out*) раздава́ть [-да́ть]; **~ justice** отправля́ть [-а́вить] правосу́дие; **~ with** обходи́ться [обойти́сь], отка́зываться [-за́ться]

disperse [dɪ'spɜ:s] разгоня́ть [разогна́ть]; рассе́ивать(ся) [-е́ять(ся)]; (*spread*) распространя́ть [-ни́ть]

dispirit [dɪ'spɪrɪt] удруча́ть [-чи́ть]; приводи́ть в уны́ние

displace [dɪs'pleɪs] (*take the place of*) заня́ть ме́сто, замеща́ть [замести́ть]

display [dɪs'pleɪ] **1.** (*exhibit*) выставля́ть [вы́ставить]; *courage, etc.* проявля́ть [-яви́ть]; **2.** вы́ставка; проявле́ние; *comput.* диспле́й

displeas|**e** [dɪs'pli:z] вызыва́ть [вы́звать] недово́льство, не [по]нра́виться (Д); быть не по вку́су (Д); **~ed** [-d] недово́льный; **~ure** [dɪs'pleʒə] недово́льство

dispos|**al** [dɪs'pəʊzl] *of troops, etc.* расположе́ние; (*removal*) удале́ние; **put at s.o.'s ~** предоста́вить в чьё-л. распоряже́ние; **~e** [dɪs'pəʊz] *v/t.* располага́ть [-ложи́ть] (В); *v/i.* **~ of** распоряжа́ться [-яди́ться] (Т); **~ed** [-d] располо́женный; настро́енный; (*be inclined to*) быть скло́нным; **~ition** [dɪspə'zɪʃn] расположе́ние; хара́ктер; предрасположе́ние (к Д), скло́нность (к Д)

disproportionate [dɪsprə'pɔ:ʃənət] □ непропорциона́льный, несоразме́рный

disprove [dɪs'pru:v] опроверга́ть [-ве́ргнуть]

dispute [dɪs'pju:t] **1.** (*discuss*) обсужда́ть [-уди́ть]; (*call into question*) оспа́ривать [оспо́рить]; (*argue*) [по]спо́рить; **2.** диспу́т, деба́ты *m/pl.*; поле́мика; диску́ссия

disqualify [dɪs'kwɒlɪfaɪ] дисквалифици́ровать (*im*)*pf.*; лиша́ть пра́ва

disquiet [dɪs'kwaɪət] [о]беспоко́ить

disregard [dɪsrɪ'gɑ:d] **1.** пренебреже́ние; игнори́рование; **2.** игнори́ровать (*im*)*pf.*; пренебрега́ть [-бре́чь]

(Т)

disreput|**able** [dɪs'repjʊtəbl] □ *behavio(u)r* дискредити́рующий; по́льзующийся дурно́й репута́цией; **~e** [dɪsrɪ'pju:t] дурна́я сла́ва

disrespect [dɪsrɪ'spekt] неуваже́ние; **~ful** [-fl] □ непочти́тельный

dissatis|**faction** [dɪsætɪs'fækʃn] недово́льство; неудовлетворённость *f*; **~factory** [-tərɪ] неудовлетвори́тельный; **~fy** [dɪs'sætɪsfaɪ] не удовлетворя́ть [-ри́ть]

dissect [dɪ'sekt] *anat.* вскрыва́ть; *fig.* анализи́ровать

dissent [dɪ'sent] **1.** несогла́сие; **2.** расходи́ться во взгля́дах, мне́ниях

dissimilar [dɪ'sɪmɪlə] □ непохо́жий, несхо́дный, разноро́дный

dissipat|**e** ['dɪsɪpeɪt] (*disperse*) рассе́ивать [-е́ять]; (*spend, waste*) растра́чивать [-тра́тить]; **~ion** [dɪsɪ'peɪʃn]: *life of* **~** беспу́тный о́браз жи́зни

dissociate [dɪ'səʊʃɪeɪt] разобща́ть [-щи́ть] отмежёвываться [-ева́ться] (от Р)

dissolut|**e** ['dɪsəlu:t] □ распу́щенный; беспу́тный; **~ion** [dɪsə'lu:ʃn] *of marriage, agreement* расторже́ние; *parl.* ро́спуск; *of firm, etc.* ликвида́ция, расформирова́ние

dissolve [dɪ'zɒlv] *v/t. parl. etc.* распуска́ть [-усти́ть]; *salt, etc.* растворя́ть [-ри́ть]; *marriage, agreement* расторга́ть [-о́ргнуть]; аннули́ровать (*im*)*pf.*; *v/i.* растворя́ться [-ри́ться]

dissonant ['dɪsənənt] нестро́йный, диссони́рующий

dissuade [dɪ'sweɪd] отгова́ривать [-вори́ть] (*from* от Р)

distan|**ce** ['dɪstəns] расстоя́ние; *sport* диста́нция; даль *f*; *of time* промежу́ток, пери́од; *in the* **~** вдали́; вдалеке́; *keep s.o. at a* **~** держа́ть кого́-л. на расстоя́нии; **~t** [-t] □ да́льний, далёкий; отдалённый; *fig.* (*reserved*) сде́ржанный, холо́дный

distaste [dɪs'teɪst] отвраще́ние; **~ful**

D

[-fl] □ неприя́тный (на В, **to** Д)

distend [dɪ'stend] разду́(ва́)ть(ся), наду́(ва́)ть(ся)

distil [dɪ'stɪl] *chem.* перегоня́ть [-гна́ть], дистиллирова́ть (*im*)*pf*.; **∼led water** дистиллиро́ванная вода́; **∼lery** [-əгɪ] перего́нный заво́д

distinct [dɪ'stɪŋkt] □ (*different*) разли́чный, осо́бый, индивидуа́льный; (*clear*) отчётливый; (*definite*) определённый; **∼ion** [dɪs'tɪŋkʃn] разли́чие; (*hono(u)r*) честь; **draw a ∼ between** де́лать разли́чие ме́жду (Т); **writer of ∼** изве́стный писа́тель; **∼ive** [-tɪv] □ отличи́тельный, характе́рный

distinguish [dɪ'stɪŋgwɪʃ] различа́ть [-чи́ть]; отлича́ть [-чи́ть]; **∼ o.s.** отличи́ться [-чи́ться]; **∼ed** [-t] выдаю́щийся, изве́стный; *guest* почётный

distort [dɪ'stɔːt] искажа́ть [искази́ть] (*a. fig.*)

distract [dɪ'strækt] отвлека́ть [отвле́чь]; **∼ion** [dɪ'strækʃn] отвлече́ние; (*amusement*) развлече́ние

distress [dɪ'stres] **1.** огорче́ние, го́ре; *naut.* бе́дствие; (*suffering*) страда́ние; (*poverty*) нужда́, нищета́; **∼ signal** сигна́л бе́дствия; **2.** (*upset*) огорча́ть [-чи́ть], расстра́ивать [-ро́ить]

distribut|e [dɪ'strɪbjuːt] распределя́ть [-ли́ть]; (*hand out*) разд(ав)а́ть; *printed matter* распространя́ть [-ни́ть]; **∼ion** [dɪstrɪ'bjuːʃn] распределе́ние; разда́ча; распростране́ние

district ['dɪstrɪkt] райо́н; о́круг; **election ∼** избира́тельный о́круг

distrust [dɪs'trʌst] **1.** недове́рие; (*suspicion*) подозре́ние; **2.** не доверя́ть (Д); **∼ful** [-fl] □ недове́рчивый; подозри́тельный; **∼ of o.s.** неуве́ренный в себе́

disturb [dɪ'stɜːb] [по]беспоко́ить; (*worry*) взволнова́ть; *peace, etc.* наруша́ть [-у́шить]; **∼ance** [-əns] шум, трево́га, волне́ние; *pl.* волне́ния *n/pl.*

disuse [dɪs'juːz] неупотребле́ние; **fall into ∼** вы́йти из употребле́ния; *of law, etc.* не применя́ться, не испо́льзоваться

ditch [dɪtʃ] кана́ва, ров

dive [daɪv] **1.** ныря́ть [нырну́ть]; погружа́ться [-узи́ться]; [-гнуть] в во́ду; *ae.* пики́ровать (*im*)*pf*.; **2.** прыжо́к в во́ду; погруже́ние; пики́рование; (*disreputable bar, etc.*) прито́н, погребо́к; **make a ∼ for** броса́ться [бро́ситься]; **∼r** ['daɪvə] водола́з; ныря́льщик *m*, -ица *f*; *sport* спортсме́н по прыжка́м в во́ду

diverge [daɪ'vɜːdʒ] расходи́ться [разойти́сь] (*a. fig.*); (*turn away*) отклоня́ться [-ни́ться]; **∼nce** [-əns] расхожде́ние; отклоне́ние; **∼nt** [-ənt] расходя́щийся; **∼ opinions** ра́зные мне́ния

diverse [daɪ'vɜːs] □ разли́чный, разнообра́зный; (*different*) ино́й; **∼ion** [daɪ'vɜːʃən] (*amusement*) развлече́ние; (*turning away*) отклоне́ние; **∼ity** [-sɪtɪ] разнообра́зие; разли́чие

divert [daɪ'vɜːt] *attention* отвлека́ть [-е́чь]; (*amuse*) развлека́ть [-е́чь]

divid|e [dɪ'vaɪd] *v/t. math.* [раз]дели́ть; (*share out*) разделя́ть [-ли́ть]; *v/i.* [раз]дели́ться; разделя́ться [-ли́ться]; *math.* дели́ться без оста́тка; **∼end** ['dɪvɪdend] *fin.* дивиде́нд; *math.* дели́мое

divine [dɪ'vaɪn] **1.** □ боже́ственный; **∼ service** богослуже́ние; **2.** (*guess*) уга́дывать [-да́ть]

diving ['daɪvɪŋ] ныря́ние; *sport* прыжки́ в во́ду; **∼ board** трампли́н

divinity [dɪ'vɪnɪtɪ] (*theology*) богосло́вие; (*a divine being*) божество́

divis|ible [dɪ'vɪzəbl] (раз)дели́мый; **∼ion** [dɪ'vɪʒn] деле́ние; разделе́ние; (*department*) отде́л; *mil.* диви́зия; *math.* деле́ние

divorce [dɪ'vɔːs] **1.** разво́д; **2.** (*dissolve a marriage*) расторга́ть брак (Р); разводи́ться [-вести́сь] с (Т); **be ∼d** быть в разво́де

divulge [daɪ'vʌldʒ] разглаша́ть [-ласи́ть]

dizz|iness ['dɪzɪnɪs] головокруже́ние; **∼y** ['dɪzɪ] □ головокружи́тельный; **I feel ∼** у меня́ кру́жится голова́

do [duː] *irr.* **1.** *v/t.* [с]де́лать; *duty, etc.* выполня́ть [вы́полнить]; (*arrange*) устра́ивать [-ро́ить]; *homework etc.* приготовля́ть [-то́вить]; ~ **London** осма́тривать Ло́ндон; *have done reading* ко́нчить чита́ть; *coll.* ~ **in** (*exhaust*), *a. sl.* (*kill*) уби́(ва́)ть; ~ **out** убира́ть [убра́ть]; ~ **out of** выма́нивать [вы́манить] (обма́ном); ~ **over** переде́л(ыв)ать; *with paint* покры́(ва́)ть; ~ **up** зава́рчивать [заверну́ть]; [с]де́лать ремо́нт; *coat* застёгивать [-егну́ть]; (*tie*) завя́зывать [-за́ть]; 2. *v/i.* [с]де́лать; поступа́ть [-пи́ть], де́йствовать; ~ **so as to ...** устра́ивать так, что́бы ...; *that will* ~ доста́точно, дово́льно; сойдёт; *how* ~ **you** ~? здра́вствуй(те)!; как вы пожива́ете?; ~ **well** успева́ть; хорошо́ вести́ де́ло; ~ **away with** уничтожа́ть [-о́жить]; *I could* ~ мне мог бы пригоди́ться (И); *I could* ~ **with a shave** мне не помеша́ло бы побри́ться; ~ **without** обходи́ться [обойти́сь] без (Р); ~ **be quick!** поспеши́те!, скоре́й!; ~ **you like London? – I** ~ вам нра́вится Ло́ндон? – Да

docil|e ['dəʊsaɪl] послу́шный; (*easily trained*) поня́тливый; ~**ity** [dəʊ'sɪlɪtɪ] послуша́ние; поня́тливость *f*

dock [dɒk] 1. *naut.* док; *law* скамья́ подсуди́мых; 2. *naut.* ста́вить су́дно в док; *of space vehicles* [co]стыко́ва́ться

dockyard ['dɒkjɑːd] верфь *f*

doctor ['dɒktə] *acad.* до́ктор; *med.* врач; ~**ate** [-rət] сте́пень до́ктора

doctrine ['dɒktrɪn] уче́ние, доктри́на

document 1. ['dɒkjʊmənt] докуме́нт; 2. [-ment] документи́ровать, подтвержда́ть докуме́нтами

dodge [dɒdʒ] 1. уве́ртка, уло́вка, хи́трость *f*; 2. увили́вать [-льну́ть]; [с]хитри́ть; избега́ть [-ежа́ть] (Р)

doe [dəʊ] *mst.* са́мка оле́ня

dog [dɒg] 1. соба́ка, пёс; 2. ходи́ть по пята́м (Р); *fig.* пресле́довать; ~ **collar** оше́йник

dogged ['dɒgɪd] □ упря́мый, упо́рный, насто́йчивый

dogma ['dɒgmə] до́гма; *specific* до́гмат; ~**tic** [dɒg'mætɪk] *person* догма-

ти́чный; ~**tism** ['dɒgmətɪzəm] догмати́зм

dog-tired [dɒg'taɪəd] уста́лый как соба́ка

doings ['duːɪŋz] дела́ *n/pl.*, посту́пки *m/pl.*

do-it-yourself: ~ **kit** набо́р инструме́нтов "сде́лай сам"

doleful ['dəʊlfʊl] □ ско́рбный, печа́льный

doll [dɒl] ку́кла

dollar ['dɒlə] до́ллар

domain [də'meɪn] (*estate*) владе́ние; (*realm*) сфе́ра; *fig.* о́бласть *f*

dome [dəʊm] ку́пол; (*vault*) свод

domestic [də'mestɪk] 1. дома́шний; семе́йный; 2. дома́шняя рабо́тница; слуга́ *m*; ~**ate** [-tɪkeɪt] *animal* прируча́ть [-чи́ть]

domicile ['dɒmɪsaɪl] местожи́тельство

domin|ant ['dɒmɪnənt] госпо́дствующий, преоблада́ющий; ~**ate** [-neɪt] госпо́дствовать, преоблада́ть; ~**ation** [dɒmɪ'neɪʃn] госпо́дство, преоблада́ние; ~**eer** [dɒmɪ'nɪə] вести́ себя́ деспоти́чески; ~**eering** [-rɪŋ] □ деспоти́чный, вла́стный

don [dɒn] *univ.* преподава́тель

donat|e [də'ʊneɪt] [по]же́ртвовать; ~**ion** [-ʃn] поже́ртвование

done [dʌn] 1. *pt. p. om do;* 2. *adj.* гото́вый; ~ **in** уста́лый; *well* ~(*f*) хорошо́ прожа́ренный; молоде́ц!

donkey ['dɒŋkɪ] осёл

donor ['dəʊnə] дари́тель(ница *f*) *m*; *of blood, etc.* до́нор

doom [duːm] 1. рок, судьба́; (*ruin*) ги́бель; 2. обрека́ть [-е́чь] (*to* на В)

door [dɔː] дверь *f*; *next* ~ в сосе́днем до́ме; *out of* ~s на откры́том во́здухе; ~ **handle** дверна́я ру́чка; ~**keeper** швейца́р; ~**way** вход, дверно́й проём

dope [dəʊp] наркоти́к; *sport* до́пинг; *coll.* (*blockhead*) о́лух

dormant ['dɔːmənt] *mst. fig.* безде́йствующий, спя́щий; ~ **capital** мёртвый капита́л

dormitory ['dɔːmɪtrɪ] большо́е спа́льное помеще́ние (*в школах, интернатах и т.д.*); *Am.* общежи́тие

dose [dəʊs] **1.** до́за; **2.** дози́ровать (*im*)*pf.*; дава́ть до́зами

dot [dɒt] **1.** то́чка; *come on the ~* прийти́ то́чно; **2.:** *~ the i's* ста́вить то́чки над i; *~ted line* пункти́р

dot|e [dəʊt]: *~ (up)on* души́ не ча́ять; *~ing* ['dəʊtɪŋ] о́чень лю́бящий

double ['dʌbl] **1.** двойно́й; *fig.* двоя́кий; **2.** *person* двойни́к; двойно́е коли́чество; па́рная игра́; *thea.* (*understudy*) дублёр; **3.** *v/t.* удва́ивать [удво́ить]; скла́дывать вдво́е; *~d up* скрю́чившийся; *v/i.* удва́иваться [удво́иться]; *~-breasted* двубо́ртный; *~-dealing* двуру́шничество; *~-edged* обоюдоо́стрый

doubt [daʊt] **1.** *v/t.* сомнева́ться [усомни́ться] в (П); не доверя́ть (Д); *v/i.* име́ть сомне́ния; **2.** сомне́ние; *no ~* без сомне́ния; *~ful* ['daʊtfʊl] □ сомни́тельный; *~less* ['daʊtlɪs] несомне́нно; вероя́тно

dough [dəʊ] те́сто; *~nut* ['dəʊnʌt] по́нчик

dove [dʌv] го́лубь *m*

down¹ [daʊn] пух; *dim.* пушо́к

down² [-] **1.** *adv.* вниз, внизу́; *~ to* вплоть до (Р); *it suits me ~ to the ground* меня́ э́то вполне́ устра́ивает; **2.** *prp.* вниз по (Д); вдоль по (Д); *the river* вниз по реке́; **3.** *adj.* напра́вленный вниз; *prices are ~* це́ны сни́зились; **4.** *v/t.* опуска́ть [опусти́ть]; *enemies* одоле(ва́)ть; *~-cast* удручённый; *~fall* паде́ние; *~-hearted* [daʊn'hɑːtɪd] па́вшийду́хом; *~hill* [daʊn'hɪl] вниз, под го́ру; *~pour* ли́вень *m*; *~right* **1.** *adv.* соверше́нно; пря́мо; **2.** *adj.* прямо́й; (*frank*) открове́нный; (*honest*) че́стный; *~stairs* [daʊn'steəz] вниз, внизу́; *~stream* [daʊn'striːm] вниз по тече́нию; *~town* [daʊn'taʊn] *part. Am.* в це́нтре го́рода; *~ward(s)* [-wəd(z)] вниз, кни́зу

downy ['daʊnɪ] пуши́стый, мя́гкий как пух

dowry ['daʊərɪ] прида́ное

doze [dəʊz] **1.** дремо́та; *have a ~* вздремну́ть; **2.** дрема́ть

dozen ['dʌzn] дю́жина

drab [dræb] ту́склый, однообра́зный

draft [drɑːft] **1.** = **draught;** чернови́к; *fin.* чек; су́мма, полу́ченная по че́ку; *mil.* призы́в, набо́р; *arch.* эски́з; **2.** набра́сывать [-роса́ть]; призыва́ть [призва́ть]

drag [dræg] **1.** обу́за, бре́мя *n*; **2.** *v/t.* [по]тяну́ть, [по]волочи́ть; *I could hardly ~ my feet* я е́ле волочи́л но́ги; *v/i.* [по]волочи́ться; *~ on* тяну́ться

dragon ['drægən] драко́н; *~fly* стрекоза́

drain [dreɪn] **1.** дрена́ж; *pl.* канализа́ция; *from roof* водосто́к; **2.** *v/t.* осуша́ть [-ши́ть]; *fig.* истоща́ть [-щи́ть]; *~age* ['dreɪnɪdʒ] дрена́ж; сток; канализа́ция

drake [dreɪk] се́лезень *m*

drama|tic [drə'mætɪk] (*~ally*) драмати́ческий; театра́льный; драмати́чный; *~tist* ['dræmətɪst] драмату́рг; *~tize* [-taɪz] драматизи́ровать (*im*)*pf.*

drank [dræŋk] *pt. of* **drink**

drape [dreɪp] [за]драпирова́ть; располага́ть скла́дками; *~ry* ['dreɪpərɪ] драпиро́вка; (*cloth*) тка́ни *f/pl.*

drastic ['dræstɪk] (*~ally*) реши́тельный, круто́й; сильноде́йствующий

draught [drɑːft] *chiefly Brt.* тя́га; *in room* сквозня́к; (*drink*) глото́к; (*rough copy*) черновы́к, набро́сок; *~s pl.* ша́шки *f/pl.*; → **draft,** *~ beer* бо́чковое пи́во; *~sman* [-smən] чертёжник; (*artist*) рисова́льщик *m*, -щица *f*

draw [drɔː] **1.** [*irr.*] [на]рисова́ть; [по]тяну́ть; [по]тащи́ть; *tooth* вырыва́ть [вы́рвать]; *water* черпа́ть; *attention* привлека́ть [-е́чь]; *conclusion* приходи́ть [-ийти́] (к Д); *sport* зака́нчивать [-ко́нчить] (игру́) вничью́; *~ near* приближа́ться [-ли́зиться]; *~ out* вытя́гивать [вы́тянуть]; *~ up paper* составля́ть [-а́вить]; (*stop*) остана́вливаться [-нови́ться]; **2.** (*lottery*) жеребьёвка; *sport* ничья́; *~back* ['drɔːbæk] недоста́ток; *~er* [drɔː] выдвижно́й я́щик; **~ers**: *a.* **pair of ~** *pl.* кальсо́ны *f/pl.*, *short* трусы́

drawing ['drɔːɪŋ] рису́нок; рисова́ние; чертёж; **~ board** чертёжная доска́; **~ room** гости́ная

drawn [drɔːn] *pt. p. om* **draw**

dread [dred] **1.** боя́ться, страши́ться (P); **2.** страх, боя́знь *f*; **~ful** ['dredfl] □ ужа́сный, стра́шный

dream [driːm] **1.** сон, сновиде́ние; (*reverie*) мечта́; **2.** [*a. irr.*] ви́деть во сне; мечта́ть; **~ up** приду́мывать [-мать]; воображать [-рази́ть]; **~er** [-ə] мечта́тель(ница *f*) *m*, фантазёр(ка); **~y** [-ɪ] □ мечта́тельный

dreary ['drɪərɪ] □ тоскли́вый; *weather* нена́стный; *work, etc.* ску́чный

dredge [dredʒ] землечерпа́лка

dregs [dregz] *pl.* оса́док; *of society* отбро́сы *m/pl.*; **drink to the ~** [вы́]пить до дна

drench [drentʃ] промока́ть [-мо́кнуть]; **get ~ed** промо́кнуть до ни́тки

dress [dres] **1.** пла́тье; *collect.* оде́жда; *thea.* **~ rehearsal** генера́льная репети́ция; **2.** оде́(ва́)ть(ся); (*adorn*) украша́ть(ся) [укра́сить(ся)]; *hair* де́лать причёску; *med.* перевя́зывать [-за́ть]; **~ circle** *thea.* бельэта́ж; **~er** [-ə] ку́хонный шкаф; *Am. a.* комо́д, туале́тный сто́лик

dressing ['dresɪŋ] перевя́зочный материа́л; перевя́зка; *cul.* припра́ва; **~ down** головомо́йка; **~ gown** хала́т; **~ table** туале́тный сто́лик

dressmaker портни́ха

drew ['druː] *pt. om* **draw**

dribble ['drɪbl] ка́пать; пуска́ть слю́ни

dried [draɪd] сухо́й; высо́хший

drift [drɪft] **1.** *naut.* дрейф; (*snow~*) сугро́б; *of sand* нано́с; *fig.* тенде́нция; **did you get the ~ of what he said?** ты уло́вил смысл его́ слов?; **2.** *v/t.* сноси́ть [снести́]; наноси́ть [нанести́]; *leaves, snow* мести́; *v/i.* дрейфова́ть (*im*)*pf.*; *наме*сти́; *fig. of person* плыть по тече́нию

drill [drɪl] **1.** дрель; бура́в; *tech.* бур; (*exercise*) упражне́ние; *sport* трениро́вка; **2.** [на]трениро́ва́ть

drink [drɪŋk] **1.** питьё; напи́ток; **2.** [*irr.*] [вы́]пить; пья́нствовать

drip [drɪp] ка́пать, па́дать ка́плями

drive [draɪv] **1.** езда́; пое́здка; подъе́зд (к до́му); *tech.* приво́д; *fig.* эне́ргия; си́ла; **go for a ~** пое́хать поката́ться на маши́не; **2.** [*irr.*] *v/t.* (*force along*) [по]гна́ть; *nail, etc.* вби(ва́)ть; (*convey*) вози́ть, [по]везти́; *v/i.* е́здить, [по]е́хать; ката́ться; [по]нести́сь; **~ at** намека́ть на (В)

drivel ['drɪvl] бессмы́слица, чепуха́

driven ['drɪvn] *pt. p. om* **drive**

driver ['draɪvə] *mot.* води́тель *m*, шофёр; *rail.* машини́ст; **racing ~** го́нщик

drizzle ['drɪzl] **1.** и́зморось *f*; ме́лкий дождь *m*; **2.** мороси́ть

drone [drəʊn] **1.** *zo.* тру́тень *m*; **2.** жужжа́ть; *plane* гуде́ть

droop [druːp] *v/t. head* опуска́ть [-сти́ть]; пове́сить; *v/i.* пони́кать [-и́кнуть]; *of flowers* увяда́ть [увя́нуть]

drop [drɒp] **1.** ка́пля; (*fruit ~*) ледене́ц; *in prices, etc.* паде́ние, сниже́ние; *thea.* за́навес; **2.** *v/t.* роня́ть [урони́ть]; *smoking, etc.* броса́ть [бро́сить]; **~ a p. a line** черкну́ть кому́-л. слове́чко; *v/i.* ка́пать [ка́пнуть]; спада́ть [спасть]; па́дать [упа́сть]; пони́жа́ться [-и́зиться]; *of wind* стиха́ть [сти́хнуть]; **~ in** заходи́ть [зайти́], загля́дывать [загляну́ть]

drought [draʊt] за́суха

drove [drəʊv] **1.** (*herd*) ста́до; **2.** *pt. om* **drive**

drown [draʊn] *v/t.* [у]топи́ть; *fig. sound* заглуша́ть [-ши́ть]; *v/i.* [у]тону́ть = **be ~ed**; **~ o.s.** [у]топи́ться

drows|e [draʊz] [за]дрема́ть; **~y** ['draʊzɪ] со́нный

drudge [drʌdʒ] исполня́ть ску́чную, тяжёлую рабо́ту, тяну́ть ля́мку

drug [drʌg] лека́рство; *pl.* медика́менты *m/pl.*; нарко́тик; **take ~s** употребля́ть нарко́тики; **~ addict** нарко́ма́н; **~gist** ['drʌgɪst] апте́карь *m*; **~store** *Am.* апте́ка

drum [drʌm] **1.** бараба́н; **2.** бить в бараба́н, бараба́нить

D

drunk [drʌŋk] **1.** *pt. p. om* **drink**; **2.** пьяный; **get ~** напиваться пьяным; **~ard** ['drʌŋkəd] пьяница *m/f*; **~en** ['drʌŋkən] пьяный

dry [draɪ] □ сухой, высохший; **~ as dust** скучный; **2.** [вы]сушить; [вы]сохнуть; **~ up** высушивать [высушить]; *of river etc.* высыхать [высохнуть], пересыхать [-сохнуть]; **~ cleaner's** химчистка

dual ['djuːəl] □ двойной

dubious ['djuːbɪəs] □ сомнительный, подозрительный

duchess ['dʌtʃɪs] герцогиня

duck¹ [dʌk] утка; *fig.* **a lame ~** неудачник

duck² [-] нырять [нырнуть]; окунаться [-нуться]; *(move quickly)* увёртываться [увернуться]

duckling ['dʌklɪŋ] утёнок

due [djuː] **1.** должный, надлежащий; **~ to** благодаря; **the train is ~ ...** поезд должен прибыть ...; **in ~ course** в своё время; **2.** *adv. naut. east, etc.* точно, прямо; **3.** должное; то, что причитается; **give s.o. his ~** отдавать должное кому-л.; *mst.* **~s** *pl.* сборы *m/pl.*, налоги *m/pl.*; пошлины *f/pl.*; членский взнос

duel ['djuːəl] **1.** дуэль *f*; **2.** драться на дуэли

duet [djuː'et] дуэт

dug [dʌg] *pt. и pt. p. om* **dig**

duke [djuːk] герцог

dull [dʌl] **1.** **(~y)** *(not sharp)* тупой *(a. fig.)*; *(boring)* скучный; *comm.* вялый; *day* пасмурный; **2.** притуплять(ся) [-пить(ся)]; *fig.* делать(-ся) скучным; **~ness** ['dʌlnɪs] скука; вялость *f*; тупость *f*

duly ['djuːlɪ] должным образом

dumb [dʌm] □ немой; *Am.* глупый; **~found** [dʌm'faʊnd] ошеломлять [-мить]

dummy ['dʌmɪ] *tailor's* манекен; *mil.* макет; *Brt.* **baby's ~** *(Am. pacifier)* соска, пустышка

dump [dʌmp] **1.** свалка; **2.** сбрасывать [сбросить]; сваливать [-лить]; **~ing**

comm. демпинг; **~s** *pl.*: **be down in the ~** плохое настроение

dunce [dʌns] тупица *m/f*

dune [djuːn] дюна

dung [dʌŋ] навоз

duplic|ate 1. ['djuːplɪkɪt] **a)** двойной; запасной; **b)** дубликат; копия; **in ~** в двух экземплярах; **2.** [-keɪt] снимать, делать копию с (P); удваивать [удвоить]; **~ity** [djuː'plɪsɪtɪ] двуличность *f*

dura|ble ['djʊərəbl] □ прочный; длительный; **~tion** [djʊə'reɪʃn] продолжительность *f*

during ['djʊərɪŋ] *prp.* в течение (P), во время (P)

dusk [dʌsk] сумерки; **~y** ['dʌskɪ] □ сумеречный; *skin* смуглый

dust [dʌst] **1.** пыль *f*; **2.** *(wipe)* вытирать пыль; **~bin** *Brt.* *(Am. trash can)* мусорное ведро; **~er** ['dʌstə] тряпка для вытирания пыли; **~y** ['dʌstɪ] □ пыльный

Dutch [dʌtʃ] **1.** голландец *m*, -дка *f*; **2.** голландский; **the ~** голландцы *pl.*

duty ['djuːtɪ] долг, обязанность *f*; дежурство; *fin.* пошлина; **off ~** свободный от дежурства; **~free** *adv.* беспошлинно

dwarf [dwɔːf] **1.** карлик; **2.** [по]мешать росту; казаться маленьким (по сравнению с Т)

dwell [dwel] [*irr.*] жить; **~ (up)on** останавливаться [-новиться] на (П); **~ing** ['dwelɪŋ] жилище, дом

dwelt [dwelt] *pt. и pt. p. om* **dwell**

dwindle ['dwɪndl] уменьшаться [уменьшиться], сокращаться [-ратиться]

dye [daɪ] **1.** краска; краситель; *fig.* **of the deepest ~** отъявленный; **2.** [по-, вы]красить, окрашивать [окрасить]

dying ['daɪɪŋ] *(s. die¹)* **1.** умирающий; *words* предсмертный; **2.** умирание; смерть

dynam|ic [daɪ'næmɪk] динамический; *fig.* динамичный; активный; энергичный; **~ics** [-ɪks] *mst. sg.* динамика; **~ite** ['daɪnəmaɪt] динамит

E

each [iːtʃ] ка́ждый; ~ *other* друг дру́га

eager ['iːgə] □ стремя́щийся; (*diligent*) усе́рдный; энерги́чный; **~ness** [-nɪs] пыл, рве́ние

eagle ['iːgl] орёл, орли́ца

ear [ɪə] у́хо (*pl.*: у́ши); *mus.* слух; **~drum** бараба́нная перепо́нка

earl [ɜːl] граф (англи́йский)

early ['ɜːlɪ] 1. ра́нний; (*premature*) преждевре́менный; *at the earliest* в лу́чшем слу́чае; *it is too*... *to draw conclusions* де́лать вы́воды преждевре́менно; 2. *adv.* ра́но; (*timely*) заблаговре́менно; *as ~ as* уже́, ещё; как мо́жно ра́ньше

earmark ['ɪəmɑːk] (*set aside*) предназнача́ть [-зна́чить]

earn [ɜːn] зараба́тывать [-бо́тать]; *fig.* заслу́живать [-жи́ть]

earnest ['ɜːnɪst] 1. □ серьёзный; убеждённый; и́скренний; 2. серьёзность *f*; *in* ~ серьёзно, всерьёз

earnings ['ɜːnɪŋz] за́работок

ear|phones ['ɪəfəʊnz] нау́шники *m./pl.*; **~ring** серьга́, серёжка; **~shot** преде́лы слы́шимости

earth [ɜːθ] 1. земля́, земно́й шар; (*soil*) земля́, по́чва; 2. *v/t.* (~ *up*) зары(ва́)ть; зака́пывать [закопа́ть]; *el.* заземля́ть [-ли́ть]; **~en** [-n] земляно́й; **~enware** [-nweə] гли́няная посу́да; **~ly** [-lɪ] земно́й; **~quake** [-kweɪk] землетрясе́ние; **~worm** земляно́й червь *m.*, *coll.* червя́к

ease [iːz] 1. лёгкость *f*; непринуждённость *f*; *at* ~ свобо́дно, удо́бно; *feel ill at* ~ чу́вствовать себя́ нело́вко; 2. облегча́ть [-чи́ть]; успока́ивать [-ко́ить]

easel ['iːzl] мольбе́рт

easiness ['iːzɪnɪs] → *ease 1*

east [iːst] 1. восто́к; 2. восто́чный; 3. *adv.* на восто́ку, восто́ку (*of* от Р)

Easter ['iːstə] Па́сха

easter|ly ['iːstəlɪ] с восто́ка; **~n** ['iːstən] восто́чный

eastward(s) ['iːstwəd(z)] на восто́к

easy ['iːzɪ] лёгкий; споко́йный; непринуждённый; *take it* ~! не торопи́(те)сь; споко́йнее!; ~ *chair* кре́сло; **~going** *fig.* благоду́шный; беззабо́тный

eat [iːt] 1. [*irr.*] [съ]есть; (*damage*) разъеда́ [-е́сть] (*mst.* **away**, *into*); 2. *pt. om eat 1*; **~able** ['iːtəbl] съедо́бный; **~en** ['iːtn] *pt. p. om eat 1*

eaves [iːvz] *pl.* карни́з; **~drop** подслу́ш(ив)ать

ebb [eb] 1. (*a.* ~*tide*) отли́в; *fig.* переме́на к ху́дшему; 2. *of tide* убы(ва́)ть; *fig.* ослабе(ва́)ть

ebony ['ebənɪ] чёрное де́рево

eccentric [ɪk'sentrɪk] 1. *fig.* эксцентри́чный; 2. чуда́к

ecclesiastical [ɪkliːzɪ'æstɪkl] □ духо́вный, церко́вный

echo ['ekəʊ] 1. э́хо; *fig.* отголо́сок; 2. отдава́ться э́хом

eclair [ɪ'kleə] экле́р

eclipse [ɪ'klɪps] 1. затме́ние; 2. затмева́ть [-ми́ть] (*a. fig.*); заслоня́ть [-ни́ть]

ecology [ɪ'kɒlədʒɪ] эколо́гия

econom|ic [iːkə'nɒmɪk] экономи́ческий; **~ical** [-l] эконо́мный, бережли́вый; **~ics** [-ɪks] *pl.* эконо́мика

econom|ist [ɪ'kɒnəmɪst] экономи́ст; **~ize** [-maɪz] [с]эконо́мить; **~y** [-mɪ] эконо́мия; бережли́вость *f*; *national* ~ эконо́мика страны́

ecsta|sy ['ekstəsɪ] экста́з, восто́рг; **~tic** [ɪk'stætɪk] (**~ally**) восто́рженный

eddy ['edɪ] водоворо́т

edge [edʒ] 1. край; *of knife* ле́звие, остриё; *of forest* опу́шка; *of cloth* кро́мка; *of road* обо́чина; *be on* ~ быть в не́рвном состоя́нии; 2. (*border*) окаймля́ть [-ми́ть]; ~ *one's way* ... пробира́ться [-бра́ться]; **~ways** [-weɪz], **~wise** [-waɪz] кра́ем, бо́ком

edging ['edʒɪŋ] край, кайма́, бордю́р; *of photo, etc.* оканто́вка

edible ['edɪbl] съедо́бный

E

edit ['edɪt] [от]редакти́ровать; *film* [с]монти́ровать; ~**ion** [ɪ'dɪʃn] **1.** изда́ние; ~**or** ['edɪtə] реда́ктор; ~**orial** [edɪ'tɔ:rɪəl] **1.** реда́кторский; редакцио́нный; ~ *office* реда́кция; **2.** передова́я статья́; ~**orship** ['edɪtəʃɪp]: *under the* ~ под реда́кцией

educat|e ['edjukeɪt] дава́ть образова́ние (Д); (*bring up*) воспи́тывать [-та́ть]; ~**ion** [edju'keɪʃn] образова́ние, воспита́ние; ~**ional** [edju'keɪʃnl] образова́тельный; педагоги́ческий; уче́бный

eel [i:l] у́горь *m*

effect [ɪ'fekt] **1.** (*result*) сле́дствие; результа́т; *phys.* эффе́кт; (*action*) де́йствие; (*impression*) эффе́кт, впечатле́ние; (*influence*) влия́ние; ~**s** *pl.* иму́щество; *come into* ~ вступа́ть в си́лу; *in* ~ в су́щности; *to no* ~ напра́сный; *to the* ~ сле́дующего содержа́ния; **2.** производи́ть [-вести́]; выполня́ть [вы́полнить]; соверша́ть [-ши́ть]; ~**ive** [-ɪv] эффекти́вный, действи́тельный; *tech.* поле́зный; ~**ual** [-ʃʊəl] *remedy, etc.* де́йственный, эффекти́вный

effeminate [ɪ'femɪnət] □ женоподо́бный

effervescent [efə'vesnt] **1.** шипу́чий; **2.** *fig.* бры́зжущий весе́льем

efficacy ['efɪkəsɪ] де́йственность *f*

efficien|cy [ɪ'fɪʃnsɪ] делови́тость *f*; эффекти́вность *f*; ~**t** [-nt] □ делови́тый; уме́лый, продукти́вный; эффекти́вный

effort ['efət] уси́лие; попы́тка

effrontery [ɪ'frʌntərɪ] на́глость *f*

effusive [ɪ'fju:sɪv] □ экспанси́вный; несде́ржанный

egg¹ [eg] яйцо́; *scrambled* ~**s** *pl.* яи́чница-болту́нья; *fried* ~**s** *pl.* яи́чница-глазу́нья; *hard-boiled* (*soft-boiled*) ~ яйцо́ вкруту́ю (всмя́тку); ~**shell** яи́чная скорлупа́

egg² [-] подстрека́ть [-кну́ть] (*mst.* ~ *on*)

egotism ['egəʊtɪzəm] эгои́зм, самомне́ние

Egyptian [ɪ'dʒɪpʃn] **1.** египтя́нин *m*,

-я́нка *f*; **2.** еги́петский

eight [eɪt] **1.** во́семь; **2.** восьмёрка; ~**een** [eɪ'ti:n] восемна́дцать; ~**eenth** [eɪ'ti:nθ] восемна́дцатый; ~**h** [eɪtθ] **1.** восьмо́й; **2.** восьма́я часть *f*; ~**ieth** ['eɪtɪəθ] восьмидеся́тый; ~**y** ['eɪtɪ] во́семьдесят

either ['aɪðə] **1.** *pron.* оди́н из двух; любо́й, ка́ждый; тот и́ли друго́й; и тот и друго́й, о́ба; **2.** *cj.* ~ ... *or* ... и́ли ... и́ли ...; ли́бо ... ли́бо ...; *not* (...) ~ та́кже не

ejaculate [ɪ'dʒækjʊleɪt] (*cry out*) восклица́ть [-ли́кнуть]; изверга́ть се́мя

eject [ɪ'dʒekt] (*throw out*) выгоня́ть [вы́гнать]; *from house* выселя́ть [вы́селить]; *lava* изверга́ть [-е́ргнуть]; *smoke* выпуска́ть [вы́пустить]

eke [i:k]: ~ *out* восполня́ть [-по́лнить], ~ *out a livelihood* перебива́ться кое-ка́к

elaborat|e [ɪ'læbərət] □ сло́жный; тща́тельно разрабо́танный; **2.** [-reɪt] разраба́тывать [-бо́тать]; разви́(ва́)ть; ~**ion** [ɪ,læbə'reɪʃn] разрабо́тка; разви́тие; уточне́ние

elapse [ɪ'læps] проходи́ть [пройти́], протека́ть [проте́чь]

elastic [ɪ'læstɪk] **1.** (~**ally**) эласти́чный, упру́гий; **2.** рези́нка; ~**ity** [elæ'stɪsɪtɪ] эласти́чность *f*, упру́гость *f*

elated [ɪ'leɪtɪd] □ в припо́днятом настрое́нии

elbow ['elbəʊ] **1.** ло́коть *m*; *of pipe, etc.* коле́но; *at one's* ~ под руко́й, ря́дом; **2.** прота́лкиваться [-толкну́ться]; ~ *out* выта́лкивать [вы́толкнуть]; ~**room** ме́сто, простра́нство; *fig.* свобо́да де́йствий

elder¹ ['eldə] *bot.* бузина́

elder² [-] **1.** ста́рец, ста́рший; ~**ly** ['eldəlɪ] пожило́й

eldest ['eldɪst] са́мый ста́рший

elect [ɪ'lekt] **1.** *by vote* изб(и)ра́ть; (*choose, decide*) выбира́ть [вы́брать]; реша́ть [-ши́ть]; **2.** и́збранный; ~**ion** [-kʃn] вы́боры *m/pl.*; ~**or** [-tə] избира́тель *m*; ~**oral** [-tərəl] избира́тельный; ~**orate** [-tərət] избира́тели *m/pl.*

electri|c [ɪ'lektrɪk] электри́ческий; ~ *circuit* электри́ческая цепь f; ~*cal* [-trɪk] □ электри́ческий; ~ *engineering* электроте́хника; ~*cian* [ɪlek'trɪʃn] электромонтёр

electri|city [ɪˌlek'trɪsətɪ] электри́чество; ~*fy* [ɪ'lektrɪfaɪ] электрифици́ровать (*im*)*pf*.; [на]электризова́ть (*a. fig.*)

electron [ɪ'lektrɒn] электро́н; ~*ic* [ɪlek'trɒnɪk] электро́нный; ~ *data processing* электро́нная обрабо́тка да́нных; ~*ics* электро́ника

elegan|ce ['elɪɡəns] элега́нтность f; изя́щество; ~*t* ['elɪɡənt] □ элега́нтный, изя́щный

element ['elɪmənt] элеме́нт (*a. tech., chem.*); черта́; до́ля; *the* ~*s* стихи́я; ~*s pl.* осно́вы f/pl.; *in one's* ~ в свое́й стихи́и; *there is an* ~ *of truth in this* в э́том есть до́ля пра́вды; ~*al* [elɪ'mentl] стихи́йный; ~*ary* [-trɪ] □ элемента́рный; *elementaries pl.* осно́вы f/pl.

elephant ['elɪfənt] слон

elevat|e ['elɪveɪt] поднима́ть [-ня́ть]; повыша́ть [-вы́сить]; *fig.* возвыша́ть [-вы́сить]; ~*ion* [elɪ'veɪʃn] возвыше́ние; (*elevated place*) возвы́шенность f; (*height*) высота́; ~*or* ['elɪveɪtə] *for grain* элева́тор, *for lifting loads* грузоподъёмник; *Am.* лифт

eleven [ɪ'levn] оди́ннадцать; ~*th* [-θ] 1. оди́ннадцатый; 2. оди́ннадцатая часть f

elf [elf] эльф; прока́зник

elicit [ɪ'lɪsɪt] ~ *the truth* добива́ться [-би́ться] и́стины

eligible ['elɪdʒəbl] □ име́ющий пра́во быть и́збранным; (*suitable*) подходя́щий

eliminat|e [ɪ'lɪmɪneɪt] устраня́ть [-ни́ть]; уничтожа́ть [-то́жить]; (*exclude*) исключа́ть [-чи́ть]; ~*ion* [ɪlɪmɪ-'neɪʃn] устране́ние; уничтоже́ние; *by a process of* ~ ме́тодом исключе́ния

elk [elk] *zo.* лось *m*

elm [elm] *bot.* вяз

eloquen|ce ['eləkwəns] красноре́чие; ~*t* [-t] □ красноречи́вый

else [els] ещё; кро́ме; ина́че; ино́й, дру-

го́й; *or* ~ а то; и́ли же; ~*where* [els'weə] где́-нибудь в друго́м ме́сте

elucidate [ɪ'lu:sɪdeɪt] разъясня́ть [-ни́ть]

elude [ɪ'lu:d] избега́ть [-ежа́ть] (P), уклоня́ться [-ни́ться] от (P); *of meaning* ускольза́ть [-зну́ть]

elusive [ɪ'lu:sɪv] неулови́мый

emaciated [ɪ'meɪʃɪeɪtɪd] истощённый, худо́й

email, E-mail ['i:meɪl] электро́нная по́чта

emanate ['eməneɪt] идти́ из (P); *rumours* исходи́ть (*from* из, от P)

emancipat|e [ɪ'mænsɪpeɪt] освобожда́ть [освободи́ть]; ~*ion* [ɪmænsɪ-'peɪʃn] освобожде́ние, эмансипа́ция

embankment [ɪm'bæŋkmənt] на́сыпь f; *by river or sea* на́бережная

embargo [em'bɑ:ɡəʊ] эмба́рго *n indecl.*; запре́т; *be under* ~ быть под запре́том

embark [ɪm'bɑ:k] *of goods* [по]грузи́ть(ся); *of passengers* сади́ться [сесть]; *fig.* ~ (*up*)*on* бра́ться [взя́ться] (за B); предпринима́ть [-ня́ть]

embarrass [ɪm'bærəs] смуща́ть [смути́ть]; приводи́ть [-вести́] в замеша́тельство; стесня́ть [-ни́ть]; ~*ed by lack of money* в стеснённом положе́нии; ~*ing* [-ɪŋ] □ затрудни́тельный; неудо́бный, стеснённый; ~*ment* [-mənt] (*difficulties*) затрудне́ние; смуще́ние; (*confusion*) замеша́тельство

embassy ['embəsɪ] посо́льство

embellish [ɪm'belɪʃ] украша́ть [укра́сить]

embers ['embəz] *pl.* тле́ющие у́гли *m/pl.*

embezzle [ɪm'bezl] растра́чивать [-а́тить]; ~*ment* [-mənt] растра́та

embitter [ɪm'bɪtə] озлобля́ть [озло́бить], ожесточа́ть [-чи́ть]

emblem ['embləm] эмбле́ма; си́мвол; *national* ~ госуда́рственный герб

embody [ɪm'bɒdɪ] воплоща́ть [-лоти́ть]; (*personify*) олицетворя́ть [-ри́ть]; (*include*) включа́ть [-чи́ть]

embrace [ɪm'breɪs] 1. объя́тие; 2. обнима́ть(ся) [-ня́ть(ся)]; (accept) принима́ть [-ня́ть]; (include) охва́тывать [охвати́ть]

embroider [ɪm'brɔɪdə] вы́ши(ва́)ть; ~y [-rɪ] вышива́ние; вы́шивка

embroil [ɪm'brɔɪl] запу́т(ыв)ать(ся); вя́зываться [-за́ться]

emerald ['emərəld] изумру́д

emerge [ɪ'mɜːdʒ] появля́ться [-ви́ться]; (surface) всплы(ва́)ть (a. fig.); ~ncy [-ənsɪ] чрезвыча́йная (авари́йная) ситуа́ция; in an ~ в слу́чае кра́йней необходи́мости; attr. запасно́й, вспомога́тельный; ~ landing вы́нужденная поса́дка

emigra|nt ['emɪɡrənt] эмигра́нт; ~te [-ɡreɪt] эмигри́ровать (im)pf.; ~tion [emɪ'ɡreɪʃn] эмигра́ция

eminen|ce ['emɪnəns] geogr. возвы́шенность f; fig. знамени́тость f; win ~ as a scientist стать pf. знамени́тым учёным; ~t [-ənt] □ fig. выдаю́щийся; adv. чрезвыча́йно

emit [ɪ'mɪt] sound, smell изд(ав)а́ть, испуска́ть [-усти́ть]; light излуча́ть; heat выделя́ть [вы́делить]

emoti|on [ɪ'məʊʃn] чу́вство; возбужде́ние; волне́ние; эмо́ция mst. pl.; ~onal [-ʃənl] □ эмоциона́льный; voice взволно́ванный; music, etc. волну́ющий

emperor ['empərə] импера́тор

empire ['empaɪə] импе́рия

employ [ɪm'plɔɪ] употребля́ть [-би́ть], применя́ть [-ни́ть], испо́льзовать (im)pf.; предоставля́ть, нанима́ть на рабо́ту (Д); ~ee [emplɔɪ'iː] слу́жащий [-щая], рабо́тник (-ица); ~er [ɪm'plɔɪə] нанима́тель m, работода́тель m; ~ment [-mənt] (use) примене́ние; рабо́та, заня́тие; ~ agency бюро́ по трудоустро́йству; full ~ по́лная за́нятость

empower [ɪm'paʊə] уполномо́чи(ва)ть

empress ['emprɪs] императри́ца

empt|iness ['emptɪnɪs] пустота́; ~y [-tɪ] **1.** □ пусто́й, поро́жний; coll. голо́дный; I feel ~ я го́лоден; **2.** опорожня́ть(ся) [-ни́ть(ся)]; [о]пусте́ть; liquid вылива́ть [вы́лить]; sand, etc. высыпа́ть [вы́сыпать]

enable [ɪ'neɪbl] дава́ть возмо́жность f; [с]де́лать возмо́жным (Д)

enact [ɪ'nækt] law постановля́ть [-ви́ть]; thea. игра́ть роль; ста́вить на сце́не

enamel [ɪ'næml] **1.** эма́ль f; art эма́ль, obs. фи́нифть; **2.** эмалирова́ть (im)pf.; покрыва́ть эма́лью

enamo(u)red [ɪ'næməd]: ~ of влюблённый в (В)

enchant [ɪn'tʃɑːnt] очаро́вывать [-ова́ть]; ~ment [-mənt] очарова́ние; ~ress [-rɪs] fig. обворожи́тельная же́нщина, волше́бница

encircle [ɪn'sɜːkl] окружа́ть [-жи́ть]

enclos|e [ɪn'kləʊz] (fence in) огора́живать [-роди́ть]; in letter, etc. прилага́ть [-ложи́ть]; ~ure [-ʒə] огоро́женное ме́сто; вложе́ние, приложе́ние

encompass [ɪn'kʌmpəs] окружа́ть [-жи́ть]

encore ['ɒŋkɔː] thea. **1.** бис!; **2.** крича́ть "бис"; вызыва́ть [вы́звать] на бис; (give an encore) бисова́ть

encounter [ɪn'kaʊntə] **1.** встре́ча; столкнове́ние; (contest, competition) состяза́ние; **2.** встреча́ть(ся) [-е́тить(ся)]; difficulties etc. ста́лкиваться [столкну́ться] (с Т); ната́лкиваться [натолкну́ться] (на В)

encourage [ɪn'kʌrɪdʒ] ободря́ть [-ри́ть]; поощря́ть [-ри́ть]; ~ment [-mənt] ободре́ние; поощре́ние

encroach [ɪn'krəʊtʃ] ~ (up)on вторга́ться [вто́ргнуться] в (В); rights посяга́ть (на В); time отнима́ть [-ня́ть]; ~ment [-mənt] вторже́ние

encumb|er [ɪn'kʌmbə] обременя́ть [-ни́ть]; (cram) загроможда́ть [-мозди́ть]; (hamper) затрудня́ть [-ни́ть]; [вос]препя́тствовать (Д); ~rance

E

[-brəns] бре́мя *n*; обу́за; *fig.* препя́тствие

encyclop(a)edia [ɪnsaɪklə'piːdɪə] энциклопе́дия

end [end] **1.** коне́ц, оконча́ние; цель *f*; *no ~ of* о́чень мно́го (P); *in the ~* в конце́ концо́в; *on ~* сто́ймя; *hair* ды́бом; беспреры́вно, подря́д; *to that ~* с э́той це́лью; **2.** конча́ть(ся) [ко́нчить(ся)]

endanger [ɪn'deɪndʒə] подверга́ть опа́сности

endear [ɪn'dɪə] внуша́ть любо́вь, заставля́ть полюби́ть; **~ment** [-mənt] ла́ска; *words of ~* ла́сковые слова́

endeavo(u)r [ɪn'devə] **1.** [по]пыта́ться, прилага́ть уси́лия, [по]стара́ться; **2.** попы́тка, стара́ние; *make every ~* сде́лать всё возмо́жное

end|ing ['endɪŋ] оконча́ние; **~less** ['endlɪs] □ бесконе́чный

endorse [ɪn'dɔːs] *fin.* индосси́ровать (*im*)*pf.*; (*approve*) одобря́ть [одо́брить]; **~ment** [-'dɔːsmənt] индоссаме́нт, одобре́ние

endow [ɪn'daʊ] одаря́ть [-ри́ть]; (*give*) [по]же́ртвовать; **~ment** [-mənt] поже́ртвование, дар

endur|ance [ɪn'djʊərəns] *physical* про́чность *f*; *mental* выно́сливость *f*; **~e** [ɪn'djʊə] выноси́ть [вы́нести]; терпе́ть

enema ['enɪmə] кли́зма

enemy ['enəmɪ] враг; неприя́тель *m*; проти́вник

energ|etic [enə'dʒetɪk] (**~ally**) энерги́чный; **~y** ['enədʒɪ] эне́ргия

enfold [ɪn'fəʊld] (*embrace*) обнима́ть [обня́ть]; (*wrap up*) заку́тывать [-тать]

enforce [ɪn'fɔːs] заставля́ть [-а́вить], принужда́ть [-ди́ть]; *a law* вводи́ть [ввести́]; *strengthen* уси́ли(ва)ть

engage [ɪn'geɪdʒ] *v/t.* (*employ*) нанима́ть [наня́ть]; *rooms* заброни́ровать; *in activity* занима́ть [заня́ть]; (*attract*) привлека́ть [-е́чь]; завладе́(ва́)ть; *in conversation* вовлека́ть [-е́чь]; *be ~d* быть за́нятым; быть помо́лвленным; *v/i.* (*pledge*) обя́зываться [-за́ться]; занима́ться

(*in* T); **~ment** [-mənt] обяза́тельство; встре́ча, свида́ние; помо́лвка

engaging [ɪn'geɪdʒɪŋ] □ очарова́тельный

engender [ɪn'dʒendə] *fig.* порожда́ть [породи́ть]

engine ['endʒɪn] *mot.* дви́гатель, мото́р; *rail.* парово́з; **~ driver** машини́ст

engineer [endʒɪ'nɪə] **1.** инжене́р; *naut.* меха́ник; *Am.* машини́ст; **2.** *fig.* подстра́ивать [-ро́ить]; **~ing** [-rɪŋ] машинострое́ние

English ['ɪŋglɪʃ] **1.** англи́йский; **2.** англи́йский язы́к; **~** англича́не *pl.*; **~man** [-mən] англича́нин; **~woman** [-ˌwʊmən] англича́нка

engrave [ɪn'greɪv] [вы́]гравирова́ть; *fig. in mind* запечатле́(ва́)ть; **~ing** [-ɪŋ] гравирова́ние; гравю́ра, эста́мп

engross [ɪn'grəʊs] поглоща́ть [-лоти́ть]; **~ing book** захва́тывающая кни́га

enhance [ɪn'hɑːns] *value, etc.* повыша́ть [повы́сить]; (*intensify*) уси́ли(ва)ть

enigma [ɪ'nɪgmə] зага́дка; **~tic** [enɪg'mætɪk] □ зага́дочный

enjoy [ɪn'dʒɔɪ] наслажда́ться [насла-ди́ться] (T); получа́ть [-чи́ть] удово́льствие; *~ o.s.* развлека́ться [-ле́чь]; *~ good health* облада́ть хоро́шим здоро́вьем; **~able** [-əbl] прия́тный; **~ment** [-mənt] наслажде́ние, удово́льствие

enlarge [ɪn'lɑːdʒ] увели́чи(ва)ть(-ся); распространя́ться (*on* о П); *~ one's mind* расширя́ть [-ши́рить] кругозо́р; **~ment** [-mənt] расшире́ние; *of photo, etc.* увеличе́ние

enlighten [ɪn'laɪtn] просвеща́ть [-ети́ть]; разъясня́ть [-ни́ть]; **~ment** просвеще́ние; *of a person* просвещённость *f*

enlist [ɪn'lɪst] *v/i. mil.* поступа́ть [-пи́ть] на вое́нную слу́жбу; *~ help* привле́чь на по́мощь

enliven [ɪn'laɪvn] оживля́ть [-ви́ть]

enmity ['enmɪtɪ] вражда́, неприя́знь *f*

ennoble [ɪ'nəʊbl] облагора́живать

[-ро́дить]

enorm|ity [ı'nɔ:mətı] необъя́тность *f*; *pej.* чудо́вищность *f*; преступле́ние; **~ous** [-əs] □ огро́мный, грома́дный; чудо́вищный

enough [ı'nʌf] доста́точно, дово́льно

enquire [ın'kwaıə] → **inquire**

enrage [ın'reıdʒ] [вз]беси́ть, приводи́ть в я́рость

enrapture [ın'ræptʃə] восхища́ть [-ити́ть], очаро́вывать

enrich [ın'rıtʃ] обогаща́ть [-гати́ть]

enrol(l) [ın'rəʊl] *v/t.* запи́сывать [-са́ть]; [за]регистри́ровать; *v/i.* запи́сываться [-са́ться]; **~ment** [-mənt] регистра́ция; за́пись *f*

en route [ˌɒn'ru:t] по доро́ге

ensign ['ensaın] флаг; *Am. naut.* мла́дший лейтена́нт

ensue [ın'sju:] (*follow*) [по]сле́довать; получа́ться в результа́те

ensure [ın'ʃʊə] обеспе́чивать [-чить]; (*guarantee*) руча́ться [поручи́ться] (за В)

entail [ın'teıl] влечь за собо́й, вызыва́ть [вы́звать]

entangle [ın'tæŋgl] запу́тывать(ся), (*a. fig.*)

enter ['entə] *v/t.* room, etc. входи́ть [войти́] в (В); *university* поступа́ть [-пи́ть] в (В); *in book* вноси́ть [внести́]; (*penetrate*) проника́ть [-ни́кнуть] в (В); *v/i.* входи́ть [войти́], вступа́ть [-пи́ть]

enterpris|e ['entəpraız] предприя́тие; (*quality*) предприи́мчивость *f*; **~ing** [-ıŋ] □ предприи́мчивый

entertain [entə'teın] *guests* принима́ть [-ня́ть]; (*give food to*) угоща́ть [угости́ть]; (*amuse*) развлека́ть [-ле́чь], занима́ть [заня́ть]; **~ment** [-mənt] развлече́ние; приём

enthusias|m [ın'θju:zıæzm] восто́рг; энтузиа́зм; **~t** [-æst] энтузиа́ст(ка); **~tic** [ınθju:zı'æstık] (**~ally**) восто́рженный; по́лный энтузиа́зма

entice [ın'taıs] зама́нивать [-ни́ть]; (*tempt*) соблазня́ть [-ни́ть]; **~ment** [-mənt] собла́зн; прима́нка

entire [ın'taıə] □ це́лый, весь; сплош-

ной; **~ly** [-lı] всеце́ло; соверше́нно

entitle [ın'taıtl] (*give a title to*) озагла́вливать [-ла́вить]; дава́ть пра́во (Д)

entity ['entıtı] бытие́; су́щность *f*

entrails ['entreılz] *pl.* вну́тренности *f/pl.*

entrance ['entrəns] вход, въезд; *actor's* вы́ход; (*right to enter*) до́ступ; **~ examinations** вступи́тельные экза́мены

entreat [ın'tri:t] умоля́ть; **~y** [-ı] мольба́, про́сьба

entrench [ın'trentʃ] *fig.* укореня́ться [-ни́ться]

entrust [ın'trʌst] поруча́ть [-чи́ть]; доверя́ть [-ве́рить]

entry ['entrı] вход, въезд; *of an actor on stage* вход/вы́ход; *in book* за́пись; *No* ⊘ вход (въезд) запрещён

enumerate [ı'nju:məreıt] перечисля́ть [-и́слить]

envelop [ın'veləp] (*wrap*) заку́т(ыв)ать; *of mist, etc.* оку́т(ыв)ать; **~e** ['envələʊp] конве́рт

envi|able ['envıəbl] □ зави́дный; **~ous** [-əs] □ зави́стливый

environ|ment [ın'vaıərənmənt] окружа́ющая среда́; **~mental** окружа́ющий; **~ protection** охра́на окружа́ющей среды́; **~s** [ın'vaıərənz] *pl.* окре́стности *f/pl.*

envisage [ın'vızıdʒ] представля́ть себе́; (*anticipate*) предви́деть; (*consider*) рассма́тривать [-смотре́ть]

envoy ['envɔı] (*messenger*) посла́нец; (*diplomat*) посла́нник; полномо́чный представи́тель *m*

envy ['envı] **1.** за́висть *f*; **2.** [по]зави́довать (Д)

epic ['epık] **1.** эпи́ческая поэ́ма; **2.** эпи́ческий

epicenter (-tre) ['epısentə] эпице́нтр

epidemic [epı'demık] эпиде́мия

epilogue ['epılɒg] эпило́г

episode ['epısəʊd] слу́чай, эпизо́д, происше́ствие

epitome [ı'pıtəmı] (*embodiment*) воплоще́ние *f/pl.*

epoch ['i:pɒk] эпо́ха

equable ['ekwəbl] □ ро́вный; *fig.* уравнове́шенный

equal ['i:kwəl] **1.** □ ра́вный; одина́ковый; **~ to** *fig.* спосо́бный на (В); **2.** равня́ться (Д); **~ity** [ɪ'kwɒlətɪ] ра́венство; **~ization** [i:kwəlaɪ'zeɪʃn] ура́внивание; **~ize** [-aɪz] ура́внивать [-ня́ть]

equanimity [ekwə'nɪmɪtɪ] споко́йствие, душе́вное равнове́сие

equat|ion [ɪ'kweɪʒn] *math.* уравне́ние; **~or** [-tə] эква́тор

equilibrium [i:kwɪ'lɪbrɪəm] равнове́сие

equip [ɪ'kwɪp] *office, etc.* обору́довать; *expedition, etc.* снаряжа́ть [-яди́ть]; (*provide*) снабжа́ть [-бди́ть]; **~ment** [-mənt] обору́дование; снаряже́ние

equity ['ekwɪtɪ] справедли́вость *f*; беспристра́стность *f*; *fin. pl.* обыкнове́нные а́кции *f/pl.*

equivalent [ɪ'kwɪvələnt] **1.** эквивале́нт (**to** Д); **2.** равноце́нный; равноси́льный

equivocal [ɪ'kwɪvəkəl] □ двусмы́сленный; (*questionable*) сомни́тельный

era ['ɪərə] э́ра; эпо́ха

eradicate [ɪ'rædɪkeɪt] искореня́ть [-ни́ть]

eras|e [ɪ'reɪz] стира́ть [стере́ть]; подчища́ть [-и́стить]; **~er** [-ə] *Am.* рези́нка

erect [ɪ'rekt] **1.** □ прямо́й; (*raised*) по́днятый; **2.** [по]стро́ить, воздвига́ть [-и́гнуть]; **~ion** [ɪ'rekʃn] постро́йка, сооруже́ние, строе́ние

ermine ['ɜ:mɪn] *zo.* горноста́й

erosion [ɪ'rəʊʒn] эро́зия

erotic [ɪ'rɒtɪk] эроти́ческий

err [ɜ:] ошиба́ться [-би́ться], заблужда́ться

errand ['erənd] поруче́ние

errat|ic [ɪ'rætɪk] (**~ally**) неусто́йчивый; *player, behavio(u)r* неро́вный; **~um** [e'rɑːtəm], *pl.* **~a** [-tə] опеча́тка, опи́ска

erroneous [ɪ'rəʊnɪəs] □ оши́бочный

error ['erə] оши́бка, заблужде́ние; по-

гре́шность *f* (*a. astr.*)

eruption [ɪ'rʌpʃn] изверже́ние; *on face, etc.* высыпа́ние (сы́пи); *of teeth* проре́зывание

escalator ['eskəleɪtə] эскала́тор

escapade ['eskəpeɪd] проде́лка; ша́льная вы́ходка

escape [ɪ'skeɪp] **1.** *v/i. from prison* бежа́ть; *from death* спаса́ться [спасти́сь]; *v/t. danger, etc.* избега́ть [-ежа́ть]; ускольза́ть [-зну́ть] (от Р); **his name ~s me** не могу́ припо́мнить его́ и́мени; **2.** побе́г, спасе́ние; (*leak*) уте́чка

escort 1. ['eskɔ:t] сопровожде́ние, эско́рт; *mil.* конво́й; **2.** [ɪs'kɔ:t, -ɔ:rt] сопровожда́ть, конвои́ровать

esoteric [esəʊ'terɪk] эзотери́ческий

especial [ɪ'speʃl] осо́бый; специа́льный; **~ly** [-ɪ] осо́бенно

espionage ['espɪənɑ:ʒ] шпиона́ж

essay ['eseɪ] о́черк, эссе́; (*attempt*) попы́тка; *educ.* сочине́ние

essen|ce ['esns] су́щность *f*; существо́; суть *f*; (*substance*) эссе́нция; **~tial** [ɪ'senʃl] **1.** □ суще́ственный (**to** для Р), ва́жный; **2.** *pl.* всё необходи́мое

establish [ɪ'stæblɪʃ] *the truth, etc.* устана́вливать [-нови́ть], (*set up*) учрежда́ть [-реди́ть], осно́вывать [-ова́ть]; **~ o.s.** поселя́ться [-ли́ться], устра́иваться [-ро́иться] (в П); **~ order** наводи́ть [-вести́] поря́док; **~ment** [-mənt] установле́ние; учрежде́ние; **the** 2 исте́блишмент

estate [ɪ'steɪt] (*property*) иму́щество; (*land with a large house*) име́ние; **real ~** недви́жимость *f*

esteem [ɪ'sti:m] **1.** уваже́ние; **2.** уважа́ть

estimable ['estɪməbl] досто́йный уваже́ния

estimat|e 1. ['estɪmeɪt] оце́нивать [-ни́ть]; **2.** [-mɪt] сме́та, калькуля́ция; оце́нка; **at a rough ~** в гру́бом приближе́нии; **~ion** [estɪ'meɪʃn] оце́нка; (*opinion*) мне́ние

estrange [ɪ'streɪndʒ] отта́лкивать [-толкну́ть], сде́лать чужи́м

etching ['etʃɪŋ] *craft* гравиро́вка;

product гравю́ра; травле́ние

etern|al ['ɪtɜːnl] ве́чный; неизме́нный; **~ity** [-nɪtɪ] ве́чность *f*

ether ['iːθə] эфи́р

ethic|al ['eθɪkl] □ эти́чный, эти́ческий; **~s** ['eθɪks] э́тика

etiquette ['etɪket] этике́т

euro ['jʊərəʊ] е́вро

European [jʊərə'piːən] **1.** европе́ец *m*, -пе́йка *f*; **2.** европе́йский

Eurovision ['jʊərəvɪʒn] Еврови́дение

evacuate [ɪ'vækjʊeɪt] эвакуи́ровать (*im*)*pf.*

evade [ɪ'veɪd] (*avoid*) избега́ть [-жа́ть] (P); уклоня́ться [-ни́ться] от (P); *law, etc.* обходи́ть [обойти́]

evaluat|e [ɪ'væljʊeɪt] оце́нивать [-ни́ть]; **~ion** [ɪvæljʊ'eɪʃn] оце́нка

evaporat|e [ɪ'væpəreɪt] испаря́ть(-ся) [-ри́ть(ся)]; *fig.* развева́ться [-е́яться]; **~ion** [ɪvæpə'reɪʃn] испаре́ние

evas|ion [ɪ'veɪʒn] уклоне́ние, увёртка; **~ve** [-sɪv] □ укло́нчивый

eve [iːv] кану́н; **on the ~ of** накану́не (P)

even ['iːvn] **1.** *adj.* □ (*level, smooth*) ро́вный, гла́дкий; (*equal*) ра́вный, одина́ковый; *number* чётный; **2.** *adv.* ро́вно; как раз; **not ~** да́же не; **~ though, ~ if** да́же е́сли; **3.** выра́внивать [вы́ровнять]; сгла́живать [сгла́дить]; **~ly** [-lɪ] ро́вно, по́ровну

evening ['iːvnɪŋ] ве́чер; вечери́нка; **~ dress** вече́рнее пла́тье; *man's* фрак

event [ɪ'vent] собы́тие, слу́чай; *sport* соревнова́ние; **at all ~s** во вся́ком слу́чае; **be wise after the ~** за́дним умо́м кре́пок; **in the ~ of** в слу́чае (P); **~ful** [-fʊl] по́лный собы́тий

eventual [ɪ'ventʃʊəl] возмо́жный; коне́чный; **~ly** [-ɪ] в конце́ концо́в; со вре́менем

ever ['evə] всегда́; когда́-нибудь, когда́-либо; **~ so** о́чень; **as soon as ~ I can** как то́лько я смогу́; **for ~** навсегда́; **hardly ~** почти́ не; **~green** вечнозелёный; **~lasting** [evə'lɑːstɪŋ] □ ве́чный; **~present** постоя́нный

every ['evrɪ] ка́ждый; **~ now and then**

вре́мя от вре́мени; **~ other day** че́рез день; **have ~ reason** име́ть все основа́ния; **~body** все *pl.*; ка́ждый, вся́кий; **~day** ежедне́вный; **~one** ка́ждый, вся́кий; все *pl.*; **~thing** всё; **~where** везде́, всю́ду

evict [ɪ'vɪkt] выселя́ть [вы́селить]

eviden|ce ['evɪdəns] доказа́тельство; (*sign*) при́знак; (*data*) да́нные, фа́кты; *law* ули́ка; свиде́тельское показа́ние; **in ~** в доказа́тельство; **~t** [-nt] □ очеви́дный, я́вный

evil ['iːvl] **1.** □ злой; *influence* па́губный; дурно́й, плохо́й; **2.** зло

evince [ɪ'vɪns] проявля́ть [-ви́ть]

evoke [ɪ'vəʊk] вызыва́ть [вы́звать]

evolution [iːvə'luːʃn] эволю́ция; разви́-тие

evolve [ɪ'vɒlv] разви(ва́)ться

ewe [juː] овца́

exact [ɪg'zækt] **1.** □ то́чный, аккура́тный; **2.** (*demand*) [по]тре́бовать (P); взы́скивать [-ка́ть]; **~ taxes** взима́ть нало́ги; **~ing** [-ɪŋ] тре́бовательный, взыска́тельный

exaggerate [ɪg'zædʒəreɪt] преувели́чи(ва)ть

exalt [ɪg'zɔːlt] (*make higher*) повыша́ть [повы́сить]; (*praise*) превозноси́ть [-нести́]; **~ation** [egzɔːl'teɪʃn] восто́рг

examin|ation [ɪgzæmɪ'neɪʃn] (*inspection*) осмо́тр; (*study*) иссле́дование; **by experts** эксперти́за; **in school, etc.** экза́мен; **~e** [ɪg'zæmɪn] *patient, etc.* осма́тривать [-мотре́ть], иссле́довать (*im*)*pf.*; [про]экзаменова́ть

example [ɪg'zɑːmpl] приме́р; (*sample*) образе́ц; **for ~** наприме́р

exasperate [ɪg'zɑːspəreɪt] изводи́ть [извести́]; раздража́ть [-жи́ть]; доводи́ть до бе́лого кале́ния

excavate ['ekskəveɪt] выка́пывать [вы́копать]; *archaeology* вести́ раско́пки

excavator ['ekskəveɪtə] экскава́тор

exceed [ɪk'siːd] *speed, etc.* превыша́ть [-вы́сить]; (*be greater than*) превосходи́ть [-взойти́]; **this ~s all limits!** э́то перехо́дит все грани́цы!; **~ing** [-ɪŋ]

□ превыша́ющий

excel [ɪk'sel] v/t. преуспева́ть [-пе́ть] (**in, at** T); v/i. выделя́ться [вы́делиться] (**in** T); **~lence** ['eksələns] высо́кое ка́чество; соверше́нство; **~lent** ['eksələnt] □ превосхо́дный

except [ɪk'sept] 1. исключа́ть [-чи́ть]; 2. prp. исключа́я (В); кро́ме (Р); **~ for** за исключе́нием (Р); **~ing** [-ɪŋ] prp. за исключе́нием (Р); **~ion** [ɪk'sepʃn] исключе́ние; **take ~ to** возража́ть [-рази́ть] (про́тив Р); **~ional** [-l] исключи́тельный; person незауря́дный

excess [ɪk'ses] избы́ток, изли́шек; эксце́сс; **~ fare** допла́та; **~ luggage** изли́шек багажа́: бага́ж сверх но́рмы; **~ profits** сверхпри́быль; **~ive** [-ɪv] □ чрезме́рный

exchange [ɪks'tʃeɪndʒ] 1. обме́ниваться [-ня́ться] (T); обме́нивать [-ня́ть] (**for** на В); [по]меня́ться (T); 2. обме́н; (a. 2) би́ржа; **foreign ~** иностра́нная валю́та

exchequer [ɪks'tʃekə]: **Chancellor of the 2** мини́стр фина́нсов Великобрита́нии

excise [ek'saɪz] fin. акци́з, акци́зный сбор

excit|able [ɪk'saɪtəbl] возбуди́мый; **~e** [ɪk'saɪt] возбужда́ть [-уди́ть], [вз]волнова́ть; **~ement** [-mənt] возбужде́ние, волне́ние

exclaim [ɪk'skleɪm] восклица́ть [-и́кнуть]

exclamation [eksklə'meɪʃn] восклица́ние

exclude [ɪk'sklu:d] исключа́ть [-чи́ть]

exclusi|on [ɪk'sklu:ʒn] исключе́ние; **~ve** [-sɪv] □ исключи́тельный; (sole) еди́нственный; **~ of** без; не счита́я; за исключе́нием (Р)

excrement ['ekskrɪmənt] экскреме́нты m/pl., испражне́ния n/pl.

excruciating [ɪk'skru:ʃɪeɪtɪŋ] мучи́тельный

excursion [ɪk'skɜ:ʒn] экску́рсия; **go on an ~** отпра́виться (пое́хать) на экску́рсию

excus|able [ɪk'skju:zəbl] □ прости́тельный; **~e 1.** [ɪk'skju:z] извиня́ть

[-ни́ть], проща́ть [прости́ть]; 2. [ɪk'skju:s] извине́ние; (reason) оправда́ние; (pretext) отгово́рка

execut|e ['eksɪkju:t] (carry out) исполня́ть [-о́лнить]; (fulfil) выполня́ть [вы́полнить]; (put to death) казни́ть (im)pf.; **~ion** [eksɪ'kju:ʃn] исполне́ние; выполне́ние; (capital punishment) казнь f; **~ive** [ɪg'zekjʊtɪv] 1. исполни́тельный; администрати́вный; 2. исполни́тельная власть f; (person) администра́тор

exemplary [ɪg'zempləri] образцо́вый, приме́рный

exemplify [ɪg'zemplɪfaɪ] (illustrate by example) поясня́ть приме́ром; (serve as example) служи́ть приме́ром (Р)

exempt [ɪg'zempt] 1. освобожда́ть [-боди́ть] (от Р); 2. освобождённый, свобо́дный (**of** от Р)

exercise ['eksəsaɪz] 1. упражне́ние; (drill) трениро́вка; (walk) прогу́лка. 2. [на]трениро́ва́ть(ся); patience, etc. проявля́ть [-ви́ть]; (use) [вос]по́льзоваться

exert [ɪg'zɜ:t] strength, etc. напряга́ть [-ря́чь]; influence, etc. ока́зывать [-за́ть]; **~ o.s.** прилага́ть [-ложи́ть] уси́лия; **~ion** [ɪg'zɜ:ʃn] напряже́ние, уси́лие

exhale [eks'heɪl] выдыха́ть [вы́дохнуть]

exhaust [ɪg'zɔ:st] 1. изнуря́ть [-ри́ть], истоща́ть [-щи́ть]; 2. pipe выхлопна́я труба́; вы́хлоп; **~ion** [-ʃn] истоще́ние, изнуре́ние; **~ive** [-ɪv] □ (very tiring) изнуря́ющий; study, etc. всесторо́нний; answer исче́рпывающий

exhibit [ɪg'zɪbɪt] 1. interest etc. проявля́ть [-ви́ть]; at exhibition выставля́ть [вы́ставить]; 2. экспона́т; **~ion** [eksɪ'bɪʃn] проявле́ние; вы́ставка; **~or** [ɪg'zɪbɪtə] экспоне́нт

exhilarat|e [ɪg'zɪləreɪt] оживля́ть [-ви́ть]; [вз]бодри́ть; **~ing** [-ɪŋ] weather, etc. бодря́щий

exhort [ɪg'zɔ:t] призыва́ть [-зва́ть]; увещева́ть; побужда́ть [-уди́ть] (к Д)

exigency ['eksɪdʒənsɪ] о́страя необходи́мость f

exile ['eksaɪl] **1.** lit., hist. изгна́ние, ссы́лка; изгна́нник, ссы́льный; **2.** ссыла́ть [сосла́ть]; from a country вы́сыла́ть [вы́слать]

exist [ɪg'zɪst] существова́ть, жить; **~ence** [-əns] существова́ние, жизнь f; **in ~ = ~ent** [-ənt] существу́ющий

exit ['eksɪt] вы́ход; **emergency~** запасно́й вы́ход

exodus ['eksədəs] ма́ссовый отъе́зд; Bibl. Исхо́д

exonerate [ɪg'zɒnəreɪt] опра́вдывать [-да́ть]; (free from blame) снима́ть [снять] обвине́ние; from responsibility снима́ть [снять] отве́тственность

exorbitant [ɪg'zɔːbɪtənt] □ непоме́рный, чрезме́рный

exotic [ɪg'zɒtɪk] экзоти́ческий

expan|d [ɪk'spænd] расширя́ть(ся) [-и́рить(ся), увели́чи(ва)ть(ся); (develop) разви(ва́)ть(ся); **~se** [ɪk'spæns] простра́нство; протяже́ние; **~sion** [-nʃn] расшире́ние; (spread) распростране́ние; разви́тие; **~sive** [-sɪv] □ обши́рный; fig. экспанси́вный

expect [ɪks'pekt] ожида́ть (P); (count on) рассчи́тывать, наде́яться; (think) полага́ть, ду́мать; **~ant** [-ənt]: **~ mother** бере́менная же́нщина; **~ation** [ekspek'teɪʃn] ожида́ние; (hope) mst. pl. наде́жда

expedi|ent [ɪk'spiːdɪənt] **1.** подходя́щий, целесообра́зный, соотве́тствующий; **2.** сре́дство достиже́ния це́ли; приём; **~tion** [ekspɪ'dɪʃn] экспеди́ция; (speed) быстрота́

expel [ɪk'spel] from school, etc. исключа́ть [-чи́ть] (из P)

expen|d [ɪk'spend] [из]тра́тить; [из]-расхо́довать; **~diture** [-dɪtʃə] расхо́д, тра́та; **~se** [ɪk'spens] расхо́д, тра́та; **at his~** за его́ счёт; **travel~s** командиро́вочные; **~sive** [-sɪv] □ дорого́й, дорогосто́ящий

experience [ɪk'spɪərɪəns] **1.** (жи́зненный) о́пыт; (event) слу́чай, приключе́ние; **2.** испы́тывать [испыта́ть]; (suffer) пережи(ва́)ть; **~d** [-t]

о́пытный; квалифици́рованный

experiment 1. [ɪk'sperɪmənt] о́пыт, экспериме́нт; **2.** [-ment] производи́ть о́пыты; **~al** [ɪkspperɪ'mentl] □ эксперимента́льный, про́бный

expert ['ekspɜːt] **1.** о́пытный, иску́сный; **2.** экспе́рт, знато́к, специали́ст; attr. высококвалифици́рованный

expir|ation [ekspɪ'reɪʃn] (end) оконча́ние, истече́ние; **~e** [ɪk'spraɪə] (breathe out) выдыха́ть [вы́дохнуть]; (die) умира́ть [умере́ть]; fin. истека́ть [-е́чь]

explain [ɪk'spleɪn] объясня́ть [-ни́ть]; (justify) опра́вдывать [-да́ть]

explanat|ion [eksplə'neɪʃn] объясне́ние; (justification) оправда́ние; (reason) причи́на; **~ory** [ɪk'splænətrɪ] объясни́тельный

explicable [ɪk'splɪkəbl] объясни́мый

explicit [ɪk'splɪsɪt] □ я́сный, недвусмы́сленный, то́чный

explode [ɪk'spləʊd] (blow up) взрыва́ть(ся) [взорва́ть(ся)] (a. fig); of applause etc. разража́ться [-рази́ться] (**with** T)

exploit 1. ['eksplɔɪt] по́двиг; **2.** [ɪk'splɔɪt] эксплуати́ровать; mining разраба́тывать [-бо́тать]; **~ation** [eksplɔɪ'teɪʃn] эксплуата́ция; разрабо́тка

explor|ation [eksplə'reɪʃn] иссле́дование; **~e** [ɪk'splɔː] иссле́довать (im)pf.; geol. разве́д(ыв)ать; problem, etc. изуча́ть [-чи́ть]; **~er** [-rə] иссле́дователь(ница f) m

explosi|on [ɪk'spləʊʒn] взрыв; of anger вспы́шка; **~ve** [-sɪv] **1.** □ взры́вчатый; fig. вспы́льчивый; **2.** взры́вчатое вещество́

exponent [ɪk'spəʊnənt] (advocate) сторо́нник, представи́тель m; math. показа́тель m сте́пени; (interpreter) толкова́тель m

export 1. ['ekspɔːt] э́кспорт, вы́воз; **2.** [ɪk'spɔːt] экспорти́ровать (im)pf., вывози́ть [вы́везти]; **~er** [-ə] экспортёр

expose [ɪk'spəʊz] to danger, etc. подверга́ть [-е́ргнуть]; (display) выставля́ть [вы́ставить]; (*unmask*) разоблача́ть [-чи́ть]; *phot.* экспони́ровать (*im*)*pf.*; **∼ition** [ekspə'zıʃn] вы́ставка; изложе́ние

exposure [ık'spəʊʒə] (*unmasking*) разоблаче́ние; *phot.* экспози́ция, вы́держка; возде́йствие вне́шней среды́; *die of* ∼ умере́ть от *переохлажде́ния и т.д.*

expound [ık'spaʊnd] излага́ть [изложи́ть]; (*explain*) разъясня́ть [-ни́ть]

express [ık'spres] **1.** □ (*clearly stated*) определённый, то́чно вы́раженный; (*urgent*) сро́чный; **2. ∼** (*train*) экспре́сс; **3.** *adv.* спе́шно; **∼ion** [ık'spreʃn] выраже́ние; (*quality*) вырази́тельность *f*; **∼ive** [-ıv] □ (*full of feeling*) вырази́тельный; (∼ *of joy, etc.*) выража́ющий

expulsion [ık'spʌlʃn] изгна́ние; *form school, etc.* исключе́ние; *from country* вы́сылка

exquisite [ık'skwızıt] □ изы́сканный, утончённый; *sensibility* обострённый; *torture* изощрённый

extant [ık'stænt] сохрани́вшийся

extemporaneous [ekstempə'reınıəs] □, **∼ary** [ık'stempərərı] импровизи́рованный; **∼e** [-pərı] *adv.* экспро́мтом

extend [ık'stend] *v/t.* протя́гивать [-тяну́ть]; (*spread*) распространя́ть [-ни́ть]; (*prolong*) продлева́ть [-ли́ть]; (*enlarge*) расширя́ть [-ши́рить]; *v/i.* простира́ться [простере́ться]

extension [ık'stenʃn] (*enlargement*) расшире́ние; *of knowledge etc.* распростране́ние; (*continuance*) продле́ние; *arch.* пристро́йка; **∼ve** [-sıv] □ обши́рный, простра́нный

extent [ık'stent] (*area, length*) протяже́ние; (*degree*) сте́пень *f*, ме́ра; *to the ∼ of* в разме́ре (P); *to some ∼* до изве́стной сте́пени

extenuate [ık'stenjʊeıt] (*lessen*) уменьша́ть [уме́ньшить]; (*find excuse for*) стара́ться найти́ оправда́ние; (*soften*) ослабля́ть [-а́бить]

exterior [ek'stıərıə] **1.** вне́шний, нару́жный; **2.** вне́шняя сторона́

exterminate [ek'stɜːmıneıt] (*destroy*) истребля́ть [-би́ть]; *fig.* искореня́ть [-ни́ть]

external [ek'stɜːnl] □ нару́жный, вне́шний

extinct [ık'stıŋkt] уга́сший; *species, etc.* вы́мерший; *volcano etc.* поту́хший

extinguish [ık'stıŋgwıʃ] [по]гаси́ть; [по]туши́ть; *debt* погаша́ть [погаси́ть]

extol [ık'stəʊl] превозноси́ть [-нести́]

extort [ık'stɔːt] *money* вымога́ть; *secret* выпы́тывать [вы́пытать]; **∼ion** [ık'stɔːʃn] вымога́тельство

extra ['ekstrə] **1.** доба́вочный, дополни́тельный; **∼** *charges* дополни́тельная (о)пла́та; **2.** *adv.* особо́, особенно; дополни́тельно; **3.** припла́та; **∼s** *pl.* дополни́тельные расхо́ды; побо́чные дохо́ды

extract 1. ['ekstrækt] экстра́кт; *from text* вы́держка, отры́вок; **2.** [ık'strækt] *tooth* удаля́ть [-ли́ть]; *bullet etc.* извлека́ть [-е́чь]; *chem.* экстраги́ровать; **∼ion** [-kʃn] экстраги́рование; (*ancestry, origin*) происхожде́ние

extraordinary [ık'strɔːdnrı] чрезвыча́йный, необы́чный, экстраордина́рный, выдаю́щийся

extrasensory [ekstrə'sensərı] внечу́вственный, экстрасенсо́рный

extravagance [ık'strævəgəns] экстравага́нтность *f*; (*wastefulness*) расточи́тельность *f*; (*excess*) изли́шество; **∼t** [-gənt] □ расточи́тельный; сумасбро́дный; экстравага́нтный

extreme [ık'striːm] **1.** □ кра́йний; преде́льный; чрезвыча́йный; **2.** кра́йность *f*; *go to ∼* пойти́ на кра́йние ме́ры; **∼ity** [ık'stremətı] (*end*) оконе́чность *f*, край; кра́йность *f*; кра́йняя нужда́; кра́йняя ме́ра; **∼ities** [-z] *pl.* коне́чности *f/pl.*

extricate ['ekstrıkeıt] высвобожда́ть [вы́свободить], вы́зволить *mst. pl.*; **∼** *o.s.* выпу́тываться [вы́путаться]

exuberance [ıg'zjuːbərəns] изоби́лие, избы́ток; **∼t** [-t] *vegetation* бу́йный; *speech* обильный, несдержанный; (*full of life*) полный жизни, экспансивный

exult [ɪgˈzʌlt] ликовать; торжествовать

eye [aɪ] **1.** глаз; *of needle* ушко; **with an ~ to** с целью (+ *inf.*); **catch s.o.'s ~** поймать чей-л. взгляд; обратить на себя внимание; **2.** смотреть на (В), пристально разглядывать; ~**ball** глазное яблоко; ~**brow** бровь *f*; ~...**ed** [aid] …глазый; ~**lash** ресница; ~**lid** веко; ~**sight** зрение; ~ **shadow** тени для век; ~**witness** свидетель, очевидец

F

fable [ˈfeɪbl] басня; *fig.* выдумка

fabric [ˈfæbrɪk] (*structure*) структура; (*cloth*) ткань *f*; ~**ate** [ˈfæbrɪkeɪt] (*mst. fig.*) выдумывать [выдумать]; (*falsify*) [с]фабриковать

fabulous [ˈfæbjʊləs] □ баснословный; (*excellent*) великолепный

face [feɪs] **1.** лицо, *joc. or pej.* физиономия; *of cloth* лицевая сторона; *of watch* циферблат; **on the ~ of it** с первого взгляда; **2.** *v/t.* встречать смело; смотреть в лицо (Д); стоять лицом к (Д); *of window, etc.* выходить на (В); *tech.* облицовывать [-цевать]

facetious [fəˈsiːʃəs] □ шутливый

face value номинальная стоимость; **take s.th. at (its) ~** принимать [-нять] за чистую монету

facil|itate [fəˈsɪlɪteɪt] облегчать [-чить]; ~**ity** [fəˈsɪlətɪ] лёгкость *f*; способность *f*; *of speech* плавность *f*

facing [ˈfeɪsɪŋ] *of wall, etc.* облицовка

fact [fækt] факт; **as a matter of ~** собственно говоря; **I know for a ~ that** я точно знаю, что

faction [ˈfækʃn] фракция

factor [ˈfæktə] *math.* множитель; (*contributing cause*) фактор; ~**y** [-rɪ] фабрика, завод

faculty [ˈfækəltɪ] способность *f*; *fig.* дар; *univ.* факультет

fad [fæd] (*craze*) увлечение; (*fancy*) прихоть *f*, причуда; (*fashion*) преходящая мода

fade [feɪd] увядать [увянуть]; постепенно уменьшать [уменьшить]; *of colo(u)r* [по]линять

fag [fæg] усталость, утомление

fail [feɪl] **1.** *v/i.* (*grow weak*) ослабе(ва)ть; (*be wanting in*) недост(ав)ать; потерпеть *pf.* неудачу; *at examination* провалиться [-литься]; *he ~ed to do* ему не удалось сделать (В); забы(ва)ть; *v/t. of courage, etc.* покидать [-инуть]; **2.** *su.:* **without ~** непременно, наверняка; ~**ing** [ˈfeɪlɪŋ] недостаток; слабость *f*; ~**ure** [ˈfeɪljə] неудача, неуспех; провал; банкротство; неудачник *m*, -ница *f*; *tech.* повреждение, отказ

faint [feɪnt] **1.** □ слабый; *light* тусклый; **2.** [о]слабеть; потерять сознание (**with** от Р); **3.** обморок, потеря сознания; ~**hearted** [feɪntˈhɑːtɪd] трусливый, малодушный

fair¹ [feə] **1.** *adj.* прекрасный, красивый; (*favo[u]rable*) благоприятный; *hair* белокурый; *weather* ясный; (*just*) справедливый; **2.** *adv.* честно; прямо, ясно; ~ **copy** чистовик; ~ **play** честная игра

fair² [-] ярмарка

fair|ly [ˈfeəlɪ] справедливо; (*quite*) довольно; ~**ness** [ˈfeənɪs] справедливость *f*; красота (→ **fair¹**); **in all ~** со всей справедливостью

fairy [ˈfeərɪ] фея; ~**land** сказочная страна; ~ **tale** сказка

faith [feɪθ] доверие, вера, *a. relig.*; ~**ful** [ˈfeɪθfl] верный, преданный; (*accurate*) точный, правдивый; **yours ~ly** преданный Вам; ~**less** [ˈfeɪθlɪs] □ вероломный

fake [feɪk] *sl.* **1.** подделка, фальшивка;

2. подде́л(ыв)ать

falcon ['fɔ:lkən] со́кол

fall [fɔ:l] **1.** паде́ние; (*decline*) упа́док; (*declivity, slope*) обры́в, склон; *Am.* о́сень *f*; (*mst.* ~**s** *pl.*) водопа́д; **2.** [*irr.*] па́дать [упа́сть]; спада́ть [спасть]; *of water* убы(ва́)ть; ~ **back** отступа́ть [-пи́ть]; ~ **ill** *или* **sick** заболе(ва́)ть; ~ **out** [по]ссо́риться; ~ **short of** не оправда́ть (ожида́ний); не достига́ть [-и́чь] *a.* [-и́гнуть] (це́ли); ~ **short** уступа́ть в чём-л., не хвата́ть [-ти́ть]; ~ **to** принима́ться [-ня́ться] за (В)

fallacious [fə'leɪʃəs] □ оши́бочный, ло́жный

fallacy ['fæləsɪ] заблужде́ние, оши́бочный вы́вод

fallen ['fɔ:lən] *pt. p. om* **fall**

falling ['fɔ:lɪŋ] паде́ние; пониже́ние

fallout ['fɔ:ləʊt]: *radioactive* ~ радиоакти́вные оса́дки

fallow ['fæləʊ] *adj.* вспа́ханный под пар

false [fɔ:ls] □ ло́жный, оши́бочный; *coin* фальши́вый; *friend* веро́ломный; *teeth* иску́сственный; ~**hood** ['fɔ:lshʊd] ложь *f*; (*falseness*) лжи́вость *f*

falsi|fication [fɔ:lsɪfɪ'keɪʃn] подде́лка; *of theories, etc.* фальсифика́ция; ~**fy** ['fɔ:lsɪfaɪ] подде́л(ыв)ать; фальсифици́ровать

falter ['fɔ:ltə] *in walking* дви́гаться неуве́ренно; *in speech* запина́ться [запну́ться]; *fig.* колеба́ться

fame [feɪm] сла́ва, изве́стность *f*; ~**d** [feɪmd] изве́стный, знамени́тый; **be** ~ **for** сла́виться (Т)

familiar [fə'mɪlɪə] □ бли́зкий, хорошо́ знако́мый; (*usual*) привы́чный; ~**ity** [fəmɪlɪ'ærətɪ] (*of manner*) *a.* pej. фамилья́рность *f*; (*knowledge*) осведомлённость *f*; ~**ize** [fə'mɪlɪəraɪz] ознакомля́ть [-ко́мить]

family ['fæmɪlɪ] семья́, семе́йство; ~ **tree** родосло́вное де́рево

fami|ne ['fæmɪn] го́лод; ~**sh**: **I feel** ~**ed** я умира́ю от го́лода

famous ['feɪməs] □ знамени́тый

fan¹ [fæn] **1.** ве́ер; *tech.* вентиля́тор; **2.:**

~ **o.s.** обма́хивать(ся) [-хну́ть(ся)] ве́ером

fan² [-] *sport* боле́льщик *m*, -щица *f*, фана́т; (*admirer*) покло́нник *m*, -ница *f*

fanatic [fə'nætɪk] **1.** (*a.* ~**al** [-ɪkəl] □) фанати́чный; **2.** фана́тик *m*, -ти́чка *f*

fanciful ['fænsɪfl] □ прихотли́вый, причу́дливый

fancy ['fænsɪ] **1.** фанта́зия, воображе́ние; (*whim*) при́хоть *f*; (*love*) пристра́стие; (*inclination*) скло́нность *f*; **2.** *prices* фантасти́ческий; ~ **goods** *pl.* мо́дные това́ры *m/pl.*; **3.** вообража́ть [-рази́ть]; представля́ть [-а́вить] себе́; [по]люби́ть; [за]хоте́ть; **just** ~**!** предста́вьте себе́!

fang [fæŋ] клык

fantas|tic [fæn'tæstɪk] (~**ally**) причу́дливый, фантасти́чный; *coll.* невероя́тный; потряса́ющий; ~**y** ['fæntəsɪ] фанта́зия, воображе́ние

far [fɑ:] *adj.* да́льний, далёкий, отдалённый; *adv.* далеко́; гора́здо; **as** ~ **as** до (Р); **as** ~ **as I know** наско́лько мне изве́стно; **inso**~ (*Brt.* **in so** ~) **as** поско́льку; ~ **away** далеко́

fare [feə] пла́та за прое́зд; ~**well** [feə'wel, feɑr-] **1.** проща́й(те)!; **2.** проща́ние

farfetched [fɑ:'fetʃt] *fig.* притя́нутый за́ уши

farm [fɑ:m] **1.** фе́рма; **2.** обраба́тывать зе́млю; ~**er** ['fɑ:mə] фе́рмер; ~**house** жило́й дом на фе́рме; ~**ing** заня́тие се́льским хозя́йством; фе́рмерство; ~**stead** ['fɑ:msted] уса́дьба

far-off ['fɑ:rɒf] далёкий

farthe|r ['fɑ:ðə] **1.** *adv.* да́льше; **2.** *adj.* бо́лее отдалённый; ~**st** [-ðɪst] **1.** *adj.* са́мый далёкий, са́мый да́льний; **2.** *adv.* да́льше всего́

fascinat|e ['fæsɪneɪt] очаро́вывать [-ова́ть], пленя́ть [-ни́ть]; ~**ion** [fæsɪ'neɪʃn] очарова́ние

fashion ['fæʃn] **1.** (*prevailing style*) мо́да; стиль *m*; (*manner*) о́браз, мане́ра; **in (out of)** ~ (не)мо́дный; **2.** придава́ть фо́рму, вид (Д *into* Р); ~**able** ['fæʃnəbl] мо́дный

fast¹ [fɑːst] (*fixed, firm*) про́чный, кре́пкий, твёрдый; (*quick*) бы́стрый; **my watch is ~** мои́ часы́ спеша́т

fast² [-] **1.** (*going without food*) пост; **2.** пости́ться

fasten ['fɑːsn] *v/t.* (*fix*) прикрепля́ть [-пи́ть]; (*tie*) привя́зывать [-за́ть]; *coat, etc.* застёгивать [-тегну́ть]; *door* запира́ть [-пере́ть]; *v/i.* застёгиваться [застегну́ться]; застёгивать(ся) [-тегну́ть(ся)]; ~ **upon** *fig.* ухвати́ться за (В); ~**er** [-ə] застёжка

fast food фаст-фу́д

fastidious [fæ'stɪdɪəs] □ разбо́рчивый; *about food* приверéдливый

fat [fæt] **1.** жи́рный; *person* ту́чный; **2.** жир; са́ло

fatal ['feɪtl] роково́й, фата́льный; (*causing death*) смерте́льный; ~**ity** [fə'tælətɪ] (*doom*) обречённость *f*; (*destiny*) фата́льность *f*; (*caused by accident*) же́ртва; смерть *f*

fate [feɪt] рок, судьба́

father ['fɑːðə] оте́ц; ~**hood** [-hʊd] отцо́вство; ~**-in-law** ['fɑːðərɪnlɔː] *husband's* свёкор; *wife's* тесть *m*; ~**less** [-lɪs] оста́вшийся без отца́; ~**ly** [-lɪ] оте́ческий

fathom ['fæðəm] *fig.* вника́ть [вни́кнуть] в (В), понима́ть [поня́ть]

fatigue [fə'tiːg] **1.** утомле́ние, уста́лость *f*; **2.** утомля́ть [-ми́ть]

fat‖**ness** ['fætnɪs] жи́рность *f*; ~**ten** ['fætn] *animal* отка́рмливать [откорми́ть]; [рас]толсте́ть

fatuous ['fætʃʊəs] □ бессмы́сленный, глу́пый

faucet ['fɔːsɪt] *esp. Am.* водопрово́дный кран

fault [fɔːlt] (*shortcoming*) недоста́ток; *tech.* неиспра́вность *f*, дефе́кт; (*blame*) вина́; **find ~ with** прид(и)ра́ться к (Д); **be at ~** быть вино́вным; ~**finder** приди́ра *m/f*; ~**less** ['fɔːltlɪs] □ безупре́чный; ~**y** ['fɔːltɪ] □ *thing* с бра́ком, с дефе́ктом; *method* поро́чный

favo(u)r ['feɪvə] **1.** благоскло́нность *f*,

расположе́ние; одолже́ние, любе́зность *f*; **do s.o. a ~** оказа́ть *pf.* кому́-л. любе́зность; **2.** (*approve*) одобря́ть [-ри́ть]; (*regard with goodwill*) хорошо́ относи́ться к (Д); *opportunity* удо́бный; ~**able** [-rəbl] □ благоприя́тный; ~**ite** ['feɪvərɪt] **1.** люби́мец *m*, -мица *f*, фавори́т; **2.** люби́мый

fawn [fɔːn] све́тло-кори́чневый цвет

fax [fæks] **1.** факс; **2.** передава́ть [-да́ть] по фа́ксу

fear [fɪə] **1.** страх, боя́знь *f*; (*apprehension*) опасе́ние; **2.** боя́ться (Р) **for ~ of** из-за боя́зни; ~**ful** ['fɪəfl] □ стра́шный, ужа́сный; ~**less** ['fɪəlɪs] бесстра́шный

feasible ['fiːzəbl] (*capable of being done*) выполни́мый, осуществи́мый, возмо́жный

feast [fiːst] банке́т; пир, пи́ршество; *eccl.* церко́вный *или* престо́льный пра́здник

feat [fiːt] по́двиг

feather ['feðə] перо́, **show the white ~** *coll.* прояви́ть тру́сость *f*; ~**brained** пустоголо́вый

feature ['fiːtʃə] **1.** черта́; осо́бенность *f*, сво́йство; *Am.* выдаю́щаяся газе́тная статья́; ~**s** *pl.* черты́ лица́; **2.** *in story* фигури́ровать; *of a film* пока́зывать [-за́ть]; **the film ~s a new actor as** ... в фи́льме с уча́стием но́вого актёра в ро́ли ...

February ['fɛbrʊərɪ] февра́ль *m*

fed [fed] *pt. и pt. p. om* **feed**; **I am ~ up with** ... мне надое́л (-ла, -ло)

federa‖**l** ['fedərəl] федера́льный; *in names of states* федерати́вный; ~**tion** [fedə'reɪʃn] федера́ция

fee [fiː] *doctor's, etc.* гонора́р; *member's* взнос; *for tuition* пла́та

feeble ['fiːbl] □ сла́бый, хи́лый

feed [fiːd] **1.** *agric.* корм, фура́ж; *baby's* еда́, кормле́ние; *of a machine* пита́ние; **2.** [*irr.*] *v/t.* [по]корми́ть; пита́ть, подава́ть; *v/i.* пита́ться, корми́ться; (*graze*) пасти́сь; ~**back** *tech.* обра́тная связь; ~**ing bottle** де́тский рожо́к

feel [fiːl] **1.** [*irr.*] [по]чу́вствовать

(себя́); (experience) испы́тывать [-та́ть]; by contact ощуща́ть [ощути́ть]; (touch) [по]тро́гать; (grope) нащу́п(ыв)ать; ~ like doing быть скло́нным сде́лать; 2.: get the ~ of привыка́ть [-ы́кнуть]; ~ing ['fiːlɪŋ] чу́вство, ощуще́ние

feet [fiːt] pl. om foot 1

feign [feɪn] притворя́ться [-ри́ться], симули́ровать (im)pf.

feint [feɪnt] (sham offensive) финт, диве́рсия

fell [fel] 1. pt. om fall; 2. tree, etc. [с]руби́ть

fellow ['feləʊ] па́рень; (companion) това́рищ; professional колле́га, сотру́дник; of a college член сове́та; ~-countryman сооте́чественник; ~ship [-ʃɪp] това́рищество

felt¹ [felt] pt. и pt. p. om feel

felt² [~] во́йлок, фетр

female ['fiːmeɪl] 1. же́нский; 2. же́нщина; zo. са́мка

feminine ['femɪnɪn] □ же́нский; же́нственный

fen [fen] боло́то, топь f

fence [fens] 1. забо́р, и́згородь f, огра́да; sit on the ~ занима́ть нейтра́льную пози́цию; 2. v/t. отгора́живать [-роди́ть]; v/i. sport фехтова́ть

fencing ['fensɪŋ] 1. и́згородь f, забо́р, огра́да; sport фехтова́ние; 2. attr. фехтова́льный

fender ['fendə] (fire screen) ками́нная решётка; of car, Am. крыло́

ferment 1. ['fɜːment] заква́ска, ферме́нт; chem.. броже́ние (a. fig.); 2. [fə'ment] вызыва́ть броже́ние; броди́ть; ~ation [fɜːmen'teɪʃn] броже́ние

fern [fɜːn] па́поротник

ferocilous [fə'rəʊʃəs] □ свире́пый; dog злой; ~ty [fə'rɒsətɪ] свире́пость f

ferret ['ferɪt] 1. zo. хорёк; 2. [по]ры́ться, [по]ша́рить; ~ out выи́скивать [вы́искать]; secret разню́хивать [-хать]; вы́ведать pf.

ferry ['ferɪ] 1. (place for crossing river, etc.) перево́з, перепра́ва; (boat) паро́м; 2. перевози́ть [-везти́]; ~man перево́зчик

fertile ['fɜːtaɪl] □ soil плодоро́дный; humans, animals плодови́тый (a. fig.); ~ imagination бога́тое воображе́ние; ~ity [fə'tɪlətɪ] плодоро́дие; плодови́тость f; ~ize ['fɜːtɪlaɪz] удобря́ть [удо́брить]; оплодотворя́ть [-ри́ть]; ~izer ['fɜːtɪlaɪzə] удобре́ние

fervent ['fɜːvənt] горя́чий, пы́лкий

fervo(u)r ['fɜːvə] жар, пыл, страсть f

fester ['festə] гнои́ться

festival ['festəvl] пра́здник; фестива́ль m; ~e ['festɪv] □ пра́здничный; ~ity [fe'stɪvətɪ] пра́зднество; торжество́

fetch [fetʃ] сходи́ть, съе́здить за (Т); приноси́ть [-нести́]; ~ing [-ɪŋ] □ привлека́тельный

fetter ['fetə] 1. mst. ~s pl. пу́ты f/pl.; fig. око́вы f/pl., у́зы f/pl.; 2. fig. свя́зывать [-за́ть] по рука́м и нога́м

feud [fjuːd] family вражда́ f

feudal ['fjuːdl] □ феода́льный

fever ['fiːvə] лихора́дка, жар; ~ish [-rɪʃ] □ лихора́дочный

few [fjuː] немно́гие; немно́го, ма́ло (P); a ~ не́сколько (P); a good ~ дово́льно мно́го

fiancé(e) [fɪ'ɒnseɪ] жени́х (неве́ста)

fiasco [fɪ'æskəʊ] прова́л, по́лная неуда́ча, фиа́ско

fib [fɪb] 1. вы́думка, непра́вда; 2. прив(и)ра́ть

fiber, Brt. fibre ['faɪbə] волокно́, нить f

fickle ['fɪkl] непостоя́нный

fiction ['fɪkʃn] вы́мысел, вы́думка; худо́жественная литерату́ра, белетри́стика; science ~ нау́чная фанта́стика; ~al [-l] □ вы́мышленный

fictitious [fɪk'tɪʃəs] □ подло́жный, фикти́вный; вы́мышленный

fiddle ['fɪdl] coll. 1. скри́пка; fig. a cheat жу́льничество; 2. игра́ть на скри́пке; fig. обма́нывать

fidelity [fɪ'delətɪ] ве́рность f, пре́данность f; (accuracy) то́чность f

fidget ['fɪdʒɪt] coll. 1. непосе́да; ёрзать, верте́ться; ~y [-ɪ] суетли́вый, беспоко́йный, не́рвный; child непосе́дливый

field [fiːld] по́ле; (meadow) луг; fig. область; **~ events** лёгкая атле́тика; **~ glasses** полево́й бино́кль *m*; **~ of vision** по́ле зре́ния; **~work** *geol., etc.* рабо́та в по́ле

fiend [fi:nd] дья́вол; *person* злоде́й; **~ish** ['fi:ndıʃ] □ дья́вольский, жесто́кий, злой

fierce [fıəs] □ свире́пый; *frost, etc.* лю́тый; *wind, etc.* си́льный; **~ness** ['fıəsnıs] свире́пость *f*, лю́тость *f*

fif|teen [fıf'ti:n] пятна́дцать; **~teenth** [-θ] пятна́дцатый; **~th** [fıfθ] **1.** пя́тый; **2.** пя́тая часть *f*; **~tieth** ['fıftııθ] пятидеся́тый; **~ty** ['fıftı] пятьдеся́т

fig [fıg] инжи́р

fight [faıt] **1.** *mil.* сраже́ние, бой; *between persons* дра́ка; (*struggle*) борьба́; **~ show~** быть гото́вым к борьбе́; **2.** [*irr.*] *v/t.* боро́ться про́тив (P); дра́ться (с T); *v/i.* сража́ться [срази́ться]; (*wage war*) воева́ть, боро́ться; **~er** ['faıtə] боре́ц; *fig.* боре́ц; **~er plane** истреби́тель *m*; **~ing** ['faıtıŋ] сраже́ние, бой; дра́ка; *attr.* боево́й

figment ['fıgmənt]: **~ of imagination** плод воображе́ния

figurative ['fıgjʊrətıv] □ перено́сный, метафори́ческий

figure ['fıgə] **1.** фигу́ра; *math.* число́; ци́фра; (*diagram etc.*) рису́нок; *coll.* (*price*) цена́; **2.** *v/t.* представля́ть себе́; рассчи́тывать [-ита́ть]; *Am.* счита́ть, полага́ть; *v/i.* фигури́ровать

filch [fıltʃ] [у]кра́сть; *coll.* [у-, с]тащи́ть (*from* у P)

file¹ [faıl] **1.** *tool* напи́льник; (*nail ~*) пи́лочка (для ногте́й); **2.** (*a. ~ down*) подпи́ливать [-ли́ть]

file² [-] **1.** (*folder*) па́пка; *of papers* подши́вка; *for reference* картоте́ка; *computer* файл; **2.** регистри́ровать (*im*)*pf.*; подшива́ть к де́лу

filial ['fılıəl] □ сыно́вний, доче́рний

fill [fıl] **1.** наполня́ть(ся) [-о́лнить(ся)]; *tooth* [за]пломби́ровать; (*satisfy*) удовлетворя́ть [-ри́ть]; *Am. an order* выполня́ть [вы́полнить]; **~ in** заполня́ть [-о́лнить]; **2.** доста́точное коли́чество; *eat one's ~* нае́сться до́сыта

fillet ['fılıt] *cul.* филе́(й) *n indecl.*

filling ['fılıŋ] наполне́ние; (*зубна́я*) пло́мба; *cul.* фарш, начи́нка; *mot.* **~ station** бензозапра́вочная ста́нция

film [fılm] **1.** (*фото*) плёнка; *cine.* фильм; (*thin layer*) плёнка **2.** производи́ть киносъёмку (P); снима́ть [снять]; экранизи́ровать (*im*)*pf.*

filter ['fıltə] **1.** фильтр; **2.** [про-] фильтрова́ть; **~-tipped** с фи́льтром

filth [fılθ] грязь *f*; **~y** ['fılθı] □ гря́зный (*a. fig.*); **~ weather** гну́сная пого́да

fin [fın] *zo.* плавни́к

final ['faınl] **1.** □ заключи́тельный; оконча́тельный; **2.** *sport* фина́л; **~s** *univ.* выпускны́е экза́мены; **~ly** [-nlı] в конце́ концо́в; (*in conclusion*) в заключе́ние

financ|e ['faınæns] **1. ~es** *pl.* фина́нсы *m/pl.*; де́ньги; **2.** *v/t.* финанси́ровать (*im*)*pf.*; **~ial** [faı'nænʃl] фина́нсовый; **~ier** [-sıə] финанси́ст

finch [fıntʃ] *zo.* зя́блик

find [faınd] [*irr.*] находи́ть (найти́); *by searching* оты́скивать [-ка́ть]; (*discover*) обнару́живать [-ить]; (*consider*) счита́ть [счесть]; *rhet.* обрета́ть [обрести́]; заст(ав)а́ть; **2.** нахо́дка; **~ing** ['faındıŋ] *law* реше́ние; *pl.* вы́воды

fine¹ [faın] □ то́нкий, изя́щный; прекра́сный; *not to put too ~ a point on it* говоря́ напрями́к

fine² [-] **1.** штраф; пе́ня; **2.** [о]штрафова́ть

finesse [fı'nes] делика́тность *f*, утончённость *f*; *at cards, etc.* иску́сный манёвр

finger ['fıŋgə] па́лец; *not to lift a ~* па́лец о па́лец не уда́рить; **2.** тро́гать; *an instrument* перебира́ть па́льцами; **~print** отпеча́ток па́льцев

finish ['fınıʃ] **1.** *v/t.* конча́ть [ко́нчить]; (*complete*) заверша́ть [-ши́ть]; (*make complete*) отде́л(ыв)ать; *v/i.* конча́ться [ко́нчиться]; *sport* финиши́ровать; **2.** коне́ц; (*polish*) отде́лка; *sport* фи́ниш

Finn [fın] финн, фи́нка, **~ish 1.** фи́нский; **2.** фи́нский язы́к

fir [fɜː] ель *f*, пи́хта; **~ cone** ['fɜːkəʊn]

еловая шишка

fire [faɪə] 1. огонь *m*; **be on ~** гореть; 2. *v/t.* (*set fire to*) зажигать [зажечь], поджигать [-жечь]; *stove* [за]топить; *fig.* воспламенять [-нить]; (*dismiss*) увольнять [уволить]; *v/i.* (*shoot*) стрелять [выстрелить]; **~ alarm** ['faɪərəlɑːm] пожарная тревога; **~ brigade**, *Am.* **~department** пожарная команда; **~ engine** ['faɪərendʒɪn] пожарная машина; **~ escape** ['faɪərɪskeɪp] пожарная лестница; **~ extinguisher** ['faɪərɪkstɪŋgwɪʃə] огнетушитель *m*; **~ fighter** пожарный; **~place** камин; **~plug** пожарный кран, гидрант; **~proof** огнеупорный; **~side** место около камина; **~ station** пожарное депо; **~wood** дрова *n/pl.*; **~works** *pl.* фейерверк

firing ['faɪərɪŋ] (*shooting*) стрельба

firm¹ [fɜːm] фирма

firm² [-] □ крепкий, плотный, твёрдый; (*resolute*) устойчивый; **~ness** ['fɜːmnɪs] твёрдость *f*

first [fɜːst] 1. *adj.* первый; **at ~ sight** с первого взгляда; **in the ~ place** во-первых; 2. *adv.* сперва, сначала; впервые; скорее, **at ~** сначала; **~ of all** прежде всего; 3. начало; **the ~** первое число; **from the ~** с самого начала; **~born** первенец; **~class** *quality* первоклассный; *travel* первым классом; **~ly** ['fɜːstlɪ] во-первых; **~rate** превосходный; *int.* прекрасно!

fiscal ['fɪskl] фискальный, финансовый

fish [fɪʃ] 1. рыба; *coll.* **odd** (или **queer**) **~** чудак; 2. ловить рыбу; **~ for compliments** напрашиваться на комплименты; **~ out** выудить; **~bone** рыбная кость *f*

fisherman ['fɪʃəmən] рыбак, рыболов

fishing ['fɪʃɪŋ] рыбная ловля; **~ line** леса; **~ rod** удочка; (*without line*) удилище; **~ tackle** рыболовные принадлежности *f/pl.*

fiss|ion ['fɪʃn] *phys.* расщепление; **~ure** ['fɪʃə] трещина, расселина

fist [fɪst] кулак

fit¹ [fɪt] 1. годный, подходящий; (*healthy*) здоровый; (*deserving*) достойный; 2. *v/t.* подгонять [-догнать] (**to** к Д); (*be suitable for*) подходить [подойти] к (Д); приспособлять [-пособить] (**for, to** к Д); **~ out** (*equip*) снаряжать [-ядить]; (*supply*) снабжать [-бдить]; *v/i.* (*suit*) годиться (*of dress* сидеть; приспособляться [приспособиться]

fit² [-] *med.* припадок, приступ; *of generosity, etc.* порыв; **by ~s and starts** урывками; **give s.o. a ~** потрясти *pf.*

fit|ful ['fɪtfl] □ судорожный, порывистый; **~ter** [-ə] механик, монтёр; **~ting** [-ɪŋ] 1. □ подходящий, годный; 2. установка; монтаж; *of clothes* примерка; **~tings** *pl.* арматура

five [faɪv] 1. пять; 2. *in cards, bus number, etc.*; *school mark* пятёрка

fix [fɪks] 1. устанавливать [-новить]; (*make fast*) укреплять [-пить]; *attention, etc.* сосредоточивать [-точить], останавливать [-новить] (на П); (*repair*) починять [-нить]; *Am.* (*prepare*) приготавливать [-товить]; *Am.* hair *etc.* приводить в порядок; **~ up** организовать (*im*)*pf.*; улаживать [уладить]; (*arrange*) устраивать [-роить]; *v/i.* затверде(ва)ть; останавливаться [-новиться] (*on* на П); 2. *coll.* дилемма, затруднительное положение; **~ed** [fɪkst] (*adv.* **~edly** ['fɪksɪdlɪ]) неподвижный; **~ture** ['fɪkstʃə] приспособление; арматура; (*equipment*) оборудование; **lighting ~** осветительное устройство

fizzle ['fɪzl] шипеть

flabby ['flæbɪ] □ вялый, *fig.* слабохарактерный

flag¹ [flæg] флаг, знамя *n*; **~ of convenience** *naut.* удобный флаг

flag² [flæg] 1. (**~stone**) плита; 2. мостить плитами

flagrant ['fleɪgrənt] □ вопиющий

flagstaff флагшток

flair [fleə] чутьё, нюх; (*ability*) способности *f/pl.*

flake [fleɪk] 1. **~s of** *snow* снежинки

f/pl.; pl. хло́пья *m/pl.*; 2. ~ **off** [об]лупи́ться, шелуши́ться

flame [fleɪm] 1. пла́мя *n*; ого́нь *m*; *fig.* страсть *f*; 2. горе́ть, пламене́ть; пыла́ть

flan [flæn] откры́тый пиро́г; ола́дья

flank [flæŋk] 1. бок, сторона́; *mil.* фланг; 2. быть располо́женным сбо́ку, на фла́нге (Р); грани́чить (с Т), примыка́ть (к Д)

flannel ['flænl] шерстяна́я флане́ль *f*; ~s [-z] *pl.* флане́левые брю́ки *f/pl.*

flap [flæp] 1. *of wings* взмах; (*sound*) хло́панье; *of hat* у́хо; **get into a** ~ засуети́ться *pf.*, панико́вать; взма́хивать [-хну́ть]; 2. *v/t.* (*give a light blow to*) шлёпать [-пну́ть]; легко́ ударя́ть; *v/i.* свиса́ть; *of flag* развева́ться [-ве́яться]

flare [fleə] 1. горе́ть я́рким пла́менем; ~ **up** вспы́хивать [-хну́ть]; *fig.* вспыли́ть *pf.*; 2. вспы́шка пла́мени; сигна́льная раке́та

flash [flæʃ] 1. → *flashy*; 2. вспы́шка; *fig.* про́блеск; *in a* ~ мгнове́нно; 3. сверка́ть [-кну́ть]; вспы́хивать [-хну́ть]; пронести́сь *pf.* (*a.* ~ **by**); ~*light phot.* вспы́шка; *Am.* карма́нный фона́рик *m*; ~**y** показно́й; безвку́сный

flask [flɑːsk] фля́жка

flat [flæt] 1. □ (*level*) пло́ский; (*smooth*) ро́вный; (*dull*) ску́чный; *voice* глухо́й; *fall* ~ не вызыва́ть [вы́звать] интере́са; не име́ть успе́ха; ~ **tire** (*Brt.* **tyre**) спу́щенная ши́на; 2. (*apartment*) кварти́ра; пло́скость *f*; *land* равни́на, ни́зина; *mus.* бемо́ль *m*; ~**iron** утю́г; ~**ten** ['flætn] де́лать(ся) пло́ским, ро́вным

flatter ['flætə] [по]льсти́ть (Д); *I am* ~*ed* я польщена́; ~**er** [-rə] льстец *m*, льсти́ца *f*; ~**ing** [-rɪŋ] ле́стный; ~**y** [-rɪ] лесть *f*

flaunt [flɔːnt] выставля́ть [вы́ставить] на пока́з, афиши́ровать

flavo(u)r ['fleɪvə] 1. (*taste*) вкус; *fig.* при́вкус; 2. приправля́ть [-ра́вить]; придава́ть запах, при́вкус (Д); ~**ing** [-rɪŋ] припра́ва; ~**less** [-lɪs] безвку́с-

ный

flaw [flɔː] (*crack*) тре́щина, щель *f*; *in character, etc.* недоста́ток; (*defect*) дефе́кт, изъя́н; ~**less** ['flɔːlɪs] безупре́чный

flax [flæks] лён

flea [fliː] блоха́

fled [fled] *pt. u pt. p. om* **flee**

flee [fliː] [*irr.*] бежа́ть, спаса́ться бе́гством

fleece [fliːs] 1. ове́чья шерсть *f*; 2. [o]стри́чь; *fig.* обдира́ть (ободра́ть)

fleet[1] [fliːt] □ бы́стрый

fleet[2] [-] флот

flesh [fleʃ] *soft or edible parts of animal bodies* мя́со; *body as opposed to mind or soul* плоть *f*; *of fruit or plant* мя́коть *f*; ~**y** [-ɪ] мяси́стый; то́лстый

flew [fluː] *pt. om* **fly**

flexib|ility [fleksə'bɪlətɪ] ги́бкость *f*; ~**le** ['fleksəbl] □ ги́бкий; *fig.* податли́вый, усту́пчивый

flicker ['flɪkə] 1. *of light* мерца́ние; *of movement* трепета́ние; 2. мерца́ть; трепета́ть *of smile* мелька́ть [-кну́ть]

flight[1] [flaɪt] полёт, перелёт; *of birds* ста́я; ~ **number** но́мер ре́йса

flight[2] [-] бе́гство; **put to** ~ обраща́ть в бе́гство

flighty ['flaɪtɪ] □ ве́треный

flimsy ['flɪmzɪ] (*not strong*) непро́чный; (*thin*) то́нкий; ~ **argument** малоубеди́тельный до́вод

flinch [flɪntʃ] вздра́гивать [вздро́гнуть]; отпря́дывать [отпря́нуть]

fling [flɪŋ] 1. бросо́к; весе́лье; **have a** ~ кутну́ть, пожи́ть в своё удово́льствие; 2. [*irr.*] *v/i.* кида́ться [ки́нуться], броса́ться [бро́ситься]; *v/t.* (*throw*) кида́ть [ки́нуть], броса́ть [бро́сить]; ~ **open** распа́хивать [-хну́ть]

flint [flɪnt] кре́мень *m*

flippan|cy ['flɪpənsɪ] легкомы́слие; ~**t** □ легкомы́сленный

flirt [flɜːt] 1. коке́тка; 2. флиртова́ть, коке́тничать; ~**ation** [flɜː'teɪʃn] флирт

flit [flɪt] порха́ть [-хну́ть] (*a. fig.*); *of smile, etc.* пробежа́ть

float [fləʊt] 1. *on fishing line* поплаво́к; 2. *v/t. timber* сплавля́ть [-а́вить]; *fin.* вводи́ть [ввести́] пла́вающий курс; *v/i. of object* пла́вать, [по]плы́ть; держа́ться на воде́; *fig.* плыть по тече́нию

flock ['flɒk] 1. *of sheep* ста́до; *of birds* ста́я; 2. стека́ться [сте́чься]; держа́ться вме́сте

flog [flɒg] [вы́]поро́ть; ~ *a dead horse* стара́ться возроди́ть безнаде́жно устаре́лое де́ло

flood [flʌd] 1. (*a.* ~ *tide*) прили́в, подъём воды́; (*inundation*) наводне́ние, полово́дье, разли́в; *Bibl.* **the** 2 всеми́рный пото́п; 2. поднима́ться [-ня́ться], выступа́ть из берего́в; (*inundate*) затопля́ть [-пи́ть]; *the market* наводня́ть [-ни́ть]; ~**gate** шлюз

floor [flɔ:] 1. пол; (*stor(e)y*) эта́ж; **take the** ~ *parl.* взять *pf.* сло́во; 2. насти́ла́ть пол; *coll.* (*knock down*) сбива́ть [сбить] с ног; *fig.* (*nonplus*) [по]ста́вить в тупи́к; ~**ing** ['flɔ:rɪŋ] насти́лка поло́в(2)

flop [flɒp] 1. шлёпаться [-пну́ться]; плю́хать(ся) [-хнуть(-ся)]; *Am.* потерпе́ть *pf.* фиа́ско; *sl.* прова́л; 2. ~ **disk** *comput.* ги́бкий диск; ~**py** [-ɪ]:

florid ['flɒrɪd] □ цвети́стый (*a. fig.*)

florist ['flɒrɪst] продаве́ц цвето́в

flounce [flaʊns] *out of room* броса́ться [бро́ситься]

flounder[1] *zo.* ['flaʊndə] ка́мбала

flounder[2] [-] *esp. in water* бара́хтаться; *fig.* [за]пу́таться

flour [flaʊə] мука́

flourish ['flʌrɪʃ] *v/i.* пы́шно расти́, (*prosper*) процвета́ть, преуспева́ть; *v/t.* (*wave*) разма́хивать (T)

flout [flaʊt] попира́ть [попра́ть]; пренебрега́ть [-ре́чь] (T)

flow [fləʊ] 1. тече́ние; пото́к; (*a. of speech*) струя́; *of sea* прпли́в; 2. течь; струи́ться; ли́ться

flower ['flaʊə] цвето́к; *fig.* цвет; *in* ~ в цвету́; 2. цвести́; ~**y** [-rɪ] цвети́стый

flown [fləʊn] *pt. p. om* **fly**

flu [flu:] = *influenza coll.* грипп

fluctuat|e ['flʌktʃʊeɪt] колеба́ться; ~**ion** [flʌktʃʊ'eɪʃn] колеба́ние

flue [flu:] дымохо́д

fluen|cy ['flu:ənsɪ] *fig.* пла́вность *f*, бе́глость *f*; ~**t** [-t] □ пла́вный, бе́глый; **she speaks** ~ **German** она́ бе́гло говори́т по-неме́цки

fluff [flʌf] пух, пушо́к; ~**y** ['flʌfɪ] пуши́стый

fluid ['flu:ɪd] 1. жи́дкость *f*; 2. жи́дкий; *fig.* неопределённый

flung [flʌŋ] *pt. и pt. p. om* **fling**

flurry ['flʌrɪ] волне́ние, сумато́ха

flush [flʌʃ] 1. румя́нец; *of shame* кра́ска; *of feeling* прили́в; 2. *v/t. toilet* спуска́ть [-сти́ть] во́ду (в убо́рной); (*rinse or wash clean*) промыва́ть [-мы́ть]; *v/i.* [по]красне́ть

fluster ['flʌstə] 1. суета́, волне́ние; 2. [вз]волнова́ть(ся)

flute [flu:t] *mus.* фле́йта

flutter ['flʌtə] 1. порха́ние; *of leaves, a. fig.* тре́пет; *fig.* волне́ние; 2. *v/i.* маха́ть [-хну́ть]; *in the wind* развева́ться; порха́ть [-хну́ть]

flux [flʌks] *fig.* тече́ние; пото́к; *in a state of* ~ в состоя́нии непреры́вного измене́ния

fly [flaɪ] 1. му́ха; *a* ~ *in the ointment* ло́жка дёгтя в бо́чке мёда; 2. [*irr.*] лета́ть, [по]лете́ть; пролета́ть [-ете́ть]; (*hurry*) [по]спеши́ть; *of flag* поднима́ть [-ня́ть]; *ae.* пилоти́ровать; ~ *at* набра́сываться [-ро́ситься] (с бра́нью) на (B); ~ *into a passion* вспы́льть *pf.*

flying ['flaɪɪŋ] лета́тельный; лётный; ~ *saucer* лета́ющая таре́лка; ~ *visit* мимолётный визи́т

fly|over путепрово́д; эстака́да; ~**weight** *boxer* наилегча́йший вес; ~**wheel** махови́к

foal [fəʊl] жеребёнок

foam [fəʊm] 1. пе́на; ~ *rubber* пенорези́на; 2. [вс]пе́ниться; *of horse* взмы́ли(ва)ться; ~**y** ['fəʊmɪ] пе́нящийся; взмы́ленный

focus ['fəʊkəs] 1. *phot., phys.* фо́кус; 2. быть в фо́кусе; сосредото́чи(ва)ть (*a. fig.*)

fodder ['fɒdə] фура́ж, корм

foe [fəu] враг

fog [fɒg] **1.** тума́н; (*bewilderment*) замеша́тельство; **2.** [за]тума́нить; *fig.* напуска́ть [-сти́ть] тума́ну; озада́чи(ва)ть; **~gy** ['fɒgɪ] □ тума́нный

foible ['fɔɪbl] *fig.* сла́бость *f*

foil¹ [fɔɪl] (*thin metal*) фольга́; (*contrast*) противопоставле́ние

foil² [-] **1.** расстра́ивать пла́ны (P); **2.** рапи́ра

fold [fəuld] **1.** скла́дка, сгиб; **2.** *v/t.* скла́дывать [сложи́ть]; сгиба́ть [согну́ть]; *one's arms* скре́щивать [-ести́ть]; **~er** ['fəuldə] *for papers* па́пка; брошю́ра

folding ['fəuldɪŋ] складно́й; **~ doors** двуство́рчатые две́ри; **~ chair** складно́й стул; **~ umbrella** складно́й зо́нтик

foliage ['fəulɪdʒ] листва́

folk [fəuk] наро́д, лю́ди *m/pl.*; **~lore** ['fəuklɔː] фолькло́р; **~song** наро́дная пе́сня

follow ['fɒləu] сле́довать (за Т *or* Д); (*watch*) следи́ть (за Т); (*pursue*) пресле́довать (B); (*engage in*) занима́ться [-ня́ться] (Т); (*understand*) понима́ть [-ня́ть]; **~ suit** сле́довать приме́ру; **~er** ['fɒləuə] после́дователь(ница *f*) *m*; (*admirer*) покло́нник; **~ing** ['fɒləuɪŋ] сле́дующий

folly ['fɒlɪ] безрассу́дство, глу́пость *f*, безу́мие

fond [fɒnd] □ не́жный, лю́бящий, **be ~ of** люби́ть (B)

fondle ['fɒndl] [при]ласка́ть; **~ness** [-nɪs] не́жность *f*, любо́вь *f*

food [fuːd] пи́ща, еда́; **~stuffs** *pl.* (пищевы́е) проду́кты *m/pl.*

fool [fuːl] **1.** дура́к, глупе́ц; **make a ~ of s.o.** [о]дура́чить кого́-л.; **2.** *v/t.* обма́нывать [-ну́ть]; *v/i.* [по]дура́читься; **~ about** валя́ть дурака́

fool|ery ['fuːlərɪ] дура́чество; **~hardy** ['fuːlhɑːdɪ] □ безрассу́дно хра́брый; **~ish** ['fuːlɪʃ] глу́пый, неразу́мный; **~ishness** [-nɪs] глу́пость *f*; **~proof** безопа́сный; безотка́зный

foot [fut] **1.** (*pl.* **feet**) нога́, ступня́; (*base*) основа́ние; *of furniture* но́жка;

on ~ пешко́м; **2.** *v/t.* (*mst.* **~ up**) подсчи́тывать [-ита́ть]; **~ the bill** заплати́ть по счёту; **~ it** идти́ пешко́м; **~ball** футбо́л; **~fall** шаг; звук шаго́в; **~gear** *coll.* о́бувь *f*; **~hold** опо́ра (*a. fig.*)

footing ['futɪŋ] опо́ра; *on a friendly ~* быть на дру́жеской ноге́; *lose one's ~* оступа́ться [-пи́ться]

foot|lights *pl. thea.* ра́мпа; **~path** тропи́нка; тропа́; **~print** след; **~sore** со стёртыми нога́ми; **~step** по́ступь *f*; шаг; *follow in s.o.'s ~s* идти́ по чьи́м-л. стопа́м; **~wear** о́бувь *f*

for [fə; *strong* fɔː] *prp. mst.* для (P); ра́ди (P); за (B); в направле́нии (P), к (D); из-за (P), по причи́не (P), всле́дствие; в тече́ние (P); в продолже́ние (P); **~ three days** в тече́ние трёх дней; уже́ три дня; вме́сто (P); в обме́н на (B); **~ all that** несмотря́ на всё э́то; **~ my part** с мое́й стороны́; **2.** *cj.* так как, потому́ что, и́бо

forbad(e) [fə'bæd] *pt. om* **forbid**

forbear [fɔː'beə] [*irr.*] (*be patient*) быть терпели́вый; (*refrain from*) возде́рживаться [-жа́ться] (*from* от P)

forbid [fə'bɪd] [*irr.*] запреща́ть [-ети́ть]; **~den** [-n] *pt. p. om* **forbid**; **~ing** [-ɪŋ] □ (*threatening*) угрожа́ющий

forbor|e [fɔː'bɔː] *pt. om* **forbear**, **~ne** [-n] *pt. p. om* **forbear**

force [fɔːs] **1.** си́ла; (*violence*) наси́лие; (*constraint*) принужде́ние; (*meaning*) смысл, значе́ние; *armed* **~s** *pl.* вооружённые си́лы *f/pl.*; *come into* **~** вступа́ть в си́лу; **2.** заставля́ть [-а́вить], принужда́ть [-уди́ть]; (*get by force*) брать си́лой; *join* **~s** объединя́ть [-ни́ть] уси́лия; **~ open** взла́мывать [взлома́ть]; **~d** [-t]: **~ landing** вы́нужденная поса́дка; **~ful** [-fl] □ си́льный, де́йственный; *argument* убеди́тельный

forcible ['fɔːsəbl] □ (*using force*) наси́льственный; (*convincing*) убеди́тельный

ford [fɔːd] **1.** брод; **2.** переходи́ть вброд

fore [fɔː] **1.** *adv.* впереди́; **2.** *adj.* переdний; ~bode [fɔ:'bəʊd] предвещать; (have a feeling) предчувствовать; ~boding предчувствие; ~cast 1. ['fɔ:-kɑ:st] предсказание; weather ~ прогноз погоды; 2. [fɔ:'kɑ:st] [irr. (cast)] [c]делать (давать [дать]) прогноз; предсказывать [-казать] ~father предок; ~finger указательный палец; ~gone [fɔ:'gɒn]: it's a conclusion это предрешённый исход; ~ground передний план; ~head ['fɔrɪd] лоб

foreign ['fɒrɪn] иностранный; Brt. the 2 Office Министерство иностранных дел; ~ policy внешняя политика; ~er [-ə] иностранец m, -нка f

fore|lock ['fɔ:lɒk] прядь волос на лбу; ~man бригадир; мастер; ~most передний, передовой; ~runner предвестник m, -ица f; ~see [fɔ:'si:] [irr. (see)] предвидеть; ~sight ['fɔ:saɪt] предвидение; (provident care) предусмотрительность f

forest ['fɒrɪst] лес

forestall [fɔ:'stɔ:l] (avert) предупреждать [-упредить]; (do s.th. first) опережать [-дить]

forest|er ['fɒrɪstə] лесник, лесничий; ~ry [-trɪ] лесничество, лесоводство

fore|taste ['fɔ:teɪst] 1. предвкушение; 2. предвкушать [-усить]; ~tell [fɔ:'tel] [irr. (tell)] предсказать [-зать]

forever [fə'revə] навсегда

forfeit ['fɔ:fɪt] 1. штраф; in game фант; 2. [по]платиться (Т); right утрачивать [-атить]

forgave [fə'geɪv] pt. om forgive

forge¹ [fɔ:dʒ] (mst. ~ ahead) настойчиво продвигаться вперёд

forge² [-] 1. кузница; 2. ковать; signature, etc. поддел(ыв)ать; ~ry ['fɔ:dʒərɪ] подделка; of document подлог

forget [fə'get] [irr.] забы(ва)ть; ~ful [-fl] □ забывчивый; ~-me-not [-mɪnɒt] незабудка

forgiv|e [fə'gɪv] [irr.] прощать [простить]; ~en [fə'gɪvən] pt. p. om ~; ~eness [-nɪs] прощение; ~ing [-ɪŋ] всепрощающий; □ великодушный, снисходительный

forgo [fɔ:'gəʊ] [irr. (go)] воздержи-

ваться [-жаться] от (P), отказываться [-заться] от (P)

forgot, ~ten [fə'gɒt(n)] pt. a. pt. p. om forget

fork [fɔ:k] вилка; agric. вилы f/pl.; mus. камертон; of road разветвление

forlorn [fə'lɔ:n] заброшенный, несчастный

form [fɔ:m] 1. форма; фигура; (document) бланк; Brt. educ. класс; matter of ~ чистая формальность; 2. образовывать(ся) [-овать(ся)]; составлять [-авить]; (create) создавать [-ать]; (organize) организовывать [-вать]; [с]формировать

formal ['fɔ:ml] □ формальный; официальный; ~ity [fɔ:'mælətɪ] формальность f

formation [fɔ:'meɪʃn] образование; формирование; mil. строй; (structure) строение

former ['fɔ:mə] прежний, бывший; предшествующий; the ~ первый; ~ly [-lɪ] прежде

formidable ['fɔ:mɪdəbl] □ грозный; size громадный; (difficult) трудный

formula ['fɔ:mjʊlə] формула; ~te [-leɪt] формулировать (im)pf., pf. a. [c-]

forsake [fə'seɪk] [irr.] оставлять [-авить], покидать [-инуть]

forswear [fɔ:'sweə] [irr. (swear)] (give up) отказываться [-заться] от (P)

fort [fɔ:t] mil. форт

forth [fɔ:θ] adv. вперёд; дальше; впредь; and so~ и так далее; ~coming предстоящий

fortieth ['fɔ:tɪɪθ] сороковой; сороковая часть f

forti|fication [fɔ:tɪfɪ'keɪʃn] укрепление; ~fy ['fɔ:tɪfaɪ] mil. укреплять [-пить]; fig. подкреплять [-пить]; ~ o.s. подкрепляться [-питься] (with Т); ~tude [-tju:d] сила духа, стойкость f

fortnight ['fɔ:tnaɪt] две недели f/pl.

fortress ['fɔ:trɪs] крепость f

fortuitous [fɔ:'tju:ɪtəs] □ случайный

fortunate ['fɔ:tʃənət] счастливый, удачный; I was ~ enough мне посчастли́вилось; **~ly** *adv.* к сча́стью

fortune ['fɔːtʃən] судьба́; (*prosperity*) бога́тство, состоя́ние; **good** (**bad**) **~** (не)уда́ча; **~ teller** гада́лка

forty ['fɔːtɪ] со́рок

forward ['fɔːwəd] **1.** *adj.* пере́дний; (*familiar*) развя́зный, де́рзкий; *spring* ра́нний; **2.** *adv.* вперёд, да́льше; впредь; **3.** *sport* напада́ющий, фо́рвард; **4.** перес(ы́)ла́ть, направля́ть [-а́вить] (по но́вому а́дресу)

forwent [fɔː'went] *pt. om* **forgo**

foster ['fɒstər] воспи́тывать [-ита́ть]; (*look after*) присма́тривать [-мотре́ть] (за Т); *fig. hope etc.* пита́ть; (*cherish*) леле́ять; (*encourage*) поощря́ть [-ри́ть]; благоприя́тствовать (Д)

fought [fɔːt] *pt. и pt. p. om* **fight**

foul [faʊl] **1.** □ (*dirty*) гря́зный; (*loathsome*) отврати́тельный (*a. weather*); нече́стный; **2.** *sport* наруше́ние пра́вил; **~ play** гру́бая игра́, **3.** [за]па́чкать(ся); (*pollute*) загрязня́ть [-ни́ть], допусти́ть *pf.* наруше́ние

found [faʊnd] **1.** *pt. и pt. p. om* **find**; **2.** (*lay the foundation of*) закла́дывать [заложи́ть]; (*establish*) осно́вывать (основа́ть); учрежда́ть [-еди́ть]

foundation [faʊn'deɪʃn] фунда́мент, осно́ва; *for research, etc.* фонд

founder ['faʊndə] основа́тель(ница *f*) *m*; *of society* учреди́тель(ница *f*) *m*

foundry ['faʊndrɪ] *tech.* лите́йный цех

fountain ['faʊntɪn] фонта́н; **~ pen** авторучка

four [fɔː] **1.** четы́ре; **2.** четвёрка (→ **five 2.**); **~teen** [,fɔː'tiːn] четы́рнадцать; **~teenth** [-θ] четы́рнадцатый; **~th** [fɔːθ] **1.** четвёртый; **2.** че́тверть *f*

fowl [faʊl] дома́шняя пти́ца

fox [fɒks] **1.** лиси́ца, лиса́; **2.** [с]хитри́ть; обма́нывать [-ну́ть]; *the question* **~ed me** вопро́с поста́вил меня́ в тупи́к; **~y** ['fɒksɪ] хи́трый

foyer ['fɔɪeɪ] фойе́ *n indecl.*

fraction ['frækʃn] *math.* дробь *f*; (*small part or amount*) части́ца

fracture ['fræktʃə] **1.** тре́щина, изло́м;

med. перело́м; **2.** [с]лома́ть (*a. med.*)

fragile ['frædʒaɪl] хру́пкий (*a. fig.*), ло́мкий

fragment ['frægmənt] обло́мок, оско́лок; *of text* отры́вок; **~ary** [-əri] фрагмента́рный; (*not complete*) отры́вочный

fragran|ce ['freɪɡrəns] арома́т; **~t** [-t] □ арома́тный

frail [freɪl] *in health* хру́пкий; хи́лый, боле́зненный; *morally* сла́бый

frame [freɪm] **1.** скеле́т, о́стов; телосложе́ние; *of picture, etc.* ра́мка, ра́ма; *of spectacles* опра́ва; **~ of mind** настрое́ние; **2.** (*construct*) [по]стро́ить, выраба́тывать [вы́работать]; вставля́ть в ра́му; **~work** *tech.* ра́ма; карка́с; *fig.* структу́ра; ра́мки *f/pl*.

franchise ['fræntʃaɪz] пра́во уча́ствовать в вы́борах; *comm.* привиле́гия; лице́нзия

frank [fræŋk] □ и́скренний, открове́нный

frankfurter ['fræŋkfɜːtə] соси́ска

frankness ['fræŋknɪs] открове́нность *f*

frantic ['fræntɪk] (**~ally**) безу́мный; *efforts, etc.* отча́янный

fratern|al [frə'tɜːnl] □ бра́тский; *adv.* по-бра́тски; **~ity** [-nəti] бра́тство; *Am. univ.* студе́нческая организа́ция

fraud [frɔːd] обма́н, моше́нничество; **~ulent** ['frɔːdjʊlənt] □ обма́нный, моше́ннический

fray[1] [freɪ] дра́ка; (*quarrel*) ссо́ра

fray[2] [-] обтрёпаться

freak [friːk] *of nature* капри́з, причу́да; *person, animal* уро́д; (*enthusiast*) фана́т; *film* **~** кинома́н

freckle ['frekl] весну́шка; **~d** [-d] весну́шчатый

free [friː] **1.** □ *com.* свобо́дный, во́льный; (*not occupied*) незаня́тый; (**~ of charge**) беспла́тный; **give s.o. a ~ hand** предоста́вить по́лную свобо́ду де́йствий; **he is ~ to** *inf.* во́лен (+ *inf.*); **make ~ to** *inf.* позволя́ть себе́; **set ~** выпуска́ть на свобо́ду; **2.** освобожда́ть [-боди́ть]; **~dom** ['friːdəm] свобо́да;

~holder свобо́дный со́бственник; **⚥mason** масо́н; **~style** sport во́льный стиль; **~ trade area** свобо́дная экономи́ческая зо́на

freez|e [fri:z] [irr.] v/i. замерза́ть [замёрзнуть]; (congeal) засты(ва́)ть; мёрзнуть; v/t. замора́живать [-ро́зить]; **~er** ['fri:zə] морози́льник; **~ing 1.** ☐ леденя́щий; **2.** замора́живание; замерза́ние; **~ point** то́чка замерза́ния

freight [freɪt] **1.** фрахт, груз; (cost) сто́имость перево́зки; **2.** [по]грузи́ть; [за]фрахтова́ть; **~car** Am. rail. това́рный ваго́н; **~ train** Am. това́рный по́езд/соста́в

French [frentʃ] **1.** францу́зский; **take ~ leave** уйти́, не проща́ясь (или по-англи́йски); **2.** францу́зский язы́к; **the ~** францу́зы pl.; **~man** ['frentʃmən] францу́з; **~woman** ['frentʃwumən] францу́женка

frenz|ied ['frenzɪd] безу́мный, нейсто́вый; **~y** [-zɪ] безу́мие, нейстовство́

frequen|cy ['fri:kwənsɪ] частота́ (a. phys.); ча́стое повторе́ние; **~t 1.** [-t] ☐ ча́стый; **2.** [fri:'kwent] регуля́рно посеща́я

fresh [freʃ] ☐ све́жий; но́вый; чи́стый; Am. развя́зный, де́рзкий; **~ water** пре́сная вода́; **make a ~ start** нача́ть pf. всё снача́ла; **~en** ['freʃn] освежа́ть [-жи́ть]; of the wind [по]свеже́ть; **~man** [-mən] (first year student) первоку́рсник; **~ness** [-nɪs] све́жесть f

fret [fret] **1.** волне́ние, раздраже́ние; **2.** беспоко́ить(ся), [вз]волнова́ть(ся); (wear away) подта́чивать [-точи́ть]

fretful ['fretfl] ☐ раздражи́тельный, капри́зный

friction ['frɪkʃn] тре́ние (a. fig.)

Friday ['fraɪdɪ] пя́тница

fridge [frɪdʒ] coll. холоди́льник

friend [frend] прия́тель(ница f) m, друг, подру́га; **make ~s** подружи́ться; **~ly** [-lɪ] дру́жеский; **~ship** [-ʃɪp] дру́жба

frigate ['frɪgət] фрега́т

fright [fraɪt] испу́г; fig. (scarecrow) пу́гало, страши́лище; **~en** ['fraɪtn] [ис-

пуга́ть; (**~en away**) вспу́гивать [-гну́ть]; **~ed at** или **of** испу́ганный (Т); **~ful** [-fl] ☐ стра́шный, ужа́сный

frigid ['frɪdʒɪd] ☐ холо́дный

frill [frɪl] обо́рка

fringe [frɪndʒ] **1.** бахрома́; of hair чёлка; of forest опу́шка; **~ benefits** дополни́тельные льго́ты; **2.** отде́лывать бахромо́й; with trees, etc. окаймля́ть [-ми́ть]

frisk [frɪsk] резви́ться; **~y** ['frɪskɪ] ☐ ре́звый, игри́вый

fritter ['frɪtə]: **~ away** транжи́рить; растра́чиваться

frivol|ity [frɪ'vɒlətɪ] легкомы́слие; фриво́льность f; **~ous** ['frɪvələs] ☐ легкомы́сленный, несерьёзный

frizzle ['frɪzl] of hair завива́ть(ся) [-ви́ть(ся)]; with a sizzle жа́рить(ся) с шипе́нием

fro [frəu]: **to and ~** взад и вперёд

frock [frɒk] да́мское или де́тское пла́тье; monk's habit ря́са

frog [frɒg] лягу́шка

frolic ['frɒlɪk] **1.** ша́лость f; весе́лье; резви́ться; **~some** [-səm] ☐ игри́вый, ре́звый

from [frɒm; strong frɒm] prp. от (P); из (P); с (P); по (Д); **defend ~** защища́ть от (P); **~ day to day** со дня на́ день

front [frʌnt] **1.** фаса́д; пере́дняя сторона́; mil. фронт; **in ~ of** пе́ред (Т); впереди́ (P); **2.** пере́дний; **3.** (face) выходи́ть на (В) (a. **~ on**); **~al** ['frʌntl] ло́бовый; anat. ло́бный; attack, etc. фронта́льный; **~ier** ['frʌntɪə] **1.** грани́ца; **2.** пограни́чный

frost [frɒst] **1.** моро́з; **2.** plants поби́ть моро́зом; **~bite** обмороже́ние; **~y** ['frɒstɪ] моро́зный; fig. (unfriendly) ледяно́й

froth [frɒθ] **1.** пе́на; **2.** [вс-, за]пе́нить(ся); **~y** ['frɒθɪ] пе́нистый

frown [fraun] **1.** хму́рый взгляд; **2.** v/i. [на]хму́риться; **~ on** относи́ться [-нести́сь] неодобри́тельно

froze [frəuz] pt. om freeze; **~n** [-n] **1.** pt. p. om freeze; **2.** замёрзший; meat, etc. заморо́женный

frugal ['fru:gl] ☐ person бережли́вый;

meal скро́мный; *with money etc.* эконо́мный

fruit [fruːt] **1.** плод (*a. fig.*); фрукт *mst. pl.*; **dried~** сухофру́кты; **2. bear~** плодоно́сить, дава́ть плоды́; **~ful** ['fruːtfl] *fig.* плодотво́рный; **~less** [-lɪs] □ бесплодный

frustrat|e [frʌ'streit] *plans* расстра́ивать [-ро́ить]; *efforts* де́лать тще́тным; **~ed** [-ɪd] обескура́женный, неудовлетворённый; **~ion** [frʌ'streiʃn] расстро́йство, *of hopes* круше́ние

fry [frai] [за-, под]жа́рить(ся); **~ing pan** ['fraiɪŋpæn] сковорода́

fudge [fʌdʒ] (*sweet*) пома́дка

fuel ['fjuːəl] **1.** то́пливо; *mot.* горю́чее; **add~ to the fire** подлива́ть ма́сла в ого́нь

fugitive ['fjuːdʒətɪv] (*runaway*) бегле́ц; *from danger, persecution, etc.* бе́женец *m*, -нка *f*

fulfil(l) [ful'fɪl] выполня́ть [вы́полнить], осуществля́ть [-ви́ть]; **~ment** [-mənt] осуществле́ние, выполне́ние

full [ful] **1.** □ по́лный; *hour* це́лый; **2.** *adv.* вполне́; как раз; о́чень; **3.** *in~* по́лностью; **to the~** в по́лной ме́ре; **~dress** пара́дная фо́рма; **~-fledged** вполне́ опери́вшийся; *fig.* зако́нченный; полнопра́вный; **~scale** [ful'skeɪl] в по́лном объёме

fumble ['fʌmbl] (*feel about*) ша́рить; (*rummage*) ры́ться; **~ for words** поды́скивать слова́

fume [fjuːm] **1.** дым; (*vapour*) испаре́ние; **2.** дыми́ть(ся); *fig.* возмуща́ться

fumigate ['fjuːmɪgeɪt] оку́ривать

fun [fʌn] весе́лье; заба́ва; **have~** хорошо́ провести́ вре́мя; **make~ of** высме́ивать [вы́смеять] (B)

function ['fʌŋkʃn] **1.** фу́нкция, назначе́ние; **2.** функциони́ровать, де́йствовать

fund [fʌnd] запа́с; *fin.* капита́л, фонд; **~s** *pl.* (*resources*) фо́нды *m/pl.*; **public~** госуда́рственные сре́дства

fundament|al [fʌndə'mentl] □ основно́й, коренно́й, суще́ственный; **~als**

pl. осно́вы *f/pl.*

funeral ['fjuːnərəl] по́хороны *f/pl.*; *attr.* похоро́нный

funnel ['fʌnl] воро́нка; *naut.* дымова́я труба́

funny ['fʌnɪ] □ заба́вный, смешно́й; (*strange*) стра́нный

fur [fɜː] мех; (*skin with~*) шку́р(к)а; **~ coat** шу́ба; **~s** *pl.* меха́ *m/pl.*, мехово́е това́ры *m/pl.*, пушни́на

furious ['fjuərɪəs] □ (*violent*) бу́йный; (*enraged*) взбешённый

furl [fɜːl] *sails* свёртывать [сверну́ть]; *umbrella* скла́дывать [сложи́ть]

fur-lined ['fɜːlaɪnd] подби́тый ме́хом

furnace ['fɜːnɪs] горн; печь *f*

furnish ['fɜːnɪʃ] (*provide*) снабжа́ть [снабди́ть] (**with** T); *room, etc.* обставля́ть [-а́вить], мебли́ровать (*im*)*pf.*; **~ings** обстано́вка; дома́шние принадле́жности

furniture ['fɜːnɪtʃər] ме́бель *f*, обстано́вка

furrier ['fʌrɪə] скорня́к

furrow ['fʌrəu] *agric.* борозда́; (*groove*) колея́

further ['fɜːðə] **1.** да́льше, да́лее; зате́м; кро́ме того́; **2.** соде́йствовать, спосо́бствовать (Д); **~ance** [-rəns] продвиже́ние (*of* P), соде́йствие (*of* Д); **~more** [fɜːðə'mɔː] *adv.* к тому́ же, кро́ме того́

furthest ['fɜːðɪst] са́мый да́льний

furtive ['fɜːtɪv] □ скры́тый, та́йный; **~ glance** взгляд укра́дкой

fury ['fjuərɪ] неи́стовство, я́рость *f*; **fly into a~** прийти́ в я́рость

fuse[1] [fjuːz] *el.* пла́вкий предохрани́тель *m*, *coll.* про́бка

fuse[2] [-]: *the lights have~d* про́бки перегоре́ли

fuss [fʌs] *coll.* **1.** суета́; (*row*) шум, сканда́л; **make a~** подня́ть *pf.* шум; **make a~ of s.o.** носи́ться с ке́м-л.; **2.** [за]суети́ться; [вз]волнова́ться (*about* из-за P)

futile ['fjuːtaɪl] бесполе́зный, тще́тный

future ['fjuːtʃə] **1.** бу́дущий; **2.** бу́дущее, бу́дущность *f*; *in the near~*

F

в ближа́йшее вре́мя; *there is no ~ in it* э́то бесперспекти́вно

fuzzy ['fʌzɪ] (*blurred*) сму́тный; (*fluffy*) пуши́стый

G

gab [gæb]: *the gift of the ~* хорошо́ подве́шенный язы́к
gabardine ['gæbədiːn] габарди́н
gabble ['gæbl] тарато́рить
gable ['geɪbl] *arch.* фронто́н
gad [gæd]: ~ *about* шля́ться, шата́ться
gadfly ['gædflaɪ] *zo.* сле́пень *m*
gadget ['gædʒɪt] приспособле́ние; *coll.* техни́ческая нови́нка
gag [gæg] **1.** *for stopping mouth* кляп; (*joke*) шу́тка, остро́та; **2.** затыка́ть рот (Д); заста́вить *pf.* замолча́ть
gaiety ['geɪətɪ] весёлость *f*
gaily ['geɪlɪ] *adv. om gay* ве́село; (*brightly*) я́рко
gain [geɪn] **1.** (*profit*) при́быль *f*; (*winnings*) вы́игрыш; (*increase*) прирост; **2.** выи́грывать [вы́играть]; приобрета́ть [-ести́]; ~ *weight* [по]полне́ть
gait [geɪt] похо́дка
galaxy ['gæləksɪ] гала́ктика; *fig.* плея́да
gale [geɪl] шторм, си́льный ве́тер
gall [gɔːl] **1.** *med.* жёлчь *f*; *bitterness* жёлчность *f*; (*bad temper*) злоба́; **2.** раздража́ть [-жи́ть]
gallant ['gælənt] **1.** гала́нтный; **2.** *adj.* ['gælənt] □ хра́брый, до́блестный
gall bladder жёлчный пузы́рь
gallery ['gælərɪ] галере́я; *thea.* балко́н; *coll.* галёрка
galley ['gælɪ] *naut.* ка́мбуз
gallon ['gælən] галло́н
gallop ['gæləp] **1.** гало́п; **2.** скака́ть гало́пом
gallows ['gæləʊz] *sg.* ви́селица
gamble ['gæmbl] **1.** аза́ртная игра́; риско́ванное предприя́тие; **2.** игра́ть в аза́ртные и́гры; *on stock exchange* игра́ть; ~**r** [-ə] картёжник, игро́к
gambol ['gæmbl] **1.** прыжо́к; **2.** пры́гать, скака́ть

game [geɪm] **1.** игра́; *of chess, etc.* па́ртия; *of tennis* гейм; (*wild animals*) дичь *f*; ~**s** *pl.* состяза́ния *n/pl.*, и́гры *f/pl.*; *beat s.o. at his own ~* бить кого́-л. его́ со́бственным ору́жием; **2.** *coll.* охо́тно гото́вый (сде́лать что́-л.); **3.** игра́ть на де́ньги; ~**ster** [-stə] игро́к, картёжник
gander ['gændə] гуса́к
gang [gæŋ] **1.** *of workers* брига́да; *of criminals* ба́нда; **2.** ~ *up* объедини́ться *pf.*
gangster ['gæŋstə] га́нгстер
gangway ['gæŋweɪ] *naut.* схо́дни; *ae.* трап; (*passage*) прохо́д
gaol [dʒeɪl] тюрьма́; → *jail*
gap [gæp] *in text, knowledge* пробе́л; (*cleft*) брешь *f*, щель *f*, *fig. between ideas, etc.* расхожде́ние
gape [geɪp] разева́ть рот; [по]глазе́ть; зия́ть
garage ['gæraːʒ] гара́ж
garbage ['gɑːbɪdʒ] отбро́сы *m/pl.*; му́сор; ~ *chute* мусоропрово́д
garden ['gɑːdn] **1.** сад; *kitchen ~* огоро́д; **2.** занима́ться садово́дством; ~**er** [-ə] садо́вник, садово́д; ~**ing** [-ɪŋ] садово́дство
gargle ['gɑːgl] **1.** полоска́ть го́рло; **2.** полоска́ние для го́рла
garish ['geərɪʃ] бро́ский, крича́щий; я́ркий
garland ['gɑːlənd] гирля́нда, вено́к
garlic ['gɑːlɪk] чесно́к
garment ['gɑːmənt] предме́т оде́жды
garnish ['gɑːnɪʃ] **1.** (*decoration*) украше́ние, *mst. cul.*; **2.** украша́ть [укра́сить]; гарни́ровать
garret ['gærɪt] манса́рда
garrison ['gærɪsn] гарнизо́н
garrulous ['gærʊləs] □ болтли́вый
gas [gæs] **1.** газ; *Am.* бензи́н, горю́чее;

~bag *coll.* болту́н; пустоме́ля; **2.** отравля́ть га́зом

gash [gæʃ] **1.** глубо́кая ра́на, разре́з; **2.** наноси́ть глубо́кую ра́ну (Д)

gas lighter га́зовая зажига́лка

gasoline, gasolene ['gæsəli:n] *mot. Am.* бензи́н

gasp [gɑ:sp] задыха́ться [задохну́ться]; лови́ть во́здух

gas station *Am.* автозапра́вочная ста́нция; **~ stove** га́зовая плита́

gastri|c ['gæstrɪk] желу́дочный; **~ ulcer** я́зва желу́дка; **~tis** [gæ'straɪtɪs] гастри́т

gate [geɪt] воро́та *n/pl.*; *in fence* кали́тка; **~way** воро́та *n/pl.*; вход; подворо́тня

gather ['gæðə] *v/t.* соб(и)ра́ть; *harvest* снима́ть [снять]; *flowers* [на-, co]рва́ть; *fig.* де́лать вы́вод; **~ speed** набира́ть ско́рость; *v/i.* соб(и)ра́ться; **~ing** [-rɪŋ] собра́ние; *social* встре́ча; *med.* нары́в

gaudy ['gɔ:dɪ] □ я́ркий, крича́щий, безвку́сный

gauge [geɪdʒ] **1.** *tech.* кали́бр; измери́тельный прибо́р; *fuel* **~** *mot.* бензиноме́р; **2.** измеря́ть [-е́рить]; градуи́ровать (*im*)*pf.*; *fig. person* оце́нивать [-ни́ть]

gaunt [gɔ:nt] □ исхуда́лый, изможде́нный; *place* забро́шенный, мра́чный

gauze [gɔ:z] ма́рля

gave [geɪv] *pt. om* **give**

gawky ['gɔ:kɪ] неуклю́жий

gay [geɪ] весёлый; *colo(u)r* я́ркий, пёстрый; гомосексуа́льный

gaze [geɪz] **1.** при́стальный взгляд; **2.** при́стально смотре́ть

gazette [gə'zet] *official* бюллете́нь *m*, ве́стник

gear [gɪə] **1.** механи́зм; приспособле́ния *n/pl.*; *tech.* шестерня́; зубча́тая переда́ча; *mot.* переда́ча; ско́рость *f*; (*equipment*) принадле́жности *f/pl.*; (*belongings*) ве́щи *f/pl.*; **change ~** переключи́ть переда́чу; **in ~** включённый, де́йствующий; **2.** приводи́ть в движе́ние; включа́ть [-чи́ть]

geese [gi:s] *pl. om* **goose**

gem [dʒem] драгоце́нный ка́мень *m*; *fig.* сокро́вище

gender ['dʒendə] *gr.* род

gene [dʒi:n] *biol.* ген

general ['dʒenərəl] **1.** □ о́бщий; обы́чный; (*in all parts*) повсеме́стный; (*chief*) гла́вный; генера́льный; **~ election** всео́бщие вы́боры *m/pl.*; **2.** *mil.* генера́л; **~ization** [dʒenrəlar'zeɪʃn] обобще́ние; **~ize** ['dʒenrəlaɪz] обобща́ть [-щи́ть]; **~ly** [-lɪ] вообще́; обы́чно

generat|e ['dʒenəreɪt] порожда́ть [-роди́ть]; производи́ть [-вести́]; *el.* выраба́тывать [вы́работать]; **~ion** [dʒenə'reɪʃn] поколе́ние; **~or** ['dʒenəreɪtə] генера́тор

gener|osity [dʒenə'rɒsətɪ] великоду́шие; *with money, etc.* ще́дрость *f*; **~ous** ['dʒenərəs] □ великоду́шный, ще́дрый

genetics [dʒɪ'netɪks] гене́тика

genial ['dʒi:nɪəl] □ *climate* тёплый, мя́гкий; до́брый, серде́чный

genius ['dʒi:nɪəs] ге́ний; тала́нт, гениа́льность *f*

genocide ['dʒenəsaɪd] геноци́д

genre ['ʒɑ:nrə] жанр

gentle ['dʒentl] □ мя́гкий; кро́ткий; ти́хий; не́жный; *animals* сми́рный; *breeze* лёгкий; **~man** джентльме́н; господи́н; **~manlike, ~manly** [-lɪ] воспи́танный; **~ness** [-nɪs] мя́гкость *f*; доброта́

genuine ['dʒenjʊɪn] □ (*real*) по́длинный; (*sincere*) и́скренний, неподде́льный

geography [dʒɪ'ɒgrəfɪ] геогра́фия

geology [dʒɪ'ɒlədʒɪ] геоло́гия

geometry [dʒɪ'ɒmɪtrɪ] геоме́трия

germ [dʒɜ:m] микро́б; (*embryo*) заро́дыш (*a. fig.*)

German ['dʒɜ:mən] **1.** герма́нский, неме́цкий; **~ silver** мельхио́р; **2.** не́мец, не́мка; неме́цкий язы́к

germinate ['dʒɜ:mɪneɪt] дава́ть ростки́, прораста́ть [-расти́]

gesticulat|e [dʒe'stɪkjʊleɪt] жестикули́ровать; **~ion** [-stɪkjʊ'leɪʃn] жестикуля́ция

gesture ['dʒestʃə] жест (*a. fig.*)

get [get] [*irr.*] **1.** *v/t.* (*obtain*) дост(ав)я́ть; (*receive*) получа́ть [-чи́ть]; (*earn*) зараба́тывать [-бо́тать]; (*buy*) покупа́ть, купи́ть; (*fetch*) приноси́ть [-нести́]; (*induce*) заставля́ть [-ста́вить]; *I have got to ...* мне ну́жно, я до́лжен; **~ one's hair cut** [по]стри́чься; **2.** *v/i.* (*become, be*) [с]де́латься, станови́ться [стать]; **~ ready** [при]гото́виться; **~ about** (*travel*) разъезжа́ть; *after illness* начина́ть ходи́ть; **~ abroad** *of rumo(u)rs* распространя́ться [-ни́ться]; **~ across** [с]де́лать [-а́вить] поня́ть; **~ ahead** продвига́ться вперёд; **~ at** доб(и)ра́ться до (Р); **~ away** уд(и)ра́ть, уходи́ть [уйти́]; **~ down** *from shelf* снима́ть [снять]; *from train* сходи́ть [сойти́]; **~ in** входи́ть [войти́]; **~ on well with a p.** хорошо́ ла́дить с ке́м-л.; **~ out** вынима́ть [вы́нуть]; **~ to hear** (*know, learn*) узн(ав)а́ть; **~ up** вст(ав)а́ть; **~up** ['getʌp] (*dress*) наря́д

geyser ['giːzə] **1.** ге́йзер; **2.** *Brt.* га́зовая коло́нка

ghastly ['gɑːstlɪ] ужа́сный

gherkin ['gɜːkɪn] огу́рчик; *pickled ~s* корнишо́ны

ghost [gəʊst] при́зрак, привиде́ние; дух (*a. eccl.*); *fig.* тень *f*, лёгкий след; **~like** ['gəʊstlaɪk], **~ly** [-lɪ] похо́жий на привиде́ние, при́зрачный

giant ['dʒaɪənt] **1.** велика́н, гига́нт; **2.** гига́нтский

gibber ['dʒɪbə] говори́ть невня́тно; **~ish** [-rɪʃ] тараба́рщина

gibe [dʒaɪb] *v/i.* насмеха́ться (*at* над Т)

gidd|iness ['gɪdɪnɪs] *med.* головокруже́ние; легкомы́слие; **~y** ['gɪdɪ] □ испы́тывающий головокруже́ние; (*not serious*) легкомы́сленный; *I feel ~* у меня́ кру́жится голова́; **~ height** головокружи́тельная высота́

gift [gɪft] дар, пода́рок; спосо́бность *f*, тала́нт (*of* к Д); **~ed** ['gɪftɪd] одарённый, спосо́бный

gigantic [dʒaɪ'gæntɪk] (**~ally**) гига́нтский, грома́дный

giggle ['gɪgl] **1.** хихи́канье; **2.** хихи́кать [-кнуть]

gild [gɪld] [*irr.*] [по]золоти́ть

gill [gɪl] *zo.* жа́бра

gilt [gɪlt] **1.** позоло́та; **2.** позоло́ченный

gin [dʒɪn] (*machine or alcoholic beverage*) джин

ginger ['dʒɪndʒə] **1.** имби́рь *m*; **2.** **~ up** *coll.* подстёгивать [-стегну́ть], оживля́ть [-ви́ть]; **~bread** имби́рный пря́ник; **~ly** [-lɪ] осторо́жный, ро́бкий

gipsy ['dʒɪpsɪ] цыга́н(ка)

giraffe [dʒɪ'rɑːf] жира́ф

girder ['gɜːdə] (*beam*) ба́лка

girdle ['gɜːdl] (*belt*) по́яс, куша́к; (*corset*) корсе́т

girl [gɜːl] де́вочка, де́вушка; **~friend** подру́га; **~hood** [-hʊd] де́вичество; **~ish** □ деви́чий

giro ['dʒaɪrəʊ] *banking* безнали́чная опера́ция

girth [gɜːθ] обхва́т, разме́р; *for saddle* подпру́га

gist [dʒɪst] суть *f*

give [gɪv] [*irr.*] **1.** *v/t.* да(ва́)ть; *as gift* [по]дари́ть; (*hand over*) передава́ть [-да́ть]; (*pay*) [за]плати́ть; *pleasure* доставля́ть [-а́вить]; **~ birth to** роди́ть; **~ away** отд(ав)а́ть; *coll.* выда(ва́)ть, пред(ав)а́ть; **~ in application** под(ав)а́ть; **~ off** *smell* изд(ав)а́ть; **~ up** отка́зываться [-за́ться] от (Р); **2.** *v/i.* **~** (*in*) уступа́ть [-пи́ть]; **~ into** выходи́ть на (В); **~ out** конча́ться [ко́нчиться]; обесси́леть *pf.*; **~n** ['gɪvn] **1.** *pt. p. om give*; **2.** *fig.* да́нный; (*disposed*) скло́нный (*to* к Д)

glaci|al ['gleɪsɪəl] □ леднико́вый; **~er** ['glæsɪə] ледни́к

glad [glæd] □ дово́льный; ра́достный, весёлый; *I am ~* я рад(а); **~ly** охо́тно, **~den** ['glædn] [об]ра́довать

glade [gleɪd] поля́на

gladness ['glædnɪs] ра́дость *f*

glamo|rous ['glæmərəs] обая́тельный, очарова́тельный; **~(u)r** ['glæmə] очарова́ние

glance [glɑːns] **1.** бы́стрый взгляд; **2.** (*slip*) скользи́ть [-зну́ть] (*mst. ~*

off); **~ at** взгляну́ть на (В); **~ back** огля́дываться [-ну́ться]; **~ through** просма́тривать [-смо-тре́ть]

gland [glænd] же́леза

glare [gleə] **1.** осле́пи́тельно сверка́ть; (*stare*) серди́то смотре́ть; **2.** серди́тый *or* свире́пый взгляд; осле́пи́тельный блеск

glass [glɑːs] **1.** стекло́; стака́н; *for wine* рю́мка; (*looking ~*) зе́ркало; (*a pair of*) **~es** pl. очки́ n/pl.; **2.** attr. стекля́нный; **~house** Brt. (*greenhouse*) тепли́ца; Am. (*place where glass is made*) стеко́льный заво́д; **~y** ['glɑːsɪ] □ зерка́льный; *eyes* тускло́й

glaz|e [gleɪz] **1.** глазу́рь f; **2.** глазиро́вать (*im*)pf.; *windows* застекля́ть [-ли́ть]; **~ier** ['gleɪzɪə] стеко́льщик

gleam [gliːm] **1.** мя́гкий, сла́бый свет; про́блеск, луч; **2.** поблёскивать

glean [gliːn] v/t. fig. *information, etc.* тща́тельно собира́ть

glee [gliː] ликова́ние

glib [glɪb] □ *tongue* бо́йкий; **~ excuse** благови́дный предло́г

glide [glaɪd] **1.** скользи́ть, пла́вно дви́гаться; **2.** пла́вное движе́ние; **~er** ['glaɪdə] ae. планёр

glimmer ['glɪmə] **1.** мерца́ние, ту́склый свет; **2.** мерца́ть, ту́скло свети́ть

glimpse [glɪmps] **1.:** *at a ~* с пе́рвого взгля́да; *catch a ~* = v. **glimpse; 2.** [у]ви́деть ме́льком

glint [glɪnt] **1.** блеск; **2.** блесте́ть

glisten ['glɪsn], **glitter** ['glɪtə] блесте́ть, сверка́ть, сия́ть

gloat [gləʊt] злора́дствовать

global ['gləʊbl] глоба́льный, всеми́рный

globe [gləʊb] шар; земно́й шар; гло́бус; **~trotter** [-trɒtə] зая́длый путеше́ственник

gloom [gluːm] мрак; *throw a ~ over ...* поверга́ть [-ве́ргнуть] в уны́ние; **~y** ['gluːmɪ] □ мра́чный, угрю́мый

glori|fy ['glɔːrɪfaɪ] прославля́ть [-а́вить]; **~ous** ['glɔːrɪəs] □ великоле́пный, чуде́сный

glory ['glɔːrɪ] **1.** сла́ва; **2.** торжество-

ва́ть; (*take pride*) горди́ться (**in** Т)

gloss [glɒs] **1.** вне́шний блеск; гля́нец; (*explanatory comment*) поясне́ние, толкова́ние; **2.** наводи́ть гля́нец на (В); **~ over** приукра́шивать [-кра́сить]; обойти́ молча́нием

glossary ['glɒsərɪ] глосса́рий; *at end of book* слова́рь n

glossy ['glɒsɪ] □ *hair* блестя́щий; *photo, etc.* гля́нцевый

glove [glʌv] перча́тка; **~ compartment** mot. бардачо́к

glow [gləʊ] **1.** (*burn*) горе́ть; *of coals* тлеть; *with happiness* сия́ть; **2.** за́рево; *on face* румя́нец; **~worm** светлячо́к

glucose ['gluːkəʊs] глюко́за

glue [gluː] **1.** клей; **2.** [с]кле́ить; *be ~d to* быть прико́ванным (к Д)

glum [glʌm] мра́чный, хму́рый

glut [glʌt] избы́ток; затова́ривание

glutton ['glʌtn] обжо́ра m/f; **~y** [-ɪ] обжо́рство

gnash [næʃ] [за]скрежета́ть

gnat [næt] кома́р; (*midge*) мо́шка

gnaw [nɔː] глода́ть; грызть (*a.* fig.)

gnome [nəʊm] гном, ка́рлик

go [gəʊ] **1.** [*irr.*] ходи́ть, идти́; (*pass*) проходи́ть (пройти́); (*leave*) уходи́ть [уйти́]; *by car, etc.* е́здить, [по]е́хать; (*become*) [с]де́латься; (*function*) рабо́тать; *let ~* отпуска́ть [отпусти́ть]; выпуска́ть из рук; **~ to see** заходи́ть [зайти́] (к Д), навеща́ть [-ести́ть]; **~ at** набра́сываться [-ро́ситься] на (В); **~ by** проходи́ть (пройти́) ми́мо; (*be guided by*) руково́дствоваться (Т); **~ for** идти́ [пойти́] за (Т); **~ for a walk** пойти́ на прогу́лку; **~ in for** занима́ться [-ня́ться]; **~ on** продолжа́ть [-до́лжить]; идти́ да́льше; **~ through with** доводи́ть до конца́ (В); **~ without** обходи́ться (обойти́сь) без (Р); **2.** ходьба́, движе́ние; coll. эне́ргия; *on the* ~ на ходу́; на нога́х; *no* ~ coll. не вы́йдет; не пойдёт; *in one* ~ с пе́рвой попы́тки; в одно́м захо́де; *have a ~ at* [по]про́бовать (В)

goad [gəʊd] побужда́ть [побуди́ть]; подстрека́ть [-кну́ть]

goal [gəʊl] цель f; sport воро́та n/pl.;

G

гол; ~**keeper** врата́рь *m*

goat [gəʊt] козёл, коза́

gobble ['gɒbl] есть жа́дно, бы́стро

go-between ['gəʊbɪtwiːn] посре́дник

goblin ['gɒblɪn] домово́й

god [gɒd] (*deity*) бог; (*supreme being*) (**God**) Бог; божество́; *fig.* куми́р; **thank God!** сла́ва Бо́гу!; ~**child** кре́стник *m*, -ница *f*; ~**dess** ['gɒdɪs] боги́ня; ~**father** крёстный оте́ц; ~**forsaken** ['-fəseɪkən] бо́гом забы́тый; забро́шенный; ~**less** ['-lɪs] безбо́жный; ~**mother** крёстная мать *f*

goggle ['gɒgl] 1. тара́щить глаза́; 2. (*a pair of*) ~**s** *pl.* защи́тные очки́ *n/pl.*

going ['gəʊɪŋ] 1. де́йствующий; **be ~ to** *inf.* наме́реваться, собира́ться (+ *inf.*); ~ **concern** процвета́ющее предприя́тие; 2. (*leave*) ухо́д; отъе́зд; ~**s-on** [gəʊɪŋz'ɒn]: **what** ~! ну и дела́!

gold [gəʊld] 1. зо́лото; 2. золото́й; ~**en** ['gəʊldən] золото́й; ~**finch** *zo.* щего́л

golf [gɒlf] гольф

gondola ['gɒndələ] гондо́ла

gone [gɒn] *pt. u. p. om* **go**

good [gʊd] хоро́ший; (*kind*) до́брый; (*suitable*) го́дный, (*beneficial*) поле́зный; ~ **for colds** помога́ет при просту́де; **Good Friday** *relig.* Страстна́я пя́тница; **be ~ at** быть спосо́бным к (Д); 2. добро́, бла́го; по́льза; ~**s** *pl.* това́р; **that's no** ~ э́то бесполе́зно; **for** ~ навсегда́!, проща́йте!; ~**by(e)** [gʊd'baɪ] 1. до свида́ния!, проща́йте!; 2. проща́ние; ~**natured** доброду́шный; ~**ness** ['-nɪs] доброта́; *int.* Го́споди!; ~**will** доброжела́тельность *f*

goody ['gʊdɪ] *coll.* конфе́та, ла́комство

goose [guːs], *pl.* **geese** [giːs] гусь *m*

gooseberry ['gʊzbərɪ] крыжо́вник (*no pl.*)

goose|flesh, *a.* ~**pimples** *pl. fig.* гуси́ная ко́жа, мура́шки

gorge [gɔːdʒ] (*ravine*) у́зкое уще́лье

gorgeous ['gɔːdʒəs] великоле́пный

gorilla [gə'rɪlə] гори́лла

gory ['gɔːrɪ] □ окрова́вленный, крова́вый

gospel ['gɒspəl] Ева́нгелие

gossip ['gɒsɪp] 1. спле́тня; спле́тник *m*, -ница *f*; 2. [на]спле́тничать

got [gɒt] *pt. u. pt. p. om* **get**

Gothic ['gɒθɪk] готи́ческий

gourmet ['gʊəmeɪ] гурма́н

gout [gaʊt] *med.* пода́гра

govern ['gʌvn] *v/t.* (*rule*) пра́вить, (*administer*) управля́ть (Т); ~**ess** [-ənɪs] гуверна́нтка; ~**ment** [-ənmənt] прави́тельство; управле́ние; *attr.* прави́тельственный; ~**or** [-ənə] губерна́тор; *coll.* (*boss*) хозя́ин; шеф

gown [gaʊn] пла́тье; *univ.* ма́нтия

grab [græb] *coll.* схва́тывать [-ати́ть]

grace [greɪs] 1. гра́ция, изя́щество; 2. *fig.* украша́ть [украси́ть]; удоста́ивать [-сто́ить]; ~**ful** ['greɪsfl] □ грацио́зный, изя́щный; ~**fulness** [-nɪs] грацио́зность *f*, изя́щество

gracious ['greɪʃəs] □ любе́зный; благоскло́нный; (*merciful*) ми́лостивый; **goodness** ~! Го́споди!

gradation [grə'deɪʃn] града́ция, постепе́нный перехо́д

grade [greɪd] 1. сте́пень *f*; (*rank*) ранг; (*quality*) ка́чество; *Am. educ.* класс; (*slope*) укло́н; 2. [рас]сортирова́ть

gradient ['greɪdɪənt] укло́н; **steep** ~ круто́й спуск *и.* подъём

gradua|l ['grædʒʊəl] □ постепе́нный; ~**te** 1. [-eɪt] градуи́ровать (*im)pf.*, наноси́ть деле́ния; конча́ть университе́т; *Am.* конча́ть (любо́е) уче́бное заведе́ние; 2. [-ɪt] *univ.* выпускни́к университе́та; ~**tion** [grædʒʊ'eɪʃn] градуиро́вка; *Am.* оконча́ние (вы́сшего) уче́бного заведе́ния

graft [grɑːft] 1. *hort.* (*scion*) черено́к; приви́вка; 2. приви(ва́)ть; *med.* переса́живать ткань *f*

grain [greɪn] зерно́; (*cereals*) хле́бные зла́ки *m/pl.*; (*particle*) крупи́нка; *fig.* **against the** ~ не по нутру́

gramma|r ['græmə] грамма́тика; ~**tical** [grə'mætɪkəl] □ граммати́ческий

gram(me) [græm] грамм

granary ['grænərɪ] амба́р; жи́тница *a. fig.*

grand [grænd] 1. □ *view, etc.* вели́чественный; *plans, etc.* грандио́зный; *we had a ~ time* мы прекра́сно прове́ли вре́мя; 2. *mus.* (*a. ~ piano*) роя́ль *m*; ~**child** ['grænt∫aɪld] внук, вну́чка; ~**eur** ['grændʒə] грандио́зность *f*; вели́чие

grandiose ['grændɪəus] □ грандио́зный

grandparents *pl.* де́душка и ба́бушка

grant [grɑ:nt] **1.** предоставля́ть [-а́вить]; (*admit as true*) допуска́ть [-сти́ть]; **2.** дар; субси́дия; *student's* стипе́ндия; *take for ~ed* принима́ть [приня́ть] как само́ собо́й разуме́ющееся

granul|ated ['grænjʊleɪtɪd] гранули́рованный; ~**e** ['grænju:l] зёрнышко

grape [greɪp] *collect.* виногра́д; *a bunch of ~s* гроздь виногра́да; *a ~* виногра́дина; ~**fruit** грейп-фру́т

graph [grɑ:f] гра́фик; ~**ic** ['græfɪk] графи́ческий; нагля́дный; *description* я́ркий; *~ arts pl.* гра́фика; ~**ite** ['græfaɪt] графи́т

grapple ['græpl]: *~ with* боро́ться с (T); *fig. difficulties* пыта́ться преодоле́ть

grasp [grɑ:sp] **1.** хвата́ть [схвати́ть] (*by* за В); *in one's hand* заж(им)а́ть; хвата́ться [схвати́ться] (*at* за В); **2.** понима́ть [поня́ть]; *it's beyond my ~* э́то вы́ше моего́ понима́ния; *she kept the child's hand in her* ~ она́ кре́пко держа́ла ребёнка за́ руку

grass [grɑ:s] трава́; (*pasture*) па́стбище; ~**hopper** ['-hɒpə] кузне́чик; *~ widow* ['-wɪdəʊ] соло́менная вдова́; ~**y** ['-ɪ] травяно́й

grate [greɪt] **1.** (*fireplace*) решётка; **2.** *cheese, etc.* [на]тере́ть; *teeth* [за]скрежета́ть; *~ on fig.* раздража́ть [-жи́ть] (В)

grateful ['greɪtfl] □ благода́рный

grater ['greɪtə] тёрка

grati|fication [grætɪfɪ'keɪ∫n] удовлетворе́ние; ~**fy** ['grætɪfaɪ] удовлетворя́ть [-ри́ть]; (*indulge*) потака́ть (Д)

grating[1] ['greɪtɪŋ] □ скрипу́чий, ре́зкий

grating[2] [-] решётка

gratitude ['grætɪtju:d] благода́рность *f*

gratuit|ous [grə'tju:ɪtəs] □ беспла́тный, безвозме́здный; ~**y** [-ətɪ] посо́бие

grave[1] [greɪv] □ серьёзный, ве́ский; *illness, etc.* тяжёлый

grave[2] [-] моги́ла

gravel ['grævl] гра́вий

graveyard кла́дбище

gravitation [grævɪ'teɪ∫n] притяже́ние; тяготе́ние (*a. fig.*)

gravity ['grævətɪ] серьёзность *f*; *of situation* тя́жесть *f*, опа́сность *f*

gravy ['greɪvɪ] (мясна́я) подли́вка

gray [greɪ] се́рый; → *Brt.* **grey**

graze[1] [greɪz] пасти́(сь)

graze[2] [-] заде́(ва́)ть; (*scrape*) [по]цара́пать

grease [gri:s] **1.** жир; *tech.* консисте́нтная сма́зка; **2.** [gri:z] сма́з(ы)в)ать

greasy ['gri:sɪ] □ жи́рный; *road* ско́льзкий

great [greɪt] □ вели́кий, большо́й; (*huge*) огро́мный; *coll.* великоле́пный; ~**coat** *mil.* шине́ль *f*; ~**grandchild** [greɪt'grænt∫aɪld] пра́внук *m*, -у́чка *f*; ~**ly** [-lɪ] о́чень, си́льно; ~**ness** [-nɪs] вели́чие

greed [gri:d] жа́дность *f*; ~**y** ['gri:dɪ] □ жа́дный (*of,* for к Д)

Greek [gri:k] **1.** грек *m*, греча́нка *f*; **2.** гре́ческий

green [gri:n] **1.** зелёный; (*unripe*) незре́лый; *fig.* нео́пытный; **2.** зелёный цвет, зелёная кра́ска; (*grassy plot*) лужа́йка; ~**s** *pl.* зе́лень *f*, о́вощи *m/pl.*; ~**grocery** овощно́й магази́н; ~**house** тепли́ца, оранжере́я; ~**ish** ['gri:nɪ∫] зеленова́тый

greet [gri:t] *guests, etc.* приве́тствовать; [по]здоро́ваться; ~**ing** ['gri:tɪŋ] приве́тствие; приве́т

grenade [grɪ'neɪd] *mil.* грана́та

grew [gru:] *pt. of* **grow**

grey [greɪ] **1.** се́рый; *hair* седо́й; **2.** се́рый цвет, се́рая кра́ска; **3.** посере́ть; *turn ~* [по]седе́ть; ~**hound** борза́я

grid [grɪd] решётка

grief [griːf] го́ре; *come to* ~ потерпе́ть *pf.* неуда́чу, попа́сть *pf.* в беду́

griev|ance ['griːvns] оби́да; *(complaint)* жа́лоба; *nurse a* ~ затаи́ть оби́ду; ~**e** [griːv] горева́ть; *(cause grief to)* огорча́ть [-чи́ть]; ~**ous** ['griːvəs] □ го́рестный, печа́льный

grill [gril] 1. (электро)гри́ль; *(on cooker)* решётка; жа́реное на решётке в гри́ле мя́со; 2. жа́рить на решётке (в гри́ле); ~**room** гриль-ба́р

grim [grim] □ жесто́кий; *smile, etc.* мра́чный

grimace [gri'meis] 1. грима́са, ужи́мка; 2. грима́сничать

grim|e [graim] грязь *f*; ~**y** ['graimi] □ запа́чканный, гря́зный

grin [grin] 1. усме́шка; 2. усмеха́ться [-хну́ться]

grind [graind] *[irr.]* 1. [с]моло́ть; разма́лывать [-моло́ть]; *to powder* растира́ть [растере́ть]; *(sharpen)* [на]точи́ть; *fig.* зубри́ть; 2. разма́лывание; тяжёлая, ску́чная рабо́та; ~**stone** точи́льный ка́мень *m*; *keep one's nose to the* ~ труди́ться без о́тдыха

grip [grip] 1. *(handle)* ру́чка, рукоя́тка; *(understanding)* понима́ние; *fig.* тиски́ *m/pl.*; 2. *(take hold of)* схва́тывать [схвати́ть]; *fig.* овладева́ть внима́нием (P)

gripe [graip] ворча́ние; *(colic pains)* ко́лики *f/pl.*

gripping ['gripiŋ] захва́тывающий

grisly ['grizli] ужа́сный

gristle ['grisl] хрящ

grit [grit] 1. песо́к, гра́вий; *coll.* твёрдость хара́ктера; ~**s** *pl.* овся́ная крупа́; 2. [за]скрежета́ть (Т)

grizzly ['grizli] 1. се́рый; *hair* с про́седью; 2. североамерика́нский медве́дь *m*, гри́зли *m indecl.*

groan [grəʊn] 1. о́хать [о́хнуть]; *with pain, etc.* [за]стона́ть; 2. стон

grocer|ies ['grəʊsəriz] *pl.* бакале́я, ~**y** [-ri] бакале́йный отде́л

groggy ['grɒgi] нетвёрдый на нога́х; *after illness* сла́бый

groin [grɔin] *anat.* пах

groom [gruːm] 1. ко́нюх; *(bride~)* жени́х; 2. уха́живать за (ло́шадью); хо́лить; *well* ~**ed** хоро́шо и тща́тельно оде́тый, опря́тный ухо́женный

groove [gruːv] желобо́к; *tech.* паз; *fig.* рути́на, привы́чка, колея́

grope [grəʊp] идти́ о́щупью; нащу́п(ыв)ать (*a. fig.*)

gross [grəʊs] 1. □ *(flagrant)* вопию́щий; *(fat)* ту́чный; *(coarse)* гру́бый; *fin.* валово́й, бру́тто; 2. ма́сса, гросс

grotesque [grəʊ'tesk] гроте́скный

grotto ['grɒtəʊ] грот

grouch [graʊtʃ] *Am. coll.* 1. дурно́е настрое́ние; 2. быть не в ду́хе; ~**y** [-i] ворчли́вый

ground[1] [graʊnd] *pt. u pt. p. om* **grind**; ~ *glass* ма́товое стекло́

ground[2] [-] 1. *mst.* земля́, по́чва; *(area of land)* уча́сток земли́; площа́дка; *(reason)* основа́ние; ~**s** *pl. adjoining house* сад, парк; *on the* ~**(s)** на основа́нии (P); *stand one's* ~ уде́рживать свои́ пози́ции, проявля́ть твёрдость; 2. обосно́вывать [-нова́ть]; *el.* заземля́ть [-ли́ть]; *(teach)* обуча́ть осно́вам предме́та; ~ *floor* [graʊnd'flɔ:] *Brt.* пе́рвый эта́ж; ~**less** [-lis] □ беспричи́нный, необосно́ванный; ~**nut** ара́хис; ~**work** фунда́мент, осно́ва

group [gruːp] 1. гру́ппа; 2. соб(и)-ра́ться [с]группирова́ть(ся)

grove [grəʊv] ро́ща, лесо́к

grovel ['grɒvl] *fig.* пресмыка́ться; зай́скивать

grow [grəʊ] *[irr.]* *v/i.* расти́; выраста́ть [вы́расти]; *(become)* [с]де́латься, станови́ться [стать]; *v/t. bot.* выра́щивать [вы́растить]; культиви́ровать (*im*)*pf.*

growl [graʊl] [за]рыча́ть

grow|n [grəʊn] *pt. p. om* **grow**; ~**nup** ['grəʊnʌp] взро́слый; ~**th** [grəʊθ] рост; *med.* о́пухоль *f*

grub [grʌb] 1. личи́нка; 2. *(dig in dirt)* ры́ться; ~**by** ['grʌbi] гря́зный

grudge [grʌdʒ] 1. неохо́та, недово́льство; *(envy)* за́висть *f*; 2. [по]зави́довать (Д, в П); неохо́тно дава́ть; [по]жале́ть

gruff [grʌf] □ рéзкий; грýбый; *voice* хри́плый

grumble ['grʌmbl] [за]ворчáть; (*complain*) [по]жáловаться; *of thunder etc.* [за]грохотáть; ~r [-ə] *fig.* ворчýн(ья *f* / *m*)

grunt [grʌnt] хрю́кать [-кнуть]; *of person* [про]бурчáть

guarant|ee [gærən'tiː] **1.** гарáнтия; поручи́тельство; **2.** гаранти́ровать (*im*)*pf.*; ручáться за (В); ~or [gærən'tɔː] *law* поручи́тель (-ница *f*) *m*; ~y ['gærənti] гарáнтия

guard [gɑːd] **1.** охрáна; *mil.* карáул; *rail.* проводни́к; ~s *pl.* гвáрдия; **be on one's ~** быть начеку́; **2.** *v/t.* охранять [-ни́ть]; сторожи́ть; (*protect*) защищáть [защити́ть] (*from* от Р); *v/i.* [по]беречься, остерегáться [-речься] (*against* Р); ~ian ['gɑːdiən] *law* опекýн; ~ianship [-ʃɪp] *law* опекýнство

guess [ges] **1.** догáдка, предположéние; **2.** отгáдывать [-дáть], угáдывать [-дáть]; *Am.* считáть, полагáть

guest [gest] гóсть(я *f*) *m*; ~house пансио́н

guffaw [gə'fɔː] хóхот

guidance ['gaidns] руково́дство

guide [gaid] **1.** *for tourists* экскурсово́д, гид; **2.** направлять [-рáвить]; руководи́ть (Т); ~book путеводи́тель *m*

guile [gail] хи́трость *f*, ковáрство; ~ful ['gailfl] □ ковáрный; ~less [-lıs] □ простодýшный

guilt [gilt] винá, вино́вность *f*; ~less ['giltlıs] невино́вный; ~y ['gilti] □ вино́вный, винова́тый

guise [gaiz]: *under the ~ of* под ви́дом (Р)

guitar [gi'tɑː] гитáра

gulf [gʌlf] зали́в; *fig.* пропасть *f*

gull¹ [gʌl] чáйка

gull² [-] обмáнывать [-нýть]; [о]дурáчить

gullet ['gʌlit] пищево́д; (*throat*) гло́тка

gullible ['gʌlibl] легкове́рный

gulp [gʌlp] **1.** жáдно глотáть; **2.** глото́к; *at one ~* зáлпом

gum¹ [gʌm] деснá

gum² [-] **1.** клей; *chewing ~* жевáтельная рези́нка; **2.** склéи(ва)ть

gun [gʌn] ору́дие, пýшка; (*rifle*) ружьё; (*pistol*) пистолéт; ~boat каноне́рка; ~man банди́т; ~ner *mil.*, *naut.* ['gʌnə] артиллери́ст, канони́р, пулемётчик; ~powder по́рох

gurgle ['gɜːgl] *of water* [за]бýлькать

gush [gʌʃ] **1.** си́льный пото́к; ~ *of enthusiasm* взрыв энтузиáзма; **2.** хлы́нуть *pf.*; ли́ться пото́ком; *fig.* бýрно изливáть чýвства

gust [gʌst] *of wind* поры́в

gusto ['gʌstəʊ] смак; *with ~* с больши́м энтузиáзмом

gut [gʌt] кишкá; ~s *pl.* внýтренности *f*/*pl.*; *coll.* **he has plenty of ~s** он мýжественный (*or* волево́й) челове́к

gutter ['gʌtə] сто́чная канáва; *on roof* жёлоб; ~ *press* бульвáрная прéсса

guy [gai] *chiefly Brt.* (*person of grotesque appearance*) чýчело; *Am. coll.* (*fellow, person*) мáлый; пáрень *m*

guzzle ['gʌzl] жáдно пить; (*eat*) есть с жáдностью

gymnas|ium [dʒim'neiziəm] спорти́вный зал; ~tics [dʒim'næstiks] *pl.* гимнáстика

gypsy ['dʒipsi] *esp. Am.* цыгáн(ка)

gyrate [dʒai'reit] дви́гаться по кругу́, вращáться

H

haberdashery ['hæbədæ∫əri] (*goods*) галантерея; (*shop*) галантерейный магазин

habit ['hæbɪt] привычка; **~able** ['hæbɪtəbl] годный для жилья; **~ation** [hæbɪ'teɪ∫n] жильё

habitual [hə'bɪt∫uəl] обычный; (*done by habit*) привычный

hack¹ [hæk] [на-, с]рубить

hack² [~] (*horse*) наёмная лошадь *f*, кляча; (*writer*) халтурщик; *coll.* писака

hackneyed ['hæknɪd] *fig.* избитый

had [d, əd, həd; *strong* hæd] *pt. u pt. p. om* **have**

haddock ['hædək] пикша

h(a)emoglobin [hi:mə'gləubɪn] гемоглобин

h(a)emorrhage ['hemərɪdʒ] кровоизлияние

haggard ['hægəd] □ измождённый, осунувшийся

haggle ['hægl] (*bargain*) торговаться

hail¹ [heɪl]: ~ *a taxi* подозвать такси

hail² [~] **1.** град; **2.** *it ~ed today* сегодня был град; **~stone** градина

hair [heə] волос; *keep your ~ on!* спокойно!; **~cut** стрижка; **~do** причёска; **~dresser** парикмахер; **~dryer** фен; **~pin** шпилька; **~raising** страшный; **~'s breadth** минимальное расстояние; **~splitting** крохоборство; **~y** [~rɪ] волосатый

hale [heɪl] здоровый, крепкий

half [ha:f, hæf] **1.** половина; ~ *past two* половина третьего; *one and a ~* полтора *n/m*, полторы *f*, *go halves* делить пополам; *not ~! Brt. coll.* ещё бы!; а как же!; **2.** полу...; половинный; **3.** почти; наполовину; **~caste** метис; **~hearted** □ равнодушный, вялый; **~length** (*a. ~portrait*) поясной портрет; **~penny** ['heɪpnɪ] полпенни *n indecl.*; **~time** *sport* конец тайма; **~way** на полпути; **~witted** полоумный

halibut ['hælɪbət] палтус

hall [hɔ:l] зал; холл, вестибюль *m*; (*entrance ~*) прихожая; *college* (*residence*) общежитие для студентов

hallow ['hæləu] освящать [-ятить]

halo ['heɪləu] *astr.* ореол (*a. fig.*); *of saint* нимб

halt [hɔ:lt] **1.** (*temporary stop*) привал, остановка; *come to a ~* остановиться *pf.*; **2.** останавливать(ся) [-новить(ся)]; делать привал; *mst. fig.* (*hesitate*) колебаться; запинаться [запнуться]

halve [ha:v] **1.** делить пополам; **2. ~s** [ha:vz, hævz] *pl. om* **half**

ham [hæm] (*pig thigh*) окорок, (*meat of pig thigh*) ветчина

hamburger ['hæmbɜ:gə] булочка с котлетой, гамбургер

hamlet ['hæmlɪt] деревушка

hammer ['hæmə] **1.** молоток; *sledge ~* молот; **2.** ковать молотом; бить молотком; (*knock*) [по-]стучать; (*form by ~ing*) выковывать [выковать]; **~ into s.o.'s head** вбивать [вбить] кому-л. в голову

hammock ['hæmək] гамак

hamper¹ ['hæmpə] корзина с крышкой

hamper² [~] [вос]препятствовать; [по]мешать (Д)

hand [hænd] **1.** рука; (*writing*) почерк; *of watch* стрелка; (*worker*) рабочий; *at ~* под рукой; *a good* (*poor*) *~ at* (не-)искусный в (П); *change ~s* переходить [-ейти] из рук в руки; *~ and glove* в тесной связи; *lend a ~* помогать [-мочь]; *off ~* экспромтом; *on ~ comm.* имеющийся в продаже; в распоряжении; *on the one ~* с одной стороны; *on the other ~* с другой стороны; *~to~* рукопашный; *come to ~* попадаться [-пасться] под руку; **2.** ~ *down* оставлять потомству; ~ *in* вручать [-чить]; ~ *over* перед(ав)ать; **~bag** дамская сумочка; **~brake** *mot.* ручной тормоз;

~cuff нару́чник; **~ful** ['hændfl] горсть *f, coll.* "наказа́ние"; **she's a real ~** она́ су́щее наказа́ние

handicap ['hændıkæp] **1.** поме́ха; *sport* гандика́п; **2.** ста́вить в невы́годное положе́ние; **~ped: physically ~** с физи́ческим недоста́тком; **mentally ~** у́мственно отста́лый

handi|craft ['hændıkrɑːft] ручна́я рабо́та; ремесло́; **~work** ручна́я рабо́та; **is this your ~?** *fig.* э́то твои́х рук де́ло?

handkerchief ['hæŋkətʃıf] носово́й плато́к

handle ['hændl] **1.** ру́чка; *of tool, etc.* рукоя́тка; **2.** держа́ть в рука́х, тро́гать или брать рука́ми; (*deal with*) обходи́ться [обойти́сь] с (Т); обраща́ться (Т)

hand|made [hænd'meıd] ручно́й рабо́ты; **~shake** рукопожа́тие; **~some** ['hænsəm] краси́вый; (*generous*) ще́дрый; (*large*) поря́дочный; **~writing** по́черк; **~y** ['hændı] удо́бный; (*nearby*) бли́зкий

hang [hæŋ] **1.** [*irr.*] *v/t.* ве́шать [пове́сить]; *lamp, etc.* подве́шивать [-ве́сить]; (*pt. и pt. p.* **~ed**) ве́шать [пове́сить]; *v/i.* висе́ть; **~ about, ~ around** слоня́ться, около́ниваться; **~ on** держа́ть(ся) (в За); *fig.* упо́рствовать; **~ on!** подожди́те мину́тку!; **2.: get the ~ of** понима́ть [-ня́ть]; разобра́ться [разбира́ться]

hangar ['hæŋə] анга́р

hanger ['hæŋə] *for clothes* ве́шалка

hangings ['hæŋıŋz] *pl.* драпиро́вки *f/pl.,* занаве́ски *f/pl.*

hangover ['hæŋəʊvə] *from drinking* похме́лье; *survival* пережи́ток

haphazard [hæp'hæzəd] **1.** науда́чу, наобу́м; **2.** □ случа́йный

happen ['hæpən] случа́ться [-чи́ться], происходи́ть [произойти́]; отка́зываться [-за́ться]; **he~ed to be at home** он оказа́лся до́ма; **it so ~ed that ...** случи́лось так, что ...; **~ (up)on** случа́йно встре́тить; **~ing** ['hæpənıŋ] слу́чай, собы́тие

happi|ly ['hæpılı] счастли́во, к сча́стью; **~ness** [-nıs] сча́стье

happy ['hæpı] □ *com.* счастли́вый; (*fortunate*) уда́чный; **~-go-lucky** беспе́чный

harangue [hə'ræŋ] разглаго́льствовать

harass ['hærəs] [за]трави́ть; (*pester*) изводи́ть [-вести́]; [из]му́чить

harbo(u)r ['hɑːbər] **1.** га́вань *f,* порт; **~ duties: physically** порто́вые сбо́ры; **2.** (*give shelter to*) дать убе́жище (Д), приюти́ть; *fig.* зата́ивать [-и́ть]

hard [hɑːd] **1.** *adj. com.* твёрдый, жёсткий; (*strong*) кре́пкий; (*difficult*) тру́дный; тяжёлый; **~ cash** нали́чные *pl.* (де́ньги); **~ currency** твёрдая валю́та; **~ of hearing** туго́й на́ ухо; **2.** *adv.* твёрдо; кре́пко; си́льно; упо́рно; с трудо́м; **~ by** бли́зко, ря́дом; **~ up** в затрудни́тельном фина́нсовом положе́нии; **~-boiled** [hɑːd'bɔıld] → **egg**, *fig.* бесчу́вственный, чёрствый; *Am.* хладнокро́вный; **~-disk** жёсткий диск; **~en** ['hɑːdn] затвердева́ть, [за]тверде́ть; *fig.* закаля́ть(ся) [-ли́ть(ся)]; **~-headed** [hɑːd'hedıd] □ практи́чный, тре́звый; **~-hearted** [hɑːd'hɑːtıd] бесчу́вственный; **~ly** ['hɑːdlı] с тру-до́м, едва́, едва́ ли; **~ship** [-ʃıp] невзго́ды; тру́дности; (*lack of money*) нужда́; **~ware** *comput.* аппара́тное обеспе́чение; **~y** ['hɑːdı] □ сме́лый, отва́жный; (*able to bear hard work, etc.*) выно́сливый

hare [heə] за́яц; **~brained** опроме́тчивый; (*foolish*) глу́пый

harm [hɑːm] **1.** вред, зло; (*damage*) уще́рб; **2.** [по]вреди́ть (Д); **~ful** ['hɑːmfl] □ вре́дный, па́губный; **~less** [-lıs] □ безвре́дный, безоби́дный

harmon|ious [hɑː'məʊnıəs] □ гармони́чный, стро́йный; **~ize** ['hɑːmənaız] *v/t.* гармонизи́ровать (*im*)*pf.*; приводи́ть в гармо́нию; *v/i.* гармони́ровать; **~y** [-nı] гармо́ния, созву́чие; (*agreement*) согла́сие

harness ['hɑːnıs] **1.** у́пряжь *f,* сбру́я; **2.** запряга́ть [запря́чь]

harp [hɑːp] **1.** а́рфа; **2.** игра́ть на а́рфе; **~ (up)on** тверди́ть, завести́ *pf.* волы́нку о (П)

harpoon [hɑːˈpuːn] гарпу́н, острога́

harrow [ˈhærəʊ] *agric.* **1.** борона́; **2.** [вз]борони́ть; *fig.* [из]му́чить; **~ing** [-ɪŋ] *fig.* мучи́тельный

harsh [hɑːʃ] ре́зкий; жёсткий; (*stern*) стро́гий, суро́вый; *to taste* те́рпкий

harvest [ˈhɑːvɪst] **1.** *of wheat, etc.* жа́тва, убо́рка; *of apples, etc.* сбор; урожа́й; **bumper ~** небыва́лый урожа́й; **2.** собира́ть урожа́й

has [z, əz, həz;, *strong* hæz] 3rd p. sg. pres. om **have**

hash [hæʃ] ру́бленое мя́со; *fig.* пу́таница

hast|e [heɪst] спе́шка; поспе́шность *f*, торопли́вость *f*; **make ~** [по]спеши́ть; **~en** [ˈheɪsn] спеши́ть, [по]торопи́ться; (*speed up*) ускоря́ть [-о́рить]; **~y** [ˈheɪstɪ] □ поспе́шный; необду́манный

hat [hæt] шля́па; *without brim* ша́пка; **talk through one's ~** нести́ чушь *f*

hatch [hætʃ] *naut.*, *ae.* люк

hatchet [ˈhætʃɪt] топо́рик

hat|e [heɪt] **1.** не́нависть *f*; **2.** ненави́деть; **~ful** [ˈheɪtfl] ненави́стный; **~red** [ˈheɪtrɪd] не́нависть *f*

haught|iness [ˈhɔːtɪnɪs] надме́нность *f*, высокоме́рие; **~y** [-tɪ] □ надме́нный, высокоме́рный

haul [hɔːl] **1.** перево́зка; (*catch*) уло́в; **2.** тяну́ть; перевози́ть [-везти́]; **~age** [-ɪdʒ] транспортиро́вка, доста́вка

haunch [hɔːntʃ] бедро́

haunt [hɔːnt] **1.** *of ghost* появля́ться [-ви́ться] в (П); (*frequent*) ча́сто посеща́ть; **2.** люби́мое ме́сто; *of criminals, etc.* прито́н; **~ed look** затра́вленный вид

have [v, əv, həv;, *strong* hæv] **1.** [*irr.*] *v/t.* име́ть; **I ~ to do** я до́лжен сде́лать; **one's hair cut** [по-] стри́чься; **he will ~ it that …** он наста́ивает на том, чтобы (+ *inf.*); **I had better go** мне лу́чше уйти́; **I had rather go** я предпочёл бы уйти́; **~ about one** име́ть при себе́; **~ it your own way** поступа́й как зна́ешь; *opinion* ду́май, что хо́чешь; **2.** *v/aux.* вспомога́тельный

глаго́л для образова́ния перфе́ктной фо́рмы: **I ~ come** я пришёл

havoc [ˈhævək] опустоше́ние; (*destruction*) разруше́ние; **play ~ with** вноси́ть [внести́] беспоря́док/ха́ос в (В); разру́шить *pf.*

hawk [hɔːk] (*a. pol.*) я́стреб

hawker [ˈhɔːkə] у́личный торго́вец

hawthorn [ˈhɔːθɔːn] боя́рышник

hay [heɪ] се́но; **~fever** се́нная лихора́дка; **~loft** сенова́л; **~stack** стог се́на

hazard [ˈhæzəd] **1.** риск; (*danger*) опа́сность *f*; **2.** рискова́ть [-кну́ть]; **~ous** [ˈhæzədəs] □ риско́ванный

haze [heɪz] дымка, тума́н

hazel [ˈheɪzl] **1.** (*tree*) оре́шник; **2.** (*colo[u]r*) ка́рий; **~nut** лесно́й оре́х

hazy [ˈheɪzɪ] □ тума́нный; *fig.* сму́тный

H-bomb водоро́дная бо́мба

he [ɪ, hɪ;, *strong* hiː] **1.** *pron. pers.* он; **~ who …** тот, кто …; **2. ~-** … *перед названием животного обозначает самца*

head [hed] **1.** *com.* голова́; *of government, etc.* глава́; *of department, etc.* руководи́тель *m*, нача́льник; *of bed* изголо́вье; *of coin* лицева́я сторона́, орёл; **come to a ~** *fig.* дости́гнуть *pf.* крити́ческой ста́дии; **get it into one's ~ that …** вбить себе́ в го́лову, что …; **2.** гла́вный; **3.** *v/t.* возглавля́ть; **~ off** (*prevent*) предотвраща́ть [-ати́ть]; **~ for** *v/i.* направля́ться [-а́виться]; держа́ть курс на (В); **~ache** [ˈhedeɪk] головна́я боль *f*; **~dress** го́ловно́й убо́р; **~ing** [-ɪŋ] загла́вие; **~land** мыс; **~light** *mot.* фа́ра; **~line** (газе́тный) заголо́вок; **~long** *adj.* опроме́тчивый; *adv.* опроме́тчиво; очертя́ го́лову; **~master** дире́ктор шко́лы; **~phone** нау́шник; **~quarters** *pl.* штаб; *of department, etc.* гла́вное управле́ние; **~strong** своево́льный, упря́мый; **~way: make ~** де́лать успе́хи, продвига́ться; **~y** [ˈhedɪ] □ опьяня́ющий; *with success* опьянённый

heal [hiːl] зале́чивать [-чи́ть], исцеля́ть [-ли́ть]; (*a. ~ up*) зажи(ва́)ть

health [helθ] здоро́вье; **~ful** [-fl] □ целе́бный; **~resort** куро́рт; **~y** [ˈhelθɪ] здоро́вый; (*good for health*) поле́зный

heap [hi:p] **1.** ку́ча, гру́да; *fig.* ма́сса, у́йма; **2.** нагроможда́ть [-мозди́ть]; *of food, etc.* накла́дывать [-ложи́ть]

hear [hɪə] [*irr.*] [у]слы́шать; [по-]слу́шать; ~ **s.o. out** вы́слушать *pf.*; ~**d** [hɜːd] *pt. u pt. p. om* **hear**, ~**er** [ˈhɪərə] слу́шатель(ница *f*) *m*; ~**ing** [-ɪŋ] слух; *law* слу́шание де́ла; *within* ~ в преде́ле слы́шимости; ~**say** [ˈhɪəseɪ] слу́хи, то́лки

heart [hɑːt] се́рдце; му́жество; (*essence*) суть *f*; (*innermost part*) сердцеви́на; *of forest* глубина́; ~**s** *pl.* че́рви *f/pl.*; *fig.* се́рдце, душа́; *by* ~ наизу́сть; *lose* ~ па́дать ду́хом; *take* ~ воспря́нуть ду́хом; *take to* ~ принима́ть бли́зко к се́рдцу; ~**attack** серде́чный при́ступ; ~**broken** уби́тый го́рем; ~**burn** изжо́га; ~**en** [ˈhɑːtn] ободря́ть [-ри́ть]; ~**felt** душе́вный, и́скренний

hearth [hɑːθ] оча́г (*a. fig.*)

heart|less [ˈhɑːtlɪs] □ бессерде́чный; ~**rending** [-rendɪŋ] душераздира́ющий; ~**to-**~ дру́жеский; ~**y** [ˈhɑːtɪ] □ дру́жеский, серде́чный; (*healthy*) здоро́вый

heat [hi:t] **1.** *com.* жара́, жар; *fig.* пыл; *sport* забе́г, заплы́в, заезд; **2.** нагре́ва́)ть(ся); *fig.* [раз]горячи́ть; ~**er** [ˈhi:tə] обогрева́тель

heath [hi:θ] ме́стность *f*, поро́сшая ве́реском; (*waste land*) пу́стошь *f*; *bot.* ве́реск

heathen [ˈhi:ðn] **1.** язы́чник; **2.** язы́ческий

heating [ˈhi:tɪŋ] обогрева́ние; отопле́ние

heave [hi:v] **1.** подъём; **2.** [*irr.*] *v/t.* (*haul*) поднима́ть [-ня́ть]; *v/i. of waves* вздыма́ться; (*strain*) напряга́ться [-я́чься]

heaven [hevn] небеса́ *n/pl.*, не́бо; *move* ~ *and earth* [с]де́лать всё возмо́жное; ~**ly** [-lɪ] небе́сный; *fig.* великоле́пный

heavy [ˈhevɪ] □ *com.* тяжёлый; *crop* оби́льный; *sea* бу́рный; *sky* мра́чный; неуклю́жий; ~**weight** *sport* тяжелове́с

heckle [ˈhekl] прерыва́ть замеча́ниями; задава́ть ка́верзные вопро́сы

hectic [ˈhektɪk] *activity* лихора́дочный; ~ *day* напряжённый день *m*

hedge [hedʒ] **1.** жива́я и́згородь *f*; **2.** *v/t.* огора́живать и́згородью; *v/i.* (*evade*) уклоня́ться от прямо́го отве́та; уви́ливать [увильну́ть]; ~**hog** *zo.* ёж

heed [hi:d] **1.** внима́ние, осторо́жность *f*; *take no* ~ *of* не обраща́ть внима́ния на (В); **2.** обраща́ть внима́ние на (В); ~**less** [-lɪs] □ небре́жный; необду́манный; ~ *of danger* не ду́мая об опа́сности

heel [hi:l] **1.** *of foot* пя́тка; *of shoe* каблу́к; *head over* ~ вверх торма́шками; *down at* ~ *fig.* неря́шливый; **2.** поста́вить *pf.* набо́йку (на В)

hefty [ˈheftɪ] *fellow* здорове́нный; *blow* си́льный

height [haɪt] высота́; *person's* рост; (*high place*) возвы́шенность *f*; *fig.* верх; ~**en** [ˈhaɪtn] *interest* повыша́ть [повы́сить]; (*make more intense*) уси́ли(ва)ть

heir [eə] насле́дник; ~**ess** [ˈeərɪs, ˈeərəs] насле́дница

held [held] *pt. u pt. p. om* **hold**

helicopter [ˈhelɪkɒptə] вертолёт

hell [hel] ад; *attr.* а́дский; *raise* ~ подня́ть ужа́сный крик; ~**ish** [-ɪʃ] а́дский

hello [həˈləʊ] *coll.* приве́т; *tel.* алло́!

helm [helm] *naut.* штурва́л; *fig.* корми́ло

helmet [ˈhelmɪt] шлем

helmsman [ˈhelmzmən] *naut.* рулево́й

help [help] **1.** *com.* по́мощь *f*; *there is no* ~ *for it !* ничего́ не поде́лаешь!; **2.** *v/t.* помога́ть (помо́чь) (Д); ~ *yourself to fruit* бери́те фру́кты; *I could not* ~ *laughing* я не мог не рассмея́ться; *v/i.* помога́ть [-мо́чь]; ~**er** [ˈhelpə] помо́щник (-и́ца); ~**ful** [ˈhelpfl] поле́зный; ~**ing** [ˈhelpɪŋ] *of food* по́рция; *have another* ~ взять *pf.* ещё (*of*Р); ~**less** [ˈhelplɪs] □ беспо́мощный; ~**lessness** [ˈhelplɪsnɪs] беспомощность *f*

hem [hem] **1.** рубе́ц; *of skirt* подо́л; **2.** подруба́ть [-би́ть]; **~ in** окружа́ть [-жи́ть]

hemisphere ['hemɪsfɪə] полуша́рие

hemlock ['hemlɒk] *bot.* болиголо́в

hemp [hemp] конопля́; *(fibre)* пенька́

hen [hen] ку́рица

hence [hens] отсю́да; сле́довательно; *a year* **~** че́рез год; **~forth** [hens'fɔːθ], **~forward** [hens'fɔːwəd] с э́того вре́мени, впредь

henpecked ['henpekt] находя́щийся под башмако́м у жены́

her [ə, hə; *strong* hɜː] *pers. pron. (ко́свенный паде́ж от* **she**) её; ей

herb [hɜːb] (целе́бная) трава́; (пря́ное) расте́ние

herd [hɜːd] **1.** ста́до; *fig.* толпа́; **2.** *v/t.* пасти́ (скот); *v/i.:* **~ together** [с]толпи́ться; **~sman** ['hɜːdzmən] пасту́х

here [hɪə] здесь, тут; сюда́; вот; **~'s to you !** за ва́ше здоро́вье!

here|**after** [hɪər'ɑːftə] в бу́дущем; **~by** э́тим, настоя́щим; таки́м о́бразом

heredit|**ary** [hɪ'redɪtrɪ] насле́дственный; **~y** [-tɪ] насле́дственность *f*

here|**upon** [hɪərə'pɒn] вслед за э́тим; **~with** при сём

heritage ['herɪtɪdʒ] насле́дство; насле́дие (*mst. fig.*)

hermetic [hɜː'metɪk] (**~ally**) гермети́ческий

hermit ['hɜːmɪt] отше́льник

hero ['hɪərəʊ] геро́й; **~ic** [-'rəʊɪk] (**~ally**) геро́ический, геро́йский; **~ine** ['herəʊɪn] геро́иня; **~ism** [-ɪzəm] герои́зм

heron ['herən] *zo.* ца́пля

herring ['herɪŋ] сельдь *f*; *cul.* селёдка

hers [hɜːz] *pron. poss.* её

herself [hɜː'self] сама́; себя́, -ся, -сь

hesitat|**e** ['hezɪteɪt] [по]колеба́ться; *in speech* запина́ться [запну́ться]; **~ion** [hezɪ'teɪʃn] колеба́ние; запина́ние

hew [hjuː] [*irr.*] руби́ть; разруба́ть [-би́ть]; *(shape)* высека́ть [вы́сечь]

hey [heɪ] эй!

heyday ['heɪdeɪ] *fig.* зени́т, расцве́т

hicc|**up, ~ough** ['hɪkʌp] **1.** ико́та; **2.** ика́ть [икну́ть]

hid [hɪd], **hidden** ['hɪdn] *pt. и pt. p. от* **hide**

hide [haɪd] [*irr.*] [с]пря́тать(ся); *(conceal)* скры(ва́)ть; **~-and-seek** [haɪdn-'siːk] пря́тки

hideous ['hɪdɪəs] ☐ отврати́тельный, уро́дливый

hiding-place потаённое ме́сто, укры́тие

hi-fi ['haɪfaɪ] высо́кая то́чность воспроизведе́ния зву́ка

high [haɪ] **1.** ☐ *adj. com.* высо́кий; *(lofty)* возвы́шенный; *wind* си́льный; *authority* вы́сший, верхо́вный; *meat* с душко́м; *it's* **~** *time* давно́ пора́; **~ spirits** *pl.* припо́днятое настрое́ние; **2.** *adv.* высоко́; **~ aim ~** высоко́ ме́тить; **~brow** интеллектуа́л; **~-class** первокла́ссный; **~-grade** высо́кого ка́чества; **~-handed** своево́льный; вла́стный; **~lands** *pl.* гори́стая ме́стность *f*

high|**light** выдаю́щийся моме́нт; **~ly** ['haɪlɪ] о́чень, весьма́; **speak ~ of** высоко́ отзыва́ться о (П); **~-minded** возвы́шенный, благоро́дный; **~-rise building** высо́тное зда́ние; **~-strung** о́чень чувстви́тельный; напряжённый; **~way** гла́вная доро́га, шоссе́; *fig.* прямо́й путь *m*; **~ code** пра́вила доро́жного движе́ния

hijack ['haɪdʒæk] *plane* угоня́ть [-на́ть]; *train, etc.* соверша́ть [-ши́ть] налёт; **~er** [-ə] уго́нщик

hike [haɪk] *coll.* **1.** прогу́лка; похо́д; **2.** путеше́ствовать пешко́м; **~r** ['haɪkə] пе́ший тури́ст

hilarious [hɪ'leərɪəs] ☐ весёлый, смешно́й; *coll.* умори́тельный

hill [hɪl] холм; **~billy** *Am.* ['hɪlbɪlɪ] челове́к из глуби́нки; **~ock** ['hɪlək] хо́лмик; **~side** склон холма́; **~y** [-ɪ] холми́стый

hilt [hɪlt] рукоя́тка (*сабли и т.д.*)

him [ɪm;, *strong* hɪm] *pers. pron. (ко́свенный паде́ж от* **he**) его́, ему́; **~self** [hɪm'self] сам; себя́, -ся, -сь

hind [haɪnd] за́дний; **~ leg** за́дняя нога́

hinder ['hɪndə] **1.** препя́тствовать (Д);

2. *v/t.* [по]меша́ть

hindrance ['hɪndrəns] поме́ха, препя́тствие

hinge [hɪndʒ] **1.** *of door* пе́тля; шарни́р; *fig.* сте́ржень *m*, суть *f*; **2. ~ upon** *fig.* зави́сеть от (P)

hint [hɪnt] **1.** намёк; **2.** намека́ть [-кну́ть] (*at* на В)

hip[1] [hɪp] бедро́; **~ pocket** за́дний карма́н

hip[2] [-] я́года шипо́вника

hippopotamus [hɪpə'pɒtəməs] гиппопота́м, бегемо́т

hire ['haɪə] **1.** *worker* наём; *car, TV, etc.* прока́т; **2.** нанима́ть [наня́ть]; *room, etc.* снима́ть [снять]; брать [взять] напрока́т; **~ out** сдава́ть в прока́т; **~ purchase** поку́пка в рассро́чку

his [ɪz, *strong* hɪz] *poss. pron.* его́, свой

hiss [hɪs] *v/i.* [за-, про]шипе́ть; *v/t.* освисты́вать [-ста́ть]

histor|**ian** [hɪ'stɔːrɪən] исто́рик; **~ic**(**al** □) [hɪs'tɒːrɪk(l)] истори́ческий; **~y** ['hɪstərɪ] исто́рия

hit [hɪt] **1.** уда́р; попада́ние; *thea., mus.* успе́х; *direct* **~** прямо́е попада́ние; **2.** [*irr.*] удáря́ть [уда́рить]; поража́ть [порази́ть]; *target* попада́ть [попа́сть] в (В); **~ town, the beach, etc.** *Am. coll.* (*arrive*) прибы́(ва́)ть в, на (В); *coll.* **~ it off with** [по]ла́дить с (Т); **~ (up)on** находи́ть [найти́] (В); **~ in the eye** *fig.* броса́ться [бро́ситься] в глаза́

hitch [hɪtʃ] **1.** толчо́к, рыво́к; *fig.* препя́тствие; **2.** зацепля́ть(ся) [-пи́ть(ся)], прицепля́ть(ся) [-пи́ть(ся)]; **~hike** *mot.* е́здить автосто́пом

hither ['hɪðər] *lit.* сюда́; **~to** [-'tuː] *lit.* до сих пор

hive [haɪv] **1.** у́лей; (*of bees*) рой пчёл; *fig.* людско́й мураве́йник; **2.** жить вме́сте

hoard [hɔːd] **1.** (скры́тый) запа́с, склад; **2.** накопля́ть [-пи́ть]; запаса́ть [-сти́] (*of*); *secretly* припря́т(ыв)ать

hoarfrost ['hɔːfrɒst] и́ней

hoarse [hɔːs] □ хри́плый, си́плый

hoax [həʊks] **1.** обма́н, ро́зыгрыш; **2.** подшу́чивать [-ути́ть] над (Т), разы-грыва́ть [-ра́ть]

hobble ['hɒbl] *v/i.* прихра́мывать

hobby ['hɒbɪ] *fig.* хо́бби *n indecl.*, люби́мое заня́тие

hock [hɒk] (*wine*) рейнве́йн

hockey ['hɒkɪ] хокке́й

hoe [həʊ] *agric.* **1.** ца́пка; **2.** ца́пать

hog [hɒg] свинья́ (*a. fig.*); бо́ров

hoist [hɔɪst] **1.** *for goods* подъёмник; поднима́ть [-ня́ть]

hold [həʊld] **1.** *naut.* трюм; *catch* (*or* *get, lay, take*) **~ of** схва́тывать [схвати́ть] (В); *keep* **~ of** уде́рживать [-жа́ть] (В); **2.** [*irr.*] *v/t.* держа́ть(ся); (*sustain*) выде́рживать [вы́держать]; (*restrain*) остана́вливать [-нови́ть]; *meeting, etc.* проводи́ть [-вести́]; *attention* завладе(ва́)ть; занима́ть [-ня́ть]; (*contain*) вмеща́ть [вмести́ть]; (*think*) счита́ть; **~ one's own** отста́ивать свою́ пози́цию; **~ talks** вести́ перегово́ры; **~ the line!** *tel.* не ве́шайте тру́бку; **~ over** откла́дывать [отложи́ть]; **~ up** (*support*) подде́рживать [-жа́ть]; (*delay*) заде́рживать [-жа́ть]; остановить с це́лью грабежа́; **3.** *v/i.* остана́вливаться [-нови́ться]; *of weather* держа́ться; **~ forth** разглаго́льствовать; **~ good** (*or* *true*) име́ть си́лу; **~ off** держа́ться поода́ль; **~ on** держи́ться за (В); **~ to** приде́рживаться (P); **~er** [-ə] аренда́тор; владе́лец; **~ing** [-ɪŋ] уча́сток земли́; владе́ние; **~up** *Am.* налёт, ограбле́ние

hole [həʊl] дыра́, отве́рстие; *in ground* я́ма; *of animals* нора́; *coll. fig.* затрудни́тельное положе́ние; *pick* **~s in** находи́ть недоста́тки в (П); придира́ться [придра́ться]

holiday ['hɒlədɪ] пра́здник, официа́льный день о́тдыха; о́тпуск; **~s** *pl. educ.* кани́кулы *f/pl.*

hollow ['hɒləʊ] **1.** □ пусто́й, по́лый; *cheeks* ввали́вшийся; *eyes* впа́лый; **2.** по́лость *f*; *in tree* дупло́; (*small valley*) лощи́на; **3.** выда́лбливать [вы́долбить]

holly ['hɒlɪ] остроли́ст, па́дуб

holster ['həʊlstə] кобура́

holy ['həʊlɪ] свято́й, свяще́нный; ♀

Week Страстна́я неде́ля

homage ['hɒmɪdʒ] уваже́ние; *do* (*or* *pay, render*) ~ отдава́ть дань уваже́ния (*to* Д)

home [həʊm] 1. дом, жили́ще; ро́дина; *at* ~ до́ма; *maternity* ~ роди́льный дом; 2. *adj.* дома́шний; вну́тренний; отéчественный; ~ *industry* отéчественная промы́шленность *f*; ♀ *Office* министе́рство вну́тренних дел; ♀ *Secretary* мини́стр вну́тренних дел; 3. *adv.* домо́й; *hit* (*or strike*) ~ попа́сть *pf.* в цель *f*; ~**less** [-lɪs] бездо́мный; ~**like** ую́тный; непринуждённый; ~**ly** [-lɪ] *fig.* просто́й, обы́денный; дома́шний; *Am.* (*plain-looking*) некраси́вый; ~**made** дома́шнего изготовле́ния; ~**sickness** тоска́ по ро́дине; ~**ward(s)** [-wəd(z)] домо́й

homicide ['hɒmɪsaɪd] уби́йство; уби́йца *m/f*

homogeneous [hɒmə'dʒiːnɪəs] □ одноро́дный, гомоге́нный

honest ['ɒnɪst] □ че́стный; ~**y** [-ɪ] че́стность *f*

honey ['hʌnɪ] мёд; (*mode of address*) дорога́я; ~**comb** ['hʌnɪkəʊm] со́ты *f/pl.*; ~**moon** 1. медо́вый ме́сяц; 2. проводи́ть медо́вый ме́сяц

honorary ['ɒnərərɪ] почётный

hono(u)r ['ɒnə] 1. честь *f*; (*respect*) почёт; *f. mil., etc.* по́честь *f*; 2. чтить, почита́ть; *fin.* *check*/*Brt.* *cheque* опла́чивать [-лати́ть]; ~**able** ['ɒnərəbl] □ почётный, благоро́дный; (*upright*) че́стный

hood [hʊd] (*covering for head*) капюшо́н; *Am.* (*for car engine*) капо́т

hoodwink ['hʊdwɪŋk] обма́нывать [-ну́ть]

hoof [huːf] копы́то

hook [huːk] 1. крюк, крючо́к; *by* ~ *or* *by crook* пра́вдами и непра́вдами, так и́ли ина́че; 2. зацепля́ть [-пи́ть]; *dress. etc.* застёгивать(ся) [-стегну́ть(ся)]

hoop [huːp] о́бруч; *make s.o. jump* *through* ~*s* подверга́ть кого́-л. тяжёлому испыта́нию

hoot [huːt] 1. ши́канье; *mot.* сигна́л; 2.

v/i. оши́кивать [-кать]; дава́ть сигна́л, сигна́лить; *v/t.* (*a.* ~ *down*) освисты́вать [-иста́ть]

hop¹ [hɒp] *bot.* хмель *m*

hop² [-] 1. прыжо́к; *keep s.o. on the* ~ не дава́ть кому́-л. поко́я; 2. на одно́й ноге́

hope [həʊp] 1. наде́жда; *past* ~ безнадёжный; *raise* ~ обнадё́жи(ва)ть; 2. наде́яться (*for* на В); ~**ful** [-fl] (*promising*) подаю́щий наде́жды; (*having hope*) наде́ющийся; ~**less** [-lɪs] безнадёжный

horde [hɔːd] орда́; по́лчища; *pl.* то́лпы *f/pl.*

horizon [hə'raɪzn] горизо́нт; *fig.* кругозо́р

hormone ['hɔːməʊn] гормо́н

horn [hɔːn] *animal's* рог; звуково́й сигна́л; *mus* рожо́к; ~ *of plenty* рог изоби́лия

hornet ['hɔːnɪt] *zo.* ше́ршень *m*

horny ['hɔːnɪ] *hands* мозо́листый

horoscope ['hɒrəskəʊp] гороско́п; *cast a* ~ составля́ть [-а́вить] гороско́п

horr|**ible** ['hɒrəbl] □ стра́шный, ужа́сный; *old* ['hɒrɪd] ужа́сный; (*repelling*) проти́вный; ~**ify** ['hɒrɪfaɪ] ужаса́ть [-сну́ть]; шоки́ровать; ~**or** ['hɒrə] у́жас

hors d'œuvres [ɔː'dɜːv] *pl.* заку́ски *f/pl.*

horse [hɔːs] ло́шадь *f*, конь *m*; *get on a* ~ сесть *pf.* на ло́шадь; *dark* ~ тёмная лоша́дка; ~**back: on** ~ верхо́м; ~ *laugh* *coll.* гру́бый, гро́мкий хо́хот; ~**man** вса́дник; ~**power** лошади́ная си́ла; ~**race** ска́чки *f/pl.*; ~**radish** хрен; ~**shoe** подко́ва

horticulture ['hɔːtɪkʌltʃə] садово́дство

hose [həʊz] (*pipe*) шланг

hosiery ['həʊzɪərɪ] чуло́чные изде́лия *n/pl.*

hospice ['hɒspɪs] *med.* хо́спис

hospitable [hɒs'pɪtəbl] □ гостеприи́мный

hospital ['hɒspɪtl] больни́ца; *mil.* го́спиталь *m*; ~**ity** [hɒspɪ'tælətɪ] гостеприимство; **~ize** ['hɒspɪtəlaɪz] госпитализи́ровать

host[1] [həʊst] хозя́ин; *act as ~* быть за хозя́ина

host[2] [-] мно́жество, *coll.* ма́сса, тьма́

hostage ['hɒstɪdʒ] зало́жник *m*, -ница *f*

hostel ['hɒstl] общежи́тие; (*youth ~*) турба́за

hostess ['həʊstɪs] хозя́йка (→ *host*)

hostil|e ['hɒstaɪl] вражде́бный; **~ity** [hɒ'stɪlətɪ] вражде́бность *f*; вражде́бный акт; *pl. mil.* вое́нные де́йствия

hot [hɒt] горя́чий; *summer* жа́ркий; *fig.* пы́лкий; **~bed** парни́к; **~ dog** *fig.* бу́лочка с горя́чей соси́ской

hotchpotch ['hɒtʃpɒtʃ] *fig.* вся́чина, смесь *f*

hotel [həʊ'tel] оте́ль *m*, гости́ница

hot|headed опроме́тчивый; **~house** оранжере́я, тепли́ца; **~ spot** *pol.* горя́чая то́чка; **~water bottle** гре́лка

hound [haʊnd] **1.** го́нчая; **2.** *fig.* [за]трави́ть

hour [aʊə] час; вре́мя; *24 ~s* су́тки; *rush ~* часы́ пик; **~ly** [-lɪ] ежеча́сный

house [haʊs] **1.** *com.* дом; зда́ние; *parl.* пала́та; *apartment ~* многокварти́рный дом; **2.** [haʊz] *v/t.* поселя́ть [-ли́ть]; помеща́ть [-ести́ть]; (*give shelter to*) приюти́ть pf.; *v/i.* помеща́ться [-ести́ться]; **~hold** дома́шний круг; семья́; **~holder** домовладе́лец; **~keeper** эконо́мка; дома́шняя хозя́йка; **~keeping: do the ~** вести́ дома́шнее хозя́йство; **~warming** новосе́лье; **~wife** домохозя́йка

housing ['haʊzɪŋ] обеспе́чение жильём; **~ conditions** жили́щные усло́вия

hove [həʊv] *pt. и pt. p. от* **heave**

hovel ['hɒvl] лачу́га, хиба́рка

hover ['hɒvə] *of bird* пари́ть; *ae.* кружи́ть(ся); **~craft** су́дно на возду́шной поду́шке

how [haʊ] как?, каки́м о́бразом?; **~ about …?** как насчёт (P) …?; **~ever** [haʊ'evə] **1.** *adv.* как бы ни; **2.** *cj.* одна́ко, и всё же

howl [haʊl] **1.** вой, завыва́ние; **2.** [за]выть; **~er** ['haʊlə] *sl.* гру́бая оши́бка; ля́псус

hub [hʌb] *of wheel* ступи́ца; *fig. of activity* центр; *of the universe* пуп земли́

hubbub ['hʌbʌb] шум; *coll.* го́мон, гам

huddle ['hʌdl] **1.** *of things* [с]вали́ть в ку́чу; **~ together** *of people* сби́ться pf. в ку́чу; **2.** ку́ча; *of people* су́толока, сумато́ха

hue[1] [hju:] отте́нок

hue[2] [-]: **~ and cry** крик, шум

huff [hʌf] раздраже́ние; *get into a ~* оби́деться

hug [hʌg] **1.** объя́тие; **2.** обнима́ть [-ня́ть]; *fig.* быть приве́рженным; **o.s.** поздравля́ть [-áвить] себя́

huge [hju:dʒ] □ огро́мный, грома́дный

hulk [hʌlk] *fig.* у́валень

hull [hʌl] *bot.* шелуха́, скорлупа́; *naut.* ко́рпус

hum [hʌm] [за]жужжа́ть; (*sing*) напева́ть; *coll.* **make things ~** вноси́ть оживле́ние в рабо́ту

human ['hju:mən] **1.** челове́ческий; **2.** *coll.* челове́к; **~e** [hju:'meɪn] гума́нный, челове́чный; **~eness** гума́нность *f*; **~itarian** [hju:mænɪ'teərɪən] гума́ни́ст; гума́нный; **~ity** [hju:'mænətɪ] челове́чество; **~kind** [hju:mən-'kaɪnd] род челове́ческий; **~ly** [hju:mən-] по-челове́чески

humble ['hʌmbl] **1.** □ (*not self-important*) смире́нный, скро́мный; (*lowly*) просто́й; **2.** унижа́ть [уни́зить]; смиря́ть [-ри́ть]

humbug ['hʌmbʌg] (*deceit*) надува́тельство; (*nonsense*) чепуха́

humdrum ['hʌmdrʌm] однообра́зный, ску́чный

humid ['hju:mɪd] сыро́й, вла́жный; **~ity** [hju:'mɪdətɪ] вла́жность *f*

humiliat|e [hju:'mɪlɪeɪt] унижа́ть [уни́зить]; **~ion** [hju:mɪlɪ'eɪʃn] униже́ние

humility [hju:'mɪlətɪ] смире́ние

humorous ['hju:mərəs] □ юмористи́ческий

H

humo(u)r ['hjuːmə] 1. юмор, шутли́вость *f*; (*mood*) настрое́ние; **out of ~** не в ду́хе; 2. (*indulge*) потака́ть (Д); (*indulge*) ублажа́ть [-жи́ть]

hump [hʌmp] 1. горб; 2. [с]го́рбить(ся)

hunch [hʌntʃ] 1. горб; (*intuitive feeling*) чутьё, интуи́ция; **have a ~ that** у меня́ тако́е чу́вство, что ...; 2. [с]го́рбить(ся) (*a. up*); **~back** горбу́н(ья)

hundred ['hʌndrəd] 1. сто; 2. со́тня; **~th** [-θ] со́тый; со́тая часть *f*; **~weight** це́нтнер

hung [hʌŋ] *pt. и pt. p. om* hang

Hungarian [hʌŋ'geərɪən] 1. венгр *m*, -ге́рка *f*; 2. венге́рский

hunger ['hʌŋɡə] 1. го́лод; *fig.* жа́жда; 2. *v/i.* голода́ть; быть голо́дным; *fig. desire* жа́ждать (**for** P)

hungry ['hʌŋɡrɪ] □ голо́дный; **get ~** проголода́ться

hunk [hʌŋk] ломо́ть *m*; *of meat* большо́й кусо́к

hunt [hʌnt] 1. охо́та; (*search*) по́иски *m/pl.* (**for** P); 2. охо́титься на (В) *or* за (Т); **~ out** *or* **up** отыскивать [-ка́ть]; **~ for** *fig.* охо́титься за (Р *or* В); **~er** ['hʌntə] охо́тник; **~ing grounds** охо́тничьи уго́дья

hurdle ['hɜːdl] барье́р; **~s** ска́чки с препя́тствиями; бег с препя́тствиями

hurl [hɜːl] 1. си́льный бросо́к; 2. швыря́ть [-рну́ть], мета́ть [метну́ть]

hurricane ['hʌrɪkən] урага́н

hurried ['hʌrɪd] торопли́вый

hurry ['hʌrɪ] 1. торопли́вость *f*, поспе́шность *f*; **be in no ~** не спеши́ть; **what's the ~?** зачём спеши́ть?; 2. *v/t.* [по]торопи́ть; *v/i.* [по]спеши́ть (*a. ~ up*)

hurt [hɜːt] [*irr.*] (*injure*) ушиба́ть

[-би́ть] (*a. fig.*); причиня́ть боль *f*; боле́ть

husband ['hʌzbənd] муж; (*spouse*) супру́г

hush [hʌʃ] 1. тишина́, молча́ние; 2. ти́ше!; 3. установи́ть *pf.* тишину́; **~ up facts** скры(ва́)ть; **the affair was ~ed up** де́ло замя́ли

husk [hʌsk] 1. *bot.* шелуха́; 2. очища́ть от шелухи́, [об]лущи́ть; **~y** ['hʌskɪ] □ (*hoarse*) си́плый; охри́плый; (*burly*) ро́слый

hustle ['hʌsl] 1. *v/t.* (*push*) толка́ть [-кну́ть]; пиха́ть [пихну́ть]; (*hurry*) [по]торопи́ть; *v/i.* толка́ться; [по]торопи́ться; 2. толкотня́; **~ and bustle** шум и толкотня́

hut [hʌt] хижина

hutch [hʌtʃ] *for rabbits, etc.* кле́тка

hyacinth ['haɪəsɪnθ] гиаци́нт

hybrid ['haɪbrɪd] гибри́д; *animal* по́месь *f*

hydro ['haɪdrə] водо...; **~electric power station** гидро(электро-) ста́нция; **~foil** су́дно на подво́дных кры́льях; **~gen** ['haɪdrədʒən] водоро́д; **~phobia** ['haɪdrə'fəubɪə] бе́шенство; **~plane** ['haɪdrəpleɪn] гидропла́н

hygiene ['haɪdʒiːn] гигие́на

hymn [hɪm] (церко́вный) гимн

hyphen ['haɪfn] дефи́с; **~ate** [-feɪt] писа́ть через чёрточку

hypnotize ['hɪpnətaɪz] [за]гипнотизи́ровать

hypo|chondriac [haɪpə'kɒndrɪæk] ипохо́ндрик; **~crisy** [hɪ'pɒkrəsɪ] лицеме́рие; **~crite** ['hɪpəkrɪt] лицеме́р; **~critical** [hɪpə'krɪtɪkl] лицеме́рный; нейскренний; **~thesis** [haɪ'pɒθəsɪs] гипотеза, предположе́ние

hyster|ical [hɪ'sterɪkl] истери́чный; **~ics** [hɪ'sterɪks] *pl.* исте́рика

I

I [aɪ] *pers. pron.* я; **feel cold** мне хо́лодно; **you and ~** мы с ва́ми

ice [aɪs] **1.** лёд; **2.** замора́живать [-ро́зить]; *cul.* глазирова́ть (*im*)*pf.*; **~ over** покрыва́ть(ся) льдом; **~ age** леднико́вый пери́од; **~box** *Am.* холоди́льник; **~breaker** ледоко́л; **~ cream** моро́женое; **~d** охлаждённый; *cake* глазиро́ванный; **~ hockey** хокке́й; **~ rink** като́к

icicle ['aɪsɪkl] сосу́лька

icing ['aɪsɪŋ] *cul.* са́харная глазу́рь *f*

icon ['aɪkən] ико́на

icy ['aɪsɪ] ☐ ледяно́й (*a. fig.*)

idea [aɪˈdɪə] (*concept*) иде́я; (*notion*) поня́тие, представле́ние; (*thought*) мысль *f*; **~l** [-l] **1.** ☐ идеа́льный; **2.** идеа́л

identi|cal [aɪˈdentɪkl] ☐ тот (же) са́мый; тожде́ственный; иденти́чный, одина́ковый; **~fication** [aɪˌdentɪfɪˈkeɪʃn] определе́ние; опозна(ва́)ние; установле́ние ли́чности; **~fy** [-faɪ] определя́ть [-ли́ть]; опозн(ав)а́ть; устана́вливать ли́чность *f* (P); **~ty** [-tɪ]; **prove s.o.'s ~** установи́ть *pf.* ли́чность *f*; **~ty card** удостовере́ние ли́чности

idiom ['ɪdɪəm] идио́ма; (*language*) наре́чие, го́вор, язы́к

idiot ['ɪdɪət] идио́т *m*, -ка *f*; **~ic** [ɪdɪˈɒtɪk] (**-ally**) идио́тский

idle ['aɪdl] **1.** неза́нятый; безрабо́тный; лени́вый; *question* пра́здный; (*futile*) тще́тный; *tech.* безде́йствующий; холосто́й; **2.** *v/t.* проводи́ть (вре́-мя) без де́ла (*mst.* **~ away**); *v/i.* лени́ться, безде́льничать; **~ness** [-nɪs] пра́здность *f*; безде́лье; **~r** [-ə] безде́льник *m*, -ица *f*, лентя́й *m*, -ка *f*

idol ['aɪdl] и́дол, *fig.* куми́р; **~ize** ['aɪdəlaɪz] боготвори́ть

idyl(l) [l] иди́ллия

if [ɪf] *cj.* е́сли; е́сли бы; (= *whether*) ли: **I don't know ~ he knows** не зна́ю, зна́ет ли он …; **~ I were you …** на ва́шем ме́сте

ignit|e [ɪgˈnaɪt] зажига́ть [-же́чь]; загора́ться [-ре́ться], воспламеня́ться [-ни́ться]; **~ion** [ɪgˈnɪʃn] *mot.* зажига́ние

ignoble [ɪgˈnəʊbl] ☐ ни́зкий, неблагоро́дный

ignor|ance ['ɪgnərəns] неве́жество; *of intent, etc.* неве́дение; **~ant** [-rənt] неве́жественный; несве́дущий; **~e** [ɪgˈnɔː] игнори́ровать

ill [ɪl] **1.** *adj.* больно́й; дурно́й; **~ omen** дурно́е предзнаменова́ние; **2.** *adv.* едва́ ли; пло́хо; **3.** зло, вред

ill-advised неблагоразу́мный; **~-bred** невоспи́танный

illegal [ɪˈliːgl] ☐ незако́нный

illegible [ɪˈledʒəbl] ☐ неразбо́рчивый

illegitimate [ɪlɪˈdʒɪtɪmət] ☐ незако́нный; *child* незаконнорождённый

ill|-fated злосча́стный, злополу́чный; **~-founded** необосно́ванный; **~-humo(u)red** раздражи́тельный

illiterate [ɪˈlɪtərət] ☐ негра́мотный

ill|-mannered невоспи́танный, гру́бый; **~-natured** ☐ зло́бный, недоброжела́тельный

illness ['ɪlnɪs] боле́знь *f*

ill|-timed несвоевре́менный, неподходя́щий; **~-treat** пло́хо обраща́ться с (Т)

illumin|ate [ɪˈluːmɪneɪt] освеща́ть [-ети́ть], озаря́ть [-ри́ть]; (*enlighten*) просвеща́ть [-ети́ть]; (*cast light on*) пролива́ть свет на (В); **~ating** [-neɪtɪŋ] поучи́тельный, осветительный; **~ation** [ɪluːmɪˈneɪʃn] освеще́ние; (*display*) иллюмина́ция

illus|ion [ɪˈluːʒn] иллю́зия, обма́н чувств; **~ive** [-sɪv], **~ory** [-sərɪ] ☐ при́зрачный, иллюзо́рный

illustrat|e ['ɪləstreɪt] иллюстри́ровать (*im*)*pf.*; (*explain*) поясня́ть [-ни́ть]; **~ion** [ɪləˈstreɪʃn] иллюстра́ция; **~ive** ['ɪləstreɪtɪv] иллюстрати́вный

illustrious [ɪˈlʌstrɪəs] ☐ просла́вленный, знамени́тый

ill-will недоброжела́тельность *f*

image ['ɪmɪdʒ] о́браз; изображе́ние; (*reflection*) отраже́ние; (*likeness*) подо́бие, ко́пия

imagin|able [ɪ'mædʒɪnəbl] □ вообрази́мый; **~ary** [-nərɪ] вообража́емый; мни́мый; **~ation** [ɪmædʒɪ'neɪʃn] воображе́ние, фанта́зия; **~ative** [-dʒɪnətɪv] □ одарённый воображе́нием; **~e** [ɪ'mædʒɪn] вообража́ть [-рази́ть], представля́ть [-а́вить] себе́

imbecile ['ɪmbəsiːl] **1.** слабоу́мный; **2.** *coll.* глупе́ц

imbibe [ɪm'baɪb] (*absorb*) впи́тывать [впита́ть] (*a. fig.*); *fig. ideas, etc.* усва́ивать [усво́ить]

imita|te ['ɪmɪteɪt] подража́ть (Д); (*copy, mimic*) передра́знивать [-ни́ть]; подде́л(ыв)ать; **~tion** [ɪmɪ'teɪʃn] подража́ние; имита́ция, подде́лка; *attr.* иску́сственный

immaculate [ɪ'mækjʊlət] безукори́зненный, безупре́чный

immaterial [ɪmə'tɪərɪəl] (*unimportant*) несуще́ственный, нева́жный; (*incorporeal*) невеще́ственный, нематериа́льный

immature [ɪmə'tjʊə] незре́лый

immediate [ɪ'miːdjət] □ непосре́дственный; ближа́йший; (*urgent*) безотлага́тельный; **~ly** [-lɪ] *adv. of time, place* непосре́дственно; неме́дленно

immemorial [ɪmə'mɔːrɪəl]: **from time ~** испоко́н веко́в

immense [ɪ'mens] □ огро́мный

immerse [ɪ'mɜːs] погружа́ть [-узи́ть], окуна́ть [-ну́ть]; *fig.* **~ o.s. in** погружа́ться [-узи́ться]

immigra|nt ['ɪmɪɡrənt] иммигра́нт *m*, **-ка** *f*; **~te** [-ɡreɪt] иммигри́ровать (*im*)*pf.*; **~tion** [ɪmɪ'ɡreɪʃn] иммигра́ция

imminent ['ɪmɪnənt] грозя́щий, нави́сший; **a storm is ~** надвига́ется бу́ря

immobile [ɪ'məʊbaɪl] неподви́жный

immoderate [ɪ'mɒdərət] непоме́рный, чрезме́рный

immodest [ɪ'mɒdɪst] нескро́мный

immoral [ɪ'mɒrəl] □ безнра́вственный

immortal [ɪ'mɔːtl] бессме́ртный

immun|e [ɪ'mjuːn] невоспри́мчивый (*from* к Д); **~ity** [-ɪtɪ] *med.* иммуните́т, невоспри́мчивость *f* (*from* к Д); *dipl.* иммуните́т

imp [ɪmp] дьяволёнок, бесёнок; шалуни́шка *m/f*

impact ['ɪmpækt] уда́р; (*collision*) столкнове́ние; *fig.* влия́ние, возде́йствие

impair [ɪm'peə] (*weaken*) ослабля́ть [-а́бить]; *health* подрыва́ть [-дорва́ть]; (*damage*) поврежда́ть [-ди́ть]

impart [ɪm'pɑːt] (*give*) прид(ав)а́ть; (*make known*) сообща́ть [-щи́ть]

impartial [ɪm'pɑːʃl] □ беспристра́стный, непредвзя́тый

impassable [ɪm'pɑːsəbl] □ непроходи́мый; *for vehicles* непрое́зжий

impassive [ɪm'pæsɪv] □ споко́йный, бесстра́стный

impatien|ce [ɪm'peɪʃns] нетерпе́ние; **~t** [-nt] □ нетерпели́вый

impeccable [ɪm'pekəbl] (*flawless*) безупре́чный

impede [ɪm'piːd] [вос]препя́тствовать (Д)

impediment [ɪm'pedɪmənt] поме́ха

impel [ɪm'pel] (*force*) вынужда́ть [вы́нудить]; (*urge*) побужда́ть [-уди́ть]

impending [ɪm'pendɪŋ] предстоя́щий, надвига́ющийся

impenetrable [ɪm'penɪtrəbl] □ непроходи́мый; непроница́емый (*a. fig.*); *fig.* непостижи́мый

imperative [ɪm'perətɪv] □ *manner, voice* повели́тельный, вла́стный; (*essential*) кра́йне необходи́мый

imperceptible [ɪmpə'septəbl] неощути́мый; незаме́тный

imperfect [ɪm'pɜːfɪkt] □ несоверше́нный; (*faulty*) дефе́ктный

imperial [ɪm'pɪərɪəl] □ импе́рский; (*majestic*) вели́чественный

imperil [ɪm'perəl] подверга́ть [-ве́ргнуть] опа́сности

imperious [ɪm'pɪərɪəs] □ (*commanding*) вла́стный; (*haughty*) высокоме́рный

impermeable [ɪm'pɜːmɪəbl] непроница́емый

impersonal [ɪmˈpɜːsənl] *gr.* безли́чный; безли́кий; объекти́вный

impersonate [ɪmˈpɜːsəneɪt] исполня́ть роль *f* (P), выдава́ть себя́ за; изобража́ть [-ази́ть]

impertinen|ce [ɪmˈpɜːtɪnəns] де́рзость *f*.; **~t** [-nənt] □ де́рзкий

imperturbable [ɪmpəˈzʒːbəbl] □ невозмути́мый

impervious [ɪmˈpɜːvɪəs] → **impermeable**; *fig.* глухо́й (**to** к Д)

impetu|ous [ɪmˈpetjʊəs] □ стреми́тельный; (*done hastily*) необду́манный; **~s** [ˈɪmpɪtəs] и́мпульс, толчо́к

impinge [ɪmˈpɪndʒ]: **~** (**up**)**on** [по]влия́ть, отража́ться [-зи́ться]

implacable [ɪmˈplækəbl] □ (*relentless*) неумоли́мый; (*unappeasable*) непримери́мый

implant [ɪmˈplɑːnt] *ideas, etc.* насажда́ть [насади́ть]; внуша́ть [-ши́ть]

implausible [ɪmˈplɔːzəbl] неправдоподо́бный, невероя́тный

implement [ˈɪmplɪmənt] **1.** (*small tool*) инструме́нт; *agric.* ору́дие; **2.** выполня́ть [вы́полнить]

implicat|e [ˈɪmplɪkeɪt] вовлека́ть [-е́чь], впу́т(ыв)ать; **~ion** [ɪmplɪˈkeɪʃn] вовлече́ние; скры́тый смысл, намёк

implicit [ɪmˈplɪsɪt] □ (*unquestioning*) безогово́рочный; (*suggested*) подразумева́емый; (*implied*) недоска́занный

implore [ɪmˈplɔː] умоля́ть [-ли́ть]

imply [ɪmˈplaɪ] подразумева́ть; (*insinuate*) намека́ть [-кну́ть] на (В); зна́чить

impolite [ɪmpəˈlaɪt] □ неве́жливый

impolitic [ɪmˈpɒlətɪk] □ нецелесообра́зный; неблагоразу́мный

import 1. [ˈɪmpɔːt] ввоз, и́мпорт; **~s** *pl.* ввози́мые това́ры *m/pl.*; **2.** [ɪmˈpɔːt] ввози́ть [ввезти́], импорти́ровать (*im*)*pf.*; **~ance** [ɪmˈpɔːtns] значе́ние, ва́жность *f*; **~ant** [-tnt] ва́жный, значи́тельный

importunate [ɪmˈpɔːtʃʊnət] □ назо́йливый

impose [ɪmˈpəʊz] *v/t.* навя́зывать

[-за́ть]; *a tax* облага́ть [обложи́ть]; **~ a fine** наложи́ть штраф; *v/i.* **~ upon** злоупотребля́ть [-би́ть] (Т); **~ing** [-ɪŋ] внуши́тельный, впечатля́ющий

impossib|ility [ɪmpɒsəˈbɪlətɪ] невозмо́жность *f*; **~le** [ɪmˈpɒsəbl] □ невозмо́жный; (*unbearable*) *coll.* несно́сный

impostor [ɪmˈpɒstə] шарлата́н; самозва́нец

impoten|ce [ˈɪmpətəns] бесси́лие, сла́бость *f*; *med.* импоте́нция; **~t** [-tənt] бесси́льный, сла́бый; импоте́нтный

impoverish [ɪmˈpɒvərɪʃ] доводи́ть до нищеты́; *fig.* обедня́ть [-ни́ть]

impracticable [ɪmˈpræktɪkəbl] □ неисполни́мый, неосуществи́мый

impractical [ɪmˈpræktɪkl] □ непракти́чный

impregnate [ˈɪmpregneɪt] (*saturate*) пропи́тывать [-пита́ть]; (*fertilize*) оплодотворя́ть [-твори́ть]

impress [ɪmˈpres] отпеча́т(ыв)ать; (*fix*) запечатле́(ва́)ть; (*bring home*) внуша́ть [-ши́ть] (**on** Д); производи́ть впечатле́ние на (В); **~ion** [ɪmˈpreʃn] впечатле́ние; *typ.* о́ттиск; **I am under the ~ that** у меня́ тако́е впечатле́ние, что ...; **~ionable** [ɪmˈpreʃənəbl] впечатли́тельный; **~ive** [ɪmˈpresɪv] □ внуши́тельный, впечатля́ющий

imprint [ɪmˈprɪnt] **1.** *in memory, etc.* запечатле́(ва́)ть; **2.** отпеча́ток

imprison [ɪmˈprɪzn] сажа́ть [посади́ть]/заключа́ть [-чи́ть] в тюрьму́; **~ment** [-mənt] тюре́мное заключе́ние

improbable [ɪmˈprɒbəbl] □ невероя́тный, неправдоподо́бный

improper [ɪmˈprɒpə] неуме́стный; (*indecent*) непристо́йный; (*incorrect*) непра́вильный

improve [ɪmˈpruːv] *v/t.* улучша́ть [улу́чшить]; [у]соверше́нствовать; *v/i.* улучша́ться [улу́чшиться]; [у]соверше́нствоваться; **~ upon** улучша́ть [улу́чшить] (В); **~ment** [-mənt] улучше́ние; усоверше́нствование

improvise [ˈɪmprəvaɪz] импровизи́ровать (*im*)*pf.*

imprudent [ɪm'pru:dnt] □ неблагоразу́мный; неосторо́жный

impuden|ce ['ɪmpjʊdəns] на́глость *f*; де́рзость *f*; **~t** [-dənt] на́глый; де́рзкий

impulse ['ɪmpʌls] и́мпульс, толчо́к; (*sudden inclination*) поры́в

impunity [ɪm'pju:nɪtɪ] безнака́занность *f*; **with ~** безнака́занно

impure [ɪm'pjʊə] нечи́стый; гря́зный (*a. fig.*); (*indecent*) непристо́йный; *air* загрязнённый; (*mixed with s.th.*) с при́месью

impute [ɪm'pju:t] припи́сывать [-са́ть] (Д/В)

in [ɪn] **1.** *prp.* в, во (П *or* В); **~ number** в коли́честве (Р), число́м в (В); **~ itself** само́ по себе́; **~ 1949** в 1949-ом (в ты́сяча девятьсо́т со́рок девя́том) году́; **cry out ~ alarm** закрича́ть в испу́ге (*or* от стра́ха); **~ the street** на у́лице; **~ my opinion** по моему́ мне́нию, помо́ему; **~ English** по-англи́йски; **a novel ~ English** рома́н на англи́йском языке́; **~ thousands** ты́сячами; **the circumstances** в э́тих усло́виях; **~ this manner** таки́м о́бразом; **~ a word** одни́м сло́вом; **be ~ power** быть у вла́сти; **be engaged ~ reading** занима́ться чте́нием; **2.** *adv.* внутри́; внутрь; **she's ~ for an unpleasant surprise** её ожида́ет неприя́тный сюрпри́з; *coll.*: **be ~ with** быть в хоро́ших отноше́ниях с (Т)

inability [ɪnə'bɪlɪtɪ] неспосо́бность *f*

inaccessible [ɪnæk'sesəbl] □ недосту́пный; непристу́пный

inaccurate [ɪn'ækjərət] □ нето́чный

inactiv|e [ɪn'æktɪv] □ безде́ятельный; безде́йствующий; **~ity** [ɪnæk'tɪvɪtɪ] безде́ятельность *f*; ине́ртность *f*

inadequate [ɪn'ædɪkwɪt] □ (*insufficient*) недоста́точный; (*not capable*) неспосо́бный; *excuse* неубеди́тельный

inadmissible [ɪnəd'mɪsəbl] недопусти́мый, неприе́млемый

inadvertent [ɪnəd'vɜ:tənt] □ невнима́тельный; неумы́шленный; (*unintentional*) ненаме́ренный

inalienable [ɪn'eɪlɪənəbl] □ неотъе́млемый

inane [ɪ'neɪn] □ (*senseless*) бессмы́сленный; (*empty*) пусто́й

inanimate [ɪn'ænɪmət] □ неодушевлённый; (*lifeless*) безжи́зненный

inappropriate [ɪnə'prəʊprɪət] неуме́стный, несоотве́тствующий

inapt [ɪn'æpt] □ неспосо́бный; (*not suitable*) неподходя́щий

inarticulate [ɪnɑː'tɪkjʊlət] □ нечленоразде́льный, невня́тный

inasmuch [ɪnəz'mʌtʃ]: **~ as** *adv.* так как; в виду́ того́, что; поско́льку

inattentive [ɪnə'tentɪv] невнима́тельный

inaugura|te [ɪ'nɔ:gjʊreɪt] *launch* откры́(ва́)ть; (*install as president*) вводи́ть в до́лжность; **~tion** [ɪnɔːgjʊ'reɪʃn] вступле́ние в до́лжность, инаугура́ция; (*торже́ственное*) откры́тие

inborn [ɪn'bɔ:n] врождённый, приро́ждённый

incalculable [ɪn'kælkjʊləbl] □ неисчисли́мый, бессчётный; *person* капри́зный, ненадёжный

incapa|ble [ɪn'keɪpəbl] □ неспосо́бный (*of* к Д *or* на В); **~citate** [ɪnkə'pæsɪteɪt] де́лать неспосо́бным, непригодным

incarnate [ɪn'kɑ:nɪt] воплощённый, олицетворённый

incautious [ɪn'kɔ:ʃəs] □ неосторо́жный, опроме́тчивый

incendiary [ɪn'sendɪərɪ] *mil., fig.* зажига́тельный

incense¹ ['ɪnsens] ла́дан

incense² [ɪn'sens] приводи́ть в я́рость

incentive [ɪn'sentɪv] сти́мул

incessant [ɪn'sesnt] □ непреры́вный

inch [ɪntʃ] дюйм; *fig.* пядь *f*; **by~es** ма́ло-пома́лу

inciden|ce ['ɪnsɪdəns]: **high~ of** большо́е коли́чество слу́чаев; **~t** [-t] слу́чай; происше́ствие; *mil., dipl.* инциде́нт; **~tal** [ɪnsɪ'dentl] □ случа́йный; побо́чный; прису́щий (Д); *pl.* непредви́денные расхо́ды *m/pl.*; **~tally**

случа́йно; ме́жду про́чим; попу́тно

incinerate [ɪnˈsɪnəreɪt] испепеля́ть [-ли́ть]; сжига́ть [сжечь]

incis|ion [ɪnˈsɪʒn] разре́з, надре́з; **~ive** [ɪnˈsaɪsɪv] □ о́стрый; *criticism, etc.* ре́зкий

incite [ɪnˈsaɪt] (*instigate*) подстрека́ть [-кну́ть]; (*move to action*) побужда́ть [-уди́ть]

inclement [ɪnˈklemənt] суро́вый, холо́дный

inclin|ation [ɪnklɪˈneɪʃn] (*slope*) накло́н, укло́н; (*mental leaning*) скло́нность *f*; **~e** [ɪnˈklaɪn] **1.** *v/i.* склоня́ться [-ни́ться]; *a. fig.* быть скло́нным к (Д); *v/t.* наклоня́ть [-ни́ть], склоня́ть [-ни́ть] (*a. fig.*); **2.** накло́н

inclose [ɪnˈkləʊz] → **enclose**

inclu|de [ɪnˈkluːd] включа́ть [-чи́ть]; содержа́ть; **~sive** [-sɪv] □ включа́ющий в себя́, содержа́щий; *from Monday to Friday* **~** с понеде́льника до пя́тницы включи́тельно

incoheren|ce [ɪnkəʊˈhɪərəns] несвя́зность *f*; непосле́довательность *f*; **~t** [-t] □ несвя́зный; (*not consistent*) непосле́довательный

income [ˈɪŋkʌm] дохо́д

incomparable [ɪnˈkɒmprəbl] □ (*not comparable*) несравни́мый; *matchless* несравне́нный

incompatible [ɪŋkəmˈpætəbl] несовмести́мый

incompetent [ɪnˈkɒmpɪtənt] □ несве́дущий, неуме́лый; *specialist* некомпете́нтный; *law* недееспосо́бный

incomplete [ɪŋkəmˈpliːt] □ непо́лный; (*unfinished*) незако́нченный

incomprehensible [ɪnkɒmprɪˈhensəbl] □ непоня́тный, непостижи́мый

inconceivable [ɪŋkənˈsiːvəbl] □ невообрази́мый

incongruous [ɪnˈkɒŋɡrʊəs] □ (*out of place*) неуме́стный; (*absurd*) неле́пый; (*incompatible*) несовмести́мый

inconsequential [ɪnkɒnsɪkwəntʃl] □ несуще́ственный

inconsidera|ble [ɪŋkənˈsɪdərəbl] □ незначи́тельный, нева́жный; **~te** [-rɪt] □ невнима́тельный (*to* к Д);

(*rash*) необду́манный

inconsisten|cy [ɪnkənˈsɪstənsɪ] непосле́довательность *f*, противоре́чие; **~t** [-tənt] □ непосле́довательный, противоречи́вый

inconsolable [ɪnkənˈsəʊləbl] □ безуте́шный

inconvenien|ce [ɪŋkənˈviːnɪəns] **1.** неудо́бство; **2.** причиня́ть [-ни́ть] неудо́бство; [по]беспоко́ить; **~t** [-nɪənt] □ неудо́бный, затрудни́тельный

incorporat|e [ɪnˈkɔːpəreɪt] объединя́ть(ся) [-ни́ть(ся)]; включа́ть [-чи́ть] (*into* в В); **~ed** [-reɪtɪd] зарегистри́рованный в ка́честве юриди́ческого лица́

incorrect [ɪŋkəˈrekt] □ непра́вильный

incorrigible [ɪnˈkɒrɪdʒəbl] □ неисправи́мый

increase [ɪnˈkriːs] **1.** увели́чи(ва)ть(ся); [вы́]расти; *of wind, etc.* уси́ли(ва)ть(ся); **2.** [ˈɪnkriːs] рост; увеличе́ние; приро́ст

incredible [ɪnˈkredəbl] □ невероя́тный; неимове́рный

incredul|ity [ɪnkrɪˈdjuːlətɪ] недове́рчивость *f*; **~ous** [ɪnˈkredjʊləs] □ недове́рчивый

increment [ˈɪŋkrəmənt] приро́ст

incriminate [ɪnˈkrɪmɪneɪt] инкримини́ровать (*im*)*pf.*; *law* обвиня́ть в преступле́нии

incrustation [ɪnkrʌˈsteɪʃn] инкруста́ция

incubator [ˈɪŋkʊbeɪtə] инкуба́тор

incur [ɪnˈkɜː] навлека́ть [-вле́чь] на себя́; **~ losses** понести́ *pf.* убы́тки

incurable [ɪnˈkjʊərəbl] неизлечи́мый; *fig.* неисправи́мый

indebted [ɪnˈdetɪd] *for money* в долгу́ (*a. fig.*); *fig.* обя́занный

indecen|cy [ɪnˈdiːsnsɪ] непристо́йность *f*, прили́чие; **~t** [-snt] □ неприли́чный

indecisi|on [ɪndɪˈsɪʒn] нереши́тельность *f*; (*hesitation*) колеба́ние; **~ve** [-ˈsaɪsɪv] нереши́тельный; не реша́ющий; **~ evidence** недоста́точно убеди́тельные доказа́тельства

indecorous [ɪnˈdekərəs] □ неприли́чный; некорре́ктный

indeed [ɪnˈdiːd] в са́мом де́ле, действи́тельно; неуже́ли!

indefensible [ɪndɪˈfensəbl] □ *mil.* незащити́мая пози́ция; (*unjustified*) не име́ющий оправда́ния; *fig.* несостоя́тельный

indefinite [ɪnˈdefɪnət] □ неопределённый (*a. gr.*); неограни́ченный

indelible [ɪnˈdeləbl] □ неизглади́мый

indelicate [ɪnˈdelɪkət] □ неделика́тный; нескро́мный; *remark* беста́ктный

indemnity [ɪnˈdemnɪtɪ] гара́нтия возмеще́ния убы́тков; компенса́ция

indent [ɪnˈdent] *v/t. typ.* нач(ин)а́ть с кра́сной строки́; *v/i. comm.* [с]де́лать зака́з на (В)

independen|ce [ɪndɪˈpendəns] незави́симость *f*, самостоя́тельность *f*; **~t** [-t] □ незави́симый, самостоя́тельный

indescribable [ɪndɪsˈkraɪbəbl] □ неопису́емый

indestructible [ɪndɪsˈtrʌktəbl] □ неразруши́мый

indeterminate [ɪndɪˈtɜːmɪnət] □ неопределённый; (*vague, not clearly seen*) нея́сный

index [ˈɪndeks] и́ндекс, указа́тель *m*; показа́тель *m*; **~ finger** указа́тельный па́лец

India [ˈɪndɪə]: **~ rubber** каучу́к; рези́на; **~n** [-n] **1.** *of India* инди́йский; *of North America* инде́йский; **~ corn** кукуру́за; **~ summer** ба́бье ле́то; **2.** инди́ец, индиа́нка; *of North America* инде́ец, индиа́нка

indicat|e [ˈɪndɪkeɪt] ука́зывать [-за́ть]; (*show*) пока́зывать [-за́ть]; (*make clear*) д(ав)а́ть поня́ть; означа́ть *impf.*; **~ion** [ɪndɪˈkeɪʃn] (*sign*) знак, при́знак; **~or** [ˈɪndɪkeɪtə] стре́лка; *mot.* сигна́л поворо́та, *coll.* мига́лка

indifferen|ce [ɪnˈdɪfrəns] равноду́шие, безразли́чие; **~t** [-t] □ равноду́шный, безразли́чный; **~ actor** посре́дственный актёр

indigenous [ɪnˈdɪdʒɪnəs] тузе́мный; ме́стный

indigest|ible [ɪndɪˈdʒestəbl] □ *fig.* неудобовари́мый; **~ion** [-tʃən] расстро́йство желу́дка

indign|ant [ɪnˈdɪɡnənt] негоду́ющий; **~ation** [ɪndɪɡˈneɪʃn] негодова́ние; **~ity** [ɪnˈdɪɡnɪtɪ] униже́ние, оскорбле́ние

indirect [ˈɪndɪrekt] □ непрямо́й; *route* око́льный; *answer* укло́нчивый; **~ taxes** ко́свенные нало́ги

indiscre|et [ɪndɪsˈkriːt] □ нескро́мный; (*tactless*) беста́ктный; **~tion** [-ˈskreʃn] нескро́мность *f*; беста́ктность *f*

indiscriminate [ɪndɪsˈkrɪmɪnət] □ неразбо́рчивый

indispensable [ɪndɪsˈpensəbl] □ необходи́мый, обяза́тельный

indispos|ed [ɪndɪsˈpəʊzd] (*disinclined*) нераспо́ложенный; нездоро́вый; **~ition** [ˈɪndɪspəˈzɪʃn] нежела́ние; недомога́ние

indisputable [ɪndɪsˈpjuːtəbl] неоспори́мый, бесспо́рный

indistinct [ɪndɪsˈtɪŋkt] □ нея́сный, неотчётливый; *speech* невня́тный

individual [ɪndɪˈvɪdʒʊəl] **1.** □ индивидуа́льный; характе́рный; (*separate*) отде́льный; **2.** индиви́дуум, ли́чность *f*; **~ity** [-vɪdjʊˈælətɪ] индивидуа́льность *f*

indivisible [ɪndɪˈvɪzəbl] недели́мый

indolen|ce [ˈɪndələns] лень *f*; **~t** [-t] лени́вый

indomitable [ɪnˈdɒmɪtəbl] □ неукроти́мый

indoor [ˈɪndɔː] вну́тренний; **~s** [ɪnˈdɔːz] в до́ме

indorse → **endorse**

indubitable [ɪnˈdjuːbɪtəbl] □ несомне́нный

induce [ɪnˈdjuːs] заставля́ть [-а́вить]; (*bring about*) вызыва́ть [вы́звать]; **~ment** [-mənt] сти́мул, побужде́ние

indulge [ɪnˈdʌldʒ] *v/t.* доставля́ть удово́льствие (Д **with** Т); (*spoil*) балова́ть; потво́рствовать (Д); *v/i.* **~ in** увлека́ться [-е́чься] (Т); пред(ав)а́ться (Д); **~nce** [-əns] потво́рство; **~nt** [-ənt] □ снисходи́тельный; нетребовательный; потворствующий

industri|al [ɪn'dʌstrɪəl] ☐ промышленный; производственный; **~alist** [-ɪst] промышленник; **~ous** [ɪn'dʌstrɪəs] трудолюбивый

industry ['ɪndəstrɪ] промышленность *f*, индустрия; трудолюбие

inedible [ɪn'edɪbl] несъедобный

ineffect|ive [ɪnɪ'fektɪv], **~ual** [-tʃʊəl] ☐ безрезультатный; неэффективный

inefficient [ɪnɪ'fɪʃnt] ☐ *person* неспособный, неумелый; *method*, *etc.* неэффективный

inelegant [ɪn'elɪgənt] ☐ неэлегантный

ineligible [ɪn'elɪdʒəbl] **be ~ for** не иметь права (на В)

inept [ɪ'nept] ☐ неуместный, неподходящий; неумелый

inequality [ɪnɪ'kwɒlətɪ] неравенство

inert [ɪ'nɜːt] ☐ инертный; (*sluggish*) вялый; **~ia** [ɪ'nɜːʃə], **~ness** [ɪ'nɜːtnɪs] инерция; вялость *f*

inescapable [ɪnɪ'skeɪpəbl] ☐ неизбежный

inessential [ɪn'əsenʃl] ☐ несущественный

inestimable [ɪn'estɪməbl] ☐ неоценимый

inevitable [ɪn'evɪtəbl] ☐ неизбежный, неминуемый

inexact [ɪnɪg'zækt] ☐ неточный

inexhaustible [ɪnɪg'zɔːstəbl] ☐ неистощимый, неисчерпаемый

inexorable [ɪn'eksərəbl] ☐ неумолимый, непреклонный

inexpedient [ɪnɪk'spiːdɪənt] ☐ нецелесообразный

inexpensive [ɪnɪk'spensɪv] ☐ недорогой, дешёвый

inexperience [ɪnɪk'spɪərɪəns] неопытность *f*; **~d** [-t] неопытный

inexplicable [ɪnɪk'splɪkəbl] ☐ необъяснимый, непонятный

inexpressible [ɪnɪk'spresəbl] ☐ невыразимый, неописуемый

inextinguishable [ɪnɪk'stɪŋgwɪʃəbl] ☐ неугасимый

inextricable [ɪnɪk'strɪkəbl] ☐ запутанный

infallible [ɪn'fæləbl] ☐ безошибочный, непогрешимый; *method* надёжный

infam|ous ['ɪnfəməs] ☐ постыдный, позорный, бесчестный; **~y** [-mɪ] бесчестье, позор; (*infamous act*) низость *f*; подлость *f*

infan|cy ['ɪnfənsɪ] младенчество; **~t** [-t] младенец

infantile ['ɪnfəntaɪl] младенческий; *behaviour* инфантильный

infantry ['ɪnfəntrɪ] пехота

infatuated [ɪn'fætjʊeɪtɪd]: **be ~ with** быть без ума от (Р)

infect [ɪn'fekt] заражать [-разить]; **~ion** [ɪn'fekʃn] инфекция; **~ious** [-ʃəs] ☐, **~ive** [-tɪv] инфекционный, заразный; *fig.* заразительный

infer [ɪn'fɜː] делать вывод; (*imply*) подразумевать; **~ence** ['ɪnfərəns] вывод, заключение

inferior [ɪn'fɪərɪə] **1.** (*subordinate*) подчинённый; (*worse*) худший, неполноценный; *goods* низкого качества; **2.** подчинённый; **~ity** [ɪnfɪərɪ'ɒrətɪ] низкое качество (положение); неполноценность *f*; **~ complex** комплекс неполноценности

infernal [ɪn'fɜːnl] ☐ *mst. fig.* адский

infertile [ɪn'fɜːtaɪl] бесплодный (*a. fig.*); неплодородный

infest [ɪn'fest]: **be ~ed** кишеть (Т)

infidelity [ɪnfɪ'delətɪ] неверность *f* (**to** Д)

infiltrate ['ɪnfɪltreɪt] (*enter secretly*) проникать [-икнуть]; просачиваться [-сочиться]

infinite ['ɪnfɪnət] ☐ бесконечный, безграничный; **~y** [ɪn'fɪnətɪ] бесконечность *f*; безграничность *f*

infirm [ɪn'fɜːm] ☐ немощный, дряхлый; **~ary** [-ərɪ] больница; **~ity** [-ətɪ] немощь *f*

inflam|e [ɪn'fleɪm] воспламенять(-ся) [-йть(ся)]; *med.* воспалять(ся) [-лить(ся)]; **~ed** [-d] воспалённый

inflamma|ble [ɪn'flæməbl] ☐ воспламеняющийся; **~tion** [ɪnflə'meɪʃn] *med.* воспаление; **~tory** [ɪn'flæmətrɪ] *speech* подстрекательский; *med.* воспалительный

inflat|e [ɪnˈfleɪt] наду(ва́)ть; *tyre* нака́чивать [-ча́ть]; *prices* взви́нчивать [-нти́ть]; ~**ion** [ɪnˈfleɪʃn] *of balloon, etc.* надува́ние; *econ.* инфля́ция

inflexible [ɪnˈfleksəbl] □ неги́бкий; *fig.* непрекло́нный, непоколеби́мый

inflict [ɪnˈflɪkt] *a blow, etc.* наноси́ть [-нести́]; *pain* причиня́ть [-ни́ть]; *views, etc.* навя́зывать(ся)

influen|ce [ˈɪnfluəns] **1.** влия́ние, возде́йствие; **2.** [по]влия́ть на (В); возде́йствовать на (В) (*im*)*pf.*; ~**tial** [ɪnfluˈenʃl] влия́тельный

influenza [ɪnfluˈenzə] грипп

influx [ˈɪnflʌks] прито́к; *of visitors* напльı́в

inform [ɪnˈfɔːm] *v/t.* информи́ровать (*im*)*pf.*, уведомля́ть [уве́домить] (*of* о П); *v/i.* доноси́ть [-нести́] (*against* на В); **keep s.o. ~ed** держа́ть в ку́рсе дел

inform|al [ɪnˈfɔːml] □ неофициа́льный; *conversation* непринуждённый; ~**ality** [ɪnfɔːˈmælɪtɪ] несоблюде́ние форма́льностей; непринуждённость *f*

inform|ation [ɪnfəˈmeɪʃn] информа́ция, све́дения *n/pl.*; спра́вка *f*; ~**ative** [ɪnˈfɔːmətɪv] информи́рующий; содержа́тельный; (*educational*) поучи́тельный

infrequent [ɪnˈfriːkwənt] □ ре́дкий

infringe [ɪnˈfrɪndʒ] наруша́ть [-ру́шить] (*a.* ~ *upon*)

infuriate [ɪnˈfjʊərɪeɪt] [вз]беси́ть

ingen|ious [ɪnˈdʒiːnɪəs] □ изобрета́тельный; ~**uity** [ɪndʒɪˈnjuːɪtɪ] изобрета́тельность *f*; ~**uous** [ɪnˈdʒenjʊəs] □ (*frank*) чистосерде́чный; (*lacking craft or subtlety*) простоду́шный; просто́й, бесхи́тростный

ingratitude [ɪnˈɡrætɪtjuːd] неблагода́рность *f*

ingredient [ɪnˈɡriːdɪənt] составна́я часть *f*, ингредие́нт (*a. cul.*)

inhabit [ɪnˈhæbɪt] населя́ть; обита́ть; жить в (П);~**ant** [-ɪtənt] жи́тель(ница *f*) *m*, обита́тель(ница *f*) *m*

inhal|ation [ɪnhəˈleɪʃn] *med.* ингаля-

ция; ~**e** [ɪnˈheɪl] вдыха́ть [вдохну́ть]

inherent [ɪnˈhɪərənt] □ прису́щий

inherit [ɪnˈherɪt] насле́довать (*im*)*pf.*; *fig.* унасле́довать *pf.*; ~**ance** [-ɪtəns] насле́дство (*a. fig.*)

inhibit [ɪnˈhɪbɪt] сде́рживать [сдержа́ть], [вос]препя́тствовать (Д); ~**ion** [ɪnˈhɪbɪʃn] *med.* торможе́ние

inhospitable [ɪnˈhɒspɪtəbl] □ негостеприи́мный

inhuman [ɪnˈhjuːmən] □ бесчелове́чный; античелове́ческий

inimitable [ɪˈnɪmɪtəbl] □ неподража́емый; (*peerless*) несравне́нный

initial [ɪˈnɪʃl] **1.** нача́льный, первонача́льный; **2.** нача́льная бу́ква; ~**s** *pl.* инициа́лы *m/pl.*; ~**te** [-ɪeɪt] вводи́ть [ввести́]; *into a secret* посвяща́ть [-вяти́ть]; (*start*) положи́ть *pf.* нача́ло (Д); ~**tive** [ɪˈnɪʃɪtɪv] инициати́ва; ~**tor** [-ʃɪeɪtə] инициа́тор

inject [ɪnˈdʒekt] *med.* [c]де́лать инъе́кцию; ~**ion** [-ʃn] инъе́кция, впры́скивание, уко́л

injur|e [ˈɪndʒə] [по]вреди́ть, поврежда́ть [-еди́ть]; *in war, etc.* ра́нить (*im*)*pf.*; (*wrong*) обижа́ть [-и́деть]; ~**ious** [ɪnˈdʒʊərɪəs] вре́дный; ~**y** [ˈɪndʒərɪ] оскорбле́ние; поврежде́ние, ра́на; *sport* тра́вма

injustice [ɪnˈdʒʌstɪs] несправедли́вость *f*

ink [ɪŋk] черни́ла *n/pl.*

inkling [ˈɪŋklɪŋ] намёк (на В); (*suspicion*) подозре́ние

inland [ˈɪnlənd] **1.** вну́тренняя террито́рия страны́; **2.** вну́тренний; **3.** [ɪnˈlænd] внутрь, внутри́ (страны́)

inlay [ɪnˈleɪ] инкруста́ция

inlet [ˈɪnlet] у́зкий зали́в, бу́хта; впускно́е отве́рстие

inmate [ˈɪnmeɪt] *of hospital* больно́й, пацие́нт, обита́тель; *of prison* заключённый

inmost [ˈɪnməʊst] глубоча́йший, *thoughts* сокрове́ннейший

inn [ɪn] гости́ница, тракти́р

innate [ɪˈneɪt] □ врождённый, приро́дный

inner [ˈɪnə] вну́тренний; ~**most**

[-məust] → *inmost*

innocen|ce ['ɪnəsns] *law* невино́вность *f*; неви́нность *f*; простота́; ~t [-snt] □ неви́нный; *law* невино́вный

innocuous [ɪ'nɒkjuəs] □ безвре́дный; *remark* безоби́дный

innovation [ɪnə'veɪʃn] нововведе́ние, но́вшество

innuendo [ɪnju:'endəu] ко́свенный намёк, инсинуа́ция

innumerable [ɪ'nju:mərəbl] □ бессчётный, бесчи́сленный

inoculate [ɪ'nɒkjuleɪt] [c]де́лать приви́вку (Д от Р)

inoffensive [ɪnə'fensɪv] безоби́дный, безвре́дный

inopportune [ɪn'ɒpətju:n] □ несвоевре́менный, неподходя́щий

inordinate [ɪn'nɔ:dɪnət] непоме́рный, чрезме́рный

in-patient ['ɪnpeɪʃnt] стациона́рный больно́й

inquest ['ɪnkwest] *law* рассле́дование, выясне́ние причи́н сме́рти

inquir|e [ɪn'kwaɪə] *v/t.* спра́шивать [-роси́ть]; *v/i.* узн(ав)а́ть; наводи́ть [-вести́] спра́вки (*about, after, for* о П; *of* у Р); ~ *into* выясня́ть, рассле́довать (*im*)*pf.*; ~**ing** [-rɪŋ] □ *mind* пытли́вый; ~**y** [-rɪ] рассле́дование, сле́дствие; (*question*) вопро́с; *make inquiries* наводи́ть спра́вки

inquisitive [ɪn'kwɪzɪtɪv] □ любозна́тельный; любопы́тный

insan|e [ɪn'seɪn] □ психи́чески больно́й; *fig.* безу́мный; ~**ity** [ɪn'sænɪtɪ] психи́ческое заболева́ние; безу́мие

insatiable [ɪn'seɪʃəbl] □ ненасы́тный; (*greedy*) жа́дный

inscribe [ɪn'skraɪb] (*write*) надпи́сывать [-са́ть] (*in, on* В/Т *or* В на П)

inscription [ɪn'skrɪpʃn] на́дпись *f*

inscrutable [ɪn'skru:təbl] □ непостижи́мый, зага́дочный

insect ['ɪnsekt] насеко́мое; ~**icide** [ɪn'sektɪsaɪd] инсектици́д

insecure [ɪnsɪ'kjuə] □ ненадёжный; (*not safe*) небезопа́сный

insens|ible [ɪn'sensəbl] □ *to touch, etc.* нечувстви́тельный; потеря́вший

созна́ние; (*unsympathetic*) бесчу́вственный; ~**itive** [-ɪtɪv] нечувстви́тельный; невоспри́мчивый

inseparable [ɪn'seprəbl] □ неразлу́чный; неотдели́мый (*from* от Р)

insert [ɪn'sɜ:t] вставля́ть [-а́вить]; *advertisement* помеща́ть [-ести́ть]; ~**ion** [ɪn'sɜ:ʃn] *of lace, etc.* вста́вка; (*announcement*) объявле́ние

inside [ɪn'saɪd] **1.** вну́тренняя сторона́; вну́тренность *f*; *of clothing* изна́нка; *turn ~ out* вы́вернуть *pf.* на изна́нку; *he knows his subject ~ out* он зна́ет свой предме́т назубо́к; **2.** *adj.* вну́тренний; **3.** *adv.* внутрь, внутри́; **4.** *prp.* внутри́ (Р)

insidious [ɪn'sɪdɪəs] □ преда́тельский, кова́рный

insight ['ɪnsaɪt] проница́тельность *f*; интуи́ция

insignificant [ɪnsɪg'nɪfɪkənt] незначи́тельный, малова́жный

insincere [ɪnsɪn'sɪə] неи́скренний

insinuat|e [ɪn'sɪnjueɪt] намека́ть [-кну́ть] на (В); ~ *o.s. fig.* вкра́дываться [вкра́сться]; ~**ion** [ɪnsɪnjʊ'eɪʃn] инсинуа́ция

insipid [ɪn'sɪpɪd] безвку́сный, пре́сный

insist [ɪn'sɪst]: ~ (*up*)*on* наста́ивать [-стоя́ть] на (П); ~**ence** [-əns] насто́йчивость *f*; ~**ent** [-ənt] насто́йчивый

insolent ['ɪnsələnt] □ высокоме́рный; на́глый

insoluble [ɪn'sɒljubl] нераствори́мый; *fig.* неразреши́мый

insolvent [ɪn'sɒlvənt] неплатёжеспосо́бный

insomnia [ɪn'sɒmnɪə] бессо́нница

inspect [ɪn'spekt] осма́тривать [осмотре́ть]; производи́ть [-вести́] инспе́кцию; ~**ion** [ɪn'spekʃn] осмо́тр; инспе́кция

inspir|ation [ɪnspə'reɪʃn] вдохнове́ние; воодушевле́ние; ~**e** [ɪn'spaɪə] *fig.* вдохновля́ть [-ви́ть]; *hope* вселя́ть [-ли́ть]; *fear* внуша́ть [-ши́ть]

install [ɪn'stɔ:l] устана́вливать [-нови́ть]; *tech.* [c]монти́ровать; ~**ation**

[ɪnstə'leɪʃn] установка

instalment [ɪn'stɔːlmənt] очередной взнос (при покупке в рассрочку); часть романа и т.д., публикуемого в нескольких номерах

instance ['ɪnstəns] случай; пример; **for ~** например

instant ['ɪnstənt] **1.** □ немедленный, безотлагательный; **2.** мгновение; момент; **~aneous** [ɪnstən'teɪnɪəs] мгновенный; **~or ~ly** ['ɪnstəntlɪ] немедленно, тотчас

instead [ɪn'sted] взамен, вместо; **~ of** вместо (P)

instep ['ɪnstep] подъём (ноги)

instigat|e ['ɪnstɪɡeɪt] (*urge on*) побуждать (-удить); (*incite*) подстрекать [-кнуть]; **~or** [-ə] подстрекатель(-ница *f*) *m*

instil(l) [ɪn'stɪl] *fig.* внушать [-шить] (*into* Д)

instinct ['ɪnstɪŋkt] инстинкт; **~ive** [-'stɪŋktɪv] □ инстинктивный

institut|e ['ɪnstɪtjuːt] научное учреждение, институт; **2.** (*set up*) учреждать [-едить]; (*found*) основывать [-вать]; **~ion** [ɪnstɪ'tjuːʃn] учреждение; *educational* **~** учебное заведение

instruct [ɪn'strʌkt] обучать [-чить], [на]учить; [про]инструктировать (*im*)*pf.*; **~ion** [ɪn'strʌkʃn] обучение; инструкция; **~ive** [-tɪv] □ поучительный; **~or** [-tə] руководитель *m*, инструктор; (*teacher*) преподаватель *m*

instrument ['ɪnstrʊmənt] инструмент; *fig.* орудие; прибор, аппарат; **~al** [ɪn'struːmentl] □ служащий средством; *gr.* творительный

insubordinate [ɪnsə'bɔːdɪnət] (*not submissive*) непокорный

insufferable [ɪn'sʌfrəbl] □ невыносимый, нестерпимый

insufficient [ɪnsə'fɪʃnt] недостаточный

insula|r ['ɪnsjʊlə] □ островной; *fig.* замкнутый; **~te** [-leɪt] *el.* изолировать (*im*)*pf.*; **~tion** [ɪnsjʊ'leɪʃn] *el.* изоляция; **~ tape** изоляционная лента

insulin ['ɪnsjʊlɪn] инсулин

insult 1. ['ɪnsʌlt] оскорбление; **2.** [ɪn'sʌlt] оскорблять [-бить]

insur|ance [ɪn'ʃʊərəns] страхование; (*sum insured*) сумма страхования, *coll.* страховка; **~ company** страховая компания; **~e** [ɪn'ʃʊə] [за]страховать(ся)

insurgent [ɪn'sɜːdʒənt] повстанец; мятежник

insurmountable [ɪnsə'maʊntəbl] непреодолимый

insurrection [ɪnsə'rekʃn] восстание

intact [ɪn'tækt] целый, невредимый

intangible [ɪn'tændʒəbl] □ неосязаемый; *fig.* неуловимый

integr|al ['ɪntɪɡrəl] □ неотъемлемый; (*whole*) целый, цельностный; **~ part** неотъемлемая часть; **~rate**[-ɡreɪt] объединять [-нить]; *math.* интегрировать (*im*)*pf.*; **~rity** [ɪn'teɡrɪtɪ] честность *f*; (*entireness*) цельностность *f*

intellect ['ɪntəlekt] ум, интеллект; **~ual** [ɪntɪ'lektjʊəl] **1.** □ интеллектуальный, умственный; **~ property** интеллектуальная собственность; **2.** интеллигент *m*, -ка *f*; **~s** *pl.* интеллигенция

intelligence [ɪn'telɪdʒəns] ум, рассудок, интеллект; *mil.* **~ service** разведывательная служба, разведка

intellig|ent [ɪn'telɪdʒənt] умный; *coll.* смышлёный; **~ible** [-dʒəbl] □ понятный

intend [ɪn'tend] намереваться, собираться; (*mean*) иметь в виду; **~ for** (*destine for*) предназначать [-значить] для (P)

intense [ɪn'tens] □ сильный; интенсивный, напряжённый

intensify [ɪn'tensɪfaɪ] усили(ва)ть(ся); интенсифицировать (*im*)*pf.*

intensity [ɪn'tensətɪ] интенсивность *f*, сила; *of colo(u)r* яркость *f*

intent [ɪn'tent] **1.** □ погружённый (*on* в В); поглощённый (*on* Т); *look* внимательный, пристальный; **2.** намерение, цель *f*; **to all ~s and purposes** в сущности, на самом деле; **~ion** [ɪn'tenʃn] намерение; **~ional** [-ʃənl] □

(пред)наме́ренный, умы́шленный

inter... ['ɪntə] *pref.* меж…, между…; пере…; взаимо…

interact [ɪntər'ækt] взаимоде́йствовать

intercede [ɪntə'si:d] [по]хода́тайствовать; *in order to save* заступа́ться [-пи́ться]

intercept [ɪntə'sept] *letter, etc.* перехва́тывать [-хвати́ть]; *(listen in on)* подслу́шивать [-шать]

intercession [ɪntə'seʃn] хода́тайство

interchange [ɪntə'tʃeɪndʒ] **1.** *v/t.* обме́ниваться [-ня́ться] (T); **2.** обме́н

intercom ['ɪntəkɒm] вну́тренняя телефо́нная связь, се́лектор

intercourse ['ɪntəkɔːs] *social* обще́ние; *sexual* полово́е сноше́ния *n/pl.*

interest ['ɪntrəst] **1.** интере́с; заинтересо́ванность *f* (*in* в П); (*advantage, profit*) по́льза, вы́года; *fin.* проце́нты *m/pl.* **~ rate** ста́вка проце́нта; **2.** интересова́ть; заинтересо́вывать [-сова́ть]; **~ing** [-ɪŋ] □ интере́сный

interface ['ɪntəfeɪs] стык, *comput.* интерфе́йс; *fig.* взаимосвя́зь *f*

interfere [ɪntə'fɪə] вме́шиваться [-ша́ться] (*in* в В); (*hinder*) [по]меша́ть (*with* Д); **~nce** [-rəns] вмеша́тельство; поме́ха

interim ['ɪntərɪm] **1.** промежу́ток вре́мени; *in the* ~ тем вре́менем; **2.** вре́менный, промежу́точный

interior [ɪn'tɪərɪə] **1.** вну́тренний; **~ decorator** оформи́тель интерье́ра; **2.** вну́тренняя часть *f*; *of house* интерье́р; вну́тренние о́бласти страны́; *pol.* вну́тренние дела́ *n/pl.*

interjection [ɪntə'dʒekʃn] восклица́ние; *gr.* междоме́тие

interlace [ɪntə'leɪs] переплета́ть(ся) [-плести́(сь)]

interlock [ɪntə'lɒk] сцепля́ть(ся) [-пи́ть(ся)]; соединя́ть(ся) [-ни́ть(ся)]

interlocutor [ɪntə'lɒkjʊtə] собесе́дник

interlude ['ɪntəluːd] *thea.* антра́кт; *mus., fig.* интерлю́дия

intermedia|ry [ɪntə'miːdɪərɪ] **1.** по-

сре́днический; **2.** посре́дник; **~te** [-'miːdɪət] □ промежу́точный

interminable [ɪn'tɜːmɪnəbl] □ бесконе́чный

intermingle [ɪntə'mɪŋgl] сме́шивать(ся) [-ша́ть(ся)]; обща́ться

intermission [ɪntə'mɪʃn] переры́в, па́уза

intermittent [ɪntə'mɪtənt] □ преры́вистый

intern [ɪn'tɜːn] интерни́ровать (*im*)*pf.*

internal [ɪn'tɜːnl] □ вну́тренний

international [ɪntə'næʃnl] □ междунаро́дный, интернациона́льный; **~ law** междунаро́дное пра́во; **♀ Monetary Fund** Междунаро́дный валю́тный фонд

Internet ['ɪntənet] *comput.* Интерне́т

interplanetary [ɪntə'plænətrɪ] межплане́тный

interpose [ɪntə'pəʊz] *v/t.* вставля́ть [-а́вить], вкли́ни(ва)ться (*между* Т); *v/i.* станови́ться [стать] (*between* между Т); (*interfere*) вме́шиваться [-ша́ться] (*in* в В)

interpret [ɪn'tɜːprɪt] объясня́ть [-ни́ть], истолко́вывать [-кова́ть]; переводи́ть [-вести́] (у́стно); **~ation** [ɪntɜːprɪ'teɪʃn] толкова́ние, интерпрета́ция, объясне́ние; **~er** [ɪn'tɜːprɪtə] перево́дчик (-ица *f*) *m*

interrogat|e [ɪn'terəgeɪt] допра́шивать [-роси́ть]; **~ion** [ɪnterə'geɪʃn] допро́с; **~ive** [ɪntə'rɒgətɪv] □ вопроси́тельный (*a. gr.*)

interrupt [ɪntə'rʌpt] прер(ы)ва́ть; **~ion** [-'rʌpʃn] переры́в

intersect [ɪntə'sekt] пересека́ть(ся) [-се́чь(ся)]; **~ion** [-kʃn] пересече́ние

intersperse [ɪntə'spɜːs] разбра́сывать [-броса́ть], рассыпа́ть; **~ with jokes** пересыпа́ть шу́тками

intertwine [ɪntə'twaɪn] сплета́ть(ся) [-ести́(сь)]

interval ['ɪntəvl] *of time* интерва́л, промежу́ток; *of space* расстоя́ние; *thea.* антра́кт; *in school* переме́на

interven|e [ɪntə'viːn] вме́шиваться [-ша́ться]; вступа́ться [-пи́ться]; **~tion** [-'venʃn] интерве́нция; вмеша́-

тельство

interview ['intəvju:] **1.** интервью *n indecl.*; *for a job* собеседование; **2.** брать [взять] интервью; проводить [-вести] собеседование

intestine [ɪn'testɪn] кишка; ~s *pl.* кишки *f/pl.*, кишечник

intima|cy ['ɪntɪməsɪ] интимность *f*, близость *f*; ~**te 1.** [-meɪt] сообщать [-щить]; (*hint*) намекать [-кнуть] на (В); **2.** [-mɪt] □ интимный, личный; близкий; ~**tion** [ɪntɪ'meɪʃn] сообщение; намёк

intimidate [ɪn'tɪmɪdeɪt] [ис]пугать; *by threats* запугивать [-гать]

into ['ɪntʊ, ɪntə] *prp.* в, во (В); *translate ~ English* переводить [-вести] на английский язык

intolera|ble [ɪn'tɒlərəbl] □ (*unbearable*) невыносимый, нестерпимый; ~**nt** [-rənt] □ (*lacking forbearance, bigoted*) нетерпимый

intonation [ɪntə'neɪʃn] интонация

intoxica|te [ɪn'tɒksɪkeɪt] опьянять [-нить] (*a. fig.*); ~**tion** [ɪntɒksɪ'keɪʃn] опьянение

intractable [ɪn'træktəbl] □ упрямый; неподатливый

intravenous [ɪntrə'viːnəs] □ внутривенный

intrepid [ɪn'trepɪd] бесстрашный, отважный

intricate ['ɪntrɪkɪt] □ сложный, запутанный

intrigu|e [ɪn'triːg] **1.** интрига; (*love affair*) любовная связь *f*; **2.** интриговать; [за]интриговать, [за]интересовать; ~**ing** [-ɪŋ] интригующий; *coll.* интересный

intrinsic [ɪn'trɪnsɪk] (~**ally**) внутренний; (*inherent*) свойственный, присущий

introduc|e [ɪntrə'djuːs] вводить [ввести]; (*acquaint*) представлять [-авить]; ~**tion** [-'dʌkʃn] (*preface*) введение; представление; *mus.* интродукция; ~**tory** [-'dʌktərɪ] вступительный, вводный

intru|de [ɪn'truːd] *into s.o.'s private life* вторгаться [вторгнуться];

появляться [-виться] некстати; ~**der** [-ə] человек, пришедший некстати, навязчивый человек; ~**sion** [-uːʒn] вторжение; появление без приглашения; *sorry for the ~* простите за беспокойство

intrust [ɪn'trʌst] → **entrust**

intuition [ɪntjuː'ɪʃn] интуиция

inundate ['ɪnʌndeɪt] затоплять [-пить], наводнять [-нить]

invade [ɪn'veɪd] *mil.* вторгаться [вторгнуться]; *of tourists, etc.* наводнять [-нить]; ~ *s.o.'s privacy* нарушить чьё-л. уединение; ~**r** [-ə] захватчик

invalid 1. [ɪn'vælɪd] недействительный, не имеющий законной силы; *argument* несостоятельный; **2.** ['ɪnvəlɪd] инвалид; ~**ate** [ɪn'vælɪdeɪt] сделать недействительным

invaluable [ɪn'væljʊəbl] □ неоценимый

invariable [ɪn'veərɪəbl] □ неизменный

invasion [ɪn'veɪʒn] вторжение

invent [ɪn'vent] (*create*) изобретать [-брести]; *story* выдумывать [выдумать]; ~**ion** [ɪn'venʃn] изобретение; выдумка; (*faculty*) изобретательность *f*; ~**ive** [-tɪv] □ изобретательный; ~**or** [-tə] изобретатель *m*; ~**ory** ['ɪnvəntrɪ] инвентарная опись *f*

inverse [ɪn'vɜːs] обратный; *in ~ order* в обратном порядке

invert [ɪn'vɜːt] переворачивать [-вернуть]; (*put in the opposite position*) переставлять [-авить]; ~**ed commas** кавычки

invest [ɪn'vest] *money* вкладывать [вложить]; *fig. with authority, etc.* облекать [облечь] (*with* Т); инвестировать

investigat|e [ɪn'vestɪgeɪt] расследовать (*im*)*pf.*; (*study*) исследовать (*im*)*pf.*; ~**ion** [ɪnvestɪ'geɪʃn] (*inquiry*) расследование; *law* следствие; исследование

invest|ment [ɪn'vestmənt] вложение денег, инвестирование; (*sum*) инвестиция, вклад; ~**or** [ɪn'vestə] вкла́дчик, инве́стор

inveterate [ɪn'vetərət] (*deep-rooted*) закорене́лый; *coll. smoker, etc.* зая́длый; ~ **prejudices** глубоко́ укорени́вшиеся предрассу́дки

invidious [ɪn'vɪdɪəs] □ вызыва́ющий оби́ду, за́висть; *remark* оби́дный

invigorate [ɪn'vɪgəreɪt] дава́ть си́лы (Д); бодри́ть

invincible [ɪn'vɪnsəbl] непобеди́мый

inviolable [ɪn'vaɪələbl] □ неруши́мый; неприкоснове́нный; ~ **right** неруши́мое пра́во

invisible [ɪn'vɪzəbl] неви́димый

invit|ation [ɪnvɪ'teɪʃn] приглаше́ние; ~**e** [ɪn'vaɪt] приглаша́ть [-ласи́ть]

invoice ['ɪnvɔɪs] *comm.* накладна́я, счёт-факту́ра

invoke [ɪn'vəʊk] взыва́ть [воззва́ть] о (П)

involuntary [ɪn'vɒləntrɪ] □ (*forced*) вы́нужденный; (*contrary to choice*) нево́льный; (*done unconsciously*) непроизво́льный

involve [ɪn'vɒlv] вовлека́ть [-е́чь]; впут(ыв)ать

invulnerable [ɪn'vʌlnərəbl] □ неуязви́мый

inward ['ɪnwəd] **1.** вну́тренний; **2.** *adv.* (*mst.* ~**s** [-z]) внутрь; вну́тренне

iodine ['aɪədiːn] йод

irascible [ɪ'ræsəbl] □ раздражи́тельный

irate [aɪ'reɪt] гне́вный

iridescent [ɪrɪ'desnt] ра́дужный

iris ['aɪərɪs] *anat.* ра́дужная оболо́чка; *bot.* и́рис

Irish ['aɪərɪʃ] **1.** ирла́ндский; **2.** *the* ~ ирла́ндцы *m/pl.*

irksome ['ɜːksəm] надое́дливый; раздража́ющий

iron ['aɪən] **1.** желе́зо; утю́г; *have many* ~ *s in the fire* бра́ться сра́зу за мно́го дел; **2.** желе́зный; **3.** [вы́]утю́жить, [вы́]гла́дить

ironic(al □) [aɪ'rɒnɪk(l)] ирони́ческий

iron|ing ['aɪənɪŋ] **1.** гла́женье; ве́щи для гла́женья; **2.** гла́дильный; ~**board** гла́дильная доска́; ~**mongery** ['aɪənmʌŋgərɪ] металлоизде́лия; ~**works**

mst. sg. металлурги́ческий заво́д

irony ['aɪərənɪ] иро́ния

irrational [ɪ'ræʃənl] неразу́мный; иррациона́льный (*a. math.*)

irreconcilable [ɪ'rekənsaɪləbl] □ непримири́мый; *ideas, etc.* несовмести́мый

irrecoverable [ɪrɪ'kʌvərəbl] □: ~ *losses* невосполни́мые поте́ри

irrefutable [ɪrɪ'fjuːtəbl] □ неопровержи́мый

irregular [ɪ'regjʊlə] □ непра́вильный (*a. gr.*); (*disorderly*) беспоря́дочный; (*not regular*) нерегуля́рный; ~ *features* непра́вильные черты́ лица́

irrelevant [ɪ'reləvənt] □ не относя́щийся к де́лу; не име́ющий значе́ния

irreparable [ɪ'repərəbl] □ непоправи́мый

irreplaceable [ɪrɪ'pleɪsəbl] незамени́мый

irreproachable [ɪrɪ'prəʊtʃəbl] □ безукори́зненный, безупре́чный

irresistible [ɪrɪ'zɪstəbl] □ неотрази́мый; *desire, etc.* непреодоли́мый

irresolute [ɪ'rezəluːt] □ нереши́тельный

irrespective [ɪrɪ'spektɪv] безотноси́тельный (*of* к Д); незави́симый (*of* от Р)

irresponsible [ɪrɪ'spɒnsəbl] □ безотве́тственный

irreverent [ɪ'revərənt] □ непочти́тельный

irrevocable [ɪ'revəkəbl] □ безвозвра́тный, бесповоро́тный

irrigate ['ɪrɪgeɪt] ороша́ть [ороси́ть]

irrita|ble ['ɪrɪtəbl] □ раздражи́тельный; ~**te** [-teɪt] раздража́ть [-жи́ть]; ~**tion** [ɪrɪ'teɪʃn] раздраже́ние

Islam [ɪz'lɑːm] исла́м; ~**ic** [ɪz'læmɪk] исла́мский

is [ɪz] *3rd p. sg. pres. om* **be**

island ['aɪlənd] о́стров; ~**er** [-ə] островитя́нин *m*, -тя́нка *f*

isle [aɪl] о́стров; ~**t** [aɪ'lɪt] острово́к

isolat|e ['aɪsəleɪt] изоли́ровать (*im*)*pf.*; (*separate*) отделя́ть [-ли́ть]; ~**ed**: *in* ~ *cases* в отде́льных слу́чаях;

~**ion** [aɪsə'leɪʃn] изоля́ция; уедине́ние
issue ['ɪʃuː] **1.** (*a. flowing out*) вытека́-
ние; *law* (*offspring*) пото́мство; (*publication*) вы́пуск, изда́ние; (*outcome*)
исхо́д, результа́т; *of money* эми́ссия;
be at ~ быть предме́том спо́ра; *point
at* ~ предме́т обсужде́ния; **2.** *v/i. of
blood* те́чь (**from** из P); вытека́ть
[вы́течь] (**from** из P); *of sound* изд(а-
ва́)ть; *v/t. book, etc.* выпуска́ть [вы́пу-
стить], изд(ав)а́ть
isthmus ['ɪsməs] переше́ек
it [ɪt] *pres. pron.* он, она́, оно́; э́то; ~ *is
cold* хо́лодно; ~ *is difficult to say* ...
тру́дно сказа́ть
Italian [ɪ'tæljən] **1.** италья́нский; **2.**

италья́нец *m*, -нка *f*; **3.** италья́нский
язы́к
italics [ɪ'tælɪks] *typ.* курси́в
itch [ɪtʃ] **1.** чесо́тка; зуд (*a. fig.*); **2.**
чеса́ться; *be ~ing to* inf. горе́ть жела́-
нием (+ *inf.*)
item ['aɪtem] **1.** (*single article*) пункт,
пара́граф; *on agenda* вопро́с; *on programme* но́мер; (*object*) предме́т
itinerary [aɪ'tɪnərərɪ] маршру́т
its [ɪts] *poss. pron. om* **it** его́, её, свой
itself [ɪt'self] (*sam m*, сама́ *f*) само́;
себя́, -с, -сь; себе́; *in* ~ само́ по себе́;
само́ собо́й; (*separately*) отде́льно
ivory ['aɪvərɪ] слоно́вая кость *f*
ivy ['aɪvɪ] плющ

J

jab [dʒæb] *coll.* **1.** толка́ть [-кну́ть];
ты́кать [ткну́ть]; (*stab*) пыря́ть
[-рну́ть]; **2.** тычо́к, пино́к; (*prick*)
уко́л (*a. coll. injection*)
jabber ['dʒæbə] болта́ть, тарато́рить
jack [dʒæk] **1.** *cards* вале́т; *mot.* домкра́т; *Union* ♀ госуда́рственный флаг
Соединённого короле́вства; **2.** ~ *up*
поднима́ть домкра́том; ~**ass** осёл;
дура́к
jackdaw ['dʒækdɔː] га́лка
jacket ['dʒækɪt] *lady's* жаке́т; *man's*
пиджа́к; *casual* ку́ртка
jack|knife складно́й нож; *fig.* (*dive*)
прыжо́к в во́ду согну́вшись; ~**-of-
-all-trades** ма́стер на все ру́ки
jade [dʒeɪd] *min.* нефри́т
jagged ['dʒægɪd] зу́бчатый; ~ *rocks*
о́стрые ска́лы
jail [dʒeɪl] **1.** тюрьма́; тюре́мное за-
ключе́ние; **2.** *v/t.* заключа́ть [-чи́ть]
в тюрьму́; ~**er** ['dʒeɪlə] тюре́мный
надзира́тель
jam¹ [dʒæm] варе́нье, джем, пови́дло
jam² [-] **1.** да́вка, сжа́тие; *traffic* ~ за-
то́р, про́бка; *be in a* ~ быть в затрудни́тельном положе́нии; **2.** заж(и-
м)а́ть; (*pinch*) защемля́ть [-ми́ть];

(*push into confined space*) набива́ть
битко́м; (*block*) загроможда́ть [-мозди́ть]; *v/i.* закли́ни(ва)ть
jangle ['dʒæŋgl] издава́ть [-да́ть] ре́з-
кий звук
janitor ['dʒænɪtə] дво́рник
January ['dʒænjuərɪ] янва́рь *m*
Japanese [dʒæpə'niːz] **1.** япо́нский; **2.**
япо́нец *m*, -нка *f*; *the* ~ *pl.* япо́нцы *pl.*
jar¹ [dʒɑː] (*vessel, usu. of glass*) ба́нка
jar² [-] **1.** *v/i.* толка́ть [-кну́ть]; *v/i.* ре́-
зать слух; **2.** толчо́к; (*shock*) потрясе́-
ние
jaundice ['dʒɔːndɪs] *med.* желту́ха;
fig. жёлчность *f*; ~**d** [-t] желту́шный;
fig. зави́стливый
jaunt [dʒɔːnt] пое́здка, прогу́лка; *let's
go for a* ~ *to London* дава́й-ка съе́з-
дим в Ло́ндон; ~**y** ['dʒɔːntɪ] □ бес-
пе́чный; бо́йкий
javelin ['dʒævlɪn] *sport* копьё
jaw [dʒɔː] че́люсть *f*; ~**s** *pl.* рот; *animal's* пасть *f*; ~**bone** челюстна́я кость *f*
jazz [dʒæz] джаз
jealous ['dʒeləs] □ ревни́вый; зави́ст-
ливый; ~**y** [-ɪ] ре́вность *f*; за́висть *f*
jeans [dʒiːnz] *pl.* джи́нсы *pl.*

jeep® [dʒiːp] *mil.* джип, вездехо́д

jeer [dʒɪə] 1. насме́шка, издёвка; 2. насмеха́ться, глуми́ться (*at* над Т)

jelly ['dʒelɪ] 1. желе́ *n indecl.*; (*aspic*) сту́день *m*; 2. засты́(ва́)ть; **~fish** меду́за

jeopardize ['dʒepədaɪz] подверга́ть опа́сности, [по]ста́вить под угро́зу

jerk [dʒɜːk] 1. рыво́к; толчо́к; **the car stopped with a ~** маши́на ре́зко останови́лась; 2. ре́зко толка́ть или дёргать; дви́гаться толчка́ми; **~y** ['dʒɜːkɪ] □ отры́вистый; *movement* судо́рожный; (*bumpy*) тря́ский; **~ily** *adv.* рывка́ми

jersey ['dʒɜːzɪ] *fabric, garment* джерси́ *indecl.*

jest [dʒest] 1. шу́тка; **in ~** в шу́тку; 2. [по]шути́ть

jet [dʒet] 1. *of water, gas, etc.* струя́; 2. бить струёй; 3. *ae.* реакти́вный самолёт; *attr.* реакти́вный

jetty ['dʒetɪ] *naut.* при́стань *f*

Jew [dʒuː] евре́й(-ка *f*) *m*

jewel ['dʒuːəl] драгоце́нный ка́мень *m.*; **~(l)er** [-ə] ювели́р; **~(le)ry** [-rɪ] драгоце́нности *f/pl.*

Jew|ess ['dʒuːɪs] евре́йка; **~ish** [-ɪʃ] евре́йский

jiffy ['dʒɪfɪ] *coll.* миг, мгнове́ние

jigsaw ['dʒɪgsɔː]: **~ (puzzle)** составна́я карти́нка-зага́дка

jilt [dʒɪlt] бро́сить *pf.*

jingle ['dʒɪŋgl] 1. звон, звя́канье; 2. [за]звене́ть, звя́кать [-кнуть]

jitters ['dʒɪtəz] не́рвное возбужде́ние; **she's got the ~** она́ трясётся от стра́ха

job [dʒɒb] рабо́та, труд; де́ло; **by the ~** сде́льно; **it's a good ~ ...** хорошо́, что ...; **it's just the ~** э́то то, что ну́жно; **know one's ~** знать своё де́ло; **~ber** ['dʒɒbə] занима́ющийся случа́йной рабо́той; бро́кер, ма́клер

jockey ['dʒɒkɪ] жоке́й

jocose [dʒəʊ'kəʊs] шутли́вый; *mood* игри́вый

jocular ['dʒɒkjʊlə] шутли́вый

jog [dʒɒg] 1. толчо́к (*a. fig.*); тря́ская езда́; 2. *v/t.* толка́ть [-кну́ть]; *v/i.*

(*mst. ~ along.*) бе́гать (бежа́ть) трусцо́й; трясти́сь; *fig.* понемно́гу продвига́ться; **~ger** люби́тель *m* оздорови́тельного бе́га

join [dʒɔɪn] 1. *v/t.* (*connect*) соединя́ть [-ни́ть], присоединя́ть [-ни́ть]; *a company* присоединя́ться [-ни́ться] к (Д); вступи́ть в чле́ны (Р); **~ hands** объединя́ться [-ни́ться]; бра́ться за́ руки; *v/i.* соединя́ться [-ни́ться]; (*unite*) объединя́ться [-ни́ться]; **~ in** присоединя́ться [-ни́ться] к (Д); **~ up** поступа́ть [-и́ть] на вое́нную слу́жбу; 2. соедине́ние; *tech.* шов

joiner ['dʒɔɪnə] столя́р

joint [dʒɔɪnt] 1. *tech.* соедине́ние; стык; *anat.* суста́в; *of meat* кусо́к мя́са для жа́рения; **put out of ~** вы́вихнуть *pf.*; 2. □ объедине́нный; о́бщий; **~ owners** совладе́льцы; **~ venture** совме́стное предприя́тие; **~ stock** акционе́рный капита́л; **~ company** акционе́рное о́бщество

jok|e [dʒəʊk] 1. шу́тка, остро́та; 2. *v/i.* [по]шути́ть; поддра́знивать [-ни́ть]; **~ing apart ...** если говори́ть серьёзно; шу́тки в сто́рону; **~er** ['dʒəʊkə] шутни́к *m*, -ни́ца *f*

jolly ['dʒɒlɪ] 1. весёлый, ра́достный; 2. *adv.* о́чень; **it's ~ hard ...** черто́вски тру́дно ...

jolt [dʒəʊlt] 1. трясти́ [тряхну́ть], встря́хивать [-хну́ть]; толчо́к; *fig.* встря́ска

jostle ['dʒɒsl] 1. толка́ть(ся); тесни́ть(ся); 2. толчо́к; *in crowd* толкотня́, да́вка

jot [dʒɒt] 1. ничто́жное коли́чество, йо́та; **not a ~ of truth** ни ка́пли пра́вды; 2. **~ down** бе́гло наброса́ть *pf.*, кра́тко записа́ть *pf.*

journal ['dʒɜːnl] 1. журна́л; дневни́к; **~ism** ['dʒɜːnəlɪzəm] журнали́стика; **~ist** [-ɪst] журнали́ст

journey ['dʒɜːnɪ] 1. пое́здка, путеше́ствие; **go on a ~** отпра́виться *pf.* в путеше́ствие; 2. путеше́ствовать

jovial ['dʒəʊvɪəl] весёлый, общи́тельный

joy [dʒɔɪ] ра́дость *f*, удово́льствие; **~ful** ['dʒɔɪfl] □ ра́достный, весёлый; **~less** [-lɪs] □ безра́достный; **~ous** [-əs] □ ра́достный, весёлый

jubil|ant ['dʒuːbɪlənt] лику́ющий; **~ee** ['dʒuːbɪliː] юбиле́й

judge [dʒʌdʒ] **1.** судья́ *m* (*a. sport*); *art* знато́к, цени́тель *m*; *in competition* член жюри́, *pl.* жюри́ *pl. indecl.*; **2.** *v/i.* суди́ть; быть арби́тром в спо́ре; **~ for yourself ...** посуди́ сам ...; *v/t.* суди́ть о (П); (*decide the merit of*) оце́нивать [-ни́ть]; (*condemn*) осужда́ть [осуди́ть], порица́ть

judg(e)ment ['dʒʌdʒmənt] *law* пригово́р, реше́ние суда́; сужде́ние; (*good sense*) рассуди́тельность *f*, (*opinion*) мне́ние, взгляд

judicial [dʒuːˈdɪʃl] □ суде́бный

judicious [dʒuːˈdɪʃəs] □ здравомы́слящий, рассуди́тельный; **~ness** [-nɪs] рассуди́тельность *f*

judo ['dʒuːdəʊ] дзюдо́ *n indecl.*

jug [dʒʌg] (*vessel*) кувши́н *m*; *sl.* (*prison*) тюрьма́

juggle ['dʒʌgl] **1.** фо́кус, трюк; **2.** жонгли́ровать (*a. fig.*); **~r** [-ə] жонглёр

juic|e [dʒuːs] сок; **~y** ['dʒuːsɪ] □ со́чный; *gossip, etc.* сма́чный, пика́нтный

July [dʒuˈlaɪ] ию́ль *m*

jumble ['dʒʌmbl] **1.** пу́таница, беспоря́док; **2.** толка́ться; переме́шивать(ся); дви́гаться беспоря́дочным о́бразом; *chiefly Brt.* **~sale** благотвори́тельная распрода́жа

jump [dʒʌmp] **1.** прыжо́к; скачо́к (*a. fig.*); **2.** *v/i.* пры́гать [-гнуть]; скака́ть; **~ at an offer, etc.** охо́тно приня́ть *pf.*, ухва́тываться [ухвати́ться] за (В); **~ to conclusions** де́лать поспе́шные вы́воды; **~ to one's feet** вскочи́ть *pf.* (на́ ноги); **the strange noise made me ~** э́тот стра́нный звук заста́вил меня́ вздро́гнуть; *v/t.* перепры́гивать [-гнуть]

jumper¹ ['dʒʌmpə] (*horse, athlete*) прыгу́н

jumper² [-] (*garment*) дже́мпер

jumpy ['dʒʌmpɪ] не́рвный

junct|ion ['dʒʌŋkʃn] соедине́ние (*a. el.*); *rail.* железнодоро́жный у́зел; (*crossroads*) перекрёсток; **~ure** [-ktʃə]: **at this ~** в э́тот моме́нт

June [dʒuːn] ию́нь *m*

jungle ['dʒʌŋgl] джу́нгли *f/pl.*; густы́е за́росли *f/pl.*

junior ['dʒuːnɪə] **1.** *in age, rank* мла́дший; моло́же (**to** Р или чем И); **2.** (*person*) мла́дший

junk [dʒʌŋk] ру́хлядь *f*, хлам, отбро́сы *m/pl.*

junta ['dʒʌntə] ху́нта

juris|diction [dʒʊərɪsˈdɪkʃn] отправле́ние правосу́дия; юрисди́кция; **~prudence** [dʒʊərɪsˈpruːdəns] юриспруде́нция

juror ['dʒʊərə] *law* прися́жный

jury ['dʒʊərɪ] *law* прися́жные *m/pl.*; *in competiton* жюри́ *n indecl.*; **~man** прися́жный; член жюри́

just [dʒʌst] **1.** □ *adj.* справедли́вый; (*exact*) ве́рный, то́чный; **2.** *adv.* то́чно, как раз, и́менно; то́лько что; пря́мо; **~ now** сейча́с, сию́ мину́ту; то́лько что

justice ['dʒʌstɪs] справедли́вость *f*, *law* правосу́дие; судья́ *m*

justifiable ['dʒʌstɪfaɪəbl] опра́вданный

justification [dʒʌstɪfɪˈkeɪʃn] оправда́ние; (*ground*) основа́ние

justify ['dʒʌstɪfaɪ] опра́вдывать [-да́ть]

justly ['dʒʌstlɪ] справедли́во

justness ['dʒʌstnɪs] справедли́вость *f*

jut [dʒʌt] (*a. ~ out*) выступа́ть, выда(ва́)ться

juvenile ['dʒuːvənaɪl] ю́ный, ю́ношеский; *delinquent* несовершенноле́тний

K

kaleidoscope [kə'laɪdəskəʊp] калейдоско́п (*a. fig.*)

kangaroo [kæŋgə'ru:] кенгуру́ *m/f indecl.*

karate [kə'rɑːtɪ] карате́

keel [ki:l] 1. киль *m*; 2. ~ **over** опроки́дывать(ся) [-и́нуть(ся)]

keen [ki:n] □ (*sharp*) о́стрый (*a. fig.*); (*acute*) проница́тельный; (*intense*) си́льный; (*enthusiastic*) стра́стный; **be ~ on** о́чень люби́ть (В), стра́стно увлека́ться (Т)

keep [ki:p] 1. содержа́ние; (*food*) пропита́ние; **for ~s** *coll.* навсегда́; 2. [*irr.*] *v/t.* сот держа́ть; сохраня́ть [-ни́ть]; храни́ть; (*manage*) содержа́ть; *diary* вести́; *word* [с]держа́ть; ~ **company with** подде́рживать знако́мство с (Т); уха́живать за (Т); ~ **waiting** заставля́ть ждать; ~ **in** не выпуска́ть (**from** к Д); *hat, etc.* не снима́ть; ~ **up** подде́рживать [-жа́ть]; 3. *v/i.* держа́ться; уде́рживаться (-жа́ться) (**from** от Р); (*remain*) ост(ав)а́ться; *of food* не по́ртиться; ~ **doing** продолжа́ть де́лать; ~ **away** держа́ться в отдале́нии; ~ **from** держа́ться [-жа́ться] от (Р); ~ **off** держа́ться в стороне́ от (Р); ~ **on** (*talk*) продолжа́ть говори́ть; ~ **to** приде́рживаться (Р); ~ **up** держа́ться бо́дро; ~ **up with** держа́ться наравне́ с (Т), идти́ в но́гу с (Т)

keep|er ['ki:pə] (*custodian*) храни́тель *m*; ~**ing** ['ki:pɪŋ] хране́ние; содержа́ние; **be in** (**out of**) ~ **with ...** (не) соотве́тствовать (Д); ~**sake** ['ki:pseɪk] сувени́р, пода́рок на па́мять

keg [keg] бочо́нок

kennel ['kenl] конура́

kept [kept] *pt. и pt. p. от* **keep**

kerb(stone) ['kɜːb(stəʊn)] поре́брик

kerchief ['kɜːtʃɪf] (головно́й) плато́к; косы́нка

kernel ['kɜːnl] зерно́, зёрнышко; *of nut* ядро́; *fig.* суть *f*

kettle ['ketl] ча́йник; **that's a different ~ of fish** э́то совсе́м друго́е де́ло; ~**drum** лита́вра

key [ki:] 1. ключ (*a. fig.*); код; *mus., tech.* кла́виш(а); *mus.* ключ, тона́льность *f*; *fig.* тон; 2. *mus.* настра́ивать [-ро́ить]; ~ **up** *fig.* придава́ть реши́мость (Д); **be ~ed up** быть в взви́нченном состоя́нии; ~**board** клавиату́ра; ~**hole** замо́чная сква́жина; ~**note** основна́я но́та ключа́; *fig.* основна́я мысль *f*; ~**stone** *fig.* краеуго́льный ка́мень *m*

kick [kɪk] 1. *with foot* уда́р; пино́к; *coll.* (*stimulus, pleasure*) удово́льствие; 2. *v/t.* ударя́ть [уда́рить]; *horse* брыка́ть [-кну́ть]; ~ **out** (*eject, dismiss*) выгоня́ть [вы́гнать]; вышвы́ривать [вы́швырнуть]; *v/i.* брыка́ться [-кну́ться], ляга́ться [лягну́ться]; (*complain, resist*) [вос]проти́виться

kid [kɪd] 1. козлёнок; (*leather*) ла́йка; *coll.* ребёнок; 2. *coll.* (*pretend*) притворя́ться [-ри́ться]; (*deceive as a joke*) шутли́во обма́нывать [-ну́ть]

kidnap ['kɪdnæp] похища́ть [-хи́тить]; ~(**p**)**er** [-ə] похити́тель *m*; (*extortionist*) вымога́тель *m*

kidney ['kɪdnɪ] *anat.* по́чка; ~ **bean** фасо́ль *f*; ~ **machine** *annapam* иску́сственная по́чка

kill [kɪl] уби(ва́)ть; (*slaughter*) заби(-ва́)ть; *fig.* [по]губи́ть; ~ **time** убива́ть вре́мя; ~**er** ['kɪlə] уби́йца *m/f.*; ~**ing** [-ɪŋ] (*exhausting*) уби́йственный; (*amusing*) умори́тельный; **the work is really ~** рабо́та про́сто на изно́с

kin [kɪn] родня́; **next of ~** ближа́йшие ро́дственники

kind [kaɪnd] 1. □ до́брый, серде́чный; 2. сорт, разнови́дность *f*; род; **nothing of the ~** ничего́ подо́бного; **pay in ~** плати́ть нату́рой; *fig.* отблагодари́ть; *for bad deed* [от]плати́ть той же моне́той; ~**hearted** добросерде́чный

kindle ['kɪndl] разжига́ть [-же́чь]; воспламеня́ть [-ни́ть]; *interest* возбужда́ть [-ди́ть]

kindling ['kɪndlɪŋ] расто́пка

kind|ly ['kaɪndlɪ] до́брый; **~ness** [-nɪs] доброта́; до́брый посту́пок; **do a ~** оказа́ть(ыв)ать кому́-л. любе́зность *f*

kindred ['kɪndrɪd] **1.** ро́дственный; **2.** родня́; ро́дственники

king [kɪŋ] коро́ль *m*; **~dom** ['kɪŋdəm] короле́вство; *bot. zo.* (расти́тельное, живо́тное) ца́рство; **~ly** [-lɪ] короле́вский, ца́рственный

kink [kɪŋk] *in metal* изги́б; *fig., in character* стра́нность *f*; причу́да

kin|sman ['kɪnzmən] родство́; **~sman** ['kɪnzmən] ро́дственник

kiosk ['ki:ɒsk] кио́ск; *Brt.* **telephone ~** телефо́нная бу́дка

kip [kɪp] *chiefly Brt. coll. (bed)* ко́йка; *(sleep)* сон; **~ down** [по]кема́рить; устро́иться; вздремну́ть *pf.*

kiss [kɪs] **1.** поцелу́й; **2.** [по]целова́ть(ся)

kit [kɪt] *mil.* ли́чное снаряже́ние; **first-aid ~** апте́чка; *tool* **~** набо́р инструме́нтов; компле́кт принадле́жностей

kitchen ['kɪtʃɪn] ку́хня

kite [kaɪt] (бума́жный) змей

kitten ['kɪtn] котёнок

knack [næk] уме́ние, сноро́вка; **get the ~** научи́ться *pf.* (**of** Д), приобрести́ *pf.* на́вык

knapsack ['næpsæk] ра́нец, рюкза́к

knave [neɪv] *cards* вале́т

knead [ni:d] [с]меси́ть

knee [ni:] коле́но; **~cap** *anat.* коле́нная ча́шка; **~l** [ni:l] *[irr.]* станови́ться на коле́ни; стоя́ть на коле́нях (**to** пе́ред Т)

knelt [nelt] *pt. и pt. p. от* **kneel**

knew [nju:] *pt. от* **know**

knickknack ['nɪknæk] безделу́шка

knife [naɪf] **1.** *(pl.* **knives**) нож; **2.** зака́лывать [заколо́ть] ножо́м

knight [naɪt] **1.** ры́царь *m*; *chess* конь *m*; **2.** *modern use* жа́ловать ти́тул; **~ly** [-lɪ] ры́царский *(a. fig.)*

knit [nɪt] *[irr.]* [с]вяза́ть; *(~ together) med.* сраста́ться [срасти́сь]; **~ one's brows** хму́рить бро́ви; **~ting** ['nɪtɪŋ] **1.** вяза́ние; **2.** вяза́льный

knives [naɪvz] *pl. om* **knife**

knob [nɒb] *(swelling)* ши́шка; *(door ~)* ру́чка; *on radio, etc.* кно́пка

knock [nɒk] **1.** стук; *on the head, etc.* уда́р; **2.** ударя́ть(ся) [уда́рить(ся)]; [по]стуча́ть(ся); *coll.* **~ about** разъезжа́ть по све́ту; **~ down** сбива́ть с ног; *mot.* сбить *pf.* маши́ной; **be ~ed down** быть сби́тым маши́ной; **~ off work** прекраща́ть рабо́ту; **~ off** стря́хивать [-хну́ть], смахива́ть [-хну́ть]; **~ out** выбива́ть, выка́лчивать [вы́колотить]; *sport.* нокаути́ровать *(im)pf.*; **~ over** сбива́ть [сбить] с ног; *object* опроки́дывать [-ки́нуть]; **~out** нока́ут *(a. ~ blow)*

knoll [nəʊl] холм, буго́р

knot [nɒt] **1.** у́зел; *in wood* сук, сучо́к; **get tied up in ~s** запу́тываться [-таться]; **2.** завя́зывать у́зел *(or* узло́м); спу́т(ыв)ать; **~ty** ['nɒtɪ] узлова́тый; сучкова́тый; *fig.* тру́дный

know [nəʊ] *[irr.]* знать; быть знако́мым с (Т); *(recognize)* узн(ав)а́ть; **~ French** говори́ть пофранцу́зски; **be in the ~** быть в ку́рсе де́ла; **come to ~** узн(ав)а́ть; **know-how** уме́ние; *tech.* но́у-ха́у; **~ing** ['nəʊɪŋ] □ ло́вкий, хи́трый; *look* многозначи́тельный; **~ledge** ['nɒlɪdʒ] зна́ние; **to my ~** по мои́м све́дениям; **~n** [nəʊn] *pt. p. от* **know**; **come to be ~** сде́латься *pf.* изве́стным; **make ~** объявля́ть [-ви́ть]

knuckle ['nʌkl] **1.** суста́в па́льца руки́; **2.** **~ down, ~ under** уступа́ть [-пи́ть]; подчиня́ться [-ни́ться]

Koran [kə'rɑːn] Кора́н

L

label ['leɪbl] **1.** ярлы́к (*a. fig.*); этике́тка; *tie-on* би́рка; *stick-on* накле́йка; **2.** накле́ивать/привя́зывать ярлы́к на (В)/к (Д) (*a. fig.*)

laboratory [ləˈbɒrətrɪ] лаборато́рия; **~ assistant** лабора́нт *m*, -ка *f*

laborious [ləˈbɔːrɪəs] □ тру́дный

labo(u)r ['leɪbə] **1.** труд; рабо́та; (*childbirth*) ро́ды *pl.*; *forced* ~ принуди́тельные рабо́ты *f/pl.*; **~ exchange** би́ржа труда́; **2.** рабо́тать; прилага́ть уси́лия; **~ed** [-d] вы́мученный; тру́дный; **~er** [-rə] рабо́чий; **~-intensive** трудоёмкий

lace [leɪs] **1.** кру́жево; (*shoe* ~) шнуро́к; **2.** [за]шнурова́ть

lacerate ['læsəreɪt] раздира́ть [разодра́ть]; (*cut*) разреза́ть [-ре́зать]

lack [læk] **1.** недоста́ток, нехва́тка; отсу́тствие (Р); **2.** испы́тывать недоста́ток, нужду́ в (П); не хвата́ть [-ти́ть], недостава́ть; *he* ~*s courage* у него́ не хвата́ет му́жества

lacquer ['lækə] **1.** лак; **2.** [от]лакирова́ть, покрыва́ть [-ы́ть] ла́ком

lad [læd] (*boy*) ма́льчик; (*fellow*) па́рень *m*; (*youth*) ю́ноша *m*

ladder ['lædə] приставна́я ле́стница, стремя́нка; *in stocking* спусти́вшаяся петля́

laden ['leɪdn] нагружённый; *fig.* обременённый

ladies, ladies (room), the ladies' ['leɪdɪz] же́нский туале́т; *coll.* (*lavatory*) же́нская убо́рная

ladle ['leɪdl] **1.** *tech.* ковш; черпа́к; *for soup* поло́вник; **2.** отче́рпывать [отчерпну́ть]; *soup* разли(ва́)ть (*a.* ~ *out*)

lady ['leɪdɪ] да́ма; *title* ле́ди *f indecl.*; **~bird** бо́жья коро́вка

lag [læg] (*trail*) тащи́ться (сза́ди); отст(ав)а́ть (*a.* ~ *behind*)

laggard ['lægəd] медли́тельный, вя́лый челове́к; отстаю́щий

lagoon [ləˈguːn] лагу́на

laid [leɪd] *pt.* и *pt. p. om* **lay**

lain [leɪn] *pt. p. om* **lie**²

lair [leə] ло́говище, берло́га

lake [leɪk] о́зеро

lamb [læm] **1.** ягнёнок; (*food*) бара́нина; **2.** [о]ягни́ться; **~skin** овчи́на, ове́чья шку́ра

lame [leɪm] **1.** □ хромо́й; *fig. excuse* сла́бый, неубеди́тельный; **2.** [из]-уве́чить, [ис]кале́чить

lament [ləˈment] **1.** сетова́ние, жа́лоба; **2.** [по]се́товать, опла́к(ив)ать; **~able** ['læməntəbl] жа́лкий; печа́льный; **~ation** [læmənˈteɪʃn] жа́лоба, плач

lamp [læmp] ла́мпа; *in street* фона́рь *m*

lampoon [læmˈpuːn] па́сквиль *m*

lamppost фона́рный столб

lampshade абажу́р

land [lænd] **1.** земля́; (*not sea*) су́ша; (*soil*) земля́, по́чва; (*country*) страна́; **~ register** земе́льный рее́стр; *travel by* ~ е́хать (е́здить) су́шей/назе́мным тра́нспортом; **2.** *of ship passengers* выса́живать(ся) [вы́садить(ся)]; *of aircraft* приземля́ться [-ли́ться]

landing ['lændɪŋ] вы́садка; *ae.* приземле́ние, поса́дка; при́стань *f*

land|lady хозя́йка; **~lord** хозя́ин; **~mark** ориенти́р; *fig.* (*turning point*) ве́ха; **~owner** землевладе́лец; **~scape** ['lændskeɪp] ландша́фт, пейза́ж; **~slide** о́ползень *m*

lane [leɪn] тропи́нка; *in town* переу́лок; *of traffic* ряд

language ['læŋgwɪdʒ] язы́к (речь); *strong* ~ си́льные выраже́ния *n/pl.*, брань *f*

languid ['læŋgwɪd] □ то́мный

languish ['læŋgwɪʃ] (*lose strength*) [за]ча́хнуть; (*pine*) тоскова́ть, томи́ться

languor ['læŋgə] апати́чность *f*; томле́ние; то́мность *f*

lank [læŋk] □ высо́кий и худо́й; *hair* прямо́й; **~y** ['læŋkɪ] □ долговя́зый

lantern ['læntən] фона́рь *m*

lap¹ [læp] **1.** по́ла; *anat.* коле́ни *n/pl;* *fig.* ло́но; *sport.* круг; **2.** перекры́(ва́)ть

lap² [-] *v/t.* (*drink*) [вы́]лака́ть; жа́дно пить; *v/i.* плеска́ться

lapel [lə'pel] ла́цкан

lapse [læps] **1.** *of time* ход; (*slip*) оши́бка, про́мах, *moral* паде́ние; **2.** [в]пасть; приня́ться *pf.* за ста́рое; (*expire*) истека́ть [умо́лкнуть]; **~ into silence** умолка́ть [умо́лкнуть]

larceny ['lɑːsənɪ] кра́жа, воровство́

lard [lɑːd] топлёное свино́е са́ло

larder ['lɑːdə] кладова́я

large [lɑːdʒ] □ большо́й; (*substantial*) кру́пный; (*too big*) вели́к; **at ~** на свобо́де; (*in full*) [lɑːdʒɪ] в значи́тельной сте́пени; в основно́м, гла́вным о́бразом; **~scale** кру́пный, крупномасшта́бный

lark [lɑːk] жа́воронок; *fig.* шу́тка, прока́за, заба́ва

larva ['lɑːvə] *zo.* личи́нка

laryngitis [lærɪn'dʒaɪtɪs] ларинги́т

larynx ['lærɪŋks] горта́нь *f*

lascivious [lə'sɪvɪəs] □ похотли́вый

laser ['leɪzə] ла́зер

lash [læʃ] **1.** плеть *f;* (*whip*) кнут; (*blow*) уда́р; (*eye~*) ресни́ца; **2.** хлеста́ть [-тну́ть]; (*fasten*) привя́зывать [-за́ть]; *fig.* бичева́ть

lass, lassie [læs, 'læsɪ] де́вушка, де́вочка

lassitude ['læsɪtjuːd] уста́лость *f*

last¹ [lɑːst] **1.** *adj.* после́дний; про́шлый; кра́йний; **~ but one** предпосле́дний; **~ night** вчера́ ве́чером; **2.** коне́ц; **at~** наконе́ц; **at long~** в конце́ концо́в; **3.** *adv.* в после́дний раз; по́сле всех; в конце́

last² [-] продолжа́ться [-до́лжиться]; [про]дли́ться; (*suffice*) хвата́ть [-ти́ть]; (*hold out*) сохраня́ться [-ни́ться]

lasting ['lɑːstɪŋ] □ дли́тельный; *peace* про́чный

lastly ['lɑːstlɪ] наконе́ц

latch [lætʃ] **1.** щеко́лда, задви́жка; замо́к с защёлкой; **2.** запира́ть [запере́ть]

late [leɪt] по́здний; (*delayed*) запозда́лый; (*former*) неда́вний; (*deceased*) поко́йный; *adv.* по́здно; **at (the) ~st** не поздне́е; **of ~** после́днее вре́мя; **be~** опа́здывать [опозда́ть]; **~ly** ['leɪtlɪ] неда́вно; в после́днее вре́мя

latent ['leɪtnt] скры́тый

lateral ['lætərəl] □ боково́й

lathe [leɪð] тока́рный стано́к

lather ['lɑːðə] **1.** мы́льная пе́на; **2.** *v/t.* намы́ли(ва)ть; *v/i.* мы́литься, намы́ли(ва)ться

Latin ['lætɪn] **1.** лати́нский язы́к; **2.** лати́нский; **~American** латиноамерика́нец, -нский

latitude ['lætɪtjuːd] *geogr., astr.* широта́; *fig.* свобо́да де́йствий

latter ['lætə] после́дний; второ́й; **~ly** [-lɪ] в после́днее вре́мя

lattice ['lætɪs] решётка (*a.* **~work**)

laudable ['lɔːdəbl] □ похва́льный

laugh [lɑːf] **1.** смех; **2.** смея́ться; **~ at a p.** высме́ивать [вы́смеять] (В), смея́ться над (Т); **~able** ['lɑːfəbl] □ смешно́й; **~ter** ['lɑːftə] смех

launch [lɔːntʃ] **1.** ка́тер; мото́рная ло́дка; **2.** *rocket* запуска́ть [-сти́ть]; *boat* спуска́ть [-сти́ть]; *fig.* пуска́ть в ход; **~ing** [-ɪŋ] → **launch** 2; **~ing pad** пускова́я устано́вка; **~ing site** пускова́я площа́дка

laundry ['lɔːndrɪ] пра́чечная; бельё для сти́рки *or* из сти́рки

laurel ['lɒrəl] лавр

lavatory ['lævətrɪ] убо́рная

lavender ['lævəndə] лава́нда

lavish ['lævɪʃ] **1.** □ ще́дрый, расточи́тельный; **2.** расточа́ть [-чи́ть]

law [lɔː] зако́н; пра́вило; *law* пра́во; юриспруде́нция; **lay down the ~** кома́ндовать; **~abiding** законопослу́шный, соблюда́ющий зако́н; **~ court** суд; **~ful** ['lɔːfl] □ зако́нный; **~less** ['lɔːlɪs] □ *person* непоко́рный; *state* анархи́чный

lawn¹ [lɔːn] (*linen*) бати́ст

lawn² [-] (*grassy area*) лужа́йка, газо́н; **~ chair** *Am.* шезло́нг; **~ mower** газонокоси́лка

law|suit ['lɔ:su:t] суде́бный проце́сс; **~yer** ['lɔ:jə] юри́ст; адвока́т

lax [læks] □ вя́лый; ры́хлый; (*careless*) небре́жный; (*not strict*) нестро́гий; **~ative** ['læksətɪv] слаби́тельное

lay[1] [leɪ] **1.** *pt. om lie*[2]; **2.** (*secular*) све́тский

lay[2] [-] **1.** положе́ние, направле́ние; **2.** [*irr.*] *v/t.* класть [положи́ть]; *blame* возлага́ть [-ложи́ть]; *table* накрыва́(ть); **~ in stocks** запаса́ться [запасти́сь (*of* Т); **~ low** (*knock down*) повали́ть *pf.*; **I was laid low by a fever** меня́ свали́ла лихора́дка; **~ off** увольня́ть [-ли́ть]; **~ out** выкла́дывать [вы́ложить]; *park, etc.* разбива́(ть); **~ up** (*collect and store*) [на]копи́ть; прико́вывать к посте́ли; *v/i. of hen* [с]нести́сь; держа́ть пари́ (*a.* **~ a wager**)

layer ['leɪə] слой, пласт, наслое́ние

layman ['leɪmən] миря́нин; (*amateur*) неспециали́ст, люби́тель *m*

lay|-off сокраще́ние ка́дров; **~out** плани́ровка

lazy ['leɪzɪ] лени́вый

lead[1] [led] свине́ц

lead[2] [li:d] **1.** руково́дство; инициати́ва; *sport.* ли́дерство; (*first place*) пе́рвое ме́сто; *thea.* гла́вная роль *f*; *el.* про́вод; **2.** [*irr.*] *v/t.* води́ть, [по]вести́; приводи́ть [-вести́] (*to* к Д); (*direct*) руководи́ть (Т); *cards* ходи́ть [пойти́] с (Р *pl.*); **~ on** соблазня́ть [-ни́ть]; *v/t.* вести́; быть пе́рвым; **~ off** отводи́ть; *v/i.* нач(ин)а́ть

leaden ['ledn] свинцо́вый (*a. fig.*)

leader ['li:də] руководи́тель(ница *f*) *m*; ли́дер; *in newspaper* передова́я статья́

leading ['li:dɪŋ] **1.** руководя́щий, веду́щий; (*outstanding*) выдаю́щийся; **~ question** наводя́щий вопро́с; **2.** руково́дство; веде́ние

leaf [li:f] (*pl.:* **leaves**) лист (*bot. pl.:* ли́стья); (*leafage*) листва́; **turn over a new ~** нача́ть но́вую жизнь; **~let** ['li:flɪt] листо́вка

league [li:g] ли́га; **in ~ with** в сою́зе с (Т)

leak [li:k] **1.** течь *f*; *of gas, etc.* уте́чка (*a. fig.*); **2.** дава́ть течь, пропуска́ть во́ду; **~ out** проса́чиваться [-сочи́ться] (*a. fig.*); **~age** ['li:kɪdʒ] проса́чивание; **~y** ['li:kɪ] протека́ющий, с те́чью

lean[1] [li:n] [*irr.*] прислоня́ть(ся) [-ни́ть(ся)] (*against* к Д); опира́ться [опере́ться] (*on* на В) (*a. fig.*); наклоня́ть(ся) [-ни́ть(ся)] (*a.* **~ forward**)

lean[2] [-] то́щий, худо́й; *meat* нежи́рный

leant [lent] *chiefly Brt. pt. p. om* **lean**

leap [li:p] **1.** прыжо́к, скачо́к; **2.** [*a. irr.*] пры́гать [-гнуть], скака́ть *once* [скакну́ть]; **~t** [lept] *pt. p. om* **leap**; **~ year** високо́сный год

learn [lɜ:n] [*a. irr.*] изуча́ть [-чи́ть], [на]учи́ться (Д); **~ from** узн(ав)а́ть от (Р); **~ed** ['lɜ:nɪd] □ учёный; **~ing** [-ɪŋ] уче́ние; учёность *f*, эруди́ция; **~t** [lɜ:nt] *chiefly Brt. pt. p. om* **learn**

lease [li:s] **1.** аре́нда; (*period*) срок аре́нды; **long-term ~** долгосро́чная аре́нда, ли́зинг; **2.** сдава́ть в аре́нду; брать в аре́нду

leash [li:ʃ] поводо́к, при́вязь *f*

least [li:st] *adj.* мале́йший; наиме́ньший; *adv.* ме́нее всего́, в наиме́ньшей сте́пени; **at (the)** ~ по кра́йней ме́ре; **not in the ~** ничу́ть, ниско́лько; **to say the ~** мя́гко говоря́

leather ['leðə] **1.** ко́жа; **2.** ко́жаный

leave [li:v] **1.** разреше́ние, позволе́ние; (*absence, holiday*) о́тпуск; **2.** [*irr.*] *v/t.* оставля́ть [-а́вить]; (*abandon*) покида́ть [поки́нуть]; предоставля́ть [-а́вить]; (*bequeath, etc.*) оставля́ть; завеща́ть *im(pf)*; **~ it to me** предоста́вь(те) э́то мне; **~ off** броса́ть [бро́сить]; *v/i.* уезжа́ть [уе́хать], уходи́ть [уйти́]

leaves [li:vz] *pl. om* **leaf**

leavings ['li:vɪŋz] оста́тки *m/pl.*

lecture ['lektʃə] **1.** ле́кция; (*reproof*) нота́ция; **2.** *v/i.* чита́ть ле́кции; *v/t.* чита́ть нота́цию; отчи́тывать [-ита́ть]; **~r** [-rə] (*speaker*) докла́дчик; *professional* ле́ктор; *univ.* преподава́тель *m*

led [led] *pt. и pt. p. om* **lead**

ledge [ledʒ] вы́ступ, усту́п

ledger ['ledʒə] *fin.* гроссбу́х, бухга́л-терская кни́га

leech [liːtʃ] *zo.* пия́вка

leer [lɪə] смотре́ть и́скоса (*at* на В); де́-лать гла́зки кому́-нибудь; кри́во улы-ба́ться [улыбну́ться]

leeway ['liːweɪ] *naut.* дрейф; *fig.* **make up ~** навёрстывать упу́щенное

left[1] [left] *pt. и pt. p. от* **leave**; **be ~** ост(ав)а́ться

left[2] [~] 1. ле́вый; 2. ле́вая сторона́; **~hander** левша́ *m/f*

left-luggage|locker *rail. Brt.* автома-ти́ческая ка́мера хране́ния; **~ office** ка́мера хране́ния

leg [leg] нога́; *of table, etc.* но́жка; *of trousers* штани́на

legacy ['legəsɪ] (*bequest*) насле́дство; *fig.* (*heritage*) насле́дие

legal ['liːgl] □ зако́нный, лега́льный; правово́й; **~ize** [-gəlaɪz] узако́ни(ва)ть, легализова́ть (*im)pf.*

legend ['ledʒənd] леге́нда; **~ary** [-drɪ] легенда́рный

legible ['ledʒəbl] □ разбо́рчивый

legislat|ion [ledʒɪs'leɪʃn] законода́-тельство; **~ive** ['ledʒɪslətɪv] законо-да́тельный; **~or** [-leɪtə] законода́тель *m*

legitima|cy [lɪ'dʒɪtɪməsɪ] зако́нность *f*; **~te** 1. [-meɪt] узако́ни(ва)ть; 2. [-mɪt] зако́нный

leisure ['leʒə] досу́г; **at your ~** когда́ вам удо́бно; **~ly** *adv.* не спеша́, споко́йно; *adj.* нетороплйвый

lemon ['lemən] лимо́н; **~ade** [lemə-'neɪd] лимона́д

lend [lend] [*irr.*] ода́лживать [одолжи́ть]; *money* дава́ть взаймы́; *fig.* д(ав)а́ть, прид(ав)а́ть; **~ a hand** помога́ть [-мо́чь]

length [leŋθ] длина́; расстоя́ние; *of time* продолжи́тельность *f*; *of cloth* отре́з; **at ~** наконе́ц; *speak* подро́бно; **go to any ~s** быть гото́вым на всё; **~en** ['leŋθən] удлиня́ть(ся) [-ни́ть(ся)]; **~wise** [-waɪz] в длину́; вдоль; **~y** [-ɪ] дли́нный; *time* дли́тельный; *speech* растя́нутый; многосло́вный

lenient ['liːnɪənt] □ мя́гкий; снисходи́-тельный

lens [lenz] ли́нза; *phot.* объекти́в; *anat.* хруста́лик; **contact ~** конта́кт-ная ли́нза

lent [lent] *pt. и pt. p. от* **lend**

Lent [lent] вели́кий пост

lentil ['lentɪl] чечеви́ца

leopard ['lepəd] леопа́рд

less [les] 1. (*comp. от* **little**) ме́ньший; 2. *adv.* ме́ньше, ме́нее; 3. *prp.* ми́нус (Р); **none the ~** тем не ме́нее

lessen ['lesn] *v/t.* уменьша́ть [уме́нь-шить]; *v/i.* уменьша́ться [уме́нь-шиться]

lesser ['lesə] ме́ньший

lesson ['lesn] уро́к; *fig.* **teach s.o. a ~** проучи́ть (В) *pf.*; **let this be a ~ to you** пусть э́то послу́жит тебе́ уро́ком

lest [lest] что́бы не, как бы не

let [let] [*irr.*] оставля́ть [-а́вить]; сда-ва́ть внаём; позволя́ть [-во́лить] (Д), пуска́ть [пусти́ть]; **~ be** оста́вить *pf.* в поко́е; **~ alone** *adv.* не говоря́ уже́ о... (П); **~ down** опуска́ть [-сти́ть]; *fig.* подводи́ть [-вести́]; **~ go** выпуска́ть из рук; **~ o.s. go** дать *pf.* во́лю чу́вствам; увлека́ться [увле́чься]; **~ into** *a secret, etc.* посвяща́ть [-яти́ть] в; **~ off** *gun* стреля́ть [вы́стрелить] из (Р); *steam mst. fig.* выпуска́ть [вы́-пустить] пар; **~ out** выпуска́ть [вы́-пустить]; **~ up** *Am.* ослабе́(ва́)ть

lethal ['liːθl] смерте́льный, лета́ль-ный

lethargy ['leθədʒɪ] летарги́я; вя́лость *f*

letter ['letə] бу́ква; письмо́; **capital (small) ~** загла́вная, прописна́я (стро́чная) бу́ква; **to the ~** буква́льно; **man of ~s** литера́тор; **registered ~** зака́зно́е письмо́; **~ box** почто́вый я́щик; **~ing** [-rɪŋ] *f on gravestone, etc.* на́дпись *f; in book* разме́р и фо́рма букв

lettuce ['letɪs] сала́т

level ['levl] 1. горизонта́льный; (*even*) ро́вный; (*equal*) одина́ковый, ра́в-ный, равноме́рный; **draw ~ with** по-равня́ться *pf.* с (Т); **keep a ~ head** со-храня́ть [-ни́ть] хладнокро́вие; 2. у́ровень *m*; *fig.* масшта́б; **~ of the sea** у́ровень мо́ря; **on the ~** че́стно, правди́во; **3.** *v/t.* выра́внивать [вы́ровнять]; ура́внивать [-вня́ть]; **~ to the ground** сровня́ть *pf.* с землёй; **~ up** повыша́ть ура́внивая; *v/i.* **~ at** прице́ли(ва)ться в (В); **~crossing** переє́зд; **~headed** рассуди́тельный

lever [ˈliːvə] рыча́г

levy [ˈlevɪ]: **~ taxes** взима́ть нало́ги

lewd [ljuːd] □ похотли́вый

liability [laɪəˈbɪlətɪ] отве́тственность *f* (*a. law*); (*obligation*) обяза́тельство; (*debt*) задо́лженность *f*; *fig.* приве́рженность *f*, скло́нность *f*; **liabilities** *pl.* обяза́тельства *n/pl.*; *fin.* долги́ *m/pl.*

liable [ˈlaɪəbl] □ отве́тственный (за В); обя́занный; (*subject to*) подве́рженный; **be ~ to** быть предрасполо́женным к (Д)

liar [ˈlaɪə] лгун *m*, -ья *f*

libel [ˈlaɪbəl] **1.** клевета́; **2.** [на]клевета́ть на (В), оклевета́ть (В) *pf.*

liberal [ˈlɪbərəl] **1.** □ (*generous*) ще́дрый; (*ample*) оби́льный; *mst. pol.* либера́льный; **2.** либера́л(ка)

liberat|**e** [ˈlɪbəreɪt] освобожда́ть [-боди́ть]; **~ion** [lɪbəˈreɪʃn] освобожде́ние; **~or** [ˈlɪbəreɪtə] освободи́тель *m*

liberty [ˈlɪbətɪ] свобо́да; (*familiar or presumptuous behavio(u)r*) бесцеремо́нность *f*; **be at ~** быть свобо́дным; **take the ~ of** брать [взять] на себя́ сме́лость; **take liberties with s.o.** позволя́ть себе́ во́льности с кем-л.

librar|**ian** [laɪˈbreərɪən] библиоте́карь *m*; **~y** [ˈlaɪbrərɪ] библиоте́ка

lice [laɪs] *pl. om* **louse**

licen|**ce,** *Am. also* **~se** [ˈlaɪsəns] **1.** разреше́ние; *comm.* лице́нзия; (*freedom*) во́льность *f*; **driving ~** води́тельские права́ *n/pl.*; **2.** разреша́ть [-ши́ть]; дава́ть пра́во (В)

licentious [laɪˈsenʃəs] □ распу́щенный

lick [lɪk] **1.** обли́зывание; **2.** лиза́ть [лизну́ть], обли́зывать [-за́ть]; *coll.* (*thrash*) [по]би́ть, [по]колоти́ть; **~ into shape** привести́ *pf.* в поря́док

lid [lɪd] кры́шка; (*eye~*) ве́ко

lie¹ [laɪ] **1.** ложь *f*; **give the ~ to** обличи́ть во лжи; **2.** [со]лга́ть

lie² [~] **1.** положе́ние; направле́ние; *explore the ~ of the land* *fig.* зонди́ровать по́чву; **2.** [*irr.*] лежа́ть; быть распо́ложенным, находи́ться; (*consist*) заключа́ться; **~ ahead** предстоя́ть (Д); **~ down** ложи́ться [лечь]; **~ in wait for** поджида́ть (В) (спря́тавшись)

lieu [ljuː]: **in ~ of** вме́сто (Р)

lieutenant [lefˈtenənt] лейтена́нт

life [laɪf] жизнь *f*; (*way of ~*) о́браз жи́зни; биогра́фия; (*vitality*) жи́вость *f*; **for ~** пожи́зненный; на всю жизнь; **~ sentence** пригово́р к пожи́зненному заключе́нию; **~boat** спаса́тельная шлю́пка; **~guard** спаса́тель *m*; **~ insurance** страхова́ние жи́зни; **~ jacket** спаса́тельный жиле́т; **~less** □ безды́ха́нный, безжи́зненный; **~like** реалисти́чный; сло́вно живо́й; **~long** всю жизнь; **~time** вся жизнь *f*, це́лая жизнь *f*

lift [lɪft] **1.** лифт, *for goods, etc.* подъ-ё́мник; *fig.* (*high spirits*) воодушевле́ние; **give s.o. a ~** подвози́ть [-везти́] кого́-л.; **2.** *v/t.* поднима́ть [-ня́ть]; возвыша́ть [-вы́сить]; *sl.* [у]кра́сть; *v/i.* возвыша́ться [вы́ситься]; *of mist, etc.* поднима́ться [-ня́ться]

ligament [ˈlɪgəmənt] *anat.* свя́зка

light¹ [laɪt] **1.** свет; (*lighting*) освеще́ние; ого́нь *m*; *fig.* (*luminary*) свети́ло; **come to ~** стать изве́стным, обнару́живаться [-житься]; **will you give me a ~?** да́йте мне прикури́ть; **put a ~ to** зажига́ть [заже́чь]; **2.** све́тлый, я́сный; **3.** [*a. irr.*] *v/t.* зажига́ть [заже́чь]; освеща́ть [-ети́ть]; *v/i.* (*mst. up*) загора́ться [-ре́ться]; освеща́ться [-ети́ться]

light² [~] **1.** □ *adj.* лёгкий (*a. fig.*); **make ~ of** относи́ться несерьёзно к (Д); **travel ~** путеше́ствовать налегке́; **2. ~ on** неожи́данно натолкну́ться *pf.* на (В)

lighten [ˈlaɪtn] освеща́ть [-ети́ть]; (*become brighter*) [по]светле́ть

lighter [ˈlaɪtə] *for cigarettes, etc.* зажига́лка

light|-headed легкомы́сленный; **~hearted** □ беззабо́тный; весёлый; **~house** мая́к

lighting ['laɪtɪŋ] освеще́ние

lightness лёгкость f

lightning ['laɪtnɪŋ] мо́лния; **with ~ speed** молниено́сно; ~ **conductor**, ~ **rod** громоотво́д

lightweight sport боксёр лёгкого ве́са; легкове́сный (a. fig.)

like [laɪk] 1. похо́жий, подо́бный; ра́вный; **as ~ as two peas** похо́жи как две ка́пли воды́; **such~** подо́бный тому́, тако́й; coll. **feel~** хоте́ться (+ inf.); **what is he ~?** что он за челове́к?; 2. не́что подо́бное; **~s** pl. скло́нности f/pl., влече́ния n/pl.; **his ~** ему́ подо́бные; 3. люби́ть; [за]хоте́ть; **how do you ~ London?** как вам нра́вится Ло́ндон?; **I should ~ to know** я хоте́л бы знать

likeable ['laɪkəbl] симпати́чный

like|lihood ['laɪklɪhud] вероя́тность f; **~ly** ['laɪklɪ] вероя́тный; (suitable) подходя́щий; **he is ~ to die** он вероя́тно умрёт; **as ~ as not** вполне́ возмо́жно

like|n ['laɪkən] уподобля́ть [-о́бить]; (compare) сра́внивать [-ни́ть]; **~ness** ['laɪknɪs] схо́дство; **~wise** [-waɪz] то́же, та́кже; подо́бно

liking ['laɪkɪŋ] расположе́ние (**for** к Д); **take a ~ to** полюби́ть pf. (В)

lilac ['laɪlək] 1. сире́нь f; 2. сире́невый, лило́вый

lily ['lɪlɪ] ли́лия; **~ of the valley** ла́ндыш

limb [lɪm] коне́чность f; of tree ве́тка

lime¹ [laɪm] tree ли́па

lime² [~] и́звесть f; **~light** свет ра́мпы; fig. центр внима́ния

limit ['lɪmɪt] преде́л, грани́ца; **be ~ed to** ограни́чивать(ся) (Т); **speed ~** преде́льная ско́рость f; **time ~** ограниче́ние во вре́мени; преде́льный срок; **~ation** [lɪmɪ'teɪʃn] ограниче́ние; **~ed** ['lɪmɪtɪd]: **~ (liability) company** компа́ния с ограни́ченной отве́тственностью; **~less** ['lɪmɪtlɪs] □ безграни́чный

limp¹ [lɪmp] 1. [за]хрома́ть; 2. прихра́мывание, хромота́

limp² [~] вя́лый; сла́бый; **her body went ~** те́ло её обмя́кло

limpid ['lɪmpɪd] прозра́чный

line [laɪn] 1. ли́ния (a. rail., tel., ae); typ. строка́; in drawing черта́, штрих; (fishing ~) леса́; специа́льность f, заня́тие; **~s** pl. стро́ки; **~ of conduct** ли́ния поведе́ния; hard ~s pl. неуда́ча; in ~ with в согла́сии с (Т); **stand in ~** Am. стоя́ть в о́череди; **that's not in my ~** э́то не по мое́й ча́сти; 2. v/t. разлино́вывать [-нова́ть]; sew. класть на подкла́дку; of trees, etc. тяну́ться вдоль (Р); v/i. ~ **up** выстра́иваться [вы́строиться] (в ряд)

linear ['lɪnɪə] лине́йный

linen ['lɪnɪn] 1. полотно́; бельё; 2. льняно́й

liner ['laɪnə] naut. ла́йнер; ae. возду́шный ла́йнер

linger ['lɪŋgə] [по]ме́длить; ~ **over** заде́рживать [-жа́ться] на (П)

lingerie ['læːnʒəriː] да́мское бельё

lining ['laɪnɪŋ] of garment подкла́дка; tech. обши́вка, облицо́вка

link [lɪŋk] 1. звено́; связь f (a. fig.); соедине́ние; 2. соединя́ть [-ни́ть]

linoleum [lɪ'nəʊlɪəm] лино́леум

linseed ['lɪnsiːd]: ~ **oil** льняно́е ма́сло

lion ['laɪən] лев; **~ess** [-es] льви́ца

lip [lɪp] губа́; (edge) край; coll. (impudence) де́рзость f; **~stick** губна́я пома́да

liquid ['lɪkwɪd] 1. жи́дкий; 2. жи́дкость f

liquidat|e ['lɪkwɪdeɪt] ликвиди́ровать im(pf.); debt выпла́чивать [вы́платить]; **~ion** [lɪkwɪ'deɪʃn] ликвида́ция; выпла́та до́лга

liquor ['lɪkə] спиртно́й напи́ток

lisp [lɪsp] 1. шепеля́вость f; 2. шепеля́вить

list¹ [lɪst] 1. спи́сок, пе́речень m; 2. вноси́ть в спи́сок; составля́ть спи́сок (Р)

list² [~] 1. naut. крен; 2. [на]крени́ться

listen ['lɪsn] [по]слу́шать; (heed) прислу́ш(ив)аться (**to** к Д); ~ **in** (eavesdrop) подслу́ш(ив)ать (**to** В); слу́шать ра́дио; **~er** [-ə] слу́шатель(-

ница f) m

listless ['listlis] апати́чный, вя́лый

lit [lit] pt. и pt. p. от **light**¹

literacy ['lɪtərəsɪ] гра́мотность f

literal ['lɪtərəl] □ буква́льный, досло́вный

litera|ry ['lɪtərərɪ] литерату́рный; **~te** [-rət] гра́мотный; **~ture** ['lɪtrətʃə] литерату́ра

lithe [laɪð] ги́бкий

lithography [lɪ'θɒɡrəfɪ] литогра́фия

litre, Am. **liter** ['liːtə] литр

litter¹ ['lɪtə] **1.** помёт (припло́д); **2.** [о]щени́ться, [о]пороси́ться и т. д.

litter² [-] **1.** му́сор; **2.** [на]му́сорить, [на]сори́ть

little ['lɪtl] **1.** adj. ма́ленький, небольшо́й; time коро́ткий; **a ~ one** малы́ш; **2.** adv. немно́го, ма́ло; **3.** пустя́к; ме́лочь f; **a ~** немно́го; **~ by ~** ма́ло-пома́лу, постепе́нно; **not a ~** нема́ло

liturgy ['lɪtədʒɪ] eccl. литурги́я

live [lɪv] **1.** com. жить; существова́ть; **~ to see** дожи(ва́)ть до (P); **~ down: I'll never ~ it down** мне э́того никогда́ не забу́дут; **~ out** пережи(ва́)ть; **~ up to expectations** опра́вдывать [-да́ть] (В); **2.** [laɪv] живо́й; coals, etc. горя́щий; el. под напряже́нием; **~lihood** ['laɪvlɪhʊd] сре́дства к существова́нию; **~liness** [-nɪs] жи́вость f; оживле́ние; **~ly** ['laɪvlɪ] живо́й; оживлённый

liver ['lɪvə] anat. пе́чень f; cul. печёнка

live|s [laɪvz] pl. от **life**; **~stock** ['laɪvstɒk] дома́шний скот

livid ['lɪvɪd] ме́ртвенно-бле́дный; **~ with rage** взбешённый

living ['lɪvɪŋ] **1.** живо́й; живу́щий; существу́ющий; **2.** сре́дства существова́ния; жизнь f, о́браз жи́зни; **~ room** гости́ная

lizard ['lɪzəd] я́щерица

load [ləʊd] **1.** груз; но́ша; (weight of cares, etc.) бре́мя n; tech. нагру́зка; **2.** [на]грузи́ть; gun заряжа́ть [-ряди́ть]; fig. обременя́ть [-ни́ть]; **~ing** ['ləʊdɪŋ] погру́зка; груз

loaf¹ ['ləʊf] (pl. **loaves**) (white) бато́н; (mst. brown) буха́нка

loaf² [-] безде́льничать; шата́ться; слоня́ться без де́ла

loafer ['ləʊfə] безде́льник

loan [ləʊn] **1.** заём f; from bank ссу́да; **the book is on ~** кни́га на рука́х; **2.** дава́ть взаймы́; дава́ть [дать] ссу́ду

loath [ləʊθ] (reluctant) несклонный; **~e** [ləʊð] пита́ть отвраще́ние к (Д); **~some** ['ləʊðsəm] □ отврати́тельный

loaves [ləʊvz] pl. от **loaf**

lobby ['lɒbɪ] **1.** in hotel вестибю́ль m; parl. кулуа́ры m/pl.; (group) ло́бби n; thea. фойе́ n indecl.; **2.** parl. пыта́ться возде́йствовать на чле́нов конгре́сса

lobe [ləʊb] of ear мо́чка

lobster ['lɒbstə] ома́р

local ['ləʊkəl] **1.** □ ме́стный; **~ government** ме́стные вла́сти pl.; **2.** ме́стный жи́тель m; (a. ~ train) при́городный по́езд; **~ity** [ləʊ'kælətɪ] ме́стность f, райо́н; (neighbo(u)rhood) окре́стность f; **~ize** ['ləʊkəlaɪz] локализова́ть (im)pf.

locat|e [ləʊ'keɪt] v/t. определя́ть ме́сто (P); располага́ть [-ложи́ть] в определённом ме́сте; назнача́ть ме́сто для (P); **be ~d** быть располо́женным; **~ion** [-ʃn] ме́сто; Am. местонахожде́ние

lock¹ [lɒk] of hair ло́кон

lock² [-] **1.** замо́к; on canal шлюз; **2.** v/t. запира́ть [запере́ть]; **~ in** запира́ть [запере́ть]; v/t. запира́ться [запере́ться]

lock|er ['lɒkə] запира́ющийся шка́фчик; **~et** ['lɒkɪt] медальо́н; **~out** лока́ут; **~smith** слеса́рь m

locomotive ['ləʊkəməʊtɪv] (или ~ **engine**) локомоти́в, парово́з, теплово́з, электрово́з

locust ['ləʊkəst] саранча́

lodg|e [lɒdʒ] **1.** сторо́жка; (mst. hunting ~) охо́тничий до́мик; **2.** v/t. да(ва́)ть помеще́ние (Д); v/i. снима́ть ко́мнату; of bullet, etc. застрева́ть [-ря́ть]; **~er** ['lɒdʒə] квартира́нт m, -ка f; **~ing** ['lɒdʒɪŋ]: **live in ~s** снима́ть ко́мнату

loft [lɒft] черда́к; hay ~ сенова́л; **~y** ['lɒftɪ] □ (haughty) высокоме́рный;

building вели́чественный; *style* возвы́шенный

log [lɒg] коло́да; бревно́; ~ **cabin** бреве́нчатая хижина

loggerhead ['lɒgəhed]: *be at* ~*s* быть в ссо́ре, ссо́риться (*with* с Т)

logic ['lɒdʒɪk] ло́гика; ~**al** [ˌlɒdʒɪkl] □ логи́ческий

loin [lɔɪn] филе́йная часть *f*; ~*s pl.* поясни́ца

loiter ['lɔɪtə] слоня́ться без де́ла; (*linger*) ме́шкать

loll [lɒl] сиде́ть/стоя́ть развали́сь

lone|liness ['ləʊnlɪnɪs] одино́чество; ~**ly** [-lɪ], ~**some** [-səm] одино́кий

long[1] [lɒŋ] **1.** до́лгий срок, до́лгое вре́мя *n*; *before* ~ вско́ре; *for* ~ надо́лго; **2.** *adj.* до́лгий; ме́дленный; *in the* ~ *run* в конце́ концо́в; *be* ~ до́лго дли́ться; **3.** *adv.* до́лго; *as* ~ *ago as*... ещё ...; ~ *ago* давно́; *so*.. ! пока́ (до свида́ния)!; ~**er** до́льше; бо́льше

long[2] [-] стра́стно жела́ть, жа́ждать (*for* Р), тоскова́ть (по Д)

long-distance *attr.* да́льний; *sport* на дли́нные диста́нции; *tel.* междугоро́дный

longing ['lɒŋɪŋ] **1.** □ тоску́ющий; **2.** си́льное жела́ние, стремле́ние (к Д), тоска́ (по Д)

longitude ['lɒndʒɪtjuːd] *geogr.* долгота́

long-|sighted дальнозо́ркий; ~**suffering** многострада́льный; ~**term** долгосро́чный; ~**winded** □ многосло́вный

look [lʊk] **1.** взгляд; *in face, eyes* выраже́ние; (*appearance*) вид, нару́жность *f* (*a.* ~*s pl.*); *have a* ~ *at* th. посмотре́ть *pf.* на (В); ознако́мля́ться [-ко́миться] с (Т); **2.** *v/i.* [по]смотре́ть (*at* на В); вы́глядеть; ~ *for* иска́ть (В *or* Р); ~ *forward to* предвкуша́ть [-уси́ть] (В); с ра́достью ожида́ть (Р); ~ *into* рассма́тривать [-мотре́ть], разбира́ться [-зобра́ться]; ~ *out!* береги́сь!; ~ (*up-*)*on fig.* смотре́ть как на (В); счита́ть (за В); ~ *with disdain* смотре́ть с презре́нием; ~ *over* не замеча́ть [-е́тить];

~ *through* просма́тривать [-мотре́ть]; ~ *up in dictionary, etc.* [по]иска́ть; (*visit*) навеща́ть [-ести́ть]

looker-on [lʊkər'ɒn] зри́тель *m*; (*невольный*) свиде́тель *m*

looking glass зе́ркало

lookout ['lʊkaʊt] (*view*) вид; (*prospects*) ви́ды *m/pl.*, ша́нсы *m/pl.*; *that is my* ~ э́то моё де́ло

loom[1] [luːm] тка́цкий стано́к

loom[2] [-] мая́чить, нея́сно вырисо́вываться

loop [luːp] **1.** петля́; **2.** де́лать петлю́; закрепля́ть петлёй; ~**hole** *mst. fig.* лазе́йка

loose [luːs] □ *com.* свобо́дный; (*vague*) неопределённый; (*not close-fitting*) просто́рный; (*not tight*) болта́ющийся, шата́ющийся; (*licentious*) распу́щенный; *earth* ры́хлый; ~**n** ['luːsn] (*make loose*) ослабля́ть [-а́бить(ся)] (*untie*) развя́зывать [-за́ть]; разрыхля́ть [-ли́ть]; расша́тывать [-шата́ть]

loot [luːt] **1.** [о]гра́бить; **2.** добы́ча, награ́бленное добро́

lopsided [lɒpˈsaɪdɪd] кривобо́кий; косо́бокий

loquacious [ləˈkweɪʃəs] болтли́вый

lord [lɔːd] лорд; (*ruler, master*) повели́тель *m*; *the* 2 Госпо́дь *m*; *my* 2 [mɪˈlɔːd] мило́рд; *the* 2*'s Prayer* О́тче наш; *the* 2*'s Supper* Та́йная ве́черя; ~**ly** ['lɔːdlɪ] высокоме́рный

lorry ['lɒrɪ] *mot.* грузови́к

lose [luːz] [*irr.*] *v/t.* [по]теря́ть; *a chance, etc.* упуска́ть [-сти́ть]; *game, etc.* прои́грывать [-ра́ть]; ~ *o.s.* заблуди́ться *pf.*; *v/i.* [по]теря́ть; *sport* прои́грывать [-ра́ть]; *of watch* отст(а́в)а́ть

loss [lɒs] поте́ря, утра́та; *comm.* уще́рб, убы́ток; *at a* ~ в растеря́нности; *with no* ~ *of time* не теря́я вре́мени

lost [lɒst] *pt. и pt. p. от* **lose**; *be* ~ пропада́ть [-па́сть]; (*perish*) погиба́ть [-ги́бнуть]; *fig.* растеря́ться *pf.*; ~ *property office* стол нахо́док

lot [lɒt] (*destiny*) жре́бий; уча́сть *f*,

до́ля; *comm.* (*consignment*) па́ртия това́ров; уча́сток земли́; *coll.* ма́сса, у́йма; **draw ~s** броса́ть жре́бий; **fall to a p.'s ~** вы́пасть *pf.* на чью-л. до́лю

lotion ['ləʊʃn] лосьо́н

lottery ['lɒtərɪ] лотере́я

loud [laʊd] □ гро́мкий, зву́чный; (*noisy*) шу́мный; *colo(u)r* крикли́вый, крича́щий

lounge [laʊndʒ] **1.** (*loll*) сиде́ть разваля́сь; (*walk idly*) слоня́ться; **2.** пра́здное времяпрепровожде́ние; *thea.* фойе́ *n indecl.*; *at airport* зал ожида́ния; *in house* гости́ная

lous|e [laʊs] (*pl.:* lice) вошь *f* (*pl.:* вши); ~y['laʊzɪ] вши́вый (*a. coll. fig.*); *sl.* парши́вый

lout [laʊt] ха́мский, неотёсанный челове́к

lovable['lʌvəbl] □ привлека́тельный, ми́лый

love [lʌv] **1.** любо́вь *f*; влюблённость *f*; предме́т любви́; **give** (*or* **send**) **one's ~ to a p.** передава́ть, посыла́ть приве́т (Д); **make ~ with** влюблённый в (В); **make ~ to** быть бли́зкими; занима́ться любо́вью; **not for ~ or money** ни за что (на све́те); **2.** люби́ть; **~ to do** де́лать с удово́льствием; **~ affair** любо́вная связь; *coll.* рома́н; ~ly['lʌvlɪ] прекра́сный, чу́дный; ~r['lʌvə] (*a paramour*) любо́вник *m*, -ница *f*; возлю́бленный; (*one fond of s.th.*) люби́тель(ница *f*) *m*

loving ['lʌvɪŋ] □ лю́бящий

low¹[ləʊ] ни́зкий, невысо́кий; *fig.* сла́бый; *voice, sound, etc.* ти́хий; *behavio(u)r* ни́зкий, непристо́йный; **feel ~** быть в плохо́м настрое́нии; пло́хо себя́ чу́вствовать

low²[-] **1.** мыча́ние; **2.** [за]мыча́ть

lower¹['ləʊə] **1.** *comp. om* low **1.** ни́зший; ни́жний; **2.** *v/t. sails, etc.* спуска́ть [-сти́ть]; *eyes* опуска́ть [-сти́ть]; *prices, voice, etc.* снижа́ть [-и́зить]; *v/i.* снижа́ться [-и́зиться]

lower²['laʊə] смотре́ть угрю́мо; (*scowl*) [на]хму́риться

low-grade ни́зкого со́рта, плохо́го ка́чества; ~land ни́зменность *f*;

~-necked с глубо́ким вы́резом; ~-paid низкоопла́чиваемый; ~-spirited пода́вленный, уны́лый

loyal ['lɔɪəl] □ ве́рный, пре́данный, лоя́льный; ~ty [-tɪ] ве́рность *f*, пре́данность *f*, лоя́льность *f*

lubric|ant ['luːbrɪkənt] сма́зочное вещество́, сма́зка; ~ate [-keɪt] сма́з(ыв)ать; ~ation[luːbrɪ'keɪʃn] сма́зывание

lucid ['luːsɪd] □ я́сный; (*transparent*) прозра́чный

luck [lʌk] уда́ча, сча́стье; **good ~** счастли́вый слу́чай, уда́ча; **bad ~, hard ~, ill ~** неуда́ча; ~ily ['lʌkɪlɪ] к/по сча́стью; ~y ['lʌkɪ] □ счастли́вый, уда́чный; принося́щий уда́чу

lucrative ['luːkrətɪv] □ при́быльный, вы́годный

ludicrous ['luːdɪkrəs] □ неле́пый, смешно́й

lug [lʌg] [по]тащи́ть; *coll.* [по]волочи́ть

luggage ['lʌgɪdʒ] бага́ж

lukewarm ['luːkwɔːm] чуть тёплый; *fig.* прохла́дный

lull [lʌl] **1.** (**~ to sleep**) убаю́к(ив)ать; *fig.* успока́ивать [-ко́ить]; усыпля́ть [-пи́ть]; **2.** *in fighting, storm, etc.* вре́менное зати́шье

lullaby ['lʌləbaɪ] колыбе́льная (пе́сня)

lumber['lʌmbə] *esp. Brt.* (*junk*) хлам; *esp. Am.* пиломатериа́лы *m/pl.*

lumin|ary ['luːmɪnərɪ] *mst.* fig. свети́ло; ~ous [-nəs] □ светя́щийся, све́тлый

lump [lʌmp] **1.** глы́ба, ком; *person* чурба́н; *of sugar, etc.* кусо́к; (*swelling*) ши́шка; **~ sum** о́бщая су́мма; **a ~ in the throat** комо́к в го́рле; **2.** **~ together** [с]вали́ть в ку́чу; *v/i.* сбива́ться в ко́мья

lunatic ['luːnətɪk] *mst.* fig. сумасше́дший

lunch ['lʌntʃ] обе́д в по́лдень, ленч; **have ~** [по]обе́дать

lung [lʌŋ] лёгкое; **~s** *pl.* лёгкие *n/pl.*

lunge [lʌndʒ] **1.** *mst. in fencing* вы́пад,

удáр; **2.** *v/i.* наносúть удáр (*at* Д)

lurch¹ [lɜːtʃ] *naut.* [на]крени́ться; идти́ шатáясь

lurch² [~]: **leave a. p. in the ~** брóсить *pf.* когó-л. в бедé

lure [ljʊə] **1.** (*bait*) примáнка; *fig.* соблáзн; **2.** примáнивать [-ни́ть]; *fig.* соблазня́ть [-ни́ть]

lurid [ˈlʊərɪd] (*glaring*) крича́щий; óчень я́ркий; (*shocking*) жу́ткий, ужáсный; (*gaudy*) аляпова́тый

lurk [lɜːk] ждать притаи́вшись; скрывáться в засáде; таи́ться

luscious [ˈlʌʃəs] □ сóчный

lust [lʌst] (*sexual desire*) пóхоть *f*; (*craving*) жáжда

lust|er, *Brt.* **lustre** [ˈlʌstə] блеск; (*pendant*) лю́стра; **~rous** [ˈlʌstrəs] □ блестя́щий

lute [luːt] *mus.* лю́тня

Lutheran [ˈluːθərən] лютерáнин *m*, -áнка *f*; лютерáнский

luxur|iant [lʌgˈʒʊərɪənt] бу́йный, пы́шный; **~ious** [-rɪəs] роскóшный, пы́шный; **~y** [ˈlʌkʃərɪ] рóскошь *f*; предмéт рóскоши

lying [ˈlaɪɪŋ] **1.** *pr. p. om* lie¹ *u* lie²; **2.** *adj. от* lie (*telling lies*) лжи́вый

lymph [lɪmf] лúмфа

lynch [lɪntʃ] линчевáть

lynx [lɪŋks] *zo.* рысь *f*

lyric [ˈlɪrɪk], **~al** [-ɪkəl] □ лири́ческий; **~s** *pl.* лúрика

M

macabre [məˈkɑːbrə] мрáчный; **~ humour** чёрный ю́мор

macaroni [mækəˈrəʊnɪ] макарóны *f/pl.*

macaroon [mækəˈruːn] миндáльное печéнье

machination [mækɪˈneɪʃn] (*usu. pl.*) махинáции, кóзни *f/pl.*; интри́га

machine [məˈʃiːn] станóк; маши́на; механи́зм; *attr.* маши́нный; **~ translation** маши́нный перевóд; **~-made** маши́нного произвóдства; **~ry** [-ərɪ] маши́нное оборýдование, маши́ны

mackerel [ˈmækrəl] макрéль *f*, скýмбрия

mad [mæd] □ сумасшéдший, помéшанный; *animals* бéшеный; **be ~ about** быть без умá от (Д); **be ~ with s.o.** серди́ться на (В); **go ~** сходи́ть с умá; **drive ~** своди́ть с умá

madam [ˈmædəm] мадáм *f indecl.*; судáрыня

mad|cap сорвиголовá *m/f*; **~den** [ˈmædn] [вз]беси́ть; своди́ть с умá; раздражáть [-жи́ть]

made [meɪd] *pt. u pt. p. om* make

mad|house *fig.* сумасшéдший дом; **~man** сумасшéдший; *fig.* безýмец **~ness** [ˈmædnɪs] сумасшéствие; безýмие

magazine [mægəˈziːn] (*journal*) журнáл

maggot [ˈmægət] личи́нка

magic [ˈmædʒɪk] **1.** (*a.* **~al** [ˈmædʒɪkəl] □) волшéбный; **2.** волшебствó; **~ian** [məˈdʒɪʃn] волшéбник

magistrate [ˈmædʒɪstreɪt] судья́

magnanimous [mægˈnænɪməs] □ великодýшный

magnet [ˈmægnɪt] магни́т; **~ic** [mægˈnetɪk] (**~ally**) магни́тный; *fig.* притяга́тельный

magni|ficence [mægˈnɪfɪsns] великолéпие; **~ficent** [-snt] великолéпный; **~fy** [ˈmægnɪfaɪ] увели́чи(ва)ть; **~fying glass** лýпа; **~tude** [ˈmægnɪtjuːd] величинá; вáжность *f*; **~ of the problem** масштáбность проблéмы

mahogany [məˈhɒgənɪ] крáсное дéрево

maid [meɪd] *in hotel* гóрничная; (*house~*) домрабóтница; **old ~** стáрая дéва

maiden [ˈmeɪdn] **1.** дéвушка; **2.** незáмужняя; *fig. voyage, etc.* пе́рвый; **~name** де́вичья фами́лия; **~ly** [-lɪ] де́вичий

mail [meɪl] **1.** по́чта; *attr.* почто́вый; **2.** отправля́ть [-а́вить] по по́чте; посыла́ть по́чтой; **~box** *Am.* почто́вый я́щик; **~man** *Am.* почтальо́н; **~order** зака́з по по́чте

maim [meɪm] [ис]кале́чить

main [meɪn] **1.** гла́вная часть *f*; **~s** *pl. el., etc.* магистра́ль *f*; *in the* **~** в основно́м; **2.** гла́вный, основно́й; **~land** ['meɪnlənd] матери́к; **~ly** ['meɪnlɪ] гла́вным о́бразом; бо́льшей ча́стью; **~ road** шоссе́ *n indecl.*, магистра́ль *f*; **~spring** *fig.* дви́жущая си́ла; **~stay** *fig.* гла́вная опо́ра

maintain [meɪn'teɪn] подде́рживать [-жа́ть]; (*support*) уде́рживать [-ржа́ть]; (*preserve*) сохраня́ть [-ни́ть]; **~ that** утвержда́ть, что…; *the status quo* сохраня́ть ста́тус-кво́

maintenance ['meɪntənəns] (*up-keep*) поддержа́ние; (*preservation*) сохране́ние; *tech.* техни́ческое обслу́живание; (*child support, etc.*) содержа́ние

maize [meɪz] кукуру́за

majest|ic [mə'dʒestɪk] (**~ally**) вели́чественный; **~y** ['mædʒəstɪ] вели́чественность *f*; *His* (*Her*) ♀ его́ (её) вели́чество

major ['meɪdʒə] **1.** бо́льший; кру́пный; *mus.* мажо́рный; **~ key** мажо́рная тона́льность *f*; **2.** майо́р; *Am. univ.* о́бласть/предме́т специализа́ции; **~general** генера́л-майо́р; **~ity** [mə'dʒɒrətɪ] совершенноле́тие; большинство́; *in the* **~ of cases** в большинстве́ слу́чаев

make [meɪk] **1.** [*irr.*] *v/t. com.* [с]де́лать; (*manufacture*) производи́ть [-вести́]; (*prepare*) [при]гото́вить; (*constitute*) составля́ть [-а́вить]; *peace, etc.* заключа́ть [-чи́ть]; (*compel, cause to*) заставля́ть [-ста́вить]; **~ good** выполня́ть [вы́полнить]; *loss* возмеща́ть [-мести́ть]; **~ sure of** удостоверя́ться [-ве́риться] в (П); **~ way** уступа́ть доро́гу (*for* Д); **~ into** превраща́ть [-рати́ть], переде́л(ыв)ать

в (В); **~ out** разбира́ть [разобра́ть]; *cheque* выпи́сывать [вы́писать]; **~ over** перед(ав)а́ть; **~ up** составля́ть [-а́вить]; *a quarrel* ула́живать [ула́дить]; сде́лать макия́ж; *time* навёрстывать [наверста́ть]; = **~ up for** (*v/i.*); **~ up one's mind** реша́ться [-ши́ться]; **2.** *v/i.* направля́ться [-а́виться] (*for* к Д); **~ off** сбега́ть *pf.* (*with* с Т); **~ for** направля́ться [-а́виться]; **~ up for** возмеща́ть [-мести́ть]; *grief caused, etc.* сгла́живать [-дить], искупа́ть [-пи́ть]; **3.** моде́ль *f*; (*firm's*) ма́рка; *of British* **~** произво́дства Великобрита́нии; **~believe** фанта́зия; (*for k* Д) заме́на; подру́чное/вре́менное сре́дство; *attr.* вре́менный; **~up** соста́в; *thea.* грим, косме́тика

maladjusted [mælə'dʒʌstɪd] пло́хо приспосо́бленный; **~ child** тру́дновоспиту́емый ребёнок

malady ['mælədɪ] боле́знь *f* (*a. fig.*)

male [meɪl] **1.** мужско́й; **2.** *person* мужчи́на; *animal* саме́ц

malevolen|ce [mə'levələns] (*rejoicing in s.o.'s misfortune*) злора́дство; (*wishing evil*) недоброжела́тельность *f*; **~t** [-lənt] □ злора́дный; недоброжела́тельный

malice ['mælɪs] *of person* злой; *of act, thought, etc.* зло́ба; *bear s.o.* **~** затаи́ть *pf.* зло́бу на (В)

malicious [mə'lɪʃəs] □ зло́бный

malign [mə'laɪn] **1.** □ па́губный, вре́дный; **2.** [на]клевета́ть на (В), оклевета́ть (В); **~ant** [mə'lɪgnənt] □ зло́бный; *med.* злока́чественный

malinger [mə'lɪŋgə] притворя́ться, симули́ровать; **~er** [-rə] симуля́нт *m*, -ка *f*

mallet ['mælɪt] деревя́нный молото́к

malnutrition ['mælnjuː'trɪʃn] недоеда́ние; непра́вильное пита́ние

malt [mɔːlt] со́лод

maltreat [mæl'triːt] пло́хо обраща́ться с (Т)

mammal ['mæml] млекопита́ющее

mammoth ['mæməθ] ма́монт

man [mæn] (*pl.* **men**) челове́к; мужчина *m*; (~*kind*) челове́чество; *chess* фигу́ра; **the ~ in the street** обы́чный челове́к

manage ['mænɪdʒ] *v/i.* руководи́ть; управля́ть (T), заве́довать (T); *problem, etc.* справля́ться [-а́виться] с (T); обходи́ться [обойти́сь] (**without** без P); **~ to** (+ *inf.*) [с]уме́ть ...; **~able** [-əbl] □ *person* послу́шный; сгово́рчивый; *task etc.* выполни́мый; **~ment** [-mənt] (*control*) управле́ние; (*governing body*) правле́ние; (*managerial staff*) администра́ция; (*senior staff*) дире́кция; **~r** [-ə] ме́неджер; дире́ктор

managing ['mænɪdʒɪŋ] руководя́щий; **~ director** замести́тель дире́ктора

mandate ['mændeɪt] (*authority*) полномо́чие; *for governing a territory* манда́т; *given by voters* нака́з; *law* прика́з суда́; **~ory** ['mændətərɪ] обяза́тельный

mane [meɪn] гри́ва; *man's* копна́ воло́с

manful ['mænfl] □ му́жественный

mangle ['mæŋgl] [ис]кале́чить; [из]уро́довать; *text, etc.* искажа́ть [искази́ть]

man|handle ['mænhændl] гру́бо обраща́ться, избива́ть [-би́ть]; **~hood** ['mænhʊd] возмужа́лость *f*, зре́лый во́зраст

mania ['meɪnɪə] ма́ния; **~c** ['meɪnæk] манья́к *m*, -я́чка *f*

manicure ['mænɪkjʊə] 1. маникю́р; 2. де́лать маникю́р (Д)

manifest ['mænɪfest] 1. □ очеви́дный, я́вный; 2. *v/t.* обнару́жи(ва)ть; проявля́ть [-ви́ть]; **~ation** ['mænɪfe-'steɪʃn] проявле́ние

manifold ['mænɪfəʊld] □ (*various*) разнообра́зный, разноро́дный; (*many*) многочи́сленный

manipulate [mə'nɪpjʊleɪt] манипули́ровать; **~ion** [mənɪpjʊ'leɪʃn] манипуля́ция; *of facts* подтасо́вка

man|kind [mæn'kaɪnd] челове́чество; **~ly** [-lɪ] му́жественный; **~made** иску́сственный

mannequin ['mænɪkɪn] (*person*) мане-

кéнщица; (*dummy*) манеке́н

manner ['mænə] спо́соб, ме́тод; мане́ра; о́браз де́йствий; **~s** *pl.* уме́ние держа́ть себя́; мане́ры *f/pl.*; обы́чаи *m/pl.*; **~of** вся́кого ро́да; са́мые ра́зные; **in a ~** в не́которой сте́пени; **in this ~** таки́м о́бразом; **in such a ~ that** таки́м о́бразом, что ...; **~ed** [-d] (*displaying a particular manner*) мане́рный; (*precious*) вы́чурный; **~ly** [-lɪ] ве́жливый

maneuver, *Brt.* **manœuvre** [mə'nu:və] 1. манёвр; махина́ция; интри́га; 2. маневри́ровать

manor ['mænə] поме́стье

manpower ['mænpaʊə] рабо́чая си́ла

mansion ['mænʃn] большо́й дом; *in town* особня́к

manslaughter ['mænslɔːtə] непредумы́шленное уби́йство

mantelpiece ['mæntlpiːs] по́лка ками́на

manual ['mænjʊəl] 1. ручно́й; **~ labo(u)r** физи́ческий труд; 2. (*handbook*) руково́дство; (*textbook*) уче́бник; (*reference book*) спра́вочник; *tech.* инстру́кция (по эксплуата́ции)

manufactur|e [mænjʊ'fæktʃə] 1. изгото́вле́ние; *on large scale* произво́дство; 2. производи́ть [-вести́]; **~er** [-rə] производи́тель *m*, изготови́тель *m*; **~ing** [-rɪŋ] произво́дство; *attr.* промы́шленный

manure [mə'njʊə] 1. (*dung*) наво́з; 2. унаво́живать

many ['menɪ] 1. мно́гие, многочи́сленные; мно́го; **~ a time** мно́го раз; 2. мно́жество; **a good ~** большо́е коли́чество; **a great ~** грома́дное коли́чество; **~sided** многосторо́нний

map [mæp] 1. ка́рта; 2. наноси́ть на ка́рту; **~ out** [с]плани́ровать

maple ['meɪpl] клён

mar [mɑː] [ис]по́ртить

marathon ['mærəθən] марафо́н (*a. fig.*)

marble ['mɑːbl] мра́мор

March[1] [mɑːtʃ] март

march[2] [-] 1. *mil.* марш; похо́д; *fig. of*

events разви́тие; **2.** марширова́ть; *fig.* идти́ вперёд (*a.* ~ **on**)

mare [meə] кобы́ла; **~'s nest** иллю́зия

margarine [mɑːdʒəˈriːn] маргари́н

margin [ˈmɑːdʒɪn] край; *of page* поля́ *n/pl.*; *of forest* опу́шка; ~ **of profit** чи́стая при́быль *f*; ~**al** [-l] □ находя́щийся на краю́; ~ **notes** заме́тки на поля́х страни́цы

marigold [ˈmærɪɡəʊld] ноготки́ *m/pl.*

marine [məˈriːn] **1.** морско́й; **2.** солда́т морско́й пехо́ты; ~**r** [ˈmærɪnə] морепла́ватель *m*; моря́к, матро́с

marital [ˈmærɪtl] □ *of marriage* бра́чный; *of married persons* супру́жеский

maritime [ˈmærɪtaɪm] морско́й

mark¹ [mɑːk] *currency* ма́рка

mark² [-] **1.** ме́тка, знак; (*school~*) балл, отме́тка; (*trade~*) фабри́чная ма́рка; (*target*) мише́нь *f*; (*stain*) пятно́; (*trace*) след; **a man of ~** выдаю́щийся челове́к; **hit the ~** *fig.* попа́сть *pf.* в цель; **up to the ~** *fig.* на до́лжной высоте́; **2.** *v/t.* отмеча́ть [-е́тить] (*a. fig.*); ста́вить отме́тку в (П); ~ **off** отделя́ть [-ли́ть]; ~ **time** топта́ться на ме́сте; ~ed [mɑːkt] □ отме́ченный; (*readily seen*) заме́тный

market [ˈmɑːkə] *comput.* ма́ркер

market [ˈmɑːkɪt] **1.** ры́нок; *comm.* сбыт; **on the ~** в прода́же; ~ **economy** ры́ночная эконо́мика; **2.** продава́ть; ~**able** [-əbl] хо́дкий; ~**ing** [-ɪŋ] (*trade*) торго́вля; (*sale*) сбыт; ма́ркетинг

marksman [ˈmɑːksmən] ме́ткий стрело́к

marmalade [ˈmɑːməleɪd] (апельси́новое) варе́нье

marquee [mɑːˈkiː] большо́й шатёр

marriage [ˈmærɪdʒ] брак; (*wedding*) сва́дьба; бракосочета́ние; **civil ~** гражда́нский брак; ~**able** [-əbl] бра́чного во́зраста; ~ **certificate** свиде́тельство о бра́ке

married [ˈmærɪd] *man* жена́тый; *woman* заму́жняя; ~ **couple** супру́ги *pl.*

marrow¹ [ˈmærəʊ] ко́стный мозг; **be chilled to the ~** продро́гнуть *pf.* до

мо́зга косте́й

marrow² [-] *bot.* кабачо́к

marry [ˈmærɪ] *v/t. of parent* (*give son in marriage*) жени́ть; (*give daughter in marriage*) вы́дать *pf.* за́муж; *relig.* [об]венча́ть; *civil* сочета́ть бра́ком; *of man* жени́ться на (П); *v/i.* жени́ться; *of woman* выходи́ть [вы́йти] за́муж

marsh [mɑːʃ] боло́то

marshal [ˈmɑːʃl] **1.** ма́ршал; *Am. also* суде́бное/полице́йское должностно́е лицо́; **2.:** ~ **one's thoughts** привести́ *pf.* свои́ мы́сли в систе́му

marshy [ˈmɑːʃɪ] боло́тистый, то́пкий

marten [ˈmɑːtɪn] *zo.* куни́ца

martial [ˈmɑːʃl] □ вое́нный; во́инственный; ~ **law** вое́нное положе́ние

martyr [ˈmɑːtə] му́ченик *m*, -ница *f*; *mst. fig.* страда́лец *m*, -лица *f*

marvel [ˈmɑːvl] **1.** чу́до; **2.** удивля́ться [-ви́ться]; ~(l)ous [ˈmɑːvələs] □ изуми́тельный

mascot [ˈmæskət] талисма́н

masculine [ˈmæskjʊlɪn] мужско́й; (*manly*) му́жественный

mash [mæʃ] **1.** *cul.* пюре́ *n indecl.*; **2.** размина́ть [-мя́ть]; ~ed **potatoes** *pl.* карто́фельное пюре́ *n indecl.*

mask [mɑːsk] **1.** ма́ска; **2.** [за]маскирова́ть; (*conceal*) скрыва́ть; ~ed [-t]: ~ **ball** маскара́д

mason [ˈmeɪsn] ка́менщик; масо́н; ~**ry** [-rɪ] ка́менная (*or* кирпи́чная) кла́дка

masquerade [ˌmæskəˈreɪd] маскара́д

mass¹ [mæs] *relig.* ме́сса

mass² [-] **1.** ма́сса; **2.** соб(и)ра́ться

massacre [ˈmæsəkə] **1.** резня́; **2.** зве́рски убива́ть [уби́ть]

massage [ˈmæsɑːʒ] **1.** масса́ж; **2.** масси́ровать

massive [ˈmæsɪv] масси́вный; кру́пный

mass media *pl.* сре́дства ма́ссовой информа́ции

mast [mɑːst] *naut.* ма́чта

master [ˈmɑːstə] **1.** хозя́ин; (*teacher*) учи́тель *m*; (*expert*) ма́стер; ♀ **of Arts** маги́стр иску́сств; **2.** (*overcome*) одоле́(ва́)ть; (*gain control of*) справля́ться [-а́виться]; (*acquire knowledge of*) овладе(ва́)ть (T); **~ful** ['mɑːstəfl] вла́стный, ма́стерский; **~ key** отмы́чка; универса́льный ключ; **~piece** ['mɑːstəri] госпо́дство, власть *f*; (*skill*) мастерство́

masticate ['mæstɪkeɪt] жева́ть

mastiff ['mæstɪf] масти́ф

mat [mæt] **1.** цино́вка; *of fabric* ко́врик; *sport.* мат; **2.** *hair* слипа́ться [сли́пнуться]

match[1] [mætʃ] спи́чка

match[2] [-] **1.** ро́вня *m/f*; *sport.* матч, состяза́ние; (*marriage*) брак, па́ртия; **be a ~ for** быть ро́вней (Д); **2.** *v/t.* [с]равня́ться с (T); *colo(u)rs, etc.* подбира́ть; **well~ed couple** хоро́шая па́ра; *v/i.* соотве́тствовать; сочета́ться; **to ~ in colour, etc.** подходя́щий; **~less** ['mætʃlɪs] несравне́нный, беспо-до́бный

mate [meɪt] **1.** това́рищ; *coll. address* друг; *of animal* саме́ц (са́мка); *naut.* помо́щник капита́на; **2.** *of animals* спа́ривать(ся)

material [məˈtɪərɪəl] **1.** □ материа́льный; *evidence* веще́ственный; **2.** ма-териа́л (*a. fig.*); (*cloth*) мате́рия

matern|al [məˈtɜːnl] □ матери́нский; **~ity** [-nɪtɪ] матери́нство; **~ hospital** роди́льный дом

mathematic|ian [mæθəməˈtɪʃn] мате-ма́тик; **~s** [-ˈmætɪks] (*mst. sg.*) мате-ма́тика

matinee ['mætɪneɪ] *thea., cine.* дневно́е представле́ние

matriculate [məˈtrɪkjʊleɪt] быть при́нятым в университе́т

matrimon|ial [mætrɪˈmoʊnɪəl] □ бра́чный; супру́жеский; **~y** ['mætrɪmənɪ] супру́жество, брак

matrix ['meɪtrɪks] ма́трица

matron ['meɪtrən] матро́на; *in hospital approx.* сестра́-хозя́йка

matter ['mætə] **1.** (*substance*) веще-ство́, материа́л; (*content*) содержа́ние; (*concern*) вопро́с, де́ло; **what's the ~?** что случи́лось?, в чём де́ло?; **no ~ who ...** всё равно́, кто ...; **~ of course**

само́ собо́й разуме́ющееся де́ло; **for that ~** что каса́ется э́того; **~ of fact** факт; **as a ~ of fact** вообще́-то; **2.** име́ть значе́ние; *it does not ~* ничего́; **~-of-fact** практи́чный, делово́й

mattress ['mætrɪs] матра́с

matur|e [məˈtjʊə] **1.** □ зре́лый; *wine* вы́держанный; **2.** созре(ва́)ть; достига́ть [-ти́чь] зре́лости; **~ity** [-rɪtɪ] зре́-лость *f*

maudlin ['mɔːdlɪn] □ плакси́вый

maul [mɔːl] [рас]терза́ть; *fig.* жесто́ко критикова́ть

mauve [moʊv] розова́то-лило́вый

mawkish ['mɔːkɪʃ] □ сентимента́ль-ный

maxim ['mæksɪm] афори́зм; при́нцип

maximum ['mæksɪməm] **1.** ма́ксимум; **2.** максима́льный

May[1] [meɪ] май

may[2] [-] *[irr.]* (*модальный глагол без инфинитива*) [с]мочь; **~ I come in?** мо́жно войти́?; **you ~ want to ...** возмо́жно вы [за]хоти́те ...

maybe ['meɪbɪ] мо́жет быть

May Day ['meɪdeɪ] Первома́йский пра́здник

mayonnaise [meɪəˈneɪz] майоне́з

mayor [meə] мэр

maze [meɪz] лабири́нт; *fig.* пу́таница; **be in a ~** быть в замеша́тельстве, в раст́ерянности

me [miː, mɪ] *косвенный падеж от I*; мне, меня́; *coll.* я

meadow ['medoʊ] луг

meager, *Brt.* **meagre** ['miːgə] худо́й, то́щий; *meal, etc.* ску́дный

meal [miːl] еда́ (за́втрак, обе́д, у́жин)

mean[1] [miːn] □ по́длый, ни́зкий; (*stin-gy*) скупо́й; (*shabby*) убо́гий, жа́лкий

mean[2] [-] **1.** сре́дний; → *meantime*; **2.** середи́на; **~s** *pl.* состоя́ние, бога́тст-во; (*a. sg.*) (*way to an end*) сре́дство; спо́соб; **by all ~s** обяза́тельно; коне́ч-но; **by no ~s** пско́лько; отню́дь не ...; **by ~s of** с по́мощью (Р); посре́дством

mean[3] [-] *[irr.]* (*intend*) намерева́ться; име́ть в виду́; хоте́ть сказа́ть, подра-зумева́ть; (*destine*) предназнача́ть [-зна́чить]; зна́чить; **~ well** име́ть добрые наме́рения

meaning ['mi:nɪŋ] значе́ние; смысл; **~less** [-lɪs] бессмы́сленный

meant [ment] *pt. и pt. p. от* **mean**

mean|time, **~while** тем вре́менем; ме́жду тем

measles ['mi:zlz] *pl.* корь *f*

measure ['meʒə] **1.** ме́ра; **beyond ~** сверх ме́ры; **in great~** в большо́й сте́пени; **made to ~** сде́ланный на зака́з; **~for** approx. о́ко за о́ко; **take ~s** принима́ть [-ня́ть] ме́ры; изме́ря́ть [-е́рить]; [с]ме́рить; sew. снима́ть ме́рку с (P); **~ one's words** взве́шивать слова́; **~ment** [-mənt] разме́р; измере́ние

meat [mi:t] мя́со; fig. суть *f*; **~ball** фрика́де́лька; **~s** (*pl.*) те́фтели (*pl.*)

mechanic [mɪ'kænɪk] меха́ник; **~al** [-nɪkəl] □ механи́ческий; fig. маши́на́льный; **~al engineering** машиностро́е́ние; **~s** (*mst. sg.*) меха́ника

medal [medl] меда́ль *f*

meddle [medl] (**with, in**) вме́шиваться [-ша́ться] (в В); **~some** [-səm] □ надое́дливый

mediat|e ['mi:dɪeɪt] посре́дничать; **~ion** [mi:dɪ'eɪʃn] посре́дничество; **~or** ['mi:dɪeɪtə] посре́дник

medical ['medɪkəl] □ медици́нский; враче́бный; **~ certificate** больни́чный листо́к; медици́нское свиде́тельство; **~ examination** медици́нский осмо́тр

medicin|al [me'dɪsɪnl] □ лека́рственный; целе́бный; **~e** ['medsɪn] медици́на; лека́рство

medieval [medɪ'i:vəl] □ средневеко́вый

mediocre [mi:dɪ'əʊkə] посре́дственный

meditat|e ['medɪteɪt] *v/i.* размышля́ть; *v/t.* обду́м(ыв)ать (В); **~ion** [medɪ'teɪʃn] размышле́ние, медита́ция

medium ['mi:dɪəm] **1.** (*middle position or condition*) середи́на; (*means of effecting or transmitting*) сре́дство; (*phys., surrounding substance*) среда́; **2.** сре́дний

medley ['medlɪ] смесь *f*

meek [mi:k] □ кро́ткий, мя́гкий;

~ness ['mi:knɪs] кро́тость *f*

meet [mi:t] [*irr.*] *v/t.* встреча́ть [-е́тить]; (*become acquainted with*) [по]знако́миться с (Т); (*satisfy*) удовлетворя́ть [-ри́ть]; *debt* опла́чивать [-лати́ть]; **go to ~ a p.** встреча́ть [-е́тить] (В); **there is more to it than ~s the eye** э́то де́ло не так про́сто; *v/i.* [по]знако́миться; (*get together*) со́(и)ра́ться [-бра́ться]; **~ with** испы́тывать [-пыта́ть] (В), подверга́ться [-ве́ргнуться]; **~ing** ['mi:tɪŋ] заседа́ние; встре́ча; ми́тинг, собра́ние

melancholy ['melənkɒlɪ] **1.** уны́ние; грусть *f*; **2.** *of person* уны́лый; *of something causing sadness* гру́стный, печа́льный

mellow ['meləʊ] *person* смягча́ть(-ся) [-чи́ть(ся)]; *fruit* созре(ва́)ть

melo|dious [mɪ'ləʊdɪəs] □ мело́ди́чный; **~dy** ['melədɪ] мело́дия

melon ['melən] ды́ня

melt [melt] [рас]та́ять; *metal* [рас]пла́вить(ся); *fat* раста́пливать [-топи́ть]; fig. смягча́ть(ся) [-чи́ть(ся)]

member ['membə] член (*a. parl.*); **~ship** [-ʃɪp] чле́нство

memoirs ['memwɑ:z] *pl.* мемуа́ры *m/pl.*

memorable ['memərəbl] □ (досто́)па́мятный

memorandum [memə'rændəm] запи́ска; *dipl.* мемора́ндум

memorial [mɪ'mɔ:rɪəl] **1.** (*commemorative object, monument, etc.*) па́мятник; (*written record, athletic tournament, etc.*) мемориа́л; **2.** мемориа́льный

memorize ['meməraɪz] запомина́ть [запо́мнить]; (*learn by heart*) зау́чивать наизу́сть

memory ['memərɪ] па́мять *f* (*a. of computer*); воспомина́ние

men [men] (*pl. от* **man**) мужчи́ны *m/pl.*

menace ['menəs] **1.** угрожа́ть, грози́ть (Д; **by, with** Т); **2.** угро́за; опа́сность *f*; (*annoying person*) зану́да

mend [mend] **1.** *v/t.* [по]чини́ть; **~ one's ways** исправля́ться [-а́виться]; *v/i.*

(*improve*) улучша́ться [улу́чшиться]; *of health* поправля́ться [-а́виться]; 2. почи́нка; **on the ~** на попра́вку

mendacious [men'deɪʃəs] □ лжи́вый

meningitis [menɪn'dʒaɪtɪs] менинги́т

menstruation [menstrʊ'eɪʃn] менструа́ция

mental ['mentl] □ *of the mind* у́мственный; *illness* психи́ческий; **make a ~ note of** отме́тить *pf.* в уме́ (B); ~ **hospital** психиатри́ческая больни́ца; ~**ity** [men'tælətɪ] склад ума́; у́мственная спосо́бность; пси́хика

mention ['menʃn] 1. упомина́ние; 2. упомина́ть [-мяну́ть] (*B*or o П); **don't it!** не за что!; **not to ~** не говоря́ уж (о П)

menu ['menju:] меню́ *n indecl.*

meow, *Brt.* **miaow** [mɪ'au] [за]мяу́кать

mercenary ['mɜːsɪnərɪ] □ коры́стный

merchandise ['mɜːtʃəndaɪz] това́ры *m/pl.*

merchant ['mɜːtʃənt] торго́вец; *chiefly Brt.* ~ **bank** комме́рческий банк

merciful ['mɜːsɪfʊl] □ милосе́рдный; ~**less** [-lɪs] □ беспоща́дный

mercury ['mɜːkjʊrɪ] ртуть *f*

mercy ['mɜːsɪ] милосе́рдие; поща́да; **be at the ~ of** быть во вла́сти (P); по́лностью зави́сеть от (P)

mere [mɪə] просто́й; *a ~ child* всего́ лишь ребёнок; ~**ly** то́лько, про́сто

merge [mɜːdʒ] сли(ва́)ть(ся) (*in* с Т); объединя́ться [-ни́ться]; ~**r** ['mɜːdʒə] *comm.* слия́ние, объедине́ние

meridian [mə'rɪdɪən] *geogr.* меридиа́н

meringue [mə'ræŋ] *cul.* мере́нга

merit ['merɪt] 1. заслу́га; (*worth*) досто́инство; **judge s.o. on his ~s** оце́нивать кого́-л. по заслу́гам; 2. заслу́живать [-ужи́ть]

mermaid ['mɜːmeɪd] руса́лка

merriment ['merɪmənt] весе́лье

merry ['merɪ] □ весёлый, ра́достный; **make ~** весели́ться; ~**-go-round** карусе́ль *f*; ~**-making** весе́лье; пра́зднество

mesh [meʃ] (*one of the spaces in net, etc.*) яче́йка; ~**es** *pl.* се́ти *f/pl.*

mess¹ [mes] 1. беспоря́док; (*confu-*

sion) пу́таница; (*trouble*) непри́ятность *f*; **make a ~ of a th.** прова́ливать де́ло; 2. *v/t.* приводи́ть в беспоря́док; *v/i. coll.* ~ **about** рабо́тать кое́-как; (*tinker*) копа́ться, вози́ться

mess² [-] *mil.* столо́вая

message ['mesɪdʒ] сообще́ние; *dipl., a. attr.* посла́ние; **did you get the ~?** поня́тно? усекли́?

messenger ['mesɪndʒə] курье́р

messy ['mesɪ] неу́бранный; гря́зный; в беспоря́дке

met [met] *pt.* и *pt. p. от* **meet**

metal ['metl] мета́лл; (*road* ~) ще́бень *m*; *attr.* металли́ческий; ~**lic** [mɪ'tælɪk] металли́ческий; ~**lurgy** [mɪ'tælədʒɪ] металлу́ргия

metaphor ['metəfə] мета́фора

meteor ['mi:tɪə] метео́р; ~**ology** [mi:tɪə'rɒlədʒɪ] метеороло́гия

meter ['mi:tə] счётчик; ~ **reading** показа́ние счётчика

meter, *Brt.* **metre** ['mi:tə] метр

method ['meθəd] ме́тод, спо́соб; систе́ма, поря́док; ~**ical** [mɪ'θɒdɪkl] системате́ческий, методи́чный; (*orderly*) методи́чный

meticulous [mɪ'tɪkjʊləs] □ тща́тельный

metric ['metrɪk] (~**ally**): ~ **system** метри́ческая систе́ма

metropoli|s [mə'trɒpəlɪs] столи́ца; метропо́лия; ~**tan** [metrə'pɒlɪtən] 1. *eccl.* митрополи́т; 2. *adj.* (*of a capital*) столи́чный

mettle ['metl] си́ла хара́ктера; хра́брость *f*; бо́дрость *f*; (*endurance*) вы́носливость *f*

Mexican ['meksɪkən] 1. мексика́нский; 2. мексика́нец *m*, -нка *f*

mice [maɪs] *pl.* мы́ши *f/pl.*

micro... ['maɪkrəu] ми́кро...

microbe ['maɪkrəub] микро́б

micro|phone ['maɪkrəfəun] микрофо́н; ~**scope** ['maɪkrəskəup] микроско́п; ~**wave oven** микроволно́вая печь *f*

mid [mɪd] сре́дний; среди́нный; ~**air**: **in ~** высоко́ в во́здухе; ~**day** 1. по́лдень *m*; 2. полу́денный

middle ['mɪdl] **1.** середи́на; **2.** сре́дний; ♀ **Ages** *pl.* средневеко́вье; **~aged** [-'eɪdʒd] сре́дних лет; **~class** буржуа́зный; **~man** посре́дник; **~weight** боксёр сре́днего ве́са

middling ['mɪdlɪŋ] (*mediocre*) посре́дственный; (*medium*) сре́дний

midge [mɪdʒ] мо́шка; **~t** ['mɪdʒɪt] ка́рлик; *attr.* ка́рликовый

mid|land ['mɪdlənd] центра́льная часть страны́; **~night** по́лночь *f*; **~riff** ['mɪdrɪf] *anat.* диафра́гма; **~st** [mɪdst]: **in the ~ of** среди́ (P); **in our ~** в на́шей среде́; **~summer** [-'sʌmə] середи́на ле́та; **~way** [-'weɪ] на полпути́; **~wife** акуше́рка; **~winter** [-'wɪntə] середи́на зимы́

might[1] [maɪt] *pt. om* **may**

might[2] [-] мощь *f*; могу́щество; **with and main** и́зо всех сил; **~y** ['maɪtɪ] могу́щественный; *blow* мо́щный; *adv. coll. Am.:* **that's ~ good of you** о́чень ми́ло с ва́шей стороны́!

migrat|e [maɪ'greɪt] мигри́ровать; **~ion** [-ʃn] мигра́ция; *of birds* перелёт

mike [maɪk] *coll.* микрофо́н

mild [maɪld] □ мя́гкий; *drink, tobacco* сла́бый; (*slight*) лёгкий

mildew ['mɪldjuː] *bot.* ми́лдью *n indecl.*; *on bread* пле́сень *f*

mile [maɪl] ми́ля

mil(e)age ['maɪlɪdʒ] расстоя́ние в ми́лях

milieu ['miːljɜː] среда́, окруже́ние

milit|ary ['mɪlɪtrɪ] **1.** □ вое́нный; во́инский; ♀ **service** вое́нная слу́жба; **2.** вое́нные; вое́нные вла́сти *f/pl.*; **~ia** [mɪ'lɪʃə] мили́ция

milk [mɪlk] **1.** молоко́; **powdered ~** сгущённое молоко́; *powdered* ~ сухо́е молоко́; *whole* **~** це́льное молоко́; **2.** [по]дои́ть; **~maid** доя́рка; **~y** ['mɪlkɪ] моло́чный; ♀ **Way** Мле́чный путь *m*

mill [mɪl] **1.** ме́льница; (*factory*) фа́брика, заво́д; **2.** [с]моло́ть

millennium [mɪ'lenɪəm] тысячеле́тие

millepede ['mɪlɪpiːd] *zo.* многоно́жка

miller ['mɪlə] ме́льник

millet ['mɪlɪt] про́со

millinery ['mɪlɪnərɪ] ателье́ да́мских

шляп

million ['mɪljən] миллио́н; **~aire** [mɪljə'neə] миллионе́р; **~th** ['mɪljənθ] **1.** миллио́нный; **2.** миллио́нная часть *f*

millstone жёрнов; **be a ~ round s.o.'s neck** ка́мень на ше́е; тяжёлая отве́тственность *f*

milt [mɪlt] моло́ки *f/pl.*

mimic ['mɪmɪk] **1.** имита́тор; **2.** пароди́ровать (*im*)*pf.*; подража́ть (Д); **~ry** [-rɪ] подража́ние; *zo.* мимикри́я

mince [mɪns] **1.** *v/t. meat* пропуска́ть [-сти́ть] через мясору́бку; **he does not ~ matters** он говори́т без обиняко́в; *v/i.* говори́ть жема́нно; **2.** мясно́й фарш (*mst.* **~d meat**); **~meat** фарш из изю́ма, я́блок *и т. п.*; **~ pie** пирожо́к (→ **mincemeat**)

mincing machine мясору́бка

mind [maɪnd] **1.** ум, ра́зум; (*opinion*) мне́ние; (*intention*) наме́рение; жела́ние; па́мять *f*; **to my ~** на мой взгляд; **be out of one's ~** быть без ума́; *change one's* **~** переду́м(ыв)ать; **bear in ~** име́ть в виду́; **have a ~ to** хоте́ть (+*inf.*); **have s.th. on one's ~** беспоко́иться о чём-л.; **be in two ~s** колеба́ться, быть в нереши́тельности; **make up one's ~** реша́ться [-ши́ться]; *set one's* **~ to …** твёрдо реши́ть; **2.** (*look after*) присма́тривать [-мотре́ть] за (Т); (*heed*) остерега́ться [-ре́чься] (P); **never ~!** ничего́!; **I don't ~** (*it*) я ничего́ не име́ю про́тив; *would you* **~ taking off your hat?** бу́дьте добры́, сними́те шля́пу; **~ful** ['maɪndful] (*of*) внима́тельный к (Д); забо́тливый

mine[1] [maɪn] *pron.* мой *m*, моя́ *f*, моё *n*, мой *pl.*

mine[2] [-] **1.** рудни́к; (*coal ~*) ша́хта; *fig.* исто́чник; *mil.* ми́на; **2.** добы(ва́)ть; **~r** ['maɪnə] шахтёр, *coll.* горня́к

mineral ['mɪnərəl] **1.** минера́л; **2.** минера́льный; **~ resources** поле́зные ископа́емые

mingle ['mɪŋgl] сме́шивать(ся) [-ша́ть(ся)]

miniature ['mɪnətʃə] **1.** миниатю́ра; **2.** миниатю́рный

minibus микроавтобус

minim|ize ['mɪnɪmaɪz] доводи́ть [довести́] до ми́нимума; *fig.* преуменьша́ть [-е́ньшить]; **~um** [-ɪməm] **1.** ми́нимум; **2.** минима́льный

mining ['maɪnɪŋ] горнодобыва́ющая промы́шленность *f*

minister ['mɪnɪstə] *pol.* мини́стр; *eccl.* свяще́нник

ministry ['mɪnɪstrɪ] *pol., eccl.* министе́рство

mink [mɪŋk] *zo.* но́рка

minor ['maɪnə] **1.** (*inessential*) несуще́ственный; (*inferior in importance*) второстепе́нный; *mus.* мино́рный; **2.** несовершенноле́тний; **~ity** [maɪˈnɒrətɪ] меньшинство́

mint¹ [mɪnt] **1.** (*place*) моне́тный двор; *a ~ of money* больша́я су́мма; **2.** [от]чека́нить

mint² [-] *bot.* мя́та

minuet [mɪnjuˈet] менуэ́т

minus ['maɪnəs] **1.** *prp.* без (P), ми́нус; *it's ~ 10° now* сейча́с (на у́лице) ми́нус де́сять гра́дусов; **2.** *adj.* отрица́тельный

minute 1. [maɪˈnjuːt] □ ме́лкий; (*slight*) незначи́тельный; (*detailed*) подро́бный, дета́львый; **2.** ['mɪnɪt] мину́та; моме́нт; **~s** *pl.* протоко́л

mirac|le ['mɪrəkl] чу́до; *work ~s* твори́ть чудеса́; **~ulous** [mɪˈrækjuləs] □ чуде́сный

mirage ['mɪrɑːʒ] мира́ж

mire ['maɪə] тряси́на; (*mud*) грязь *f*

mirror ['mɪrə] **1.** зе́ркало; **2.** отража́ть [отрази́ть]

mirth [mɜːθ] весе́лье, ра́дость *f*; **~ful** [-fl] □ весёлый, ра́достный; **~less** [-lɪs] □ безра́достный

miry ['maɪərɪ] то́пкий

misadventure ['mɪsədˈventʃə] несча́стье; несча́стный слу́чай

misapply ['mɪsəˈplaɪ] непра́вильно испо́льзовать

misapprehend [mɪsæprɪˈhend] понима́ть [-ня́ть] превра́тно

misbehave [mɪsbɪˈheɪv] пло́хо вести́ себя́

miscalculate [mɪsˈkælkjuleɪt] оши-

ба́ться в расчёте, подсчёте

miscarr|iage [mɪsˈkærɪdʒ] (*failure*) неуда́ча; *med.* вы́кидыш; **~ of justice** суде́бная оши́бка; **~y** [-rɪ] терпе́ть неуда́чу; име́ть вы́кидыш

miscellaneous [mɪsəˈleɪnɪəs] □ ра́зный, сме́шанный

mischief ['mɪstʃɪf] озо́рство; прока́зы *f/pl.*; (*harm*) вред; зло; *do s.o. a ~* причиня́ть [-ни́ть] кому́-л. зло

mischievous ['mɪstʃɪvəs] □ (*injurious*) вре́дный; *mst. child* озо́рно́й; шаловли́вый

misconceive [mɪskənˈsiːv] непра́вильно поня́ть *pf.*

misconduct 1. [mɪsˈkɒndʌkt] плохо́е поведе́ние; **2.** [-kənˈdʌkt]: *~ o.s.* ду́рно вести́ себя́

misconstrue [mɪskənˈstruː] непра́вильно истолко́вывать

misdeed [mɪsˈdiːd] просту́пок

misdirect [mɪsdɪˈrekt] неве́рно напра́вить; *mail* непра́вильно адресова́ть

miser ['maɪzə] скупе́ц, скря́га *m/f*

miserable ['mɪzrəbl] □ (*wretched*) жа́лкий; (*unhappy*) несча́стный; (*squalid*) убо́гий; *meal* ску́дный

miserly ['maɪzəlɪ] скупо́й

misery ['mɪzərɪ] невзго́да, несча́стье, страда́ние; (*poverty*) нищета́

misfortune [mɪsˈfɔːtʃən] неуда́ча, несча́стье, беда́

misgiving [mɪsˈgɪvɪŋ] опасе́ние, предчу́вствие дурно́го

misguide [mɪsˈgaɪd] вводи́ть в заблужде́ние; дава́ть [дать] непра́вильный сове́т

mishap ['mɪshæp] неприя́тное происше́ствие, неуда́ча

misinform [mɪsɪnˈfɔːm] непра́вильно информи́ровать, дезинформи́ровать

misinterpret [mɪsɪnˈtɜːprɪt] неве́рно поня́ть *pf.*, истолко́вывать

mislay [mɪsˈleɪ] [*irr.* (*lay*)] положи́ть не на ме́сто; *lose* затеря́ть; *I've mislaid my pipe somewhere* я куда́-то дел свою́ тру́бку

mislead [mɪsˈliːd] [*irr.* (*lead*)] вести́ по непра́вильному пути́; вводи́ть в заблужде́ние

mismanage [mɪs'mænɪdʒ] пло́хо вести́ дела́

misplace [mɪs'pleɪs] положи́ть не на ме́сто; *p. pt.* ~**d** *fig.* неуме́стный

misprint [mɪs'prɪnt] опеча́тка

misread [mɪs'riːd] [*irr.* (**read**)] непра́вильно проче́сть *pf.*; непра́вильно истолко́вывать

misrepresent [mɪsreprɪ'zent] представля́ть в ло́жном све́те; искажа́ть [-кази́ть]

miss¹ [mɪs] де́вушка; (*as title*) мисс

miss² [-] **1.** про́мах; **give s.th. a** ~ пропусти́ть *pf.*, не сде́лать *pf.* чего́-л.; **2.** *v/t. chance* упуска́ть [-сти́ть]; *train* опа́здывать [-да́ть] на (В); (*fail to notice*) не заме́тить *pf.*; (*not find*) не заста́ть *pf.* до́ма; (*long for*) тоскова́ть по (Т, Д); *v/i.* (*fail to hit*) прома́хиваться [-хну́ться]

missile ['mɪsaɪl] раке́та; *guided* ~ управля́емая раке́та

missing ['mɪsɪŋ] отсу́тствующий, недостаю́щий; *mil.* пропа́вший без ве́сти; **be** ~ отсу́тствовать

mission ['mɪʃn] ми́ссия, делега́ция; (*task*) зада́ча; (*calling*) призва́ние

misspell [mɪs'spel] [*a. irr.* (**spell**)] [с]де́лать орфографи́ческую оши́бку; непра́вильно написа́ть

mist [mɪst] тума́н; ды́мка

mistake [mɪ'steɪk] **1.** [*irr.* (**take**)] ошиба́ться [-би́ться]; (*understand wrongly*) непра́вильно понима́ть [-ня́ть]; непра́вильно принима́ть [-ня́ть] (*for* за (В); **be** ~**n** ошиба́ться [-би́ться]; **2.** оши́бка; заблужде́ние; **by** ~ по оши́бке; ~**n** [-эн] оши́бочный, непра́вильно по́нятый; (*ill-judged*) неосмотри́тельный; неуме́стный

mister ['mɪstə] ми́стер, господи́н

mistletoe ['mɪsltəʊ] оме́ла

mistress ['mɪstrɪs] *of household, etc.* хозя́йка до́ма; (*school* ~) учи́тельница; (*a paramour*) любо́вница

mistrust [mɪs'trʌst] **1.** не доверя́ть (Д); **2.** недове́рие; ~**ful** [-fʊl] □ недове́рчивый

misty ['mɪstɪ] □ тума́нный; (*obscure*) сму́тный

misunderstand [mɪsʌndə'stænd] [*irr.* (**stand**)] непра́вильно понима́ть; ~**ing** [-ɪŋ] недоразуме́ние; (*disagreement*) размо́лвка

misuse 1. [mɪs'juːz] злоупотребля́ть [-би́ть] (Т); (*treat badly*) ду́рно обраща́ться с (Т); **2.** [-'juːs] злоупотребле́ние

mite [maɪt] (*small child*) малю́тка *m/f*

mitigate ['mɪtɪgeɪt] смягча́ть [-чи́ть]; (*lessen*) уменьша́ть [уме́ньшить]

mitten ['mɪtn] рукави́ца

mix [mɪks] [с]меша́ть(ся); переме́шивать [-ша́ть]; (*mingle with*) обща́ться; ~**ed** переме́шанный, сме́шанный; (*of different kind*) разноро́дный; ~ **up** перепу́т(ыв)ать; **be** ~ **up in** быть заме́шанным в (П); ~**ture** ['mɪkstʃə] смесь *f*

moan [məʊn] **1.** стон; **2.** [за]стона́ть

mob [mɒb] **1.** толпа́; **2.** (*throng*) [с]толпи́ться; (*besiege*) осажда́ть [-ди́ть]

mobile ['məʊbaɪl] *person, face, mind* живо́й, подви́жный; *mil.* моби́льный; ~ **phone** моби́льный телефо́н; ~**ization** [məʊbɪlaɪ'zeɪʃn] *mil., etc.* мобилиза́ция; ~**ize** ['məʊbɪlaɪz] (*a. fig.*) мобилизова́ть (*im*)*pf.*

moccasin ['mɒkəsɪn] мокаси́н

mock [mɒk] **1.** насме́шка; **2.** подде́льный; *v/t.* осме́ивать [-ея́ть]; *v/i.*; ~ **at** насмеха́ться [-ея́ться] над (Т); ~**ery** [-ərɪ] издева́тельство, осмея́ние

mode [məʊd] ме́тод, спо́соб; *tech.* режи́м; ~ **of life** о́браз жи́зни

model ['mɒdl] **1.** моде́ль *f*; *fashion* мане́кенщица; *art* нату́рщик *m*, -ица *f*; *fig.* приме́р; образе́ц; *attr.* образцо́вый; **2.** *sculpture* вы́лепить; (~ **after**, [**up**]**on**) брать приме́р

modem ['məʊdem] мо́дем

moderate 1. ['mɒdərət] □ уме́ренный; **2.** ['mɒdəreɪt] умеря́ть [уме́рить]; смягча́ть(ся) [-чи́ть(ся)]; *wind* стиха́ть [сти́хнуть]; ~**ion** [mɒdə'reɪʃn] уме́ренность *f*

modern ['mɒdən] совреме́нный; ~**ize** [-aɪz] модернизи́ровать (*im*)*pf.*

modest ['mɒdɪst] □ скро́мный; ~y [-ɪ] скро́мность f

modi|fication [mɒdɪfɪ'keɪʃn] видоизмене́ние; *mst. tech.* модифика́ция; ~fy ['mɒdɪfaɪ] видоизменя́ть [-ни́ть]; *(make less severe)* смягча́ть [-чи́ть]; модифици́ровать

modul|ate ['mɒdjʊleɪt] модули́ровать; ~e ['mɒdju:l] *math.* мо́дуль m; *(separate unit)* блок, се́кция; *(spacecraft)* мо́дульный отсе́к; *lunar ~* лу́нная ка́псула

moist [mɔɪst] вла́жный; ~en ['mɔɪsn] увлажня́ть(ся) [-ни́ть(ся)]; ~ure ['mɔɪstʃə] вла́га

molar ['məʊlə] коренно́й зуб

mold¹ [məʊld] *(Brt. mould) (fungus)* пле́сень f

mold² [-] *(Brt. mould)* 1. (лите́йная) фо́рма; 2. *tech.* отлива́ть [-ли́ть]; *fig.* [с]формирова́ть

moldy ['məʊldɪ] *(Brt. mouldy)* запле́сневелый

mole¹ [məʊl] *zo.* крот; *(secret agent)* «крот»

mole² [-] *(breakwater)* мол

mole³ [-] *on skin* ро́динка

molecule ['mɒlɪkju:l] моле́кула

molest [mə'lest] приста(ва́)ть к (Д)

mollify ['mɒlɪfaɪ] успока́ивать [-ко́ить], смягча́ть [-чи́ть]

molt [məʊlt] *(Brt. moult) zo.* [по]линя́ть

moment ['məʊmənt] моме́нт, миг, мгнове́ние; *at the ~* в да́нное вре́мя; *a great ~* ва́жное собы́тие; ~ary *(instantaneous)* мгнове́нный; *(not lasting)* кратковре́менный; ~ous [mə'mentəs] □ ва́жный; ~um [-təm] *phys.* ине́рция; дви́жущая си́ла; *gather ~* набира́ть ско́рость f; разраста́ться [-ти́сь]

monarch ['mɒnək] мона́рх; ~y [-ɪ] мона́рхия

monastery ['mɒnəstrɪ] монасты́рь m

Monday ['mʌndɪ] понеде́льник

monetary ['mʌnɪtrɪ] валю́тный; *reform, etc.* де́нежный

money ['mʌnɪ] де́ньги f/pl.; *ready* ~ нали́чные де́ньги f/pl.; *be out of* ~ не

име́ть де́нег; ~**box** копи́лка; ~**order** де́нежный перево́д

mongrel ['mʌŋgrəl] *dog* дворня́жка

monitor ['mɒnɪtə] *in class* ста́роста; *tech.* монито́р

monk [mʌŋk] мона́х

monkey ['mʌŋkɪ] 1. обезья́на; 2. *coll.* дура́читься; ~ *with* вози́ться с (Т); ~ *wrench tech.* разводно́й га́ечный ключ

mono|logue ['mɒnəlɒg] моноло́г; ~**polist** [mə'nɒpəlɪst] монополи́ст; ~**polize** [-laɪz] монополизи́ровать *(im)pf.*; ~**poly** [-lɪ] монопо́лия (P); ~**to-nous** [mə'nɒtənəs] □ моното́нный; ~**tony** [-tənɪ] моното́нность f

monsoon [mɒn'su:n] муссо́н

monster ['mɒnstə] чудо́вище; *fig.* монстр; *attr. (huge)* гига́нтский

monstro|sity [mɒn'strɒsətɪ] чудо́вищность f; ~**us** ['mɒnstrəs] □ чудо́вищный; безобра́зный

month [mʌnθ] ме́сяц; ~**ly** ['mʌnθlɪ] 1. (еже)ме́сячный; ~ *season ticket* ме́сячный проездно́й биле́т; 2. ежеме́сячный журна́л

monument ['mɒnjʊmənt] па́мятник; монуме́нт; ~**al** [mɒnjʊ'mentl] □ монумента́льный

mood [mu:d] настрое́ние

moody ['mu:dɪ] *(gloomy)* угрю́мый; *(in low spirits)* не в ду́хе; переме́нчивого настрое́ния; капри́зный

moon [mu:n] луна́, ме́сяц; *reach for the* ~ жела́ть невозмо́жного; ~**light** лу́нный свет; ~**lit** за́литый лу́нным све́том

moor¹ [mʊə] торфяни́стая ме́стность f, боло́то

moor² [-] *naut.* [при]швартова́ться

moot [mu:t]: ~ *point* спо́рный вопро́с

mop [mɒp] 1. шва́бра; ~ *of hair* копна́ воло́с; 2. мыть, протира́ть шва́брой

mope [məʊp] хандри́ть

moped ['məʊped] мопе́д

moral ['mɒrəl] 1. □ мора́льный, нра́вственный; мора́ль f, ~**s** *pl.* нра́вы m/pl.; ~**e** [mɒ'rɑ:l] *part. mil.* мора́льное состоя́ние; ~**ity** [mə'rælətɪ] мора́ль f, э́тика; ~**ize** ['mɒrəlaɪz] морализи́ровать

morato|rium [mɔrə'tɔ:riəm] *pl.*, **~ria** [-riə] *comm., pol., mil.* морато́рий

morbid ['mɔːbid] боле́зненный

more [mɔː] бо́льше; бо́лее; ещё; **~ or less** бо́лее и́ли ме́нее; **once ~** ещё раз; **no ~** бо́льше не ...; **the ~ so as ...** тем бо́лее, что ...; **~over** [mɔːr-'əuvə] кро́ме того́, бо́лее того́

morning ['mɔːniŋ] у́тро; **in the ~** у́тром; **tomorrow ~** за́втра у́тром

morose [mə'rəus] □ мра́чный

morphia ['mɔːfiə], **morphine** ['mɔːfiːn] мо́рфий

morsel ['mɔːsl] кусо́чек

mortal ['mɔːtl] **1.** □ сме́ртный; *wound* смерте́льный; **2.** сме́ртный; *ordinary* **~** просто́й сме́ртный; **~ity** [mɔː'tæləti] (*being mortal; a. ~ rate*) сме́ртность *f*

mortar ['mɔːtə] известко́вый раство́р

mortgage ['mɔːgidʒ] **1.** ссу́да (под недви́жимость); закладна́я; **2.** закла́дывать [заложи́ть]

morti|fication [mɔːtifi'keiʃn] чу́вство стыда́; **to my ~** к моему́ стыду́; **~fy** ['mɔːtifai] (*shame, humiliate*) обижа́ть [оби́деть]; унижа́ть [уни́зить]; (*cause grief*) оскорбля́ть [-би́ть]

mortuary ['mɔːtʃəri] морг

mosaic [məu'zeiik] моза́ика

Moslem ['mɒzləm] = **Muslim**

mosque [mɒsk] мече́ть *f*

mosquito [məs'kiːtəu] кома́р; *in tropics* моски́т

moss [mɒs] мох; **~y** ['-i] мши́стый

most [məust] **1.** *adj.* □ наибо́льший; **2.** *adv.* бо́льше всего́; **~ beautiful** са́мый краси́вый; **3.** наибо́льшее коли́чество; бо́льшая часть *f*; **at (the) ~** са́мое бо́льшее, не бо́льше чем; **make the ~ of ...** наилу́чшим о́бразом испо́льзовать; **the ~ I can do** всё, что я могу́ сде́лать; **~ly** ['məustli] по бо́льшей ча́сти; гла́вным о́бразом; ча́ще всего́

motel [məu'tel] моте́ль *m*

moth [mɒθ] моль *f*; мотылёк; **~-eaten** изъе́денный мо́лью

mother ['mʌðə] **1.** мать *f*; **2.** относи́ться по-матери́нски к (Д); **~hood** ['mʌðəhud] матери́нство; **~-in-law** [-rinlɔ:] (*wife's mother*) тёща; (*husband's mother*) свекро́вь *f*; **~ly** [-li] матери́нский; **~-of-pearl** [-rəv'pɜːl] перламу́тровый; **~ tongue** родно́й язы́к

motif [məu'tiːf] моти́в

motion ['məuʃn] **1.** движе́ние; *of mechanism* ход; (*proposal*) предложе́ние; **2.** *v/t.* пока́зывать жестом; *v/i.* кивать [кивну́ть] (**to** в В); **~less** [-lis] неподви́жный; **~ picture** *Am.* (кино)фи́льм

motiv|ate ['məutiveit] мотиви́ровать; **~e** ['məutiv] **1.** *of power* дви́жущий; **2.** (*inducement*) по́вод, моти́в

motley ['mɒtli] пёстрый

motor ['məutə] **1.** дви́гатель *m*, мото́р; **2.** мото́рный; **~ mechanic, ~ fitter** автомеха́ник; **3.** е́хать (везти́) на автомаши́не; **~ boat** мото́рная ло́дка; **~car** автомаши́на, *coll.* маши́на; **~cycle** мотоци́кл; **~ing** ['məutəriŋ] автомоби́льный спорт; автотури́зм; **~ist** [-rist] автомоби́ли́ст *m*, -ка *f*; **~ scooter** мотороллер; **~way** автостра́да

mottled ['mɒtld] кра́пчатый

mound [maund] (*hillock*) холм; (*heap*) ку́ча

mount¹ [maunt] возвы́шенность *f*; гора́; **2** *Everest* гора́ Эвере́ст

mount² [-] *v/i.* поднима́ться [-ня́ться]; сади́ться на ло́шадь *f*; *v/t. radio, etc.* устана́вливать [-нови́ть]; [с]монти́ровать; (*frame*) вставля́ть в ра́му (в опра́ву)

mountain ['mauntin] **1.** гора́; **2.** го́рный, наго́рный; **~eer** [maunti'niə] альпини́ст(ка); **~ous** ['mauntinəs] гори́стый

mourn [mɔːn] горева́ть; *s.b.'s death* опла́к(ив)ать; **~er** ['mɔːnə] скорбя́щий; **~ful** ['mɔːnfl] □ печа́льный, ско́рбный; **~ing** ['mɔːniŋ] тра́ур

mouse [maus] (*pl. mice*) мышь *f*

moustache [mə'stɑːʃ] = **mustache**

mouth [mauθ], *pl.* **~s** [-z] рот; *of river* у́стье; *of cave, etc.* вход; **~ organ** губна́я гармо́ника; *fig.* ру́пор; **~piece** *of pipe, etc.* мундшту́к; *fig.* ру́пор

move [muːv] *v/t. com.* дви́гать [дви́нуть]; передвига́ть [-и́нуть]; (*touch*) тро́гать [тро́нуть]; (*propose*) вноси́ть [внести́]; *v/i.* дви́гаться [дви́нуться]; (*change residence*) переезжа́ть [переє́хать]; *of events* развива́ться; *of affairs* идти́ [пойти́]; *fig. in artistic circles, etc.* враща́ться [въ езжа́ть [въе́хать]; ~ **on** дви́гаться вперёд; 2. движе́ние; переє́зд; *in game pf.* ход; *fig.* шаг; **on the** ~ на ходу́; **make a** ~ сде́лать ход; ~**ment** ['mu:vmənt] движе́ние *f* *of symphony, etc.* часть *f*

movies ['mu:vɪz] *pl.* кино́ *n indecl.*

moving ['mu:vɪŋ] □ дви́жущийся; (*touching*) тро́гательный; ~ **staircase** эскала́тор

mow [məʊ] [*irr.*] [с]коси́ть; ~**n** *pt. p. om* **mow**

Mr. ['mɪstə] → **mister**

Mrs. ['mɪsɪz] ми́ссис, госпожа́

much [mʌtʃ] *adj.* мно́го; *adv.* о́чень; **I thought as** ~ я так и ду́мал; **make** ~ **of** придава́ть [прида́ть] большо́е значе́ние; окружа́ть внима́нием; ба́ловать (B); **I am not** ~ **of a dancer** я нева́жно танцу́ю

muck [mʌk] наво́з; *fig.* дрянь *f*

mucus ['mju:kəs] слизь *f*

mud [mʌd] грязь *f*

muddle ['mʌdl] 1. *v/t.* перепу́т(ыв)ать; [с]пу́тать (*a.* ~ **up**); 2. *coll.* пу́таница, неразбери́ха; (*disorder*) беспоря́док

mud|dy ['mʌdɪ] гря́зный; ~**guard** крыло́

muffin ['mʌfɪn] сдо́бная бу́лочка

muffle ['mʌfl] *of voice, etc.* глуши́ть, заглуша́ть [-ши́ть]; (*envelop*) заку́т(ыв)ать; ~**r** [-ə] (*device for deadening sound; Am. esp. mot.*) глуши́тель *m*

mug [mʌg] кру́жка

muggy ['mʌgɪ] ду́шный, вла́жный

mulberry ['mʌlbərɪ] (*tree*) ту́товое де́рево, шелкови́ца; (*fruit*) ту́товая я́года

mule [mju:l] мул; **stubborn as a** ~ упря́мый как осёл

mull [mʌl]: ~ **over** обду́м(ыв)ать; размышля́ть [-мы́слить]

mulled [mʌld]: ~ **wine** глинтве́йн

multi|ple ['mʌltɪpl] 1. *math.* кра́тный; 2. *math.* кра́тное число́; (*repeated*) многокра́тный; *interests. etc.* разнообра́зный; ~**plication** [mʌltɪplɪ'keɪʃn] умноже́ние; увеличе́ние; ~ **table** табли́ца умноже́ния; ~**plicity** [-'plɪsətɪ] многочи́сленность *f*; (*variety*) разнообра́зие; ~**ply** ['mʌltɪplaɪ] увели́чи(ва)ть(ся); *math.* умножа́ть [-о́жить]; ~**purpose** многоцелево́й; ~**tude** [-tju:d] мно́жество, ма́сса; толпа́

mum [mʌm]: **keep** ~ пома́лкивать

mumble ['mʌmbl] [про]бормота́ть

mummy ['mʌmɪ] му́мия

mumps [mʌmps] *sg.* сви́нка

mundane [mʌndeɪn] земно́й, мирско́й; □ бана́льный; *life* прозаи́чный

municipal [mju:'nɪsɪpl] □ муниципа́льный; ~**ity** [-nɪsɪ'pælətɪ] муниципалите́т

mural ['mjʊərəl] фре́ска; стенна́я ро́спись *f*

murder ['mɜ:də] 1. уби́йство; 2. уби(ва́)ть; ~**er** [-rə] уби́йца *m/f*; ~**ous** [-rəs] □ уби́йственный

murky ['mɜ:kɪ] □ тёмный; *day* па́смурный

murmur ['mɜ:mə] 1. *of brook* журча́ние; *of voices* ти́хие зву́ки голосо́в; шёпот; 2. [за]журча́ть, шепта́ть; (*grumble*) ворча́ть

musc|le ['mʌsl] му́скул, мы́шца; ~**ular** ['mʌskjʊlə] (*brawny*) мускули́стый; му́скульный

muse[1] [mju:z] му́за

muse[2] [~] заду́м(ыв)аться (*about, on* над T)

museum [mju:'zɪəm] музе́й

mushroom ['mʌʃrum] 1. гриб; **pick** ~**s** собира́ть грибы́; 2. (*grow rapidly*) расти́ как грибы́

music ['mju:zɪk] му́зыка; музыка́льное произведе́ние; (*notes*) но́ты *f/pl.*; **face the** ~ расхлёбывать ка́шу; **set to** ~ положи́ть *pf.* на му́зыку; ~**al** ['mju:zɪkl] □ музыка́льный; мелоди́чный; ~ **hall** мю́зикхолл; эстра́дный теа́тр; зал [mju:'zɪʃn] музыка́нт

Muslim ['mʊzlɪm] мусульма́нский

muslin ['mʌzlɪn] мусли́н

musquash ['mʌskwɒʃ] онда́тра; мех

рнда́тры

mussel [mʌsl] ми́дия

must [mʌst]: *I~* я до́лжен (+ *inf.*); *I~ not* мне нельзя́; *he ~ still be there* он до́лжно́ быть всё ещё там

mustache [məˈstɑːʃ] усы́ *m/pl.*

mustard [ˈmʌstəd] горчи́ца

muster [ˈmʌstə] (*gather*) собира́ться [-бра́ться]; ~ (*up*) *one's courage* набра́ться *pf.* хра́брости, собра́ться *pf.* с ду́хом

musty [ˈmʌstɪ] за́тхлый

mutation [mjuːˈteɪʃn] *biol.* мута́ция

mut|e [mjuːt] 1. □ немо́й; 2. немо́й; ~ed [ˈ-ɪd] приглушённый

mutilat|e [ˈmjuːtɪleɪt] [из]уве́чить; ~ion [-ˈeɪʃn] уве́чье

mutin|ous [ˈmjuːtɪnəs] □ мяте́жный (*a. fig.*); ~y [-nɪ] бунт, мяте́ж

mutter [ˈmʌtə] 1. бормота́нье; (*grumble*) ворча́ние; 2. [про]бормота́ть; [про]ворча́ть

mutton [ˈmʌtn] бара́нина; *leg of ~* ба-

ра́нья нога́; ~ *chop* бара́нья отбивна́я

mutual [ˈmjuːtʃʊəl] □ обою́дный, взаи́мный; о́бщий; ~ *friend* о́бщий друг

muzzle [ˈmʌzl] 1. мо́рда, ры́ло; *of gun* ду́ло; (*for dog*) намо́рдник; 2. надева́ть намо́рдник (Д); *fig.* заста́вить *pf.* молча́ть

my [maɪ] *poss. pron.* мой *m*, моя́ *f*, моё *n*; мой *pl.*

myrtle [ˈmɜːtl] мирт

myself [maɪˈself] *refl. pron.* 1. себя́, меня́ самого́; -ся, -сь; 2. *pron. emphatic* сам; *I dit it* я сам э́то сде́лал

myster|ious [mɪˈstɪərɪəs] □ зага́дочный, таи́нственный; ~y [ˈmɪstərɪ] та́йна; *it's a ~ to me ...* остаётся для меня́ зага́дкой

mystic [ˈmɪstɪk] (*a.* ~*cal* [-kl] □) мисти́ческий; ~fy [-tfaɪ] мистифици́ровать (*im*)*pf.*; (*bewilder*) озада́чи(ва)ть

myth [mɪθ] миф

N

nab [næb] *coll.* (*arrest*) накрыва́ть [-ы́ть]; (*take unawares*) застига́ть [-и́гнуть]

nag [næg] *coll.* пили́ть

nail [neɪl] 1. *anat.* но́готь *m*; гвоздь *m*; ~ *file* пи́лка для ногте́й; 2. забива́ть гвоздя́ми; приби(ва́)ть; ~ *down* заста́вить *pf.* раскры́ть свои́ ка́рты; прижа́ть *pf* к стене́

naïve [naɪˈiːv] *or* **naive** □ наи́вный; безыску́сный

naked [ˈneɪkɪd] □ наго́й, го́лый; (*evident*) я́вный; *with the ~ eye* невооружённым гла́зом; ~ness [-nɪs] нагота́

name [neɪm] 1. и́мя *n*; (*surname*) фами́лия; *of things* назва́ние; *of* (*coll. by*) *the ~ of* по и́мени (И); *in the ~ of* и́мя (Р); от и́мени (Р); *call a p. ~s* [об]руга́ть (В); 2. наз(ы)ва́ть; дава́ть и́мя (Д); ~less [ˈneɪmlɪs] □ безымя́нный;

~ly [ˈ-lɪ] и́менно; ~plate табли́чка с фами́лией; ~sake тёзка *m/f*

nap¹ [næp] 1. коро́ткий/лёгкий сон; 2. дрема́ть [вздремну́ть]; *catch s.b.* ~*ping* заст(ав)а́ть кого́-л. враспло́х

nap² [-] *on cloth* ворс

nape [neɪp] заты́лок

napkin [ˈnæpkɪn] салфе́тка; *baby's* пелёнка

narcotic [nɑːˈkɒtɪk] 1. (~*ally*) наркоти́ческий; 2. нарко́тик

narrat|e [nəˈreɪt] расска́зывать [-за́ть]; ~ion [-ʃn] расска́з; ~ive [ˈnærətɪv] повествова́ние

narrow [ˈnærəʊ] 1. □ у́зкий; (*confinsed*) те́сный; *person, mind* ограни́ченный; 2. ~*s pl.* проли́в; 3. су́живать(ся) [су́зить(-ся)]; уменьша́ть(ся) [уме́ньшить(-ся)]; *of chances, etc.* ограничи(ва)ть; ~-minded у́зкий; с предрассу́дками

nasal ['neɪzl] □ носово́й; *voice* гнуса́вый

nasty ['nɑ:stɪ] □ (*offensive*) проти́вный; неприя́тный; гря́зный; (*spiteful*) злобный

nation ['neɪʃn] на́ция

national ['næʃnl] 1. □ национа́льный, наро́дный; госуда́рственный; 2. (*citizen*) по́дданный; ~ity [næʃə'nælətɪ] национа́льность f; гражда́нство, по́дданство; ~ize['næʃnəlaɪz] национализи́ровать (*im*)*pf.*

native ['neɪtɪv] 1. □ родно́й; (*indigenous*) тузе́мный, ме́стный, коренно́й; ~ **language** родно́й язы́к; 2. уроже́нец *m*, -нка *f*; ме́стный жи́тель

natural ['nætʃrəl] □ есте́ственный; *leather, etc.* натура́льный; ~ **sciences** есте́ственные нау́ки *f/pl.*; ~ize [-aɪz] предоставля́ть [-а́вить] гражда́нство

nature ['neɪtʃə] приро́да; хара́ктер

naught [nɔ:t] ничто́; ноль *m*; **set at** ~ во что ни ста́вить; пренебрега́ть [-бре́чь] (Т)

naughty ['nɔ:tɪ] □ непослу́шный, капри́зный

nause|a ['nɔ:zɪə] тошнота́; (*disgust*) отвраще́ние; ~ate['nɔ:zɪeɪt] *v/t.* тошни́ть; **it** ~**s me** меня́ тошни́т от э́того; вызыва́ть [вы́звать] отвраще́ние; **be** ~**d** испы́тывать отвраще́ние

nautical ['nɔ:tɪkl] морско́й

naval ['neɪvl] (вое́нно-)морско́й

nave [neɪv] *arch.* неф

navel ['neɪvl] пуп, пупо́к

naviga|ble ['nævɪgəbl] □ судохо́дный; ~**te** [-geɪt] *v/i. naut., ae.* управля́ть; *v/t. ship, plane* вести́; ~**tion** [nævɪ'geɪʃn] навига́ция; *inland* ~ речно́е судохо́дство; ~**tor**['nævɪgeɪtə] штурма́н

navy ['neɪvɪ] вое́нно-морски́е си́лы; вое́нно-морско́й флот; ~(**blue**) тёмно-си́ний

near [nɪə] 1. *adj.* бли́зкий; бли́жний; (*stingy*) скупо́й; **in the** ~ **future** в ближа́йшее вре́мя; ~ **at hand** под руко́й; 2. *adv.* ря́дом; бли́зко, недалеко́; почти́; ско́ро; 3. *prp.* о́коло (Р), у (Р); 4. приближа́ться [-ли́зиться] к (Д); ~**by** [nɪə'baɪ] близлежа́щий; ря́дом;

~**ly** ['nɪəlɪ] почти́; ~**-sighted** [nɪə-'saɪtɪd] близору́кий

neat[ni:t] □ чи́стый, опря́тный; *figure* изя́щный; стро́йный; *workmanship* иску́сный; (*undiluted*) неразба́вленный; ~**ness** ['ni:tnɪs] опря́тность *f*

necess|ary ['nesəsərɪ] 1. □ необходи́мый, ну́жный; 2. необходи́мое; ~**itate** [nɪ'sesɪteɪt] [по]тре́бовать; вынужда́ть [вы́нудить]; ~**ity** [-tɪ] необходи́мость *f*, нужда́

neck[nek] ше́я; *of bottle, etc.* го́рлышко; ~ **of land**перешеек; **risk one's** ~ рискова́ть голово́й; **stick one's** ~ **out** риско́вать; [по]ле́зть в пе́тлю; ~**band**воротни́к; ~**lace** ['-lɪs] ожере́лье; ~**tie** га́лстук

neé [neɪ] урождённая

need [ni:d] 1. на́добность *f*; потре́бность *f*, необходи́мость *f*; (*poverty*) нужда́; **be in** ~ **of** нужда́ться в (П); 2. нужда́ться в (П); **I** ~ **it** мне э́то ну́жно; **if** I ~ **be** в слу́чае необходи́мости; ~**ful** [-fl] ну́жный

needle ['ni:dl] игла́, иго́лка; (*knitting* ~) спи́ца

needless ['ni:dlɪs] □ нену́жный; ~ **to say** разуме́ется

needlework вы́шивка

needy ['ni:dɪ] □ нужда́ющийся

negat|ion [nɪ'geɪʃn] отрица́ние; ~**ive** ['negətɪv] 1. □ отрица́тельный; негати́вный; 2. *phot.* негати́в; **answer in the** ~ дава́ть [дать] отрица́тельный отве́т

neglect [nɪ'glekt] 1. пренебреже́ние; (*carelessness*) небре́жность *f*; 2. пренебрега́ть [-бре́чь] (Т); ~**ed** [-ɪd] забро́шенный; ~**ful** [-fʊl] небре́жный

negligen|ce ['neglɪdʒəns] небре́жность *f*; (*attitude*) хала́тность *f*; ~**t** [-t] небре́жный; хала́тный

negligible ['neglɪdʒəbl] □ ничто́жный, незначи́тельный

negotia|te [nɪ'gəʊʃɪeɪt] вести́ перегово́ры; догова́риваться [-вори́ться] о (П); *obstacles, etc.* преодоле(ва́)ть; ~**tion** [nɪgəʊʃɪ'eɪʃn] перегово́ры *m/pl.*; ~**tor** [nɪ'gəʊʃɪeɪtə] лицо́, веду́щее перегово́ры

Negr|ess ['niːɡrɪs] *contemptuous* афроамерика́нка, негритя́нка; ~o ['niːɡrəʊ], pl. ~oes [-z] афроамерика́нец, негр

neigh [neɪ] 1. ржа́ние; 2. [за]ржа́ть

neighbo(u)r ['neɪbə] сосе́д(ка); ~hood [-hʊd] окру́га, райо́н; ~ing [-rɪŋ] сосе́дний

neither ['naɪðə] 1. ни тот, ни друго́й; 2. *adv.* та́кже не; ~ ... *nor* ... ни ... ни ...

nephew ['nevjuː] племя́нник

nerve [nɜːv] 1. нерв; (*courage*) му́жество, хладнокро́вие; на́глость f; *get on s.b.'s ~s* де́йствовать на не́рвы; *have the ~ to* ... име́ть на́глость f; 2. придава́ть си́лы (хра́брости) (Д)

nervous ['nɜːvəs] □ не́рвный; (*highly strung*, *irritable*) нерво́зный; ~ness [-nɪs] не́рвность f, нерво́зность f

nest [nest] 1. гнездо́ (a. *fig.*); 2. вить гнездо́; ~le ['nesl] *v/i.* удо́бно устро́иться *pf.*; прижи(им)а́ться (*to*, *on*, *against* к Д); *v/t.* one's head прижи(им)а́ть (го́лову)

net¹ [net] 1. сеть f; 2. расставля́ть се́ти; пойма́ть *pf.* се́тью

net² [-] 1. не́тто *adj. indecl.*, *weight*, *profit* чи́стый; 2. приноси́ть (получа́ть) чи́стый дохо́д

nettle ['netl] 1. *bot.* крапи́ва; 2. обжига́ть крапи́вой; *fig.* раздража́ть, [рас]серди́ть

network ['netwɜːk] *tech.*, *rail*, *etc.* сеть f

neuralgia [njʊəˈrældʒə] невралги́я

neurosis [njʊəˈrəʊsɪs] невро́з

neuter ['njuːtə] *gr.* сре́дний род

neutral ['njuːtrəl] 1. □ нейтра́льный; 2. нейтра́льное госуда́рство; ~ity [njuːˈtrælətɪ] нейтралите́т; ~ize ['njuːtrəlaɪz] нейтрализова́ть (*im*)*pf.*

never ['nevə] никогда́; совсе́м не; ~ending бесконе́чный, несконча́емый; ~more никогда́ бо́льше; ~theless [ˌnevəðəˈles] тем не ме́нее; несмотря́ на э́то

new [njuː] но́вый; *vegetables*, *moon* молодо́й; *bread*, *etc.* све́жий; ~born новорождённый; ~comer вновь прибы́вший; новичо́к; ~fangled

['-fæŋɡld] новомо́дный; ~ly ['njuːlɪ] за́ново, вновь; неда́вно

news [njuːz] но́вости *f/pl.*, изве́стия *n/pl.*; *what's the ~?* что но́вого?; ~agent продаве́ц газе́т; ~paper газе́та; ~print газе́тная бума́га; ~reel киножурна́л; ~stall, ~stand газе́тный кио́ск

New Testament Но́вый заве́т

New Year Но́вый год; ~'s Eve кану́н Но́вого го́да; *Happy ~!* С Но́вым Го́дом!

next [nekst] 1. *adj.* сле́дующий; ближа́йший; ~ door to в сле́дующем доме; *fig.* чуть (ли) не, почти́; ~ to во́зле (P); *вслед за* (T); 2. *adv.* пото́м, по́сле, зате́м; в сле́дующий раз; ~ of kin ближа́йший (- шая) ро́дственник (-ица)

nibble ['nɪbl] *v/t.* обгры́з(а́)ть

nice [naɪs] □ прия́тный, ми́лый, сла́вный; (*fine*, *delicate*) то́нкий; ~ty ['naɪsətɪ] (*delicate point, detail*) то́нкости *f/pl.*, дета́ли *f/pl.*

niche [nɪtʃ] ни́ша

nick [nɪk] 1. (*notch*) зару́бка; *in the ~ of time* как раз во́время; 2. сде́лать *pf.* зару́бку в (П); *Am.* (*cheat*) обма́нывать [-ну́ть]; *Brt. coll.* (*steal*) стащи́ть *pf.*

nickel ['nɪkl] 1. *min.* ни́кель *m*; *Am.* моне́та в 5 це́нтов; 2. [от]никели́ровать

nickname ['nɪkneɪm] 1. про́звище; 2. прозыва́ть [-зва́ть]; да(ва́)ть про́звище (Д)

nicotine ['nɪkətiːn] никоти́н

niece [niːs] племя́нница

niggard ['nɪɡəd] скупе́ц; ~ly [-lɪ] скупо́й; *sum*, *etc.* жа́лкий

night [naɪt] ночь f, ве́чер; *by ~*, *at ~* но́чью; *stay the ~* переночева́ть; ~club ночно́й клуб; ~fall су́мерки *f/pl.*; ~dress, ~gown ночна́я руба́шка; ~ingale ['naɪtɪŋɡeɪl] солове́й; ~ly ['naɪtlɪ] ночно́й; *adv.* но́чью; ка́ждую ночь; ~mare кошма́р

nil [nɪl] *sport* ноль *m* or нуль *m*; ничего́

nimble ['nɪmbl] □ прово́рный, ло́вкий; *mind* живо́й

nimbus ['nɪmbəs] *eccl. art* нимб

nine [naɪn] де́вять; де́вятка; → *five*; **~pins** pl. ке́гли f/pl.; **~teen** [naɪn'tiːn] девятна́дцать; **~ty** ['naɪntɪ] девяно́сто

ninny ['nɪnɪ] coll. простофи́ля m/f

ninth [naɪnθ] **1.** девя́тый; **2.** девя́тая часть f

nip [nɪp] **1.** щипо́к; (*bite*) уку́с; (*frost*) моро́з; **there is a ~ in the air** во́здух моро́зный; **2.** щипа́ть [щипну́ть]; *finger* прищемля́ть [-ми́ть]; *flowers* поби́ть pf. моро́зом; **~ in the bud** пресека́ть в заро́дыше

nipper ['nɪpə] (*a pair of*) **~s** pl. кле́щи pl.; coll. малы́ш

nipple ['nɪpl] сосо́к

nitrate ['naɪtreɪt] нитра́т

nitrogen ['naɪtrədʒən] азо́т

no [nəʊ] **1.** adj. никако́й; **in ~ time** в мгнове́ние о́ка; **~ one** никто́; **2.** adv. нет; **3.** отрица́ние

Nobel prize [nəʊ'bel] Но́белевская пре́мия

nobility [nəʊ'bɪlɪtɪ] дворя́нство; благоро́дство

noble ['nəʊbl] **1.** □ благоро́дный; (*highborn*) зна́тный; **~ metal** благоро́дный мета́лл; **2.** = **~man** титуло́ванное лицо́, дворяни́н

nobody ['nəʊbədɪ] pron. никто́; su. ничто́жный челове́к

nocturnal [nɒk'tɜːnl] ночно́й

nod [nɒd] **1.** кива́ть голово́й; (*doze*) дрема́ть; coll. (*drowse*) клева́ть но́сом; **2.** киво́к голово́й

noise [nɔɪz] шум; (*din*) гро́хот; *make a* **~** fig. поднима́ть [-ня́ть] шум; **~less** ['nɔɪzlɪs] □ бесшу́мный

noisy ['nɔɪzɪ] □ шу́мный; *child* шумли́вый

nomin|al ['nɒmɪnl] □ номина́льный; gr. именно́й; **~ value** номина́льная цена́; **~ate** ['nɒmɪneɪt] (*appoint*) назнача́ть [-зна́чить]; *candidate* выдвига́ть ['-инуть]; **~ation** [nɒmɪ'neɪʃn] выдвиже́ние; назначе́ние

non [nɒn] prf. не..., бес.., без...

nonalcoholic безалкого́льный

nonchalance ['nɒnʃələns] беззабо́тность f

noncommittal [nɒnkə'mɪtl]

укло́нчивый

nondescript ['nɒndɪskrɪpt] (*dull*) невзра́чный; *colo(u)r* неопределённый

none [nʌn] **1.** ничто́, никто́; ни оди́н; никако́й; **2.** ниско́лько, совсе́м не ...; **~theless** тем не ме́нее

nonentity [nɒ'nentətɪ] person ничто́жество

nonexistent несуществу́ющий

nonpayment mst. fin. неплатёж, неупла́та

nonplus [nɒn'plʌs] приводи́ть в замеша́тельство, озада́чи(ва)ть

nonpolluting [nɒnpə'luːtɪŋ] не загрязня́ющий среду́

nonprofit некомме́рческий

nonresident не прожива́ющий в да́нном ме́сте

nonsens|e ['nɒnsəns] вздор, бессмы́слица; **~ical** [nɒn'sensɪkl] бессмы́сленный

nonsmoker person некуря́щий; *Brt.* rail ваго́н для некуря́щих

nonstop безостано́вочный; ae. беспоса́дочный

noodle ['nuːdl]: **~s** pl. лапша́

nook [nʊk] укро́мный уголо́к; зако́улок; **search every ~ and cranny** обша́рить pf. все углы́ и зако́улки

noon [nuːn] по́лдень m

noose [nuːs] петля́; (*lasso*) арка́н

nor [nɔː] и не; та́кже не; ни

norm [nɔːm] но́рма; **~al** ['nɔːml] □ норма́льный; **~alize** [-əlaɪz] приводи́ть [-вести́] в но́рму; нормализова́ть (*im*)pf.

north [nɔːθ] **1.** се́вер; **2.** се́верный; **3.** adv.: **~ of** к се́веру от (P); **~-east 1.** се́веро-восто́к; **2.** се́веро-восто́чный (a. **~-eastern**; **~erly** ['nɔːðəlɪ], **~ern** ['nɔːðən]; **~ward(s)** ['nɔːθwəd(z)] adv. на се́вер; к се́веру; **~-west 1.** се́веро-за́пад; naut. норд-вест; **2.** се́веро-за́падный (a. **~-western**)

nose [nəʊz] **1.** нос; (*sense of smell, a. fig.*) чутьё; *of boat, etc.* нос; **2.** v/t. [по]ню́хать; *information* разню́х(ив)ать; **~gay** буке́т цвето́в

nostril ['nɒstrəl] ноздря́

nosy ['nəʊzɪ] *coll.* любопы́тный

not [nɒt] не

notable ['nəʊtəbl] □ примеча́тельный, знамена́тельный; *person* выдаю́щийся

notary ['nəʊtərɪ] нота́риус (*a. public* ~); **notation** [nəʊ'teɪʃn] *mus.* нота́ция; за́пись *f*

notch [nɒtʃ] **1.** зару́бка; (*mark*) ме́тка; **2.** [c]де́лать зару́бку

note [nəʊt] **1.** заме́тка; за́пись *f*; (*comment*) примеча́ние; (*bank note*) банкно́т; (*denomination*) де́нежная купю́ра; *dipl. mus.* но́та; *mus.* но́та; *man of* ~ знамени́тость *f*; ~ *worthy of* ~ досто́йный внима́ния; **2.** замеча́ть [-е́тить]; (*mention*) упомина́ть [-мяну́ть]; (*a.* ~ *down*) де́лать заме́тки, запи́сывать [-са́ть]; (*make a mental note*) отмеча́ть [-е́тить]; ~**book** записна́я кни́жка; ~**d** [-ɪd] хорошо́ изве́стный; ~**worthy** примеча́тельный

nothing ['nʌθɪŋ] ничто́, ничего́; *for* ~ зря, да́ром; *come to* ~ ни к чему́ не привести́ *pf*; *to say* ~ *of* не говоря́ уже́ о (П); *there is* ~ *like* … нет ничего́ лу́чшего, чем …

notice ['nəʊtɪs] **1.** внима́ние; извеще́ние, уведомле́ние; (*warning*) предупрежде́ние; (*announcement*) объявле́ние; *at short* ~ без предупрежде́ния; *give* ~ предупрежда́ть об увольне́нии (*or* об ухо́де); извеща́ть [-ести́ть]; **2.** замеча́ть [-е́тить]; обраща́ть внима́ние на (В); ~**able** [-əbl] □ досто́йный внима́ния, заме́тный; ~**board** доска́ объявле́ний

notification [nəʊtɪfɪ'keɪʃn] извеще́ние, сообще́ние

notify ['nəʊtɪfaɪ] извеща́ть [-ести́ть], уведомля́ть [уве́домить]

notion ['nəʊʃn] поня́тие, представле́ние

notorious [nəʊ'tɔːrɪəs] □ общеизве́стный; *pej.* пресловутый

notwithstanding [nɒtwɪθ'stændɪŋ] несмотря́ на (В), вопреки́ (Д)

nought [nɔːt] ничто́, *math.* ноль *m or* нуль *m*; *bring to* ~ своди́ть [свести́] на нет

nourish ['nʌrɪʃ] пита́ть (*a. fig.*); [на]корми́ть; *fig. hope, etc.* леле́ять; ~**ing** [-ɪŋ] пита́тельный; ~**ment** [-mənt] пита́ние; пи́ща (*a. fig.*)

novel ['nɒvl] **1.** но́вый; (*unusual*) необы́чный; **2.** рома́н; ~**ist** [-ɪst] писа́тель *m*, -ница *f*; романти́ст; ~**ty** [-tɪ] новви́нка; новизна́; (*method*) нововве́дение

November [nəʊ'vembə] ноя́брь *m*

novice ['nɒvɪs] новичо́к; *eccl.* послу́шник *m*, -ница *f*

now [naʊ] **1.** тепе́рь, сейча́с; то́тчас; *just* ~ то́лько что; ~ *and again* (*или* *then*) вре́мя от вре́мени; **2.** *cj.* когда́, раз

nowadays ['naʊədeɪz] ны́нче; в на́ши дни; в на́ше вре́мя

nowhere ['nəʊweə] нигде́, никуда́

noxious ['nɒkʃəs] □ вре́дный

nozzle ['nɒzl] *of hose* наконе́чник; *tech.* сопло́

nucle|ar ['njuːklɪə] я́дерный; ~ *pile* я́дерный реа́ктор; ~ *power plant* а́томная электроста́нция; ~**us** [-s] ядро́

nude [njuːd] го́лый, наго́й; *art.* ~ *figure* обнажённая фигу́ра

nudge [nʌdʒ] *coll.* **1.** подта́лкивать [-толкну́ть]; **2.** лёгкий толчо́к ло́ктем

nuisance ['njuːsns] неприя́тность *f*; доса́да; *fig.* надое́дливый челове́к

null [nʌl] недействи́тельный; *become* ~ *and void* утра́чивать (утра́тить) зако́нную си́лу; ~**ify** ['nʌlɪfaɪ] аннули́ровать (*im*)*pf.*; растора́ть [-то́ргнуть]

numb [nʌm] *with terror* онеме́вший, оцепене́вший; *with cold* окоченевший

number ['nʌmbə] **1.** число́; но́мер; (*figure*) ци́фра; нумерова́ть [за-]; *be in number* насчи́тывать; ~**less** [-lɪs] бесчи́сленный; ~**plate** *mot.* номерно́й знак

numeral ['njuːmərəl] **1.** *gr.* и́мя числи́тельное; (*figure*) ци́фра; **2.** цифрово́й

numerical [njuː'merɪkəl] □ числово́й; чи́сленный

numerous ['nju:mərəs] □ многочи́сленный; *in ~ cases* во мно́гих слу́чаях

nun [nʌn] мона́хиня

nunnery ['nʌnərɪ] же́нский монасты́рь *m*

nurse [nɜːs] 1. ня́ня (*a. ~maid*); медици́нская сестра́, медсестра́; 2. (*breast-feed*) [на]корми́ть гру́дью; (*take nourishment from the breast*) соса́ть грудь *f*; (*rear*) вска́рмливать; (*look after*) уха́живать за (Т); ~ry ['nɜːsərɪ] де́тская (ко́мната); *agric.* пито́мник; ~ *school* де́тский сад

nursing ['nɜːsɪŋ]: ~ *home* ча́стная лече́бница; ~ *staff* медсёстры

nurture ['nɜːtʃə] (*bring up*) воспи́тывать [-та́ть]

nut [nʌt] оре́х; *tech.* га́йка; *a hard ~ to crack* кре́пкий оре́шек; **~cracker** щипцы́ для оре́хов; **~meg** ['nʌtmeg] муска́тный оре́х

nutri|tion [nju:'trɪʃn] пита́ние; **~tious** [-ʃəs], **~tive** ['nju:trətɪv] □ пита́тельный

nut|shell оре́ховая скорлупа́; *in a ~* кра́тко, в двух слова́х; **~ty** ['nʌtɪ] *taste* име́ющий вкус оре́ха; *coll. idea, etc.* бредово́й; *person* безу́мный, психо́ванный

nylon ['naɪlɒn] нейло́н

nymph [nɪmf] ни́мфа

O

oaf [əʊf] дура́к; у́валень *m*

oak [əʊk] дуб; *attr.* дубо́вый

oar [ɔː] 1. весло́; 2. *poet.* грести́; **~sman** ['ɔːzmən] гребе́ц

oasis [əʊ'eɪsɪs] оа́зис

oat [əʊt] овёс (*mst. ~s pl.*)

oath [əʊθ] кля́тва; *mil., law* прися́га; (*curse*) руга́тельство

oatmeal ['əʊtmiːl] овся́нка

obdurate ['ɒbdjʊərət] □ (*stubborn*) упря́мый; (*unrepentant*) нераска́янный

obedien|ce [ə'biːdɪəns] повинове́ние; **~t** [-t] □ послу́шный

obelisk ['ɒbəlɪsk] обели́ск

obese [əʊ'biːs] ту́чный

obesity [əʊ'biːsətɪ] ту́чность *f*

obey [ə'beɪ] повинова́ться (*im*)*pf.* (Д); [по]слу́шаться (Р)

obituary [ə'bɪtʃʊərɪ] некроло́г

object 1. ['ɒbdʒɪkt] предме́т, вещь *f*; объе́кт; *fig.* цель *f*; наме́рение; 2. [əb'dʒekt] (*disapprove*) не одобря́ть (Р), протестова́ть; возража́ть [-рази́ть] (*to* про́тив Р); *if you don't ~* е́сли вы не возража́ете

objection [əb'dʒekʃn] возраже́ние; проте́ст; **~able** [-əbl] □ нежела́тель-

ный; (*distasteful*) неприя́тный

objective [əb'dʒektɪv] 1. □ объекти́вный; 2. объе́кт, цель *f*

obligat|ion [ɒblɪ'geɪʃn] (*promise*) обяза́тельство; (*duty*) обя́занность *f*; **~ory** [ə'blɪɡətrɪ] □ обяза́тельный

oblig|e [ə'blaɪdʒ] (*require*) обя́зывать [-за́ть]; (*compel*) вынужда́ть [-нудить]; *I was ~d to …* я был вы́нужден …; ~ *a p.* [с]де́лать одолже́ние кому́-либо; *much ~d* о́чень благода́рен (-рна); **~ing** [-ɪŋ] □ услу́жливый, любе́зный

oblique [ə'bliːk] □ косо́й; *gr.* ко́свенный

obliterate [ə'blɪtəreɪt] (*efface*) изгла́живать(ся) [-ла́дить(ся)]; (*destroy*) уничтожа́ть [-о́жить]; (*expunge*) вычёркивать [вы́черкнуть]

obliv|ion [ə'blɪvɪən] забве́ние; **~ous** [-əs] □ забы́вчивый

obnoxious [əb'nɒkʃəs] проти́вный, несно́сный

obscene [əb'siːn] □ непристо́йный

obscur|e [əb'skjʊə] 1. □ тёмный; (*not distinct*) нея́сный; *author, etc.* неизве́стный; *meaning* непоня́тный; 2. *sun* заслоня́ть [-ни́ть]; **~ity** [-ətɪ] неизве́стность *f*; *in text* нея́сное ме́сто

obsequious [əb'si:kwiəs] □ подобо-
стра́стный

observ|able [əb'zɜ:vəbl] □ заме́тный;
~ance [-vəns] *of law, etc.* соблюде́-
ние; *of anniversary, etc.* пра́зднова-
ние; **~ant**[-vənt] □ наблюда́тельный;
~ation [ɒbzə'veiʃn] наблюде́ние; на-
блюда́тельность *f*; (*comment*) за-
меча́ние; **~atory** [əb'zɜ:vətri] обсер-
вато́рия; **~e** [əb'zɜ:v] *v/t.* наблюда́ть;
fig. соблюда́ть (-юсти́); (*notice*) за-
меча́ть (-е́тить) (В); *v/i.* замеча́ть
[-е́тить]; **~er** [-ə] наблюда́тель *m*

obsess [əb'ses] □ (*seize*) *a.* **with** одер-
жи́мый (Т); **~ion** [əb'seʃn] навя́зчивая
иде́я; одержи́мость *f*

obsolete ['ɒbsəli:t] устаре́лый; *words,
etc.* устаре́вших

obstacle ['ɒbstəkl] препя́тствие

obstinate ['ɒbstənət] упря́мый; на-
сто́йчивый

obstruct [əb'strʌkt] [по]меша́ть (Д),
затрудня́ть [-ни́ть]; (*block*) згражда́ть
[-ади́ть] загора́живать [-горо-
ди́ть]; **~ion** [əb'strʌkʃn] препя́тствие,
поме́ха; загражде́ние; *law* обстру́к-
ция; **~ive** [-tɪv] препя́тствующий;
обструкцио́нный

obtain [əb'tein] *v/t.* (*receive*) получа́ть
[-чи́ть]; (*procure*) добы́(ва́)ть; (*acquire*) обрета́ть [-сти́]; **~able** [-əbl]
досту́пный; *result, etc.* достижи́мый

obtru|de [əb'tru:d] навя́зывать(ся)
[-за́ть(ся)] (*on* Д); **~sive** [-sɪv] на-
вя́зчивый

obvious ['ɒbviəs] □ очеви́дный,
я́сный, я́вный

occasion [ə'keiʒn] **1.** слу́чай; возмо́ж-
ность *f*; (*reason*) по́вод, причи́на; (*special event*) собы́тие; **on that~** в тот раз;
on the~of по слу́чаю (Р); **rise to the~**
оказа́ться *pf.* на высоте́ положе́ния;
2. причиня́ть [-ни́ть]; дава́ть по́вод
к (Д); **~al** [-ʒnl] □ случа́йный; ре́дкий

occult [ɒ'kʌlt] □ окку́льтный

occup|ant ['ɒkjʊpənt] (*inhabitant*) жи-
тель *m*, -ница *f*; (*tenant*) жиле́ц; **the~s
of the car** е́хавшие (*or* сидя́щие) в
маши́не; **~ation** [ɑkjʊ'peiʃn] *mil.* ок-

купа́ция; (*work, profession*) заня́тие,
профе́ссия; **~y** ['ɒkjʊpai] seat, *etc.* за-
нима́ть [заня́ть]; (*take possession of*)
завладе́(ва́)ть (Т); оккупи́ровать
(*im*)*pf.*

occur [ə'kɜ:] (*take place*) случа́ться
[-чи́ться]; (*be met with*) встреча́ться
[-е́титься]; **~** *to a p.* приходи́ть в го́ло-
ву; **~rence** [ə'klrəns] происше́ствие,
слу́чай

ocean ['əʊʃn] океа́н

o'clock [ə'klɒk]: **five ~** пять часо́в

ocul|ar ['ɒkjʊlə] глазно́й; **~ist** ['ɒkjʊ-
list] окули́ст, глазно́й врач

odd[ɒd] □ нечётный; *sock, etc.* непа́р-
ный; (*extra*) ли́шний; *of incomplete set*
разро́зненный; (*strange*) стра́нный;
~ity ['ɒdɪtɪ] чудакова́тость *f*; **~s**
[ɒdz] ша́нсы *m/pl.*; **be at ~ with** не ла́-
дить с (Т); **~ and ends** оста́тки *m/pl.*;
вся́кая вся́чина

odious ['əʊdiəs] нена́вистный; (*repul-
sive*) отврати́тельный

odo(u)r ['əʊdə] за́пах; арома́т

of [ɒv; *mst.* əv, v] *prp.* о, об (П); из (Р);
от (Р); *denoting cause, affiliation,
agent, quality, source; often corresponds to the genitive case in Russian;*
think ~ s.th. ду́мать о (П); **out~ charity**
из милосе́рдия; **die ~** умере́ть *pf.* от
(Р); **cheat ~** обсчи́тывать на (В); **the
battle ~ Quebec** би́тва под Квебе́ком;
proud ~ го́рдый (Т); **the roof ~ the
house** кры́ша до́ма

off [ɔ:f, ɒf] **1.** *adv.* прочь; *far ~* далеко́;
*translated into Russian mst. by verbal
prefixes;* **go ~** (*leave*) уходи́ть [уйти́];
switch ~ выключа́ть [вы́ключить];
take ~ (*remove*) снима́ть [снять]; **on
and ~, ~ and on** вре́мя от вре́мени;
be well ~ быть обеспе́ченным; **2.**
prp. с (Р), со (П) *indicates removal
from a surface;* от (Р) *indicates distance;* **3.** *adj.:* **day ~** выходно́й день;
~side *Brt.* пра́вая сторона́; *Am.* ле́вая
сторона́; **the~ season** мёртвый сезо́н

offal ['ɒfl] потроха́ *m/pl.*

offend [ə'fend] *v/t.* обижа́ть [оби́-
деть]; *feelings* оскорбля́ть [-би́ть];
v/i. наруша́ть [-у́шить] (*against* В);

~er [-ə] оби́дчик; *law* правонаруши́тель(ница *f*) *m*; **first ~** челове́к, суди́мый (соверши́вший преступле́ние) впервы́е

offen|se, *Brt.* **~ce** [ə'fens] (*transgression*) просту́пок; оби́да, оскорбле́ние; *mil.* наступле́ние

offensive [ə'fensɪv] **1.** □ (*insulting*) оскорби́тельный; оби́дный; (*disagreeable*) проти́вный; **2.** *mil.* наступле́ние

offer ['ɒfə] **1.** предложе́ние; **2.** *v/t.* предлага́ть [-ложи́ть]; **~ an explanation** дава́ть [дать] объясне́ние; **~ resistance** оказа́ть [-а́зывать] сопротивле́ние

offhand [ɒf'hænd] *manner* бесцеремо́нный; развя́зный; *adv.* без подгото́вки; **he couldn't tell me ~** ... он не смог мне сра́зу отве́тить

office ['ɒfɪs] (*position*) до́лжность *f*; слу́жба; (*premises*) конто́ра; канцеля́рия; *of doctor, dentist, etc.* кабине́т; **~** министе́рство; **~ hours** часы́ рабо́ты, приёмные часы́

officer ['ɒfɪsə] *mil.* офице́р

official [ə'fɪʃl] **1.** □ официа́льный; служе́бный; **through ~ channels** по официа́льным кана́лам; **2.** должностно́е лицо́, служа́щий; *hist.*, *a. pej.* чино́вник

officious [ə'fɪʃəs] □ назо́йливый, навя́зчивый

off|set возмеща́ть [-ести́ть]; **~shoot** побе́г; ответвле́ние; **~spring** о́трыск, пото́мок; **~-the-record** конфиденциа́льный

often ['ɒfn] ча́сто, мно́го раз; **more than not** бо́льшей ча́стью; в большинстве́ слу́чаев

ogle ['əʊgl] стро́ить гла́зки (Д)

oil [ɔɪl] **1.** (*vegetable ~*) ма́сло; (*petroleum ~*) нефть *f*; **diesel ~**, *fuel* **~** жи́дкое то́пливо; **2.** сма́з(ыв)ать; **~cloth** клеёнка; **~field** нефтяно́е месторожде́ние; **~ well** нефтяна́я сква́жина; **~y** ['ɔɪlɪ] масляни́стый, ма́сляный; *fig.* еле́йный

ointment ['ɔɪntmənt] мазь *f*

OK, okay [əʊ'keɪ] *coll.* **1.** *pred.* в поря́дке, хорошо́; **2.** *int.* хорошо́!, ла́д-

но!, идёт!; слу́шаюсь!

old [əʊld] *com.* ста́рый; (*in times*) **of ~** старину́; **~ age** ста́рость *f*; **~-fashioned** [-'fæʃnd] старомо́дный

olfactory [ɒl'fæktərɪ] обоня́тельный

olive ['ɒlɪv] *fruit* масли́на; **colo(u)r** оли́вковый цвет

Olympic [ə'lɪmpɪk]: **the ~ Games** Олимпи́йские и́гры

omelet(te) ['ɒmlɪt] омле́т

ominous ['ɒmɪnəs] □ злове́щий

omission [ə'mɪʃn] (*oversight*) упуще́ние; (*leaving out*) про́пуск

omit [ə'mɪt] пропуска́ть [-сти́ть]; (*on purpose*) опуска́ть [-сти́ть]

on [ɒn] **1.** *prp. mst.* на (П или В); **~ the wall** на стене́; **~ good authority** из досто́верного исто́чника; **~ the 1st of April** пе́рвого апре́ля; **~ his arrival** по его́ прибы́тии; **talk ~ a subject** говори́ть на те́му; **~ hearing it** услы́шав э́то; **2.** *adv.* да́льше; вперёд; да́лее; **keep one's hat ~** остава́ться в шля́пе; **have a coat ~** быть в пальто́; **and so ~** и так да́лее (и т. д.); **be ~** быть запу́щенным в ход, включённым (*и т. п.*)

once [wʌns] **1.** *adv.* раз; не́когда; когда́-то; **at ~** сейча́с же; **~ and for all** раз (и) навсегда́; **~ in a while** и́зредка; **this ~** на э́тот раз; **2.** *cj.* как то́лько

one [wʌn] **1.** *adj.* оди́н; еди́ный; еди́нственный; како́й-то; **~ day** одна́жды; **~ never knows** никогда́ не зна́ешь; **~** (*число*) оди́н; едини́ца; **the little ~s** малыши́ *m/pl.*; **another** друг дру́га; **at ~** заодно́; **~ by ~** оди́н за други́м; **I for ~** я со свое́й стороны́

onerous ['ɒnərəs] □ обремени́тельный

one|self [wʌn'self] *pron. refl.* -ся, -сь, (самого́) себя́; **~-sided** □ односторо́нний; **~-way: ~ street** у́лица с односторо́нним движе́нием

onion ['ʌnjən] лук, лу́ковица

onlooker ['ɒnlʊkə] → **looker-on**

only ['əʊnlɪ] **1.** *adj.* еди́нственный; **2.** *adv.* еди́нственно; то́лько, лишь; исключи́тельно; **~ yesterday** то́лько вчера́; **3.** *cj.* но; **~ that ...** е́сли бы не то, что ...

onset ['ɒnset] нача́ло

onslaught ['ɒnslɔːt] ата́ка, нападе́ние

onward ['ɒnwəd] **1.** *adj.* продвига́ющий; **~ movement** движе́ние вперёд; **2.** *adv.* вперёд; впереди́

ooze [uːz] [про]сочи́ться

opaque [əʊ'peɪk] □ непрозра́чный

open ['əʊpən] **1.** □ *com.* откры́тый; *(frank)* открове́нный; **~ to** досту́пный (Д); **in the ~ air** на откры́том во́здухе; **2. bring into the ~** сде́лать *pf.* достоя́нием обще́ственности; **3.** *v/t.* открыва́ть; нач(ин)а́ть; *v/i.* открыва́ться; нач(ин)а́ться; **~ into** of door открыва́ться в (В); **~on to** выходи́ть на *or* в (В); **~-handed** щедрый; **~ing** [-ɪŋ] отве́рстие; нача́ло; *of exhibition* откры́тие; **~-minded** *fig.* непредубеждённый

opera ['ɒpərə] о́пера; **~ glasses** *pl.* театра́льный бино́кль *m*

operat|e ['ɒpəreɪt] *v/t.* управля́ть (Т); *part. Am.* приводи́ть в де́йствие; *v/i. med.* опери́ровать *(im)pf.*; рабо́тать; де́йствовать; **~ion** [ɒpə'reɪʃn] де́йствие; *med., mil., comm.* опера́ция; проце́сс; **be in ~** быть в де́йствии; **~ive** ['ɒpərətɪv] □ *having force* действи́тельный; *effective* де́йственный; *working* де́йствующий; **~or** ['ɒpəreɪtə] *of a machine* управля́ющий; *tel.* опера́тор; телеграфи́ст(ка *f*) *m*

opinion [ə'pɪnjən] мне́ние; взгляд; **in my ~** по-мо́ему

opponent [ə'pəʊnənt] оппоне́нт, проти́вник

opportun|e ['ɒpətjuːn] □ благоприя́тный, подходя́щий; *timely* своевре́менный; **~ity** [ɒpə'tjuːnətɪ] удо́бный слу́чай, возмо́жность *f*

oppos|e [ə'pəʊz] противопоставля́ть [-ста́вить]; *(be against)* [вос]проти́виться (Д); **~ed** [-d] противопоста́вленный; **as ~ to** в отли́чие от (Р); **be ~** быть про́тив (Р); **~ite** ['ɒpəzɪt] **1.** □ противополо́жный; **2** *prp., adv.* напро́тив, про́тив (Р); **3.** противополо́жность *f*; **~ition** [ɒpə'zɪʃn] противопоставле́ние; сопротивле́ние; оппози́ция

oppress [ə'pres] притесня́ть [-ни́ть], угнета́ть; **~ion** [-ʃn] притесне́ние, угнете́ние; **~ive** [-sɪv] □ гнету́щий; *weather* ду́шный

optic ['ɒptɪk] глазно́й, зри́тельный; **~al** [-l] □ опти́ческий; **~ian** [ɒp'tɪʃn] о́птик

optimism ['ɒptɪmɪzəm] оптими́зм

optimistic [ɒptɪ'mɪstɪk] *person* оптимисти́чный; *prognosis, etc.* оптимисти́ческий

option ['ɒpʃn] вы́бор, пра́во вы́бора; **~al** ['ɒpʃənl] □ необяза́тельный, факультати́вный

opulence ['ɒpjʊləns] бога́тство

or [ɔː] и́ли; **~ else** ина́че; и́ли же

oracle ['ɒrəkl] ора́кул

oral ['ɔːrəl] □ у́стный; слове́сный

orange ['ɒrɪndʒ] **1.** апельси́н; ора́нжевый цвет; **2.** ора́нжевый

orator ['ɒrətə] ора́тор

orbit ['ɔːbɪt] орби́та; **put into ~** выводи́ть [-вести] на орби́ту

orchard ['ɔːtʃəd] фрукто́вый сад

orchestra ['ɔːkɪstrə] орке́стр

ordain [ɔː'deɪn] посвяща́ть в духо́вный сан

ordeal [ɔː'diːl] *fig.* испыта́ние

order ['ɔːdə] **1.** поря́док; *(command)* прика́з; *comm.* зака́з; **take (holy) ~s** принима́ть духо́вный сан; **in ~ to** что́бы; **in ~ that** с тем, что́бы; **make to ~** де́лать на зака́з; **out of ~** неиспра́вный; **2.** прика́зывать [-за́ть]; *comm.* зака́зывать [за́ть]; **~ly** [-lɪ] *(well arranged, tidy)* аккура́тный, дисциплини́рованный

ordinary ['ɔːdnrɪ] обыкнове́нный; зауря́дный; **out of the ~** необы́чный

ore ['ɔː] руда́

organ ['ɔːgən] о́рган; *mus.* орга́н; **~ic** [ɔː'gænɪk] **(~ally)** органи́ческий; *fig.* органи́чный

organ|ization [ɔːgənaɪ'zeɪʃn] организа́ция; **~ize** [ɔːgənaɪz] организова́ть *(im)pf.*; **~izer** [-ə] организа́тор

orgy ['ɔːdʒɪ] о́ргия

orient ['ɔːrɪənt] **1.:** *the* **☉** Восто́к, восто́чные стра́ны *f/pl.*; **2.** ориенти́ровать *(im)pf.*; **~al** [ɔːrɪ'entl] □ восто́чный, азиа́тский; **~ate**[ˈɔːrɪənteɪt] ориенти́ровать (*im*)*pf.*

orifice [ˈɒrɪfɪs] (*opening*) отве́рстие

origin [ˈɒrɪdʒɪn] (*source*) исто́чник; (*derivation*) происхожде́ние; (*beginning*) нача́ло

original [əˈrɪdʒənl] **1.** □ (*first*) первонача́льный; *ideas, etc.* оригина́льный; (*not a copy*) по́длинный; **2.** оригина́л, по́длинник; (*eccentric*) чуда́к; **in the~** в оригина́ле; **~ity**[ərɪdʒəˈnæltɪ] оригина́льность *f*

originat|e [əˈrɪdʒɪneɪt] *v/t.* дава́ть нача́ло (Д), порожда́ть (породи́ть); *v/i.* происходи́ть [-изойти́] (**from** от P); **~or** [-ə] инициа́тор

ornament 1. [ˈɔːnəmənt] украше́ние (*a. fig.*), орна́мент; **2.** [-ment] украша́ть [украси́ть]; **~al** [ɔːnəˈmentl] □ декорати́вный

ornate [ɔːˈneɪt] □ бога́то укра́шенный; *style* витиева́тый

orphan [ˈɔːfn] **1.** сирота́ *m/f.*; **2.** осироте́вший (*a. ~ed*); **~age** [ˈɔːfənɪdʒ] сиро́тский дом; прию́т для сиро́т

orthodox [ˈɔːθədɒks] □ ортодокса́льный; *eccl.* правосла́вный

oscillate [ˈɒsɪleɪt] □ кача́ться; (*fluctuate*), *a. fig.* колеба́ться

ostensible [ɒˈstensəbl] □ служа́щий предло́гом; мни́мый; очеви́дный

ostentatious [ɒstenˈteɪʃəs] □ показно́й

ostrich [ˈɒstrɪtʃ] *zo.* стра́ус

other [ˈʌðə] друго́й; ино́й; **the~ day** на днях; **the~ morning** неда́вно у́тром; **every~ day** че́рез день; **in~ words** други́ми слова́ми; **~wise** [-waɪz] ина́че; и́ли же

otter [ˈɒtə] *zo.* вы́дра

ought [ɔːt]: **I~ to** мне сле́довало бы; **you~ to have done it** вам сле́довало э́то сде́лать

ounce [aʊns] у́нция

our [ˈaʊə] *poss. adj.*; **~s** [ˈaʊəz] *pron. & pred. adj.* наш, на́ша, на́ше; на́ши *pl.*; **~selves** [aʊəˈselvz] *pron.* **1.** *refl.* себя́, -ся, -сь; **2.** *for emphasis* (мы) са́ми

oust [aʊst] выгоня́ть [вы́гнать], вытесня́ть [вы́теснить]

out [aʊt] *adv.* нару́жу; вон; в, на; *often translated by the prefix* вы-; **take~** вынима́ть [вы́нуть]; **have it~ with s.o.** объясни́ться *pf.* с ке́м-л.; **~ and ~** соверше́нно; **a/the way~** вы́ход; **~ size** разме́р бо́льше норма́льного; *prp.* **~ of:** из (P); вне (P); из-за (P)

out|... [aʊt] пере...; вы...; рас...; про...; воз..., вз..., из...; **~balance** [-ˈbæləns] переве́шивать [-ве́сить]; **~break** [ˈaʊtbreɪk] *of anger, etc.* вспы́шка; *of war, etc.* (внеза́пное) нача́ло; **~building** [ˈaʊtbɪldɪŋ] надво́рное строе́ние; **~burst** [-bɜːst] взрыв, вспы́шка; **~cast** [-kɑːst] отве́рженный; **~come** [-kʌm] результа́т; **~cry** [-kraɪ] кри́ки, шум; проте́ст; **~do** [aʊtˈduː] [*irr.* (**do**)] превосходи́ть [-взойти́]; **~door** [ˈaʊtdɔː] *adj.* (находя́щийся) на откры́том во́здухе; *clothes* ве́рхний; **~doors** [-ˈdɔːz] *adv.* на откры́том во́здухе; **it's cold~** на у́лице хо́лодно

outer [ˈaʊtə] вне́шний, нару́жный; **~most** [-məʊst] кра́йний; са́мый да́льний от це́нтра

out|fit [ˈaʊtfɪt] (*equipment*) снаряже́ние; (*clothes*) костю́м; **~going** [-gəʊɪŋ] уходя́щий; *letters, etc.* исходя́щий; *person* общи́тельный; уживчивый; **~grow** [aʊtˈgrəʊ] [*irr.* (**grow**)] *clothes* выраста́ть [вы́расти] из (P); **~house** [-haʊs] надво́рное строе́ние; *Am.* убо́рная во дворе́

outing [ˈaʊtɪŋ] (за́городная) прогу́лка, экску́рсия

out|last [aʊtˈlɑːst] *mst. of person* пережи(ва́)ть; *of things* служи́ть (носи́ться) до́льше, чем...; **~law** [ˈaʊtlɔː] **1.** челове́к вне зако́на; **2.** объявля́ть вне зако́на; **~lay** [-leɪ] расхо́ды *m/pl.*; **~let** [-let] выпускно́е отве́рстие; вы́ход; **~line** [-laɪn] **1.** (*a. pl.*) очерта́ние, ко́нтур; **2.** де́лать набро́сок (P); **~live** [aʊtˈlɪv] пережи(ва́)ть; **~look** [ˈaʊtlʊk] вид, перспекти́ва; то́чка зре́ния, взгляд; **~lying** [-laɪŋ] отдалённый; **~number** [aʊtˈnʌmbə] превосходи́ть чи́сленностью; **~patient** амбулато́рный больно́й; **☨patient De-**

partment поликли́ника при больни́це; **~pouring** ['-pɔ:rɪŋ] *mst. pl.* излия́ние (чувств); **~put** [-pʊt] (*production*) вы́пуск; проду́кция; (*productivity*) производи́тельность *f*

outrage ['aʊtreɪdʒ] **1.** наруше́ние прили́чий; безобра́зие; возмути́тельное явле́ние; **2.** оскорбля́ть [-би́ть] возмуща́ть [-ути́ть]; изнаси́ловать; **~ous** [aʊt'reɪdʒəs] □ возмути́тельный; безобра́зный; сканда́льный

outright ['aʊtraɪt] откры́то, пря́мо, реши́тельно; **~run** [aʊt'rʌn] [*irr.* (**run**)] перегоня́ть [-гна́ть], опережа́ть [-реди́ть]; **~set** [-set] нача́ло; *from the ~* с са́мого нача́ла; **~shine** [aʊt'ʃaɪn] [*irr.* (**shine**)] затмева́ть [-ми́ть]; **~side** [aʊtsaɪd] нару́жная сторона́; (*surface*) пове́рхность *f*; вне́шний вид; *at the ~* са́мое бо́льшее; **2.** ['aʊtsaɪd] нару́жный, вне́шний; кра́йний; **3.** *adv.* нару́жу; снару́жи; на (откры́том) во́здухе; **4.** *prp.* вне (P); **~sider** [aʊt'saɪdə] посторо́нний (челове́к); **~skirts** [aʊtskз:ts] *pl.* окра́ина; (*surface*) снару́жи; **~spoken** [aʊt'spəʊkən] □ открове́нный; **~standing** [aʊt'stændɪŋ] *fig.* выдаю́щийся; *bill* неопла́ченный; **~stretch** [aʊt'stretʃ] протя́гивать [-тяну́ть]; **~strip** [-'strɪp] опережа́ть [-реди́ть]; (*surpass*) превосходи́ть [-взойти́]

outward ['aʊtwəd] **1.** вне́шний, нару́жный; *during the ~ journey (to)* … во вре́мя пое́здки туда́ (в B); **2.** *adv.* (*mst.* **~s** [-z]) нару́жу; за преде́лы

outweigh [aʊt'weɪ] превосходи́ть ве́сом; переве́шивать [переве́сить]

oven ['ʌvn] *in bakery, industry, etc.* печь *f*; *in stove* духо́вка

over ['əʊvə] **1.** *adv. usually translated by verbal prefixes:* пере-…; вы-…; про-…; сно́ва; вдоба́вок; сли́шком; *and above* в доба́вле́ние, к тому́ же; (*all*) *~ again* сно́ва, ещё раз; *~ and ~ (again)* сно́ва и сно́ва; **~** переи́тывать [-чита́ть] *it's all* всё ко́нчено; **2.** *prp.* над (T); по (Д); за (B); свы́ше (P); сверх (P) че́рез (B); о(б) (П); *all ~ the town* по всему́ го́роду

over|… ['əʊvə] *pref.* сверх…; над…; пере…; чрезме́рно; **~act** [əʊvə'ækt] переи́грывать [-гра́ть]; **~all** ['əʊvərɔ:l] *working clothes* хала́т; **~s** комбинезо́н, *coll.* спецо́вка; **~awe** [əʊvə'ɔ:] внуша́ть [-ши́ть] благогове́йный страх; **~balance** [əʊvə'bæləns] теря́ть равнове́сие; *fig.* переве́шивать [-ве́сить]; **~bearing** [əʊvə'beərɪŋ] □ вла́стный; **~board** ['əʊvəbɔ:d] *naut.* за́ борт, за бо́ртом; **~cast** [əʊvə'kɑ:st] покры́тый облака́ми; па́смурный; **~charge** [əʊvə'tʃɑ:dʒ] брать [взять] сли́шком мно́го (*for* за B); **~coat** ['əʊvəkəʊt] пальто́ *n indecl.*; **~come** [əʊvə'kʌm] [*irr.* (**come**)] (*surmount*) преодоле́(ва́)ть, (*defeat*) побежда́ть [-еди́ть]; **~crowd** [əʊvə'kraʊd] переполня́ть [-по́лнить]; **~do** [əʊvə'du:] [*irr.* (**do**)] *meat, etc.* пережа́ри(ва)ть; (*go too far*) переусе́рдствовать (*im*)*pf.*; **~draw** [əʊvə'drɔ:] [*irr.* (**draw**)] *~ one's account* превы́сить *pf.* креди́т в ба́нке; **~dress** [əʊvə'dres] оде́(ва́)ться; сли́шком наря́дно; **~due** [əʊvə'dju:] *payment* просро́ченный; *the bus is 5 minutes ~* авто́бус опа́здывает на пять мину́т; **~eat** [əʊvə'i:t] перееда́ть [-е́сть]; **~flow** [əʊvə'fləʊ] [*irr.* (**flow**)] *v/t.* затопля́ть [-пи́ть]; *v/i.* перели(ва́)ться; **2.** ['əʊvəfləʊ] наводне́ние; разли́в; **~grow** [əʊvə'grəʊ] [*irr.* (**grow**)] *with weeds* зараста́ть [-ти́]; **~hang** [əʊvə'hæŋ] [*irr.* (**hang**)] *v/i.* нависа́ть [-и́снуть]; **~haul** [əʊvə'hɔ:l] (*repair*) (капита́льно) [от]ремонти́ровать; **~head 1.** [əʊvə'hed] *adv.* над голово́й, наверху́; **2.** ['əʊvəhed] *adj.* ве́рхний; **3.** **~s** ['əʊvəhedz] *pl.* comm накладны́е расхо́ды *m/pl.*; **~hear** [əʊvə'hɪə] [*irr.* (**hear**)] подслу́ш(ив)ать; неча́янно услы́шать; **~lap** [əʊvə'læp] *v/i.* заходи́ть оди́н на друго́й; *fig.* совпада́ть; **~lay** [əʊvə'leɪ] [*irr.* (**lay**)] *tech.* покры́(ва́)ть; **~load** [əʊvə'ləʊd] перегружа́ть [-узи́ть]; **~look** [əʊvə'lʊk] *of windows, etc.* выходи́ть на (B); (*not notice*) пропуска́ть [-сти́ть]; упуска́ть [-сти́ть]; **~pay** [əʊvə'peɪ] [*irr.* (**pay**)] перепла́чивать [-лати́ть]; **~power** [əʊvə'raʊə]

пересили(ва)ть; **~rate** ['əʊvə-'reɪt] переоце́нивать [-ни́ть]; **~reach** [əʊvə-'riːtʃ] перехитри́ть *pf.*; **~ o.s.** брать сли́шком мно́го на себя́; **~ride** [əʊvə-'raɪd] [*irr.* (*ride*)] *fig.* отверга́ть [-éргнуть]; **~run** [əʊvə'rʌn] [*irr.* (*run*)] перелива́ться че́рез край; **~seas** [əʊvə-'siːz] **1.** иностра́нный, заграни́чный; **2.** за рубежо́м, за грани́цей; **~seer** ['əʊvəsɪə] надсмо́трщик; **~shadow** [əʊvə'ʃædəʊ] *fig.* затмева́ть [-ми́ть]; **~sight** [-saɪt] недосмо́тр; **~sleep** [əʊvə'sliːp] [*irr.* (*sleep*)] прос(ы)па́ть; **~state** [əʊvə'steɪt] преувели́чи(ва)ть; **~statement** [əʊvə'steɪtmənt] преувеличе́ние; **~strain** [əʊvə'streɪn] **1.** переутомле́ние; **2.** переутомля́ть [-ми́ть]; **~take** [əʊvə'teɪk] [*irr.* (*take*)] обгоня́ть [обогна́ть]; *of events* засти́гнуть *pf.* враспло́х; **~tax** [əʊvə'tæks] облага́ть чрезме́рным нало́гом; *fig. strength, etc.* перенапряга́ть [-ря́чь]; **don't~ my patience** не испы́тывай моё терпе́ние; **~throw** [əʊvə'θrəʊ] [*irr.* (*throw*)] сверга́ть [све́ргнуть]; **~time** ['əʊvətaɪm] **1.** сверхуро́чная рабо́та; **2.** *adv.* сверхуро́чно
overture ['əʊvətjʊə] *mus.* увертю́ра
over|turn [əʊvə'tɜːn] опроки́дывать

[-и́нуть]; **~whelm** [əʊvə'welm] (*crush*) подавля́ть [-ви́ть]; пересили(ва)ть; **~ed with grief** уби́тый го́рем; **~work** ['əʊvəwɜːk] **1.** переутомле́ние; **2.** [əʊvə'wɜːk] переутомля́ть(ся) [-ми́ть(ся)]; **~wrought** [əʊvə'rɔːt] в состоя́нии кра́йнего возбужде́ния; *nerves* перенапряжённый
owe [əʊ] быть до́лжным (Д/В); быть обя́занным (Д/Т)
owing ['əʊɪŋ] до́лжный; неупла́ченный; **~ to** *prp.* благодаря́ (Д)
owl [aʊl] сова́
own [əʊn] **1.** свой, со́бственный; родно́й; **my ~** моя́ со́бственность *f*; **a house of one's ~** со́бственный дом; **hold one's ~** не сдава́ть свои́ пози́ции; **3.** владе́ть (Т); (*admit, confess*) призна(ва́)ть (В); **~ to** призна(ва́)ться в (П)
owner ['əʊnə] владе́лец *m*, -лица *f*; хозя́ин; **~ship** [-ʃɪp] со́бственность *f*
ox [ɒks], *pl.* **oxen** ['ɒksn] вол, бык
oxid|e ['ɒksaɪd] о́кись *f*; **~ize** ['ɒksɪdaɪz] окисля́ть(ся) [-ли́ть(ся)]
oxygen ['ɒksɪdʒən] кислоро́д
oyster ['ɔɪstə] у́стрица

P

pace [peɪs] **1.** (*step*) шаг; (*speed*) темп, ско́рость *f*; **2.** *v/t.* ме́рить шага́ми; *v/i.* [за]шага́ть; *room* ходи́ть взад и вперёд; **set the ~** задава́ть темп
pacify ['pæsɪfaɪ] умиротворя́ть [-ри́ть]; *rebellion* усмиря́ть [-ри́ть]
pack [pæk] **1.** *of cigarettes, etc.,* па́чка; *of papers* ки́па; *cards* коло́да; *of* свора; *of wolves* ста́я; **2.** *v/t.* (*often ~ up*) упако́вывать [-кова́ть]; укла́дываться [уложи́ться]; (*fill*) заполня́ть [запо́лнить]; наби(ва́)ть; (*a. ~ off*) выпрова́живать [вы́проводить]; отгружа́ть [отгрузи́ть]; **~age** ['pækɪdʒ] (*parcel*) паке́т, свёрток, упако́вка; **~ tour** туристи́ческая пое́здка, ком-

плексное турне́; **~er** ['pækə] упако́вщик *m*, -ица *f*; **~et** ['pækɪt] паке́т; па́чка; **small ~ mail** бандеро́ль *f*
pact [pækt] пакт, догово́р
pad [pæd] **1.** мя́гкая прокла́дка; (*writing ~*) блокно́т; **2.** подби(ва́)ть, наби(ва́)ть (ва́той *и т. д.*); *fig.* **~ out** перегружа́ть [-узи́ть]
paddle ['pædl] **1.** гребо́к; байда́рочное весло́; **2.** грести́; плыть на байда́рке
paddling pool ['pædlɪŋ] *coll.* лягуша́тник
paddock ['pædək] вы́гон
padlock ['pædlɒk] вися́чий замо́к
pagan ['peɪgən] **1.** язы́чник; **2.** язы́ческий

page [peɪdʒ] страни́ца

pageant ['pædʒənt] карнава́льное (пра́здничное) ше́ствие; пы́шное зре́лище

paid [peɪd] pt. и pt. p. от pay

pail [peɪl] ведро́

pain [peɪn] 1. боль f; ~s pl. (often sg.) страда́ния n/pl.; on ~ of под стра́хом (P); be in ~ испы́тывать боль; spare no ~s приложи́ть все уси́лия; take ~s [по]стара́ться; 2. причиня́ть боль (Д); ~ful ['peɪnfl] □ боле́зненный; мучи́тельный; ~less ['~lɪs] □ безболе́зненный; ~staking ['peɪnzteɪkɪŋ] усе́рдный, стара́тельный

paint [peɪnt] 1. кра́ска; "Wet ℒ" Осторо́жно, окра́шено; 2. [по]кра́сить; ~brush кисть f; ~er ['peɪntə] art худо́жник; (decorator) маля́р; ~ing ['peɪntɪŋ] (art or occupation) жи́вопись f; (work of art) карти́на

pair [peə] 1. па́ра; a ~ of scissors но́жницы f/pl.; 2. (~ off) соединя́ть(ся) по дво́е; раздели́ть pf. на па́ры; biol. спа́ривать(ся)

pal [pæl] прия́тель(ница f) m; coll. ко́реш

palace ['pælɪs] дворе́ц

palate ['pælɪt] anat. нёбо; fig. вкус

pale [peɪl] 1. □ бле́дный; ~ ale све́тлое пи́во; 2. [по]бледне́ть

paleness ['peɪlnɪs] бле́дность f

palette ['pælɪt] пали́тра

pall [pɔːl] v/i. приеда́ться [-е́сться]

palliate ['pælɪeɪt] pain облегча́ть [-чи́ть]

pallid ['pælɪd] □ бле́дный; ~or [-lə] бле́дность f

palm¹ [pɑːm] 1. of hand ладо́нь f; 2. ~ off on s.b. coll. подсо́вывать [подсу́нуть]; fig. pej. всу́чивать [-чи́ть] (Д)

palm² [-], ~tree па́льма; ℒ Sunday Ве́рбное воскресе́нье

palpable ['pælpəbl] □ осяза́емый; ощути́мый; fig. очеви́дный, я́вный

palpitat|e ['pælpɪteɪt] with fear, etc. трепета́ть; of heart си́льно би́ться; ~ion [pælpɪ'teɪʃn] сердцебие́ние

paltry ['pɔːltrɪ] □ пустяко́вый, ничто́жный

pamper ['pæmpə] [из]ба́ловать

pamphlet ['pæmflɪt] памфле́т

pan [pæn] (saucepan) кастрю́ля; (frying ~) сковорода́, (-ро́дка)

pan... [-] pref. пан...; обще...

panacea [pænə'sɪə] панаце́я

pancake ['pænkeɪk] блин; without yeast бли́нчик; small and thick ола́дья

pandemonium [pændɪ'məʊnɪəm] смяте́ние; fig. столпотворе́ние

pander ['pændə] потво́рствовать (to Д)

pane [peɪn] (око́нное) стекло́

panel ['pænl] 1. arch. пане́ль f; mot. прибо́рная доска́; 2. обшива́ть пане́лями

pang [pæŋ] внеза́пная о́страя боль f; ~s of conscience угрызе́ния со́вести

panic ['pænɪk] пани́ческий; 2. па́ника; ~-stricken [-strɪkən] охва́ченный па́никой

pansy ['pænzɪ] bot. аню́тины гла́зки m/pl.

pant [pænt] задыха́ться; тяжело́ дыша́ть; вздыха́ть; стра́стно жела́ть (for, after P)

panties ['pæntɪz] (a pair of ~) women's тру́сики; children's штани́шки

pantry ['pæntrɪ] кладова́я

pants [pænts] pl. (a pair of ~) трусы́; Am. брю́ки m/pl.

papal ['peɪpəl] □ па́пский

paper ['peɪpə] 1. бума́га; (news~) газе́та; (wall~) обо́и m/pl.; нау́чный докла́д; докуме́нт; 2. окле́ивать [окле́ить] обо́ями; ~back кни́га в мя́гком переплёте; ~ bag куле́к; ~clip скре́пка; ~work канцеля́рская рабо́та

paprika ['pæprɪkə] кра́сный пе́рец

par [pɑː] ра́венство; (recognized or face value) номина́льная сто́имость f; at ~ по номина́лу; be on a ~ with быть наравне́, на одно́м у́ровне с (Т)

parable ['pærəbl] при́тча

parachut|e ['pærəʃuːt] парашю́т; ~ist [-ɪst] парашюти́ст

parade [pə'reɪd] 1. mil. пара́д; make a ~ of выставля́ть напока́з; 2. щеголя́ть

paradise ['pærədaɪs] рай

paradox ['pærədɒks] парадо́кс; ~ical

[-ɪkl] парадоксáльный

paraffin ['pærəfɪn] *chiefly Brt.* керосúн; (~ *wax*) парафúн

paragon ['pærəgən] образéц; ~ *of virtue* образéц добродéтели

paragraph ['pærəgrɑːf] абзáц; газéтная замéтка

parallel ['pærəlel] 1. параллéльный; 2. параллéль *f* (*a. fig.*); *geogr.* параллéль *f*; **without** ~ несравнúмый; 3. быть паралле́льным с (T), (*compare*) проводúть [-вестú] паралле́ль ме́жду; срáвнивать [-нúть]

paraly|se *Am.* ~**ze** ['pærəlaɪz] парализовáть (*im*)*pf.* (*a. fig.*); ~**sis** [pə'rælɪsɪs] *med.* парали́ч

paramount ['pærəmaʊnt]: *of ~ importance* первостепéнной вáжности

parapet ['pærəpɪt] парапéт

paraphernalia [pærəfə'neɪlɪə] *pl.* лúчные вéщи *f/pl.*, принадлéжности

parasite ['pærəsaɪt] парази́т (*a. fig.*)

paratroops ['pærətruːps] *pl.* парашю́тно-десáнтные войскá *n/pl.*

parcel ['pɑːsl] 1. пакéт; *mail* посы́лка; 2. (*mst.* ~ *out*) *land* делúть на учáстки; (*mst.* ~ *up*) упакóвывать [-овáть]

parch [pɑːtʃ] иссушáть [-шúть]; *of sun* опаля́ть [-лúть]; *my throat is* ~*ed* у меня пересóхло в гóрле

parchment [pɑːtʃmənt] пергáмент

pardon ['pɑːdn] 1. прощéние; *law* помúлование; прощáть [простúть]; помúловать *pf.*; ~**able** [-əbl] □ прости́тельный

pare [peə] (*peel*) [по]чи́стить; (*cut*) обрезáть [-рéзать]; *fig.* [о-, по-] стричь; *fig. expenses* урéз(ыв)ать

parent ['peərənt] *mst. pl.* родúтели *m/pl.*; ~**age** [-ɪdʒ] происхождéние; ~**al** [pə'rentl] □ родúтельский

parenthe|sis [pə'renθəsɪs], *pl.* ~**ses** [-siːz] ввóдное слóво *or* предложéние; *pl. typ.* (кру́глые) скóбки *f/pl.*

paring ['peərɪŋ] кожурá, кóрка, шелухá; ~*s pl.* обрéзки *m/pl.*; *of vegetables, fruit* очúстки *f/pl.*

parish ['pærɪʃ] 1. церкóвный прихóд; 2. прихóдский; ~**ioners** [pə'rɪʃənəz] прихожáне *pl.*

parity ['pærɪtɪ] рáвенство; равноцéнность *f; fin.* паритéт

park [pɑːk] 1. (*public garden*) парк; *for vehicles* стоя́нка; 2. *mot.* парковáть, стáвить на стоя́нку; ~**ing** ['pɑːkɪŋ] автостоя́нка; *No* ℘ стоя́нка запрещенá

parlance ['pɑːləns]: *in common* ~ в обихóдной рéчи

parliament ['pɑːləmənt] парлáмент; ~**ary** [pɑːlə'mentərɪ] парлáментский

parlo(u)r ['pɑːlə] *in house* гости́ная; *Am., for services* ателье́ *n indecl.*; ~ *games* кóмнатные úгры

parody ['pærədɪ] парóдия

parole [pə'rəʊl] чéстное слóво; усло́вно-досро́чное освобождéние

parquet ['pɑːkeɪ] паркéт

parrot ['pærət] 1. попугáй; 2. повторя́ть как попугáй

parry ['pærɪ] (*ward off*) отражáть [-разúть], пари́ровать (*a. fig.*)

parsimonious [pɑːsɪ'məʊnɪəs] □ скупóй

parsley ['pɑːslɪ] петрýшка

parsnip ['pɑːsnɪp] пастернáк

parson ['pɑːsn] приходскóй свящéнник, пáстор

part [pɑːt] 1. часть *f*, дóля; учáстие; *thea. a. fig. rôle* роль *f*; мéстность *f*, край; *mus.* пáртия; *in these* ~*s* в э́тих краях; *take in good* ~ не обúдеться *pf.*, приня́ть *pf.* спокóйно; *take* ~ принимáть [-ня́ть] учáстие; *for my* (*own*) ~ с моéй стороны́; *in* ~ части́чно; *on the* ~ *of* со стороны́ (P); 2. *adv.* части́чно, отчáсти; 3. *v/t.* разделя́ть [-лúть]; ~ *the hair* дéлать пробóр; *v/i.* разлучáться [-чи́ться], расст(ав)áться (*with, from* с T)

partial ['pɑːʃl] □ части́чный; (*not indifferent*) пристрáстный; неравнодýшный (*to* к Д); *I'm* ~ *to peaches* я люблю́ пéрсики

particip|ant [pɑː'tɪsɪpənt] учáстник *m*, -ица *f*; ~**ate** [-peɪt] учáствовать (*in* в П); ~**ation** [-'peɪʃn] учáстие

particle ['pɑːtɪkl] части́ца

particular [pə'tɪkjʊlə] 1. □ особéнный; осóбый; (*hard to satisfy*) разбóрчивый; *in this* ~ *case* в дáнном слу́чае; **for no ~ reason** без осо́бой причи́ны; **2.** подро́бность *f*, дета́ль *f*; **in ~** в осо́бенности; **~ly** [pə'tɪkjʊləlɪ] осо́бенно

parting ['pɑːtɪŋ] **1.** (*separation*) разлу́ка; (*farewell*) проща́ние; *in hair* пробо́р; **2.** проща́льный

partisan [pɑːtɪ'zæn] **1.** (*adherent*) сторо́нник *m*, -ица *f*; *mil.* партиза́н *m*; **2.** партиза́нский

partition [pɑː'tɪʃn] **1.** (*division*) разде́л; (*separating structure*) перегоро́дка; **2.:** **~ off** отгора́живать [-ради́ть]

partly ['pɑːtlɪ] ча́стью, отча́сти

partner ['pɑːtnə] **1.** *in crime* соуча́стник *m*, -ица *f*; *comm.* компаньо́н, партнёр; *sport, etc.* партнёр; **2.** быть партнёром; **~ship** [-ʃɪp] парнёрство; (*marriage*) сою́з, това́рищество, компа́ния

part-owner совладе́лец

partridge ['pɑːtrɪdʒ] куропа́тка

part-time непо́лный рабо́чий день; *attr.* не по́лностью за́нятый; **~ worker** рабо́чий, за́нятый непо́лный рабо́чий день

party ['pɑːtɪ] *pol.* па́ртия; (*team*) отря́д; (*group*) гру́ппа, компа́ния, *law* сторона́; уча́стник (**to** в П); (*social gathering*) вечери́нка

pass ['pɑːs] **1.** прохо́д; *mountain* перева́л; (*permit*) про́пуск; беспла́тный биле́т; *univ.* посре́дственная сда́ча экза́мена; *cards, sport* пас; **2.** *v/i.* проходи́ть [пройти́]; (*drive by*) проезжа́ть [-е́хать]; переходи́ть (**from ... to ...** из (Р) ... в (В) ...); *cards* пасова́ть; **~ as, for** счита́ться (Т), слыть (Т); **~ away** умира́ть [умере́ть]; **~ by** проходи́ть ми́мо; **~ into** переходи́ть [перейти́] в (В); **~ off** *of pain, etc.* проходи́ть [пройти́]; **~ on** идти́ да́льше; **~ out** (*faint*) [по]теря́ть созна́ние; **3.** *v/t.* проходи́ть [пройти́]; проезжа́ть [-е́хать]; минова́ть (*im*)*pf.*; *exam* сдать *pf.*; обгоня́ть [обогна́ть], опережа́ть [-реди́ть]; переправля́ть(ся) [-а́вить(ся)] че́рез (В); (*a. ~ on*) перед(ав)а́ть; *sentence* выноси́ть [вы́нести]; *time* проводи́ть [-вести́]; *law* принима́ть [-ня́ть]; **~able**

['pɑːsəbl] *road, etc.* проходи́мый; (*tolerable*) сно́сный

passage ['pæsɪdʒ] прохо́д; *of time* тече́ние; перее́зд, перепра́ва; *ae.* перелёт; *crossing by ship* пла́вание, рейс; (*corridor*) коридо́р; *from book* отры́вок

passenger ['pæsɪndʒə] пассажи́р; **~ train** пассажи́рский по́езд

passer-by [pɑːsə'baɪ] прохо́жий

passion ['pæʃn] *strong emotion, desire* страсть *f*; (*anger*) гнев; **♀ Week** Страстна́я неде́ля; **~ate** [-ɪt] □ стра́стный, пы́лкий

passive ['pæsɪv] □ пасси́вный; *gr.* **the ~ voice** страда́тельный зало́г

passport ['pɑːspɔːt] па́спорт

password ['pɑːswɜːd] паро́ль *m*

past [pɑːst] **1.** *adj.* про́шлый; мину́вший; **for some time ~** за после́днее вре́мя; **2.** *adv.* ми́мо; **3.** *prp.* за (Т); по́сле (Р); ми́мо (Р); свы́ше (Р); **half ~ two** полови́на тре́тьего; **~ endurance** нестерпи́мый; **~ hope** безнадёжный; **4.** про́шлое

paste [peɪst] **1.** (*glue*) клей; **2.** кле́ить, прикле́и(ва)ть

pastel ['pæstl] (*crayon*) пасте́ль *f*

pasteurize ['pæstəraɪz] пастеризова́ть (*im*)*pf.*

pastime ['pɑːstaɪm] времяпрепровожде́ние

pastor ['pɑːstə] па́стор *m*; **~al** [-rəl] *of shepherds or country life* пастора́льный; *of clergy* па́сторский

pastry ['peɪstrɪ] (*dough*) те́сто; (*tart*) пиро́жное; **~ cook** конди́тер

pasture ['pɑːstʃə] **1.** па́стбище; вы́гон; **2.** пасти́(сь)

pat [pæt] **1.** похло́пывание; **2.** *on back* похло́п(ыв)ать; [по]гла́дить; **3.** кста́ти; как раз подходя́щий; **~ answer** гото́вый отве́т (*a. fig.* шабло́нный)

patch [pætʃ] **1.** *on clothes* запла́та; *of colo(u)r* пятно́; клочо́к земли́; **2.** [за]лата́ть; [по]чини́ть; **~ up a quarrel** ула́живать [-а́дить] ссо́ру

patent ['peɪtnt] **1.** (*obvious*) я́вный; запатенто́ванный; **~ leather** лакиро́ванная ко́жа; **2.** (*a.* **letters ~** *pl.*) пате́нт; **3.**

[за]патентова́ть; **~ee** [peɪtn'tiː] владе́лец пате́нта

patern|al [pə'tɜːnl] □ отцо́вский; (*fatherly*) оте́ческий; **~ity** [-nəti] отцо́вство

path [pɑːθ], *pl.* **~s** [pɑːðz] тропи́нка, доро́жка

pathetic [pə'θetɪk] жа́лкий; печа́льный; тро́гательный

patien|ce ['peɪʃns] терпе́ние; **~t** [-nt] 1. □ терпели́вый; 2. больно́й *m*, -на́я *f*, пацие́нт *m*, -тка *f*

patriot ['pætrɪət] патрио́т; **~ism** ['-ɪzəm] патриоти́зм

patrol [pə'trəʊl] *mil.* 1. патру́ль *m*; 2. патрули́ровать

patron ['peɪtrən] (*supporter, sponsor*) покрови́тель *m*; (*customer*) клие́нт, покупа́тель *m*; **~age** ['pætrənɪdʒ] *support* покрови́тельство; **~ize** [-naɪz] покрови́тельствовать; (*be condescending*) снисходи́тельно относи́ться к (Д)

patter ['pætə] говори́ть скорогово́ркой; [про]бормота́ть; *of rain* бараба́нить; *of feet* топота́ть

pattern ['pætn] 1. образе́ц; (*way*) о́браз; (*design*) узо́р; 2. де́лать по образцу́ (**on** P)

paunch [pɔːntʃ] брюшко́

pauper ['pɔːpə] ни́щий *m*, -щая *f*

pause [pɔːz] 1. па́уза, переры́в; 2. [с]де́лать па́узу

pave [peɪv] [вы]мости́ть; **~ the way for** *fig.* прокла́дывать [проложи́ть] путь; **~ment** ['peɪvmənt] тротуа́р

pavilion [pə'vɪlɪən] павильо́н

paw [pɔː] 1. ла́па (*coll a.* = **hand**); 2. тро́гать ла́пой

pawn¹ [pɔːn] *chess* пе́шка

pawn² [-] 1. зало́г, закла́д; **in ~** в закла́де; 2. закла́дывать [заложи́ть]; **~broker** владе́лец ломба́рда; ростовщи́к; **~shop** ломба́рд

pay [peɪ] 1. (о)пла́та, упла́та; *wages* зарпла́та; 2. [*irr.*] *v/t.* [за]плати́ть; *bill, etc.* опла́чивать [оплати́ть]; **~ a visit** посеща́ть [-ети́ть], (*official*) наноси́ть [-нести́] визи́т; **~ attention to** обраща́ть внима́ние на (В); **~ down** пла-

ти́ть нали́чными; *v/i.* (*be profitable*) окупа́ться [-пи́ться] (*a. fig.*); **~ for** [у-, за]плати́ть за (В), опла́чивать; *fig.* [по]плати́ться за (В); **~able** ['peɪəbl] опла́чиваемый подлежа́щий упла́те; **~day** день зарпла́ты; *coll.* полу́чка; **~ing** ['peɪɪŋ] вы́годный; **~ment** ['-mənt] упла́та, опла́та, платёж

pea [piː] *bot.* горо́х; горо́шина; **~s** *pl.* горо́х; *attr.* горо́ховый

peace [piːs] мир; споко́йствие; **~able** ['piːsəbl] миролюби́вый, ми́рный; **~ful** ['-fl] □ ми́рный, споко́йный; **~maker** миротво́рец

peach [piːtʃ] пе́рсик

peacock ['piːkɒk] павли́н

peak [piːk] *of mountain* верши́на (*a. fig.*); *of cap* козырёк; **~ of summer** разга́р ле́та; *attr.* максима́льный; вы́сший

peal [piːl] 1. звон колоколо́в; *of thunder* раска́т; **~ of laughter** взрыв сме́ха; 2. звони́ть

peanut ['piːnʌt] ара́хис

pear [peə] гру́ша

pearl [pɜːl] *collect.* же́мчуг; жемчу́жина *a. fig.*; *attr.* жемчу́жный; **~ barley** перло́вая крупа́, *coll.* перло́вка

peasant ['peznt] 1. крестья́нин *m*, -я́нка *f*; 2. крестья́нский; **~ry** [-ri] крестья́нство

peat [piːt] торф

pebble ['pebl] га́лька

peck [pek] клева́ть [клю́нуть]

peckish ['pekɪʃ] *coll.* голо́дный; **feel ~** хоте́ть есть

peculiar [pɪ'kjuːlɪə] □ (*distinctive*) своеобра́зный; осо́бенный; (*strange*) стра́нный; (*characteristic*) сво́йственный (Д); **~ity** [pɪkjuːlɪ'ærətɪ] осо́бенность *f*; стра́нность *f* сво́йство

peddler *or* Brt. **pedlar** ['pedlə] разно́счик; у́личный торго́вец

pedal ['pedl] 1. педа́ль *f*; 2. е́хать на велосипе́де

pedestal ['pedɪstl] пьедеста́л (*a. fig.*);

~rian [pɪ'destrɪən] 1. пешехо́д; 2. пешехо́дный; **~rian crossing** перехо́д

pedigree ['pedɪgriː] родосло́вная; происхожде́ние

peek [pi:k] → *peep*

peel [pi:l] 1. кóрка, кóжица, шелухá; 2. *(a. ~ off)* v/t. снимáть кóжицу, кóрку, шелухý с (P); *fruit, vegetables* [по]чи́стить; v/i. [об]лупи́ться; *of skin* сходи́ть [сойти́]

peep¹ [pi:p] [про]пищáть

peep² [-] 1. взгляд укрáдкой; **have a ~** взглянýть *pf.*; 2. взгляну́ть *pf.* укрáдкой; **~ in** загля́дывать [-яну́ть]; **~hole** *in door* глазóк

peer¹ [pɪə]: **~ at** всмáтриваться [всмотрéться]

peer² [-] рóвня *m/pf.*; пэр; **~less** [ˈpɪəlɪs] несравнéнный

peevish [ˈpiːvɪʃ] □ брюзгли́вый

peg [peg] 1. кóлышек; *for coats, etc.* вéшалка; *(clothes ~)* прищéпка; *fig.* **take a p. down a ~** сбивáть спесь с когó-л.; 2. прикрепля́ть кóлышком; отмечáть кóлышками; **~ away** *impf. only, coll.* укáлывать; упóрно рабóтать

pellet [ˈpelɪt] шáрик; *(pill)* пилю́ля; *collect.* дробь *f*

pell-mell [pelˈmel] впереме́шку

pelt¹ [pelt] кóжа, шку́ра

pelt² [-] *(throw at)* забрáсывать [-росáть]; v/i. *of rain, etc.* барабáнить

pelvis [ˈpelvɪs] *anat.* таз

pen [pen] 1. ру́чка; **ballpoint ~** шáриковая ру́чка; **fountain ~** авторýчка; 2. [на]писáть

penal [ˈpiːnl] уголóвный; **~ offence**, *Am.* **-se** уголóвное преступлéние; **~ize** [ˈpiːnəlaɪz] накáзывать [-зáть]; **~ty** [ˈpenltɪ] наказáние; *sport.* пенáльти; *attr.* штрафнóй

pence [pens] *pl. om* **penny**

pencil [ˈpensl] 1. карандáш; **in ~** карандашóм; 2. *(draw)* [на]рисовáть; писáть карандашóм

pendant [ˈpendənt] кулóн; брелóк

pending [ˈpendɪŋ] 1. *law* ожидáющий решéния; 2. *prp.* (вплоть до (P)

pendulum [ˈpendjʊləm] мáятник

penetra|ble [ˈpenɪtrəbl] □ проницáемый; **~te** [-treɪt] проникáть [-ни́кнуть] в (B); *(pervade)* прони́зывать [-зáть]; *fig.* вникáть (вни́кнуть) в (B); **~ting** [ˈtreɪtɪŋ] *(acute)* проницá-

тельный; *sound, etc.* пронзи́тельный; **~tion** [penɪˈtreɪʃn] проникновéние; проницáтельность *f*

peninsula [pəˈnɪnsjʊlə] полуóстров

peniten|ce [ˈpenɪtəns] раскáяние; покáяние; **~t** [-nt] □ кáющийся; **~tiary** [penɪˈtenʃərɪ] исправи́тельный дом; тюрьмá

penknife [ˈpennaɪf] перочи́нный нож

pen name псевдони́м

pennant [ˈpenənt] вы́мпел

penniless [ˈpenɪlɪs] без копéйки

penny [ˈpenɪ] пéнни *n indecl.*, пенс; **cost a pretty ~** влетéть *pf.* в копéечку

pen pal друг по перепи́ске

pension 1. [ˈpenʃn] пéнсия; *(disability ~)* пéнсия по инвали́дности; 2. v/t. назнáчить *pf.* пéнсию; **(~ off)** увольня́ть на пéнсию; **~er** [ˈpenʃənə] пенсионéр(ка)

pensive [ˈpensɪv] □ заду́мчивый

pent [pent] заклю́ченный; **~up** *anger, etc.* накопи́вшийся; подáвленный

penthouse [ˈpenthaʊs] кварти́ра; вы́строенная на кры́ше дóма

people [ˈpiːpl] 1. *(race, nation)* нарóд; *(persons generally)* лю́ди *m/pl.*; *(inhabitants)* населéние; 2. заселя́ть [-ли́ть]; *country* населя́ть [-ли́ть]

pepper [ˈpepə] 1. пéрец; 2. [по-, на]пéрчить; **~mint** *bot.* пéречная мя́та; **~y** [-rɪ] напéрченный; *fig.* вспы́льчивый, раздражи́тельный

per [pɜː] по (Д), чéрез (B), посрéдством (P); за (B); **~ annum** в год, ежегóдно; **~cent** процéнт

perambulator [pəˈræmbjʊleɪtə] дéтская коля́ска

perceive [pəˈsiːv] *(visually)* замечáть [-éтить]; *(discern)* различáть [-чи́ть]; *mentally* понимáть [-ня́ть]; осозн(ав)áть; *through senses* [по-] чу́вствовать; ощущáть [-ути́ть]

percentage [pəˈsentɪdʒ] процéнт

percepti|ble [pəˈseptəbl] □ ощути́мый, различи́мый; **~on** [-ʃn] восприя́тие

perch¹ [pɜːtʃ] *zo.* óкунь *m*

perch² [-] сади́ться [сесть]; усáживаться [усéсться]

percolator ['pɜːkəleɪtə] кофева́рка

percussion [pə'kʌʃn] уда́р; *mus. collect.* уда́рные инструме́нты

peremptory [pə'remptərɪ] безапелляцио́нный, категори́чный, (*manner*) вла́стный

perennial [pə'renɪəl] □ *fig.* ве́чный, неувяда́емый; *bot.* многоле́тний

perfect ['pɜːfɪkt] **1.** □ соверше́нный; (*exact*) то́чный; **2.** [pə'fekt] [у]соверше́нствовать; **~ion** [-ʃn] соверше́нство

perfidious [pə'fɪdɪəs] □ *lit.* вероло́мный

perforate ['pɜːfəreɪt] перфори́ровать (*im*)*pf.*

perform [pə'fɔːm] исполня́ть [-о́лнить] (*a. thea.*); *thea., mus.* игра́ть [сыгра́ть]; **~ance** [-əns] исполне́ние (*a. thea.*); *thea.* спекта́кль *m*; *sport.* достиже́ние; **~er** [-ə] исполни́тель(ница *f*) *m*

perfume ['pɜːfjuːm] *liquid* духи́ *m/pl.*; (*smell, bouquet*) арома́т, (*fragrance*) благоуха́ние

perfunctory [pə'fʌŋktərɪ] □ (*automatic*) машина́льный; *fig.* (*careless*) небре́жный; (*superficial*) пове́рхностный

perhaps [pə'hæps] мо́жет быть

peril ['perəl] опа́сность *f*; **~ous** [-əs] □ опа́сный

period ['pɪərɪəd] пери́од; эпо́ха; (*full stop*) то́чка, коне́ц; **~ic** [pɪərɪ'ɒdɪk] периоди́ческий; **~ical** [-dɪkl] **1.** → *periodic*; **2.** периоди́ческое изда́ние

periphery [pə'rɪfərɪ] окру́жность *f*; *fig.* перифери́я

perish ['perɪʃ] погиба́ть [-и́бнуть]; **~able** ['perɪʃəbl] □ *food* скоропо́ртящийся; **~ing** [-ɪŋ]: *it's ~ here* здесь жу́тко хо́лодно

perjur|e ['pɜːdʒə]: **~ o.s.** лжесвиде́тельствовать; **~y** [-rɪ] лжесвиде́тельство

perk [pɜːk] *coll.: mst.* **~ up** *v/i.* оживля́ться [-ви́ться]; **~y** ['pɜːkɪ] □ живо́й; (*self-assured*) самоуве́ренный

permanen|ce ['pɜːmənəns] постоя́нство; **~t** [-nt] постоя́нный, неизме́нный; **~ address** постоя́нный а́дрес; **~ wave** зави́вка «перма́не́нт»

permea|ble ['pɜːmɪəbl] проница́емый; **~te** [-mɪeɪt] проника́ть [-и́кнуть]; пропи́тывать [-ита́ть]

permissi|ble [pə'mɪsəbl] □ допусти́мый; **~on** [-ʃn] разреше́ние

permit 1. [pə'mɪt] разреша́ть [-ши́ть], позволя́ть [-во́лить]; допуска́ть [-усти́ть]; *weather ~ting* е́сли пого́да позво́лит; **2.** ['pɜːmɪt] разреше́ние; (*document*) про́пуск

pernicious [pə'nɪʃəs] □ па́губный, вре́дный

perpendicular [pɜːpən'dɪkjʊlə] □ перпендикуля́рный

perpetrate ['pɜːpɪtreɪt] соверша́ть [-ши́ть]

perpetu|al [pə'petʃʊəl] □ постоя́нный, ве́чный; **~ate** [-ʃʊeɪt] увекове́чи(ва)ть

perplex [pə'pleks] озада́чи(ва)ть, сбива́ть с то́лку; **~ity** [-ətɪ] озада́ченность *f*; недоуме́ние

perquisite ['pɜːkwɪzɪt] побо́чное преиму́щество; льго́та

persecut|e ['pɜːsɪkjuːt] пресле́довать; **~ion** [pɜːsɪ'kjuːʃn] пресле́дование

persever|ance [pɜːsɪ'vɪərəns] насто́йчивость *f*, упо́рство; **~e** [-'vɪə] *v/i.* упо́рно продолжа́ть (*in* B)

persist [pə'sɪst] упо́рствовать (*in* в П); **~ence** [-əns] насто́йчивость *f*; **~ent** [-ənt] □ насто́йчивый; (*unceasing*) беспреста́нный

person ['pɜːsn] лицо́, ли́чность *f*; персо́на, осо́ба; *pleasant ~* прия́тный челове́к; **~age** [-ɪdʒ] ва́жная персо́на; *lit.* персона́ж; **~al** [-l] □ ли́чный, персона́льный; **~ality** [pɜːsə'nælətɪ] ли́чность *f*; **~ify** [pə'sɒnɪfaɪ] (*give human qualities*) олицетворя́ть [-ри́ть]; (*embody, exemplify*) воплоща́ть [-лоти́ть]; **~nel** [pɜːsə'nel] персона́л, штат; **~ department** отде́л ка́дров

perspective [pə'spektɪv] перспекти́ва; (*view*) вид

perspir|ation [pɜːspə'reɪʃn] поте́ние; пот; **~e** [pə'spaɪə] [вс]поте́ть

persua|de [pə'sweɪd] убежда́ть [убедить]; ~**sion** [-ʒn] убежде́ние; убеди́тельность *f*; ~**sive** [-sɪv] □ убеди́тельный

pert [pɜːt] □ де́рзкий

pertain [pəˈteɪn] (*relate*) име́ть отноше́ние (к Д); (*belong*) принадлежа́ть

pertinacious [pɜːtɪˈneɪʃəs] □ упря́мый; (*determined*) настойчивый

pertinent [ˈpɜːtɪnənt] уме́стный; относя́щийся к де́лу

perturb [pəˈtɜːb] [вз]волнова́ть, [о]беспоко́ить

perusal [pəˈruːzl] внима́тельное прочте́ние; рассмотре́ние

pervade [pəˈveɪd] *of smell, etc.* распространя́ться [-ни́ться] по (Д)

pervers|e [pəˈvɜːs] □ превра́тный, отклоня́ющийся от но́рмы; извращённый; ~**ion** [ʃn] *med.* извраще́ние

pervert 1. [pəˈvɜːt] извраща́ть [-рати́ть]; совраща́ть [-рати́ть]; 2. [ˈpɜːvɜːt] извраще́нец

pest [pest] *fig.* я́зва, бич; *zo.* вреди́тель *m*; ~**er** [ˈ-ə] докуча́ть (Д); надоеда́ть [-е́сть] (Д); ~**icide** [ˈ-tɪsaɪd] пестици́д

pet [pet] 1. дома́шнее живо́тное; (*favourite*) люби́мец, ба́ловень *m*; 2. люби́мый; ~ *name* ласка́тельное и́мя; 3. ба́ловать; ласка́ть

petal [ˈpetl] *bot.* лепесто́к

petition [pəˈtɪʃn] 1. проше́ние, хода́тайство; 2. обраща́ться [-ати́ться] с проше́нием; хода́тайствовать

petrol [ˈpetrəl] *chiefly Brt.* бензи́н

petticoat [ˈpetɪkəʊt] ни́жняя ю́бка; комбина́ция

petty [ˈpetɪ] □ ме́лкий; (*small-minded*) ме́лочный

petulant [ˈpetjʊlənt] раздражи́тельный, капри́зный

pew [pjuː] церко́вная скамья́

phantom [ˈfæntəm] фанто́м, при́зрак; иллю́зия

pharmacy [ˈfɑːməsɪ] фарма́ция; (*drugstore*) апте́ка

phase [feɪz] фа́за; пери́од, эта́п

phenomen|on [fəˈnɒmɪnən], *pl.* ~**a** [-nə] явле́ние; феноме́н

phial [ˈfaɪəl] пузырёк

philologist [fɪˈlɒlədʒɪst] фило́лог

philosoph|er [fɪˈlɒsəfə] фило́соф; ~**ize** [-faɪz] философствовать; ~**y** [-fɪ] филосо́фия

phlegm [flem] мокро́та; (*sluggishness*) флегмати́чность *f*

phone [fəʊn] → **telephone**

phonetics [fəˈnetɪks] *pl.* фоне́тика

phon(e)y [ˈfəʊnɪ] *coll.* (*false*) фальши́вый, неесте́ственный

phosphorus [ˈfɒsfərəs] фо́сфор

photograph [ˈfəʊtəgrɑːf] 1. фотогра́фия, сни́мок; 2. [с]фотографи́ровать; ~**er** [fəˈtɒgrəfə] фото́граф; ~**y** [-fɪ] фотогра́фия

phrase [freɪz] 1. фра́за, выраже́ние; 2. выража́ть [вы́разить]; [с]формули́ровать

physic|al [ˈfɪzɪkəl] □ физи́ческий; материа́льный; ~**ian** [fɪˈzɪʃn] врач; ~**ist** [ˈ-sɪst] физик; ~**s** [ˈfɪzɪks] *sg.* физика

physique [fɪˈziːk] телосложе́ние

pianist [ˈpɪənɪst] пиани́ст

piano [pɪˈænəʊ] *upright* пиани́но; *grand* ~ роя́ль *m*; ~ *concerto* конце́рт для роя́ля с орке́стром

pick [pɪk] 1. вы́бор; (*tool*) кирка́; 2. выбира́ть [вы́брать]; *nose* ковыря́ть в (П); *flowers, fruit* соби(-)ра́ть; (*pluck*) срыва́ть [сорва́ть]; ~ *out* выбира́ть [вы́брать]; ~ *up* подбира́ть [подобра́ть]; поднима́ть [-ня́ть]; (*collect s.o.*) заезжа́ть [зае́хать] за (Т); ~**aback** [ˈpɪkəbæk], = **piggyback** [ˈpɪgɪbæk], на спине́; на зако́рках; *give me a* ~ посади́ меня́ на пле́чи; ~**axe** кирка́

picket [ˈpɪkɪt] 1. (*stake*) кол; *mil.* заста́ва; пост; *of strikers, etc.* пике́т; 2. пикети́ровать

picking [ˈpɪkɪŋ] *of fruit* сбор; ~**s** *pl.* оста́тки *m/pl.*, объе́дки *m/pl.*

pickle [ˈpɪkl] 1. мари́над; *pl.* пи́кули *f/pl.*; *coll.* беда́; неприя́тности *f/pl.*; *be in a* ~ вли́пнуть *pf.*; 2. [за-] марино́ва́ть; ~**d herring** марино́ванная селёдка

pickup (*van*) пика́п

pictorial [pɪkˈtɔːrɪəl] иллюстри́рованный; *art* изобрази́тельный

picture ['pɪktʃə] **1.** карти́на; **~s** pl. (generally) жи́вопись f; chiefly Brt. кино́ indecl.; **put in the~** вводи́ть [ввести́] в курс де́ла; **~ gallery** карти́нная галере́я; **~ (post)card** откры́тка с ви́дом; **2.** (depict) изобража́ть [-рази́ть]; (describe) опи́сывать [-са́ть]; (imagine) вообража́ть [-рази́ть]; **~ to o.s.** представля́ть [-а́вить] себе́; **~sque** [pɪktʃə'resk] живопи́сный

pie [paɪ] пиро́г; small пирожо́к

piece [piːs] **1.** кусо́к, часть f; (fragment) обры́вок, обло́мок; (single article) вещь f; предме́т; шту́ка; **~ of advice** сове́т; **~ of news** но́вость f; **by the~** пошту́чно; **give a ~ of one's mind** выска́зывать своё мне́ние; **take to~s** разбира́ть на ча́сти; **2.: ~ together** соединя́ть в одно́ це́лое, собира́ть из кусо́чков; **~meal** по частя́м, уры́вками; **~work** сде́льная рабо́та

pier [pɪə] naut. пирс; of bridge усто́й, бык; (breakwater) волноло́м; (wharf) при́стань f

pierce [pɪəs] пронза́ть [-зи́ть]; прока́лывать [-коло́ть]; of cold прони́зывать [-за́ть]

piety ['paɪətɪ] благоче́стие; набо́жность f

pig [pɪg] свинья́

pigeon ['pɪdʒɪn] го́лубь m; **~hole 1.** отделе́ние (пи́сьменного стола́ u m. n.); **2.** раскла́дывать по я́щикам; fig. откла́дывать в до́лгий я́щик

pig|headed [pɪg'hedɪd] упря́мый; **~skin** свина́я ко́жа; **~sty** свина́рник; **~tail** коси́чка, коса́

pike [paɪk] (fish) щу́ка

pile [paɪl] **1.** ку́ча, гру́да; (stack) шта́бель m; **2.** скла́дывать [сложи́ть]; сва́ливать в ку́чу

piles pl. med. геморро́й

pilfer ['pɪlfə] ворова́ть; стяну́ть pf.

pilgrim ['pɪlgrɪm] пало́мник; **~age** ['pɪlgrɪmɪdʒ] пало́мничество

pill [pɪl] табле́тка; **bitter ~** fig. го́рькая пилю́ля

pillage ['pɪlɪdʒ] мародёрство

pillar ['pɪlə] столб, коло́нна; Brt. **~box** почто́вый я́щик

pillion ['pɪljən] on motorcycle за́днее сиде́нье

pillow ['pɪləʊ] поду́шка; **~case**, **~slip** на́волочка

pilot ['paɪlət] **1.** ae. пило́т; naut. ло́цман; **2.** naut. проводи́ть [-вести́]; ae. пилоти́ровать

pimple ['pɪmpl] пры́щик

pin [pɪn] **1.** була́вка; **hair ~** шпи́лька; Brt. **drawing ~** (Am. thumbtack) кно́пка; **2.** прика́лывать [-коло́ть]; **~ down** припере́ть pf. к сте́нке; **~ one's hopes on** возлага́ть [-ложи́ть] наде́жды на (В)

pinafore ['pɪnəfɔː] пере́дник

pincers ['pɪnsəz] pl. кле́щи f/pl.; (tweezers) пинце́т

pinch [pɪntʃ] **1.** щипо́к; of salt, etc. щепо́тка; fig. стеснённое положе́ние; **at a ~** в кра́йнем слу́чае; **2.** v/t. щипа́ть [щипну́ть]; (squeeze) прищемля́ть [-ми́ть]; v/i. [по]скупи́ться; of shoes жать

pine[1] [paɪn]: **~ away** [за]ча́хнуть; **~ for** тоскова́ть по (П)

pine[2] [-] bot. сосна́; **~apple** анана́с; **~ cone** сосно́вая ши́шка

pinion ['pɪnjən] tech. (cogwheel) шестерня́

pink [pɪŋk] **1.** bot. гвозди́ка; ро́зовый цвет; **2.** ро́зовый

pinnacle ['pɪnəkl] arch. островоконе́чная ба́шенка; of mountain верши́на; fig. верх

pint [paɪnt] пи́нта

pioneer [paɪə'nɪə] **1.** пионе́р; первопрохо́дец m; **2.** прокла́дывать путь m (for Д)

pious ['paɪəs] □ на́божный

pip [pɪp] of fruit ко́сточка, зёрнышко

pipe [paɪp] труба́; smoker's тру́бка; mus. ду́дка; **2.: ~ down** замолча́ть pf.; **~dream** несбы́точная мечта́; **~line** трубопрово́д; нефтепрово́д; **~r** ['paɪpə] mst. волы́нщик

piping ['paɪpɪŋ]: **~ hot** о́чень горя́чий

piquant ['piːkənt] пика́нтный (a. fig.)

pique [piːk] **1.** доса́да; **2.** (nettle) раздража́ть; вызыва́ть доса́ду; (wound) уязвля́ть [-ви́ть] заде́(ва́)ть

pira|cy ['paɪərəsɪ] пира́тство (*a. in publishing*); **~te** [-rət] **1.** пира́т

pistol ['pɪstl] пистоле́т

piston ['pɪstən] *tech.* по́ршень *m*; **~ stroke** ход по́ршня

pit [pɪt] я́ма; *mining* ша́хта; *thea.* оркестро́вая я́ма

pitch¹ [pɪtʃ] смола́; (*tar*) дёготь *m*; **as black as ~** чёрный как смоль

pitch² [-] (*degree*) сте́пень *f*; *mus.* высота́ то́на; *naut.* ки́левая ка́чка; *tech.* (*slope*) накло́н; *tech.* (*thread*) шаг резьбы́; *sport* по́ле, площа́дка; **2.** *v/t.* (*set up camp, tent, etc.*) разби(ва́)ть; (*throw*) броса́ть [бро́сить]; *naut.* кача́ть; **~ into** набра́сываться [-ро́ситься] на (В)

pitcher ['pɪtʃə] (*jug*) кувши́н; (*sport*) подаю́щий

pitchfork ['pɪtʃfɔːk] ви́лы *f/pl.*

pitfall ['pɪtfɔːl] *fig.* лову́шка

pith [pɪθ] *bot.* сердцеви́на; *fig.* су́щность *f*, суть *f*; **~y** ['pɪθɪ] *fig.* сжа́тый; содержа́тельный

pitiable ['pɪtɪəbl] □ (*arousing pity*) несча́стный; (*arousing contempt*) жа́лкий

pitiful ['pɪtɪfl] □ (*arousing compassion*) жа́лостливый; (*arousing contempt*) жа́лкий

pitiless ['pɪtɪlɪs] □ безжа́лостный

pittance ['pɪtəns] гроши́

pity ['pɪtɪ] **1.** жа́лость *f* (*for* к Д), **it is a ~** жаль; **2.** [по]жале́ть

pivot ['pɪvət] **1.** ось *f* враще́ния; *fig.* сте́ржень *m*; **2.** враща́ться ([**up**]**on** вокру́г Р)

pizza ['piːtsə] пи́цца

placard ['plækɑːd] плака́т

placate [plə'keɪt] умиротворя́ть [-ри́ть]

place [pleɪs] **1.** ме́сто; го́род, селе́ние; дом; (*station*) до́лжность *f*; **give ~ to** уступа́ть ме́сто (Д); **in ~ of** вме́сто (Р); **in ~s** места́ми; **out of ~** неуме́стный; **2.** [по]ста́вить, класть [положи́ть]; *orders, etc.* размеща́ть [-ести́ть]; *article, etc.* помеща́ть [-ести́ть]; **I can't ~ her** не могу́ вспо́мнить, отку́да я её зна́ю

placid ['plæsɪd] □ споко́йный

plagiar|ism ['pleɪdʒərɪzəm] плагиа́т; **~ize** [-raɪz] занима́ться плагиа́том

plague [pleɪg] **1.** (*pestilence*) чума́ *fig.* (*calamity*) бе́дствие; (*scourge*) бич; **2.** [из]му́чить; *coll.* надоеда́ть [-е́сть] (Д)

plaice [pleɪs] ка́мбала

plaid [plæd] шотла́ндка; плед

plain [pleɪn] **1.** просто́й; поня́тный, я́сный; (*obvious*) очеви́дный; обыкнове́нный; (*smooth, level*) гла́дкий, ро́вный; **2.** *adv.* я́сно; открове́нно; **3.** *geogr.* равни́на; **~spoken** прямо́й

plaint|iff ['pleɪntɪf] исте́ц *m*, исти́ца *f*; **~ive** ['pleɪntɪv] □ жа́лобный, зауны́вный

plait [plæt] **1.** коса́; **2.** заплета́ть [-ести́]

plan [plæn] **1.** план, прое́кт; **2.** [за]плани́ровать; составля́ть план; *fig.* намеча́ть [-е́тить]; (*intend*) намерева́ться

plane¹ [pleɪn] **1.** пло́ский; **2.** пло́скость *f*; *math.* прое́кция; *ae.* самолёт; *fig.* у́ровень *m*

plane² [-] **1.** (*tool*) руба́нок; **2.** [вы́]строга́ть

planet ['plænɪt] плане́та

plank [plæŋk] **1.** доска́; **2.** настила́ть *or* обшива́ть до́сками

plant [plɑːnt] **1.** расте́ние; *tech.* заво́д, фа́брика; **2.** *tree* сажа́ть [посади́ть]; [по]ста́вить; **~ation** [plæn'teɪʃən] планта́ция; насажде́ние

plaque [plɑːk] (*wall ornament*) таре́лка; *on door, etc.* доще́чка, табли́чка; **memorial ~** мемориа́льная доска́

plasma ['plæzmə] пла́зма

plaster ['plɑːstə] **1.** *for walls* штукату́рка; *med.* пла́стырь *m*; (*mst. ~ of Paris*) гипс; **sticking ~** *med.* лейкопла́стырь; **2.** [о]штукату́рить; накла́дывать пла́стырь на (В)

plastic ['plæstɪk] (**~ally**) **1.** пласти́ческий; **2.** пластма́сса, пла́стик; **~ surgery** пласти́ческая хирурги́я

plate [pleɪt] **1.** (*dish*) таре́лка; (*metal tableware*) посу́да; (*sheet of glass, metal, etc.*) лист; *on door* доще́чка; **silver ~** столо́вое серебро́; **2.** покрыва́ть метáллом

plateau ['plætəʊ] платó *n indecl.*

platform ['plætfɔ:m] *rail.* перрóн, платфóрма; *for speakers* трибýна; *on bus, etc.* площáдка; *pol.* полити́ческая прогрáмма

platinum ['plætinəm] плáтина; *attr.* плáтиновый

platitude ['plætitju:d] банáльность *f*; истáсканное выражéние

platoon [plə'tu:n] *mil.* взвод

platter ['plætə] блюдо

plausible ['plɔ:zəbl] □ правдоподóбный; *of excuse, argument, etc.* благови́дный

play [pleɪ] **1.** игрá; пьéса; *fair ~* чéстная игрá; **2.** игрáть [сыгрáть] (в **В**, *mus.* на П); (*direct*) направля́ть [-вить]; **~ off** *fig.* разы́грывать [-рáть]; стрáвливать [стрáвить] (*against* с Т); **~ed out** вы́дохшийся; **~bill** театрáльная афи́ша; **~er** ['pleɪə] игрóк; актёр; **~mate** товáрищ по и́грам, друг дéтства; **~ful** ['pleɪfl] □ игри́вый; **~goer** ['-ɡəʊə] театрáл; **~ground** дéтская площáдка; **~house** теáтр; **~pen** дéтский манéж; **~thing** игрýшка; **~wright** ['-raɪt] драматýрг

plea [pli:] прóсьба, мольбá; *law* заявлéние в судé; *on the ~* (*of или that ...*) под предлóгом (Р *or* что ...)

plead [pli:d] *v/i.:* **~ for** вступáться [-пи́ться] за (В); говори́ть за (В); **~ guilty** признавáть себя́ вино́вным; *v/t. in court* защищáть [-ити́ть]; приводи́ть в оправдáние

pleasant ['pleznt] □ прия́тный

please [pli:z] [по]нрáвиться (Д); угождáть [угоди́ть] (Д); *if you ~* с вáшего позволéния; изво́льте!; ~ *come in!* войди́те, пожáлуйста!; доставля́ть удово́льствие (Д); *be ~d to do* дéлать с удово́льствием; *be ~d with* быть дово́льным (Т); **~d** [pli:zd] дово́льный

pleasing ['pli:zɪŋ] □ прия́тный

pleasure ['pleʒə] удово́льствие, наслаждéние; *attr.* развлекáтельный, увесели́тельный; *at your ~* по вáшему желáнию

pleat [pli:t] **1.** склáдка; **2.** дéлать склáдки на (П)

pledge [pledʒ] **1.** залóг, заклáд; (*promise*) обещáние; **2.** заклáдывать [заложи́ть]; обещáть; (*vow*) [по]кля́сться; обя́зываться [-зáться]; *he ~d himself* он связáл себя́ обещáнием

plenary ['pli:nərɪ] пленáрный

plenipotentiary [plenɪpə'tenʃərɪ] полномóчный представи́тель *m*

plentiful ['plentɪfl] □ оби́льный

plenty ['plentɪ] **1.** изоби́лие; ~ *of* мнóго (Р); **2.** *coll.* вполнé; довóльно

pleurisy ['plʊərɪsɪ] плеври́т

pliable ['plaɪəbl] □ ги́бкий; *fig.* подáтливый, мя́гкий

pliancy ['plaɪənsɪ] ги́бкость *f*

pliers ['plaɪəz] *pl.* плоскогýбцы *m/pl.*

plight [plaɪt] плохóе положéние, состоя́ние

plod [plɒd] (*a.* ~ *along, on*) [по]тащи́ться; корпéть (*at* над Т)

plot [plɒt] **1.** учáсток земли́, деля́нка; (*conspiracy*) зáговор; *lit.* фáбула, сюжéт; **2.** *v/i.* готóвить зáговор; *v/t. on map* наноси́ть [нанести́]; замышля́ть [-ы́слить]; интриговáть

plow, *Brt.* **plough** [plaʊ] **1.** плуг; **2.** [вс]пахáть; *fig.* [из]борозди́ть; **~land** пахóтная земля́; пáшня

pluck [plʌk] **1.** *coll.* смéлость *f*, мýжество; **2.** *flowers* срывáть [сорвáть]; *fowl* ощи́пывать [-пáть]; ~ *at* дёргать [дёрнуть] (В); хватáться [схвати́ть(ся)] за (В); ~ *up courage* собрáться *pf.* с дýхом; **~y** ['plʌkɪ] смéлый, отвáжный

plug [plʌɡ] **1.** зáты́чка; *in bath, etc.* прóбка; *el.* штéпсель *m*; ~ *socket* штéпсельная розéтка; **2.** *v/t. stop up* затыкáть [заткнýть]; ~ *in* включáть [-чи́ть]

plum [plʌm] сли́ва; *attr.* сли́вовый

plumage ['plu:mɪdʒ] оперéние

plumb [plʌm] *adv.* (*exactly*) тóчно; пря́мо, как раз

plumb|er ['plʌmə] сантéхник, *coll.* водопровóдчик; **~ing** [-ɪŋ] *in house* водопровóд и канализáция

plummet ['plʌmɪt] свинцóвый отвéс;

on fishing line грузи́ло

plump¹ [plʌmp] (*chubby*) пу́хлый; (*somewhat fat*) по́лный; *poultry* жи́рный

plump² [-] **1.** □ *coll.* реши́тельный; **2.** бу́хаться [-хнуться]; **3.** *adv. coll.* пря́мо, без обиняко́в

plunder ['plʌndə] [o]гра́бить

plunge [plʌndʒ] **1.** (*dive*) ныря́ть [нырну́ть]; *hand, etc.* окуна́ть [-ну́ть]; **2.** ныря́ние; погруже́ние; **take the ~** [с]де́лать реши́тельный шаг

plural ['pluərəl] *gr.* мно́жественное число́; (*multiple*) многочи́сленный

plush [plʌʃ] плюш

ply² [plaɪ] *v/t.* with questions засыпа́ть [засы́пать], забра́сывать [-роса́ть]; *v/i.* курси́ровать

ply² [-] слой: **~wood** фане́ра

pneumatic [njuː'mætɪk] (**~ally**) пневмати́ческий

pneumonia [njuː'məʊnɪə] воспале́ние лёгких, пневмони́я

poach¹ [pəʊtʃ] браконье́рствовать

poach² [-]: **~ed egg** яйцо́-пашо́т

poacher ['pəʊtʃə] браконье́р

PO Box (= *Post Office Box*) почто́вый я́щик (п/я)

pocket ['pɒkɪt] **1.** карма́н; (*air~*) возду́шная я́ма; **2.** класть в карма́н; *fig.* appropriate прикарма́ни(ва)ть; *pride* подавля́ть [-ви́ть]; *insult* прогла́тывать [-лоти́ть]; **3.** карма́нный

pod [pɒd] **1.** *of seed* стручо́к; **2.** *shell* v/t. лу́щить

poem ['pəʊɪm] поэ́ма; стихотворе́ние

poet ['pəʊɪt] поэ́т; **~ess** [-əs] поэте́сса; **~ic(al** □) [pəʊ'etɪk(əl)] поэти́ческий; **~ry** ['pəʊɪtrɪ] поэ́зия

poignan|cy ['pɔɪnjənsɪ] острота́; **~t** [-nt] о́стрый; тро́гательный; *fig.* мучи́тельный

point [pɔɪnt] **1.** (*dot*) то́чка; (*item*) пункт; *on thermometer* гра́дус, деле́ние; (*essence*) смысл, суть де́ла; *sport* очко́; (*sharp end*) остриё; о́стрый коне́ц; *rail* стре́лка; **~ of view** то́чка зре́ния; **the ~ is that ...** де́ло в том, что ...; **make a ~ of** + *ger.* поста́вить себе́ зада́чей (+ *inf.*); **in ~ of** в отноше́нии (P);

off the ~ не (относя́щийся) к де́лу; **be on the ~ of** + *ger.* соб(и)ра́ться (+ *inf.*); **win on ~s** выи́грывать по очка́м; **to the ~** к де́лу (относя́щийся); *a sore ~* больно́й вопро́с; *that's beside the ~* э́то не при чём; **2.** *v/t.:* **one's finger** пока́зывать па́льцем (*at* на В); заостря́ть [-ри́ть]; (*often ~ out*) ука́зывать [-за́ть]; *~ a weapon at* направля́ть [-ра́вить] ору́жие на (В); *v/i.:* **~ at** ука́зывать [-за́ть] на (В); **~ to** быть напра́вленным на (В); **~blank**: *ask ~* спра́шивать в упо́р; *refuse ~* категори́чески отказа́ть(ся) *pf.*; **~ed** ['pɔɪntɪd] □ остроконе́чный; о́стрый; *fig.* ко́лкий; **~er** ['pɔɪntə] *m*; *teacher's* ука́зка; *dog* по́йнтер; **~less** ['-lɪs] бессмы́сленный

poise [pɔɪz] **1.** равнове́сие; *carriage* оса́нка; **2.** *v/i.* баланси́ровать

poison ['pɔɪzn] **1.** яд, отра́ва; **2.** отравля́ть [-ви́ть]; **~ous** [-əs] (*fig. a.*) ядови́тый

poke [pəʊk] **1.** толчо́к, тычо́к; **2.** *v/t.* (*prod*) ты́кать [ткнуть]; толка́ть [-кну́ть]; сова́ть [су́нуть]; *fire* меша́ть кочерго́й; **~ fun at** подшу́чивать [-шути́ть] над (Т); *v/i.* сова́ть нос (*into* в В); (*grope for*) иска́ть о́щупью (*for* B or P)

poker ['pəʊkə] кочерга́

poky ['pəʊkɪ] те́сный; убо́гий

polar ['pəʊlə] поля́рный; **~ bear** бе́лый медве́дь *m*; **~ity** [pəʊ'lærətɪ] поля́рность *f*

pole¹ [pəʊl] (*of planet; a. elec.*) по́люс

pole² [-] (*post; a. in sport*) шест

Pole³ [-] поля́к *m*, по́лька *f*

polemic [pə'lemɪk] (*a.* **~al** [-mɪkl] □) полеми́чный, полеми́ческий; **~s** [-s] поле́мика

police [pə'liːs] **1.** поли́ция; **2.** соде́ржать поря́док в (П); **~man** полице́йский; **~ station** полице́йский уча́сток

policy¹ ['pɒləsɪ] поли́тика; ли́ния поведе́ния

policy² [-]: *insurance ~* страхово́й по́лис

Polish¹ ['pəʊlɪʃ] по́льский

polish² ['pɒlɪʃ] **1.** полиро́вка; *fig.* лоск; **2.** [от]полирова́ть; *floor* натира́ть

[-ерéть]; shoes почúстить; fig. наводúть [-вестú] лоск

polite [pə'laɪt] □ вéжливый; **~ness** [-nɪs] вéжливость f

politic|al [pə'lɪtɪkl] □ политúческий; **~ian** [pɒlɪ'tɪʃən] полúтик, политúческий дéятель; **~s** ['pɒlətɪks] pl. полúтика

poll [pəʊl] 1. голосовáние; (elections) вы́боры; **opinion ~** опрóс общéственного мнéния; 2. v/t. receive votes получáть [-чúть]; v/i. голосовáть

pollen ['pɒlən] пыльцá

polling ['pəʊlɪŋ] 1. → poll; 2.: **~ station** избирáтельный учáсток

pollute [pə'lu:t] загрязня́ть [-нúть]; осквернять [-нúть]

pollution [pə'lu:ʃn] загрязнéние

polyethylene [pɒlɪ'eθɪliːn] or Brt.

polythene ['pɒlɪθiːn] полиэтилéн

polyp ['pɒlɪp] zo., **~us** [-əs] med. полúп

pomegranate ['pɒmɪɡrænɪt] гранáт

pommel ['pɒml] of sword голóвка; of saddle лукá; v/t. = **pummel**

pomp [pɒmp] пóмпа; великолéпие

pompous ['pɒmpəs] □ напы́щенный, помпéзный

pond [pɒnd] пруд

ponder ['pɒndə] v/t. обдýм(ыв)ать; v/i. задýм(ыв)аться; **~ous** [-rəs] □ fig. тяжелéсный

pontoon [pɒn'tuːn] понтóн; **~ bridge** понтóнный мост

pony ['pəʊnɪ] horse пóни m indecl.

poodle ['puːdl] пýдель m

pool [puːl] 1. (puddle) лýжа; (pond) пруд; (swimming ~) плáвательный бассéйн; 2. cards банк; billards пул; comm. фонд; v/t. объединя́ть в óбщий фонд; склáдываться [сложúться] (**with** с Т)

poor [pʊə] □ бéдный; неимýщий; (unfortunate) несчáстный; (scanty) скýдный; (bad) плохóй; **~ly** ['pʊəlɪ] adj. нездорóвый

pop [pɒp] 1. (explosive sound) хлопóк; coll. (fizzy drink) шипýчка; 2. v/t. (put) совáть [сýнуть]; of cork v/i. хлóпать [-пнуть]; **~ across** to a shop, etc.

сбегáть; **~ in** заскочúть, забежáть

popcorn ['pɒpkɔːn] попкóрн; воздýшная кукурýза

pope [pəʊp] (рúмский) пáпа m

poplar ['pɒplə] тóполь m

poppy ['pɒpɪ] мак

popula|ce ['pɒpjʊləs] (the masses) мáссы; (the common people) простóй нарóд; населéние; **~r** [-lə] (of the people) нарóдный; (generally liked) популя́рный; **~rity** [-'lærətɪ] популя́рность f

populat|e ['pɒpjʊleɪt] населя́ть [-лúть]; **~ion** [pɒpjʊ'leɪʃn] населéние

populous ['pɒpjʊləs] □ многолю́дный

porcelain ['pɔːsəlɪn] фарфóр

porch [pɔːtʃ] крыльцó; пóртик; Am. верáнда

pore¹ [pɔː] пóра

pore² [-] problem размышля́ть, book корпéть (**over** над Т)

pork [pɔːk] свинúна

pornography [pɔː'nɒɡrəfɪ] порногрáфия

porous ['pɔːrəs] □ пóристый

porridge ['pɒrɪdʒ] овся́ная кáша

port¹ [pɔːt] гáвань f, порт; naut. (left side) лéвый борт

port² [-] портвéйн

portable ['pɔːtəbl] портатúвный

portal ['pɔːtl] arch. портáл

portend [pɔː'tend] предвещáть

portent ['pɔːtent] предвéстник, предзнаменовáние

porter ['pɔːtə] вахтёр; in hotel швейцáр; rail, etc. носúльщик; Am. on train проводнúк

portion ['pɔːʃn] 1. часть f, of food, etc. пóрция; 2. (share out) [раз-] делúть

portly ['pɔːtlɪ] дорóдный

portrait ['pɔːtrɪt] портрéт; **~ist** [-ɪst] портретúст

portray [pɔː'treɪ] рисовáть (писáть) портрéт с (Р); изображáть [-разúть]; (describe) опúсывать [-сáть]; **~al** [-əl] изображéние; описáние

pose [pəʊz] 1. пóза; 2. for an artist позúровать; question (по)стáвить; **~ as** выдавáть себя́ за (В)

position [pə'zɪʃn] ме́сто; положе́ние; пози́ция; состоя́ние; то́чка зре́ния

positive ['pɒzətɪv] 1. □ положи́тельный, позити́вный; (*sure*) уве́ренный; (*definite*) определённый; 2. *phot.* позити́в

possess [pə'zes] *quality* облада́ть (Т); *things* владе́ть (Т); *fig.* овладе́(ва́)ть (Т); **be ~ed** быть одержи́мым; **~ion** [-zeʃn] владе́ние; **take ~ of** завладе́(ва́)ть (Т); облада́ние; *fig.* одержи́мость *f*; **~or** [-zesə] владе́лец; облада́тель *m*

possib|ility [pɒsə'bɪlətɪ] возмо́жность *f*; **~le** ['pɒsəbl] возмо́жный; **~ly** [-ɪ] возмо́жно; *if I ~ can* е́сли у меня́ бу́дет возмо́жность *f*

post[1] [pəʊst] столб

post[2] [-] 1. (*mail*) по́чта; *mil.* (*duty station*) пост; (*appointment, job*) до́лжность *f*; 2. *v/t.* отправля́ть по по́чте

postage ['pəʊstɪdʒ] почто́вая опла́та; **~ stamp** почто́вая ма́рка

postal ['pəʊstl] □ почто́вый; **~ order** де́нежный почто́вый перево́д

post|card откры́тка; **~code** почто́вый и́ндекс

poster ['pəʊstə] афи́ша, плака́т

poste restante [pəʊst'rɪstænt] *chiefly Brt.* до востре́бования

posterior [pɒ'stɪərɪə] (*subsequent*) после́дующий; (*behind*) за́дний; (*buttocks*) зад

posterity [pɒ'sterətɪ] пото́мство

post-free *chiefly Brt.* → **postpaid**

postgraduate [pəʊst'grædʒʊət] аспира́нт(ка); (*not working for degree*) стажёр; **~ study** аспиранту́ра

posthumous ['pɒstjʊməs] посме́ртный; *child* рождённый по́сле сме́рти отца́

post|man почтальо́н; **~mark** 1. почто́вый ште́мпель *m*; 2. [за]штемпелева́ть; **~master** нача́льник почто́вого отделе́ния

postmortem [pəʊst'mɔːtəm] вскры́тие, аутопси́я

post|office отделе́ние свя́зи, *coll.* по́чта; **~box** абонеме́нтный почто́вый я́щик; *general ~ office* (гла́вный) почта́мт; **~paid** опла́ченный отправи́телем

postpone [pəʊs'pəʊn] отсро́чи(ва)ть, откла́дывать [отложи́ть]; **~ment** [-mənt] отсро́чка

postscript ['pəʊsskrɪpt] постскри́птум

postulate 1. ['pɒstjʊlət] постула́т; 2. [-leɪt] постули́ровать (*im*)*pf.*

posture ['pɒstʃə] (*attitude*) по́за; (*carriage*) оса́нка

postwar [pəʊst'wɔː] послевое́нный

posy ['pəʊzɪ] буке́т цвето́в

pot [pɒt] 1. горшо́к; котело́к; **~s of money** ку́ча де́нег; 2. *plants* сажа́ть в горшо́к; *jam, etc.* заготовля́ть впрок, [за]консерви́ровать

potato [pə'teɪtəʊ] (*single*) карто́фелина; **~es** [-z] *pl.* карто́фель *m*; *coll.* карто́шка; **~ crisps** хрустя́щий карто́фель

pot-belly брю́хо, пу́зо

poten|cy ['pəʊtnsɪ] эффекти́вность *f*; (*sexual*) поте́нция; *of drink* кре́пость *f*; **~t** [-tnt] □ эффекти́вный; кре́пкий; **~tial** [pə'tenʃl] 1. потенциа́льный, возмо́жный; 2. потенциа́л

pothole ['pɒthəʊl] вы́боина, ры́твина

potion ['pəʊʃn] зе́лье; *love ~* любо́вный напи́ток

pottery ['pɒtərɪ] керами́ческие (*or* гонча́рные) изде́лия *n/pl.*

pouch [paʊtʃ] су́мка (*a. biol.*); мешо́чек

poultry ['pəʊltrɪ] дома́шняя пти́ца

pounce [paʊns] 1. прыжо́к; 2. набра́сываться [-ро́ситься] ([*up*]*on* на В)

pound[1] [paʊnd] (*weight*) фунт; (*money*) **~** (*sterling*) фунт сте́рлингов (*abbr.* £)

pound[2] [-] (*ис-*, *рас*]толо́чь; (*strike*) колоти́ть; **~ to pieces** разби́ть *pf.*

pour [pɔː] *v/t.* лить; **~ out** налива́ть; *dry substance* сы́пать, насыпа́ть [насы́пать]; *v/i.* ли́ться; [по]сыпа́ться **~ing** [-rɪŋ]: **~ rain** проливно́й дождь *m*

pout [paʊt] *v/i.* [на]ду́ться; **~ one's lips** наду́(ва́)ть гу́бы

poverty ['pɒvətɪ] бе́дность *f*

powder ['paʊdə] 1. порошо́к; (*face ~*) пу́дра; (*gun~*) по́рох; 2. [ис]толо́чь;

[на]пу́дрить(ся); посыпа́ть [посы́-
пать]; ~ **compact** пу́дреница

power ['pauə] си́ла; мощь f; tech. мо́щ-
ность f; atomic, etc. эне́ргия; pol. дер-
жа́ва; власть f; law полномо́чие; math
сте́пень f; **mental ~s** у́мственные спо-
со́бности; **~ful** [-fl] мо́щный, мо-
гу́щественный; си́льный; **~less** [-lɪs]
бесси́льный; ~ **plant**, ~ **station** элек-
тростáнция

powwow ['pauwau] совещáние, со-
брáние

practica|ble ['præktɪkəbl] □ реáль-
ный, осуществи́мый; **~l** [-kl] прак-
ти́ческий; mind, person, etc. практи́чный, факти́ческий; ~ **joke** ро́зы-
грыш

practice ['præktɪs] прáктика; (training) упражне́ние, трениро́вка; (habit) привы́чка; (custom) обы́чай; **in ~**
факти́чески; **put into ~** осуществля́ть
[-ви́ть]

practice, Brt. **practise** [-] v/t. приме-
ня́ть [-ни́ть]; medicine, etc. зани-
мáться [-ня́ться] (Т); упражня́ться в
(П); практикова́ть; v/i. упражня́ться;
~d [-t] о́пытный

practitioner [præk'tɪʃənə]: **general ~**
врач-терапéвт

praise [preɪz] 1. похвалá; 2. [по]хва-
ли́ть

praiseworthy ['preɪzwɜ:ðɪ] досто́й-
ный похвалы́

prance [prɑ:ns] of child пры́гать; of
horse гарцева́ть

prank [præŋk] вы́ходка, прока́за

prattle ['prætl] болтáть; of baby лепе-
тáть

prawn [prɔ:n] zo. креве́тка

pray [preɪ] [по]моли́ться; [по]проси́ть

prayer [preə] моли́тва; **Lord's ~** О́тче
наш; ~ **book** моли́твенник

pre... [pri:, pri] до...; пред...

preach [pri:tʃ] пропове́довать; **~er**
['pri:tʃə] пропове́дник

precarious [prɪ'keəriəs] (uncertain)
ненадёжный; (dangerous) опа́сный

precaution [prɪ'kɔːʃn] предосторóж-
ность f; **take ~s** принимáть [-ня́ть]
мéры предосторóжности

precede [prɪ'si:d] предшéствовать
(Д); **~nce** ['presɪdəns] пер-
воочерёдность, приорите́т; **~nt** ['pre-
sɪdənt] прецеде́нт

precept ['pri:sept] наставлéние

precinct ['pri:sɪŋkt] предéл; Am. (electoral ~) избирáтельный óкруг; **~s** pl.
окрéстности f/pl.

precious ['preʃəs] 1. □ драгоцéнный;
~ **metals** благорóдные металлы; 2.
coll. adv. óчень

precipi|ce ['presɪpɪs] прóпасть f; **~tate**
1. [prɪ'sɪpɪteɪt] ввергáть [-éргнуть];
(hasten) ускорять [-óрить]; 2. [-tɪt]
a) □ (rash) опромéтчивый; (violently
hurried) стреми́тельный; b) chem.
осáдок; **~tous** [prɪ'sɪpɪtəs] □ (steep)
крутóй; обры́вистый

precis|e [prɪ'saɪs] □ тóчный; tech.
прецизиóнный; **~ion** [-'sɪʒn]
тóчность f

preclude [prɪ'klu:d] исключáть зарáнее; (prevent) предотвращáть [-ра-
ти́ть] (В); (hinder) [по]мешáть (Д)

precocious [prɪ'kəuʃəs] □ не по го-
дáм развитóй

preconceive ['pri:kən'si:v] пред-
ставля́ть себé зарáнее; **~d** [-d] пред-
взя́тый

preconception [pri:kən'sepʃn] пред-
взя́тое мнéние

precondition [pri:kən'dɪʃn] предвари́-
тельное услóвие

predatory ['predətrɪ] хи́щный

predecessor ['pri:dɪsesə] предшéст-
венник [-ица]

predestine [pri:'destɪn] предопре-
деля́ть [-ли́ть]; **~d** предопределён-
ный

predetermine [pri:dɪ'tɜ:mɪn] предо-
пределя́ть [-ли́ть]

predicament [prɪ'dɪkəmənt] нелóвкое
положéние; серьёзное затруднéние

predicate ['predɪkət] gr. сказу́емое;
утверждáть [-ди́ть]

predict [prɪ'dɪkt] предскáзывать
[-зáть]; **~ion** [-kʃn] предсказáние

predilection [pri:dɪ'lekʃn] склóнность
f, пристрáстие (for к Д)

predispose [pri:dɪs'pəuz] предраспо-

лага́ть [-ложи́ть]
predomina|nce [prɪ'dɒmɪnəns] гос-
по́дство, преоблада́ние; **~nt** [-nənt]
□ преоблада́ющий, домини́-
рующий; **~te** [-neɪt] госпо́дствовать,
преоблада́ть (**over** над Т)
preeminent [priː'emɪnənt] превосхо-
дя́щий; выдаю́щийся
prefabricated [priː'fæbrɪkeɪtɪd]: **~
house** сбо́рный до́м
preface ['prefɪs] **1.** предисло́вие; **2.**
начина́ть [-ча́ть] (В **with**, с Р); снабжа́ть
предисло́вием
prefect ['priːfekt] префе́кт
prefer [prɪ'fɜː] предпочита́ть [-по-
че́сть]; (*put forward*) выдвига́ть
[вы́двинуть]; **~able** ['prefrəbl] □ пред-
почти́тельный; **~ence** [-rəns] пред-
почте́ние; **~ential** [prefə'renʃl] □
предпочти́тельный; *econ.* льго́тный
prefix ['priːfɪks] префикс, приста́вка
pregnan|cy ['pregnənsɪ] бере́мен-
ность *f*; **~t** [-nənt] □ бере́менная;
fig. чрева́тый; **~ pause** многозна-
чи́тельная па́уза
prejudice ['predʒudɪs] **1.** предрассу́-
док; предубежде́ние; **2.** предубеж-
да́ть [-ди́ть]; (*harm*) [по]вреди́ть, на-
носи́ть уще́рб (Д)
preliminary [prɪ'lɪmɪnərɪ] **1.** □ предва-
ри́тельный; **2.** подготови́тельное
мероприя́тие
prelude ['preljuːd] *mus.* прелю́дия (*a.
fig.*)
prematur|e ['premətjuə] преждевре́-
менный; **~ baby** недоно́шенный
ребёнок
premeditation [priːmedɪ'teɪʃn] пред-
наме́ренность *f*
premier ['premɪə] пе́рвый, гла́вный;
премье́р-мини́стр
première ['premɪeə] премье́ра
premises ['premɪsɪz] *pl.* помеще́ние
premium ['priːmɪəm] (*reward*) награ́-
да; *payment* пре́мия; **at a ~** вы́ше но-
мина́льной сто́имости; в большо́м
спро́се
premonition [preːmə'nɪʃn] пред-
чу́вствие
preoccup|ied [priː'ɒkjupaɪd] оза-

бо́ченный; **~y** [-paɪ] поглоща́ть внима́-
ние (Р); занима́ться [-ня́ться] (**with**
Т)
prepaid [priː'peɪd] зара́нее
опла́ченный; **carriage ~** доста́вка
опла́чена
preparat|ion [prepə'reɪʃn] приготов-
ле́ние; подгото́вка; *med.* препара́т;
~ory [prɪ'pærətrɪ] предвари́тельный;
подготови́тельный; **~ to leaving** пе́-
ред тем как уйти́
prepare [prɪ'peə] *v/t. of surprise, etc.*
пригота́вливать [-то́вить]; *of dinner,
etc.* [при]гото́вить; (*for an exam, etc.*)
подгота́вливать [-то́вить]; *v/i.* [при]-
гото́виться; подгота́вливаться [-то́-
виться] (**for** к Д); **~d** [-d] □ гото́вый;
подгото́вленный
prepondera|nce [prɪ'pɒndərəns] пе-
реве́с; **~nt** [-rənt] име́ющий переве́с;
~ntly [-lɪ] преиму́щественно
prepossessing [priːpə'zesɪŋ] □ рас-
полага́ющий; привлека́тельный
preposterous [prɪ'pɒstərəs] неле́пый,
абсу́рдный
prerequisite [priː'rekwɪzɪt] предпо-
сы́лка, непреме́нное усло́вие
presage ['presɪdʒ] предвеща́ть; пред-
чу́вствовать
preschool [priː'skuːl] дошко́льный
prescribe [prɪ'skraɪb] предпи́сывать
[-писа́ть]; *med.* пропи́сывать [-пи-
са́ть]
prescription [prɪ'skrɪpʃn] предписы́-
вание; распоряже́ние; *med.* реце́пт
presence ['prezns] прису́тствие; **~ of
mind** прису́тствие ду́ха
present[1] ['preznt] **1.** □ прису́т-
ствующий; (*existing now*) тепе́решний,
настоя́щий; (*given*) да́нный; **2.** насто-
я́щее вре́мя; **at ~** сейча́с; в да́нное
вре́мя; **for the ~** пока́; на э́тот раз
present[2] [prɪ'zent] (*introduce, etc.*)
представля́ть [-а́вить]; *gift* преподно-
си́ть[-нести́]; *petition* под(ав)а́ть
(проше́ние); *a play* [по]ста́вить; *ticket*
предъявля́ть [-ви́ть]
present[3] ['preznt] пода́рок
presentation [prezn'teɪʃn] представ-
ле́ние, презента́ция; (*exposition*) из-

ложе́ние
presentiment [prɪ'zentɪmənt] предчу́вствие

presently ['prezntlɪ] вско́ре; сейча́с

preservati|on [prezə'veɪʃn] охра́на, сохране́ние; сохра́нность *f*; **~ve** [prɪ'zɜːvətɪv] консерва́нт

preserve [prɪ'zɜːv] 1. сохраня́ть [-ни́ть]; предохраня́ть [-ни́ть]; *vegetables, etc.* консерви́ровать; 2. (*mst. pl.*) консе́рвы *m/pl.*; варе́нье; (*game* ~) запове́дник

preside [prɪ'zaɪd] председа́тельствовать (*over* на П)

presiden|cy ['prezɪdənsɪ] президе́нтство; **~t** [-dənt] президе́нт

press [pres] 1. печа́ть *f*, пре́сса; (*crowd*) толпа́; *coll.* да́вка; *tech.* пресс; 2. *v/t.* жать; дави́ть; *button* наж(и)ма́ть; (*force*) навя́зывать [-за́ть] (*on* Д); *I am ~ed for time* меня́ поджима́ют сро́ки; у меня́ ма́ло вре́мени; **~ for** наста́ивать [настоя́ть] на (П); **~ on** дви́гаться да́льше; **~ card** журнали́стское удостовере́ние; **~ing** ['presɪŋ] сро́чный, неотло́жный; (*insistent*) настоя́тельный; **~ure** ['preʃə] давле́ние (*a. fig.*); сжа́тие

prestig|e [pre'stiːʒ] прести́ж; **~ious** [pre'stɪdʒəs] (*having prestige*) влия́тельный; *hono(u)red* уважа́емый

presum|able [prɪ'zjuːməbl] предположи́тельный; **~e** [prɪ'zjuːm] *v/t.* предполага́ть [-ложи́ть]; *v/i.* полага́ть; (*dare*) осме́ли(ва)ться; **~ (up)on** злоупотребля́ть [-би́ть] (Т); *he ~s too much* он сли́шком мно́го себе́ позволя́ет

presumpt|ion [prɪ'zʌmpʃn] предположе́ние; *law* презу́мпция; **~uous** [-tʃʊəs] самонадея́нный, переступа́ющий грани́цы чего́-л.

presuppos|e [priːsə'pəʊz] предполага́ть [-ложи́ть]; **~ition** [priːsʌpə'zɪʃn] предположе́ние

pretend [prɪ'tend] притворя́ться [-ри́ться]; [с]де́лать вид

pretense, *Brt.* **pretence** [prɪ'tens] (*false show*) притво́рство; (*pretext*) предло́г

preten|sion [prɪ'tenʃn] прете́нзия, притяза́ние (*to* на В); **~tious** [-ʃəs] претенцио́зный

pretext ['priːtekst] предло́г

pretty ['prɪtɪ] 1. □ краси́вый; прия́тный; хоро́шенький; 2. *adv.* дово́льно, весьма́; *be sitting ~* хорошо́ устро́ился

prevail [prɪ'veɪl] одолева́ть [-ле́ть] (*over* В); преоблада́ть; превали́ровать; (*over* над Т *or* среди́ Р); **~ (up)on s.b. to do s.th.** убеди́ть *pf.* кого́-л. что́-л. сде́лать; **~ing** [-ɪŋ] госпо́дствующий, преоблада́ющий

prevalent ['prevələnt] □ распространённый

prevaricate [prɪ'værɪkeɪt] уклоня́ться от прямо́го отве́та, уви́ливать [-льну́ть]

prevent [prɪ'vent] предотвраща́ть [-ати́ть]; (*hinder*) [по]меша́ть (Д); *crime* предупрежда́ть [-упреди́ть]; **~ion** [prɪ'venʃn] предупрежде́ние; предотвраще́ние; **~ive** [-tɪv] 1. □ предупреди́тельный; профилакти́ческий; 2. *med.* профилакти́ческое сре́дство

pre|view ['priːvjuː] *of film, etc* предвари́тельный просмо́тр

previous ['priːvɪəs] □ предыду́щий; (*premature*) преждевре́менный; **~ to** до (Р); **~ly** [-lɪ] пре́жде (Р); пе́ред (Т)

prewar ['priː'wɔː] довое́нный

prey [preɪ] 1. добы́ча; (*fig., victim*) же́ртва; *beast* (*bird*) *of* ~ хи́щный зверь *m.* (хи́щная пти́ца); 2.: **~ (up)on** охо́титься (на В); *fig.* терза́ть

price [praɪs] 1. цена́; 2. (*value*) оце́нивать [-ни́ть]; назнача́ть це́ну (Д); **~less** ['-lɪs] бесце́нный

prick [prɪk] 1. уко́л; шип; *of conscience* угрызе́ния *n/pl.*; 2. *v/t.* коло́ть [кольну́ть]; **~ up one's ears** навостри́ть у́ши; *v/i.* коло́ться; **~le** ['prɪkl] шип, колю́чка; **~ly** ['-lɪ] (*having prickles or thorns*) колю́чий; (*causing stinging sensation*) ко́лкий; (*touchy*) оби́дчивый

pride [praɪd] 1. го́рдость *f*; *take* ~ *in* горди́ться (Т); 2.: ~ *o.s.* горди́ться ([*up*]*on* Т)

priest [pri:st] свяще́нник

prim [prim] □ чо́порный

prima|cy ['praiməsi] пе́рвенство; **~ry** [-ri] первонача́льный; *colours, etc.* основно́й; нача́льный; *geol.* перви́чный; *of ~ importance* первостепе́нной ва́жности

prime [praim] 1. □ *(main)* гла́вный, основно́й; *(original)* первонача́льный; перви́чный; *(excellent)* превосхо́дный; **~ minister** премье́рмини́стр; 2. *fig.* расцве́т; *in one's ~* в расцве́те сил; 3. *v/t.* снабжа́ть информа́цией; ната́скивать

primer ['praimə] *(schoolbook)* буква́рь *m*; *(paint)* грунто́вка

primeval [prai'mi:vl] □ первобы́тный

primitive ['primitiv] первобы́тный; примити́вный

primrose ['primrəuz] при́мула

prince [prins] *(son of royalty)* принц; князь *m*; **~ss** [prin'ses] *(daughter of sovereign)* принце́сса; *(wife of nonroyal prince)* княги́ня; *(daughter of nonroyal prince and princess)* княжна́

principal ['prinsəpl] 1. □ гла́вный, основно́й; 2. *univ.* ре́ктор; *of school* дире́ктор шко́лы; *fin.* основно́й капита́л; *thea.* веду́щий актёр

principle ['prinsəpl] при́нцип; пра́вило; *on ~* из при́нципа; *a matter of ~* де́ло при́нципа

print [print] 1. *typ.* печа́ть *f*; о́ттиск; *(type)* шрифт; *(imprint)* след, отпеча́ток *(a. photo)*; *art* гравю́ра; *out of ~* тиражо́м распро́дан; 2. *v/t.* [на-]печа́тать; *phot.* отпеча́т(ыв)ать; *fig.* запечатле́(ва́)ть *(on* на П); **~er** ['printə] печа́тник; *comput.* при́нтер

printing ['printiŋ] печа́тание; печа́тное де́ло; **~ of 50,000 copies** тира́ж в 50 000 экземпля́ров; *attr.* печа́тный; **~ office** типогра́фия

prior ['praiə] 1. предше́ствующий *(to* Д); 2. *adv.:* **~ to** до (Р); **~ity** [prai'prəti] приорите́т; очерёдность *f*; *of top ~* первостепе́нной ва́жности

prism ['prizəm] при́зма

prison ['prizn] тюрьма́; **~er** [-ə] заключённый; *(~ of war)* военнопле́нный

privacy ['praivəsi] *(seclusion)* уедине́ние; ли́чная/ча́стная жизнь

private ['praivit] 1. □ ча́стный; *(personal)* ли́чный; *(secluded)* уединённый; *conversation* с гла́зу на глаз; 2. *mil.* рядово́й; *in ~* конфиденциа́льно; *keep s.th. ~* держа́ть в та́йне

privation [prai'veiʃn] лише́ние, нужда́

privatize ['praivitaiz] приватизи́ровать

privilege ['privilidʒ] привиле́гия; льго́та; **~d** привилегиро́ванный

privy ['privi]: **~ to** посвящённый в (В)

prize¹ [praiz]: **~ open** вскрыва́ть [-ры́ть], взла́мывать [-лома́ть]

prize² [-] 1. пре́мия, приз; трофе́й; *in lottery* вы́игрыш; 2. удосто́енный пре́мии; 3. высоко́ цени́ть; **~fighter** боксёр-профессиона́л; **~ winner** призёр; лауреа́т

pro [prəu] *pl.* **pros:** **the ~s and cons** до́воды за и про́тив

probab|ility [prɒbə'biləti] вероя́тность *f*; **~le** ['prɒbəbl] вероя́тный

probation [prə'beiʃn] испыта́тельный срок; *law* усло́вное освобожде́ние

probe [prəub] *med.* 1. зонд; 2. зонди́ровать; *into problem* глубоко́ изуча́ть [-чи́ть]

problem ['prɒbləm] пробле́ма; вопро́с; *(difficulty)* тру́дность *f*; зада́ча; **~atic(al** □) [prɒblə'mætik(əl)] проблемати́чный

procedure [prə'si:dʒə] процеду́ра

proceed [prə'si:d] отправля́ться да́льше; приступа́ть [-пи́ть] *(to* к Д); *(act)* поступа́ть [-пи́ть]; продолжа́ть [-до́лжить] *(with* В); **~ from** исходи́ть из (Р); **~ing** [-iŋ] посту́пок; **~s** *pl. law* судопроизво́дство; *(scientific publication)* запи́ски *f/pl.,* труды́ *m/pl.;* **~s** ['prəusi:dz] дохо́д, вы́ручка

process ['prəuses] 1. проце́сс *(a. law);* *in the ~* в хо́де; *in the ~ of construction* стро́ящийся; 2. *tech.* обраба́тывать [-бо́тать]; **~ing** [-iŋ] *of data, etc.* обрабо́тка; *of food* перерабо́тка; **~ion** [-ʃn] проце́ссия; **~or** [-ə] *comput.* проце́ссор

proclaim [prə'kleɪm] провозглаша́ть [-ласи́ть]; *war, etc.* объявля́ть [-ви́ть]

proclamation [prɒklə'meɪʃn] объявле́ние, провозглаше́ние

procrastinate [prəʊ'kræstɪneɪt] (*delay*) *v/i.* оття́гивать [-яну́ть], (*put off*) откла́дывать [отложи́ть]; (*drag out*) тяну́ть

procure [prə'kjʊə] *v/t.* дост(ав)а́ть

prod [prɒd] **1.** тычо́к, толчо́к; **2.** ты́кать (ткнуть); толка́ть [-кну́ть], *fig.* подстрека́ть [-кну́ть]

prodigal ['prɒdɪgl] расточи́тельный; *the ♀ Son* блу́дный сын

prodig|ious [prə'dɪdʒəs] □ удиви́тельный; (*huge*) грома́дный; **~y** ['prɒdɪdʒɪ] чу́до; *child* ~ вундерки́нд

produc|e 1. [prə'dju:s] (*show*) предъявля́ть [-ви́ть]; (*proof, etc.*) представля́ть [-а́вить]; производи́ть [-вести́]; *film, etc.* [по]ста́вить; *sound* изд(ав)а́ть; **2.** ['prɒdju:s] проду́кция, проду́кт; **~er** [prə'dju:sə] *of goods* производи́тель *m*; *thea.* режиссёр; *cine.* продю́сер

product ['prɒdʌkt] проду́кт; изде́лие; **~ion** [prə'dʌkʃn] произво́дство; проду́кция; *thea.* постано́вка; *mass* ~ ма́ссовое произво́дство; **~ive** [prə'dʌktɪv] □ производи́тельный, *fig.* продукти́вный; *soil* плодоро́дный; *writer* плодови́тый; **~ivity** [prɒdʌk'tɪvətɪ] (*efficiency*) продукти́вность *f*, (*rate of production*) производи́тельность *f*

profane [prə'feɪn] (*desecrate*) оскверня́ть [-ни́ть]

profess [prə'fes] (*declare*) заявля́ть [-ви́ть]; (*claim*) претендова́ть на (В); *I don't* ~ *to be an expert on this subject* я не счита́ю себя́ специали́стом в э́той о́бласти; **~ion** [prə'feʃn] профе́ссия; **~ional 1.** □ профессиона́льный; **2.** специали́ст; профессиона́л (*a. sport*); **~or** [-sə] профе́ссор

proffer ['prɒfə] предлага́ть [-ложи́ть]

proficien|cy [prə'fɪʃnsɪ] овладе́ние; о́пытность *f*; уме́ние; **~t** [-ʃnt] □ уме́лый, иску́сный

profile ['prəʊfaɪl] про́филь *m*

profit ['prɒfɪt] **1.** *comm.* при́быль *f*;

вы́года, по́льза; *gain* ~ *from* извле́чь *pf.* по́льзу из (Р); **2.** *v/t.* приноси́ть по́льзу (Д); *v/i.* ~ *by* [вос]по́льзоваться (Т); извлека́ть по́льзу из (Р); **~able** [-əbl] при́быльный; вы́годный; поле́зный; **~eer** [prɒfɪ'tɪə] спекуля́нт; **sharing** уча́стие в при́были

profound [prə'faʊnd] □ глубо́кий; (*thorough*) основа́тельный; **~ly** о́чень, глубоко́

profus|e [prə'fju:s] □ оби́льный; ще́дрый; **~ion** [prə'fju:ʒn] изоби́лие

progeny ['prɒdʒənɪ] пото́мство

prognosis [prɒg'nəʊsɪs] прогно́з

program(me) ['prəʊgræm] **1.** програ́мма; **2.** программи́ровать; *comput.* **~er** [-ə] программи́ст

progress 1. ['prəʊgres] прогре́сс; продвиже́ние; *in studies* успе́хи *m/pl.*; *be in* ~ развива́ться, вести́сь; **2.** [prə'gres] продвига́ться вперёд; [с]де́лать успе́хи; **~ive** [-sɪv] □ передово́й, прогресси́вный; *illness, disease* прогресси́рующий; ~ *taxation* прогресси́вный нало́г

prohibit [prə'hɪbɪt] запреща́ть [-ети́ть]; **~ion** [prəʊɪ'bɪʃn] запреще́ние; **~ive** [prə'hɪbətɪv] □ запрети́тельный

project 1. ['prɒdʒekt] прое́кт (*a. arch.*); план; **2.** [prə'dʒekt] *v/t. light* броса́ть [бро́сить]; (*plan*) [с-, за]проекти́ровать; *v/i.* (*jut out*) выда(ва́)ться; **~ile** [prə'dʒektaɪl] снаря́д

prolific [prə'lɪfɪk] (**~ally**) *writer, etc.* плодови́тый

prolix ['prəʊlɪks] □ многосло́вный

prologue ['prəʊlɒg] проло́г

prolong [prə'lɒŋ] продлева́ть [-ли́ть]; *law* пролонги́ровать

promenade [prɒmə'nɑːd] **1.** прогу́лка; ме́сто для прогу́лки; *along waterfront* на́бережная; *in park* алле́я; **2.** прогу́ливаться [-ля́ться]

prominent ['prɒmɪnənt] (*conspicuous*) □ ви́дный, заме́тный; (*jutting out*) выступа́ющий; *fig.* (*outstanding*) выдаю́щийся

promiscuous [prə'mɪskjʊəs] □ неразбо́рчивый; огу́льный; *sexually* сексуа́льно распу́щенный

promis|e ['prɒmɪs] 1. обеща́ние; *make a ~* [по]обеща́ть; *show great ~* подава́ть больши́е наде́жды; 2. обеща́ть (*im*)*pf.*, *pf. a.* [по-]; **~ing** [-ɪŋ] □ *fig.* перспекти́вный; подаю́щий наде́жды

promontory ['prɒməntrɪ] мыс

promot|e [prə'məʊt] (*further*) спо-со́бствовать (*im*)*pf.*, *pf. a.* [по-] (Д); соде́йствовать (*im*)*pf.*, *pf. a.* [по-] (Д); (*establish*) учрежда́ть [-ди́ть]; (*advance in rank, station, etc.*) повыша́ть по слу́жбе; *mil.* присво́ить (очередно́е) зва́ние (Р); **~ion** [prə'məʊʃn] *in position* повыше́ние; продвиже́ние

prompt [prɒmpt] 1. □ бы́стрый; *reply* неме́дленный; 2. побужда́ть [-уди́ть]; внуша́ть [-ши́ть]; (*suggest*) подска́зывать [-за́ть] (Д); **~ness** ['prɒmptnɪs] быстрота́; прово́рство

promulgate ['prɒmʌlgeɪt] обнаро́довать; провозглаша́ть [-аси́ть]

prone [prəʊn] □ (*face down*) (лежа́щий) ничко́м; **~ to** скло́нный к (Д); *he is ~ to colds* он легко́ простужа́ется

prong [prɒŋ] *agric.* **~s** *pl.* ви́лы *f/pl.*

pronounce [prə'naʊns] (*articulate*) произноси́ть [-нести́]; (*proclaim*) объявля́ть [-ви́ть]; (*declare*) заявля́ть [-ви́ть]

pronunciation [prənʌnsɪ'eɪʃn] произноше́ние

proof [pruːf] 1. доказа́тельство; (*test*) испыта́ние; прове́рка; *typ.* корректу́ра; 2. (*impervious*) непроница́емый; **~reader** корре́ктор

prop [prɒp] 1. подпо́рка; *fig.* опо́ра; 2. подпира́ть [-пере́ть]; **~ against** приста́влять [-вить] к (Д); прислони́ть

propagate ['prɒpəgeɪt] размножа́ть(ся) [-о́жить(ся)]; (*spread*) распространя́ть(ся) [-ни́ть(ся)]

propel [prə'pel] продвига́ть вперёд; **~ s.o. towards** подтолкну́ть *pf.* кого́-л. к (Д); **~ler** [-ə] пропе́ллер; *naut.* гребно́й винт

propensity [prə'pensətɪ] предрас-

положенность *f*; скло́нность *f*

proper ['prɒpə] □ (*own, peculiar*) сво́йственный, прису́щий; подходя́щий; пра́вильный; (*decent, seemly*) прили́чный; **~ty** [-tɪ] со́бственность *f*; (*quality*) сво́йство; *intellectual ~* интеллектуа́льная со́бственность

prophe|cy ['prɒfəsɪ] проро́чество; **~sy** [-saɪ] [на]проро́чить

prophet ['prɒfɪt] проро́к

prophylactic [prɒfɪ'læktɪk] 1. профилакти́ческий; 2. профила́ктика

proportion [prə'pɔːʃn] 1. пропо́рция; соразме́рность *f*; (*size*) до́ля, часть *f*; **~s** *pl.* разме́ры *m/pl*; 2. соразмеря́ть [-ме́рить]; **~al** [-l] пропорциона́льный

propos|al [prə'pəʊzl] предложе́ние; **~e** [prə'pəʊz] *v/t.* предлага́ть [-ложи́ть]; *v/i. marriage* сде́лать *pf.* предложе́ние; (*intend*) намерева́ться, предполага́ть; **~ition** [prɒpə'zɪʃn] (*offer*) предложе́ние

propound [prə'paʊnd] предлага́ть на обсужде́ние, выдвига́ть [-инуть]

propriet|ary [prə'praɪətrɪ]: **~ rights** права́ со́бственности; **~ name** фи́рменное назва́ние; **~or** [-ətə] владе́лец *m*, -лица *f*; **~y** [-ətɪ] уме́стность *f*, присто́йность *f*

propulsion [prə'pʌlʃn] движе́ние вперёд

prosaic [prə'zeɪk] (**~ally**) *fig.* проза́ичный

prose [prəʊz] 1. про́за; 2. проза́ический; *fig.* проза́ичный

prosecut|e ['prɒsɪkjuːt] пресле́довать в суде́бном поря́дке; **~ion** [prɒsɪ'kjuːʃn] суде́бное разбира́тельство; **~or** ['prɒsɪkjuːtə] *law* обвини́тель *m*; *public ~* прокуро́р

prospect 1. ['prɒspekt] перспекти́ва, вид (*a. fig.*); 2. [prə'spekt] *geol.* разве́д(ыв)ать (*for* на В); **~ive** [prə'spektɪv] □ бу́дущий, ожида́емый; **~us** [-təs] проспе́кт

prosper ['prɒspə] *v/i.* процвета́ть; преуспева́ть; **~ity** [prɒ'sperətɪ] процвета́ние; благополу́чие; *fig.* расцвет; **~ous** ['prɒspərəs] состоя́тельный; процвета́ющий

prostitute ['prɒstɪtjuːt] проститу́тка

prostrat|e ['prɒstreɪt] (*lying flat*) распростёртый; (*without srength*) обесси́ленный; **~** *with grief* сло́мленный го́рем; **~ion** [-ʃn] *fig.* изнеможе́ние

prosy ['prəʊzɪ] □ *fig.* прозаи́чный; бана́льный

protect [prə'tekt] защища́ть [-ити́ть]; [пред]охраня́ть [-ни́ть] (*from* от P); **~ion** [prə'tekʃn] защи́та; **~ive** [-tɪv] защи́тный; предохрани́тельный; **~or** [-tə] защи́тник; (*patron*) покрови́тель *m*

protest 1. ['prəʊtest] проте́ст; 2. [prə'test] *v/t.* (*declare*) заявля́ть [-ви́ть], утвержда́ть; *v/i.* [за]протестова́ть

Protestant ['prɒtɪstənt] 1. протеста́нт *m*, -ка *f*; 2. протеста́нтский

protestation [prɒtə'steɪʃn] торже́ственное заявле́ние

protocol ['prəʊtəkɒl] протоко́л (*a. dipl.*)

prototype ['prəʊtətaɪp] прототи́п

protract [prə'trækt] тяну́ть (В *or* с Т); продолжа́ть [-до́лжить]; **~ed** затяжно́й

protru|de [prə'truːd] выдава́ться нару́жу, торча́ть; **~ding** [-ɪŋ] выступа́ющий; **~** *eyes* глаза́ навы́кате; **~sion** [-ʒn] вы́ступ

protuberance [prə'tjuːbərəns] вы́пуклость *f*

proud [praʊd] □ го́рдый (*of* Т)

prove [pruːv] *v/t.* дока́зывать [-за́ть]; *v/i.*; **~ o.s. to be** ока́зываться [-за́ться]

proverb ['prɒvɜːb] посло́вица

provide [prə'vaɪd] *v/t.* снабжа́ть [-бди́ть]; предоставля́ть [-а́вить]; *law* ста́вить усло́вием; предусма́тривать [-мотре́ть]; *v/i.*: **~** *for one's family* обеспе́чивать [-чить] свою́ семью́; **~d** (*that*) при усло́вии (что)

providen|ce ['prɒvɪdəns] провиде́ние; (*prudence*) предусмотри́тельность *f*; **~t** [-dənt] □ предусмотри́тельный

provin|ce ['prɒvɪns] о́бласть *f*; прови́нция; *fig.* сфе́ра де́ятельности;

~cial [prə'vɪnʃl] 1. провинциа́льный; 2. провинциа́л *m*, -ка *f*

provision [prə'vɪʒn] снабже́ние; обеспе́чение; *law of contract, etc.* положе́ние; **~s** *pl.* проду́кты; **~al** [-ʒnl] □ предвари́тельный; ориентиро́вочный; вре́менный

proviso [prə'vaɪzəʊ] усло́вие

provocat|ion [prɒvə'keɪʃn] вы́зов; провока́ция; **~ive** [prə'vɒkətɪv] *behaviour* вызыва́ющий; *question, etc.* провокацио́нный

provoke [prə'vəʊk] (с)провоци́ровать; (*stir up*) возбужда́ть [-буди́ть]; (*cause*) вызыва́ть [вы́звать]; (*make angry*) [рас]серди́ть

prowl [praʊl] кра́сться; броди́ть

proximity [prɒk'sɪmətɪ] бли́зость *f*

proxy ['prɒksɪ] (*authorization*) полномо́чие; (*substitute*) замести́тель; **~ vote** голосова́ние по дове́ренности; дове́ренность *f*

prude [pruːd] ханжа́

pruden|ce ['pruːdns] благоразу́мие; (*forethought*) предусмотри́тельность *f*; осторо́жность *f*; **~t** [-nt] □ благоразу́мный; осторо́жный; **~ housekeeper** бережли́вая хозя́йка

prudery ['pruːdərɪ] ханжество

prune¹ [pruːn] черносли́в

prune² [-] *agric.* подреза́ть [-ре́зать], обреза́ть [обре́зать]; *fig.* сокраща́ть [-рати́ть]

pry¹ [praɪ] подгля́дывать [-яде́ть]; **~ into** сова́ть нос в (В)

pry² [-]: *Am.* **~ open** → *prize¹*

psalm [sɑːm] псало́м

pseudonym ['sjuːdənɪm] псевдони́м

psychiatrist [saɪ'kaɪətrɪst] психиа́тр

psychic ['saɪkɪk], **~al** [-kɪkl] □ психи́ческий

psycholog|ical [saɪkə'lɒdʒɪkl] психологи́ческий; **~ist** [saɪ'kɒlədʒɪst] психо́лог; **~y** [-dʒɪ] психоло́гия

pub [pʌb] паб, пивно́й бар

puberty ['pjuːbətɪ] полова́я зре́лость *f*

public ['pʌblɪk] 1. □ публи́чный, обще́ственный; госуда́рственный; коммуна́льный; **~ convenience** общéственный туале́т; ~ *figure* госуда́рственный де́ятель; ~ *opinion* обще́ственное мне́ние; ~ *house* пивна́я; ~ *spirit* обще́ственное созна́ние; 2. пу́блика; обще́ственность f; ~*ation* [pʌblɪ'keɪʃn] опубликова́ние; изда́ние; *monthly* ~ ежеме́сячник; ~*ity* [pʌb'lɪsətɪ] гла́сность f; (*advertising*) рекла́ма

publish ['pʌblɪʃ] [о]публикова́ть, изд(ав)а́ть; оглаша́ть [огласи́ть]; ~*ing house* изда́тельство; ~*er* [-ə] изда́тель m; ~*s* pl. изда́тельство

pucker ['pʌkə] 1. [с]мо́рщить(ся); *frown* [на]сму́пить(ся); 2. морщи́на

pudding ['pʊdɪŋ] пу́динг; *black* ~ кровяна́я колбаса́

puddle ['pʌdl] лу́жа

puff [pʌf] 1. *of wind* дунове́ние; *of smoke* клуб; 2. v/t. (~ *out*) наду́(ва́)ть; ~*ed eyes* распу́хшие глаза́ m/pl.; v/i. дуть поры́вами; пыхте́ть; ~ *away at* попы́хивать (T); ~ *out* наду́(ва́)ться; ~*paste* слоёное те́сто; ~*y* ['pʌfɪ] запыха́вшийся; *eyes* отёкший; *face* одутлова́тый

pug [pʌg]: ~ *dog* мопс

pugnacious [pʌg'neɪʃəs] драчли́вый

pug-nosed ['pʌgnəʊzd] курно́сый

puke [pjuːk] 1. рво́та; 2. v/i. [вы]рвать

pull [pʊl] 1. тя́га (a. fig.); (*inhalation of smoke*) затя́жка; 2. [по]тяну́ть; (*drag*) таска́ть, [по]тащи́ть (~ *out*) выдёргивать [вы́дернуть]; (*tug*) дёргать [-рнуть]; ~ *down* (*demolish*) сноси́ть [снести́]; ~ *out* (*move away*) отойти́); *med.* ~ *through* fig. спаса́ть [-сти́]; (*recover*) поправля́ться [-а́виться]; ~ *o.s. together* взять pf. себя́ в ру́ки; ~ *up* подтя́гивать [-яну́ть]; *car, etc.* остана́вливать(ся) [-нови́ть(ся)]

pulley ['pʊlɪ] tech. блок; шкив

pullover ['pʊləʊvə] пуло́вер

pulp [pʌlp] *of fruit* мя́коть f; *of wood* древе́сная ма́сса; fig. бесфо́рменная ма́сса

pulpit ['pʊlpɪt] ка́федра

puls|ate [pʌl'seɪt] пульси́ровать; би́ться; ~*e* [pʌls] пульс; tech. и́мпульс

pumice ['pʌmɪs] пе́мза

pummel ['pʌml] [по]колоти́ть, [по]би́ть

pump [pʌmp] 1. насо́с; 2. кача́ть; ~ *out* выка́чивать [вы́качать]; ~ *up* нака́чивать [-ча́ть]

pumpkin ['pʌmpkɪn] ты́ква

pun [pʌn] 1. каламбу́р; игра́ слов; 2. [с]каламбу́рить

punch [pʌntʃ] 1. tech. пробо́йник; *for perforating* компо́стер; (*blow with fist*) уда́р кулако́м; 2. ~ *hole* проби́(ва́)ть; [про]компости́ровать; (*hit with fist*) бить кулако́м

punctilious [pʌŋk'tɪlɪəs] педанти́чный; щепети́льный до мелоче́й

punctual ['pʌŋktʃʊəl] □ пунктуа́льный; ~*ity* [pʌŋktʃʊ'ælətɪ] пунктуа́льность f

punctuat|e ['pʌŋktʃʊeɪt] ста́вить зна́ки препина́ния; fig. прерыва́ть [-рва́ть]; ~*ion* [pʌŋktʃʊ'eɪʃn] пунктуа́ция; ~ *mark* знак препина́ния

puncture ['pʌŋktʃə] 1. *tyre* прокол; *med.* пу́нкция; 2. прока́лывать [-коло́ть]

pungen|cy ['pʌndʒənsɪ] острота́, е́дкость f; ~*t* [-nt] о́стрый, е́дкий (a. fig.)

punish ['pʌnɪʃ] нака́зывать [-за́ть]; ~*able* [-əbl] наказу́емый; ~*ment* [-mənt] наказа́ние

puny ['pjuːnɪ] кро́хотный; тщеду́шный

pupil[1] ['pjuːpl] *of eye* зрачо́к

pupil[2] [-] учени́к m, -и́ца f

puppet ['pʌpɪt] ку́кла, марионе́тка (a. fig.); ~ *show* ку́кольное представле́ние

puppy ['pʌpɪ] щено́к; coll. (*greenhorn*) молокосо́с

purchas|e ['pɜːtʃəs] 1. поку́пка, заку́пка; 2. покупа́ть [купи́ть]; приобрета́ть [-рести́]; ~*er* [-ə] покупа́тель m, -ница f; ~*ing* [-ɪŋ]: ~ *power* покупа́тельная спосо́бность

pure [pjʊə] □ чи́стый; ~*bred* ['pjʊəbred] чистокро́вный, поро́дистый

purgat|ive ['pɜːgətɪv] слаби́тельное; ~*ory* [-trɪ] чисти́лище

purge [pɜːdʒ] очища́ть [очи́стить]

purify ['pjʊərɪfaɪ] очища́ть [очи́стить]

purity ['pjʊərɪtɪ] чистота́

purl [pɜːl] *of water* журча́ть

purple ['pɜːpl] **1.** пурпу́рный; багро́вый; **2.** *turn* ~ [по]багрове́ть

purport ['pɜːpət] смысл, суть *f*

purpose ['pɜːpəs] **1.** наме́рение, цель *f*; целеустремлённость *f*; *on* ~ наме́ренно, наро́чно; *to the* ~ кста́ти; к де́лу; *to no* ~ напра́сно; **2.** име́ть це́лью; намерева́ться [наме́риться]; ~**ful** [-fl] □ целеустремлённый; целеустремлённый; ~**less** [-lɪs] □ бесце́льный; ~**ly** [-lɪ] наро́чно

purr [pɜː] [за]мурлы́кать

purse [pɜːs] **1.** кошелёк; *Am.* (*handbag*) су́мочка; *public* ~ казна́; **2.** *lips* поджима́ть [-жа́ть]

pursuance [pə'sjuːəns]: выполне́ние; *in* (*the*) ~ *of one's duty* приисполне́нии свои́х обя́занностей

pursu|e [pə'sjuː]: (*go after*) пресле́довать (В); (*work at*) занима́ться [заня́ться] (Т); (*continue*) продолжа́ть [-до́лжить]; ~**er** [-ə] пресле́дователь *m*, -ница *f*; ~**it** [pə'sjuːt] пресле́дование; пого́ня *f*; *mst.* ~**s** *pl.* заня́тие

pus [pʌs] *med.* гной

push [pʊʃ] **1.** толчо́к; (*pressure*) давле́ние; напо́р; (*effort*) уси́лие; *of person* напо́ристость *f*; *at a* ~ при необходи́мости; **2.** толка́ть [-кну́ть]; нажи(м)а́ть (на В); продвига́ть(ся) [-ви́нуть(ся)] (*a.* ~ *on*); ~ *into* *fig.* заставля́ть [-а́вить]; ~ *one's way* прота́лкиваться [протолка́ться]; ~**button** *el.* нажи́мная кно́пка; ~**chair** де́тская *or* прогу́лочная (*invalid's* инвали́дная) коля́ска

puss(y) ['pʊs(ɪ)] ко́шечка, ки́ска

put [pʊt] [*irr.*] **1.** класть [положи́ть]; [по]ста́вить; сажа́ть; [по]сади́ть; *question, etc.* зад(ав)а́ть; *into pocket, etc.* сова́ть [су́нуть]; (*express*) выража́ть

[-азить]; (*explain*) объясня́ть [-ни́ть]; ~ *across a river, etc.* перевози́ть [-везти́]; ~ *back* ста́вить на ме́сто; ста́вить наза́д; ~ *by money* откла́дывать [отложи́ть]; ~ *down* (*rebellion*) подавля́ть [-ви́ть]; (*write down*) запи́сывать [-са́ть]; (*set down*) положи́ть, [по]ста́вить; (*attribute*) припи́сывать [-са́ть]; (*to* Д); ~ *forth* проявля́ть [-ви́ть]; *shoots* пуска́ть [пусти́ть]; ~ *in* вставля́ть [-а́вить]; всо́вывать [всу́нуть]; ~ *off* откла́дывать [отложи́ть]; ~ *on dress, etc.* наде(ва́)ть; (*feign*) притворя́ться; (*exaggerate*) преувели́чивать [-чить]; *weight* приба́вить [-а́вить]; ~ *out* выкла́дывать [вы́ложить]; (*extend*) протя́гивать [-тяну́ть]; *fire* [по]туши́ть; ~ *through* *tel.* соединя́ть [-ни́ть] (*to* С Т); ~ *to* приба́вить [-ба́вить]; ~ *to death* казни́ть (*im*)*pf.*; ~ *up building* [по]стро́ить, возводи́ть [-вести́]; *prices* повыша́ть [-ы́сить]; дава́ть [дать] приста́нище; **2.** *v/i.*: ~ *to sea* [вы]ходи́ть в мо́ре; ~ *in* *naut.* заходи́ть в порт; ~ *up at* остана́вливаться [останови́ться] в (П); ~ *up with* *fig.* мири́ться с (Т)

putrefy ['pjuːtrɪfaɪ] [с]гнить; разлага́ться [-ложи́ться]

putrid ['pjuːtrɪd] □ гнило́й; (*ill-smelling*) воню́чий

putty ['pʌtɪ] **1.** зама́зка; **2.** зама́з(ыв)ать

puzzle ['pʌzl] **1.** недоуме́ние; зага́дка, головоло́мка; *crossword* ~ кроссво́рд; **2.** *v/t.* озада́чи(ва)ть; ста́вить в тупи́к; ~ *out* разгада́ть распу́т(ыв)ать; *v/i.* би́ться (*over* над Т); ~**r** [-ə] *coll.* головоло́мка, кре́пкий оре́шек

pygmy ['pɪgmɪ] пигме́й

pyjamas [pə'dʒɑːməz] *pl.* пижа́ма

pyramid ['pɪrəmɪd] пирами́да

python ['paɪθn] пито́н

Q

quack¹ [kwæk] кря́кать [-кнуть]

quack² [-] (*sham doctor*) шарлата́н

quadrangle ['kwɒdræŋgl] четырёхуго́льник

quadru|ped ['kwɒdrʊped] четвероно́гое живо́тное; **~ple** ['kwɒdrʊpl] □ учетверённый

quagmire ['kwægmaɪə] тряси́на

quail [kweɪl] (*falter*) дро́гнуть *pf.*; (*funk*) [с]тру́сить

quaint [kweɪnt] причу́дливый, стра́нный, курьёзный

quake [kweɪk] [за]трясти́сь; [за-] дрожа́ть; дро́гнуть *pf.*; *stronger* содрога́ться [-гну́ться]

quali|fication [kwɒlɪfɪ'keɪʃn] квалифика́ция; (*restriction*) огово́рка, ограниче́ние; **~fy** ['kwɒlɪfaɪ] *v/t.* квалифици́ровать (*im*)*pf.*; огова́ривать [-вори́ть]; ограни́чи(ва)ть; (*modify*) уточня́ть [-ни́ть]; (*describe*) оце́нивать [-ни́ть] (*as* Т); *v/i.* подгота́вливаться [-гото́виться] (*for* к Д); **~ty** [-tɪ] ка́чество; сво́йство

qualm [kwɑːm] сомне́ние

quandary ['kwɒndərɪ]: *be in a* ~ не знать как поступи́ть

quantity ['kwɒntətɪ] коли́чество; *math.* величина́; мно́жество

quarantine ['kwɒrəntiːn] 1. каранти́н; 2. подверга́ть каранти́ну; содержа́ть в каранти́не

quarrel ['kwɒrəl] 1. ссо́ра, перебра́нка; 2. [по]ссо́риться; **~some** □ [-səm] сварли́вый

quarry ['kwɒrɪ] 1. карье́р, каменоло́мня; 2. добы́(ва́)ть, разраба́тывать

quart [kwɔːt] ква́рта

quarter ['kwɔːtə] 1. че́тверть *f*, четвёртая часть; (*three months*) кварта́л; (*place*) ме́сто, сторона́; ~s *pl. mil.* каза́рмы *f/pl.*; *fig.* исто́чники *m/pl.*; *from all* ~s со всех сторо́н; ~ *past two* че́тверть тре́тьего; 2. дели́ть на четы́ре ча́сти; (*give lodgings*) a. *mil.*

расквартиро́вывать [-ирова́ть]; **~ly** [-lɪ] 1. кварта́льный; 2. (*periodical*) ежекварта́льный журна́л

quartet(te) [kwɔː'tet] *mus.* кварте́т

quartz [kwɔːts] кварц; *attr.* ква́рцевый

quash [kwɒʃ] (*cancel*) отменя́ть, анну́ли́ровать (*im*)*pf.*; (*crush*) подавля́ть [-дави́ть]

quaver ['kweɪvə] 1. дрожь *f*; *mus.* восьма́я но́та; 2. говори́ть дрожа́щим го́лосом

quay [kiː] при́стань *f*

queasy ['kwiːzɪ] □ *I feel* ~ меня́ тошни́т

queen [kwiːn] короле́ва; *chess* ферзь *m*; *cards* да́ма

queer [kwɪə] стра́нный, эксцентри́чный; *sl.* (*a. su.*) гомосексуа́льный; гомосексуали́ст

quench [kwentʃ] *thirst* утоля́ть [-ли́ть]; *fire* [по]туши́ть; (*cool*) охлажда́ть [охлади́ть]

querulous ['kwerʊləs] □ ворчли́вый

query ['kwɪərɪ] 1. вопро́с; (*doubt*) сомне́ние; вопроси́тельный знак; 2. спра́шивать [спроси́ть]; выража́ть ['-разить] сомне́ние

quest [kwest] по́иски *m/pl.*; *in* ~ *of* в по́исках

question ['kwestʃən] 1. вопро́с; сомне́ние; пробле́ма; *beyond (all)* ~ вне вся́кого сомне́ния; *in* ~ о кото́ром идёт речь; *call into* ~ подверга́ть сомне́нию; *settle a* ~ реши́ть *pf.* вопро́с; *that is out of the* ~ об э́том не мо́жет быть и ре́чи; 2. расспра́шивать [-роси́ть]; задава́ть вопро́с (Д); (*interrogate*) допра́шивать [-проси́ть]; подверга́ть сомне́нию; **~able** [-əbl] сомни́тельный; **~naire** [kwestʃə'neə] анке́та; *for polls, etc.* вопро́сник

queue [kjuː] 1. о́чередь *f*, хвост; (*mst.* ~ *up*) станови́ться в о́чередь

quibble ['kwɪbl] 1. (*evasion*) увёртка; спор из-за пустяко́в; 2. (*evade*) уклоня́ться [-ни́ться]; (*argue*) спо́рить из-за пустяко́в

quick [kwɪk] **1.** (*lively*) живо́й; (*fast*) бы́стрый, ско́рый; *hands, etc.* прово́рный; *ear* о́стрый; *eye* зо́ркий; **2.** чувстви́тельное ме́сто; *cut to the ~* заде́вать за живо́е; **~en** ['kwɪkən] *v/t.* ускоря́ть [-о́рить]; (*liven*) оживля́ть [-ви́ть]; *v/i.* ускоря́ться [-о́риться]; оживля́ться [-ви́ться]; **~ness** ['kwɪknɪs] быстрота́; оживлённость *f*; *of mind* сообрази́тельность *f*; **~sand** зыбу́чий песо́к *m/pl.*; **~silver** ртуть *f*; **~witted** [-'wɪtɪd] нахо́дчивый

quiet ['kwaɪət] **1.** □ (*calm*) споко́йный, ти́хий; (*noiseless*) бесшу́мный; *keep s.th. ~* ума́лчивать [умолча́ть] (о П); **2.** поко́й; тишина́; *on the ~* тайко́м, втихомо́лку; **3.** успока́ивать(ся) [-ко́ить(ся)]

quill [kwɪl] пти́чье перо́; *of porcupine, etc.* игла́

quilt [kwɪlt] **1.** стёганое одея́ло; **2.** [вы́]стега́ть; **~ed** ['-ɪd] стёганый

quince [kwɪns] *fruit, tree* айва́

quinine [kwɪ'ni:n] *pharm.* хини́н

quintuple ['kwɪntjupl] пятикра́тный

quip [kwɪp] острота́; ко́лкость *f*

quirk [kwɜːk] причу́да

quit [kwɪt] **1.** покида́ть [-и́нуть]; оставля́ть [-а́вить]; (*stop*) прекраща́ть [-ати́ть]; *give notice to ~* под(ав)а́ть заявле́ние об ухо́де; **2.** свобо́дный, отде́лавшийся (*of* от Р)

quite [kwaɪt] вполне́, соверше́нно, совсе́м; (*rather*) дово́льно; *~ a hero* настоя́щий геро́й; *~ (so)!* так!, соверше́нно ве́рно!

quits [kwɪts]: *we are ~* мы с ва́ми кви́ты

quiver ['kwɪvə] [за]дрожа́ть, [за-] трепета́ть

quiz [kwɪz] **1.** (*interrogation*) опро́с; (*written or oral test*) прове́рка зна́ний; *entertainment* виктори́на; **2.** расспра́шивать [-роси́ть], опра́шивать [опроси́ть]

quizzical ['kwɪzɪkl] *look* насме́шливый

quorum ['kwɔːrəm] *parl.* кво́рум

quota ['kwəutə] до́ля, часть *f*, кво́та

quotation [kwəu'teɪʃn] цита́та; цити́рование

quote [kwəut] [про]цити́ровать

R

rabbi ['ræbaɪ] равви́н

rabbit ['ræbɪt] кро́лик

rabble ['ræbl] сброд; чернь *f*

rabid ['ræbɪd] □ неи́стовый, я́ростный; бе́шеный

rabies ['reɪbi:z] бе́шенство

race[1] [reɪs] ра́са; (*breed*) поро́да

race[2] [-] **1.** состяза́ние в ско́рости; бег; го́нки *f/pl.*; *horse ~s pl.* ска́чки *f/pl.*; бега́ *m/pl.*; **2.** (*move at speed*) [по]мча́ться; *compete* состяза́ться в ско́рости; уча́ствовать в ска́чках *и т.п.*; **~course** ипподро́м; **~track** *sport* трек; *for cars, etc.* автомотодро́м

racial ['reɪʃl] ра́совый

rack [ræk] **1.** ве́шалка; *for dishes* суши́лка; (*shelves*) стелла́ж, по́лка; *rail. luggage ~* се́тка для веще́й; *go to ~ and ruin* пойти́ пра́хом; погиба́ть [-и́бнуть]; разоря́ться [-ри́ться]; **2.** *~ one's brains* лома́ть себе́ го́лову

racket[1] ['rækɪt] те́ннисная раке́тка

racket[2] [-] шум, гам; *Am.* рэ́кет; **~eer** [rækə'tɪə] афери́ст; *Am.* вымога́тель *m*, рэкети́р

racy ['reɪsɪ] □ пика́нтный; колори́тный; риско́ванный

radar ['reɪdɑː] рада́р; радиолока́тор

radian|ce ['reɪdɪəns] сия́ние; **~t** [-nt] □ (*transmitted by radiation*) лучи́стый; (*shining, resplendent*) сия́ющий, лучеза́рный

radiat|e ['reɪdɪeɪt] излуча́ть [-чи́ть]; **~ion** [reɪdɪ'eɪʃn] излуче́ние; **~or** ['reɪdieitə] излучатель m; *mot.* радиатор; *for heating* батаре́я, радиа́тор

radical ['rædɪkl] 1. □ *pol.* радика́льный; (*fundamental*) коренно́й; 2. *math.* ко́рень m; *pol.* радика́л

radio ['reɪdɪəʊ] n *in indecl.*; ~ *show* радиопостано́вка; ~ *set* радиоприёмник; ~*therapy* рентгенотерапия; 2. передава́ть по ра́дио; ~*active* радиоакти́вный; ~*waste* радиоакти́вные отхо́ды; ~*activity* радиоакти́вность *f*; ~*graph* [-grɑ:f] рентге́новский сни́мок

radish ['rædɪʃ] ре́дька; (*red*) реди́ска; ~*es* pl. реди́с *collect.*

radius ['reɪdɪəs] ра́диус; *within a ~ of* в ра́диусе (P)

raffle ['ræfl] 1. *v/t.* разы́грывать в лотере́е; *v/i.* уча́ствовать в лотере́е; 2. лотере́я

raft [rɑ:ft] 1. плот; 2. *timber* сплавля́ть [-а́вить]; ~*er* [-ə] *arch.* стропи́ло

rag [ræg] тря́пка; ~*s* pl. тряпьё, ве́тошь *f*; лохмо́тья *m/pl.*

ragamuffin ['rægəmʌfɪn] оборва́нец; у́личный мальчи́шка

rage [reɪdʒ] 1. я́рость *f*, гнев; (*vogue*) пова́льное увлече́ние; *it is all the ~* э́то после́дний крик мо́ды; 2. [вз]беси́ться; *of storm, etc.* бушева́ть

ragged ['rægɪd] □ неро́вный; *clothes* рва́ный

ragout ['ræguː] *cul.* рагу́

raid [reɪd] 1. *mil.* налёт; *by police* обла́ва; 2. соверша́ть [-ши́ть] налёт на (B); *mil.* вторга́ться [вто́ргнуться] в (B)

rail[1] [reɪl] 1. (*hand~*) пери́ла *n/pl.*; (*fence*) огра́да; *rail* рельс; *naut.* по́ручень m; *fig.* сби́ться с pf. пути́; 2. е́хать по желе́зной доро́ге

rail[2] [-] [вы́]руга́ть, [вы́]брани́ть (*at, against* B)

railing ['reɪlɪŋ] огра́да; пери́ла *n/pl.*

railroad ['reɪlrəʊd] *chiefly Am.*, **railway** [-weɪ] желе́зная доро́га

rain [reɪn] 1. дождь m; 2. *it's ~ing* идёт дождь; *fig.* [по]сы́паться; ~*bow* ра́дуга; ~*coat* *Am.* дождеви́к, плащ; ~*fall*

коли́чество оса́дков; ~*y* ['reɪnɪ] дожди́вый; *fig.* **for a ~ day** на чёрный день m

raise [reɪz] (*often ~ up*) поднима́ть [-ня́ть]; *monument* воздвига́ть [-и́гнуть]; (*elevate*) возвыша́ть [-ы́сить]; (*bring up*) воспи́тывать [-ита́ть]; *laughter, suspicion, etc.* вызыва́ть [вы́звать]; *money* добы́(ва́)ть, собира́ть; *increase* повыша́ть [-вы́сить]

raisin ['reɪzn] изю́минка; *pl.* изю́м *collect.*

rake[1] [reɪk] 1. *agric.* гра́бли *f/pl.*; 2. *v/t.* сгреба́ть [-ести́]; разгреба́ть [-ести́]; *fig.* ~ *for* тща́тельно иска́ть (B *or* P)

rake[2] [-] пове́са, распу́тник

rally ['rælɪ] 1. (*gather*) собира́ть(ся [собра́ться]); *fig.* собра́ться pf. с си́лами; овладе́(ва́)ть собо́й (*rouse*) воодушевля́ть [-шеви́ть]; (*recover*) оправля́ться [опра́виться]; 2. *Am.* ма́ссовый ми́тинг; *sport* ра́лли

ram [ræm] 1. бара́н; *astr.* Ове́н; 2. [про]тара́нить; заби́(ва́)ть; ~ *home* вдолби́ть pf. в го́лову

rambl|e ['ræmbl] 1. прогу́лка; 2. (*wander*) броди́ть; (*speak incoherently*) говори́ть бессвя́зно; ~*er* [-ə] праздноша́тающийся; (*plant*) ползу́чее расте́ние; ~*ing* [-ɪŋ] бродя́чий; бессвя́зный; *town* беспоря́дочно разбро́санный; ползу́чий

ramify ['ræmɪfaɪ] развётвля́ться [-етви́ться]

ramp [ræmp] скат, укло́н; ~*ant* ['ræmpənt] *plants* бу́йный; *sickness, etc.* свире́пствующий; *fig.* (*unrestrained*) необу́зданный

rampart ['ræmpɑːt] крепостно́й вал

ramshackle ['ræmʃækl] ве́тхий; обветша́лый

ran [ræn] *pt. om* run

ranch [rænt∫] ра́нчо n *indecl.* фе́рма

rancid ['rænsɪd] □ прого́рклый

ranco(u)r ['ræŋkə] зло́ба

random ['rændəm] 1. *at* ~ нау́га́д, наобу́м; 2. сде́ланный (вы́бранный *и т.д.*) нау́да́чу; случа́йный

rang [ræŋ] *pt. om* ring

range [reɪndʒ] 1. ряд; *of mountains*

цепь *f*; (*extent*) преде́л, амплиту́да; диапазо́н (*a. mus.*); *mil.* (*shooting ~*) стре́льбище; **2.** *v/t.* выстра́ивать в ряд; располага́ть [-ложи́ть]; *v/i.* выстра́иваться в ряд, располага́ться [-ложи́ться]; *of land* простира́ться; (*wander*) броди́ть

rank [ræŋk] **1.** ряд; *mil.* шере́нга; (*status*) зва́ние, чин; катего́рия; **~ and file** рядово́й соста́в; *fig.* обыкнове́нные лю́ди; **2.** *v/t.* стро́ить в шере́нгу; выстра́ивать в ряд; классифици́ровать (*impf.*); (*consider*) счита́ть; *v/i.* стро́иться в шере́нгу; равня́ться (**with** Д); **3.** *vegetation* бу́йный

rankle ['ræŋkl] (*fester*) гнои́ться; причиня́ть [-ни́ть] гнев, боль *f*

ransack ['rænsæk] (*search*) [по-]ры́ться в (П); (*plunder*) [о]гра́бить

ransom ['rænsəm] вы́куп

rant [rænt] разглаго́льствовать

rap [ræp] **1.** лёгкий уда́р; *at door, etc.* стук; *fig.* **not a ~** ни гроша́; **2.** ударя́ть [уда́рить]; [по]стуча́ть

rapacious [rə'peɪʃəs] □ жа́дный; *animal* хи́щный; **~ty** [rə'pæsɪtɪ] жа́дность *f*; хи́щность *f*

rape [reɪp] **1.** изнаси́лование; **2.** [из]наси́ловать

rapid ['ræpɪd] **1.** □ бы́стрый, ско́рый; **2. ~s** *pl.* поро́ги *m/pl.*; **~ity** [rə'pɪdətɪ] быстрота́ ско́рость *f*

rapt [ræpt] (*carried away*) восхищённый; (*engrossed*) поглощённый; **~ure** ['ræptʃə] восто́рг, экста́з; **go into ~s** приходи́ть в восто́рг

rare [reə] □ ре́дкий; *air* разрежённый; *undercooked* недожа́ренный; **at ~ intervals** ре́дко

rarity ['reərətɪ] ре́дкость *f*; *thing* рарите́т

rascal ['rɑːskl] моше́нник; *child coll.* плути́шка

rash[1] [ræʃ] □ опроме́тчивый; необду́манный

rash[2] [-] *med.* сыпь *f*

rasp [rɑːsp] **1.** (*grating sound*) скре́жет; **2.** скрежета́ть; **~ing voice** скрипу́чий го́лос

raspberry ['rɑːzbrɪ] мали́на

rat [ræt] кры́са; **smell a ~** [по]чу́ять недо́брое

rate[1] [reɪt] **1.** но́рма; ста́вка; (*tax*) ме́стный нало́г; разря́д; (*speed*) ско́рость *f*; **at any ~** во вся́ком слу́чае; **~ of exchange** (валю́тный) курс; **~ of profit** но́рма при́были; **interest ~** проце́нтная ста́вка; **birth ~** рожда́емость *f*; **death ~** сме́ртность *f*; **2.** оце́нивать [-ни́ть]; расце́нивать [-ни́ть]; *fin.* облага́ться нало́гом; **~ among** счита́ться среди́ (Р)

rate[2] [-] (*scold*) брани́ть [вы́бранить] [от]руга́ть

rather ['rɑːðə] скоре́е; предпочти́тельно; верне́е; дово́льно; **I had ~....** я предпочёл бы …; *int.* ещё бы!

ratify ['rætɪfaɪ] ратифици́ровать (*impf.*); утвержда́ть [-рди́ть]

rating ['reɪtɪŋ] (*valuing*) оце́нка; су́мма нало́га; класс; *in opinion poll* рейтинг

ratio ['reɪʃɪəʊ] соотноше́ние, пропо́рция; коэффицие́нт

ration ['ræʃn] **1.** рацио́н; паёк; **2.** норми́ровать вы́дачу (Р)

rational ['ræʃnl] □ рациона́льный; разу́мный; **~ity** [ræʃə'nælətɪ] рациона́льность *f*; разу́мность *f*; **~ize** ['ræʃnəlaɪz] (*give reasons for*) опра́вдывать [-да́ть]; (*make mare efficient*) рационализи́ровать (*impf.*)

rattle ['rætl] **1.** треск; *of window* дребезжа́ние; *of talk* трескотня́; (*baby's toy*) погрему́шка; **2.** [за]дребезжа́ть; *of train, etc.* [про]громыха́ть; *of pots, etc.* [за]греме́ть (Т); говори́ть без у́молку; **~ off** отбараба́нить *pf.*; **~snake** грему́чая змея́

ravage ['rævɪdʒ] **1.** опустоше́ние; **2.** опустоша́ть [-ши́ть], разоря́ть [-ри́ть]

rave [reɪv] бре́дить (*a. fig.*), говори́ть бессвя́зно; (*rage*) неи́стовствовать; **~ about** быть без ума́ от (Р)

ravel ['rævl] *v/t.* запу́т(ыв)ать; распу́т(ыв)ать; *v/i.* запу́т(ыв)аться; (*a. ~ out*) распол-за́ться по швам

raven ['reɪvn] во́рон

ravenous ['rævənəs] прожо́рливый; *feel* ~ быть голо́дным как волк

ravine [rə'vi:n] овра́г, лощи́на

raving ['reɪvɪŋ]: *he's* ~ *mad* он совсе́м спя́тил

ravish ['rævɪʃ] приводи́ть в восто́рг; ~**ing** [-ɪŋ] восхити́тельный

raw [rɔ:] □ сыро́й; *hide, etc.* необрабо́танный; *(inexperienced)* нео́пытный; *knee, etc.* обо́дранный; ~**boned** худо́й, костля́вый; ~ **material** сырьё

ray [reɪ] луч; *fig.* про́блеск

rayon ['reɪɒn] иску́сственный шёлк, виско́за

raze [reɪz]: ~ *to the ground* разруша́ть до основа́ния

razor ['reɪzə] бри́тва; ~ **blade** ле́звие бри́твы

re... [ri:] *pref.* (приша́ет сло́ву значе́ния:) сно́ва, за́ново, ещё раз, обра́тно

reach [ri:tʃ] **1.** *beyond* ~ вне преде́лов досяга́емости; *within easy* ~ побли́зости; под руко́й; *within* ~ *financially* досту́пный; **2.** *v/t.* достига́ть [-и́гнуть] (Р); доезжа́ть [дойти́] до (Р); *of forest, land, etc.* простира́ться [-стере́ться] до (Р); *(pass)* протя́гивать [-яну́ть]; *(get to)* дост(ав)а́ть до (Р); *v/i.* протя́гивать ру́ку (*for* за Т)

react [rɪ'ækt] реаги́ровать; ~ *against idea, plan, etc.* возража́ть [-зи́ть] (про́тив Р)

reaction [rɪ'ækʃn] реа́кция; ~**ary** [-ʃənrɪ] **1.** реакцио́нный; **2.** реакционе́р

read 1. [ri:d] [*irr.*] [про]чита́ть; *(study)* изуча́ть [-чи́ть]; *(interpret)* истолко́вывать [-кова́ть]; *of instrument* пока́зывать [-за́ть]; *of text* гласи́ть; ~ *to s.o.* чита́ть кому́-л. вслух; **2.** [red] **a)** *pt. и pt. p. от* **read 1.**; **b)** *adj.*: *well-*~ начи́танный; ~**able** ['-əbl] разбо́рчивый; интере́сный; *(legible)* чёткий; ~**er** ['-ə] чита́тель(ница *f*) *m*; *(reciter)* чтец; *univ.* ле́ктор

readily ['redɪlɪ] *adv.* охо́тно; без труда́; легко́; ~**ness** [-nɪs] гото́вность *f*; подгото́вленность *f*

reading ['ri:dɪŋ] чте́ние; *(interpreta-*

tion) толкова́ние, понима́ние; *parl.* чте́ние (законопрое́кта); ~ *lamp* насто́льная ла́мпа; ~ *room* чита́льный зал

readjust [ri:ə'dʒʌst] *tech.* отрегули́ровать; приспоса́бливать [-со́бить]; *of attitude situation, etc.* пересма́тривать [-смотре́ть]; ~**ment** [-mənt] регулиро́вка; приспособле́ние

ready ['redɪ] □ гото́вый; *money* нали́чный; *make (или get)* ~ [при]гото́вить(ся); ~**made** гото́вый

reaffirm [ri:ə'fɜ:m] вновь подтвержда́ть

reagent [ri:'eɪdʒənt] *chem.* реакти́в

real [rɪəl] □ действи́тельный; реа́льный; настоя́щий; ~ *estate* недви́жимость *f*; ~**ity** [rɪ'ælɪtɪ] действи́тельность *f*; ~**ization** [rɪəlaɪ'zeɪʃn] понима́ние, осозна́ние; *(implementation)* осуществле́ние, реализа́ция (*a. comm.*); ~**ize** ['rɪəlaɪz] представля́ть себе́; осуществля́ть [-ви́ть]; осозн(ав)а́ть; сообража́ть [-ази́ть]; реализова́ть (*im*)*pf.*

realm [relm] короле́вство; ца́рство; *fig.* сфе́ра; *be in the* ~ *of fantasy* из о́бласти фанта́зии

reanimate [ri:'ænɪmeɪt] оживля́ть [-ви́ть]; воскреша́ть, [-еси́ть]

reap [ri:p] [с]жать; *fig.* пож(ин)а́ть; ~**er** ['-ə] *machine* жа́тка

reappear ['ri:ə'pɪə] сно́ва появля́ться

reappraisal [ri:ə'preɪzl] переоце́нка

rear [rɪə] **1.** *v/t.* воспи́тывать [-та́ть]; *(breed)* выра́щивать [вы́растить]; *v/i. of horse* станови́ться на дыбы́; **2.** за́дняя сторона́; *mil.* тыл; *at the ~ of, in the ~ of* позади́ (Р); **3.** за́дний; ты́льный; ~ *admiral* контрадмира́л

rearm [ri:'ɑ:m] перевооружа́ть(ся) [-жи́ть(ся)]

rearrange [ri:ə'reɪndʒ] перестра́ивать [-стро́ить]; *timetable, etc.* изменя́ть [-ни́ть], переде́лывать [-лать]; *furniture* переставля́ть [-ста́вить]

reason ['ri:zn] **1.** *(intellectual capability)* ра́зум, рассу́док; *(cause)* основа́ние, причи́на; *(sense)* смысл; *by* ~ *of* по причи́не (Р); *for this* ~ поэ́тому;

R

it stands to ~ that ... я́сно, что ...,
очеви́дно, что ...; 2. *v/i.* рассужда́ть
[-уди́ть]; ~ **out** разга́дывать [-да́ть];
проду́мать *pf.* до конца́; ~ **out of** разубежда́ть [-еди́ть] в (П); ~**able** [-əbl]
□ (благо)разу́мный; (*moderate*) уме́ренный; ~**ing** [-ɪŋ] рассужде́ние

reassure [riːə'ʃʊə] успока́ивать
[-ко́ить], ободря́ть [-ри́ть]

rebate ['riːbeɪt] *comm.* ски́дка; вы́чет

rebel 1. ['rebl] бунтовщи́к *m*, -и́ца *f*; *fig.* бунта́рь *m*; 2.
[-] (*a.* ~**lious** [rɪ'beljəs]) мяте́жный; 3.
[rɪ'bel] восст(ав)а́ть; бунтова́ть
[взбунтова́ться]; ~**lion** [rɪ'beljən] восста́ние; (*riot*) бунт

rebirth [riː'bɜːθ] возрожде́ние

rebound [rɪ'baʊnd] 1. отска́кивать
[-скочи́ть]; ~ **on** *fig.* обора́чиваться
[оберну́ться] (про́тив Р); 2. рикоше́т;
отско́к

rebuff [rɪ'bʌf] 1. отпо́р; ре́зкий отка́з;
2. дава́ть отпо́р (Д)

rebuild [riː'bɪld] [*irr.* (**build**)] сно́ва [по]стро́ить; реконструи́ровать; перестра́ивать [-стро́ить]

rebuke [rɪ'bjuːk] 1. упрёк; вы́говор; 2.
упрека́ть [-кну́ть], де́лать вы́говор
(Д)

recall [rɪ'kɔːl] 1. *of diplomat, etc.* отзы́в; *beyond ~* безвозвра́тно, бесповоро́тно; 2. отзыва́ть [отозва́ть]; (*revoke*) отменя́ть [-ни́ть]; (*remind*) напомина́ть [-о́мнить]; (*call to mind*)
вспомина́ть [-о́мнить] (В)

recapture [riː'kæptʃə] *territory* взять
обра́тно; освобожда́ть [-боди́ть]; ~
the atmosphere воссоздава́ть [-да́ть]
атмосфе́ру

recede [rɪ'siːd] (*move back*) отступа́ть
[-пи́ть]; (*move away*) удаля́ться
[-ли́ться]

receipt [rɪ'siːt] (*document*) распи́ска,
квита́нция; (*receiving*) получе́ние;
cul. реце́пт; ~**s** *pl.* прихо́д

receive [rɪ'siːv] получа́ть [-чи́ть];
guests, etc. принима́ть [-ня́ть]; *news,
ideas* воспринима́ть [-ня́ть]; ~**r** [-ə] получа́тель *m*, -ница *f*; *tel.* телефо́нная
тру́бка; *radio* приёмник

recent ['riːsnt] □ неда́вний; све́жий;
но́вый; *in ~ years* в после́дние го́ды;
~**ly** [-lɪ] неда́вно

receptacle [rɪ'septəkl] вмести́лище

reception [rɪ'sepʃn] получе́ние;
приём; ~ **desk** *in hotel* регистра́ция;
in hospital регистрату́ра; ~**ist** [-ənɪst]
регистра́тор

receptive [rɪ'septɪv] □ восприи́мчивый (к Д)

recess [rɪ'ses] *parl.* кани́кулы *f/pl.*;
(*break*) переры́в; *arch.* ни́ша; ~**es**
pl. fig. глуби́ны *f/pl.*; ~**ion** [-ʃn] *econ.*
спад

recipe ['resəpɪ] *cul.* реце́пт

recipient [rɪ'sɪpɪənt] получа́тель *m*,
-ница *f*

reciproc|al [rɪ'sɪprəkl] взаи́мный,
обою́дный; ~**ate** [-keɪt] отвеча́ть
[-ве́тить] взаи́мностью; (*interchange*)
обме́ниваться [-ня́ться]; ~**ity** [resɪ'prɒsətɪ] взаи́мность *f*

recit|al [rɪ'saɪtl] чте́ние, деклама́ция;
(*account*) повествова́ние, расска́з;
mus. со́льный; ~**ation** [resɪ'teɪʃn] деклама́ция; ~**e** [rɪ'saɪt] [про]деклами́ровать

reckless ['reklɪs] □ безрассу́дный;
опроме́тчивый; беспе́чный

reckon ['rekən] *v/t.* счита́ть;
причисля́ть [-чи́слить] (*among* к
Д); счита́ть [счесть] за (В); ~ **up** подсчи́тывать *pf.*; *v/i.* (*consider*) счита́ть, ду́мать, предполага́ть [-ложи́ть]; ~ (**up**)-
on *fig.* рассчи́тывать на (В); *a man to
be ~ed with* челове́к, с кото́рым сле́дует счита́ться; ~**ing** [-ɪŋ] подсчёт;
счёт; распла́та

reclaim [rɪ'kleɪm] [по]тре́бовать обра́тно; *waste* утилизи́ровать; *land* осва́ивать [-во́ить]; *neglected land* рекультиви́ровать

recline [rɪ'klaɪn] отки́дывать(ся)
[-и́нуть(ся)]; полулежа́ть

recluse [rɪ'kluːs] отше́льник *m*, -и́ца *f*

recogni|tion [rekəg'nɪʃn] (*realization*)
осозна́ние; узнава́ние; призна́ние
(Р); *change beyond ~* изменя́ться
[-ни́ться] до неузнава́емости; *gain ~*
доби́ться *pf.* призна́ния; ~**ze** ['rek-

əgnaiz] узн(ав)а́ть; призн(ав)а́ть

recoil [rɪ'kɔɪl] **1.** *mil.* отда́ча; **2.** отска́кивать [-скочи́ть], отпря́нуть *pf.*; *of gun* отдава́ть [-да́ть]

recollect [rekə'lekt] вспомина́ть [вспо́мнить] (B); *as far as I can* ~ наско́лько я по́мню; ~**ion** [rekə'lekʃn] воспомина́ние, па́мять *f* (*of* о П)

recommend [rekə'mend] рекомендова́ть (*im)pf.*, *pf. a.* [по-], [по]сове́товать; ~**ation** [rekəmen'deɪʃn] рекоменда́ция

recompense ['rekəmpens] **1.** вознагражде́ние; компенса́ция; *as or in* ~ в ка́честве компенса́ции (*for* за B); **2.** вознагражда́ть [-ради́ть]; отпла́чивать [отплати́ть] (Д); *for a loss, etc.* компенси́ровать, возмеща́ть [-мести́ть]

reconcil|e ['rekənsaɪl] примиря́ть [-ри́ть] (*to* с Т); ула́живать [ула́дить]; ~ **o.s.** примиря́ться [-ри́ться]; ~**iation** [rekənsɪlɪ'eɪʃn] примире́ние; ула́живание

recon|naissance [rɪ'kɒnəsns] *mil.* разве́дка; ~**noitre** [rekə'nɔɪtə] производи́ть разве́дку; разве́д(ыв)ать

reconsider [riːkən'sɪdə] пересма́тривать [-мотре́ть]

reconstruct [riːkəns'trʌkt] восстана́вливать [-нови́ть]; перестра́ивать [-стро́ить]; ~**ion** [-'strʌkʃn] реконстру́кция; восстановле́ние

record 1. ['rekɔːd] за́пись *f*; *sport* реко́рд; *of meeting* протоко́л; *place on* ~ запи́сывать [-са́ть]; граммофо́нная пласти́нка, диск; репута́ция; *library* фоноте́ка; ~ **office** госуда́рственный архи́в; *off the* ~ неофициа́льно; *on* ~ зарегистри́рованный; *attr.* реко́рдный; *in* ~ *time* в реко́рдно коро́ткое вре́мя; **2.** [rɪ'kɔːd] [за]писывать [-са́ть], [за]регистри́ровать; ~**er** [rɪ'kɔːdə] регистра́тор; (*instrument*) самопи́сец; ~**ing** [-ɪŋ] за́пись *f* (*a. mus.*)

recount [rɪ'kaʊnt] расска́зывать [-за́ть]

recourse [rɪ'kɔːs]: *have* ~ *to* прибега́ть [-бе́гнуть] к (P)

recover [rɪ'kʌvə] *v/t.* получа́ть обра́т-

но; верну́ть *pf.*; *waste* утилизи́ровать, регенери́ровать; *v/i. from illness* оправля́ться [-а́виться]; ~**y** [-rɪ] восстановле́ние; выздоровле́ние; *economic* ~ восстановле́ние наро́дного хозя́йства

recreation [rekrɪ'eɪʃn] о́тдых; развлече́ние

recrimination [rɪkrɪmɪ'neɪʃn] контробвине́ние

recruit [rɪ'kruːt] **1.** *mil.* новобра́нец; *fig.* новичо́к; **2.** [взять] на вое́нную слу́жбу; *new players* наб(и)ра́ть; *for work* [за]вербова́ть

rectangle ['rektæŋgl] прямоуго́льник

recti|fy ['rektɪfaɪ] (*put right*) исправля́ть [-а́вить]; ~**tude** ['rektɪtjuːd] прямота́, че́стность *f*

rector ['rektə] *univ.* ре́ктор; *eccl.* па́стор, свяще́нник; ~**y** [-rɪ] дом свяще́нника

recumbent [rɪ'kʌmbənt] лежа́чий

recuperate [rɪ'kjuːpəreɪt] восстана́вливать си́лы; оправля́ться [опра́виться]

recur [rɪ'kɜː] (*be repeated*) повторя́ться [-и́ться]; (*go back to s.th.*) возраща́ться [-рати́ться] (*to* к Д); *of ideas, event* приходи́ть сно́ва на ум, на па́мять; (*happen again*) происходи́ть вновь; ~**rence** [rɪ'kʌrəns] повторе́ние; ~**rent** [-rənt] □ повторя́ющийся; периоди́ческий; *med.* возвра́тный

recycling [riː'saɪklɪŋ] перерабо́тка; повто́рное испо́льзование

red [red] **1.** кра́сный; ~ *herring fig.* отвлече́ние внима́ния; ℒ *Cross* Кра́сный Крест; ~ *tape* волоки́та, бюрократи́зм; **2.** кра́сный цвет

red|breast ['redbrest] мали́новка; ~**den** ['redn] [по]красне́ть

redeem [rɪ'diːm] (*make amends*) искупа́ть [-пи́ть]; (*get back*) выкупа́ть [вы́купить]; спаса́ть [-сти́]; ~**er** [-ə] спаси́тель *m*

red-handed [red'hændɪd]: *catch a p.* ~ пойма́ть *pf.* кого́-л. на ме́сте преступле́ния

red-hot [red'hɒt] накалённый докрас-

F

на; горя́чий; *fig.* взбешённый

redirect [ri:dɪˈrekt] *letter* переадресо́-
вывать [-ва́ть]

red-letter [red'letə]: ~ **day** счастли́вый
день; кра́сный день календаря́

redness ['rednɪs] краснота́

redouble [riːˈdʌbl] удва́ивать(ся)
[удво́ить(ся)]

redress [rɪˈdres] **1.** *errors, etc.* исправ-
ле́ние; *law* возмеще́ние; **2.** ис-
правля́ть [-а́вить]; возмеща́ть [-ести́-
ти́ть]

reduc|e [rɪˈdjuːs] *in size* понижа́ть
[-и́зить]; *prices, etc.* снижа́ть
[-и́зить]; доводи́ть [довести́] (**to** до
P); *pain* уменьша́ть [уме́ньшить];
(*lessen*) сокраща́ть [-рати́ть]; уре́з(ы-
в)ать; **~tion** [rɪˈdʌkʃn] сниже́ние,
ски́дка; уменьше́ние; сокраще́ние;
of picture, etc. уме́ньшенная ко́пия

redundant [rɪˈdʌndənt] □ изли́шний;
be made ~ быть уво́ленным

reed [riːd] тростни́к; камы́ш

reeducation [riːedjuˈkeɪʃn] переобу-
че́ние

reef [riːf] *geogr. naut.* риф

reek [riːk] **1.** вонь *f*; за́тхлый за́пах; **2.**
v/i. дыми́ться; (неприя́тно) па́хнуть
(*of* T)

reel [riːl] **1.** кату́шка; *for film, etc.* бо-
би́на; **2.** *v/i.* [за]кружи́ться, [за]вер-
те́ться; (*stagger*) шата́ться [шат-
ну́ться]; *my head ~ed* у меня́ закружи́-
лась голова́; *v/t.* [на]мота́ть; ~ **off** раз-
ма́тывать [-мота́ть]; *fig.* отбараба́-
нить *pf.*

reelect [riːɪˈlekt] переизб(и)ра́ть

reenter [riːˈentə] сно́ва входи́ть в (В)

reestablish [riːɪˈstæblɪʃ] восстана́в-
ливать [-нови́ть]

refer [rɪˈfɜː]: ~ **to** *v/t.* относи́ть [отне-
сти́] (к Д); (*direct*) направля́ть [-ра́-
вить], отсыла́ть [отосла́ть] (к Д);
(*hand over*) передава́ть на рассмо-
тре́ние (Д); (*attribute*) припи́сывать
[-са́ть]; *v/i.* (*allude to*) ссыла́ться [со-
сла́ться] на (В); (*relate*) относи́ться
[отнести́сь] к (Д); **~ee** [refəˈriː] *sport*
судья́ *m*; *football* арби́тр (*a. fig.*); *boxing* ре́фери *m indecl.*; **~ence** ['refrəns]

спра́вка; *in book* ссы́лка; (*testimonial*)
рекоменда́ция; (*allusion*) упомина́-
ние; (*relationship*) отноше́ние; **in ~
to** относи́тельно (P); ~ **book** спра́воч-
ник; ~ **library** спра́вочная библиоте́-
ка; **make ~ to** ссыла́ться [сосла́ться]
на (В)

referendum [refəˈrendəm] рефере́н-
дум

refill [riːˈfɪl] наполня́ть сно́ва; по-
полня́ть(ся) [-по́лнить(ся)]

refine [rɪˈfaɪn] *tech.* очища́ть
[очи́стить]; *sugar* рафини́ровать
(*im*)*pf.*; *fig.* де́лать(ся) бо́лее
утончённым; ~ (**up**)**on** [у]соверше́н-
ше́нствовать; **~d** [-d] *person* рафини́-
рованный; *style, etc.* изы́сканный,
утончённый; очи́щенный; **~ry** [-əri]
for sugar са́харный заво́д

reflect [rɪˈflekt] *v/t.* отража́ть [отра-
зи́ть]; *v/i.* ~ (**up**)**on**: броса́ть тень на
(В); (*meditate on*) размышля́ть [-ы́с-
лить] о (П); (*tell on*) отража́ться [-ра-
зи́ться] на (В); **~ion** [rɪˈflekʃn] отра-
же́ние; отсве́т; размышле́ние, обду́-
мывание; *fig.* тень *f*

reflex ['riːfleks] рефле́кс

reforest [riːˈfɒrɪst] восстана́вливать
[-нови́ть] лес

reform [rɪˈfɔːm] **1.** рефо́рма; **2.** рефор-
ми́ровать (*im*)*pf.*; *of person* ис-
правля́ть(ся); **~ation** [refəˈmeɪʃn]
преобразова́ние; исправле́ние; *hist.*
the ~ Реформа́ция; **~er** [-mə] рефор-
ма́тор

refraction [rɪˈfrækʃn] *phys.* рефра́к-
ция, преломле́ние

refrain¹ [rɪˈfreɪn] *v/i.* возде́рживаться
[-жа́ться] (**from** от P)

refrain² [-] припе́в, рефре́н

refresh [rɪˈfreʃ] освежа́ть [-жи́ть];
with food or drink подкрепля́ть(ся)
[-пи́ться]; **~ment** [-mənt] еда́; питьё

refrigerat|e [rɪˈfrɪdʒəreɪt] замора́жи-
вать [-ро́зить]; (*cool*) охлажда́ть(ся)
[охлади́ть(ся)]; **~ion** [rɪfrɪdʒəˈreɪʃn]
замора́живание; охлажде́ние; **~or**
[rɪˈfrɪdʒəreɪtə] холоди́льник; *of van,
ship, etc.* рефрижера́тор

refuel [riːˈfjʊəl] *mot.* заправля́ться

[-áвиться] (горю́чим)

refuge ['refju:dʒ] убе́жище; *take ~* укрыва́ться [-ы́ться]; ~e [refju'dʒi:] бе́женец *m*, -нка *f*

refund [rɪ'fʌnd] возмеща́ть расхо́ды (Д); возвраща́ть [-рати́ть]

refusal [rɪ'fju:zl] отка́з

refuse 1. [rɪ'fju:z] *v/t.* отка́зываться [-за́ться] от (Р); отка́зывать [-за́ть] в (П); (*deny*) отверга́ть [отве́ргнуть]; *v/i.* отка́зываться [-за́ться]; **2.** ['refju:s] отбро́сы *m/pl.*; му́сор; *~ dump* сва́лка

regain [rɪ'geɪn] получа́ть обра́тно; сно́ва достига́ть; *strength* восстана́вливать [-нови́ть]

regal ['ri:gəl] □ короле́вский, ца́рственный

regale [rɪ'geɪl] *v/t.* угоща́ть [угости́ть]; *v/i.* наслажда́ться [-ди́ться]

regard [rɪ'gɑ:d] **1.** внима́ние; уваже́ние; *with ~ to* по отноше́нию к (Д); *kind ~s* серде́чный приве́т; **2.** [по]смотре́ть на (В); (*consider*) счита́ть; рассма́тривать (*as* как); (*concern*) каса́ться; относи́ться [отнести́сь] к (Д); *as ~s ...* что каса́ется (Р); *~ing* [-ɪŋ] относи́тельно (Р); *~less* [-lɪs] *adv.*: *~ of* несмотря́ на (В), незави́симо от (Р)

regent ['ri:dʒənt] ре́гент

regime [reɪ'ʒi:m] режи́м

regiment ['redʒɪmənt] полк

region ['ri:dʒən] о́бласть *f (a. administrative*); райо́н; *large* регио́н; *~al* [-l] □ областно́й; райо́нный; региона́льный

register ['redʒɪstə] **1.** журна́л; (*written record*) за́пись *f*, *tech.*, *mus.* реги́стр; **2.** регистри́ровать(ся) (*im*)*pf.*, *pf. a.* [за-]; заноси́ть в спи́сок; *mail* посыла́ть заказны́м; (*show*) пока́зывать [-за́ть]

registrar [redʒɪ'strɑ:] регистра́тор; слу́жащий регистрату́ры; *~ation* [redʒɪ'streɪʃn] регистра́ция; *~y* ['redʒɪstrɪ]: *~ office* загс

regret [rɪ'gret] **1.** сожале́ние; **2.** [по]жале́ть (*that ...* что ...); сожале́ть о (П); *~ful* [-fl] □ по́лный сожале́ния; опеча́ленный; *~table* [-əbl] □ приско́рбный

regular ['regjʊlə] □ пра́вильный; регуля́рный (*army a.*), постоя́нный; *~ity* [regjʊ'lærətɪ] регуля́рность *f*

regulat|e ['regjʊleɪt] [у]регули́ровать, упоря́дочи(ва)ть; *tech.* [от-] регули́ровать; *~ion* [regjʊ'leɪʃn] регули́рование; (*rule*) пра́вило

rehabilitation [ri:əbɪlɪ'teɪʃn] реабилита́ция; трудоустро́йство; перевоспита́ние

rehears|al [rɪ'hɜ:sl] *thea., mus.* репети́ция; *~e* [rɪ'hɜ:s] *thea.* [про]репети́ровать

reign [reɪn] **1.** ца́рствование; *fig.* власть *f*; **2.** ца́рствовать; *fig.* цари́ть

reimburse [ri:ɪm'bɜ:s] возвраща́ть [-рати́ть]; возмеща́ть [-мести́ть] расхо́ды (Д)

rein [reɪn] вожжа́ *f*; *fig.* узда́

reindeer ['reɪndɪə] се́верный оле́нь *m*

reinforce [ri:ɪn'fɔ:s] уси́ливать [уси́лить]; укрепля́ть [-пи́ть]; *mil.* подкрепля́ть [-пи́ть] (*a. fig.*); *~ment* [-mənt] усиле́ние; *mil.* подкрепле́ние

reinstate [ri:ɪn'steɪt] восстана́вливать [-нови́ть] (*в права́х и т.д.*)

reiterate [ri:'ɪtəreɪt] повторя́ть [-ри́ть]

reject [rɪ'dʒekt] **1.** *idea, etc.* отверга́ть [отве́ргнуть]; (*refuse to accept*) отка́зываться [-за́ться] от (Р); *proposal* отклоня́ть [-ни́ть]; *goods* бракова́ть; **2.** ['ri:dʒekt] брак; *~s* брако́ванный това́р; *~ion* [rɪ'dʒekʃn] отка́з; брако́вка

rejoic|e [rɪ'dʒɔɪs] *v/t.* [об]ра́довать; *v/i.* [об]ра́доваться (*at, in* Д); *~ing* [-ɪŋ] (*часто ~ings pl.*) весе́лье

rejoin [rɪ'dʒɔɪn] возража́ть [-рази́ть]; *~der* [-də] отве́т; возраже́ние

rejuvenate [rɪ'dʒu:vəneɪt] омола́живать(ся) [омолоди́ть(ся)]

relapse [rɪ'læps] **1.** *law, med.* рециди́в; **2.** *into bad habits, etc.* верну́ться *pf.*; *~ into silence* (сно́ва) умолка́ть

relate [rɪ'leɪt] *v/t.* расска́зывать

[-за́ть]; (*connect*) свя́зывать [-за́ть], соотноси́ть [-ти́ть]; *v/i.* относи́ться [отнести́сь]; ~d [-ɪd] (*connected*) свя́занный; состоя́щий в родстве́ (**to** с Т)

relation [rɪ'leɪʃn] отноше́ние; связь *f*; родство́; ро́дственник *m*, -ица *f*; *in*~ по отноше́нию к (Д); ~ship [-ʃɪp] связь; родство́

relative ['relətɪv] 1. □ относи́тельный; (*comparative*) сравни́тельный; ~ **to** относя́щийся к (Д); 2. ро́дственник *m*, -ица *f*

relax [rɪ'læks] *v/t.* ослабля́ть [-а́бить]; *muscles* расслабля́ть [-а́бить]; *v/i.* [o]сла́бнуть; расслабля́ться [-а́биться]; ~**ation** [rɪlæk'seɪʃn] ослабле́ние; расслабле́ние; (*amusement*) развлече́ние

relay [rɪ'leɪ] 1. сме́на; *sport* эстафе́та; *attr.* эстафе́тный; *el.* реле́ *n indecl.*; 2. *radio* ретрансли́ровать (*im*)*pf.*

release [rɪ'liːs] 1. освобожде́ние; вы́свобожде́ние; избавле́ние; *of film* вы́пуск; 2. (*set free*) освобожда́ть [-боди́ть]; высвобожда́ть [вы́свободить]; (*relieve*) избавля́ть [-а́вить]; (*issue*) выпуска́ть [вы́пустить]; (*let go*) отпуска́ть [-сти́ть]

relegate ['relɪgeɪt] отсыла́ть [отосла́ть], низводи́ть [-вести́]; направля́ть [-ра́вить] (**to** к Д); *sport* переводи́ть [-вести́]

relent [rɪ'lent] смягча́ться [-чи́ться]; ~**less** [-lɪs] □ безжа́лостный

relevant ['reləvənt] уме́стный; относя́щийся к де́лу

reliab|**ility** [rɪlaɪə'bɪlətɪ] надёжность *f*; достове́рность *f*; ~**le** [rɪ'laɪəbl] надёжный; достове́рный

reliance [rɪ'laɪəns] дове́рие; уве́ренность *f*

relic ['relɪk] пережи́ток; рели́квия

relief [rɪ'liːf] облегче́ние; (*assistance*) по́мощь *f*; посо́бие; подкрепле́ние; *in shiftwork* сме́на; *geogr* релье́ф; **to my** ~ к моему́ облегче́нию; ~ **fund** фонд по́мощи

relieve [rɪ'liːv] облегча́ть [-чи́ть]; (*free*) освобожда́ть [-боди́ть]; (*help*) ока́зывать по́мощь *f* (Д), выруча́ть

[вы́ручить]; *of shift* сменя́ть [-ни́ть]; (*soften*) смягча́ть [-чи́ть]; ~ **one's feelings** отвести́ *pf.* ду́шу

religion [rɪ'lɪdʒən] рели́гия

religious [rɪ'lɪdʒəs] □ религио́зный; (*conscientious*) добросо́вестный

relinquish [rɪ'lɪŋkwɪʃ] *hope, etc.* оставля́ть [-а́вить]; *habit* отка́зываться [-за́ться] (от Р); ~ **one's rights** уступа́ть [-пи́ть] права́

relish ['relɪʃ] 1. вкус; при́вкус; *cul.* припра́ва; 2. наслажда́ться [-лади́ться] (Т); получа́ть удово́льствие от (Р); придава́ть вкус (Д); **eat with** ~ есть с аппети́том

reluctan|**ce** [rɪ'lʌktəns] нежела́ние; неохо́та, нерасположе́ние; ~**t** [-nt] □ неохо́тный; (*offering resistance*) сопротивля́ющийся

rely [rɪ'laɪ]: ~ (*up*)*on* полага́ться [-ложи́ться] на (В), наде́яться на (В); (*depend on*) зави́сеть от (Р)

remain [rɪ'meɪn] ост(ав)а́ться; *it* ~**s to be seen** э́то ещё вы́яснится; ещё посмо́трим; ~**der** [-də] оста́ток

remark [rɪ'maːk] 1. (*notice, I made no* ~ я ничего́ не сказа́ла; 2. (*notice, say*) замеча́ть [-е́тить]; выска́зываться (*on* о П); ~**able** [rɪ'maːkəbl] (*of note*) замеча́тельный; (*extraordinary*) удиви́тельный

remedy ['remədɪ] 1. сре́дство, лека́рство; ме́ра (*for* про́тив Р); 2. (*put right*) исправля́ть [-а́вить]

rememb|**er** [rɪ'membə] по́мнить; (*recall*) вспомина́ть [-о́мнить]; ~ **me to** ... переда́й(те) приве́т (Д); ~**rance** [-brəns] (*recollection*) па́мять *f*, воспомина́ние; (*memento*) сувени́р

remind [rɪ'maɪnd] напомина́ть [-о́мнить] (Д; *of* о П *or* В); ~**er** [-ə] напомина́ние

reminiscence [remɪ'nɪsns] воспомина́ние

remiss [rɪ'mɪs] □ неради́вый; небре́жный; хала́тный; ~**ion** [rɪ'mɪʃn] (*forgiveness*) проще́ние; освобожде́ние от до́лга; (*abatement*) уменьше́ние; *med.* реми́ссия

remit [rɪ'mɪt] *goods* перес(ы)ла́ть;

money переводить [-вести]; *(abate)* уменьшать(ся) [уменьшить(ся)]; **~tance** [~əns] денежный перевод

remnant ['remnənt] *of cloth* остаток; *of food* остатки

remodel [ri:'mɒdl] перестраивать [-строить]

remonstrate ['remənstreɪt] протестовать; увещевать (**with** B)

remorse [rɪ'mɔ:s] угрызения (*n/pl.*) совести; раскаяние; **~less** [-lɪs] □ безжалостный

remote [rɪ'məʊt] □ отдалённый; дальний; **~ control** дистанционное управление; *I haven't got the ~st idea* не имею ни малейшего понятия

remov|al [rɪ'mu:vl] переезд; *of threat, etc.* устранение; *from office* смещение; **~ van** фургон для перевозки мебели; **~e** [rɪ'mu:v] *v/t.* удалять [-лить]; уносить [унести]; передвигать [-инуть]; *(take off)* снимать [снять]; *(take away)* уб(и-) рать; *(dismiss)* снимать [снять]; *v/i.* переезжать [переехать]; **~ers** [-əz] firm трансагентство; *personnel* перевозчики

remunerat|e [rɪ'mju:nəreɪt] вознаграждать [-радить]; *(pay)* оплачивать [оплатить]; **~ive** [rɪ'mju:-'nərətɪv] □ *(profitable)* выгодный

Renaissance [rɪ'neɪsns] эпоха Возрождения; Ренессанс; ☿ *(revival)* возрождение

render ['rendə] *(service)* оказывать [оказать]; *(represent)* изображать [-разить]; *mus.* исполнять [-олнить]; *(translate)* переводить [перевести]; *(give as due)* возд(ав)ать

renew [rɪ'nju:] возобновлять [-новить]; **~al** [-əl] возобновление

renounce [rɪ'naʊns] отказываться [-заться] от (P); *(disown)* отрекаться [отречься] от (P)

renovate ['renəveɪt] восстанавливать [-новить]; обновлять [обновить]

renown [rɪ'naʊn] слава; известность *f*; **~ed** [-d] □ прославленный, известный

rent[1] [rent] прореха; дыра

rent[2] [~] **1.** *for land* арендная плата; *for*

apartment квартирная плата; **2.** *(occupy for ~)* взять в наём; *(let for ~)* сдать в наём; **~al** [rentl] *(rate of rent)* арендная плата

renunciation [rɪnʌnsɪ'eɪʃn] отречение; отказ *(of* от P)

reopen [ri:'əʊpən] открывать [-рыть] вновь; **~ negotiations** возобновлять [-новить] переговоры

repair [rɪ'peə] **1.** починка, ремонт; *in good ~* в исправном состоянии; **2.** [по]чинить, [от]ремонтировать; *(make amends for)* исправлять [-авить]

reparation [repə'reɪʃn] возмещение; *pol.* репарация

repartee [repɑ:'ti:] остроумный ответ

repay [*irr.* (**pay**)] [rɪ'peɪ] *(reward)* отблагодарить (**for** за B); отдавать долг (Д); возмещать [-естить]; **~ment** [-mənt] *of money* возврат; возмещение

repeal [rɪ'pi:l] аннулировать *(im)pf.*; отменять [-нить]

repeat [rɪ'pi:t] **1.** повторять(ся) [-рить(ся)]; **2.** повторение; **~ed** [-ɪd]: **~ efforts** неоднократные усилия

repel [rɪ'pel] отталкивать [оттолкнуть]; *mil.* отражать [-разить], отбивать [-бить]

repent [rɪ'pent] раскаиваться [-каяться] *(of* в П); **~ance** [-əns] раскаяние; **~ant** [-ənt] кающийся

repercussion [ri:pə'kʌʃn] *of sound* отзвук; *fig.* последствие

repertoire ['repətwɑ:] репертуар

repetition [repɪ'tɪʃn] повторение

replace [rɪ'pleɪs] ставить, класть обратно; *(change for another)* заменять [-нить]; *(take place of)* замещать [-естить], заменять [-нить]; **~ment** [-mənt] замещение, замена

replenish [rɪ'plenɪʃ] пополнять [-олнить]; **~ment** [-mənt] пополнение *(a. mil.)*

replete [rɪ'pli:t] наполненный; насыщенный

replica ['replɪkə] точная копия

reply [rɪ'plaɪ] **1.** ответ (**to** на B); **2.** отвечать [-етить]; *(retort)* возражать

report [rɪˈpɔːt] **1.** (*account*) отчёт сообще́ние; *mil.* донесе́ние; *official* докла́д; (*hearsay*) молва́, слух; (*on* о П); **2.** сообща́ть [-щи́ть] (В *or* о П); *mil.* доноси́ть [-нести́] о (П); сде́лать *pf.* докла́д; докла́дывать [доложи́ть]; **~ for work** яви́ться *pf.* на рабо́ту; **~er** [-ə] репортёр

repos|e [rɪˈpəʊz] о́тдых; переды́шка; **~itory** [rɪˈpɒsɪtrɪ] склад; храни́лище

represent [reprɪˈzent] представля́ть [-а́вить]; изобража́ть [-рази́ть]; *thea.* исполня́ть роль *f* (Р); **~ation** [-zən'teɪʃn] изображе́ние; *parl.* представи́тельство; *thea.* представле́ние; постано́вка; **~ative** [reprɪˈzentətɪv] **1.** □ (*typical*) характе́рный; *parl.* представи́тельный; **2.** представи́тель *m*, -ница *f*; *House of* **~s** *pl. Am. parl.* пала́та представи́телей

repress [rɪˈpres] подавля́ть [-ви́ть]; **~ion** [rɪˈpreʃn] подавле́ние

reprimand [ˈreprɪmɑːnd] **1.** вы́говор; **2.** де́лать вы́говор (Д)

reprint [riːˈprɪnt] **1.** перепеча́тка; **2.** перепеча́тывать [-та́ть]

reprisal [rɪˈpraɪzl] отве́тное де́йствие

reproach [rɪˈprəʊtʃ] **1.** упрёк, уко́р; (**~ a p. with a th.**) упрека́ть [-кну́ть] (кого́-л. в чём-л.)

reprobate [ˈreprəbeɪt] негодя́й, распу́тник

reproduc|e [riːprəˈdjuːs] воспроизводи́ть [-извести́]; (*beget*) размножа́ться [-о́житься]; **~tion** [-ˈdʌkʃn] воспроизведе́ние; *of offspring* размноже́ние; (*copy*) репроду́кция

reproof [rɪˈpruːf] вы́говор; порица́ние

reprove [rɪˈpruːv] де́лать вы́говор (Д)

reptile [ˈreptaɪl] пресмыка́ющееся

republic [rɪˈpʌblɪk] респу́блика; **~an** [-ɪkən] **1.** республика́нский; **2.** республика́нец *m*, -нка *f*

repudiate [rɪˈpjuːdɪeɪt] (*disown*) отрека́ться [-ре́чься] от (Р); (*reject*) отверга́ть [-ве́ргнуть]

repugnan|ce [rɪˈpʌgnəns] отвраще́ние; **~t** [-nənt] □ отта́лкивающий, отврати́тельный

repuls|e [rɪˈpʌls] *mil.* отбива́ть [-би́ть], отража́ть [отрази́ть]; (*alienate*) отта́лкивать [оттолкну́ть]; **~ive** [-ɪv] □ отта́лкивающий; омерзи́тельный

reput|able [ˈrepjʊtəbl] □ уважа́емый; почте́нный; *company, firm, etc.* соли́дный; **~ation** [repjʊˈteɪʃn] репута́ция; **~e** [rɪˈpjuːt] репута́ция; **~ed** [rɪˈpjuːtɪd] изве́стный; (*supposed*) предполага́емый; **be ~** (**to be ...**) слыть за (В)

request [rɪˈkwest] **1.** тре́бование; про́сьба; **2.** [по]проси́ть (В *or* Р *or* о П)

require [rɪˈkwaɪə] (*need*) нужда́ться в (П); (*demand*) [по]тре́бовать (Р); **~d** [-d] ну́жный; (*compulsory*) обяза́тельный; **~ment** [-mənt] нужда́; тре́бование; потре́бность *f*; **meet the ~s** отвеча́ть тре́бованиям

requisit|e [ˈrekwɪzɪt] **1.** необходи́мый; **2. ~es** *pl.* всё необходи́мое, ну́жное; **sports ~** спорти́вное снаряже́ние; **~ion** [rekwɪˈzɪʃn] зая́вка, тре́бование

requital [rɪˈkwaɪtl] (*recompense*) вознагражде́ние; (*avenging*) возме́здие

requite [rɪˈkwaɪt] отпла́чивать [-лати́ть] (Д *for* за В); (*avenge*) [ото]мсти́ть за (В)

rescue [ˈreskjuː] **1.** освобожде́ние; спасе́ние; **come to s.o.'s ~** прийти́ кому́-л. на по́мощь *f*; **2.** освобожда́ть [-боди́ть]; спаса́ть [-сти́]; **~ party** гру́ппа спаса́телей

research [rɪˈsɜːtʃ] иссле́дование

resembl|ance [rɪˈzembləns] схо́дство (**to** с Т); **~e** [rɪˈzembl] походи́ть на (В), име́ть схо́дство с (Т)

resent [rɪˈzent] возмуща́ться [-мути́ться]; негодова́ть на (В); обижа́ться [оби́деться] за (В); **I ~ his familiarity** меня́ возмуща́ет его́ фамилья́рность; **~ful** [-fl] □ оби́женный; возмущённый; **~ment** [-mənt] негодова́ние; чу́вство оби́ды

reservation [rezəˈveɪʃn] огово́рка; *for game* запове́дник; *for tribes* резерва́ция; (*booking*) предвари́тельный зака́з; **without ~** без вся́ких огово́рок, безоговорочно

reserve [rɪ'zɜːv] 1. запас; *fin.* резервный фонд; резерв; (*reticence*) сдержанность *f*; скрытность *f*; 2. сберегать [-речь]; (*keep back*) приберегать [-речь], откладывать [отложить]; (*book*) заказывать [-зать]; *for business purposes* [за]бронировать; оставлять за собой; *I ~ the right to ...* я оставляю за собой право ...; **~d** [-d] □ скрытный; заказанный заранее

reside [rɪ'zaɪd] жить, проживать; **~nce** ['rezɪdəns] местожительство; *official* резиденция; **~nt** [-dənt] 1. проживающий, живущий; 2. оседлый, постоянный житель *m*; *in hotel* постоялец

residu|al [rɪ'zɪdjuəl] остаточный; **~e** ['rezɪdjuː] остаток; (*sediment*) осадок

resign [rɪ'zaɪn] *v/t. right, etc.* отказываться [-заться] от; *hope* оставлять [-авить]; *rights* уступать [-пить]; *o.s. to* покоряться [-риться] (Д); *v/i.* уходить в отставку; **~ation** [rezɪg'neɪʃn] отставка; уход с работы

resilien|ce [rɪ'zɪlɪəns] упругость *f*, эластичность *f*; **~t** [-nt] упругий, эластичный; *person* жизнестойкий

resin ['rezɪn] смола

resist [rɪ'zɪst] сопротивляться (Д); противостоять (Д); **~ance** [-əns] сопротивление; *to colds, etc.* сопротивляемость *f*; **~ant** [-ənt] сопротивляющийся; *heat-~* жаростойкий; *fire-~* огнеупорный

resolut|e ['rezəluːt] □ решительный; **~ion** [rezə'luːʃn] (*motion*) резолюция, решительность *f*, решимость *f*; *make a ~* решать [-шить]

resolve [rɪ'zɒlv] 1. *v/t. fig.* решать [решить]; *problem, etc.* разрешать [-шить]; *v/i.* решать(ся) [решить(ся)]; **~** (*up*)*on* решаться [-шиться] на (В); 2. решение; **~d** [-d] полный решимости

resonance ['rezənəns] резонанс

resonant ['rezənənt] □ звучащий; резонирующий; *be ~ with* быть созвучным

resort [rɪ'zɔːt] 1. (*health ~*) курорт; (*expedient*) надежда; *in the last ~* в край-

нем случае; 2. **~ to**: прибегать [-егнуть] к (Д); обращаться [-атиться] к (Д)

resound [rɪ'zaʊnd] [про]звучать; оглашать(ся) [огласить(ся)]

resource [rɪ'sɔːs] **~s** *pl.* ресурсы *m/pl.*; возможность *f*; находчивость *f*; **~ful** [-fl] □ находчивый

respect [rɪ'spekt] 1. (*esteem*) уважение; (*relation*) отношение; *in this ~* в этом отношении; **~s** *pl.* привет; 2. *v/t.* уважать, почитать; *you must ~ his wishes* вы обязаны считаться с его пожеланиями; **~able** [-əbl] □ приличный, порядочный; респектабельный; *part. comm.* солидный; **~ful** [-fl] □ вежливый, почтительный; **~ing** [-ɪŋ] относительно (Р); **~ive** [-ɪv] □ соответствующий; *we went to our ~ places* мы разошлись по своим местам; **~ively** [-ɪvlɪ] соответственно

respirat|ion [respə'reɪʃn] дыхание; вдох и выдох; **~or** ['respəreɪtə] респиратор

respite ['respaɪt] передышка; (*reprieve*) отсрочка

respond [rɪ'spɒnd] отвечать [-етить]; **~ to** реагировать на; отзываться [отозваться] на (В)

response [rɪ'spɒns] ответ; *fig.* отклик; реакция

responsi|bility [rɪspɒnsə'bɪlətɪ] ответственность *f*; **~ble** [rɪ'spɒnsəbl] □ ответственный (*for* за В, *to* перед Т)

rest[1] [rest] 1. отдых, покой; (*stand*) подставка; опора; 2. *v/i.* отдыхать [отдохнуть]; (*remain*) оставаться; (*lean*) опираться [опереться] (*on* на В); **~ against** прислонять [-нить]; *fig.* **~** (*up*)*on* основываться [-оваться] на (П); *v/t.* давать отдых (Д)

rest[2] [-] остаток

restaurant ['restrɒnt] ресторан; **~ car** вагон-ресторан

restful ['restfl] спокойный

restive ['restɪv] □ строптивый, упрямый

restless ['restlɪs] непоседливый, неугомонный; *night, etc.* беспокойный

restoration [restə'reɪʃn] *arch., hist.*

реставра́ция; восстановле́ние

restore [rɪ'stɔ:] восстана́вливать [-нови́ть]; (*return*) возвраща́ть [-рати́ть]; (*reconvert*) реставри́ровать (*im*)*pf*.; ~ **to health** выле́чивать [вы́лечить]

restrain [rɪ'streɪn] сде́рживать [-жа́ть]; уде́рживать; *feelings* подавля́ть [-ви́ть]; ~**t** [-t] сде́ржанность *f*; (*restriction*) ограниче́ние; (*check*) обузда́ние

restrict [rɪ'strɪkt] ограни́чи(ва)ть; ~**ion** [-ʃn] ограниче́ние

result [rɪ'zʌlt] **1.** результа́т, исхо́д; (*consequence*) сле́дствие; **2.** явля́ться [яви́ться] сле́дствием (*from* P); ~ *in* приводи́ть [-вести́] к (Д), конча́ться ['-читься]

resum|e [rɪ'zju:m] (*renew*) возобновля́ть [-ви́ть]; (*continue*) продолжа́ть [-лжи́ть]; ~ *one's seat* верну́ться на своё ме́сто; ~ *classes* возобнови́ть *pf*. заня́тия

resurrection [rezə'rekʃn] *of custom, etc.* воскреше́ние; *the* ♀ Воскресе́ние

resuscitate [rɪ'sʌsɪteɪt] *med.* приводи́ть [-вести́] в созна́ние

retail ['ri:teɪl] **1.** ро́зничная прода́жа; *goods sold by* ~ това́ры, продаю́щиеся в ро́зницу; *attr.* ро́зничный; **2.** продава́ть(ся) в ро́зницу

retain [rɪ'teɪn] (*preserve*) сохраня́ть [-ни́ть]; (*hold*) уде́рживать [-жа́ть]

retaliat|e [rɪ'tælɪeɪt] отпла́чивать [-лати́ть] (тем же); ~**ion** [rɪtælɪ'eɪʃn] отпла́та, возме́здие; *in* ~ *for* в отве́т на

retard [rɪ'tɑ:d] (*check*) заде́рживать [-жа́ть]; замедля́ть [-е́длить]; ~**ed** [-ɪd]: *mentally* ~ *child* у́мственно отста́лый ребёнок

retention [rɪ'tenʃn] удержа́ние; сохране́ние

retentive [rɪ'tentɪv]: ~ *memory* хоро́шая па́мять *f*

reticent ['retɪsnt] скры́тный; молчали́вый

retinue ['retɪnju:] сви́та, сопровожда́ющие ли́ца

retir|e [rɪ'taɪə] *v/t.* увольня́ть с рабо́ты; *v/i.* выходи́ть в отста́вку; *because of age* уходи́ть [уйти́] на пе́нсию;

(*withdraw*) удаля́ться [-ли́ться]; (*seclude o.s.*) уединя́ться [-ни́ться]; ~**ed** [-d] (*secluded*) уединённый; отставно́й, в отста́вке; ~**ement** [-mənt] отста́вка; ухо́д на пе́нсию; уедине́ние; ~ *age* пенсио́нный во́зраст; ~**ing** [-ɪŋ] скро́мный, засте́нчивый

retort [rɪ'tɔ:t] **1.** ре́зкий (*or* нахо́дчивый) отве́т; возраже́ние; **2.** *to a biting remark* [от]пари́ровать; возража́ть [-рази́ть]

retrace [rɪ'treɪs] просле́живать [-еди́ть]; ~ *one's steps* возвраща́ться тем же путём

retract [rɪ'trækt] отрека́ться [отре́чься] от (P); *one's words, etc.* брать наза́д; (*draw in*) втя́гивать [втяну́ть]

retraining [ri:'treɪnɪŋ] переподгото́вка

retreat [rɪ'tri:t] **1.** отступле́ние (*part. mil.*); (*place of privacy or safety*) приста́нище; **2.** (*walk away*) уходи́ть [уйти́]; удаля́ться [-ли́ться]; *part. mil.* отступа́ть [-пи́ть]

retrench [rɪ'trentʃ] сокраща́ть [-рати́ть]; [с]эконо́мить

retrieve [rɪ'tri:v] **1.** (*get back*) брать [взять] обра́тно; (*restore*) восстана́вливать [-нови́ть]; (*put right*) исправля́ть [-а́вить]

retro... ['retrəu] обра́тно...; ~**active** [retrəu'æktɪv] име́ющий обра́тную си́лу; ~**grade** ['retrəugreɪd] реакцио́нный; ~**spect** ['retrəuspekt] ретроспекти́ва; ~**spective** [retrəu'spektɪv] □ ретроспекти́вный; *law* име́ющий обра́тную си́лу

return [rɪ'tз:n] **1.** возвраще́ние; возвра́т; *fin.* оборо́т; дохо́д, при́быль *f*; результа́т вы́боров; *many happy* ~**s** *of the day* поздравля́ю с днём рожде́ния; *in* ~ в обме́н (*for* за В); в отве́т; *by* ~ *of post* с обра́тной по́чтой; *tax* ~ нало́говая деклара́ция; ~ *ticket* обра́тный биле́т; **2.** *v/i.* возвраща́ться [-рати́ться]; верну́ться *pf*.; *v/t.* возвраща́ть [-рати́ть]; верну́ть *pf*.; присыла́ть наза́д; (*reply*) отвеча́ть [-е́тить]; ~ *s.o.'s kindness* отблагодари́ть за доброту́

reunion [ri:'ju:nɪən] *of friends, etc.*

встре́ча; *of family* сбор всей семьи́; *(reuniting)* воссоедине́ние

revaluation [ri:væljʊ'eɪʃn] переоце́нка; *of currency* ревалва́ция

reveal [ri'vi:l] обнару́жи(ва)ть; *secret, etc.* откры́(ва́)ть; **~ing** [-ɪŋ] *fig.* показа́тельный

revel ['revl] пирова́ть; упи(ва́)ться *(in* T)

revelation [revə'leɪʃn] открове́ние *(a. eccl.)*; *(disclosure)* разоблаче́ние; откры́тие

revelry ['revlrɪ] разгу́л; *(binge)* пиру́шка; кутёж

revenge [rɪ'vendʒ] **1.** месть *f, sport* рева́нш; отме́стка; *in~ for* в отме́стку за (В); **2.** [ото]мсти́ть за (В); **~ful** [-fl] мсти́тельный

revenue ['revənju:] дохо́д; *of state* госуда́рственные дохо́ды; *Internal,* **(Brt.) Inland** ℒ Нало́говое управле́ние

reverberate [rɪ'vɜ:bəreɪt] отража́ть(ся) [отрази́ть(ся)]

revere [rɪ'vɪə] уважа́ть, почита́ть; **~nce** ['revərəns] почте́ние

reverent ['revərənt] почти́тельный; по́лный благогове́ния

reverie ['revərɪ] мечты́ *f/pl.*; мечта́ние

revers|al [rɪ'vɜ:sl] измене́ние; **~e** [rɪ'vɜ:s] **1.** обра́тная сторона́; *of paper* оборо́т, оборо́тная сторона́ *(a. fig.)*; *(opposite)* противополо́жное; **~s** *pl.* превра́тности *f/pl.*; **2.** обра́тный; противополо́жный; **3.** изменя́ть [-ни́ть]; повора́чивать наза́д; *mot.* дава́ть за́дний ход; *law* отменя́ть [-ни́ть]

revert [rɪ'vɜ:t] *to former state or question* возвраща́ться [-ти́ться]

review [rɪ'vju:] **1.** *(survey)* обзо́р; *law* пересмо́тр; *(journal)* обозре́ние; *of book* реце́нзия; **2.** пересма́тривать [-смотре́ть]; писа́ть реце́нзию о (П)

revis|e [rɪ'vaɪz] пересма́тривать [-смотре́ть]; *(correct)* исправля́ть [-а́вить]; **~ion** [rɪ'vɪʒn] пересмо́тр; *(reworking)* перерабо́тка; испра́вленное изда́ние

reviv|al [rɪ'vaɪvl] возрожде́ние; *of trade, etc.* оживле́ние; **~e** [rɪ'vaɪv]

приходи́ть *or* приводи́ть в чу́вство; *(liven up)* оживля́ть(ся) [-ви́ть(ся)]; ожи(ва́)ть

revoke [rɪ'vəʊk] *v/t. (repeal)* отменя́ть [-ни́ть]; *promise* брать [взять] наза́д

revolt [rɪ'vəʊlt] **1.** восста́ние; бунт; **2.** *v/i.* восста́(ва́)ть *(a. fig.)*; *v/t. fig.* отта́лкивать [оттолкну́ть]

revolution [revə'lu:ʃn] *(revolving)* враще́ние; *(one complete turn)* оборо́т; *pol.* револю́ция; **~ary** [-ʃənərɪ] **1.** революцио́нный; **2.** революционе́р *m*, -ка *f*; **~ize** [-aɪz] революционизи́ровать *(im)pf.*

revolve [rɪ'vɒlv] *v/i.* враща́ться; *v/t.* враща́ть; обду́м(ыв)ать; **~ a problem in one's mind** всесторо́нне обду́мывать пробле́му; **~er** [-ə] револьве́р; **~ing** [-ɪŋ] враща́ющийся; **~ door** враща́ющаяся дверь *f*

reward [rɪ'wɔ:d] **1.** награ́да; вознагражде́ние; **2.** вознагражда́ть [-ради́ть]; награжда́ть [-ради́ть]; **~ing** [-ɪŋ]: **~ work** благода́рная рабо́та

rewrite [ri:'raɪt] *[irr. (write)]* переписы́вать [-са́ть]

rhapsody ['ræpsədɪ] рапсо́дия

rheumatism ['ru:mətɪzəm] ревмати́зм

rhinoceros ['raɪnɒsərəs] носоро́г

rhubarb ['ru:ba:b] реве́нь *m*

rhyme [raɪm] **1.** ри́фма; *(рифмо́ванный) стих*; **without ~ or reason** нет никако́го смы́сла; ни с того́, ни с сего́; **2.** рифмова́ть(ся) *(with* с T)

rhythm ['rɪðəm] ритм; **~ic(al)** [-mɪk(l)] ритми́чный, ритми́ческий

rib [rɪb] ребро́

ribald ['rɪbəld] гру́бый; непристо́йный; скабрёзный

ribbon ['rɪbən] ле́нта; *mil.* о́рденская ле́нта; **tear to ~s** изорва́ть в кло́чья

rice [raɪs] рис; *attr.* ри́совый

rich [rɪtʃ] □ бога́тый *(in* T); *(splendid)* роско́шный; *soil* плодоро́дный; *food* жи́рный; *colo(u)r* со́чный; **get ~** разбога́теть; **~es** ['rɪtʃɪz] *pl.* бога́тство; сокро́вища *n/pl.*

rick [rɪk] *agric.* скирда́

ricket|s ['rɪkɪts] *pl.* рахи́т; **~y** [-ɪ] рахити́чный; *chair. etc.* ша́ткий

rid [rɪd] [*irr.*] избавля́ть [-а́вить] (*of* от P); **get~ of** отде́л(ыв)аться от (P), избавля́ться [-а́виться] от (P)

ridden ['rɪdn] *pt. p. om* ride

riddle¹ ['rɪdl] зага́дка; **ask a ~** задава́ть зага́дку

riddle² [-] (*sieve*) **1.** си́то, решето́; **2.** изреше́чивать [-шети́ть]

ride [raɪd] **1.** *on horseback* езда́ верхо́м; *for pleasure* прогу́лка; **2.** [*irr.*] *v/i. in car, on horseback, etc.* е́здить, [по]е́хать; ката́ться верхо́м; *v/t.* [по]е́хать на (П); **~r** [-ə] вса́дник *m*, -и́ца *f*; *in circus* нае́здник *m*, -и́ца *f*

ridge [rɪdʒ] го́рный кряж, хребе́т; *on rooftop* конёк

ridicul|e ['rɪdɪkjuːl] **1.** осмея́ние, насме́шка; **2.** высме́ивать [вы́смеять]; **~ous** [rɪ'dɪkjələs] ☐ неле́пый, смешно́й; **don't be ~!** не говори́ ерунду́!

riding ['raɪdɪŋ] верхова́я езда́

rife [raɪf]: **~ with** изоби́лующий (Т)

riffraff ['rɪfræf] подо́нки, отбро́сы (о́бщества) *m/pl.*

rifle [raɪfl] винто́вка; *for hunting* ружьё; **~man** *mil.* стрело́к

rift [rɪft] тре́щина, рассе́лина; *fig.* разры́в; *geol.* разло́м

rig [rɪg] **1.** *naut.* осна́стка; *coll.* наря́д; (*oil ~*) бурова́я вы́шка; **2.** оснаща́ть [оснасти́ть]; *coll.* наряжа́ть [-яди́ть]; **~ging** ['rɪgɪŋ] *naut.* такела́ж, сна́сти *f/pl.*

right [raɪt] **1.** ☐ (*correct*) пра́вильный, ве́рный; (*suitable*) подходя́щий, ну́жный; пра́вый; **be ~** быть пра́вым; **put ~** приводи́ть в поря́док; **2.** *adv.* пря́мо; пра́вильно; справедли́во; как раз; **~ away** сра́зу, сейча́с же; **~ on** пря́мо вперёд; **3.** пра́во; справедли́вость *f*; пра́вда; **by ~** на основа́нии (P); **on** (*or to*) **the ~** напра́во; **4.** приводи́ть в поря́док; (*correct*) исправля́ть [-вить]; **~eous** ['raɪtʃəs] ☐ пра́ведный; **~ful** [-fl] ☐ справедли́вый; зако́нный; **~ly** [-lɪ] пра́вильно; справедли́во

rigid ['rɪdʒɪd] ☐ негну́щийся, неги́бкий, жёсткий; *fig.* суро́вый; непрекло́нный; **be ~ with fear** оцепене́ть от стра́ха; **~ity** [rɪ'dʒɪdətɪ] жёсткость

f; непрекло́нность *f*

rigo(u)r ['rɪgə] суро́вость *f*; стро́гость *f*

rigorous ['rɪgərəs] ☐ *climate* суро́вый; *measures* стро́гий

rim [rɪm] ободо́к; *of wheel* о́бод; *of glasses* опра́ва

rind [raɪnd] *of fruit* кожура́; *of cheese, etc.* ко́рка

ring¹ [rɪŋ] **1.** (*of bells*) звон, звоно́к; **2.** [*irr.*] [за]звуча́ть; *at door* [по-] звони́ть; **~ s.o. up** позвони́ть *pf.* кому́-л. по телефо́ну; **~ s a bell** э́то мне что́-то напомина́ет

ring² [-] **1.** кольцо́; круг; *sport* ринг; **2.** (*mst. ~ in, round, about*) окружа́ть [-жи́ть]; **~leader** зачи́нщик *m*, -и́ца *f*; **~let** ['rɪŋlɪt] коле́чко; ло́кон; **~ road** кольцева́я доро́га

rink [rɪŋk] като́к

rinse [rɪns] [вы]полоска́ть; *dishes* сполосну́ть *pf.*

riot ['raɪət] **1.** беспоря́дки *m/pl.*; *of colo(u)rs* бу́йство; **run ~** шу́мно весели́ться, разгуля́ться *pf.*; **2.** принима́ть уча́стие в беспоря́дках, волне́ниях; бу́йствовать

rip [rɪp] **1.** (*tear*) [по]рва́ть; **2.** проре́ха

ripe [raɪp] ☐ зре́лый (*a. fig.*); спе́лый; гото́вый; **the time is ~ for ...** пришло́ вре́мя ...; **~n** ['-ən] созре(ва́)ть, [по]спе́ть

ripple ['rɪpl] **1.** рябь *f*, зыбь *f*; (*sound*) журча́ние; **2.** покрыва́ть(ся) ря́бью, журча́ть

rise [raɪz] **1.** повыше́ние; *of sun* восхо́д; *of road, etc.* подъём; *geogr.* возвы́шенность *f*; *of river* исто́к; **2.**, [*irr.*] поднима́ться [-ня́ться]; всходи́ть; *of river* брать нача́ло; **~** быть в состоя́нии, спра́виться с (Т); **~n** ['rɪzn] *pt. p. om* rise

rising ['raɪzɪŋ] возвыше́ние; восста́ние; восхо́д

risk [rɪsk] **1.** риск; **run a** (*or the*) **~** рискова́ть [-кну́ть]; **2.** (*venture*) отва́живаться на (В); рискова́ть [-кну́ть] (Т); **~y** ['-ɪ] ☐ риско́ванный

rit|e [raɪt] обря́д, церемо́ния; **~ual** ['rɪtʃʊəl] **1.** ритуа́льный; **2.** ритуа́л

rival ['raɪvəl] **1.** сопе́рник *m*, -ница *f*;

comm. конкуре́нт; **2.** сопе́рничающий; **3.** сопе́рничать с (Т); ~**ry** [-rɪ] сопе́рничество; соревнова́ние

river ['rɪvə] река́; ~**bed** ру́сло реки́; ~**mouth** у́стье реки́; ~**side** бе́рег реки́; *attr.* прибре́жный

rivet ['rɪvɪt] **1.** заклёпка; **2.** заклёпывать [-лепа́ть]; *fig.* прико́вывать [-ова́ть] (В к Д)

road [rəud] доро́га; путь *m*; ~ *accident* доро́жное происше́ствие, ава́рия; ~**side** обо́чина; ~**sign** доро́жный знак

roam [rəum] *v/t.* броди́ть по (Д); *v/i.* стра́нствовать

roar [rɔ:] **1.** *of storm, lion* [за]реве́ть; *of cannon* [за]грохота́ть; ~ *with laughter* пока́тываться со́ смеху; **2.** рёв; гро́хот

roast [rəust] **1.** *mus.* [из]жа́рить(ся); **2.** жа́реный; ~ *meat* жарко́е

rob [rɒb] [о]гра́бить; *fig.* лиша́ть [-ши́ть] (*of*); ~**ber** ['-ə] граби́тель *m*; ~**bery** ['-ərɪ] грабёж

robe [rəub] *magistrate's* ма́нтия; (*bath* ~) хала́т

robin ['rɒbɪn] мали́новка

robot ['rəubɒt] ро́бот

robust [rəu'bʌst] □ кре́пкий, здоро́вый

rock[1] [rɒk] скала́; утёс; го́рная поро́да; ~ *crystal* го́рный хруста́ль *m*

rock[2] [-] **1.** *mus.* рок; **2.** *v/t.* кача́ть [-чну́ть]; *strongly* [по]шатну́ть; *to sleep* убаю́к(ив)ать; *v/i.* кача́ться; ~ *with laughter* трясти́ от сме́ха

rocket ['rɒkɪt] раке́та; *attr.* раке́тный

rocking chair кача́лка

rocky ['rɒkɪ] (*full of rocks*) камени́стый; скали́стый

rod [rɒd] *tech.* сте́ржень *m*; прут *m*; *for fishing* уди́лище; *piston* ~ шток

rode [rəud] *pt. om* **ride**

rodent ['rəudənt] грызу́н

roe[1] [rəu] *zo.* косу́ля

roe[2] [-] икра́; *soft* ~ моло́ки *f/pl.*

rogue [rəug] моше́нник; плут; ~**ish** ['rəugɪʃ] плутова́тый

role [rəul] *thea.* роль *f* (*a. fig.*)

roll [rəul] **1.** *of cloth, paper, etc.* руло́н; (*list*) спи́сок; *of thunder* раска́т; (*bread* ~) бу́лочка; *naut.* бортова́я ка́чка; **2.** *v/t.* ката́ть, [по]кати́ть; *dough* раска́тывать [-ката́ть]; *metal* прока́тывать [-ката́ть]; ~ *up* свёртывать [сверну́ть]; [с]ката́ть(ся); *v/i.* ката́ться, валя́ться (*in* в П); *of thunder* грохота́ть [-хотну́ть]; ~**er** ['rəulə] ро́лик; вал; ~ *skates* ро́ликовые коньки́

rollick ['rɒlɪk] шу́мно весели́ться

rolling ['rəulɪŋ] (*hilly*) холми́стый; ~ *mill tech.* прока́тный стан; ~ *pin* скалка́; ~ *stone person* перекати́по́ле

Roman ['rəumən] **1.** ри́мский; ~ *numeral* ри́мская ци́фра; **2.** ри́млянин *m*, -янка *f*

romance [rəu'mæns] **1.** *mus.* рома́нс; (*tale*) рома́н (*a. love affair*); **2.** *fig.* приукра́шивать действи́тельность; фантази́ровать; стро́ить возду́шные за́мки; **3.** ♀ рома́нский

romantic [rəu'mæntɪk] (~**ally**) **1.** рома́нти́чный; **2.** ~**ist** [-tɪsɪst] рома́нтик; ~**ism** [-tɪsɪzəm] романти́зм; рома́нтика

romp [rɒmp] вози́ться, шу́мно игра́ть

roof [ru:f] кры́ша; ~ *of the mouth* нёбо; ~**ing** [-ɪŋ] **1.** кро́вельный материа́л; **2.** кро́вля; ~ *felt* толь *m*

rook[1] [ruk] *bird* грач

rook[2] [-] *coll.* **1.** моше́нник; **2.** обма́нывать [-ну́ть]

rook[3] [-] *chess* ладья́

room [ru:m, rum] ко́мната; ме́сто; простра́нство; *make* ~ *for* освободи́ть ме́сто для (Р); ~**mate** това́рищ по ко́мнате; ~**y** ['ru:mɪ] □ просто́рный

roost [ru:st] **1.** насе́ст; **2.** уса́живаться на насе́ст; *fig.* устра́иваться на́ ночь; ~**er** ['-ə] пету́х

root [ru:t] **1.** ко́рень *m*; *get to the* ~ добра́ться *pf.* до су́ти (Р); *take* ~ пуска́ть ко́рни; укореня́ться [-ни́ться]; **2.** ~ *out* выка́рбивать с ко́рнем (*a. fig.*); (*find*) разы́скивать [-ка́ть]; *stand* ~**ed to the spot** стоя́ть как вко́панный; ~**ed** [-ɪd] укорени́вшийся

rope [rəup] **1.** кана́т; верёвка; *mst. naut.* трос; *of pearls* ни́тка; *know the* ~**s** *pl.* знать все хо́ды и вы́ходы; *show the* ~**s** *pl.* вводи́ть [ввести́] в суть де́ла; **2.**

связывать верёвкой; привязывать канатом; (mst. ~ off) отгородить канатом

rosary ['rəʊzəri] eccl. чётки f/pl.
rose[1] [rəʊz] róза; ро́зовый цвет
rose[2] [-] pt. om rise
rosin ['rɒzɪn] канифо́ль f
rostrum ['rɒstrəm] ка́федра; трибу́на
rosy ['rəʊzɪ] □ ро́зовый; румя́ный; fig. ра́дужный
rot [rɒt] 1. гние́ние; гниль f; 2. v/t. [с]гнои́ть; v/i. сгни(ва́)ть, [с]гнить
rota|ry ['rəʊtərɪ] враща́тельный; ~te [rəʊ'teɪt] враща́ть(ся); (alternate) чередова́ть(ся); ~tion [rəʊ'teɪʃn] враще́ние; чередова́ние
rotten ['rɒtn] □ гнило́й; испо́рченный; a. sl. отврати́тельный
rouge [ru:ʒ] румя́на n/pl.
rough [rʌf] 1. □ (crude) гру́бый; (uneven) шерша́вый, шерохова́тый; (violent) бу́рный; (inexact) приблизи́тельный; ~ and ready сде́ланный кое-как, на́спех; грубова́тый; 2.: ~ it обходи́ться без обы́чных удо́бств; ~en ['rʌfn] де́лать(ся) гру́бым, шерохова́тым; ~ly ['-lɪ] гру́бо, приблизи́тельно; ~ speaking гру́бо говоря́; ~ness ['-nɪs] гру́бость f; гру́бость f
round [raʊnd] 1. □ кру́глый; кругово́й; ~ trip пое́здка в о́ба конца́; 2. adv. круго́м, вокру́г; обра́тно; (often ~ about) вокру́г да о́коло; all year ~ кру́глый год; 3. prp. вокру́г, круго́м (P); за (B or T); по (Д); 4. круг; цикл; of talks тур; sport ра́унд; doctor's обхо́д; 5. v/t. закругля́ть [-ли́ть]; огиба́ть [обогну́ть]; ~ up окружа́ть [-жи́ть]; v/i. закругля́ться [-ли́ться]; ~about ['raʊndəbaʊt] 1. way око́льный; 2. mot. кольцева́я тра́нспортная развя́зка; at fair карусе́ль f; ~ish ['raʊndɪʃ] кругло́ватый; ~up of cattle заго́н скота́; обла́ва
rous|e [raʊz] v/t. (waken) [раз]буди́ть; fig. возбужда́ть [-уди́ть]; воодушевля́ть [-ви́ть]; ~ o.s. встряхну́ться pf.; v/i. просыпа́ться [-сну́ться]; ~ing ['raʊzɪŋ] возбужда́ющий; cheers бу́рный

rout [raʊt] обраща́ть в бе́гство
route [ru:t] путь m; маршру́т
routine [ru:'ti:n] 1. режи́м, поря́док; рути́на; 2. рути́нный
rove [rəʊv] скита́ться; броди́ть
row[1] [rəʊ] ряд
row[2] [raʊ] coll. гвалт; (quarrel) ссо́ра
row[3] [rəʊ] грести́; ~boat гребна́я ло́дка; ~er ['rəʊə] гребе́ц
royal ['rɔɪəl] □ короле́вский; великоле́пный; ~ty [-tɪ] член(ы) короле́вской семьи́; а́вторский гонора́р
rub [rʌb] v/t. тере́ть; протира́ть [-тере́ть]; натира́ть [натере́ть]; ~ in втира́ть [втере́ть]; ~ out стира́ть [стере́ть]; ~ up [от]полирова́ть; (freshen) освежа́ть [-жи́ть]; v/i. тере́ться (against о В); fig. ~ along проби(ва́)ться с трудо́м
rubber ['rʌbə] каучу́к; рези́на; (eraser) рези́нка; (contraceptive) противозача́точное сре́дство; презервати́в; cards ро́ббер; attr. рези́новый
rubbish ['rʌbɪʃ] му́сор, хлам; fig. вздор; глу́пости f/pl.
rubble ['rʌbl] (debris) обло́мки; ще́бень m
ruby ['ru:bɪ] руби́н; руби́новый цвет
rucksack ['rʌksæk] рюкза́к
rudder ['rʌdə] naut. руль m
ruddy ['rʌdɪ] я́рко-кра́сный; cheeks румя́ный
rude [ru:d] □ неотёсанный; гру́бый; неве́жливый; fig. health кре́пкий; ~ awakening неприя́тное откры́тие; го́рькое разочарова́ние
rudiment ['ru:dɪmənt] biol. рудиме́нт; ~s pl. осно́вы f/pl.; ~s of knowledge элемента́рные зна́ния
rueful ['ru:fl] □ печа́льный
ruffian ['rʌfɪən] громи́ла, хулига́н
ruffle ['rʌfl] 1. sew. сбо́рка; on water рябь f; 2. hair [взъ]еро́шить; water ряби́ть; fig. наруша́ть споко́йствие (P), [вс]трево́жить
rug [rʌg] плед; on floor ковёр, ко́врик; ~ged ['rʌgɪd] неро́вный; шерохова́тый; terrain пересечённый; features гру́бые, ре́зкие
ruin ['ru:ɪn] 1. ги́бель f; разоре́ние; of

hopes, etc. круше́ние; *mst.* **~s** *pl.* развали́ны *f/pl.*, руи́ны *f/pl.*; **2.** [по]губи́ть; разоря́ть [-ри́ть]; разруша́ть [-у́шить]; *dishono(u)r* [о]бесче́стить; **~ous** ['ru:ɪnəs] □ губи́тельный; разори́тельный; разру́шенный

rul|e [ru:l] **1.** пра́вило; правле́ние; власть *f; for measuring* лине́йка; **as a ~** обы́чно; **2.** *v/t.* управля́ть (Т); *(give as decision)* постановля́ть [-ви́ть], **~ out** исключа́ть [-чи́ть]; *v/i.* ца́рствовать; **~er** ['ru:lə] прави́тель *m*

rum [rʌm] ром

Rumanian [ru:'meɪnɪən] **1.** румы́нский; **2.** румы́н *m*, -ка *f*

rumble ['rʌmbl] **1.** громыха́ние; гро́хот; **2.** [за]громыха́ть; [за]грохота́ть; *of thunder* [за]греме́ть

rumina|nt ['ru:mɪnənt] жва́чное; **~te** [-neɪt] *fig.* размышля́ть

rummage ['rʌmɪdʒ] *v/t.* переры(ва́)ть; *v/i.* ры́ться; **~ sale** благотвори́тельная распрода́жа

rumo(u)r ['ru:mə] **1.** слух; молва́; **2.:** *it is ~ed that …* хо́дят слу́хи, что …

rump [rʌmp] огу́зок

rumple ['rʌmpl] (с)мять; *hair* [взъ]еро́шить

run [rʌn] **1.** *[irr.] v/i. com* бе́гать, [по]бежа́ть; [по]те́чь; *of colo(u)rs, etc.* расплы(ва́)ться; *of engine* рабо́тать; *text* гласи́ть; **~ across a p.** случа́йно встре́тить (В); **~ away** убега́ть [убежа́ть]; **~ down** сбега́ть [сбежа́ть]; *of watch, etc.* остана́вливаться [-ови́ться]; истоща́ться [-щи́ться]; **~ dry** иссяка́ть [-я́кнуть]; **~ for** *parl.* выставля́ть свою́ кандидату́ру на (В); **~ into** впада́ть в (В); *debt* залеза́ть [-ле́зть]; *person* встреча́ть [-е́тить]; **~ on** продолжа́ться [-до́лжиться]; говори́ть без умо́лку; **~ out, ~ short** конча́ться [ко́нчиться]; **~ through** прочита́ть бе́гло *pf.; capital* прома́тывать [-мота́ть]; **~ to** *(reach)* достига́ть [-и́гнуть]; *up to* доходи́ть [дойти́] до (Р); **2.** *v/t.* пробега́ть [-бежа́ть] *(расстоя́ние); water* налива́ть; *business* вести́; *(drive in)* вонза́ть [-зи́ть]; *department, etc.* руководи́ть; прово-

ди́ть [-вести́] (Т, *over* по Д); *car* сбива́ть [сбить]; **~ down** *fig.* поноси́ть (В); *(tire)* переутомля́ть [-ми́ть]; **~ over** переезжа́ть [-е́хать], сби(ва́)ть; *прочита́ть бе́гло pf.;* **~ up** *prices* взду(ва́)ть; *building* возводи́ть [-вести́]; **~ up a bill a** [за]должа́ть (Д); **3.** бег; пробе́г; *of mechanism* рабо́та, де́йствие; *of time* тече́ние, ход; ряд; *(outing)* пое́здка, прогу́лка; руково́дство; **the common ~** обыкнове́нные лю́ди *m/pl.; thea.* **have a ~ of 20 nights** два́дцать вечеро́в подря́д; **in the long ~** со вре́менем; в конце́ концо́в

run|about ['rʌnəbaʊt] *mot.* малолитра́жка; **~away** бегле́ц

rung[1] [rʌŋ] *pt. p. om* **ring**

rung[2] [-] ступе́нька стремя́нки

runner ['rʌnə] бегу́н; *of sledge* по́лоз; *of plant* побе́г; **~up** [-'ʌp] *sport* занима́ющий второ́е ме́сто

running ['rʌnɪŋ] **1.** бегу́щий; *track* бегово́й; **two days ~** два дня подря́д; **2.** бе́ганье; *of person* бег; *of horses* бега́ *m/pl.;* **~ board** подно́жка; **~ water** *in nature* прото́чная вода́; *in man-made structures* водопрово́д

runway ['rʌnweɪ] *ae.* взлётно-поса́дочная полоса́

rupture ['rʌptʃə] **1.** разры́в; *(hernia)* гры́жа; **2.** разрыва́ть [разорва́ть] *(a. fig.);* про́р(ы)ва́ть

rural ['rʊərəl] □ се́льский, дереве́нский

rush[1] [rʌʃ] **1.** *bot.* тростни́к, камы́ш; **~ mat** цино́вка

rush[2] [-] **1.** *(influx)* напли́в; **~ hours** *pl.* часы́ пик; **2.** *v/i.* мча́ться; броса́ться [бро́ситься]; носи́ться, [по-] нести́сь; **~ into** броса́ться необду́манно в (В); *v/t.* мчать

rusk [rʌsk] суха́рь *m*

Russian ['rʌʃn] **1.** ру́сский; **2.** ру́сская; ру́сский язы́к

rust [rʌst] **1.** ржа́вчина; **2.** [за]ржаве́ть

rustic ['rʌstɪk] **(~ally)** дереве́нский; *(simple)* просто́й; *(rough)* гру́бый

rustle ['rʌsl] **1.** [за]шелесте́ть; **2.** ше́лест, шо́рох

rust|proof ['rʌstpruːf] нержаве́ющий;

R

~y ['rʌstɪ] заржа́вленный, ржа́вый
rut [rʌt] колея́ (a. fig.)
ruthless ['ru:θlɪs] безжа́лостный

rye [raɪ] bot. рожь f; ~ **bread** ржано́й хлеб

S

sabbatical [sə'bætɪkl]: ~ **leave** univ. академи́ческий о́тпуск
saber, Brt. **sabre** ['seɪbə] са́бля, ша́шка
sable ['seɪbl] со́боль m; (fur) со́болий мех
sabotage ['sæbətɑ:ʒ] 1. сабота́ж; 2. саботи́ровать (B)
sack[1] [sæk] 1. разграбле́ние; 2. [раз]гра́бить
sack[2] [-] 1. мешо́к; 2. класть, ссыпа́ть в мешо́к; coll. (dismiss) увольня́ть [-ли́ть]; ~**cloth**, ~**ing** ['sækɪŋ] мешкови́на
sacrament ['sækrəmənt] act or rite таи́нство; (Eucharist) прича́стие
sacred ['seɪkrɪd] □ свято́й; свяще́нный; mus. духо́вный
sacrifice ['sækrɪfaɪs] 1. же́ртва; (offering to a deity) жертвоприноше́ние; at a ~ с убы́тками; 2. [по]же́ртвовать
sacrilege ['sækrɪlɪdʒ] святота́тство, кощу́нство
sad [sæd] □ печа́льный, гру́стный; in a ~ state в плаче́вном состоя́нии
sadden ['sædn] о[пе]ча́лить(ся)
saddle ['sædl] 1. седло́; 2. [о]седла́ть; fig. взва́ливать [-ли́ть] (s.o. with sth. что-нибудь на кого-нибудь); обременя́ть [-ни́ть]
sadism ['seɪdɪzm] сади́зм
sadness ['sædnɪs] печа́ль f, грусть f
safe [seɪf] 1. □ невреди́мый; надёжный; безопа́сный; ~ **and sound** цел и невреди́м; in ~ **hands** в надёжных рука́х; 2. сейф; ~**guard** 1. гара́нтия; 2. охраня́ть [-ни́ть]; гаранти́ровать
safety ['seɪftɪ] 1. безопа́сность f; надёжность f; 2. безопа́сный; ~ **belt** реме́нь m безопа́сности, привязно́й ре-

ме́нь m; ~ **pin** англи́йская була́вка; ~ **razor** безопа́сная бри́тва; ~ **valve** предохрани́тельный кла́пан
saffron ['sæfrən] шафра́н
sag [sæg] of roof, etc. оседа́ть [-се́сть], прогиба́ться [-гну́ться]; of cheeks, etc. обвиса́ть [-и́снуть]; her spirits ~**ged** она́ упа́ла ду́хом
sage[1] [seɪdʒ] мудре́ц
sage[2] [-] bot. шалфе́й
said [sed] pt. и pt. p. от **say**
sail [seɪl] 1. па́рус; пла́вание под паруса́ми; 2. v/i. идти́ под паруса́ми; (travel over) пла́вать, [по]плы́ть, отплы́(ва́)ть; v/t. (control navigation of) управля́ть; пла́вать по (Д); ~**boat** па́русная ло́дка; ~**ing** [-ɪŋ] пла́вание; it wasn't plain ~всё бы́ло не так про́сто; ~**or** [-ə] моря́к, матро́с; be a (good) bad ~ (не) страда́ть морско́й боле́знью; ~**plane** планёр
saint [seɪnt] свято́й; ~**ly** ['seɪntlɪ] adj. свято́й
sake [seɪk]: for the ~ of ра́ди (Р); for my ~ ра́ди меня́
sal|**able** ['seɪləbl] хо́дкий (това́р)
salad ['sæləd] сала́т
salary ['sælərɪ] окла́д, за́работная пла́та
sale [seɪl] прода́жа; (clearance ~) распрода́жа; аукцио́н; be for ~, be on ~ име́ться в прода́же
sales|**man** продаве́ц; door-to-door коммивояжёр; ~**woman** продавщи́ца
saline ['seɪlaɪn] соляно́й; солёный
saliva [sə'laɪvə] слюна́
sallow ['sæləʊ] complexion нездоро́вый; желтова́тый
salmon ['sæmən] лосо́сь m; flesh лосо́си́на

salon ['sælɒn]: *beauty* ~ косметический салон

saloon [sə'luːn] зал; *naut.* салон; бар, пивная; *Brt.* (*car*) седан

salt [sɔːlt] **1.** соль *f*; *fig.* остроумие; *take s.th. with a grain of* ~ относиться к чему-л. скептически; **2.** солёный; **3.** [по]солить; засаливать [-солить]; ~ *cellar* солонка; ~*y* ['sɔːltɪ] солёный

salutary ['sæljʊtrɪ] □ благотворный; полезный для здоровья

salut|ation [sælju:'teɪʃn] приветствие; ~**e** [sə'luːt] **1.** *mil.* отдание чести; воинское приветствие; *with weapons* салют; **2.** приветствовать; отдавать честь *f* (Д)

salvage ['sælvɪdʒ] **1.** *of ship, property, etc.* спасение; (*what is saved*) спасённое имущество; (*scrap*) утиль *m*; *paper* макулатура; *naut.* подъём; **2.** спасать [спасти]

salvation [sæl'veɪʃn] спасение; ♀ *Army* Армия спасения

salve [sælv] **1.** успокоительное средство; **2.** *conscience* успокаивать [-коить]

salvo ['sælvəʊ] *of guns* залп; *fig.* взрыв аплодисментов

same [seɪm]: *the* ~ тот же самый; та же самая; то же самое; *all the* ~ тем не менее, всё-таки; *it is all the* ~ *to me* мне всё равно

sample ['sɑːmpl] **1.** проба; образчик, образец; *fig.* пример; **2.** [по]пробовать; отбирать образцы (Р); *wine, etc.* дегустировать

sanatorium [sænə'tɔːrɪəm] санаторий

sanct|ion ['sæŋkʃn] **1.** (*permission*) разрешение; (*approval*) одобрение; *official* санкция; *apply* ~ *against* применять [-нить] санкции против (Р); **2.** санкционировать (*im*)*pf.*; давать [дать] согласие, разрешение; ~**uary** [-tʃʊərɪ] (*holy place*) святилище; (*refuge*) убежище

sand [sænd] **1.** песок; (~*bank*) отмель *f*; *of desert* пески *m/pl.* ~**s** *pl.* песчаный пляж; **2.** (*sprinkle with* ~) посыпать песком; (*polish*) протирать [-ереть] песком

sandal ['sændl] сандалия; (*lady's a.*) босоножки *f/pl.*

sandpaper наждачная бумага

sandwich ['sænwɪdʒ] **1.** бутерброд, сандвич; **2.**: ~ *between* втискивать [-нуть] между (Т)

sandy ['sændɪ] песчаный; песочный; песочного цвета

sane [seɪn] нормальный; *fig.* здравый, разумный; здравомыслящий

sang [sæŋ] *pt. om* sing

sanguine ['sæŋgwɪn] жизнерадостный, сангвинический

sanitary ['sænɪtrɪ] □ санитарный; гигиенический; ~ *napkin* гигиеническая прокладка

sanitation [sænɪ'teɪʃn] санитарные условия; *for sewage* канализация

sanity ['sænətɪ] психическое здоровье; здравый ум

sank [sæŋk] *pt. om* sink

sap [sæp] **1.** *of plants* сок; *fig.* жизненные силы *f/pl.*; **2.** истощать [-щить]; *confidence* подрывать [подорвать]; ~*less* ['sæplɪs] истощённый; ~*ling* ['sæplɪŋ] молодое деревцо

sapphire ['sæfaɪə] *min.* сапфир

sappy ['sæpɪ] сочный; *fig.* полный сил

sarcasm ['sɑːkæzm] сарказм

sardine [sɑː'diːn] сардин(к)а; *packed like* ~*s* как сельди в бочке

sardonic [sɑ'dɒnɪk] (~*ally*) сардонический

sash [sæʃ] кушак, пояс

sash window подъёмное окно

sat [sæt] *pt. u pt. p. om* sit

satchel ['sætʃəl] сумка, ранец

sateen [sə'tiːn] сатин

satellite ['sætəlaɪt] *celestial* спутник (*a. spacecraft*)

satiate ['seɪʃɪeɪt] пресыщать [-ытить]; насыщать [-ытить]; ~*d* [-ɪd] сытый

satin ['sætɪn] атлас

satir|e ['sætaɪə] сатира; ~*ical* [sə'tɪrɪkl] сатирический; ~*ist* ['sætərɪst] сатирик; ~*ize* [-raɪz] высмеивать [высмеять]

satisfaction [sætɪs'fækʃn] удовлетворение

S

satisfactory [sætɪsˈfæktərɪ] удовле-
твори́тельный

satisfy [ˈsætɪsfaɪ] удовлетворя́ть
[-ри́ть]; *hunger, etc.* утоля́ть [-ли́ть];
obligations выполня́ть [вы́полнить];
(convince) убежда́ть [убеди́ть]

saturate [ˈsætʃəreɪt] *chem.* насыща́ть
[-ы́тить]; пропи́тывать [-ита́ть]; *we
came home ~d* пока мы добежа́ли
до́ дому, мы промо́кли

Saturday [ˈsætədɪ] суббо́та

sauce [sɔːs] со́ус; *(gravy)* подли́вка;
coll. (impudence) де́рзость *f*; **~pan**
кастрю́ля; **~r** [ˈsɔːsə] блю́дце

saucy [ˈsɔːsɪ] *coll.* де́рзкий

sauerkraut [ˈsaʊəkraʊt] ки́слая капу́-
ста

sauna [ˈsɔːnə] са́уна

saunter [ˈsɔːntə] 1. прогу́ливаться; 2.
прогу́лка

sausage [ˈsɒsɪdʒ] *(frankfurter)* соси́с-
ка; *(salami, etc.)* колбаса́; *(polony,
saveloy)* сарде́лька

savage [ˈsævɪdʒ] 1. □ ди́кий; *(cruel)*
жесто́кий; *(ferocious)* свире́пый; 2.
дика́рь *m*, -арка *f*; *fig.* зверь *m*; **~ry**
[-rɪ] ди́кость *f*; жесто́кость *f*

save [seɪv] спаса́ть [спасти́]; из-
бавля́ть [-ба́вить] *(from* от *T)*;
strength, etc. сберега́ть [-ре́чь]; *(put
by)* [с]копи́ть, откла́дывать [отло-
жи́ть]; *time, money, etc.* [с]экономить

saving [ˈseɪvɪŋ] 1. □ *(redeeming)* спа-
си́тельный; 2. *(rescue)* спасе́ние; **~s**
pl. сбереже́ния *n/pl.*

savings bank сберега́тельная ка́сса

savio(u)r [ˈseɪvjə] спаси́тель *m*; **the ~**
Спаси́тель *m*

savo(u)r [ˈseɪvə] 1. *(taste)* вкус; *fig.*
при́вкус; 2. *(enjoy)* смакова́ть; **~ of**
па́хнуть (Т); *fig.* отдава́ть (Т); **~y**
[-rɪ] вку́сный; пика́нтный, о́стрый

saw[1] [-] *pt. om* **see**

saw[2] [-] 1. пила́; 2. *[irr.]* пили́ть; **~dust**
опи́лки *f/pl.*; **~mill** лесопи́лка; лесо-
пи́льный заво́д; **~n** [sɔːn] *pt. p. om* **saw**

say [seɪ] *[irr.]* говори́ть [сказа́ть];
that is to ~ то́ есть, те; *you don't ~!* не-
ужéли!; *I ~!* послу́шай(те)!; *he is said
to be ...* говоря́т, что он ...; *I dare ~ ...*

наве́рно (вполне́) возмо́жно ...; *they
~ ...* говоря́т ...; 2. име́ть значе́ние;
сказа́ть *pf.* своё мне́ние, сказа́ть *pf.* своё
сло́во; **~ing** [ˈseɪɪŋ] погово́рка

scab [skæb] *on a sore* струп

scaffolding [ˈskæfəldɪŋ] *arch.* леса́
m/pl.

scald [skɔːld] 1. ожо́г; 2. [о]шпа́рить;
обва́ривать [-ри́ть]

scale[1] [skeɪl] 1. *of fish, etc.* чешу́йка
(collect.: чешуя́); *inside kettles, etc.* на́-
кипь *f*; 2. *fish* [по]чи́стить; *of skin* ше-
луши́ться

scale[2] [-] *(a pair of)* **~s** *pl.* весы́ *m/pl.*

scale[3] [-] 1. масшта́б; *(size)* разме́р; *in
grading* шкала́; *mus.* га́мма; 2.: **~ up**
постепе́нно увели́чивать; **~ down** по-
степе́нно уменьша́ть в масшта́бе

scallop [ˈskɒləp] *mollusk* гребешо́к

scalp [skælp] ко́жа головы́; *hist.*
скальп

scamp [skæmp] 1. шалу́н; безде́льник;
2. рабо́тать ко́е-как; **~er** [-ə] бежа́ть
поспе́шно; **~ away, off** уд(и)ра́ть

scandal [ˈskændl] сканда́л; *(gossip)*
спле́тни *f/pl.*; *it's a ~!* позо́р!;
~ize [-dəlaɪz] возмуща́ть [-ти́ть]; шо-
ки́ровать *impf.*; **~ous** [-ləs] □ позо́р-
ный; сканда́льный; *(defamatory)* кле-
ветни́ческий; *(shocking)* ужа́сный

scant, scanty [skænt, ˈskæntɪ] ску́д-
ный; недоста́точный

scapegoat [ˈskeɪpɡəʊt] козёл от-
пуще́ния

scar [skɑː] 1. шрам; рубе́ц; 2. *v/t.* по-
крыва́ться рубца́ми; *his face was
~red* лицо́ его́ бы́ло покры́то шра́ма-
ми; *v/i.* [за]рубцева́ться

scarce [skeəs] недоста́точный; ску́д-
ный; *(rare)* ре́дкий; *goods* дефици́т-
ный; *make o.s. ~* убира́ться
[убра́ться]; **~ly** [-lɪ] едва́ ли, как
то́лько; едва́; **~ity** [-sətɪ] нехва́тка;
ре́дкость *f*

scare [skeə] 1. [на-, ис]пуга́ть; отпу́ги-
вать [-гну́ть] *(a. ~ away)*; 2. испу́г; па́-
ника; **~crow** пу́гало; *a. fig.* чу́чело

scarf [skɑːf] шарф; *(head~)* плато́к,
косы́нка

scarlet [ˈskɑːlɪt] 1. а́лый цвет; 2. а́лый;

~ fever скарлати́на

scathing ['skeɪðɪŋ] ре́зкий; язви́тельный

scatter ['skætə] разбра́сывать [-броса́ть] (*a.* **~ about, around**); рассыпа́ть(ся) [-ы́пать(ся)]; *clouds, etc.* рассе́ивать(ся) [-е́ять(ся)]; *crowd* разбега́ться [-жа́ться]

scenario [sɪ'nɑːrɪəʊ] сцена́рий

scene [siːn] сце́на; вид; ме́сто де́йствия; **behind the ~s** за кули́сами (*a. fig.*); **make a ~** устро́ить *pf.* сце́ну, сканда́л; **~ry** ['siːnərɪ] *thea.* декора́ции *f/pl.*; пейза́ж

scent [sent] **1.** арома́т, за́пах; (*perfume*) духи́ *m/pl.*; *hunt.* след; чутьё; нюх; **follow the wrong ~** идти́ по ло́жному следу́; **2.** *danger, etc.* [по]чу́ять; [на]души́ть

schedule ['ʃedjuːl] **1.** *of charges* спи́сок, пе́речень *m*; *of work* гра́фик, план; (*timetable*) расписа́ние; **a full ~** больша́я програ́мма; **2.** составля́ть расписа́ние (P); (*plan*) назнача́ть [назна́чить], намеча́ть [-е́тить]

scheme [skiːm] **1.** схе́ма; план; прое́кт; (*plot*) интри́га. **2.** *v/t.* [за]проекти́ровать; *v/i* плести́ интри́ги

schnitzel ['ʃnɪtzl] шни́цель *m*

scholar ['skɒlə] учёный; (*holder of scholarship*) стипендиа́т; **~ly** [-lɪ] *adj.* учёный; **~ship** [-ʃɪp] учёность *f*, эруди́ция; (*grant-in-aid*) стипе́ндия

school [skuːl] **1.** шко́ла; **at ~** в шко́ле; **secondary** (*Am.* **high**) **~** сре́дняя шко́ла; **2.** [на]учи́ть; приуча́ть [-чи́ть]; **~boy** шко́льник; **~fellow** шко́льный това́рищ; **~girl** шко́льница; **~ing** ['skuːlɪŋ] обуче́ние в шко́ле; **~master** учи́тель *m*; **~mate** → **schoolfellow**; **~mistress** учи́тельница; **~room** кла́ссная ко́мната

science ['saɪəns] нау́ка

scientific [saɪən'tɪfɪk] (**~ally**) нау́чный

scientist ['saɪəntɪst] учёный

scintillate ['sɪntɪleɪt] и́скриться; сверка́ть [-кну́ть]; мерца́ть; **scintillating wit** блестя́щее остроу́мие

scissors ['sɪzəz] *pl.* (*a* **pair of ~**) но́жницы *f/pl.*

sclerosis [sklə'rəʊsɪs] *med.* склеро́з

scoff [skɒf] **1.** насме́шка; **2.** смея́ться (*at* над Т)

scold [skəʊld] [вы́-, от]руга́ть, [вы́-] брани́ть; отчи́тывать [-чита́ть]

scone [skɒn] бу́лочка

scoop [skuːp] **1.** сово́к; *for liquids* черпа́к, ковш; *in newspaper* сенсацио́нная но́вость *f*; заче́рпывать [-пну́ть]

scooter ['skuːtə] *child's* самока́т; *mot.* мото700ро́ллер

scope [skəʊp] кругозо́р; разма́х; охва́т; просто́р; *of activity* сфе́ра; **outside the ~** за преде́лами (**of** P)

scorch [skɔːtʃ] *v/t.* обжига́ть [обже́чь]; [с]пали́ть; *coll.* бе́шено нести́сь; **~er** ['-ə] *coll.* (*hot day*) зно́йный день

score [skɔː] **1.** (*cut*) зару́бка; *sport* счёт; *mus.* партиту́ра; **~s** *pl.* мно́жество; **on the ~ of**, **on** *this* ~, **on** *that* ~ на э́тот счёт, по э́тому по́воду; **what's the ~?** како́й счёт?; **2.** отмеча́ть [-е́тить]; засчи́тывать [-ита́ть]; выи́грывать [вы́играть]; забива́ть гол; *mus.* оркестрова́ть (*im*)*pf.*; *chiefly Am.* [вы́]брани́ть; **~board** табло́ *n indecl.*

scorn [skɔːn] **1.** презре́ние; **2.** презира́ть [-зре́ть]; *advice* пренебрега́ть [-ре́чь]; **~ful** ['skɔːnfl] □ *pers.* надме́нный; *look, etc.* презри́тельный

Scotch [skɒtʃ] **1.** шотла́ндский; **2.** шотла́ндский диале́кт; (*whiskey*) шотла́ндское ви́ски; **the ~** шотла́ндцы *m/pl.*; **~man** шотла́ндец; *trademark* **~ tape** кле́йкая ле́нта, скотч; **~woman** шотла́ндка

scot-free [skɒt'friː] невреди́мый; (*unpunished*) безнака́занный

scoundrel ['skaʊndrəl] негодя́й, подле́ц

scour[1] ['skaʊə] *v/t.* [вы́]чи́стить; *pan* начища́ть [начи́стить]; *with water* промыва́ть [про]мы́ть

scour[2] ['-] *area* прочёсывать [-чеса́ть] (В); *v/i.* ры́скать (*a.* **about**)

scourge [skɜːdʒ] **1.** бич (*a. fig.*); бе́дствие; **2.** [по]кара́ть

scout [skaʊt] 1. разведчик (*a. ae.*); *Boy*
2s *pl.* скауты *m/pl.*; 2. производить
разведку; ~ *about for* [по]искать (В)

scowl [skaʊl] 1. хмурый вид; 2. [на]
хмуриться; ~ *at* хмуро посмотреть
pf. на (В)

scraggy ['skrægɪ] тощий

scram [skræm] *coll.*: ~! убирайся!

scramble ['skræmbl] 1. [вс]карабкаться; бороться (*for* за В); ~*d eggs*
pl. яичница-болтунья; 2. свалка,
борьба; карабканье

scrap [skræp] 1. *of paper* клочок, кусочек; *of cloth* лоскуток; (*cutting*)
вырезка; (*waste*) лом; вторичное
сырьё; ~*s pl.* остатки *m/pl.*; *of food*
объедки *m/pl.*; 2. (*throw away*) выбрасывать [выбросить]

scrap|e [skreɪp] 1. скобление; *on knee,
etc.* царапина; (*predicament*) затруднение; 2. скоблить; скрести(сь); соскребать [-ести] (*mst.* ~ *off*); отчищать [-истить]; (*touch*) заде(ва)ть;
~ *together* money наскрести

scrap iron железный лом

scrappy ['skræpɪ] отрывочный

scratch [skrætʃ] царапина; *start from*
~ начинать[-чать] с нуля; [о]царапать; ~
out (*erase*) вычёркивать
[вычеркнуть]

scrawl [skrɔːl] 1. каракули *f/pl.*; 2. написать *pf.* неразборчиво

scream [skriːm] 1. вопль *m*; крик; ~*s of
laughter* взрывы смеха; 2. пронзительно кричать

screech [skriːtʃ] 1. крик; визг; 2. пронзительно кричать; взвизгивать
[-гнуть]

screen [skriːn] 1. ширма; экран (*a.
cine*); ~ *adaptation* экранизация;
adapt for the ~ экранизировать; *the*
~ кино *n indecl.*; 2. (*protect*) прикры(ва)ть; заслонять [-нить]; *film* показывать на экране; просеивать [-еять];
(*investigate*) проверять [-ерить]

screw [skruː] 1. шуруп; винт; 2. привинчивать [-нтить] (*mst.* ~ *on*); ~ *together* скреплять винтами; ~ *up* завинчивать [-нтить]; *one's face* [с]морщить; ~*driver* отвёртка

scribble ['skrɪbl] 1. каракули *f/pl.*; 2.
написать *pf.* небрежно

scrimp [skrɪmp]: ~ *and save* всячески
экономить

script [skrɪpt] *cine.* сценарий; ~*writer*
сценарист

Scripture ['skrɪptʃə]: *Holy* ~ Священное писание

scroll [skrəʊl] свиток; (*list*) список

scrub[1] [skrʌb] куст; ~*s pl.* кустарник;
заросль *f*

scrub[2] [-] мыть [вымыть]

scrubby ['skrʌbɪ] *plant* (*stunted*)
чахлый

scruffy ['skrʌfɪ] грязный; неопрятный

scrup|le ['skruːpl] сомнения *n/pl.*;
~*ulous* ['skruːpjʊləs] [-] щепетильный; (*thorough*) скрупулёзный; (*conscientious*) добросовестный

scrutin|ize ['skruːtɪnaɪz] внимательно
рассматривать [-мотреть]; *case, etc.*
тщательно изучать [-чить]; ~*y*
['skruːtɪnɪ] испытующий
взгляд; всесторонняя проверка; внимательное изучение

scud [skʌd] *of clouds* нестись; *of yacht*
скользить

scuffle ['skʌfl] 1. потасовка, драка; 2.
[по]драться

sculptor ['skʌlptə] скульптор

sculpture ['skʌlptʃə] 1. скульптура; 2.
[из]ваять; *in stone* высекать
[высечь]; *in wood* резать [вырезать]

scum [skʌm] пена; *fig.* подонки *m/pl.*

scurf [skɜːf] перхоть *f*

scurry ['skʌrɪ] быстро бегать; суетливо двигаться; сновать (туда и сюда);
they scurried for shelter они бросились в укрытие

scurvy ['skɜːvɪ] *med.* цинга

scythe [saɪð] коса

sea [siː] море; *attr.* морской; *be at* ~ *fig.*
не знать, что делать; недоумевать;
~*faring* ['siːfeərɪŋ] мореплавание;
~*going* ['siːgəʊɪŋ] *ship* мореходный

seal[1] [siːl] *zo.* тюлень *m*

seal[2] [-] 1. печать *f*; (*leaden* ~) пломба;
2. *letter* запеча́т(ыв)ать; скреплять
печатью; *room* опеча́т(ыв)ать

sea level у́ровень *m* мо́ря

sealing ['siːlɪŋ] *tech.* уплотне́ние; ~ **wax** сургу́ч

seam [siːm] **1.** шов (*a. tech.*); рубе́ц; *geol.* пласт; **2.** сши(ва́)ть

sea|man моря́к; матро́с; ~**plane** гидросамолёт

searing ['sɪərɪŋ]: ~ **pain** жгу́чая боль *f*

search [sɜːtʃ] **1.** по́иски *m/pl.*; *by police* о́быск; ро́зыск; **in** ~ **of** в по́исках (P); ~ **party** поиско́вая гру́ппа; **2.** *v/t.* иска́ть; обы́скивать [-ка́ть]; ~ **me!** не име́ю поня́тия; *v/i.* разы́скивать [-ка́ть] (**for** B); ~**ing** [-ɪŋ] тща́тельный; *look* испыту́ющий; ~**light** прожёктор; ~ **warrant** о́рдер на о́быск

sea|shore морско́й бе́рег; ~**sick** страда́ющий морско́й боле́знью; ~**side** примо́рье; взмо́рье; **go to the** ~ пое́хать *pf.* на мо́ре; *attr.* примо́рский; ~ **resort** морско́й куро́рт

season ['siːzn] **1.** вре́мя го́да; пери́од; сезо́н; *holiday* ~ пери́од отпуско́в; *apricots are in* ~ **now** абрико́сы сейча́с созре́ли; **with the compliments of the** ~ с лу́чшими пожела́ниями к пра́зднику; **2.** *v/t. food* приправля́ть [-а́вить]; *wood.* выде́рживать [вы́держать]; ~**able** [-əbl] □ своевре́менный; по сезо́ну; ~**al** [-zənl] □ сезо́нный; ~**ing** [-zənɪŋ] припра́ва; ~ **ticket** сезо́нный биле́т

seat [siːt] **1.** *in car* сиде́нье; (*garden* ~) скамья́; *thea., etc.* ме́сто; *take a* ~ сесть *pf.*; *take one's* ~ занима́ть [-ня́ть] своё ме́сто; **2.** уса́живать [усади́ть]; (*hold*) вмеща́ть [вмести́ть]; ~**ed** [-ɪd] сидя́щий; *be* ~ сиде́ть, сади́ться [сесть]

sea|weed морска́я во́доросль *f*; ~**worthy** го́дный к пла́ванию

secede [sɪ'siːd] отделя́ться [-ли́ться]; отка́лываться [отколо́ться]

seclu|de [sɪ'kluːd] изоли́ровать (**from** от P); ~ **o.s.** уединя́ться [-ни́ться]; ~**ded** [-ɪd] уединённый; изоли́рованный; ~**sion** [-'kluːʒn] уедине́ние

second ['sekənd] **1.** ~ второ́й; втори́чный; уступа́ющий (**to** Д); **on** ~ **thoughts** по зре́лому размышле́нию; **2.** секу́нда; *a split* ~ до́ля секу́нды;

мгнове́ние; **3.** (*support*) подде́рживать [-жа́ть]; ~**ary** [-rɪ] □ втори́чный; второстепе́нный; побо́чный; ~ *education* сре́днее образова́ние; ~**hand** поде́ржанный; *information* из вторы́х рук; ~ *bookshop* букинисти́ческий магази́н; ~**ly** [-lɪ] во-вторы́х; ~**rate** второсо́ртный; *hotel* второразря́дный; *writer, etc.* посре́дственный

secre|cy ['siːkrəsɪ] *of person* скры́тность *f*; секре́тность *f*; ~**t** ['siːkrɪt] **1.** □ та́йный; секре́тный; **2.** та́йна, секре́т; **in** ~ секре́тно, тайко́м; *be in on the* ~ быть посвящённым в секре́т; *keep a* ~ храни́ть та́йну

secretary ['sekrətrɪ] секрета́рь *m*, *coll.* секрета́рша; мини́стр

secret|e [sɪ'kriːt] *med.* выделя́ть [вы́делить]; ~**ion** [-'kriːʃn] выделе́ние

secretive ['siːkrətɪv] скры́тный

section ['sekʃn] (*cut*) сече́ние, разре́з; (*part*) часть *f*; *of orange* до́лька; *in newspaper* отде́л; *of book* разде́л; ~**al** [-ʃənl] разбо́рный, секцио́нный

sector ['sektə] се́ктор

secular ['sekjʊlə] □ *noneccl.* све́тский; *of this world* мирско́й

secur|e [sɪ'kjʊə] **1.** □ (*safe*) безопа́сный; (*reliable*) надёжный; (*firm*) про́чный; уве́ренный; *I feel* ~ *about my future* я уве́рена в своём бу́дущем; **2.** (*make fast*) закрепля́ть [-пи́ть]; обеспе́чи(ва)ть; (*make safe*) обезопа́сить *pf.*; (*get*) дост(ав)а́ть; ~**ity** [-rətɪ] безопа́сность *f*; надёжность *f*; обеспе́чение; зало́г; ~**ities** *pl.* це́нные бума́ги *f/pl.*

sedate [sɪ'deɪt] □ степе́нный

sedative ['sedətɪv] *mst. med.* успока́ивающее сре́дство

sedentary ['sedntrɪ] □ сидя́чий

sediment ['sedɪmənt] оса́док

seduc|e [sɪ'djuːs] соблазня́ть [-ни́ть]; ~**tive** [sɪ'dʌktɪv] □ соблазни́тельный

see [siː] (*irr.*) *v/i.* [у]ви́деть; ~ я понима́ю; ~ *about a th.* [по]забо́титься о (П); ~ *through a p.* ви́деть кого́-л. наскво́зь; *v/t.* [у]ви́деть; *film, etc.* [по]смотре́ть; замеча́ть [-е́тить]; понимáть [-нять]; посещáть [-етить]; ~ *a p.* **home** провожáть кого-нибудь домóй; ~ **off** провожáть [-водить]; ~ **to** позабóтиться (о П); заня́ться *pf.* (Т); ~ *a* **th. through** доводить [довести] чтó-нибудь до концá; **live to** ~ дожи́(-вá)ть до (Р)

seed [si:d] **1.** сéмя *n* (*a. fig.*); *of grain* зернó; *collect.* семенá *n/pl.*; *of apple, etc.* зёрнышко; (*offspring*) *mst. Bibl.* потóмство; **2.** *v/t.* засевáть [засéять]; [по]сéять; ~**ling** ['si:dlɪŋ] *agric.* сéянец; (*tree*) сáженец; ~**s** *pl.* рассáда *collect.*; ~**y** ['si:dɪ] напóлненный семенáми; (*shabby*) потрёпанный, обноси́вшийся; *coll.* не в фóрме; нездорóвый

seek [si:k] [*irr.*] *mst. fig.* искáть (Р); ~ **advice** обращáться за совéтом; ~ **after** добивáться (Р); ~ **out** разы́скивать [-ыскáть]; оты́скивать [-кáть]

seem [si:m] [по]казáться; ~**ing** ['-ɪŋ] □ кáжущийся; мни́мый; ~**ingly** ['-ɪŋlɪ] пови́димому; ~**ly** ['-lɪ] подобáющий; присто́йный

seen [si:n] *pt. p. om* **see**

seep [si:p] просáчиваться [-сочи́ться]

seesaw ['si:sɔ:] доскá-качéли *f/pl.*

seethe [si:ð] бурли́ть; *fig.* кипéть

segment ['segmənt] *math.* сегмéнт, отрéзок; *of orange* дóлька; (*part*) кусóк, часть *f*

segregate ['segrɪgeɪt] отделя́ть [-ли́ть]

seismic ['saɪzmɪk] сейсми́ческий

seiz|e [si:z] (*take hold of*) хватáть [схвати́ть]; (*take possession of*) захвáтывать [захвати́ть]; ухвати́ться за (В) *pf.* (*a. fig.*); *property* конфисковáть (*im*)*pf.*; *fig. of feeling* охвати́ть [-ти́ть]; ~**ure** ['si:ʒə] *med.* при́ступ

seldom ['seldəm] *adv.* рéдко, почти́ никогдá

select [sɪ'lekt] отбирáть [отобрáть]; *s.th. to match* подбирáть [подобрáть]; **2.** отбóрный; (*exclusive*) и́збранный; ~**ion** [sɪ'lekʃn] вы́бор; подбóр; отбóр

self [self] **1.** *pron.* сам; себя́; *coll.* = **myself** *etc.* я сам *и т.д.*; **2.** *su.* (*pl.* **selves** [selvz]) ли́чность *f*; ~**assured** само-

увéренный; ~**centered**, *Brt.* **-centred** эгоцентри́чный; ~**command** самооблáдание; ~**conceit** самомнéние; ~**conscious** застéнчивый; ~**contained** *person* самостоя́тельный; *lodgings, etc.* отдéльный; *fig.* зáмкнутый; ~**control** самооблáдание; ~**defence** (-nse): **in** ~ при самозащи́те; ~**determination** самоопределéние; ~**evident** очеви́дный; ~**interest** своекоры́стие; ~**ish** ['selfɪʃ] эгоисти́чный; ~**possession** самооблáдание; ~**reliant** полагáющийся на самогó себя́; ~**seeking** своекоры́стный; ~**service** самообслу́живание; ~**willed** своевóльный

sell [sel] [*irr.*] прод(ав)áть; торговáть; ~ **off**, ~ **out** распрод(ав)áть; ~**er** ['selə] продавéц (-вщи́ца)

semblance ['sembləns] подóбие; вид; **put on a** ~ **of ...** притворя́ться [-ри́ться]

semi... ['semɪ...] полу...; ~**final** полуфинáл

seminary ['semɪnərɪ] семинáрия

semolina [semə'li:nə] мáнная крупá; *cooked* мáнная кáша

senate ['senɪt] сенáт; *univ.* совéт

senator ['senətə] сенáтор

send [send] [*irr.*] пос(ы)лáть; отправля́ть [-áвить]; ~ **for** пос(ы)- лáть за (Т); *for signal, etc.* посылáть [-слáть]; *invitations* разосылáть [рассылáть]; ~ **up** вызывáть повышéние (Р); ~ **word** сообщáть [-щи́ть]; ~**er** [-ə] отправи́тель *m*

senile ['si:naɪl] стáрческий

senior ['si:nɪə] **1.** стáрший; ~ **partner** *comm.* главá фи́рмы; **2.** стáрше; **he is my** ~ **by a year** он стáрше меня́ нá год; ~**ity** [si:nɪ'ɒrətɪ] старшинствó

sensation [sen'seɪʃn] ощущéние; чу́вство; сенсáция; **cause a** ~ вызывáть ['-звать] сенсáцию; ~**al** [-ʃənl] □ сенсацио́нный

sense [sens] **1.** чу́вство; ощущéние; смысл; значéние; **common** ~ здрáвый смысл; **bring a p. to his** ~**s** *pl. fig.* образу́мить *pf.* когó-л.; **make** ~ имéть смысл; быть поня́тным; **2.** ощущáть [ощути́ть], [по]чу́вствовать

senseless ['senslis] □ бессмы́сленный; (*unconscious*) без созна́ния

sensibility [sensə'bɪlətɪ] чувстви́тельность f

sensible ['sensəbl] □ (благо)разу́мный; здравомы́слящий; (*that can be felt*) ощути́мый, заме́тный; **be** ~ **of** созн(ав)а́ть (В)

sensitiv|e ['sensətɪv] □ чувстви́тельный (**to** к Д); ~**ity** [sensə'tɪvətɪ] чувстви́тельность f (**to** к Д)

sensual ['sensʊəl] □ чу́вственный

sent [sent] *pt. и pt. p. om* **send**

sentence ['sentəns] **1.** *law* пригово́р; *gr.* предложе́ние; **serve one's** ~ отбы́вать наказа́ние; **2.** пригова́ривать [-говори́ть]

sententious [sen'tenʃəs] дидакти́чный; нравоучи́тельный

sentiment ['sentɪmənt] чу́вство; (*opinion*) мне́ние; → ~**ality**, ~**al** [sentɪ'mentl] сентимента́льный; ~**ality** [sentɪmen'tælɪtɪ] сентимента́льность f

sentry ['sentrɪ] *mil.* часово́й

separa|ble ['sepərəbl] □ отдели́мый; ~**te 1.** □ ['seprɪt] отде́льный; осо́бый; *pol.* сепара́тный; **2.** ['sepəreɪt] отделя́ть(ся) [-ли́ть(ся)]; (*part*) разлуча́ть(ся) [-чи́ть(ся)]; (*go different ways*) расходи́ться [разойти́сь]; ~**tion** [sepə'reɪʃn] разлу́ка; расстава́ние; ~**tism** ['sepərətɪzm] сепарати́зм; ~**tist** ['sepərətɪst] сепарати́ст

September [sep'tembə] сентя́брь m

sequel ['si:kwəl] *of story* продолже́ние; (*result, consequence*) после́дствие

sequence ['si:kwəns] после́довательность f; (*series*) ряд, цикл

serenade [serə'neɪd] серена́да

seren|e [sɪ'ri:n] □ безо́блачный (*a. fig.*); я́сный; безмяте́жный; споко́йный; ~**ity** [sɪ'renətɪ] споко́йствие; безмяте́жность f; безо́блачность f

serf [sɜːf] *hist.* крепостно́й

sergeant ['sɑːdʒənt] *mil.* сержа́нт

serial ['sɪərɪəl] □ поря́дковый; сери́йный; после́довательный; ~ **number** сери́йный но́мер

series ['sɪəri:z] *sg. a. pl.* се́рия; (*number*) ряд; *of goods* па́ртия

serious ['sɪərɪəs] □ серьёзный; **be** ~ серьёзно говори́ть; ~**ness** [-nɪs] серьёзность f

sermon ['sɜːmən] про́поведь f

serpent ['sɜːpənt] змея́; ~**ine** [-aɪn] изви́листый

servant ['sɜːvənt] слуга́ m; служа́нка; прислу́га; **civil** ~ госуда́рственный слу́жащий

serve [sɜːv] **1.** *v/t.* [по]служи́ть (Д); *dinner, ball in tennis, etc.* под(ав)а́ть; *in shops, etc.* обслу́живать [-жи́ть]; *law* вруча́ть [-чи́ть] (**on** Д); *sentence* отбы(ва́)ть; (*it*) ~**s him right** так ему́ и на́до; ~ **out** выд(ав)а́ть, разд(ав)а́ть; *v/i.* [по]служи́ть (*a. mil.*) (*as* Т); **2.** *tennis*; пода́ча

service ['sɜːvɪs] **1.** слу́жба; *in hotel, etc.* обслу́живание; услу́га; (*a. divine* ~) богослуже́ние; (*train, etc.* ~) сообще́ние; *tennis:* пода́ча; *tech.* техобслу́живание; **the** ~**s** *pl.* а́рмия, флот и вое́нная авиа́ция; **be at a p.'s** ~ быть к чьи́м-либо услу́гам; ~ **station** ста́нция техобслу́живания; **2.** *Am. tech.* [от]ремонти́ровать; ~**able** ['sɜːvɪsəbl] □ поле́зный; про́чный

serviette [sɜːvɪ'et] салфе́тка

servile ['sɜːvaɪl] подобостра́стный

servitude ['sɜːvɪtjuːd] ра́бство; **penal** ~ ка́торжные рабо́ты, отбы́тие сро́ка наказа́ния

session ['seʃn] *parl.* се́ссия; *law, etc.* заседа́ние

set [set] **1.** [*irr.*] *v/t.* (*adjust*) [по]ста́вить; *place* класть [положи́ть]; помеща́ть (-сти́ть); *homework, etc.* зад(ав)а́ть; *cine.* вставля́ть в ра́му; уса́живать [усади́ть] (**to** за В); *med.* вправля́ть [-а́вить]; ~ **a p. laughing** [рас]смеши́ть кого́-л.; ~ **sail** отпра́виться *pf.* в пла́вание; ~ **aside** откла́дывать [отложи́ть]; ~ **store by** высоко́ цени́ть (В); счита́ть ва́жным (В); ~ **forth** излага́ть [изложи́ть]; ~ **off** отправля́ться [-виться]; ~ **up** учрежда́ть [-еди́ть]; устра́ивать [-ро́ить]; **2.** *v/i. astr.* заходи́ть [зайти́], сади́ться [сесть]; *of jelly* застыі(ва́)ть; **~ about a th.** принима́ться [-ня́ться] за что́-л.; **~ out → ~ off.**; **to work** бра́ться [взя́ться] за рабо́ту; **~ o.s. up as** выдава́ть себя́ за (B); **3.** неподви́жный; *time* определённый; *rules* устано́вленный; *smile* засты́вший; *(rigid)* твёрдый; **hard~** нужда́ющийся; **4.** набо́р; компле́кт; *of furniture* гарниту́р; *(tea~, etc.)* серви́з; *(радио-)*приёмник; *(group)* круг; *tennis*: сет; *thea.* декора́ции

setback ['setbæk] заде́ржка; неуда́ча; *in production* спад

settee [se'tiː] кушетка

setting ['setɪŋ] *of jewels* опра́ва; *thea.* декора́ции; *fig.* окружа́ющая обстано́вка; *of sun* захо́д

settle ['setl] *v/t.* поселя́ть [-ли́ть]; приводи́ть в поря́док; *nerves*: успока́ивать [-ко́ить]; *question* реша́ть [-и́ть]; *(arrange)* устра́ивать [-ро́ить], ула́живать [-а́дить]; заселя́ть [-ли́ть]; *bill* опла́чивать [-ати́ть]; *v/i. (often ~ down)* поселя́ться [-ли́ться]; устра́иваться [-ро́иться]; уса́живаться [усе́сться]; приходи́ть к соглаше́нию; *of dust, etc.* оседа́ть [осе́сть]; *of weather* устана́вливаться [-нови́ться]; **reach a ~** достига́ть [-ти́чь] соглаше́ния; **~r** ['setlə] поселе́нец

set-to ['settu] сва́тка; *coll.* потасо́вка; *verbal* перепа́лка

seven ['sevn] семь; семёрка → *five*; **~teen(th)** [sevn'tiːn(θ)] семна́дцать [-тый]; **~th** ['sevnθ] **1.** □ седьмо́й; **2.** седьма́я часть *f*; **~tieth** ['sevntɪθ] семидеся́тый; **~ty** ['sevntɪ] се́мьдесят

sever ['sevə] *v/t. (cut)* разреза́ть [-е́зать]; разрыва́ть [-зорва́ть] *(a. fig.)*; *v li.* [по]рва́ть(ся)

several ['sevrəl] не́сколько (P); *(some)* не́которые *pl.*; □ отде́льный; **they went their ~ ways** ка́ждый пошёл свое́й доро́гой; **~ly** по отде́льности

severe [sɪ'vɪə] *(strict, stern)* стро́гий,

суро́вый *(a. of climate)*; *(violent, strong)* си́льный; *competition* жесто́кий; *losses* кру́пный; **~ity** [sɪ'verətɪ] стро́гость *f*; суро́вость *f*

sew [səʊ] [*irr.*] [с]шить; **~ on** пришива́ть [-ши́ть]

sewer ['sjuːə] канализацио́нная труба́; **~age** ['sjuːəːrɪdʒ] канализа́ция

sewing ['səʊɪŋ] шитьё; *attr.* шве́йный; **~n** [səʊn] *pt. p. om* **sew**

sex [seks] пол; секс; **~ual** ['seksjʊəl] □ полово́й; сексуа́льный

shabby ['ʃæbɪ] □ *clothes* потёртый; *building, etc.* убо́гий; *behavio(u)r* по́длый; *excuse* жа́лкий

shack [ʃæk] *Am.* лачу́га, хиба́рка

shackle ['ʃækl]: **~s** *pl. (fetters)* око́вы *f/pl.*

shade [ʃeɪd] **1.** тень *f*; *(hue)* отте́нок; *(lamp~)* абажу́р; *fig.* нюа́нс; *paint* те́ни *f/pl.*; **2.** заслоня́ть [-ни́ть]; затеня́ть [-ни́ть]; [за-] штрихова́ть

shadow ['ʃædəʊ] **1.** тень *f*; *(ghost)* при́зрак; **2.** *(follow)* та́йно следи́ть за (T); **~y** [-ɪ] тени́стый; *(indistinct)* сму́тный, нея́сный

shady ['ʃeɪdɪ] тени́стый; *coll.* тёмный, сомни́тельный; *side* тенево́й

shaft [ʃɑːft] *tech.* вал

shaggy ['ʃægɪ] косма́тый

shake [ʃeɪk] **1.** [*irr.*] *v/t.* трясти́ (B or T); тряхну́ть (T) *pf.*; встря́хивать [-хну́ть]; *of explosion* потряса́ть [-сти́] *(a. fig.)*; *faith* [по]колеба́ть; *finger, fist* [по]грози́ть; **~ hands** пожа́ть ру́ку друг дру́гу, обменя́ться рукопожа́тием; **~ one's head** покача́ть *pf.* голово́й; *v/i.* [за]трясти́сь; [за]дрожа́ть *(with, at* от P); **2.** дрожь *f*; потрясе́ние; **~n** ['ʃeɪkən] **1.** *p. pt. om* **shake**; **2.** *adj.* потрясённый

shaky ['ʃeɪkɪ] □ *on one's legs* нетвёрдый; *hands* трясу́щийся; *(not firm)* ша́ткий; **my German is ~** я пло́хо зна́ю неме́цкий язы́к

shall [ʃæl] [*irr.*] *v/aux.* вспом., глаго́л, образу́ющий бу́дущее *(1-е лицо́ единственного и множественного числа)*: **I ~ do** я бу́ду де́лать, я сде́лаю

shallow ['ʃæləʊ] **1.** ме́лкий; *fig.* повёрхностный; 2.: *the ~s* мелково́дье

sham [ʃæm] **1.** притво́рный; подде́льный; **2.** притво́рство; подде́лка; притво́рщик *m*; **3.** *v/t.* симули́ровать *(im)pf.*; *v/i.* притворя́ться [-ти́ться]

shamble [ʃæmbl] волочи́ть но́ги

shambles [ʃæmblz] *(disorder)* беспоря́док

shame [ʃeɪm] **1.** стыд; позо́р; *for ~!* сты́дно!; *what a ~!* кака́я жа́лость!; *it's a ~ that ...* жаль, что ...; *put to ~* [при]сты́дить; **2.** [при-] стыди́ть; [о]срами́ть; **~faced** [ʃeɪmfeɪst] □ пристыжённый, винова́тый вид; **~ful** [ʃeɪmfl] □ посты́дный; позо́рный; **~less** [ʃeɪmlɪs] □ бессты́дный

shampoo [ʃæmˈpuː] **1.** шампу́нь *m*; мытьё головы́; **2.** мыть шампу́нем

shamrock [ʃæmrɒk] трили́стник

shank [ʃæŋk] *anat.* го́лень *f*

shape [ʃeɪp] **1.** фо́рма; *(outline)* очерта́ние; **2.** *v/t.* созд(ав)а́ть; придава́ть фо́рму, вид (Д); *v/i.* [с]формирова́ться; **~less** [-lɪs] бесфо́рменный; **~ly** [-lɪ] хорошо́ сло́женный

share [ʃeə] **1.** до́ля, часть *f*; *(participation)* уча́стие; *fin.* а́кция; *go~s pl.* плати́ть по́ровну; *have no ~ in* не име́ть отноше́ния (к Д); **2.** *v/t.* [по]дели́ться (Т); *v/i.* уча́ствовать (*in* в П); **~holder** акционе́р

shark [ʃɑːk] аку́ла *(a. fig.)*

sharp [ʃɑːp] **1.** □ *com.* о́стрый *(a. fig.)*; *fig. (clear in shape)* отчётливый; *turn* круто́й; *(biting)* е́дкий; *pain* ре́зкий; *voice* пронзи́тельный; *remark* ко́лкий; *coll.* продувно́й; **2.** *adv.* кру́то; то́чно; *at 2 o'clock ~* ро́вно в два часа́; *look ~!* жи́во!; **3.** *mus.* дие́з; **~en** [ˈʃɑːpən] [на]точи́ть; заостри́ть [-ри́ть]; **~ener** [ˈʃɑːpənə] *(pencil ~)* точи́лка; **~ness** [ˈʃɑːpnɪs] острота́; ре́зкость *f*; **~sighted** зо́ркий; **~witted** остроу́мный

shatter [ˈʃætə] разбива́ть вдре́безги; *hope* разруша́ть [-ру́шить]; *health* расстра́ивать [-ро́ить]

shave [ʃeɪv] **1.** [*irr.*] [по]бри́ть(ся); *plank* [вы́]строгать; **2.** бритьё; *have a ~* [по]бри́ться; *have a close ~* едва́

избежа́ть опа́сности; **~n** [ˈʃeɪvn] бри́тый

shaving [ˈʃeɪvɪŋ] **1.** бритьё; **~s** *pl.* стру́жки *f/pl.*; **~ cream** крем для бритья́

shawl [ʃɔːl] шаль *f*, головно́й плато́к

she [ʃiː] **1.** она́; **2.** же́нщина; **she-...** са́мка; **she-wolf** волчи́ца

sheaf [ʃiːf] *agric.* сноп; *of paper* свя́зка

shear [ʃɪə] **1.** [*irr.*] *sheep* [о]стри́чь; *fig.* обдира́ть как ли́пку; **2. ~s** *pl.* (больши́е) но́жницы *f/pl.*

sheath [ʃiːθ] но́жны *f/pl.*; **~e** [ʃiːð] вкла́дывать в но́жны

sheaves [ʃiːvz] *pl. om* **sheaf**

shed[1] [ʃed] [*irr.*] *hair, etc.* [по]теря́ть; *tears, blood* пролива́ть; *clothes, skin* сбра́сывать [сбро́сить]; **~ new light on s.th.** пролива́ть [-ли́ть] свет (на В)

shed[2] [-] сара́й

sheen [ʃiːn] блеск; *reflected* о́тблеск

sheep [ʃiːp] овца́; **~dog** овча́рка; **~ish** [ˈʃiːpɪʃ] глупова́тый; ро́бкий; **~skin** овчи́на; **~ coat, ~ jacket** дублёнка, полушубок

sheer [ʃɪə] *(absolute)* полне́йший; *(diaphanous)* прозра́чный; *(steep)* отве́сный; *by ~ chance* по чи́стой случа́йности; *~ nonsense* абсолю́тная чепуха́; *~ waste of time* бесполе́зная тра́та вре́мени

sheet [ʃiːt] простыня́; *of paper, metal* лист; *of water, snow* широ́кая полоса́; *~ iron* листово́е желе́зо; *~ lightning* зарни́ца

shelf [ʃelf] по́лка; *of rock* усту́п; *sea* шельф

shell [ʃel] **1.** *(nut~)* скорлупа́; *of mollusc* ра́ковина; *of tortoise* па́нцирь *m*; *tech.* ко́рпус; **2.** *eggs* очища́ть [очи́стить] от скорлупы́; *peas* лущи́ть; *mil.* обстре́ливать [-ля́ть]; **~fish** моллю́ск

shelter [ˈʃeltə] **1.** *bulding, etc.* прию́т *(a. fig.)*, кров; убе́жище *(a. mil.)*; **2.** *v/t.* приюти́ть *pf.*; *v/i.* *(a. take~)* укры(ва́)ться; приюти́ться *pf.*

shelve [ʃelv] *fig.* откла́дывать в до́лгий я́щик

shelves [ʃelvz] *pl. om* **shelf**

shepherd [ˈʃepəd] **1.** пасту́х; **2.** *sheep*

пасти́; *people* [про]вести́

sherry ['ʃerɪ] хе́рес

shield [ʃiːld] **1.** щит; защи́та; *ozone~* озо́нный слой; **2.** заслоня́ть [-ни́ть] (*from* от P)

shift [ʃɪft] **1.** *at work* сме́на; (*change*) измене́ние; (*move*) сдвиг; *make ~ to* ухитря́ться [-ри́ться]; дово́льствоваться (*with*T); **2.** *v/t.* [по]меня́ть; перемеща́ть [-мести́ть]; *v/i.* извора́чиваться [извернуться]; перемеща́ть [-мести́ться]; *~ for o.s.* обходи́ться без по́мощи; **~y** ['ʃɪftɪ] ско́льзкий, *fig.* изворо́тливый, ло́вкий; *~ reply* укло́нчивый ответ

shilling ['ʃɪlɪŋ] ши́ллинг

shin [ʃɪn] *anat.* го́лень f

shine [ʃaɪn] **1.** сия́ние; свет; блеск, гля́нец; [*irr.*] сия́ть; свети́ть; блесте́ть; (*polish*) [от]полирова́ть; *shoes* [по]чи́стить; *fig.* блиста́ть

shingle ['ʃɪŋgl] (*gravel*) га́лька

shiny ['ʃaɪnɪ] □ (*polished*) начи́щенный; *through wear* лосня́щийся; (*bright*) блестя́щий

ship [ʃɪp] **1.** су́дно, кора́бль m; **2.** (*carry*) перевози́ть [-везти́]; *~board: on~* на корабле́; *~building* судостро́ение; *~ment* ['ʃɪpmənt] груз; погру́зка; *~owner* судовладе́лец; *~ping* ['ʃɪpɪŋ] (*loading*) погру́зка; (*transport*) перево́зка; (*ship traffic*) судохо́дство; *~wreck* **1.** кораблекруше́ние; **2.** потерпе́ть *pf.* кораблекруше́ние; *~yard* верфь f

shirk [ʃɜːk] увиливать [-льну́ть] (от P); *~er* ['ʃɜːkə] ло́дырь m; увиливающий (от P)

shirt [ʃɜːt] руба́шка, соро́чка; *woman's also* блу́зка; *~sleeves: in one's ~* без пиджака́

shiver ['ʃɪvə] **1.** дрожь f; **2.** [за]дрожа́ть

shoal¹ [ʃəʊl] мелково́дье; мель f

shoal² [-] *of fish* ста́я, костя́к

shock [ʃɒk] **1.** *fig.* потрясе́ние; *med.* шок; **2.** *fig.* потряса́ть [-ясти́]; шоки́ровать; *~ absorber* *mot.* амортиза́тор; *~ing* ['ʃɒkɪŋ] □ сканда́льный; ужа́сный; потряса́ющий

shod [ʃɒd] *pt. и pt. p. от* **shoe**

shoddy ['ʃɒdɪ] *goods, etc.* дрянно́й

shoe [ʃuː] **1.** ту́фля; *heavy* башма́к; *above ankle* полуботи́нок; (*horse~*) подко́ва; **2.** [*irr.*] обу(ва́)ть; *horse* подко́вывать [-кова́ть]; *~horn* рожо́к; *~lace* шнуро́к для боти́нок; *~maker* сапо́жник; *~ polish* крем для о́буви

shone [ʃɒn] *pt. и pt. p. от* **shine**

shook [ʃʊk] *pt. от* **shake**

shoot [ʃuːt] **1.** *bot.* росто́к, побе́г; **2.** [*irr.*] *v/t.* стреля́ть; (*kill*) [за]стрели́ть *pf.*; (*execute by shooting*) расстре́ливать [-ля́ть]; *cine.* снима́ть [снять], засня́ть *pf.*; *v/i.* стреля́ть [вы́стрелить]; *of pain* дёргать [~несь]; *~ along, past* проноси́ться [-нести́сь]; промелькну́ть *pf.*; *~ ahead* ри́нуться вперёд; *~er* ['ʃuːtə] стрело́к

shooting ['ʃuːtɪŋ] стрельба́; *hunt.* охо́та; *cine.* съёмка; *~ star* па́дающая звезда́

shop [ʃɒp] **1.** магази́н; (*work~*) мастерска́я; *talk~* говори́ть о рабо́те со свои́ми колле́гами; **2.** де́лать поку́пки (*mst.* **go ~ping**); *~keeper* владе́лец магази́на; *~per* ['ʃɒpə] покупа́тель m; *~ping* ['-ɪŋ]: *~ centre (-ter)* торго́вый центр; *~ window* витри́на

shore [ʃɔː] бе́рег; взмо́рье; побере́жье; *on the ~* на́ берег, на берегу́

shorn [ʃɔːn] *pt. p. от* **shear**

short [ʃɔːt] коро́ткий; (*brief*) кра́ткий; *in height* невысо́кий; (*insufficient*) недоста́точный; (*not complete*) непо́лный; *answer* ре́зкий, сухо́й; *pastry* песо́чный; *in ~* коро́че говоря́; вкра́тце; *fall ~ of* уступа́ть в чём-л.; *expectations, etc.* не опра́вдывать [-да́ть]; *cut ~* прер(ы)ва́ть; *run ~* иссяка́ть [-я́кнуть]; *stop ~ of* не доезжа́ть [дое́хать], не доходи́ть [дойти́] до (P) (*a. fig.*); *~age* ['ʃɔːtɪdʒ] нехва́тка, дефици́т; *~ circuit* коро́ткое замыка́ние; потряса́ющий; изъя́н; *~coming* недоста́ток; изъя́н; *~cut* кратча́йший путь m; *~en* ['ʃɔːtn] *v/t.* сокраща́ть [-рати́ть]; укора́чивать [-роти́ть]; *v/i.* сокраща́ться [-рати́ться]; укора́чиваться [-роти́ться]; ~hand стеногра́фия; ~ly ['ʃɔːtlɪ] *adv.* вско́ре; ~s [-s] *pl.* шо́рты; ~sighted близору́кий; ~term краткоско́рочный; ~ wave коротковолно́вый; ~winded страда́ющий одышкой

shot [ʃɒt] **1.** *pt. u pt. p. om* shoot; **2.** вы́стрел; *collect.* дробь *f*, дроби́нка (*mst. small* ~); *pers.* стрело́к; *sport* ядро́; *stroke, in ball games* уда́р; *phot.* сни́мок; *med.* инъе́кция; *have a* ~ сде́лать *pf.* попы́тку; *coll.* **not by a long** ~ отню́дь не; ~gun дробови́к

should [ʃʊd, ʃəd] *pt. om* shall

shoulder ['ʃəʊldə] **1.** плечо́; **2.** взва́ливать на пле́чи; *fig.* брать на себя́; ~blade *anat.* лопа́тка; ~ strap брете́лька; *mil.* пого́н

shout [ʃaʊt] **1.** крик; во́зглас; **2.** [за]крича́ть (кри́кнуть); [на]крича́ть (*at* на В)

shove [ʃʌv] **1.** толчо́к; **2.** толка́ть [-кну́ть]; ~ *off* ста́лкивать [столкну́ть]; отта́лкивать [оттолкну́ть]

shovel ['ʃʌvl] **1.** (*spade*) лопа́та; *for use in home* сово́к; **2.** греба́ть лопа́той

show [ʃəʊ] **1.** [*irr.*] *v/t.* (*manifest*) ока́зывать [-за́ть]; (*exhibit*) выставля́ть [вы́ставить]; *interest, etc.* проявля́ть [-ви́ть]; (*prove*) дока́зывать [-за́ть]; ~ *in* вводи́ть [ввести́]; ~ *up* (*expose*) разоблача́ть [-чи́ть] *v/i. coll.* (*appear*) появля́ться [-ви́ться]; ~ *off* [по]щего́льть; пуска́ть пыль в глаза́; **2.** (*spectacle*) зре́лище; (*exhibition*) вы́ставка; (*outward appearance*) ви́димость *f*; *thea.* спекта́кль *m*; ~case витри́на

shower ['ʃaʊə] **1.** ли́вень *m*; душ; *take a* ~ принима́ть [-ня́ть] душ; **2.** ли́ться ли́внем; *fig.* осыпа́ть [осы́пать]; *questions* засыпа́ть [-пать]; ~y ['ʃaʊərɪ] дождли́вый

show|n [ʃəʊn] *pt. p. om* show; ~room вы́ставочный зал; ~ window *Am.* витри́на; ~y ['ʃəʊɪ] показно́й

shrank [ʃræŋk] *pt. om* shrink

shred [ʃred] **1.** *of cloth* лоскуто́к; *of paper* клочо́к; *tear to* ~s разорва́ть [разрыва́ть] в кло́чья; **2.** [*irr.*] ре́зать, рвать на клочки́; *cul.* [на]шинкова́ть

shrewd [ʃruːd] проница́тельный; *in business* де́льный, расчётливый

shriek [ʃriːk] **1.** визг, крик, вопль *m*; **2.** [за]вопи́ть, [за]визжа́ть

shrill [ʃrɪl] □ пронзи́тельный, ре́зкий

shrimp [ʃrɪmp] *zo.* креве́тка; *coll. pers.* сморчо́к

shrine [ʃraɪn] святы́ня

shrink [ʃrɪŋk] [*irr.*] (*become smaller*) сокраща́ться [-рати́ться]; *of wood, etc.* усыха́ть [усо́хнуть]; *of cloth* сади́ться [сесть]; *recoil* отпря́нуть

shrivel ['ʃrɪvl] смо́рщи(ва)ть(ся); съё-жи(ва)ться

shroud [ʃraʊd] **1.** са́ван; *fig.* покро́в; **2.** оку́т(ыв)ать (*a. fig.*)

shrub [ʃrʌb] куст; ~s *pl.* куста́рник

shrug [ʃrʌg] пож(им)а́ть плеча́ми

shrunk [ʃrʌŋk] *pt. u pt. p. om* shrink (*a. ~en*)

shudder ['ʃʌdə] **1.** дрожа́ть *impf.*; содрога́ться [-гну́ться]; *I* ~ *to think* я содрога́юсь при мы́сли об э́том; **2.** дрожь *f*

shuffle ['ʃʌfl] **1.** ша́ркать; *cards* [пере]тасова́ть; ~ *off responsibility* перекла́дывать [переложи́ть] отве́тственность на други́х; **2.** ша́рканье; тасо́вка

shun [ʃʌn] избега́ть [-ежа́ть] (Р)

shunt [ʃʌnt] *fig. coll.* (*postpone*) откла́дывать [отложи́ть]

shut [ʃʌt] [*irr.*] **1.** закры́(ва́)ть(ся), затворя́ть(ся) [-ри́ть(ся)]; ~ *down* (*close*) закрыва́ть [-ры́ть]; ~ *up!* замолчи́!; **2.** закры́тый; ~ter *m*; *phot.* затво́р

shuttle ['ʃʌtl] (*device for weaving*) челно́к; ~ *service* челно́чные ре́йсы; при́городный по́езд

shy [ʃaɪ] *animal* пугли́вый; *person* засте́нчивый

shyness ['ʃaɪnɪs] засте́нчивость *f*

Siberian [saɪˈbɪərɪən] **1.** сиби́рский; **2.** сибиря́к *m*, -я́чка *f*

sick [sɪk] **1.** больно́й (*of* Т); чу́вствующий тошноту́; уста́вший (*of* от П); *I am* ~ *of* ... мне надое́ло (+ *inf.*, И); *I feel* ~ меня́ тошни́т; ~en ['sɪkən] *v/i.* заболе(ва́)ть; [за]ча́хнуть;

~ *at* чу́вствовать отвраще́ние к (Д); *v/t.* де́лать больны́м; вызыва́ть тошноту́ у (P)

sickle ['sɪkl] серп

sick|-leave: *I am on* ~ я на больни́чном; ~**ly** ['sɪklɪ] боле́зненный; (*causing nausea*) тошнотво́рный; (*puny*) хи́лый; ~**ness** ['sɪknɪs] боле́знь *f*; тошнота́; ~ *pay* вы́плата по больни́чному листу́

side [saɪd] **1.** *com.* сторона́; бок; (*edge*) край; ~ *by* ~ бок о́ бок; *to be on the safe* ~ на вся́кий слу́чай; *on the one* ~ ... *on the other* ~ с одно́й стороны́ ... с друго́й стороны́; *take the* ~ *of* примыка́ть к той и́ли ино́й стороне́ (P); **2.** *attr.* боково́й; *effect, etc.* побо́чный; **3.** ~ *with* встать *pf.* на сто́рону (P); ~**board** буфе́т, серва́нт; ~**car** *mot.* коля́ска мотоци́кла; ~**light** *mot.* подфа́рник; ~**long:** ~ *glance* взгляд и́скоса; ~**walk** *Am.* тротуа́р

siding ['saɪdɪŋ] *rail.* запа́сный путь *m*

sidle ['saɪdl] подходи́ть бочко́м

siege [siːdʒ] оса́да; *lay* ~ *to* осажда́ть [осади́ть]

sieve [sɪv] си́то

sift [sɪft] просе́ивать [-е́ять]; *fig.* [про]анализи́ровать

sigh [saɪ] **1.** вздох; **2.** вздыха́ть [вздохну́ть]

sight [saɪt] **1.** зре́ние; вид; взгляд; (*spectacle*) зре́лище; *of gun* прице́л; ~**s** *pl.* достопримеча́тельности *f/pl.*; *catch* ~ *of* уви́деть, заме́тить (P); *lose* ~ *of* потеря́ть из ви́ду; **2.** уви́деть *pf.*; ~**seeing** ['saɪtsiːɪŋ] осмо́тр достопримеча́тельностей

sign [saɪn] **1.** знак; при́знак; симпто́м; *over a shop* вы́веска; *as a* ~ *of* в знак (P); **2.** *v/i.* подава́ть знак (Д); *v/t.* подпи́сывать [-са́ть]

signal ['sɪɡnəl] **1.** сигна́л; **2.** [по]дава́ть сигна́л; подава́ть [-да́ть] знак; [про]сигна́лить

signature ['sɪɡnətʃə] по́дпись *f*

sign|board вы́веска; ~**er** ['saɪnə] лицо́ подписа́вшее како́й-либо докуме́нт

signet ['sɪɡnɪt]: ~ *ring* кольцо́ с печа́ткой

signific|ance [sɪɡ'nɪfɪkəns] значе́ние; ~**ant** [-kənt] значи́тельный; *look* многозначи́тельный; ва́жный

signify ['sɪɡnɪfaɪ] зна́чить, означа́ть

signpost доро́жный указа́тель *m*

silence ['saɪləns] **1.** молча́ние; тишина́; безмо́лвие; ~*!* ти́хо!; **2.** заста́вить *pf.* молча́ть; заглуши́ть [-ши́ть]; ~**r** [-ə] *mot.* глуши́тель *m*

silent ['saɪlənt] безмо́лвный; молчали́вый; (*noiseless*) бесшу́мный

silk [sɪlk] **1.** шёлк; **2.** (*made of silk*) шёлковый; ~**en** ['sɪlkən] (*resembling silk*) шелкови́стый; ~**worm** шелкови́чный червь *m*; ~**y** ['sɪlkɪ] шелкови́стый

sill [sɪl] *of window* подоко́нник

silly ['sɪlɪ] □ глу́пый; *don't be* ~ не валя́й дурака́

silt [sɪlt] **1.** ил; **2.** зайли́ваться (*mst.* ~ *up*)

silver ['sɪlvə] **1.** серебро́; **2.** (*made of silver*) сере́бряный; ~**y** [-rɪ] серебри́стый

similar ['sɪmɪlə] □ схо́дный (с Т), похо́жий (на В); подо́бный, аналоги́чный; ~**ity** [sɪmɪ'lærətɪ] схо́дство; подо́бие

simile ['sɪmɪlɪ] сравне́ние

simmer ['sɪmə] ме́дленно кипе́ть; держа́ть на ме́дленном огне́

simple ['sɪmpl] □ просто́й; несло́жный; ~**-hearted** простоду́шный; наи́вный; ~**ton** [-tən] проста́к

simpli|city [sɪm'plɪsətɪ] простота́; простоду́шие; ~**fy** ['sɪmplɪfaɪ] упроща́ть [-ости́ть]

simply ['sɪmplɪ] про́сто

simulate ['sɪmjʊleɪt] симули́ровать (*im*)*pf.*; притворя́ться [-ори́ться]

simultaneous [sɪml'teɪnɪəs] □ одновреме́нный; ~ *interpretation* синхро́нный перево́д; ~ *interpreter* перево́дчик-синхрони́ст

sin [sɪn] **1.** грех; **2.** согреша́ть [-ши́ть], [по]греши́ть

since [sɪns] **1.** *prp.* с (P); **2.** *adv.* с тех пор; ... тому́ наза́д; **3.** *cj.* с тех пор, как; так как; поско́льку

sincer|e [sɪn'sɪə] □ и́скренний; ~**ely:**

yours ~ и́скренне Ваш, *formal* с глубо́ким уваже́нием; ~ity [sɪn'serətɪ] и́скренность *f*

sinew ['sɪnjuː] сухожи́лие; ~**y** [-ɪ] жи́листый

sinful ['sɪnfl] □ гре́шный

sing [sɪŋ] [*irr.*] [с]петь; ~ *s.o.'s praises* петь кому́-л. дифира́мбы

singe [sɪndʒ] опаля́ть [-ли́ть]

singer ['sɪŋə] певе́ц *m*, певи́ца *f*

single ['sɪŋgl] **1.** □ еди́нственный; одино́чный; (*alone*) одино́кий; (*not married*) холосто́й, незаму́жняя; *in ~ file* гусько́м; **2.**: ~ *out* отбира́ть [отобра́ть]; ~**breasted** однобо́ртный; ~**handed** самостоя́тельно, без посторо́нней по́мощи; ~**minded** целеустремлённый; ~**t** ['sɪŋglɪt] ма́йка

singular ['sɪŋgjʊlə] необыча́йный; стра́нный; *gr.* еди́нственный; ~**ity** [sɪŋgju'lærətɪ] осо́бенность *f*, необыча́йность *f*

sinister ['sɪnɪstə] злове́щий

sink [sɪŋk] **1.** [*irr.*] *v/i.* (*fall*) опуска́ться [-сти́ться] (*a. of sun, etc.*); [за-, по-, у]тону́ть; *fig.* погружа́ться [-узи́ться]; (*subside*) оседа́ть [осе́сть]; ~ *or swim* будь что бу́дет; *v/t.* затопля́ть [-пи́ть]; **2.** *in kitchen* ра́ковина

sinless ['sɪnlɪs] безгре́шный

sinner ['sɪnə] гре́шник *m*, -ица *f*

sip [sɪp] пить ма́ленькими глотка́ми

siphon ['saɪfn] сифо́н

sir [sɜː] *form of address* су́дарь *m*; ♀ сэр

siren ['saɪərən] сире́на

sirloin ['sɜːlɔɪn] филе́йная часть

sister ['sɪstə] сестра́; ~**in-law** [-rɪnlɔː] сестра́ му́жа (жены́); ~**ly** [-lɪ] се́стринский

sit [sɪt] [*irr.*] *v/i.* сиде́ть; *of assembly* заседа́ть; ~ *down* сади́ться [сесть]; ~ *for paint.* пози́ровать; ~ *for an examination* сдава́ть экза́мен

site [saɪt] ме́сто, местоположе́ние; *building* ~ строи́тельная площа́дка

sitting ['sɪtɪŋ] заседа́ние; ~ *room* гости́ная

situat|ed ['sɪtjʊeɪtɪd] располо́женный; ~**ion** [sɪtʃʊ'eɪʃn] положе́ние; ситуа́ция; (*job*) ме́сто

six [sɪks] **1.** шесть; **2.** шестёрка; ~**teen** [sɪk'stiːn] шестна́дцать; ~**teenth** [sɪk'stiːnθ] шестна́дцатый; ~**th** [sɪksθ] шесто́й; **2.** шеста́я часть *f*; ~**tieth** ['sɪkstɪɪθ] шестидеся́тый; ~**ty** ['sɪkstɪ] шестьдеся́т

size [saɪz] **1.** величина́; *of books, etc.* форма́т; (*dimension*) разме́р (*a. of shoes, clothing*); **2.** ~ *up* определи́ть взве́сить *fig.* оцени́ть *pf.*, поня́ть *pf.*

siz(e)able ['saɪzəbl] поря́дочного разме́ра

sizzle ['sɪzl] шкворча́ть, шипе́ть

skat|e [skeɪt] **1.** конёк (*pl.*: коньки́); **2.** ката́ться на конька́х; ~**er** ['skeɪtə] конькобе́жец *m*, -жка *f*

skein [skeɪn] мото́к пря́жи

skeleton ['skelɪtn] *anat.* скеле́т; *tech.* о́стов, карка́с; ~ *key* отмы́чка

skeptic, *Brt.* **sceptic** ['skeptɪk] ске́птик; ~**al** [-tɪkl] □ скепти́ческий

sketch [sketʃ] **1.** эски́з, набро́сок; де́лать набро́сок, эски́з (P); ~**y** ['-ɪ] пове́рхностный

ski [skiː] **1.** (*pl.* ~ *или* ~s) лы́жа; **2.** ходи́ть на лы́жах

skid [skɪd] **1.** *mot.* юз, зано́с; *of wheels* буксова́ние; **2.** *v/i.* буксова́ть; идти́ [пойти́] ю́зом; *of person* скользи́ть

skillful, *Brt.* **skilful** ['skɪlfl] □ иску́сный, уме́лый

skill [skɪl] мастерство́, уме́ние; ~**ed** [-d] квалифици́рованный, иску́сный

skim [skɪm] *cream, scum, etc.* снима́ть [снять]; (*glide*) скользи́ть [-зну́ть] по (Д); (*read*) просма́тривать [-смотре́ть]; ~ *over* бе́гло прочи́тывать; ~**med milk** снято́е молоко́

skimp [skɪmp] эконо́мить; [по]скупи́ться (*on* на В); ~**y** ['skɪmpɪ] □ ску́дный

skin [skɪn] **1.** ко́жа; (*hide*) шку́ра; *of apricot, etc.* кожура́; **2.** *v/t.* сдира́ть ко́жу, шку́ру с (Р); *deep* пове́рхностный; ~**diver** акваланги́ст; ~**flint** скря́га *m*; ~**ny** ['skɪnɪ] то́щий; ~**tight** в обтя́жку

skip [skɪp] **1.** прыжо́к, скачо́к; **2.** *v/i.* [по]скака́ть; *fig.* переска́кивать

[-скочи́ть] (*from* с [P]); (*to* на [B]); *v/t.* (*omit*) пропуска́ть [-сти́ть]

skipper ['skɪpə] капита́н

skirmish ['skɜːmɪʃ] *mil.* сты́чка (*a. fig.*)

skirt [skɜːt] **1.** (*waist-down garment or part of a dress*) ю́бка; *of coat* пола́; (*edge*) край, окра́ина; **2.** *v/t.* обходи́ть [обойти́]; объезжа́ть [-е́хать]

skit [skɪt] сати́ра, паро́дия

skittle ['skɪtl] ке́гля; *play* (*at*) *~s pl.* игра́ть в ке́гли; *~ alley* кегельба́н

skulk [skʌlk] кра́сться

skull [skʌl] че́реп

sky [skaɪ] не́бо (небеса́ *pl.*); *praise to the skies* расхва́ливать до небе́с; *out of a clear ~* как гром среди́ я́сного не́ба; *~lark* **1.** жа́воронок; **2.** выки́дывать шту́чки; *~light* светово́й люк; *~line* горизо́нт; *of buildings, etc.* очерта́ние; *~scraper* небоскрёб; *~ward(s)* ['skaɪwəd(z)] к не́бу

slab [slæb] плита́

slack [slæk] **1.** (*remiss*) неради́вый; *behavio(u)r* расхля́банный; (*loose*) сла́бый; (*slow*) ме́дленный; *rope, etc.* сла́бо натя́нутый; (*a. comm.*) вя́лый; **2.** *naut. of rope* слабина́; *~s pl.* брю́ки *f/pl.*; **3.** = *~en* [slækn] ослабля́ть [-а́бить]; [о]сла́бнуть; замедля́ть [-е́длить]

slain [sleɪn] *p. pt. om* **slay**

slake [sleɪk] *thirst* утоля́ть [-ли́ть]

slalom ['slɑːləm] сла́лом

slam [slæm] **1.** хло́панье; **2.** хло́пать [-пнуть] (Т); захло́пывать(ся) [-пнуть(ся)]

slander ['slɑːndə] **1.** клевета́; **2.** [на]клевета́ть; *~ous* [-rəs] □ клеветни́ческий

slang [slæŋ] сленг; жарго́н

slant [slɑːnt] склон, укло́н (*a. fig.*); то́чка зре́ния; *~ed* [-ɪd] (*biased*) тенденцио́зный; *~ing* [-ɪŋ] □ *adj.* накло́нный; косо́й

slap [slæp] **1.** шлепо́к; *~ in the face* пощёчина; **2.** шлёпать [-пнуть]; *on back, etc.* хло́пать [-пнуть]

slash [slæʃ] **1.** разре́з; **2.** (*wound*) [по]ра́нить; *with whip, etc.* [ис]полосова́ть

[полосну́ть]

slate [sleɪt] сла́нец; *for roof* ши́фер

slattern ['slætən] неря́ха

slaughter ['slɔːtə] **1.** убо́й (скота́); *fig.* резня́, кровопроли́тие; **2.** [за-] ре́зать; забива́ть [-би́ть]; *~house* бо́йня

Slav [slɑːv] **1.** славяни́н *m*, -я́нка *f*; **2.** славя́нский

slave [sleɪv] **1.** раб *m*, -ы́ня *f*; *attr.* ра́бский; **2.** рабо́тать как ка́торжник

slav|ery ['sleɪvərɪ] ра́бство; *~ish* [-vɪʃ] □ ра́бский

slay [sleɪ] [*irr.*] уби(ва́)ть

sled [sled], **sledge¹** [sledʒ] са́ни *f/pl.*; *child's* са́нки *f/pl.*

sledge² [-] (*~ hammer*) кузне́чный мо́лот

sleek [sliːk] **1.** □ *animal's coat* гла́дкий и блестя́щий; *manner* вкра́дчивый

sleep [sliːp] **1.** [*irr.*] *v/i.* [по]спа́ть; *~ like a log* спать мёртвым сном; *~ on it* отложи́ть *pf.* до за́втра; *v/t.* дава́ть (кому́-нибудь) ночле́г; *put to ~ animal* усыпля́ть [-пи́ть]; **2.** сон; *~er* ['-ə] спя́щий; *rail* спа́льный ваго́н; *~ing* ['-ɪŋ]: *~ bag* спа́льный мешо́к; *~ pill* табле́тка снотво́рного; *~ car rail.* спа́льный ваго́н; *~less* [-lɪs] □ бессо́нный; *~walker* луна́тик; *~y* ['-ɪ] □ со́нный, *coll.* за́спанный

sleet [sliːt] мо́крый снег; *~y* ['sliːtɪ] сля́котный

sleeve [sliːv] рука́в; *tech.* му́фта; втýлка

sleigh [sleɪ] са́ни *f/pl.*

sleight [slaɪt] (*mst. ~ of hand*) ло́вкость *f* (рук)

slender ['slendə] □ стро́йный; то́нкий; (*scanty*) скýдный

slept [slept] *pt. и pt. p. om* **sleep**

sleuth [sluːθ] *joc.* сы́щик, детекти́в

slew [sluː] *pt. om* **slay**

slice [slaɪs] **1.** ло́моть *m, dim.* ло́мтик; (*part*) часть *f*; **2.** [на]ре́зать ло́мтиками

slick [slɪk] *coll.* гла́дкий; *Am.* хи́трый, ско́льзкий

slid [slɪd] *pt. и pt. p. om* **slide**

slide [slaɪd] **1.** [*irr.*] скользи́ть [-зну́ть]; ката́ться по льду; вдвига́ть [-и́нуть], всо́вывать [всу́нуть] (*into* в B); **let things ~** относи́ться ко всему́ спустя́ рукава́; **2.** *photo.* диапозити́в, слайд; **3.** скольже́ние; *for children* де́тская го́рка; (*land~*) о́ползень *m*; **~ rule** логарифми́ческая лине́йка

slight [slaɪt] **1.** □ (*thin and delicate*) то́нкий, хру́пкий; незначи́тельный; сла́бый; **not the ~est idea** ни мале́йшего представле́ния; **2.** (*disrespect*) пренебреже́ние; **3.** обижа́ть [-и́деть]; унижа́ть [-и́зить]

slim [slɪm] (*slender*) то́нкий, то́ненький; *person* стро́йный; **~ hope** сла́бая наде́жда

slim|e [slaɪm] (*mud*) жи́дкая грязь *f*; (*silt*) ил; **~y** ['slaɪmɪ] сли́зистый, ско́льзкий

sling [slɪŋ] **1.** *bandage* пе́ревязь; **2.** *throw* [*irr.*] швыря́ть [швырну́ть]

slink [slɪŋk] [*irr.*] кра́сться; **~ off** потихо́ньку отходи́ть [отойти́]

slip [slɪp] **1.** [*irr.*] *v/i.* скользи́ть; поскользну́ться *pf.*; *out of hands* выска́льзывать [вы́скользнуть]; *of wheels* буксова́ть; *v/t.* сова́ть [су́нуть] *one's attention* ускольза́ть [-зну́ть]; **~ a p.'s memory** вы́лететь из головы́ (P); **~ on** (**off**) наде́ва́ть(ся), сбра́сывать [сбро́сить]; **2.** скольже́ние; *of paper* поло́ска; про́мах; оши́бка; *in writing* опи́ска; (*petticoat*) комбина́ция; (*pillowcase*) на́волочка; **give a p. the ~** ускольза́ть [-зну́ть] от (P); **~ of the tongue** огово́рка; **~per** ['slɪpə] ко́мнатная ту́фля; **~pery** ['slɪpərɪ] ско́льзкий; (*not safe*) ненаде́жный; **~shod** ['slɪpʃɒd] неря́шливый; (*careless*) небре́жный; **~t** [slɪpt] *pt. и pt. p. om* **slip**

slit [slɪt] **1.** разре́з; щель *f*; **2.** [*irr.*] разре́зать в длину́

sliver ['slɪvə] *of wood* ще́пка; *of glass* оско́лок

slogan ['sləʊgən] ло́зунг

slop [slɒp] **1.:** **~s** *pl.* помо́и *m/pl.*; **2.** (*spill*) проли́ва(ва)ть; расплёскивать(-ся) [-еска́ть(ся)]

slop|e [sləʊp] **1.** накло́н, склон, скат; **2.** клони́ться; име́ть накло́н; **~ing** ['-ɪŋ] пока́тый

sloppy ['slɒpɪ] (*slovenly*) неря́шливый; (*careless*) небре́жный; сентимента́льный

slot [slɒt] щель *f*; про́резь *f*; паз; (*place or job*) ме́сто

sloth [sləʊθ] лень *f*, ле́ность *f*; *zo.* лени́вец

slot machine иго́рный (торго́вый) автома́т

slouch [slaʊtʃ] **1.** [c]суту́литься; *when sitting* [c]горби́ться; **~ about, around** слоня́ться без де́ла; **2.** суту́лость *f*

slovenly ['slʌvnlɪ] неря́шливый

slow [sləʊ] **1.** ме́дленный; медли́тельный; (*dull in mind*) тупо́й; *trade* вя́лый; *watch* отст(ав)а́ть; **2.** (*a.* **down, up**) замедля́ть(ся) [заме́длить(ся)]; **~poke** (*or chiefly Brt.* **~coach**) копу́ша; **~-witted** тупо́й, тупова́тый

slug [slʌg] слизня́к

slug|gard ['slʌgəd] лежебо́ка *m/f.*; **~ish** ['slʌgɪʃ] ме́дленный, вя́лый

sluice [sluːs] шлюз

slum [slʌm] *mst.* **~s** *pl.* трущо́бы

slumber ['slʌmbə] **1.** дремо́та; сон; **2.** дрема́ть; спать

slump [slʌmp] **1.** *of prices, demand* ре́зкое паде́ние; **2.** ре́зко па́дать; *into a chair, etc.* тяжело́ опуска́ться

slung [slʌŋ] *pt. и pt. p. om* **sling**

slunk [slʌŋk] *pt. и pt. p. om* **slink**

slur [slɜː] **1.** *in speech* невня́тная речь; *on reputation, etc.* пятно́; **2.** *v/t.* говори́ть невня́тно; **~ over** ума́лчивать [-молча́ть], опуска́ть [-сти́ть]; *fig. coll.* сма́зывать [сма́зать]

slush [slʌʃ] сля́коть *f*; та́лый снег

sly [slaɪ] □ хи́трый; лука́вый; **on the ~** тайко́м

smack¹ [smæk] **~ of** име́ть (при́-) вкус; [-кну́ть] (T)

smack² [-] **1.** (*kiss*) зво́нкий поцелу́й; (*slap*) шлепо́к; **2.** *lips* чмо́кать [-кнуть]; хло́пать [-пнуть] (T); шлёпать [-пнуть]

small [smɔːl] *com.* ма́ленький, небольшо́й; *mistakes, etc.* ме́лкий; незначи́тельный; **~ change** ме́лочь *f*; **~ fry** ме́лкая ры́бешка; **~ of the back**

S

anat. поясни́ца; *in the ~ hours* под у́тро; в предрассве́тные часы́; *~ arms pl.* стрелко́вое ору́жие; *~pox med.* о́спа; *~talk* лёгкий, бессодержа́тельный разгово́р; све́тская болтовня́

smart [smɑːt] **1.** □ *blow* ре́зкий, си́льный; (*clever*) ло́вкий; у́мный; (*stylish*) элега́нтный; (*witty*) остроу́мный; (*fashionable*) мо́дный; **2.** боль *f*; **3.** боле́ть, садни́ть; *fig.* страда́ть; **~ness** ['smɑːtnɪs] наря́дность *f*, элега́нтность *f*; ло́вкость *f*

smash [smæʃ] **1.** *v/t. enemy* сокруша́ть [-ши́ть] *a. fig.*; разбива́ть вдре́безги; *v/i.* разби́(ва́)ться; ста́лкиваться [столкну́ться] (*into* с T); **~up** (*collision*) столкнове́ние; катастро́фа

smattering ['smætərɪŋ] пове́рхностное зна́ние; небольшо́е коли́чество чего́-то

smear [smɪə] **1.** пятно́; мазо́к (*a. med.*); **2.** [на]ма́зать, изма́з(ыв)ать

smell [smel] **1.** за́пах; *sense* обоня́ние; **2.** [*irr.*] [по]чу́вствовать за́пах; *of animal* [по]чу́ять (B); (*a. ~ at*) [по]ню́хать (B); *~ of* па́хнуть (T)

smelt[1] [smelt] *pt. u pt. p. om* **smell**

smelt[2] [~] выплавля́ть [вы́плавить]

smile [smaɪl] **1.** улы́бка; **2.** улыба́ться [-бну́ться]

smirk [smɜːk] ухмыля́ться [-льну́ться]

smite [smaɪt] [*irr.*] (*afflict*) поража́ть [-рази́ть]; *she was smitten with sorrow* она́ была́ уби́та го́рем

smith [smɪθ] *black~* кузне́ц

smithereens ['smɪðə'riːnz] *break into ~* разбива́ть [-би́ть] вдре́безги

smithy ['smɪðɪ] ку́зница

smitten ['smɪtn] *pt. p. om* **smite**

smock [smɒk] *child's* де́тский хала́тик; *woman's* же́нская [крестья́нская] блу́за

smoke [sməʊk] **1.** дым; *have a ~* покури́ть *pf.*; *go up in ~* ко́нчиться *pf.* ниче́м; **2.** кури́ть; [на]дыми́ть; (*emit ~*) [за]дыми́ться; *tobacco, etc.* выку́ривать [вы́курить] (*a. ~ out*); **~dried** копчёный; **~less** ['-lɪs] безды́мный; **~r** ['-ə] куря́щий; *rail coll.* ваго́н для

куря́щих; **~stack** дымова́я труба́

smoking ['sməʊkɪŋ] куря́щий; *~ compartment rail.* купе́ для куря́щих; *~ room* ко́мната для куре́ния

smoky ['sməʊkɪ] ды́мный; наку́ренный

smolder, *Brt.* **smoulder** ['sməʊldə] тлеть

smooth [smuːð] **1.** □ гла́дкий; *take-off, etc.* пла́вный; (*calm*) споко́йный; (*ingratiating*) вкра́дчивый; (*flattery*) льсти́вый; **2.** прила́живать [-ла́дить]; *~ out* разгла́живать [-ла́дить]; *fig.* (*a. ~ over*) смягча́ть [-чи́ть]; *differences* сгла́живать [-а́дить]

smote [sməʊt] *pt. om* **smite**

smother ['smʌðə] [за]души́ть; *anger, etc.* подави́ть *pf.*

smudge [smʌdʒ] **1.** [за]па́чкать(ся); **2.** гря́зное пятно́

smug [smʌg] самодово́льный

smuggle ['smʌgl] занима́ться контраба́ндой; провози́ть контраба́ндой; *~r* [-ə] контрабанди́ст *m*, -ка *f*

smut [smʌt] **1.** (*soot*) са́жа, ко́поть *f*; (*fungus, crop disease*) головня́; (*obscene language*) непристо́йность *f*; *a talk ~* нести́ похабщину

smutty ['smʌtɪ] □ гря́зный

snack [snæk] лёгкая заку́ска; *have a ~* перекуси́ть; *~ bar* заку́сочная

snag [snæg] *fig.* препя́тствие; *there's a ~* в э́том загво́здка

snail [sneɪl] *zo.* ули́тка; *at a ~'s pace* ме́дленно как черепа́ха

snake [sneɪk] *zo.* змея́

snap [snæp] **1.** (*noise*) щелчо́к; треск; (*fastener*) кно́пка, застёжка; *coll.* (*photo*) сни́мок; *fig.* (*zest*) жи́вость; *cold ~* внеза́пное похолода́ние; **2.** *v/i.* (*break*) [с]лома́ться; (*make a sharp noise*) щёлкать [-кнуть]; (*snatch*) ухва́тываться [ухвати́ться] (*at* за B); *of a dog, a. fig.* огрыза́ться [-зну́ться] (*at* на B); (*break, as a string, etc.*) [по]рва́ться; (*close, as a fastener*) защёлкивать [защёлкнуть]; *phot.* де́лать сни́мок (P); *~ out of it!* бро́с(те)!, встряхни́тесь!; *~ up* (*buy up*) раскупа́ть [-пи́ть]; **~dragon** льви́ный зев;

~ **fastener** кно́пка (застёжка); ~**pish** ['snæpɪʃ] □ раздражи́тельный; ~**py** ['snæpɪ] *coll.* энерги́чный; живо́й; **make it** ~ ! поживе́е; ~**shot** *phot.* сни́мок

snare [sneə] **1.** сило́к; *fig.* лову́шка, западня́; **2.** лови́ть [пойма́ть] силка́ми *m/pl.*

snarl [snɑːl] **1.** рыча́ние; **2.** [про-] рыча́ть; *fig.* огрыза́ться [-зну́ться]

snatch [snætʃ] **1.** рыво́к; (*a grab*) хвата́ние; (*fragment*) обры́вок; кусо́чек; **2.** хвата́ть [схвати́ть]; (~ *away*) вырыва́ть [-рвать]; ~ **at** хвата́ться [схвати́ться] за (В); ~ **up** подхва́тывать [-хвати́ть]

sneak [sniːk] **1.** *v/i.* (*move stealthily*) кра́сться; ~ **up** подкра́дываться [-ра́сться]; *v/t.* (*take in a furtive way, as a look, a smoke, etc.*) стащи́ть *pf.*, укра́сть *pf.*; **2.** (*telltale*) я́бедник *m*, -ица *f*; ~**ers** ['sniːkəz] *Am.* полуке́ды *f/pl.*; (*running shoes*) кроссо́вки *f/pl.*

sneer [snɪə] **1.** (*contemptuous smile*) презри́тельная усме́шка; насме́шка; **2.** насме́шливо улыба́ться; насмеха́ться, глуми́ться (*at* над Т)

sneeze [sniːz] **1.** чиха́нье; **2.** чиха́ть [чихну́ть]

snicker ['snɪkə] хихи́кать [-кнуть]; *of horses* ржать

sniff [snɪf] *v/t.* [по]ню́хать; *of dog* учу́ять; *v/i.* шмы́гать [-гну́ть] но́сом

snigger ['snɪgə] → **snicker**

snip [snɪp] **1.** (*piece cut off*) обре́зок; кусо́к; (*cut*) надре́з; **2.** (*trim*) подреза́ть [-ре́зать]; (*cut out*) выре́зывать [вы́резать]

sniper ['snaɪpə] сна́йпер

snivel ['snɪvl] хны́кать; (*after crying*) всхли́пывать [-пнуть]; *coll.* распуска́ть со́пли

snob [snɒb] сноб; ~**bery** ['snɒbərɪ] сноби́зм

snoop [snuːp] подгля́дывать, выню́хивать, чужи́е та́йны

snooze [snuːz] *coll.* **1.** лёгкий, коро́ткий сон; **2.** дрема́ть, вздремну́ть *pf.*

snore [snɔː] [за]храпе́ть

snorkel ['snɔːkl] шно́ркель *m*

snort [snɔːt] фы́ркать [-кнуть]; *of horse* [за]храпе́ть

snout [snaʊt] *pig's* ры́ло; *dog's, etc.* мо́рда

snow [snəʊ] **1.** снег; **2.** *it is* ~**ing** идёт снег; **be covered with** ~ быть занесённым сне́гом; **be** ~**ed under with work** быть зава́ленным рабо́той; ~**ball** снежо́к; ~**drift** сугро́б; ~**fall** снегопа́д; ~**flake** снежи́нка; ~ **plow**, *Brt.* ~**plough** снегоочисти́тель *m*; ~**storm** вью́га; ~**white** белосне́жный; ~**y** ['snəʊɪ] □ сне́жный

snub [snʌb] **1.** *fig.* оса́живать [осади́ть]; **2.** пренебрежи́тельное обхожде́ние; ~**nosed** курно́сый

snug [snʌg] □ ую́тный; ~**gle** ['snʌgl] (ла́сково) приж(им)а́ться (**up to** к Д)

so [səʊ] так; ита́к; таки́м о́бразом; **I hope** ~ я наде́юсь, что да; **Look, it's raining.** 2 **it is.** Смотри́, идёт дождь. Да, действи́тельно; **you are tired,** ~ **am I** вы уста́ли и я то́же; ~ **far** до сих пор

soak [səʊk] *v/t.* [за]мочи́ть; (*draw in*) впи́тывать [впита́ть]; *v/i.* промока́ть; ~ **in** проси́тываться [-пита́ться]; ~ **through** проса́чиваться [-сочи́ться]; **get** ~**ed to the skin** промо́кнуть до ни́тки

soap [səʊp] **1.** мы́ло; **2.** намы́ли(ва)ть; ~**dish** мы́льница; ~**suds** мы́льная пе́на; ~**y** ['səʊpɪ] □ мы́льный

soar [sɔː] (*fly high*) пари́ть; *of birds* взмыва́ть [-ыть]; *of prices* подска́кивать [-кочи́ть]

sob [sɒb] **1.** всхлип; рыда́ние; **2.** [за]рыда́ть; разрыда́ться *pf.*

sober ['səʊbə] **1.** □ тре́звый (*a. fig.*); **2.** *fig.* отрезвля́ть [-ви́ть]; **have a** ~**ing effect** [по]де́йствовать отрезвля́юще; ~ **up** протрезвля́ться [-ви́ться]

so-called ['səʊ'kɔːld] так называ́емый

sociable ['səʊʃəbl] □ общи́тельный

social ['səʊʃl] **1.** □ обще́ственный; социа́льный; ~ **security** социа́льное обеспе́чение; **2.** вечери́нка

socialism ['səʊʃəlɪzəm] социали́зм

society [sə'saɪətɪ] о́бщество; *comm.*

компа́ния; (*the public, the community*) обще́ственность *f*; (*association*) объедине́ние

sociology [ˌsəʊsɪˈɒlədʒɪ] социоло́гия

sock [sɒk] носо́к

socket [ˈsɒkɪt] *of eye* впа́дина; *for bulb* патро́н; *for wall* розе́тка; *tech.* штепсельное гнездо́

soda [ˈsəʊdə] со́да; (*drink*) газиро́ванная вода́

sodden [ˈsɒdn] промо́кший

soft [sɒft] □ *com.* мя́гкий; не́жный; ти́хий; нея́ркий; (*unmanly*) изне́женный; (*weak in mind*) *coll.* придуркова́тый; ~ **drink** безалкого́льный напи́ток; **~en** [ˈsɒfn] смягча́ть(ся) [-чи́ть(ся)]; **~hearted** мягкосерде́чный; **~ware** *comput.* програ́ммное обеспе́чение

soggy [ˈsɒgɪ] сыро́й; пропи́танный водо́й

soil [sɔɪl] 1. (*earth*) по́чва, земля́ (*a. fig. country*); 2. (*dirty*) [за]па́чкать(ся)

solace [ˈsɒlɪs] утеше́ние

solar [ˈsəʊlə] со́лнечный; ~ **eclipse** со́лнечное затме́ние

sold [səʊld] *pt. u pt. p. om* **sell**

solder [ˈsɒldə] 1. припо́й; 2. пая́ть; запа́ивать [запая́ть]

soldier [ˈsəʊldʒə] солда́т

sole¹ [səʊl] □ еди́нственный; (*exclusive*) исключи́тельный

sole² [-] 1. *of foot* ступня́; *of shoe* подмётка; 2. ста́вить подмётку на (В)

sole³ [-] *zo.* ка́мбала

solely [ˈsəʊllɪ] исключи́тельно, еди́нственно

solemn [ˈsɒləm] □ *event, etc.* торже́ственный; серьёзный; (*pompous*) напы́щенный; **~ity** [səˈlemnətɪ] торже́ственность *f*; **~ize** [ˈsɒləmnaɪz]: ~ *a marriage* сочета́ть бра́ком

solicit [səˈlɪsɪt] *help, etc.* проси́ть; **~or** [-ə] *law Brt.* адвока́т, юрисконсу́льт; **~ous** [-əs] □ (*considerate*) забо́тливый; ~ *of* стремя́щийся к (Д); **~ude** [-juːd] забо́тливость *f*, забо́та

solid [ˈsɒlɪd] 1. □ твёрдый; (*firm*) про́чный; (*unbroken*) сплошно́й; масси́вный; (*sound, reliable*) соли́дный;

(*dependable*) надёжный; (*unanimous*) единогла́сный; (*united*) сплочённый; *a ~ hour* це́лый час; *on ~ ground fig.* на твёрдой по́чве; ~ *gold* чи́стое зо́лото; 2. *phys.* твёрдое те́ло; **~arity** [sɒlɪˈdærətɪ] солида́рность *f*

soliloquy [səˈlɪləkwɪ] моноло́г

solit|ary [ˈsɒlɪtrɪ] □ (*lonely*) одино́кий; (*secluded*) уединённый; **~ude** [-tjuːd] одино́чество, уедине́ние

solo [ˈsəʊləʊ] *n indecl.*; **~ist** [ˈsəʊləʊɪst] соли́ст *m*, -ка *f*

solu|ble [ˈsɒljʊbl] раствори́мый; *fig.* (*solvable*) разреши́мый; **~tion** [səˈluːʃn] (*process*) растворе́ние; (*result of process*) раство́р

solv|e [sɒlv] реша́ть [реши́ть], разреша́ть [-ши́ть]; **~ent** [ˈvənt] 1. *fin.* платёжеспосо́бный; *chem.* растворя́ющий; 2. раствори́тель *m*

somb|er, *Brt.* **~re** [ˈsɒmbə] □ мра́чный; угрю́мный; *clothes* тёмный

some [sʌm, səm] не́кий; како́й-то; како́й-нибудь; не́сколько; не́которые; о́коло (Р); ~ *20 miles* миль два́дцать; *in ~ degree*, *to ~ extent* до изве́стной сте́пени; **~body** [ˈsʌmbədɪ] кто́-то; кто́-нибудь; **~how** [ˈsʌmhaʊ] ка́к-то; ка́к-нибудь; ~ *or other* так или ина́че; **~one** [ˈsʌmwʌn] → **somebody**

somersault [ˈsʌməsɔːlt] кувырка́ние; *in air* са́льто *n indecl.*; *turn ~s pl.* кувыря́ться, [с]де́лать са́льто, *turn a ~* кувыркну́ться *pf.*

some|thing [ˈsʌmθɪŋ] что́-то; что́-нибудь; кое-что́; ~ *like* приблизи́тельно; что́-то вро́де (Р): *is ~ the matter?* что́-нибудь не в поря́дке?; **~time** когда́-то, когда́-нибудь, когда́-либо; **~times** иногда́; **~what** слегка́, немно́го; до не́которой сте́пени; **~where** где́-то, куда́-то; где́-нибудь, куда́-нибудь

son [sʌn] сын, *dim.* сыно́к; (*pl.*: сыновья́ *f*; *rhet.*: сыны́)

sonata [səˈnɑːtə] сона́та

song [sɒŋ] пе́сня, *dim.* пе́сенка; рома́нс; *coll. for a ~* за бесце́нок; **~bird** пе́вчая пти́ца**

son-in-law зять *m*

sonorous ['sɒnərəs] □ зву́чный

soon [su:n] ско́ро, вско́ре; ра́но; *as ~ as* как то́лько; *~er* ['su:nə] скоре́е; *no ~ … than* едва́ …, как; *no ~ said than done* ска́зано – сде́лано; *the ~ the better* чем скоре́е, тем лу́чше

soot [sut] са́жа *f*; ко́поть *f*

soothe [su:ð] успока́ивать [-ко́ить] (*a. fig.*); *fig.* утеша́ть [уте́шить]

sooty ['suti] □ закопчённый; чёрный как са́жа

sophist|icated [sə'fɪstɪkeɪtɪd] изы́сканный; *person* све́тский, искушённый; *machinery* сло́жный; *argument* изощрённый

soporific [sɒpə'rɪfɪk] снотво́рное

sordid ['sɔ:dɪd] □ *condition* убо́гий; *behavio(u)r, etc.* гну́сный

sore [sɔ:] **1.** □ (*tender*) чувстви́тельный; *point* боле́зненный; (*painful*) больно́й, воспалённый; (*aggrieved*) оби́женный; *she has a ~ throat* у неё боли́т го́рло; **2.** боля́чка; *from rubbing* натёртое ме́сто; (*running ~*) гноя́щаяся ра́н(к)а

sorrel ['sɒrəl] *bot.* щаве́ль *m*

sorrow ['sɒrəʊ] го́ре, печа́ль *f*; (*regret*) сожале́ние; *to my great ~* к моему́ вели́кому сожале́нию; *~ful* ['sɒrəʊful] печа́льный, ско́рбный

sorry ['sɒrɪ] □ по́лный сожале́ния; *~? mst. Brt.* прости́те, не расслы́шал(а), *coll.* что?; (*I am*) (*so*) *~!* мне о́чень жаль! винова́т!; *I feel ~ for you* мне вас жаль; *I'm ~ to say that …* к сожале́нию, я …; *say ~* извиня́ться [-ни́ться]

sort [sɔ:t] **1.** род, сорт; *people of all ~s pl.* лю́ди вся́кого разбо́ра; *~ of coll.* как бу́дто; *be out of ~s pl.* быть не в ду́хе; пло́хо чу́вствовать себя́; **2.** сортирова́ть; *~ out* разбира́ть [разобра́ть]; рассортиро́вывать [-ирова́ть]

so-so ['səʊsəʊ] *coll.* так себе́, нева́жно

SOS [esəʊ'es] СОС: сигна́л бе́дствия в а́збуке мо́рзе

souffle ['su:fleɪ] суфле́ *n indecl.*

sought [sɔ:t] *pt. u pt. p. om* **seek**

soul [səʊl] душа́ (*a. fig.*); (*person*) челове́к, душа́

sound¹ [saʊnd] □ (*healthy*) здоро́вый, кре́пкий, (*firm*) про́чный; (*sensible*) здра́вый; *in mind* норма́льный; *comm.* надёжный; *sleep* глубо́кий: *be ~ asleep* кре́пко спать

sound² [-] **1.** звук, шум; *mus.* звуча́ние; **2.** звуча́ть (*a. fig.*); разд(ав)а́ться; *fig.* [про]зонди́ровать; *patient's chest* выслу́шивать [вы́слушать]; *~ barrier* звуково́й барье́р; *~ing* ['saʊndɪŋ] *naut.* проме́р глубины́ воды́; *~less* [-lɪs] □ беззву́чный; *~proof* звуконепроница́емый; *~track* звуково́е сопровожде́ние

soup [su:p] суп; *~ plate* глубо́кая таре́лка; *~ spoon* столо́вая ло́жка

sour ['saʊə] □ ки́слый; (*bad-tempered*) раздражи́тельный; *~ cream* смета́на; *fig.* угрю́мый; *turn ~* закиса́ть [-и́снуть]; прокиса́ть [-и́снуть]

source [sɔ:s] исто́к; исто́чник (*mst. fig.*)

south [saʊθ] **1.** юг; **2.** ю́жный; *~east* ю́го-восто́к; **2.** ю́го-восто́чный (*a. ~ern*)

souther|ly ['sʌðəlɪ], *~n* ['sʌðən] ю́жный; *~ner* ['sʌðənə] южа́нин, южа́нка

southernmost са́мый ю́жный

southward, *~ly* ['saʊθwəd, -lɪ], *~s* [-dz] *adv.* к ю́гу, на юг

south|west 1. ю́го-за́пад; **2.** ю́гоза́падный (*a. ~erly, ~ern*); *~wester* ю́го-западный ве́тер

souvenir [su:və'nɪə] сувени́р

sovereign ['sɒvrɪn] **1.** суvере́нный; **2.** госуда́рь *m*; мона́рх; (*coin*) сове́рен; *~ty* [-tɪ] суверените́т

Soviet ['səʊvɪet] **1.** сове́т; **2.** сове́тский

sow¹ [saʊ] *zo.* свинья́; (*breeding ~*) свинома́тка

sow² [səʊ] [*irr.*] [по]се́ять; засева́ть [засе́ять]; *~n* [səʊn] *pt. p. om* **sow²**

soya beans ['sɔɪə] со́евые бобы́ *m/pl.*

spa [spɑ:] куро́рт с минера́льными исто́чниками

space [speɪs] простра́нство; ме́сто; промежу́ток; *of time* срок; *attr.* кос-

spacecraft 536

мический; **~craft** косми́ческий кора́бль m

spacing ['speisiŋ]: *type s.th. in double* ~ печа́тать че́рез два интерва́ла

spacious ['speiʃəs] просто́рный; обши́рный; вмести́тельный

spade [speid] лопа́та; **~s** *cards* пи́ки *f/pl.*; **~work** предвари́тельная (кропотли́вая) рабо́та

spaghetti [spə'geti] *pl.* спаге́тти *indecl.*

span [spæn] 1. *of bridge* пролёт; коро́ткое расстоя́ние и́ли вре́мя; 2. перекрыва́ть [-кры́ть] стро́ить мост че́рез (B); измеря́ть [-е́рить]

spangle ['spæŋgl] 1. блёстка; 2. украша́ть блёстками; *fig.* усе́ивать [усе́ять]

Spaniard ['spænjəd] испа́нец *m*, -нка *f*

spaniel ['spænjəl] спание́ль *m*

Spanish ['spæniʃ] испа́нский

spank [spæŋk] *coll.* 1. шлёпать [-пнуть]; отшлёпать; 2. шлепо́к

spanking ['spæŋkiŋ] *breeze* све́жий

spare [speə] □ 1. (*reserve*) запасно́й; (*surplus*) ли́шний, свобо́дный; (*thin*) худоща́вый; ~ *time* свобо́дное вре́мя *n*; 2. (~ *part*) запасна́я часть *f*; 3. *life* [по]щади́ть; (*grudge*) [по]жале́ть; (*save*) [с]бере́чь; *time* уделя́ть [-ли́ть]; (*save from*) избавля́ть [-а́вить] от (P)

sparing ['speəriŋ] □ эконо́мный; (*frugal*) скупо́й; *he is* ~ *of praise* он скуп на похвалы́

spark [spɑːk] 1. и́скра (*a. fig.*); 2. [за]искри́ться; ~(ing) *plug mot.* зажига́тельная свеча́

sparkle ['spɑːkl] 1. и́скра; (*process*) сверка́ние; 2. [за]искри́ться, [за]сверка́ть; *sparkling wine* игри́стое вино́

sparrow ['spærəʊ] воробе́й

sparse [spɑːs] □ ре́дкий; (*scattered*) разбро́санный; **~ly** [-li] ~ *populated* малонаселённый

spasm [spæzəm] спа́зма, су́дорога; ~ *of coughing* при́ступ ка́шля; **~odic(al** □) [spæz'mɒdik(əl)] су́дорожный

spat [spæt] *pt. u pt. p. om* spit

spatter ['spætə] бры́згать [-знуть];

with mud забры́згать, обры́згать гря́зью; (*spill*) расплёскивать [-плеска́ть]

spawn [spɔːn] 1. икра́; 2. мета́ть икру́; *multiply* [рас]плоди́ться

speak [spiːk] [*irr.*] *v/i.* говори́ть; [по]говори́ть (*with, to* с T); разгова́ривать; ~ *out* выска́зываться [вы́сказаться] открове́нно; ~ *up* говори́ть гро́мко; (*express, as opinion, etc.*) выска́зывать [вы́сказать]; *v/t. the truth, etc.* говори́ть [сказа́ть]; **~er** ['spiːkə] выступа́ющий; докла́дчик; ора́тор; *parl.* спи́кер

spear [spiə] 1. копьё; острога́; 2. пронза́ть копьём; *fish* бить острого́й

special ['speʃl] □ специа́льный; (*exceptional*) осо́бенный; осо́бый; ~ *delivery* сро́чная доста́вка; ~ *powers* чрезвыча́йные полномо́чия; **~ist** [-ʃlist] специали́ст; **~ity** [speʃi'ælɪti] → **specialty**; **~ize** ['speʃəlaiz] специализи́ровать(ся) (*im*)*pf.* (в П *or* по Д); **specialty** ['speʃəlti] осо́бенность *f*; специа́льность *f*

species ['spiːʃiːz] вид; разнови́дность *f*; *human* ~ челове́ческий род

specific [spə'sifik] (~*ally*) характе́рный; специфи́ческий; осо́бый; (*definite*) определённый; ~ *gravity* уде́льный вес; **~fy** ['spesifai] огова́ривать [-вори́ть]; то́чно определя́ть; (*stipulate*) предусма́тривать [-мотре́ть], обусла́вливать [-сло́вить]; **~men** ['spesimən] образе́ц, обра́зчик; экземпля́р

specious ['spiːʃəs] □ *excuse* благови́дный; показно́й

speck [spek] *of dirt, dust, etc.* пя́тнышко; *of colo(u)r* кра́пинка

spectacle ['spektəkl] (*show*) зре́лище; **~s** [-z] *pl.* (*glasses*) очки́ *n/pl.*

spectacular [spek'tækjʊlə] □ эффе́ктный; *coll.* потряса́ющий

spectator [spek'teɪtə] зри́тель *m*, -ни́ца *f*

spect|er, *Brt.* **~re** ['spektə] при́зрак

spectrum ['spektrəm] спектр

speculat|e ['spekjʊleɪt] (*consider*) размышля́ть [-ы́слить]; *fin.* спекули́ровать (*in* T); ~ion [spekjʊ'leɪʃn] размышле́ние; (*supposition*) предположе́ние; *fin.* спекуля́ция; ~ive ['spekjʊlətɪv] (*given to theory*) умозри́тельный; *fin.* спекуляти́вный; ~or ['spekjʊleɪtə] спекуля́нт

sped [sped] *pt. и pt. p. от* **speed**

speech [spiːtʃ] речь *f*; ~less ['spiːtʃlɪs] немо́й; онеме́вший; *I was* ~ я лиши́лся да́ра ре́чи

speed [spiːd] **1.** ско́рость *f*, быстрота́; *mot.* ско́рость *f*; *at full* ~ на по́лной ско́рости; **2.** [*irr.*] *v/i.* [по-] спеши́ть; бы́стро идти́; ~ *by* промча́ться *pf.* ми́мо; *v/t.* ~ *up* ускоря́ть [-о́рить]; ~ing ['-ɪŋ] *mot.* превыше́ние ско́рости; ~limit разреша́емая ско́рость *f*; ~ometer [spiː'dɒmɪtə] *mot.* спидо́метр; ~y ['spiːdɪ] □ бы́стрый

spell¹ [spel] **1.** (*коро́ткий*) пери́од; *a cold* ~ пери́од холо́дной пого́ды; *for a* ~ на вре́мя; *rest for a* ~ немно́го передохну́ть *pf.*

spell² [-] писа́ть, произноси́ть по бу́квам; *fig.* (*signify, bode*) сули́ть

spell³ [-] ча́ры *f/pl.*; очарова́ние; ~bound очаро́ванный

spelling ['spelɪŋ] правописа́ние; орфогра́фия

spelt [spelt] *chiefly Brt. pt. и pt. p. от* **spell**

spend [spend] [*irr.*] *money* [по]тра́тить, [из]расхо́довать; *time* проводи́ть [-вести́]; ~thrift ['spendθrɪft] мот, расточи́тель *m*, -ница *f*

spent [spent] *pt. и pt. p. от* **spend**; **2.** *adj.* (*exhausted*) истощённый, измо́танный

sperm [spɜːm] спе́рма

spher|e [sfɪə] шар; сфе́ра; *celestial* небе́сная сфе́ра; *fig.* о́бласть *f*, сфе́ра; по́ле де́ятельности; ~ical ['sferɪkl] □ сфери́ческий

spice [spaɪs] **1.** спе́ция, пря́ность *f*; *fig.* при́вкус; при́месь *f*; **2.** приправля́ть [-а́вить]

spick and span ['spɪkən'spæn] (*spotlessly clean*) сверка́ющий чистото́й; с иго́лочки

spicy ['spaɪsɪ] □ пря́ный; *fig.* пика́нт-

ный

spider ['spaɪdə] *zo.* пау́к

spike [spaɪk] **1.** (*point*) острие́; *on shoe* шип; *bot.* ко́лос; **2.** снабжа́ть шипа́ми; (*pierce*) пронза́ть [-зи́ть]

spill [spɪl] [*irr.*] *v/t.* проли́(ва́)ть; *powder* рассыпа́ть [-ы́пать]; *v/i.* проли́(ва́)ться

spilt [spɪlt] *pt. и pt. p. от* **spill**

spin [spɪn] **1.** [*irr.*] *yarn* [с]пря́сть; (~ *round*) крути́ться; [за]кружи́ть(ся); верте́ться; ~ *when fishing* лови́ть ры́бу спи́ннингом; *my head is* ~ning у меня́ кру́жится голова́; ~ *a yarn* расска́зывать исто́рию/небыли́цы; ~ *round* оберну́ться *pf.*; **2.** круже́ние; бы́страя езда́

spinach ['spɪnɪdʒ] шпина́т

spinal ['spaɪnl] спинно́й; ~ *column* позвоно́чный столб, спинно́й хребе́т; ~ *cord* спинно́й мозг

spine [spaɪn] *anat.* позвоно́чник; *bot.* колю́чка; ~less ['-lɪs] *fig.* бесхребе́тный

spinning| mill пряди́льная фа́брика; ~ **wheel** пря́лка

spinster ['spɪnstə] (*old maid*) ста́рая де́ва; *law* (*unmarried woman*) незаму́жняя же́нщина

spiny ['spaɪnɪ] (*prickly*) колю́чий

spiral ['spaɪərəl] **1.** □ спира́льный; ~ **staircase** винтова́я ле́стница; **2.** спира́ль *f*

spire ['spaɪə] *arch.* шпиль *m*

spirit ['spɪrɪt] **1.** *coll.* дух, душа́; (*ghost*) привиде́ние; (*enthusiasm*) воодушевле́ние; (*alcohol*) спирт; ~s *pl.* (*high* припо́днятое, *low* пода́вленное) настрое́ние; спиртны́е напи́тки *m/pl.*; **2.** ~ *away*, *off* та́йно похища́ть; ~ed [-ɪd] (*lively*) живо́й; (*courageous*) сме́лый; (*energetic*) энерги́чный; ~ *argument* жа́ркий спор; ~less [-lɪs] вя́лый; ро́бкий; безжи́зненный

spiritual ['spɪrɪtʃʊəl] □ духо́вный; ~ism [-ɪzəm] спирити́зм

spit¹ [spɪt] **1.** (*spittle*) слюна́; плево́к; *fig.* подо́бие; **2.** [*irr.*] плева́ть [плю́нуть]; *of fire* рассыпа́ть и́скры; *of cat* шипе́ть; *of rain* мороси́ть; *the*

~ting image of s.o. то́чная ко́пия кого́-л.

spit² [-] *geogr.* коса́, о́тмель *f; cul.* ве́ртел

spite [spaɪt] **1.** зло́ба, злость *f;* **in ~ of** не смотря́ на (В); **2.** досажда́ть [досади́ть]; **~ful** [ˈspaɪtful] зло́бный

spitfire [ˈspɪtfaɪə] вспы́льчивый челове́к

spittle [ˈspɪtl] слюна́; плево́к

splash [splæʃ] **1.** бры́зги *f/pl.* (*mst.* **~es** pl.); плеск; **2.** бры́згать [-знуть]; забры́згать *pf.;* плеска́ть(ся) [-сну́ть]

spleen [spliːn] *anat.* селезёнка; *fig.* раздраже́ние

splend|id [ˈsplendɪd] □ великоле́пный, роско́шный; **~o(u)r** [-də] блеск, великоле́пие

splice [splaɪs] *rope* сплета́ть [сплести́]; *wood* соединя́ть [-ни́ть]; *tape, etc.* скле́ивать [-ить]

splint [splɪnt] *med.* ши́на; **put an arm in a ~** накла́дывать ши́ну на (В); **~er** [ˈsplɪntə] **1.** *of stone* оско́лок; *of wood* ще́пка; *in skin* зано́за; **2.** расщепля́ть(ся) [-пи́ть(ся)]; раска́лываться [-коло́ться]

split [splɪt] **1.** (*crack, fissure*) тре́щина; щель *f; fig.* раско́л; **2.** расщеплённый; раско́лотый; **3.** [*irr.*] *v/t.* раска́лывать [-коло́ть]; расщепля́ть [-пи́ть]; (*divide*) [раз]дели́ть; **~ hairs** вдава́ться в то́нкости; спо́рить о пустяка́х; **~ one's sides laughing** надрыва́ться от сме́ха; *v/i.* раска́лываться [-коло́ться]; раздели́ться *pf.;* (*burst*) ло́паться [ло́пнуть]; **~ting** [ˈsplɪtɪŋ] *headache* ужа́сный

splutter [ˈsplʌtə] → **sputter**

spoil¹ [spɔɪl] **1.** (*a.* **~s** *pl.*) добы́ча

spoil² [-] [*irr.*] [ис]по́ртить; *food* [ис]по́ртиться; *child* [из]балова́ть

spoke¹ [spəuk] *of wheel* спи́ца; *of ladder* ступе́нька, перекла́дина

spoke² [-] *pt. om* **speak**; **~n** [ˈspəukən] *pt. p. om* **speak**; **~sman** [ˈspəuksmən] представи́тель *m*

sponge [spʌndʒ] **1.** гу́бка; **2.** *v/t.* вытира́ть и́ли мыть гу́бкой; **~ up** впи́тывать гу́бкой; *v/i. fig.* парази́т; жить

на чужо́й счёт; **~ cake** бискви́т; **~r** [ˈspʌndʒə] нахле́бник (-ница)

spongy [ˈspʌndʒɪ] гу́бчатый

sponsor [ˈspɒnsə] **1.** спо́нсор; (*guarantor*) поручи́тель *m,* -ница *f;* **2.** руча́ться [поручи́ться] за (В); рекомендова́ть; финанси́ровать

spontaneous [spɒnˈteɪnɪəs] □ *behavio(u)r, talk* непосре́дственный; непринуждённый; спонта́нный; **~ generation** самозарожде́ние

spook [spuːk] привиде́ние; **~y** [ˈ-ɪ] жу́ткий

spool [spuːl] *in sewing machine* шпу́лька; *in tape-recorder* боби́на; *of film, etc.* кату́шка

spoon [spuːn] **1.** ло́жка; **2.** черпа́ть ло́жкой; **~ful** [ˈspuːnfl] ло́жка (ме́ра)

spore [spɔː] спо́ра

sport [spɔːt] **1.** спорт; *attr.* спорти́вный; (*amusement, fun*) развлече́ние, заба́ва; (*good ~*) *sl.* молоде́ц; **~s** *pl.* спорти́вные и́гры *f/pl.;* **~s ground** спорти́вная площа́дка; **2.** *v/i.* игра́ть, весели́ться, резви́ться; *v/t. coll.* щеголя́ть (Т); **~sman** [ˈspɔːtsmən] спортсме́н

spot [spɒt] **1.** *com.* пятно́; *small* кра́пинка; (*place*) ме́сто; *coll.* (*small quantity*) немно́жко; **be in a ~** быть в тру́дном положе́нии; **on the ~** на ме́сте; сра́зу, неме́дленно; **2.** [за-, пере]па́чкать; (*detect*) обнару́жи(ва)ть; *coll.* (*identify*) опозн(ав)а́ть; **~less** [ˈspɒtlɪs] □ безупре́чный; незапя́тнанный; **~light** прожéктор; *fig.* центр внима́ния; **~ty** [ˈspɒtɪ] пятни́стый; *face* прыщева́тый

spouse [spauz] супру́г *m,* -а *f*

spout [spaut] **1.** *water* струя́; *of teapot, etc.* но́сик; **2.** ли́ться струёй; бить струёй; *coll.* (*speak*) разглаго́льствовать

sprain [spreɪn] **1.** *med.* растяже́ние; **2.** растя́гивать [-тяну́ть]

sprang [spræŋ] *pt. om* **spring**

sprawl [sprɔːl] (*a.* **~ out**) растя́гивать(ся) [-яну́ть(ся)]; *in a chair* разва́ливаться [-ли́ться]; *bot.* бу́йно разраста́ться

spray¹ [spreɪ] **1.** водяна́я пыль f; бры́зги f/pl.; (*instrument*) пульвериза́тор, распыли́тель m (*a.* **~er**); **2.** распыля́ть [-ли́ть]; опры́скивать [-скать], обры́зг(ив)ать

spray² [-] (*cluster, bunch*) кисть f, гроздь f

spread [spred] **1.** [*irr.*] v/t. (*a.* **~ out**) расстила́ть [разостла́ть]; *news* распространя́ть [-ни́ть]; *butter* нама́з(ыв)ать (T); *wings* расправля́ть [-а́вить]; **~ the table** накры(ва́)ть на стол; v/i. *of fields* простира́ться *pf.*; *of fire, etc.* распространя́ться [-ни́ться]; **2.** *pt. и pt. p. от* **spread 1**; **3.** распростране́ние; протяже́ние

spree [spri:] весе́лье; (*drinking*) кутёж; **go on a shopping ~** отпра́виться по магази́нам; накупи́ть вся́кой вся́чины

sprig [sprɪg] ве́точка, побе́г

sprightly ['spraɪtlɪ] (*lively*) живо́й, оживлённый, (*cheerful*) весёлый; бо́дрый

spring [sprɪŋ] **1.** (*leap*) прыжо́к, скачо́к; (*mineral ~, etc.*) ключ; (*a.* **~time**) весна́; *tech.* пружи́на; *of vehicle* рессо́ра; *fig.* моти́в; **2.** [*irr.*] v/t. (*explode*) взрыва́ть [взорва́ть]; *a leak* дава́ть течь f; v/i. (*jump*) пры́гать [-гнуть]; **to one's feet** вска́кивать [вскочи́ть]; *bot.* появля́ться [-ви́ться]; **~ aside** отскочи́ть *pf.* в сто́рону; **~ up** *fig.* возника́ть [-ни́кнуть]; **~ board** трампли́н; **~ tide** весна́; **~y** ['sprɪŋɪ] □ упру́гий

sprinkl||e ['sprɪŋkl] *liquid* бры́згать [-знуть]; обры́згивать [-знуть]; *sand, sugar* посыпа́ть [-ы́пать]; **~ing** [-ɪŋ]: *a* немно́го

sprint [sprɪnt] *sport* **1.** спринт; **2.** *sport* бежа́ть с максима́льной ско́ростью на коро́ткую диста́нцию; **he ~ed past us** он промча́лся ми́мо

sprout [spraʊt] **1.** *of plant* пуска́ть ростки́; *of seeds* прораста́ть [-расти́]; **2.** *bot.* росто́к

spruce¹ [spru:s] □ (*neat*) опря́тный; (*smart*) наря́дный

spruce² [-] *bot.* ель f

sprung [sprʌŋ] *pt. и pt. p. от* **spring**

spry [spraɪ] (*lively*) живо́й; (*nimble*) подви́жный

spun [spʌn] *pt. и pt. p. от* **spin**

spur [spɜ:] **1.** шпо́ра; *fig.* побужде́ние; **act on the ~ of the moment** де́йствовать не разду́мывая; **2.** пришпо́ривать; побужда́ть [-уди́ть]; **~ on** спеши́ть; *fig.* подстёгивать [-егну́ть]

spurious ['spjʊərɪəs] □ подде́льный; фальши́вый

spurn [spɜ:n] отверга́ть, отказа́ться *pf.* с презре́нием

spurt [spɜ:t] **1.** *of liquid* бить струёй; *of flame* выбра́сывать [вы́бросить]; **2.** *water* струя́; (*gust*) поры́в ве́тра; *sport* рыво́к (*a. fig.*)

sputter ['spʌtə] **1.** бры́зги f/pl.; шипе́ние; **2.** *of fire* [за]треща́ть, [за]шипе́ть; бры́згаться слюно́й при разгово́ре; говори́ть бы́стро и бессвя́зно

spy [spaɪ] **1.** шпио́н m, -ка f; **2.** шпио́нить, следи́ть (**on** за Т); (*notice*) заме́тить *pf.*

squabble ['skwɒbl] **1.** перебра́нка, ссо́ра; **2.** [по]вздо́рить

squad [skwɒd] *of workers* брига́да; отря́д; (*a. mil.*) гру́ппа, кома́нда (*a. sport*); **~ car** *Am.* патру́льная маши́на; **~ron** ['skwɒdrən] *mil.* эскадро́н; *ae.* эскадри́лья; *naut.* эска́дра

squalid ['skwɒlɪd] □ убо́гий

squall [skwɔ:l] **1.** *of wind* шквал; вопль m, крик; **2.** [за]вопи́ть

squander ['skwɒndə] прома́тывать [-мота́ть], [рас]транжи́рить

square [skweə] **1.** □ квадра́тный; *shoulders, right angles, etc.* прямо́й; (*fair, honest*) прямо́й, че́стный; **2.** квадра́т; (*town ~*) пло́щадь f; **3.** v/t. де́лать прямоуго́льным; (*pay*) опла́чивать [оплати́ть]; (*bring into accord*) согласо́вывать [-сова́ть]; v/i. согласо́вываться [-сова́ться]

squash [skwɒʃ] **1.** фрукто́вый напи́ток; (*crush*) да́вка, толчея́; **2.** разда́вливать [-дави́ть]

squat [skwɒt] **1.** призе́мистый; **2.** де́ть на ко́рточках; **~ down** при́ *pf.* на корточки

squawk [skwɔːk] **1.** *bird's* пронзи́тельный крик; **2.** пронзи́тельно крича́ть

squeak [skwiːk] [про]пища́ть; *of shoes, etc.* скрипе́ть

squeal [skwiːl] [за]визжа́ть; *sl.* доноси́ть [донести́]

squeamish ['skwiːmɪʃ] □ (*too scrupulous*) щепети́льный; оби́дчивый; *about food, etc.* приверёдливый; (*fastidious*) брезгли́вый

squeeze [skwiːz] **1.** сж(им)а́ть; (*clench*) сти́скивать [-снуть]; *lemon, etc.* выжима́ть [вы́жать]; *fig. money* вымога́ть (*from* у Р); **2.** сжа́тие; пожа́тие; давле́ние; да́вка; **~r** ['skwiːzə] выжима́лка

squelch [skweltʃ] хлюпать

squint [skwɪnt] коси́ть; *at the sun* [со]щу́риться

squirm [skwɜːm] извива́(ва́)ться, [с]ко́рчиться

squirrel ['skwɪrəl] бе́лка

squirt [skwɜːt] **1.** струя́; *coll.* (*a nobody*) вы́скочка *m/f.*; **2.** бры́згать [-знуть]; бить то́нкой струёй

stab [stæb] **1.** уда́р; **2.** *v/t. to death* зака́лывать [заколо́ть]; *v/i.* (*wound*) наноси́ть уда́р (*at* Д)

stabili|ty [stə'bɪlətɪ] усто́йчивость *f,* *fin.* стаби́льность *f;* про́чность *f;* **~ze** ['steɪbəlaɪz] стабилизи́ровать (*im*)*pf.;* **~zer** ['steɪbəlaɪzə] *tech.* стабилиза́тор

stable¹ ['steɪbl] □ усто́йчивый; *situation, etc.* стаби́льный

stable² [~] коню́шня

stack [stæk] **1.** *of hay* стог; *of wood* шта́бель *m; of books* сто́пка; ку́ча; **2.** скла́дывать [сложи́ть]

stadium ['steɪdɪəm] *sport* стадио́н

staff [stɑːf] **1.** (*flag~*) дре́вко; (*body of employees*) штат, персона́л; ***editorial~*** редколле́гия; **2.** набира́ть [-ра́ть] персона́л; укомплекто́вывать [-това́ть]

stag [stæg] *zo.* оле́нь-саме́ц

stage [steɪdʒ] **1.** сце́на, подмо́стки *m/pl.; for singer, etc.* эстра́да; *fig.* ста́[дия, эта́п; **2.** [по]ста́вить; **~ manager** [ре]жиссёр

stagger ['stægə] *v/i.* шата́ть(ся) [(по)-

шатну́ться]; *v/t. fig.* потряса́ть [-ясти́]; поража́ть [порази́ть]; **~ing** [-ɪŋ] потряса́ющий

stagna|nt ['stægnənt] □ *water* стоя́чий; **~te** [stæg'neɪt] заста́иваться [застоя́ться]; *fig. mst. econ.* быть в состоя́нии засто́я

staid [steɪd] □ уравнове́шенный, степе́нный; сде́ржанный

stain [steɪn] **1.** пятно́ (*a. fig.*); **2.** [за]па́чкать; *fig.* [за]пятна́ть; **~ed glass** цветно́е стекло́; **~ed-glass window** витра́ж; **~less** ['steɪnlɪs] *steel* нержаве́ющий

stair [steə] ступе́нька; **~s** *pl.* ле́стница; **~case, ~way** ле́стница; ле́стничная кле́тка

stake [steɪk] **1.** *wooden* кол; (*bet*) ста́вка; *be at* ~ *fig.* быть поста́вленным на ка́рту; **2.** *money* ста́вить (*on* на В)

stale [steɪl] □ несве́жий; *air* спёртый; *joke* изби́тый; *bread* чёрствый; *news* устаре́вший

stalemate ['steɪlmeɪt] *chess* пат; *fig.* тупи́к

stalk [stɔːk] **1.** сте́бель *m; of leaf* черено́к; **2.** *v/i.* ва́жно ше́ствовать, го́рдо выступа́ть

stall [stɔːl] **1.** *for animals* сто́йло; *in market mst. Brt.* прила́вок; кио́ск, ларёк; *thea.* ме́сто в парте́ре; **2.:** **the engine ~ed** мото́р загло́х

stallion ['stælɪən] жеребе́ц

stalwart ['stɔːlwət] ро́слый, кре́пкий; *supporter* сто́йкий

stamina ['stæmɪnə] выно́сливость *f*

stammer ['stæmə] **1.** заика́ться [-кну́ться]; запина́ться [запну́ться]; **2.** заика́ние

stamp [stæmp] **1.** штамп, ште́мпель *m,* печа́ть *f; fig.* отпеча́ток, печа́ть *f; for letter* ма́рка; *of feet* то́панье; **~ collector** филатели́ст; **2.** [про]штампова́ть; [по]ста́вить ште́мпель *m,* печа́ть *f;* то́пать ного́й

stampede [stæm'piːd] **1.** пани́ческое бе́гство; **2.** обраща́ть(ся) в пани́ческое бе́гство

stand [stænd] **1.** [*irr.*] *v/i. com.* стоя́ть; простаивать [-стоя́ть]; (~ *still*) остана́вливаться [-нови́ться]; (~ *fast*) держа́ться; устоя́ть *pf*.; ~ *against* [вос]проти́виться, сопротивля́ться (Д); ~ *aside* [по]сторони́ться; ~ *by* прису́тствовать; *fig.* быть наготове; подде́рживать; [-жа́ть]; ~ *for* быть кандида́том (Р); стоя́ть за (В); зна́чить; ~ *out* выделя́ться [вы́делиться] (*against* на П); ~ *over* оставля́ться нерешённым; ~ *up* вст(ав)а́ть, поднима́ться [-ня́ться]; ~ *up for* защища́ть [-ити́ть]; **2.** *v/t.* [по]ста́вить; (*bear*) выде́рживать [вы́держать], вы́носи́ть [вы́нести]; *coll* (*treat*) угоща́ть [угости́ть] (Т); **3.** остано́вка; сопротивле́ние; то́чка зре́ния; стенд, кио́ск; пози́ция; ме́сто; (*support*) подста́вка; (*rostrum*) трибу́на; *make a ~ against* сопротивля́ться (Д)

standard ['stændəd] **1.** зна́мя *n*, флаг; но́рма, станда́рт; образе́ц *m*; ~ *of living* жи́зненный у́ровень *m*; **2.** станда́ртный; образцо́вый; ~**ize** [-aız] стандартизи́ровать (*im*)*pf.*

standby ['stændbaı] **1.** опо́ра; **2.** *tech.*, *fin.* резе́рвный

standing ['stændıŋ] **1.** (*posture, etc.*) стоя́чий; *permanent* постоя́нный; **2.** (*rank, reputation*) положе́ние; (*duration*) продолжи́тельность *f*

stand|offish [stænd'ɒfıʃ] за́мкнутый; надме́нный; ~**point** то́чка зре́ния; ~**still** остано́вка; *the work came to a ~* рабо́та останови́лась; *bring to a ~* останови́ть, засто́порить

stank [stæŋk] *pt. om* **stink**

stanza ['stænzə] строфа́

staple ['steıpl] основно́й; ~ *diet* осно́ва пита́ния

star [stɑː] **1.** звезда́ (*a. fig.*); *fig.* судьба́; *the ~s and Stripes* *pl.* *Am.* национа́льный флаг США; *thank one's lucky ~s* благодари́ть судьбу́; **2.** игра́ть гла́вную роль *f*

starboard ['stɑːbəd] *naut.* пра́вый борт

starch [stɑːtʃ] **1.** крахма́л; **2.** [на]крахма́лить

stare [steə] **1.** при́стальный взгляд; **2.** смотре́ть при́стально; уста́виться

pf.; (*at* на В)

stark [stɑːk] (*stiff*) окочене́лый; (*utter*) соверше́нный; *adv.* соверше́нно

starling ['stɑːlıŋ] скворе́ц

starry ['stɑːrı] звёздный

start [stɑːt] **1.** нача́ло; *of train, etc.* отправле́ние; *sport* старт; *give a ~* вздро́гнуть *pf.* *give s.o. a ~* испуга́ть кого́-л.; *give s.o. a ~ in life* помо́чь *pf.* кому́-л. встать на́ ноги; **2.** *v/i. at a sound, etc.* вздра́гивать [-ро́гнуть]; *from one's seat, etc.* вска́кивать [вскочи́ть]; отправля́ться в путь; *sport* стартова́ть (*im*)*pf.*; начина́ться; *v/t.* (*set going*) пуска́ть (пусти́ть); *sport* дава́ть старт (Д); *fig.* нач(ин)а́ть; учрежда́ть [-еди́ть]; побужда́ть [-уди́ть] (~ *a p. doing* кого́-л. де́лать); ~**er** ['stɑːtə] *mot.* стартёр

startl|e [stɑːtl] (*alarm*) трево́жить (*take aback*) поража́ть [порази́ть]; [ис-, на]пуга́ть; ~**ing** ['stɑːtlıŋ] порази́тельный

starv|ation [stɑːveıʃən] го́лод; голода́ние; ~**e** [stɑːv] голода́ть; умира́ть с го́лоду; мори́ть го́лодом; ~ *for* *fig.* жа́ждать (Р)

state [steıt] **1.** состоя́ние; (*station in life*) положе́ние; госуда́рство (*pol. a.* ♀); (*member of federation*) штат; *attr.* госуда́рственный; *get into a* ~ разне́рвничаться *pf.*, разволнова́ться *pf.*; ~ *of emergency* чрезвыча́йное положе́ние; **2.** заявля́ть [-ви́ть]; конста́ти́ровать (*im*)*pf.*; [с]формули́ровать; (*set forth*) излага́ть (изложи́ть); ~**ly** [-lı] вели́чественный; ~**ment** [-mənt] утвержде́ние; официа́льное заявле́ние; *fin.* отчёт; ~**room** *naut.* отде́льная каю́та; ~**sman** ['steıtsmən] госуда́рственный де́ятель *m*

static ['stætık] *el.* стати́ческий; неподви́жный; (*stable*) стаби́льный

station ['steıʃn] **1.** *radio, el., rail.* ста́[ция; (*building*) вокза́л; р[...]меща́ть [-ести́ть] (*a. mil.*); ['steıʃənrı] неподви́жный; с[...]на́рный; ~**ery** [-] канцеля́рск[...]ры *m/pl.*

statistics [stəˈtɪstɪks] стати́стика

statue [ˈstætʃuː] ста́туя

stature [ˈstætʃə] рост; масшта́б, кали́бр

status [ˈsteɪtəs] положе́ние; **~ quo** ста́тус-кво

statute [ˈstætʃuːt] стату́т; зако́н; законода́тельный акт; *pl.* уста́в

staunch [stɔːntʃ] *supporter* ве́рный; непоколеби́мый

stay [steɪ] **1.** пребыва́ние, визи́т; *law* отсро́чка; **2.** *v/t. law* приостана́вливать [-нови́ть]; *v/i.* (*remain*) ост(а)ва́ться; *as guest at hotel, etc.* остана́вливаться [-нови́ться], жить (*at* в П), [по]гости́ть

stead [sted]: *in a person's* ~ вме́сто кого́-нибудь; **~fast** [ˈstedfɑːst] сто́йкий, непоколеби́мый

steady [ˈstedɪ] **1.** □ (*balanced*) усто́йчивый; *look, etc.* при́стальный; (*regular*) постоя́нный; равноме́рный; (*stable*) уравнове́шенный; **2.** де́лать(ся) усто́йчивым; приводи́ть в равнове́сие; *adv.* ~*!* осторо́жно!

steak [steɪk] *of beef* бифште́кс; (*fillet* ~) вы́резка

steal [stiːl] [*irr.*] *v/t.* [с]ворова́ть, [у]кра́сть; *v/i.* кра́сться, прокра́дываться [-ра́сться]

stealth [stelθ]: *by* ~ укра́дкой, тайко́м; ~**y** [ˈstelθɪ] □ та́йный; бесшу́мный; *glance* взгляд укра́дкой; ~ *steps* краду́щиеся шаги́

steam [stiːm] **1.** пар; **2.** *attr.* парово́й; **3.** *v/i.* (*move by steam*) *of train* идти́; *of ship* пла́вать; [по]плы́ть; *get* ~*ed up* запоте́ть *pf.*; *fig.* [вз]волнова́ться; *v/t.* вари́ть на пару́; пари́ть; выпа́ривать [вы́парить]; ~**er** [ˈstiːmə] *naut.* парохо́д; *cul.* скорова́рка; ~**y** [ˈstiːmɪ] насы́щенный па́ром; *glass* запоте́вший

steel [stiːl] **1.** сталь *f*; **2.** стально́й (*a.* ~**y**); ~ *o.s.* для собра́ть всё му́жество; ожесточа́ться [-чи́ться]; ~**works** сталелите́йный заво́д

steep [stiːp] круто́й; *coll. price* сли́шком высо́кий

steeple [stiːpl] шпиль *m*; *with bell* коло-

локо́льня; ~**chase** ска́чки с препя́тствиями

steer [stɪə] пра́вить рулём; *naut., etc.* управля́ть (Т); ~**ing** [ˈ-ɪŋ]: ~ *wheel naut.* штурва́л; *mot.* рулево́е колесо́, *coll.* бара́нка; ~**sman** [ˈstɪəzmən] рулево́й

stem[1] [stem] **1.** *bot.* сте́бель *m*; *gr.* осно́ва; **2.** *v/i.* (*arise*) происходи́ть [-изойти́]

stem[2] [-] (*stop, check*) заде́рживать [-жа́ть]

stench [stentʃ] злово́ние

stencil [ˈstensl] трафаре́т

stenographer [steˈnɒgrəfə] стеногра́фи́ст *m*, -ка *f*

step[1] [step] **1.** шаг (*a. fig.*); похо́дка; *of stairs* ступе́нька; (*footboard*) подно́жка; *fig.* ме́ра; *it's only a* ~ *from here* отсю́да руко́й пода́ть; ~ *by* ~ постепе́нно; *a rushed* ~ необду́манный шаг; *take* ~*s* принима́ть [-ня́ть] ме́ры; *tread in the* ~*s of fig.* идти́ по стопа́м (Р); ~*s pl.* стремя́нка; **2.** *v/i.* шага́ть [шагну́ть], ступа́ть [-пи́ть]; ходи́ть, идти́ [пойти́]; ~ *aside* посторони́ться *pf.*; ~ *back* отступи́ть *pf.* наза́д, отойти́ *pf.*; ~ *up v/t.* (*increase*) повыша́ть [-ы́сить]

step[2] [-]: ~**daughter** па́дчерица; ~**father** о́тчим; ~**mother** ма́чеха

steppe [step] степь *f*

stepping-stone ка́мень *m* для перехо́да че́рез руче́й; ~ *to success* ступе́нь к успе́ху

stepson па́сынок

stereo [ˈsterɪəʊ] стереофони́ческий (про́игрыватель *m or* радиоприёмник)

stereotype [ˈsterɪətaɪp] стереоти́п

steril|e [ˈsteraɪl] беспло́дный; (*free from germs*) стери́льный; ~**ity** [steˈrɪlətɪ] беспло́дие; стери́льность *f*; ~**ize** [ˈsterəlaɪz] стерилизова́ть (*im*)*pf.*

sterling [ˈstɜːlɪŋ]: *the pound* ~ фунт сте́рлингов

stern[1] [stɜːn] □ стро́гий, суро́вый

stern[2] [-] *naut.* корма́

stevedore [ˈstiːvɪdɔː] до́кер; порто́вый грузчи́к

stew [stju:] 1. [c]туши́ть(ся); 2. тушёное мя́со; *be in a ~* волнова́ться, беспоко́иться

steward ['stjuəd] *naut., ae.* стю́ард, бортпроводни́к; **~ess** ['stjuədis] стюарде́сса, бортпроводни́ца

stick[1] [stik] па́лка; (*walking ~*) трость *f*; **~s for fire** хво́рост

stick[2] [-] *irr.*] *v/i.* прикле́и(ва)ться, прилипа́ть [-ли́пнуть]; (*become fixed*) застрева́ть [-ря́ть]; завяза́ть [-я́знуть]; *at home* торча́ть; ~ *to* приде́рживаться [-жа́ться] (P); ~ *at nothing* не остана́вливаться ни пе́ред чем; ~ *out, ~ up* торча́ть; стоя́ть торчко́м; *v/t.* вка́лывать [вколо́ть]; *fork, etc.* втыка́ть [воткну́ть]; *stamp* накле́ивать [-е́ить]; прикле́и(ва)ть; *coll.* (*bear*) терпе́ть, вы́терпеть *pf.*; **~ing plaster** лейкопла́стырь *m*

sticky ['stiki] ли́пкий, кле́йкий; *come to a ~ end* пло́хо ко́нчить *pf.*

stiff [stif] □ жёсткий, неги́бкий; *lock, etc.* туго́й; тру́дный; *relations* натя́нутый; ~ *with cold* окочене́ть *pf.* от хо́лода; **~en** ['stifn] *of starch, etc.* [за]густе́ть

stifle ['staifl] задыха́ться [задохну́ться]; *rebellion* подавля́ть [-ви́ть]

stigma ['stigmə] *fig.* пятно́, клеймо́

still [stil] 1. *adj.* ти́хий; неподви́жный; 2. *adv.* ещё, всё ещё; 3. *cj.* всё же, одна́ко; 4. (*make calm*) успока́ивать [-ко́ить]; **~born** мертворождённый; ~ *life* натюрмо́рт; **~ness** ['stilnis] тишина́

stilted ['stiltid] *style* высокопа́рный

stimul|ant ['stimjulənt] *med.* возбужда́ющее сре́дство; *fig.* сти́мул; **~ate** [-leit] (*excite*) возбужда́ть [-уди́ть], стимули́ровать (*a. fig.*); поощря́ть [-ри́ть]; **~ating** стимули́рующий, вдохновля́ющий; **~us** [-ləs] сти́мул

sting [stiŋ] 1. (*organ*) жа́ло; (*bite*) уку́с; о́страя боль *f*; *fig.* ко́лкость *f*; 2. [*irr.*] [у]жа́лить; *of nettle* жечь(ся); (*smart, burn*) садни́ть; *fig.* уязвля́ть [-ви́ть]

sting|iness ['stindʒinis] ска́редность *f*; **~y** ['stindʒi] скупо́й

stink [stiŋk] 1. вонь *f*; 2. [*irr.*] воня́ть

stint [stint] 1. (*fixed amount*) но́рма; 2. (*keep short*) ограни́чи(ва)ть; [по]скупи́ться на (В); *she doesn't ~ herself* она́ себе́ ни в чём не отка́зывает

stipulat|e ['stipjuleit] ста́вить усло́вия; обусло́вливать [-вить]; *the ~d sum* огово́ренная [-вить] су́мма; **~ion** [stipju'leiʃn] усло́вие

stir [stз:] 1. шевеле́ние (*excitement*) суета́, суматоха; движе́ние; *fig.* оживле́ние; *create a ~* наде́лать *pf.* мно́го шу́ма; 2. *leaves, etc.* шевели́ть(ся) [-льну́ть(ся)]; *tea, etc.* [по]меша́ть; [вз]волнова́ть; ~ *up* (*excite*) возбужда́ть [-уди́ть]; размеши́вать [-ша́ть]

stirrup ['stirəp] стре́мя *n* (*pl.*: стремена́)

stitch [stitʃ] *sew.* стежо́к; *in knitting* петля́; *med.* шов; 2. [с]шить, проши(ва́)ть

stock [stɔk] 1. (*supply*) запа́с; *live ~* поголо́вье скота́, скота́, скот; *capital ~* уставно́й капита́л; *take ~ of* де́лать переучёт (P), производи́ть инвентариза́цию; *fig.* крити́чески оце́нивать; 2. *size* станда́ртный; *joke, etc.* изби́тый; 3. (*supply*) снабжа́ть [-бди́ть]

stock|breeder животново́д; **~broker** биржево́й ма́клер; бро́кер; ~ **exchange** фо́ндовая би́ржа; **~holder** *Am.* акционе́р

stocking ['stɔkiŋ] чуло́к

stock|taking переучёт, инвентариза́ция; **~y** ['stɔki] корена́стый

stoic ['stəuik] 1. сто́ик; 2. сто́ический

stole [stəul] *pt. om steal*; **~n** ['stəulən] *pt. p. om steal*

stolid ['stɔlid] □ флегмати́чный

stomach ['stʌmək] 1. желу́док; живо́т; *it turns my ~* от э́того меня́ тошни́т; 2. *fig.* переноси́ть [-нести́]

stone [stəun] 1. ка́мень *m*; *of fruit* ко́сточка; *leave no ~ unturned* [с]де́лать всё возмо́жное; 2. ка́менный; 3. броса́ть ка́мни, броса́ться камня́ми; *fruit* вынима́ть ко́сточки из (P); **~-deaf** соверше́нно глухо́й; **~ware** гонча́рные изде́лия *n/pl.*

stony ['stəuni] камени́стый; *fig.* ка́менный

S

stood [stʊd] *pt. и pt. p. om* **stand**

stool [stu:l] (*seat*) табуре́тка; (*f(a)eces*) стул

stoop [stu:p] **1.** *v/i.* наклоня́ться [-ни́ться], нагиба́ться [нагну́ться]; (*be bent*) [c]суту́литься; *fig.* унижа́ться [уни́зиться] (**to** до P); *v/t.* суту́лить; **2.** суту́лость *f*

stop [stɒp] **1.** *v/t.* затыка́ть [заткну́ть] (*a.* ~ **up**), заде́л(ыв)ать; *tooth* [за]пломби́ровать; (*prevent*) уде́рживать [-жа́ть]; (*cease*) прекраща́ть [-крати́ть]; (*halt*) остана́вливать [-нови́ть]; ~ **it!** прекрати́!; *v/i.* перест(ав)а́ть; (*stay*) остана́вливаться [-нови́ться]; (*finish*) прекраща́ться [-рати́ться]; конча́ться [ко́нчиться]; **2.** остано́вка; па́уза; заде́ржка; *tech.* упо́р; *gr.* (*a.* **full** ~) то́чка; ~**page** ['stɒpidʒ] остано́вка, прекраще́ние рабо́ты; *tech.* про́бка, засоре́ние; ~**per** ['stɒpə] про́бка; ~**ping** ['stɒpiŋ] (зубна́я) пло́мба

storage ['stɔ:ridʒ] хране́ние; *place* склад

store [stɔ:] **1.** запа́с; склад; *Am.* магази́н; (*department* ~) универма́г; **in** ~ нагото́ве; про запа́с; **2.** храни́ть на скла́де; (*put by*) запаса́ть [-сти́]; ~**house** склад; *fig.* сокро́вищница; ~**keeper** *Am.* хозя́ин магази́на

stor(e)y ['stɔ:ri] эта́ж

stork [stɔ:k] а́ист

storm [stɔ:m] **1.** бу́ря; *at sea* шторм; *mil.* штурм; **a** ~ **in a teacup** бу́ря в стака́не воды́; **2.** бушева́ть; *mil.* штурмова́ть (*a. fig.*); ~**y** ['-ri] □ бу́рный (*a. fig.*); штормово́й

story ['stɔ:ri] (*account*) расска́з, исто́рия; *lit.* расска́з; *longer* по́весть *f*; *cine.* сюже́т; *in newspaper* статья́

stout [staʊt] **1.** □ *thing* кре́пкий, про́чный; (*sturdy*) пло́тный; (*fat*) ту́чный; (*brave*) отва́жный; **2.** кре́пкое тёмное пи́во

stove [stəʊv] печь *f*, пе́чка; (*ку́хонная*) плита́

stow [stəʊ] (*pack*) укла́дывать [уложи́ть]; ~**away** *naut.* безбиле́тный пассажи́р

straggl|e ['strægl] *of houses* быть разбро́санным; (*drop behind*) отст(а)ва́ть; ~**ing** [-iŋ] разбро́санный; беспоря́дочный

straight [streit] **1.** *adj.* прямо́й; че́стный; (*undiluted*) неразба́вленный; **put** ~ приводи́ть в поря́док; **2.** *adv.* пря́мо; сра́зу; ~**en** ['streitn] выпрямля́ть(ся) [вы́прямить(ся)]; ~**out** приводи́ть в поря́док; ~**forward** [-'fɔ:wəd] □ че́стный, прямо́й, открове́нный

strain[1] [strein] поро́да; сорт; черта́ хара́ктера

strain[2] [~] напряже́ние; *tech.* (*force*) нагру́зка; перенапряже́ние (*a. med.*); *mus. mst.* ~**s** *pl.* напе́в, мело́дия; **2.** *v/t.* натя́гивать [натяну́ть]; напряга́ть [-я́чь]; (*filter*) проце́живать [-еди́ть]; (*exhaust*) переутомля́ть [-ми́ть]; *med.* растя́гивать [-яну́ть] *v/i.* напряга́ться [-я́чься]; тяну́ться (**after** за T); тяну́ть изо всех сил (**at** B); ~ стара́ться; ~**er** ['streinə] (*colander*) дуршла́г; (*sieve*) си́то; цеди́лка

strait [streit] проли́в; ~**s** *pl.* затрудни́тельное положе́ние; ~**ened** ['streitnd]: **be in** ~ **circumstances** оказа́ться *pf.* в стеснённом положе́нии

strand [strænd] *of hair* прядь *f*; *of cable* жи́ла; ~**ed** [-id]: **be** ~ *fig.* оказа́ться *pf.* без средств

strange [streindʒ] □ стра́нный; (*alien*) чужо́й; (*unknown*) незнако́мый; ~**r** ['streindʒə] незнако́мец *m*, -мка *f*; посторо́нний (челове́к)

strangle ['stræŋgl] [за]души́ть

strap [stræp] **1.** *on watch, etc.* реме́шок; (*shoulder* ~) брете́лька; *mil.* пого́н; **2.** стя́гивать ремнём

stratagem ['strætədʒəm] уло́вка; хи́трость *f*

strategic [strə'ti:dʒik] (~**ally**) стратеги́ческий; ~**y** ['strætidʒi] страте́гия

strat|um ['stra:təm], *pl.* ~**a** [-tə] *geol.* пласт; *social* слой

straw [strɔ:] **1.** соло́ма; соло́минка; **the last** ~ после́дняя ка́пля; **2.** соло́менный; ~**berry** ['-bri] клубни́ка; (*a. wild* ~) земляни́ка

stray [strei] **1.** сбива́ться с пути́, заблуди́ться *pf.*; забрести́ *pf.*; *of thoughts, affections* блужда́ть; *2.* (*a.* **~ed**) заблуди́вшийся; бездо́мный; *dog, cat* бродя́чий; *bullet* шальна́я пу́ля

streak [striːk] поло́ска *f.*; *fig.* черта́ *f.*; **~s of grey** про́седь *f*

stream [striːm] **1.** пото́к (*a. fig.*); (*brook*) руче́й *m*; (*jet*) струя́ *f*; **2.** *v/i.* [по]те́чь; *poet.* струи́ться; *of flag, etc.* развева́ться

streamline *v/t.* придава́ть [прида́ть] обтека́емую фо́рму; упрости́ть [упрости́ть]; *fig.* рационализи́ровать

street [striːt] у́лица; *attr.* у́личный; **not up my** ~ не по мое́й части; ~ **lamp** у́личный фона́рь *m*; ~**car** *Am.* трамва́й

strength [streŋθ] си́ла *f.*; *of cloth, etc.* про́чность *f.*; *of alcohol, etc.* кре́пость *f.*; **on the** ~ **of** на основа́нии (P); ~**en** ['streŋθən] *v/t.* уси́ли(ва)ть; укрепля́ть [-пи́ть]; *v/i.* уси́ли(ва)ть

strenuous ['strenjʊəs] энерги́чный; *day, work* напряжённый, тяжёлый

stress [stres] **1.** напряже́ние (*a. tech.*); (*accent*) ударе́ние *n.*; подчёркивать [-черкну́ть]; ста́вить ударе́ние на (П)

stretch [stretʃ] **1.** *v/t.* (~ *tight*) натя́гивать [-яну́ть]; (*make wider or longer*) растя́гивать [-яну́ть]; *neck* вытя́гивать [вы́тянуть]; протя́гивать [-яну́ть]; (*mst.* ~ **out**); **a point** допуска́ть [-сти́ть] натя́жку, преувели́чи(ва)ть; *v/i.* тяну́ться, растя́гиваться [-яну́ться]; **2.** растя́гивание; напряже́ние; *of road* отре́зок; натя́жка; преувеличе́ние; (*level area*) простра́нство; промежу́ток вре́мени; ~**er** ['stretʃə] носи́лки *f/pl*

strew [struː] [*irr.*] посыпа́ть [посы́пать]; (*litter, scatter*) разбра́сывать [-роса́ть]

stricken ['strɪkən] *pt. p. om* **strike**

strict [strɪkt] (*exact*) то́чный; (*severe*) стро́гий

stride [straɪd] **1.** [*irr.*] шага́ть [шагну́ть]; ~ **over** переша́гивать [-гну́ть]; **2.** большо́й шаг; **take** (**s.th.**) **in one's** ~ *fig.* легко́ добива́ться своего́; легко́ переноси́ть [-нести́]

strident ['straɪdnt] □ ре́зкий, скрипу́чий; пронзи́тельный

strike [straɪk] **1.** забасто́вка; **be on** ~ бастова́ть; **2.** [*irr.*] *v/t.* ударя́ть [уда́рить]; *coins, etc.* [от]чека́нить; *fig.* поража́ть [порази́ть]; находи́ть [найти́]; *a bargain* заключа́ть [-чи́ть]; *a pose* принима́ть [-ня́ть]; ~ **up** *acquaintance* познако́миться; *v/i. of clock* [про]би́ть; [за]бастова́ть; ~ **home** *fig.* попада́ть в са́мую то́чку; ~**r** ['straɪkə] забасто́вщик (-и́ца)

striking ['straɪkɪŋ] □ порази́тельный; ~ **changes** рази́тельные переме́ны

string [strɪŋ] **1.** бечёвка; верёвка; *mus.* струна́ *f.*; *of pearls* ни́тка *f.*; **~s** *pl. mus.* стру́нные инструме́нты *m/pl.*; **pull ~s** испо́льзовать свои́ свя́зи; **2.** [*irr.*] *beads* нани́зывать [-за́ть]; ~ **band** стру́нный орке́стр

stringent ['strɪndʒənt] *rules* стро́гий; (*which must be obeyed*) обяза́тельный

strip [strɪp] **1.** сдира́ть [содра́ть] (*a.* ~ **off**); *bark* обдира́ть [ободра́ть]; разде́(ва́)ть(ся); *of rank, etc.* лиша́ть [лиши́ть] (**of** P); (*rob*) [о]гра́бить; **2.** полоса́, поло́ска; **landing** ~ взлётно-поса́дочная полоса́

stripe [straɪp] полоса́ *f.*; *mil.* наши́вка

strive [straɪv] [*irr.*] [по]стара́ться; стреми́ться (**for, after** к Д); ~**n** ['strɪvn] *pt. p. om* **strive**

strode [strəʊd] *pt. om* **stride**

stroke [strəʊk] **1.** уда́р (*a. med.*); *of pen, etc.* штрих; *of brush* мазо́к; **at one** ~ одни́м ма́хом; ~ **of luck** уда́ча; **2.** [по-] гла́дить

stroll [strəʊl] **1.** прогу́ливаться [-ля́ться]; **2.** прогу́лка

strong [strɒŋ] □ *com.* си́льный; про́чный; *tea, etc.* кре́пкий; *cheese* о́стрый; *argument* убеди́тельный; **a ~ point** си́льная сторона́; ~**hold** *fig.* опло́т; ~**willed** реши́тельный; упря́мый

strove [strəʊv] *pt. om* **strive**

struck [strʌk] *pt. и pt. p. om* **strike**

structure ['strʌktʃə] структу́ра (*a. phys.*); *social* строй; *arch.* строе́ние

(a. phys.), сооруже́ние

struggle ['strʌgl] **1.** боро́ться; вся́чески стара́ться; би́ться (**with** над Т); **~ through** с трудо́м пробива́ться; **2.** борьба́

strung [strʌŋ] pt. и pt. p. om **string**

stub [stʌb] **1.** of cigarette оку́рок; of pencil огры́зок; **2.** one's toe уда́риться [уда́риться] (**against** о В)

stubble ['stʌbl] стерня́; of beard щети́на

stubborn ['stʌbən] □ упря́мый; непода́тливый; efforts, etc. упо́рный

stuck [stʌk] pt. и pt. p. om **stick**, **~up** coll. высокоме́рный; зано́счивый

stud [stʌd] **1.** (collar~) за́понка; (press-~) кно́пка; on boots шип; **2.** усе́ивать [усе́ять] (Т)

student ['stju:dnt] студе́нт m, -ка f

studied ['stʌdɪd] answer, remark обду́манный; insult преднаме́ренный; умы́шленный

studio ['stju:dɪəu] сту́дия; artist's ателье́ n indecl., мастерска́я

studious ['stju:dɪəs] □ нарочи́тый; приле́жный

study ['stʌdɪ] **1.** изуче́ние; (research) иссле́дование; (room) кабине́т; paint. этю́д, эски́з; **2.** учи́ться (Д) [-чи́ть]; иссле́довать (im)pf.

stuff [stʌf] **1.** материа́л; вещество́; (cloth) ткань f, мате́рия; **~ and nonsense** чепуха́; **2.** v/t. (fill) наби(ва́)ть; cul. фарширова́ть, начиня́ть [-ни́ть]; (shove into) засо́вывать [засу́нуть]; (overeat) объеда́ться [объе́сться]; **~ing** ['stʌfɪŋ] наби́вка; cul. начи́нка; **~y** ['stʌfɪ] □ спёртый, ду́шный

stumble ['stʌmbl] спотыка́ться [-ткну́ться]; in speech запина́ться [запну́ться]; **~ upon** натыка́ться [наткну́ться] на (В)

stump [stʌmp] **1.** of tree пень m; of tail, etc. обру́бок; of cigarette оку́рок; **2.** v/t. coll. ста́вить в тупи́к; v/i. тяжело́ ступа́ть; **~y** ['stʌmpɪ] призе́мистый

stun [stʌn] оглуша́ть [-ши́ть] (a. fig.); fig. ошеломля́ть [-ми́ть]

stung [stʌŋ] pt. и pt. p. om **sting**

stunk [stʌŋk] pt. и pt. p. om **stink**

stunning ['stʌnɪŋ] coll. сногсшиба́тельный

stunt [stʌnt] трюк

stupefy ['stju:pɪfaɪ] ошеломля́ть [-ми́ть]; поража́ть [порази́ть]; with drug одурма́нить; **~id** ['stju:pɪd] □ глу́пый, тупо́й; **~idity** [stju:'pɪdətɪ] глу́пость f

sturdy ['stɜ:dɪ] си́льный, кре́пкий; здоро́вый; thing про́чный

sturgeon ['stɜ:dʒən] осётр; cul. осетри́на

stutter ['stʌtə] заика́ться

stye [staɪ] on eyelid ячме́нь m

style [staɪl] стиль m; (fashion) мо́да; фасо́н; life ~ о́браз жи́зни

stylish ['staɪlɪʃ] □ мо́дный; элега́нтный, coll. сти́льный

suave [swɑ:v] гла́дкий; обходи́тельный; мя́гкий в обраще́нии

sub... [sʌb] mst. под...; суб...

subconscious [sʌb'kɒnʃəs] **1.** подсозна́тельный; **2.** подсозна́ние; подсозна́тельное

subdivision [sʌbdɪ'vɪʒn] подразделе́ние; of a group a. се́кция

subdue [səb'dju:] (conquer, subjugate) покоря́ть [-ри́ть]; подавля́ть [-ви́ть]; (reduce) уменьша́ть [уме́ньшить]

subject ['sʌbdʒɪkt] **1.** подчинённый; подвла́стный; fig. **~ to** подлежа́щий (Д); **she is ~ to colds** она́ подве́ржена просту́дам; **2.** adv.: **~ to** при усло́вии (Р); **3.** pol. по́дданный; in school предме́т; of novel сюже́т; (a. **~ matter**) те́ма; **drop the ~** переве́сти pf. разгово́р на другу́ю те́му; **4.** [səb'dʒekt] подчиня́ть [-ни́ть]; fig. подверга́ть [-е́ргнуть]

subjugate ['sʌbdʒugeɪt] (entral(l)) порабоща́ть [-бори́ть]; покоря́ть [-ри́ть]

sublease [sʌb'li:s] субаре́нда

sublime [sə'blaɪm] □ возвы́шенный

submachine [sʌbmə'ʃi:n]: **~ gun** автома́т

submarine [sʌbmə'ri:n] naut. подво́дная ло́дка, субмари́на

submerge [səb'mɜ:dʒ] погружа́ть(ся) [-узи́ть(ся)]; затопля́ть [-пи́ть]

submiss|ion [səb'mıʃn] подчине́ние; поко́рность f; *of documents, etc.* представле́ние; **~ive** [səb'mısıv] □ поко́рный

submit [səb'mıt] *(give in)* покоря́ться [-ри́ться] (Д); *(present)* представля́ть [-а́вить]

subordinate 1. [sə'bɔːdɪnət] подчинённый; *gr.* прида́точный; **2.** [-] подчинённый (-ённая); **3.** [sə'bɔːdɪneıt] подчиня́ть [-ни́ть]

subscribe [səb'skraıb] *v/t. (donate)* [по]же́ртвовать; *v/i.* подде́рживать [-жа́ть] *(to* B); *magazine, etc.* подпи́сываться [-са́ться] *(to* B); **~r** [-ə] подпи́счик m, -чица f; *tel.* абоне́нт m

subscription [səb'skrıpʃn] подпи́ска; *to series of concerts, etc.* абонеме́нт; *to club* чле́нские взно́сы

subsequent ['sʌbsıkwənt] □ после́дующий; **~ly** впосле́дствии

subservient [səb'sɜːvıənt] подобостра́стный; *(serving to promote)* соде́йствующий *(to* Д)

subsid|e [səb'saıd] *of temperature* спада́ть [спасть]; *of water* убы(ва́)ть; *of wind* утиха́ть [ути́хнуть]; *of passions* уле́чься *pf.*; **~iary** [səb'sıdıərı] **1.** □ вспомога́тельный; **2.** филиа́л, доче́рняя компа́ния; **~ize** ['sʌbsıdaız] субсиди́ровать *(im)pf.*; **~y** ['sʌbsıdı] субси́дия

subsist [səb'sıst] *(exist)* существова́ть; жить *(on* на B); *(eat)* пита́ться *(on* Т); **~ence** [-əns] существова́ние; *means of* ~ сре́дства к существова́нию

substance ['sʌbstəns] вещество́; *(gist)* су́щность f, суть f; *(content)* содержа́ние

substantial [səb'stænʃl] □ существенный, ва́жный; *(strongly made)* про́чный; *(considerable)* значи́тельный; *meal* сы́тный

substantiate [səb'stænʃıeıt] обосно́вывать [-нова́ть]; дока́зывать справедли́вость (P); *(confirm)* подтвержда́ть [-рди́ть]

substitut|e ['sʌbstıtjuːt] **1.** заменя́ть [-ни́ть]; *at work* замеща́ть [-ести́ть]

(for B); **2.** заме́на; *(thing)* суррога́т; **~ion** [sʌbstı'tjuːʃn] заме́на

subterfuge ['sʌbtəfjuːdʒ] уве́ртка, уло́вка

subterranean [sʌbtə'reınıən] □ подзе́мный

subtle ['sʌtl] □ то́нкий; утончённый; *(elusive)* неулови́мый

subtract [səb'trækt] *math.* вычита́ть [вы́честь]

suburb ['sʌbɜːb] при́город; предме́стье; *(outskirts)* окра́ина; **~an** [sə'bɜːbən] при́городный

subvention [səb'venʃn] субве́нция, дота́ция

subversive [sʌb'vɜːsıv] *fig.* подрывно́й

subway ['sʌbweı] подзе́мный перехо́д; *Am. rail.* метро́(полите́н) *n indecl.*

succeed [sək'siːd] [по]сле́довать за (Т); *(take the place of)* быть пре́емником (P); достига́ть це́ли; *(do well)* преуспе(ва́)ть

success [sək'ses] успе́х; *(good fortune)* уда́ча; **~ful** [sək'sesfl] □ успе́шный; уда́чный; *person* уда́чливый; *businessman* преуспева́ющий; **~ion** [-'seʃn] после́довательность f; *(series)* ряд; *in* ~ оди́н за други́м; подря́д; **~ive** [-'sesıv] □ после́дующий, сле́дующий; **~or** [-'sesə] *at work* пре́емник m, -ница f; *to throne* насле́дник m, -ница f

succinct [sək'sınkt] кра́ткий, сжа́тый

succulent ['sʌkjulənt] со́чный

succumb [sə'kʌm] *to temptation, etc.* подд(ав)а́ться *(to* Д); *to pressure, etc.* не выде́рживать [вы́держать] *(to* P)

such [sʌtʃ] тако́й; *pred.* тако́в, -á и *т.д.*; *~ a man* тако́й челове́к; *~ as* тако́й, как ...; как наприме́р; **~ as**

suck [sʌk] соса́ть; выса́сывать [вы́сосать] *(a.* ~ *out)*; вса́сывать [всоса́ть] *(a.* ~ *in)*; **~er** ['sʌkə] *Am. coll.* проста́к; **~le** ['sʌkl] корми́ть гру́дью; **~ling** ['sʌklıŋ] грудно́й ребёнок; *animal* сосу́н(о́к)

suction ['sʌkʃn] **1.** *tech.* вса́сывание; **2.**

attr. всасывающий

sudden ['sʌdn] □ внеза́пный; *all of a ~* внеза́пно, вдруг

suds [sʌdz] *pl.* мы́льная пе́на

sue [sjuː] *v/t.* предъявля́ть [-ви́ть] иск кому́-л.; *v/i.* возбужда́ть де́ло (*for* о П)

suede [sweɪd] за́мша

suffer ['sʌfə] *v/i.* [по]страда́ть (*from* от P *or* T); *v/t.* (*undergo, endure*) [по]терпе́ть; *~er* [-rə] страда́лец *m*, -лица *f*; *~ing* [-rɪŋ] страда́ние

suffice [sə'faɪs] хвата́ть [-ти́ть], быть доста́точным; *~ it to say that* доста́точно сказа́ть, что …

sufficient [sə'fɪʃnt] □ доста́точный

suffocate ['sʌfəkeɪt] *v/t.* [за]души́ть; *v/i.* задыха́ться [задохну́ться]

suffrage ['sʌfrɪdʒ] избира́тельное пра́во

sugar ['ʃʊgə] **1.** са́хар; *granulated ~* са́харный песо́к; *lump ~* (са́хар-) рафина́д; **2.** са́харный; **3.** *tea, etc.* положи́ть са́хар; *~y* [-rɪ] *fig.* при́торный, слаща́вый

suggest [sə'dʒest] (*propose*) предлага́ть [-ложи́ть]; *solution* подска́зывать [-за́ть]; наводи́ть на мысль *f* о (П); [по]сове́товать; *~ion* [-ʃən] сове́т, предложе́ние; (*hint*) намёк; *~ive* [-ɪv] □ (*giving food for thought*) наводя́щий на размышле́ние; (*improper*) непристо́йный; *joke* двусмы́сленный

suicide ['suːɪsaɪd] самоуби́йство; *commit ~* поко́нчить *pf.* с собо́й

suit [suːt] **1.** (*a. ~ of clothes*) костю́м; *cards* масть *f*; *law* суде́бное де́ло, иск; **2.** *v/t.* (*adapt*) приспоса́бливать [-собить] (*to, with* к Д); соотве́тствовать (Д); удовлетвори́ть; (*be convenient or right*) устра́ивать [-ро́ить]; подходи́ть [подойти́] (Д); *~ yourself* поступа́й как зна́ешь; *v/i.* (*be appropriate*) подходи́ть, годи́ться; *~able* ['suːtəbl] □ подходя́щий, соотве́тствующий; *~case* чемода́н

suite [swiːt] *mus.* сюи́та; *in hotel* но́мер-люкс; *of furniture* гарниту́р

suited ['suːtɪd] подходя́щий

sulfur, *Brt.* **sulphur** ['sʌlfə] *chem.* се́ра; *~ic* [sʌl'fjuərɪk] се́рный

sulk [sʌlk] **1.** [на]ду́ться; быть не в ду́хе; **2.:** *~s* [-s] *pl.* плохо́е настрое́ние; *~y* ['sʌlkɪ] □ наду́тый

sullen ['sʌlən] угрю́мый, мра́чный; *sky* па́смурный

sultry ['sʌltrɪ] ду́шный, зно́йный

sum [sʌm] **1.** су́мма; ито́г; *in ~* ко́ротко говоря́; *~s pl.* арифме́тика; **2.** (*a. ~ up*) *math.* скла́дывать [сложи́ть]; *fig.* подводи́ть ито́г

summar|ize ['sʌməraɪz] сумми́ровать (*im*)*pf.*; подводи́ть [-вести́] ито́г; написа́ть *pf.* резюме́; *~y* [-rɪ] сво́дка; анно-та́ция, резюме́ *n indecl.*

summer ['sʌmə] ле́то; *in ~* ле́том; *~y* [-rɪ] ле́тний

summit ['sʌmɪt] верши́на (*a. fig.*); *pol.* са́ммит, встре́ча в верха́х; *fig.* преде́л

summon ['sʌmən] соз(ы)ва́ть (собра́ние *и т. n.*); *law* вызыва́ть [вы́звать]; *~s* [-z] вы́зов в суд; *law* суде́бная пове́стка

sumptuous ['sʌmptʃuəs] роско́шный, пы́шный

sun [sʌn] **1.** со́лнце; **2.** со́лнечный; **3.** гре́ть(ся) на со́лнце; *~bathe* загора́ть; *~burn* зага́р; *painful* со́лнечный ожо́г

Sunday ['sʌndɪ] воскресе́нье

sundown захо́д со́лнца

sundry ['sʌndrɪ] ра́зный; *all and ~* все без исключе́ния

sunflower ['sʌnflaʊə] подсо́лнечник

sung [sʌŋ] *pt. p. om* **sing**

sunglasses *pl.* тёмные очки́ *n/pl.*

sunk [sʌŋk] *pt. p. om* **sink**

sunken ['sʌŋkən] *fig.* впа́лый

sun|ny ['sʌnɪ] □ со́лнечный; *~rise* восхо́д со́лнца; *~set* захо́д со́лнца, зака́т; *~shade* зо́нт(ик) от со́лнца; *~shine* со́лнечный свет; *in the ~* на со́лнце; *~stroke* *med.* со́лнечный уда́р; *~tan* зага́р; *~tanned* загоре́лый

super... ['suːpə] *pref.*: пе́ре…, пре…; сверх…; над…; *~* су́пер…

super ['suːpə] замеча́тельный; *~!* здо́рово!

superb [suː'pɜːb] великоле́пный, превосхо́дный

super|cilious [suːpəˈsɪlɪəs] □ высокомерный; **~ficial** [suːpəˈfɪʃl] □ поверхностный; **~fluous** [suːˈpɜːfluəs] лишний, излишний; **~human** сверхчеловеческий; **~intend** [suːpərɪnˈtend] (*watch*) надзирать за (Т); (*direct*) руководить (Т); **~intendent** [-ənt] руководитель *m*

superior [suːˈpɪərɪə] **1.** □ *in rank* высший, старший; *in quality* превосходный; превосходящий (**to** В); **~ smile** надменная улыбка; *eccl.* настоятель *m*, -ница *f*; *of a convent* **Mother/Father** ♀ игуменья/игумен; **~ity** [suːpɪərɪˈɒrətɪ] *of quality, quantity, etc.* превосходство; *of rank* старшинство

super|lative [suːˈpɜːlətɪv] **1.** □ высочайший; величайший; **2.** *gr.* превосходная степень *f*; **~man** [ˈsuːpəmæn] супермен; **~market** [ˈsuːpəmɑːkɪt] универсам (= *универсальный магазин самообслуживания*); **~sede** [suːpəˈsiːd] (*replace*) заменять [-нить]; (*displace*) вытеснять [вытеснить], *fig.* (*overtake*) обгонять [обогнать]; **~sonic** [suːpəˈsɒnɪk] сверхзвуковой; **~stition** [suːpəˈstɪʃn] суеверие; **~stitious** [-ˈstɪʃəs] суеверный; **~vene** [-ˈviːn] следовать за чём-либо; **~vise** [ˈsuːpəvaɪz] надзирать (Т); **~vision** [suːpəˈvɪʒn] надзор; **~visor** [ˈsuːpəvaɪzə] надзиратель *m*, -ница *f*

supper [ˈsʌpə] ужин; **the Last ♀** Тайная Вечеря

supplant [səˈplɑːnt] вытеснять [вытеснить] (В)

supple [ˈsʌpl] гибкий (*a. fig.*)

supplement 1. [ˈsʌplɪmənt] (*addition*) дополнение; *to a periodical* приложение; **2.** [-ˈment] дополнять [дополнить]; **~ary** [sʌplɪˈmentərɪ] дополнительный, добавочный

supplier [səˈplaɪə] поставщик

supply [səˈplaɪ] **1.** снабжать [-бдить] (**with** Т); *goods* поставлять [-авить]; *information, etc.* предоставлять [-авить]; **2.** снабжение; поставка; (*stock*) запас; **supplies** *pl.* (*food*) продовольствие; **~ and demand** спрос и предложение

support [səˈpɔːt] поддержка; *phys., tech.* опора (*a. fig.*); **2.** подпирать [-переть]; *a candidature, etc.* поддерживать [-жать]; *one's family, etc.* содержать

suppose [səˈpəʊz] (*assume*) предполагать [-ложить]; (*imagine*) полагать; *coll.* **~ we do so?** а если мы это сделаем?; **he's ~d to be back today** он должен сегодня вернуться

supposed [səˈpəʊzd] □ предполагаемый; **~ly** [səˈpəʊzɪdlɪ] предположительно; якобы

supposition [sʌpəˈzɪʃn] предположение

suppress [səˈpres] *uprising, yawn, etc.* подавлять [-вить]; (*ban*) запрещать [-етить]; *laugh, anger, etc.* сдерживать [-жать]; **~ion** [səˈpreʃn] подавление

suprem|acy [suːˈpreməsɪ] превосходство; **~e** [suːˈpriːm] □ *command, etc.* верховный; (*greatest*) высочайший

surcharge [ˈsɜːtʃɑːdʒ] (*extra charge*) приплата, доплата

sure [ʃʊə] □ *com.* верный; (*certain*) уверенный; (*safe*) безопасный; надёжный; *Am.* **~!** конечно; **make ~ that ...** выяснить *pf.*, убедиться *pf.*, проверить *pf.*; **~ly** [ˈʃʊəlɪ] несомненно

surf [sɜːf] прибой

surface [ˈsɜːfɪs] поверхность *f*; **on the ~** *fig.* чисто внешне; на первый взгляд; **~ mail** обычной почтой

surfing [ˈsɜːfɪŋ] сёрфинг

surge [sɜːdʒ] **1.** волна; **2.** *of waves* вздыматься; *of crowd* подаваться [-даться] вперёд; *of emotions* [на]хлынуть *pf.*

surg|eon [ˈsɜːdʒən] хирург; **~ery** [ˈsɜːdʒərɪ] хирургия; операция; *Brt.* приёмная (врача); **~ hours** приёмные часы

surgical [ˈsɜːdʒɪkl] □ хирургический

surly [ˈsɜːlɪ] □ неприветливый; хмурый; угрюмый

surmise [səˈmaɪz] **1.** предположение; **2.** предполагать [-ложить]

surmount [sə'maʊnt] преодоле(ва́)ть, превозмога́ть [-мо́чь]

surname ['sɜːneɪm] фами́лия

surpass [sə'pɑːs] *expectations, etc.* превосходи́ть [-взойти́]

surplus ['sɜːpləs] **1.** изли́шек; (*remainder*) оста́ток; **2.** изли́шний; ли́шний

surprise [sə'praɪz] **1.** удивле́ние; *event, present, etc.* неожи́данность f, сюрпри́з; *attr.* неожи́данный; **2.** удивля́ть [-ви́ть]; (*take unawares*) застава́ть враспло́х

surrender [sə'rendə] **1.** сда́ча; капитуля́ция; **2.** *v/t.* сда(ва́)ть; *one's rights* отка́зываться [-за́ться] от (P); *v/i.* сд(ав)а́ться

surround [sə'raʊnd] окружа́ть [-жи́ть]; **~ing** [-ɪŋ] окружа́ющий; **~ings** [-ɪŋz] *pl.* окре́стности *f/pl.*; (*environment*) среда́, окруже́ние

survey [sɜː'veɪ] **1.** (*look at, examine*) обозре(ва́)ть; осма́тривать [осмотре́ть]; производи́ть [-вести́] топографи́ческую съёмку; **2.** ['sɜːveɪ] осмо́тр; (*study*) обзо́р; топографи́ческая съёмка; *attr.* обзо́рный; **~or** [sə'veɪə] земле́мер; топо́граф

surviv|al [sə'vaɪvl] выжива́ние; (*relic*) пережи́ток; **~e** [sə'vaɪv] *v/t.* пережи́(ва́)ть *mst. pf.*; *v/i.* остава́ться в живы́х, вы́жи(ва́)ть; *of custom* сохраня́ться [-ни́ться]; **~or** [sə'vaɪvə] оста́вшийся в живы́х

susceptible [sə'septəbl] □ восприи́мчивый (**to** к Д); (*sensitive*) чувстви́тельный; (*easily enamo(u)red*) влюбчивый

suspect 1. [sə'spekt] подозрева́ть, запода́зривать [-до́зрить] (**of** в П); *the truth of, etc.* сомнева́ться [усомни́ться] в (П); (*think*) предполага́ть; **2.** ['sʌspekt] подозри́тельный; подозрева́емый

suspend [sə'spend] подве́шивать [-е́сить]; (*stop for a time*) приостана́вливать [-нови́ть]; вре́менно прекраща́ть; **~ed** [-ɪd] подвесно́й; **~ers** [-əz] *pl. Am.* подтя́жки *f/pl.*

suspens|e [sə'spens] напряжённое внима́ние; (*uneasy uncertainty*) со-

стоя́ние неизве́стности, неопределённости; **in ~** напряжённо, в напряже́нии; **~ion** [sə'spenʃn] прекраще́ние; **~ bridge** вися́чий мост

suspicio|n [sə'spɪʃn] подозре́ние; *trace, nuance* оттёнок; **~us** [-ʃəs] □ подозри́тельный

sustain [sə'steɪn] (*support*) подпира́ть [-пере́ть], подде́рживать [-жа́ть] (*a. fig.*); *law* подтвержда́ть [-рди́ть]; вы́держивать [вы́держать]; (*suffer*) выноси́ть [вы́нести], испы́тывать [испыта́ть]

sustenance ['sʌstɪnəns] пи́ща; сре́дства к существова́нию

swaddle ['swɒdl] [с-, за]пелена́ть

swagger ['swægə] ходи́ть с ва́жным ви́дом; (*brag*) [по]хва́стать (*a.* -ся)

swallow¹ ['swɒləʊ] *zo.* ла́сточка

swallow² [-] глото́к; глота́ть; прогла́тывать [-лоти́ть]

swam [swæm] *pt. om* swim

swamp [swɒmp] **1.** боло́то, топь *f*; **2.** затопля́ть [-пи́ть], залива́ть; **~y** ['swɒmpɪ] боло́тистый

swan [swɒn] ле́бедь *m*

swap [swɒp] *coll.* **1.** обме́нивать(ся) [-ня́ть(ся)]; [по]меня́ть(ся); **2.** обме́н

swarm [swɔːm] **1.** *of bees* рой; *of birds* ста́я; толпа́; **2.** *of bees* рои́ться; кише́ть (**with** Т); *crowds ~ed into the cinema* толпа́ хлы́нула в кинотеа́тр

swarthy ['swɔːðɪ] сму́глый

sway [sweɪ] **1.** кача́ние; (*influence*) влия́ние; **2.** кача́ть(ся) [качну́ть(ся)]; *fig.* [по]влия́ть, склони́ть на свою́ сто́рону

swear [sweə] [*irr.*] (*take an oath*) [по]кля́сться (**by** Т); (*curse*) [вы́-] руга́ться; **~word** руга́тельство

sweat [swet] **1.** пот; **2.** [*irr.*] *v/i.* [вс]поте́ть; исполня́ть тяжёлую рабо́ту; *v/t.* заставля́ть поте́ть; **~ blood** *coll.* рабо́тать как вол; **~er** ['swetə] сви́тер; **~y** ['swetɪ] потный

Swede [swiːd] швед *m*, -ка *f*

swede [-] *bot.* брю́ква

Swedish ['swiːdɪʃ] шве́дский

sweep [swiːp] **1.** [*irr.*] мести́, подметать [-ести́]; *chimney* [по]чи́стить; (*rush*) проноси́ться [-нести́сь] (*a. ~ past, along*); **~ s.o. off his feet** вскружи́ть кому́-л. го́лову; **2.** *of arm* взмах; (*curve*) изги́б; **make a clean ~ (of)** отде́л(ыв)аться (от P); **~er** ['swiːpə]: **road ~** подмета́льная маши́на; **~ing** ['swiːpɪŋ] □ *gesture* широ́кий; *accusation* огу́льный; *changes* радика́льный, широкомасшта́бный; **~ings** [-z] *pl.* му́сор

sweet [swiːt] **1.** □ сла́дкий; *air* све́жий; *water* пре́сный; *person* ми́лый; **have a ~ tooth** быть сластёной; **2.** конфе́та; **~s** *pl.* сла́сти *f/pl.*; **~en** ['swiːtn] подсла́щивать [-ласти́ть]; **the pill** позолоти́ть *pf.* пилю́лю; **~heart** возлю́бленный (-енная)

swell [swel] **1.** [*irr.*] *v/i.* [о-, при-, рас]пу́хнуть; *of cheek* разду́(ва)ться; *of wood* набуха́ть [-у́хнуть]; *of sound* нараста́ть [-сти́]; *v/t.* (*increase*) увели́чи(ва)ть; **2.** *coll.* (*fashionable*) шика́рный; (*excellent*) великоле́пный; **3.** *coll.* франт; **~ing** ['swelɪŋ] о́пухоль *f*, *slight* припу́хлость *f*

swelter ['sweltə] изнемога́ть от жары́

swept [swept] *pt. и pt. p. от* **sweep**

swerve [swɜːv] свора́чивать [сверну́ть] в сто́рону; *of car, etc.* ре́зко сверну́ть *pf.*

swift [swift] □ бы́стрый, ско́рый; **~ness** ['-nɪs] быстрота́

swill [swil] **1.** (*slops*) помо́и *m/pl.*; **2.** [про]полоска́ть, опола́скивать [-лосну́ть] (*a. ~ out*)

swim [swim] **1.** [*irr.*] пла́вать, [по]плы́ть; перепл(ы)(ва́)ть (*a. ~ across*); **my head ~s** у меня́ голова́ кру́жится; **2.** пла́вание; **be in the ~** быть в ку́рсе дел; **~mer** ['-ə] плове́ц *m*, -вчи́ха *f*; **~ming** [-ɪŋ] пла́вание; **~ pool** пла́вательный бассе́йн; **~ trunks** пла́вки *pl.*; **~suit** купа́льный костю́м

swindle ['swɪndl] **1.** обма́нывать [-ну́ть], наду́(ва́)ть; **2.** обма́н, надува́тельство; **~r** [-ə] моше́нник

swine [swaɪn] *coll. fig.* свинья́

swing [swɪŋ] **1.** [*irr.*] кача́ть(ся) [качну́ть(ся)]; *hands* разма́хивать;

feet болта́ть; (*hang*) висе́ть; **2.** кача́ние; разма́х; взмах; ритм; каче́ли *f/pl.*; **in full ~** в по́лном разга́ре; **go with a ~** проходи́ть о́чень успе́шно; **~ door** дверь *f*, открыва́ющаяся в любу́ю сто́рону

swipe [swaɪp] уда́рить; *joc.* (*steal*) стащи́ть

swirl [swɜːl] **1.** *in dance, etc.* кружи́ть(ся); *of dust, etc.* клуби́ться; *of water* крути́ться; **2.** водоворо́т

Swiss [swɪs] швейца́рский; **2.** швейца́рец *m*, -рка *f*; **the ~** *pl.* швейца́рцы *m/pl.*

switch [swɪtʃ] **1.** *el.* выключа́тель *m*; *radio, TV* переключа́тель *m*; **2.** (*whip*) хлеста́ть [-стну́ть]; *el.* переключа́ть [-чи́ть] (*often ~ over*) (*a. fig.*); *fig.* **the conversation** переводи́ть [-вести́] разгово́р (на В); **~ on** *el.* включа́ть [-чи́ть]; **~ off** выключа́ть [вы́ключить]; **~board** *tel.* коммута́тор

swollen ['swəʊlən] *pt. p. от* **swell**

swoon [swuːn] **1.** о́бморок; **2.** па́дать в о́бморок

swoop [swuːp] (*a. ~ down*), ри́нуться; (*suddenly attack*) налета́ть [-ете́ть] (*on* на В)

sword [sɔːd] шпа́га; меч

swore [swɔː] *pt. от* **swear**

sworn [swɔːn] *pt. p. от* **swear**, *adj. enemy* закля́тый

swum [swʌm] *pt. p. от* **swim**

swung [swʌŋ] *pt. и pt. p. от* **swing**

syllable ['sɪləbl] слог

syllabus ['sɪləbəs] уче́бный план

symbol ['sɪmbl] си́мвол, усло́вное обозначе́ние; **~ic(al)** [sɪm'bɒlɪk(l)] символи́ческий; **~ism** ['sɪmbəlɪzəm] символи́зм

symmetr|ical [sɪ'metrɪkl] □ симметри́чный; **~y** ['sɪmɪtrɪ] симме́три

sympath|etic [sɪmpə'θetɪk] (**~ally**) сочу́вственный; **~ize** ['sɪmpəθaɪz] [по]сочу́вствовать (**with** Д); **~y** ['sɪmpəθɪ] сочу́вствие (**with** к Д)

symphony ['sɪmfənɪ] симфо́ния

symptom ['sɪmptəm] симпто́м

synchron|ize ['sɪŋkrənaɪz] *v/i.* совпада́ть по вре́мени; *v/t. actions* синхронизи́ровать (*im*)*pf.*; **~ous** [-nəs] □ синхро́нный

syndicate ['sɪndɪkət] синдика́т

synonym ['sɪnənɪm] сино́ним; **~ous** [sɪ'nɒnɪməs] синоними́ческий

synopsis [sɪ'nɒpsɪs] кра́ткое изложе́ние, сино́псис

synthe|sis ['sɪnθesɪs] си́нтез; **~tic** [sɪn'θetɪk] синтети́ческий

syringe [sɪ'rɪndʒ] шприц

syrup ['sɪrəp] сиро́п

system ['sɪstəm] систе́ма; **~atic** [sɪstə'mætɪk] (**~ally**) системати́ческий

T

tab [tæb] *for hanging garment* ве́шалка; *mil.* наши́вка, петли́ца

table ['teɪbl] стол; (*list of data, etc.*) табли́ца; **~ of contents** оглавле́ние; **~cloth** ска́терть *f*; **~ d'hôte** ['tɑːbl'dout] табльдо́т; о́бщий стол; **~ lamp** насто́льная ла́мпа; **~spoon** столо́вая ло́жка

tablet ['tæblɪt] *med.* табле́тка; *of soap* кусо́к; мемориа́льная доска́

table tennis насто́льный те́ннис

taboo [tə'buː] табу́ *n indecl.*

tacit ['tæsɪt] □ подразумева́емый; молчали́вый; **~urn** ['tæsɪtɜːn] □ неразгово́рчивый

tack [tæk] **1.** гвоздик с широ́кой шля́пкой; (*thumb~*) *Am.* кно́пка; **~ing** *sew.* намётка; **2.** *v/t.* прикрепля́ть гво́здиками и/или кно́пками; *sewing* смётывать [смета́ть]

tackle ['tækl] **1.** (*equipment*) принадле́жности *f/pl.*; *for fishing* снасть *f*; **2.** (*deal with*) энерги́чно бра́ться за (В); *problem* би́ться над (Т)

tact [tækt] такт, такти́чность *f*; **~ful** ['tæktful] такти́чный

tactics ['tæktɪks] *pl.* та́ктика

tactless ['tæktlɪs] □ беста́ктный

tag [tæg] **1.** би́рка, этике́тка; *fig.* изби́тое выраже́ние; *price* **~** це́нник; **2.: ~ along** сле́довать по пята́м; тащи́ться сза́ди

tail [teɪl] **1.** хвост; *of coat* фа́лда; пола́; *of coin* обра́тная сторона́; *heads or* **~s?** орёл и́ли ре́шка?; **2.** *v/t.* (*follow*) сле́довать, тащи́ться (*after* за Т); *Am. coll. of police* высле́живать [вы́сле-

дить]; *v/i.* тяну́ться верени́цей; **~ off** (*fall behind*) отст(ав)а́ть; **~coat** фрак; **~light** *mot.* за́дний фона́рь *m*/свет

tailor ['teɪlə] портно́й; **~-made** сде́ланный по зака́зу

take [teɪk] **1.** [*irr.*] *v/t.* брать [взять]; *medicine, etc.* принима́ть [-ня́ть]; [съ]есть; [вы́]пить; *seat* занима́ть [заня́ть]; *phot.* снима́ть [снять]; *time* отнима́ть [-ня́ть]; *I~ it that* я полага́ю, что …; **~ in hand** взять *pf.* в свои́ ру́ки; **~ o.s. in hand** взять *pf.* себя́ в ру́ки; **~ pity on** сжа́литься *pf.* над (Т); **~ place** случа́ться [-чи́ться], происходи́ть (произойти́); **~ a rest** отдыха́ть (отдохну́ть); **~ a hint** поня́ть *pf.* намёк; **~ a seat** сади́ться [сесть]; **~ a taxi** брать [взять] такси́; **~ a view** выска́зывать свою́ то́чку зре́ния; **~ a walk** [по]гуля́ть, прогу́ливаться [-ля́ться]; **~ down** снима́ть [снять]; запи́сывать [-са́ть]; **~ for** принима́ть [-ня́ть] за (В); **~ from** брать [взять] у Р; **~ in** (*deceive*) обма́нывать [-ну́ть]; (*understand*) поня́ть *pf.*; **~ off** *coat, etc.* снима́ть [снять]; **~ out** вынима́ть [вы́нуть]; **~ to pieces** разбира́ть [разобра́ть]; **~ up** бра́ться [взя́ться] за (В); *space, time* занима́ть [заня́ть], отнима́ть [отня́ть]; **2.** *v/i.* (*have the intended effect*) [по]де́йствовать; (*be a success*) име́ть успе́х; **~ after** походи́ть на (В); **~ off** *ae.* взлета́ть [-ете́ть]; **~ over** принима́ть дела́ (*from* от Р); **~ to** пристрасти́ться к (Д) *pf.*; привяза́ться к (Д) *pf.*; **~n** ['teɪkən] *pt. p. om* **take**; **be ~ ill** заболе(ва́)ть; **~off**

['teɪkəf] (*impersonation*) подража́ние; *ae.* взлёт

takings ['teɪkɪŋz] *pl. comm.* вы́ручка; сбор

tale [teɪl] расска́з, по́весть *f*; (*false account*) вы́думка; (*unkind account*) спле́тня; **tell ~s** спле́тничать

talent ['tælənt] тала́нт; **~ed** [-ɪd] тала́нтливый

talk [tɔːk] **1.** разгово́р, бесе́да; **~s** *pl. pol.* перегово́ры; **there is ~ that …** говоря́т, что …; **2.** [по]говори́ть; разгова́ривать; [по]бесе́довать; **~ative** ['tɔːkətɪv] разгово́рчивый; **~er** ['tɔːkə] **1.** говоря́щий; говорли́вый челове́к

tall [tɔːl] высо́кий; **~ order** чрезме́рное тре́бование; **~ story** *coll.* небыли́ца; неправдоподо́бная исто́рия

tally ['tælɪ] соотве́тствовать (**with** Д)

tame [teɪm] **1.** □ *animal* ручно́й, приручённый; (*submissive*) поко́рный; (*dull*) ску́чный; **2.** прируча́ть [-чи́ть]

tamper ['tæmpə]: **~ with** тро́гать; копа́ться; *document* подде́л(ыв)ать (В); **someone has ~ed with my luggage** кто́-то копа́лся в моём багаже́

tan [tæn] **1.** (*sun~*) зага́р; **2.** загара́ть

tang [tæŋ] (*taste*) ре́зкий при́вкус; (*smell*) за́пах

tangent ['tændʒənt] *math.* каса́тельная; **go** (*a.* **fly**) **off at a ~** ре́зко отклони́ться *pf.*

tangerine [tændʒə'riːn] мандари́н

tangible ['tændʒəbl] □ осяза́емый, ощути́мый

tangle ['tæŋgl] **1.** пу́таница, неразбери́ха; **2.** запу́т(ыв)ать(ся)

tank [tæŋk] цисте́рна; бак; *mil.* танк, *attr.* та́нковый; **gas(oline) ~**, *Brt.* **petrol ~** бензоба́к

tankard ['tæŋkəd] высо́кая кру́жка

tanker ['tæŋkə] *naut.* та́нкер; *mot.* автоцисте́рна

tantalize ['tæntəlaɪz] дразни́ть; [за-, из]му́чить

tantrum ['tæntrəm] *coll.* вспы́шка гне́ва *или* раздраже́ния; **throw a ~** закати́ть *pf.* исте́рику

tap¹ [tæp] **1.** *for water, gas* кран; **2.**: **~ for**

money выпра́шивать де́ньги у Р; **~ for information** выу́живать [-удить] информа́цию

tap² [-] **1.** [по]стуча́ть; [по]хло́пать; **2.** лёгкий стук; **~ dance** чечётка

tape [teɪp] тесьма́; *sport* фи́нишная ле́нточка; магни́тная ле́нта; **sticky ~** ли́пкая ле́нта; **~ measure** ['teɪpmeʒə] руле́тка; *of cloth* сантиме́тр

taper ['teɪpə] *v/i.* су́живаться к концу́; *v/t.* заостря́ть [-ри́ть]

tape recorder магнитофо́н

tapestry ['tæpɪstrɪ] гобеле́н

tar [tɑː] **1.** дёготь *m*; *for boats* смола́; **2.** [вы́]смоли́ть

tardy ['tɑːdɪ] □ (*slow-moving*) медли́тельный; (*coming or done late*) запозда́лый

target ['tɑːgɪt] цель *f* (*a. fig.*); мише́нь *f* (*a. fig.*)

tariff ['tærɪf] тари́ф

tarnish ['tɑːnɪʃ] *fig.* [о]поро́чить; *v/i. of metal* [по]тускне́ть; **~ed reputation** запя́тнанная репута́ция

tarpaulin [tɑː'pɔːlɪn] брезе́нт

tart¹ [tɑːt] откры́тый пиро́г с фру́ктами; сла́дкая ватру́шка

tart² [-] ки́слый, те́рпкий; *fig.* ко́лкий

tartan ['tɑːtn] шотла́ндка

task [tɑːsk] (*problem*) зада́ча; (*job*) зада́ние; **set a ~** дать *pf.* зада́ние; **take to ~** отчи́тывать [-ита́ть]; **~ force** *mil.* операти́вная гру́ппа

taste [teɪst] **1.** вкус; **have a ~ for** люби́ть, знать толк (в П); **2.** [по]про́бовать; *fig.* испы́тывать [-пыта́ть]; **~ sweet** быть сла́дким на вкус; **~ful** ['teɪstfl] □ (*сде́ланный*) со вку́сом; изя́щный; **~less** [-lɪs] безвку́сный

tasty ['teɪstɪ] □ вку́сный

tatter|ed ['tætəd] изно́шенный, изо́рванный; **~s** *pl.* лохмо́тья *n/pl.*; **tear to ~s** разорва́ть в кло́чья; *fig.* разбива́ть [-би́ть] в пух и прах

tattle ['tætl] болтовня́

tattoo [tə'tuː] (*design on skin*) татуиро́вка

taught [tɔːt] *pt. и pt. p. от* **teach**

taunt [tɔːnt] **1.** насме́шка, ко́лкость *f*; **2.** говори́ть ко́лкости (Д), дразни́ть

taut [tɔːt] (*stretched tight*) туго натянутый; *nerves* взвинченный

tawdry ['tɔːdrɪ] □ безвкусный; кричащий

tawny ['tɔːnɪ] рыжевато-коричневый

tax [tæks] 1. налог (*on* на В); *income*~ подоходный налог; ~ *evasion* уклонение от уплаты налога; *value added* ~ налог на добавочную стоимость *f*; 2. облагать налогом; *one's strength* чрезмерно напрягать; ~ *s.o.'s patience* испытывать чьё-л. терпение; ~ *a p. with a th.* обвинять [-нить] кого-л. в чём-л.; ~**ation** [tæk'seɪʃn] обложение налогом; взимание налога

taxi ['tæksɪ] = ~**cab** такси *n indecl.*

taxpayer ['tækspeɪə] налогоплательщик

tea [tiː] чай; *make* (*the*) ~ заваривать [-рить] чай

teach [tiːtʃ] [*irr.*] [на]учить, обучать [-чить]; *a subject* преподавать; ~**er** ['tiːtʃə] учитель *m*, -ница *f*; *univ.* преподаватель *m*, -ница *f*

teacup ['tiːkʌp] чайная чашка

team [tiːm] 1. *sport* команда; *of workers* бригада; ~ *spirit* чувство локтя; 2.: ~ *up* сотрудничать; ~**work** совместная работа

teapot ['tiːpɒt] чайник (для заварки)

tear¹ [teə] 1. [*irr.*] дыра, прореха; 2. [по]рвать(ся); разрыва́ть(ся) [разорвать(ся)]; *fig.* раздирать(ся); (*go at great speed*) [по]мчаться; *country torn by war* страна, раздираемая войной

tear² [tɪə] слеза (*pl.* слёзы)

tearful ['tɪəfl] □ слезливый; *eyes* полный слёз

tease [tiːz] 1. человек, любящий поддразнивать; 2. *coll.* дразнить; подшучивать; ~**r** [-ə] *coll.* головоломка

teat [tiːt] сосок

technic|al ['teknɪkl] □ технический; ~**ality** [teknɪ'kælətɪ] техническая деталь *f*; формальность *f*; ~**ian** [tek-'nɪʃn] техник

technique [tek'niːk] техника; метод, способ

technology [tek'nɒlədʒɪ] технология; технологические науки *f/pl.*

tedious ['tiːdɪəs] □ скучный, утомительный

tedium ['tiːdɪəm] утомительность *f*; скука

teem [tiːm] изобиловать, кишеть (*with* Т)

teenager ['tiːneɪdʒə] подросток; юноша *m* / девушка *f* до двадцати лет

teeth [tiːθ] *pl. om* **tooth**; ~**e** [tiːð]: *the child is teething* у ребёнка прорезаются зубы

teetotal(l)er [tiː'təʊtlə] трезвенник

telecommunications [telɪkəmjuːnɪ-'keɪʃnz] *pl.* средства дальней связи

telegram ['telɪgræm] телеграмма

telegraph ['telɪgrɑːf] 1. телеграф; 2. телеграфировать (*im*)*pf.*; 3. *attr.* телеграфный

telephone ['telɪfəʊn] 1. телефон; звонить по телефону; ~ *booth* телефон-автомат; ~ *directory* телефонный справочник

telescop|e ['telɪskəʊp] телескоп; ~**ic** [telɪs'kɒpɪk] телескопический; ~ *aerial* выдвижная антенна

teletype ['telɪtaɪp] телетайп

television ['telɪvɪʒn] телевидение

telex ['teleks] телекс

tell [tel] [*irr.*] *v/t.* говорить [сказать]; (*relate*) рассказывать [-зать]; (*distinguish*) отличать [-чить]; ~ *a p. to do a th.* велеть кому-л. что-л. сделать; ~ *off coll.* [вы]бранить; *v/i.* (*affect*) сказываться [-заться]; (*know*) знать; *how can I* ~? откуда мне знать?; ~**er** ['telə] *esp. Am.* кассир (в банке); ~**ing** ['telɪŋ] □ многоговорящий, многозначительный; ~**tale** ['telteɪl] ябеда *m & f*

telly ['telɪ] *chiefly Brt. coll.* телик

temper ['tempə] 1. *steel* закалять [-лить] (*a. fig.*); 2. нрав; (*mood*) настроение; (*irritation, anger*) раздражение, гнев; *he has a quick* ~ он вспыльчив; ~**ament** ['tempræmənt] темперамент; ~**amental** [temprə-'mentl] □ темпераментный; ~**ate** ['tempərət] □ *climate* умеренный; *behavio(u)r* сдержанный; ~**ature**

['temprətʃə] температу́ра

tempest ['tempist] бу́ря; **~uous** □
[tem'pestʃuəs] бу́рный (*a. fig.*)

temple¹ [templ] храм

temple² [-] *anat.* висо́к

tempo ['tempəʋ] темп

tempor|ary ['temprərɪ] □ вре́менный;
~ize [-raɪz] стара́ться вы́играть
вре́мя, тяну́ть вре́мя

tempt [tempt] искуша́ть [-уси́ть], со-
блазня́ть [-ни́ть]; (*attract*) привле-
ка́ть [-е́чь]; **~ation** [temp'teɪʃn] ис-
куше́ние, собла́зн; **~ing** ['-tɪŋ] □ за-
ма́нчивый, соблазни́тельный

ten [ten] **1.** де́сять; **2.** деся́ток

tenable ['tenəbl]: *not a ~ argument* ар-
гуме́нт, не выде́рживающий кри́ти-
ки

tenaci|ous [tɪ'neɪʃəs] □ це́пкий; **~
memory** хоро́шая па́мять *f*; **~ty**
[tɪ'næsətɪ] це́пкость *f*, насто́йчивость
f

tenant ['tenənt] *of land* аренда́тор; *of
flat* кварти́рант

tend [tend] *v/i.* быть скло́нным (**to** к
Д); **~ prices ~ to rise during the holiday season** в пери́од о́тпусков це́ны
обы́чно повыша́ются; уха́живать за
(Т); присма́тривать [-мотре́ть]; *tech.*
обслу́живать [-и́ть]; **~ency** ['tendənsɪ]
тенде́нция; *of person* скло́нность *f*

tender ['tendə] **1.** □ *com.* не́жный; **~
spot** больно́е (уязви́мое) ме́сто; **2.**
comm. те́ндер; **3.** предлага́ть [-ло-
жи́ть]; *documents* представля́ть
[-а́вить]; *apologies, etc.* приноси́ть
[-нести́]; **~-hearted** [-'hɑːtɪd] мягко-
серде́чный; **~ness** [-nɪs] не́жность *f*

tendon ['tendən] *anat.* сухожи́лие

tendril ['tendrəl] *bot.* у́сик

tenement ['tenəmənt]: **~ house** мно-
гокварти́рный дом

tennis ['tenɪs] те́ннис

tenor ['tenə] *mus.* те́нор; (*general
course*) тече́ние, направле́ние; *of life*
укла́д; (*purport*) о́бщий смысл

tens|e [tens] **1.** *gr.* вре́мя *n*; **2.** натя́ну-
тый; *muscles, atmosphere, etc.* на-
пряжённый; **~ion** ['tenʃn] напряже́-
ние; натяже́ние; *pol.* напряжённость

f

tent [tent] пала́тка, шатёр

tentacle ['tentəkl] *zo.* щу́пальце

tentative ['tentətɪv] □ (*trial*) про́б-
ный; (*provisional*) предвари́тель-
ный

tenterhooks ['tentəhʋks]: *be on ~* си-
де́ть как на иго́лках; *keep s.o. on ~*
держа́ть кого́-л. в неизве́стности

tenth [tenθ] **1.** деся́тый; **2.** деся́тая
часть *f*

tenure ['tenjʋə] пребыва́ние в долж-
ности; пра́во владе́ния землёй;
срок владе́ния

tepid ['tepid] □ теплова́тый; *fig.* про-
хла́дный

term [tɜːm] **1.** (*period*) срок; *univ.* се-
ме́стр; *ling.* те́рмин; *school* че́тверть;
~s *pl.* усло́вия; *be on good* (*bad*) **~s**
быть в хоро́ших (плохи́х) отноше́-
ниях; *come to ~s* прийти́ *pf.* к со-
глаше́нию; **2.** (*call*) наз(ы)ва́ть;
(*name*) [на]именова́ть

termina|l ['tɜːmɪnl] **1.** □ коне́чный; **2.**
el. кле́мма, зажи́м; *Am. rail.* ко-
не́чная ста́нция; *air* ~ аэровокза́л;
bus ~ автовокза́л; **~te** [-neɪt]
конча́ть(ся) [ко́нчить(ся)]; *~ a contract* расто́ргнуть *pf.* контра́кт; **~tion**
[tɜːmɪ'neɪʃn] оконча́ние; коне́ц

terminus ['tɜːmɪnəs] *rail., bus* ко-
не́чная ста́нция

terrace ['terəs] терра́са; **~s** *pl. sport*
трибу́ны стадио́на; **~d** [-t] располо́-
женный терра́сами

terrestrial [te'restrɪəl] □ земно́й

terrible ['terəbl] □ ужа́сный, стра́ш-
ный

terri|fic [tə'rɪfɪk] (**~ally**) *coll.* по-
тряса́ющий, великоле́пный; **~fy**
['terɪfaɪ] *v/t.* ужаса́ть [-сну́ть]

territor|ial [terɪ'tɔːrɪəl] □ террито-
риа́льный; **~y** ['terɪtrɪ] террито́рия

terror ['terə] у́жас; (*violence*) терро́р;
~ize [-raɪz] терроризова́ть (*im*)*pf.*

terse [tɜːs] □ (*concise*) сжа́тый

test [test] **1.** испыта́ние (*a. fig.*); про́ба;
контро́ль *m*; *in teaching* контро́льная
рабо́та; (*check*) прове́рка; *attr.* испы-
та́тельный; про́бный; *nuclear* **~s**

T

я́дерные испыта́ния; **2.** подверга́ть испыта́нию, прове́рке

testament ['testəmənt] *law* завеща́ние; *Old* (*New*) ♎ Ве́тхий (Но́вый) заве́т

testify ['testɪfaɪ] *law* дава́ть показа́ние (*to* в по́льзу Р, *against* про́тив Р); свиде́тельствовать (*to* о П)

testimon|ial [testɪ'məʊnɪəl] рекоменда́ция, характери́стика; **~y** ['testɪmənɪ] *law* свиде́тельские показа́ния; *fig.* свиде́тельство

test pilot лётчик-испыта́тель *m*

test tube *chem.* проби́рка

tête-à-tête [teɪtɑː'teɪt] с гла́зу на́ глаз

tether ['teðə]: *come to the end of one's ~* дойти́ *pf.* до ру́чки

text [tekst] текст; **~book** уче́бник

textile ['tekstaɪl] **1.** тексти́льный; **2. ~s** *coll.* тексти́ль *m*

texture ['tekstʃə] *of cloth* тексту́ра; *of mineral, etc.* структу́ра

than [ðæn, ðən] чем, не́жели; *more ~ ten* бо́льше десяти́

thank [θæŋk] **1.** [по]благодари́ть (В); *~ you* благодарю́ вас; **2. ~s** *pl.* спаси́бо!; *~s to* благодаря́ (Д); *~ful* ['-fl] □ благода́рный; *~less* ['-lɪs] □ неблагода́рный

that [ðæt, ðət] **1.** *pron.* тот, та, то; те *pl.*; (*a.* э́тот *и т. д.*); кото́рый *и т. д.*; **2.** *cj.* что; чтобы

thatch [θætʃ]: *~ed roof* соло́менная кры́ша

thaw [θɔː] **1.** о́ттепель *f*; (*melting*) та́яние; **2.** *v/i.* [рас]та́ять; (*a. ~ out*) отта́ивать [отта́ять]

the [ðə, ... ðг, ... ðɪ] [ðí: *перед гласными* ði, *перед согласными* ðə] **1.** определённый арти́кль; **2.** *adv.* *~ ... ~ ...* чем ..., тем ...

theat|er, *Brt.* **theatre** ['θɪətə] теа́тр; *fig.* аре́на; *operating ~* операцио́нная; *~ of war* теа́тр вое́нных де́йствий; *~rical* □ [θɪ'ætrɪkl] театра́льный (*a. fig.*); сцени́ческий

theft [θeft] воровство́; кра́жа

their [ðeə] *poss. pron.* (*om* **they**) их; свой, своя́, своё, свои́ *pl.*; *~s* [ðeəz] *poss. pron. pred.* их, свой *и т.д*

them [ðəm, ðem] *pron.* (*косвенный падеж от* **they**) их, им

theme [θiːm] те́ма

themselves [ðəm'selvz] *pron. refl.* себя́, -ся; *emphatic* са́ми

then [ðen] **1.** *adv.* тогда́; пото́м, зате́м; *from ~ on* с тех пор; *by ~* к тому́ вре́мени; **2.** *cj.* тогда́, в тако́м слу́чае; зна́чит; **3.** *adj.* тогда́шний

thence *lit* [ðens] отту́да; с того́ вре́мени; *fig.* отсю́да, из э́того

theology [θɪ'ɒlədʒɪ] богосло́вие

theor|etic(al) □ [θɪə'retɪk(l)] теорети́ческий; *~ist* ['θɪərɪst] теоре́тик; *~y* ['θɪərɪ] тео́рия

there [ðeə] там, туда́; *~!* (ну) вот!; *~ she is* вон она́; *~ is*, *~ are* [ðə'rɪz, ðə'rɑː] есть, име́ется; име́ются; *~about(s)* [ðeərə'baʊt(s)] поблизо́сти; (*approximately*) о́коло э́того, приблизи́тельно; *~after* [ðeər'ɑːftə] по́сле того́; *~by* ['ðeə'baɪ] посре́дством э́того, таки́м о́бразом; *~fore* ['ðeəfɔː] поэ́тому; сле́довательно; *~upon* ['ðeərə'pɒn] сра́зу же; тут; всле́дствие того́

thermo|meter [θə'mɒmɪtə] термо́метр, гра́дусник; *~nuclear* [θɜːməʊ'njuːklɪə] термоя́дерный; *~s* ['θɜːməs] (*or ~ flask*) те́рмос

these [ðiːz] *pl. om* **this**

thes|is ['θiːsɪs], *pl. ~es* [-siːz] те́зис; диссерта́ция

they [ðeɪ] *pers. pron.* они́

thick [θɪk] **1.** □ *com.* то́лстый; *fog, hair, etc.* густо́й; *voice* хри́плый; *coll.* (*stupid*) глу́пый; *that's a bit ~* э́то уж сли́шком; **2.** *fig.* гу́ща; *in the ~ of* в са́мой гу́ще Р; *~en* ['θɪkən] утолща́ть(ся) [утолщи́ть(ся)]; *of darkness, fog, etc.* сгуща́ть(ся) [сгусти́ть(ся)]; *~et* ['θɪkɪt] ча́ща; *of bushes* за́росли *f/pl.*; *~-headed* тупоголо́вый, тупоу́мный; *~ness* ['θɪknɪs] толщина́; (*density*) густота́; *~set* [θɪk'set] *person* корена́стый; *~-skinned* (*a. fig.*) толстоко́жий

thie|f [θiːf], *pl. ~ves* [θiːvz] вор; *~ve* [θiːv] *v/i.* ворова́ть

thigh [θaɪ] бедро́

thimble ['θɪmbl] напёрсток

thin [θɪn] **1.** □ *com.* тонкий; *person* худой, худощавый; *hair* редкий; *soup* жидкий; **2.** делать(ся) тонким, утончаться(ся) [-читься(ся)]; [по]редеть; [по]худеть

thing [θɪŋ] вещь *f;* предмет; дело; ~**s** *pl.* (belongings) вещи *f/pl.;* (luggage) багаж; (clothes) одежда *f/pl.;* for painting, etc. принадлежности *f/pl.;* **the ~ is that** дело в том, что ...; **the very ~** как раз то, что нужно; **~s are getting better** положение улучшается

think [θɪŋk] [irr.] *v/i.* [по]думать (of, about о П); abstractly мыслить; (presume) полагать; (remember) вспоминать [вспомнить] (of о П); (intend) намереваться (+ inf.); (devise) придум(ыв)ать (of B); *v/t.* считать [счесть]; ~ **a lot of** высоко ценить; быть высокого мнения о (П)

third [θɜːd] **1.** третий; **2.** треть *f*

thirst [θɜːst] **1.** жажда (a. fig.); **2.** жаждать (for, after P) (part. fig.); ~**y** ['-ɪ]: *I am ~* я хочу пить

thirt|**een** [θɜːˈtiːn] тринадцать; ~**eenth** [θɜːˈtiːnθ] тринадцатый; ~**ieth** ['θɜːtɪɪθ] тридцатый; ~**y** ['θɜːtɪ] тридцать

this [ðɪs] demonstrative pron. (pl. **these**) этот, эта, это; эти *pl.;* ~ **morning** сегодня утром; **one of these days** как-нибудь, когда-нибудь

thistle ['θɪsl] чертополох

thorn [θɔːn] bot. шип, колючка; ~**y** ['θɔːnɪ] колючий; fig. тяжёлый, тернистый

thorough ['θʌrə] □ основательный, тщательный; (detailed) детальный, подробный; ~**ly** adv. основательно, досконально; ~**bred** чистокровный; ~**fare** улица, магистраль *f;* "**No 2**" "Проезда нет"

those [ðəʊz] pl. om that

though [ðəʊ] conj. хотя; даже если бы, хотя бы; adv. тем не менее, однако; всё-таки; **as** ~ как будто, словно

thought [θɔːt] **1.** pt. u pt. p. om **think**; **2.** мысль *f;* мышление; (contemplation) размышление; (care) забота; вни-

мательность *f;* ~**ful** ['θɔːtfl] □ задумчивый; (considerate) заботливый; внимательный (of к Д); ~**less** ['θɔːtlɪs] □ (careless) беспечный; необдуманный; невнимательный (of к Д)

thousand ['θaʊznd] тысяча; ~**th** ['θaʊznθ] **1.** тысячный; **2.** тысячная часть *f*

thrash [θræʃ] [вы]пороть; избивать [-бить]; fig. (defeat) побеждать [-едить]; ~ **out** тщательно обсуждать [-удить]; ~**ing** ['θræʃɪŋ]: **give s.o. a good** ~ основательно поколотить *pf.* кого-л.

thread [θred] **1.** нитка, нить *f;* fig. нить *f;* of a screw, etc. резьба; **2.** needle продевать нитку в (В); beads нанизывать [-зать]; ~**bare** ['θredbeə] потёртый, изношенный; потрёпанный; fig. (hackneyed) избитый

threat [θret] угроза; ~**en** ['θretn] *v/t.* (при)грозить, угрожать (Д with Т); *v/i.* грозить

three [θriː] **1.** три; **2.** тройка → **five;** ~**fold** ['θriːfəʊld] тройной; adv. втройне; ~**ply** трёхслойный

thresh [θreʃ] agric. обмолотить *pf.*

threshold ['θreʃhəʊld] порог

threw [θruː] pt. om **throw**

thrice [θraɪs] трижды

thrift [θrɪft] бережливость *f,* экономность *f;* ~**y** ['θrɪftɪ] □ экономный, бережливый

thrill [θrɪl] **1.** *v/t.* [вз]волновать; приводить в трепет, [вз]будоражить; *v/i.* (за)трепетать (with от Р); [вз]волноваться; **2.** трепет; глубокое волнение; нервная дрожь *f;* ~**er** ['θrɪlə] детективный or приключенческий роман or фильм, триллер; ~**ing** ['θrɪlɪŋ] захватывающий; news потрясающий

thrive [θraɪv] [irr.] of business процветать; of person преуспевать; of plants разрастаться; ~**n** ['θrɪvn] pt. p. om **thrive**

throat [θrəʊt] горло; **clear one's** ~ откашливаться [-ляться]

throb [θrɒb] **1.** пульсировать; сильно биться; **2.** пульсация; биение, fig. трепет

throes [θrəʊz]: *be in the ~ of* в ходе, в процессе

throne [θrəʊn] трон, престол

throng [θrɒŋ] **1.** толпа; **2.** [с]толпиться; (*fill*) заполнять [-о́лнить]; *people ~ed to the square* народ толпой валил на площадь *f*

throttle ['θrɒtl] [за]души́ть; (*fill*) (*regulate*) дроссели́ровать

through [θruː] **1.** через (В); сквозь (В); по (Д); *adv.* наскво́зь; от начала до конца́; **2.** *train, etc.* прямо́й; *be ~ with s.o.* порвать с кем-л.; *put ~ tel.* соедини́ть *pf.* (с Т); **~out** [θruː'aʊt] **1.** *prp.* через (В); по всему, всей …; **2.** повсю́ду; по всех отноше́ниях

throve [θrəʊv] *pt. om* **thrive**

throw [θrəʊ] **1.** [*irr.*] бросать [бросить], кидать [ки́нуть]; *discus, etc.* метать [метну́ть]; *~ away* выбра́сывать ['-росить]; (*forgo*) упускать [-сти́ть]; *~ over* перебра́сывать [-бросить]; *~ light on s.th.* пролива́ть [-ли́ть] свет на (В); **2.** бросо́к; броса́ние; *~n* [-n] *pt. om* **throw**

thru *Am.* = **through**

thrush [θrʌʃ] дрозд

thrust [θrʌst] **1.** толчо́к; *mil.* уда́р; **2.** [*irr.*] (*push*) толкать [-кну́ть]; (*poke*) ты́кать [ткну́ть]; *~ o.s. into fig.* втира́ться [втере́ться] в (В); *~ upon a p.* навя́зывать [-зать] (Д)

thud [θʌd] глухо́й звук *or* стук

thug [θʌg] головоре́з

thumb [θʌm] **1.** большо́й па́лец (руки́); **2.** *book* перели́стывать [-стать]; *~ a lift coll.* голосова́ть (на доро́ге)

thump [θʌmp] **1.** глухо́й стук; тяжёлый уда́р; **2.** стуча́ть [-у́кнуть]

thunder ['θʌndə] **1.** гром; **2.** [за]греме́ть; *fig.* мета́ть гро́мы и мо́лнии; *~bolt* уда́р мо́лнии; *~clap* уда́р гро́ма; *~ous* ['θʌndərəs] □ (*very loud*) громово́й, оглуша́ющий; *~storm* гроза́; *~struck fig.* как гро́мом поражённый

Thursday ['θɜːzdɪ] четве́рг

thus [ðʌs] так, таки́м о́бразом

thwart [θwɔːt] *plans, etc.* меша́ть, расстра́ивать [-ро́ить]; *be ~ed at every turn* встреча́ть препя́тствия на каж-

дом шагу́

tick¹ [tɪk] *zo.* клещ

tick² [~] **1.** *of clock* ти́канье; **2.** *v/i.* ти́кать

tick³ [~] *mark* га́лочка; *~ off* отмеча́ть га́лочкой

ticket ['tɪkɪt] **1.** биле́т; *price~* этике́тка с цено́й; *cloakroom~* номеро́к; *round trip* (*Brt. return*) ~ обра́тный биле́т; *~ office* биле́тная ка́сса

tickle ['tɪkl] (по)щекота́ть; *~ish* [-ɪʃ] □ *fig.* щекотли́вый

tidal ['taɪdl]: *~ wave* прили́вная волна́

tidbit [tɪdbɪt], *Brt.* **titbit** ['tɪtbɪt] ла́комый кусо́чек; *fig.* пика́нтная но́вость *f*

tide [taɪd] **1.** *low ~* отли́в; *high ~* прили́в; *fig.* тече́ние; направле́ние; **2.** *fig. ~ over: will this ~ you over till Monday?* Это вам хва́тит до понеде́льника?

tidy ['taɪdɪ] **1.** опря́тный; аккура́тный; *sum* значи́тельный; **2.** уб(и)ра́ть; приводи́ть в поря́док

tie [taɪ] **1.** га́лстук; *sport* ничья́; *~s pl.* (*bonds*) у́зы *f/pl.*; **2.** *v/t.* knot, etc. завя́зывать [-зать]; *together* свя́зывать [-зать]; *v/i.* сыгра́ть *pf.* вничью́

tier [tɪə] я́рус

tiff [tɪf] *coll.* размо́лвка

tiger ['taɪgə] тигр

tight [taɪt] □ туго́й; туго натя́нутый; (*fitting too closely*) те́сный; *coll.* (*drunk*) подвы́пивший; *coll. ~ spot fig.* затрудни́тельное положе́ние; *~en* ['taɪtn] стя́гивать(ся) [стяну́ть(ся)] (*a. ~ up*); *belt, etc.* затя́гивать [-яну́ть]; *screw* подтя́гивать [-яну́ть]; *~fisted* скупо́й; *~s* [taɪts] *pl.* колго́тки

tigress ['taɪgrɪs] тигри́ца

tile [taɪl] **1.** *for roof* черепи́ца; *for walls, etc.* облицо́вочная пли́тка, *decorative* изразе́ц; **2.** покрыва́ть черепи́цей; облицо́вывать пли́ткой

till¹ [tɪl] ка́сса

till² [~] **1.** *prp.* до P+; **2.** *cj.* пока́

till³ [~] *agric.* возде́л(ыв)ать (В); [вс]па́хивать

tilt [tɪlt] **1.** накло́нное положе́ние, наклон; *at full* ~ на по́лной ско́рости; 2. наклоня́ть(ся) [-ни́ть(ся)]

timber ['tɪmbə] лесоматериа́л, строево́й лес

time [taɪm] 1. *com.* вре́мя *n*; (*suitable* ~) пора́; (*term*) срок; *at the same* ~ в то же вре́мя; *beat* ~ отбива́ть такт; *for the* ~ *being* пока́, на вре́мя; *in* (or *on*) ~ во́время; *next* ~ в сле́дующий раз; *what's the* ~? кото́рый час?; 2. (уда́чно) выбира́ть вре́мя для P; ~ *limit* преде́льный срок; ~*r* ['taɪmə] та́ймер; ~*ly* ['taɪmlɪ] своевре́менный; ~*saving* эконо́мящий вре́мя; ~*table rail* расписа́ние

timid ['tɪmɪd] □ ро́бкий

tin [tɪn] 1. о́лово; (*container*) консе́рвная ба́нка; 2. консерви́ровать

tinfoil ['tɪnfɔɪl] фольга́

tinge [tɪndʒ] 1. слегка́ окра́шивать; *fig.* придава́ть отте́нок (Д); 2. лёгкая окра́ска; *fig.* отте́нок

tingle ['tɪŋgl] испы́тывать *или* вызыва́ть пока́лывание (в онеме́вших коне́чностях), пощи́пывание (на моро́зе), звон в уша́х *и т. п.*

tinker ['tɪŋkə] вози́ться (*with* с Т)

tinkle ['tɪŋkl] звя́кать [-кнуть]

tin|ned консерви́рованный; ~ *opener* консе́рвный нож

tinsel ['tɪnsl] мишура́

tint [tɪnt] 1. кра́ска; (*shade*) отте́нок; 2. слегка́ окра́шивать; *hair* подкра́шивать

tiny ['taɪnɪ] □ о́чень ма́ленький, крошечный

tip¹ [tɪp] (то́нкий) коне́ц, наконе́чник; *of finger, etc.* ко́нчик

tip² [-] 1. информа́ция, (*hint*) намёк; (*advice*) рекоменда́ция, осно́ванная на малодосту́пной информа́ции; 2. дава́ть на чай (Д); дава́ть информа́цию (Д), рекомендова́ть

tip³ [-] опроки́дывать [-и́нуть]

tipple ['tɪpl] *coll.* вы́пи(ва́)ть, пить

tipsy ['tɪpsɪ] подвы́пивший

tiptoe ['tɪptəu]: *on* ~ на цы́почках

tire¹ (*Brt.* **tyre**) ши́на; *flat* ~ спу́щенная ши́на

tire² [taɪə] утомля́ть [-ми́ть]; уста́(-ва́)ть; ~*d* [-d] уста́лый; ~*less* ['-lɪs] неутоми́мый; ~*some* ['-səm] утоми́тельный; (*pesky*) надое́дливый; (*boring*) ску́чный

tissue ['tɪʃuː] ткань *f* (*a. biol.*); ~ *paper* папиро́сная бума́га

title ['taɪtl] загла́вие, назва́ние; (*person's status*) ти́тул; зва́ние; ~ *holder sport* чемпио́н; ~ *page* титу́льный лист

titter ['tɪtə] 1. хихи́канье; 2. хихи́кать [-кнуть]

tittle-tattle ['tɪtltætl] спле́тни *f/pl.*, болтовня́

to [tə, ... tu, ... tuː] *prp. indicating direction, aim* к (Д); в (В); на (В); *introducing indirect object, corresponds to the Russian dative case*: ~ *me etc.* мне *и т. д.*; ~ *and fro adv.* взад и вперёд; *показатель инфинитива*: ~ *work* рабо́тать; *I weep* ~ *think of it* я пла́чу, ду́мая об э́том

toad [təud] жа́ба; ~*stool* пога́нка

toast [təust] 1. гре́нок; (*drink*) тост; 2. де́лать гре́нки; поджа́ри(ва)ть; *fig.* (*warm o.s.*) гре́ть(ся); пить за (В); ~*er* [-ə] то́стер

tobacco [tə'bækəu] таба́к; ~*nist's* [tə'bækənɪsts] таба́чный магази́н

toboggan [tə'bɒgən] 1. са́ни *f/pl.*; *children's* са́нки; 2. ката́ться на саня́х, са́нках

today [tə'deɪ] сего́дня; настоя́щее вре́мя; *from* ~ с сего́дняшнего дня; *a month* ~ че́рез ме́сяц

toe [təu] па́лец (на ноге́); *of boot, sock* носо́к

toffee ['tɒfɪ] ири́ска; *soft* тяну́чка

together [tə'geðə] вме́сте

togs [tɒgs] *pl. coll.* оде́жда

toil [tɔɪl] 1. тяжёлый труд; 2. усиленно труди́ться; тащи́ться, идти́ с трудо́м

toilet ['tɔɪlɪt] туале́т; ~ *paper* туале́тная бума́га

token ['təukən] знак; *as a* ~ *of* в знак чего́-то; ~ *payment* символи́ческая пла́та

told [təuld] *pt. и pt. p. om* **tell**

tolera|ble ['tɒlərəbl] □ терпи́мый; (*fairly good*) сно́сный; ~*nce* [-rəns] терпи́мость *f*; ~nt [-rənt] □ терпи́мый; ~te [-reɪt] (вы-, по)терпе́ть, допуска́ть [-сти́ть]

toll [təʊl] (*tax*) по́шлина, сбор; *fig.* дань *f*; ~gate ме́сто, где взима́ются сбо́ры; заста́ва

tom [tɒm]: ~ *cat* кот

tomato [tə'mɑːtəʊ], *pl.* ~es [-z] помидо́р, тома́т

tomb [tuːm] моги́ла

tomboy ['tɒmbɔɪ] сорване́ц (о де́вочке)

tomfoolery [tɒm'fuːlərɪ] дура́чество

tomorrow [tə'mɒrəʊ] за́втра

ton [tʌn] *metric* то́нна

tone [təʊn] **1.** *mus., paint., fig.* тон; интона́ция; **2.**: ~ *down* смягча́ть(ся) [-чи́ть]; ~ *in with* гармони́ровать (с Т)

tongs [tɒŋz] *pl.* щипцы́ *m/pl.*, кле́щи, *a.* клещи́ *f/pl.*

tongue [tʌŋ] язы́к; *hold your ~!* молчи́(те)!

tonic ['tɒnɪk] *med.* тонизи́рующее сре́дство; ~ *water* то́ник

tonight [tə'naɪt] сего́дня ве́чером

tonnage ['tʌnɪdʒ] *naut.* тонна́ж; (*freight carrying capacity*) грузоподъёмность *f*; (*duty*) ва́жный сбор

tonsil ['tɒnsl] *anat.* гла́нда, минда́лина

too [tuː] та́кже, то́же; *of degree* сли́шком; о́чень; (*moreover*) бо́лее того́; к тому́ же; *there was ground frost last night, and in June ~!* вчера́ но́чью – за́морозки на по́чве, и э́то ию́не!

took [tʊk] *pt. om* **take**

tool [tuːl] (рабо́чий) инструме́нт; *fig.* ору́дие

toot [tuːt] **1.** гудо́к; **2.** дать гудо́к; *mot.* проси́гна́ли(зи́рова)ть

tooth [tuːθ] (*pl.* **teeth**) зуб; ~ache зубна́я боль *f*; ~brush зубна́я щётка; ~less ['tuːθlɪs] □ беззу́бый; ~paste зубна́я па́ста

top [tɒp] **1.** ве́рхняя часть *f*; верх; *of mountain* верши́на; *of head, tree* маку́шка; (*lid*) кры́шка; *leafy top of root vegetable* ботва́; *at the ~ of one's voice* во весь го́лос; *on ~* наверху́; *on ~ of all this* в доверше́ние всего́; в доба́вок ко всему́; **2.** вы́сший, пе́рвый; *speed, etc.*

максима́льный; **3.** (*cover*) покры́(ва́)ть; *fig.* (*surpass*) превыша́ть [-ы́сить]

topic ['tɒpɪk] те́ма; ~al [-kl] актуа́льный, злободне́вный

top-level: ~ *negotiations* перегово́ры на вы́сшем у́ровне

topple ['tɒpl] [с]вали́ть; опроки́дывать(ся) [-и́нуть(ся)] (*a.* ~ *over*)

topsy-turvy ['tɒpsɪ'tɜːvɪ] □ (*пере*-)вёрнутый вверх дном

torch [tɔːtʃ] фа́кел; *electric* ~ электри́ческий фона́рь *m*; *chiefly Brt.* (*flashlight*) карма́нный фона́рик

tore [tɔː] *pt. om* **tear**

torment 1. ['tɔːment] муче́ние, му́ка; **2.** [tɔː'ment] [из-, за]му́чить

torn [tɔːn] *pt. p. om* **tear**

tornado [tɔː'neɪdəʊ] торна́до (*indecl.*); смерч *m*; (*hurricane*) урага́н

torpedo [tɔː'piːdəʊ] **1.** торпе́да; **2.** торпеди́ровать (*im*)*pf.* (*a. fig.*)

torpid ['tɔːpɪd] □ (*inactive, slow*) вя́лый, апати́чный

torrent ['tɒrənt] пото́к (*a. fig.*)

torrid ['tɒrɪd] жа́ркий, зно́йный

tortoise ['tɔːtəs] *zo.* черепа́ха

tortuous ['tɔːtʃʊəs] (*winding*) изви́листый; *fig.* (*devious*) укло́нчивый, нейскренний

torture ['tɔːtʃə] **1.** пы́тка (*a. fig.*); **2.** пыта́ть; [из-, за]му́чить

toss [tɒs] (*fling*) броса́ть [бро́сить]; *in bed* беспоко́йно мета́ться; *head* вски́дывать [-и́нуть]; *coin* подбра́сывать [-ро́сить] (*mst.* ~ *up*)

tot [tɒt] (*child*) малы́ш

total ['təʊtl] **1.** □ (*complete*) по́лный, абсолю́тный; *war* тота́льный; *number* о́бщий; **2.** су́мма; ито́г; *in* ~ в ито́ге; **3.** подводи́ть ито́г, подсчи́тывать [-ита́ть]; (*amount to*) составля́ть в ито́ге; (*equal*) равня́ться (Д); ~itarian [təʊtælɪ'teərɪən] тоталита́рный; ~ly [-lɪ] по́лностью, соверше́нно

totter ['tɒtə] идти́ нетвёрдой похо́дкой; (*shake*) шата́ться [(по)шатну́ться]; (*be about to fall*) разруша́ться

touch [tʌtʃ] **1.** (*sense*) осяза́ние; (*con-*

tact) прикоснове́ние; *fig.* конта́кт, связь *f*; **a ~** (*a little*) чу́точка; (*a trace*) при́месь *f*; *of illness* лёгкий при́ступ; штрих; **2.** тро́гать [тро́нуть] (В) (*a. fig.*); прикаса́ться [-косну́ться], притра́гиваться [-тро́нуться] к (Д); *fig. subject, etc.* каса́ться [косну́ться] (Р); затра́гивать [-ро́нуть]; **be ~ed** *fig.* быть тро́нутым; **~ up** поправля́ть [-а́вить]; **~ing** ['tʌtʃɪŋ] тро́гательный; **~y** ['tʌtʃɪ] □ оби́дчивый

tough [tʌf] **1.** *meat, etc.* жёсткий (*a. fig.*); (*strong*) про́чный; *person* вы́носливый; *job, etc.* тру́дный; **2.** хулига́н; **~en** [tʌfn] де́лать(ся) жёстким

tour [tʊə] **1.** пое́здка, экску́рсия, тур; *sport, thea.* турне́ *n indecl.*; *a. thea.* га- стро́ли *f/pl.*; **2.** соверша́ть путеше́- ствие *или* турне́ по (Д); путеше́ство- вать (**through** по Д); гастроли́ровать; **~ist** ['tʊərɪst] тури́ст *m*, -ка *f*; **~ agency** туристи́ческое аге́нтство

tournament ['tʊənəmənt] турни́р

tousle ['taʊzl] взъеро́ши(ва)ть, рас- трёпывать (-репа́ть)

tow [təʊ] *naut.* **1.** букси́р; **take in ~** брать на букси́р; **with all her kids in ~** со все́- ми детьми́; **2.** букси́ровать

toward(s) [təˈwɔːdz, twɔːdʒ] *prp.* (*di- rection*) по направле́нию к (Д); (*rela- tion*) к (Д), по отноше́нию к (Д); (*purpose*) для (Р), на (В)

towel ['taʊəl] полоте́нце

tower ['taʊə] **1.** ба́шня; **2.** воз- выша́ться (**above, over** над Т) (*a. fig.*)

town [taʊn] **1.** го́род; **2.** *attr.* городско́й; **~ council** городско́й сове́т; **~ hall** ра́- туша; **~ dweller** горожа́нин *m*, -нка *f*; **~sfolk** ['taʊnsfəʊk], **~speople** ['taʊnzpiːpl] *pl.* горожа́не *m/pl.*

toxic ['tɒksɪk] токси́ческий

toy [tɔɪ] **1.** игру́шка; **2.** *attr.* иг- ру́шечный; **3.** игра́ть, забавля́ться; **~ with** (*consider*) поду́мывать

trace [treɪs] **1.** след; (*very small quan- tity*) следы́, незначи́тельное коли́чество; **2.** (*draw*) [на]черти́ть; (*lo- cate*) выслежива́ть [вы́следить] (В); (*follow*) просле́живать [-еди́ть] (В)

track [træk] **1.** след; (*rough road*) про-

сёлочная доро́га; (*path*) тропи́нка; *for running* бегова́я доро́жка; *for mo- tor racing* трек; *rail* коле́я; **be on the right** (**wrong**) **~** быть на пра́вильном (ло́жном) пути́; **2.** следи́ть за (Т); про- сле́живать [-еди́ть] (В); **~ down** вы- сле́живать [вы́следить] (В)

tract [trækt] простра́нство, полоса́ зе- мли́; *anat.* тракт; **respiratory ~** дыха́- тельные пути́

tractable ['træktəbl] *person* сго́- во́рчивый

tract|ion ['trækʃn] тя́га; **~ engine** тяга́ч; **~or** ['træktə] тра́ктор

trade [treɪd] **1.** профе́ссия; ремесло́; торго́вля; **2.** торго́вля (**in** T; **with** с T); (*exchange*) обме́нивать [-ня́ть] (**for** на В); **~** использование (*im)pf.*; **~mark** фабри́чная ма́рка; **~r** ['treɪdə] торго́вец; **~sman** ['treɪdzmən] торго́- вец; (*shopkeeper*) владе́лец магази́на; **~(s) union** [treɪd(z)'juːnɪən] проф- сою́з

tradition [trəˈdɪʃn] (*custom*) тради́ция, обы́чай; (*legend*) преда́ние; **~al** [-ʃənl] □ традицио́нный

traffic ['træfɪk] **1.** движе́ние (у́личное, железнодоро́жное *и т. д.*); (*vehicles*) тра́нспорт; (*trading*) торго́вля; **~ jam** зато́р у́личного движе́ния; **~ lights** *pl.* светофо́р; **~ police** ГАИ (госу- да́рственная автомоби́льная инспе́к- ция)

tragedy ['trædʒədɪ] траге́дия

tragic(al) □ ['trædʒɪk(l)] траги́ческий, траги́чный

trail [treɪl] **1.** след; (*path*) тропа́; **2.** *v/t.* (*pull*) тащи́ть, волочи́ть; (*track*) идти́ по сле́ду (Р); *v/i.* тащи́ться, во- лочи́ться; *bot.* ви́ться; **~er** ['treɪlə] *mot.* прице́п, тре́йлер

train [treɪn] **1.** по́езд; (*retinue*) сви́та; *film star's* толпа́ (покло́нников); **by ~** по́ездом; **freight ~** това́рный соста́в; **suburban ~** при́городный по́езд, *coll.* электри́чка; **~ of thought** ход мы́слей; **2.** (*bring up*) воспи́тывать [-та́ть]; приуча́ть [-чи́ть]; (*coach*) [на]трени- рова́ть(ся); обуча́ть [-чи́ть]; *lions, etc.* [вы́]дрессирова́ть

trait [treɪt] (характе́рная) черта́

traitor ['treɪtə] преда́тель *m*, изме́нник

tram [træm], **~car** ['træmkɑ:] трамва́й, ваго́н трамва́я

tramp [træmp] **1.** (*vagrant*) бродя́га *m*; (*hike*) путеше́ствие пешко́м; *of feet* то́пот; звук тяжёлых шаго́в; **2.** тяжело́ ступа́ть; тащи́ться с трудо́м; то́пать; броди́ть; **~le** ['træmpl] (*crush underfoot*) топта́ть; тяжело́ ступа́ть; **~ down** затапты́вать [-топта́ть]

trance [trɑ:ns] транс

tranquil ['træŋkwɪl] □ споко́йный; **~(l)ity** [træŋ'kwɪlətɪ] споко́йствие; **~(l)ize** ['træŋkwɪlaɪz] успока́ивать(ся) [-ко́ить(ся)]; **~(l)izer** ['træŋkwɪlaɪzə] транквилиза́тор

transact [træn'zækt] заключа́ть [-чи́ть] сде́лку, вести́ дела́ с (T); **~ion** [-'zækʃn] сде́лка; **~s** *pl.* (*proceedings*) труды́ *m/pl.* нау́чного о́бщества

transatlantic [trænzət'læntɪk] трансатланти́ческий

transcend [træn'send] выходи́ть [вы́йти] за преде́лы; *expectations, etc.* превосходи́ть [-взойти́], превыша́ть [-ы́сить]

transfer 1. [træns'fɜ:] *v/t.* переноси́ть [-нести́], перемеща́ть [-мести́ть]; *ownership* перед(ав)а́ть; *to another job, town, team, etc.* переводи́ть [-вести́]; *v/i. Am., of passengers* переса́живаться [-се́сть]; **2.** ['trænsfə:] перено́с; *comm.* трансфе́рт; перево́д; *Am.* переса́дка; **~able** [træns'fɜ:rəbl] с пра́вом переда́чи; переводи́мый

transfigure [træns'fɪgə] видоизменя́ть [-ни́ть]; *with joy, etc.* преобража́ть [-рази́ть]

transfixed [træns'fɪkst]: **~ with fear** ско́ванный стра́хом

transform [træns'fɔ:m] превраща́ть [-врати́ть]; преобразо́вывать [-зова́ть]; **~ation** [-fə'meɪʃn] преобразова́ние; превраще́ние; **~er** [-'fɔ:mə] трансформа́тор

transfusion [træns'fju:ʒn]: **blood ~** перелива́ние кро́ви

transgress [trænz'gres] *v/t. law, etc.* преступа́ть [-пи́ть]; *agreement* наруша́ть [-у́шить]; *v/i.* (*sin*) [co]греши́ть; **~ion** [-'greʃn] просту́пок; *of law, etc.* наруше́ние

transient ['trænzɪənt] → **transitory**; *Am., a.* (*temporary guest/lodger*) вре́менный жиле́ц; челове́к/скита́лец, и́щущий себе́ рабо́ту

transit ['trænzɪt] прое́зд; *of goods* перево́зка; транзи́т; **he is here in ~** он здесь прое́здом

transition [træn'zɪʃn] перехо́д; перехо́дный пери́од

transitory ['trænsɪtrɪ] мимолётный; преходя́щий

translat|e [træns'leɪt] переводи́ть [-вести́] (*from* с Р, *into* на В); *fig.* (*interpret*) [ис]толкова́ть; объясня́ть [-ни́ть]; **~ion** [-'leɪʃn] перево́д; **~or** [-leɪtə] перево́дчик *m*, -чица *f*

translucent [trænz'lu:snt] полупрозра́чный

transmission [trænz'mɪʃn] переда́ча (*a. radio & tech.*); *radio, TV* трансля́ция

transmit [trænz'mɪt] перед(ав)а́ть (*a. radio, TV*, *a.* трансли́ровать); *heat* проводи́ть *impf.*; **~ter** [-ə] переда́тчик (*a. radio, TV*)

transparent [træns'pærənt] □ прозра́чный (*a. fig.*)

transpire [træn'spaɪə] *fig.* вы́ясниться *pf.*, оказа́ться *pf.*; *coll.* случа́ться [-чи́ться]

transplant [træns'plɑ:nt] **1.** переса́живать [-сади́ть]; *fig. people* переселя́ть [-ли́ть]; **2.** ['trænsplɑ:nt] *med.* переса́дка

transport 1. [træn'spɔ:t] перевози́ть [-везти́]; транспорти́ровать *im(pf.)*; *fig.* увлека́ть [-е́чь]; восхища́ть [-ити́ть]; **2.** ['trænspɔ:t] тра́нспорт; перево́зка; *of joy, delight, etc.* **be in ~s** быть вне себя́ (*of* от Р); **~ation** [trænspɔ:'teɪʃn] перево́зка, транспортиро́вка

transverse ['trænzvɜ:s] □ попере́чный; **~ly** попере́к

trap [træp] **1.** ловушка, западня (*a. fig.*); капкан; **2.** *fig.* (*lure*) заманить *pf.* в ловушку; **fall into a ~** попасть *pf.* в ловушку; (*fall for the bait*) попасться *pf.* на удочку; **~door** опускная дверь *f*

trapeze [trəˈpiːz] трапеция

trappings [ˈtræpɪŋz] *pl.* (*harness*) сбруя; *fig.* **the ~ of office** внешние атрибуты служебного положения

trash [træʃ] хлам; (*waste food*) отбросы *m/pl.*; *fig.* дрянь *f*; *book* макулатура; (*nonsense*) вздор, ерунда; **~y** [ˈtræʃɪ] □ дрянной

travel [ˈtrævl] **1.** *v/i.* путешествовать; ездить, [по]ехать; (*move*) передвигаться [-инуться]; *of light, sound* распространяться (-ниться); *v/t.* объезжать [-ездить, -ехать]; проезжать [-ехать] (… *км в час и т. п.*); **2.** путешествие; *tech.* ход; (пере)движение; **~(l)er** [-ə] путешественник *m*, -ица *f*

traverse [trəˈvɜːs] **1.** пересекать [-сечь]; (*pass through*) проходить [пройти] (В); **2.** поперечина

travesty [ˈtrævəstɪ] пародия

trawler [ˈtrɔːlə] траулер

tray [treɪ] поднос

treacher|ous [ˈtretʃərəs] □ (*disloyal*) предательский, вероломный; (*unreliable*) ненадёжный; **~ weather** коварная погода; **~y** [-rɪ] предательство, вероломство

treacle [ˈtriːkl] патока; (*chiefly Brt., molasses*) меласса

tread [tred] **1.** [*irr.*] ступать [-пить]; **~ down** затаптывать [затоптать]; **~ lightly** *fig.* действовать осторожно, тактично; **2.** поступь *f*, походка; *of stairs* ступенька; *of tire, Brt. tyre* протектор

treason [ˈtriːzn] (государственная) измена

treasure [ˈtreʒə] **1.** сокровище; **2.** хранить; (*value greatly*) дорожить; **~r** [-rə] казначей

treasury [ˈtreʒərɪ] сокровищница; *Brt.* **the ⁀** Казначейство

treat [triːt] **1.** *v/t. chem.* обрабатывать

[-ботать]; *med.* лечить; (*stand a drink, etc.*) угощать [угостить] (**to** Т); (*act towards*) обращаться [обратиться] с (Т), обходиться [обойтись] с (Т); *v/i.* **~ of** рассматривать [-мотреть], обсуждать [-удить] (В); **~ for … with** лечить (от Р, Т); **2.** (*pleasure*) удовольствие, наслаждение; **this is my ~** за всё плачу я!; я угощаю!

treatise [ˈtriːtɪz] научный труд

treatment [ˈtriːtmənt] *chem., tech.* обработка (Т); *med.* лечение; (*handling*) обращение (**of** с Т)

treaty [ˈtriːtɪ] договор

treble [ˈtrebl] **1.** тройной, утроенный; **2.** тройное количество; *mus.* дискант; **3.** утраивать(ся) [утроить(ся)]

tree [triː] дерево; **family ~** родословное дерево

trellis [ˈtrelɪs] решётка; шпалера

tremble [ˈtrembl] [за]дрожать, [за]трястись (**with** от Р)

tremendous [trɪˈmendəs] □ громадный; страшный; *coll.* огромный, потрясающий

tremor [ˈtremə] дрожь *f*; **~s** *pl.* подземные толчки

tremulous [ˈtremjʊləs] □ дрожащий; (*timid*) трепетный, робкий

trench [trentʃ] канава; *mil.* траншея, окоп

trend [trend] **1.** направление (*a. fig.*); *fig.* (*course*) течение; (*style*) стиль *m*; (*tendency*) тенденция; **2.** иметь тенденцию (**towards** к Д); склоняться

trendy [ˈtrendɪ] *coll.* стильный; модный

trespass [ˈtrespəs] зайти *pf.* на чужую территорию; (*sin*) совершать проступок; (*encroach*) злоупотреблять [-бить] (**on** Т); **~ on s.o.'s time** посягать на чьё-л. время

trial [ˈtraɪəl] (*test, hardship*) испытание, проба; *law* судебное разбирательство; суд; *attr.* пробный, испытательный; **on ~** под судом; **give a p. a ~** взять кого-л. на испытательный срок

triang|le [ˈtraɪæŋgl] треугольник; **~ular** [traɪˈæŋgjʊlə] □ треугольный

tribe [traɪb] пле́мя *n*; *pej.* компа́ния; братва́

tribune ['trɪbjuːn] (*platform*) трибу́на; (*person*) трибу́н

tribut|ary ['trɪbjʊtərɪ] *geogr.* прито́к; ~e ['trɪbjuːt] дань *f* (*a. fig.*); **pay ~ to** *fig.* отдава́ть до́лжное (Д)

trice [traɪs]: *in a* ~ вмиг, ми́гом

trick [trɪk] **1.** (*practical joke*) шу́тка, *child's* ша́лость *f*; *done to amuse* фо́кус, трюк; (*device*) уло́вка; (*special skill*) сноро́вка; **do the** ~ подейтвовать *pf.*, дости́чь *pf.* це́ли; **2.** (*deceive*) обма́нывать [-ну́ть]; наду(ва́)ть; ~ery ['trɪkərɪ] надува́тельство, обма́н

trickle ['trɪkl] течь стру́йкой; (*ooze*) сочи́ться

trick|ster ['trɪkstə] обма́нщик; ~y ['trɪkɪ] □ (*sly*) хи́трый; (*difficult*) сло́жный, тру́дный; ~ *customer* скользкий тип

tricycle ['traɪsɪkl] трёхколёсный велосипе́д

trifl|e ['traɪfl] **1.** пустя́к; ме́лочь *f*; *a* ~ *fig., adv.* немно́жко; **2.** *v/i.* занима́ться пустяка́ми; относи́ться несерьёзно к (Д); *he is not to be* ~*d with* с ним шу́тки пло́хи; *v/t.* ~ *away* зря тра́тить; ~ing ['traɪflɪŋ] пустя́чный, пустяко́вый

trigger ['trɪgə] **1.** *mil.* спусково́й крючо́к; **2.** (*start*) дава́ть [дать] нача́ло; вызыва́ть ['-зва́ть] (В)

trill [trɪl] **1.** трель *f*; **2.** выводи́ть трель

trim [trɪm] **1.** *figure* аккура́тный, ла́дный; *garden* приведённый в поря́док; **2.** *naut.* (у́гол накло́нения су́дна) дифферент; *in good* ~ в поря́дке; **3.** *hair, etc.* подреза́ть [-е́зать], подстрига́ть [-и́чь]; *dress* отде́л(ыв)ать; *hedge* подра́внивать [-ровня́ть]; ~ming ['trɪmɪŋ] *mst.* ~s *pl.* отде́лка; *cul.* припра́ва, гарни́р

trinket ['trɪŋkɪt] безделу́шка

trip [trɪp] **1.** пое́здка; экску́рсия; **2.** *v/i.* идти́ легко́ и бы́стро; (*stumble*) спотыка́ться [споткну́ться] (*a. fig.*); *v/t.* подставля́ть подно́жку (Д)

tripartite [traɪˈpɑːtaɪt] *agreement* трёхсторо́нний; состоя́щий из трёх часте́й

tripe [traɪp] *cul.* рубе́ц

triple ['trɪpl] тройно́й; утро́енный; ~ts ['trɪplɪts] *pl.* тро́йня *sg.*

tripper ['trɪpə] *coll.* экскурса́нт

trite [traɪt] □ бана́льный, изби́тый

triumph ['traɪəmf] **1.** триу́мф; торжество́; **2.** (*be victorious*) побежда́ть [-ди́ть]; (*celebrate victory*) торжествова́ть, восторжествова́ть *pf.* (*over* над Т); ~al [traɪˈʌmfl] триумфа́льный; ~ant [traɪˈʌmfənt] победоно́сный; торжеству́ющий

trivial ['trɪvɪəl] □ ме́лкий, пустяко́вый; тривиа́льный

trod [trɒd] *pt. om* **tread**; ~**den** ['trɒdn] *pt. p. om* **tread**

trolley ['trɒlɪ] теле́жка; *Am. streetcar* трамва́й; ~**bus** тролле́йбус

trombone [trɒmˈbəʊn] *mus.* тромбо́н

troop [truːp] **1.** (*group*) гру́ппа, толпа́; **2.** дви́гаться толпо́й; ~ *away*, ~ *off* удаля́ться [-ли́ться]; *we all* ~*ed to the museum* мы всей гру́ппой пошли́ в музе́й; ~**s** *pl.* войска́ *n/pl.*

trophy ['trəʊfɪ] трофе́й

tropic ['trɒpɪk] тро́пик; ~**s** *pl.* тро́пики *m/pl.*; ~**al** □ [-pɪkəl] тропи́ческий

trot [trɒt] **1.** *of horse* рысь *f*; бы́стрый шаг; *keep s.o. on the* ~ не дава́ть кому́-л. поко́я; **2.** бежа́ть трусцо́й

trouble ['trʌbl] **1.** (*worry*) беспоко́йство; (*anxiety*) волне́ние; (*cares*) забо́ты *f/pl.*, хло́поты *f/pl.*; (*difficulties*) затрудне́ния *n/pl.*; беда́; *get into* ~ попа́сть *pf.* в беду́; *take the* ~ стара́ться, прилага́ть уси́лия; **2.** [по]беспоко́ить(ся); [по]тревожить; [по]проси́ть; утружда́ть; *don't* ~! не утружда́й(те) себя́!; ~**some** [-səm] тру́дный, причиня́ющий беспоко́йство; ~**shooter** [-ˈʃuːtə] авари́йный монтёр; уполномо́ченный по урегули́рованию конфли́ктов

troupe [truːp] *thea.* тру́ппа

trousers ['traʊzəz] *pl.* брю́ки *f/pl.*

trout [traʊt] форе́ль *f*

truant ['truːənt] *pupil* прогу́льщик; *play* ~ прогу́ливать уро́ки

truce [truːs] переми́рие

truck [trʌk] **1.** (*barrow*) теле́жка; *Am.*

(*motorvehicle*) грузови́к; *Brt. rail.* грузова́я платфо́рма; **2.** *mst. Am.* перевози́ть на грузовика́х

truculent ['trʌkjʊlənt] (*fierce*) свире́пый; (*cruel*) жесто́кий; агресси́вный

trudge [trʌdʒ] идти́ с трудо́м; таска́ться, [по]тащи́ться; *I had to ~ to the station on foot* пришло́сь тащи́ться на ста́нцию пешко́м

true [tru:] ве́рный, пра́вильный; (*real*) настоя́щий; *it is ~* э́то пра́вда; *come ~* сбы(ва́)ться; *~ to life* реалисти́ческий; (*genuine*) правди́вый; *portrait, etc.* как живо́й

truism ['tru:ɪzəm] трюи́зм

truly ['tru:lɪ] *he was ~ grateful* он был и́скренне благода́рен; *Yours ~* (*at close of letter*) пре́данный Вам

trump [trʌmp] **1.** (*card*) ко́зырь *m*; **2.** бить ко́зырной ка́ртой

trumpet ['trʌmpɪt] **1.** труба́; *blow one's own ~* расхва́ливать себя́; **2.** [за-, про]труби́ть; *fig.* раструби́ть *pf.*; *~er* [-ə] труба́ч

truncheon ['trʌntʃən] *policeman's* дуби́нка

trunk [trʌŋk] *of tree* ствол; *anat.* ту́ловище; *elephant's* хо́бот; *Am. mot.* бага́жник; (*large suitcase*) сунду́к; *pair of ~s* трусы́; *~ call tel.* вы́зов по междугоро́дному телефо́ну; *~ road* маги-стра́ль *f*

trust [trʌst] **1.** дове́рие; ве́ра; *comm.* конце́рн, трест; *on ~* на ве́ру; в креди́т; *position of ~* отве́тственное положе́ние; **2.** *v/t.* [по]ве́рить (Д); доверя́ть [-е́рить] (Д *with* В); *v/i.* полага́ться [положи́ться] (*in, to* на В); наде́яться (*in, to* на В); наде́юсь, они́ соглася́тся; *~ee* [trʌs-'ti:] опеку́н; попечи́тель *m*; довери́тельный со́бственник; *~ful* ['trʌstfl] □, *~ing* ['trʌstɪŋ] дове́рчивый; *~worthy* [-wɜː:ðɪ] заслу́живающий дове́рия; надёжный

truth [tru:θ] пра́вда; (*verity*) и́стина; *~ful* ['tru:θfl] □ *person* правди́вый; *statement, etc. a.* ве́рный

try [traɪ] **1.** (*sample*) [по]про́бовать; (*attempt*) [по]пыта́ться; [по]стара́ться;

(*tire, strain*) утомля́ть [-ми́ть]; *law* суди́ть; (*test*) испы́тывать [испыта́ть]; *~ on* примеря́ть [-е́рить]; *~ one's luck* попыта́ть *pf.* сча́стья; **2.** попы́тка; *~ing* ['traɪɪŋ] тру́дный; тяжёлый; (*annoying*) раздража́ющий

T-shirt ['ti:ʃɜːt] ма́йка (с коро́ткими рукава́ми), футбо́лка

tub [tʌb] (*barrel*) ка́дка; (*wash~*) лоха́нь *f*; *coll.* (*bath~*) ва́нна

tube [tju:b] труба́, тру́бка; *Brt.* (*subway*) метро́ *n indecl.*; *of paint, etc.* тю́бик; *inner ~ mot.* ка́мера

tuber ['tju:bə] *bot.* клу́бень *m*

tuberculosis [tju:bɜːkjʊ'ləʊsɪs] туберкулёз

tubular ['tju:bjʊlə] □ тру́бчатый

tuck [tʌk] **1.** *on dress* скла́дка, сбо́рка; **2.** де́лать скла́дки; засо́вывать [-су́-нуть]; (*hide*) [с]пря́тать; *~ in shirt* запра́вить *pf.*; *to food* упи́сывать; *~ up sleeves* засу́чивать [-чи́ть]

Tuesday ['tju:zdɪ] вто́рник

tuft [tʌft] *of grass* пучо́к; *of hair* хохо́л

tug [tʌg] **1.** (*pull*) рыво́к; *naut.* букси́р; **2.** тащи́ть [тяну́ть]; (*a. tug at*) дёргать [дёрнуть]

tuition [tju:'ɪʃn] обуче́ние

tulip ['tju:lɪp] тюльпа́н

tumble ['tʌmbl] **1.** *v/i.* (*fall*) па́дать [упа́сть]; (*overturn*) опроки́дываться [-и́нуться]; *into bed* повали́ться; *~ to* (*grasp, realize*) разгада́ть *pf.*, поня́ть *pf.*; **2.** паде́ние; *~down* полуразру́шенный; *~r* [-ə] (*glass*) стака́н

tummy ['tʌmɪ] *coll.* живо́т; *baby's* живо́тик

tumo(u)r ['tju:mə] о́пухоль *f*

tumult ['tju:mʌlt] (*uproar*) шум и кри́ки; сумато́ха; си́льное волне́ние; *~uous* [tju:'mʌltjʊəs] шу́мный, бу́йный; взволно́ванный

tuna ['tju:nə] туне́ц

tune [tju:n] **1.** мело́дия, моти́в; *in ~ piano* настро́енный; *in ~ with* сочета́ющийся, гармони́рующий; *out of ~* расстро́енный; *sing out of ~* фальши́вить; **2.** настра́ивать [-ро́ить]; (*a. ~ in*) *radio* настра́ивать (*to* на В); *~ful* ['tju:nfl] □ мелоди́чный

tunnel ['tʌnl] **1.** туннéль *m* (*a.* тоннéль *m*); **2.** проводи́ть туннéль (под Т, сквозь В)

turbid ['tɜ:bɪd] (*not clear*) му́тный; *fig.* тума́нный

turbot ['tɜ:bət] па́лтус

turbulent ['tɜ:bjʊlənt] бу́рный (*a. fig.*); *mob, etc.* бу́йный

tureen [tə'ri:n] су́пница

turf [tɜ:f] дёрн; (*peat*) торф; (*races*) ска́чки *f/pl.*; **the** ~ ипподро́м

Turk [tɜ:k] ту́рок *m*, турча́нка *f*

turkey ['tɜ:kɪ] индю́к *m*, индéйка *f*

Turkish ['tɜ:kɪʃ] **1.** туре́цкий; ~ **delight** раха́т-луку́м; **2.** туре́цкий язы́к

turmoil ['tɜ:mɔɪl] смяте́ние; волне́ние; беспоря́док

turn [tɜ:n] **1.** *v/t.* (*round*) враща́ть, верте́ть; *head, etc.* пова́рачивать [повернýть]; (*change*) превраща́ть [-рати́ть]; (*direct*) направля́ть [-ра́вить]; ~ **a corner** заверну́ть *pf.* за угол; ~ **down suggestion** отверга́ть [-éргнуть]; (*fold*) загиба́ть [загну́ть]; ~ **off** *tap* закры́(ва́)ть; *light, gas, etc.* выключа́ть [вы́ключить]; ~ **on** *tap* откры́(ва́)ть; включа́ть [-чи́ть]; ~ **out** выгоня́ть [вы́гнать]; *of job, etc.* увольня́ть [уво́лить]; *goods* выпуска́ть [вы́пустить]; ~ **over** перевёртывать [-верну́ть]; *fig.* перед(ав)а́ть; ~ **up** *collar, etc.* поднима́ть; **2.** *v/i.* враща́ться, верте́ться; пова́рачиваться [поверну́ться]; станови́ться [стать]; превраща́ться [-рати́ться]; ~ **pale, red, etc.** побледнéть *pf.*, покрасне́ть *pf.*, *и т. д.*; ~ **about** обора́чиваться [оберну́ться]; ~ **in** (*inform on*) доноси́ть [-нести́]; (*go to bed*) ложи́ться спать; ~ **out** ока́зываться [-за́ться]; ~ **to** принима́ться [-ня́ться] за (В); обраща́ться [обрати́ться] к (Д); ~ **up** появля́ться [-ви́ться]; ~ **upon** обраща́ться [обрати́ться] про́тив (Р); **3.** *su.* поворо́т; изги́б; переме́на; услу́га; *of speech* оборо́т; *coll.* (*shock*) испу́г; **at every** ~ на ка́ждом шагу́, постоя́нно; **in** ~**s** по о́череди; **it is my** ~ моя́ о́чередь *f*; **take** ~**s** де́лать поочерёдно; **in his** ~ в свою́ о́чередь; **do s.o. a good** ~ оказа́ть *pf.* кому́-л. услу́гу; ~**er** ['tɜ:nə] то́карь *m*

turning ['tɜ:nɪŋ] *of street, etc.* поворо́т; ~ **point** *fig.* поворо́тный пункт; перело́м; *fig.* кри́зис

turnip ['tɜ:nɪp] *bot.* рéпа

turn|out ['tɜ:naʊt] *econ.* вы́пуск, проду́кция; число́ уча́ствующих на собра́нии, голосова́нии, и. т. д.; ~**over** ['tɜ:nəʊvə] *comm.* оборо́т; *of goods* товарооборо́т; ~**stile** ['tɜ:nstaɪl] турнике́т

turpentine ['tɜ:pəntaɪn] скипида́р

turquoise ['tɜ:kwɔɪz] *min.* бирюза́; бирюзо́вый цвет

turret ['tʌrɪt] ба́шенка

turtle ['tɜ:tl] *zo.* черепа́ха

tusk [tʌsk] *zo.* би́вень *m*

tussle ['tʌsl] потасо́вка; дра́ка

tussock ['tʌsək] ко́чка

tutor ['tju:tə] **1.** (*private teacher*) репети́тор; *Brt. univ.* преподава́тель *m*, -ница *f*; **2.** дава́ть ча́стные уро́ки; обуча́ть [-чи́ть]; ~**ial** [tju:'tɔ:rɪəl] *univ.* консульта́ция

tuxedo [tʌk'si:dəʊ] *Am.* смо́кинг

twaddle ['twɒdl] **1.** пуста́я болтовня́; **2.** пустосло́вить

twang [twæŋ] **1.** *of guitar* звон; (*mst. nasal* ~) гнуса́вый го́лос; **2.** звене́ть

tweak [twi:k] **1.** щипо́к; **2.** ущипну́ть

tweed [twi:d] твид

tweezers ['twi:zəz] *pl.* пинцéт

twelfth [twelfθ] двена́дцатый

twelve [twelv] двена́дцать

twent|ieth ['twentɪɪθ] двадца́тый; ~**y** ['twentɪ] два́дцать

twice [twaɪs] два́жды; вдво́е; **think** ~ хорошо́ обду́мать

twiddle ['twɪdl] *in hands* верте́ть; (*play*) игра́ть (Т); ~ **one's thumbs** *fig.* безде́льничать

twig [twɪg] вéточка, прут

twilight ['twaɪlaɪt] су́мерки *f/pl.*

twin [twɪn] близне́ц; ~ **towns** города́-побрати́мы

twine [twaɪn] **1.** бечёвка, шпага́т; **2.** [с]вить; *garland* [с]плести́; *of plants* обви́(ва́)ть(ся)

twinge [twɪndʒ] при́ступ бо́ли; ~ **of**

conscience угрызе́ния со́вести *f/pl.*

twink|le ['twɪŋkl] **1.** мерца́ние, мига́ние; *of eyes* и́скорки; **2.** [за]мерца́ть; мига́ть; искри́ться; **~ling** [-ɪŋ] *in the ~ of an eye* в мгнове́ние о́ка

twirl [twɜːl] верте́ть, крути́ть

twist [twɪst] **1.** круче́ние; (~ *together*) скру́чивание; *of road, etc.* изги́б; *fig.* (*change*) поворо́т; *of ankle* вы́вих; **2.** [с]крути́ть; повора́чивать [-верну́ть], [с]ви́ться; сплета́ть(ся) [-ести́(сь)]; ~ *the facts* искажа́ть [-ази́ть] фа́кты

twit [twɪt] *coll.* болва́н

twitch [twɪtʃ] **1.** подёргивание; **2.** подёргиваться

twitter ['twɪtə] **1.** щебет; **2.** [за]щебета́ть (*a. of little girls*), чири́кать [-кнуть]; *be in a ~* дрожа́ть

two [tuː] два, две; дво́е; па́ра; *in ~* на́двое, попола́м; *put ~ and ~ together* смекну́ть в чём де́ло *pf.*; *the ~ of them* они́ о́ба; **2.** дво́йка; → *five*, в ~*s* попа́рно; ~*-faced* *fig.* двули́чный; ~*fold* ['tuːfəʊld] **1.** двойно́й; **2.** *adv.*

вдво́е; ~*pence* ['tʌpəns] два пе́нса; ~*-stor(e)y* двухэта́жный; ~*-way* двусторо́нний

type [taɪp] **1.** тип; *of wine, etc.* сорт; *typ.* шрифт; *true to ~* типи́чный; **2.** печа́тать на маши́нке; ~*writer* пи́шущая маши́нка

typhoid ['taɪfɔɪd] (*a. ~ fever*) брюшно́й тиф

typhoon [taɪ'fuːn] тайфу́н

typhus ['taɪfəs] сыпно́й тиф

typi|cal ['tɪpɪkl] типи́чный; ~*fy* [-faɪ] служи́ть типи́чным приме́ром для (P)

typist ['taɪpɪst] машини́стка; *short-hand ~* (машини́стка)-стенографи́ст(ка)

tyrann|ical [tɪ'rænɪkəl] □ тирани́ческий; ~*ize* ['tɪrənaɪz] тира́нить; ~*y* ['tɪrənɪ] тирани́я

tyrant ['taɪrənt] тира́н

tyre ['taɪə] → *tire*

tzar [zɑː] → *czar*

U

ubiquitous [juː'bɪkwɪtəs] □ вездесу́щий *a. iro.*

udder ['ʌdə] вы́мя *n*

UFO ['juːfəʊ] НЛО

ugly ['ʌglɪ] □ уро́дливый, безобра́зный (*a. fig.*); ~ *customer* ме́рзкий/ опа́сный тип

ulcer ['ʌlsə] я́зва

ulterior [ʌl'tɪərɪə]: ~ *motive* за́дняя мысль *f*

ultimate ['ʌltɪmɪt] □ после́дний; коне́чный; (*final*) оконча́тельный; ~*ly* [-lɪ] в конце́ концо́в

ultra... ['ʌltrə] *pref.* сверх..., у́льтра...

umbrage ['ʌmbrɪdʒ]: *take ~ at* обижа́ться [оби́деться] на (В)

umbrella [ʌm'brelə] зо́нтик; *telescopic ~* складно́й зо́нтик

umpire ['ʌmpaɪə] **1.** *sport* судья́ *m*, арби́тр; **2.** суди́ть

un... [ʌn] *pref.* (*придаёт отрица́тельное или противополо́жное значе́ние*) не..., без...

unable [ʌn'eɪbl] неспосо́бный; *be ~* быть не в состоя́нии, не [с]мочь

unaccountabl|e [ʌnə'kaʊntəbl] □ необъясни́мый, непостижи́мый; ~*y* [-blɪ] по непоня́тной причи́не

unaccustomed [ʌnə'kʌstəmd] не привы́кший; (*not usual*) непривы́чный

unacquainted [ʌnə'kweɪntɪd]: ~ *with* незнако́мый с (Т); не зна́ющий (Р)

unaffected [ʌnə'fektɪd] □ (*genuine*) непритво́рный, и́скренний; (*not affected*) не(за)тро́нутый (*by* Т)

unaided [ʌn'eɪdɪd] без посторо́нней по́мощи

unalterable [ʌn'ɔːltərəbl] □ неизме́нный

unanimous [juː'nænɪməs] □ единоду́шный; *in voting* единогла́сный

unanswerable [ʌnˈɑːnsərəbl] □ *argument* неопроверж́имый

unapproachable [ʌnəˈprəʊtʃəbl] □ (*physically inaccessible*) непристу́пный; *person* недосту́пный

unasked [ʌnˈɑːskt] непро́шеный; *I did this* ~ я э́то сде́лал по свое́й инициати́ве

unassisted [ʌnəˈsɪstɪd] без посторо́нней по́мощи, самостоя́тельно

unassuming [ʌnəˈsjuːmɪŋ] скро́мный, непритяза́тельный

unattractive [ʌnəˈtræktɪv] непривлека́тельный

unauthorized [ʌnˈɔːθəraɪzd] нераз-реш́ённый; *person* посторо́нний

unavail|able [ʌnəˈveɪləbl] не име́ющийся в нали́чии; отсу́тствующий; **these goods are ~ at present** э́тих това́ров сейча́с нет; ~ing [-lɪŋ] бесполе́зный

unavoidable [ʌnəˈvɔɪdəbl] неизбе́жный

unaware [ʌnəˈweə] не зна́ющий, не подозрева́ющий (*of* Р); *be ~ of* ничего́ не знать о (П); не замеча́ть [-е́тить] (P); ~s [-z]: *catch s.o.* ~ застава́ть [-ста́ть] кого́-л. враспло́х

unbalanced [ʌnˈbælənst] неуравнове́шенный (*a. mentally*)

unbearable [ʌnˈbeərəbl] невыноси́мый, нестерпи́мый

unbecoming [ʌnbɪˈkʌmɪŋ] □ (*inappropriate*) неподходя́щий; (*unseemly*) неподоба́ющий; *clothes* не иду́щий к лицу́

unbelie|f [ʌnbɪˈliːf] неве́рие; ~vable [ˈʌnbɪˈliːvəbl] невероя́тный

unbend [ʌnˈbend] [*irr.* (**bend**)] выпрямля́ть(ся) [вы́прямить(ся)]; *fig.* станови́ться непринуждённым; ~ing [-ɪŋ] □ *fig.* чи́стый; *fig.* непрекло́нный

unbias(s)ed [ʌnˈbaɪəst] □ беспристра́стный

unbind [ʌnˈbaɪnd] [*irr.* (**bind**)] развя́зывать [-за́ть]

unblemished [ʌnˈblemɪʃt] чи́стый; *fig.* незапя́тнанный

unblushing [ʌnˈblʌʃɪŋ] безза-сте́нчивый

unbolt [ʌnˈbəʊlt] отпира́ть [-пере́ть]

unbounded [ʌnˈbaʊndɪd] □ неограни́ченный; беспреде́льный

unbroken [ʌnˈbrəʊkn] (*whole*) неразби́тый; *record* непоби́тый; (*uninterrupted*) непреры́вный

unburden [ʌnˈbɜːdn]: ~ **o.s.** излива́ть [-ли́ть] ду́шу

unbutton [ʌnˈbʌtn] расстёгивать [расстегну́ть]

uncalled-for [ʌnˈkɔːldfɔː] непро́шеный; неуме́стный

uncanny [ʌnˈkænɪ] □ сверхъесте́ственный; жу́ткий, пуга́ющий

uncared [ʌnˈkeəd]: ~**for** забро́шенный

unceasing [ʌnˈsiːsɪŋ] □ непрекраща́ющийся, беспреры́вный

unceremonious [ʌnserɪˈməʊnɪəs] бесцеремо́нный

uncertain [ʌnˈsɜːtn] неуве́ренный; *plans, etc.* неопределённый; неизве́стный; *it is* ~ *whether he will be there* неизве́стно, бу́дет ли он там; ~ *weather* переме́нчивая пого́да; ~ty [-tɪ] неуве́ренность *f*; неизве́стность *f*; неопределённость *f*

unchanging [ʌnˈtʃeɪndʒɪŋ] □ неизме́нный

uncharitable [ʌnˈtʃærɪtəbl] □ немилосе́рдный; ~ *words* жесто́кие слова́

unchecked [ʌnˈtʃekt] беспрепя́тственный; (*not verified*) непрове́ренный

uncivil [ʌnˈsɪvl] неве́жливый; ~ized [ʌnˈsɪvɪlaɪzd] нецивилизо́ванный

uncle [ˈʌŋkl] дя́дя *m*

unclean [ʌnˈkliːn] □ нечи́стый

uncomfortable [ʌnˈkʌmfətəbl] неудо́бный; *fig.* нело́вкий

uncommon [ʌnˈkɒmən] □ (*remarkable*) необыкнове́нный; (*unusual*) необы́чный; (*rare*) ре́дкий

uncommunicative [ʌnkəˈmjuːnɪkətɪv] неразгово́рчивый, сде́ржанный; скры́тный

uncomplaining [ʌnkəmˈpleɪnɪŋ] безро́потный

uncompromising [ʌnˈkɒmprəmaɪzɪŋ] □ бескомпроми́ссный

unconcerned [ʌnkənˈsɜːnd]: **be ~ about** относи́ться равноду́шно, безразли́чно (к Д)

unconditional [ʌnkənˈdɪʃənl] □ безоговоро́чный, безусло́вный

unconquerable [ʌnˈkɒŋkrəbl] □ непобеди́мый

unconscious [ʌnˈkɒnʃəs] □ (*not intentional*) бессозна́тельный; потеря́вший созна́ние; **be ~ of** не созна(ва́)ть P; **the ~** подсозна́ние; ~ness [-nɪs] бессозна́тельное состоя́ние

unconstitutional [ʌnkɒnstɪˈtjuːʃnl] □ противоре́чащий конститу́ции; неконституцио́нный

uncontrollable [ʌnkənˈtrəʊləbl] □ неудержи́мый; неуправля́емый

unconventional [ʌnkənˈvenʃənl] □ (*free in one's ways*) чу́ждый усло́вности; (*unusual*) необы́чный, эксцентри́чный; (*original*) нешабло́нный

uncork [ʌnˈkɔːk] отку́пори(ва)ть

uncount|able [ʌnˈkaʊntəbl] бесчи́сленный; ~ed [-tɪd] несчётный

uncouth [ʌnˈkuːθ] (*rough*) грубый

uncover [ʌnˈkʌvə] *face, etc.* откры(ва́)ть; снима́ть кры́шку с (P); *head* обнажа́ть [-жи́ть]; *fig. plot, etc.* раскрыва́ть [-ы́ть]

uncult|ivated [ʌnˈkʌltɪveɪtɪd] *land* невозде́ланный; *plant* ди́кий; *person* неразвито́й; некульту́рный

undamaged [ʌnˈdæmɪdʒd] неповреждённый

undaunted [ʌnˈdɔːntɪd] □ (*fearless*) неустраши́мый

undecided [ʌndɪˈsaɪdɪd] □ нереши́нный; (*in doubt*) нереши́тельный

undeniable [ʌndɪˈnaɪəbl] □ неоспори́мый; несомне́нный

under [ˈʌndə] **1.** *adv.* ни́же; внизу́; вниз; **2.** *prp.* под (В, Т); ни́же (P); ме́ньше (P); при (П); **3.** *pref.* ни́же..., под..., недо...; **4.** ни́жний; ни́зший; ~**bid** [ʌndəˈbɪd] [*irr.* (**bid**)] предлага́ть бо́лее ни́зкую це́ну, чем (И); ~**brush** [-brʌʃ] подле́сок; ~**carriage** [-kærɪdʒ] шасси́ *n indecl.*; ~**clothing** [-kləʊðɪŋ]

ни́жнее бельё; ~**cut** [-kʌt] сбива́ть це́ну; ~**done** [ʌndəˈdʌn] недожа́ренный; *cake* непропечённый; ~**estimate** [ʌndərˈestɪmeɪt] недооце́нивать [-и́ть]; ~**fed** [-fed] недоко́рмленный, истощённый от недоеда́ния; ~**go** [ʌndəˈɡəʊ], *irr.* (**go**)] испы́тывать [испыта́ть]; *criticism, etc.* подверга́ться [-е́ргнуться] (Д); ~**graduate** [ʌndəˈɡrædʒʊət] студе́нт *m*, -ка *f*; ~**ground** [-ɡraʊnd] **1.** подзе́мный; *pol.* подпо́льный; **2.** метро́(полите́н) *n indecl.*; (*movement*) подпо́лье; ~**hand** [ʌndəˈhænd] **1.** та́йный, закули́сный; **2.** *adv.* тайно, за спино́й; ~**lie** [ʌndəˈlaɪ], *irr.* (**lie**)] лежа́ть в осно́ве (P); ~**line** [ʌndəˈlaɪn] подчёркивать [-черкну́ть]; ~**mine** [ʌndəˈmaɪn] подрыва́ть [подорва́ть]; ~**neath** [ʌndəˈniːθ] **1.** *prp.* под (Т/В); **2.** *adv.* вниз, внизу́; ~**rate** [ʌndəˈreɪt] недооце́нивать [-и́ть]; ~**secretary** [ʌndəˈsekrətrɪ] замести́тель *m*, помо́щник мини́стра (в А́нглии и США); ~**signed** [ʌndəˈsaɪnd] нижеподписа́вшийся; ~**stand** [ʌndəˈstænd], *irr.* (**stand**)] *com.* понима́ть [поня́ть]; подразумева́ть (*by* под Т); **make o.s. understood** уме́ть объясни́ться; (*make o.s. responsible for*) брать на себя́; обя́зываться (-за́ться); ~**standable** [ʌndəˈstændəbl] поня́тный; ~**standing** [ʌndəˈstændɪŋ] понима́ние; взаимопонима́ние; (*agreement*) договорённость *f*; **come to an ~** договори́ться *pf.*; ~**state** [ʌndəˈsteɪt] преуменьша́ть [-ме́ньшить]; ~**stood** [ʌndəˈstʊd] *pt. и pt. p. om* **understand**; ~**take** [ʌndəˈteɪk] [*irr.* (**take**)] предпринима́ть [-ня́ть]; (*make o.s. responsible for*) брать на себя́; обя́зываться (-за́ться); ~**taker** [-teɪkə] содержа́тель *m* похоро́нного бюро́; ~**taking** [ʌndəˈteɪkɪŋ] предприя́тие; ~**tone** [-təʊn]: *in an ~* вполго́лоса; ~**value** [ʌndəˈvæljuː] недооце́нивать [-и́ть]; ~**wear** [-weə] ни́жнее бельё; ~**write** [ʌndəˈraɪt] [*irr.* (**write**)] [за]страхова́ть; ~**writer** [-raɪtə] поручи́тель-гара́нт; страхова́тель *m*

undeserved [ʌndɪˈzɜːvd] □ незаслу́женный

undesirable [ʌndɪˈzaɪərəbl] □ неже-

u

ла́тельный; *moment, etc.* неудо́бный, неподходя́щий

undisciplined [ʌnˈdɪsɪplɪnd] недисципли́ни́рованный

undiscriminating [ʌndɪsˈkrɪmɪneɪtɪŋ] неразбо́рчивый

undisguised [ʌndɪsˈgaɪzd] □ откры́тый, я́вный; незамаскиро́ванный

undivided [ʌndɪˈvaɪdɪd] неразделённый; *attention* по́лный

undo [ʌnˈduː] [*irr.* (**do**)] *string, etc.* развя́зывать [-за́ть]; *buttons, zip* расстёгивать [расстегну́ть]; (*destroy*) погуби́ть *pf.*; **~ing** [-ɪŋ]: *that was my ~* э́то погуби́ло меня́

undoubted [ʌnˈdaʊtɪd] несомне́нный, беспо́рный

undreamed-of, **undreamt-of** [ʌnˈdremtɒv] невообрази́мый, неожи́данный

undress [ʌnˈdres] раздева́ть(ся); **~ed** [-st] неоде́тый

undue [ʌnˈdjuː] □ (*excessive*) чрезме́рный

undulating [ˈʌndjʊleɪtɪŋ] *geogr.* холми́стый

unduly [ʌnˈdjuːlɪ] чересчу́р, чрезме́рно

unearth [ʌnˈɜːθ] вырыва́ть из земли́; *fig.* (*discover*) раска́пывать [-копа́ть]; **~ly** [ʌnˈɜːθlɪ] (*not terrestrial*) неземно́й; (*supernatural*) сверхъесте́ственный; (*weird*) стра́нный; *time* чересчу́р ра́нний (час)

uneas|iness [ʌnˈiːzɪnɪs] беспоко́йство, трево́га; **~y** [ʌnˈiːzɪ] □ беспоко́йный, трево́жный

uneducated [ʌnˈedjʊkeɪtɪd] необразо́ванный

unemotional [ʌnɪˈməʊʃənl] бесстра́стный; неэмоциона́льный

unemploy|ed [ʌnɪmˈplɔɪd] безрабо́тный; **~ment** [-mənt] безрабо́тица

unending [ʌnˈendɪŋ] □ несконча́емый, бесконе́чный

unendurable [ʌnɪnˈdjʊərəbl] нестерпи́мый

unequal [ʌnˈiːkwəl] □ нера́вный; *length, weight* разли́чный; *be ~ to* не в си́лах; *task, etc.* не по плечу́;

~led [-d] непревзойдённый

unerring [ʌnˈɜːrɪŋ] безоши́бочный

uneven [ʌnˈiːvn] □ неро́вный; *temper* неуравнове́шенный

uneventful [ʌnɪˈventfl] □ без осо́бых собы́тий/приключе́ний

unexpected [ʌnɪksˈpektɪd] □ неожи́данный

unexposed [ʌnɪkˈspəʊzd] *film* неэкспони́рованный

unfailing [ʌnˈfeɪlɪŋ] □ ве́рный, надёжный; *interest* неизме́нный; *patience, etc.* неистощи́мый, беспреде́льный

unfair [ʌnˈfeə] □ несправедли́вый; *play, etc.* нече́стный

unfaithful [ʌnˈfeɪθfl] □ неве́рный; (*violating trust*) вероло́мный; *to the original* нето́чный

unfamiliar [ʌnfəˈmɪlɪə] незнако́мый; *surroundings* непривы́чный

unfasten [ʌnˈfɑːsn] *door* открыва́ть [-ы́ть]; *buttons, etc.* расстёгивать [расстегну́ть]; *knot* развя́зывать [-за́ть]; **~ed** [-d] расстёгнутый; *door* неза́пертый

unfavo(u)rable [ʌnˈfeɪvərəbl] □ неблагоприя́тный; *reports, etc.* отрица́тельный

unfeeling [ʌnˈfiːlɪŋ] □ бесчу́вственный

unfinished [ʌnˈfɪnɪʃt] незако́нченный

unfit [ʌnˈfɪt] него́дный, неподходя́щий; *~ for service* него́ден к вое́нной слу́жбе

unflagging [ʌnˈflægɪŋ] неослабева́ющий

unfold [ʌnˈfəʊld] развёртывать(ся) [-верну́ть(ся)]; *plans, secret, etc.* раскры́(ва́)ть

unforeseen [ʌnfɔːˈsiːn] непредви́денный

unforgettable [ʌnfəˈgetəbl] □ незабыва́емый

unfortunate [ʌnˈfɔːtʃənɪt] несча́стный; неуда́чный; (*unlucky*) неуда́чливый; **~ly** [-lɪ] к несча́стью; к сожале́нию

unfounded [ʌnˈfaʊndɪd] необосно́-

ванный

unfriendly [ʌn'frendlɪ] недружелю́бный; непривéтливый

unfruitful [ʌn'fruːtfl] □ неплодоро́дный; *fig.* беспло́дный

unfurl [ʌn'fɜːl] развёртывать [разверну́ть]

ungainly [ʌn'geɪnlɪ] нескла́дный

ungodly [ʌn'ɡɒdlɪ]: нечести́вый; *he woke us up at an ~ hour* он разбуди́л нас безбо́жно ра́но

ungovernable [ʌn'ɡʌvənəbl] □ неуправля́емый; *temper, etc.* неукроти́мый, необу́зданный

ungracious [ʌn'ɡreɪʃəs] □ *(not polite)* невéжливый

ungrateful [ʌn'ɡreɪtfl] □ неблагода́рный

unguarded [ʌn'ɡɑːdɪd] □ неохраня́емый, незащищённый; *fig.* неосторо́жный

unhampered [ʌn'hæmpəd] беспрепя́тственный

unhappy [ʌn'hæpɪ] □ несча́стный

unharmed [ʌn'hɑːmd] *thing* неповреждённый; *person* невреди́мый

unhealthy [ʌn'helθɪ] □ нездоро́вый, болéзненный; *coll. (harmful)* врéдный

unheard-of [ʌn'hɜːdɒv] неслы́ханный

unhesitating [ʌn'hezɪteɪtɪŋ] □ реши́тельный; **~ly** [-lɪ] не колéблясь

unholy [ʌn'həʊlɪ] поро́чный; *coll.* жу́ткий, ужа́сный

unhoped-for [ʌn'həʊptfɔː] неожи́данный

unhurt [ʌn'hɜːt] невреди́мый, цéлый

uniform ['juːnɪfɔːm] **1.** □ одина́ковый; *(alike all over)* единообра́зный, одноро́дный; **2.** фо́рма, фо́рменная одéжда; **~ity** [juːnɪ'fɔːmətɪ] единообра́зие, одноро́дность *f*

unify ['juːnɪfaɪ] объединя́ть [-ни́ть]; унифици́ровать *(im)pf.*

unilateral [juːnɪ'lætrəl] односторо́нний

unimaginable [ʌnɪ'mædʒɪnəbl] □ невообрази́мый

unimportant [ʌnɪm'pɔːtənt] □ нева́жный

uninhabit|able [ʌnɪn'hæbɪtəbl] непри́го́дный для жилья́; **~ed** [-tɪd] *house* нежило́й; необита́емый

uninjured [ʌn'ɪndʒəd] непострада́вший; невреди́мый

unintelligible [ʌnɪn'telɪdʒəbl] □ непоня́тный; *hand writing* неразбо́рчивый, нево́льный

unintentional [ʌnɪn'tenʃənl] □ ненамéренный, неумы́шленный

uninteresting [ʌn'ɪntrəstɪŋ] □ неинтерéсный

uninterrupted [ʌnɪntə'rʌptɪd] □ непреры́вный, беспреры́вный

uninvited [ʌnɪn'vaɪtɪd] неприглашённый; *pej.* незва́ный; *come* ~ прийти́ *pf.* без приглашéния; **~ing** [-tɪŋ] непривлека́тельный; *food* неаппети́тный

union ['juːnɪən] союз; *(trade ~)* профсою́з; 2 **Jack** брита́нский национа́льный флаг

unique ['juːniːk] еди́нственный в своём ро́де, уника́льный

unison ['juːnɪzn] унисо́н; гармо́ния; в по́лном согла́сии; *act in* ~ дéйствовать сла́женно

unit ['juːnɪt] *mil.* часть *f*, подразделéние; *math.* едини́ца; *tech.* агрега́т; ~ *furniture* секцио́нная мéбель; **~e** [juː'naɪt] *in marriage* сочета́ть у́зами бра́ка; соединя́ть(ся) [-ни́ть(ся)]; объединя́ть(ся) [-ни́ть(ся)]; **~y** ['juːnətɪ] еди́нство

univers|al [juːnɪ'vɜːsl] □ *agreement, etc.* всео́бщий; всеми́рный; *mst. tech.* универса́льный; **~e** ['juːnɪvɜːs] мир, вселéнная; **~ity** [juːnɪ'vɜːsətɪ] университéт

unjust [ʌn'dʒʌst] □ несправедли́вый; **~ified** [ʌn'dʒʌstɪfaɪd] неопра́вданный

unkempt [ʌn'kempt] *(untidy)* беспоря́дочный; неопря́тный; *hair* растрёпанный

unkind [ʌn'kaɪnd] □ недо́брый

unknown [ʌn'nəʊn] неизвéстный; **~ to me** *adv.* без моего́ вéдома

unlace [ʌn'leɪs] расшнуро́вывать [-ова́ть]

U

unlawful [ʌn'lɔːfl] □ незако́нный

unless [ən'les, ʌn'les] *cj.* е́сли не

unlike [ʌn'laɪk] **1.** непохо́жий на (B); *it's quite ~ her* э́то совсе́м на неё не похо́же; **2.** *prp.* в отли́чие от (P); **~ly** [ʌn'laɪklɪ] неправдоподо́бный, невероя́тный; маловероя́тный; *his arrival today is ~* маловероя́тно, что он прие́дет сего́дня

unlimited [ʌn'lɪmɪtɪd] неограни́ченный

unload [ʌn'ləʊd] выгружа́ть [вы́грузить], разгружа́ть [-узи́ть]; *mil. a weapon* разряжа́ть [-яди́ть]

unlock [ʌn'lɒk] отпира́ть [отпере́ть]; **~ed** [-t] неза́пертый

unlooked-for [ʌn'lʊktfɔː] неожи́данный, непредви́денный

unlucky [ʌn'lʌkɪ] □ неуда́чный, несчастли́вый; *I was ~* мне не повезло́; *be ~* (*bring ill-luck*) приноси́ть несча́стье

unmanageable [ʌn'mænɪdʒəbl] □ неуправля́емый; *child, problem* тру́дный

unmanly [ʌn'mænlɪ] нему́жественный; не по-мужски́; трусли́вый

unmarried [ʌn'mærɪd] нежена́тый, холосто́й; *woman* незаму́жняя

unmask [ʌn'mɑːsk] *fig.* разоблача́ть [-чи́ть]

unmatched [ʌn'mætʃt] не име́ющий себе́ ра́вного, непревзойдённый

unmerciful [ʌn'mɜːsɪfl] безжа́лостный

unmerited [ʌn'merɪtɪd] незаслу́женный

unmistakable [ʌnmɪs'teɪkəbl] □ ве́рный, очеви́дный; несомне́нный; (*clearly recognizable*) легко́ узнава́емый

unmitigated [ʌn'mɪtɪgeɪtɪd] несмягчённый; *fig.* отъя́вленный, по́лный, абсолю́тный

unmoved [ʌn'muːvd] оста́вшийся равноду́шным; бесчу́вственный; *he was ~ by her tears* её слёзы не тро́нули его́

unnatural [ʌn'nætʃrəl] □ неесте́ственный; (*contrary to nature*) противоесте́ственный

unnecessary [ʌn'nesəsrɪ] □ нену́жный, ли́шний; (*excessive*) изли́шний

unnerve [ʌn'nɜːv] обесси́ливать; лиша́ть прису́тствия ду́ха, реши́мости

unnoticed [ʌn'nəʊtɪst] незаме́ченный

unobserved [ʌnəb'zɜːvd] незаме́ченный

unobtainable [ʌnəb'teɪnəbl]: *~ thing* недосту́пная вещь *f*

unobtrusive [ʌnəb'truːsɪv] ненавя́зчивый

unoccupied [ʌn'ɒkjʊpaɪd] неза́нятый

unoffending [ʌnə'fendɪŋ] безоби́дный

unofficial [ʌnə'fɪʃl] неофициа́льный

unopened [ʌn'əʊpənd] неоткры́тый; *letter* нераспеча́танный

unopposed [ʌnə'pəʊzd] не встреча́ющий сопротивле́ния

unpack [ʌn'pæk] распако́вывать [-ова́ть]

unpaid [ʌn'peɪd] *debt* неупла́ченный; *work* неопла́ченный

unparalleled [ʌn'pærəleld] беспримéрный; *success, kindness* необыкнове́нный

unpardonable [ʌn'pɑːdənəbl] □ непрости́тельный

unperturbed [ʌnpə'tɜːbd] невозмути́мый

unpleasant [ʌn'pleznt] □ неприя́тный; **~ness** [-nɪs] неприя́тность *f*

unpopular [ʌn'pɒpjʊlə] непопуля́рный; *make o.s. ~* лиша́ть [-ши́ть] себя́ популя́рности

unpractical [ʌn'præktɪkəl] непракти́чный

unprecedented [ʌn'presɪdəntɪd] □ беспрецеде́нтный; *courage* беспримéрный

unprejudiced [ʌn'predʒʊdɪst] □ непредубеждённый; непредвзя́тый

unprepared [ʌnprɪ'peəd] неподгото́вленный; без подгото́вки

unpretentious [ʌnprɪ'tenʃəs] □ скро́мный, без прете́нзий

unprincipled [ʌn'prɪnsəpld] беспринци́пный

U

цийпный

unprofitable [ʌn'prɒfɪtəbl] невы́год-
ный; *enterprise* нерента́бельный

unpromising [ʌn'prɒmɪsɪŋ] малообе-
ща́ющий; *the crops look ~* вряд ли
бу́дет хоро́ший урожа́й

unproved [ʌn'pru:vd] недока́занный

unprovoked [ʌnprə'vəʊkt] неспрово-
ци́рованный

unqualified [ʌn'kwɒlɪfaɪd] неквали-
фици́рованный; некомпете́нтный;
denial, etc. безоговоро́чный; *success,
etc.* реши́тельный; безграни́чный

unquestionable [ʌn'kwestʃənəbl] не-
сомне́нный, неоспори́мый

unravel [ʌn'rævəl] распу́т(ыв)ать (*a.
fig.*); (*solve*) разга́дывать [-да́ть]

unreal [ʌn'rɪəl] нереа́льный

unreasonable [ʌn'ri:znəbl] □ не(благо)разу́мный; безрассу́дный; *price,
etc.* чрезме́рный

unrecognizable [ʌn'rekəgnaɪzəbl] □
неузнава́емый

unrelated [ʌnrɪ'leɪtɪd] *people* не
ро́дственники; *ideas, facts, etc.* не
име́ющий отноше́ния; не свя́занные
(ме́жду собо́й)

unrelenting [ʌnrɪ'lentɪŋ] □ неумоли́-
мый; *it was a week of ~ activity* всю
неде́лю мы рабо́тали без переды́ш-
ки

unreliable [ʌnrɪ'laɪəbl] ненадёжный

unrelieved [ʌnrɪ'li:vd] ~ *boredom* не-
облегчённая ску́ка; ~ *sadness* неиз-
бы́вная грусть *f*

unremitting [ʌnrɪ'mɪtɪŋ] □ беспре-
ры́вный; *pain, etc.* неослабева́ющий

unreserved [ʌnrɪ'zɜ:vd] □ *seat, etc.*
незаброни́рованный; *support, etc.*
безоговоро́чный

unrest [ʌn'rest] *social, political* волне́-
ния, беспоря́дки; (*disquiet*) беспо-
ко́йство

unrestrained [ʌnrɪs'treɪnd] □ *behavi-
o(u)r* несде́ржанный; *anger, etc.* не-
обу́зданный

unrestricted [ʌnrɪs'trɪktɪd] неогра-
ни́ченный

unrewarding [ʌnrɪ'wɔ:dɪŋ] неблаго-
да́рный

unripe [ʌn'raɪp] незре́лый, неспе́лый

unrival(l)ed [ʌn'raɪvld] непревзойдённый; не име́ющий сопе́рников

unroll [ʌn'rəʊl] развёртывать [-вер-
ну́ть]

unruffled [ʌn'rʌfld] *sea, etc.* гла́дкий;
person невозмути́мый

unruly [ʌn'ru:lɪ] непослу́шный; непо-
ко́рный; бу́йный

unsafe [ʌn'seɪf] □ (*not dependable*)
ненадёжный; (*dangerous*) опа́сный

unsal(e)able [ʌn'seɪləbl] *goods* нехо́д-
кий

unsanitary [ʌn'sænɪtərɪ] антисани-
та́рный

unsatisfactory [ʌnsætɪs'fæktərɪ] □
неудовлетвори́тельный

unsavo(u)ry [ʌn'seɪvərɪ] невку́сный;
неприя́тный; (*offensive*) отврати́-
тельный

unscathed [ʌn'skeɪðd] невреди́мый

unscrew [ʌn'skru:] отви́нчивать(-ся)
[-нти́ть(ся)]; выви́нчивать [-вер-
ну́ть]

unscrupulous [ʌn'skru:pjʊləs] □ бес-
принци́пный; неразбо́рчивый в
сре́дствах

unseasonable [ʌn'si:zənəbl] □ (*ill-
-timed*) несвоевре́менный; не по се-
зо́ну

unseemly [ʌn'si:mlɪ] неподоба́ющий;
(*indecent*) непристо́йный

unseen [ʌn'si:n] (*invisible*) неви́ди-
мый; (*not seen*) неви́данный

unselfish [ʌn'selfɪʃ] □ бескоры́стный

unsettle [ʌn'setl] *person* расстра́и-
вать [-ро́ить]; ~d [-d] *weather* не-
усто́йчивый; *problem, etc.* нерешён-
ный; *bill* неопла́ченный

unshaken [ʌn'ʃeɪkən] непоколеби́-
мый

unshaven [ʌn'ʃeɪvn] небри́тый

unshrinkable [ʌn'ʃrɪŋkəbl] безуса́-
дочный

unsightly [ʌn'saɪtlɪ] непригля́дный

unskil(l)**ful** [ʌn'skɪlfl] □ неуме́лый,
неиску́сный; ~ed [ʌn'skɪld] неквали-
фици́рованный

unsociable [ʌn'səʊʃəbl] необщи́тель-
ный

U

unsolicited [ʌnsə'lɪsɪtɪd] непрóшенный

unsophisticated [ʌnsə'fɪstɪkeɪtɪd] безыскýсный, бесхúтростный; простóй, простодýшный

unsound [ʌn'saʊnd] □ *health* нездорóвый; *views* не(достáточно) обоснóванный; *judg(e)ment* шáткий; лишённый прóчности

unsparing [ʌn'speərɪŋ] □ (*unmerciful*) беспощáдный; (*profuse*) щéдрый; ~ **efforts** неустáнные усилия

unspeakable [ʌn'spiːkəbl] □ невыразúмый; (*terrible*) ужáсный

unstable [ʌn'steɪbl] □ неустóйчивый; *phys., chem.* нестóйкий

unsteady [ʌn'stedɪ] □ → **unstable**; *hand* трясýщийся; *steps* нетвёрдый; шáткий; непостоянный

unstudied [ʌn'stʌdɪd] невыýченный; естéственный, непринуждённы

unsuccessful [ʌnsək'sesfl] □ неудáчный, безуспéшный; неудáчливый

unsuitable [ʌn'suːtəbl] □ неподходящий

unsurpassed [ʌnsə'pɑːst] непревзойдённый

unsuspect|ed [ʌnsəs'pektɪd] □ неожúданный; **~ing** [-ɪŋ] неподозревáемый (**of** о П)

unsuspicious [ʌnsə'sprɪʃəs] □ *person* неподозревáющий; довéрчивый

unswerving [ʌn'swɜːvɪŋ] □ неуклóнный

untangle [ʌn'tæŋgl] распýт(ыв)ать

untarnished [ʌn'tɑːnɪʃt] *reputation* незапятнанный

untenable [ʌn'tenəbl] *theory etc.* несостоятельный

unthink|able [ʌn'θɪŋkəbl] немыслимый; **~ing** [-ɪŋ] □ бездýмный; опромéтчивый

untidy [ʌn'taɪdɪ] □ неопрятный, неаккурáтный; *room* неýбранный

untie [ʌn'taɪ] развязывать [-зáть]; *one thing from another* отвязывать [-зáть]

until [ən'tɪl] **1.** *prp.* до (Р); *not* ~ *Sunday* не рáнее воскресéнья; **2.** *cj.* (до тех пор) покá … (не) …

untimely [ʌn'taɪmlɪ] несвоеврéменный; ~ *death* безврéменная кончúна

untiring [ʌn'taɪərɪŋ] □ неутомúмый

untold [ʌn'təʊld] (*not told*) нерассказанный; (*incalculable*) несмéтный, несчётный

untouched [ʌn'tʌtʃt] нетрóнутый

untroubled [ʌn'trʌbld]: необеспокóенный; ~ *life* безмятéжная жизнь f

untrue [ʌn'truː] □ невéрный; *this is* ~ это непрáвда

untrustworthy [ʌn'trʌstwɜːðɪ] не заслýживающий довéрия

unus|ed 1. [ʌn'juːzd] (*new*) не бывший в употреблéнии; (*not used*) неиспóльзованный; **2.** [ʌn'juːst] непривыкший (**to** к Д); **~ual** [ʌn'juːʒʊəl] □ необыкновéнный, необычный

unvarnished [ʌn'vɑːnɪʃt] *fig.* неприкрáшенный

unvarying [ʌn'veərɪŋ] □ неизменяющийся, неизмéнный

unveil [ʌn'veɪl] *statute, monument* открыв(á)ть

unwanted [ʌn'wɒntɪd] *child* нежелáнный; ненýжный

unwarranted [ʌn'wɒrəntɪd] □ неразрешённый, неоправданный; *criticism, etc.* незаслýженный

unwavering [ʌn'weɪvərɪŋ] □ непоколебúмый; ~ *look* прúстальный взгляд

unwell [ʌn'wel] □ нездорóвый; *he is* ~ ему нездорóвится; *feel* ~ невáжно (плóхо) себя чýвствовать

unwholesome [ʌn'həʊlsəm] неблаготвóрный; (*harmful*) врéдный

unwieldy [ʌn'wiːldɪ] □ *carton, etc.* громóздкий

unwilling [ʌn'wɪlɪŋ] □ несклóнный, нежелáющий; нерасполóженный; *be* ~ *to do s.th.* не хотéть чтó-то сдéлать

unwise [ʌn'waɪz] □ неразýмный

unwittingly [ʌn'wɪtɪŋlɪ] невóльно, непреднамéренно

unworthy [ʌn'wɜːðɪ] □ недостóйный

unwrap [ʌn'ræp] развёртывать(ся) [-вернýть(ся)]

U

unyielding [ʌnˈjiːldɪŋ] □ неподатливый, неуступчивый

unzip [ʌnˈzɪp] расстёгивать [-егнуть]; *come ~ped* расстегнуться *pf.*

up [ʌp] **1.** *adv.* вверх, наверх, наверху; выше; *fig.* **be ~ to the mark** быть в форме, на высоте; **be ~ against a task** стоять перед задачей; **~ to** вплоть до (P); **it is ~ to me (to do)** мне приходится (делать); **what's ~?** *coll.* что случилось?, в чём дело?; **what is he ~ to?** чем он занимается?; **2.** *prp.* вверх по (Д); по направлению к (Д); **~ the river** вверх по реке; **3.** *su.* the **~s and downs** *fig.* превратности судьбы; **4.** *vb. coll.* поднимать [-нять]; *prices* повышать [-ысить]

up|braid [ʌpˈbreɪd] [вы]бранить; **~bringing** [ˈʌpbrɪŋɪŋ] воспитание; **~date** [ʌpˈdeɪt] модернизировать; *person* держать в курсе дела; **~heaval** [ʌpˈhiːvl] earthquake, etc. сдвиг; *fig.* глубокие (революционные) перемены; **~hill** [ʌpˈhɪl] (идущий) в гору; *fig.* тяжёлый; **~hold** [ʌpˈhəʊld] *irr.* support поддерживать [-жать]; **~holster** [ʌpˈhəʊlstə] оби(ва́)ть; **~holstery** [-stərɪ] обивка

up|keep [ˈʌpkiːp] содержание; *cost* стоимость *f* содержания; **~lift 1.** [ˈʌplɪft] душевный подъём; **2.** [ʌpˈlɪft] поднимать [-нять]

upon [əˈpɒn] → **on**

upper [ˈʌpə] верхний; высший; *gain* the **~ hand** одержи́вать [одержа́ть] верх (над Т); **~most** [-məʊst] самый верхний; наивысший; **be ~ in one's mind** стоять на первом месте, быть главным

uppish [ˈʌpɪʃ] *coll.* надменный

upright [ˈʌpraɪt] □ прямой (*a. fig.*), вертикальный; *adv. a.* стоймя; **~ piano** пианино *n indecl.*

up|rising [ˈʌpraɪzɪŋ] восстание; **~roar** [ˈʌprɔː] шум, *coll.* гам; **~roarious** [ʌpˈrɔːrɪəs] □ (*noisy*) шумный; (*funny*) ужасно смешной

up|root [ʌpˈruːt] вырывать с корнем; *fig.* **I don't want to ~ myself again** я не хочу снова переезжать; **~set** [ʌpˈset]

[*irr.* (**set**)] (*knock over*) опрокидывать(ся) [-инуть(ся)]; *person, plans, etc.* расстраивать [-ро́ить]; **~shot** [ˈʌpʃɒt] итог, результат; **the ~ of it was that ...** кончилось тем, что ...; **~side: ~ down** [ʌpsaɪdˈdaʊn] вверх дном; **~stairs** [ʌpˈsteəz] вверх (по лестнице), наверх(у); **~start** [ˈʌpstɑːt] выскочка *m/f;* **~stream** [ʌpˈstriːm] вверх по течению; **~to-date** [ʌptəˈdeɪt] современный; **bring s.o. ~** вводить [ввести] кого́л. в курс дела; **~turn** [ʌpˈtɜːn] сдвиг к лучшему; улучшение; **~ward(s)** [ˈʌpwədz] вверх, наверх; **~ of** свыше, больше

urban [ˈɜːbən] городской; **~e** [ɜːbˈeɪn] вежливый; (*refined*) изысканный; (*suave*) обходительный

urchin [ˈɜːtʃɪn] мальчишка *m*

urge [ɜːdʒ] **1.** (*try to persuade*) убеждать [-едить]; подгонять [подогнать], (*often ~ on*) **2.** стремление, желание, толчок *fig.;* **~ncy** [ˈɜːdʒənsɪ] (*need*) настоятельность *f;* (*haste*) срочность *f;* настойчивость *f;* **~nt** [ˈɜːdʒənt] □ срочный; настоятельный, настойчивый

urin|al [ˈjʊərɪnl] писсуар; **~ate** [-rɪneɪt] [по]мочиться; **~e** [-rɪn] моча

urn [ɜːn] урна

us [əs, ... ʌs] *pers. pron.* (*косвенный падеж от* **we**) нас, нам, нами

usage [ˈjuːzɪdʒ] употребление; (*custom*) обычай

use 1. [juːs] употребление; применение; пользование; (*usefulness*) польза; (*habit*) привычка; (*of*) *no ~* бесполезный; **come into ~** войти в употребление; **for general ~** для общего пользования; **what's the ~ ...?** какой смысл ...?, что толку ...?; **2.** [juːz] употреблять [-бить]; **~ up** использовать (Т); воспользоваться (Т) *pf.;* использовать (*im*)*pf.;* (*treat*) обращаться с (Т), обходиться [обойтись] с (Т); *I* **~d to do, был, бывало, часто делал; be ~d to** привыкший к (Д); **~ful** [ˈjuːsfl] □ полезный; пригодный; **come in ~** пригодиться; **~less** [ˈjuːslɪs] □ бесполезный; непригодный, не-

U

го́дный; ~r ['juːzə] по́льзователь *m*; (*customer*) потреби́тель *m*; *of library, etc.* чита́тель *m*

usher ['ʌʃə] (*conduct*) проводи́ть [-вести́]; (~ *in*) вводи́ть [ввести́]; ~ette [-'ret] билетёрша

usual ['juːʒʊəl] □ обыкнове́нный, обы́чный

usurp [juːˈzəːp] узурпи́ровать (*im*)*pf.*; ~er [juːˈzəːpə] узурпа́тор

utensil [juːˈtensl] (*mst. pl.* ~s) инструме́нт; посу́да; *kitchen* ~s ку́хонные принадле́жности *f/pl.*

utility [juːˈtɪlətɪ] (*usefulness*) поле́зность *f*; *public utilities* коммуна́ль-

ные услу́ги/предприя́тия

utiliz|ation [juːtəlaɪˈzeɪʃn] испо́льзование, утилиза́ция; ~e ['juːtəlaɪz] испо́льзовать (*im*)*pf.*, утилизи́ровать (*im*)*pf.*

utmost ['ʌtməʊst] кра́йний, преде́льный; *do one's* ~ сде́лать *pf.* всё возмо́жное; *at the* ~ са́мое бо́льшее

utter ['ʌtə] **1.** ~ *fig.* по́лный; соверше́нный; **2.** *sounds* изд(ав)а́ть; *words* произноси́ть [-нести́]; ~ance [-ərəns] выска́зывание; *give* ~ **to** вы́сказывать [-сказать]; *emotion* дать вы́ход (Д)

U-turn ['juːtɜːn] *mot.* разворо́т

V

vacan|cy ['veɪkənsɪ] (*emptiness*) пустота́; (*unfilled job*) вака́нсия; *in hotel* свобо́дная ко́мната; ~t ['veɪkənt] □ неза́нятый, вака́нтный; пусто́й; *look, mind, etc.* отсу́тствующий

vacat|e [vəˈkeɪt] *house, hotel room, etc.* освобожда́ть [-боди́ть]; ~ion [vəˈkeɪʃn, *Am.* veɪˈkeɪʃən] *univ.* кани́кулы *f/pl.*; *Am.* (*holiday*) о́тпуск; *be on* ~ быть в о́тпуске

vaccin|ate ['væksɪneɪt] *med.* [c]де́лать приви́вку; ~ation [væksɪˈneɪʃn] приви́вка; ~e ['væksiːn] вакци́на

vacillate ['væsəleɪt] колеба́ться

vacuum ['vækjʊəm] *phys.* ва́куум (*a. fig.*); ~ *cleaner* пылесо́с; ~ *flask* те́рмос; ~-*packed* в ва́куумной упако́вке

vagabond ['vægəbɒnd] бродя́га *m*

vagrant ['veɪgrənt] бродя́га *m*

vague [veɪg] неопределённый, нея́сный, сму́тный; *I haven't the* ~*st idea of ...* я не име́ю ни мале́йшего представле́ния о (П)

vain [veɪn] □ (*useless*) тще́тный, напра́сный; (*conceited*) тщесла́вный; *in* ~ напра́сно, тще́тно; ~*glorious* [veɪnˈglɔːrɪəs] тщесла́вный; (*boastful*) хвастли́вый

valet ['vælɪt, 'væleɪ] камерди́нер

valiant ['vælɪənt] *rhet.* хра́брый, до́блестный

valid ['vælɪd] *law* действи́тельный (*a. of ticket, etc.*), име́ющий си́лу; *of an argument, etc.* ве́ский, обосно́ванный

valley ['vælɪ] доли́на

valo(u)r ['vælə] *rhet.* до́блесть *f*

valuable ['væljʊəbl] **1.** □ це́нный; **2.** ~*s pl.* це́нности *f/pl.*

valuation [væljʊˈeɪʃn] оце́нка

value ['væljuː] **1.** це́нность *f*; *comm.* сто́имость *f*; *math.* величина́; *put* (*or* *set*) *little* ~ *on* невысоко́ цени́ть; **2.** оце́нивать [-и́ть] (В); цени́ть (В); дорожи́ть (Т); ~*less* ['væljuːlɪs] ничего́ не сто́ящий

valve ['vælv] *tech.* ве́нтиль *m*, кла́пан (*a. anat.*)

van [væn] автофурго́н; *rail.* бага́жный *or* това́рный ваго́н

vane [veɪn] (*weathercock*) флю́гер; *of propeller* ло́пасть *f*

vanguard ['vænɡɑːd]: *be in the* ~ быть в пе́рвых ряда́х; *fig.* аванга́рд

vanilla [vəˈnɪlə] вани́ль

vanish ['vænɪʃ] исчеза́ть [-е́знуть]

vanity ['vænətɪ] тщесла́вие; ~ *bag* (су́мочка-)косме́ти́чка

vanquish ['væŋkwɪʃ] побежда́ть

[-еди́ть]

vantage ['vɑːntɪdʒ]: ~ **point** удо́бное для обзо́ра ме́сто; вы́годная пози́ция

vapid ['væpɪd] □ пло́ский; пре́сный; *fig.* неинтере́сный

vaporize ['veɪpəraɪz] испаря́ть(ся) [-ри́ть(ся)]

vapo(u)r ['veɪpə] пар

varia|ble ['veərɪəbl] **1.** □ непостоя́нный, изме́нчивый; **2.** *math.* переме́нная величина́; **~nce** [-rɪəns]: **be at ~** расходи́ться во мне́ниях; быть в противоре́чии; **~nt** [-rɪənt] вариа́нт; **~tion** [veərɪ'eɪʃn] измене́ние; *mus.* вариа́ция

varie|d ['veərɪd] □ → **various**; **~gated** ['veərɪgeɪtɪd] разноцве́тный, пёстрый; **~ty** [və'raɪətɪ] разнообра́зие; *(sort)* сорт, разнови́дность *f*; ряд, мно́жество; **for a ~ of reasons** по ря́ду причи́н; **~ show** варьете́; эстра́дное представле́ние

various ['veərɪəs] ра́зный, *(of different sorts)* разли́чный; разнообра́зный; **~ly** [-lɪ] по-ра́зному

varnish ['vɑːnɪʃ] **1.** лак; *fig. (gloss)* лоск; **2.** покрыва́ть ла́ком

vary ['veərɪ] *(change)* изменя́ть(ся) [-ни́ть(ся)]; *(be different)* разни́ться; *of opinion* расходи́ться [разойти́сь]; *(diversify)* разнообра́зить

vase [vɑːz] ва́за

vast [vɑːst] □ обши́рный, грома́дный

vat [væt] чан; бо́чка, ка́дка

vault [vɔːlt] **1.** свод; *(tomb, crypt)* склеп; *(cellar)* подва́л, по́греб; **2.** *(a. ~ over)* перепры́гивать [-гнуть]

veal [viːl] теля́тина; *attr.* теля́чий

veer [vɪə] *of wind* меня́ть направле́ние; *views, etc.* изменя́ть [-ни́ть]; **the car ~ed to the right** маши́ну занесло́ впра́во

vegeta|ble ['vedʒtəbl] **1.** о́вощ; **~s** *pl.* зе́лень *f*, о́вощи *m/pl.*; **2.** *oil* расти́тельный; овощно́й; **~ garden** огоро́д; **~ marrow** кабачо́к; **~rian** [vedʒɪ'teərɪən] **1.** вегетариа́нец *m*, -нка *f*; **2.** вегетариа́нский; **~tion** [vedʒɪ'teɪʃn] расти́тельность *f*

vehemen|ce ['viːəməns] си́ла; стра́ст-

ность *f*; **~t** [-t] си́льный; стра́стный; *protests, etc.* бу́рный

vehicle ['viːɪkl] автомаши́на, авто́бус *и т. д. (любое тра́нспортное сре́дство)*; *fig.* сре́дство; *med.* перено́счик

veil [veɪl] **1.** вуа́ль *f*; *of mist* пелена́; *fig.* заве́са; *bridal ~* фата́; **2.** закрыва́ть вуа́лью; *fig.* завуали́ровать; *in mist* оку́тывать

vein [veɪn] ве́на; *geol.* жи́ла; *fig.* жи́лка; *(mood)* настрое́ние

velocity [vɪ'lɒsətɪ] ско́рость *f*

velvet ['velvɪt] ба́рхат; *attr.* ба́рхатный; **~y** [-ɪ] ба́рхатный *(fig.)*; бархати́стый

vend|or ['vendə] *(у́личный)* продаве́ц *m*, -вщи́ца *f*

veneer [və'nɪə] фане́ра; *fig.* фаса́д

venerable ['venərəbl] □ почте́нный; *eccl. title* преподо́бный

venereal [və'nɪərɪəl] венери́ческий

Venetian [və'niːʃn] венециа́нский; **~ blinds** жалюзи́ *n indecl.*

vengeance ['vendʒəns] месть *f*

venom ['venəm] *(part.* змеи́ный*)* яд *(a. fig.)*; *fig.* зло́ба; **~ous** [-əs] □ ядови́тый *(a. fig.)*

vent [vent] **1.** вентиляцио́нное отве́рстие; *(air ~)* отду́шина; **give~to** изли(ва́)ть (В); **2.** *fig.* изли(ва́)ть (В), дава́ть вы́ход (Д)

ventilat|e ['ventɪleɪt] прове́три(ва)ть; *fig., of question* обсужда́ть [-уди́ть], выясня́ть [вы́яснить]; **~ion** [ventɪ'leɪʃn] вентиля́ция

venture ['ventʃə] **1.** риско́ванное предприя́тие; **at a ~** науга́д; **joint ~** совме́стное предприя́тие; **2.** рискова́ть [-кну́ть] (Т); отва́жи(ва)ться на (В) *(a. ~ upon)*

veracious [və'reɪʃəs] правди́вый

veranda(h) [və'rændə] вера́нда

verb|al ['vɜːbl] □ слове́сный; *(oral)* у́стный; *gr.* отглаго́льный; **~atim** [vɜː'beɪtɪm] досло́вно, сло́во в сло́во; **~ose** [vɜː'bəʊs] □ многосло́вный

verdict ['vɜːdɪkt] *law* верди́кт; **what's your ~, doctor?** каково́ Ва́ше мне́ние, до́ктор?

verdure ['vɜːdʒə] зе́лень f

verge [vɜːdʒ] **1.** (*edge*) край; *of forest* опу́шка; *of flower bed* бордю́р; *fig.* грань f; **on the ~ of** на гра́ни (P); **2.:** **~ (up)on** грани́чить с (T)

veri|fy ['verɪfaɪ] проверя́ть [-е́рить]; (*bear out*) подтвержда́ть [-рди́ть]; **~table** ['verɪtəbl] □ настоя́щий, и́стинный

vermin ['vɜːmɪn] *coll.* вреди́тели *m/pl.*; (*lice, etc.*) парази́ты *m/pl.*

vermouth ['vɜːməθ] ве́рмут

vernacular [və'nækjʊlə] *language* родно́й; ме́стный диале́кт

versatile ['vɜːsətaɪl] □ разносторо́нний; (*having many uses*) универса́льный

verse [vɜːs] стих *m/pl.*; (*line*) строка́; (*stanza*) строфа́; **~d** [vɜːst] о́пытный, све́дущий; **she is well ~ in English history** она́ хорошо́ зна́ет англи́йскую исто́рию

version ['vɜːʃn] вариа́нт; (*account of an event, etc.*) ве́рсия; (*translation*) перево́д

vertebral ['vɜːtɪbrəl]: **~ column** позвоно́чник

vertical ['vɜːtɪkəl] □ вертика́льный; *cliff, etc.* отве́сный

vertigo ['vɜːtɪgəʊ] головокруже́ние

verve [vɜːv] энтузиа́зм; подъём

very ['verɪ] **1.** *adv.* о́чень; **the ~ best** са́мое лу́чшее; **2.** *adj.* настоя́щий, су́щий; (*in emphasis*) са́мый; **the ~ same** тот са́мый; **the ~ thing** и́менно то, что ну́жно; **the ~ thought** уже́ одна́ мысль f, сама́ мысль f; **the ~ stones** да́же ка́мни *m/pl.*

vessel ['vesl] сосу́д (*a. anat.*); *naut.* су́дно, кора́бль *m*

vest [vest] жиле́т; *chiefly Brt.* ма́йка

vestibule ['vestɪbjuːl] вестибю́ль *m*

vestige ['vestɪdʒ] (*remains*) след, оста́ток; **there is not a ~ of truth in this** в э́том нет и до́ли пра́вды

veteran ['vetərən] **1.** ветера́н; **2.** *attr.* ста́рый; (*experienced*) о́пытный

veterinary ['vetrɪnərɪ] **1.** ветерина́р (*mst.* **~ surgeon**); **2.** ветерина́рный

veto ['viːtəʊ] **1.** ве́то *n indecl.*; **2.** налага́ть [-ложи́ть] ве́то на (B)

vex [veks] досажда́ть [досади́ть], раздража́ть [-жи́ть]; **~ation** [vek'seɪʃn] доса́да, неприя́тность f; **~atious** [vek'seɪʃəs] доса́дный; **~ed** ['vekst] *person* раздосо́́ванный; *question* спо́рный; больно́й

via ['vaɪə] че́рез (B)

viable ['vaɪəbl] жизнеспосо́бный

vial ['vaɪəl] пузырёк

vibrat|e [vaɪ'breɪt] вибри́ровать; **~ion** [-ʃn] вибра́ция

vice[1] [vaɪs] поро́к

vice[2] [-] *chiefly Brt.* → **vise**

vice[3] [-] *pref.* ви́це…; **~ president** ви́це-президе́нт

vice versa [vaɪsɪ'vɜːsə] наоборо́т

vicinity [vɪ'sɪnətɪ] (*neighbo[u]rhood*) окре́стность f; бли́зость f; **in the ~** недалеко́ (**of** от P)

vicious ['vɪʃəs] □ поро́чный; злой; **~ circle** поро́чный круг

vicissitude [vɪ'sɪsɪtjuːd]: *mst.* **~s** *pl.* превра́тности f/pl.

victim ['vɪktɪm] же́ртва; **~ize** [-tɪmaɪz] (*for one's views, etc.*) пресле́довать

victor ['vɪktə] победи́тель *m*; **~ious** [vɪk'tɔːrɪəs] □ победоно́сный; **~y** ['vɪktərɪ] побе́да

video ['vɪdɪəʊ] ви́део; **~ camera** видеока́мера; **~ cassette** видеокассе́та; **~ recorder** видеомагнитофо́н, *coll.* ви́дик

vie [vaɪ] сопе́рничать

view [vjuː] **1.** вид (**of** на B); по́ле зре́ния; (*opinion*) взгляд; (*intention*) наме́рение; **in ~ of** ввиду́ P; **on ~** (вы́ставленный) для обозре́ния; **with a ~ to** или **of** + *ger.* с наме́рением (+ *inf.*); **have in ~** име́ть в виду́; **2.** (*examine*) осма́тривать [осмотре́ть]; (*consider*) рассма́тривать [-мотре́ть]; (*look at*) [по]смотре́ть на (B); **~point** то́чка зре́ния

vigil|ance ['vɪdʒɪləns] бди́тельность f; **~ant** [-lənt] □ бди́тельный

vigo|rous ['vɪgərəs] □ си́льный, энерги́чный; **~(u)r** ['vɪgə] си́ла, эне́ргия

vile [vaɪl] □ ме́рзкий, ни́зкий

villa ['vɪlə] ви́лла

village ['vɪlɪdʒ] село́, дере́вня; *attr.* се́льский, дереве́нский; **~r** [-ə] се́льский (-кая) жи́тель *m* (-ница f)

villian ['vɪlən] злодей, негодяй

vim [vɪm] энергия, сила

vindic|ate ['vɪndɪkeɪt] (*prove*) доказывать [-зать]; (*justify*) оправдывать [-дать]; **~tive** [vɪn'dɪktɪv] □ мстительный

vine [vaɪn] виноградная лоза; **~gar** ['vɪnɪgə] уксус; **~ growing** виноградарство; **~yard** ['vɪnjəd] виноградник

vintage ['vɪntɪdʒ] сбор винограда; вино урожая определённого года; **~ wine** марочное вино

violat|e ['vaɪəleɪt] *law, promise, etc.* нарушать [-ушить]; (*rape*) [из]насиловать; **~ion** [vaɪə'leɪʃn] нарушение

violen|ce ['vaɪələns] насилие; *outbreak of* **~** беспорядки *m/pl.*; **~t** [-nt] □ (*strong*) сильный, мощный, неистовый; *quarrel, etc.* яростный; *of death* насильственный

violet ['vaɪələt] фиалка, фиолетовый цвет

violin [vaɪə'lɪn] скрипка

viper ['vaɪpə] гадюка

virgin ['vɜːdʒɪn] **1.** девственница; *the Blessed* ♀ Дева Мария, Богородица; **2.** □ девственный (*a.* **~al**); **~ity** [və'dʒɪnətɪ] девственность *f*

Virgo ['vɜːgəʊ] *in the zodiac* Дева

viril|e ['vɪraɪl] (*sexually potent*) вирильный; полный энергии, мужественный; **~ity** [vɪ'rɪlətɪ] мужественность *f*; (*potency*) мужская сила

virtu|al ['vɜːtʃʊəl] □ фактический; **~e** ['vɜːtjuː] добродетель *f*; (*advantage*) достоинство; *in or by* **~** *of* благодаря, в силу (P); **~ous** ['vɜːtʃʊəs] □ добродетельный; (*chaste*) целомудренный

virulent ['vɪrʊlənt] □ *of poison* смертельный; *of illness* свирепый, опасный; *fig.* злобный

virus ['vaɪərəs] вирус; *attr.* вирусный

visa ['viːzə] виза; *entry* (*exit*) **~** въездная (выездная) виза

viscount ['vaɪkaʊnt] виконт

viscous ['vɪskəs] □ вязкий; *liquid* тягучий, густой

vise [vaɪs] *tech.* тиски *m/pl.*

visibility [vɪzə'bɪlətɪ] □ видимость *f*

visible ['vɪzəbl] *apparent, evident* видимый; *conspicuous, prominent* видный; *fig., obvious* явный, очевидный

vision ['vɪʒn] (*eyesight*) зрение; (*mental picture*) видение; *fig.* проницательность *f*; *field of* **~** поле зрения; *my* **~** *of the events is different* моё видение этих событий иное; **~ary** ['vɪʒənərɪ] провидец *m*, -дица *f*; (*one given to reverie*) мечтатель *m*, -ница *f*

visit ['vɪzɪt] **1.** *v/t. person* навещать [-естить]; *museum, etc.* посещать [-етить]; *v/i.* ходить в гости; (*stay*) гостить; **2.** посещение, визит; **~ing** [-ɪŋ]: **~ card** визитная карточка; **~ hours** приёмные часы; **~or** ['vɪzɪtə] посетитель *m*, -ница *f*, гость *m*, -я *f*

vista ['vɪstə] перспектива (*a. fig.*); (*view*) вид

visual ['vɪʒʊəl] зрительный; наглядный; **~ aids** наглядные пособия; **~ize** [-aɪz] представлять себе, мысленно видеть

vital ['vaɪtl] □ жизненный; (*essential*) насущный, существенный; *person, style* живой; **~s**, **~ parts** *pl.* жизненно важные органы *m/pl.*; **~ity** [vaɪ'tælətɪ] жизненная сила; энергия; живость *f*; *the child is full of* **~** ребёнок полон сил

vitamin ['vaɪtəmɪn, *Brt.* 'vɪtəmɪn] витамин; **~ deficiency** авитаминоз

vivid ['vɪvɪd] □ *fig.* живой, яркий

vixen ['vɪksn] лиса, лисица

vocabulary [və'kæbjʊlərɪ] словарь *m*, список слов; *person's* запас слов

vocal ['vəʊkl] □ голосовой; (*talkative*) разговорчивый; *mus.* вокальный; **~ cords** голосовые связки

vocation [və'keɪʃn] призвание; профессия; **~al** [-l] □ профессиональный

vogue [vəʊg] мода; популярность *f*; *be in* **~** быть в моде

voice [vɔɪs] **1.** голос; *at the top of one's* **~** во весь голос; *give* **~** *to* выражать [выразить] (B); **2.** выражать [выразить]

void [vɔɪd] **1.** пусто́й; лишённый (*of* P); *law* недействи́тельный; **2.** пустота́; пробе́л

volatile ['vɒlətaɪl] *chem.* лету́чий; *fig.* изме́нчивый

volcano [vɒl'keɪnəʊ] (*pl.* **volcanoes**) вулка́н

volition [və'lɪʃn] во́ля

volley ['vɒlɪ] *of shots* залп; *fig. of questions, etc.* град; **~ball** волейбо́л

voltage ['vəʊltɪdʒ] *el.* напряже́ние

voluble ['vɒljʊbl] разгово́рчивый, говорли́вый

volum|e ['vɒljuːm] объём; (*book*) том; (*capacity*) ёмкость *f*, вмести́тельность *f*; *fig. of sound, etc.* си́ла, полнота́; **~ control** *radio, T.V.* регуля́тор зву́ка; **~inous** [və'luːmɪnəs] □ объёмистый; обши́рный

volunt|ary ['vɒləntrɪ] □ доброво́льный; **~eer** [vɒlən'tɪə] **1.** доброво́лец; **2.** *v/i.* вызыва́ться [вы́зваться] (*for* на В); идти́ доброво́льцем; *v/t.* help, *etc.* предлага́ть [-ложи́ть]

voluptu|ary [və'lʌptʃʊərɪ] □ сластолю́бец; **~ous** [-ʃʊəs] □ сладостра́стный

vomit ['vɒmɪt] **1.** рво́та; **2.** [вы́]рвать: **he is ~ing** его́ рвёт

voraci|ous [və'reɪʃəs] □ прожо́рливый, жа́дный; **~ reader** ненасы́тный чита́тель; **~ty** [və'ræsɪtɪ] прожо́рливость *f*

vortex ['vɔːteks] *mst. fig.* водоворо́т; *of wind mst. fig.* вихрь

vote [vəʊt] **1.** голосова́ние; (*vote cast*) го́лос; пра́во го́лоса; во́тум; (*decision*) реше́ние; **cast a ~** отдава́ть го́лос (*for* за В; *against* про́тив P); **~ of no confidence** во́тум недове́рия; **put to the ~** поста́вить *pf.* на голосова́ние; **2.** *v/i.* голосова́ть (*im*)*pf.*, *pf. a.* [про-] (*for* за В; *against* про́тив P); *v/t.* голосова́ть (*im*)*pf.*, *pf. a.* [про-]; **~r** ['vəʊtə] избира́тель *m*, -ница *f*

voting ['vəʊtɪŋ] **1.** голосова́ние; **2.** избира́тельный; **~ paper** избира́тельный бюллете́нь

vouch [vaʊtʃ]: **~ for** руча́ться [поручи́ться] за (В); **~er** ['vaʊtʃə] (*receipt*) распи́ска; *fin.* ва́учер

vow [vaʊ] **1.** обе́т, кля́тва; **2.** *v/t.* [по]кля́сться в (П)

vowel ['vaʊəl] гла́сный

voyage ['vɔɪɪdʒ] **1.** путеше́ствие водо́й, пла́вание; **2.** путеше́ствовать мо́рем

vulgar ['vʌlgə] □ (*unrefined*) вульга́рный; (*low*) по́шлый; (*common*) широко́ распространённый

vulnerable ['vʌlnərəbl] □ *fig. position* уязви́мый; *person* рани́мый

vulture ['vʌltʃə] *zo.* гриф; *fig.* стервя́тник

W

wad [wɒd] *of cotton, paper* комо́к; *of banknotes* па́чка

waddle ['wɒdl] ходи́ть вперева́лку

wade [weɪd] *v/t.* переходи́ть вброд; *v/i.* проб(и)ра́ться (*through* по Д *or* че́рез В)

wafer ['weɪfə] *relig.* обла́тка; ва́фля

waffle ['wɒfl] *cul.* ва́фля

waft [wɒft, wɑːft] **1.** *of wind* дунове́ние; *of air* струя́; **2.** доноси́ться [-нести́сь]

wag [wæg] **1.** (*joker*) шутни́к; **2.** ма-ха́ть [махну́ть] (Т); *of dog* виля́ть [вильну́ть] хвосто́м; **~ one's finger** грози́ть па́льцем

wage[1] [weɪdʒ]: **~ war** вести́ войну́

wage[2] *mst.* **~s** [weɪdʒɪz] *pl.* за́работная пла́та, зарпла́та; **~ freeze** замора́живание за́работной пла́ты

wag(g)on ['wægən] *mst.* ваго́н, теле́га; *rail.* *Brt.* това́рный ваго́н, *open* ваго́н-платфо́рма

waif [weɪf] *homeless* бездо́мный ребёнок; безприз́орного; *neglected* забро́шенный ребёнок

wail [weɪl] 1. вопль *m*; вой; (*lament*) причита́ние; *of wind* завыва́ние; 2. [за]вопи́ть; выть, завы́(ва́)ть; причита́ть

waist [weɪst] та́лия; **stripped to the ~** го́лый по по́яс; **~coat** ['weɪskout, 'weskət] *chiefly Brt.* (*vest*) жиле́т

wait [weɪt] *v/i.* ждать (*for* B or P), ожида́ть (*for* P), подожда́ть *pf.* (*for* B or P); (*часто*: ~ **at table**) обслу́живать [-жи́ть] (B); **well, we'll have to** ~ **and see** что ж, поживём-уви́дим; **I'll** ~ **up for you** я не ля́гу, подожду́ тебя́; *v/t.* выжида́ть [вы́ждать] (B); **~er** ['weɪtə] официа́нт

waiting ['weɪtɪŋ] ожида́ние; ~ **room** приёмная; *rail.* зал ожида́ния

waitress ['weɪtrɪs] официа́нтка

waive [weɪv] *a claim, right, etc.* отка́зываться [-за́ться] от (P)

wake [weɪk] 1.: **hunger brought disease in its** ~ го́лод повлёк за собо́й эпиде́мию; 2. [*irr.*] *v/i.* бо́дрствовать; (*mst.* ~ **up**) просыпа́ться [просну́ться], *fig.* пробужда́ться [-уди́ться]; *v/t.* [раз]буди́ть; *fig.* пробужда́ть [-уди́ть]; *desire, etc.* возбужда́ть [-уди́ть]; **~ful** ['weɪkfl] □ бессо́нный; (*vigilant*) бди́тельный; **~n** ['weɪkən] → **wake 2**

walk [wɔːk] 1. *v/i.* ходи́ть, идти́ (пойти́); (*stroll*) гуля́ть, прогу́ливаться; ~ **away** отходи́ть [отойти́]; ~ **in(to)** входи́ть [войти́]; ~ **off** уходи́ть [уйти́]; ~ **out** выходи́ть [вы́йти]; ~ **over** (*cross*) переходи́ть (перейти́); ~ **up** подходи́ть [-дойти́]; 2. ходьба́; (*gait*) похо́дка; прогу́лка пешко́м; (*path*) тропа́, алле́я; ~ **of life** сфе́ра де́ятельности; профе́ссия

walking ['wɔːkɪŋ] 1. ходьба́; 2.: ~ **dictionary** ходя́чая энциклопе́дия; ~ **stick** трость *f*

walk|out ['wɔːk'aut] забасто́вка; **~over** лёгкая побе́да

wall [wɔːl] 1. стена́; (*side, unit*) сте́нка; **drive s.o. up the** ~ доводи́ть кого́-л. до исступле́ния; 2. обноси́ть стено́й; ~ **up** заде́л(ыв)ать (*дверь и т. п.*)

wallet ['wɒlɪt] бума́жник

wallflower желтофио́ль *f*; *fig.* де́вушка, оста́вшаяся без партнёра (на та́нцах, и т. д.)

wallop ['wɒləp] *coll.* [по]би́ть, [по-, от]колоти́ть

wallow ['wɒləu] валя́ться

wallpaper *obl m/pl.*

walnut ['wɔːlnʌt] *bot.* гре́цкий оре́х

walrus ['wɔːlrəs] *zo.* морж

waltz [wɔːls] 1. вальс; 2. танцева́ть вальс

wan [wɒn] □ бле́дный, ту́склый

wander ['wɒndə] броди́ть; блужда́ть (*a. of gaze, thoughts, etc.*)

wane [weɪn]: **be on the** ~ *of moon* убы́(ва́)ть, быть на убы́ле; *of popularity, etc.* уменьша́ться [-шиться], снижа́ться [-и́зиться]

wangle ['wæŋgl] заполучи́ть хи́тростью; *coll.* вы́клянчить

want [wɒnt] 1. (*lack*) недоста́ток (*of* P or в П); (*poverty*) нужда́; (*need*) потре́бность *f*; 2. *v/i.* **be** ~**ing: he is** ~**ing in patience** ему́ недостаёт терпе́ния; ~ **for** нужда́ться в (П); *v/t.* [за]хоте́ть (P *a.* B); [по]жела́ть (P *a.* B); нужда́ться в (Д); **he** ~**s energy** ему́ недостаёт эне́ргии; **what do you** ~? вам ну́жно?; **you** ~ **to see a doctor** вам сле́дует обрати́ться к врачу́; ~**ed** [-ɪd] (в объявле́ниях) тре́буется, *law* разы́скивается

wanton ['wɒntən] □ (*debauched*) распу́тный; *of cruelty* бессмы́сленный

war [wɔː] 1. война́; *fig.* борьба́; **be at** ~ воева́ть с (Т); **make** ~ вести́ войну́ ([up]on с Т); 2. *attr.* вое́нный; ~ **memorial** па́мятник солда́там, поги́бшим на войне́

warble ['wɔːbl] *of birds* издава́ть тре́ли; *of person* залива́ться пе́сней

ward [wɔːd] 1. находя́щийся под опе́кой; *hospital* пала́та; 2. ~ (**off**) *blow* отража́ть [отрази́ть], *danger, illness* отвраща́ть [-рати́ть]; ~**er** ['wɔːdə] *in prison* надзира́тель; тюре́мный контролёр; ~**robe** ['wɔːdrəub] платяно́й шкаф; (*clothes*) гардеро́б

ware [weə] *in compds.* посу́да; ~**s** *pl.*

W

това́р(ы pl.) изде́лия

warehouse ['weəhaʊs] склад

war|fare ['wɔːfeə] война́, веде́ние войны́; **~head** [-hed] боеголо́вка

warm [wɔːm] **1.** □ тёплый (a. fig.); fig. горя́чий; person серде́чный; **2.** тепло́; **3.** [на-, ото-, со]гре́ть, нагре́(ва́)ть(ся), согре́(ва́)ться (a. ~ up); his words...ed my heart его́ слова́ согре́ли мою́ ду́шу; **~th** [-θ] тепло́; теплота́ (a. fig.)

warn [wɔːn] предупрежда́ть [-реди́ть] (of, against о П); caution предостерега́ть [-стере́чь] (of against от Р); **~ing** ['wɔːnɪŋ] предупрежде́ние; предостереже́ние

warp [wɔːp] of wood [по]коро́бить(ся); fig. извраща́ть [-рати́ть]; (distort) искажа́ть [искази́ть]; **~ed mind** извращённый ум

warrant ['wɒrənt] **1.** (justification) оправда́ние; fin. гара́нтия, руча́тельство; (~ to arrest) о́рдер на аре́ст; **2.** опра́вдывать [-да́ть]; руча́ться [поручи́ться] за (В); (guarantee) гаранти́ровать (im)pf.; **~y** [-ɪ] гара́нтия; руча́тельство

warrior ['wɒrɪə] poet. во́ин

wart [wɔːt] борода́вка

wary ['weərɪ] □ осторо́жный

was [wəz, ... wɒz] pt. om be

wash [wɒʃ] **1.** v/t. floor, dishes [вы-, по]мы́ть; face умы́ть pf.; wound, etc. промы́(ва́)ть; clothes [вы́]стира́ть; v/i. [вы́]мы́ться, умы́ться pf.; стира́ться; that won't ~ coll. не пройдёт; э́тому никто́ не пове́рит; **2.** мытьё; сти́рка; (articles for washing) бельё; of waves прибо́й; mouth ~ полоска́ние; **~basin** ра́ковина; **~er** ['wɒʃə] (washing machine) стира́льная маши́на; tech. ша́йба, прокла́дка; **~ing** ['wɒʃɪŋ] **1.** мытьё; сти́рка; (articles) бельё; **2.** стира́льный; **~ powder** стира́льный порошо́к

washroom ['wɒʃrʊm] Am. euph. (lavatory) убо́рная

wasp [wɒsp] оса́

waste [weɪst] **1.** (loss) поте́ря; (wrong use) изли́шняя тра́та; (domestic) от-

бро́сы m/pl.; tech. отхо́ды m/pl.; **lay ~** опустоша́ть [-щи́ть]; **~ of time** напра́сная тра́та вре́мени; **2.** ~**land** пусты́рь m, plot of ground пу́стошь f; **3.** ~ money, etc. [по-, рас]тра́тить зря; time [по]теря́ть; v/i. resources истоща́ться [-щи́ть-ся]; **~ful** ['weɪstfl] □ расточи́тельный; ~ **paper** испо́льзованная нену́жная бума́га; for pulping макулату́ра; **~paper basket** корзи́на для нену́жных бума́г

watch¹ [wɒtʃ] (wrist~) нару́чные часы́ m/pl.; ва́хта

watch² v/i.: ~ **for** chance, etc. выжида́ть [вы́ждать] (В); ~ **out!** осторо́жно!; v/t. (look after) смотре́ть за; (observe) наблюда́ть, следи́ть за (Т); **~dog** сторожева́я соба́ка; **~ful** [-fl] бди́тельный; **~maker** часовщи́к; **~man** [-mən] вахтёр

water ['wɔːtə] **1.** вода́; ~**s** pl. во́ды f/pl.; **drink the ~s** пить минера́льные во́ды; **throw cold ~ on s.o.** охлади́ть pf. пыл, отрезви́ть pf.; attr. водяно́й; во́дный; водо...; **2.** v/t. поли(ва́)ть; animals [на]пои́ть (a. ~ **down**) разбавля́ть водо́й; fig. чересчу́р смягча́ть; v/i. of eyes слези́ться; **it makes my mouth ~** от э́того у меня́ слю́нки теку́т; ~**colo(u)r** акваре́ль; ~**fall** водопа́д; ~ **heater** (kettle) кипяти́льник

watering ['wɔːtərɪŋ]: ~ **can** ле́йка; ~ **place** for animals водопо́й; (spa) куро́рт на во́дах

water| level у́ровень воды́; ~ **lily** водяна́я ли́лия, кувши́нка; ~ **main** водопрово́дная магистра́ль; ~**melon** арбу́з; ~ **polo** во́дное по́ло n indecl.; ~**proof 1.** непромока́емый; **2.** непромока́емый плащ m; ~ **supply** водоснабже́ние; ~**tight** водонепроница́емый; fig. of alibi, etc. неопроверж́имый; ~**way** во́дный путь m; фарва́тер; ~**works** pl. a., sg. систе́ма водоснабже́ния; ~**y** ['wɔːtərɪ] водяни́стый

wave [weɪv] **1.** of hand взмах, взмах; **2.** v/t. [по]маха́ть, де́лать знак (Т); hair зави(ва́)ть; ~ **a p. away** де́лать знак кому́-либо, что́бы он удали́лся; отстраня́ть [-ни́ть] же́стом; ~ **aside**

W

fig. отмáхиваться [-хнýться] от (P); *v/i.* of flags развевáться; *of hair* вúться; *of corn, grass* колыхáться; *of boughs* качáться; ~length длинá волны́

waver ['weivə] [по]колебáться; *of flames* колыхáться [-хнýться]; *of troops, voice* дрóгнуть *pf.*

wavy ['weivi] волни́стый

wax¹ [wæks] воск; *in ear* серá; *attr.* восковóй

wax² [-] [*irr.*] *of moon* прибы́(вá)ть

way [wei] *mst.* дорóга, путь *m*; (*direction*) сторонá, направлéние; мéтод, спóсоб; (*custom, habit*) обы́чай, привы́чка; (*a.* ~*s pl.*) óбраз жи́зни; поведéние; ~ **in, out** вход, вы́ход; **in a** ~ в извéстном смы́сле; **in many** ~**s** во мнóгих отношéниях; **this** ~ сюдá; **by the** ~ кстáти, мéжду прóчим; **by** ~ **of** в кáчестве (P); (*through*) чéрез; **in the** ~ *fig.* поперёк дорóги; **on the** ~ в пути́, по дорóге; **out of the** ~ находя́щийся в сторонé; (*unusual*) необы́чный; необыкновéнный; **under** ~ на ходý; **give** ~ уступáть [-пи́ть] (Д); **have one's** ~ добивáться своегó; настáивать на своём; **keep out of s.o.'s** ~ не попадáться комý-л.; **lead the** ~ идти́ впереди́, [по]вести́; **lose the** ~ заблуди́ться *pf.*; ~lay [wei'lei] [*irr.* (*lay*)] подстерегáть [-рéчь]; ~side [-] обóчина; 2. придорóжный; ~ward ['weiwəd] □ своенрáвный

we [wi, ... wi:] *pers. pron.* мы

weak [wi:k] □ слáбый; ~en ['wi:kən] *v/t.* ослаблять [-áбить] *v/i.* [о]слабéть; ~ling ['wi:kliŋ] физи́чески слáбый *or* слабовóльный человéк; ~ly [-li] *adv.* слáбо; ~ness [-nis] слáбость *f*

wealth [welθ] богáтство; (*profusion*) изоби́лие; ~y ['welθi] □ богáтый

wean [wi:n] отнимáть от груди́; отучáть [-чи́ть] (*from, of* от P)

weapon ['wepən] орýжие (*a. fig.*)

wear [weə] 1. [*irr.*] *v/t.* hat, glasses, etc. носи́ть; (*a.* ~ **away, down, off**) стирáть [стерéть]; изнáшивать (*fig.* изнуря́ть [-ри́ть] *mst.* ~ **out**); *v/i.* clothes но-

си́ться; ~ **on** мéдленно тянýться; **2.** (*a.* ~ **and tear**, *part. tech.*) изнóс; **men's** (**ladies'**) ~ мужскáя (жéнская) одéжда

wear|iness ['wiərinis] устáлость *f*; утомлённость *f*; ~isome [-səm] □ (*tiring*) утоми́тельный; (*boring*) скýчный; ~y ['wiəri] 1. утомлённый; 2. утоми́ть(ся) [-ми́ть(ся)]; *v/i.* наскýчить *pf.*

weasel ['wi:zl] *zo.* лáска

weather ['weðə] 1. погóда; **be a bit under the** ~ невáжно себя́ чýвствовать; быть в плохóм настроéнии; 2. *v/t. of rocks* изнáшивать [-носи́ть]; *a storm* вы́держать [вы́держать] (*a. fig.*); *v/i.* вывéтриваться [вы́ветриться]; ~**beaten**, ~**worn** *face* обвéтренный; *person* пострадáвший от непогóды; ~ **forecast** прогнóз погóды

weav|e [wi:v] [*irr.*] [со]ткáть; [с]плести́; *fig. story* сочиня́ть [-ни́ть]; ~er ['wi:və] ткач *m*, ткачи́ха *f*

web [web] *spider's* паути́на; **a** ~ **of lies** паути́на лжи

wed [wed] *of woman* выходи́ть зáмуж (за B); *of man* жени́ться (*im*)*pf.* (на П); сочетáться брáком; ~ding ['wediŋ] 1. свáдьба; 2. свáдебный; ~ding ring обручáльное кольцó

wedge [wedʒ] клин; **drive a** ~ **between** *fig.* вби(вá)ть клин мéжду (T); 2. (*a.* ~ **in**) вкли́нивать(ся) [-ни́ть(ся)]; ~ **o.s.** вти́скиваться [вти́снуться]

wedlock ['wedlɒk] брак

Wednesday ['wenzdi] средá

wee [wi:] крóшечный, малю́сенький; ~ **hours** предрассвéтные часы́

weed [wi:d] 1. сорня́к; 2. [вы́]полоть; ~**killer** гербици́д; ~y ['wi:di] зарóсший сорнякóм; *coll. fig. person* тóщий, долговя́зый

week [wi:k] недéля; **by the** ~ понедéльно; **for** ~**s on end** цéлыми недéлями; **this day a** ~ недéлю томý назáд; чéрез недéлю; ~**day** бýдний день *m*; ~**end** [wi:k'end] суббóта и воскресéнье, уикéнд; ~ly ['wi:kli] 1. еженедéльный; 2. еженедéльник

weep [wi:p] [*irr.*] [за]плáкать; ~ing

['wi:pɪŋ] *person* пла́чущий; *willow* плаку́чий

weigh [weɪ] *v/t.* взве́шивать [-е́сить] (*a. fig.*); ~ **anchor** поднима́ть я́корь; ~**ed down** отягощённый; *v/i.* взве́шиваться [-е́ситься]; *fig.* име́ть вес, значе́ние; ~ (**up)on** тяготе́ть над (T)

weight [weɪt] **1.** вес; (*heaviness*) тя́жесть *f*; (*object for weighing*) ги́ря; *sport* шта́нга; *of responsibility* бре́мя *n*; влия́ние; **2.** отягоща́ть [-готи́ть]; *fig.* обременя́ть [-ни́ть]; ~**y** ['weɪtɪ] □ тяжёлый; тру́дный; *fig.* ва́жный, ве́ский

weird [wɪəd] (*uncanny*) таи́нственный; стра́нный

welcome ['welkəm] **1.** приве́тствие; *you are* ~ *to* + *inf.* я охо́тно позволя́ю вам (+ *inf.*); (*you are*) ~ né за что!; ~! добро́ пожа́ловать!; **2.** (*wanted*) жела́нный; (*causing gladness*) прия́тный; **3.** (*greet*) приве́тствовать (*a. fig.*); (*receive*) ра́душно принима́ть

weld [weld] *tech.* сва́ривать [-и́ть]

welfare ['welfeə] *of nation* благосостоя́ние; *of person* благополу́чие; *Am.* социа́льная по́мощь *f*

well[1] [wel] исто́чник; *fig.* исто́чник; (*stairwell*) пролёт; *tech.* бурова́я сква́жина; **2.** хлы́нуть *pf.*

well[2] [-wel] **1.** хорошо́; ~ *off* состоя́тельный; *I am not* ~ мне нездоро́вится; **2.** *int.* ну! *or* ну, …; ~**-being** ['-'bi:ɪŋ] благополу́чие; ~**-bred** ['-'bred] (хорошо́) воспи́танный; ~**-built** ['-'bɪlt] хорошо́ сло́жённый; ~**-founded** ['-'faundɪd] обосно́ванный; ~**-kept** ['-'kept] *garden* ухо́женный; *secret* тща́тельно храни́мый; ~**-read** ['-'red] начи́танный; *in history, etc.* хорошо́ зна́ющий; ~**-timed** ['-'taɪmd] своевре́менный; ~**-to-do** [-tə'du:] состоя́тельный, зажи́точный; ~**-worn** ['-'wɔːn] поно́шенный; *fig.* изби́тый

Welsh [welʃ] **1.** уэ́льский, валли́йский; **2.** валли́йский язы́к; *the* ~ валли́йцы *m/pl.*

welter ['weltə] *of ideas* сумбу́р

went [went] *pt. om* **go**

wept [wept] *pt. и pt. p. om* **weep**

were [wə, wɜː] *pt. om* **be**

west [west] **1.** за́пад; **2.** за́падный; **3.** *adv.* к за́паду, на за́пад; ~ *of* к за́паду от (P); ~**erly** ['westəlɪ], ~**ern** ['westən] за́падный; ~**ward(s)** ['westwəd(z)] на за́пад

wet [wet] **1.** дождли́вая пого́да; *don't go out in* ~ не выходи́ под дождь; **2.** мо́крый; *weather* сыро́й; дождли́вый; "Ⓢ *Paint*" "окра́шено"; *get* ~ *through* наскво́зь промо́кнуть *pf.*; **2.** [*irr.*] [на]мочи́ть, нама́чивать [-мочи́ть]

whale [weɪl] кит

wharf [wɔːf] прича́л, при́стань *f*

what [wɒt] **1.** что?; ско́лько …?; **2.** то, что; что; ~ *about …?* что но́вого о …?; ну ка́к …?; ~ *for?* заче́м? ~ *a pity* … кака́я жа́лость …; **3.** ~ *with* … из-за (P), отча́сти от (P); **4.** како́й; ~**(so)ever** [wɒt(sou)'evə] како́й бы ни; что́ бы ни; *there is no doubt whatever* нет никако́го сомне́ния

wheat [wiːt] пшени́ца

wheel [wiːl] **1.** колесо́; *mot.* руль *m*; **2.** *pram, etc.* ката́ть, [по]кати́ть; ~ *into* вка́тывать [-ти́ть]; ~ *round* повора́чивать(ся) [поверну́ть(ся)]; ~**barrow** та́чка; ~**chair** инвали́дная коля́ска

wheeze [wiːz] хрипе́ть; дыша́ть с при́свистом

when [wen] **1.** когда́?; **2.** *conj.* когда́, в то вре́мя как, как то́лько; тогда́ как

whenever [wen'evə] вся́кий раз когда́; когда́ бы ни

where [weə] где, куда́; *from* ~ отку́да; ~**about(s)** **1.** [weərə'baut(s)] где?; **2.** ['weərəbaut(s)] местонахожде́ние; ~**as** [weər'æz] тогда́ как; поско́льку; ~**by** [weə'baɪ] посре́дством чего́; ~**in** [weər'ɪn] в чём; ~**of** [weər'ɒv] из кото́рого; о кото́ром; о чём; ~**upon** [weərə'pɒn] по́сле чего́

wherever [weər'evə] где бы ни; куда́ бы ни

wherewithal [weəwɪ'ðɔːl] необходи́мые сре́дства *n/pl.*

whet [wet] [на]точи́ть; *fig.* возбуж-

дать [-удить]
whether ['weðə] … ли; *or not* так и́ли
ина́че; в любо́м слу́чае
which [wɪtʃ] **1.** кото́рый?; како́й?; **2.**
кото́рый; что; *ever* [-'evə] како́й
уго́дно, како́й бы ни …
whiff [wɪf] *of air* дунове́ние, струя́;
(*smell*) за́пах; *of pipe, etc.*
while [waɪl] **1.** вре́мя *n*, промежу́ток
вре́мени; *after a* че́рез не́которое
вре́мя; *a little (long) ago* недавно́
(давно́); *in a little* ~ ско́ро; *for a* ~ на
вре́мя; *coll. worth* ~ сто́ящий затра́-
ченного труда́; **2.** *away time* прово-
ди́ть [-вести́]; **3.** (*a. whilst* [waɪlst])
пока́, в то вре́мя как; тогда́ как
whim [wɪm] при́хоть *f*, капри́з
whimper ['wɪmpə] [за]хны́кать
whim|sical ['wɪmzɪkl] □ прихотли́-
вый, причу́дливый; *sy* ['wɪmzɪ]
при́хоть *f*; причу́да
whine [waɪn] [за]скули́ть; [за]хны́-
кать
whip [wɪp] **1.** *v/t.* хлеста́ть [-стну́ть];
(*punish*) [вы́]сечь; *eggs, cream* сби-
(ва́)ть; ~ *out gun, etc.* выхва́тывать
['-хватить]; ~ *up* расшеве́ливать
[-ли́ть]; подстёгивать [-стегну́ть];
v/i.: *I'll whip round to the neighbo(u)rs*
я то́лько сбе́гаю к сосе́дям; **2.** плеть;
кнут, (*a. riding* ~) хлыст
whippet ['wɪpɪt] *zo.* го́нчая
whipping ['wɪpɪŋ] (*punishment*) по́р-
ка
whirl [wɜːl] **1.** *of dust* вихрь *m*; круже́-
ние; *my head is in a* ~ у меня́ голова́
идёт кру́гом; **2.** кружи́ть(ся); *pool*
водоворо́т; *wind* смерч
whisk [wɪsk] **1.** (*egg* ~) муто́вка; **2.** *v/t.*
cream, etc. сби(ва́)ть; (*remove*) сма́хи-
вать [-хну́ть]; *v/i. of mouse, etc.*
юркать [юркнуть]; *ers* ['wɪskəz] *pl.*
zo. усы́ *m/pl.*; (*side-*~) бакенба́рды
f/pl.
whiskey, *Brt.* **whisky** ['wɪskɪ] ви́ски *n*
indecl.
whisper ['wɪspə] **1.** шёпот; **2.** шепта́ть
[шепну́ть]
whistle ['wɪsl] **1.** свист; свисто́к (*a. instrument*); **2.** свисте́ть [сви́стнуть]

white [waɪt] **1.** *com.* бе́лый; (*pale*)
бле́дный; ~ *coffee* ко́фе с молоко́м;
~ *lie* ложь *f* во спасе́ние; **2.** бе́лый
цвет; *of eye, egg* бело́к; *n* ['waɪn]
[по]беле́ть; (*turn white*) [по]беле́ть;
ness ['waɪtnɪs] белизна́; *wash* **1.** по-
бе́лка; **2.** [по]бели́ть; *fig.* обеля́ть
[-ли́ть]
whitish ['waɪtɪʃ] бел(ес)ова́тый
Whitsun ['wɪtsn] *relig.* Тро́ица
whiz(z) [wɪz] *of bullets, etc.* свисте́ть; ~
past промча́ться *pf.* ми́мо
who [huː] *pron.* **1.** кто?; **2.** кото́рый;
кто; тот, кто …; *pl.*: те, кто
whoever [huː'evə] *pron.* кто бы ни …;
(*who ever*) кто то́лько; кото́рый бы
ни …
whole [həʊl] **1.** □ (*complete, entire*) це́-
лый, весь; (*intact, undamaged*) це́-
лый; ~ *milk* це́льное молоко́; ~ *number* це́лое число́; **2.** це́лое; всё *n*; ито́г;
on the ~ (*entity, totality*) в це́лом;
hearted □ и́скренний, от всего́
се́рдца; *sale* **1.** (*mst.* ~ *trade*) о́птовая
торго́вля; **2.** о́птовый; *fig.* (*indiscriminate*) огу́льный; ~ *dealer* о́птовый
торго́вец; **3.** о́птом; *some* ['həʊlsəm]
□ поле́зный, здоро́вый
wholly ['həʊlɪ] *adv.* целико́м, всеце́л-
по́лностью
whom [huːm] *pron.* (*вини́тельный
паде́ж от* **who**) кого́ *и т. д.*; кото́ро-
го *и т. д.*
whoop [huːp]: ~ *of joy* ра́достный во́з-
глас; *ing cough* ['huːpɪŋ kɒf] *med.*
коклю́ш
whose [huːz] (*роди́тельный паде́ж
от* **who**) чей *m*, чья *f*, чьё *n*, чьи
pl.; *relative pron. mst.*: кото́рого, кото́-
рой; ~ *father* оте́ц кото́рого
why [waɪ] **1.** *adv.* почему́?, отчего́?, за-
че́м?; **2.** *int.* да ведь …; что ж…
wick [wɪk] фити́ль *m*
wicked ['wɪkɪd] □ (*malicious*) злой,
зло́бный; (*depraved*) бессо́вестный;
(*immoral*) безнра́вственный
wicker ['wɪkə]: ~ *basket* плетёная кор-
зи́нка; ~ *chair* плетёный стул
wide [waɪd] *a.* □ *and adv.* широ́кий;
обши́рный; широко́; далеко́, далеко́

W

(*of* от P); **~ awake** бди́тельный; осмотри́тельный; **three feet ~** три фу́та в ширину́, ширино́й в три фу́та; **~ of the mark** далёкий от и́стины; не по существу́; **~n** ['waɪdn] расширя́ть(ся) [-и́рить(ся)]; **~spread** распространённый

widow ['wɪdəʊ] вдова́; **grass ~** соло́менная вдова́; *attr.* вдо́вий; **~er** [-ə] вдове́ц

width [wɪdθ] ширина́; (*extent*) широта́

wield [wi:ld] *lit.* владе́ть (Т); держа́ть в рука́х

wife [waɪf] жена́; (*spouse*) супру́га

wig [wɪg] пари́к

wild [waɪld] **1.** □ ди́кий; *flowers* полево́й; *sea* бу́рный; *behavio(u)r* бу́йный; **be ~ about s.o.** *or* **s.th.** быть без ума́ в ди́ком восто́рге от кого́-л. *or* чего́-л.; **run ~** расти́ без присмо́тра; **talk ~** говори́ть не ду́мая; **2. ~, ~s** [-z] ди́кая ме́стность *f*; де́бри *f/pl.*; **~cat strike** неофициа́льная забасто́вка; **~erness** ['wɪldənɪs] пусты́ня, ди́кая ме́стность *f*; **~fire:** **like ~fire** с быстрото́й мо́лнии; **~fowl** дичь *f*

wile [waɪl] *mst.* **~s** *pl.* хи́трость *f*; уло́вка

wil(l)ful ['wɪlfl] упря́мый, своево́льный; (*intentional*) преднаме́ренный

will [wɪl] **1.** во́ля; (*willpower*) си́ла во́ли; (*desire*) жела́ние; *law* (*testament*) завеща́ние; **with a ~** энерги́чно; **2.** [*irr.*] *v/aux.:* **he ~ come** он придёт; **3.** завеща́ть (*im*)*pf.*; [по]жела́ть, [за]хоте́ть; **~ o.s. compel** заставля́ть [-ста́вить] себя́

willing ['wɪlɪŋ] □ *to help, etc.* гото́вый (**to** на B *or* + *inf.*); **~ness** [-nɪs] гото́вность *f*

willow ['wɪləʊ] *bot.* и́ва

wilt [wɪlt] □ *of flowers* [за]вя́нуть; *of person* [по]ни́кнуть; раскиса́ть [-ки́снуть]

wily ['waɪlɪ] □ хи́трый, кова́рный

win [wɪn] [*irr.*] *v/t.* побежда́ть [-еди́ть]; выи́грывать; *victory* оде́рживать [-жа́ть]; *prize* получа́ть [-чи́ть]; **~ a p. over** угова́ривать [-вори́ть]; склони́ть кого́-л. на свою́ сто́рону; *v/i.*

выи́грывать [вы́играть]; оде́рживать побе́ду

wince [wɪns] вздра́гивать [вздро́гнуть]

winch [wɪntʃ] лебёдка; во́рот

wind[1] [wɪnd] ве́тер; (*breath*) дыха́ние; *of bowels, etc.* га́зы *m/pl.;* *mus.* духовы́е инструме́нты *m/pl.* **let me get my ~ back** подожди́, я отдышу́сь; **get ~ of** *s.th.* [по]чу́ять; узна́ть *pf.*, проню́хать *pf.;* **second ~** второе дыха́ние

wind[2] [waɪnd] [*irr.*] *v/t.* нама́тывать [намота́ть]; обма́тывать [обмота́ть]; *of plant* обви(ва́)ть; **~ up** *watch* заводи́ть [завести́]; *comm.* ликвиди́ровать (*im*)*pf.;* *discussion, etc.* зака́нчивать [зако́нчить]; *v/i.* нама́тываться [намота́ться]; обви(ва́)ться

winding ['waɪndɪŋ] **1.** изги́б, изви́лина; (*act of ~*) нама́тывание; *el.* обмо́тка; **2.** изви́листый; **~ stairs** *pl.* винтова́я ле́стница

wind instrument духово́й инструме́нт

windmill ветряна́я ме́льница

window ['wɪndəʊ] окно́; (*shop ~*) витри́на; **~ dressing** оформле́ние витри́ны; *fig.* показу́ха *coll.;* **~sill** [-sɪl] подоко́нник

wind|pipe ['wɪndpaɪp] *anat.* трахе́я; **~shield**, *Brt.* **~screen** *mot.* ветровое стекло́

windy ['wɪndɪ] □ ве́треный; *fig.* (*wordy*) многосло́вный; *chiefly Brt. coll.* **get ~** стру́сить *pf.*

wine [waɪn] вино́; **~ glass** бока́л; рю́мка

wing [wɪŋ] (*a. arch.*) крыло́; *thea.* **~s** *pl.* кули́сы *f/pl.;* **take ~** полете́ть *pf.;* **on the ~** в полёте; **take s.o. under one's ~** взять *pf.* кого́-л. под своё кры́лышко

wink [wɪŋk] **1.** (*moment*) миг; *coll.* **not get a ~ of sleep** не сомкну́ть *pf.* глаз; **2.** морга́ть [-гну́ть], мига́ть [мигну́ть]; **~ at** подми́гивать [-гну́ть] (Д); *fig.* (*connive*) смотре́ть сквозь па́льцы на (B)

win|ner ['wɪnə] победи́тель m, -ница f; *in some competitions* призёр; лауреа́т; **Nobel Prize ~** лауреа́т Нобелевской пре́мии; **~ning** ['wɪnɪŋ] **1.** (*on way to winning*) выи́грывающий; побежда́ющий; (*having won*) вы́игравший, победи́вший; *fig.* (*attractive, persuasive*) обая́тельный (*a.* **~some** [-səm]); **2. ~s** *pl.* вы́игрыш

wint|er ['wɪntə] **1.** зима́; *attr.* зи́мний; **2.** проводи́ть зи́му, (пере-, про)зимова́ть; **~ry** ['wɪntrɪ] зи́мний

wipe [waɪp] вытира́ть [вы́тереть]; *tears* утира́ть [утере́ть]; **~ off** стира́ть [стере́ть]; **~ out** (*destroy*) уничтожа́ть [-о́жить]; **~r** ['waɪpə] (*windshield ~*, *Brt.* windscreen ~) стеклоочисти́тель; *coll.* дво́рник

wire ['waɪə] **1.** про́волока; *el.* про́вод; *coll.* телегра́мма; **2.** [c]де́лать прово́дку; телеграфи́ровать (*im*)*pf.*; **~ netting** про́волочная се́тка

wiry ['waɪərɪ] *person* жи́листый; *hair* жёсткий

wisdom ['wɪzdəm] му́дрость f; **~ tooth** зуб му́дрости

wise[1] [waɪz] му́дрый; благоразу́мный; **~crack** *coll.* остро́та

wise[2] [-] *in no ~* нико́им о́бразом

wish [wɪʃ] **1.** жела́ние; пожела́ние (*a.* greetings); **2.** [по]жела́ть (P) (*a.* ~ *for*); ~ *well* (*ill*) жела́ть добра́ (зла); **~ful** ['wɪʃfl] □ **~ thinking** *in context* принима́ть жела́емое за действи́тельное

wisp [wɪsp] *of smoke* стру́йка; *of hair* прядь f

wistful ['wɪstfl] □ заду́мчивый, тоскли́вый

wit [wɪt] *verbal felicity* (*mental astuteness*) ум, ра́зум (*a.* **~s** *pl.*); остросло́в; *be at one's ~'s end* в отчча́янии; *I'm at my ~s end* пря́мо ум за ра́зум захо́дит; *be scared out of one's ~s* испуга́ться до́ сме́рти

witch [wɪtʃ] колду́нья; ве́дьма; **~craft** колдовство́; **~hunt** охо́та за ве́дьмами

with [wɪð] с (T), со (T); (*because of*) от (P); у (P); при (П); ~ *a knife* ножо́м, ~ *pen* ру́чкой

withdraw [wɪð'drɔː] [*irr.* (**draw**)] *v/t.*
убира́ть; *quickly* одёргивать [-рнуть]; *money from banks* брать [взять]; брать наза́д; *from circulation* изыма́ть [изъя́ть]; *troops* выводи́ть [-вести]; *v/i.* удаля́ться [-ли́ться]; *mil.* отходи́ть [отойти́]; **~al** [-əl] изъя́тие; удале́ние; *mil.* отхо́д; вы́вод; **~n** *person* за́мкнутый

wither ['wɪðə] *v/i.* [за]вя́нуть; *of colo(u)r* [по]бле́кнуть; *v/t.* crops погуби́ть *pf.*; **~ed hopes** увя́дшие наде́жды

withhold [wɪð'həʊld] [*irr.* (**hold**)] (*refuse to give*) отка́зывать [-за́ть] в (П); *information* скры(ва́)ть (*from* от P); **~in** [-'ɪn] **1.** *lit. adv.* внутри́; **2.** *prp.* в (П), в преде́лах (P); внутри́ (P); **~ call** в преде́лах слы́шимости; **~out** [-'aʊt] **1.** *lit. adv.* вне, снару́жи; **2.** *prp.* без (P); вне (P); *it goes* **~** *saying* ... само́ собо́й разуме́ется; **~stand** [-'stænd] [*irr.* (**stand**)] выде́рживать [вы́держать] про тивосто(я́)ть (Д)

witness ['wɪtnɪs] **1.** свиде́тель m, -ница f; очеви́дец m, -дица f; *bear* **~** свиде́тельствовать (*to, of* о П); **2.** свиде́тельствовать о (П); быть свиде́телем (P); *signature, etc.* заверя́ть [-е́рить]

wit|ticism ['wɪtɪsɪzəm] остро́та; **~ty** ['wɪtɪ] □ остроу́мный

wives [waɪvz] *pl. om* **wife**

wizard ['wɪzəd] волше́бник, маг

wizened ['wɪznd] *old lady* вы́сохший; *apple, etc.* смо́рщенный

wobble ['wɒbl] кача́ться, шата́ться

woe [wəʊ] го́ре; **~begone** ['wəʊbɪgɒn] удручённый

woke [wəʊk] *pt. om* **wake**; **~n** ['wəʊkən] *pt. p. om* **wake**

wolf [wʊlf] **1.** волк; **2. ~ down** есть бы́стро и с жа́дностью; на́спех проглоти́ть

wolves [wʊlvz] *pl. om* **wolf**

woman ['wʊmən] же́нщина; *old* ~ стару́ха; ~ *doctor* же́нщина-врач, **~ish** [-ɪʃ] □ женоподо́бный, ба́бий; **~kind** [-'kaɪnd] *collect.* же́нщины f *pl.*; **~ly** [-lɪ] же́нственный

womb [wuːm] *anat.* ма́тка; чре́во ма́тери

women ['wɪmɪn] *pl. om* **woman**; **~folk**

[-fəuk] же́нщины *f/pl.*

won [wʌn] *pt.* и *pt. p. om* **win**

wonder ['wʌndə] **1.** удивле́ние, изумле́ние; (*miracle*) чу́до; **2.** удивля́ться [-ви́ться] (*at* Д); **I ~** интере́сно, хоте́лось бы знать; **~ful** [-fl] □ удиви́тельный, замеча́тельный

won't [wəunt] не бу́ду *и т. д.*; не хочу́ *и т. д.*

wont [-]: **be ~** име́ть обыкнове́ние

woo [wuː] уха́живать за (Т)

wood [wʊd] лес; (*material*) де́рево, лесоматериа́л; (*fire~*) дрова́ *n/pl.*; **dead ~** сухосто́й; *fig.* балла́ст; *attr.* лесно́й, деревя́нный/дровяно́й; **~cut** гравю́ра на де́реве; *fig.* безжи́зненный; **~cutter** дровосе́к; **~ed** ['wʊdɪd] леси́стый; **~en** ['wʊdn] деревя́нный; *fig.* безжи́зненный; **~pecker** [-pekə] дя́тел; **~winds** [-wɪndz] деревя́нные духовы́е инструме́нты *m/pl.*; **~work** деревя́нные изде́лия *n/pl.*; *of building* деревя́нные ча́сти *f/pl.*; **~y** ['wʊdɪ] леси́стый

wool [wʊl] шерсть *f*; *attr.* шерстяно́й; **~gathering** ['wʊlgæðərɪŋ] *fig.* мечта́тельность; вита́ние в облака́х; **~(l)en** ['wʊlɪn] шерстяно́й; **~ly** ['wʊlɪ] **1.** (*like wool*) шерсти́стый; *thoughts* нея́сный; **2.** **woollies** *pl.* шерстяны́е изде́лия *n/pl.*; *esp.* бельё

word [wɜːd] **1.** *mst.* сло́во; разгово́р; (*news*) изве́стия, но́вости; (*promise*) обеща́ние, сло́во; **~s** *pl. mus.* слова́ *n/pl.*; *fig.* (*angry argument*) кру́пный разгово́р; **in a ~** сло́вом; **in other ~s** други́ми слова́ми; **~ of hono(u)r** че́стное сло́во; **2.** формули́ровать (*im*)*pf., pf. a.* [с-]; **~ing** ['wɜːdɪŋ] формулиро́вка

wordy ['wɜːdɪ] □ многосло́вный

wore [wɔː] *pt. om* **wear 1**

work [wɜːk] **1.** рабо́та; труд; де́ло; заня́тие; *art, lit.* произведе́ние, сочине́ние; *attr.* рабо́то...; рабо́чий; **~s** *pl.* механи́зм; (*construction*) строи́тельные рабо́ты *f/pl.*; (*mill*) заво́д; (*factory*) фа́брика; **all in a day's ~** де́ло привы́чное; **be out of ~** быть безрабо́тным; **I'm sure it's his ~** уве́рен, э́то де́ло его́ рук; **set to ~** бра́ться за рабо́ту;

2. *v/i.* рабо́тать; занима́ться [-ня́ться] (*have effect*) де́йствовать; *v/t.* [*irr.*] *land, etc.* обраба́тывать [-бо́тать]; [*regular vb.*] *mine, etc.* разраба́тывать [-бо́тать]; приводи́ть в де́йствие; **~ one's way through crowd** проби(ва́)ться, с трудо́м пробива́ть себе́ доро́гу (*both a. fig.*); **~ off debt** отраба́тывать [-бо́тать]; *anger* успока́иваться [-ко́иться]; **~ out** *problem* реша́ть [реши́ть]; *plan* разраба́тывать [-бо́тать]; *agreement* составля́ть [-вить]; [*a. irr.*]; **~ up** (*excite*) возбужда́ть; *coll.* взбудора́жи(ва)ть; **don't get ~ed up** споко́йно

work|able ['wɜːkəbl] осуществи́мый; приго́дный; приго́дный для обрабо́тки; **~aday** (*time worked for payment*) бу́дний; повседне́вный; **~day** бу́день *m*; **~er** ['wɜːkə] *manual* рабо́чий; рабо́тник (-и́ца); **~ing** ['wɜːkɪŋ] рабо́чий; рабо́тающий; **in ~ order** в рабо́чем состоя́нии; **~ capital** оборо́тный капита́л

workman ['wɜːkmən] рабо́тник; **~ship** мастерство́; (*signs of skill*) отде́лка

work|shop ['wɜːkʃɒp] мастерска́я; *in factory* цех

world [wɜːld] *com.* мир, свет; *attr.* мирово́й, всеми́рный; *fig.* **a ~ of difference** огро́мная ра́зница; **come into the ~** роди́ться, появи́ться *pf.* на свет; **come up in the ~** преуспе́(ва́)ть (в жи́зни); сде́лать карье́ру; **it's a small ~** мир те́сен; **champion of the ~** чемпио́н ми́ра

wordly ['wɜːldlɪ] све́тский

world power мирова́я держа́ва

worldwide ['wɜːldwaɪd] всеми́рный

worm [wɜːm] **1.** червя́к, червь *m*; *med.* глист; **2.** выве́дывать (вы́ведать), вы́пы́тывать [вы́пытать] (*out of* у Р); **~ o.s.** *fig.* вкра́дываться [вкра́сться] (*into* в В)

worn [wɔːn] *pt. p. om* **wear**, **~-out** [wɔːn-ˈaʊt] изно́шенный; *fig.* изму́ченный

worry ['wʌrɪ] **1.** беспоко́йство; трево́га; (*care*) забо́та; **2.** беспоко́ить(ся); (*bother with questions, etc.*) надоеда́ть [-е́сть] (Д); (*pester*) пристава́ть к (Д);

W

[за]му́чить; **she'll ~ herself to death!** она́ совсе́м изведёт себя́!

worse [wɜ:s] ху́дший; *adv.* ху́же; *of pain, etc.* сильне́е; **from bad to ~** всё ху́же и ху́же; **~n** ['wɜ:sn] ухудша́ть(ся) [уху́дшить(ся)]

worship ['wɜ:ʃɪp] **1.** *relig.* богослуже́ние; **2.** поклоня́ться (Д); (*love*) обожа́ть; **~per** [-ə] покло́нник *m*, -ица *f*

worst [wɜ:st] (са́мый ху́дший, наиху́дший); *adv.* ху́же всего́; **if the ~ comes to the ~** в са́мом ху́дшем слу́чае; **the ~ of it is that ...** ху́же всего́ то, что …

worth [wɜ:θ] **1.** сто́ящий; заслу́живающий; **be ~** заслу́живать, сто́ить; **2.** цена́; сто́имость *f*; це́нность *f*; **idea of little ~** иде́я, не име́ющая осо́бой це́нности; **~less** ['wɜ:θlɪs] ничего́ не сто́ящий; не име́ющий це́нности; **~while** ['wɜ:θ'waɪl] *coll.* сто́ящий; **be ~** име́ть смысл; **be not ~** не сто́ить труда́; **~y** ['wɜ:ðɪ] □ досто́йный (**of** P); заслу́живающий (**of** B)

would [wʊd] (*pt. om* **will**) *v/aux.*: **he ~ do it** он сде́лал бы э́то; он обы́чно э́то де́лал

wound[1] [wu:nd] **1.** ра́на, ране́ние; **2.** ра́нить (*im*)*pf.*; заде́(ва́)ть

wound[2] [waʊnd] *pt. u pt. p. om* **wind**

wove ['wəʊv] *pt. om* **weave**; **~n** ['wəʊvn] *pt. p. om* **weave**

wrangle ['ræŋgl] **1.** пререка́ния *n/pl.*, **2.** пререка́ться

wrap [ræp] *v/t.* (ча́сто **~ up**) завёртывать [заверну́ть]; *in paper* обёртывать [оберну́ть]; закут(ыв)ать; *fig.* окут(ыв)ать; **be ~ped up in thought**, *etc.* быть погружённым в (В); *v/i.* **~ up** закут(ыв)аться; **~per** ['ræpə] обёртка; **~ping** ['ræpɪŋ] упако́вка; обёртка

wrath [rɔ:θ] гнев

wreath [ri:θ], *pl.* **~s** [ri:ðz] *placed on coffin* вено́к; гирля́нда; *fig. of smoke* кольцо́, коле́чко

wreck [rek] **1.** (*destruction*) *esp. of ship* круше́ние; ава́рия; катастро́фа; *involving person, vehicle, etc.* разва́лина; **2.** *building, plans* разруша́ть [-у́шить];

car разби́ть *pf.*; **be ~ed** потерпе́ть *pf.* круше́ние; **~age** ['rekɪdʒ] (*remains*) обло́мки

wrench [rentʃ] **1.** (*spanner*) га́ечный ключ; **give a ~** дёрнуть *pf.*; **2.** вырыва́ть [-рвать]; *joint* выви́хивать [вы́вихнуть]; *fig.*, (*distort*) *facts, etc.* искажа́ть [искази́ть]; **~ open** взла́мывать [взлома́ть]

wrest [rest] вырыва́ть [вы́рвать] (**from** у Р) (*a. fig.*); **~le** ['resl] *mst. sport* боро́ться [-ли́ть]; **~ling** [-lɪŋ] борьба́

wretch [retʃ]: **poor ~** бедня́га

wretched ['retʃɪd] □ несча́стный; (*pitiful*) жа́лкий

wriggle ['rɪgl] *of worm, etc.* изви́ва́ться; **~ out of** уклоня́ться [-ни́ться] от (Р), выкру́чиваться [вы́крутиться] из (Р)

wring [rɪŋ] [*irr.*] скру́чивать [-ути́ть]; *one's hands* лома́ть (*a. ~ out*) *of washing, etc.* выжима́ть [вы́жать]; *money* вымога́ть (**from** у Р); *confession* вы́рвать *pf.* (**from** у Р)

wrinkle ['rɪŋkl] **1.** *in skin* морщи́на; *in dress* скла́дка; **2.** [с]мо́рщить(ся)

wrist [rɪst] запя́стье; **~ watch** ручны́е (*or* нару́чные) часы́ *m/pl.*

write [raɪt] [*irr.*] [на]писа́ть; **~ down** запи́сывать [-са́ть]; **~ out** *check, Brt. cheque, etc.* выпи́сывать [вы́писать]; **~ off** (*cancel*) спи́сывать [-са́ть]; **~r** ['raɪtə] писа́тель *m*, -ница *f*

writhe [raɪð] *with pain* [с]ко́рчиться

writing ['raɪtɪŋ] **1.** *process* писа́ние; (*composition*) письмо́; (*literatúrное) произведе́ние, сочине́ние; (*a. hand ~*) по́черк; **in ~** пи́сьменно; **2.** пи́сьменный; **~ paper** пи́счая бума́га

written ['rɪtn] **1.** *pt. p. om* **write**; **2.** пи́сьменный

wrong [rɒŋ] **1.** □ (*not correct*) непра́вильный, оши́бочный; не тот (, кото́рый ну́жен); **be ~** быть непра́вым; **go ~** *of things* не получа́ться [-чи́ться], срыва́ться [сорва́ться]; (*make a mistake*) сде́лать *pf.* оши́бку; **come at the ~ time** прийти́ *pf.* не во́время; *adv.* непра́вильно, не так; **2.** непра́вота́; непра́вильность *f*; (*injustice, unjust* *action*) оби́да; несправедли́вость *f*; зло; **know right from~** отлича́ть добро́ от зла; **3.** поступа́ть несправедли́во с (Т); обижа́ть [оби́деть]; **~doer** [~du:ə] гре́шник *m*, -ница*f*; престу́пник *m*, -ница *f*; правонаруши́тель; **~ful** ['rɒŋfl] □ (*unlawful*) незако́нный;

(*unjust*) несправедли́вый
wrote [rəut] *pt. om* **write**
wrought [rɔːt] *pt. и pt. p. om* **work 2** [*irr.*]: **~ iron** кова́ное желе́зо
wrung [rʌŋ] *pt. и pt. p. om* **wring**
wry [raɪ] □ *smile* криво́й; *remark* переко́шенный; ирони́ческий

X

xerox ['zɪərɒks] **1.** ксе́рокс; **2.** ксерокопи́ровать
Xmas ['krɪsməs, 'eksməs] → **Christmas**
X-ray ['eksreɪ] **1.** рентге́новские лучи́ *m/pl.*; рентгеногра́мма; **2.** просве́чивать [просвети́ть] рентге́новскими луча́ми; [с]де́лать рентге́н
xylophone ['zaɪləfəun] ксилофо́н

Y

yacht [jɒt] **1.** я́хта; **2.** плыть на я́хте; **~ing** ['jɒtɪŋ] па́русный спорт
yankee ['jæŋki] *coll.* я́нки *m indecl.*
yap [jæp] **1.** тя́вкать [-кнуть]; болта́ть
yard¹ [jɑːd] двор
yard² [-] ярд; измери́тельная лине́йка; **~stick** *fig.* мери́ло, ме́рка
yarn [jɑːn] пря́жа; *coll. fig.* расска́з; **spin a ~** плести́ небыли́цы
yawn [jɔːn] **1.** зево́та; **2.** зева́ть [зевну́ть]; *fig.* (*be wide open*) зия́ть
year [jɪə, jɜː] год (*pl.* года́, го́ды, ле́та *n/pl.*); **he is six ~s old** ему́ шесть лет; **~ly** [-lɪ] ежего́дный
yearn [jɜːn] тоскова́ть (**for, after** по Д)
yeast [jiːst] дро́жжи *f/pl.*
yell [jel] **1.** пронзи́тельный крик; **2.** пронзи́тельно крича́ть, (*howl*) [за]вопи́ть
yellow ['jeləu] **1.** жёлтый; *coll.* (*cowardly*) трусли́вый; **~ press** жёлтая пре́сса; **2.** [по]желте́ть; **~ed** [-d] пожелте́вший; **~ish** [-ɪʃ] желтова́тый
yelp [jelp] **1.** лай, визг; **2.** [за]визжа́ть, [за]ла́ять
yes [jes] да; нет: **you don't like tea? –**

Yes, I do Вы не лю́бите чай? – Нет, люблю́
yesterday ['jestədɪ] вчера́
yet [jet] **1.** *adv.* ещё, всё ещё; уже́; до сих пор; да́же; тем не ме́нее; **as ~** пока́, до сих пор; **not ~** ещё не(т); **2.** *cj.* одна́ко, всё же, несмотря́ на э́то
yield [jiːld] **1.** *v/t.* (*give*) приноси́ть [-нести́]; (*surrender*) сда(ва́)ть; *v/i.* уступа́ть [-пи́ть] (**to** Д); подд(ав)а́ться; сд(ав)а́ться; **2.** *agric.* урожа́й; *fin.* дохо́д; **~ing** ['jiːldɪŋ] □ *fig.* усту́пчивый
yog|a ['jəugə] (*system*) йо́га; **~i** [-gɪ] йог
yog(h)urt ['jɒgət] йо́гурт
yoke [jəuk] ярмо́ (*a. fig.*); иго; *for carrying, buckets, pails, etc.* коромы́сло
yolk [jəuk] желто́к
you [jə, … ju, … ju:] *pron. pers.* ты, вы; тебя́, вас; тебе́, вам (*часто* **to ~**) *n m. д.*; **~ and I (me)** мы с ва́ми
young [jʌŋ] **1.** □ молодо́й; *person* ю́ный; **2. the ~** молодёжь *f*; *zo.* детёныши *m/pl.*; **~ster** ['jʌŋstə] подро́сток, ю́ноша *m*

your [jə, … jɔ:] *pron. poss.* твой *m*, твоя́ *f*, твоё *n*, твои́ *pl.*; ваш *m*, ва́ша *f*, ва́ше *n*, ва́ши *pl.*; **~s** [jɔ:z] *pron. poss. absolute form* твой *m*, твоя́ *f* и *m. д.*; **~self** [jɔ:'self], *pl.* **~selves** [-'selvz] сам *m*, сама́ *f*, само́ *n*, са́ми *pl.*; себя́, -ся

youth [ju:θ] *collect.* молодёжь *f*, (*boy*) ю́ноша *m*, мо́лодость *f*, **in my ~** в мо́лодости (*or* в ю́ности); **~ful** ['ju:θfl] □ ю́ношеский; (*looking young*) моложа́вый

Z

zeal [zi:l] рве́ние, усе́рдие; **~ous** ['zeləs] □ рья́ный, усе́рдный, ре́вностный

zenith ['zeniθ] зени́т (*a. fig.*)

zero ['zɪərəu] нуль *m* (*a.* ноль *m*); **10˚ below** (**above**) **~** де́сять гра́дусов моро́за (тепла́) *or* ни́же (вы́ше) нуля́

zest [zest] (*gusto*) жар; **~ for life** жизнера́достность; любо́вь к жи́зни

zigzag ['zɪgzæg] зигза́г

zinc [zɪŋk] цинк; *attr.* ци́нковый

zip [zɪp] (*sound of bullets*) свист; *coll.* эне́ргия; **~ code** почто́вый и́ндекс; **~**

fastener = **~per** ['zɪpə] (застёжка-)-мо́лния

zone [zəun] зо́на (*a. pol.*); *geogr.* по́яс; (*region*) райо́н

zoo [zu:] зооса́д, зоопа́рк

zoolog|ical [zəuə'lɒdʒɪkl] □ зоологи́ческий; **~ gardens** → **zoo**; **~y** [zəu'ɒlədʒɪ] зооло́гия

zoom [zu:m] **1.** (*hum, buzz*) жужжа́ние; *ae.*, (*vertical climb*) свеча́, го́рка; **2.** [про]жужжа́ть; *ae.* [с]де́лать свечу́/го́рку; **~ lens** объекти́в с переме́нным фо́кусным расстоя́нием

Appendix

Important Russian Abbreviations

авт. *авто́бус* bus

АЗС *автозапра́вочная ста́нция* filling station

акад. *акаде́мик* academician

АТС *автомати́ческая телефо́нная ста́нция* telephone exchange

АЭС *а́томная электроста́нция* nuclear power station

б-ка *библиоте́ка* library

б. *бы́вший* former, ex-

БСЭ *Больша́я сове́тская энциклопе́дия* Big Soviet Encyclopedia

в. *век* century

вв. *века́* centuries

ВВС *вое́нно-возду́шные си́лы* Air Forces

ВИЧ *ви́рус имунодефици́та челове́ка* HIV (human immunodeficiency virus)

вм. *вме́сто* instead of

ВОЗ *Всеми́рная организа́ция здравоохране́ния* WHO (World Health Organization)

ВС *Верхо́вный Сове́т* *hist.* Supreme Soviet; *вооружённые си́лы* the armed forces

вуз *вы́сшее уче́бное заведе́ние* university, college

г *грамм* gram(me)

г. 1. *год* year; 2. *го́род* city

га *гекта́р* hectare

ГАИ *Госуда́рственная автомоби́льная инспе́кция* traffic police

ГАТТ *Генера́льное соглаше́ние по тамо́женным тари́фам и торго́вле* GATT (General Agreement on Tariffs and Trade)

гг. *го́ды* years

г-жа *госпожа́* Mrs

глав... *in compounds* *гла́вный* chief, main

главвра́ч *гла́вный врач* head physician

г-н *господи́н* Mr

гос... *in compounds* *госуда́рственный* state, public

гр. *граждани́н* citizen

ГУМ *Госуда́рственный универ-* *са́льный магази́н* department store

дир. *дире́ктор* director

ДК *Дом культу́ры* House of Culture

доб. *доба́вочный* additional

доц. *доце́нт* lecturer, reader, assistant professor

д-р *до́ктор* doctor

ЕС *Европе́йский сою́з* EU (European Union)

ЕЭС *Европе́йское экономи́ческое соо́бщество* EEC (European Economic Community)

ж.д. *желе́зная доро́га* railroad, railway

зав. *заве́дующий* head of ...

загс *отде́л за́писей гражда́нского состоя́ния* registrar's (registry) office

зам. *замести́тель* deputy, assistant

и др. *и други́е* etc.

им. *и́мени* called

и мн. др. *и мно́гие други́е* and many (much) more

ИНТЕРПОЛ *Междунаро́дная организа́ция уголо́вной поли́ции* INTERPOL

и пр., и проч. *и про́чее* etc

ИТАР *Информацио́нное телегра́фное аге́нтство Росси́и* ITAR (Information Telegraph Agency of Russia)

и т.д. *и так да́лее* and so on

и т.п. *и тому́ подо́бное* etc.

к. *копе́йка* kopeck

кг *килогра́мм* kg (kilogram[me])

кв. 1. *квадра́тный* square; 2. *кварти́ра* apartment, flat

км/час *киломе́тров в час* km/h (kilometers per hour)

колхо́з *коллекти́вное хозя́йство* collective farm, kolkhoz

коп. *копе́йка* kopeck

к.п.д. *коэффицие́нт поле́зного де́йствия* efficiency

КПСС *Коммунисти́ческая па́ртия Сове́тского Сою́за* hist. C.P.S.U. (Communist Party of the Soviet Union)

куб. *куби́ческий* cubic

л.с. *лошади́ная си́ла* h.p. (horse power)

МАГАТЭ *Междунаро́дное аге́нтство по а́томной эне́ргии* IAEA (International Atomic Energy Agency)

МБР *Министе́рство безопа́сности Росси́и* Ministry of Security of Russia

МВД *Министе́рство вну́тренних дел* Ministry of Internal Affairs

МВФ *Междунаро́дный валю́тный фонд* IMF (International Monetary Fund)

МГУ *Моско́вский госуда́рственный университе́т* Moscow State University

МИД *Министе́рство иностра́нных дел* Ministry of Foreign Affairs

МО *Министе́рство оборо́ны* Ministry of Defence

МОК *Междунаро́дный олимпи́йский комите́т* IOC (International Olympic Committee)

МОТ *Междунаро́дная организа́ция труда́* ILO (International Labor Organization)

м.пр. *ме́жду про́чим* by the way, incidentally; among other things

МХАТ *Моско́вский худо́жественный академи́ческий теа́тр* Academic Artists' Theater, Moscow

напр. *наприме́р* for instance

№ *но́мер* number

НА́ТО *Североатланти́ческий сою́з* NATO (North Atlantic Treaty Organization)

НЛО *неопо́знанный лета́ющий объе́кт* UFO (unidentified flying object)

н.э. *на́шей э́ры* A.D.

о. *о́стров* island

обл. *о́бласть* region

ОБСЕ *Организа́ция по безо-*

па́сности и сотру́дничеству в Евро́пе OSCE (Organisation on Security and Cooperation in Europe)

о-во *о́бщество* society

оз. *о́зеро* lake

ОНО *отде́л наро́дного образова́ния* Department of Popular Education

ООН *Организа́ция Объедине́нных На́ций* UNO (United Nations Organization)

отд. *отде́л* section, **отделе́ние** department

ОПЕК *Организа́ция стран-экспортёров не́фти* OPEC (Organization of Petroleum Exporting Countries)

п. *пункт* point, paragraph

пер. *переу́лок* lane

ПК *персона́льный компью́тер* PC (personal computer)

пл. *пло́щадь* f square; area (a. math.)

проф. *профе́ссор* professor

р. 1. *река́* river; **2.** *рубль* m r(o)uble

райко́м *райо́нный комите́т* district committee (Sov.)

РИА *Росси́йское информацио́нное аге́нство* Information Agency of Russia

РФ *Росси́йская Федера́ция* Russian Federation

с.г. *сего́ го́да* (of) this year

след. *сле́дующий* following

см *сантиме́тр* cm. (centimeter)

с.м. *сего́ ме́сяца* (of) this month

см. *смотри́* see

СНГ *Содру́жество незави́симых госуда́рств* CIS (Commonwealth of Independent States)

СП *совме́стное предприя́тие* joint venture

СПИД *синдро́м преобретённого имунодефици́та* AIDS (acquired immune deficiency syndrome)

ср. *сравни́* cf. (compare)

СССР *Сою́з Сове́тских Социалисти́ческих Респу́блик* hist. U.S.S.R. (Union of Soviet Socialist

Republics)

ст. *ста́нция* station

стенгазе́та *стенна́я газе́та* wall newspaper

с., стр. *страни́ца* page

с.х. *се́льское хозя́йство* agriculture

с.-х. *сельскохозя́йственный* agricultural

США *Соединённые Шта́ты Аме́рики* U.S.A (United States of America)

т *то́нна* ton

т. 1. *това́рищ* comrade; **2.** *том* volume

ТАСС *Телегра́фное аге́нтство Сове́тского Сою́за* hist. TASS (Telegraph Agency of the Soviet Union)

т-во *това́рищество* company, association

т. е. *то есть* i.e. (that is)

тел. *телефо́н* telephone

т.к. *так как* cf. *так*

т. наз. *так называ́емый* so-called

тов. → *т. 1*

торгпре́дство *торго́вое представи́тельство* trade agency

тт. *тома́* volumes

тыс. *ты́сяча* thousand

ул. *у́лица* street

ФБР *Федера́льное бюро́ рассле́дований* FBI (Federal Bureau of Investigation)

ФИФА *Междунаро́дная ассоциа́ция футбо́льных о́бществ* FIFA (Fédération Internationale de Football)

ФРГ *Федерати́вная Респу́блика Герма́ния* Federal Republic of Germany

ЦБР *Центра́льный банк Росси́и* Central Bank of Russia

ЦПКиО *Центра́льный парк культу́ры и о́тдыха* Central Park for Culture and Recreation

ЦРУ *Центра́льное разве́дывательное управле́ние* CIA (Central Intelligence Agency)

ЮАР *Ю́жно-Африка́нская Респу́блика* South African Republic

ЮНЕСКО *Организа́ция Объединённых на́ций по вопро́сам образова́ния, нау́ки и культу́ры* UNESCO (United Nations Educational, Scientific and Cultural Organization)

Important American and British Abbreviations

AC *alternating current* переме́нный ток

A/C *account (current)* теку́щий счёт

acc(t). *account* отчёт; счёт

AEC *Atomic Energy Commission* Коми́ссия по а́томной эне́ргии

AFL-CIO *American Federation of Labor & Congress of Industrial Organizations* Америка́нская федера́ция труда́ и Конгре́сс произво́дственных профсою́зов, АФТ/КПП

AL, Ala. *Alabama* Алаба́ма (штат в США)

Alas. *Alaska* Аля́ска (штат в США)

a.m. *ante meridiem (= before noon)* до полу́дня

AP *Associated Press* Ассоши'йтед пресс

AR *Arkansas* Арка́нзас (штат в США)

ARC *American Red Cross* Америка́нский Кра́сный Крест

Ariz. *Arizona* Аризо́на (штат в США)

ATM *automated teller machine* банкома́т

AZ *Arizona* Аризо́на (штат в США)

BA *Bachelor of Arts* бакала́вр иску́сств

BBC. *British Broadcasting Corporation* Брита́нская радиовеща́тельная корпора́ция

B/E *Bill of Exchange* ве́ксель *m*, тра́тта

BL *Bachelor of Law* бакала́вр пра́ва

B/L *bill of lading* коносаме́нт; тра́нспортная накладна́я

BM *Bachelor of Medicine* бакала́вр медици́ны

BOT *Board of Trade* министе́рство торго́вли (Великобрита́нии)

BR *British Rail* Брита́нская желе́зная доро́га

Br(it). *Britain* Великобрита́ния; *British* брита́нский, англи́йский

Bros. *brothers* бра́тья *pl.* (в назва́ниях фирм)

c. 1. *cent(s)* цент (америка́нская моне́та); **2.** *circa* приблизи́тельно, о́коло; **3.** *cubic* куби́ческий

CA *California* Калифо́рния (штат в США)

C/A *current account* теку́щий счёт

Cal(if). *California* Калифо́рния (штат в США)

Can. *Canada* Кана́да; *Canadian* кана́дский

CIA *Central Intelligence Agency* Центра́льное разве́дывательное управле́ние, ЦРУ

CID *Criminal Investigation Department* кримина́льная поли́ция

c.i.f. *cost, insurance, freight* цена́, включа́ющая сто́имость, расхо́ды по страхова́нию и фрахт

CIS *Commonwealth of Independent States* содру́жество незави́симых госуда́рств, СНГ

c/o *care of* че́рез, по а́дресу (на́дпись на конве́ртах)

Co. *Company* о́бщество, компа́ния

COD *cash (am. collect) on delivery* нало́женный платёж, упла́та при доста́вке

Colo. *Colorado* Колора́до (штат в США)

Conn. *Connecticut* Конне́ктикут (штат в США)

cwt *hundredweight* ха́ндредвейт

DC 1. *direct current* постоя́нный ток; **2.** *District of Columbia* федера́льный о́круг Колу́мбия (с америка́нской столи́цей)

Del. *Delaware* Де́лавэр (штат в США)

dept. *Department* отде́л; управле́ние; министе́рство; ве́домство

disc. *discount* ски́дка; ди́сконт, учёт векселе́й

div. *dividend* дивиде́нд

DJ 1. *disc jockey* диск-жоке́й; **2.** *dinner jacket* смо́кинг

dol. *dollar* до́ллар

DOS *disk operating system* ди́скова́я операцио́нная систе́ма

doz. *dozen* дю́жина

dpt. *Department* отде́л; управле́ние; министе́рство; ве́домство

E 1. *East* восто́к; *Eastern* восто́чный; **2.** *English* англи́йский

E. & O.E. *errors and omissions excepted* исключа́я оши́бки и про́пуски

EC *European Community* Европе́йское Сообще́ство, ЕС

ECOSOC *Economic and Social Council* Экономи́ческий и социа́льный сове́т, ООН

ECU *European Currency Unit* Европе́йская де́нежная едини́ца, ЭКЮ

EEC *European Economic Community* Европе́йское экономи́ческое сообще́ство, ЕЭС

e.g. *exempli gratia* (лат. = *for instance*) напр. (наприме́р)

Enc. *enclosure(s)* приложе́ние (-ния)

Esq. *Esquire* эсква́йр (ти́тул дворяни́на, должностно́го лица́; обы́чно ста́вится в письме́ по́сле фами́лии)

etc. & c. *et cetera, and so on* и так да́лее

EU *European Union* Европе́йский сою́з

f *feminine* же́нский; *gram.* же́нский род; *foot* фут, *feet* фу́ты; *following* сле́дующий

FBI *Federal Bureau of Investigation* федера́льное бюро́ рассле́дований (в США)

FIFA *Fédération Internationale de Football Association* Междунаро́дная федера́ция футбо́льных о́бществ, ФИФА

Fla. *Florida* флори́да (штат в США)

F.O. *Foreign Office* министе́рство иностра́нных дел

fo(l) *folio* фо́лио *indecl. n* (форма́т в пол-листа́); лист (бухга́лтерской кни́ги)

f.o.b. *free on board* франко-борт, ФОБ

fr. *franc(s)* фра́нк(и)

FRG *Federal Republic of Germany* Федерати́вная Респу́блика Герма́ния, ФРГ

  foot фут, *feet* фу́ты

g. *gram(me)* грамм

GA (Ga.) *Georgia* Джо́рджия (штат в США)

GATT *General Agreement on Tariffs and Trade* Генера́льное соглаше́ние по тамо́женным тари́фам и торго́вле

GB *Great Britain* Великобрита́ния

GI *government issue* *fig.* америка́нский солда́т

GMT *Greenwich Mean Time* сре́днее вре́мя по гри́нвичскому меридиа́ну

gr. *gross* бру́тто

gr.wt. *gross weight* вес бру́тто

h. *hour(s)* час(ы́)

HBM. *His (Her) Britannic Majesty* Его́ (Её) Брита́нское Вели́чество

H.C. *House of Commons* Пала́та о́бщин (в Великобрита́нии)

hf. *half* полови́на

HIV *human immunodeficiency virus* ВИЧ

HL *House of Lords* пала́та ло́рдов (в Великобрита́нии)

HM *His (Her) Majesty* Его́ (Её) Вели́чество

HMS *His (Her) Majesty's Ship* кора́бль англи́йского вое́нно-морско́го фло́та

HO *Home Office* министе́рство вну́тренних дел (в А́нглии)

HP, hp *horsepower* лошади́ная си́ла (едини́ца мо́щности)

HQ, Hq *Headquarters* штаб

HR *House of Representatives* пала́та представи́телей (в США)

HRH *His (Her) Royal Highness* Его́ (Её) Короле́вское Высо́чество

hrs. *hours* часы́

IA, Ia. *Iowa* Айо́ва (штат в США)

IAEA *International Atomic Energy Agency* Междунаро́дное аге́нтство по а́томной эне́ргии, МАГАТЭ

ID *identification* удостовере́ние ли́чности

Id(a). *Idaho* Айдахо (штат в США)

i.e., ie *id est* (лат. = *that is to say*) т.е. (то есть)

IL, Ill. *Illinois* Иллино́йс (штат в США)

IMF *International Monetary Fund* Междунаро́дный валю́тный фонд ООН

in. *inch(es)* дю́йм(ы)

Inc., inc. *incorporated* объединённый; зарегистри́рованный как корпора́ция

incl. *inclusive, including* включи́тельно

Ind. *Indiana* Индиа́на (штат в США)

inst. *instant* с.м. (сего́ ме́сяца)

INTERPOL *International Criminal Police Organization* Междунаро́дная организа́ция уголо́вной поли́ции, ИНТЕРПОЛ

IOC *International Olympic Committee* Междунаро́дный олимпи́йский комите́т, МОК

IQ *intelligence quotient* коэффици́ент у́мственных спосо́бностей

Ir. *Ireland* Ирла́ндия; *Irish* ирла́ндский

JP *Justice of the Peace* мирово́й судья́

Jnr, Jr, jun., junr *junior* мла́дший

Kan(s). *Kansas* Канза́с (штат в США)

KB *kilobyte* килоба́йт

kg *kilogram(me)s.* килогра́мм, кг

km *kilometer, -tre* киломе́тр

kW, kw *kilowatt* килова́тт

KY, Ky *Kentucky* Кенту́кки (штат в США)

l. *litre* литр

L *pound sterling* фунт сте́рлингов

La. *Louisiana* Луизиа́на (штат в США)

LA *1. Los Angeles* Лос-Анджелес; *2. Australian pound* австрали́йский фунт (де́нежная едини́ца)

lb., lb *pound* фунт (ме́ра ве́са)

L/C *letter of credit* аккредити́в

LP *Labour Party* лейбори́стская па́ртия

Ltd, ltd *limited* с ограни́ченной отве́тственностью

m. *1. male* мужско́й; *2. meter, -tre* метр; *3. mile* ми́ля; *4. minute* мину́та

MA *Master of Arts* маги́стр иску́сств

Mass. *Massachusetts* Массачу́сетс (штат в США)

max. *maximum* ма́ксимум

MD *medicinae doctor* (лат. = *Doctor of Medicine*) до́ктор медици́ны

Md. *Maryland* Мэ́риленд (штат в США)

ME, Me. *Maine* Мэн (штат в США)

mg. *milligram(me)(s)* миллигра́мм

Mich. *Michigan* Мичига́н (штат в США)

Minn. *Minnesota* Миннесо́та (штат в США)

Miss. *Mississippi* Миссиси́пи (штат в США)

mm. *millimeter* миллиме́тр

MO *1. Missouri* Миссу́ри (штат в США); *2. money order* де́нежный перево́д по по́чте

Mont. *Montana* Монта́на (штат в США)

MP *1. Member of Parliament* член парла́мента; *2. military police* вое́нная поли́ция

mph *miles per hour* (сто́лько-то) миль в час

Mr *Mister* ми́стер, господи́н

Mrs *originally Mistress* ми́ссис, госпожа́

MS *1. Mississippi* Миссиси́пи (штат в США); *2. manuscript* ру́копись *f*; *3. motorship* теплохо́д

N *north* се́вер; *northern* се́верный

NATO *North Atlantic Treaty Organization* Североатланти́ческий сою́з, НАТО

NC, N.C. *North Carolina* Се́верная Кароли́на (штат в США)

ND, N.D. *North Dakota* Се́верная Дако́та (штат в США)

NE *1. Nebraska* Небра́ска (штат в США); *2. northeast* се́веро-восто́к

Neb(r). *Nebraska* Небра́ска (штат в США)

Nev. *Nevada* Нева́да (штат в США)

NH, N.H *New Hampshire* Нью-хэ́мпшир (штат в США)

NJ, N.J *New Jersey* Нью-Дже́рси (штат в США)

NM, N.M(ex). *New Mexico* Нью-Ме́ксико (штат в США)

nt.wt. *net weight* вес не́тто, чи́стый вес

NW *northwestern* се́веро-за́падный
NY, N.Y. *New York* Нью-Йо́рк (штат в США)
NYC, N.Y.C. *New York City* Нью-Йо́рк (го́род)

OH *Ohio* Ога́йо (штат в США)
OHMS *On His (Her) Majesty's Service* состоя́щий на короле́вской (госуда́рственной или вое́нной) слу́жбе; служе́бное де́ло
OK 1. *okay* всё в поря́дке, всё пра́вильно; утверждено́, согласо́вано; 2. *Oklahoma* Оклахо́ма (штат в США)
Okla. *Oklahoma* Оклахо́ма (штат в США)
OR, Ore(g). *Oregon* Орего́н (штат в США)
OSCE *Organisation on Security and Cooperation in Europe* Организа́ция по безопа́сности и сотру́дничеству в Евро́пе, ОБСЕ

p *Brt penny, pence* пе́нни, пенс
p. *page* страни́ца; *part* часть, ч.
PA, Pa. *Pennsylvania* Пенсильва́ния (штат в США)
p.a. *per annum* (лат.) в год; ежего́дно
PC 1. *personal computer* персона́льный компью́тер; 2. *police constable* полице́йский
p.c. *per cent* проце́нт, проце́нты
pd. *paid* упла́чено; опла́ченный
Penn(a). *Pennsylvania* Пенсильва́ния (штат в США)
per pro(c). *per procurationem* (= *by proxy*) по дове́ренности
p.m., pm *post meridiem* (= *after noon*) ...часо́в (часа́) дня
PO 1. *post office* почто́вое отделе́ние; 2. *postal order* де́нежный перево́д по по́чте
POB *post office box* почто́вый абоне́нтный я́щик
POD *pay on delivery* нало́женный платёж
Pres. *president* президе́нт
Prof. *professor* проф. профе́ссор
PS *Postscript* постскри́птум, припи́ска
PTO., p.t.o. *please turn over* см. н/об. (смотри́ на оборо́те)

RAF *Royal Air Force* вое́нно-возду́шные си́лы Великобрита́нии
RAM *random access memory* операти́вное запомина́ющее устро́йство, ОЗУ
ref. *reference* ссы́лка, указа́ние
regd *registered* зарегистри́рованный; заказно́й
reg.ton *register ton* реги́стровая то́нна
Rev., Revd *Reverend* преподо́бный
RI, R.I. *Rhode Island* Род-А́йленд (штат в США)
RN *Royal Navy* вое́нно-морско́й флот Великобрита́нии
RP *reply paid* отве́т опла́чен

S *south* юг; *southern* ю́жный
s 1. *second* секу́нда; 2. *hist. shilling* ши́ллинг
SA 1. *South Africa* Ю́жная А́фрика; 2. *Salvation Army* А́рмия спасе́ния
SC, S.C. *South Carolina* Ю́жная Кароли́на (штат в США)
SD, S.D(ak). *South Dakota* Ю́жная Дако́та (штат в США)
SE 1. *southeast* юго-восто́к; *southeastern* юго-восто́чный; 2. *Stock Exchange* фо́ндовая би́ржа (в Ло́ндоне)
Soc. *society* о́бщество
Sq. *Square* пло́щадь *f*
sq. *square...* квадра́тный
SS *steamship* парохо́д
stg. *sterling* фунт сте́рлингов
suppl. *supplement* дополне́ние, приложе́ние
SW *southwest* юго-за́пад; *southwestern* юго-за́падный

t *ton* то́нна
TB *tuberculosis* туберкулёз, ТБ
tel. *telephone* телефо́н, тел.
Tenn. *Tennessee* Те́ннесси (штат в США)
Tex. *Texas* Теха́с (штат в США)
TU *trade(s) union* тред-юнио́н профессиона́льный сою́з
TUC *Trade Unions Congress* конгре́сс (брита́нских) тред-юнио́нов

UK *United Kingdom* Соединённое Короле́вство (А́нглия, Шотла́ндия, Уэльс и Се́верная Ирла́ндия)

UFO *unidentified flying object* неопо́знанные лета́ющие объе́кты, НЛО

UN *United Nations* Объединённые На́ции

UNESCO *United Nations Educational, Scientific, and Cultural Organization* Организа́ция Объединённых На́ций по вопро́сам просвеще́ния, нау́ки и культу́ры, ЮНЕ́СКО

UNSC *United Nations Security Council* Сове́т Безопа́сности ООН

UP *United Press* телегра́фное аге́нтство „Юна́йтед Пресс"

US(A) *United States (of America)* Соединённые Шта́ты (Аме́рики)

USW *ultrashort wave* у́льтракоро́ткие во́лны, УКВ

UT, Ut. *Utah* Ю́та (штат в США)

V *volt(s)* во́льт(ы) В

VA, Va. *Virginia* Вирджи́ния (штат в США)

VCR *video cassette recorder* видеомагнитофо́н

viz. *videlicet* (лат.) а и́менно

vol. *volume* том

vols *volumes* тома́ *pl*

VT, Vt. *Vermont* Вермо́нт (штат в США)

W 1. *west* за́пад; *western* за́падный; **2.** *watt* ватт, Вт

WA, Wash. *Washington* Вашингто́н (штат в США)

W.F.T.U. *World Federation of Trade Unions* Всеми́рная федера́ция профессиона́льных сою́зов, ВФП

WHO *World Health Organization* Всеми́рная организа́ция здравоохране́ния, ВОЗ

Wis(c). *Wisconsin* Виско́нсин (штат в США)

wt., wt *weight* вес

WV, W Va. *West Virginia* За́падная Вирги́ния (штат в США)

WWW *World-Wide Web* всеми́рная паути́на

WY, Wyo. *Wyoming* Ва́йоминг (штат в США)

Xmas *Christmas* Рождество́

yd(s) *yard(s)* ярд(ы)

YMCA *Young Men's Christian Association* Христиа́нская ассоциа́ция молоды́х люде́й

YWCA *Young Women's Christian Association* Христиа́нская ассоциа́ция молоды́х (де́вушек)

Russian Geographical Names

Австра́лия f Australia
А́встрия f Austria
Азербайджа́н m Azerbaijan
А́зия f Asia
Алба́ния f Albania
А́льпы pl. the Alps
Аля́ска f Alaska
Аме́рика f America
А́нглия f England
Антаркти́да f the Antarctic Continent, Antarctica
Анта́рктика f Antarctic
Аргенти́на f Argentina
А́рктика f Arctic (Zone)
Арме́ния f Armenia
Атла́нтика f, **Атланти́ческий океа́н** m the Atlantic (Ocean)
Афганиста́н m Afghanistan
Афи́ны pl. Athens
А́фрика f Africa

Байка́л m (Lake) Baikal
Балти́йское мо́ре the Baltic Sea
Ба́ренцево мо́ре the Barents Sea
Белору́ссия f Byelorussia
Бе́льгия f Belgium
Бе́рингово мо́ре the Bering Sea
Бе́рингов проли́в the Bering Straits
Болга́рия f Bulgaria
Бо́сния f Bosnia
Брита́нские острова́ the British Isles
Брюссе́ль m Brussels
Будапе́шт m Budapest
Бухаре́ст m Bucharest

Варша́ва f Warsaw
Вашингто́н m Washington
Великобрита́ния f Great Britain
Ве́на f Vienna
Ве́нгрия f Hungary
Вене́ция f Venice
Во́лга f the Volga

Гаа́га f the Hague
Герма́ния f Germany
Гимала́и pl. the Himalayas
Гонко́нг m Hong Kong
Гренла́ндия f Greenland
Гре́ция f Greece
Гру́зия f Georgia (Caucasus)

Да́ния f Denmark
Днепр m Dniepr
Донба́сс m (Доне́цкий бассе́йн) the Donbas, the Donets Basin
Дуна́й m the Danube

Евро́па f Europe
Еги́пет m [-пта] Egypt
Енисе́й m the Yenisei

Иерусали́м m Jerusalem
Изра́иль m Israel
И́ндия f India
Ира́к m Iraq
Ира́н m Iran
Ирла́ндия f Ireland; Eire
Исла́ндия f Iceland
Испа́ния f Spain
Ита́лия f Italy

Кавка́з m the Caucasus
Казахста́н m Kasakhstan
Каи́р m Cairo
Камча́тка f Kamchatka
Кана́да f Canada
Каре́лия f Karelia
Карпа́ты pl. the Carpathians
Каспи́йское мо́ре the Caspian Sea
Кёльн m Cologne
Ки́ев m Kiev
Кипр m Cyprus
Коре́я f Korea
Крым m [в -ý] the Crimea
Кузба́сс m Кузне́цкий бассе́йн the Kuzbas, the Kuznetsk Basin

Ла́дожское о́зеро Lake Ladoga
Ла-Ма́нш m the English Channel
Ленингра́д m Leningrad (hist.)
Лива́н m Lebanon
Литва́ f Lithuania
Ла́твия f Latvia

Ме́ксика f Mexico
Молдо́ва f Moldova
Монго́лия f Mongolia
Москва́ f Moscow

Нева́ f the Neva
Нидерла́нды pl. the Netherlands
Норве́гия f Norway

Нью-Йóрк *m* New York

Палестúна *f* Palestine
Парúж *m* Paris
Пóльша *f* Poland
Прáга *f* Prague

Рейн *m* Rhine
Рим *m* Rome
Россúйская Федерáция *f* Russian Federation
Россúя *f* Russia
Румы́ния *f* Romania

Санкт-Петербýрг *m* St. Petersburg
Сéверный Ледовúтый океáн *the* Arctic Ocean
Сибúрь *f* Siberia
Стокгóльм *m* Stockholm
Соединённые Штáты Амéрики *pl. the* United States of America

Тéмза *f the* Thames
Таджикистáн *m* Tajikistan

Туркменистáн *f* Turkmenistan
Тýрция *f* Turkey

Узбекистáн *m* Uzbekistan
Украúна *f the* Ukraine
Урáл *m the* Urals

Финля́ндия *f* Finland
Фрáнция *f* France

Чёрное мóре *the* Black Sea
Чечня́ *f* Chechnia
Чéшская Респýблика *f the* Czech Republic

Швейцáрия *f* Switzerland
Швéция *f* Sweden

Эдинбýрг *m* Edinburgh
Эстóния *f* Estonia

Ю́жно-Африкáнская Респýблика *f the* South African Republic

English Geographical Names

Afghanistan [æf'gænɪstɑːn] Афганиста́н

Africa ['æfrɪkə] А́фрика

Alabama [ˌæləˈbæmə] Алаба́ма (штат в США)

Alaska [əˈlæskə] Аля́ска (штат в США)

Albania [ælˈbeɪnjə] Алба́ния

Alps [ælps] the А́льпы

Amazon [ˈæməzn] the Амазо́нка

America [əˈmerɪkə] Аме́рика

Antarctica [æntˈɑːktɪkə] the Анта́рктика

Arctic [ˈɑːktɪk] the А́рктика

Argentina [ˌɑːdʒənˈtiːnə] Аргенти́на

Arizona [ˌærɪˈzəʊnə] Аризо́на (штат в США)

Arkansas [ˈɑːkənsɔː] Арка́нзас (штат и река́ в США)

Asia [ˈeɪʃə] А́зия; *Middle ~* Сре́дняя А́зия

Athens [ˈæθɪnz] г. Афи́ны

Atlantic Ocean [ətˌlæntɪkˈəʊʃn] the Атланти́ческий океа́н

Australia [ɒˈstreɪljə] Австра́лия

Austria [ˈɒstrɪə] А́встрия

Baikal [baɪˈkæl] о́зеро Байка́л

Balkans [ˈbɔːlkənz] the Балка́ны

Baltic Sea [ˌbɔːltɪkˈsiː] the Балти́йское мо́ре

Barents Sea [ˈbæːrəntsiː] the Ба́ренцево мо́ре

Belfast [ˌbelˈfɑːst] г. Бе́лфаст

Belgium [ˈbeldʒəm] Бе́льгия

Bering Sea [ˌbeərɪŋˈsiː] the Бе́рингово мо́ре

Berlin [bɜːˈlɪn] г. Берли́н

Birmingham [ˈbɜːmɪŋəm] г. Би́рмингем

Black Sea [ˌblækˈsiː] the Чёрное мо́ре

Bosnia [ˈbɒznɪə] Бо́сния

Boston [ˈbɒstən] г. Босто́н

Brazil [brəˈzɪl] Брази́лия

Britain [ˈbrɪtn] (*Great* Велико) Брита́ния

Brussels [ˈbrʌslz] г. Брю́ссель

Bucharest [ˌbuːkəˈrest] г. Бухаре́ст

Bulgaria [bʌlˈgeərɪə] Болга́рия

Byelorussia [bɪˌeləʊˈrʌʃə] Белору́ссия, Белару́сь

Cairo [ˈkaɪrəʊ] г. Каи́р

Calcutta [kælˈkʌtə] г. Кальку́тта

California [ˌkʌlɪˈfɔːnjə] Калифо́рния (штат в США)

Cambridge [ˈkeɪmbrɪdʒ] г. Ке́мбридж

Canada [ˈkænədə] Кана́да

Cape Town [ˈkeɪptaʊn] г. Ке́йптаун

Carolina [ˌkærəˈlaɪnə] Кароли́на (*North* Се́верная, *South* Ю́жная)

Caspian Sea [ˌkæspɪənˈsiː] the Каспи́йское мо́ре

Caucasus [ˈkɔːkəsəs] the Кавка́з

Ceylon [sɪˈlɒn] о. Цейло́н

Chechnia [ˈtʃetʃnɪə] Чечня́

Chicago [ʃɪˈkɑːgəʊ, *Am.* ʃɪˈkɔːgəʊ] г. Чика́го

Chile [ˈtʃɪlɪ] Чи́ли

China [ˈtʃaɪnə] Кита́й

Colorado [ˌkɒləˈrɑːdəʊ] Колора́до (штат в США)

Columbia [kəˈlʌmbɪə] Колу́мбия (река́, го́род, админ. округ)

Connecticut [kəˈnetɪkət] Конне́ктикут (река́ и штат в США)

Copenhagen [ˌkəʊpnˈheɪgən] г. Копенга́ген

Cordilleras [ˌkɔːdɪˈljeərəz] the Кордилье́ры (го́ры)

Croatia [krəʊˈeɪʃə] Хорва́тия

Cuba [ˈkjuːbə] Ку́ба

Cyprus [ˈsaɪprəs] о. Кипр

Czech Republic [ˌtʃek rɪˈpʌblɪk] the Че́шская Респу́блика

Dakota [dəˈkəʊtə] Дако́та *North* Се́верная, *South* Ю́жная (шта́ты в США)

Danube [ˈdænjuːb] р. Дуна́й

Delaware [ˈdeləweə] Де́лавер (штат в США)

Denmark [ˈdenmɑːk] Да́ния

Detroit [dəˈtrɔɪt] г. Детро́йт

Dover [ˈdəʊvə] г. Дувр

Dublin [ˈdʌblɪn] г. Ду́блин

Edinburgh [ˈedɪnbərə] г. Э́динбург

Egypt [ˈiːdʒɪpt] Еги́пет

Eire [ˈeərə] Эйре

England [ˈɪŋglənd] А́нглия

Europe [ˈjʊərəp] Евро́па

Finland ['fɪnlənd] Финля́ндия
Florida ['flɔrɪdə] Фло́рида
France [frɑːns] Фра́нция

Geneva [dʒɪ'niːvə] г. Жене́ва
Georgia ['dʒɔːdʒə] Джо́рджия (штат в США); Гру́зия
Germany ['dʒɜːmənɪ] Герма́ния
Gibraltar [dʒɪ'brɔːltə] Гибра́лтар
Glasgow ['glɑːzgəʊ] г. Гла́зго
Greece ['griːs] Гре́ция
Greenwich ['grenɪtʃ] Гри́н(в)ич

Hague ['heɪg] the г. Га́ага
Harwich ['hærɪdʒ] г. Ха́ридж
Hawaii [hə'waiiː] Гава́йи (о́стров, штат в США)
Helsinki ['helsɪŋkɪ] г. Хе́льсинки
Himalaya [ˌhɪmə'leɪə] the г. Гимала́и
Hiroshima [hɪ'rɒʃɪmə] г. Хиро́сима
Hollywood ['hɒlɪwʊd] г. Го́лливуд
Hungary ['hʌŋgərɪ] Ве́нгрия

Iceland ['aɪslənd] Исла́ндия
Idaho ['aɪdəhəʊ] Айда́хо (штат в США)
Illinois [ˌɪlə'nɔɪ] Йллино́йс (штат в США)
India ['ɪndjə] Йндия
Indiana [ˌɪndɪ'ænə] Индиа́на (штат в США)
Indian Ocean [ˌɪndjən'əʊʃən] the Инди́йский океа́н
Iowa ['aɪəʊə] Айо́ва (штат в США)
Iran [ɪ'rɑːn] Ира́н
Iraq [ɪ'rɑːk] Ира́к
Ireland ['aɪələnd] Ирла́ндия
Israel ['ɪzreɪəl] Изра́иль
Italy ['ɪtəlɪ] Ита́лия

Japan [dʒə'pæn] Япо́ния
Jersey ['dʒɜːzɪ] о. Дже́рси
Jerusalem [dʒə'ruːsələm] г. Иерусали́м

Kansas ['kænzəs] Ка́нзас (штат в США)
Kentucky [ken'tʌkɪ] Генту́кки (штат в США)
Kiev ['kiːev] г. Ки́ев
Korea [kə'rɪə] Коре́я
Kosovo ['kɒsəvəʊ] Ко́сово
Kremlin ['kremlɪn] Кремль
Kuwait [kʊ'weɪt] Куве́йт

Latvia ['lætvɪə] Ла́твия
Libya ['lɪbɪə] Ли́вия
Lithuania [ˌlɪθjuː'eɪnjə] Литва́
Lisbon ['lɪzbən] г. Лиссабо́н
Liverpool ['lɪvəpuːl] г. Ли́верпул
London ['lʌndən] г. Ло́ндон
Los Angeles [lɒs'ændʒɪliːz] г. Лос-А́нджелес
Louisiana [luːˌiːzɪ'ænə] Луизиа́на (штат в США)
Luxembourg ['lʌksəmbɜːg] г. Люксембу́рг

Madrid [mə'drɪd] г. Мадри́д
Maine [meɪn] Мэн (штат в США)
Malta ['mɔːltə] Ма́льта (о. и госуда́рство)
Manitoba [ˌmænɪ'təʊbə] Манито́ба
Maryland ['meərɪlənd] Мэ́риленд (штат в США)
Massachusetts [ˌmæsə'tʃuːsɪts] Массачу́сетс (штат в США)
Melbourne ['melbən] г. Ме́льбурн
Mexico ['meksɪkəʊ] Ме́ксика
Michigan ['mɪʃɪgən] Ми́чиган (штат в США)
Minnesota [ˌmɪnɪ'səʊtə] Миннесо́та (штат в США)
Minsk [mɪnsk] г. Минск
Mississippi [ˌmɪsɪ'sɪpɪ] Миссиси́пи (река́ и штат в США)
Missouri [mɪ'zʊərɪ] Миссу́ри (река́ и штат в США)
Moldova [mɒl'dəʊvə] Молдо́ва
Montana [mɒn'tænə] Монта́на (штат в США)
Montreal [ˌmɒntrɪ'ɔːl] г. Монреа́ль
Moscow ['mɒskəʊ] г. Москва́
Munich ['mjuːnɪk] г. Мю́нхен

Nebraska [nə'bræskə] Небра́ска (штат в США)
Netherlands ['neðələndz] the Нидерла́нды
Nevada [nə'vɑːdə] Нева́да (штат в США)
Newfoundland ['njuːfəndlənd] о. Ньюфа́ундленд
New Hampshire [ˌnjuː'hæmpʃə] Нью-Хэ́мпшир (штат в США)
New Jersey [ˌnjuː'dʒɜːzɪ] Нью-Дже́рси (штат в США)
New Mexico [ˌnjuː'meksɪkəʊ] Нью-Ме́ксико (штат в США)

New Orleans [ˌnjuː'ɔːlɪənz] г. Нόвый Орлеάн

New York [ˌnjuː'jɔːk] Нью-Йόрк (город и штат в США)

New Zealand [ˌnjuː'ziːlənd] Нόвая Зелάндия

Niagara [naɪ'æɡərə] the р. Ниагάра, Ниагάрские водопάды

Nile [naɪl] the р. Нил

North Sea [ˌnɔːθ'siː] the Сéверное мόре

Norway ['nɔːweɪ] Норвéгия

Ohio [əʊ'haɪəʊ] Огάйо (река и штат в США)

Oklahoma [ˌəʊklə'həʊmə] Оклахόма (штат в США)

Oregon ['ɒrɪɡən] Орегόн (штат в США)

Oslo ['ɒzləʊ] г. Осло

Ottawa ['ɒtəwə] г. Оттάва

Oxford ['ɒksfəd] г. Óксфорд

Pacific Ocean [pə,sɪfɪk'əʊʃn] Тйхий океάн

Pakistan [ˌpɑːkɪ'stɑːn] Пакистάн

Paris ['pærɪs] г. Парйж

Pennsylvania [ˌpensɪl'veɪnjə] Пенсильвάния (штат в США)

Philippines ['fɪlɪpiːnz] the Филиппйны

Poland ['pəʊlənd] Пόльша

Portugal ['pɔːtʃʊɡl] Португάлия

Pyrenees [ˌpɪrə'niːz] the Пиренéйские гόры

Quebec [kwɪ'bek] г. Квебéк

Rhine [raɪn] the р. Рейн

Rhode Island [ˌrəʊd'aɪlənd] Род-Áйленд (штат в США)

Rome [rəʊm] г. Рим

Romania [ruː'meɪnjə] Румы́ния

Russia ['rʌʃə] Россйя

Saudi Arabia [ˌsaʊdɪə'reɪbɪə] Саýдовская Арάвия

Scandinavia [ˌskændɪ'neɪvjə] Скандинάвия

Scotland ['skɒtlənd] Шотлάндия

Seoul [səʊl] г. Сеул

Serbia ['sɜːbɪə] Сéрбия

Siberia [saɪ'bɪərɪə] Сибйрь

Singapore [ˌsɪŋə'pɔː] Сингапýр

Spain [speɪn] Испάния

Stockholm ['stɒkhəʊm] г. Стокгόльм

St Petersburg [snt'piːtəzbɜːɡ] г. Санкт-Петербýрг

Stratford ['strætfəd] -on-Avon ['eɪvən] г. Стрάтфорд-на-Эйвоне

Sweden [swiːdn] Швéция

Switzerland ['swɪtsələnd] Швейцάрия

Sydney ['sɪdnɪ] г. Сйдней

Taiwan [ˌtaɪ'wɑːn] Тайвάнь

Teh(e)ran [ˌteə'rɑːn] г. Тегерάн

Tennessee [ˌtenə'siː] Теннесй (река и штат в США)

Texas ['teksəs] Тéхас (штат в США)

Thames [temz] the р. Тéмза

Turkey ['tɜːkɪ] Тýрция

Ukraine [juː'kreɪn] the Украйна

Urals ['jʊərəlz] the Урάльские гόры

Utah ['juːtɑː] Юта (штат в США)

Venice ['venɪs] г. Венéция

Vermont [vɜː'mɒnt] Вермонт (штат в США)

Vienna [vɪ'enə] г. Вéна

Vietnam [ˌviːet'næm] Вьетнάм

Virginia [və'dʒɪnjə] **West** Зάпадная Вирджйния (штат в США)

Warsaw ['wɔːsɔː] г. Варшάва

Washington ['wɒʃɪŋtən] Вάшингтон (город и штат в США)

Wellington ['welɪŋtən] г. Вéллингтон (столица Новой Зеландии)

White Sea [ˌwaɪt'siː] the Бéлое мόре

Wimbledon ['wɪmbldən] г. Уймблдон

Wisconsin [wɪs'kɒnsɪn] Вискόнсин (река и штат в США)

Worcester ['wʊstə] г. Вýстер

Wyoming [waɪ'əʊmɪŋ] Вайόминг (штат в США)

Yugoslavia [ˌjuːɡəʊ'slɑːvjə] Югослάвия

Zurich ['zʊərɪk] г. Цю́рих

Numerals

Cardinals

0 ноль & нуль *m* naught, zero
1 оди́н *m*, одна́ *f*, одно́ *n* one
2 два *m/n*, две *f* two
3 три three
4 четы́ре four
5 пять five
6 шесть six
7 семь seven
8 во́семь eight
9 де́вять nine
10 де́сять ten
11 оди́ннадцать eleven
12 двена́дцать twelve
13 трина́дцать thirteen
14 четы́рнадцать fourteen
15 пятна́дцать fifteen
16 шестна́дцать sixteen
17 семна́дцать seventeen
18 восемна́дцать eighteen
19 девятна́дцать nineteen
20 два́дцать twenty
21 два́дцать оди́н *m* (одна́ *f*, одно́ *n*) twenty-one
22 два́дцать два *m/n* (две *f*) twenty-two
23 два́дцать три twenty-three

30 три́дцать thirty
40 со́рок forty
50 пятьдеся́т fifty
60 шестьдеся́т sixty
70 се́мьдесят seventy
80 во́семьдесят eighty
90 девяно́сто ninety
100 сто (а *и́ли* one) hundred
200 две́сти two hundred
300 три́ста three hundred
400 четы́реста four hundred
500 пятьсо́т five hundred
600 шестьсо́т six hundred
700 семьсо́т seven hundred
800 восемьсо́т eight hundred
900 девятьсо́т nine hundred
1000 (одна́) ты́сяча *f* (а *и́ли* one) thousand
60140 шестьдеся́т ты́сяч сто со́рок sixty thousand one hundred and forty
1 000 000 (оди́н) миллио́н *m* (а *и́ли* one) million
1 000 000 000 (оди́н) миллиа́рд *m* milliard, *Am.* billion

Ordinals

1st пе́рвый first
2nd второ́й second
3rd тре́тий third
4th четвёртый fourth
5th пя́тый fifth
6th шесто́й sixth
7th седьмо́й seventh
8th восьмо́й eighth
9th девя́тый ninth
10th деся́тый tenth
11th оди́ннадцатый eleventh
12th двена́дцатый twelfth
13th трина́дцатый thirteenth
14th четы́рнадцатый fourteenth
15th пятна́дцатый fifteenth
16th шестна́дцатый sixteenth
17th семна́дцатый seventeenth
18th восемна́дцатый eighteenth
19th девятна́дцатый nineteenth

20th двадца́тый twentieth
21st два́дцать пе́рвый twenty-first
22nd два́дцать второ́й twenty-second
23rd два́дцать тре́тий twenty-third
30th тридца́тый thirtieth
40th сороково́й fortieth
50th пятидеся́тый fiftieth
60th шестидеся́тый sixtieth
70th семидеся́тый seventieth
80th восьмидеся́тый eightieth
90th девяно́стый ninetieth
100th со́тый (one) hundredth
200th двухсо́тый two hundredth
300th трёхсо́тый three hundredth
400th четырёхсо́тый four hundredth

500th пятисо́тый five hundredth	
600th шестисо́тый six hundredth	
700th семисо́тый seven hundredth	
800th восьмисо́тый eight hundredth	
900th девятисо́тый nine hundredth	

1000th ты́сячный (one) thousandth

60 140th шестьдесят ты́сяч сто сороково́й sixty thousand one hundred and fortieth

1 000 000th миллио́нный millionth

American and British Weights and Measures

1. Linear Measure

1 inch (in.) дюйм = 2,54 см
1 foot (ft) фут = 30,48 см
1 yard (yd) ярд = 91,44 см

2. Nautical Measure

1 fathom (fm) морская сажень = 1,83 м
1 cable('s) length кабельтов = 183 м, в США = 120 морским саженям = 219 м
1 nautical mille (n. m.) *or* **1 knot** морская миля = 1852 м

3. Square Measure

1 square inch (sq. in.) квадратный дюйм = 6,45 кв. см
1 square foot (sq. ft) квадратный фут = 929,03 кв. см
1 square yard (sq. yd) квадратный ярд = 8361,26 кв. см
1 square rod (sq. rd) квадратный род = 25,29 кв. м
1 rood (ro.) руд = 0,25 акра
1 acre (a.) акр = 0,4 га
1 square mile (sq. ml, *Am.* **sq. mi.)** квадратная миля = 259 га

4. Cubic Measure

1 cubic inch (cu. in.) кубический дюйм = 16,387 куб. см
1 cubic foot (cu. ft) кубический фут = 28 316,75 куб. см
1 cubic yard (cu. yd) кубический ярд = 0,765 куб. м
1 register ton (reg. tn) регистровая тонна = 2,832 куб. см

5. British Measure of Capacity
Dry and Liquid Measure

Меры жидких и сыпучих тел
1 imperial gill (gl, gi.) стандартный джилл = 0,142 л
1 imperial pint (pt) стандартная пинта = 0,568 л
1 imperial quart (qt) стандартная кварта = 1,136 л
1 imperial gallon (Imp. gal.) стандартный галлон = 4,546 л

Dry Measure

1 imperial peck (pk) стандартный пек = 9,092 л
1 imperial bushel (bu., bsh.) стандартный бушель = 36,36 л
1 imperial quarter (qr) стандартная четверть = 290,94 л

Liquid Measure

1 imperial barrel (bbl., bl) стандартный баррель = 1,636 гл

6. American Measure of Capacity
Dry Measure

1 U.S. dry pint американская сухая пинта = 0,551 л
1 U.S. dry quart американская сухая кварта = 1,1 л
1 U.S. dry gallon американский сухой галлон = 4,4 л
1 U.S. peck американский пек = 8,81 л
1 U.S. bushel американский бушель = 35,24 л

Liquid Measure

1 U.S. liquid gill американский джилл (жидкости) = 0,118 л
1 U.S. liquid pint американская пинта (жидкости) = 0,473 л
1 U.S. liquid quart американская кварта (жидкости) = 0,946 л
1 U.S. gallon американский галлон (жидкости) = 3,785 л
1 U.S. barrel американский баррель = 119 л
1 U.S. barrel petroleum американский баррель нефти = 158,97 л

7. Avoirdupois Weight

1 grain (gr.) гран = 0,0648 г
1 dram (dr.) драхма = 1,77 г
1 ounce (oz) унция = 28,35 г
1 pound (lb.) фунт = 453,⁷

1 quarter (qr) че́тверть = 12,7 кг, в США = 11,34 кг

1 hundredweight (cwt) це́нтнер = 50,8 кг, в США = 45,36 кг

1 stone (st.) стон = 6,35 кг

1 ton (tn, t) = 1016 кг (тж long ton: tn. l.), в США = 907,18 кг (тж short ton: tn. sh.)

Some Russian First Names

Алекса́ндр *m*, Alexander
dim: Са́ня, Са́ша, Шу́ра, Шу́рик
Алекса́ндра *f*, Alexandra
dim: Са́ня, Са́ша, Шу́ра
Алексе́й *m*, Alexis
dim: Алёша, Лёша
Анастаси́я *f*, coll. Наста́сья, Anastasia
dim: На́стя, Настёна, Та́ся
Анато́лий *m* Anatoly
dim: То́лик, То́ля
Андре́й *m* Andrew
dim: Андре́йка, Андрю́ша
А́нна *f* Ann, Anna
dim: Аннушка, Аню́та, Аня, Нюра, Нюша, Нюся
Анто́н *m* Antony
dim: Анто́ша, То́ша
Антони́на *f* Antoni(n)a
dim: То́ня
Арка́дий *m* Arcady
dim: Арка́ша, Адик
Арсе́ний *m* Arseny
dim: Арсю́ша
Бори́с *m* Boris
dim: Бо́ря, Бори́ска
Вади́м *m* Vadim
dim: Ди́ма, Ва́дик, Ва́дя
Валенти́н *m* Valentine
dim: Ва́ля
Валенти́на *f* Valentine
dim: Ва́ля, Валю́ша, Ти́на
Вале́рий *m* Valery
dim: Вале́ра, Ва́ля, Вале́рик
Вале́рия *f* Valeria
dim: Ле́ра, Леру́ся
Варва́ра *f* Barbara
dim: Ва́ря, Варю́ша
Васи́лий *m* Basil
dim: Ва́ся, Василёк
Ве́ра *f* Vera
dim: Веру́ся, Веру́ша
Ви́ктор *m* Victor
dim: Ви́тя, Витю́ша
Викто́рия *f* Victoria
dim: Ви́ка
Влади́мир *m* Vladimir
dim: Во́ва, Володя
Владисла́в *m* Vladislav
dim: Вла́дя, Вла́дик, Сла́ва, Сла́вик
Все́волод *m* Vsevolod
dim: Се́ва

Вячесла́в *m* Viacheslav
dim: Сла́ва, Сла́вик
Гали́на *f* Galina
dim: Га́ля, Га́лочка
Генна́дий *m* Gennady
dim: Ге́на, Ге́ня, Ге́ша
Гео́ргий *m* **Его́р** *m* George, Egor
dim: Го́ша, Жо́ра/Его́рка
Григо́рий *m* Gregory
dim: Гри́ша, Гри́ня
Да́рья *f* Daria
dim: Да́ша, Дашу́ля, Да́шенька
Дени́с *m* Denis
dim: Дени́ска
Дми́трий *m* Dmitry
dim: Ди́ма, Ми́тя, Митю́ша
Евге́ний *m* Eugene
dim: Же́ня
Евге́ния *f* Eugenia
dim: Же́ня
Екатери́на *f* Catherine
dim: Ка́тя, Катю́ша
Еле́на *f* Helen
dim: Ле́на, Алёнка, Алёна, Алёнушка, Лёля
Елизаве́та *f* Elizabeth
dim: Ли́за, Ли́занька
Заха́р *m* Zachary
dim: Заха́рка
Зинаи́да *f* Zinaida
dim: Зи́на, Зину́ля
Зо́я *f* Zoe
dim: Зо́енька
Ива́н *m* John
dim: Ва́ня, Ваню́ша
И́горь *m* Igor
dim: Игорёк, Га́рик
Илья́ *m* Elijah, Elias
dim: Илю́ша
Иннке́нтий *m* Innokenty
dim: Ке́ша
Ио́сиф *m* **О́сип** *m* Joseph
dim: Ося
Ири́на *f* Irene
dim: Ира, Ири́нка, Ири́ша, Иру́ся
Кири́лл *m* Cyril
dim: Кири́лка, Кирю́ша
Кла́вдия *f* Claudia
dim: Кла́ва, Кла́ша, Кла́вочка
Константи́н *m* Constantine
dim: Ко́ка, Ко́стя
Ксе́ния *f* **Акси́нья** *f* Xer

dim: Ксе́ня, Ксю́ша
Кузьма́ *m* Cosmo
dim: Ку́зя
Лари́са *f* Larisa
dim: Лари́ска, Ла́ра, Ло́ра
Лев *m* Leo
dim: Лёва, Лёвушка
Леони́д *m* Leonid
dim: Лёня
Ли́дия *f* Lydia
dim: Ли́да, Лиду́ся, Лиду́ша
Любо́вь *f* Lubov (Charity)
dim: Лю́ба, Люба́ша
Людми́ла *f* Ludmila
dim: Лю́да, Лю́ся, Ми́ла
Мака́р *m* Macar
dim: Мака́рка, Мака́рушка
Макси́м *m* Maxim
dim: Макси́мка, Макс
Маргари́та *f* Margaret
dim: Ри́та, Марго́(ша)
Мари́на *f* Marina
dim: Мари́нка, Мари́ша
Мари́я *f* **Ма́рья** *f* Maria
dim: Мари́йка, Мару́ся, Ма́ня,
   Ма́ша, Ма́шенька
Марк *m* Mark
dim: Марку́ша, Марку́ся
Матве́й *m* Mathew
dim: Матве́йка, Матю́ша, Мо́тя
Михаи́л *m* Michael
dim: Миха́лка, Ми́ша, Мишу́ля
Наде́жда *f* Nadezhda (Hope)
dim: На́дя, Надю́ша
Ната́лия *f coll.* **Ната́лья** *f* Natalia
dim: Ната́ша, На́та, Нату́ля,
   Нату́ся, Та́та
Ники́та *m* Nikita
dim: Ни́ка, Ники́тка, Ники́ша
Никола́й *m* Nicholas
dim: Ни́ка, Никола́ша, Ко́ля
Ни́на *f* Nina
dim: Нину́ля, Нину́ся
Окса́на *f* Oxana
dim: Кса́на
Оле́г *m* Oleg
dim: Олёжка
О́льга *f* Olga
dim: О́ля, Олю́шка, Олю́та
...ел *m* Paul

dim: Па́влик, Павлу́ша, Па́ша
Пётр *m* Peter
dim: Петру́ша, Пе́тя
Поли́на *f* Pauline
dim: Поли́нка, По́ля, Па́ша
Раи́са *f* Raisa
dim: Ра́я, Раю́ша
Ростисла́в *m* Rostislav
dim: Ро́стик, Ро́ся, Сла́ва, Сла́вик
Русла́н *m* Ruslan
dim: Русла́нчик, Ру́сик
Светла́на *f* Svetlana
dim: Светла́нка, Све́та
Святосла́в *m* Sviatoslav
dim: Сла́ва
Семён *m* Simeon, Simon
dim: Сёма, Се́ня
Серге́й *m* Serge
dim: Сергу́ня, Серёжа, Серж
Станисла́в *m* Stanislav
dim: Ста́сик, Сла́ва
Степа́н *m* Stephen
dim: Степа́ша, Стёпа
Степани́да *f* Stephanie
dim: Стёша
Тама́ра *f* Tamara
dim: То́ма
Татья́на *f* Tatiana
dim: Та́ня, Таню́ша, Та́та
Тимофе́й *m* Timothy
dim: Ти́ма, Тимо́ша
Фёдор *m* Theodore
dim: Фе́дя, Федю́ля(ня)
Фе́ликс *m* Felix
dim: Фе́ля
Фили́пп *m* Philip
dim: Фи́ля, филю́ша
Эдуа́рд *m* Edward
dim: Э́дик, Э́дя
Э́мма *f* Emma
dim: Э́ммочка
Ю́лия *f* Julia
dim: Ю́ля
Ю́рий *m* Yuri
dim: Ю́ра, Ю́рочка, Юра́ша
Я́ков *m* Jacob
dim: Я́ша, Я́шенька, Яшу́ня
Яросла́в *m* Yaroslav
dim: Сла́ва (ик)

Grammatical Tables

Conjugation and Declension

The following two rules relative to the spelling of endings in Russian inflected words must be observed:

1. Stems terminating in г, к, х, ж, ш, ч, щ are never followed by ы, ю, я, but by **и, у, а**.

2. Stems terminating in ц are never followed by и, ю, я, but by **ы, у, а**.

Besides these, a third spelling rule, dependent on phonetic conditions, i.e. the position of stress, is likewise important:

3. Stems terminating in ж, ш, ч, ц can be followed by an o in the ending only if the syllable in question bears the stress; otherwise, i.e. in unstressed position, **e** is used instead.

A. Conjugation

Prefixed forms of the perfective aspect are represented by adding the prefix in angle brackets, e.g.: <про>читáть = читáть *impf.*, прочитáть *pf.*

Personal endings of the present (and perfective future) tense:

1st conjugation:	-ю (-у)	-ешь	-ет	-ем	-ете	-ют (-ут)
2nd conjugation:	-ю (-у)	-ишь	-ит	-им	-ите	-ят (-ат)

Reflexive:

1st conjugation:	-юсь (-усь)	-ешься	-ется	-емся	-етесь	-ются (-утся)
2nd conjugation:	-юсь (-усь)	-ишься	-ится	-имся	-итесь	-ятся (-атся)

Suffixes and endings of the other verbal forms:

imp.	-й(те)	-и(те)	-ь(те)	
reflexive	-йся (-йтесь)	-ись (-итесь)	-ься (-ьтесь)	
	m	*f*	*n*	*pl.*
p. pr. a.	-щий(ся)	-щая(ся)	-щее(ся)	-щие(ся)
g. pr.	-я(сь)	-а(сь)		
p. pr. p.	-мый	-мая	-мое	-мые
short form	-м	-ма	-мо	-мы
pt.	-л	-ла	-ло	-ли
	-лся	-лась	-лось	-лись
p. pt. a.	-вший(ся)	-вшая(ся)	-вшее(ся)	-вшие(с
g. pt.	-в(ши)	-вши(сь)		
p. pt. p.	-нный	-нная	-нное	-нн
	-тый	-тая	-тое	-т
short form	-н	-на	-но	-
	-т	-та	-то	

Stress:

a) There is *no change of stress unless the final syllable of the infinitive is stressed*, i. e. in all forms of the verb stress remains invariably on the root syllable accentuated in the infinitive, e.g.: пла́кать. The forms of пла́кать correspond to paradigm [3], except for the stress, which is always on пла́-. The imperative of such verbs also differs from the paradigms concerned: it is in **-ь(те)** provided their stem ends in **one consonant** only, e.g.: пла́кать – пла́чь(те), ве́рить – ве́рь(те); and in **-и(те)** (unstressed!) in cases of **two and more consonants** preceding the imperative ending, e.g.: по́мнить – по́мни(те). Verbs with a vowel stem termination, however, generally form their imperative in **-й(те)**: успоко́ить – успоко́й(те).

b) The prefix вы- in perfective verbs always bears the stress: вы́полнить (but *impf.*: выполня́ть). Imperfective (iterative) verbs with the suffix -ыв-/-ив- are always stressed on the syllable preceding the suffix: пока́зывать (but *pf.* показа́ть), спра́шивать (but *pf.* спроси́ть).

c) In the past participle passive of verbs in **-а́ть (-я́ть)**, there is usually a shift of stress back onto the root syllable as compared with the infinitive (see paradigms [1]–[4], [6], [7], [28]). With verbs in **-éть** and **-и́ть** such a shift may occur as well, very often in agreement with a parallel accent shift in the 2nd p.sg. present tense, e.g.: [про]смотре́ть: [про]смотрю́, смо́тришь – просмо́тренный; see also paradigms [14]–[16] as against [13]: [по]ми-ри́ть: [по]мирю́, -и́шь – помирённый. In this latter case the short forms of the participles are stressed on the last syllable throughout: -ённый: -ён, -ена́, -ено́, -ены́. In the former examples, however, the stress remains on the same root syllable as in the long form: -'енный: -'ен, -'ена, -'ено, -'ены.

(*a*) present, (*b*) future, (*c*) imperative, (*d*) present participle active, (*e*) present participle passive, (*f*) present gerund, (*g*) preterite, (*h*) past participle active, (*i*) past participle passive, (*j*) past gerund.

Verbs in **-ать**

1   <про>**чита́ть**
(*a*), <(*b*)>   <про>чита́ю, -а́ешь, -а́ют
(*c*)   <про>чита́й(те)!
(*d*)   чита́ющий
(*e*)   чита́емый
(*f*)   чита́я
(*g*)   <про>чита́л, -а, -о, -и
(*h*)   <про>чита́вший
(*i*)   прочи́танный
(*j*)   прочита́в

2   <по>**трепа́ть**
             (with л after б, в, м, п, ф)
<(*b*)>   <по>треплю́, -е́плешь, -е́плют
         <по>трепли́(те)!
         тре́плющий
         –
         ...репля́
         ...>трепа́л, -а, -о, -и

(*h*)   <по>трепа́вший
(*i*)   <по>трёпанный
(*j*)   потрепа́в

3   <об>**глода́ть**
       (with changing consonant:
             г, д, з > ж
             к, т > ч
             х, с > ш
             ск, ст > щ)
(*a*), <(*b*)>   <об>гложу́, -о́жешь, -о́жут
(*c*)   <об>гложи́(те)!
(*d*)   гло́жущий
(*e*)   –
(*f*)   гложа́
(*g*)   <об>глода́л, -а, -о, -и
(*h*)   <об>глода́вший
(*i*)   обгло́данный
(*j*)   обглода́в

4 <по>**держа́ть**
      (with preceding ж, ш, ч, щ)
(a), <(b)> <по>держу́, -е́ржишь,
            -е́ржат
(c)   <по>держи́(те)!
(d)   <по>держа́щий
(e)   –
(f)   держа́
(g)   <по>держа́л, -а, -о, -и
(h)   <по>держа́вший
(i)   поде́ржанный
(j)   подержа́в

Verbs in **-авать**

5   дава́ть
(a)   даю́, даёшь, даю́т
(c)   дава́й(те)!
(d)   даю́щий
(e)   дава́емый
(f)   дава́я
(g)   дава́л, -а, -о, -и
(h)   дава́вший
(i)   –
(j)   –

Verbs in **-евать**

      (е. = -ю́, -ёшь, etc.)
6   <на>**малева́ть**
(a), <(b)> <на>малю́ю, -ю́ешь,
            -ю́ют
(c)   <на>малю́й(те)!
(d)   малю́ющий
(e)   малю́емый
(f)   малю́я
(g)   <на>малева́л, -а, -о, -и
(h)   <на>малева́вший
(i)   намалёванный
(j)   намалева́в

Verbs in **-овать**

(and in **-евать** with preceding ж, ш,
ч, щ, ц)
7   <на>**рисова́ть**
      (е. = -ю́, -ёшь, etc.)
(a), <(b)> <на>рису́ю, -у́ешь, -у́ют
(c)   <на>рису́й(те)!
(d)   рису́ющий
(e)   рису́емый
(f)   рису́я
(g)   <на>рисова́л, -а, -о, -и
(h)   <на>рисова́вший

(i)   нарисо́ванный
(j)   нарисова́в

Verbs in **-еть**

8   <по>**жале́ть**
(a), <(b)> <по>жале́ю, -е́ешь,
            -е́ют
(c)   <по>жале́й(те)!
(d)   жале́ющий
(e)   жале́емый
(f)   жале́я
(g)   <по>жале́л, -а, -о, -и
(h)   <по>жале́вший
(i)   ...ённый
      (e.g.: одолённый)
(j)   пожале́в

9   <по>**смотре́ть**
(a), <(b)> <по>смотрю́, -о́тришь,
            -о́трят
(c)   <по>смотри́(те)!
(d)   смо́трящий
(e)   –
(f)   смотря́
(g)   <по>смотре́л, -а, -о, -и
(h)   <по>смотре́вший
(i)   ...о́тренный (e.g.: про-
      смо́тренный)
(j)   посмотре́в

10   <по>**терпе́ть**
      (with л after б, в, м, п, ф)
(a), <(b)> <по>терплю́, -е́рпишь,
            -е́рпят
(c)   <по>терпи́(те)!
(d)   терпя́щий
(e)   терпи́мый
(f)   терпя́
(g)   <по>терпе́л, -а, -о, -и
(h)   <по>терпе́вший
(i)   ...ённый (e.g.: претер-
      пенный)
(j)   потерпе́в

11   <по>**лете́ть**
      (with changing consonant:
            г, з > ж
            к, т > ч
            х, с > ш
            ск, ст > щ)
(a), <(b)> <по>лечу́, -ети́шь, -ети́
(c)   <по>лети́(те)
(d)   летя́щий

(e) –
(f) летя́
(g) <по>лете́л, -а, -о, -и
(h) <по>летéвший
(i) ...енный (*e.g.*: ве́рченный)
(j) полете́в(ши)

Verbs in **-ереть**

12   <по>**тере́ть**
(*st.* = -ешь, -ет, *etc.*)
(a), <(b)> <по>тру́, -трёшь, -тру́т
(c) <по>три́(те)!
(d) тру́щий
(e) –
(f) –
(g) <по>тёр, -ла, -ло, -ли
(h) <по>тёрший
(i) потёртый
(j) потере́в

Verbs in **-ить**

13   <по>**мири́ть**
(a), <(b)> <по>мирю́, -ри́шь, -ря́т
(c) <по>мири́(те)!
(d) миря́щий
(e) мири́мый
(f) миря́
(g) <по>мири́л, -а, -о, -и
(h) <по>мири́вший
(i) помирённый
(j) помири́в(ши)

14   <по>**люби́ть**
(with л after б, в, м, п, ф)
(a), <(b)> <по>люблю́, -ю́бишь, -ю́бят
(c) <по>люби́(те)!
(d) лю́бящий
(e) люби́мый
(f) любя́
(g) <по>люби́л, -а, -о, -и
(h) <по>люби́вший
(i) ...лю́бленный (*e.g.*: возлю́бленный)
(j) полюби́в

15   <по>**носи́ть**
(with changing consonant see No 11)
(a), <(b)> <по>ношу́, -о́сишь, -о́сят
      <по>носи́(те)!
      но́сящий

(e) носи́мый
(f) нося́
(g) <по>носи́л, -а, -о, -и
(h) <по>носи́вший
(i) поно́шенный
(j) поноси́в

16   <на>**кроши́ть**
(with preceding ж, ш, ч, щ)
(a), <(b)> <на>крошу́, -о́шишь, -о́шат
(c) <на>кроши́(те)!
(d) кроша́щий
(e) кроши́мый
(f) кроша́
(g) <на>кроши́л, -а, -о, -и
(h) <на>кроши́вший
(i) накро́шенный
(j) накроши́в

Verbs in **-оть**

17   <за>**коло́ть**
(a), <(b)> <за>колю́, -о́лешь, -о́лют
(c) <за>коли́(те)!
(d) ко́лющий
(e) –
(f) –
(g) <за>коло́л, -а, -о, -и
(h) <за>коло́вший
(i) зако́лотый
(j) заколо́в

Verbs in **-уть**

18   <по>**ду́ть**
(a), <(b)> <по>ду́ю, -у́ешь, -у́ют
(c) <по>ду́й(те)!
(d) ду́ющий
(e) –
(f) ду́я
(g) <по>ду́л, -а, -о, -и
(h) <по>ду́вший
(i) ...ду́тый (*e.g.*: разду́тый)
(j) поду́в

19   <по>**тяну́ть**
(a), <(b)> <по>тяну́, -я́нешь, -я́нут
(c) <по>тяни́(те)!
(d) тя́нущий
(e) –
(f) –
(g) <по>тяну́л, -а, -о, -и
(h) <по>тяну́вший

(i)	потя́нутый
(j)	потяну́в

20   <co>**гну́ть**
    (*st.* = -ешь, -ет, *etc.*)

(a), <*(b)*>	<со>гну́, -нёшь, -ну́т
(c)	<со>гни́(те)!
(d)	гну́щий
(e)	–
(f)	–
(g)	<со>гну́л, -а, -о, -и
(h)	<со>гну́вший
(i)	со́гнутый
(j)	согну́в

21   <за>**мёрзнуть**

(a), <*(b)*>	<за>мёрзну, -нешь, -нут
(c)	<за>мёрзни(те)!
(d)	мёрзнущий
(e)	–
(f)	–
(g)	<за>мёрз, -зла, -о, -и
(h)	<за>мёрзший
(i)	...нутый (*e.g.*: возвдви́гнутый)
(j)	замёрзши

Verbs in **-ыть**

22   <по>**кры́ть**

(a), <*(b)*>	<по>кро́ю, -бешь, -бют
(c)	<по>кро́й(те)!
(d)	кро́ющий
(e)	–
(f)	кро́я
(g)	<по>кры́л, -а, -о, -и
(h)	<по>кры́вший
(i)	<по>кры́тый
(j)	покры́в

23   <по>**плы́ть**
    (*st.* = -ешь, -ет, *etc.*)

(a), <*(b)*>	<по>плыву́, -вёшь, -ву́т
(c)	<по>плыви́(те)!
(d)	плыву́щий
(e)	–
(f)	плывя́
(g)	<по>плы́л, -а́, -о, -и
(h)	<по>плы́вший
(i)	...плы́тый (*e.g.*: проплы́тый)
(j)	поплы́в

Verbs in **-зти́, -зть (-сти)**

24   <по>**везти́**
  (-с[т]- = -с[т]-instead of -з- through-out)
    (*st.* = -ешь, -ет, *etc.*)

(a), <*(b)*>	<по>везу́, -зёшь, -зу́т
(c)	<по>вези́(те)!
(d)	везу́щий
(e)	везо́мый
(f)	везя́
(g)	<по>вёз, -везла́, -о́, -и́
(h)	<по>вёзший
(i)	повезённый
(j)	повезя́

Verbs in **-сти́, -сть**

25   <по>**вести́**
  (-т- = -т- instead of -д- throughout)
    (*st.* = -ешь, -ет, *etc.*)

(a), <*(b)*>	<по>веду́, -дёшь, -ду́т
(c)	<по>веди́(те)!
(d)	веду́щий
(e)	ведо́мый
(f)	ведя́
(g)	<по>вёл, -вела́, -о́, -и́
(h)	<по>вéдший
(i)	поведённый
(j)	поведя́

Verbs in **-чь**

26   <по>**влечь**

(a), <*(b)*>	<по>влеку́, -ечёшь, -еку́т
(c)	<по>влеки́(те)!
(d)	влеку́щий
(e)	влеко́мый
(f)	–
(g)	<по>влёк, -екла́, -о́, -и́
(h)	<по>влёкший
(i)	...влечённый (*e.g.*: увлечённый)
(j)	повлёкши

Verbs in **-ять**

27   <рас>**та́ять**
    (*e.* = -ю, -ёшь, -ёт, *etc.*)

(a), <*(b)*>	<рас>та́ю, -áешь, -áют
(c)	<рас>та́й(те)!
(d)	та́ющий
(e)	–
(f)	та́я

(g)	<рас>та́ял, -а, -о, -и		(c)	<по>теря́й(те)!	
(h)	<рас>та́явший		(d)	теря́ющий	
(i)	...а́янный (*e.g.*: обла́ян-		(e)	теря́емый	
	ный)		(f)	теря́я	
(j)	раста́яв		(g)	<по>теря́л, -а, -о, -и	
			(h)	<по>теря́вший	
28	<по>**теря́ть**		(i)	поте́рянный	
(a), <(b)>	<по>теря́ю, -я́ешь, -я́ют		(j)	потеря́в	

B. Declension

Noun

a) Succession of the six cases (horizontally): nominative, genitive, dative, accusative, instrumental and prepositional in the singular and (thereunder) the plural. *With nouns denoting animate beings (persons and animals) there is a coincidence of endings in the accusative and genitive both singular and plural of the masculine, but only in the plural of the feminine and neuter genders.* This rule also applies, of course, to adjectives as well as various pronouns and numerals that must in syntactical connections agree with their respective nouns.

b) Variants of the following paradigms are pointed out in notes added to the individual declension types or, if not, mentioned after the entry word itself.

Masculine nouns:

		N	G	D	A	I	P
1	ви́д	-	-а	-у	-	-ом	-е
		-ы	-ов	-ам	-ы	-ами	-ах

Note: Nouns in -ж, -ш, -ч, -щ have in the *g/pl.* the ending -ей.

2	реб	**-ёнок**	-ёнка	-ёнку	-ёнка	-ёнком	-ёнке
		-я́та	-я́т	-я́там	-я́т	-я́тами	-я́тах

3	слу́ча	**-й**	-я	-ю	-й	-ем	-е
		-и	-ев	-ям	-и	-ями	-ях

Notes: Nouns in -ий have in the *prpos/sg.* the ending -ии.
When *e.*, the ending of the *instr/sg.* is -ём, and of the *g/pl.* -ёв.

4	про́фил	**-ь**	-я	-ю	-ь	-ем	-е
		-и	-ей	-ям	-и	-ями	-ях

Note: When *e.*, the ending of the *instr/sg.* is -ём.

Feminine nouns:

5	рабо́т	**-а**	-ы	-е	-у	-ой	-е
		-ы	-	-ам	-ы	-ами	-ах

6	неде́л	**-я**	-и	-е	-ю	-ей	-е
		-и	-ь	-ям	-и	-ями	-ях

Notes: Nouns in -ья have in the *g/pl.* the ending -ий (unstressed) or -éй (stressed), the latter being also the ending of nouns in -éя. Nouns in -я with preceding vowel terminate in the *g/pl.* in -й (for -ий see also No. 7). When *e.*, the ending of the *instr/sg.* is -ёй (-ёю).

| 7 | а́рми | **-я** | -и | -и | -ю | -ей | -и |
| | | -и | -й | -ям | -и | -ями | -ях |

| 8 | тетра́д | **-ь** | -и | -и | -ь | -ью | -и |
| | | -и | -ей | -ям | -и | -ями | -ях |

Neuter nouns:

| 9 | блю́д | **-о** | -а | -у | -о | -ом | -е |
| | | -а | - | -ам | -а | -ами | -ах |

| 10 | по́л | **-е** | -я | -ю | -е | -ем | -е |
| | | -я | -éй | -я́м | -е | -я́ми | -я́х |

Note: Nouns in -ье have in the *g/pl.* the ending -ий. In addition, they do not shift their stress.

| 11 | учи́лищ | **-е** | -а | -у | -е | -ем | -е |
| | | -а | - | -ам | -а | -ами | -ах |

| 12 | жела́ни | **-е** | -я | -ю | -е | -ем | -и |
| | | -я | -й | -ям | -я | -ями | -ях |

| 13 | вре́м | **-я** | -ени | -ени | -я | -енем | -ени |
| | | -ена́ | -ён | -ена́м | -ена́ | -ена́ми | -ена́х |

Adjective
also ordinal numbers, etc.

Notes

a) Adjectives in **-ский** have no predicative (short) forms.

b) Variants of the following paradigms have been recorded with the individual entry words.

		m	*f*	*n*	*pl.*	
14	бе́л	**-ый(-о́й)**	**-ая**	**-ое**	**-ые**	
		-ого	-ой	-ого	-ых	
		-ому	-ой	-ому	-ым	
		-ый	-ую	-ое	-ые	long form
		-ым	-ой	-ым	-ыми	
		-ом	-ой	-ом	-ых	
		-	-а́	-о (*a.* -о́)	-ы (*a.* -ы́)	short form

15	си́н	**-ий**	**-яя**	**-ее**	**-ие**	
		-его	-ей	-его	-их	
		-ему	-ей	-ему	-им	
		-ий	-юю	-ее	-ие	long form
		-им	-ей	-им	-ими	
		-ем	-ей	-ем	-их	
		-(ь)	-я	-е	-и	short form
16	стро́г	**-ий**	**-ая**	**-ое**	**-ие**	
		-ого	-ой	-ого	-их	
		-ому	-ой	-ому	-им	
		-ий	-ую	-ое	-ие	long form
		-им	-ой	-им	-ими	
		-ом	-ой	-ом	-их	
		-	-а́	-о	-и (*a.* -й)	short form
17	то́щ	**-ий**	**-ая**	**-ее**	**-ие**	
		-его	-ей	-его	-их	
		-ему	-ей	-ему	-им	
		-ий	-ую	-ее	-ие	long form
		-им	-ей	-им	-ими	
		-ем	-ей	-ем	-их	
		-	-а	-е (-о́)	-и	short form
18	оле́н	**-ий**	**-ья**	**-ье**	**-ьи**	
		-ьего	-ьей	-ьего	-ьих	
		-ьему	-ьей	-ьему	-ьим	
		-ий	-ью	-ье	-ьи	
		-ьим	-ьей	-ьим	-ьими	
		-ьем	-ьей	-ьем	-ьих	
19	дя́дин	-	**-а**	**-о**	**-ы**	
		-а	-ой	-а	-ых	
		-у	-ой	-у	-ым	
		-	-у	-о	-ы	
		ым	-ой	-ым	-ыми	
		-ом[1]	-ой	-ом	-ых	

[1] Masculine surnames in -ов, -ев, -ин, -ын have the ending -е.

Pronoun

20	**я**	меня́	мне	меня́	мной (мно́ю)	мне
	мы	нас	нам	нас	на́ми	
21	**ты**	тебя́	тебе́	тебя́	тобой (тобо́ю)	тебе́
	вы	вас	вам	вас	ва́ми	вас
22	**он**	его́	ему́	его́	им	нём
	она́	её	ей	её	е́ю (ей)	ней
	оно́	его́	ему́	его́	им	нём
	они́	их	им	их	и́ми	них

Note: After prepositions the oblique forms receive an н-prothesis, e.g.: для него́, с не́ю (ней).

| 23 | **кто** | кого́ | кому́ | кого́ | кем | ком |
| | **что** | чего́ | чему́ | что | чем | чём |

Note: In combinations with ни-, не- a preposition separates such compounds, e.g. ничто́: ни от чего́, ни к чему́.

24	**мой**	моего́	моему́	мой	мои́м	моём
	моя́	мое́й	мое́й	мою́	мое́й	мое́й
	моё	моего́	моему́	моё	мои́м	моём
	мои́	мои́х	мои́м	мой	мои́ми	мои́х

25	**наш**	на́шего	на́шему	наш	на́шим	на́шем
	на́ша	на́шей	на́шей	на́шу	на́шим	на́шей
	на́ше	на́шего	на́шему	на́ше	на́шим	на́шем
	на́ши	на́ших	на́шим	на́ши	на́шими	на́ших

26	**чей**	чьего́	чьему́	чей	чьим	чьём
	чья	чьей	чьей	чью	чьей	чьей
	чьё	чьего́	чьему́	чьё	чьим	чьём
	чьи	чьих	чьим	чьи	чьи́ми	чьих

27	**э́тот**	э́того	э́тому	э́тот	э́тим	э́том
	э́та	э́той	э́той	э́ту	э́той	э́той
	э́то	э́того	э́тому	э́то	э́тим	э́том
	э́ти	э́тих	э́тим	э́ти	э́тими	э́тих

28	**тот**	того́	тому́	тот	тем	том
	та	той	той	ту	той	той
	то	того́	тому́	то	тем	том
	те	тех	тем	те	те́ми	тех

29	**сей**	сего́	сему́	сей	сим	сём
	сия́	сей	сей	сию́	сей	сей
	сие́	сего́	сему́	сие́	сим	сём
	сии́	сих	сим	сий	си́ми	сих

30	**сам**	самого́	самому́	самого́	сами́м	само́м
	сама́	само́й	само́й	саму́, самоё	само́й	само́й
	само́	самого́	самому́	само́	сами́м	само́м
	са́ми	сами́х	сами́м	сами́х	сами́ми	сами́х

31	**весь**	всего́	всему́	весь	всем	всём
	вся	всей	всей	всю	всей	всей
	всё	всего́	всему́	всё	всем	всём
	все	всех	всем	все	все́ми	всех

| 32 | **не́сколь-**
ко | не́сколь-
ких | не́сколь-
ким | не́сколь-
ко | не́сколь-
кими | не́сколь-
ких |

Numeral

33	**оди́н**	одного́	одному́	оди́н	одни́м	одно́м
	одна́	одно́й	одно́й	одну́	одно́й	одно́й
	одно́	одного́	одному́	одно́	одни́м	одно́м
	одни́	одни́х	одни́м	одни́	одни́ми	одни́х

34	**два**	**две**	**три**	**четы́ре**
	двух	двух	трёх	четырёх
	двум	двум	трём	четырём
	два	две	три	четы́ре
	двумя́	двумя́	тремя́	четырьмя́
	двух	двух	трёх	четырёх

35	**пять**	**пятна́дцать**	**пятьдеся́т**	**сто**	**со́рок**
	пяти́	пятна́дцати	пяти́десяти	ста	сорока́
	пяти́	пятна́дцати	пяти́десяти	ста	сорока́
	пять	пятна́дцать	пятьдеся́т	сто	со́рок
	пятью́	пятна́дцатью	пятью́десятью	ста	сорока́
	пяти́	пятна́дцати	пяти́десяти	ста	сорока́

36	**две́сти**	**три́ста**	**четы́реста**	**пятьсо́т**
	двухсо́т	трёхсо́т	четырёхсо́т	пятисо́т
	двумста́м	трёмста́м	четырёмста́м	пятиста́м
	две́сти	три́ста	четы́реста	пятьсо́т
	двумяста́ми	тремяста́ми	четырьмяста́ми	пятьюста́ми
	двухста́х	трёхста́х	четырёхста́х	пятиста́х

37	**о́ба**	**о́бе**	**дво́е**	**че́тверо**
	обо́их	обе́их	двои́х	четверы́х
	обо́им	обе́им	двои́м	четверы́м
	о́ба	о́бе	дво́е	че́тверо
	обо́ими	обе́ими	двои́ми	четверы́ми
	обо́их	обе́их	двои́х	четверы́х